A Woman's Place in the World

SIX VICTORIAN TRAVEL NARRATIVES BY WOMEN

A Woman's Place in the World

SIX VICTORIAN TRAVEL NARRATIVES BY WOMEN

Edited with an Introduction by
Haley Ruffner

WHITLOCK PUBLISHING
Alfred, NY

Original publication dates:
Travels in West Africa by Mary Kingsley, 1897
Among the Tibetans, Isabella Bird, 1894
Across Patagonia, Lady Florence Dixie, 1880
Safar Nameh, Persian Pictures, Gertrude Bell,1894
A White Woman in Central Africa, Helen Caddick, 1900
Eastern Life, Present and Past, Harriet Martineau, 1848

First Whitlock Publishing edition 2019

Whitlock Publishing
Alfred, New York

Editorial matter @ Haley Ruffner

ISBN: 978-1-943115-34-1

Cover art from Wikimedia Commons
Image: *Landscape with Walkers* by Anton Hansch, 1847

CONTENTS

Introduction i

Chronology vi

Bibliography ix

Acknowledgements and Note on the Text xi

Biography of Mary Kingsley 1

Travels in West Africa 6

Biography of Isabella Bird..380

Among the Tibetans..384

Biography of Lady Florence Dixie 443

Across Patagonia...447

Biography of Gertrude Bell...590

Safar Nameh, Persian Pictures 593

Biography of Helen Caddick..691

A White Woman in Central Africa 696

Biography of Harriet Martineau..800

Eastern Life, Present and Past 803

Suggested Reading 1111

INTRODUCTION

WHEN WE THINK OF FAMOUS TRAVELERS in history, we think of Christopher Columbus, Marco Polo, and Lewis and Clark. We think of young white men setting out from their countries' shores to discover the world, oceans, and continents open and waiting for them. We think of men lured by the promise of discovering their fortunes and winning fame in far-away lands as they impose their cultures onto places with already-rich histories. Maps were drawn in the footprints of male adventurers whose voices would dominate the literary canon at the expense of the countries they visited.

As a genre, travel fiction has also been historically male-dominated, reinforcing the idea of separate gendered spheres even in literature. We remember *The Odyssey*, Huckleberry Finn's adventures down the Mississippi, and *Around the World in Eighty Days*, all supporting the male worldview that the outside world belonged to them in its entirety; a woman's destiny was to tend to her household and wait for her husband's return. Her place in the world was a limited one, confined on all fronts by history, literature, and societal pressure.

The ideal Victorian woman was passive, silent, and domestic. The Victorian era marked the height of the corset's popularity in women's fashion, the perfect garment for restricting women's activity and lung capacity. Poems like Tennyson's 1832 "The Lady of Shalott," and the 1852 Millais painting of Ophelia drowning romanticize the figure of the female body, whose beauty is enhanced by her reduction to an object—the Lady of Shalott is allowed to exist peacefully as long as she goes about domestic tasks in her castle, but she is punished when she tries to leave that sphere.

The authors anthologized in this volume exist in stark opposition to the literary, artistic, and fashion conventions of their time. They overcame their lack of access to the same education their male peers enjoyed and escaped the domestic sphere to encounter and interact with different parts of the world. Each preceded by an author biography, these six works were all written by British women in the late nineteenth century. Each author travels to non-English speaking countries outside of Europe, many of which were colonized by England and under some degree of European political control. The interaction of these women travelers, an oppressed group in Western society, with other oppressed groups of people, provides the basis for a relationship made complicated through having in common a lower social standing than white men, while maintaining the barrier formed by British exceptionalism and white supremacy. Viewing history through the lens of a marginalized writer allows the reader to recognize common threads of privilege, oppression, and gendered perspectives.

The Western world tends to glorify these authors as heroines. In celebrating their courage and ability to break gender norms, history often ignores their complicity in dehumanizing other cultures and people of color. They were early champions of white feminism, excluding voices from women of color from their narratives or filtering them to further a political stance. Some of them recognized the damage colonization had on the cultures they visited, but even in praising the native people's art, societal structure, or way of life, they could not avoid revealing their casual racism and belief in British exceptionalism.

Some of these authors were more progressive than others, but they share the common denominator of being impossible to classify under one description. Harriet Martineau, who lost her hearing at an early age, wrote for disabled peoples' healthcare and rights, helped to preserve ancient Egyptian culture, and was an abolitionist—but she also argued for treating Egyptian people like children and described the governor of Thebes as "apish." Mary Kingsley, who pioneered the practice of anthropological fieldwork, lived with cannibalistic tribes of people and defended some of their ways of life, also used the n-word in her work and claimed that "I did not do anything without the assistance of the superior sex." Helen Caddick wrote frankly about the damage British colonization did to African people and their environment, but lacked the resources and drive to make change.

These authors' destinations, non-English-speaking countries outside of Europe, were considered dangerous because of their "otherness." Some of these women traveled purely for the sake of seeing new places, some for mission trips, and some for anthropological or sociological work, but they share the culpability of upholding and, in some cases, even strengthening the dichotomy between white Europeans and everyone else. Most of the authors anthologized here sought only to observe and report, not to elicit change or impose their beliefs on others, but even so their lenses of experience are colored by racism.

Although the term did not exist until more recently, the idea of the white feminist savior is rooted in narratives like some of the ones anthologized here wherein Western women, taught to pity women of other cultures and lifestyles, feel compelled to "save" them without any conversation with or input from the

INTRODUCTION

people they impose their help on. These authors report on countries saturated with European colonialists and missionaries, commenting on the "civilizing" process that seemed, even to them, to be doing more harm than good. In her narrative *A White Woman in Central Africa*, Helen Caddick writes: "We English are an odd mixture, we send out large sums for missions, and then permit and encourage such a show in London as 'Savage Africa,' which must thoroughly demoralise the natives, and undo years of patient work."

This almost-playful dismissal of English cruelty and dehumanization masquerading under the guise of religion as "an odd mixture" points to a larger and ongoing issue in Western societies—in recognizing marginalized people's struggles while simultaneously viewing them as subhuman, Caddick's concern for their welfare never develops beyond vague written apprehension. Caddick's passive reaction is likely suppressed, at least in part, because of her political powerlessness at home as a woman. She had the freedom to travel alone across the world, but upon returning to the bounds of English society, she would have been reduced to a comparatively domestic sphere.

The work these women did—building hospitals, preserving Egyptian culture, providing literary representation of strong women traveling, identifying new plants and animals—was inarguably important work, but the circumstances that made their work necessary was nearly always directly linked to European imperialism. The fish Mary Kingsley "discovered" were very likely already well-known to Africans who had fished the rivers for generations. The cultural preservation these authors worked towards was only necessary because European colonization destroyed ancient cultures. Missionary work tried to overwrite centuries-old tradition with Bible verses, rampant tourism defaced monuments and broke down rich history into fun facts on a white family's vacation itinerary, and historically-rich villages were razed to make way for European-style buildings.

During the mid-1800s, ethnology and anthropology began to compete with each other for academic dominance between young and old members of the European Ethnological Society. Ethnology, rooted in the belief that different races of people were biologically unequal in development and mental faculties, began to give way to the anthropological perspective of studying humankind's behaviors as a whole rather than pitting its different cultures against each other. Fieldwork in either of these areas of study was uncommon during the nineteenth century, making Mary Kingsley a pioneer of anthropological fieldwork despite her misguided views exaggerating the racial and sexual differences between people. She argued for immersing oneself in other cultures in order to best understand them, eschewing the traditional route of watching from afar. She writes, "…unless you have lived among the natives you can never

iii

get to know them. At first you see nothing but a confused stupidity and crime; but when you get to see—well! ...you see things worth seeing."

The context of the American Civil War also provided insight into the intensifying debate between whether humanity as a whole was worth looking at, or whether racial differences merited an entire area of study. In her text, Kingsley uses the n-word twice, which is worth examining because the word had largely fallen out of use among her contemporaries and might have been surprising to her readers. In combining progressive attitudes and multidisciplinary interests with outdated, degrading tenets in certain matters, these works encourage examination of how seemingly conflicting viewpoints align.

These women travelers and writers chipped away at stereotypes by not only traversing lands previously considered inaccessible to them, but documenting them in their own voices. Readers must acknowledge both the progress they made for women's rights and the ways in which they reinforced white supremacy, the effects of which remain relevant today in discussions of intersectionality in feminism. In traveling as part of a marginalized group and interacting with other marginalized groups, their connections are inextricably wound together in common struggles that they face with varying degrees of privilege.

HALEY RUFFNER, APRIL 2019
ALFRED, NY

CHRONOLOGY

1802   Harriet Martineau is born on June 12.

1807   American inventor Robert Fulton creates the first successful steamboat.

1831   Isabella Bird is born on October 15.

1832   Martineau publishes *Illustrations of Political Economy*, her first commissioned novel, and despite low expectations, it outsells Charles Dickens' work.

1833   England passes the Slavery Abolition Act.

1834   Martineau visits the United States to meet with abolitionists, and three years later publishes Society in America condemning slavery and the state of women's education.

1845   Helen Caddick is born.

1855   Lady Florence Dixie is born on May 24.

1862   Mary Kingsley is born on October 13.

1868   Gertrude Bell is born on July 14.

       The modern typewriter and QWERTY keyboard are invented.

1869   Mark Twain's *The Innocents Abroad* is published, beginning a new style of comic travel writing.

       Girton College at Cambridge opens for female students.

1873	Jules Verne's *Around the World in Eighty Days* is published, blending science fiction with travel writing.
1874	The London School of Economics begins admitting women.
1876	Martineau dies of bronchitis.
1878	Dixie leaves her newborn son at home and travels with her husband, brother, and other male friends to Patagonia.
1880	Dixie publishes *Across Patagonia*.
1883	Reports are published of an assassination attempt on Lady Florence Dixie due to her political views and activism, but no conviction is made due to lack of evidence.
1885	The Berlin West Africa Conference convenes to produce the Berlin Treaty, a guide for European invasion and partitioning of Africa.
1889	Bird, close to 60 years old, sails to India to visit missions and build a women's hospital.
1890	Bird becomes the first woman to be awarded the Honorary Fellowship of the Royal Scottish Geographical Society.
1892	Bird becomes the first woman to be admitted into the Royal Geographic Society.
	Bell travels to Persia for the first time to visit her uncle. In the next twelve years, she crosses Arabia six more times.
1893	Kingsley arrives in Sierra Leone on her first voyage to Africa.
1894	Bird publishes *Among the Tibetans*.
1894	Bell publishes *Persian Pictures*.
	Kingsley returns to Africa on her second trip with more support and supplies from England.
1895	Dixie becomes President of the British Ladies' Football Club.
1897	Kingsley publishes *Travels in West Africa*, an immediate bestseller.
1899	Rudyard Kipling writes "The White Man's Burden," a poem about the racial responsibilities of white imperialists.

1900	Kingsley dies of typhoid fever in Cape Town while volunteering as a nurse for Boer prisoners of war in the Second Boer War. She is buried at sea by her request.
	Caddick publishes *A White Woman in Central Africa*.
1901	The Alpine mountain Gertrudspitze is named for Bell after she is the first ever to scale it with her guides.
1904	Bird dies in her home in the midst of planning another trip to China.
1905	Dixie dies of diptheria in her home.
1920	The 19th Amendment is passed in the United States, granting women the right to vote.
1926	Bell is found dead in her home, having overdosed on sleeping pills.

BIBLIOGRAPHY

Ablow, Rachel. "Harriet Martineau and the Impersonality of Pain." Victorian Studies, vol. 56, no. 4, Summer 2014, pp. 675–697. EBSCOhost, doi:10.2979/victorianstudies.56.4.675.

Belasco, Susan. "Harriet Martineau's Black Hero and the American Antislavery Movement." Nineteenth-Century Literature, vol. 55, no. 2, 2000, pp. 157–194. JSTOR, www.jstor.org/stable/2903113.

"Bell (Gertrude) Archive." Archives Hub, archiveshub.jisc.ac.uk/search/archives/74e845fa-b746-3598-8c8e-cebd02f786b7.

Birkett, Deborah. "West Africa's Mary Kingsley." History Today, vol. 37, no. 5, May 1987, p. 10. EBSCOhost.

Encyclopedia of War Journalism (2nd Edition), edited by Mitchel Roth, Grey House Publishing, 2010. ProQuest Ebook Central.

Birmingham City Council. "Helen Caddick and Her Diaries." Birmingham City Council, Birmingham City Council, 22 Jan. 2018, birmingham.gov.uk/info/50165/birmingham_connection/1581/helen_caddick_and_her_diaries.

"Florence Douglas Dixie." Contemporary Authors Online, Gale, 2001. Literature Resource Center.

"Gertrude Bell." Britannica Academic, Encyclopædia Britannica, 30 Jan. 2009. academic.eb.com/levels/collegiate/article/Gertrude-Bell/15231.

"Harriet Martineau." Britannica Academic, Encyclopædia Britannica, 21 Dec. 2006. academic.eb.com/levels/collegiate/article/Harriet-Martineau/51172.

MacGowan, Doug. "Attack on Lady Florence Dixie: 'Saved by Her St Bernard.'" Historic Mysteries, 11 Feb. 2017, historicmysteries.com/lady-florence-dixie/.

Said, Edward W. *Orientalism.* Random House, Inc., 1978.

Scarce, Jennifer. "Isabella Bird Bishop (1831–1904) and Her Travels in Persia and Kurdistan in 1890." Iranian Studies, vol. 44, no. 2, 2011, pp. 243–250. JSTOR, jstor.org/stable/23033327.

Sharp, John. "Who Was. . . Mary Kingsley?" Biologist, vol. 49, no. 4, Aug. 2002, p. 179. EBSCOhost.

Stocking, George W., Jr. *Victorian Anthropology.* The Free Press, 1987.

Tarabay, Jamie. "Gertrude Bell, a Masterful Spy and Diplomat." NPR, NPR, 12 July 2006, npr.org/templates/story/story.php?storyId=5552563.

Tiryakian, Edward A. "White Women In Darkest Africa: Marginals As Observers In No-Woman's Land." Civilisations, vol. 41, no. 1/2, 1993, pp. 209–238. JSTOR, jstor.org/stable/41229831.

Wolf, James. "A Woman Passing Through: Helen Caddick and the Maturation of the Empire in British Central Africa." Journal of Popular Culture, vol. 30, no. 3, Winter 1996, pp. 35–55. EBSCOhost, doi:10.1111/j.0022-3840.1996.00035.x.

Workman, Nancy V. "Gertrude Bell and the Poetics of Translation: 'The Divan of Hafez.'" English Literature in Transition, 1880-1920, vol. 53, no. 2, Apr. 2010, pp. 182–203. EBSCOhost, doi:10.2487/elt.53.2(2010)0058.

Yale, Pat. "Gertrude of Arabia: The Great Adventurer May Finally Get Her Museum." The Guardian, Guardian News and Media, 9 Aug. 2016, theguardian.com/culture/2016/aug/09/gertrude-of-arabia-gertrude-bell-home-museum-redcar.

Acknowledgements

Thank you to Dr. Grove for challenging me and offering your guidance and wisdom throughout the course of this project. Thank you to Dr. Mayberry, Dr. Reginio, Dr. Ryan, and Dr. Myers for your input, reassurance, and for believing in me.

Thank you to my family for your endless support and encouragement.

Thank you to my grandfather, Harry Hurd, for offering to take me trail riding whenever you thought I was spending too much time in the computer lab.

Note on the Text

Based on original texts, this volume reflects the grammatical conventions and viewpoints of the nineteenth century. Archaic spellings and phrasings were preserved in order to maintain the authenticity of the literature. Obvious typographical errors have been corrected.

Only Part I of Harriet Martineau's narrative *Eastern Life, Present and Past* is included in this volume due to length constraints. Parts II and III are public domain materials and accessible for free online in facsimile form.

BIOGRAPHY OF MARY KINGSLEY

Mary Kingsley was born in London on October 13, 1862 into a family of novelists, doctors, and travelers. Her father, George Kingsley, worked in the medical field, which brought him away from home frequently on excursions throughout Europe and North America. During his time in North America, he was invited to participate in the U.S. Army expedition into Sioux territory. Weather prevented him from joining Custer's forces (and saved him from their consequent slaughter), but his experience with how thoroughly white invaders dehumanized Native Americans likely influenced his daughter's later writings on British imperialism.

Kingsley had little formal schooling as a child, but educated herself through voracious reading in her father's extensive library. She reportedly eschewed the popular novels of her era, more interested in explorers' memoirs than Jane Austen. By 1881, her family had moved to Cambridge, and Kingsley was enrolled there as a student of medicine while her brother Charles studied law.

In 1882, both of Kingsley's parents were ill and bedridden, limiting her travel and educational opportunities while she cared for them. Her father died of a fever contracted while traveling, and her mother followed a few months after. Left with 8,600 euros for her inheritance, her parents' deaths gave her the freedom and the means to explore the world. At the time of her father's death, he had started writing a book grounded in African religion and law, so she undertook her first journeys with the intention of finishing his work.

Kingsley's travels included expeditions to the Canary Islands, Cabinda, Angola, Nigeria, Equatorial Guinea, and the French Congo, including a visit to the reportedly cannibalistic Fang people in Gabon. She also climbed Mount Cameroon, a 13,250-foot ascent, via a route never before traversed by a European.

Her background in medicine and science, combined with the assortment of knowledge gleaned from her father's library, provided the basis for her study of, in her words, "fish and fetish." This phrase, a humorous underrating of her

1

work, refers to her documentation of Africa's flora and fauna as well as her ethnological tendencies in studying the religious and legal practices of different tribes. She collected specimens of over eighty fish and reptiles, all of biological interest and some previously undiscovered. Several of the newfound fish species were named after her.

The views and political stances she brought back to England with her were somewhat unexpected. Hailed as a "New Woman" upon stepping off a cargo ship back onto English soil, she was quick to distance herself from the women's rights movement. She favored separate spheres for men and women, citing a need not for women to be able to join men's travel societies, but for them to create their own, as discussion was best fostered within same-sex groups. "Women like myself know many things no man can know about the heathen," she wrote to the Royal Geographical Society's secretary, "and no doubt men do ditto." In angry response to a Daily Telegraph article linking her travels to the New Woman feminist concept, Kingsley wrote to the editor saying, "I did not do anything without the assistance of the superior sex." When asked about women's suffrage, she called it a minor issue, redirecting concern towards British trading rights in Africa, although some scholars argue that her lack of identification with women's movements may have been an attempt to gain wider readership for her books.

These ideals of separation paralleled Kingsley's views of the relationship between men and women, and Europeans and Africans. "I feel certain that a black man is no more an underdeveloped white man than a rabbit is an underdeveloped hare, and the mental difference between the races is very similar to that between men and women among ourselves," she wrote. She condemned missionaries for trying to "civilize" native Africans, believing that better understanding and studying their ways of life was more effective than trying to gloss over the differences between races and assimilate Africans and Europeans together.

Kingsley's adherence to traditional Victorian values carried over into her clothing choices—even traversing rivers in dugout canoes, traipsing through thick brush, and weathering extreme temperatures, she dressed in full-length skirts and petticoats and wore a tight corset, high collar, and fur bonnet. Despite the obvious drawbacks of such a dress code, she even claimed practicality in some cases. After falling into a game pit trap and landing on sharpened sticks at the bottom, she wrote, "It is at these times you realize the blessings of a good thick skirt." She defended her mode of dress vehemently as a facet of her status as a lady, which was often attacked in response to her anti-missionary stance; critics would claim she had fallen in with the native Africans' "savage" ways.

By the mid-1890s, Kingsley's reputation as a political activist had grown through her methods of writing to government officials' wives, arguing powerful men to her side and letting them fight her battles for her, and continuing to write. Her final book, West African Studies, published in 1899, attacked the Crown Colony system whereby Britain imperialist policy dismantled all pre-existing African social structures. In its place, she offered a solution in which, although British technology and trade would still be implemented in Africa, the system of government would operate with a council of African chiefs to give opinions and offer their input.

In March of 1900, Kingsley made her final voyage to Cape Town, South Africa to volunteer as a nurse in the Second Boer War, caring for Boer prisoners of war. There, at only thirty-eight years old, she fell ill with typhoid and, after months of sickness, went off to die alone. She requested a burial at sea, and her final send-off reflected an irony always present in her sense of humor—her coffin, pushed out to sea, refused to sink, and had to be drawn back in and an anchor added to finish the sea burial.

Travels in West Africa

Congo Français, Corisco and Cameroons

BY

Mary H. Kingsley

To my brother, C. G. Kingsley this book is dedicated.

CONTENTS

PREFACE..9

PREFACE TO THE ABRIDGED EDITION OF TRAVELS IN WEST

AFRICA...10

INTRODUCTION...13

CHAPTER I

Liverpool to Sierra Leone and the Gold Coast.....................20

CHAPTER II

Fernando Po and the Bubis..34

CHAPTER III

Voyage Down Coast..54

CHAPTER IV

The Ogowé...64

CHAPTER V

The Rapids of the Ogowé..83

CHAPTER VI

Lembarene 101

CHAPTER VII

On the Way From Kangwe to Lake Ncovi...........................124

CHAPTER VIII

From Ncovi to Esoon..142

CHAPTER IX

From Esoon to Agonjo 167

CHAPTER X

Bush Trade and Fan Customs 177

CHAPTER XI

Down the Rembwé...192

CHAPTER XII

Fetish 204

CHAPTER XIII

Fetish - (Continued)...222

CHAPTER XIV

Fetish—(Continued) 237

CHAPTER XV

Fetish—(Continued) 250

CHAPTER XVI

Fetish—(Concluded)...262

CHAPTER XVII

Ascent of the Great Peak of Cameroons......................................280

CHAPTER XVIII

The Great Peak of Cameroons—(Continued)...............................291

CHAPTER XIX

The Great Peak of Cameroons—(Continued)...............................301

CHAPTER XX

The Great Peak of Cameroons—(Concluded) 308

CHAPTER XXI

Trade and Labour in West Africa...319

CHAPTER XXII

Disease in West Africa 362

APPENDIX

The Invention of the Cloth Loom 372

PREFACE

To THE READER.—What this book wants is not a simple Preface but an apology, and a very brilliant and convincing one at that. Recognising this fully, and feeling quite incompetent to write such a masterpiece, I have asked several literary friends to write one for me, but they have kindly but firmly declined, stating that it is impossible satisfactorily to apologise for my liberties with Lindley Murray and the Queen's English. I am therefore left to make a feeble apology for this book myself, and all I can personally say is that it would have been much worse than it is had it not been for Dr. Henry Guillemard, who has not edited it, or of course the whole affair would have been better, but who has most kindly gone through the proof sheets, lassoing prepositions which were straying outside their sentence stockade, taking my eye off the water cask and fixing it on the scenery where I meant it to be, saying firmly in pencil on margins "No you don't," when I was committing some more than usually heinous literary crime, and so on. In cases where his activities in these things may seem to the reader to have been wanting, I beg to state that they really were not. It is I who have declined to ascend to a higher level of lucidity and correctness of diction than I am fitted for. I cannot forbear from mentioning my gratitude to Mr. George Macmillan for his patience and kindness with me,—a mere jungle of information on West Africa. Whether you my reader will share my gratitude is, I fear, doubtful, for if it had not been for him I should never have attempted to write a book at all, and in order to excuse his having induced me to try I beg to state that I have written only on things that I know from personal experience and very careful observation. I have never accepted an explanation of a native custom from one person alone, nor have I set down things as being prevalent customs from having seen a single instance. I have endeavoured to give you an honest account of the general state and manner of life in Lower Guinea and some description of the various types of country there. In reading this section you must make allowances for my love of this sort of country, with its great forests and rivers and its animistic-minded inhabitants, and for my ability to be more comfortable there than in England. Your superior culture-instincts may militate against your enjoying West Africa, but if you go there you will find things as I have said.

January, 1897.

PREFACE TO THE ABRIDGED EDITION OF TRAVELS IN WEST AFRICA

WHEN ON MY RETURN TO ENGLAND from my second sojourn in West Africa, I discovered, to my alarm, that I was, by a freak of fate, the sea-serpent of the season, I published, in order to escape from this reputation, a very condensed, much abridged version of my experiences in Lower Guinea; and I thought that I need never explain about myself or Lower Guinea again. This was one of my errors. I have been explaining ever since; and, though not reconciled to so doing, I am more or less resigned to it, because it gives me pleasure to see that English people can take an interest in that land they have neglected. Nevertheless, it was a shock to me when the publishers said more explanation was required. I am thankful to say the explanation they required was merely on what plan the abridgment of my first account had been made. I can manage that explanation easily. It has been done by removing from it certain sections whole, and leaving the rest very much as it first stood. Of course it would have been better if I had totally reformed and rewritten the book in pellucid English; but that is beyond me, and I feel at any rate this book must be better than it was, for there is less of it; and I dimly hope critics will now see that there is a saving grace in disconnectedness, for owing to that disconnectedness whole chapters have come out without leaving holes.

As for the part that is left in, I have already apologised for its form, and I cannot help it, for Lower Guinea is like what I have said it is. No one who knows it has sent home contradictions of my description of it, or its natives, or their manners or customs, and they have had by now ample time and opportunity. The only complaints I have had regarding my account from my fellow West Coasters have been that I might have said more. I trust my forbearance will send a thrill of gratitude through readers of the 736-page edition.

There is, however, one section that I reprint, regarding which I must say a few words. It is that on the trade and labour problem in West Africa, particularly the opinion therein expressed regarding the liquor traffic. This part has brought down on me much criticism from the Missionary Societies and their friends; and I beg gratefully to acknowledge the honourable fairness with which the controversy has been carried on by the great Wesleyan Methodist Mission to the Gold Coast and the Baptist Mission to the Congo. It has not ended in our agreement on this point, but it has raised my esteem of Missionary Societies considerably; and anyone interested in this matter I beg to refer to the Baptist Magazine for October, 1897. Therein will be found my answer, and the comments on it by a competent missionary authority; for the rest of this matter I beg all readers of this book to bear in mind that I confine myself to speaking only of the bit of Africa I know—West Africa. During this past summer I attended a meeting at which Sir George Taubman Goldie spoke, and was much struck with the truth of what he said on the difference of different African regions. He divided Africa into three zones: firstly, that region where white races could colonise in the true sense of the word, and form a great native-born white population, namely, the region of the Cape; secondly, a region where the white race could colonise, but to a less extent— an extent analogous to that in India—namely, the highlands of Central East Africa and parts of Northern Africa; thirdly, a region where the white races cannot colonise in a true sense of the word, namely, the West African region, and in those regions he pointed out one of the main elements of prosperity and advance is the native African population. I am quoting his words from memory, possibly imperfectly; but there is very little reliable printed matter to go on when dealing with Sir George Taubman Goldie, which is regrettable because he himself is an experienced and reliable authority. I am however quite convinced that these aforesaid distinct regions are regions that the practical politician dealing with Africa must recognise, and keep constantly in mind when attempting to solve the many difficulties that that great continent presents, and sincerely hope every reader of this work will remember that I am speaking of that last zone, the zone wherein white races cannot colonise in a true sense of the word, but which is nevertheless a vitally important region to a great manufacturing country like England, for therein are vast undeveloped markets wherein she can sell her manufactured goods and purchase raw material for her manufactures at a reasonable rate.

Having a rooted, natural, feminine hatred for politics I have no inclination to become diffuse on them, as I have on the errors of other people's cooking or ideas on decoration. I know I am held to be too partial to France in West Africa; too fond of pointing out her brilliant achievements there, too fond of saying the native is as happy, and possibly happier, under her rule than under ours; and also that I am given to a great admiration for Germans; but this is just like any common-sense Englishwoman. Of course I am devoted to my own John; but still Monsieur is brave, bright, and fascinating; Mein Herr is possessed of courage and commercial ability in the highest degree, and, besides, he takes such a lot of trouble to know the real truth about things, and tells them to you so calmly and carefully—and our own

John—well, of course, he is everything that's good and great, but he makes a shocking fool of himself at times, particularly in West Africa.

I should enjoy holding what one of my justly irritated expurgators used to call one of my little thanksgiving services here, but I will not; for, after all, it would be impossible for me to satisfactorily thank those people who, since my publication of this book, have given me help and information on the subject of West Africa. Chief amongst them have been Mr. A. L. Jones, Sir. R. B. N. Walker, Mr. Irvine, and Mr. John Holt. I have not added to this book any information I have received since I wrote it, as it does not seem to me fair to do so. My only regret regarding it is that I have not dwelt sufficiently on the charm of West Africa; it is so difficult to explain such things; but I am sure there are amongst my readers people who know by experience the charm some countries exercise over men—countries very different from each other and from West Africa. The charm of West Africa is a painful one: it gives you pleasure when you are out there, but when you are back here it gives you pain by calling you. It sends up before your eyes a vision of a wall of dancing white, rainbow-gemmed surf playing on a shore of yellow sand before an audience of stately coco palms; or of a great mangrove-watered bronze river; or of a vast aisle in some forest cathedral: and you hear, nearer to you than the voices of the people round, nearer than the roar of the city traffic, the sound of the surf that is breaking on the shore down there, and the sound of the wind talking on the hard palm leaves and the thump of the natives' tom-toms; or the cry of the parrots passing over the mangrove swamps in the evening time; or the sweet, long, mellow whistle of the plantain warblers calling up the dawn; and everything that is round you grows poor and thin in the face of the vision, and you want to go back to the Coast that is calling you, saying, as the African says to the departing soul of his dying friend, "Come back, come back, this is your home."

M. H. KINGSLEY.

October, 1897.

[NOTE.—The following chapters of the first edition are not included in this edition:—Chap. ii., The Gold Coast; Chap. iv., Lagos Bar; Chap. v., Voyage down Coast; Chap. vi., Libreville and Glass; Chap. viii., Talagouga; Chap. xvi., Congo Français; Chap. xvii., The Log of the Lafayette; Chap. xviii., From Corisco to Gaboon; Chap. xxviii., The Islands in the Bay of Amboises; Appendix ii., Disease in West Africa; Appendix iii., Dr. A. Günther on Reptiles and Fishes; Appendix iv., Orthoptera, Hymenoptera, and Hemiptera.]

INTRODUCTION

Relateth the various causes which impelled the author to embark upon the voyage.

I T WAS IN 1893 THAT, for the first time in my life, I found myself in possession of five or six months which were not heavily forestalled, and feeling like a boy with a new half-crown, I lay about in my mind, as Mr. Bunyan would say, as to what to do with them. "Go and learn your tropics," said Science. Where on earth am I to go? I wondered, for tropics are tropics wherever found, so I got down an atlas and saw that either South America or West Africa must be my destination, for the Malayan region was too far off and too expensive. Then I got Wallace's Geographical Distribution and after reading that master's article on the Ethiopian region I hardened my heart and closed with West Africa. I did this the more readily because while I knew nothing of the practical condition of it, I knew a good deal both by tradition and report of South East America, and remembered that Yellow Jack was endemic, and that a certain naturalist, my superior physically and mentally, had come very near getting starved to death in the depressing society of an expedition slowly perishing of want and miscellaneous fevers up the Parana.

My ignorance regarding West Africa was soon removed. And although the vast cavity in my mind that it occupied is not even yet half filled up, there is a great deal of very curious information in its place. I use the word curious advisedly, for I think many seemed to translate my request for practical hints and advice into an advertisement that "Rubbish may be shot here." This same information is in a state of great confusion still, although I have made heroic efforts to codify it. I find, however, that it can almost all be got in under the following different headings, namely and to wit: -

The dangers of West Africa.

The disagreeables of West Africa.

The diseases of West Africa.

The things you must take to West Africa.

The things you find most handy in West Africa.

The worst possible things you can do in West Africa.

I inquired of all my friends as a beginning what they knew of West Africa. The majority knew nothing. A percentage said, "Oh, you can't possibly go there; that's where Sierra Leone is, the white man's grave, you know." If these were pressed further, one occasionally found that they had had relations who had gone out there after having been "sad trials," but, on consideration of their having left not only West Africa, but this world, were now forgiven and forgotten.

I next turned my attention to cross-examining the doctors. "Deadliest spot on earth," they said cheerfully, and showed me maps of the geographical distribution of disease. Now I do not say that a country looks inviting when it is coloured in Scheele's green or a bilious yellow, but these colours may arise from lack of artistic gift in the cartographer. There is no mistaking what he means by black, however, and black you'll find they colour West Africa from above Sierra Leone to below the Congo. "I wouldn't go there if I were you," said my medical friends, "you'll catch something; but if you must go, and you're as obstinate as a mule, just bring me—" and then followed a list of commissions from here to New York, any one of which—but I only found that out afterwards.

All my informants referred me to the missionaries. "There were," they said, in an airy way, "lots of them down there, and had been for many years." So to missionary literature I addressed myself with great ardour; alas! only to find that these good people wrote their reports not to tell you how the country they resided in was, but how it was getting on towards being what it ought to be, and how necessary it was that their readers should subscribe more freely, and not get any foolishness into their heads about obtaining an inadequate supply of souls for their money. I also found fearful confirmation of my medical friends' statements about its unhealthiness, and various details of the distribution of cotton shirts over which I did not linger.

From the missionaries it was, however, that I got my first idea about the social condition of West Africa. I gathered that there existed there, firstly the native human beings—the raw material, as it were—and that these were led either to good or bad respectively by the missionary and the trader. There were also the Government representatives, whose chief business it was to strengthen and consolidate the missionary's work, a function they carried on but indifferently well. But as for those traders! well, I put them down under the dangers of West Africa at once. Subsequently I came across the good old Coast yarn of how, when a trader from that region went thence, it goes without saying where, the Fallen Angel without a moment's hesitation vacated the infernal throne

(Milton) in his favour. This, I beg to note, is the marine form of the legend. When it occurs terrestrially the trader becomes a Liverpool mate. But of course no one need believe it either way—it is not a missionary's story.

Naturally, while my higher intelligence was taken up with attending to these statements, my mind got set on going, and I had to go. Fortunately I could number among my acquaintances one individual who had lived on the Coast for seven years. Not, it is true, on that part of it which I was bound for. Still his advice was pre-eminently worth attention, because, in spite of his long residence in the deadliest spot of the region, he was still in fair going order. I told him I intended going to West Africa, and he said, "When you have made up your mind to go to West Africa the very best thing you can do is to get it unmade again and go to Scotland instead; but if your intelligence is not strong enough to do so, abstain from exposing yourself to the direct rays of the sun, take 4 grains of quinine every day for a fortnight before you reach the Rivers, and get some introductions to the Wesleyans; they are the only people on the Coast who have got a hearse with feathers."

My attention was next turned to getting ready things to take with me. Having opened upon myself the sluice gates of advice, I rapidly became distracted. My friends and their friends alike seemed to labour under the delusion that I intended to charter a steamer and was a person of wealth beyond the dreams of avarice. This not being the case, the only thing to do was to gratefully listen and let things drift.

Not only do the things you have got to take, but the things you have got to take them in, present a fine series of problems to the young traveller. Crowds of witnesses testified to the forms of baggage holders they had found invaluable, and these, it is unnecessary to say, were all different in form and material.

With all this embarras de choix I was too distracted to buy anything new in the way of baggage except a long waterproof sack neatly closed at the top with a bar and handle. Into this I put blankets, boots, books, in fact anything that would not go into my portmanteau or black bag. From the first I was haunted by a conviction that its bottom would come out, but it never did, and in spite of the fact that it had ideas of its own about the arrangement of its contents, it served me well throughout my voyage.

It was the beginning of August '93 when I first left England for "the Coast." Preparations of quinine with postage partially paid arrived up to the last moment, and a friend hastily sent two newspaper clippings, one entitled "A Week in a Palm-oil Tub," which was supposed to describe the sort of accommodation, companions, and fauna likely to be met with on a steamer going to West Africa, and on which I was to spend seven to The Graphic contributor's one; the other from The Daily Telegraph, reviewing a French book of "Phrases in common use" in Dahomey. The opening sentence in the latter was, "Help, I am drowning." Then came the inquiry, "If a man is not a thief?" and then another cry, "The boat is upset." "Get up, you lazy scamps," is the next exclamation, followed almost immediately by the question, "Why has not this man been buried?" "It is fetish that has killed him, and he must lie here exposed with nothing on him until only the bones remain," is the cheerful answer. This sounded discouraging to a person whose occupation would necessitate going about considerably in boats, and whose fixed desire was to study fetish. So with a feeling of foreboding gloom I left London for Liverpool—none the more cheerful for the matter-of-fact manner in which the steamboat agents had informed me that they did not issue return tickets by the West African lines of steamers. I will not go into the details of that voyage here, much as I am given to discursiveness. They are more amusing than instructive, for on my first voyage out I did not know the Coast, and the Coast did not know me and we mutually terrified each other. I fully expected to get killed by the local nobility and gentry; they thought I was connected with the World's Women's Temperance Association, and collecting shocking details for subsequent magic-lantern lectures on the liquor traffic; so fearful misunderstandings arose, but we gradually educated each other, and I had the best of the affair; for all I had got to teach them was that I was only a beetle and fetish hunter, and so forth, while they had to teach me a new world, and a very fascinating course of study I found it. And whatever the Coast may have to say against me—for my continual desire for hair-pins, and other pins, my intolerable habit of getting into water, the abominations full of ants, that I brought into their houses, or things emitting at unexpectedly short notice vivid and awful stenches—they cannot but say that I was a diligent pupil, who honestly tried to learn the lessons they taught me so kindly, though some of those lessons were hard to a person who had never previously been even in a tame bit of tropics, and whose life for many years had been an entirely domestic one in a University town.

One by one I took my old ideas derived from books and thoughts based on imperfect knowledge and weighed them against the real life around me, and found them either worthless or wanting. The greatest recantation I had to make I made humbly before I had been three months on the Coast in 1893. It was of my idea of the traders. What I had expected to find them was a very different thing to what I did find them; and of their kindness to me I can never sufficiently speak, for on that voyage I was utterly out of touch with the governmental circles, and utterly dependent on the traders, and the most useful lesson of all the lessons I learnt on the West Coast in 1893 was that I could trust them. Had I not learnt this very thoroughly I could never have gone out again and carried out the voyage I give you a sketch of in this book.

Thanks to "the Agent," I have visited places I could never otherwise have seen; and to the respect and affection in which he is held by the native, I owe it that I have done so in safety. When I have arrived off his factory in a steamer or canoe unexpected, unintroduced, or turned up equally unheralded out of the bush in a dilapidated state, he has always received me with that gracious hospitality which must have given him, under Coast conditions, very real trouble and inconvenience—things he could have so readily found logical excuses against entailing upon himself for the sake of an individual whom he had never seen before—whom he most likely would never see again—and whom it was no earthly profit to him to see then. He has bestowed himself—Allah only knows where—on his small trading vessels so that I might have his one cabin. He has fished me out of sea and fresh water with boat-hooks; he has continually given me good advice, which if I had only followed would have enabled me to keep out of water and any other sort of affliction; and although he holds the meanest opinion of my intellect for going to such a place as West Africa for beetles, fishes and fetish, he has given me the greatest assistance in my work. The value of that work I pray you withhold judgment on, until I lay it before you in some ten volumes or so mostly in Latin. All I know that is true regarding West African facts, I owe to the traders; the errors are my own.

To Dr. Günther, of the British Museum, I am deeply grateful for the kindness and interest he has always shown regarding all the specimens of natural history that I have been able to lay before him; the majority of which must have had very old tales to tell him. Yet his courtesy and attention gave me the thing a worker in any work most wants—the sense that the work was worth doing—and sent me back to work again with the knowledge that if these things interested a man like him, it was a more than sufficient reason for me to go on collecting them. To Mr. W. H. F. Kirby I am much indebted for his working out my small collection of certain Orders of insects; and to Mr. Thomas S. Forshaw, for the great help he has afforded me in revising my notes.

It is impossible for me even to catalogue my debts of gratitude still outstanding to the West Coast. Chiefly am I indebted to Mr. C. G. Hudson, whose kindness and influence enabled me to go up the Ogowé and to see as much of Congo Français as I have seen, and his efforts to take care of me were most ably seconded by Mr. Fildes. The French officials in "Congo Français" never hindered me, and always treated me with the greatest kindness. You may say there was no reason why they should not, for there is nothing in this fine colony of France that they need be ashamed of any one seeing; but I find it is customary for travellers to say the French officials throw obstacles in the way of any one visiting their possessions, so I merely beg to state this was decidedly not my experience; although my deplorable ignorance of French prevented me from explaining my humble intentions to them.

The Rev. Dr. Nassau and Mr. R. E. Dennett have enabled me, by placing at my disposal the rich funds of their knowledge of native life and idea, to amplify any deductions from my own observation. Mr. Dennett's work I have not dealt with in this work because it refers to tribes I was not amongst on this journey, but to a tribe I made the acquaintance with in my '93 voyage—the Fjort. Dr. Nassau's observations I have referred to. Herr von Lucke, Vice-governor of Cameroon, I am indebted to for not only allowing me, but for assisting me by every means in his power, to go up Cameroons Peak, and to the Governor of Cameroon, Herr von Puttkamer, for his constant help and kindness. Indeed so great has been the willingness to help me of all these gentlemen, that it is a wonder to me, when I think of it, that their efforts did not project me right across the continent and out at Zanzibar. That this brilliant affair did not come off is owing to my own lack of enterprise; for I did not want to go across the continent, and I do not hanker after Zanzibar, but only to go puddling about obscure districts in West Africa after raw fetish and fresh-water fishes.

I owe my ability to have profited by the kindness of these gentlemen on land, to a gentleman of the sea—Captain Murray. He was captain of the vessel I went out on in 1893, and he saw then that my mind was full of errors that must be eradicated if I was going to deal with the Coast successfully; and so he eradicated those errors and replaced them with sound knowledge from his own stores collected during an acquaintance with the West Coast of over thirty years. The education he has given me has been of the greatest value to me, and I sincerely hope to make many more voyages under him, for I well know he has still much to teach and I to learn.

Last, but not least, I must chronicle my debts to the ladies. First to those two courteous Portuguese ladies, Donna Anna de Sousa Coutinho e Chichorro and her sister Donna Maria de Sousa Coutinho, who did so much for me in Kacongo in 1893, and have remained, I am proud to say, my firm friends ever since. Lady MacDonald and Miss Mary Slessor I speak of in this book, but only faintly sketch the pleasure and help they have afforded me; nor have I fully expressed my gratitude for the kindness of Madame Jacot of Lembarene, or Madame Forget of Talagouga. Then there are a whole list of nuns belonging to the Roman Catholic Missions on the South West Coast, ever cheery and charming companions; and Frau Plehn, whom it was a continual pleasure to see in Cameroons, and discourse with once again on things that seemed so far off then—art, science, and literature; and Mrs. H. Duggan, of Cameroons too, who used, whenever I came into that port to rescue me from fearful states of starvation for toilet necessaries, and lend a sympathetic and intelligent ear to the "awful sufferings" I had gone through, until Cameroons became to me a thing to look forward to.

When in the Canaries in 1892, I used to smile, I regretfully own, at the conversation of a gentleman from the Gold Coast who was up there recruiting after a bad fever. His conversation consisted largely of anecdotes of friends of his, and nine times in ten he used to say, "He's dead now." Alas! my own conversation may be smiled at now for the same cause. Many of my friends mentioned even in this very recent account of the Coast "are dead now." Most of those I learnt to know in 1893; chief among these is my old friend Captain Boler, of Bonny, from whom I first learnt a certain power of comprehending the African and his form of thought.

I have great reason to be grateful to the Africans themselves—to cultured men and women among them like Charles Owoo, Mbo, Sanga Glass, Jane Harrington and her sister at Gaboon, and to the bush natives; but of my experience with them I give further details, so I need not dwell on them here.

I apologise to the general reader for giving so much detail on matters that really only affect myself, and I know that the indebtedness which all African travellers have to the white residents in Africa is a matter usually very lightly touched on. No doubt my voyage would seem a grander thing if I omitted mention of the help I received, but—well, there was a German gentleman once who evolved a camel out of his inner consciousness. It was a wonderful thing; still, you know, it was not a good camel, only a thing which people personally unacquainted with camels could believe in. Now I am ambitious to make a picture, if I make one at all, that people who do know the original can believe in—even if they criticise its points—and so I give you details a more showy artist would omit.

CHAPTER I

LIVERPOOL TO SIERRA LEONE AND THE GOLD COAST

Setting forth how the voyager departs from England in a stout vessel and in good company, and reaches in due course the Island of the Grand Canary, and then the Port of Sierra Leone: to which is added some account of this latter place and the comeliness of its women. Wherein also some description of Cape Coast and Accra is given, to which are added divers observations on supplies to be obtained there.

The West Coast of Africa is like the Arctic regions in one particular, and that is that when you have once visited it you want to go back there again; and, now I come to think of it, there is another particular in which it is like them, and that is that the chances you have of returning from it at all are small, for it is a Belle Dame sans merci.

I succumbed to the charm of the Coast as soon as I left Sierra Leone on my first voyage out, and I saw more than enough during that voyage to make me recognise that there was any amount of work for me worth doing down there. So I warned the Coast I was coming back again and the Coast did not believe me; and on my return to it a second time displayed a genuine surprise, and formed an even higher opinion of my folly than it had formed on our first acquaintance, which is saying a good deal.

During this voyage in 1893, I had been to Old Calabar, and its Governor, Sir Claude MacDonald, had heard me expatiating on the absorbing interest of the Antarctic drift, and the importance of the collection of fresh-water fishes and so on. So when Lady MacDonald heroically decided to go out to him in Calabar, they most kindly asked me if I would join her, and make my time fit hers for starting on my second journey. This I most willingly did. But I fear that very sweet and gracious lady suffered a great deal of apprehension at the prospect of spending a month on board ship with a person so devoted to science as to go down the West Coast in its pursuit. During the earlier days of our voyage she would attract my attention to all sorts of marine objects overboard, so as to amuse me. I used to look at them, and think it would be the death of me if I had to work like this, explaining meanwhile aloud that "they were very interesting, but Haeckel had done them, and I was out after fresh-water fishes from a river north of the Congo this time," fearing all the while that she felt me unenthusiastic for not flying over into the ocean to secure the specimens.

However, my scientific qualities, whatever they may amount to, did not blind this lady long to the fact of my being after all a very ordinary individual, and she told me so—not in these crude words, indeed, but nicely and kindly—whereupon, in a burst of gratitude to her for understanding me, I appointed myself her honorary aide-de-camp on the spot, and her sincere admirer I shall remain for ever, fully recognising that her courage in going to the Coast was far greater than my own, for she had more to lose had fever claimed her, and she was in those days by no means under the spell of Africa. But this is anticipating.

It was on the 23rd of December, 1894, that we left Liverpool in the Batanga, commanded by my old friend Captain Murray, under whose care I had made my first voyage. On the 30th we sighted the Peak of Teneriffe early in the afternoon. It displayed itself, as usual, as an entirely celestial phenomenon. A great many people miss seeing it. Suffering under the delusion that El Pico is a terrestrial affair, they look in vain somewhere about the level of their own eyes, which are striving to penetrate the dense masses of mist that usually enshroud its slopes by day, and then a friend comes along, and gaily points out to the newcomer the glittering white triangle somewhere near the zenith. On some days the Peak stands out clear from ocean to summit, looking every inch and more of its 12,080 ft.; and this is said by the Canary fishermen to be a certain sign of rain, or fine weather, or a gale of wind; but whenever and however it may be seen, soft and dream-like in the sunshine, or melodramatic and bizarre in the moonlight, it is one of the most beautiful things the eye of man may see.

Soon after sighting Teneriffe, Lançarote showed, and then the Grand Canary. Teneriffe is perhaps the most beautiful, but it is hard to judge between it and Grand Canary as seen from the sea. The superb cone this afternoon stood out a deep purple against a serpent-green sky, separated from the brilliant blue ocean by a girdle of pink and gold cumulus, while Grand Canary and Lançarote looked as if they were formed from fantastic-shaped sunset cloud-banks that by some spell had been solidified. The general colour of the mountains of Grand Canary, which rise peak after peak until they culminate in the Pico de las

Nieves, some 6,000 feet high, is a yellowish red, and the air which lies among their rocky crevices and swathes their softer sides is a lovely lustrous blue.

Just before the sudden dark came down, and when the sun was taking a curve out of the horizon of sea, all the clouds gathered round the three islands, leaving the sky a pure amethyst pink, and as a good-night to them the sun out-lined them with rims of shining gold, and made the snow-clad Peak of Teneriffe blaze with star-white light. In a few minutes came the dusk, and as we neared Grand Canary, out of its cloud-bank gleamed the red flash of the lighthouse on the Isleta, and in a few more minutes, along the sea level, sparkled the five miles of irregularly distributed lights of Puerto de la Luz and the city of Las Palmas.

We reached Sierra Leone at 9 A.M. on the 7th of January, and as the place is hardly so much in touch with the general public as the Canaries are {14} I may perhaps venture to go more into details regarding it. The harbour is formed by the long low strip of land to the north called the Bullam shore, and to the south by the peninsula terminating in Cape Sierra Leone, a sandy promontory at the end of which is situated a lighthouse of irregular habits. Low hills covered with tropical forest growth rise from the sandy shores of the Cape, and along its face are three creeks or bays, deep inlets showing through their narrow entrances smooth beaches of yellow sand, fenced inland by the forest of cotton-woods and palms, with here and there an elephantine baobab.

The first of these bays is called Pirate Bay, the next English Bay, and the third Kru Bay. The wooded hills of the Cape rise after passing Kru Bay, and become spurs of the mountain, 2,500 feet in height, which is the Sierra Leone itself. There are, however, several mountains here besides the Sierra Leone, the most conspicuous of them being the peak known as Sugar Loaf, and when seen from the sea they are very lovely, for their form is noble, and a wealth of tropical vegetation covers them, which, unbroken in its continuity, but endless in its variety, seems to sweep over their sides down to the shore like a sea, breaking here and there into a surf of flowers.

It is the general opinion, indeed, of those who ought to know that Sierra Leone appears at its best when seen from the sea, particularly when you are leaving the harbour homeward bound; and that here its charms, artistic, moral, and residential, end. But, from the experience I have gained of it, I have no hesitation in saying that it is one of the best places for getting luncheon in that I have ever happened on, and that a more pleasant and varied way of spending an afternoon than going about its capital, Free Town, with a certain Irish purser, who is as well known as he is respected among the leviathan old negro ladies, it would be hard to find. Still it must be admitted it is rather hot.

Free Town its capital is situated on the northern base of the mountain, and extends along the sea-front with most business-like wharves, quays, and warehouses. Viewed from the harbour, "The Liverpool of West Africa," {15} as it is called, looks as if it were built of gray stone, which it is not. When you get ashore, you will find that most of the stores and houses—the majority of which, it may be remarked, are in a state of acute dilapidation—are of painted wood, with corrugated iron roofs. Here and there, though, you will see a thatched house, its thatch covered with creeping plants, and inhabited by colonies of creeping insects.

Some of the stores and churches are, it is true, built of stone, but this does not look like stone at a distance, being red in colour—unhewn blocks of the red stone of the locality. In the crannies of these buildings trailing plants covered with pretty mauve or yellow flowers take root, and everywhere, along the tops of the walls, and in the cracks of the houses, are ferns and flowering plants. They must get a good deal of their nourishment from the rich, thick air, which seems composed of 85 per cent. of warm water, and the remainder of the odours of Frangipani, orange flowers, magnolias, oleanders, and roses, combined with others that demonstrate that the inhabitants do not regard sanitary matters with the smallest degree of interest.

There is one central street, and the others are neatly planned out at right angles to it. None of them are in any way paved or metalled. They are covered in much prettier fashion, and in a way more suitable for naked feet, by green Bahama grass, save and except those which are so nearly perpendicular that they have got every bit of earth and grass cleared off them down to the red bed-rock, by the heavy rain of the wet season.

In every direction natives are walking at a brisk pace, their naked feet making no sound on the springy turf of the streets, carrying on their heads huge burdens which are usually crowned by the hat of the bearer, a large limpet-shaped affair made of palm leaves. While some carry these enormous bundles, others bear logs or planks of wood, blocks of building stone, vessels containing palm-oil, baskets of vegetables, or tin tea-trays on which are folded shawls. As the great majority of the native inhabitants of Sierra Leone pay no attention whatever to where they are going, either in this world or the next, the confusion and noise are out of all proportion to the size of the town; and when, as frequently happens, a section of actively perambulating burden-bearers charge recklessly into a sedentary section, the members of which have dismounted their loads and squatted themselves down beside them, right in the middle of the fair way, to have a friendly yell with some acquaintances, the row becomes terrific.

In among these crowds of country people walk stately Mohammedans, Mandingoes, Akers, and Fulahs of the Arabised tribes of the Western Soudan. These are lithe, well-made men, and walk with a peculiarly fine, elastic carriage. Their graceful garb consists of a long white loose-sleeved shirt, over which they wear either a long black mohair or silk gown, or a deep bright blue affair, not altogether unlike a University gown, only with more stuff in it and more folds. They are undoubtedly the gentlemen of the Sierra Leone native population, and they are becoming an increasing faction in the town, by no means to the pleasure of the Christians.

But to the casual visitor at Sierra Leone the Mohammedan is a mere passing sensation. You neither feel a burning desire to laugh with, or at him, as in the case of the country folks, nor do you wish to punch his head, and split his coat up his back—things you yearn to do to that perfect flower of Sierra Leone culture, who yells your bald name across the street at you, condescendingly informs you that you can go and get letters that are waiting for you, while he smokes his cigar and lolls in the shade, or in some similar way displays his second-hand rubbishy white culture—a culture far lower and less dignified than that of either the stately Mandingo or the bush chief. I do not think that the Sierra Leone dandy really means half as much insolence as he shows; but the truth is he feels too insecure of his own real position, in spite of all the "side" he puts on, and so he dare not be courteous like the Mandingo or the bush Fan.

It is the costume of the people in Free Town and its harbour that will first attract the attention of the newcomer, notwithstanding the fact that the noise, the smell, and the heat are simultaneously making desperate bids for that favour. The ordinary man in the street wears anything he may have been able to acquire, anyhow, and he does not fasten it on securely. I fancy it must be capillary attraction, or some other partially-understood force, that takes part in the matter. It is certainly neither braces nor buttons. There are, of course, some articles which from their very structure are fairly secure, such as an umbrella with the stick and ribs removed, or a shirt. This last-mentioned treasure, which usually becomes the property of the ordinary man from a female relative or admirer taking in white men's washing, is always worn flowing free, and has such a charm in itself that the happy possessor cares little what he continues his costume with—trousers, loin cloth, red flannel petticoat, or rice-bag drawers, being, as he would put it, "all same for one" to him.

The ladies are divided into three classes; the young girl you address as "tee-tee"; the young person as "seester"; the more mature charmer as "mammy"; but I do not advise you to employ these terms when you are on your first visit, because you might get misunderstood. For, you see, by addressing a mammy as seester, she might think either that you were unconscious of her dignity as a married lady—a matter she would soon put you right on—or that you were flirting, which of course was totally foreign to your intention, and would make you uncomfortable. My advice is that you rigidly stick to missus or mammy. I have seen this done most successfully.

The ladies are almost as varied in their costume as the gentlemen, but always neater and cleaner; and mighty picturesque they are too, and occasionally very pretty. A market-woman with her jolly brown face and laughing brown eyes—eyes all the softer for a touch of antimony—her ample form clothed in a lively print overall, made with a yoke at the shoulders, and a full long flounce which is gathered on to the yoke under the arms and falls fully to the feet; with her head done up in a yellow or red handkerchief, and her snowy white teeth gleaming through her vast smiles, is a mighty pleasant thing to see, and to talk to. But, Allah! the circumference of them!

The stone-built, white-washed market buildings of Free Town have a creditably clean and tidy appearance considering the climate, and the quantity and variety of things exposed for sale—things one wants the pen of a Rabelais to catalogue. Here are all manner of fruits, some which are familiar to you in England; others that soon become so to you in Africa. You take them as a matter of course if you are outward bound, but on your call homeward (if you make it) you will look on them as a blessing and a curiosity. For lower down, particularly in "the Rivers," these things are rarely to be had, and never in such perfection as here; and to see again lettuces, yellow oranges, and tomatoes bigger than marbles is a sensation and a joy.

One of the chief features of Free Town are the jack crows. Some writers say they are peculiar to Sierra Leone, others that they are not, but both unite in calling them Picathartes gymnocephalus. To the white people who live in daily contact with them they are turkey buzzards; to the natives, Yubu. Anyhow they are evil-looking fowl, and no ornament to the roof-ridges they choose to sit on. The native Christians ought to put a row of spikes along the top of their cathedral to keep them off; the beauty of that edifice is very far from great, and it cannot carry off the effect produced by the row of these noisome birds as they sit along its summit, with their wings arranged at all manner of different angles in an "all gone" way. One bird perhaps will have one straight out in front, and the other casually disposed at right-angles, another both straight out in front, and others again with both hanging hopelessly down, but none with them neatly and tidily folded up, as decent birds' wings should be. They all give the impression of having been extremely drunk the previous evening, and of having subsequently fallen into some sticky abomination—into blood for choice. Being the scavengers of Free Town, however, they are respected by the local authorities and preserved; and the natives tell me you never see either a young or a dead one. The latter is a thing you would not expect, for half of them look as if they could not live through the afternoon. They also told me that when you got close to them, they had a "'trong, 'trong 'niff; 'niff too much." I did not try, but I am quite willing to believe this statement.

The other animals most in evidence in the streets are, first and foremost, goats and sheep. I have to lump them together, for it is exceedingly difficult to tell one from the other. All along the Coast the empirical rule is that sheep carry their tails down, and goats carry their tails up; fortunately you need not worry much anyway, for they both "taste rather like the nothing that the world was made of," as Frau Buchholtz says, and own in addition a fibrous texture, and a certain twang. Small cinnamon-coloured cattle are to be got here, but horses there are practically none. Now and again some one who does not see why a horse should not live here as well as at Accra or Lagos imports one, but it always shortly dies. Some say it is because the natives who get their living by hammock-carrying poison them, others say the tsetse fly finishes them off; and others, and these I believe are right, say that entozoa are the cause. Small, lean, lank yellow dogs with very erect ears lead an awful existence, afflicted by many things, but beyond all others by the goats, who, rearing their families in the grassy streets, choose to think the dogs intend attacking them. Last, but not least, there is the pig—a rich source of practice to the local lawyer.

Cape Coast Castle and then Accra were the next places of general interest at which we stopped. The former looks well from the roadstead, and as if it had very recently been white-washed. It is surrounded by low, heavily-forested hills, which rise almost from the seashore, and the fine mass of its old castle does not display its dilapidation at a distance. Moreover, the three stone forts of Victoria, William, and Macarthy, situated on separate hills commanding the town, add to the general appearance of permanent substantialness so different from the usual ramshackledom of West Coast settlements. Even when you go ashore and have had time to recover your senses, scattered by the surf experience, you find this substantialness a true one, not a mere visual delusion produced by painted wood as the seeming substantialness of Sierra Leone turns out to be when you get to close quarters with it. It causes one some mental effort to grasp the fact that Cape Coast has been in European hands for centuries, but it requires a most unmodern power of credence to realise this of any other settlement on the whole western seaboard until you have the pleasure of seeing the beautiful city of San Paul de Loanda, far away down south, past the Congo.

My experience of Cape Coast on this occasion was one of the hottest, but one of the pleasantest I have ever been through on the Gold Coast. The former attribute was due to the climate, the latter to my kind friends, Mr. Batty, and Mr. and Mrs. Dennis Kemp. I was taken round the grand stone-built houses with their high stone-walled yards and sculpture-decorated gateways, built by the merchants of the last century and of the century before, and through the great rambling stone castle with its water-tanks cut in the solid rock beneath it, and its commodious accommodation for slaves awaiting shipment, now almost as obsolete as the guns it mounts, but not quite so, for these cool and roomy chambers serve to house the native constabulary and their extensive families.

This being done, I was taken up an unmitigated hill, on whose summit stands Fort William, a pepper-pot-like structure now used as a lighthouse. The view from the top was exceedingly lovely and extensive. Beneath, and between us and the sea, lay the town in the blazing sun. In among its solid stone build-ings patches of native mud-built huts huddled together as though they had been shaken down out of a sack into the town to serve as dunnage. Then came the snow-white surf wall, and across it the blue sea with our steamer rolling to and fro on the long, regular swell, impatiently waiting until Sunday should be over and she could work cargo. Round us on all the other sides were wooded hills and valleys, and away in the distance to the west showed the white town and castle of Elmina and the nine-mile road thither, skirting the surf-bound seashore, only broken on its level way by the mouth of the Sweet River. Over all was the brooding silence of the noonday heat, broken only by the dulled thunder of the surf.

After seeing these things we started down stairs, and on reaching ground descended yet lower into a sort of stone-walled dry moat, out of which opened clean, cool, cellar-like chambers tunnelled into the earth. These, I was informed, had also been constructed to keep slaves in when they were the staple export of the Gold Coast. They were so refreshingly cool that I lingered looking at them and their massive doors, ere being marched up to ground level again, and down the hill through some singularly awful stenches, mostly arising from rubber, into the big Wesleyan church in the middle of the town. It is a building in the terrible Africo-Gothic style, but it compares most favourably with the cathedral at Sierra Leone, particularly internally, wherein, indeed, it far surpasses that structure. And then we returned to the Mission House and spent a very pleas-ant evening, save for the knowledge (which amounted in me to remorse) that, had it not been for my edification, not one of my friends would have spent the day toiling about the town they know only too well. The Wesleyan Mission on the Gold Coast, of which Mr. Dennis Kemp was at that time chairman, is the largest and most influential Protestant mission on the West Coast of Africa, and it is now, I am glad to say, adding a technical department to its scholastic and religious one. The Basel Mission has done a great deal of good work in giving technical instruction to the natives, and practically started this most important branch of their education. There is still an almost infinite amount of this work to be done, the African being so strangely deficient in mechanical culture; in-finitely more so, indeed, in this than in any other particular.

After leaving Cape Coast our next port was Accra which is one of the five West Coast towns that look well from the sea. The others don't look well from anywhere. First in order of beauty comes San Paul de Loanda; then Cape Coast with its satellite Elmina, then Gaboon, then Accra with its satellite Christiansborg, and lastly, Sierra Leone.

What there is of beauty in Accra is oriental in type. Seen from the sea, Fort St. James on the left and Christiansborg Castle on the right, both almost on shore level, give, with an outcrop of sandy dwarf cliffs, a certain air of balance and strength to the town, though but for these and the two old castles, Accra would be but a poor place and a flimsy, for the rest of it is a mass of rubbishy mud and palm-leaf huts, and corrugated iron dwellings for the Europeans.

Corrugated iron is my abomination. I quite understand it has points, and I do not attack from an æsthetic standpoint. It really looks well enough when it is painted white. There is, close to Christiansborg Castle, a patch of bungalows and offices for officialdom and wife that from a distance in the hard bright sunshine looks like an encampment of snow-white tents among the coco palms, and pretty enough withal. I am also aware that the corrugated-iron roof is an advantage in enabling you to collect and store rain-water, which is the safest kind of water you can get on the Coast, always supposing you have not painted the aforesaid roof with red oxide an hour or two before so collecting, as a friend of mine did once. But the heat inside those iron houses is far greater than inside mud-walled, brick, or wooden ones, and the alternations of temperature more sudden: mornings and evenings they are cold and clammy; draughty they are always, thereby giving you chill which means fever, and fever in West Africa means more than it does in most places.

Going on shore at Accra with Lady MacDonald gave me opportunities and advantages I should not otherwise have enjoyed, such as the hospitality of the Governor, luxurious transport from the landing place to Christiansborg Castle, a thorough inspection of the cathedral in course of erection, and the strange and highly interesting function of going to a tea-party at a police station to meet a king,—a real reigning king,—who kindly attended with his suite and displayed an intelligent interest in photographs. Tackie (that is His Majesty's name) is an old, spare man, with a subdued manner. His sovereign rights are acknowledged by the Government so far as to hold him more or less responsible for any iniquity committed by his people; and as the Government do not allow him to execute or flagellate the said people, earthly pomp is rather a hollow thing to Tackie.

On landing I was taken in charge by an Assistant Inspector of Police, and after a scrimmage for my chief's baggage and my own, which reminded me of a long ago landing on the distant island of Guernsey, the inspector and I got into a 'rickshaw, locally called a go-cart. It was pulled in front by two government negroes and pushed behind by another pair, all neatly attired in white jackets and knee breeches, and crimson cummerbunds yards long, bound round their middles. Now it is an ingrained characteristic of the uneducated negro, that he cannot keep on a neat and complete garment of any kind. It does not matter what that garment may be; so long as it is whole, off it comes. But as soon as that garment becomes a series of holes, held together by filaments of rag, he keeps it upon him in a manner that is marvellous, and you need have no further anxiety on its behalf. Therefore it was but natural that the governmental cummerbunds, being new, should come off their wearers several times in the course of our two mile trip, and as they wound riskily round the legs of their running wearers, we had to make halts while one end of the cummerbund was affixed to a tree-trunk and the other end to the man, who rapidly wound himself up in it again with a skill that spoke of constant practice.

The road to Christiansborg from Accra, which runs parallel to the sea and is broad and well-kept, is in places pleasantly shaded with pepper trees, eucalyptus, and palms. The first part of it, which forms the main street of Accra, is remarkable. The untidy, poverty-stricken native houses or huts are no credit to their owners, and a constant source of anxiety to a conscientious sanitary inspector. Almost every one of them is a shop, but this does not give rise to the animated commercial life one might imagine, owing, I presume, to the fact that every native inhabitant of Accra who has any money to get rid of is able recklessly to spend it in his own emporium. For these shops are of the store nature, each after his kind, and seem homogeneously stocked with tin pans, loud-patterned basins, iron pots, a few rolls of cloth and bottles of American rum. After passing these there are the Haussa lines, a few European houses, and the cathedral; and when nearly into Christiansborg, a cemetery on either side of the road. That to the right is the old cemetery, now closed, and when I was there, in a disgracefully neglected state: a mere jungle of grass infested with snakes. Opposite to it is the cemetery now in use, and I remember well my first visit to it under the guidance of a gloomy Government official, who said he always walked there every afternoon, "so as to get used to the place before staying permanently in it,"—a rank waste of time and energy, by the way, as subsequent events proved, for he is now safe off the Gold Coast for good and all.

He took me across the well-kept grass to two newly dug graves, each covered with wooden hoods in a most business-like way. Evidently those hoods were regular parts of the cemetery's outfit. He said nothing, but waved his hand with a "take-your-choice,-they-are-both-quite-ready" style. "Why?" I queried laconically. "Oh! we always keep two graves ready dug for Europeans. We have to bury very quickly here, you know," he answered. I turned at bay. I had had already a very heavy dose of details of this sort that afternoon and was disinclined to believe another thing. So I said, "It's exceedingly wrong to do a thing like that, you only frighten people to death. You can't want new-dug graves daily. There are not enough white men in the whole place to keep the institution up." "We do," he replied, "at any rate at this season. Why, the other day we had two white men to bury before twelve o'clock, and at four, another dropped in on a steamer."

"At 4.30," said a companion, an exceedingly accurate member of the staff. "How you fellows do exaggerate!" Subsequent knowledge of the Gold Coast has convinced me fully that the extra funeral being placed half-an-hour sooner than it occurred is the usual percentage of exaggeration you will be able to find in stories relating to the local mortality. And at Accra, after I left it, and all along the Gold Coast, came one of those dreadful epidemic outbursts sweeping away more than half the white population in a few weeks.

But to return to our state journey along the Christiansborg road. We soon reached the castle, an exceedingly roomy and solid edifice built by the Danes, and far better fitted for the climate than our modern dwellings, in spite of our supposed advance in tropical hygiene. We entered by the sentry-guarded great gate into the courtyard; on the right hand were the rest of the guard; most of them asleep on their mats, but a few busy saying Dhikr, etc., towards Mecca, like the good Mohammedans these Haussas are, others winding themselves into their cummerbunds. On the left hand was Sir Brandford Griffiths' hobby—a choice and select little garden, of lovely eucharis lilies mostly in tubs, and rare and beautiful flowers brought by him from his Barbadian home; while shading it and the courtyard was a fine specimen of that superb thing of beauty—a flamboyant tree—glorious with its delicate-green acacia-like leaves and vermilion and yellow flowers, and astonishing with its vast beans. A flight of stone stairs leads from the courtyard to the upper part of the castle where the living rooms are, over the extensive series of cool tunnel-like slave barracoons, now used as store chambers. The upper rooms are high and large, and full of a soft pleasant light and the thunder of the everlasting surf breaking on the rocky spit on which the castle is built.

From the day the castle was built, now more than a hundred years ago, the surf spray has been swept by the on-shore evening breeze into every chink and cranny of the whole building, and hence the place is mouldy—mouldy to an extent I, with all my experience in that paradise for mould, West Africa, have never elsewhere seen. The matting on the floors took an impression of your foot as a light snowfall would. Beneath articles of furniture the cryptogams attained a size more in keeping with the coal period than with the nineteenth century.

The Gold Coast is one of the few places in West Africa that I have never felt it my solemn duty to go and fish in. I really cannot say why. Seen from the sea it is a pleasant looking land. The long lines of yellow, sandy beach backed by an almost continuous line of blue hills, which in some places come close to the beach, in other places show in the dim distance. It is hard to think that it is so unhealthy as it is, from just seeing it as you pass by. It has high land and has not those great masses of mangrove-swamp one usually, at first, associates with a bad fever district, but which prove on acquaintance to be at any rate no worse than this well-elevated open-forested Gold Coast land. There are many things to be had here and in Lagos which tend to make life more tolerable, that you cannot have elsewhere until you are south of the Congo. Horses, for example, do fairly well at Accra, though some twelve miles or so behind the town there is a belt of tsetse fly, specimens of which I have procured and had identified at the British Museum, and it is certain death to a horse, I am told, to take it to Aburi.

The food-supply, although bad and dear, is superior to that you get down south. Goats and sheep are fairly plentiful. In addition to fresh meat and tinned you are able to get a quantity of good sea fish, for the great West African Bank, which fringes the coast in the Bight of Benin, abounds in fish, although the native cook very rarely knows how to cook them. Then, too, you can get more fruit and vegetables on the Gold Coast than at most places lower down: the plantain, {28} not least among them and very good when allowed to become ripe, and then cut into longitudinal strips, and properly fried; the banana, which surpasses it when served in the same manner, or beaten up and mixed with rice, butter, and eggs, and baked. Eggs, by the way, according to the great mass of native testimony, are laid in this country in a state that makes them more fit for electioneering than culinary purposes, and I shall never forget one tribe I was once among, who, whenever I sat down on one of their benches, used to smash eggs round me for ju-ju. They meant well. But I will nobly resist the temptation to tell egg stories and industriously catalogue the sour-sop, guava, grenadilla, aubergine or garden-egg, yam, and sweet potato.

The sweet potato should be boiled, and then buttered and browned in an oven, or fried. When cooked in either way I am devoted to them, but in the way I most frequently come across them I abominate them, for they jeopardise my existence both in this world and the next. It is this way: you are coming home from a long and dangerous beetle-hunt in the forest; you have battled with mighty beetles the size of pie dishes, they have flown at your head, got into your hair and then nipped you smartly. You have been also considerably stung and bitten by flies, ants, etc., and are most likely sopping wet with rain, or with the wading of streams, and you are tired and your feet go low along the ground, and it is getting, or has got, dark with that ever-deluding tropical rapidity, and then you for your sins get into a piece of ground which last year was a native's farm, and, placing one foot under the tough vine of a surviving sweet potato, concealed by rank herbage, you plant your other foot on another portion of the same vine. Your head you then deposit promptly in some prickly ground crop, or against a tree stump, and then, if there is human blood in you, you say d--n!

Then there are also alligator-pears, limes, and oranges. There is something about those oranges I should like to have explained. They are usually green and sweetish in taste, nor have they much white pith, but now and again you get a big bright yellow one from those trees that have been imported, and these are very pithy and in full possession of the flavour of verjuice. They have also got the papaw on the Coast, the Carica papaya of botanists. It is an insipid fruit. To the newcomer it is a dreadful nuisance, for no sooner does an old coaster set eyes on it than he straightway says, "Paw-paws are awfully good for the digestion, and even if you just hang a tough fowl or a bit of goat in the tree among the leaves, it gets tender in no time, for there is an awful lot of pepsine in a paw-paw,"—which there is not, papaine being its active principle. After hearing this hymn of praise to the papaw some hundreds of times, it palls, and you usually arrive at this tired feeling about the thing by the time you reach the Gold Coast, for it is a most common object, and the same man will say the same thing about it a dozen times a day if he gets the chance. I got heartily sick of it on my first voyage out, and rashly determined to check the old coaster in this habit of his, preparatory to stamping the practice out. It was one of my many failures. I soon met an old coaster with a papaw fruit in sight, and before he had time to start, I boldly got away with "The paw-paw is awfully good for the digestion," hoping that this display of knowledge would impress him and exempt me from hearing the rest of the formula. But no. "Right you are," said he solemnly. "It's a powerful thing is the paw-paw. Why, the other day we had a sad case along here. You know what a nuisance young assistants are, bothering about their chop, and scorpions in their beds and boots, and what not and a half, and then, when you have pulled them through these, and often enough before, pegging out with fever, or going on the fly in the native town. Did you know poor B---? Well! he's dead now, had fever and went off like a babe in eight hours though he'd been out fourteen years for A--- and D---. They sent him out a new book-keeper, a tender young thing with a dairymaid complexion and the notion that he'd got the indigestion. He fidgeted about it something awful. One night there was a big paw-paw on the table for evening chop, and so B---, who was an awfully good chap, told him about how good it was for the digestion. The book-keeper said his trouble always came on two hours after eating, and asked if he might take a bit of the thing to his room. 'Certainly,' says B---, and as the paw-paw wasn't cut at that meal the book-keeper quietly took it off whole with him.

"In the morning time he did not turn up. B---, just before breakfast, went to his room and he wasn't there, but he noticed the paw-paw was on the bed and that was all, so he thought the book-keeper must have gone for a walk, being, as it were, a bit too tender to have gone on the fly as yet. So he just told the store clerk to tell the people to return him to the firm when they found him straying around lost, and thought no more about it, being, as it was, mail-day, and him busy.

"Well! Fortunately the steward boy put that paw-paw on the table again for twelve o'clock chop. If it hadn't been for that, not a living soul would have known the going of the book-keeper. For when B--- cut it open, there, right inside it, were nine steel trouser-buttons, a Waterbury watch, and the poor young fellow's keys. For you see, instead of his digesting his dinner with that paw-paw, the paw-paw took charge and digested him, dinner and all, and when B--- interrupted it, it was just getting a grip on the steel things. There's an awful lot of pepsine in a paw-paw, and if you hang, etc., etc."

I collapsed, feebly murmuring that it was very interesting, but sad for the poor young fellow's friends.

"Not necessarily," said the old coaster. So he had the last word, and never again will I attempt to alter the ways of the genuine old coaster. What you have got to do with him is to be very thankful you have had the honour of knowing him.

Still I think we do over-estimate the value of the papaw, although I certainly did once myself hang the leg of a goat no mortal man could have got tooth into, on to a papaw tree with a bit of string for the night. In the morning it was clean gone, string and all; but whether it was the pepsine, the papaine, or a purloining pagan that was the cause of its departure there was no evidence to show. Yet I am myself, as Hans Breitmann says, "still skebdigal" as to the papaw, and I dare say you are too.

But I must forthwith stop writing about the Gold Coast, or I shall go on telling you stories and wasting your time, not to mention the danger of letting out those which would damage the nerves of the cultured of temperate climes, such as those relating to the youth who taught himself French from a six months' method book; of the man who wore brass buttons; the moving story of three leeches and two gentlemen; the doctor up a creek; and the reason why you should not eat pork along here because all the natives have either got the guinea-worm, or kraw-kraw or ulcers; and then the pigs go and—dear me! it was a near thing that time. I'll leave off at once.

CHAPTER II

FERNANDO PO AND THE BUBIS

GIVING SOME ACCOUNT OF THE OCCUPATION OF THIS ISLAND BY THE WHITES AND THE MANNERS AND CUSTOMS OF THE BLACKS PECULIAR TO IT.

OUR OUTWARD VOYAGE REALLY TERMINATED AT CALABAR, and it terminated gorgeously in fireworks and what not, in honour of the coming of Lady MacDonald, the whole settlement, white and black, turning out to do her honour to the best of its ability; and its ability in this direction was far greater than, from my previous knowledge of Coast conditions, I could have imagined possible. Before Sir Claude MacDonald settled down again to local work, he and Lady MacDonald crossed to Fernando Po, still in the Batanga, and I accompanied them, thus getting an opportunity of seeing something of Spanish official circles.

I had heard sundry noble legends of Fernando Po, and seen the coast and a good deal of the island before, but although I had heard much of the Governor, I had never met him until I went up to his residence with Lady MacDonald and the Consul-General. He was a delightful person, who, as a Spanish naval officer, some time resident in Cuba, had picked up a lot of English, with a strong American accent clinging to it. He gave a most moving account of how, as soon as his appointment as Governor was announced, all his friends and acquaintances carefully explained to him that this appointment was equivalent to execution, only more uncomfortable in the way it worked out. During the outward voyage this was daily confirmed by the stories told by the sailors and merchants personally acquainted with the place, who were able to support their information with dates and details of the decease of the victims to the climate.

Still he kept up a good heart, but when he arrived at the island he found his predecessor had died of fever; and he himself, the day after landing, went down with a bad attack and he was placed in a bed—the same bed, he was mournfully informed, in which the last Governor had expired. Then he did believe, all in one awful lump, all the stories he had been told, and added to their horrors a few original conceptions of death and purgatory, and a lot of transparent semi-formed images of his own delirium. Fortunately both prophecy and personal conviction alike miscarried, and the Governor returned from the jaws of death. But without a moment's delay he withdrew from the Port of Clarence and went up the mountain to Basile, which is in the neighbourhood of the highest native village, where he built himself a house, and around it a little village of homes for the most unfortunate set of human beings I have ever laid eye on. They are the remnant of a set of Spanish colonists, who had been located at some spot in the Spanish possessions in Morocco, and finding that place unfit to support human life, petitioned the Government to remove them and let them try colonising elsewhere.

The Spanish Government just then had one of its occasional fits of interest in Fernando Po, and so shipped them here, and the Governor, a most kindly and generous man, who would have been a credit to any country, established them and their families around him at Basile, to share with him the advantages of the superior elevation; advantages he profoundly believed in, and which he has always placed at the disposal of any sick white man on the island, of whatsoever nationality or religion. Undoubtedly the fever is not so severe at Basile as in the lowlands, but there are here the usual drawbacks to West African high land, namely an over supply of rain, and equally saturating mists, to say nothing of sudden and extreme alternations of temperature, and so the colonists still fall off, and their children die continuously from the various entozoa which abound upon the island.

When the Governor first settled upon the mountain he was very difficult to get at for business purposes, and a telephone was therefore run up to him from Clarence through the forest, and Spain at large felt proud at this dashing bit of enterprise in modern appliance. Alas! the primæval forests of Fernando Po were also charmed with the new toy, and they talked to each other on it with their leaves and branches to such an extent that a human being could not get a word in edgeways. So the Governor had to order the construction of a road along the course of the wire to keep the trees off it, but unfortunately the telephone is still an uncertain means of communication, because another interruption in its usefulness still afflicts it, namely the indigenous natives' habit of stealing bits out of its wire, for they are fully persuaded that they cannot be found out in their depredations provided they take sufficient care that they are not caught in the act. The Governor is thus liable to be cut off at any moment in the middle of a conversation with Clarence, and the amount of "Hellos" "Are you theres?" and "Speak louder, pleases" in Spanish that must at such times be poured out and wasted in the lonely forests before the break is realised and an unfortunate man sent off as a messenger, is terrible to think of.

But nothing would persuade the Governor to come a mile down towards Clarence until the day he should go there to join the vessel that was to take him home, and I am bound to say he looked as if the method was a sound one, for he was an exceedingly healthy, cheery-looking man.

Fernando Po is said to be a comparatively modern island, and not so very long ago to have been connected with the mainland, the strait between them being only nineteen miles across, and not having any deep soundings. {37} I fail to see what grounds there are for these ideas, for though Fernando Po's volcanoes are not yet extinct, but merely have their fires banked, yet, on the other hand, the island has been in existence sufficiently long to get itself several peculiar species of animals and plants, and that is a thing which takes time. I myself do not believe that this island was ever connected with the continent, but arose from the ocean as the result of a terrific upheaval in the chain of volcanic activity which runs across the Atlantic from the Cameroon Mountains in a SSW. direction to Anno Bom island, and possibly even to the Tristan da Cunha group midway between the Cape and South America.

These volcanic islands are all of extreme beauty and fertility. They consist of Fernando Po (10,190 ft.); Principe (3000 ft.); San Thomé (6,913 ft.); and Anno Bom (1,350 ft.). San Thomé and Principe are Portuguese possessions, Fernando Po and Anno Bom Spanish, and they are all exceedingly unhealthy. San Thomé is still called "The Dutchman's Church-yard," on account of the devastation its climate wrought among the Hollanders when they once occupied it; as they seem, at one time or another, to have occupied all Portuguese possessions out here, during the long war these two powers waged with each other for supremacy in the Bights, a supremacy that neither of them attained to. Principe is said to be the most unhealthy, and the reason of the difference in this particular between Principe and Anno Bom is said to arise from the fact that the former is on the Guinea Current—a hot current—and Anno Bom on the Equatorial, which averages 10° cooler than its neighbour.

The shores of San Thomé are washed by both currents, and the currents round Fernando Po are in a mixed and uncertain state. It is difficult, unless you have haunted these seas, to realise the interest we take down there in currents; particularly when you are navigating small sailing boats, a pursuit I indulge in necessarily from my fishing practices. Their effect on the climate too is very marked. If we could only arrange for some terrific affair to take place in the bed of the Atlantic, that would send that precious Guinea current to the place it evidently comes from, and get the cool Equatorial alongside the mainland shore, West Africa would be quite another place.

Fernando Po is the most important island as regards size on the West African coast, and at the same time one of the most beautiful in the world. It is a great volcanic mass with many craters, and culminates in the magnificent cone, Clarence Peak, called by the Spaniards, Pico de Santa Isabel, by the natives of the island O Wassa. Seen from the sea or from the continent it looks like an immense single mountain that has floated out to sea. It is visible during clear weather (and particularly sharply visible in the strange clearness you get after a tornado) from a hundred miles to seawards, and anything more perfect than Fernando Po when you sight it, as you occasionally do from far-away Bonny Bar, in the sunset, floating like a fairy island made of gold or of amethyst, I cannot conceive. It is almost equally lovely at close quarters, namely from the mainland at Victoria, nineteen miles distant. Its moods of beauty are infinite; for the most part gentle and gorgeous, but I have seen it silhouetted hard against tornado-clouds, and grandly grim from the upper regions of its great brother Mungo. And as for Fernando Po in full moonlight—well there! you had better go and see it yourself.

The whole island is, or rather I should say was, heavily forested almost to its peak, with a grand and varied type of forest, very rich in oil palms and tree-ferns, and having an undergrowth containing an immense variety and quantity of ferns and mosses. Sugar-cane also grows wild here, an uncommon thing in West Africa. The last botanical collection of any importance made from these forests was that of Herr Mann, and its examination showed that Abyssinian genera and species predominated, and that many species similar to those found in the mountains of Mauritius, the Isle de Bourbon, and Madagascar, were present. The number of European plants (forty-three genera, twenty-seven species) is strikingly large, most of the British forms being represented chiefly at the higher elevations. What was more striking was that it showed that South African forms were extremely rare, and not one of the characteristic types of St. Helena occurred.

Cocoa, coffee, and cinchona, alas! flourish in Fernando Po, as the coffee suffers but little from the disease that harasses it on the mainland at Victoria, and this is the cause of the great destruction of the forest that is at present taking place. San Thomé, a few years ago, was discovered by its surprised neighbours to be amassing great wealth by growing coffee, and so Fernando Po and Principe immediately started to amass great wealth too, and are now hard at work with gangs of miscellaneous natives got from all parts of the Coast save the Kru. For to the Kruboy, "Panier," as he calls "Spaniard," is a name of horror worse even than Portugee, although he holds "God made white man and God made black man, but dem debil make Portugee," and he also remembers an unfortunate affair that occurred some years ago now, in connection with coffee-growing.

A number of Krumen engaged themselves for a two years' term of labour on the Island of San Thomé, and when they arrived there, were set to work on coffee plantations by the Portuguese. Now agricultural work is "woman's palaver," but nevertheless the Krumen made shift to get through with it, vowing the while no doubt, as they hopefully notched away the moons on their tally-sticks, that they would never let the girls at home know that they had been hoeing. But when their moons were all complete, instead of being sent home with their pay to "We country," they were put off from time to time; and month after month went by and they were still on San Thomé, and still hoeing. At last the home-sick men, in despair of ever getting free, started off secretly in ones and twos to try and get to "We country" across hundreds of miles of the storm-haunted Atlantic in small canoes, and with next to no provisions. The result was a tragedy, but it might easily have been worse; for a few, a very few, were picked up alive by English vessels and taken back to their beloved "We country" to tell the tale. But many a canoe was found with a dead Kruboy or so in it; and many a one which, floating bottom upwards, graphically spoke of madness caused by hunger, thirst, and despair having driven its occupants overboard to the sharks.

My Portuguese friends assure me that there was never thought of permanently detaining the boys, and that they were only just keeping them until other labourers arrived to take their place on the plantations. I quite believe them, for I have seen too much of the Portuguese in Africa to believe that they would, in a wholesale way, be cruel to natives. But I am not in the least surprised that the poor Krumen took the Portuguese logo and amanhã for Eternity itself, for I have frequently done so.

The greatest length of the island lies N.E. and S.W., and amounts to thirty-three miles; the mean breadth is seventeen miles. The port, Clarence Cove, now called Santa Isabel by the Spaniards—who have been giving Spanish names to all the English-named places without any one taking much notice of them— is a very remarkable place, and except perhaps Gaboon the finest harbour on the West Coast. The point that brings Gaboon anchorage up in line with Clarence Cove is its superior healthiness; for Clarence is a section of a circle, and its shores are steep rocky cliffs from 100 to 200 feet high, and the place, to put it very mildly, exceedingly hot and stuffy. The cove is evidently a partly submerged crater, the submerged rim of the crater is almost a perfect semi-circle seawards—having on it 4, 5, 7, 8, and 10 fathoms of water save almost in the centre of the arc where there is a passage with 12 to 14 fathoms. Inside, in the crater, there is deeper water, running in places from 30 to 45 fathoms, and outside the submerged rim there is deeper water again, but rocky shoals abound. On the top of the shore cliffs stands the dilapidated little town of Clarence, on a plateau that falls away slightly towards the mountain for about a mile, when the ground commences to rise into the slopes of the Cordillera. On the narrow beach, tucked close against the cliffs, are a few stores belonging to the merchants, where goods are placed on landing, and there is a little pier too, but as it is usually having something done to its head, or else is closed by the authorities because they intend doing something by and by, the chances are against its being available for use. Hence it usually comes about that you have to land on the beach, and when you have done this you make your way up a very steep path, cut in the cliffside, to the town. When you get there you find yourself in the very dullest town I know on the Coast. I remember when I first landed in Clarence I found its society in a flutter of expectation and alarm not untinged with horror. Clarence, nay, the whole of Fernando Po, was about to become so rackety and dissipated as to put Paris and Monte Carlo to the blush. Clarence was going to have a café; and what was going to go on in that café I shrink from reciting.

I have little hesitation now in saying this alarm was a false one. When I next arrived in Clarence it was just as sound asleep and its streets as weed-grown as ever, although the café was open. My idea is that the sleepiness of the place infected the café and took all the go out of it. But again it may have been that the inhabitants were too well guarded against its evil influence, for there are on the island fifty-two white laymen, and fifty-four priests to take charge of them {44} - the extra two being, I presume, to look after the Governor's conduct, although this worthy man made a most spirited protest against this view when I suggested it to him; and in addition to the priests there are several missionaries of the Methodist mission, and also a white gentleman who has invented a new religion. Anyhow, the café smoulders like a damp squib.

When you spend the day on shore and when, having exhausted the charms of the town,—a thing that usually takes from between ten minutes to a quarter of an hour,—you apply to an inhabitant for advice as to the disposal of the rest of your shore leave, you are told to "go and see the coals." You say you have not come to tropical islands to see a coal heap, and applying elsewhere for advice you probably get the same. So, as you were told to "go and see the coals" when you left your ship, you do as you are bid. These coals, the remnant of the store that was kept here for the English men-of-war, were left here when the naval station was removed. The Spaniards at first thought of using them, and ran a tram-way from Clarence to them. But when the tramway was finished, their activity had run out too, and to this day there the coals remain. Now and again some one has the idea that they are quite good, and can be used for a steamer, and some people who have tried them say they are all right, and others say they are all wrong. And so the end of it will be that some few thousand years hence there will be a serious quarrel among geologists on the strange pocket of coal on Fernando Po, and they will run up continents, and raise and lower oceans to explain them, and they will doubtless get more excitement and pleasure out of them than you can nowadays.

The history of the English occupation of Fernando Po seems often misunderstood, and now and then one hears our Government reviled for handing it over to the Spaniards. But this was unavoidable, for we had it as a loan from Spain in 1827 as a naval station for our ships, at that time energetically commencing to suppress the slave trade in the Bights; the idea being that this island would afford a more healthy and convenient spot for a naval depot than any port on the coast itself.

More convenient Fernando Po certainly was, but not more healthy, and ever since 1827 it has been accumulating for itself an evil reputation for unhealthiness which is only languishing just at present because there is an interval between its epidemics—fever in Fernando Po, even more than on the mainland, having periodic outbursts of a more serious type than the normal intermittent and remittent of the Coast. Moreover, Fernando Po shares with Senegal the undoubted yet doubtful honour of having had regular yellow fever. In 1862 and 1866 this disease was imported by a ship that had come from Havana. Since then it has not appeared in the definite South American form, and therefore does not seem to have obtained the foothold it has in Senegal, where a few years ago all the money voted for the keeping of the Fête Nationale was in one district devoted by public consent to the purchase of coffins, required by an overwhelming outbreak of Yellow Jack.

In 1858 the Spanish Government thinking, presumably, that the slave trade was suppressed enough, or at any rate to a sufficiently inconvenient extent, re-claimed Fernando Po, to the horror of the Baptist missionaries who had settled in Clarence apparently under the erroneous idea that the island had been definitely taken over by the English. This mission had received from the West African Company a large grant of land, and had collected round it a gathering of Sierra Leonians and other artisan and trading Africans who were attracted to Clarence by the work made by the naval station; and these people, with the English traders who also settled here for a like reason, were the founders of Clarence Town. The declaration of the Spanish Government stating that only Roman Catholic missions would be countenanced caused the Baptists to abandon their possessions and withdraw to the mainland in Ambas Bay, where they have since remained, and nowadays Protestantism is represented by a Methodist Mission which has a sub-branch on the mainland on the Akwayafe River and one on the Qua Ibo.

The Spaniards, on resuming possession of the island, had one of their attacks of activity regarding it, and sent out with Don Carlos Chacon, who was to take over the command, four Jesuit priests, a secretary, a commissariat officer, a custom-house clerk, and a transport, the Santa Maria, with a number of emigrant families. This attempt to colonise Fernando Po should have at least done the good of preventing such experiments ever being tried again with women and children, for of these unfortunate creatures—for whom, in spite of its being the wet season, no houses had been provided—more than 20 per cent. died in the space of five months. Mr. Hutchinson, who was English Consul at the time, tells us that "In a very short time gaunt figures of men, women, and children might be seen crawling through the streets, with scarcely an evidence of life in their faces, save the expression of a sort of torpid carelessness as to how soon it might be their turn to drop off and die. The Portino, a steamer, carried back fifty of them to Cadiz, who looked when they embarked more like living skeletons of skin and bone than animated human beings." {47} I quote this not to cast reproach on the Spanish Government, but merely to give a fact, a case in point, of the deadly failure of endeavours to colonise on the West Coast, a thing which is even now occasionally attempted, always with the same sad results, though in most cases these attempts are now made by religious but misinformed people under Bishop Taylor's mission.

The Spaniards did not entirely confine their attention to planting colonists in a ready-made state on the island. As soon as they had settled themselves and built their barracks and Government House, they set to work and cleared away the bush for an area of from four to six miles round the town. The ground soon became overgrown again, but this clearing is still perceptible in the different type of forest on it, and has enabled the gardens and little plantations round Clarence to be made more easily. My Spanish friends assure me that the Portuguese, who discovered the island in 1471, {48a} and who exchanged it and Anno Bom in 1778 to the Spaniards for the little island of Catalina and the colony of Sacramento in South America, did not do anything to develop it. When they, the Spaniards, first entered into possession they at once set to work to colonise and clear. Then the colonisation scheme went to the bad, the natives poisoned the wells, it is said, and the attention of the Spaniards was in those days turned, for some inscrutable reason, to the eastern shores of the island—a district now quite abandoned by whites, on account of its unhealthiness—and they lost in addition to the colonists a terrible quantity of their sailors, in Concepcion Bay. {48b} A lull then followed, and the Spaniards willingly lent the place to the English as aforesaid. They say we did nothing except establish Clarence as a headquarters, which they consider to have been a most excellent enterprise, and import the Baptist Mission, which they hold as a less estimable undertaking; but there! that's nothing to what the Baptist Mission hold regarding the Spaniards. For my own part, I wish the Spaniards better luck this time in their activity, for in directing it to plantations they are on a truer and safer road to wealth than they have been with their previous importations of Cuban political prisoners and ready-made families of colonists, and I hope they will send home those unfortunate wretches they have there now, and commence, in their expected two years, to reap the profits of the coffee and cocoa. Certainly the chances are that they may, for the soil of Fernando Po is of exceeding fertility; Mr. Hutchinson says he has known Indian corn planted here on a Monday evening make its appearance four inches above ground on the following Wednesday morning, within a period, he carefully says, of thirty-six hours. I have seen this sort of thing over in Victoria, but I like to get a grown, strong man, and a Consul of Her Britannic Majesty, to say it for me.

Having discoursed at large on the various incomers to Fernando Po we may next turn to the natives, properly so-called, the Bubis. These people, although presenting a series of interesting problems to the ethnologist, both from their insular position, and their differentiation from any of the mainland peoples, are still but little known. To a great extent this has arisen from their exclusiveness, and their total lack of enthusiasm in trade matters, a thing that differentiates them more than any other characteristic from the mainlanders, who, young and old, men and women, regard trade as the great affair of life, take to it as soon as they can toddle, and don't even leave it off at death, according to their own accounts of the way the spirits of distinguished traders still dabble and interfere in market matters. But it is otherwise with the Bubi. A little rum, a few beads, and finish—then he will turn the rest of his attention to catching porcupines, or the beautiful little gazelles, gray on the back, and white underneath, with which the island abounds. And what time he may have on hand after this, he spends in building houses and making himself hats. It is only his utterly spare moments that he employs in making just sufficient palm oil from the rich supply of nuts at his command to get that rum and those beads of his. Cloth he does not want; he utterly fails to see what good the stuff is, for he abhors clothes. The Spanish authorities insist that the natives who come into the town should have something on, and so they array themselves in a bit of cotton cloth, which before they are out of sight of the town on their homeward way, they strip off and stuff into their baskets, showing in this, as well as in all other particulars, how uninfluencible by white culture they are. For the Spaniards, like the Portuguese, are great sticklers for clothes and insist on their natives wearing them—usually with only too much success. I shall never forget the yards and yards of cotton the ladies of Loanda wore; and not content with making cocoons of their bodies, they wore over their heads, as a mantilla, some dozen yards or so of black cloth into the bargain. Moreover this insistence on drapery for the figure is not merely for towns; a German officer told me the other day that when, a week or so before, his ship had called at Anno Bom, they were simply besieged for "clo', clo', clo';" the Anno Bomians explaining that they were all anxious to go across to Principe and get employment on coffee plantations, but that the Portuguese planters would not engage them in an unclothed state.

You must not, however, imagine that the Bubi is neglectful of his personal appearance. In his way he is quite a dandy. But his idea of decoration goes in the direction of a plaster of "tola" pomatum over his body, and above all a hat. This hat may be an antique European one, or a bound-round handkerchief, but it is more frequently a confection of native manufacture, and great taste and variety are displayed in its make. They are of plaited palm leaf—that's all you can safely generalise regarding them—for sometimes they have broad brims, sometimes narrow, sometimes no brims at all. So, too, with the crown. Sometimes it is thick and domed, sometimes non-existent, the wearer's hair aglow with red-tail parrots' feathers sticking up where the crown should be. As a general rule these hats are much adorned with oddments of birds' plumes, and one chief I knew had quite a Regent-street Dolly Varden creation which he used to affix to his wool in a most intelligent way with bonnet-pins made of wood. These hats are also a peculiarity of the Bubi, for none of the mainlanders care a row of pins for hats, except "for dandy," to wear occasionally, whereas the Bubi wears his perpetually, although he has by no means the same amount of sun to guard against owing to the glorious forests of his island.

For earrings the Bubi wears pieces of wood stuck through the lobe of the ear, and although this is not a decorative habit still it is less undecorative than that of certain mainland friends of mine in this region, who wear large and necessarily dripping lumps of fat in their ears and in their hair. His neck is hung round with jujus on strings—bits of the backbones of pythons, teeth, feathers, and antelope horns, and occasionally a bit of fat in a bag. Round his upper arm are bracelets, preferably made of ivory got from the mainland, for celluloid bracelets carefully imported for his benefit he refuses to look at. Often these bracelets are made of beads, or a circlet of leaves, and when on the war-path an armlet of twisted grass is always worn by the men. Men and women alike wear armlets, and in the case of the women they seem to be put on when young, for you see puffs of flesh growing out from between them. They are not entirely for decoration, serving also as pockets, for under them men stick a knife, and women a tobacco pipe, a well-coloured clay. Leglets of similar construction are worn just under the knee on the right leg, while around the body you see belts of tshibbu, small pieces cut from Achatectonia shells, which form the native currency of the island. These shells are also made into veils worn by the women at their wedding.

This native coinage-equivalent is very interesting, for such things are exceedingly rare in West Africa. The only other instance I personally know of a tribe in this part of the world using a native-made coin is that of the Fans, who use little bundles of imitation axe-heads. Dr. Oscar Baumann, who knows more than any one else about these Bubis, thinks, I believe, that these bits of Achatectonia shells may have been introduced by the runaway Angola slaves in the old days, who used to fly from their Portuguese owners on San Thomé to the Spaniards on Fernando Po. The villages of the Bubis are in the forest in the interior of the island, and they are fairly wide apart. They are not a sea-beach folk, although each village has its beach, which merely means the place to which it brings its trade, these beaches being usually the dwelling places of the so-called Portos, {51} negroes, who act as middle-men between the Bubis and the whites.

You will often be told that the Bubis are singularly bad house-builders, indeed that they make no definite houses at all, but only rough shelters of branches. This is, however, a mistake. Shelters of this kind that you come across are merely the rough huts put up by hunters, not true houses. The village is usually fairly well built, and surrounded with a living hedge of stakes. The houses inside this are four-cornered, the walls made of logs of wood stuck in edgeways, and surmounted by a roof of thatch pitched at an extremely stiff angle, and the whole is usually surrounded with a dug-out drain to carry off surface water. These houses, as usual on the West Coast, are divisible into two classes—houses of assembly, and private living houses. The first are much the larger. The latter are very low, and sometimes ridiculously small, but still they are houses and better than those awful Loango grass affairs you get on the Congo.

Herr Baumann says that the houses high up on the mountain have double walls between which there is a free space; an arrangement which may serve to minimise the extreme draughtiness of an ordinary Bubi house—a very necessary thing in these relatively chilly upper regions. I may remark on my own account that the Bubi villages do not often lie right on the path, but, like those you have to deal with up the Calabar, some little way off it. This is no doubt for the purpose of concealing their whereabouts from strangers, and it does it successfully too, for many a merry hour have I spent dodging up and down a path trying to make out at what particular point it was advisable to dive into the forest thicket to reach a village. But this cultivates habits of observation, and a short course of this work makes you recognise which tree is which along miles of a bush path as easily as you would shops in your own street at home.

The main interest of the Bubi's life lies in hunting, for he is more of a sportsman than the majority of mainlanders. He has not any big game to deal with, unless we except pythons—which attain a great size on the island—and crocodiles. Elephants, though plentiful on the adjacent mainland, are quite absent from Fernando Po, as are also hippos and the great anthropoid apes; but of the little gazelles, small monkeys, porcupines, and squirrels he has a large supply, and in the rivers a very pretty otter (Lutra poensis) with yellow brown fur often quite golden underneath; a creature which is, I believe, identical with the Angola otter.

The Bubis use in their hunting flint-lock guns, but chiefly traps and nets, and, I am told, slings. The advantage of these latter methods are, I expect, the same as on the mainland, where a distinguished sportsman once told me: "You go shoot thing with gun. Berrah well—but you no get him thing for sure. No, sah. Dem gun make nize. Berrah well. You fren hear dem nize and come look him, and you hab to go share what you done kill. Or bad man hear him nize, and he come look him, and you no fit to get share—you fit to get kill yusself. Chii! chii! traps be best." I urged that the traps might also be robbed. "No, sah," says he, "them bian (charm) he look after them traps, he fit to make man who go tief swell up and bust."

The Bubis also fish, mostly by basket traps, but they are not experts either in this or in canoe management. Their chief sea-shore sport is hunting for the eggs of the turtles who lay in the sand from August to October. These eggs—about 200 in each nest—are about the size of a billiard-ball, with a leathery envelope, and are much valued for food, as are also the grubs of certain beetles got from the stems of the palm-trees, and the honey of the wild bees which abound here.

Their domestic animals are the usual African list; cats, dogs, sheep, goats, and poultry. Pigs there are too, very domestic in Clarence and in a wild state in the forest. These pigs are the descendants of those imported by the Spaniards, and not long ago became such an awful nuisance in Clarence that the Government issued instructions that all pigs without rings in their noses - i.e. all in a condition to grub up back gardens—should be forthwith shot if found abroad. This proclamation was issued by the governmental bellman thus:—"I say—I say—I say—I say. Suppose pig walk—iron no live for him nose! Gun shoot. Kill him one time. Hear re! hear re!"

However a good many pigs with no iron living in their noses got adrift and escaped into the interior, and have flourished like the green bay-tree, destroying the Bubi's plantation and eating his yams, while the Bubi retaliating kills and eats them. So it's a drawn battle, for the Bubi enjoys the pig and the pig enjoys the yams, which are of singular excellence in this island and celebrated throughout the Bight. Now, I am told, the Government are firmly discouraging the export of these yams, which used to be quite a little branch of Fernando Po trade, in the hope that this will induce the native to turn his attention to working in the coffee and cacao plantations. Hope springs eternal in the human breast, for the Bubi has shown continually since the 16th century that he takes no interest in these things whatsoever. Now and again a man or woman will come voluntarily and take service in Clarence, submit to clothes, and rapidly pick up the ways of a house or store. And just when their owner thinks he owns a treasure, and begins to boast that he has got an exception to all Bubidom, or else that he knows how to manage them better than other men, then a hole in that man's domestic arrangements suddenly appears. The Bubi has gone, without giving a moment's warning, and without stealing his master's property, but just softly and silently vanished away. And if hunted up the treasure will be found in his or her particular village—clothes-less, comfortable, utterly unconcerned, and unaware that he or she has lost anything by leaving Clarence and Civilisation. It is this conduct that gains for the Bubi the reputation of being a bigger idiot than he really is.

For West Africans their agriculture is of a fairly high description—the noteworthy point about it, however, is the absence of manioc. Manioc is grown on Fernando Po, but only by the Portos. The Bubi cultivated plants are yams (Dioscorea alata), koko (Colocasia esculenta - the taro of the South Seas,) and plantains. Their farms are well kept, particularly those in the grass districts by San Carlos Bay. The yams of the Cordillera districts are the best flavoured, but those of the east coast the largest. Palm-oil is used for domestic purposes in the usual ways, and palm wine both fresh and fermented is the ordinary native drink. Rum is held in high esteem, but used in a general way in moderation as a cordial and a treat, for the Bubi is, like the rest of the West African natives, by no means an habitual drunkard. Gin he dislikes. {55}

And I may remark you will find the same opinion in regard to the Dualla in Cameroons river—on the undeniable authority of Dr. Buchner, and my own extensive experience of the West Coast bears it out.

Physically the Bubis are a fairly well-formed race of medium height; they are decidedly inferior to the Benga or the Krus, but quite on a level with the Effiks. The women indeed are very comely: their colour is bronze and their skin the skin of the Bantu. Beards are not uncommon among the men, and these give their faces possibly more than anything else, a different look to the faces of the Effiks or the Duallas. Indeed the people physically most like the Bubis that I have ever seen, are undoubtedly the Bakwiri of Cameroons Mountain, who are also liable to be bearded, or possibly I should say more liable to wear beards, for a good deal of the African hairlessness you hear commented on—in the West African at any rate—arises from his deliberately pulling his hair out—his beard, moustache, whiskers, and, occasionally, as among the Fans, his eyebrows.

Dr. Baumann, the great authority on the Bubi language says it is a Bantu stock. {56} I know nothing of it myself save that it is harsh in sound. Their method of counting is usually by fives but they are notably weak in arithmetical ability, differing in this particular from the mainlanders, and especially from their Negro neighbours, who are very good at figures, surpassing the Bantu in this, as indeed they do in most branches of intellectual activity.

But the most remarkable instance of inferiority the Bubis display is their ignorance regarding methods of working iron. I do not know that iron in a native state is found on Fernando Po, but scrap-iron they have been in touch with for some hundreds of years. The mainlanders are all cognisant of native methods of working iron, although many tribes of them now depend entirely on European trade for their supply of knives, etc., and this difference between them and the Bubis would seem to indicate that the migration of the latter to the island must have taken place at a fairly remote period, a period before the iron-working tribes came down to the coast. Of course, if you take the Bubi's usual explanation of his origin, namely that he came out of the crater on the top of Clarence Peak, this argument falls through; but he has also another legend, one moreover which is likewise to be found upon the mainland, which says he was driven from the district north of the Gaboon estuary by the coming of the M'pongwe to the coast, and as this legend is the more likely of the two I think we may accept it as true, or nearly so. But what adds another difficulty to the matter is that the Bubi is not only unlearned in iron lore, but he was learned in stone, and up to the time of the youth of many Porto-negroes on Fernando Po, he was making and using stone implements, and none of the tribes within the memory of man have done this on the mainland. It is true that up the Niger and about Benin and Axim you get polished stone celts, but these are regarded as weird affairs,—thunderbolts— and suitable only for grinding up and making into medicine; there is no trace in the traditions of these places, as far as I have been able to find, of any time at which stone implements were in common use, and certainly the M'pongwe have not been a very long time on the coast, for their coming is still remembered in their traditions. The Bubi stone implements I have seen twice, but on neither occasion could I secure one, and although I have been long promised specimens from Fernando Po, I have not yet received them. They are difficult to procure, because none of the present towns are on really old sites, the Bubi, like most Bantus, moving pretty frequently, either because the ground is witched, demonstrated by outbreaks of sickness, or because another village-full of his fellow creatures, or a horrid white man plantation-making, has come too close to him. A Roman Catholic priest in Ka Congo once told me a legend he laughed much over, of how a fellow priest had enterprisingly settled himself one night in the middle of a Bubi village with intent to devote the remainder of his life to quietly but thoroughly converting it. Next morning, when he rose up, he found himself alone, the people having taken all their portable possessions and vanished to build another village elsewhere. The worthy Father spent some time chivying his flock about the forest, but in vain, and he returned home disgusted, deciding that the Creator, for some wise purpose, had dedicated the Bubis to the Devil.

The spears used by this interesting people are even to this day made entirely of wood, and have such a Polynesian look about them that I intend some time or other to bring some home and experiment on that learned Polynesian-culture-expert, Baron von Hügel, with them:—intellectually experiment, not physically, pray understand.

The pottery has a very early-man look about it, but in this it does not differ much from that of the mainland, which is quite as poor, and similarly made without a wheel, and sun-baked. Those pots of the Bubis I have seen have, however, not had the pattern (any sort of pattern does, and it need not be carefully done) that runs round mainland pots to "keep their souls in" - i.e. to prevent their breaking up on their own account.

The basket-work of the Bubis is of a superior order: the baskets they make to hold the palm oil are excellent, and will hold water like a basin, but I am in doubt whether this art is original, or imported by the Portuguese runaway slaves, for they put me very much in mind of those made by my old friends the Kabinders, from whom a good many of those slaves were recruited. I think there is little doubt that several of the musical instruments own this origin, particularly their best beloved one, the elibo. This may be described as a wooden bell having inside it for clappers several (usually five) pieces of stick threaded on a bit of wood jammed into the dome of the bell and striking the rim, beyond which the clappers just protrude. These bells are very like those you meet with in Angola, but I have not seen on the island, nor does Dr. Baumann cite having seen, the peculiar double bell of Angola—the engongui. The Bubi bell is made out of one piece of wood and worked—or played—with both hands. Dr. Baumann says it is customary on bright moonlight nights for two lines of men to sit facing each other and to clap—one can hardly call it ring—these bells vigorously, but in good time, accompanying this performance with a monotonous song, while the delighted women and children dance round. The learned doctor evidently sees the picturesqueness of this practice, but notes that the words of the songs are not "tiefsinnige" (profound), as he has heard men for hours singing "The shark bites the Bubi's hand," only that over and over again and nothing more. This agrees with my own observations of all Bantu native songs. I have always found that the words of these songs were either the repetition of some such phrase as this, or a set of words referring to the recent adventures or experiences of the singer or the present company's little peculiarities; with a very frequent chorus, old and conventional.

The native tunes used with these songs are far superior, and I expect many of them are very old. They are often full of variety and beauty, particularly those of the M'pongwe and Igalwa, of which I will speak later.

The dances I have no personal knowledge of, but there is nothing in Baumann's description to make one think they are distinct in themselves from the mainland dances. I once saw a dance at Fernando Po, but that was among Portos, and it was my old friend the Batuco in all its beauty. But there is a distinct peculiarity about the places the dances are held on, every village having a kept piece of ground outside it which is the dancing place for the village—the ballroom as it were; and exceedingly picturesque these dances must be, for they are mostly held during the nights of full moon. These kept grounds remind one very much of the similar looking patches of kept grass one sees in villages in Ka Congo, but there is no similarity in their use, for the Ka Congo lawns are of fetish, not frivolous, import.

The Bubis have an instrument I have never seen in an identical form on the mainland. It is made like a bow, with a tense string of fibre. One end of the bow is placed against the mouth, and the string is then struck by the right hand with a small round stick, while with the left it is scraped with a piece of shell or a knife-blade. This excruciating instrument, I warn any one who may think of living among the Bubis, is very popular. The drums used are both the Dualla form—all wood—and the ordinary skin-covered drum, and I think if I catalogue fifes made of wood, I shall have nearly finished the Bubi orchestra. I have doubts on this point because I rather question whether I may be allowed to refer to a very old bullock hide—unmounted—as a musical instrument without bringing down the wrath of musicians on my head. These stiff, dry pelts are much thought of, and played by the artistes by being shaken as accompaniments to other instruments—they make a noise, and that is after all the soul of most African instrumental music. These instruments are all that is left of certain bullocks which many years ago the Spaniards introduced, hoping to improve the food supply. They seemed as if they would have flourished well on the island, on the stretches of grass land in the Cordillera and the East, but the Bubis, being great sportsmen, killed them all off.

The festivities of the Bubis—dances, weddings, feasts, etc.,—at which this miscellaneous collection of instruments are used in concert, usually take place in November, the dry season; but the Bubi is liable to pour forth his soul in the bosom of his family at any time of the day or night, from June to January, and when he pours it forth on that bow affair it makes the lonely European long for home.

Divisions of time the Bubi can hardly be said to have, but this is a point upon which all West Africans are rather weak, particularly the Bantu. He has, however, a definite name for November, December, and January—the dry season months—calling them Lobos.

The Fetish of these people, although agreeing on broad lines with the Bantu Fetish, has many interesting points, as even my small knowledge of it showed me, and it is a subject that would repay further investigation; and as by fetish I always mean the governing but underlying ideas of a man's life, we will commence with the child. Nothing, as far as I have been able to make out, happens to him, for fetish reasons, when he first appears on the scene. He receives at birth, as is usual, a name which is changed for another on his initiation into the secret society, this secret society having also, as usual, a secret language. About the age of three or five years the boy is decorated, under the auspices of the witch doctor, with certain scars on the face. These scars run from the root of the nose across the cheeks, and are sometimes carried up in a curve on to the forehead.

Tattooing, in the true sense of the word, they do not use much, but they paint themselves, as the mainlanders do, with a red paint made by burning some herb and mixing the ash with clay or oil, and they occasionally—whether for ju-ju reasons or for mere decoration I do not know—paint a band of yellow clay round the chest; but of the Bubi secret society I know little, nor have I been able to find any one who knows much more. Hutchinson, {61} in his exceedingly amusing description of a wedding he was once present at among these people, would lead one to think the period of seclusion of the women's society was twelve months.

The chief god or spirit, O Wassa, resides in the crater of the highest peak, and by his name the peak is known to the native. Another very important spirit, to whom goats and sheep are offered, is Lobe, resident in a crater lake on the northern slope of the Cordilleras, and the grass you sometimes see a Bubi wearing is said to come from this lake and be a ju-ju of Lobe's. Dr. Baumann says that the lake at Riabba from which the spirit Uapa rises is more holy, and that he is small, and resides in a chasm in a rock whose declivity can only be passed by means of bush ropes, and in the wet season he is not get-at-able at all. He will, if given suitable offerings, reveal the future to Bubis, but Bubis only. His priest is the King of all the Bubis, upon whom it is never permitted to a white man, or a Porto, to gaze. Baumann also gives the residence of another important spirit as being the grotto at Banni. This is a sea-cave, only accessible at low water in calm weather. I have heard many legends of this cave, but have never had an opportunity of seeing it, or any one who has seen it first hand.

The charms used by these people are similar in form to those of the mainland Bantu, but the methods of treating paths and gateways are somewhat peculiar. The gateways to the towns are sometimes covered by freshly cut banana leaves, and during the religious feast in November, the paths to the villages are barred across with a hedge of grass which no stranger must pass through.

The government is a peculiar one for West Africa. Every village has its chief, but the whole tribe obey one great chief or king who lives in the crater-ravine at Riabba. This individual is called Moka, but whether he is now the same man referred to by Rogoszinsky, Mr. Holland, and the Rev. Hugh Brown, who attempted to interview him in the seventies, I do not feel sure, for the Bubis are just the sort of people to keep a big king going with a variety of individuals. Even the indefatigable Dr. Baumann failed to see Moka, though he evidently found out a great deal about the methods of his administration and formed a very high opinion of his ability, for he says that to this one chief the people owe their present unity and orderliness; that before his time the whole island was in a state of internecine war: murder was frequent, and property unsafe. Now their social condition, according to the Doctor's account, is a model to Europe, let alone Africa. Civil wars have been abolished, disputes between villages being referred to arbitration, and murder is swiftly and surely punished. If the criminal has bolted into the forest and cannot be found, his village is made responsible, and has to pay a fine in goats, sheep and tobacco to the value of 16 pounds. Theft is extremely rare and offences against the moral code also, the Bubis having an extremely high standard in this matter, even the little children having each a separate sleeping hut. In old days adultery was punished by cutting off the offender's hand. I have myself seen women in Fernando Po who have had a hand cut off at the wrist, but I believe those were slave women who had suffered for theft. Slaves the Bubis do have, but their condition is the mild, poor relation or retainer form of slavery you find in Calabar, and differs from the Dualla form, for the slaves live in the same villages as their masters, while among the Duallas, as among most Bantu slave-holding tribes, the slaves are excluded from the master's village and have separate villages of their own. For marriage ceremonies I refer you to Mr. Hutchinson. Burial customs are exceedingly quaint in the southern and eastern districts, where the bodies are buried in the forest with their heads just sticking out of the ground. In other districts the body is also buried in the forest, but is completely covered and an erection of stones put up to mark the place.

Little is known of all West African fetish, still less of that of these strange people. Dr. Oscar Baumann brought to bear on them his careful unemotional German methods of observation, thereby giving us more valuable information about them and their island than we otherwise should possess. Mr. Hutchinson resided many years on Fernando Po, in the capacity of H. B. M.'s Consul, with his hands full of the affairs of the Oil Rivers and in touch with the Portos of Clarence, but he nevertheless made very interesting observations on the natives and their customs. The Polish exile and his courageous wife who ascended Clarence Peak, Mr. Rogoszinsky, and another Polish exile, Mr. Janikowski, about complete our series of authorities on the island. Dr. Baumann thinks they got their information from Porto sources—sources the learned Doctor evidently regards as more full of imagination than solid fact, but, as you know, all African travellers are occasionally in the habit of pooh-poohing each other, and I own that I myself have been chiefly in touch with Portos, and that my knowledge of the Bubi language runs to the conventional greeting form:—"I-pori?" "Porto." "Ke Soko?'" "Hatsi soko":—"Who are you?" "Porto." "What's the news?" "No news."

Although these Portos are less interesting to the ethnologist than the philanthropist, they being by-products of his efforts, I must not leave Fernando Po without mentioning them, for on them the trade of the island depends. They are the middlemen between the Bubi and the white trader. The former regards them with little, if any, more trust than he regards the white men, and his view of the position of the Spanish Governor is that he is chief over the Portos. That he has any headship over Bubis or over the Bubi land—Itschulla as he calls Fernando Po—he does not imagine possible. Baumann says he was once told by a Bubi: "White men are fish, not men. They are able to stay a little while on land, but at last they mount their ships again and vanish over the horizon into the ocean. How can a fish possess land?" If the coffee and cacao thrive on Fernando Po to the same extent that they have already thriven on San Thomé there is but little doubt that the Bubis will become extinct; for work on plantations, either for other people, or themselves, they will not, and then the Portos will become the most important class, for they will go in for plantations. Their little factories are studded all round the shores of the coast in suitable coves and bays, and here in fairly neat houses they live, collecting palm-oil from the Bubis, and making themselves little cacao plantations, and bringing these products into Clarence every now and then to the white trader's factory. Then, after spending some time and most of their money in the giddy whirl of that capital, they return to their homes and recover. There is a class of them permanently resident in Clarence, the city men of Fernando Po, and these are very like the Sierra Leonians of Free Town, but preferable. Their origin is practically the same as that of the Free Towners. They are the descendants of liberated slaves set free during the time of our occupation of the island as a naval depot for suppressing the slave trade, and of Sierra Leonians and Accras who have arrived and settled since then. They have some of the same "Black gennellum, Sar" style about them, but not developed to the same ridiculous extent as in the Sierra Leonians, for they have not been under our institutions. The

"Nanny Po" ladies are celebrated for their beauty all along the West Coast, and very justly. They are not however, as they themselves think, the most beautiful women in this part of the world. Not at least to my way of thinking. I prefer an Elmina, or an Igalwa, or a M'pongwe, or—but I had better stop and own that my affections have got very scattered among the black ladies on the West Coast, and I no sooner remember one lovely creature whose soft eyes, perfect form and winning, pretty ways have captivated me than I think of another. The Nanny Po ladies have often a certain amount of Spanish blood in them, which gives a decidedly greater delicacy to their features—delicate little nostrils, mouths not too heavily lipped, a certain gloss on the hair, and a light in the eye. But it does not improve their colour, and I am assured that it has an awful effect on their tempers, so I think I will remain, for the present, the faithful admirer of my sable Ingramina, the Igalwa, with the little red blossoms stuck in her night-black hair, and a sweet soft look and word for every one, but particularly for her ugly husband Isaac the "Jack Wash."

CHAPTER III

VOYAGE DOWN COAST

WHEREIN THE VOYAGER BEFORE LEAVING THE RIVERS DISCOURSES ON
DANGERS, TO WHICH IS ADDED SOME ACCOUNT OF MANGROVE SWAMPS
AND THE CREATURES THAT ABIDE THEREIN.

I LEFT CALABAR IN MAY and joined the Benguela off Lagos Bar. My voyage
down coast in her was a very pleasant one and full of instruction, for Mr.
Fothergill, who was her purser, had in former years resided in Congo
Français as a merchant, and to Congo Français I was bound with an empty
hold as regards local knowledge of the district. He was one of that class of men,
of which you most frequently find representatives among the merchants, who
do not possess the power so many men along here do possess (a power that
always amazes me), of living for a considerable time in a district without taking
any interest in it, keeping their whole attention concentrated on the point of
how long it will be before their time comes to get out of it. Mr. Fothergill
evidently had much knowledge and experience of the Fernan Vaz district and
its natives. He had, I should say, overdone his experiences with the natives, as
far as personal comfort and pleasure at the time went, having been nearly killed
and considerably chivied by them. Now I do not wish a man, however much I
may deplore his total lack of local knowledge, to go so far as this. Mr. Fothergill gave his accounts of these incidents calmly, and in an undecorated way that
gave them a power and convincingness verging on being unpleasant, although
useful, to a person who was going into the district where they had occurred, for
one felt there was no mortal reason why one should not personally get involved
in similar affairs. And I must here acknowledge the great subsequent service
Mr. Fothergill's wonderfully accurate descriptions of the peculiar characteristics
of the Ogowé forests were to me when I subsequently came to deal with these

forests on my own account, as every district of forest has peculiar characteristics of its own which you require to know. I should like here to speak of West Coast dangers because I fear you may think that I am careless of, or do not believe in them, neither of which is the case. The more you know of the West Coast of Africa, the more you realise its dangers. For example, on your first voyage out you hardly believe the stories of fever told by the old Coasters. That is because you do not then understand the type of man who is telling them, a man who goes to his death with a joke in his teeth. But a short experience of your own, particularly if you happen on a place having one of its periodic epidemics, soon demonstrates that the underlying horror of the thing is there, a rotting corpse which the old Coaster has dusted over with jokes to cover it so that it hardly shows at a distance, but which, when you come yourself to live alongside, you soon become cognisant of. Many men, when they have got ashore and settled, realise this, and let the horror get a grip on them; a state briefly and locally de-scribed as funk, and a state that usually ends fatally; and you can hardly blame them. Why, I know of a case myself. A young man who had never been outside an English country town before in his life, from family reverses had to take a situation as book-keeper down in the Bights. The factory he was going to was in an isolated out-of-the-way place and not in a settlement, and when the ship called off it, he was put ashore in one of the ship's boats with his belongings, and a case or so of goods. There were only the firm's beach-boys down at the surf, and as the steamer was in a hurry the officer from the ship did not go up to the factory with him, but said good-bye and left him alone with a set of naked sav-ages as he thought, but really of good kindly Kru boys on the beach. He could not understand what they said, nor they what he said, and so he walked up to the house and on to the verandah and tried to find the Agent he had come out to serve under. He looked into the open-ended dining-room and shyly round the verandah, and then sat down and waited for some one to turn up. Sundry natives turned up, and said a good deal, but no one white or comprehensible, so in desperation he made another and a bolder tour completely round the verandah and noticed a most peculiar noise in one of the rooms and an infin-ity of flies going into the venetian shuttered window. Plucking up courage he went in and found what was left of the white Agent, a considerable quantity of rats, and most of the flies in West Africa. He then presumably had fever, and he was taken off, a fortnight afterwards, by a French boat, to whom the natives signalled, and he is not coming down the Coast again. Some men would have died right out from a shock like this.

But most of the new-comers do not get a shock of this order. They ei-ther die themselves or get more gradually accustomed to this sort of thing, when they come to regard death and fever as soldiers, who on a battle-field sit down, and laugh and talk round a camp fire after a day's hard battle, in which they have seen their friends and companions falling round them; all the time knowing that to-morrow the battle comes again and that to-morrow night they themselves may never see.

It is not hard-hearted callousness, it is only their way. Michael Scott put this well in Tom Cringle's Log, in his account of the yellow fever during the war in the West Indies. Fever, though the chief danger, particularly to people who go out to settlements, is not the only one; but as the other dangers, except perhaps domestic poisoning, are incidental to pottering about in the forests, or on the rivers, among the unsophisticated tribes, I will not dwell on them. They can all be avoided by any one with common sense, by keeping well out of the districts in which they occur; and so I warn the general reader that if he goes out to West Africa, it is not because I said the place was safe, or its dangers over-rated. The cemeteries of the West Coast are full of the victims of those people who have said that Coast fever is "Cork fever," and a man's own fault, which it is not; and that natives will never attack you unless you attack them: which they will—on occasions.

My main aim in going to Congo Français was to get up above the tide line of the Ogowé River and there collect fishes; for my object on this voyage was to collect fish from a river north of the Congo. I had hoped this river would have been the Niger, for Sir George Goldie had placed at my disposal great facilities for carrying on work there in comfort; but for certain private reasons I was disinclined to go from the Royal Niger Protectorate into the Royal Niger Company's territory; and the Calabar, where Sir Claude MacDonald did everything he possibly could to assist me, I did not find a good river for me to collect fishes in. These two rivers failing me, from no fault of either of their own presiding genii, my only hope of doing anything now lay on the South West Coast river, the Ogowé, and everything there depended on Mr. Hudson's attitude towards scientific research in the domain of ichthyology. Fortunately for me that gentleman elected to take a favourable view of this affair, and in every way in his power assisted me during my entire stay in Congo Français. But before I enter into a detailed description of this wonderful bit of West Africa, I must give you a brief notice of the manners, habits and customs of West Coast rivers in general, to make the thing more intelligible.

There is an uniformity in the habits of West Coast rivers, from the Volta to the Coanza, which is, when you get used to it, very taking. Excepting the Congo, the really great river comes out to sea with as much mystery as possible; lounging lazily along among its mangrove swamps in a what's-it-matter-when-one-comes-out and where's-the-hurry style, through quantities of channels inter-communicating with each other. Each channel, at first sight as like the other as peas in a pod, is bordered on either side by green-black walls of mangroves, which Captain Lugard graphically described as seeming "as if they had lost all count of the vegetable proprieties, and were standing on stilts with their branches tucked up out of the wet, leaving their gaunt roots exposed in midair." High-tide or low-tide, there is little difference in the water; the river, be it broad or narrow, deep or shallow, looks like a pathway of polished metal; for it is as heavy weighted with stinking mud as water e'er can be, ebb or flow, year out and year in. But the difference in the banks, though an unending alternation between two appearances, is weird.

At high-water you do not see the mangroves displaying their ankles in the way that shocked Captain Lugard. They look most respectable, their foliage rising densely in a wall irregularly striped here and there by the white line of an aërial root, coming straight down into the water from some upper branch as straight as a plummet, in the strange, knowing way an aërial root of a mangrove does, keeping the hard straight line until it gets some two feet above water-level, and then spreading out into blunt fingers with which to dip into the water and grasp the mud. Banks indeed at high water can hardly be said to exist, the water stretching away into the mangrove swamps for miles and miles, and you can then go, in a suitable small canoe, away among these swamps as far as you please.

This is a fascinating pursuit. But it is a pleasure to be indulged in with caution; for one thing, you are certain to come across crocodiles. Now a crocodile drifting down in deep water, or lying asleep with its jaws open on a sand-bank in the sun, is a picturesque adornment to the landscape when you are on the deck of a steamer, and you can write home about it and frighten your relations on your behalf; but when you are away among the swamps in a small dug-out canoe, and that crocodile and his relations are awake—a thing he makes a point of being at flood tide because of fish coming along—and when he has got his foot upon his native heath—that is to say, his tail within holding reach of his native mud—he is highly interesting, and you may not be able to write home about him—and you get frightened on your own behalf; for crocodiles can, and often do, in such places, grab at people in small canoes. I have known of several natives losing their lives in this way; some native villages are approachable from the main river by a short cut, as it were, through the mangrove swamps, and the inhabitants of such villages will now and then go across this way with small canoes instead of by the constant channel to the village, which is almost always winding. In addition to this unpleasantness you are liable—until you realise the danger from experience, or have native advice on the point—to get tide-trapped away in the swamps, the water falling round you when you are away in some deep pool or lagoon, and you find you cannot get back to the main river. Of course if you really want a truly safe investment in Fame, and really care about Posterity, and Posterity's Science, you will jump over into the black batter-like, stinking slime, cheered by the thought of the terrific sensation you will produce 20,000 years hence, and the care you will be taken of then by your fellow-creatures, in a museum. But if you are a mere ordinary person of a retiring nature, like me, you stop in your lagoon until the tide rises again; most of your attention is directed to dealing with an "at home" to crocodiles and mangrove flies, and with the fearful stench of the slime round you. What little time you have over you will employ in wondering why you came to West Africa, and why, after having reached this point of folly, you need have gone and painted the lily and adorned the rose, by being such a colossal ass as to come fooling about in mangrove swamps.

Still, even if your own peculiar tastes and avocations do not take you in small dug-out canoes into the heart of the swamps, you can observe the difference in the local scenery made by the flowing of the tide when you are on a vessel stuck on a sand-bank, in the Rio del Rey for example. Moreover, as you will have little else to attend to, save mosquitoes and mangrove flies, when in such a situation, you may as well pursue the study. At the ebb gradually the foliage of the lower branches of the mangroves grows wet and muddy, until there is a great black band about three feet deep above the surface of the water in all directions; gradually a network of gray-white roots rises up, and below this again, gradually, a slope of smooth and lead-grey slime. The effect is not in the least as if the water had fallen, but as if the mangroves had, with one accord, risen up out of it, and into it again they seem silently to sink when the flood comes. But by this more safe, if still unpleasant, method of observing mangrove-swamps, you miss seeing in full the make of them, for away in their fastnesses the mangroves raise their branches far above the reach of tide line, and the great gray roots of the older trees are always sticking up in mid-air. But, fringing the rivers, there is always a hedge of younger mangroves whose lower branches get immersed.

At corners here and there from the river face you can see the land being made from the waters. A mud-bank forms off it, a mangrove seed lights on it, and the thing's done. Well! not done, perhaps, but begun; for if the bank is high enough to get exposed at low water, this pioneer mangrove grows. He has a wretched existence though. You have only got to look at his dwarfed attenuated form to see this. He gets joined by a few more bold spirits and they struggle on together, their network of roots stopping abundance of mud, and by good chance now and then a consignment of miscellaneous débris of palm leaves, or a floating tree-trunk, but they always die before they attain any considerable height. Still even in death they collect. Their bare white stems remaining like a net gripped in the mud, so that these pioneer mangrove heroes may be said to have laid down their lives to make that mud-bank fit for colonisation, for the time gradually comes when other mangroves can and do colonise on it, and flourish, extending their territory steadily; and the mud-bank joins up with, and becomes a part of, Africa.

Right away on the inland fringe of the swamp—you may go some hundreds of miles before you get there—you can see the rest of the process. The mangroves there have risen up, and dried the mud to an extent that is more than good for themselves, have over civilised that mud in fact, and so the brackish waters of the tide—which, although their enemy when too deep or too strong in salt, is essential to their existence—cannot get to their roots. They have done this gradually, as a mangrove does all things, but they have done it, and down on to that mud come a whole set of palms from the old mainland, who in their early colonisation days go through similarly trying experiences. First the screw-pines come and live among them; then the wine-palm and various creepers, and then the oil-palm; and the débris of these plants being greater and making better soil than dead mangroves, they work quicker and the mangrove is doomed. Soon the salt waters are shut right out, the mangrove dies, and that bit of Africa is made. It is very interesting to get into these regions; you see along the river-bank a rich, thick, lovely wall of soft-wooded plants, and behind this you find great stretches of death;—miles and miles sometimes of gaunt white mangrove skeletons standing on gray stuff that is not yet earth and is no longer slime, and through the crust of which you can sink into rotting putrefaction. Yet, long after you are dead, buried, and forgotten, this will become a forest of soft-wooded plants and palms; and finally of hard-wooded trees. Districts of this description you will find in great sweeps of Kama country for example, and in the rich low regions up to the base of the Sierra del Cristal and the Rumby range.

You often hear the utter lifelessness of mangrove-swamps commented on; why I do not know, for they are fairly heavily stocked with fauna, though the species are comparatively few. There are the crocodiles, more of them than any one wants; there are quantities of flies, particularly the big silent mangrove-fly which lays an egg in you under the skin; the egg becomes a maggot and stays there until it feels fit to enter into external life. Then there are "slimy things that crawl with legs upon a slimy sea," and any quantity of hopping mud-fish, and crabs, and a certain mollusc, and in the water various kinds of cat-fish. Birdless they are save for the flocks of gray parrots that pass over them at evening, hoarsely squarking; and save for this squarking of the parrots the swamps are silent all the day, at least during the dry season; in the wet season there is no silence night or day in West Africa, but that roar of the descending deluge of rain that is more monotonous and more gloomy than any silence can be. In the morning you do not hear the long, low, mellow whistle of the plantain-eaters calling up the dawn, nor in the evening the clock-bird nor the Handel-Festival-sized choruses of frogs, or the crickets, that carry on their vesper controversy of "she did"—"she didn't" so fiercely on hard land.

But the mangrove-swamp follows the general rule for West Africa, and night in it is noisier than the day. After dark it is full of noises; grunts from I know not what, splashes from jumping fish, the peculiar whirr of rushing crabs, and quaint creaking and groaning sounds from the trees; and—above all in eeriness—the strange whine and sighing cough of crocodiles.

Great regions of mangrove-swamps are a characteristic feature of the West African Coast. The first of these lies north of Sierra Leone; then they occur, but of smaller dimensions—just fringes of river-outfalls—until you get to Lagos, when you strike the greatest of them all:—the swamps of the Niger outfalls (about twenty-three rivers in all) and of the Sombreiro, New Calabar, Bonny, San Antonio, Opobo (false and true), Kwoibo, Old Calabar (with the Cross Akwayafe Qwa Rivers) and Rio del Rey Rivers. The whole of this great stretch of coast is a mangrove-swamp, each river silently rolling down its great mass of mud-laden waters and constituting each in itself a very pretty problem to the navigator by its network of intercommunicating creeks, and the sand and mud bar which it forms off its entrance by dropping its heaviest mud; its lighter mud is carried out beyond its bar and makes the nasty-smelling brown soup of the South Atlantic Ocean, with froth floating in lines and patches on it, for miles to seaward.

In this great region of swamps every mile appears like every other mile until you get well used to it, and are able to distinguish the little local peculiarities at the entrance of the rivers and in the winding of the creeks, a thing difficult even for the most experienced navigator to do during those thick wool-like mists called smokes, which hang about the whole Bight from November till May (the dry season), sometimes lasting all day, sometimes clearing off three hours after sunrise.

The upper or north-westerly part of the swamp is round the mouths of the Niger, and it successfully concealed this fact from geographers down to 1830, when the series of heroic journeys made by Mungo Park, Clapperton, and the two Landers finally solved the problem—a problem that was as great and which cost more men's lives than even the discovery of the sources of the Nile.

That this should have been so may seem very strange to us who now have been told the answer to the riddle; for the upper waters of this great river were known of before Christ and spoken of by Herodotus, Pliny and Ptolemy, and its mouths navigated continuously along by the seaboard by trading vessels since the fifteenth century, but they were not recognised as belonging to the Niger. Some geographers held that the Senegal or the Gambia was its outfall; others that it was the Zaire (Congo); others that it did not come out on the West Coast at all, but got mixed up with the Nile in the middle of the continent, and so on. Yet when you come to know the swamps this is not so strange. You find on going up what looks like a big river—say Forcados, two and a half miles wide at the entrance and a real bit of the Niger. Before you are up it far great, broad, business-like-looking river entrances open on either side, showing wide rivers mangrove-walled, but two-thirds of them are utter frauds which will ground you within half an hour of your entering them. Some few of them do communicate with other main channels to the great upper river, and others are main channels themselves; but most of them intercommunicate with each other and lead nowhere in particular, and you can't even get there because of their shallowness. It is small wonder that the earlier navigators did not get far up them in sailing ships, and that the problem had to be solved by men descending the main stream of the Niger before it commences to what we in Devonshire should call "squander itself about" in all these channels. And in addition it must be remembered that the natives with whom these trading vessels dealt, first for slaves, afterwards for palm-oil, were not, and are not now, members of the Lo family of savages. Far from it: they do not go in for "gentle smiles," but for murdering any unprotected boat's crew they happen to come across, not only for a love of sport but to keep white traders from penetrating to the trade-producing interior, and spoiling prices. And the region is practically foodless.

The rivers of the great mangrove-swamp from the Sombreiro to the Rio del Rey are now known pretty surely not to be branches of the Niger, but the upper regions of this part of the Bight are much neglected by English explorers. I believe the great swamp region of the Bight of Biafra is the greatest in the world, and that in its immensity and gloom it has a grandeur equal to that of the Himalayas.

Take any man, educated or not, and place him on Bonny or Forcados River in the wet season on a Sunday—Bonny for choice. Forcados is good. You'll keep Forcados scenery "indelibly limned on the tablets of your mind when a yesterday has faded from its page," after you have spent even a week waiting for the Lagos branch-boat on its inky waters. But Bonny! Well, come inside the bar and anchor off the factories: seaward there is the foam of the bar gleaming and wicked white against a leaden sky and what there is left of Breaker Island. In every other direction you will see the apparently endless walls of mangrove, unvarying in colour, unvarying in form, unvarying in height, save from perspective. Beneath and between you and them lie the rotting mud waters of Bonny River, and away up and down river, miles of rotting mud waters fringed with walls of rotting mud mangrove-swamp. The only break in them—one can hardly call it a relief to the scenery—are the gaunt black ribs of the old hulks, once used as trading stations, which lie exposed at low water near the shore, protruding like the skeletons of great unclean beasts who have died because Bonny water was too strong even for them.

Raised on piles from the mud shore you will see the white-painted factories and their great store-houses for oil; each factory likely enough with its flag at half-mast, which does not enliven the scenery either, for you know it is because somebody is "dead again." Throughout and over all is the torrential downpour of the wet-season rain, coming down night and day with its dull roar. I have known it rain six mortal weeks in Bonny River, just for all the world as if it were done by machinery, and the interval that came then was only a few wet days, where-after it settled itself down to work again in the good West Coast water-spout pour for more weeks.

While your eyes are drinking in the characteristics of Bonny scenery you notice a peculiar smell—an intensification of that smell you noticed when near-ing Bonny, in the evening, out at sea. That's the breath of the malarial mud, laden with fever, and the chances are you will be down to-morrow. If it is near evening time now, you can watch it becoming incarnate, creeping and crawling and gliding out from the side creeks and between the mangrove-roots, laying itself upon the river, stretching and rolling in a kind of grim play, and finally crawling up the side of the ship to come on board and leave its cloak of moisture that grows green mildew in a few hours over all. Noise you will not be much troubled with: there is only that rain, a sound I have known make men who are sick with fever well-nigh mad, and now and again the depressing cry of the curlews which abound here. This combination is such that after six or eight hours of it you will be thankful to hear your shipmates start to work the winch. I take it you are hard up when you relish a winch. And you will say—let your previous experience of the world be what it may—Good Heavens, what a place!

Five times have I been now in Bonny River and I like it. You always do get to like it if you live long enough to allow the strange fascination of the place to get a hold on you; but when I first entered it, on a ship commanded by Captain Murray in '93, in the wet season, i.e. in August, in spite of the confidence I had by this time acquired in his skill and knowledge of the West Coast, a sense of horror seized on me as I gazed upon the scene, and I said to the old Coaster who then had charge of my education, "Good Heavens! what an awful accident. We've gone and picked up the Styx." He was evidently hurt and said, "Bonny was a nice place when you got used to it," and went on to discourse on the last epidemic here, when nine men out of the resident eleven died in about ten days from yellow fever. Next to the scenery of "a River," commend me for cheerfulness to the local conversation of its mangrove-swamp region; and every truly important West African river has its mangrove-swamp belt, which extends inland as far as the tide waters make it brackish, and which has a depth and extent from the banks depending on the configuration of the country. Above this belt comes uniformly a region of high forest, having towards the river frontage clay cliffs, sometimes high, as in the case of the Old Calabar at Adiabo, more frequently dwarf cliffs, as in the Forcados up at Warree, and in the Ogowé,—for a long stretch through Kama country. After the clay cliffs region you come to a region of rapids, caused by the river cutting its way through a mountain range; such ranges are the Pallaballa, causing the Livingstone rapids of the Congo; the Sierra del Cristal, those of the Ogowé, and many lesser rivers; the Rumby and Omon ranges, those of the Old Calabar and Cross Rivers.

Naturally in different parts these separate regions vary in size. The mangrove-swamp may be only a fringe at the mouth of the river, or it may cover hundreds of square miles. The clay cliffs may extend for only a mile or so along the bank, or they may, as on the Ogowé, extend for 130. And so it is also with the rapids: in some rivers, for instance the Cameroons, there are only a few miles of them, in others there are many miles; in the Ogowé there are as many as 500; and these rapids may be close to the river mouth, as in most of the Gold Coast rivers, save the Ancobra and the Volta; or they may be far in the interior, as in the Cross River, where they commence at about 200 miles; and on the Ogowé, where they commence at about 208 miles from the sea coast; this depends on the nearness or remoteness from the coast line of the mountain ranges which run down the west side of the continent; ranges (apparently of very different geological formations), which have no end of different names, but about which little is known in detail. {80}

And now we will leave generalisations on West African rivers and go into particulars regarding one little known in England, and called by its owners, the French, the greatest strictly equatorial river in the world—the Ogowé.

CHAPTER IV

THE OGOWÉ

WHEREIN THE VOYAGER GIVES EXTRACTS FROM THE LOG OF THE MOVÉ AND OF THE ÉCLAIREUR, AND AN ACCOUNT OF THE VOYAGER'S FIRST MEETING WITH "THOSE FEARFUL FANS," ALSO AN AWFUL WARNING TO ALL YOUNG PERSONS WHO NEGLECT THE STUDY OF THE FRENCH LANGUAGE.

ON THE 20TH OF MAY I reached Gaboon, now called Libreville—the capital of Congo Français, and, thanks to the kindness of Mr. Hudson, I was allowed a passage on a small steamer then running from Gaboon to the Ogowé River, and up it when necessary as far as navigation by steamer is possible—this steamer is, I deeply regret to say, now no more. As experiences of this kind contain such miscellaneous masses of facts, I am forced to commit the literary crime of giving you my Ogowé set of experiences in the form of diary.

June 5th, 1895.—Off on Mové at 9.30. Passengers, Mr. Hudson, Mr. Woods, Mr. Huyghens, Père Steinitz, and I. There are black deck-passengers galore; I do not know their honourable names, but they are evidently very much married men, for there is quite a gorgeously coloured little crowd of ladies to see them off. They salute me as I pass down the pier, and start inquiries. I say hastily to them: "Farewell, I'm off up river," for I notice Mr. Fildes bearing down on me, and I don't want him to drop in on the subject of society interest. I expect it is settled now, or pretty nearly. There is a considerable amount of mild uproar among the black contingent, and the Mové firmly clears off before half the good advice and good wishes for the black husbands are aboard. She is a fine little vessel; far finer than I expected. The accommodation I am getting is excellent. A long, narrow cabin, with one bunk in it and pretty nearly everything one can wish for, and a copying press thrown in. Food is excellent, society charming, captain and engineer quite acquisitions. The saloon is square and roomy for the size of the vessel, and most things, from rowlocks to teapots, are kept under the seats in good nautical style. We call at the guard-ship to pass our papers, and then steam ahead out of the Gaboon estuary to the south, round Pongara Point, keeping close into the land. About forty feet from shore there is a good free channel for vessels with a light draught which if you do not take, you have to make a big sweep seaward to avoid a reef. Between four and five miles below Pongara, we pass Point Gombi, which is fitted with a lighthouse, a lively and conspicuous structure by day as well as night. It is perched on a knoll, close to the extremity of the long arm of low, sandy ground, and is painted black and white, in horizontal bands, which, in conjunction with its general figure, give it a pagoda-like appearance.

Alongside it are a white-painted, red-roofed house for the lighthouse keeper, and a store for its oil. The light is either a flashing or a revolving or a stationary one, when it is alight. One must be accurate about these things, and my knowledge regarding it is from information received, and amounts to the above. I cannot throw in any personal experience, because I have never passed it at night-time, and seen from Glass it seems just steady. Most lighthouses on this Coast give up fancy tricks, like flashing or revolving, pretty soon after they are established. Seventy-five per cent. of them are not alight half the time at all. "It's the climate." Gombi, however, you may depend on for being alight at night, and I have no hesitation in saying you can see it, when it is visible, seventeen miles out to sea, and that the knoll on which the lighthouse stands is a grass-covered sand cliff, about forty or fifty feet above sea-level. As we pass round Gombi point, the weather becomes distinctly rough, particularly at lunch-time. The Mové minds it less than her passengers, and stamps steadily along past the wooded shore, behind which shows a distant range of blue hills. Silence falls upon the black passengers, who assume recumbent positions on the deck, and suffer. All the things from under the saloon seats come out and dance together, and play puss-in-the-corner, after the fashion of loose gear when there is any sea on. As the night comes down, the scene becomes more and more picturesque. The moonlit sea, shimmering and breaking on the darkened shore, the black forest and the hills silhouetted against the star-powdered purple sky, and, at my feet, the engine-room stoke-hole, lit with the rose-coloured glow from its furnace, showing by the great wood fire the two nearly naked Krumen stokers, shining like polished bronze in their perspiration, as they throw in on to the fire the billets of red wood that look like freshly-cut chunks of flesh. The white engineer hovers round the mouth of the pit, shouting down directions and ever and anon plunging down the little iron ladder to carry them out himself. At intervals he stands on the rail with his head craned round the edge of the sun deck to listen to the captain, who is up on the little deck above, for there is no telegraph to the engines, and our gallant commander's voice is not strong. While the white engineer is roosting on the rail, the black engineer comes partially up the ladder and gazes hard at me; so I give him a wad of tobacco, and he plainly regards me as inspired, for of course that was what he wanted. Remember that whenever you see a man, black or white, filled with a nameless longing, it is tobacco he requires. Grim despair accompanied by a gusty temper indicates something wrong with his pipe, in which case offer him a straightened-out hairpin. The black engineer having got his tobacco, goes below to the stoke-hole again and smokes a short clay as black and as strong as himself. The captain affects an immense churchwarden. How he gets through life, waving it about as he does, without smashing it every two minutes, I cannot make out.

At last we anchor for the night just inside Nazareth Bay, for Nazareth Bay wants daylight to deal with, being rich in low islands and sand shoals. We crossed the Equator this afternoon.

June 6th.—Off at daybreak into Nazareth Bay. Anxiety displayed by navigators, sounding taken on both sides of the bows with long bamboo poles painted in stripes, and we go "slow ahead" and "hard astern" successfully, until we get round a good-sized island, and there we stick until four o'clock, high water, when we come off all right, and steam triumphantly but cautiously into the Ogowé. The shores of Nazareth Bay are fringed with mangroves, but once in the river the scenery soon changes, and the waters are walled on either side with a forest rich in bamboo, oil and wine-palms. These forest cliffs seem to rise right up out of the mirror-like brown water. Many of the highest trees are covered with clusters of brown-pink young shoots that look like flowers, and others are decorated by my old enemy the climbing palm, now bearing clusters of bright crimson berries. Climbing plants of other kinds are wreathing everything, some blossoming with mauve, some with yellow, some with white flowers, and every now and then a soft sweet heavy breath of fragrance comes out to us as we pass by. There is a native village on the north bank, embowered along its plantations with some very tall cocoa-palms rising high above them.

The river winds so that it seems to close in behind us, opening out in front fresh vistas of superb forest beauty, with the great brown river stretching away unbroken ahead like a broad road of burnished bronze. Astern, it has a streak of frosted silver let into it by the Move's screw. Just about six o'clock, we run up to the Fallaba, the Move's predecessor in working the Ogowé, now a hulk, used as a depot by Hatton and Cookson. She is anchored at the entrance of a creek that runs through to the Fernan Vaz; some say it is six hours' run, others that it is eight hours for a canoe; all agree that there are plenty of mosquitoes.

The Fallaba looks grimly picturesque, and about the last spot in which a person of a nervous disposition would care to spend the night. One half of her deck is dedicated to fuel logs, on the other half are plank stores for the goods, and a room for the black sub-trader in charge of them. I know that there must be scorpions which come out of those logs and stroll into the living room, and goodness only knows what one might not fancy would come up the creek or rise out of the floating grass, or the limitless-looking forest. I am told she was a fine steamer in her day, but those who had charge of her did not make allowances for the very rapid rotting action of the Ogowé water, so her hull rusted through before her engines were a quarter worn out; and there was nothing to be done with her then, but put a lot of concrete in, and make her a depot, in which state of life she is very useful, for during the height of the dry season, the Mové cannot get through the creek to supply the firm's Fernan Vaz factories.

Subsequently I heard much of the Fallaba, which seems to have been a celebrated, or rather notorious, vessel. Every one declared her engines to have been of immense power, but this I believe to have been a mere local superstition; because in the same breath, the man who referred to them, as if it would have been quite unnecessary for new engines to have been made for H.M.S. Victorious if those Fallaba engines could have been sent to Chatham dockyard, would mention that "you could not get any pace up on her"; and all who knew her sadly owned "she wouldn't steer," so naturally she spent the greater part of her time on the Ogowé on a sand-bank, or in the bush. All West African steamers have a mania for bush, and the delusion that they are required to climb trees. The Fallaba had the complaint severely, because of her defective steering powers, and the temptation the magnificent forest, and the rapid currents, and the sharp turns of the creek district, offered her; she failed, of course—they all fail—but it is not for want of practice. I have seen many West Coast vessels up trees, but never more than fifteen feet or so.

The trade of this lower part of the Ogowé, from the mouth to Lembarene, a matter of 130 miles, is almost nil. Above Lembarene, you are in touch with the rubber and ivory trade.

This Fallaba creek is noted for mosquitoes, and the black passengers made great and showy preparations in the evening time to receive their onslaught, by tying up their strong chintz mosquito bars to the stanchions and the cook-house. Their arrangements being constantly interrupted by the white engineer making alarums and excursions amongst them; because when too many of them get on one side the Mové takes a list and burns her boilers. Conversation and atmosphere are full of mosquitoes. The decision of widely experienced sufferers amongst us is, that next to the lower Ogowé, New Orleans is the worst place for them in this world.

The day closed with a magnificent dramatic beauty. Dead ahead of us, up through a bank of dun-coloured mist rose the moon, a great orb of crimson, spreading down the oil-like, still river, a streak of blood-red reflection. Right astern, the sun sank down into the mist, a vaster orb of crimson, and when he had gone out of view, sent up flushes of amethyst, gold, carmine and serpent-green, before he left the moon in undisputed possession of the black purple sky.

Forest and river were absolutely silent, but there was a pleasant chatter and laughter from the black crew and passengers away forward, that made the Move seem an island of life in a land of death. I retired into my cabin, so as to get under the mosquito curtains to write; and one by one I heard my companions come into the saloon adjacent, and say to the watchman: "You sabe six o'clock? When them long arm catch them place, and them short arm catch them place, you call me in the morning time." Exit from saloon—silence—then: "You sabe five o'clock? When them long arm catch them place, and them short arm catch them place, you call me in the morning time." Exit—silence—then: "You sabe half-past five o'clock? When them long arm—" Oh, if I were a watchman! Anyhow, that five o'clocker will have the whole ship's company roused in the morning time.

June 7th.—Every one called in the morning time by the reflex row from the rousing of the five o'clocker. Glorious morning. The scene the reversal of that of last night. The forest to the east shows a deep blue-purple, mounted on a background that changes as you watch it from daffodil and amethyst to rose-pink, as the sun comes up through the night mists. The moon sinks down among them, her pale face flushing crimson as she goes; and the yellow-gold sunshine comes, glorifying the forest and gilding the great sweep of tufted papyrus growing alongside the bank; and the mist vanishes, little white flecks of it lingering among the water reeds and lying in the dark shadows of the forest stems. The air is full of the long, soft, rich notes of the plantain warblers, and the uproar consequent upon the Move taking on fuel wood, which comes alongside in canoe loads from the Fallaba.

Père Steinitz and Mr. Woods are busy preparing their respective canoes for their run to Fernan Vaz through the creek. Their canoes are very fine ones, with a remarkably clean run aft. The Père's is quite the travelling canoe, with a little stage of bamboo aft, covered with a hood of palm thatch, under which you can make yourself quite comfortable, and keep yourself and your possessions dry, unless something desperate comes on in the way of rain.

By 10.25 we have got all our wood aboard, and run off up river full speed. The river seems broader above the Fallaba, but this is mainly on account of its being temporarily unencumbered with islands. A good deal of the bank we have passed by since leaving Nazareth Bay on the south side has been island shore, with a channel between the islands and the true south bank.

The day soon grew dull, and looked threatening, after the delusive manner of the dry season. The climbing plants are finer here than I have ever before seen them. They form great veils and curtains between and over the trees, often hanging so straight and flat, in stretches of twenty to forty feet or so wide, and thirty to sixty or seventy feet high, that it seems incredible that no human hand has trained or clipped them into their perfect forms. Sometimes these curtains are decorated with large bell-shaped, bright-coloured flowers, sometimes with delicate sprays of white blossoms. This forest is beyond all my expectations of tropical luxuriance and beauty, and it is a thing of another world to the forest of the Upper Calabar, which, beautiful as it is, is a sad dowdy to this. There you certainly get a great sense of grimness and vastness; here you have an equal grimness and vastness with the addition of superb colour. This forest is a Cleopatra to which Calabar is but a Quaker. Not only does this forest depend on flowers for its illumination, for there are many kinds of trees having their young shoots, crimson, brown-pink, and creamy yellow: added to this there is also the relieving aspect of the prevailing fashion among West African trees, of wearing the trunk white with here and there upon it splashes of pale pink lichen, and vermilion-red fungus, which alone is sufficient to prevent the great mass of vegetation from being a monotony in green.

All day long we steam past ever-varying scenes of loveliness whose component parts are ever the same, yet the effect ever different. Doubtless it is wrong to call it a symphony, yet I know no other word to describe the scenery of the Ogowé. It is as full of life and beauty and passion as any symphony Beethoven ever wrote: the parts changing, interweaving, and returning. There are leit motifs here in it, too. See the papyrus ahead; and you know when you get abreast of it you will find the great forest sweeping away in a bay-like curve behind it against the dull gray sky, the splendid columns of its cotton and red woods looking like a façade of some limitless inchoate temple. Then again there is that stretch of sword-grass, looking as if it grew firmly on to the bottom, so steady does it stand; but as the Mové goes by, her wash sets it undulating in waves across its broad acres of extent, showing it is only riding at anchor; and you know after a grass patch you will soon see a red dwarf clay cliff, with a village perched on its top, and the inhabitants thereof in their blue and red cloths standing by to shout and wave to the Mové, or legging it like lamp-lighters from the back streets and the plantation to the river frontage, to be in time to do so, and through all these changing phases there is always the strain of the vast wild forest, and the swift, deep, silent river.

At almost every village that we pass—and they are frequent after the Fallaba—there is an ostentatious display of firewood deposited either on the bank, or on piles driven into the mud in front of it, mutely saying in their uncivilised way, "Try our noted chunks: best value for money"—(that is to say, tobacco, etc.), to the Mové or any other little steamer that may happen to come along hungry for fuel.

We stayed a few minutes this afternoon at Ashchyouka, where there came off to us in a canoe an enterprising young Frenchman who has planted and tended a coffee plantation in this out-of-the-way region, and which is now, I am glad to hear, just coming into bearing. After leaving Ashchyouka, high land showed to the N.E., and at 5.15, without evident cause to the uninitiated, the Mové took to whistling like a liner. A few minutes later a factory shows up on the hilly north bank, which is Woermann's; then just beyond and behind it we see the Government Post; then Hatton and Cookson's factory, all in a line. Opposite Hatton and Cookson's there was a pretty little stern-wheel steamer nestling against the steep clay bank of Lembarene Island when we come in sight, but she instantly swept out from it in a perfect curve, which lay behind her marked in frosted silver on the water as she dropt down river. I hear now she was the Éclaireur, the stern-wheeler which runs up and down the Ogowé in connection with the Chargeurs Réunis Company, subsidised by the Government, and when the Mové whistled, she was just completing taking on 3,000 billets of wood for fuel. She comes up from the Cape (Lopez) stoking half wood and half coal as far as Njole and back to Lembarene; from Lembarene to the sea downwards she does on wood. In a few minutes we have taken her berth close to the bank, and tied up to a tree. The white engineer yells to the black engineer "Tom-Tom: Haul out some of them fire and open them drains one time," and the stokers, with hooks, pull out the glowing logs on to the iron deck in front of the furnace door, and throw water over them, and the Mové sends a cloud of oil-laden steam against the bank, coming perilously near scalding some of her black admirers assembled there. I dare say she felt vicious because they had been admiring the Éclaireur.

After a few minutes, I am escorted on to the broad verandah of Hatton and Cookson's factory, and I sit down under a lamp, prepared to contemplate, until dinner time, the wild beauty of the scene. This idea does not get carried out; in the twinkling of an eye I am stung all round the neck, and recognise there are lots too many mosquitoes and sandflies in the scenery to permit of contemplation of any kind. Never have I seen sandflies and mosquitoes in such appalling quantities. With a wild ping of joy the latter made for me, and I retired promptly into a dark corner of the verandah, swearing horribly, but internally, and fought them. Mr. Hudson, Agent-general, and Mr. Cockshut, Agent for the Ogowé, walk up and down the beach in front, doubtless talking cargo, apparently unconscious of mosquitoes; but by and by, while we are having dinner, they get their share. I behave exquisitely, and am quite lost in admiration of my own conduct, and busily deciding in my own mind whether I shall wear one of those plain ring haloes, or a solid plate one, à la Cimabue, when Mr. Hudson says in a voice full of reproach to Mr. Cockshut, "You have got mosquitoes here, Mr. Cockshut." Poor Mr. Cockshut doesn't deny it; he has got four on his forehead and his hands are sprinkled with them, but he says: "There are none at Njole," which we all feel is an absurdly lame excuse, for Njole is some ninety miles above Lembarene, where we now are. Mr. Hudson says this to him, tersely, and feeling he has utterly crushed Mr. Cockshut, turns on me, and utterly failing to recognise me as a suffering saint, says point blank and savagely, "You don't seem to feel these things, Miss Kingsley." Not feel them, indeed! Why, I could cry over them. Well! that's all the thanks one gets for trying not to be a nuisance in this world.

After dinner I go back on to the Mové for the night, for it is too late to go round to Kangwe and ask Mme. Jacot, of the Mission Evangelique, if she will take me in. The air is stiff with mosquitoes, and saying a few suitable words to them, I dash under the mosquito bar and sleep, lulled by their shrill yells of baffled rage.

June 8th.—In the morning, up at five. Great activity on beach. Mové synchronously taking on wood fuel and discharging cargo. A very active young French pastor from the Kangwe mission station is round after the mission's cargo. Mr. Hudson kindly makes inquiries as to whether I may go round to Kangwe and stay with Mme. Jacot. He says: "Oh, yes," but as I find he is not M. Jacot, I do not feel justified in accepting this statement without its having personal confirmation from Mme. Jacot, and so, leaving my luggage with the Mové, I get them to allow me to go round with him and his cargo to Kangwe, about three-quarters of an hour's paddle round the upper part of Lembarene Island, and down the broad channel on the other side of it. Kangwe is beautifully situated on a hill, as its name denotes, on the mainland and north bank of the river. Mme. Jacot most kindly says I may come, though I know I shall be a fearful nuisance, for there is no room for me save M. Jacot's beautifully neat, clean, tidy study. I go back in the canoe and fetch my luggage from the Mové; and say good-bye to Mr. Hudson, who gave me an immense amount of valuable advice about things, which was subsequently of great use to me, and a lot of equally good warnings which, if I had attended to, would have enabled me to avoid many, if not all, my misadventures in Congo Français.

I camped out that night in M. Jacot's study, wondering how he would like it when he came home and found me there; for he was now away on one of his usual evangelising tours. Providentially Mme. Jacot let me have the room that the girls belonging to the mission school usually slept in, to my great relief, before M. Jacot came home.

I will not weary you with my diary during my first stay at Kangwe. It is a catalogue of the collection of fish, etc., that I made, and a record of the continuous, never-failing kindness and help that I received from M. and Mme. Jacot, and of my attempts to learn from them the peculiarities of the region, the natives, and their language and customs, which they both know so well and manage so admirably. I daily saw there what it is possible to do, even in the wildest and most remote regions of West Africa, and recognised that there is still one heroic form of human being whose praise has never adequately been sung, namely, the missionary's wife.

Wishing to get higher up the Ogowé, I took the opportunity of the river boat of the Chargeurs Réunis going up to the Njole on one of her trips, and joined her.

June 22nd. - Éclaireur, charming little stern wheel steamer, exquisitely kept. She has an upper and a lower deck. The lower deck for business, the upper deck for white passengers only. On the upper deck there is a fine long deck-house, running almost her whole length. In this are the officers' cabins, the saloon and the passengers' cabins (two), both large and beautifully fitted up. Captain Verdier exceedingly pleasant and constantly saying "N'est-ce pas?" A quiet and singularly clean engineer completes the white staff.

The passengers consist of Mr. Cockshut, going up river to see after the sub-factories; a French official bound for Franceville, which it will take him thirty-six days, go as quick as he can, in a canoe after Njole; a tremendously lively person who has had black water fever four times, while away in the bush with nothing to live on but manioc, a diet it would be far easier to die on under the circumstances. He is excellent company; though I do not know a word he says, he is perpetually giving lively and dramatic descriptions of things which I cannot but recognise. M. S---, with his pince-nez, the Doctor, and, above all, the rapids of the Ogowé, rolling his hands round and round each other and clashing them forward with a descriptive ejaculation of "Whish, flash, bum, bum, bump," and then comes what evidently represents a terrific fight for life against terrific odds. Wish to goodness I knew French, for wishing to see these rapids, I cannot help feeling anxious and worried at not fully understanding this dramatic entertainment regarding them. There is another passenger, said to be the engineer's brother, a quiet, gentlemanly man. Captain argues violently with every one; with Mr. Cockshut on the subject of the wicked waste of money in keeping the Mové and not shipping all goods by the Éclaireur, "N'est-ce pas?" and with the French official on goodness knows what, but I fancy it will be pistols for two and coffee for one in the morning time. When the captain feels himself being worsted in argument, he shouts for support to the engineer and his brother. "N'est-ce pas?" he says, turning furiously to them. "Oui, oui, certainement," they say dutifully and calmly, and then he, refreshed by their support, dashes back to his controversial fray. He even tries to get up a row with me on the subject of the English merchants at Calabar, whom he asserts have sworn a kind of blood oath to ship by none but British and African Company's steamers. I cannot stand this, for I know my esteemed and honoured friends the Calabar traders would ship by the Flying Dutchman or the Devil himself if either of them would take the stuff at 15 shillings the ton. We have, however, to leave off this row for want of language, to our mutual regret, for it would have been a love of a fight.

Soon after leaving Lembarene Island, we pass the mouth of the chief southern affluent of the Ogowé, the Ngunie; it flows in unostentatiously from the E.S.E., a broad, quiet river here with low banks and two islands (Walker's Islands) showing just off its entrance. Higher up, it flows through a mountainous country, and at Samba, its furthest navigable point, there is a wonderfully beautiful waterfall, the whole river coming down over a low cliff, surrounded by an amphitheatre of mountains. It takes the Éclaireur two days steaming from the mouth of the Ngunie to Samba, when she can get up; but now, in the height of the long dry season neither she nor the Mové can go because of the sandbanks; so Samba is cut off until next October. Hatton and Cookson have factories up at Samba, for it is an outlet for the trade of Achango land in rubber and ivory, a trade worked by the Akele tribe, a powerful, savage and difficult lot to deal with, and just in the same condition, as far as I can learn, as they were when Du Chaillu made his wonderful journeys among them. While I was at Lembarene, waiting for the Éclaireur, a notorious chief descended on a Ngunie sub-factory, and looted it. The wife of the black trading agent made a gallant resistance, her husband was away on a trading expedition, but the chief had her seized and beaten, and thrown into the river. An appeal was made to the Doctor then Administrator of the Ogowé, a powerful and helpful official, and he soon came up with the little canoniere, taking Mr. Cockshut with him and fully vindicated the honour of the French flag, under which all factories here are.

The banks of the Ogowé just above Lembarene Island are low; with the forest only broken by village clearings and seeming to press in on those, ready to absorb them should the inhabitants cease their war against it. The blue Ntyankâlâ mountains of Achango land show away to the E.S.E. in a range. Behind us, gradually sinking in the distance, is the high land on Lembarene Island.

Soon we run up alongside a big street of a village with four high houses rising a story above the rest, which are strictly ground floor; it has also five or six little low open thatched huts along the street in front. {96} These may be fetish huts, or, as the captain of the Sparrow would say, "again they mayn't." For I have seen similar huts in the villages round Libreville, which were store places for roof mats, of which the natives carefully keep a store dry and ready for emergencies in the way of tornadoes, or to sell. We stop abreast of this village. Inhabitants in scores rush out and form an excited row along the vertical bank edge, several of the more excited individuals falling over it into the water.

Yells from our passengers on the lower deck. Yells from inhabitants on shore. Yells of vite, vite from the Captain. Dogs bark, horns bray, some exhilarated individual thumps the village drum, canoes fly out from the bank towards us. Fearful scrimmage heard going on all the time on the deck below. As soon as the canoes are alongside, our passengers from the lower deck, with their bundles and their dogs, pour over the side into them. Canoes rock wildly and wobble off rapidly towards the bank, frightening the passengers because they have got their best clothes on, and fear that the Éclaireur will start and upset them altogether with her wash.

On reaching the bank, the new arrivals disappear into brown clouds of wives and relations, and the dogs into fighting clusters of resident dogs. Happy, happy day! For those men who have gone ashore have been away on hire to the government and factories for a year, and are safe home in the bosoms of their families again, and not only they themselves, but all the goods they have got in pay. The remaining passengers below still yell to their departed friends; I know not what they say, but I expect it's the Fan equivalent for "Mind you write. Take care of yourself. Yes, I'll come and see you soon," etc., etc. While all this is going on, the Éclaireur quietly slides down river, with the current, broadside on as if she smelt her stable at Lembarene. This I find is her constant habit whenever the captain, the engineer, and the man at the wheel are all busy in a row along the rail, shouting overside, which occurs whenever we have passengers to land. Her iniquity being detected when the last canoe load has left for the shore, she is spun round and sent up river again at full speed.

We go on up stream; now and again stopping at little villages to land passengers or at little sub-factories to discharge cargo, until evening closes in, when we anchor and tie up at O'Saomokita, where there is a sub-factory of Messrs. Woermann's, in charge of which is a white man, the only white man between Lembarene and Njole. He comes on board and looks only a boy, but is really aged twenty. He is a Frenchman, and was at Hatton and Cookson's first, then he joined Woermann's, who have put him in charge of this place. The isolation for a white man must be terrible; sometimes two months will go by without his seeing another white face but that in his looking-glass, and when he does see another, it is only by a fleeting visit such as we now pay him, and to make the most of this, he stays on board to dinner.

June 23rd.—Start off steaming up river early in the morning time. Land ahead showing mountainous. Rather suddenly the banks grow higher. Here

and there in the forest are patches which look like regular hand-made plantations, which they are not, but only patches of egombie-gombie trees, showing
that at this place was once a native town. Whenever land is cleared along here,
this tree springs up all over the ground. It grows very rapidly, and has great
leaves something like a sycamore leaf, only much larger. These leaves growing
in a cluster at the top of the straight stem give an umbrella-like appearance
to the affair; so the natives call them and an umbrella by the same name, but
whether they think the umbrella is like the tree or the tree is like the umbrella,
I can't make out. I am always getting myself mixed over this kind of thing
in my attempts "to contemplate phenomena from a scientific standpoint," as
Cambridge ordered me to do. I'll give the habit up. "You can't do that sort
of thing out here—It's the climate," and I will content myself with stating the
fact, that when a native comes into a store and wants an umbrella, he asks for
an egombie-gombie.

The uniformity of the height of the individual trees in one of these patches
is striking, and it arises from their all starting fair. I cannot make out other
things about them to my satisfaction, for you very rarely see one of them in
the wild bush, and then it does not bear a fruit that the natives collect and use,
and then chuck away the stones round their domicile. Anyhow, there they are
all one height, and all one colour, and apparently allowing no other vegetation
to make any headway among them. But I found when I carefully investigated
egombie-gombie patches that there were a few of the great, slower-growing
forest trees coming up amongst them, and in time when these attain a sufficient
height, their shade kills off the egombie-gombie, and the patch goes back into
the great forest from which it came. The frequency of these patches arises from
the nomadic habits of the chief tribe in these regions, the Fans. They rarely
occupy one site for a village for any considerable time on account—firstly, of
their wasteful method of collecting rubber by cutting down the vine, which
soon stamps it out of a district; and, secondly, from their quarrelsome ways. So
when a village of Fans has cleared all the rubber out of its district, or has made
the said district too hot to hold it by rows with other villages, or has got itself
very properly shelled out and burnt for some attack on traders or the French
flag in any form, its inhabitants clear off into another district, and build another
village; for bark and palm thatch are cheap, and house removing just nothing;
when you are an unsophisticated cannibal Fan you don't require a pantechnicon
van to stow away your one or two mushroom-shaped stools, knives, and cooking-pots, and a calabash or so. If you are rich, maybe you will have a box with
clothes in as well, but as a general rule all your clothes are on your back. So your
wives just pick up the stools and the knives and the cooking-pots, and the box,
and the children toddle off with the calabashes. You have, of course, the gun to

carry, for sleeping or waking a Fan never parts with his gun, and so there you are "finish," as M. Pichault would say, and before your new bark house is up, there grows the egombie-gombie, where your house once stood. Now and again, for lack of immediate neighbouring villages to quarrel with, one end of a village will quarrel with the other end. The weaker end then goes off and builds itself another village, keeping an eye lifting for any member of the stronger end who may come conveniently into its neighbourhood to be killed and eaten. Meanwhile, the egombie-gombie grows over the houses of the empty end, pretending it's a plantation belonging to the remaining half. I once heard a new-comer hold forth eloquently as to how those Fans were maligned. "They say," said he, with a fine wave of his arm towards such a patch, "that these people do not till the soil—that they are not industrious—that the few plantations they do make are ill-kept—that they are only a set of wandering hunters and cannibals. Look there at those magnificent plantations!" I did look, but I did not alter my opinion of the Fans, for I know my old friend egombie-gombie when I see him.

This morning the French official seems sad and melancholy. I fancy he has got a Monday head (Kipling), but he revives as the day goes on. As we go on, the banks become hills and the broad river, which has been showing sheets of sandbanks in all directions, now narrows and shows only neat little beaches of white sand in shallow places along the bank. The current is terrific. The Éclaireur breathes hard, and has all she can do to fight her way up against it. Masses of black weathered rock in great boulders show along the exposed parts of both banks, left dry by the falling waters. Each bank is steep, and quantities of great trees, naked and bare, are hanging down from them, held by their roots and bush-rope entanglement from being swept away with the rushing current, and they make a great white fringe to the banks. The hills become higher and higher, and more and more abrupt, and the river runs between them in a gloomy ravine, winding to and fro; we catch sight of a patch of white sand ahead, which I mistake for a white painted house, but immediately after doubling round a bend we see the houses of the Talagouga Mission Station. The Éclaireur forthwith has an hysteric fit on her whistle, so as to frighten M. Forget and get him to dash off in his canoe to her at once. Apparently he knows her, and does not hurry, but comes on board quietly. I find there will be no place for me to stay at at Njole, so I decide to go on in the Éclaireur and use her as an hotel while there, and then return and stay with Mme. Forget if she will have me. I consult M. Forget on this point. He says, "Oh, yes," but seems to have lost something of great value recently, and not to be quite clear where. Only manner, I suppose. When M. Forget has got his mails he goes, and the Éclaireur goes on; indeed, she has never really stopped, for the water is too deep to anchor in here, and the terrific current would promptly whisk the steamer down out of Talagouga gorge were she to leave off fighting it. We run on up past Talagouga Island, where the river broadens out again a little, but not much, and reach Njole by nightfall, and tie up to a tree by Dumas' factory beach. Usual uproar, but as Mr. Cockshut says, no mosquitoes. The mosquito belt ends abruptly at O'Soamokita.

Next morning I go ashore and start on a walk. Lovely road, bright yellow clay, as hard as paving stone. On each side it is most neatly hedged with pine-apples; behind these, carefully tended, acres of coffee bushes planted in long rows. Certainly coffee is one of the most lovely of crops. Its grandly shaped leaves are like those of our medlar tree, only darker and richer green, the berries set close to the stem, those that are ripe, a rich crimson; these trees, I think, are about three years old, and just coming into bearing; for they are covered with full-sized berries, and there has been a flush of bloom on them this morning, and the delicious fragrance of their stephanotis-shaped and scented flowers lingers in the air. The country spreads before me a lovely valley encompassed by purple-blue mountains. Mount Talagouga looks splendid in a soft, infinitely deep blue, although it is quite close, just the other side of the river. The road goes on into the valley, as pleasantly as ever and more so. How pleasant it would be now, if our government along the Coast had the enterprise and public spirit of the French, and made such roads just on the remote chance of stray travellers dropping in on a steamer once in ten years or so and wanting a walk. Observe extremely neatly Igalwa built huts, people sitting on the bright clean ground outside them, making mats and baskets. "Mboloani," say I. "Ai! Mbolo," say they, and knock off work to stare. Observe large wired-in enclosures on left-hand side of road—investigate—find they are tenanted by animals—goats, sheep, chickens, etc. Clearly this is a jardin d'acclimatation. No wonder the colony does not pay, if it goes in for this sort of thing, 206 miles inland, with simply no public to pay gate-money. While contemplating these things, hear awful hiss. Serpents! No, geese. Awful fight. Grand things, good, old-fashioned, long skirts are for Africa! Get through geese and advance in good order, but somewhat rapidly down road, turn sharply round corner of native houses. Turkey cock—terrific turn up. Flight on my part forwards down road, which is still going strong, now in a northerly direction, apparently indefinitely. Hope to goodness there will be a turning that I can go down and get back by, without returning through this ferocious farmyard. Intent on picking up such an outlet, I go thirty yards or so down the road. Hear shouts coming from a clump of bananas on my left. Know they are directed at me, but it does not do to attend to shouts always. Expect it is only some native with an awful knowledge of English, anxious to get up my family history—therefore accelerate pace. More shouts, and louder, of "Madame Gacon! Madame Gacon!"

and out of the banana clump comes a big, plump, pleasant-looking gentleman, clad in a singlet and a divided skirt. White people must be attended to, so advance carefully towards him through a plantation of young coffee, apologising humbly for intruding on his domain. He smiles and bows beautifully, but—horror!—he knows no English, I no French. Situation très inexplicable et très interessante, as I subsequently heard him remark; and the worst of it is he is evidently bursting to know who I am, and what I am doing in the middle of his coffee plantation, for his it clearly is, as appears from his obsequious bodyguard of blacks, highly interested in me also. We gaze at each other, and smile some more, but stiffly, and he stands bareheaded in the sun in an awful way. It's murder I'm committing, hard all! He, as is fitting for his superior sex, displays intelligence first and says, "Interpreter," waving his hand to the south. I say "Yes," in my best Fan, an enthusiastic, intelligent grunt which any one must understand. He leads the way back towards those geese—perhaps, by the by, that is why he wears those divided skirts—and we enter a beautifully neatly built bamboo house, and sit down opposite to each other at a table and wait for the interpreter who is being fetched. The house is low on the ground and of native construction, but most beautifully kept, and arranged with an air of artistic feeling quite as unexpected as the rest of my surroundings. I notice upon the walls sets of pictures of terrific incidents in Algerian campaigns, and a copy of that superb head of M. de Brazza in Arab headgear. Soon the black minions who have been sent to find one of the plantation hands who is supposed to know French and English, return with the "interpreter." That young man is a fraud. He does not know English—not even coast English—and all he has got under his precious wool is an abysmal ignorance darkened by terror; and so, after one or two futile attempts and some frantic scratching at both those regions which an African seems to regard as the seats of intellectual inspiration, he bolts out of the door. Situation terrible! My host and I smile wildly at each other, and both wonder in our respective languages what, in the words of Mr. Squeers as mentioned in the classics—we "shall do in this 'ere most awful go." We are both going mad with the strain of the situation, when in walks the engineer's brother from the Éclaireur. He seems intensely surprised to find me sitting in his friend the planter's parlour after my grim and retiring conduct on the Éclaireur on my voyage up. But the planter tells him all, sousing him in torrents of words, full of the violence of an outbreak of pent-up emotion. I do not understand what he says, but I catch "très inexplicable" and things like that. The calm brother of the engineer sits down at the table, and I am sure tells the planter something like this: "Calm yourself, my friend, we picked up this curiosity at Lembarene. It seems quite harmless." And then the planter calmed, and mopped a perspiring brow, and so did I, and we smiled more freely, feeling the mental atmosphere had become less tense and cooler. We both simply beamed on our deliverer, and the planter gave him lots of things to drink. I had nothing about me except a head of tobacco in my pocket, which I did not feel was a suitable offering. Now the engineer's brother, although he would not own to it, knew English, so I told him how the beauty of the road had lured me on, and how I was interested in coffee-planting, and how much I admired the magnificence of this plantation, and all the enterprise and energy it represented.

"Oui, oui, certainement," said he, and translated. My friend the planter seemed charmed; it was the first sign of anything approaching reason he had seen in me. He wanted me to have eau sucrée more kindly than ever, and when I rose, intending to bow myself off and go, geese or no geese, back to the Éclaireur, he would not let me go. I must see the plantation, toute la plantation. So presently all three of us go out and thoroughly do the plantation, the most well-ordered, well-cultivated plantation I have ever seen, and a very noble monument to the knowledge and industry of the planter. For two hot hours these two perfect gentlemen showed me over it. I also behaved well, for petticoats, great as they are, do not prevent insects and catawumpuses of sorts walking up one's ankles and feeding on one as one stands on the long grass which has been most wisely cut and laid round the young trees for mulching. This plantation is of great extent on the hill-sides and in the valley bottom, portions of it are just coming into bearing. The whole is kept as perfectly as a garden, amazing as the work of one white man with only a staff of unskilled native labourers—at present only eighty of them. The coffee planted is of three kinds, the Elephant berry, the Arabian, and the San Thomé. During our inspection, we only had one serious misunderstanding, which arose from my seeing for the first time in my life tree-ferns growing in the Ogowé. There were three of them, evidently carefully taken care of, among some coffee plants. It was highly exciting, and I tried to find out about them. It seemed, even in this centre of enterprise, unlikely that they had been brought just "for dandy" from the Australasian region, and I had never yet come across them in my wanderings save on Fernando Po. Unfortunately, my friends thought I wanted them to keep, and shouted for men to bring things and dig them up; so I had a brisk little engagement with the men, driving them from their prey with the point of my umbrella, ejaculating Kor Kor, like an agitated crow. When at last they understood that my interest in the ferns was scientific, not piratical, they called the men off and explained that the ferns had been found among the bush, when it was being cleared for the plantation.

Ultimately, with many bows and most sincere thanks from me, we parted, providentially beyond the geese, and I returned down the road to Njole, where I find Mr. Cockshut waiting outside his factory. He insists on taking me to the Post to see the Administrator, and from there he says I can go on to the Éclaireur from the Post beach, as she will be up there from Dumas'. Off we go up the road which skirts the river bank, a dwarf clay cliff, overgrown with vegetation, save where it is cleared for beaches. The road is short, but exceedingly pretty; on the other side from the river is a steep bank on which is growing a plantation of cacao. Lying out in the centre of the river you see Njole Island, a low, sandy one, timbered not only with bush, but with orange and other fruit trees; for formerly the Post and factories used to be situated on the island—now only their trees remain for various reasons, one being that in the wet season it is a good deal under water. Everything is now situated on the mainland north bank, in a straggling but picturesque line; first comes Woermann's factory, then Hatton and Cookson's, and John Holt's, close together with a beach in common in a sweetly amicable style for factories, who as a rule firmly stockade themselves off from their next door neighbours. Then Dumas' beach, a little native village, the cacao patch and the Post at the up river end of things European, an end of things European, I am told, for a matter of 500 miles. Immediately beyond the Post is a little river falling into the Ogowé, and on its further bank a small village belonging to a chief, who, hearing of the glories of the Government, came down like the Queen of Sheba—in intention, I mean, not personal appearance—to see it, and so charmed has he been that here he stays to gaze on it.

Although Mr. Cockshut hunted the Administrator of the Ogowé out of his bath, that gentleman is exceedingly amiable and charming, all the more so to me for speaking good English. Personally, he is big, handsome, exuberant, and energetic. He shows me round with a gracious enthusiasm, all manner of things—big gorilla teeth and heads, native spears and brass-nail-ornamented guns; and explains, while we are in his study, that the little model canoe full of Kola nuts is the supply of Kola to enable him to sit up all night and work. Then he takes us outside to see the new hospital which he, in his capacity as Administrator, during the absence of the professional Administrator on leave in France, has granted to himself in his capacity as Doctor; and he shows us the captive chief and headmen from Samba busily quarrying a clay cliff behind it so as to enlarge the governmental plateau, and the ex-ministers of the ex-King of Dahomey, who are deported to Njole, and apparently comfortable and employed in various non-menial occupations. Then we go down the little avenue of cacao trees in full bearing, and away to the left to where there is now an encampment of Adoomas, who have come down as a convoy from Franceville, and are going back with another under the command of our vivacious fellow passenger, who, I grieve to see, will have a rough time of it in the way of accommodation in those narrow, shallow canoes which are lying with their noses tied to the bank, and no other white man to talk to. What a blessing he will be conversationally to Franceville when he gets in. The Adooma encampment is very picturesque, for they have got their bright-coloured chintz mosquito-bars erected as tents.

Dr. Pélessier then insists on banging down monkey bread-fruit with a stick, to show me their inside. Of course they burst over his beautiful white clothes. I said they would, but men will be men. Then we go and stand under the two lovely odeaka trees that make a triumphal-arch-like gateway to the Post's beach from the river, and the Doctor discourses in a most interesting way on all sorts of subjects. We go on waiting for the Éclaireur, who, although it is past four o'clock, is still down at Dumas' beach. I feel nearly frantic at detaining the Doctor, but neither he nor Mr. Cockshut seem in the least hurry. But at last I can stand it no longer. The vision of the Administrator of the Ogowé, worn out, but chewing Kola nut to keep himself awake all night while he finishes his papers to go down on the Éclaireur to-morrow morning, is too painful; so I say I will walk back to Dumas' and go on the Éclaireur there, and try to liberate the Administrator from his present engagements, so that he may go back and work. No good! He will come down to Dumas' with Mr. Cockshut and me. Off we go, and just exactly as we are getting on to Dumas' beach, off starts the Éclaireur with a shriek for the Post beach. So I say good-bye to Mr. Cockshut, and go back to the Post with Dr. Pélessier, and he sees me on board, and to my immense relief he stays on board a good hour and a half, talking to other people, so it is not on my head if he is up all night.

June 25th. - Éclaireur has to wait for the Administrator until ten, because he has not done his mails. At ten he comes on board like an amiable tornado, for he himself is going to Cape Lopez. I am grieved to see them carrying on board, too, a French official very ill with fever. He is the engineer of the canoniere and they are taking him down to Cape Lopez, where they hope to get a ship to take him up to Gaboon, and to the hospital on the Minervé. I heard subsequently that the poor fellow died about forty hours after leaving Njole at Achyouka in Kama country.

We get away at last, and run rapidly down river, helped by the terrific current. The Éclaireur has to call at Talagouga for planks from M. Gacon's sawmill. As soon as we are past the tail of Talagouga Island, the Éclaireur ties her whistle string to a stanchion, and goes off into a series of screaming fits, as only she can. What she wants is to get M. Forget or M. Gacon, or better still both, out in their canoes with the wood waiting for her, because "she cannot anchor in the depth," "nor can she turn round," and "backing plays the mischief with any ship's engines," and "she can't hold her own against the current," and—then Captain Verdier says things I won't repeat, and throws his weight passionately on the whistle string, for we are in sight of the narrow gorge of Talagouga, with the Mission Station apparently slumbering in the sun. This puts the Éclaireur in an awful temper. She goes down towards it as near as she dare, and then frisks round again, and runs up river a little way and drops down again, in violent hysterics the whole time. Soon M. Gacon comes along among the trees on the bank, and laughs at her. A rope is thrown to him, and the panting Éclaireur tied up to a tree close in to the bank, for the water is deep enough here to moor a liner in, only there are a good many rocks. In a few minutes M. Forget and several canoe loads of beautiful red-brown mahogany planks are on board, and things being finished, I say good-bye to the captain, and go off with M. Forget in a canoe, to the shore.

CHAPTER V

THE RAPIDS OF THE OGOWÉ

THE LOG OF AN ADOOMA CANOE DURING A VOYAGE UNDERTAKEN TO
THE RAPIDS OF THE RIVER OGOWÉ, WITH SOME ACCOUNT OF THE DIV-
ERS DISASTERS THAT BEFELL THEREON.

MME. FORGET RECEIVED ME MOST KINDLY, and, thanks to her ever
thoughtful hospitality, I spent a very pleasant time at Talagouga,
wandering about the forest and collecting fishes from the native fishermen: and seeing the strange forms of some of these Talagouga region fishes
and the marked difference between them and those of Lembarene, I set my
heart on going up into the region of the Ogowé rapids. For some time no
one whom I could get hold of regarded it as a feasible scheme, but, at last, M.
Gacon thought it might be managed; I said I would give a reward of 100 francs
to any one who would lend me a canoe and a crew, and I would pay the working expenses, food, wages, etc. M. Gacon had a good canoe and could spare
me two English-speaking Igalwas, one of whom had been part of the way with
MM. Allégret and Teisserès, when they made their journey up to Franceville
and then across to Brazzaville and down the Congo two years ago. He also
thought we could get six Fans to complete the crew. I was delighted, packed
my small portmanteau with a few things, got some trade goods, wound up my
watch, ascertained the date of the day of the month, and borrowed three hair-
pins from Mme. Forget, then down came disappointment. On my return from
the bush that evening, Mme. Forget said M. Gacon said "it was impossible,"
the Fans round Talagouga wouldn't go at any price above Njole, because they
were certain they would be killed and eaten by the up-river Fans. Internally
consigning the entire tribe to regions where they will get a rise in temperature,
even on this climate, I went with Mme. Forget to M. Gacon, and we talked it

over; finally, M. Gacon thought he could let me have two more Igalwas from Hatton and Cookson's beach across the river. Sending across there we found this could be done, so I now felt I was in for it, and screwed my courage to the sticking point—no easy matter after all the information I had got into my mind regarding the rapids of the River Ogowé.

I establish myself on my portmanteau comfortably in the canoe, my back is against the trade box, and behind that is the usual mound of pillows, sleeping mats, and mosquito-bars of the Igalwa crew; the whole surmounted by the French flag flying from an indifferent stick.

M. and Mme. Forget provide me with everything I can possibly require, and say that the blood of half my crew is half alcohol; on the whole it is patent they don't expect to see me again, and I forgive them, because they don't seem cheerful over it; but still it is not reassuring—nothing is about this affair, and it's going to rain. It does, as we go up the river to Njole, where there is another risk of the affair collapsing, by the French authorities declining to allow me to proceed. On we paddled, M'bo the head man standing in the bows of the canoe in front of me, to steer, then I, then the baggage, then the able-bodied seamen, including the cook also standing and paddling; and at the other extremity of the canoe—it grieves me to speak of it in this unseamanlike way, but in these canoes both ends are alike, and chance alone ordains which is bow and which is stern—stands Pierre, the first officer, also steering; the paddles used are all of the long-handled, leaf-shaped Igalwa type. We get up just past Talagouga Island and then tie up against the bank of M. Gazenget's plantation, and make a piratical raid on its bush for poles. A gang of his men come down to us, but only to chat. One of them, I notice, has had something happen severely to one side of his face. I ask M'bo what's the matter, and he answers, with a derisive laugh, "He be fool man, he go for tief plantain and done got shot." M'bo does not make it clear where the sin in this affair is exactly located; I expect it is in being "fool man." Having got our supply of long stout poles we push off and paddle on again. Before we reach Njole I recognise my crew have got the grumbles, and at once inquire into the reason. M'bo sadly informs me that "they no got chop," having been provided only with plantain, and no meat or fish to eat with it. I promise to get them plenty at Njole, and contentment settles on the crew, and they sing. After about three hours we reach Njole, and I proceed to interview the authorities. Dr. Pélessier is away down river, and the two gentlemen in charge don't understand English; but Pierre translates, and the letter which M. Forget has kindly written for me explains things and so the palaver ends satisfactorily, after a long talk. First, the official says he does not like to take the responsibility of allowing me to endanger myself in those rapids. I explain I will not hold any one responsible but myself, and I urge that a lady has been up before, a Mme. Quinee. He says "Yes, that is true, but Madame had with her a husband and many men, whereas I am alone and have only eight Igalwas and not Adoomas, the proper crew for the rapids, and they are away up river now with the convoy." "True, oh King!" I answer, "but Madame Quinee went right up to Lestourville, whereas I only want to go sufficiently high up the rapids to get typical fish. And these Igalwas are great men at canoe work, and can go in a canoe anywhere that any mortal man can go"—this to cheer up my Igalwa interpreter—"and as for the husband, neither the Royal Geographical Society's list, in their 'Hints to Travellers,' nor Messrs. Silver, in their elaborate lists of articles necessary for a traveller in tropical climates, make mention of husbands." However, the official ultimately says Yes, I may go, and parts with me as with one bent on self destruction. This affair being settled I start off, like an old hen with a brood of chickens to provide for, to get chop for my men, and go first to Hatton and Cookson's factory. I find its white Agent is down river after stores, and John Holt's Agent says he has got no beef nor fish, and is precious short of provisions for himself; so I go back to Dumas', where I find a most amiable French gentleman, who says he will let me have as much fish or beef as I want, and to this supply he adds some delightful bread biscuits. M'bo and the crew beam with satisfaction; mine is clouded by finding, when they have carried off the booty to the canoe, that the Frenchman will not let me pay for it. Therefore taking the opportunity of his back being turned for a few minutes, I buy and pay for, across the store counter, some trade things, knives, cloth, etc. Then I say goodbye to the Agent. "Adieu, Mademoiselle," says he in a for-ever tone of voice. Indeed I am sure I have caught from these kind people a very pretty and becoming mournful manner, and there's not another white station for 500 miles where I can show it off. Away we go, still damp from the rain we have come through, but drying nicely with the day, and cheerful about the chop.

The Ogowé is broad at Njole and its banks not mountainous, as at Talagouga; but as we go on it soon narrows, the current runs more rapidly than ever, and we are soon again surrounded by the mountain range. Great masses of black rock show among the trees on the hillsides, and under the fringe of fallen trees that hang from the steep banks. Two hours after leaving Njole we are facing our first rapid. Great gray-black masses of smoothed rock rise up out of the whirling water in all directions. These rocks have a peculiar appearance which puzzle me at the time, but in subsequently getting used to it I accepted it quietly and admired. When the sun shines on them they have a soft light blue haze round them, like a halo. The effect produced by this, with the forested hillsides and the little beaches of glistening white sand was one of the most perfect things I have ever seen.

We kept along close to the right-hand bank, dodging out of the way of the swiftest current as much as possible. Ever and again we were unable to force our way round projecting parts of the bank, so we then got up just as far as we could to the point in question, yelling and shouting at the tops of our voices. M'bo said "Jump for bank, sar," and I "up and jumped," followed by half the crew. Such banks! sheets, and walls, and rubbish heaps of rock, mixed up with trees fallen and standing. One appalling corner I shall not forget, for I had to jump at a rock wall, and hang on to it in a manner more befitting an insect than an insect-hunter, and then scramble up it into a close-set forest, heavily burdened with boulders of all sizes. I wonder whether the rocks or the trees were there first? there is evidence both ways, for in one place you will see a rock on the top of a tree, the tree creeping out from underneath it, and in another place you will see a tree on the top of a rock, clasping it with a network of roots and getting its nourishment, goodness knows how, for these are by no means tender, digestible sandstones, but uncommon hard gneiss and quartz which has no idea of breaking up into friable small stuff, and which only takes on a high polish when it is vigorously sanded and canvassed by the Ogowé. While I was engaged in climbing across these promontories, the crew would be busy shouting and hauling the canoe round the point by means of the strong chain provided for such emergencies fixed on to the bow. When this was done, in we got again and paddled away until we met our next affliction.

M'bo had advised that we should spend our first night at the same village that M. Allégret did: but when we reached it, a large village on the north bank, we seemed to have a lot of daylight still in hand, and thought it would be better to stay at one a little higher up, so as to make a shorter day's work for to-morrow, when we wanted to reach Kondo Kondo; so we went against the bank just to ask about the situation and character of the up-river villages. The row of low, bark huts was long, and extended its main frontage close to the edge of the river bank. The inhabitants had been watching us as we came, and when they saw we intended calling that afternoon, they charged down to the river-edge hopeful of excitement. They had a great deal to say, and so had we. After compliments, as they say, in excerpts of diplomatic communications, three of their men took charge of the conversation on their side, and M'bo did ours. To M'bo's questions they gave a dramatic entertainment as answer, after the manner of these brisk, excitable Fans. One chief, however, soon settled down to definite details, prefacing his remarks with the silence-commanding "Azuna! Azuna!" and his companions grunted approbation of his observations. He took a piece of plantain leaf and tore it up into five different sized bits. These he laid along the edge of our canoe at different intervals of space, while he told M'bo things, mainly scandalous, about the characters of the villages these bits of leaf represented, save of course about bit A, which represented his own. The interval between the bits was proportional to the interval between the villages, and the size of the bits was proportional to the size of the village. Village number four was the only one he should recommend our going to. When all was said, I gave our kindly informants some heads of tobacco and many thanks. Then M'bo sang them a hymn, with the assistance of Pierre, half a line behind him in a different key, but every bit as flat. The Fans seemed impressed, but any crowd would be by the hymn-singing of my crew, unless they were inmates of deaf and dumb asylums. Then we took our farewell, and thanked the village elaborately for its kind invitation to spend the night there on our way home, shoved off and paddled away in great style just to show those Fans what Igalwas could do.

We hadn't gone 200 yards before we met a current coming round the end of a rock reef that was too strong for us to hold our own in, let alone progress. On to the bank I was ordered and went; it was a low slip of rugged confused boulders and fragments of rocks, carelessly arranged, and evidently under water in the wet season. I scrambled along, the men yelled and shouted and hauled the canoe, and the inhabitants of the village, seeing we were becoming amusing again, came, legging it like lamp-lighters, after us, young and old, male and female, to say nothing of the dogs. Some good souls helped the men haul, while I did my best to amuse the others by diving headlong from a large rock on to which I had elaborately climbed, into a thick clump of willow-leaved shrubs. They applauded my performance vociferously, and then assisted my efforts to extricate myself, and during the rest of my scramble they kept close to me, with keen competition for the front row, in hopes that I would do something like it again. But I refused the encore, because, bashful as I am, I could not but feel that my last performance was carried out with all the superb reckless abandon of a Sarah Bernhardt, and a display of art of this order should satisfy any African village for a year at least. At last I got across the rocks on to a lovely little beach of white sand, and stood there talking, surrounded by my audience, until the canoe got over its difficulties and arrived almost as scratched as I; and then we again said farewell and paddled away, to the great grief of the natives, for they don't get a circus up above Njole every week, poor dears.

Now there is no doubt that that chief's plantain-leaf chart was an ingenious idea and a credit to him. There is also no doubt that the Fan mile is a bit Irish, a matter of nine or so of those of ordinary mortals, but I am bound to say I don't think, even allowing for this, that he put those pieces far enough apart. On we paddled a long way before we picked up village number one, mentioned in that chart. On again, still longer, till we came to village number two. Village number three hove in sight high up on a mountain side soon after, but it was getting dark and the water worse, and the hill-sides growing higher and higher into nobly shaped mountains, forming, with their forest-graced steep sides, a ravine that, in the gathering gloom, looked like an alley-way made of iron, for the foaming Ogowé. Village number four we anxiously looked for; village number four we never saw; for round us came the dark, seeming to come out on to the river from the forests and the side ravines, where for some hours we had seen it sleeping, like a sailor with his clothes on in bad weather. On we paddled, looking for signs of village fires, and seeing them not. The Erd-geist knew we wanted something, and seeing how we personally lacked it, thought it was beauty; and being in a kindly mood, gave it us, sending the lovely lingering flushes of his afterglow across the sky, which, dying, left it that divine deep purple velvet which no one has dared to paint. Out in it came the great stars blazing high above us, and the dark round us was be-gemmed with fire-flies: but we were not as satisfied with these things as we should have been; what we wanted were fires to cook by and dry ourselves by, and all that sort of thing. The Erd-geist did not understand, and so left us when the afterglow had died away, with only enough starlight to see the flying foam of the rapids ahead and around us, and not enough to see the great trees that had fallen from the bank into the water. These, when the rapids were not too noisy, we could listen for, because the black current rushes through their branches with an impatient "lish, swish"; but when there was a rapid roaring close alongside we ran into those trees, and got ourselves mauled, and had ticklish times getting on our course again. Now and again we ran up against great rocks sticking up in the black water—grim, isolated fellows, who seemed to be standing silently watching their fellow rocks noisily fighting in the arena of the white water. Still on we poled and paddled. About 8 P.M. we came to a corner, a bad one; but we were unable to leap on to the bank and haul round, not being able to see either the details or the exact position of the said bank, and we felt, I think naturally, disinclined to spring in the direction of such bits of country as we had had experience of during the afternoon, with nothing but the aid we might have got from a compass hastily viewed by the transitory light of a lucifer match, and even this would not have informed us how many tens of feet of tree fringe lay between us and the land, so we did not attempt it. One must be careful at times, or nasty accidents may follow. We fought our way round that corner, yelling defiance at the water, and dealt with succeeding corners on the vi et armisplan, breaking, ever and anon, a pole. About 9.30 we got into a savage rapid. We fought it inch by inch. The canoe jammed herself on some barely sunken rocks in it. We shoved her off over them. She tilted over and chucked us out. The rocks round being just awash, we survived and got her straight again, and got into her and drove her unmercifully; she struck again and bucked like a broncho, and we fell in heaps upon each other, but stayed inside that time—the men by the aid of their intelligent feet, I by clinching my hands into the bush rope lacing which ran round the rim of the canoe and the meaning of which I did not understand when I left Talagouga. We sorted ourselves out hastily and sent her at it again. Smash went a sorely tried pole and a paddle. Round and round we spun in an exultant whirlpool, which, in a light-hearted, maliciously joking way, hurled us tail first out of it into the current. Now the grand point in these canoes of having both ends alike declared itself; for at this juncture all we had to do was to revolve on our own axis and commence life anew with what had been the bow for the stern. Of course we were defeated, we could not go up any further without the aid of our lost poles and paddles, so we had to go down for shelter somewhere, anywhere, and down at a terrific pace in the white water we went. While hitched among the rocks the arrangement of our crew had been altered, Pierre joining M'bo in the bows; this piece of precaution was frustrated by our getting turned round; so our position was what you might call precarious, until we got into another whirlpool, when we persuaded Nature to start us right end on. This was only a matter of minutes, whirlpools being plentiful, and then M'bo and Pierre, provided with our surviving poles, stood in the bows to fend us off rocks, as we shot towards them; while we midship paddles sat, helping to steer, and when occasion arose, which occasion did with lightning rapidity, to whack the whirlpools with the flat of our paddles, to break their force. Cook crouched in the stern concentrating his mind on steering only. A most excellent arrangement in theory and the safest practical one no doubt, but it did not work out what you might call brilliantly well; though each department did its best. We dashed full tilt towards high rocks, things twenty to fifty feet above water. Midship backed and flapped like fury; M'bo and Pierre received the shock on their poles; sometimes we glanced successfully aside and flew on; sometimes we didn't. The shock being too much for M'bo and Pierre they were driven back on me, who got flattened on to the cargo of bundles which, being now firmly tied in, couldn't spread the confusion further aft; but the shock of the canoe's nose against the rock did so in style, and the rest of the crew fell forward on to the bundles, me, and themselves. So shaken up together were we several times that night, that it's a wonder to me, considering the hurry, that we sorted our-selves out correctly with our own particular legs and arms. And although we in the middle of the canoe did some very spirited flapping, our whirlpool-breaking was no more successful than M'bo and Pierre's fending off, and many a wild waltz we danced that night with the waters of the River Ogowé.

Unpleasant as going through the rapids was, when circumstances took us into the black current we fared no better. For good all-round inconvenience, give me going full tilt in the dark into the branches of a fallen tree at the pace we were going then—and crash, swish, crackle and there you are, hung up, with a bough pressing against your chest, and your hair being torn out and your clothes ribboned by others, while the wicked river is trying to drag away the canoe from under you. After a good hour and more of these experiences, we went hard on to a large black reef of rocks. So firm was the canoe wedged that we in our rather worn-out state couldn't move her so we wisely decided to "lef 'em" and see what could be done towards getting food and a fire for the remainder of the night. Our eyes, now trained to the darkness, observed pretty close to us a big lump of land, looming up out of the river. This we subsequently found out was Kembe Island. The rocks and foam on either side stretched away into the darkness, and high above us against the star-lit sky stood out clearly the summits of the mountains of the Sierra del Cristal.

The most interesting question to us now was whether this rock reef communicated sufficiently with the island for us to get to it. Abandoning conjecture; tying very firmly our canoe up to the rocks, a thing that seemed, considering she was jammed hard and immovable, a little unnecessary—but you can never be sufficiently careful in this matter with any kind of boat—off we started among the rock boulders. I would climb up on to a rock table, fall off it on the other side on to rocks again, with more or less water on them—then get a patch of singing sand under my feet, then with varying suddenness get into more water, deep or shallow, broad or narrow pools among the rocks; out of that over more rocks, etc., etc., etc.: my companions, from their noises, evidently were going in for the same kind of thing, but we were quite cheerful, because the probability of reaching the land seemed increasing. Most of us arrived into deep channels of water which here and there cut in between this rock reef and the bank, M'bo was the first to find the way into certainty; he was, and I hope still is, a perfect wonder at this sort of work. I kept close to M'bo, and when we got to the shore, the rest of the wanderers being collected, we said "chances are there's a village round here"; and started to find it. After a gay time in a rock-encumbered forest, growing in a tangled, matted way on a rough hillside, at an angle of 45 degrees, M'bo sighted the gleam of fires through the tree stems away to the left, and we bore down on it, listening to its drum. Viewed through the bars of the tree stems the scene was very picturesque. The village was just a collection of palm mat-built huts, very low and squalid. In its tiny street, an affair of some sixty feet long and twenty wide, were a succession of small fires. The villagers themselves, however, were the striking features in the picture. They were painted vermilion all over their nearly naked bodies, and were dancing enthusiastically to the good old rump-a-tump-tump-tump tune, played energetically by an old gentleman on a long, high-standing, white-and-black painted drum. They said that as they had been dancing when we arrived they had failed to hear us. M'bo secured a—well, I don't exactly know what to call it—for my use. It was, I fancy, the remains of the village club-house. It had a certain amount of palm-thatch roof and some of its left-hand side left, the rest of the structure was bare old poles with filaments of palm mat hanging from them here and there; and really if it hadn't been for the roof one wouldn't have known whether one was inside or outside it. The floor was trodden earth and in the middle of it a heap of white ash and the usual two bush lights, laid down with their burning ends propped up off the ground with stones, and emitting, as is their wont, a rather mawkish, but not altogether unpleasant smell, and volumes of smoke which finds its way out through the thatch, leaving on the inside of it a rich oily varnish of a bright warm brown colour. They give a very good light, provided some one keeps an eye on them and knocks the ash off the end as it burns gray; the bush lights' idea of being snuffed. Against one of the open-work sides hung a drum covered with raw hide, and a long hollow bit of tree trunk, which served as a cupboard for a few small articles. I gathered in all these details as I sat on one of the hard wood benches, waiting for my dinner, which Isaac was preparing outside in the street. The atmosphere of the hut, in spite of its remarkable advantages in the way of ventilation, was oppressive, for the smell of the bush lights, my wet clothes, and the natives who crowded into the hut to look at me, made anything but a pleasant combination. The people were evidently exceedingly poor; clothes they had very little of. The two head men had on old French military coats in rags; but they were quite satisfied with their appearance, and evidently felt through them in touch with European culture, for they lectured to the others on the habits and customs of the white man with great self-confidence and superiority. The majority of the village had a slight acquaintance already with this interesting animal, being, I found, Adoomas. They had made a settlement on Kembe Island some two years or so ago. Then the Fans came and attacked them, and killed and ate several. The Adoomas left and fled to the French authority at Njole and remained under its guarding shadow until the French came up and chastised the Fans and burnt their village; and the Adoomas—when things had quieted down again and the Fans had gone off to build themselves a new village for their burnt one—came back to Kembe Island and their plantain patch. They had only done this a few months before my arrival and had not had time to rebuild, hence the dilapidated state of the village. They are, I am told, a Congo region tribe, whose country lies south-west of Franceville, and, as I have already said, are the tribe used by the French authorities to take convoys up and down the Ogowé to Franceville, more to keep this route open than for transport purposes; the rapids rendering it impracticable to take heavy stores this way, and making it a thirty-six days' journey from Njole with good luck. The practical route is viâ Loango and Brazzaville. The Adoomas told us the convoy which had gone up with the vivacious Government official had had trouble with the rapids and had spent five days on Kondo Kondo, dragging up the canoes empty by means of ropes and chains, carrying the cargo that was in them along on land until they had passed the worst rapid and then repacking. They added the information that the rapids were at their worst just now, and entertained us with reminiscences of a poor young French official who had been drowned in them last year—indeed they were just as cheering as my white friends. As soon as my dinner arrived they politely cleared out, and I heard the devout M'bo holding a service for them, with hymns, in the street, and this being over they returned to their drum and dance, keeping things up distinctly late, for it was 11.10 P.M. when we first entered the village.

While the men were getting their food I mounted guard over our little possessions, and when they turned up to make things tidy in my hut, I walked off down to the shore by a path, which we had elaborately avoided when coming to the village, a very vertically inclined, slippery little path, but still the one whereby the natives went up and down to their canoes, which were kept tied up amongst the rocks. The moon was rising, illumining the sky, but not yet sending down her light on the foaming, flying Ogowé in its deep ravine. The scene was divinely lovely; on every side out of the formless gloom rose the peaks of the Sierra del Cristal. Lomba-ngawku on the further side of the river surrounded by his companion peaks, looked his grandest, silhouetted hard against the sky. In the higher valleys where the dim light shone faintly, one could see wreaths and clouds of silver-gray mist lying, basking lazily or rolling to and fro. Olangi seemed to stretch right across the river, blocking with his great blunt mass all passage; while away to the N.E. a cone-shaped peak showed conspicuous, which I afterwards knew as Kangwe. In the darkness round me flitted thousands of fire-flies and out beyond this pool of utter night flew by unceasingly the white foam of the rapids; sound there was none save their thunder. The majesty and beauty of the scene fascinated me, and I stood leaning with my back against a rock pinnacle watching it. Do not imagine it gave rise, in what I am pleased to call my mind, to those complicated, poetical reflections natural beauty seems to bring out in other people's minds. It never works that way with me; I just lose all sense of human individuality, all memory of human life, with its grief and worry and doubt, and become part of the atmosphere. M'bo, I found, had hung up my mosquito-bar over one of the hard wood benches, and going cautiously under it I lit a night-light and read myself asleep with my damp dilapidated old Horace.

Woke at 4 A.M. lying on the ground among the plantain stems, having by a reckless movement fallen out of the house. Thanks be there are no mosquitoes. I don't know how I escaped the rats which swarm here, running about among the huts and the inhabitants in the evening, with a tameness shocking to see. I turned in again until six o'clock, when we started getting things ready to go up river again, carefully providing ourselves with a new stock of poles, and subsidising a native to come with us and help us to fight the rapids.

The greatest breadth of the river channel we now saw, in the daylight, to be the S.S.W. branch; this was the one we had been swept into, and was almost completely barred by rock. The other one to the N.N.W. was more open, and the river rushed through it, a terrific, swirling mass of water. Had we got caught in this, we should have got past Kembe Island, and gone to Glory. Whenever the shelter of the spits of land or of the reefs was sufficient to allow the water to lay down its sand, strange shaped sandbanks showed, as regular in form as if they had been smoothed by human hands. They rise above the water in a slope, the low end or tail against the current; the down-stream end terminating in an abrupt miniature cliff, sometimes six and seven feet above the water; that they are the same shape when they have not got their heads above water you will find by sticking on them in a canoe, which I did several times, with a sort of automatic devotion to scientific research peculiar to me. Your best way of getting off is to push on in the direction of the current, carefully preparing for the shock of suddenly coming off the cliff end.

We left the landing place rocks of Kembe Island about 8, and no sooner had we got afloat, than, in the twinkling of an eye, we were swept, broadside on, right across the river to the north bank, and then engaged in a heavy fight with a severe rapid. After passing this, the river is fairly uninterrupted by rock for a while, and is silent and swift. When you are ascending such a piece the effect is strange; you see the water flying by the side of your canoe, as you vigorously drive your paddle into it with short rapid strokes, and you forthwith fancy you are travelling at the rate of a North-Western express; but you just raise your eyes, my friend, and look at that bank, which is standing very nearly still, and you will realise that you and your canoe are standing very nearly still too; and that all your exertions are only enabling you to creep on at the pace of a crushed snail, and that it's the water that is going the pace. It's a most quaint and unpleasant disillusionment.

Above the stretch of swift silent water we come to the Isangaladi Islands, and the river here changes its course from N.N.W., S.S.E. to north and south. A bad rapid, called by our ally from Kembe Island "Unfanga," being surmounted, we seem to be in a mountain-walled lake, and keeping along the left bank of this, we get on famously for twenty whole restful minutes, which lulls us all into a false sense of security, and my crew sing M'pongwe songs, descriptive of how they go to their homes to see their wives, and families, and friends, giving chaffing descriptions of their friends' characteristics and of their failings, which cause bursts of laughter from those among us who recognise the allusions, and how they go to their boxes, and take out their clothes, and put them on—a long bragging inventory of these things is given by each man as a solo, and then the chorus, taken heartily up by his companions, signifies their admiration and astonishment at his wealth and importance—and then they sing how, being dissatisfied with that last dollar's worth of goods they got from "Holty's," they have decided to take their next trade to Hatton and Cookson, or vice versa; and then comes the chorus, applauding the wisdom of such a decision, and extolling the excellence of Hatton and Cookson's goods or Holty's. These M'pongwe and Igalwa boat songs are all very pretty, and have very elaborate tunes in a minor key. I do not believe there are any old words to them; I have tried hard to find out about them, but I believe the tunes, which are of a limited number and quite distinct from each other, are very old. The words are put in by the singer on the spur of the moment, and only restricted in this sense, that there would always be the domestic catalogue—whatever its component details might be—sung to the one fixed tune, the trade information sung to another, and so on. A good singer, in these parts, means the man who can make up the best song—the most impressive, or the most amusing; I have elsewhere mentioned pretty much the same state of things among the Ga's and Krumen and Bubi, and in all cases the tunes are only voice tunes, not for instrumental performance. The instrumental music consists of that marvellously developed series of drum tunes—the attempt to understand which has taken up much of my time, and led me into queer company—and the many tunes played on the 'mrimba and the orchid-root-stringed harp: they are, I believe, entirely distinct from the song tunes. And these peaceful tunes my men were now singing were, in their florid elaboration very different from the one they fought the rapids to, of—So Sir—So Sur—So Sir—So Sur—Ush! So Sir, etc.

On we go singing elaborately, thinking no evil of nature, when a current, a quiet devil of a thing, comes round from behind a point of the bank and catches the nose of our canoe; wringing it well, it sends us scuttling right across the river in spite of our ferocious swoops at the water, upsetting us among a lot of rocks with the water boiling over them; this lot of rocks being however of the table-top kind, and not those precious, close-set pinnacles rising up sheer out of profound depths, between which you are so likely to get your canoe wedged in and split. We, up to our knees in water that nearly tears our legs off, push and shove the canoe free, and re-embarking return singing "So Sir" across the river, to have it out with that current. We do; and at its head find a rapid, and notice on the mountain-side a village clearing, the first sign of human habitation we have seen to-day.

Above this rapid we get a treat of still water, the main current of the Ogowé flying along by the south bank. On our side there are sandbanks with their graceful sloping backs and sudden ends, and there is a very strange and beautiful effect produced by the flakes and balls of foam thrown off the rushing main current into the quiet water. These whirl among the eddies and rush backwards and forwards as though they were still mad with wild haste, until, finding no current to take them down, they drift away into the landlocked bays, where they come to a standstill as if they were bewildered and lost and were trying to remember where they were going to and whence they had come; the foam of which they are composed is yellowish-white, with a spongy sort of solidity about it. In a little bay we pass we see eight native women, Fans clearly, by their bright brown faces, and their loads of brass bracelets and armlets; likely enough they had anklets too, but we could not see them, as the good ladies were pottering about waist-deep in the foam-flecked water, intent on breaking up a stockaded fish-trap. We pause and chat, and watch them collecting the fish in baskets, and I acquire some specimens; and then, shouting farewells when we are well away, in the proper civil way, resume our course.

The middle of the Ogowé here is simply forested with high rocks, looking, as they stand with their grim forms above the foam, like a regiment of strange strong creatures breasting it, with their straight faces up river, and their more flowing curves down, as though they had on black mantles which were swept backwards. Across on the other bank rose the black-forested spurs of Lomba-njaku. Our channel was free until we had to fight round the upper end of our bay into a long rush of strong current with bad whirlpools curving its face; then the river widens out and quiets down and then suddenly contracts—a rocky forested promontory running out from each bank. There is a little village on the north bank's promontory, and, at the end of each, huge monoliths rise from the water, making what looks like a gateway which had once been barred and through which the Ogowé had burst.

For the first time on this trip I felt discouraged; it seemed so impossible that we, with our small canoe and scanty crew, could force our way up through that gateway, when the whole Ogowé was rushing down through it. But we clung to the bank and rocks with hands, poles, and paddle, and did it; really the worst part was not in the gateway but just before it, for here there is a great whirlpool, its centre hollowed some one or two feet below its rim. It is caused, my Kembe islander says, by a great cave opening beneath the water. Above the gate the river broadens out again and we see the arched opening to a large cave in the south bank; the mountain-side is one mass of rock covered with the unbroken forest; and the entrance to this cave is just on the upper wall of the south bank's promontory; so, being sheltered from the current here, we rest and examine it leisurely. The river runs into it, and you can easily pass in at this season, but in the height of the wet season, when the river level would be some twenty feet or more above its present one, I doubt if you could. They told me this place is called Boko Boko, and that the cave is a very long one, extending on a level some way into the hill, and then ascending and coming out near a mass of white rock that showed as a speck high up on the mountain.

If you paddle into it you go "far far," and then "no more water live," and you get out and go up the tunnel, which is sometimes broad, sometimes narrow, sometimes high, sometimes so low that you have to crawl, and so get out at the other end.

One French gentleman has gone through this performance, and I am told found "plenty plenty" bats, and hedgehogs, and snakes. They could not tell me his name, which I much regretted. As we had no store of bush lights we went no further than the portals; indeed, strictly between ourselves, if I had had every bush light in Congo Français I personally should not have relished going further. I am terrified of caves; it sends a creaming down my back to think of them.

We went across the river to see another cave entrance on the other bank, where there is a narrow stretch of low rock-covered land at the foot of the mountains, probably under water in the wet season. The mouth of this other cave is low, between tumbled blocks of rock. It looked so suspiciously like a short cut to the lower regions, that I had less exploring enthusiasm about it than even about its opposite neighbour; although they told me no man had gone down "them thing." Probably that much-to-be-honoured Frenchman who explored the other cave, allowed like myself, that if one did want to go from the Equator to Hades, there were pleasanter ways to go than this. My Kembe Island man said that just hereabouts were five cave openings, the two that we had seen and another one we had not, on land, and two under the water, one of the sub-fluvial ones being responsible for the whirlpool we met outside the gateway of Boko Boko.

The scenery above Boko Boko was exceedingly lovely, the river shut in between its rim of mountains. As you pass up it opens out in front of you and closes in behind, the closely-set confused mass of mountains altering in form as you view them from different angles, save one, Kangwe—a blunt cone, evidently the record of some great volcanic outburst; and the sandbanks show again wherever the current deflects and leaves slack water, their bright glistening colour giving a relief to the scene.

For a long period we paddle by the south bank, and pass a vertical cleft-like valley, the upper end of which seems blocked by a finely shaped mountain, almost as conical as Kangwe. The name of this mountain is Njoko, and the name of the clear small river, that apparently monopolises the valley floor, is the Ovata. Our peace was not of long duration, and we were soon again in the midst of a bristling forest of rock; still the current running was not dangerously strong, for the river-bed comes up in a ridge, too high for much water to come over at this season of the year; but in the wet season this must be one of the worst places. This ridge of rock runs two-thirds across the Ogowé, leaving a narrow deep channel by the north bank. When we had got our canoe over the ridge, mostly by standing in the water and lifting her, we found the water deep and fairly quiet.

On the north bank we passed by the entrance of the Okana River. Its mouth is narrow, but, the natives told me, always deep, even in the height of the dry season. It is a very considerable river, running inland to the E.N.E. Little is known about it, save that it is narrowed into a ravine course above which it expands again; the banks of it are thickly populated by Fans, who send down a considerable trade, and have an evil reputation. In the main stream of the Ogowé below the Okana's entrance, is a long rocky island called Shandi. When we were getting over our ridge and paddling about the Okana's entrance my ears recognised a new sound. The rush and roar of the Ogowé we knew well enough, and could locate which particular obstacle to his headlong course was making him say things; it was either those immovable rocks, which threw him back in foam, whirling wildly, or it was that fringe of gaunt skeleton trees hanging from the bank playing a "pull devil, pull baker" contest that made him hiss with vexation. But this was an elemental roar. I said to M'bo: "That's a thunderstorm away among the mountains." "No, sir," says he, "that's the Alemba."

We paddled on towards it, hugging the right-hand bank again to avoid the mid-river rocks. For a brief space the mountain wall ceased, and a lovely scene opened before us; we seemed to be looking into the heart of the chain of the Sierra del Cristal, the abruptly shaped mountains encircling a narrow plain or valley before us, each one of them steep in slope, every one of them forest-clad; one, whose name I know not unless it be what is sometimes put down as Mt. Okana on the French maps, had a conical shape which contrasted beautifully with the more irregular curves of its companions. The colour down this gap was superb, and very Japanese in the evening glow. The more distant peaks were soft gray-blues and purples, those nearer, indigo and black. We soon passed this lovely scene and entered the walled-in channel, creeping up what seemed an interminable hill of black water, then through some whirlpools and a rocky channel to the sand and rock shore of our desired island Kondo Kondo, along whose northern side tore in thunder the Alemba. We made our canoe fast in a little cove among the rocks, and landed, pretty stiff and tired and considerably damp. This island, when we were on it, must have been about half a mile or so long, but during the long wet season a good deal of it is covered, and only the higher parts—great heaps of stone, among which grows a long branched willow-like shrub—are above or nearly above water. The Adooma from Kembe Island especially drew my attention to this shrub, telling me his people who worked the rapids always regarded it with an affectionate veneration; for he said it was the only thing that helped a man when his canoe got thrown over in the dreaded Alemba, for its long tough branches swimming in, or close to, the water are veritable life lines, and his best chance; a chance which must have failed some poor fellow, whose knife and leopard-skin belt we found wedged in among the rocks on Kondo Kondo. The main part of the island is sand, with slabs and tables of polished rock sticking up through it; and in between the rocks grew in thousands most beautiful lilies, their white flowers having a very strong scent of vanilla and their bright light-green leaves looking very lovely on the glistening pale sand among the black-gray rock. How they stand the long submersion they must undergo I do not know; the natives tell me they begin to spring up as soon as ever the water falls and leaves the island exposed; that they very soon grow up and flower, and keep on flowering until the Ogowé comes down again and rides roughshod over Kondo Kondo for months. While the men were making their fire I went across the island to see the great Alemba rapid, of which I had heard so much, that lay between it and the north bank. Nobler pens than mine must sing its glory and its grandeur. Its face was like nothing I have seen before. Its voice was like nothing I have heard. Those other rapids are not to be compared to it; they are wild, headstrong, and malignant enough, but the Alemba is not as they. It does not struggle, and writhe, and brawl among the rocks, but comes in a majestic springing dance, a stretch of waltzing foam, triumphant.

The beauty of the night on Kondo Kondo was superb; the sun went down and the afterglow flashed across the sky in crimson, purple, and gold, leaving it a deep violet-purple, with the great stars hanging in it like moons, until the moon herself arose, lighting the sky long before she sent her beams down on us in this valley. As she rose, the mountains hiding her face grew harder and harder in outline, and deeper and deeper black, while those opposite were just enough illumined to let one see the wefts and floating veils of blue-white mist upon them, and when at last, and for a short time only, she shone full down on the savage foam of the Alemba, she turned it into a soft silver mist. Around, on all sides, flickered the fire-flies, who had come to see if our fire was not a big relation of their own, and they were the sole representatives, with ourselves, of animal life. When the moon had gone, the sky, still lit by the stars, seeming indeed to be in itself lambent, was very lovely, but it shared none of its light with us, and we sat round our fire surrounded by an utter darkness. Cold, clammy drifts of almost tangible mist encircled us; ever and again came cold faint puffs of wandering wind, weird and grim beyond description.

I will not weary you further with details of our ascent of the Ogowé rapids, for I have done so already sufficiently to make you understand the sort of work going up them entails, and I have no doubt that, could I have given you a more vivid picture of them, you would join me in admiration of the fiery pluck of those few Frenchmen who traverse them on duty bound. I personally deeply regret it was not my good fortune to meet again the French official I had had the pleasure of meeting on the Éclaireur. He would have been truly great in his description of his voyage to Franceville. I wonder how he would have "done" his unpacking of canoes and his experiences on Kondo Kondo, where, by the by, we came across many of the ashes of his expedition's attributive fires. Well! he must have been a pleasure to Franceville, and I hope also to the good Fathers at Lestourville, for those places must be just slightly sombre for Parisians.

Going down big rapids is always, everywhere, more dangerous than coming up, because when you are coming up and a whirlpool or eddy does jam you on rocks, the current helps you off—certainly only with a view to dashing your brains out and smashing your canoe on another set of rocks it's got ready below; but for the time being it helps, and when off, you take charge and convert its plan into an incompleted fragment; whereas in going down the current is against your backing off. M'bo had a series of prophetic visions as to what would happen to us on our way down, founded on reminiscence and tradition. I tried to comfort him by pointing out that, were any one of his prophecies fulfilled, it would spare our friends and relations all funeral expenses; and, unless they went and wasted their money on a memorial window, that ought to be a comfort to our well-regulated minds. M'bo did not see this, but was too good a Christian to be troubled by the disagreeable conviction that was in the minds of other members of my crew, namely, that our souls, unliberated by funeral rites from this world, would have to hover for ever over the Ogowé near the scene of our catastrophe. I own this idea was an unpleasant one—fancy having to pass the day in those caves with the bats, and then come out and wander all night in the cold mists! However, like a good many likely-looking prophecies, those of M'bo did not quite come off, and a miss is as good as a mile. Twice we had a near call, by being shot in between two pinnacle rocks, within half an inch of being fatally close to each other for us; but after some alarming scrunching sounds, and creaks from the canoe, we were shot ignominiously out down river. Several times we got on to partially submerged table rocks, and were unceremoniously bundled off them by the Ogowé, irritated at the hindrance we were occasioning; but we never met the rocks of M'bo's prophetic soul—that lurking, submerged needle, or knife-edge of a pinnacle rock which was to rip our canoe from stem to stern, neat and clean into two pieces.

The course we had to take coming down was different to that we took coming up. Coming up we kept as closely as might be to the most advisable bank, and dodged behind every rock we could, to profit by the shelter it afforded us from the current. Coming down, fallen-tree-fringed banks and rocks were converted from friends to foes; so we kept with all our power in the very centre of the swiftest part of the current in order to avoid them. The grandest part of the whole time was coming down, below the Alemba, where the whole great Ogowé takes a tiger-like spring for about half a mile, I should think, before it strikes a rock reef below. As you come out from among the rocks in the upper rapid it gives you—or I should perhaps confine myself to saying, it gave me—a peculiar internal sensation to see that stretch of black water, shining like a burnished sheet of metal, sloping down before one, at such an angle. All you have got to do is to keep your canoe-head straight—quite straight, you understand—for any failure so to do will land you the other side of the tomb, instead of in a cheerful no-end-of-a-row with the lower rapid's rocks. This lower rapid is one of the worst in the dry season; maybe it is so in the wet too, for the river's channel here turns an elbow-sharp curve which infuriates the Ogowé in a most dangerous manner.

I hope to see the Ogowé next time in the wet season—there must be several more of these great sheets of water then over what are rocky rapids now. Just think what coming down over that ridge above Boko Boko will be like! I do not fancy however it would ever be possible to get up the river, when it is at its height, with so small a crew as we were when we went and played our knockabout farce, before King Death, in his amphitheatre in the Sierra del Cristal.

CHAPTER VI

LEMBARENE

In which is given some account of the episode of the Hippopotame, and of the voyager's attempts at controlling an Ogowé canoe; and also of the Igalwa tribe.

I say good-bye to Talagouga with much regret, and go on board the Éclaireur, when she returns from Njole, with all my bottles and belongings. On board I find no other passenger; the Captain's English has widened out considerably; and he is as pleasant, cheery, and spoiling for a fight as ever; but he has a preoccupied manner, and a most peculiar set of new habits, which I find are shared by the Engineer. Both of them make rapid dashes to the rail, and nervously scan the river for a minute and then return to some occupation, only to dash from it to the rail again. During breakfast their conduct is nerve-shaking. Hastily taking a few mouthfuls, the Captain drops his knife and fork and simply hurls his seamanlike form through the nearest door out on to the deck. In another minute he is back again, and with just a shake of his head to the Engineer, continues his meal. The Engineer shortly afterwards flies from his seat, and being far thinner than the Captain, goes through his nearest door with even greater rapidity; returns, and shakes his head at the Captain, and continues his meal. Excitement of this kind is infectious, and I also wonder whether I ought not to show a sympathetic friendliness by flying from my seat and hurling myself on to the deck through my nearest door, too. But although there are plenty of doors, as four enter the saloon from the deck, I do not see my way to doing this performance aimlessly, and what in this world they are both after I cannot think. So I confine myself to woman's true sphere, and assist in a humble way by catching the wine and Vichy water bottles, glasses, and plates of food, which at every performance are jeopardised by the members of the nobler sex starting off with a considerable quantity of the ample table cloth wrapped round their legs. At last I can stand it no longer, so ask the Captain point-blank what is the matter. "Nothing," says he, bounding out of his chair and flying out of his doorway; but on his return he tells me he has got a bet on of two bottles of champagne with Woermann's Agent for Njole, as to who shall reach Lembarene first, and the German agent has started off some time before the Éclaireur in his little steam launch.

During the afternoon we run smoothly along; the free pulsations of the engines telling what a very different thing coming down the Ogowé is to going up against its terrific current. Every now and again we stop to pick up cargo, or discharge over-carried cargo, and the Captain's mind becomes lulled by getting no news of the Woermann's launch having passed down. He communicates this to the Engineer; it is impossible she could have passed the Éclaireur since they started, therefore she must be some where behind at a subfactory, "N'est-ce pas?" "Oui, oui, certainement,"says the Engineer. The Engineer is, by these considerations, also lulled, and feels he may do something else but scan the river à la sister Ann. What that something is puzzles me; it evidently requires secrecy, and he shrinks from detection. First he looks down one side of the deck, no one there; then he looks down the other, no one there; good so far. I then see he has put his head through one of the saloon portholes; no one there; he hesitates a few seconds until I begin to wonder whether his head will suddenly appear through my port; but he regards this as an unnecessary precaution, and I hear him enter his cabin which abuts on mine and there is silence for some minutes. Writing home to his mother, think I, as I go on putting a new braid round the bottom of a worn skirt. Almost immediately after follows the sound of a little click from the next cabin, and then apparently one of the denizens of the infernal regions has got its tail smashed in a door and the heavy hot afternoon air is reft by an inchoate howl of agony. I drop my needlework and take to the deck; but it is after all only that shy retiring young man practising secretly on his clarionet.

The Captain is drowsily looking down the river. But repose is not long allowed to that active spirit; he sees something in the water—what? "Hip-popotame," he ejaculates. Now both he and the Engineer frequently do this thing, and then fly off to their guns—bang, bang, finish; but this time he does not dash for his gun, nor does the Engineer, who flies out of his cabin at the sound of the war shout "Hippopotame." In vain I look across the broad river with its stretches of yellow sandbanks, where the "hippopotame" should be, but I can see nothing but four black stumps sticking up in the water away to the right. Meanwhile the Captain and the Engineer are flying about getting off a crew of blacks into the canoe we are towing alongside. This being done the

Captain explains to me that on the voyage up "the Engineer had fired at, and hit a hippopotamus, and without doubt this was its body floating." We are now close enough even for me to recognise the four stumps as the deceased's legs, and soon the canoe is alongside them and makes fast to one, and then starts to paddle back, hippo and all, to the Éclaireur. But no such thing; let them paddle and shout as hard as they like, the hippo's weight simply anchors them. The Éclaireur by now has dropped down the river past them, and has to sweep round and run back. Recognising promptly what the trouble is, the energetic Captain grabs up a broom, ties a light cord belonging to the leadline to it, and holding the broom by the end of its handle, swings it round his head and hurls it at the canoe. The arm of a merciful Providence being interposed, the broom-tomahawk does not hit the canoe, wherein, if it had, it must infallibly have killed some one, but falls short, and goes tearing off with the current, well out of reach of the canoe. The Captain seeing this gross dereliction of duty by a Chargeur Réunis broom, hauls it in hand over hand and talks to it. Then he ties the other end of its line to the mooring rope, and by a better aimed shot sends the broom into the water, about ten yards above the canoe, and it drifts towards it. Breathless excitement! surely they will get it now. Alas, no! Just when it is within reach of the canoe, a fearful shudder runs through the broom. It throws up its head and sinks beneath the tide. A sensation of stun comes over all of us. The crew of the canoe, ready and eager to grasp the approaching aid, gaze blankly at the circling ripples round where it sank. In a second the Captain knows what has happened. That heavy hawser which has been paid out after it has dragged it down, so he hauls it on board again.

The Éclaireur goes now close enough to the hippo-anchored canoe for a rope to be flung to the man in her bows; he catches it and freezes on gallantly. Saved! No! Oh horror! The lower deck hums with fear that after all it will not taste that toothsome hippo chop, for the man who has caught the rope is as nearly as possible jerked flying out of the canoe when the strain of the Éclaireurcontending with the hippo's inertia flies along it, but his companion behind him grips him by the legs and is in his turn grabbed, and the crew holding on to each other with their hands, and on to their craft with their feet, save the man holding on to the rope and the whole situation; and slowly bobbing towards us comes the hippopotamus, who is shortly hauled on board by the winners in triumph.

My esteemed friends, the Captain and the Engineer, who of course have been below during this hauling, now rush on to the upper deck, each coatless, and carrying an enormous butcher's knife. They dash into the saloon, where a terrific sharpening of these instruments takes place on the steel belonging to the saloon carving-knife, and down stairs again. By looking down the ladder,

I can see the pink, pig-like hippo, whose colour has been soaked out by the water, lying on the lower deck and the Captain and Engineer slitting down the skin intent on gralloching operations. Providentially, my prophetic soul induces me to leave the top of the ladder and go forward—"run to win'ard," as Captain Murray would say—for within two minutes the Captain and Engineer are up the ladder as if they had been blown up by the boilers bursting, and go as one man for the brandy bottle; and they wanted it if ever man did; for remember that hippo had been dead and in the warm river-water for more than a week.

The Captain had had enough of it, he said, but the Engineer stuck to the job with a courage I profoundly admire, and he saw it through and then retired to his cabin; sand-and-canvassed himself first, and then soaked and saturated himself in Florida water. The flesh gladdened the hearts of the crew and lower-deck passengers and also of the inhabitants of Lembarene, who got dashes of it on our arrival there. Hippo flesh is not to be despised by black man or white; I have enjoyed it far more than the stringy beef or vapid goat's flesh one gets down here.

I stayed on board the Éclaireur all night; for it was dark when we reached Lembarene, too dark to go round to Kangwe; and next morning, after taking a farewell of her—I hope not a final one, for she is a most luxurious little vessel for the Coast, and the feeding on board is excellent and the society varied and charming—I went round to Kangwe.

I remained some time in the Lembarene district and saw and learnt many things; I owe most of what I learnt to M. and Mme. Jacot, who knew a great deal about both the natives and the district, and I owe much of what I saw to having acquired the art of managing by myself a native canoe. This "recklessness" of mine I am sure did not merit the severe criticism it has been subjected to, for my performances gave immense amusement to others (I can hear Lembarene's shrieks of laughter now) and to myself they gave great pleasure.

My first attempt was made at Talagouga one very hot afternoon. M. and Mme. Forget were, I thought, safe having their siestas, Oranie was with Mme. Gacon. I knew where Mme. Gacon was for certain; she was with M. Gacon; and I knew he was up in the sawmill shed, out of sight of the river, because of the soft thump, thump, thump of the big water-wheel. There was therefore no one to keep me out of mischief, and I was too frightened to go into the forest that afternoon, because on the previous afternoon I had been stalked as a wild beast by a cannibal savage, and I am nervous. Besides, and above all, it is quite impossible to see other people, even if they are only black, naked savages, gliding about in canoes, without wishing to go and glide about yourself. So I went down to where the canoes were tied by their noses to the steep bank, and finding a paddle, a broken one, I unloosed the smallest canoe. Unfortunately this was fifteen feet or so long, but I did not know the disadvantage of having, as it were, a long-tailed canoe then—I did shortly afterwards.

The promontories running out into the river on each side of the mission beach give a little stretch of slack water between the bank and the mill-race-like current of the Ogowé, and I wisely decided to keep in the slack water, until I had found out how to steer—most important thing steering. I got into the bow of the canoe, and shoved off from the bank all right; then I knelt down—learn how to paddle standing up by and by—good so far. I rapidly learnt how to steer from the bow, but I could not get up any pace. Intent on acquiring pace, I got to the edge of the slack water; and then displaying more wisdom, I turned round to avoid it, proud as a peacock, you understand, at having found out how to turn round. At this moment, the current of "the greatest equatorial river in the world," grabbed my canoe by its tail. We spun round and round for a few seconds, like a teetotum, I steering the whole time for all I was worth, and then the current dragged the canoe ignominiously down river, tail foremost.

Fortunately a big tree was at that time temporarily hanging against the rock in the river, just below the sawmill beach. Into that tree the canoe shot with a crash, and I hung on, and shipping my paddle, pulled the canoe into the slack water again, by the aid of the branches of the tree, which I was in mortal terror would come off the rock, and insist on accompanying me and the canoe, viâKama country, to the Atlantic Ocean; but it held, and when I had got safe against the side of the pinnacle-rock I wiped a perspiring brow, and searched in my mind for a piece of information regarding Navigation that would be applicable to the management of long-tailed Adooma canoes. I could not think of one for some minutes. Captain Murray has imparted to me at one time and another an enormous mass of hints as to the management of vessels, but those vessels were all pre-supposed to have steam power. But he having been the first man to take an ocean-going steamer up to Matadi on the Congo, through the terrific currents that whirl and fly in Hell's Cauldron, knew about currents, and I remembered he had said regarding taking vessels through them, "Keep all the headway you can on her." Good! that hint inverted will fit this situation like a glove, and I'll keep all the tailway I can off her. Feeling now as safe as only a human being can feel who is backed up by a sound principle, I was cautiously crawling to the tail-end of the canoe, intent on kneeling in it to look after it, when I heard a dreadful outcry on the bank. Looking there I saw Mme. Forget, Mme. Gacon, M. Gacon, and their attributive crowd of mission children all in a state of frenzy. They said lots of things in chorus. "What?" said I. They said some more and added gesticulations. Seeing I was wasting their time as I could not hear, I drove the canoe from the rock and made my way, mostly by steering, to the bank close by; and then tying the canoe firmly up I walked over the mill stream and divers other things towards my anxious friends. "You'll be drowned," they said. "Gracious goodness!" said I, "I thought that half an hour ago, but it's all right now; I can steer." After much conversation I lulled their fears regarding me, and having received strict orders to keep in the stern of the canoe, because that is the proper place when you are managing a canoe single-handed, I returned to my studies. I had not however lulled my friends' interest regarding me, and they stayed on the bank watching.

I found first, that my education in steering from the bow was of no avail; second, that it was all right if you reversed it. For instance, when you are in the bow, and make an inward stroke with the paddle on the right-hand side, the bow goes to the right; whereas, if you make an inward stroke on the right-hand side, when you are sitting in the stern, the bow then goes to the left. Understand? Having grasped this law, I crept along up river; and, by Allah! before I had gone twenty yards, if that wretch, the current of the greatest, etc., did not grab hold of the nose of my canoe, and we teetotummed round again as merrily as ever. My audience screamed. I knew what they were saying, "You'll be drowned! Come back! Come back!" but I heard them and I heeded not. If you attend to advice in a crisis you're lost; besides, I couldn't "Come back" just then. However, I got into the slack water again, by some very showy, high-class steering. Still steering, fine as it is, is not all you require and hanker after. You want pace as well, and pace, except when in the clutches of the current, I had not so far attained. Perchance, thought I, the pace region in a canoe may be in its centre; so I got along on my knees into the centre to experiment. Bitter failure; the canoe took to sidling down river broadside on, like Mr. Winkle's horse. Shouts of laughter from the bank. Both bow and stern education utterly inapplicable to centre; and so, seeing I was utterly thrown away there, I crept into the bows, and in a few more minutes I steered my canoe, perfectly, in among its fellows by the bank and secured it there. Mme. Forget ran down to meet me and assured me she had not laughed so much since she had been in Africa, although she was frightened at the time lest I should get capsized and drowned. I believe it, for she is a sweet and gracious lady; and I quite see, as she demonstrated, that the sight of me, teetotumming about, steering in an elaborate and showy way all the time, was irresistibly comic. And she gave a most amusing account of how, when she started looking for me to give me tea, a charming habit of hers, she could not see me in among my bottles, and so asked the little black boy where I was. "There," said he, pointing to the tree hanging against the rock out in the river; and she, seeing me hitched with a canoe against the rock, and knowing the danger and depth of the river, got alarmed.

Well, when I got down to Lembarene I naturally went on with my canoeing studies, in pursuit of the attainment of pace. Success crowned my efforts, and I can honestly and truly say that there are only two things I am proud of—one is that Doctor Günther has approved of my fishes, and the other is that I can paddle an Ogowé canoe. Pace, style, steering and all, "All same for one" as if I were an Ogowé African. A strange, incongruous pair of things: but I often wonder what are the things other people are really most proud of; it would be a quaint and repaying subject for investigation.

Mme. Jacot gave me every help in canoeing, for she is a remarkably clear-headed woman, and recognised that, as I was always getting soaked, any-how, I ran no extra danger in getting soaked in a canoe; and then, it being the dry season, there was an immense stretch of water opposite Andande beach, which was quite shallow. So she saw no need of my getting drowned.

The sandbanks were showing their yellow heads in all directions when I came down from Talagouga, and just opposite Andande there was sticking up out of the water a great, graceful, palm frond. It had been stuck into the head of the pet sandbank, and every day was visited by the boys and girls in canoes to see how much longer they would have to wait for the sandbank's appearance. A few days after my return it showed, and in two days more there it was, acres and acres of it, looking like a great, golden carpet spread on the surface of the centre of the clear water—clear here, down this side of Lembarene Island, because the river runs fairly quietly, and has time to deposit its mud. Dark brown the Ogowé flies past the other side of the island, the main current being deflected that way by a bend, just below the entrance of the Nguni.

There was great rejoicing. Canoe-load after canoe-load of boys and girls went to the sandbank, some doing a little fishing round its rim, others bring-ing the washing there, all skylarking and singing. Few prettier sights have I ever seen than those on that sandbank—the merry brown forms dancing or lying stretched on it: the gaudy-coloured patchwork quilts and chintz mosquito-bars that have been washed, spread out drying, looking from Kan-gwe on the hill above, like beds of bright flowers. By night when it was moonlight there would be bands of dancers on it with bush-light torches, gyrating, intermingling and separating till you could think you were looking at a dance of stars.

They commenced affairs very early on that sandbank, and they kept them up very late; and all the time there came from it a soft murmur of laughter and song. Ah me! if the aim of life were happiness and pleasure, Africa should send us missionaries instead of our sending them to her—but, fortunately for the work of the world, happiness is not. One thing I remember which struck me very much regarding the sandbank, and this was that Mme. Jacot found such pleasure in taking her work on to the verandah, where she could see it. I knew she did not care for the songs and the dancing. One day she said to me, "It is such a relief." "A relief?" I said. "Yes, do you not see that until it shows there is nothing but forest, forest, forest, and that still stretch of river? That bank is the only piece of clear ground I see in the year, and that only lasts a few weeks until the wet season comes, and then it goes, and there is nothing but forest, forest, forest, for another year. It is two years now since I came to this place; it may be I know not how many more before we go home again." I grieve to say, for my poor friend's sake, that her life at Kangwe was nearly at its end. Soon after my return to England I heard of the death of her husband from malignant fever. M. Jacot was a fine, powerful, energetic man, in the prime of life. He was a teetotaler and a vegetarian; and although constantly travelling to and fro in his district on his evangelising work, he had no foolish recklessness in him. No one would have thought that he would have been the first to go of us who used to sit round his hospitable table. His delicate wife, his two young children or I would have seemed far more likely. His loss will be a lasting one to the people he risked his life to (what he regarded) save. The natives held him in the greatest affection and respect, and his influence over them was considerable, far more profound than that of any other missionary I have ever seen. His loss is also great to those students of Africa who are working on the culture or on the languages; his knowledge of both was extensive, particularly of the little known languages of the Ogowé district. He was, when I left, busily employed in compiling a dictionary of the Fan tongue, and had many other works on language in contemplation. His work in this sphere would have had a high value, for he was a man with a University education and well grounded in Latin and Greek, and thoroughly acquainted with both English and French literature, for although born a Frenchman, he had been brought up in America. He was also a cultivated musician, and he and Mme. Jacot in the evenings would sing old French songs, Swiss songs, English songs, in their rich full voices; and then if you stole softly out on to the verandah, you would often find it crowded with a silent, black audience, listening intently.

The amount of work M. and Mme. Jacot used to get through was, to me, amazing, and I think the Ogowé Protestant mission sadly short-handed—its missionaries not being content to follow the usual Protestant plan out in West Africa, namely, quietly sitting down and keeping house, with just a few native children indoors to do the housework, and close by a school and a little church where a service is held on Sundays. The representatives of the Mission Évangélique go to and fro throughout the district round each station on evangelising work, among some of the most dangerous and uncivilised tribes in Africa, frequently spending a fortnight at a time away from their homes, on

the waterways of a wild and dangerous country. In addition to going themselves, they send trained natives as evangelists and Bible-readers, and keep a
keen eye on the trained native, which means a considerable amount of worry
and strain too. The work on the stations is heavy in Ogowé districts, because
when you have got a clearing made and all the buildings up, you have by no
means finished with the affair, for you have to fight the Ogowé forest back, as a
Dutchman fights the sea. But the main cause of work is the store, which in this
exhausting climate is more than enough work for one man alone.

Payments on the Ogowé are made in goods; the natives do not use any
coinage-equivalent, save in the strange case of the Fans, which does not
touch general trade and which I will speak of later. They have not even the
brass bars and cheetems that are in us in Calabar, or cowries as in Lagos. In
order to expedite and simplify this goods traffic, a written or printed piece of
paper is employed—practically a cheque, which is called a "bon" or "book,"
and these "bons" are cashed - i.e. gooded, at the store. They are for three
amounts. Five fura = a dollar. One fura = a franc. Desu = fifty centimes =
half a fura. The value given for these "bons" is the same from Government,
Trade, and Mission. Although the Mission Évangélique does not trade - i.e.
buy produce and sell it at a profit, its representatives have a great deal of
business to attend to through the store, which is practically a bank. All the
native evangelists, black teachers, Bible-readers and labourers on the stations
are paid off in these bons; and when any representative of the mission is
away on a journey, food bought for themselves and their canoe crews is paid
for in bons, which are brought in by the natives at their convenience, and
changed for goods at the store. Therefore for several hours every weekday
the missionary has to devote himself to store work, and store work out here is
by no means playing at shop. It is very hard, tiring, exasperating work when
you have to deal with it in full, as a trader, when it is necessary for you to
purchase produce at a price that will give you a reasonable margin of profit
over storing, customs' duties, shipping expenses, etc., etc. But it is quite
enough to try the patience of any Saint when you are only keeping store
to pay on bons, à la missionary; for each class of article used in trade—and
there are some hundreds of them—has a definite and acknowledged value,
but where the trouble comes in is that different articles have the same value;
for example, six fish hooks and one pocket-handkerchief have the same value,
or you can make up that value in lucifer matches, pomatum, a mirror, a hair
comb, tobacco, or scent in bottles.

Now, if you are a trader, certain of these articles cost you more than others, although they have an identical value to the native, and so it is to your
advantage to pay what we should call, in Cameroons, "a Kru, cheap copper,"

and you have a lot of worry to effect this. To the missionary this does not so
much matter. It makes absolutely no difference to the native, mind you; so
he is by no means done by the trader. Take powder for an example. There is
no profit on powder for the trader in Congo Français, but the native always
wants it because he can get a tremendous profit on it from his black brethren
in the bush; hence it pays the trader to give him his bon out in Boma check,
etc., better than in gunpowder. This is a fruitful spring of argument and
persuasion. However, whether the native is passing in a bundle of rubber
or a tooth of ivory, or merely cashing a bon for a week's bush catering, he is
in Congo Français incapable of deciding what he will have when it comes to
the point. He comes into the shop with a bon in his hand, and we will say,
for example, the idea in his head that he wants fish-hooks—"jupes," he calls
them—but, confronted with the visible temptation of pomatum, he hesitates,
and scratches his head violently. Surrounding him there are ten or twenty
other natives with their minds in a similar wavering state, but yet anxious to
be served forthwith. In consequence of the stimulating scratch, he remembers that one of his wives said he was to bring some Lucifer matches, another
wanted cloth for herself, and another knew of some rubber she could buy very
cheap, in tobacco, of a Fan woman who had stolen it. This rubber he knows
he can take to the trader's store and sell for pocket-handkerchiefs of a superior
pattern, or gunpowder, or rum, which he cannot get at the mission store. He
finally gets something and takes it home, and likely enough brings it back, in
a day or so, somewhat damaged, desirous of changing it for some other article
or articles. Remember also that these Bantu, like the Negroes, think externally, in a loud voice; like Mr. Kipling's 'oont, "'e smells most awful vile," and, if
he be a Fan, he accompanies his observations with violent dramatic gestures,
and let the customer's tribe or sex be what it may, the customer is sadly, sadly
liable to pick up any portable object within reach, under the shadow of his
companions' uproar, and stow it away in his armpits, between his legs, or,
if his cloth be large enough, in that. Picture to yourself the perplexities of
a Christian minister, engaged in such an occupation as storekeeping under
these circumstances, with, likely enough, a touch of fever on him and jiggers
in his feet; and when the store is closed the goods in it requiring constant
vigilance to keep them free from mildew and white ants.

Then in addition to the store work, a fruitful source of work and worry are
the schools, for both boys and girls. It is regarded as futile to attempt to get
any real hold over the children unless they are removed from the influence of
the country fashions that surround them in their village homes; therefore the
schools are boarding; hence the entire care of the children, including feeding
and clothing, falls on the missionary.

The instruction given in the Mission Évangélique Schools does not include teaching the boys trades. The girls fare somewhat better, as they get instruction in sewing and washing and ironing, but I think in this district the young ladies would be all the better for being taught cooking.

It is strange that all the cooks employed by the Europeans should be men, yet all the cooking among the natives themselves is done by women, and done abominably badly in all the Bantu tribes I have ever come across; and the Bantu are in this particular, and indeed in most particulars, far inferior to the true Negro; though I must say this is not the orthodox view. The Negroes cook uniformly very well, and at moments are inspired in the direction of palm-oil chop and fish cooking. Not so the Bantu, whose methods cry aloud for improvement, they having just the very easiest and laziest way possible of dealing with food. The food supply consists of plantain, yam, koko, sweet potatoes, maize, pumpkin, pineapple, and ochres, fish both wet and smoked, and flesh of many kinds—including human in certain districts—snails, snakes, and crayfish, and big maggot-like pupæ of the rhinoceros beetle and the Rhyncophorus palmatorum. For sweetmeats the sugar-cane abounds, but it is only used chewed au naturel. For seasoning there is that bark that tastes like an onion, an onion distinctly passé, but powerful and permanent, particularly if it has been used in one of the native-made, rough earthen pots. These pots have a very cave-man look about them; they are unglazed, unlidded bowls. They stand the fire wonderfully well, and you have got to stand, as well as you can, the taste of the aforesaid bark that clings to them, and that of the smoke which gets into them during cooking operations over an open wood fire, as well as the soot-like colour they impart to even your own white rice. Out of all this varied material the natives of the Congo Français forests produce, dirtily, carelessly and wastefully, a dull, indigestible diet. Yam, sweet potatoes, ochres, and maize are not so much cultivated or used as among the Negroes, and the daily food is practically plantain—picked while green and the rind pulled off, and the tasteless woolly interior baked or boiled and the widely distributed manioc treated in the usual way. The sweet or non-poisonous manioc I have rarely seen cultivated, because it gives a much smaller yield, and is much longer coming to perfection. The poisonous kind is that in general use; its great dahlia-like roots are soaked in water to remove the poisonous principle, and then dried and grated up, or more commonly beaten up into a kind of dough in a wooden trough that looks like a model canoe, with wooden clubs, which I have seen the curiosity hunter happily taking home as war clubs to alarm his family with. The thump, thump, thump of this manioc beating is one of the most familiar sounds in a bush village. The meal, when beaten up, is used for thickening broths, and rolled up into bolsters about a foot long and two inches in diameter, and then wrapped in plantain leaves, and tied round with tie-tie and boiled, or more properly speaking steamed, for a lot of the rolls are arranged in a brass skillet. A small quantity of water is poured over the rolls of plantain, a plantain leaf is tucked in over the top tightly, so as to prevent the steam from escaping, and the whole affair is poised on the three cooking-stones over a wood fire, and left there until the contents are done, or more properly speaking, until the lady in charge of it has delusions on the point, and the bottom rolls are a trifle burnt or the whole insufficiently cooked.

This manioc meal is the staple food, the bread equivalent, all along the coast. As you pass along you are perpetually meeting with a new named food, fou-fou on the Leeward, kank on the Windward, m'vada in Corisco, ogooma in the Ogowé; but acquaintance with it demonstrates that it is all the same—manioc.

It is a good food when it is properly prepared; but when a village has soaked its soil-laden manioc tubers in one and the same pool of water for years, the water in that pool becomes a trifle strong, and both it and the manioc get a smell which once smelt is never to be forgotten; it is something like that resulting from bad paste with a dash of vinegar, but fit to pass all these things, and has qualities of its own that have no civilised equivalent.

I believe that this way of preparing the staple article of diet is largely responsible for that dire and frequent disease "cut him belly," and several other quaint disorders, possibly even for the sleep disease. The natives themselves say that a diet too exclusively maniocan produces dimness of vision, ending in blindness if the food is not varied; the poisonous principle cannot be anything like soaked out in the surcharged water, and the meal when it is made up and cooked has just the same sour, acrid taste you would expect it to have from the smell.

The fish is boiled, or wrapped in leaves and baked. The dried fish, very properly known as stink-fish, is much preferred; this is either eaten as it is, or put into stews as seasoning, as also are the snails. The meat is eaten either fresh or smoked, boiled or baked. By baked I always mean just buried in the ground and a fire lighted on top, or wrapped in leaves and buried in hot embers.

The smoked meat is badly prepared, just hung up in the smoke of the fires, which hardens it, blackening the outside quickly; but when the lumps are taken out of the smoke, in a short time cracks occur in them, and the interior part proceeds to go bad, and needless to say maggoty. If it is kept in the smoke, as it often is to keep it out of the way of dogs and driver ants, it acquires the toothsome taste and texture of a piece of old tarpaulin.

Now I will ask the surviving reader who has waded through this dissertation on cookery if something should not be done to improve the degraded condition of the Bantu cooking culture? Not for his physical delectation only, but because his present methods are bad for his morals, and drive the man to drink, let alone assisting in riveting him in the practice of polygamy, which the missionary party say is an exceedingly bad practice for him to follow. The inter-relationship of these two subjects may not seem on the face of it very clear, but inter-relationships of customs very rarely are; I well remember M. Jacot coming home one day at Kangwe from an evangelising visit to some adjacent Fan towns, and saying he had had given to him that afternoon a new reason for polygamy, which was that it enabled a man to get enough to eat. This sounds sinister from a notoriously cannibal tribe; but the explanation is that the Fans are an exceedingly hungry tribe, and require a great deal of providing for. It is their custom to eat about ten times a day when in village, and the men spend most of their time in the palaver-houses at each end of the street, the women bringing them bowls of food of one kind or another all day long. When the men are away in the forest rubber or elephant-hunting, and have to cook their own food, they cannot get quite so much; but when I have come across them on these expeditions, they halted pretty regularly every two hours and had a substantial snack, and the gorge they all go in for after a successful elephant hunt is a thing to see—once.

There are other reasons which lead to the prevalence of this custom, beside the cooking. One is that it is totally impossible for one woman to do the whole work of a house—look after the children, prepare and cook the food, prepare the rubber, carry the same to the markets, fetch the daily supply of water from the stream, cultivate the plantation, etc., etc. Perhaps I should say it is impossible for the dilatory African woman, for I once had an Irish charwoman, who drank, who would have done the whole week's work of an African village in an afternoon, and then been quite fresh enough to knock some of the nonsense out of her husband's head with that of the broom, and throw a kettle of boiling water or a paraffin lamp at him, if she suspected him of flirting with other ladies. That woman, who deserves fame in the annals of her country, was named Harragan. She has attained immortality some years since, by falling down stairs one Saturday night from excitement arising from "the Image's" (Mr. Harragan) conduct; but we have no Mrs. Harragan in Africa. The African lady does not care a travelling whitesmith's execration if her husband does flirt, so long as he does not go and give to other women the cloth, etc., that she should have. The more wives the less work, says the African lady; and I have known men who would rather have had one wife and spent the rest of the money on themselves, in a civilised way, driven into polygamy by the women; and of course this state of affairs is most common in nonslave-holding tribes like the Fan.

Mission work was first opened upon the Ogowé by Dr. Nassau, the great pioneer and explorer of these regions. He was acting for the American Presbyterian Society; but when the French Government demanded education in

French in the schools, the stations on the Ogowé, Lembarene (Kangwe), and Talagouga were handed over to the Mission Évangélique of Paris, and have been carried on by its representatives with great devotion and energy. I am unsympathetic, in some particulars, for reasons of my own, with Christian missions, so my admiration for this one does not arise from the usual ground of admiration for missions, namely, that however they may be carried on, they are engaged in a great and holy work; but I regard the Mission Évangélique, judging from the results I have seen, as the perfection of what one may call a purely spiritual mission.

Lembarene is strictly speaking a district which includes Adânlinan lângâ and the Island, but the name is locally used to denote the great island in the Ogowé, whose native name is Nenge Ezangy; but for the sake of the general reader I will keep to the everyday term of Lembarene Island.

Lembarene Island is the largest of the islands on the Ogowé. It is some fifteen miles long, east and west, and a mile to a mile and a half wide. It is hilly and rocky, uniformly clad with forest, and several little permanent streams run from it on both sides into the Ogowé. It is situated 130 miles from the sea, at the point, just below the entrance of the N'guni, where the Ogowé commences to divide up into that network of channels by which, like all great West African rivers save the Congo, it chooses to enter the Ocean. The island, as we mainlanders at Kangwe used to call it, was a great haunt of mine, particularly after I came down from Talagouga and saw fit to regard myself as competent to control a canoe.

From Andande, the beach of Kangwe, the breadth of the arm of the Ogowé to the nearest village on the island, was about that of the Thames at Blackwall. One half of the way was slack water, the other half was broadside on to a stiff current. Now my pet canoe at Andande was about six feet long, pointed at both ends, flat bottomed, so that it floated on the top of the water; its freeboard was, when nothing was in it, some three inches, and the poor thing had seen trouble in its time, for it had a hole you could put your hand in at one end; so in order to navigate it successfully, you had to squat in the other, which immersed that to the water level but safely elevated the damaged end in the air. Of course you had to stop in your end firmly, because if you went forward the hole went down into the water, and the water went into the hole, and forthwith you foundered with all hands - i.e., you and the paddle and the calabash baler. This craft also had a strong weather helm, owing to a warp in the tree of which it had been made. I learnt all these things one afternoon, paddling round the sandbank; and the next afternoon, feeling confident in the merits of my vessel, I started for the island, and I actually got there, and associated with the natives, but feeling my arms were permanently worn out by paddling against the current, I availed myself of the offer of a gentleman to paddle me back in his canoe. He introduced himself as Samuel, and volunteered the statement that he was "a very good man." We duly settled ourselves in the canoe, he occupying the bow, I sitting in the middle, and a Mrs. Samuel sitting in the stern. Mrs. Samuel was a powerful, pretty lady, and a conscientious and continuous paddler. Mr. S. was none of these things, but an ex-Bible reader, with an amazing knowledge of English, which he spoke in a quaint, falsetto, far-away sort of voice, and that man's besetting sin was curiosity. "You be Christian, ma?" said he. I asked him if he had ever met a white man who was not. "Yes, ma," says Samuel. I said "You must have been associating with people whom you ought not to know." Samuel fortunately not having a repartee for this, paddled on with his long paddle for a few seconds. "Where be your husband, ma?" was the next conversational bomb he hurled at me. "I no got one," I answer. "No got," says Samuel, paralysed with astonishment; and as Mrs. S., who did not know English, gave one of her vigorous drives with her paddle at this moment, Samuel as near as possible got jerked head first into the Ogowé, and we took on board about two bucketfuls of water. He recovered himself, however and returned to his charge. "No got one, ma?" "No," say I furiously. "Do you get much rubber round here?" "I no be trade man," says Samuel, refusing to fall into my trap for changing conversation. "Why you no got one?" The remainder of the conversation is unreportable, but he landed me at Andande all right, and got his dollar.

The next voyage I made, which was on the next day, I decided to go by myself to the factory, which is on the other side of the island, and did so. I got some goods to buy fish with, and heard from Mr. Cockshut that the poor boy-agent at Osoamokita, had committed suicide. It was a grievous thing. He was, as I have said, a bright, intelligent young Frenchman; but living in the isolation, surrounded by savage, tiresome tribes, the strain of his responsibility had been too much for him. He had had a good deal of fever, and the very kindly head agent for Woermann's had sent Dr. Pélessier to see if he had not better be invalided home; but he told the Doctor he was much better, and as he had no one at home to go to he begged him not to send him, and the Doctor, to his subsequent regret, gave in. No one knows, who has not been to West Africa, how terrible is the life of a white man in one of these out-of-the-way factories, with no white society, and with nothing to look at, day out and day in, but the one set of objects—the forest, the river, and the beach, which in a place like Osoamokita you cannot leave for months at a time, and of which you soon know every plank and stone. I felt utterly wretched as I started home again to come up to the end of the island, and go round it and down to Andande; and paddled on for some little time, before I noticed that I was making absolutely no progress. I redoubled my exertions, and crept slowly up to some rocks projecting above the water; but pass them I could not, as the main current of the Ogowé flew in hollow swirls round them against my canoe. Several passing canoefuls of natives gave me good advice in Igalwa; but facts were facts, and the Ogowé was too strong for me. After about twenty minutes an old Fan gentleman came down river in a canoe and gave me good advice in Fan, and I got him to take me in tow—that is to say, he got into my canoe and I held on to his and we went back down river. I then saw his intention was to take me across to that disreputable village, half Fan, half Bakele, which is situated on the main bank of the river opposite the island; this I disapproved of, because I had heard that some Senegal soldiers who had gone over there, had been stripped of every rag they had on, and maltreated; besides, it was growing very late, and I wanted to get home to dinner. I communicated my feelings to my pilot, who did not seem to understand at first, so I feared I should have to knock them into him with the paddle; but at last he understood I wanted to be landed on the island and duly landed me, when he seemed much surprised at the reward I gave him in pocket-handkerchiefs. Then I got a powerful young Igalwa dandy to paddle me home.

I did not go to the island next day, but down below Fula, watching the fish playing in the clear water, and the lizards and birds on the rocky high banks; but on my next journey round to the factories I got into another and a worse disaster. I went off there early one morning; and thinking the only trouble lay in getting back up the Ogowé, and having developed a theory that this might be minimised by keeping very close to the island bank, I never gave a thought to dangers attributive to going down river; so, having by now acquired pace, my canoe shot out beyond the end rocks of the island into the main stream. It took me a second to realise what had happened, and another to find out I could not get the canoe out of the current without upsetting it, and that I could not force her back up the current, so there was nothing for it but to keep her head straight now she had bolted. A group of native ladies, who had followed my proceedings with much interest, shouted observations which I believe to have been "Come back, come back; you'll be drowned." "Good-bye, Susannah, don't you weep for me," I courteously retorted; and flew past them and the factory beaches and things in general, keenly watching for my chance to run my canoe up a siding, as it were, off the current main line. I got it at last—a projecting spit of land from the island with rocks projecting out of the water in front of it bothered the current, and after a wild turn round or so, and a near call from my terrified canoe trying to climb up a rock, I got into slack water and took a pause in life's pleasures for a few minutes. Knowing I must be near the end of the island, I went on pretty close to the bank, finally got round into the Kangwe branch of the Ogowé by a connecting creek, and after an hour's steady paddling I fell in with three big canoes going up river; they took me home as far as Fula, whence a short paddle landed me at Andande only slightly late for supper, convinced that it was almost as safe and far more amusing to be born lucky than wise.

Now I have described my circumnavigation of the island, I will proceed to describe its inhabitants. The up-river end of Lembarene Island is the most inhabited. A path round the upper part of the island passes through a succession of Igalwa villages and by the Roman Catholic missionary station. The slave villages belonging to these Igalwas are away down the north face of the island, opposite the Fan town of Fula, which I have mentioned. It strikes me as remarkable that the Igalwa, like the Dualla of Cameroons, have their slaves in separate villages; but this is the case, though I do not know the reason of it. These Igalwa slaves cultivate the plantations, and bring up the vegetables and fruit to their owners' villages and do the housework daily.

The interior of the island is composed of high, rocky, heavily forested hills, with here and there a stream, and here and there a swamp; the higher land is towards the up-river end; down river there is a lower strip of land with hillocks. This is, I fancy, formed by deposits of sand, etc., catching in among the rocks, and connecting what were at one time several isolated islands. There are no big game or gorillas on the island, but it has a peculiar and awful house ant, much smaller than the driver ant, but with a venomous, bad bite; its only good point is that its chief food is the white ants, which are therefore kept in abeyance on Lembarene Island, although flourishing destructively on the mainland banks of the river in this locality. I was never tired of going and watching those Igalwa villagers, nor were, I think, the Igalwa villagers ever tired of observing me. Although the physical conditions of life were practically identical with those of the mainland, the way in which the Igalwas dealt with them, i.e. the culture, was distinct from the culture of the mainland Fans.

The Igalwas are a tribe very nearly akin, if not ethnically identical with, the M'pongwe, and the culture of these two tribes is on a level with the highest native African culture. African culture, I may remark, varies just the same as European in this, that there is as much difference in the manners of life between, say, an Igalwa and a Bubi of Fernando Po, as there is between a Londoner and a Laplander.

The Igalwa builds his house like that of the M'pongwe, of bamboo, and he surrounds himself with European-made articles. The neat houses, fitted with windows, with wooden shutters to close at night, and with a deal door—a carpenter-made door—are in sharp contrast with the ragged ant-hill looking performances of the Akkas, or the bark huts of the Fan, with no windows, and just an extra broad bit of bark to slip across the hole that serves as a door. On going into an Igalwa house you will see a four-legged table, often covered with a bright-coloured tablecloth, on which stands a water bottle, with two clean glass-es, and round about you will see chairs—Windsor chairs. These houses have usually three, sometimes more rooms, and a separate closed-in little kitchen, built apart, wherein you may observe European-made saucepans, in addition to the ubiquitous skillet. Outside, all along the clean sandy streets, the inhabi-tants are seated. The Igalwa is truly great at sitting, the men pursuing a policy of masterly inactivity, broken occasionally by leisurely netting a fishing net, the end of the netting hitched up on to the roof thatch, and not held by a stirrup. The ladies are employed in the manufacture of articles pertaining to a higher culture—I allude, as Mr. Micawber would say, to bed-quilts and pillow-cases—the most gorgeous bed-quilts and pillow-cases—made of patchwork, and now and again you will see a mosquito-bar in course of construction, of course not made of net or muslin because of the awesome strength and ferocity of the Lem-barene strain of mosquitoes, but of stout, fair-flowered and besprigged chintzes; and you will observe these things are often being sewn with a sewing machine.

The women who may not be busy sewing are busy doing each other's hair. Hair-dressing is quite an art among the Igalwa and M'pongwe women, and their hair is very beautiful; very crinkly, but fine. It is plaited up, close to the head, partings between the plaits making elaborate parterres. Into the beds of plaited hair are stuck long pins of river ivory (hippo), decorated with black tracery and openwork, and made by their good men. A lady will stick as many of these into her hair as she can get, but the prevailing mode is to have one stuck in behind each ear, showing their broad, long heads above like two horns; they are exceedingly becoming to these black but comely ladies, verily, I think, the comeliest ladies I have ever seen on the Coast. Very black they are, blacker than many of their neighbours, always blacker than the Fans, and although their skin lacks that velvety pile of the true negro, it is not too shiny, but it is fine and usually unblemished, and their figures are charmingly rounded, their hands and feet small, almost as small as a high-class Calabar woman's, and their eyes large, lustrous, soft and brown, and their teeth as white as the sea surf and undisfigured by filing.

The native dress for men and women alike is the cloth or paun. The men wear it by rolling the upper line round the waist, and in addition they frequent-ly wear a singlet or a flannel shirt worn more Africano, flowing free. Rich men will mount a European coat and hat, and men connected with the mission or trading stations occasionally wear trousers. The personal appearance of the men does not amount to much when all's done, so we will return to the ladies. They wrap the upper hem of these cloths round under the armpits, a graceful form of drapery, but one which requires continual readjustment. The cloth is about four yards long and two deep, and there is always round the hem a border, or false hem, of turkey red twill, or some other coloured cotton cloth to the main body of the paun. In addition to the cloth there is worn, when possible, a European shawl, either one of those thick cotton cloth ones printed with Chinese-looking patterns in dull red on a dark ground, this sort is wrapped round the upper part of the body: or what is more highly esteemed is a bright, light-coloured, fancy wool shawl, pink or pale blue preferred, which being carefully folded into a roll is placed over one shoulder, and is entirely for dandy. I am thankful to say they do not go in for hats; when they wear anything on their heads it is a handkerchief folded shawl-wise; the base of the triangle is bound round the forehead just above the eyebrows, the ends carried round over the ears and tied behind over the apex of the triangle of the handkerchief, the three ends being then arranged fan-wise at the back. Add to this costume a sober-coloured silk parasol, not one of your green or red young tent-like, brutally masculine, knobby-sticked umbrellas, but a fair, lady-like parasol, which, being carefully rolled up, is carried handle foremost right in the middle of the head, also for dandy. Then a few strings of turquoise-blue beads, or imitation gold ones, worn round the shapely throat; and I will back my Igalwa or M'pongwe belle against any of those South Sea Island young ladies we nowadays hear so much about, thanks to Mr. Stevenson, yea, even though these may be wreathed with fragrant flowers, and the African lady very rarely goes in for flowers. The only time I have seen the African ladies wearing them for ornament has been among these Igalwas, who now and again stud their night-black hair with pretty little round vividly red blossoms in a most fetching way. I wonder the Africans do not wear flowers more frequently, for they are devoted to scent, both men and women.

The Igalwas are a proud race, one of the noble tribes, like the M'pongwe and the Ajumba. The women do not intermarry with lower-class tribes, and in their own tribe they are much restricted, owing to all relations on the mother's side being forbidden to intermarry. This well-known form of accounting relationships only through the mother (Mutterrecht) is in a more perfected and elaborated form among the Igalwa than among any other tribe I am personally acquainted with; brothers and cousins on the mother's side being in one class of relationship.

The father's responsibility, as regards authority over his own children, is very slight. The really responsible male relative is the mother's elder brother. From him must leave to marry be obtained for either girl, or boy; to him and the mother must the present be taken which is exacted on the marriage of a girl; and should the mother die, on him and not on the father, lies the responsibility of rearing the children; they go to his house, and he treats and regards them as nearer and dearer to himself than his own children, and at his death, after his own brothers by the same mother, they become his heirs.

Marriage among the Igalwa and M'pongwe is not direct marriage by purchase, but a certain fixed price present is made to the mother and uncle of the girl. Other propitiatory presents (Kueliki) are made, but do not count legally, and have not necessarily to be returned in case of post-nuptial differences arising leading to a divorce—a very frequent catastrophe in the social circle; for the Igalwa ladies are spirited, and devoted to personal adornment, and they are naggers at their husbands. Many times when walking on Lembarene Island, have I seen a lady stand in the street and let her husband, who had taken shelter inside the house, know what she thought of him, in a way that reminded me of some London slum scenes. When the husband loses his temper, as he surely does sooner or later, being a man, he whacks his wife—or wives, if they have been at him in a body. He may whack with impunity so long as he does not draw blood; if he does, be it never so little, his wife is off to her relations, the present he has given for her is returned, the marriage is annulled, and she can re-marry as soon as she is able.

Her relations are only too glad to get her, because, although the present has to be returned, yet the propitiatory offerings remain theirs, and they know more propitiatory offerings as well as another present will accrue with the next set of suitors. This of course is only the case with the younger women; the older women for one thing do not nag so much, and moreover they have usually children willing and able to support them. If they have not, their state is, like that of all old childless women in Africa, a very desolate one.

Infant marriage is now in vogue among the Igalwa, and to my surprise I find it is of quite recent introduction and adoption. Their own account of this retrograde movement in culture is that in the last generation—some of the old people indeed claim to have known him—there was an exceedingly ugly and deformed man who could not get a wife, the women being then, as the men are now, great admirers of physical beauty. So this man, being very cunning, hit on the idea of becoming betrothed to one before she could exercise her own choice in the matter; and knowing a family in which an interesting event was likely to occur, he made heavy presents in the proper quarters and bespoke the coming infant if it should be a girl. A girl it was, and thus, say the Igalwa, arose the custom; and nowadays, although they do not engage their wives so early as did the founder of the custom, they adopt infant marriage as an institution.

I inquired carefully, in the interests of ethnology, as to what methods of courting were in vogue previously. They said people married each other because they loved each other. I hope other ethnologists will follow this inquiry up, for we may here find a real golden age, which in other races of humanity lies away in the mists of the ages behind the kitchen middens and the Cambrian rocks. My own opinion in this matter is that the earlier courting methods of the Igalwa involved a certain amount of effort on the man's part, a thing abhorrent to an Igalwa. It necessitated his dressing himself up, and likely enough fighting that impudent scoundrel who was engaged in courting her too; and above all serenading her at night on the native harp, with its strings made from the tendrils of a certain orchid, or on the marimba, amongst crowds of mosquitoes. Any institution that involved being out at night amongst crowds of those Lembarene mosquitoes would have to disappear, let that institution be what it might.

The Igalwa are one of the dying-out coast tribes. As well as on Lembarene Island, their villages are scattered along the banks of the Lower Ogowé, and on the shores and islands of Elivá Z'Onlange. On the island they are, so far, undisturbed by the Fan invasion, and laze their lives away like lotus-eaters. Their slaves work their large plantations, and bring up to them magnificent yams, ready prepared ogooma, sweet-potatoes, papaw, etc., not forgetting that delicacy Odeaka cheese; this is not an exclusive inspiration of theirs, for the M'pongwe and the Benga use it as well. It is made from the kernel of the wild mango, a singularly beautiful tree of great size and stately spread of foliage. I can compare it only in appearance and habit of growth to our Irish, or evergreen, oak, but it is an idealisation of that fine tree. Its leaves are a softer, brighter, deeper green, and in due season (August) it is covered—not ostentatiously like the real mango, with great spikes of bloom, looking each like a gigantic head of mignonette—but with small yellow-green flowers tucked away under the leaves, filling the air with a soft sweet perfume, and then falling on to the bare shaded ground beneath to make a deep-piled carpet. I do not know whether it is a mango tree at all, for I am no botanist: but anyhow the fruit is rather like that of the mango in external appearance, and in internal still more so, for it has a disproportionately large stone. These stones are cracked, and the kernel taken out. The kernels are spread a short time in the shade to dry; then they are beaten up into a pulp with a wooden pestle, and the pulp put into a basket lined carefully with plantain leaves and placed in the sun, which melts it up into a stiff mass. The basket is then removed from the sun and stood aside to cool. When cool, the cheese can be turned out in shape, and can be kept a long time if it is wrapped round with leaves and a cloth, and hung up inside the house. Its appearance is that of almond rock, and it is cut easily with a knife; but at any period of its existence, if it is left in the sun it melts again rapidly into an oily mass.

The natives use it as a seasoning in their cookery, stuffing fish and plantains with it and so on, using it also in the preparation of a sort of sea-pie they make with meat and fish. To make this, a thing well worth doing, particularly with hippo or other coarse meat, reduce the wood fire to embers, and make plantain leaves into a sort of bag, or cup; small pieces of the meat should then be packed in layers with red pepper and odeaka in between. The tops of the leaves are then tied together with fine tie-tie, and the bundle, without any saucepan of any kind, stood on the glowing embers, the cook taking care there is no flame. The meat is done, and a superb gravy formed, before the containing plantain leaves are burnt through—plantain leaves will stand an amazing lot in the way of fire. This dish is really excellent, even when made with python, hippo, or crocodile. It makes the former most palatable; but of course it does not remove the musky taste from crocodile; nothing I know of will.

The great and important difference between the M'pongwe, {167} Igalwa, and Ajumba fetish, and the Fetish of those tribes round them, consists in their conception of a certain spirit called O Mbuiri. They have, as is constant among the Bantu races of South-West Africa, a great god—the creator, a god who has made all things, and who now no longer takes any interest in the things he has created. Their name for this god is Anyambie, which when pronounced sounds to my ears like anlynlae—the l's being very weak,—the derivation of this name, however, is from Anyima a spirit, and Mbia, good. This god, unlike other forms of the creating god in Fetish, has a viceroy or minister who is a god he has created, and to whom he leaves the government of affairs. This god is O Mbuiri or O Mbwiri, and this O Mbwiri is of very high interest to the student of comparative fetish. He has never been, nor can he ever become, a man, i.e. be born as a man, but he can transfuse with his own personality that of human beings, and also the souls of all those things we white men regard as inanimate, such as rocks, trees, etc., in a similar manner.

The M'pongwe know that his residence is in the sea, and some of them have seen him as an old white man, not flesh-colour white, but chalk white. There is another important point here, but it wants a volume to itself, so I must pass it. O Mbuiri's appearance in a corporeal form denotes ill luck, not death to the seer, but misfortune of a severe and diffused character. The ruin of a trading enterprise, the destruction of a village or a family, are put down to O Mbuiri's action. Yet he is not regarded as a malevolent god, a devil, but as an avenger, or punisher of sin; and the M'pongwe look on him as the Being to whom they primarily owe the good things and fortunes of this life, and as the Being who alone has power to govern the host of truly malevolent spirits that exist in nature.

The different instruments with which he works in the shaping of human destiny bear his name when in his employ. When acting by means of water, he is O Mbuiri Aningo; when in the weather, O Mbuiri Ngali; when in the forests, O Mbuiri Ibaka; when in the form of a dwarf, O Mbuiri Akoa, and so on.

The great difference between O Mbuiri and the lesser spirits is this:—the lesser spirits cannot incarnate themselves except through extraneous things; O Mbuiri can, he can become visible without anything beyond his own will to do so. The other spirits must be in something to become visible. This is an extremely delicate piece of Fetish which it took me weeks to work out. I think I may say another thing about O Mbuiri, though I say it carefully, and that is, that among the M'pongwe and the tribe who are the parent tribe of the M'pongwe—the now rapidly dying out Ajumba, and their allied tribe the Igalwa—O Mbuiri is a distinct entity, while among the neighbouring tribes he is a class, i.e. there are hundreds of O Mbuiri or Ibwiri, one for every remarkable place or thing, such as rock, tree, or forest thicket, and for every dangerous place in a river. Had I not observed a similar state of affairs regarding Sasabonsum, a totally different kind of spirit on the Windward coast, I should have had even greater trouble than I had, in finding a key to what seemed at first a mass of conflicting details regarding this important spirit O Mbuiri.

There is one other very important point in M'pongwe Fetish; and that is that the souls of men exist before birth as well as after death. This is indeed, as far as I have been able to find out, a doctrine universally held by the West African tribes, but among the M'pongwe there is this modification in it, which agrees strangely well with the idea I found regarding reincarnated diseases, existent among the Okÿon tribes (pure negroes). The malevolent minor spirits are capable of being born with, what we will call, a man's soul, as well as going in with the man's soul during sleep. For example, an Olâgâ may be born with a man and that man will thereby be born mad; he may at any period of his life, given certain conditions, become possessed by an evil spirit, Onlogho Abambo, Injembe, Nkandada, and become mad, or ill; but if he is born mad, or sickly, one of the evil spirits such as an Olâgâ or an Obambo, the soul of a man that has not been buried properly, has been born with him.

The rest of the M'pongwe Fetish is on broad lines common to other tribes, so I relegate it to the general collection of notes on Fetish. M'pongwe jurisprudence is founded on the same ideas as those on which West African jurisprudence at large is founded, but it is so elaborated that it would be desecration to sketch it. It requires a massive monograph.

CHAPTER VII

ON THE WAY FROM KANGWE TO LAKE NCOVI

In which the voyager goes for bush again and wanders into a
new lake and a new river.

J ULY 22ND, 1895.—LEFT KANGWE. The four Ajumba {170} did not turn
up early in the morning as had been arranged, but arrived about eight, in
pouring rain, so decided to wait until two o'clock, which will give us time to
reach their town of Arevooma before nightfall, and may perhaps give us a chance
of arriving there dry. At two we start. We go down river on the Kangwe side of
Lembarene Island, make a pause in front of the Igalwa slave town, which is on
the Island and nearly opposite the Fan town of Fula on the mainland bank, our
motive being to get stores of yam and plantain—and magnificent specimens of
both we get—and then, when our canoe is laden with them to an extent that
would get us into trouble under the Act if it ran here, off we go again. Every
canoe we meet shouts us a greeting, and asks where we are going, and we say
"Rembwé"—and they say "What! Rembwé!"—and we say "Yes, Rembwé," and
paddle on. I lay among the luggage for about an hour, not taking much interest
in the Rembwé or anything else, save my own headache; but this soon lifted,
and I was able to take notice, just before we reached the Ajumba's town, called
Arevooma. The sandbanks stretch across the river here nearly awash, so all our
cargo of yams has to be thrown overboard on to the sand, from which they can
be collected by being waded out to. The canoe, thus lightened, is able to go on a
little further, but we are soon hard and fast again, and the crew have to jump out
and shove her off about once every five minutes, and then to look lively about
jumping back into her again, as she shoots over the cliffs of the sandbanks.

When we reach Arevooma, I find it is a very prettily situated town, on the
left-hand bank of the river—clean and well kept, and composed of houses built

on the Igalwa and M'pongwe plan with walls of split bamboo and a palm thatch roof. I own I did not much care for these Ajumbas on starting, but they are evidently going to be kind and pleasant companions. One of them is a gentlemanly-looking man, who wears a gray shirt; another looks like a genial Irishman who has accidentally got black, very black; he is distinguished by wearing a singlet; another is a thin, elderly man, notably silent; and the remaining one is a strapping, big fellow, as black as a wolf's mouth, of gigantic muscular development, and wearing quantities of fetish charms hung about him. The two first mentioned are Christians; the other two pagans, and I will refer to them by their characteristic points, for their honourable names are awfully alike when you do hear them, and, as is usual with Africans, rarely used in conversation.

Gray Shirt places his house at my disposal, and both he and his exceedingly pretty wife do their utmost to make me comfortable. The house lies at the west end of the town. It is one room inside, but has, I believe, a separate cooking shed. In the verandah in front is placed a table, an ivory bundle chair and a gourd of water, and I am also treated to a calico tablecloth, and most thoughtfully screened off from the public gaze with more calico so that I can have my tea in privacy. After this meal, to my surprise Ndaka turns up. Certainly he is one of the very ugliest men—black or white—I have ever seen, and I fancy one of the best. He is now on a holiday from Kangwe, seeing to the settlement of his dead brother's affairs. The dead brother was a great man in Arevooma and a pagan, but Ndaka, the Christian Bible-reader, seems to get on perfectly with the family and is holding tonight a meeting outside his brother's house and comes with a lantern to fetch me to attend it. Of course I have to go, headache or no headache.

Most of the town was there, mainly as spectators. Ndaka and my two Christian boatmen manage the service between them, and what with the hymns and the mosquitoes the experience is slightly awful. We sit in a line in front of the house, which is brilliantly lit up—our own lantern on the ground before us acting as a rival entertainment to the house lamps inside for some of the best insect society in Africa, who after the manner of the insect world, insist on regarding us as responsible for their own idiocy in getting singed; and sting us in revenge, while we slap hard, as we howl hymns in the fearful Igalwa and M'pongwe way. Next to an English picnic, the most uncomfortable thing I know is an open-air service in this part of Africa. Service being over, Ndaka takes me over the house to show its splendours. The great brilliancy of its illumination arises from its being lit by two hanging lamps burning paraffin oil. The most remarkable point about the house is the floor, which is made of split, plaited bamboo. It gives under your feet in an alarming way, being raised some three or four feet above the ground, and I am haunted by the fear that I shall go through it and give pain to myself, and great trouble to others before I could be got out. It is a beautiful piece of workmanship, and Arevooma has every reason to be proud of it. Having admired these things, I go, dead tired and still headachy, down the road with my host who carries the lantern, through an atmosphere that has 45 per cent. of solid matter in the shape of mosquitoes; then wishing him good-night, I shut myself in, and illuminate, humbly, with a candle. The furniture of the house consists mainly of boxes, containing the wealth of Gray Shirt, in clothes, mirrors, etc. One corner of the room is taken up by great calabashes full of some sort of liquor, and there is an ivory bundle chair, a hanging mirror, several rusty guns, and a considerable collection of china basins and jugs. Evidently Gray Shirt is rich. The most interesting article to me, however, just now is the bed hung over with a clean, substantial, chintz mosquito bar, and spread with clean calico and adorned with patchwork-covered pillows. So I take off my boots and put on my slippers; for it never does in this country to leave off boots altogether at anytime and risk getting bitten by mosquitoes on the feet, when you are on the march; because the rub of your boot on the bite always produces a sore, and a sore when it comes in the Gorilla country, comes to stay.

No sooner have I carefully swished all the mosquitoes from under the bar and turned in, than a cat scratches and mews at the door—turn out and let her in. She is evidently a pet, so I take her on to the bed with me. She is a very nice cat—sandy and fat—and if I held the opinion of Pythagoras concerning wild fowl, I should have no hesitation in saying she had in her the soul of Dame Juliana Berners, such a whole-souled devotion to sport does she display, dashing out through the flaps of the mosquito bar after rats which, amid squeals from the rats and curses from her, she kills amongst the china collection. Then she comes to me, triumphant, expecting congratulations, and accompanied by mosquitoes, and purrs and kneads upon my chest until she hears another rat.

Tuesday, July 23rd.—Am aroused by violent knocking at the door in the early gray dawn—so violent that two large centipedes and a scorpion drop on to the bed. They have evidently been tucked away among the folds of the bar all night. Well "when ignorance is bliss 'tis folly to be wise," particularly along here. I get up without delay, and find myself quite well. The cat has thrown a basin of water neatly over into my bag during her nocturnal hunts; and when my tea comes I am informed a man "done die" in the night, which explains the firing of guns I heard. I inquire what he has died of, and am told "He just truck luck, and then he die." His widows are having their faces painted white by sympathetic lady friends, and are attired in their oldest, dirtiest clothes, and but very few of them; still, they seem to be taking things in a resigned spirit. These Ajumba seem pleasant folk. They play with their pretty brown children in a taking way. Last night I noticed some men and women playing a game new to me, which consisted in throwing a hoop at each other. The point was to get the hoop to fall over your adversary's head. It is a cheerful game. Quantities of the common house-fly about—and, during the early part of the morning, it rains in a gentle kind of way; but soon after we are afloat in our canoe it turns into a soft white mist.

We paddle still westwards down the broad quiet waters of the O'Rembo Vongo. I notice great quantities of birds about here—great hornbills, vividly coloured kingfishers, and for the first time the great vulture I have often heard of, and the skin of which I will take home before I mention even its approximate spread of wing. There are also noble white cranes, and flocks of small black and white birds, new to me, with heavy razor-shaped bills, reminding one of the Devonian puffin. The hornbill is perhaps the most striking in appearance. It is the size of a small, or say a good-sized hen turkey. Gray Shirt says the flocks, which are of eight or ten, always have the same quantity of cocks and hens, and that they live together "white man fashion," i.e. each couple keeping together. They certainly do a great deal of courting, the cock filling out his wattles on his neck like a turkey, and spreading out his tail with great pomp and ceremony, but very awkwardly. To see hornbills on a bare sandbank is a solemn sight, but when they are dodging about in the hippo grass they sink ceremony, and roll and waddle, looking—my man said—for snakes and the little sand-fish, which are close in under the bank; and their killing way of dropping their jaws—I should say opening their bills—when they are alarmed is comic. I think this has something to do with their hearing, for I often saw two or three of them in a line on a long branch, standing, stretched up to their full height, their great eyes opened wide, and all with their great beaks open, evidently listening for something. Their cry is most peculiar and can only be mistaken for a native horn; and although there seems little variety in it to my ear, there must be more to theirs, for they will carry on long confabulations with each other across a river, and, I believe, sit up half the night and talk scandal.

There were plenty of plantain-eaters here, but, although their screech was as appalling as I have heard in Angola, they were not regarded, by the Ajumba at any rate, as being birds of evil omen, as they are in Angola. Still, by no means all the birds here only screech and squark. Several of them have very lovely notes. There is one who always gives a series of infinitely beautiful, soft, rich-toned whistles just before the first light of the dawn shows in the sky, and one at least who has a prolonged and very lovely song. This bird, I was told in Gaboon, is called Telephonus erythropterus. I expect an ornithologist would enjoy himself here, but I cannot—and will not—collect birds. I hate to have them killed any how, and particularly in the barbarous way in which these natives kill them.

The broad stretch of water looks like a long lake. In all directions sandbanks are showing their broad yellow backs, and there will be more showing soon, for it is not yet the height of the dry. We are perpetually grounding on those which by next month will be above water. These canoes are built, I believe, more with a view to taking sandbanks comfortably than anything else; but they are by no means yet sufficiently specialised for getting off them. Their flat bottoms enable them to glide on to the banks, and sit there, without either upsetting or cutting into the sand, as a canoe with a keel would; but the trouble comes in when you are getting off the steep edge of the bank, and the usual form it takes is upsetting. So far my Ajumba friends have only tried to meet this difficulty by tying the cargo in.

I try to get up the geography of this region conscientiously. Fortunately I find Gray Shirt, Singlet, and Pagan can speak trade English. None of them, however, seem to recognise a single blessed name on the chart, which is saying nothing against the chart and its makers, who probably got their names up from M'pongwes and Igalwas instead of Ajumba, as I am trying to. Geographical research in this region is fraught with difficulty, I find, owing to different tribes calling one and the same place by different names; and I am sure the Royal Geographical Society ought to insert among their "Hints" that every traveller in this region should carefully learn every separate native word, or set of words, signifying "I don't know,"—four villages and two rivers I have come across out here solemnly set down with various forms of this statement, for their native name. Really I think the old Portuguese way of naming places after Saints, etc., was wiser in the long run, and it was certainly pleasanter to the ear. My Ajumba, however, know about my Ngambi and the Vinue all right and Elivā z'Ayzingo, so I must try and get cross bearings from these.

We have an addition to our crew this morning—a man who wants to go and get work at John Holt's sub-factory away on the Rembwé. He has been waiting a long while at Arevooma, unable to get across, I am told, because the road is now stopped between Ayzingo and the Rembwé by "those fearful Fans." "How are we going to get through that way?" says I, with natural feminine alarm. "We are not, sir," says Gray Shirt. This is what Lady MacDonald would term a chatty little incident; and my hair begins to rise as I remember what I have been told about those Fans and the indications I have already seen of its being true when on the Upper Ogowé. Now here we are going to try to get through the heart of their country, far from a French station, and without the French flag. Why did I not obey Mr. Hudson's orders not to go wandering about in a reckless way! Anyhow I am in for it, and Fortune favours the brave. The only question is: Do I individually come under this class? I go into details. It seems Pagan thinks he can depend on the friendship of two Fans he once met and did business with, and who now live on an island in Lake Ncovi—Ncovi is not down on my map and I have never heard of it before—anyhow thither we are bound now.

Each man has brought with him his best gun, loaded to the muzzle, and tied on to the baggage against which I am leaning—the muzzles sticking out each side of my head: the flint locks covered with cases, or sheaths, made of the black-haired skins of gorillas, leopard skin, and a beautiful bright bay skin, which I do not know, which they say is bush cow—but they call half a dozen things bush cow. These guns are not the "gas-pipes" I have seen up north; but decent rifles which have had the rifling filed out and the locks replaced by flint locks and converted into muzzle loaders, and many of them have beautiful barrels. I find the Ajumba name for the beautiful shrub that has long bunches of red, yellow and cream-coloured young leaves at the end of its branches is "obaa." I also learn that in their language ebony and a monkey have one name. The forest on either bank is very lovely. Some enormously high columns of green are formed by a sort of climbing plant having taken possession of light-ning-struck trees, and in one place it really looks exactly as if some one had spread a great green coverlet over the forest, so as to keep it dry. No high land showing in any direction. Pagan tells me the extinguisher-shaped juju filled with medicine and made of iron is against drowning—the red juju is "for keep foot in path." Beautiful effect of a gleam of sunshine lighting up a red sandbank till it glows like the Nibelungen gold. Indeed the effects are Turneresque to-day owing to the mist, and the sun playing in and out among it.

The sandbanks now have their cliffs to the N.N.W. and N.W. At 9.30, the broad river in front of us is apparently closed by sandbanks which run out from the banks thus: —

yellow}
S. bank bright-red} N. bank.
yellow}

Current running strong along south bank. This bank bears testimony of this also being the case in the wet season, for a fringe of torn-down trees hangs from it into the river. Pass Seke, a town on north bank, interchanging the usual observations regarding our destination. The river seems absolutely barred with sand again; but as we paddle down it, the obstructions resolve themselves into spits of sand from the north bank and the largest island in mid-stream, which also has a long tail, or train, of sandbank down river. Here we meet a pictur-esque series of canoes, fruit and trade laden, being poled up stream, one man with his pole over one side, the other with his pole over the other, making a St. Andrew's cross as you meet them end on.

Most luxurious, charming, and pleasant trip this. The men are standing up swinging in rhythmic motion their long, rich red wood paddles in perfect time to their elaborate melancholy, minor key boat song. Nearly lost with all hands. Sandbank palaver—only when we were going over the end of it, the canoe slips sideways over its edge. River deep, bottom sand and mud. This information may be interesting to the geologist, but I hope I shall not be converted by circumstances into a human sounding apparatus again to-day. Next time she strikes I shall get out and shove behind.

We are now skirting the real north bank, and not the bank of an island or islands as we have been for some time heretofore. Lovely stream falls into this river over cascades. The water is now rough in a small way and the width of the river great, but it soon is crowded again with wooded islands. There are patches and wreaths of a lovely, vermilion-flowering bush rope decorating the forest, and now and again clumps of a plant that shows a yellow and crimson spike of bloom, very strikingly beautiful. We pass a long tunnel in the bush, quite dark as you look down it—evidently the path to some native town. The south bank is covered, where the falling waters have exposed it, with hippo grass. Terrible lot of mangrove flies about, although we are more than one hundred miles above the mangrove belt. River broad again—tending W.S.W., with a broad flattened island with attributive sandbanks in the middle. The fair way is along the south bank of the river. Gray Shirt tells me this river is called the O'Rembo Vongo, or small River, so as to distinguish it from the main stream of the Ogowé which goes down past the south side of Lembarene Island, as well I know after that canoe affair of mine. Ayzingo now bears due north—and native mahogany is called "Okooma." Pass village called Welli on north bank. It looks like some gipsy caravans stuck on poles. I expect that village has known what it means to be swamped by the rising river; it looks as if it had, very hastily in the middle of some night, taken to stilts, which I am sure, from their present rickety condition, will not last through the next wet season, and then some unfortunate spirit will get the blame of the collapse. I also learn that it is the natal spot of my friend Kabinda, the carpenter at Andande. Now if some of these good people I know would only go and distinguish themselves, I might write a sort of county family history of these parts; but they don't, and I fancy won't. For example, the entrance— or should I say the exit?—of a broadish little river is just away on the south bank. If you go up this river—it runs S.E.—you get to a good-sized lake; in this lake there is an island called Adole; then out of the other side of the lake there is another river which falls into the Ogowé main stream—but that is not the point of the story, which is that on that island of Adole, Ngouta, the interpreter, first saw the light. Why he ever did—there or anywhere—Heaven only knows! I know I shall never want to write his biography.

On the western bank end of that river going to Adole, there is an Igalwa town, notable for a large quantity of fine white ducks and a clump of Indian bamboo. My informants say, "No white man ever live for this place," so I suppose the ducks and bamboo have been imported by some black trader whose natal spot this is. The name of this village is Wanderegwoma. Stuck on sandbank—I flew out and shoved behind, leaving Ngouta to do the balancing performances in the stern. This O'Rembo Vongo divides up just below here, I am told, when we have re-embarked, into three streams. One goes into the main Ogowé opposite Ayshouka in Nkami country—Nkami country commences at Ayshouka and goes to the sea—one into the Ngumbi, and one into the Nunghi—all in the Ouroungou country. Ayzingo now lies N.E. according to Gray Shirt's arm. On our river there is here another broad low island with its gold-coloured banks shining out, seemingly barring the entire channel, but there is really a canoe channel along by both banks.

We turn at this point into a river on the north bank that runs north and south—the current is running very swift to the north. We run down into it, and then, it being more than time enough for chop, we push the canoe on to a sandbank in our new river, which I am told is the Karkola. I, after having had my tea, wander off, and find behind our high sandbank, which like all the other sandbanks above water now, is getting grown over with hippo grass—a fine light green grass, the beloved food of both hippo and manatee—a forest, and entering this I notice a succession of strange mounds or heaps, made up of branches, twigs, and leaves, and dead flowers. Many of these heaps are recent, while others have fallen into decay. Investigation shows they are burial places. Among the débris of an old one there are human bones, and out from one of the new ones comes a stench and a hurrying, exceedingly busy line of ants, demonstrating what is going on. I own I thought these mounds were some kind of bird's or animal's nest. They look entirely unhuman in this desolate reach of forest. Leaving these, I go down to the water edge of the sand, and find in it a quantity of pools of varying breadth and expanse, but each surrounded by a rim of dark red-brown deposit, which you can lift off the sand in a skin. On the top of the water is a film of exquisite iridescent colours like those on a soap bubble, only darker and brighter. In the river alongside the sand, there are thousands of those beautiful little fish with a black line each side of their tails. They are perfectly tame, and I feed them with crumbs in my hand. After making every effort to terrify the unknown object containing the food—gallant bulls, quite two inches long, sidling up and snapping at my fingers—they come and feed right in the palm, so that I could have caught them by the handful had I wished. There are also a lot of those weird, semi-transparent, yellow, spotted little sandfish with cup-shaped pectoral fins, which I see they use to enable them to make their astoundingly long leaps. These fish are of a more nervous and distrustful disposition, and hover round my hand but will not come into it. Indeed I do not believe the other cheeky little fellows would allow them to.

The men, having had their rest and their pipes, shout for me, and off we go again. The Karkola {181} soon widens to about 100 feet; it is evidently very deep here; the right bank (the east) is forested, the left, low and shrubbed, one patch looking as if it were being cleared for a plantation, but no village showing. A big rock shows up on the right bank, which is a change from the clay and sand, and soon the whole character of the landscape changes. We come to a sharp turn in the river, from north and south to east and west—the current very swift. The river channel dodges round against a big bank of sword grass, and then widens out to the breadth of the Thames at Putney. I am told that a river runs out of it here to the west to Ouroungou country, and so I imagine this Karkola falls ultimately into the Nazareth. We skirt the eastern banks, which are covered with low grass with a scanty lot of trees along the top. High land shows in the distance to the S.S.W. and S.W., and then we suddenly turn up into a broad river or straith, shaping our course N.N.E. On the opposite bank, on a high dwarf cliff, is a Fan town. "All Fan now," says Singlet in anything but a gratified tone of voice.

It is a strange, wild, lonely bit of the world we are now in, apparently a lake or broad—full of sandbanks, some bare and some in the course of developing into permanent islands by the growth on them of that floating coarse grass, any joint of which being torn off either by the current, a passing canoe, or hippos, floats down and grows wherever it settles. Like most things that float in these parts, it usually settles on a sandbank, and then grows in much the same way as our couch grass grows on land in England, so as to form a network, which catches for its adopted sandbank all sorts of floating débris; so the sandbank comes up in the world. The waters of the wet season when they rise drown off the grass; but when they fall, up it comes again from the root, and so gradually the sandbank becomes an island and persuades real trees and shrubs to come and grow on it, and its future is then secured.

We skirt alongside a great young island of this class; the sword grass some ten or fifteen feet high. It has not got any trees on it yet, but by next season or so it doubtless will have. The grass is stabbled down into paths by hippos, and just as I have realised who are the road-makers, they appear in person. One immense fellow, hearing us, stands up and shows himself about six feet from us in the grass, gazes calmly, and then yawns a yawn a yard wide and grunts his news to his companions, some of whom—there is evidently a large herd—get up and stroll towards us with all the flowing grace of Pantechnicon vans in motion. We put our helm paddles hard a starboard and leave that bank.

Our hasty trip across to the bank of the island on the other side being accomplished, we, in search of seclusion and in the hope that out of sight would mean out of mind to hippos, shot down a narrow channel between semi-island sandbanks, and those sandbanks, if you please, are covered with specimens—as fine a set of specimens as you could wish for—of the West African crocodile. These interesting animals are also having their siestas, lying sprawling in all directions on the sand, with their mouths wide open. One immense old lady has a family of lively young crocodiles running over her, evidently playing like a lot of kittens. The heavy musky smell they give off is most repulsive, but we do not rise up and make a row about this, because we feel hopelessly in the wrong in intruding into these family scenes uninvited, and so apologetically pole ourselves along rapidly, not even singing. The pace the canoe goes down that channel would be a wonder to Henley Regatta. When out of ear-shot I ask Pagan whether there are many gorillas, elephants, or bush cows round here. "Plenty too much," says he; and it occurs to me that the corn-fields are growing golden green away in England; and soon there rises up in my mental vision a picture that fascinated my youth in the Fliegende Blätter, representing "Friedrich Gerstaeker auf der Reise." That gallant man is depicted tramping on a serpent, new to M. Boulenger, while he attempts to club, with the butt end of his gun, a most lively savage who, accompanied by a bison, is attacking him in front. A terrific and obviously enthusiastic crocodile is grabbing the tail of the explorer's coat, and the explorer says "Hurrah! das gibt wieder einen prächtigen Artikel für Die Allgemeine Zeitung." I do not know where in the world Gerstaeker was at the time, but I should fancy hereabouts. My vigorous and lively conscience also reminds me that the last words a most distinguished and valued scientific friend had said to me before I left home was, "Always take measurements, Miss Kingsley, and always take them from the adult male." I know I have neglected opportunities of carrying this commission out on both those banks, but I do not feel like going back. Besides, the men would not like it, and I have mislaid my yard measure.

The extent of water, dotted with sandbanks and islands in all directions, here is great, and seems to be fringed uniformly by low swampy land, beyond which, to the north, rounded lumps of hills show blue. On one of the islands is a little white house which I am told was once occupied by a black trader for John Holt. It looks a desolate place for any man to live in, and the way the crocodiles and hippo must have come up on the garden ground in the evening time could not have enhanced its charms to the average cautious man. My men say, "No man live for that place now." The factory, I believe, has been, for some trade reason, abandoned. Behind it is a great clump of dark-coloured trees. The rest of the island is now covered with hippo grass looking like a beautifully kept lawn. We lie up for a short rest at another island, also a weird spot in its way, for it is covered with a grove of only one kind of tree, which has a twisted, contorted, gray-white trunk and dull, lifeless-looking, green, hard foliage.

I learn that these good people, to make topographical confusion worse confounded, call a river by one name when you are going up it, and by another when you are coming down; just as if you called the Thames the London when you were going up, and the Greenwich when you were coming down. The banks all round this lake or broad, seem all light-coloured sand and clay. We pass out of it into a channel. Current flowing north. As we are entering the channel between banks of grass-overgrown sand, a superb white crane is seen standing on the sand edge to the left. Gray Shirt attempts to get a shot at it, but it—alarmed at our unusual appearance—raises itself up with one of those graceful preliminary curtseys, and after one or two preliminary flaps spreads its broad wings and sweeps away, with its long legs trailing behind it like a thing on a Japanese screen.

The river into which we ran zigzags about, and then takes a course S.S.E. It is studded with islands slightly higher than those we have passed, and thinly clad with forest. The place seems alive with birds; flocks of pelican and crane rise up before us out of the grass, and every now and then a crocodile slides off the bank into the water. Wonderfully like old logs they look, particularly when you see one letting himself roll and float down on the current. In spite of these interests I began to wonder where in this lonely land we were to sleep to-night. In front of us were miles of distant mountains, but in no direction the slightest sign of human habitation. Soon we passed out of our channel into a lovely, strangely melancholy, lonely-looking lake—Lake Ncovi, my friends tell me. It is exceedingly beautiful. The rich golden sunlight of the late afternoon soon followed by the short-lived, glorious flushes of colour of the sunset and the after-glow, play over the scene as we paddle across the lake to the N.N.E.— our canoe leaving a long trail of frosted silver behind her as she glides over the mirror-like water, and each stroke of the paddle sending down air with it to come up again in luminous silver bubbles—not as before in swirls of sand and mud. The lake shore is, in all directions, wreathed with nobly forested hills, indigo and purple in the dying daylight. On the N.N.E. and N.E. these come directly down into the lake; on N.W., N., S.W., and S.E. there is a band of well-forested ground, behind which they rise. In the north and north-eastern part of the lake several exceedingly beautiful wooded islands show, with gray rocky beaches and dwarf cliffs.

Sign of human habitation at first there was none; and in spite of its beauty, there was something which I was almost going to say was repulsive. The men evidently felt the same as I did. Had any one told me that the air that lay on the lake was poison, or that in among its forests lay some path to regions of utter death, I should have said—"It looks like that"; but no one said anything, and we only looked round uneasily, until the comfortable-souled Singlet made the unfortunate observation that he "smelt blood." {185} We all called him an utter fool to relieve our minds, and made our way towards the second island. When we got near enough to it to see details, a large village showed among the trees on its summit, and a steep dwarf cliff, overgrown with trees and creeping plants came down to a small beach covered with large water-washed gray stones. There was evidently some kind of a row going on in that village, that took a lot of shouting too. We made straight for the beach, and drove our canoe among its outlying rocks, and then each of my men stowed his paddle quickly, slung on his ammunition bag, and picked up his ready loaded gun, sliding the skin sheath off the lock. Pagan got out on to the stones alongside the canoe just as the inhabitants became aware of our arrival, and, abandoning what I hope was a mass meeting to remonstrate with the local authorities on the insanitary state of the town, came—a brown mass of naked humanity—down the steep cliff path to attend to us, whom they evidently regarded as an Imperial interest. Things did not look restful, nor these Fans personally pleasant. Every man among them—no women showed—was armed with a gun, and they loosened their shovel-shaped knives in their sheaths as they came, evidently regarding a fight quite as imminent as we did. They drew up about twenty paces from us in silence. Pagan and Gray Shirt, who had joined him, held out their unembarrassed hands, and shouted out the name of the Fan man they had said they were friendly with: "Kiva-Kiva." The Fans stood still and talked angrily among themselves for some minutes, and then, Silence said to me, "It would be bad palaver if Kiva no live for this place," in a tone that conveyed to me the idea he thought this unpleasant contingency almost a certainty. The Passenger exhibited unmistakable symptoms of wishing he had come by another boat. I got up from my seat in the bottom of the canoe and leisurely strolled ashore, saying to the line of angry faces "M'boloani" in an unconcerned way, although I well knew it was etiquette for them to salute first. They grunted, but did not commit themselves further. A minute after they parted to allow a fine-looking, middle-aged man, naked save for a twist of dirty cloth round his loins and a bunch of leopard and wild cat tails hung from his shoulder by a strip of leopard skin, to come forward. Pagan went for him with a rush, as if he were going to clasp him to his ample bosom, but holding his hands just off from touching the Fan's shoulder in the usual way, while he said in Fan, "Don't you know me, my beloved Kiva? Surely you have not forgotten your old friend?" Kiva grunted feelingly, and raised up his hands and held them just off touching Pagan, and we breathed again. Then Gray Shirt made a rush at the crowd and went through great demonstrations of affection with another gentleman whom he recognised as being a Fan friend of his own, and whom he had not expected to meet here. I looked round to see if there was not any Fan from the Upper Ogowé whom I knew to go for, but could not see one that I could on the strength of a previous acquaintance, and on their individual merits I did not feel inclined to do even this fashionable imitation embrace. Indeed I must say that never—even in a picture book—have I seen such a set of wild wicked-looking savages as those we faced this night, and with whom it was touch-and-go for twenty of the longest minutes I have ever lived, whether we fought—for our lives, I was going to say, but it would not have been even for that, but merely for the price of them.

Peace having been proclaimed, conversation became general. Gray Shirt brought his friend up and introduced him to me, and we shook hands and smiled at each other in the conventional way. Pagan's friend, who was next introduced, was more alarming, for he held his hands for half a minute just above my elbows without quite touching me, but he meant well; and then we all disappeared into a brown mass of humanity and a fog of noise. You would have thought, from the violence and vehemence of the shouting and gesticulation, that we were going to be forthwith torn to shreds; but not a single hand really touched me, and as I, Pagan, and Gray Shirt went up to the town in the midst of the throng, the crowd opened in front and closed in behind, evidently half frightened at my appearance. The row when we reached the town redoubled in volume from the fact that the ladies, the children, and the dogs joined in. Every child in the place as soon as it saw my white face let a howl out of it as if it had seen his Satanic Majesty, horns, hoofs, tail and all, and fled into the nearest hut, headlong, and I fear, from the continuance of the screams, had fits. The town was exceedingly filthy—the remains of the crocodile they had been eating the week before last, and piles of fish offal, and remains of an elephant, hippo or manatee—I really can't say which, decomposition was too far advanced—united to form a most impressive stench. The bark huts are, as usual in a Fan town, in unbroken rows; but there are three or four streets here, not one only, as in most cases. The palaver house is in the innermost street, and there we went, and noticed that the village view was not in the direction in which we had come, but across towards the other side of the lake. I told the Ajumba to explain we wanted hospitality for the night, and wished to hire three carriers for to-morrow to go with us to the Rembwé.

For an hour and three-quarters by my watch I stood in the suffocating, smoky, hot atmosphere listening to, but only faintly understanding, the war of words and gesture that raged round us. At last the fact that we were to be received being settled, Gray Shirt's friend led us out of the guard house—the crowd flinching back as I came through it—to his own house on the right-hand side of the street of huts. It was a very different dwelling to Gray Shirt's residence at Arevooma. I was as high as its roof ridge and had to stoop low to get through the door-hole. Inside, the hut was fourteen or fifteen feet square, unlit by any window. The door-hole could be closed by pushing a broad piece of bark across it under two horizontally fixed bits of stick. The floor was sand like the street outside, but dirtier. On it in one place was a fire, whose smoke found its way out through the roof. In one corner of the room was a rough bench of wood, which from the few filthy cloths on it and a wood pillow I saw was the bed. There was no other furniture in the hut save some boxes, which I presume held my host's earthly possessions. From the bamboo roof hung a long stick with hooks on it, the hooks made by cutting off branching twigs. This was evidently the hanging wardrobe, and on it hung some few fetish charms, and a beautiful ornament of wild cat and leopard tails, tied on to a square piece of leopard skin, in the centre of which was a little mirror, and round the mirror were sewn dozens of common shirt buttons. In among the tails hung three little brass bells and a brass rattle; these bells and rattles are not only "for dandy," but serve to scare away snakes when the ornament is worn in the forest. A fine strip of silky-haired, young gorilla skin made the band to sling the ornament from the shoulder when worn. Gorillas seem well enough known round here. One old lady in the crowd outside, I saw, had a necklace made of sixteen gorilla canine teeth slung on a pine-apple fibre string. Gray Shirt explained to me that this is the best house in the village, and my host the most renowned elephant hunter in the district.

We then returned to the canoe, whose occupants had been getting uneasy about the way affairs were going "on top," on account of the uproar they heard and the time we had been away. We got into the canoe and took her round the little promontory at the end of the island to the other beach, which is the main beach. By arriving at the beach when we did, we took our Fan friends in the rear, and they did not see us coming in the gloaming. This was all for the best, it seems, as they said they should have fired on us before they had had time to see we were rank outsiders, on the apprehension that we were coming from one of the Fan towns we had passed, and with whom they were on bad terms regarding a lady who bolted there from her lawful lord, taking with her—cautious soul!—a quantity of rubber. The only white man who had been here before in the memory of man, was a French officer who paid Kiva six dollars to take him somewhere, I was told—but I could not find out when, or what happened to that Frenchman. {189} It was a long time ago, Kiva said, but these folks have no definite way of expressing duration of time nor, do I believe, any great mental idea of it; although their ideas are, as usual with West Africans, far ahead of their language.

All the goods were brought up to my hut, and while Ngouta gets my tea we started talking the carrier palaver again. The Fans received my offer, starting at two dollars ahead of what M. Jacot said would be enough, with utter scorn, and every dramatic gesture of dissent; one man, pretending to catch Gray Shirt's words in his hands, flings them to the ground and stamps them under his feet. I affected an easy take-it-or-leave-it-manner, and looked on. A woman came out of the crowd to me, and held out a mass of slimy gray abomination on a bit of plantain leaf—smashed snail. I accepted it and gave her fish hooks. She was delighted and her companions excited, so she put the hooks into her mouth for safe keeping. I hurriedly explained in my best Fan that I do not require any more snail; so another lady tried the effect of a pine-apple. There might be no end to this, so I retired into trade and asked what she would sell it for. She did not want to sell it—she wanted to give it me; so I gave her fish hooks. Silence and Singlet interposed, saying the price for pine-apples is one leaf of tobacco, but I explained I was not buying. Ngouta turned up with my tea, so I went inside, and had it on the bed. The door-hole was entirely filled with a mosaic of faces, but no one attempted to come in. All the time the carrier palaver went on without cessation, and I went out and offered to take Gray Shirt's and Pagan's place, knowing they must want their chop, but they refused relief, and also said I must not raise the price; I was offering too big a price now, and if I once rise the Fan will only think I will keep on rising, and so make the palaver longer to talk. "How long does a palaver usually take to talk round here?" I ask. "The last one I talked," says Pagan, "took three weeks, and that was only a small price palaver." "Well," say I, "my price is for a start to-morrow—after then I have no price—after that I go away." Another hour however sees the jam made, and to my surprise I find the three richest men in this town of M'fetta have personally taken up the contract—Kiva my host, Fika a fine young fellow, and Wiki, another noted elephant hunter. These three Fans, the four Ajumba and the Igalwa, Ngouta, I think will be enough. Moreover I fancy it safer not to have an overpowering percentage of Fans in the party, as I know we shall have considerable stretches of uninhabited forest to traverse; and the Ajumba say that the Fans will kill people, i.e. the black traders who venture into their country, and cut them up into neat pieces, eat what they want at the time, and smoke the rest of the bodies for future use. Now I do not want to arrive at the Remb-wé in a smoked condition, even should my fragments be neat, and I am going in a different direction to what I said I was when leaving Kangwe, and there are so many ways of accounting for death about here—leopard, canoe capsize, elephants, etc.—that even if I were traced—well, nothing could be done then, anyhow—so will only take three Fans. One must diminish dead certainties to the level of sporting chances along here, or one can never get on.

No one, either Ajumba or Fan, knew the exact course we were to take. The Ajumba had never been this way before—the way for black traders across being viâ Lake Ayzingo, the way Mr. Goode of the American Mission once went, and the Fans said they only knew the way to a big Fan town called Efoua, where no white man or black trader had yet been. There is a path from there to the Rembwé they knew, because the Efoua people take their trade all to the Rembwé. They would, they said, come with me all the way if I would guarantee them safety if they "found war" on the road. This I agreed to do, and arranged to pay off at Hatton and Cookson's subfactory on the Rembwé, and they have "Look my mouth and it be sweet, so palaver done set." Every load then, by the light of the bush lights held by the women, we arranged. I had to unpack my bottles of fishes so as to equalise the weight of the loads. Every load is then made into a sort of cocoon with bush rope.

I was left in peace at about 11.30 P.M., and clearing off the clothes from the bench threw myself down and tried to get some sleep, for we were to start, the Fans said, before dawn. Sleep impossible—mosquitoes! lice!!—so at 12.40 I got up and slid aside my bark door. I found Pagan asleep under his mosquito bar outside, across the doorway, but managed to get past him without rousing him from his dreams of palaver which he was still talking aloud, and reconnoitred the town. The inhabitants seemed to have talked themselves quite out and were sleeping heavily. I went down then to our canoe and found it safe, high up among the Fan canoes on the stones, and then I slid a small Fan canoe off, and taking a paddle from a cluster stuck in the sand, paddled out on to the dark lake.

It was a wonderfully lovely quiet night with no light save that from the stars. One immense planet shone pre-eminent in the purple sky, throwing a golden path down on to the still waters. Quantities of big fish sprung out of the water, their glistening silver-white scales flashing so that they look like slashing swords. Some bird was making a long, low boom-booming sound away on the forest shore. I paddled leisurely across the lake to the shore on the right, and seeing crawling on the ground some large glow-worms, drove the canoe on to the bank among some hippo grass, and got out to get them.

While engaged on this hunt I felt the earth quiver under my feet, and heard a soft big soughing sound, and looking round saw I had dropped in on a hippo banquet. I made out five of the immense brutes round me, so I softly returned to the canoe and shoved off, stealing along the bank, paddling under water, until I deemed it safe to run out across the lake for my island. I reached the other end of it to that on which the village is situated; and finding a miniature rocky bay with a soft patch of sand and no hippo grass, the incidents of the Fan hut suggested the advisability of a bath. Moreover, there was no china collection in that hut, and it would be a long time before I got another chance, so I go ashore again, and, carefully investigating the neighbourhood to make certain there was no human habitation near, I then indulged in a wash in peace. Drying one's self on one's cummerbund is not pure joy, but it can be done when you put your mind to it. While I was finishing my toilet I saw a strange thing happen. Down through the forest on the lake bank opposite came a violet ball the size of a small orange. When it reached the sand beach it hovered along it to and fro close to the ground. In a few minutes another ball of similarly coloured light came towards it from behind one of the islets, and the two waver to and fro over the beach, sometimes circling round each other. I made off towards them in the canoe, thinking—as I still do—they were some brand new kind of luminous insect. When I got on to their beach one of them went off into the bushes and the other away over the water. I followed in the canoe, for the water here is very deep, and, when I almost thought I had got it, it went down into the water and I could see it glowing as it sunk until it vanished in the depths. I made my way back hastily, fearing my absence with the canoe might give rise, if discovered, to trouble, and by 3.30 I was back in the hut safe, but not so comfortable as I had been on the lake. A little before five my men are stirring and I get my tea. I do not state my escapade to them, but ask what those lights were. "Akom," said the Fan, and pointing to the shore of the lake where I had been during the night they said, "they came there, it was an 'Aku'"—or devil bush. More than ever did I regret not having secured one of those sort of two phenomena. What a joy a real devil, appropriately put up in raw alcohol, would have been to my scientific friends!

Wednesday, July 24th.—We get away about 5.30, the Fans coming in a separate canoe. We call at the next island to M'fetta to buy some more aguma. The inhabitants are very much interested in my appearance, running along the stony beach as we paddle away, and standing at the end of it until we are out of sight among the many islands at the N.E. end of Lake Ncovi. The scenery is savage; there are no terrific cliffs nor towering mountains to make it what one usually calls wild or romantic, but there is a distinction about it which is all its own. This N.E. end has beautiful sand beaches on the southern side, in front of the forested bank, lying in smooth ribbons along the level shore, and in scollops round the promontories where the hills come down into the lake. The forest on these hills, or mountains—for they are part of the Sierra del Cristal—is very dark in colour, and the undergrowth seems scant. We presently come to a narrow but deep channel into the lake coming from the eastward, which we go up, winding our course with it into a valley between the hills. After going up it a little way we find it completely fenced across with stout stakes, a space being left open in the middle, broader than the spaces between the other stakes; and over this is poised a spear with a bush rope attached, and weighted at the top of the haft with a great lump of rock. The whole affair is kept in position by a bush rope so arranged just under the level of the water that anything passing through the opening would bring the spear down. This was a trap for hippo or manatee (Ngany 'imanga), and similar in structure to those one sees set in the hippo grass near villages and plantations, which serve the double purpose of defending the vegetable supply, and adding to the meat supply of the inhabitants. We squeeze through between the stakes so as not to let the trap off, and find our little river leads us into another lake, much smaller than Ncovi. It is studded with islands of fantastic shapes, all wooded with high trees of an equal level, and with little or no undergrowth among them, so their pale gray stems look like clusters of columns supporting a dark green ceiling. The forest comes down steep hill sides to the water edge in all directions; and a dark gloomy-looking herb grows up out of black slime and water, in a bank or ribbon in front of it. There is another channel out of this lake, still to the N.E. The Fans say they think it goes into the big lake far far away, i.e., Lake Ayzingo. From the look of the land, I think this river connecting Ayzingo and Lake Ncovi wanders down this valley between the mountain spurs of the Sierra del Cristal, expanding into one gloomy lake after another. We run our canoe into a bank of the dank dark-coloured water herb to the right, and disembark into a fitting introduction to the sort of country we shall have to deal with before we see the Rembwé—namely, up to our knees in black slime.

CHAPTER VIII

FROM NCOVI TO ESOON

CONCERNING THE WAY IN WHICH THE VOYAGER GOES FROM THE IS-
LAND OF M'FETTA TO NO ONE KNOWS EXACTLY WHERE, IN DOUBTFUL
AND BAD COMPANY, AND OF WHAT THIS LED TO AND GIVING ALSO SOME
ACCOUNTS OF THE GREAT FOREST AND OF THOSE PEOPLE THAT LIVE
THEREIN.

I WILL NOT BORE YOU WITH MY DIARY in detail regarding our land journey, because the water-washed little volume attributive to this period is mainly full of reports of law cases, for reasons hereinafter to be stated; and at night, when passing through this bit of country, I was usually too tired to do anything more than make an entry such as: "5 S., 4 R. A., N.E Ebony. T. 1-50, etc., etc."—entries that require amplification to explain their significance, and I will proceed to explain.

Our first day's march was a very long one. Path in the ordinary acceptance of the term there was none. Hour after hour, mile after mile, we passed on, in the under-gloom of the great forest. The pace made by the Fans, who are infinitely the most rapid Africans I have ever come across, severely tired the Ajumba, who are canoe men, and who had been as fresh as paint, after their exceedingly long day's paddling from Arevooma to M'fetta. Ngouta, the Igalwa interpreter, felt pumped, and said as much, very early in the day. I regretted very much having brought him; for, from a mixture of nervous exhaustion aris-ing from our M'fetta experiences, and a touch of chill he had almost entirely lost his voice, and I feared would fall sick. The Fans were evidently quite at home in the forest, and strode on over fallen trees and rocks with an easy, grace-ful stride. What saved us weaklings was the Fans' appetites; every two hours they sat down, and had a snack of a pound or so of meat and aguma apiece, followed by a pipe of tobacco. We used to come up with them at these halts. Ngouta and the Ajumba used to sit down, and rest with them, and I also, for a few minutes, for a rest and chat, and then I would go on alone, thus getting a good start. I got a good start, in the other meaning of the word, on the afternoon of the first day when descending into a ravine.

I saw in the bottom, wading and rolling in the mud, a herd of five elephants. I remembered, hastily, that your one chance when charged by several elephants is to dodge them round trees, working down wind all the time, until they lose smell and sight of you, then to lie quiet for a time, and go home. It was evident from the utter unconcern of these monsters that I was down wind now, so I had only to attend to dodging, and I promptly dodged round a tree, and lay down. Seeing they still displayed no emotion on my account, and fascinated by the novelty of the scene, I crept forward from one tree to another, until I was close enough to have hit the nearest one with a stone, and spats of mud, which they sent flying with their stamping and wallowing came flap, flap among the bushes covering me.

One big fellow had a nice pair of 40 lb. or so tusks on him, singularly straight, and another had one big curved tusk and one broken one. Some of them lay right down like pigs in the deeper part of the swamp, some drew up trunkfuls of water and syringed themselves and each other, and every one of them indulged in a good rub against a tree. Presently when they had had enough of it they all strolled off up wind, through the bush in Indian file, now and then breaking off a branch, but leaving singularly little dead water for their tonnage and breadth of beam. When they had gone I rose up, turned round to find the men, and trod on Kiva's back then and there, full and fair, and fell sideways down the steep hillside until I fetched up among some roots.

It seems Kiva had come on, after his meal, before the others, and seeing the elephants, and being a born hunter, had crawled like me down to look at them. He had not expected to find me there, he said. I do not believe he gave a thought of any sort to me in the presence of these fascinating creatures, and so he got himself trodden on. I suggested to him we should pile the baggage, and go and have an elephant hunt. He shook his head reluctantly, saying "Kor, kor," like a depressed rook, and explained we were not strong enough; there were only three Fans—the Ajumba, and Ngouta did not count—and moreover that we had not brought sufficient ammunition owing to the baggage having to be carried, and the ammunition that we had must be saved for other game than elephant, for we might meet war before we met the Rembwé River.

We had by now joined the rest of the party, and were all soon squattering about on our own account in the elephant bath. It was shocking bad going—like a ploughed field exaggerated by a terrific nightmare. It pretty nearly pulled all the legs off me, and to this hour I cannot tell you if it is best to put your foot into a footmark—a young pond, I mean—about the size of the bottom of a Madeira work arm-chair, or whether you should poise yourself on the rim of the same, and stride forward to its other bank boldly and hopefully. The footmarks and the places where the elephants had been rolling were by now filled with water, and the mud underneath was in places hard and slippery. In spite of my determination to preserve an awesome and unmoved calm while among these dangerous savages, I had to give way and laugh explosively; to see the portly, powerful Pagan suddenly convert himself into a quadruped, while Gray Shirt poised himself on one heel and waved his other leg in the air to advertise to the assembled nations that he was about to sit down, was irresistible. No one made such palaver about taking a seat as Gray Shirt; I did it repeatedly without any fuss to speak of. That lordly elephant-hunter, the Great Wiki, would, I fancy, have strode over safely and with dignity, but the man who was in front of him spun round on his own axis and flung his arms round the Fan, and they went to earth together; the heavy load on Wiki's back drove them into the mud like a pile-driver. However we got through in time, and after I had got up the other side of the ravine I saw the Fan let the Ajumba go on, and were busy searching themselves for something.

I followed the Ajumba, and before I joined them felt a fearful pricking irritation. Investigation of the affected part showed a tick of terrific size with its head embedded in the flesh; pursuing this interesting subject, I found three more, and had awfully hard work to get them off and painful too for they give one not only a feeling of irritation at their holding-on place, but a streak of rheumatic-feeling pain up from it. On completing operations I went on and came upon the Ajumba in a state more approved of by Praxiteles than by the general public nowadays. They had found out about elephant ticks, so I went on and got an excellent start for the next stage.

By this time, shortly after noon on the first day, we had struck into a mountainous and rocky country, and also struck a track—a track you had to keep your eye on or you lost it in a minute, but still a guide as to direction.

The forest trees here were mainly ebony and great hard wood trees, {200} with no palms save my old enemy the climbing palm, calamus, as usual, going on its long excursions, up one tree and down another, bursting into a plume of fronds, and in the middle of each plume one long spike sticking straight up, which was an unopened frond, whenever it got a gleam of sunshine; running along the ground over anything it meets, rock or fallen timber, all alike, its long, dark-coloured, rope-like stem simply furred with thorns. Immense must be the length of some of these climbing palms. One tree I noticed that day that had hanging from its summit, a good one hundred and fifty feet above us, a long straight ropelike palm stem.

The character of the whole forest was very interesting. Sometimes for hours we passed among thousands upon thousands of gray-white columns of uniform height (about 100-150 feet); at the top of these the boughs branched out and interlaced among each other, forming a canopy or ceiling, which dimmed the light even of the equatorial sun to such an extent that no undergrowth could thrive in the gloom. The statement of the struggle for existence was published here in plain figures, but it was not, as in our climate, a struggle against climate mainly, but an internecine war from over population. Now and again we passed among vast stems of buttressed trees, sometimes enormous in girth; and from their far-away summits hung great bush-ropes, some as straight as plumb lines, others coiled round, and intertwined among each other, until one could fancy one was looking on some mighty battle between armies of gigantic serpents, that had been arrested at its height by some magic spell. All these bush-ropes were as bare of foliage as a ship's wire rigging, but a good many had thorns. I was very curious as to how they got up straight, and investigation showed me that many of them were carried up with a growing tree. The only true climbers were the calamus and the rubber vine (Landolphia), both of which employ hook tackle.

Some stretches of this forest were made up of thin, spindly stemmed trees of great height, and among these stretches I always noticed the ruins of some forest giant, whose death by lightning or by his superior height having given the demoniac tornado wind an extra grip on him, had allowed sunlight to penetrate the lower regions of the forest; and then evidently the seedlings and saplings, who had for years been living a half-starved life for light, shot up. They seemed to know that their one chance lay in getting with the greatest rapidity to the level of the top of the forest. No time to grow fat in the stem. No time to send out side branches, or any of those vanities. Up, up to the light level, and he among them who reached it first won in this game of life or death; for when he gets there he spreads out his crown of upper branches, and shuts off the life-giving sunshine from his competitors, who pale off and die, or remain dragging on an attenuated existence waiting for another chance, and waiting sometimes for centuries. There must be tens of thousands of seeds which perish before they get their chance; but the way the seeds of the hard wood African trees are packed, as it were in cases specially made durable, is very wonderful. Indeed the ways of Providence here are wonderful in their strange dual intention to preserve and to destroy; but on the whole, as Peer Gynt truly observes, "Ein guter Wirth—nein das ist er nicht."

We saw this influence of light on a large scale as soon as we reached the open hills and mountains of the Sierra del Cristal, and had to pass over those fearful avalanche-like timber falls on their steep sides. The worst of these lay between Efoua and Egaja, where we struck a part of the range that was exposed to the south-east. These falls had evidently arisen from the tornados, which from time to time have hurled down the gigantic trees whose hold on the superficial soil over the sheets of hard bed rock was insufficient, in spite of all the anchors they had out in the shape of roots and buttresses, and all their rigging in the shape of bush ropes. Down they had come, crushing and dragging down with them those near them or bound to them by the great tough climbers.

Getting over these falls was perilous, not to say scratchy work. One or another member of our party always went through; and precious uncomfortable going it was, I found, when I tried it in one above Egaja; ten or twelve feet of crashing creaking timber, and then flump on to a lot of rotten, wet débris, with more snakes and centipedes among it than you had any immediate use for, even though you were a collector; but there you had to stay, while Wiki, who was a most critical connoisseur, selected from the surrounding forest a bush-rope that he regarded as the correct remedy for the case, and then up you were hauled, through the sticks you had turned the wrong way on your down journey.

The Duke had a bad fall, going twenty feet or so before he found the rubbish heap; while Fika, who went through with a heavy load on his back, took us, on one occasion, half an hour to recover; and when we had just got him to the top, and able to cling on to the upper sticks, Wiki, who had been superintending operations, slipped backwards, and went through on his own account. The bush-rope we had been hauling on was too worn with the load to use again, and we just hauled Wiki out with the first one we could drag down and cut; and Wiki, when he came up, said we were reckless, and knew nothing of bush ropes, which shows how ungrateful an African can be. It makes the perspiration run down my nose whenever I think of it. The sun was out that day; we were neatly situated on the Equator, and the air was semisolid, with the stinking exhalations from the swamps with which the mountain chain is fringed and intersected; and we were hot enough without these things, because of the violent exertion of getting these twelve to thirteen-stone gentlemen up among us again, and the fine varied exercise of getting over the fall on our own account.

When we got into the cool forest beyond it was delightful; particularly if it happened to be one of those lovely stretches of forest, gloomy down below, but giving hints that far away above us was a world of bloom and scent and beauty which we saw as much of as earth-worms in a flower-bed. Here and there the ground was strewn with great cast blossoms, thick, wax-like, glorious cups of orange and crimson and pure white, each one of which was in itself a handful, and which told us that some of the trees around us were showing a glory of colour to heaven alone. Sprinkled among them were bunches of pure stephanotis-like flowers, which said that the gaunt bush-ropes were rubber vines that had burst into flower when they had seen the sun. These flowers we came across in nearly every type of forest all the way, for rubber abounds here.

I will weary you no longer now with the different kinds of forest and only tell you I have let you off several. The natives have separate names for seven different kinds, and these might, I think, be easily run up to nine.

A certain sort of friendship soon arose between the Fans and me. We each recognised that we belonged to that same section of the human race with whom it is better to drink than to fight. We knew we would each have killed the other, if sufficient inducement were offered, and so we took a certain amount of care that the inducement should not arise. Gray Shirt and Pagan also, their trade friends, the Fans treated with an independent sort of courtesy; but Silence, Singlet, the Passenger, and above all Ngouta, they openly did not care a row of pins for, and I have small doubt that had it not been for us other three they would have killed and eaten these very amiable gentlemen with as much compunction as an English sportsman would kill as many rabbits. They on their part hated the Fan, and never lost an opportunity of telling me "these Fan be bad man too much." I must not forget to mention the other member of our party, a Fan gentleman with the manners of a duke and the habits of a dustbin. He came with us, quite uninvited by me, and never asked for any pay; I think he only wanted to see the fun, and drop in for a fight if there was one going on, and to pick up the pieces generally. He was evidently a man of some importance from the way the others treated him; and moreover he had a splendid gun, with a gorilla skin sheath for its lock, and ornamented all over its stock with brass nails. His costume consisted of a small piece of dirty rag round his loins; and whenever we were going through dense undergrowth, or wading a swamp, he wore that filament tucked up scandalously short. Whenever we were sitting down in the forest having one of our nondescript meals, he always sat next to me and appropriated the tin. Then he would fill his pipe, and turning to me with the easy grace of aristocracy, would say what may be translated as "My dear Princess, could you favour me with a lucifer?"

I used to say, "My dear Duke, charmed, I'm sure," and give him one ready lit.

I dared not trust him with the box whole, having a personal conviction that he would have kept it. I asked him what he would do suppose I was not there with a box of lucifers; and he produced a bush-cow's horn with a neat wood lid tied on with tie tie, and from out of it he produced a flint and steel and demonstrated.

The first day in the forest we came across a snake {205} —a beauty with a new red-brown and yellow-patterned velvety skin, about three feet six inches long and as thick as a man's thigh. Ngouta met it, hanging from a bough, and shot backwards like a lobster, Ngouta having among his many weaknesses a rooted horror of snakes. This snake the Ogowé natives all hold in great aversion. For the bite of other sorts of snakes they profess to have remedies, but for this they have none. If, however, a native is stung by one he usually conceals the fact that it was this particular kind, and tries to get any chance the native doctor's medicine may give. The Duke stepped forward and with one blow flattened its head against the tree with his gun butt, and then folded the snake up and got as much of it as possible into his bag, while the rest hung dangling out. Ngouta, not being able to keep ahead of the Duke, his Grace's pace being stiff, went to the extreme rear of the party, so that other people might be killed first if the snake returned to life, as he surmised it would. He fell into other dangers from this caution, but I cannot chronicle Ngouta's afflictions in full without running this book into an old fashioned folio size. We had the snake for supper, that is to say the Fan and I; the others would not touch it, although a good snake, properly cooked, is one of the best meats one gets out here, far and away better than the African fowl.

The Fans also did their best to educate me in every way: they told me their names for things, while I told them mine. I found several European words already slightly altered in use among them, such as "Amuck"—a mug, "Alas"—a glass, a tumbler. I do not know whether their "Ami"—a person addressed, or spoken of—is French or not. It may come from "Anwe"—M'pongwe for "Ye," "You." They use it as a rule in addressing a person after the phrase they always open up conversation with, "Azuna"—Listen, or I am speaking.

They also showed me many things: how to light a fire from the pith of a certain tree, which was useful to me in after life, but they rather overdid this branch of instruction one way and another; for example, Wiki had, as above indicated, a mania for bush-ropes and a marvellous eye and knowledge of them; he would pick out from among the thousands surrounding us now one of such peculiar suppleness that you could wind it round anything, like a strip of cloth, and as strong withal as a hawser; or again another which has a certain stiffness, combined with a slight elastic spring, excellent for hauling, with the ease and accuracy of a lady who picks out the particular twisted strand of embroidery silk from a multi-coloured tangled ball. He would go into the bush after them while other people were resting, and particularly after the sort which, when split, is bright yellow, and very supple and excellent to tie round loads.

On one occasion, between Egaja and Esoon, he came back from one of these quests and wanted me to come and see something, very quietly; I went, and we crept down into a rocky ravine, on the other side of which lay one of the outermost Egaja plantations. When we got to the edge of the cleared ground, we lay down, and wormed our way, with elaborate caution, among a patch of Koko; Wiki first, I following in his trail.

After about fifty yards of this, Wiki sank flat, and I saw before me some thirty yards off, busily employed in pulling down plantains, and other depredations, five gorillas: one old male, one young male, and three females. One of these had clinging to her a young fellow, with beautiful wavy black hair with just a kink in it. The big male was crouching on his haunches, with his long arms hanging down on either side, with the backs of his hands on the ground, the palms upwards. The elder lady was tearing to pieces and eating a pine-apple, while the others were at the plantains destroying more than they ate.

They kept up a sort of a whinnying, chattering noise, quite different from the sound I have heard gorillas give when enraged, or from the one you can hear them giving when they are what the natives call "dancing" at night. I noticed that their reach of arm was immense, and that when they went from one tree to another, they squattered across the open ground in a most inelegant style, dragging their long arms with the knuckles downwards. I should think the big male and female were over six feet each. The others would be from four to five. I put out my hand and laid it on Wiki's gun to prevent him from firing, and he, thinking I was going to fire, gripped my wrist.

I watched the gorillas with great interest for a few seconds, until I heard Wiki make a peculiar small sound, and looking at him saw his face was working in an awful way as he clutched his throat with his hand violently.

Heavens! think I, this gentleman's going to have a fit; it's lost we are entirely this time. He rolled his head to and fro, and then buried his face into a heap of dried rubbish at the foot of a plantain stem, clasped his hands over it, and gave an explosive sneeze. The gorillas let go all, raised themselves up for a second, gave a quaint sound between a bark and a howl, and then the ladies and the young gentleman started home. The old male rose to his full height (it struck me at the time this was a matter of ten feet at least, but for scientific purposes allowance must be made for a lady's emotions) and looked straight towards us, or rather towards where that sound came from. Wiki went off into a paroxysm of falsetto sneezes the like of which I have never heard; nor evidently had the gorilla, who doubtless thinking, as one of his black co-relatives would have thought, that the phenomenon favoured Duppy, went off after his family with a celerity that was amazing the moment he touched the forest, and disappeared as they had, swinging himself along through it from bough to bough, in a way that convinced me that, given the necessity of getting about in tropical forests, man has made a mistake in getting his arms shortened. I have seen many wild animals in their native wilds, but never have I seen anything to equal gorillas going through bush; it is a graceful, powerful, superbly perfect hand-trapeze performance. {208}

After this sporting adventure, we returned, as I usually return from a sporting adventure, without measurements or the body.

Our first day's march, though the longest, was the easiest, though, providentially I did not know this at the time. From my Woermann road walks I judge it was well twenty-five miles. It was easiest however, from its lying for the greater part of the way through the gloomy type of forest. All day long we never saw the sky once.

The earlier part of the day we were steadily going up hill, here and there making a small descent, and then up again, until we came on to what was apparently a long ridge, for on either side of us we could look down into deep, dark, ravine-like valleys. Twice or thrice we descended into these to cross them, finding at their bottom a small or large swamp with a river running through its midst. Those rivers all went to Lake Ayzingo.

We had to hurry because Kiva, who was the only one among us who had been to Efoua, said that unless we did we should not reach Efoua that night. I said, "Why not stay for bush?" not having contracted any love for a night in a Fan town by the experience of M'fetta; moreover the Fans were not sure that after all the whole party of us might not spend the evening at Efoua, when we did get there, simmering in its cooking-pots.

Ngouta, I may remark, had no doubt on the subject at all, and regretted having left Mrs. N. keenly, and the Andande store sincerely. But these Fans are a fine sporting tribe, and allowed they would risk it; besides, they were almost certain they had friends at Efoua; and, in addition, they showed me trees scratched in a way that was magnification of the condition of my own cat's pet table leg at home, demonstrating leopards in the vicinity. I kept going, as it was my only chance, because I found I stiffened if I sat down, and they always carefully told me the direction to go in when they sat down; with their superior pace they soon caught me up, and then passed me, leaving me and Ngouta and sometimes Singlet and Pagan behind, we, in our turn, overtaking them, with this difference that they were sitting down when we did so.

About five o'clock I was off ahead and noticed a path which I had been told I should meet with, and, when met with, I must follow. The path was slightly indistinct, but by keeping my eye on it I could see it. Presently I came to a place where it went out, but appeared again on the other side of a clump of underbush fairly distinctly. I made a short cut for it and the next news was I was in a heap, on a lot of spikes, some fifteen feet or so below ground level, at the bottom of a bag-shaped game pit.

It is at these times you realise the blessing of a good thick skirt. Had I paid heed to the advice of many people in England, who ought to have known better, and did not do it themselves, and adopted masculine garments, I should have been spiked to the bone, and done for. Whereas, save for a good many bruises, here I was with the fulness of my skirt tucked under me, sitting on nine ebony spikes some twelve inches long, in comparative comfort, howling lustily to be hauled out. The Duke came along first, and looked down at me. I said, "Get a bush-rope, and haul me out." He grunted and sat down on a log. The Passenger came next, and he looked down. "You kill?" says he. "Not much," say I; "get a bush-rope and haul me out." "No fit," says he, and sat down on the log. Presently, however, Kiva and Wiki came up, and Wiki went and selected the one and only bush-rope suitable to haul an English lady, of my exact complexion, age, and size, out of that one particular pit. They seemed rare round there from the time he took; and I was just casting about in my mind as to what method would be best to employ in getting up the smooth, yellow, sandy-clay, incurved walls, when he arrived with it, and I was out in a twinkling, and very much ashamed of myself, until Silence, who was then leading, disappeared through the path before us with a despairing yell. Each man then pulled the skin cover off his gun lock, carefully looked to see if things there were all right and ready loosened his knife in its snake-skin sheath; and then we set about hauling poor Silence out, binding him up where necessary with cool green leaves; for he, not having a skirt, had got a good deal frayed at the edges on those spikes. Then we closed up, for the Fans said these pits were symptomatic of the immediate neighbourhood of Efoua. We sounded our ground, as we went into a thick plantain patch, through which we could see a great clearing in the forest, and the low huts of a big town. We charged into it, going right through the guard-house gateway, at one end, in single file, as its narrowness obliged us, and into the street-shaped town, and formed ourselves into as imposing a looking party as possible in the centre of the street. The Efouerians regarded us with much amazement, and the women and children cleared off into the huts, and took stock of us through the door-holes. There were but few men in the town, the majority, we subsequently learnt, being away after elephants. But there were quite sufficient left to make a crowd in a ring round us. Fortunately Wiki and Kiva's friends were present, and as a result of the confabulation, one of the chiefs had his house cleared out for me. It consisted of two apartments almost bare of everything save a pile of boxes, and a small fire on the floor, some little bags hanging from the roof poles, and a general supply of insects. The inner room contained nothing save a hard plank, raised on four short pegs from the earth floor.

I shook hands with and thanked the chief, and directed that all the loads should be placed inside the huts. I must admit my good friend was a villainous-looking savage, but he behaved most hospitably and kindly. From what I had heard of the Fan, I deemed it advisable not to make any present to him at once, but to base my claim on him on the right of an amicable stranger to hospitality. When I had seen all the baggage stowed I went outside and sat at the doorway on a rather rickety mushroom-shaped stool in the cool evening air, waiting for my tea which I wanted bitterly. Pagan came up as usual for tobacco to buy chop with; and after giving it to him, I and the two chiefs, with Gray Shirt acting as interpreter, had a long chat. Of course the first question was, Why was I there?

I told them I was on my way to the factory of H. and C. on the Rembwé. They said they had heard of "Ugumu," i.e., Messrs Hatton and Cookson, but they did not trade direct with them, passing their trade into towns nearer to the Rembwé, which were swindling bad towns, they said; and they got the idea stuck in their heads that I was a trader, a sort of bagman for the firm, and Gray Shirt could not get this idea out, so off one of their majesties went and returned with twenty-five balls of rubber, which I bought to promote good feeling, subsequently dashing them to Wiki, who passed them in at Ndorko when we got there. I also bought some elephant-hair necklaces from one of the chiefs' wives, by exchanging my red silk tie with her for them, and one or two other things. I saw fish-hooks would not be of much value because Efoua was not near a big water of any sort; so I held fish-hooks and traded handkerchiefs and knives.

One old chief was exceedingly keen to do business, and I bought a meat spoon, a plantain spoon, and a gravy spoon off him; and then he brought me a lot of rubbish I did not want, and I said so, and announced I had finished trade for that night. However the old gentleman was not to be put off, and after an unsuccessful attempt to sell me his cooking-pots, which were roughly made out of clay, he made energetic signs to me that if I would wait he had got something that he would dispose of which Gray Shirt said was "good too much." Off he went across the street, and disappeared into his hut, where he evidently had a thorough hunt for the precious article. One box after another was brought out to the light of a bush torch held by one of his wives, and there was a great confabulation between him and his family of the "I'm sure you had it last," "You must have moved it," "Never touched the thing," sort. At last it was found, and he brought it across the street to me most carefully. It was a bundle of bark cloth tied round something most carefully with tie tie. This being removed, disclosed a layer of rag, which was unwound from round a central article. Whatever can this be? thinks I; some rare and valuable object doubtless, let's hope connected with Fetish worship, and I anxiously watched its unpacking; in the end, however, it disclosed, to my disgust and rage, an old shilling razor. The way the old chief held it out, and the amount of dollars he asked for it, was enough to make any one believe that I was in such urgent need of the thing, that I was at his mercy regarding price. I waved it off with a haughty scorn, and then feeling smitten by the expression of agonised bewilderment on his face, I dashed him a belt that delighted him, and went inside and had tea to soothe my outraged feelings.

The chiefs made furious raids on the mob of spectators who pressed round the door, and stood with their eyes glued to every crack in the bark of which the hut was made. The next door neighbours on either side might have amassed a comfortable competence for their old age, by letting out seats for the circus. Every hole in the side walls had a human eye in it, and I heard new holes being bored in all directions; so I deeply fear the chief, my host, must have found his palace sadly draughty. I felt perfectly safe and content, however, although Ngouta suggested the charming idea that "P'r'aps them M'fetta Fan done sell we." As soon as all my men had come in, and established themselves in the inner room for the night, I curled up among the boxes, with my head on the tobacco sack, and dozed.

After about half an hour I heard a row in the street, and looking out,—for I recognised his grace's voice taking a solo part followed by choruses,—I found him in legal difficulties about a murder case. An alibi was proved for the time being; that is to say the prosecution could not bring up witnesses because of the elephant hunt; and I went in for another doze, and the town at last grew quiet. Waking up again I noticed the smell in the hut was violent, from being shut up I suppose, and it had an unmistakably organic origin. Knocking the ash end off the smouldering bush-light that lay burning on the floor, I investigated, and tracked it to those bags, so I took down the biggest one, and carefully noted exactly how the tie-tie had been put round its mouth; for these things are important and often mean a lot. I then shook its contents out in my hat, for fear of losing anything of value. They were a human hand, three big toes, four eyes, two ears, and other portions of the human frame. The hand was fresh, the others only so so, and shrivelled.

Replacing them I tied the bag up, and hung it up again. I subsequently learnt that although the Fans will eat their fellow friendly tribesfolk, yet they like to keep a little something belonging to them as a memento. This touching trait in their character I learnt from Wiki; and, though it's to their credit, under the circumstances, still it's an unpleasant practice when they hang the remains in the bedroom you occupy, particularly if the bereavement in your host's family has been recent. I did not venture to prowl round Efoua; but slid the bark door aside and looked out to get a breath of fresh air.

It was a perfect night, and no mosquitoes. The town, walled in on every side by the great cliff of high black forest, looked very wild as it showed in the starlight, its low, savage-built bark huts, in two hard rows, closed at either end by a guard-house. In both guard-houses there was a fire burning, and in their flickering glow showed the forms of sleeping men. Nothing was moving save the goats, which are always brought into the special house for them in the middle of the town, to keep them from the leopards, which roam from dusk to dawn.

Dawn found us stirring, I getting my tea, and the rest of the party their chop, and binding up anew the loads with Wiki's fresh supple bush-ropes. Kiva amused me much; during our march his costume was exceeding scant, but when we reached the towns he took from his bag garments, and attired himself so resplendently that I feared the charm of his appearance would lead me into one of those dreadful wife palavers which experience had taught me of old to dread; and in the morning time he always devoted some time to repacking. I gave a big dash to both chiefs, and they came out with us, most civilly, to the end of their first plantations; and then we took farewell of each other, with many expressions of hope on both sides that we should meet again, and many warnings from them about the dissolute and depraved character of the other towns we should pass through before we reached the Rembwé.

Our second day's march was infinitely worse than the first, for it lay along a series of abruptly shaped hills with deep ravines between them; each ravine had its swamp and each swamp its river. This bit of country must be absolutely impassable for any human being, black or white, except during the dry season. There were representatives of the three chief forms of the West African bog. The large deep swamps were best to deal with, because they make a break in the forest, and the sun can come down on their surface and bake a crust, over which you can go, if you go quickly. From experience in Devonian bogs, I knew pace was our best chance, and I fancy I earned one of my nicknames among the Fans on these. The Fans went across all right with a rapid striding glide, but the other men erred from excess of caution, and while hesitating as to where was the next safe place to plant their feet, the place that they were standing on went in with a glug. Moreover, they would keep together, which was more than the crust would stand. The portly Pagan and the Passenger gave us a fine job in one bog, by sinking in close together. Some of us slashed off boughs of trees and tore off handfuls of hard canna leaves, while others threw them round the sinking victims to form a sort of raft, and then with the aid of bush-rope, of course, they were hauled out.

The worst sort of swamp, and the most frequent hereabouts, is the deep narrow one that has no crust on, because it is too much shaded by the forest. The slopes of the ravines too are usually covered with an undergrowth of shen-ja, beautiful beyond description, but right bad to go through. I soon learnt to dread seeing the man in front going down hill, or to find myself doing so, for it meant that within the next half hour we should be battling through a patch of shenja. I believe there are few effects that can compare with the beauty of them, with the golden sunlight coming down through the upper forest's branches on to their exquisitely shaped, hard, dark green leaves, making them look as if they were sprinkled with golden sequins. Their long green stalks, which support the leaves and bear little bunches of crimson berries, take every graceful curve imaginable, and the whole affair is free from insects; and when you have said this, you have said all there is to say in favour of shenja, for those long green stalks of theirs are as tough as twisted wire, and the graceful curves go to the making of a net, which rises round you shoulder high, and the hard green leaves when lying on the ground are fearfully slippery. It is not nice going down through them, particularly when Nature is so arranged that the edge of the bank you are descending is a rock-wall ten or twelve feet high with a swamp of unknown depth at its foot; this arrangement was very frequent on the second and third day's marches, and into these swamps the shenja seemed to want to send you head first and get you suffocated. It is still less pleasant, however, going up the other side of the ravine when you have got through your swamp. You have to fight your way upwards among rough rocks, through this hard tough network of stems; and it took it out of all of us except the Fans.

These narrow shaded swamps gave us a world of trouble and took up a good deal of time. Sometimes the leader of the party would make three or four attempts before he found a ford, going on until the black, batterlike ooze came up round his neck, and then turning back and trying in another place; while the rest of the party sat upon the bank until the ford was found, feeling it was unnecessary to throw away human life, and that the more men there were paddling about in that swamp, the more chance there was that a hole in the bottom of it would be found; and when a hole is found, the discoverer is liable to leave his bones in it. If I happened to be in front, the duty of finding the ford fell on me; for none of us after leaving Efoua knew the swamps personally. I was too frightened of the Fan, and too nervous and uncertain of the stuff my other men were made of, to dare show the white feather at anything that turned up. The Fan took my conduct as a matter of course, never having travelled with white men before, or learnt the way some of them require carrying over swamps and rivers and so on. I dare say I might have taken things easier, but I was like the immortal Schmelzle, during that omnibus journey he made on his way to Flætz in the thunder-storm—afraid to be afraid. I am very certain I should have fared very differently had I entered a region occupied by a powerful and ferocious tribe like the Fan, from some districts on the West Coast, where the inhabitants are used to find the white man incapable of personal exertion, requiring to be carried in a hammock, or wheeled in a go-cart or a Bath-chair about the streets of their coast towns, depending for the defence of their settlement on a body of black soldiers. This is not so in Congo Français, and I had behind me the prestige of a set of white men to whom for the native to say, "You shall not do such and such a thing;" "You shall not go to such and such a place," would mean that those things would be done. I soon found the name of Hatton and Cookson's agent-general for this district, Mr. Hudson, was one to conjure with among the trading tribes; and the Ajumba, moreover, although their knowledge of white men had been small, yet those they had been accustomed to see were fine specimens. Mr. Fildes, Mr. Cockshut, M. Jacot, Dr. Pélessier, Père Lejeune, M. Gacon, Mr. Whittaker, and that vivacious French official, were not men any man, black or white, would willingly ruffle; and in addition there was the memory among the black traders of "that white man MacTaggart," whom an enterprising trading tribe near Fernan Vaz had had the hardihood to tackle, shooting him, and then towing him behind a canoe and slashing him all over with their knives the while; yet he survived, and tackled them again in a way that must almost pathetically have astonished those simple savages, after the real good work they had put in to the killing of him. Of course it was hard to live up to these ideals, and I do not pretend to have succeeded, or rather that I should have succeeded had the real strain been put on me.

But to return to that gorilla-land forest. All the rivers we crossed on the first, second, and third day I was told went into one or other of the branches of the Ogowé, showing that the long slope of land between the Ogowé and the Rembwé is towards the Ogowé. The stone of which the mountains were composed was that same hard black rock that I had found on the Sierra del Cristal, by the Ogowé rapids; only hereabouts there was not amongst it those great masses of white quartz, which are so prominent a feature from Talagouga upwards in the Ogowé valley; neither were the mountains anything like so high, but they had the same abruptness of shape. They look like very old parts of the same range worn down to stumps by the disintegrating forces of the torrential rain and sun, and the dense forest growing on them. Frost of course they had not been subject to, but rocks, I noticed, were often being somewhat similarly split by rootlets having got into some tiny crevice, and by gradual growth enlarged it to a crack.

Of our troubles among the timber falls on these mountains I have already spoken; and these were at their worst between Efoua and Egaja. I had suffered a good deal from thirst that day, unboiled water being my ibet and we were all very nearly tired out with the athletic sports since leaving Efoua. One thing only we knew about Egaja for sure, and that was that not one of us had a friend there, and that it was a town of extra evil repute, so we were not feeling very cheerful when towards evening time we struck its outermost plantations, their immediate vicinity being announced to us by Silence treading full and fair on to a sharp ebony spike driven into the narrow path and hurting himself.

Fortunately, after we passed this first plantation, we came upon a camp of rubber collectors—four young men; I got one of them to carry Silence's load and
show us the way into the town, when on we went into more plantations.

There is nothing more tiresome than finding your path going into a plantation, because it fades out in the cleared ground, or starts playing games with a
lot of other little paths that are running about amongst the crops, and no West
African path goes straight into a stream or a plantation, and straight out the
other side, so you have a nice time picking it up again.

We were spared a good deal of fine varied walking by our new friend the
rubber collector; for I noticed he led us out by a path nearly at right angles to
the one by which we had entered. He then pitched into a pit which was half full
of thorns, and which he observed he did not know was there, demonstrating
that an African guide can speak the truth. When he had got out, he handed
back Silence's load and got a dash of tobacco for his help; he left us to devote the
rest of his evening by his forest fire to unthorning himself, while we proceeded
to wade a swift, deepish river that crossed the path he told us led into Egaja,
and then went across another bit of forest and downhill again. "Oh, bless
those swamps!" thought I, "here's another," but no—not this time. Across the
bottom of the steep ravine, from one side to another, lay an enormous tree as
a bridge, about fifteen feet above a river, which rushed beneath it, over a boul-
der-encumbered bed. I took in the situation at a glance, and then and there I
would have changed that bridge for any swamp I have ever seen, yea, even for
a certain bush-rope bridge in which I once wound myself up like a buzzing fly
in a spider's web. I was fearfully tired, and my legs shivered under me after the
falls and emotions of the previous part of the day, and my boots were slippery
with water soaking.

The Fans went into the river, and half swam, half waded across. All the
Ajumba, save Pagan, followed, and Ngouta got across with their assistance.
Pagan thought he would try the bridge, and I thought I would watch how the
thing worked. He got about three yards along it and then slipped, but caught
the tree with his hands as he fell, and hauled himself back to my side again;
then he went down the bank and through the water. This was not calculated to
improve one's nerve; I knew by now I had got to go by the bridge, for I saw I
was not strong enough in my tired state to fight the water. If only the wretched
thing had had its bark on it would have been better, but it was bare, bald, and
round, and a slip meant death on the rocks below. I rushed it, and reached the
other side in safety, whereby poor Pagan got chaffed about his failure by the
others, who said they had gone through the water just to wash their feet.

The other side, when we got there, did not seem much worth reaching, being a swampy fringe at the bottom of a steep hillside, and after a few yards the

path turned into a stream or backwater of the river. It was hedged with thickly pleached bushes, and covered with liquid water on the top of semi-liquid mud. Now and again for a change you had a foot of water on top of fearfully slippery harder mud, and then we light-heartedly took headers into the bush, sideways, or sat down; and when it was not proceeding on the evil tenor of its way, like this, it had holes in it; in fact, I fancy the bottom of the holes was the true level, for it came near being as full of holes as a fishing-net, and it was very quaint to see the man in front, who had been paddling along knee-deep before, now plop down with the water round his shoulders; and getting out of these slippery pockets, which were sometimes a tight fit, was difficult.

However that is the path you have got to go by, if you're not wise enough to stop at home; the little bay of shrub overgrown swamp fringing the river on one side and on the other running up to the mountain side.

At last we came to a sandy bank, and on that bank stood Egaja, the town with an evil name even among the Fan, but where we had got to stay, fair or foul. We went into it through its palaver house, and soon had the usual row.

I had detected signs of trouble among my men during the whole day; the Ajumba were tired, and dissatisfied with the Fans; the Fans were in high feather, openly insolent to Ngouta, and anxious for me to stay in this delightful locality, and go hunting with them and divers other choice spirits, whom they assured me we could easily get to join us at Efoua. I kept peace as well as I could, explaining to the Fans I had not enough money with me now, because I had not, when starting, expected such magnificent opportunities to be placed at my disposal; and promising to come back next year—a promise I hope to keep—and then we would go and have a grand time of it. This state of a party was a dangerous one in which to enter a strange Fan town, where our security lay in our being united. When the first burst of Egaja conversation began to boil down into something reasonable, I found that a villainous-looking scoundrel, smeared with soot and draped in a fragment of genuine antique cloth, was a head chief in mourning. He placed a house at my disposal, quite a mansion, for it had no less than four apartments. The first one was almost entirely occupied by a bedstead frame that was being made up inside on account of the small size of the door.

This had to be removed before we could get in with the baggage at all. While this removal was being effected with as much damage to the house and the article as if it were a quarter-day affair in England, the other chief arrived. He had been sent for, being away down the river fishing when we arrived. I saw at once he was a very superior man to any of the chiefs I had yet met with. It was not his attire, remarkable though that was for the district, for it consisted of a gentleman's black frock-coat such as is given in the ivory bundle, a bright blue felt sombrero hat, an ample cloth of Boma check; but his face and general bearing was distinctive, and very powerful and intelligent; and I knew that Egaja, for good or bad, owed its name to this man, and not to the mere sensual, brutal-looking one. He was exceedingly courteous, ordering his people to bring me a stool and one for himself, and then a fly-whisk to battle with the evening cloud of sand-flies. I got Pagan to come and act as interpreter while the rest were stowing the baggage, etc. After compliments, "Tell the chief," I said, "that I hear this town of his is thief town."

"Better not, sir," says Pagan.

"Go on," said I, "or I'll tell him myself."

So Pagan did. It was a sad blow to the chief.

"Thief town, this highly respectable town of Egaja! a town whose moral conduct in all matters (Shedule) was an example to all towns, called a thief town! Oh, what a wicked world!"

I said it was; but I would reserve my opinion as to whether Egaja was a part of the wicked world or a star-like exception, until I had experienced it myself. We then discoursed on many matters, and I got a great deal of interesting fetish information out of the chief, which was valuable to me, because the whole of this district had not been in contact with white culture; and altogether I and the chief became great friends.

Just when I was going in to have my much-desired tea, he brought me his mother—an old lady, evidently very bright and able, but, poor woman, with the most disgusting hand and arm I have ever seen. I am ashamed to say I came very near being sympathetically sick in the African manner on the spot. I felt I could not attend to it, and have my tea afterwards, so I directed one of the canoe-shaped little tubs, used for beating up the manioc in, to be brought and filled with hot water, and then putting into it a heavy dose of Condy's fluid, I made her sit down and lay the whole arm in it, and went and had my tea. As soon as I had done I went outside, and getting some of the many surrounding ladies to hold bush-lights, I examined the case. The whole hand was a mass of yellow pus, streaked with sanies, large ulcers were burrowing into the fore-arm, while in the arm-pit was a big abscess. I opened the abscess at once, and then the old lady frightened me nearly out of my wits by gently subsiding, I thought dying, but I soon found out merely going to sleep. I then washed the abscess well out, and having got a lot of baked plantains, I made a big poultice of them, mixed with boiling water and more Condy in the tub, and laid her arm right in this; and propping her up all round and covering her over with cloths I requisitioned from her son, I left her to have her nap while I went into the history of the case, which was that some forty-eight hours ago she had been wading along the bank, catching crawfish, and had been stung by "a fish like a snake"; so I presume the ulcers were an old-standing palaver. The hand had been a good deal torn by the creature, and the pain and swelling had been so great she had not had a minute's sleep since. As soon as the poultice got chilled I took her arm out and cleaned it again, and wound it round with dressing, and had her ladyship carried bodily, still asleep, into her hut, and after rousing her up, giving her a dose of that fine preparation, pil. crotonis cum hydrargi, saw her tucked up on her own plank bedstead for the night, sound asleep again. The chief was very anxious to have some pills too; so I gave him some, with firm injunctions only to take one at the first time. I knew that that one would teach him not to take more than one forever after, better than I could do if I talked from June to January. Then all the afflicted of Egaja turned up, and wanted medical advice. There was evidently a good stiff epidemic of the yaws about; lots of cases of dum with the various symptoms; ulcers of course galore; a man with a bit of a broken spear head in an abscess in the thigh; one which I believe a professional enthusiast would call a "lovely case" of filaria, the entire white of one eye being full of the active little worms and a ridge of surplus population migrating across the bridge of the nose into the other eye, under the skin, looking like the bridge of a pair of spectacles. It was past eleven before I had anything like done, and my men had long been sound asleep, but the chief had conscientiously sat up and seen the thing through. He then went and fetched some rolls of bark cloth to put on my plank, and I gave him a handsome cloth I happened to have with me, a couple of knives, and some heads of tobacco and wished him goodnight; blockading my bark door, and picking my way over my sleeping Ajumba into an inner apartment which I also blockaded, hoping I had done with Egaja for some hours. No such thing. At 1.45 the whole town was roused by the frantic yells of a woman. I judged there was one of my beauties of Fans mixed up in it, and there was, and after paying damages, got back again by 2.30 A.M., and off to sleep again instantly. At four sharp, whole town of Egaja plunged into emotion, and worse shindy. I suggested to the Ajumba they should go out; but no, they didn't care a row of pins if one of our Fans did get killed, so I went, recognising Kiva's voice in high expostulation. Kiva, it seems, a long time ago had a transaction in re a tooth of ivory with a man who, unfortunately, happened to be in this town to-night, and Kiva owed the said man a coat. {223}

Kiva, it seems, has been spending the whole evening demonstrating to his creditor that, had he only known they were to meet, he would have brought the coat with him—a particularly beautiful coat—and the reason he has not paid it before is that he has mislaid the creditor's address. The creditor says he has called repeatedly at Kiva's village, that notorious M'fetta, and Kiva has never been at home; and moreover that Kiva's wife (one of them) stole a yellow dog of great value from his (the creditor's) canoe. Kiva says, women will be women, and he had gone off to sleep thinking the affair had blown over and the bill renewed for the time being. The creditor had not gone to sleep; but sat up thinking the affair over and remembered many cases, all cited in full, of how Kiva had failed to meet his debts; also Kiva's brother on the mother's side and uncle ditto; and so has decided to foreclose forthwith on the debtor's estate, and as the estate is represented by and consists of Kiva's person, to take and seize upon it and eat it.

It is always highly interesting to observe the germ of any of our own institutions existing in the culture of a lower race. Nevertheless it is trying to be hauled out of one's sleep in the middle of the night, and plunged into this study. Evidently this was a trace of an early form of the Bankruptcy Court; the court which clears a man of his debt, being here represented by the knife and the cooking pot; the whitewashing, as I believe it is termed with us, also shows, only it is not the debtor who is whitewashed, but the creditors doing themselves over with white clay to celebrate the removal of their enemy from his sphere of meretricious activity. This inversion may arise from the fact that whitewashing a creditor who was about to be cooked would be unwise, as the stuff would boil off the bits and spoil the gravy. There is always some fragment of sound sense underlying African institutions. Kiva was, when I got out, tied up, talking nineteen to the dozen; and so was every one else; and a lady was working up white clay in a pot.

I dare say I ought to have rushed at him and cut his bonds, and killed people in a general way with a revolver, and then flown with my band to the bush; only my band evidently had no flying in them, being tucked up in the hut pretending to be asleep, and uninterested in the affair; and although I could have abandoned the band without a pang just then, I could not so lightheartedly fly alone with Kiva to the bush and leave my fishes; so I shouted Azuna to the Bankruptcy Court, and got a Fan who spoke trade English to come and interpret for me; and from him I learnt the above stated outline of the proceedings up to the time. Regarding the original iniquity of Kiva, my other Fans held the opinion that the old Scotch lady had regarding certain passages in the history of the early Jews—that it was a long time ago, and aiblins it was no true.

Fortunately for the reader it is impossible for me to give in full detail the proceedings of the Court. I do not think if the whole of Mr. Pitman's school of shorthand had been there to take them down the thing could possibly have been done in word-writing. If the late Richard Wagner, however, had been present he could have scored the performance for a full orchestra; and with all its weird grunts and roars, and pistol-like finger clicks, and its elongated words and thigh slaps, it would have been a masterpiece.

I got my friend the chief on my side; but he explained he had no jurisdiction, as neither of the men belonged to his town; and I explained to him, that as the proceedings were taking place in his town he had a right of jurisdiction ipso facto. The Fan could not translate this phrase, so we gave it the chief raw; and he seemed to relish it, and he and I then cut into the affair together, I looking at him with admiration and approval when he was saying his say, and after his "Azuna" had produced a patch of silence he could move his tongue in, and he similarly regarding me during my speech for the defence. We neither, I expect, understood each other, and we had trouble with our client, who would keep pleading "Not guilty," which was absurd. Anyhow we produced our effect, my success arising from my concluding my speech with the announcement that I would give the creditor a book on Hatton and Cookson for the coat, and I would deduct it from Kiva's pay.

But, said the Court: "We look your mouth and it be sweet mouth, but with Hatton and Cookson we can have no trade." This was a blow to me. Hatton and Cookson was my big Ju Ju, and it was to their sub-factory on the Rembwé that I was bound. On inquiry I elicited another cheerful little fact which was they could not deal with Hatton and Cookson because there was "blood war on the path that way." The Court said they would take a book on Holty, but with Holty i.e. Mr. John Holt, I had no deposit of money, and I did not feel justified in issuing cheques on him, knowing also he could not feel amiable towards wandering scientists, after what he had recently gone through with one. Not that I doubt for one minute but that his representatives would have honoured my book; for the generosity and helpfulness of West African traders is unbounded and long-suffering. But I did not like to encroach on it, all the more so from a feeling that I might never get through to refund the money. So at last I paid the equivalent value of the coat out of my own trade-stuff; and the affair was regarded by all parties as satisfactorily closed by the time the gray dawn was coming up over the forest wall. I went in again and slept in snatches until I got my tea about seven, and then turned out to hurry my band out of Egaja. This I did not succeed in doing until past ten. One row succeeded another with my men; but I was determined to get them out of that town as quickly as possible, for I had heard so much from perfectly reliable and experienced people regarding the treacherousness of the Fan. I feared too that more cases still would be brought up against Kiva, from the résumé of his criminal career I had had last night, and I knew it was very doubtful whether my other three Fans were any better than he. There was his grace's little murder affair only languishing for want of evidence owing to the witnesses for the prosecution being out elephant-hunting not very far away; and Wiki was pleading an alibi, and a twin brother, in a bad wife palaver in this town. I really hope for the sake of Fan morals at large, that I did engage the three worst villains in M'fetta, and that M'fetta is the worst town in all Fan land, inconvenient as this arrangement was to me personally. Anyhow, I felt sure my Pappenheimers would take a lot of beating for good solid crime, among any tribe anywhere. Moreover, the Ajumba wanted meat, and the Fans, they said, offered them human. I saw no human meat at Egaja, but the Ajumba seem to think the Fans eat nothing else, which is a silly prejudice of theirs, because the Fans do. I think in this case the Ajumba thought a lot of smoked flesh offered was human. It may have been; it was in neat pieces; and again, as the Captain of the late s.s. Sparrow would say, "it mayn't." But the Ajumba have a horror of cannibalism, and I honestly believe never practise it, even for fetish affairs, which is a rare thing in a West African tribe where sacrificial and ceremonial cannibalism is nearly universal. Anyhow the Ajumba loudly declared the Fans were "bad men too much," which was impolitic under existing circumstances, and inexcusable, because it by no means arose from a courageous defiance of them; but the West African! Well! "'E's a devil an' a ostrich an' a orphan child in one."

The chief was very anxious for me to stay and rest, but as his mother was doing wonderfully well, and the other women seemed quite to understand my directions regarding her, I did not feel inclined to risk it. The old lady's farewell of me was peculiar: she took my hand in her two, turned it palm upwards, and spat on it. I do not know whether this is a constant form of greeting among the Fan; I fancy not. Dr. Nassau, who explained it to me when I saw him again down at Baraka, said the spitting was merely an accidental by-product of the performance, which consisted in blowing a blessing; and as I happened on this custom twice afterwards, I feel sure from observation he is right.

The two chiefs saw us courteously out of the town as far as where the river crosses the out-going path again, and the blue-hatted one gave me some charms "to keep my foot in path," and the mourning chief lent us his son to see us through the lines of fortification of the plantation. I gave them an equal dash, and in answer to their question as to whether I had found Egaja a thief-town, I said that to call Egaja a thief-town was rank perjury, for I had not lost a thing while in it; and we parted with mutual expression of esteem and hopes for another meeting at an early date.

The defences of the fine series of plantations of Egaja on this side were most intricate, to judge from the zigzag course our guide led us through them. He explained they had to be because of the character of the towns towards the Rembwé. After listening to this young man, I really began to doubt that the Cities of the Plain had really been destroyed, and wondered whether some future revision committee will not put transported for destroyed. This young man certainly hit off the character of Sodom and Gomorrah to the life, in describing the towns towards the Rembwé, though he had never heard Sodom and Gomorrah named. He assured me I should see the difference between them and Egaja the Good, and I thanked him and gave him his dash when we parted; but told him as a friend, I feared some alteration must take place, and some time elapse before he saw a regular rush of pilgrim worshippers of Virtue coming into even Egaja the Good, though it stood just as good a chance and better than most towns I had seen in Africa.

We went on into the gloom of the Great Forest again; that forest that seemed to me without end, wherein, in a lazy, hazy-minded sort of way, I expected to wander through by day and drop in at night to a noisy savage town for the rest of my days.

We climbed up one hill, skirted its summit, went through our athletic sports over sundry timber falls, and struck down into the ravine as usual. But at the bottom of that ravine, which was exceeding steep, ran a little river free from swamp. As I was wading it I noticed it had a peculiarity that distinguished it from all the other rivers we had come through; and then and there I sat down on a boulder in its midst and hauled out my compass. Yes, by Allah! it's going north-west and bound as we are for Rembwé River. I went out the other side of that river with a lighter heart than I went in, and shouted the news to the boys, and they yelled and sang as we went on our way.

All along this bit of country we had seen quantities of rubber vines, and between Egaja and Esoon we came across quantities of rubber being collected. Evidently there was a big camp of rubber hunters out in the district very busy. Wiki and Kiva did their best to teach me the trade. Along each side of the path we frequently saw a ring of stout bush rope, raised from the earth on pegs about a foot to eighteen inches. On the ground in the middle stood a calabash, into which the ends of the pieces of rubber vine were placed, the other ends being supported by the bush rope ring. Round the outside of some of these rings was a slow fire, which just singes the tops of the bits of rubber vine as they project over the collar or ring, and causes the milky juice to run out of the lower end into the calabash, giving out as it does so a strong ammoniacal smell. When the fire was alight there would be a group of rubber collectors sitting round it watching the cooking operations, removing those pieces that had run dry and placing others, from a pile at their side, in position. On either side of the path we continually passed pieces of rubber vine cut into lengths of some two feet or so, and on the top one or two leaves plaited together, or a piece of bush rope tied into a knot, which indicated whose property the pile was.

The method of collection employed by the Fan is exceedingly wasteful, because this fool of a vegetable Landolphia florida (Ovariensis) does not know how to send up suckers from its root, but insists on starting elaborately from seeds only. I do not, however, see any reasonable hope of getting them to adopt more economical methods. The attempt made by the English houses, when the rubber trade was opened up in 1883 on the Gold Coast, to get the more tractable natives there to collect by incisions only, has failed; for in the early days a man could get a load of rubber almost at his own door on the Gold Coast, and now he has to go fifteen days' journey inland for it. When a Fan town has exhausted the rubber in its vicinity, it migrates, bag and baggage, to a new part of the forest. The young unmarried men are the usual rubber hunters. Parties of them go out into the forest, wandering about in it and camping under shelters of boughs by night, for a month and more at a time, during the dry seasons, until they have got a sufficient quantity together; then they return to their town, and it is manipulated by the women, and finally sold, either to the white trader, in districts where he is within reach, or to the M'pongwe trader who travels round buying it and the collected ivory and ebony, like a Norfolk higgler. In districts like these I was in, remote from the M'pongwe trader, the Fans carry the rubber to the town nearest to them that is in contact with the black trader, and sell it to the inhabitants, who in their turn resell it to their next town, until it reaches him. This passing down of the rubber and ivory gives rise between the various towns to a series of commercial complications which rank with woman palaver for the production of rows; it being the sweet habit of these Fans to require a life for a life, and to regard one life as good as another. Also rubber trade and wife palavers sweetly intertwine, for a man on the kill in re a wife palaver knows his best chance of getting the life from the village he has a grudge against lies in catching one of that village's men when he may be out alone rubber hunting. So he does this thing, and then the men from the victim's village go and lay for a rubber hunter from the killer's village; and then of course the men from the killer's village go and lay for rubber hunters from victim number one's village, and thus the blood feud rolls down the vaulted chambers of the ages, so that you, dropping in on affairs, cannot see one end or the other of it, and frequently the people concerned have quite forgotten what the killing was started for. Not that this discourages them in the least. Really if Dr. Nassau is right, and these Fans are descendants of Adam and Eve, I expect the Cain and Abel killing palaver is still kept going among them.

Wiki, being great on bush rope, gave me much information regarding rubber, showing me the various other vines besides the true rubber vine, whose juice, mingled with the true sap by the collector when in the forest, adds to the weight; a matter of importance, because rubber is bought by weight. The other adulteration gets done by the ladies in the villages when the collected sap is handed over to them to prepare for the markets.

This preparation consists of boiling it in water slightly, and adding a little salt, which causes the gummy part to separate and go to the bottom of the pot, where it looks like a thick cream. The water is carefully poured off this deposit, which is then taken out and moulded, usually in the hands; but I have seen it run into moulds made of small calabashes with a stick or piece of iron passing through, so that when the rubber is set this can be withdrawn. A hole being thus left the balls can be threaded on to a stick, usually five on one stick, for convenience of transport. It is during the moulding process that most of the adulteration gets in. Down by the side of many of the streams there is a white chalky-looking clay which is brought up into the villages, powdered up, and then hung up over the fire in a basket to attain a uniform smuttiness; it is then worked into the rubber when it is being made up into balls. Then a good chunk of Koko, Arum esculentum(Koko is better than yam, I may remark, because it is heavier), also smoked approximately the right colour, is often placed in the centre of the rubber ball. In fact, anything is put there, that is hopefully regarded as likely to deceive the white trader. So great is the adulteration, that most of the traders have to cut each ball open. Even the Kinsembo rubber, which is put up in clusters of bits shaped like little thimbles formed by rolling pinches of rubber between the thumb and finger, and which one would think difficult to put anything inside of, has to be cut, because "the simple children of nature" who collect it and bring it to that "swindling white trader" struck upon the ingenious notion that little pieces of wood shaped like the thimbles and coated by a dip in rubber were excellent additions to a cluster.

The pure rubber, when it is made, looks like putty, and has the same dusky-white colour; but, owing to the balls being kept in the huts in baskets in the smoke, and in wicker-work cages in the muddy pools to soak up as much water as possible before going into the hands of the traders, they get almost inky in colour.

CHAPTER IX

FROM ESOON TO AGONJO

In which the Voyager sets forth the beauties of the way from Esoon to N'dorko, and gives some account of the local Swamps.

Our next halting place was Esoon, which received us with the usual row, but kindly enough; and endeared itself to me by knowing the Rembwé, and not just waving the arm in the air, in any direction, and saying "Far, far plenty bad people live for that side," as the other towns had done. Of course they stuck to the bad people part of the legend; but I was getting quite callous as to the moral character of new acquaintances, feeling sure that for good solid murderous rascality several of my old Fan acquaintances, and even my own party, would take a lot of beating; and yet, one and all, they had behaved well to me. Esoon gave me to understand that of all the Sodoms and Gomorrahs that town of Egaja was an easy first, and it would hardly believe we had come that way. Still Egaja had dealt with us well. However I took less interest—except, of course, as a friend, in some details regarding the criminal career of Chief Blue-hat of Egaja—in the opinion of Esoon regarding the country we had survived, than in the information it had to impart regarding the country we had got to survive on our way to the Big River, which now no longer meant the Ogowé, but the Rembwé. I meant to reach one of Hatton and Cookson's sub-factories there, but—strictly between ourselves—I knew no more at what town that factory was than a Kindergarten Board School child does. I did not mention this fact; and a casual observer might have thought that I had spent my youth in that factory, when I directed my inquiries to the finding out the very shortest route to it. Esoon shook its head. "Yes, it was close, but it was impossible to reach Uguma's factory." "Why?" "There was blood war on the path." I said it was no war of mine. But Esoon said, such was the appalling depravity of the next town on the road, that its inhabitants lay in wait at day with loaded guns and shot on sight any one coming up the Esoon road, and that at night they tied strings with bells on across the road and shot on hearing them. No one had been killed since the first party of Esoonians were fired on at long range, because no one had gone that way; but the next door town had been heard by people who had been out in the bush at night, blazing down the road when the bells were tinkled by wild animals. Clearly that road was not yet really healthy.

The Duke, who as I have said before, was a fine courageous fellow, ready to engage in any undertaking, suggested I should go up the road—alone by myself—first—a mile ahead of the party—and the next town, perhaps, might not shoot at sight, if they happened to notice I was something queer; and I might explain things, and then the rest of the party would follow. "There's nothing like dash and courage, my dear Duke," I said, "even if one display it by deputy, so this plan does you great credit; but as my knowledge of this charming language of yours is but small, I fear I might create a wrong impression in that town, and it might think I had kindly brought them a present of eight edible heathens—you and the remainder of my followers, you understand." My men saw this was a real danger, and this was the only way I saw of excusing myself. It is at such a moment as this that the Giant's robe gets, so to speak, between your legs and threatens to trip you up. Going up a forbidden road, and exposing yourself as a pot shot to ambushed natives would be jam and fritters to Mr. MacTaggart, for example; but I am not up to that form yet. So I determined to leave that road severely alone, and circumnavigate the next town by a road that leaves Esoon going W.N.W., which struck the Rembwé by N'dorko, I was told, and then follow up the bank of the river until I picked up the sub-factory. Subsequent experience did not make one feel inclined to take out a patent for this plan, but at the time in Esoon it looked nice enough.

Some few of the more highly cultured inhabitants here could speak trade English a little, and had been to the Rembwé, and were quite intelligent about the whole affair. They had seen white men. A village they formerly occupied nearer the Rembwé had been burnt by them, on account of a something that had occurred to a Catholic priest who visited it. They were, of course, none of them personally mixed up in this sad affair, so could give no details of what had befallen the priest. They knew also "the Mové," which was a great bond of union between us. "Was I a wife of them Mové white man," they inquired—"or them other white man?" I civilly said them Mové men were my tribe, and they ought to have known it by the look of me. They discussed my points of resemblance to "the Mové white man," and I am ashamed to say I could not forbear from smiling, as I distinctly recognised my friends from the very racy description of their personal appearance and tricks of manner given by a lively Esoonian belle who had certainly met them. So content and happy did I become under these soothing influences, that I actually took off my boots, a thing I had quite got out of the habit of doing, and had them dried. I wanted to have them rubbed with palm oil, but I found, to my surprise, that there was no palm oil to be had, the tree being absent, or scarce in this region, so I had to content myself with having them rubbed with a piece of animal fat instead. I chaperoned my men, while among the ladies of Esoon—a forward set of minxes—with the vigilance of a dragon; and decreed, like the Mikado of Japan, "that whosoever leered or winked, unless connubially linked, should forthwith be beheaded," have their pay chopped, I mean; and as they were beginning to smell their pay, they were careful; and we got through Esoon without one of them going into jail; no mean performance when you remember that every man had a past—to put it mildly.

Esoon is not situated like the other towns, with a swamp and the forest close round it; but it is built on the side of a fairly cleared ravine among its plantain groves. When you are on the southern side of the ravine, you can see Esoon looking as if it were hung on the hillside before you. You then go through a plantation down into the little river, and up into the town—one long, broad, clean-kept street. Leaving Esoon you go on up the hill through another plantation to the summit. Immediately after leaving the town we struck westwards; and when we got to the top of the next hill we had a view that showed us we were dealing with another type of country. The hills to the westward are lower, and the valleys between them broader and less heavily forested, or rather I should say forested with smaller sorts of timber. All our paths took us during the early part of the day up and down hills, through swamps and little rivers, all flowing Rembwé-wards. About the middle of the afternoon, when we had got up to the top of a high hill, after having had a terrible time on a timber fall of the first magnitude, into which four of us had fallen, I of course for one, I saw a sight that made my heart stand still. Stretching away to the west and north, winding in and out among the feet of the now isolated mound-like mountains, was that never to be mistaken black-green forest swamp of mangrove; doubtless the fringe of the River Rembwé, which evidently comes much further inland than the mangrove belt on the Ogowé. This is reasonable and as it should be, though it surprised me at the time; for the great arm of the sea which is called the Gaboon is really a fjord, just like Bonny and Opobo rivers, with several rivers falling into it at its head, and this fjord brings the sea water further inland. In addition to this the two rivers, the 'Como (Nkâmâ) and Rembwé that fall into this Gaboon, with several smaller rivers, both bring down an inferior quantity of fresh water, and that at nothing like the tearing, tide-beating back pace of the Ogowé. As my brother would say, "It's perfectly simple if you think about it;" but thinking is not my strong point. Anyhow I was glad to see the mangrove-belt; all the gladder because I did not then know how far it was inland from the sea, and also because I was fool enough to think that a long line I could see, running E. and W. to the north of where I stood, was the line of the Rembwé river; which it was not, as we soon found out. Cheered by this pleasing prospect, we marched on forgetful of our scratches, down the side of the hill, and down the foot slope of it, until we struck the edge of the swamp. We skirted this for some mile or so, going N.E. Then we struck into the swamp, to reach what we had regarded as the Rembwé river. We found ourselves at the edge of that open line we had seen from the mountain. Not standing, because you don't so much as try to stand on mangrove roots unless you are a born fool, and then you don't stand long, but clinging, like so many monkeys, to the net of aërial roots which surrounded us, looking blankly at a lake of ink-black slime. It was half a mile across, and some miles long. We could not see either the west or east termination of it, for it lay like a rotten serpent twisted between the mangroves. It never entered into our heads to try to cross it, for when a swamp is too deep for mangroves to grow in it, "No bottom lib for them dam ting," as a Kruboy once said to me, anent a small specimen of this sort of ornament to a landscape. But we just looked round to see which direction we had better take. Then I observed that the roots, aërial and otherwise, were coated in mud, and had no leaves on them, for a foot above our heads. Next I noticed that the surface of the mud before us had a sort of quiver running through it, and here and there it exhibited swellings on its surface, which rose in one place and fell in another. No need for an old coaster like me to look at that sort of thing twice to know what it meant, and feeling it was a situation more suited to Mr. Stanley than myself, I attempted to emulate his methods and addressed my men. "Boys," said I, "this beastly hole is tidal, and the tide is coming in. As it took us two hours to get to this sainted swamp, it's time we started out, one time, and the nearest way. It's to be hoped the practice we have acquired in mangrove roots in coming, will enable us to get up sufficient pace to get out on to dry land before we are all drowned." The boys took the hint. Fortunately one of the Ajumbas had been down in Ogowé, it was Gray Shirt, who "sabed them tide palaver." The rest of them, and the Fans, did not know what tide meant, but Gray Shirt hustled them along and I followed, deeply regretting that my ancestors had parted prematurely with prehensile tails, for four limbs, particularly when two of them are done up in boots and are not sufficient to enable one to get through a mangrove swamp network of slimy roots rising out of the water, and swinging lines of aërial ones coming down to the water à la mangrove, with anything approaching safety. Added to these joys were any quantity of mangrove flies, a broiling hot sun, and an atmosphere three-quarters solid stench from the putrefying ooze all round us. For an hour and a half thought I, Why did I come to Africa, or why, having come, did I not know when I was well off and stay in Glass? Before these problems were settled in my mind we were close to the true land again, with the water under us licking lazily among the roots and over our feet.

We did not make any fuss about it, but we meant to stick to dry land for some time, and so now took to the side of a hill that seemed like a great bubble coming out of the swamp, and bore steadily E. until we found a path. This path, according to the nature of paths in this country, promptly took us into another swamp, but of a different kind to our last—a knee-deep affair, full of beautiful palms and strange water plants, the names whereof I know not. There was just one part where that abomination, pandanus, had to be got through, but, as swamps go, it was not at all bad. I ought to mention that there were leeches in it, lest I may be thought too enthusiastic over its charms. But the great point was that the mountains we got to on the other side of it, were a good solid ridge, running, it is true, E. and W., while we wanted to go N.; still on we went waiting for developments, and watching the great line of man-grove-swamp spreading along below us to the left hand, seeing many of the lines in its dark face, which betokened more of those awesome slime lagoons that we had seen enough of at close quarters.

About four o'clock we struck some more plantations, and passing through these, came to a path running north-east, down which we went. I must say the forest scenery here was superbly lovely. Along this mountain side cliff to the mangrove-swamp the sun could reach the soil, owing to the steepness and abruptness and the changes of curves of the ground; while the soft steamy air which came up off the swamp swathed everything, and although unpleasantly strong in smell to us, was yet evidently highly agreeable to the vegetation. Love-ly wine palms and rafia palms, looking as if they had been grown under glass, so deliciously green and profuse was their feather-like foliage, intermingled with giant red woods, and lovely dark glossy green lianes, blooming in wreaths and festoons of white and mauve flowers, which gave a glorious wealth of beauty and colour to the scene. Even the monotony of the mangrove-belt alongside gave an additional charm to it, like the frame round a picture.

As we passed on, the ridge turned N. and the mangrove line narrowed between the hills. Our path now ran east and more in the middle of the forest, and the cool shade was charming after the heat we had had earlier in the day. We crossed a lovely little stream coming down the hillside in a cascade; and then our path plunged into a beautiful valley. We had glimpses through the trees of an amphitheatre of blue mist-veiled mountains coming down in a crescent before us, and on all sides, save due west where the mangrove-swamp came in. Never shall I forget the exceeding beauty of that valley, the foliage of the trees round us, the delicate wreaths and festoons of climbing plants, the graceful delicate plumes of the palm trees, interlacing among each other, and showing through all a background of soft, pale, purple-blue mountains and forest, not really far away, as the practised eye knew, but only made to look so by the mist, which has this trick of giving suggestion of immense space without destroying the beauty of detail. Those African misty forests have the same marvellous distinctive quality that Turner gives one in his greatest pictures. I am no artist, so I do not know exactly what it is, but I see it is there. I luxuriated in the exquisite beauty of that valley, little thinking or knowing what there was in it besides beauty, as Allah "in mercy hid the book of fate." On we went among the ferns and flowers until we met a swamp, a different kind of swamp to those we had heretofore met, save the little one last mentioned. This one was much larger, and a gem of beauty; but we had to cross it. It was completely furnished with characteristic flora. Fortunately when we got to its edge we saw a woman crossing before us, but unfortunately she did not take a fancy to our appearance, and instead of staying and having a chat about the state of the roads, and the shortest way to N'dorko, she bolted away across the swamp. I noticed she carefully took a course, not the shortest, although that course immersed her to her armpits. In we went after her, and when things were getting unpleasantly deep, and feeling highly uncertain under foot, we found there was a great log of a tree under the water which, as we had seen the lady's care at this point, we deemed it advisable to walk on. All of us save one, need I say that one was myself? effected this with safety. As for me, when I was at the beginning of the submerged bridge, and busily laying about in my mind for a definite opinion as to whether it was better to walk on a slippy tree trunk bridge you could see, or on one you could not, I was hurled off by that inexorable fate that demands of me a personal acquaintance with fluvial and paludial ground deposits; whereupon I took a header, and am thereby able to inform the world, that there is between fifteen and twenty feet of water each side of that log. I conscientiously went in on one side, and came up on the other. The log, I conjecture, is odum or ebony, and it is some fifty feet long; anyhow it is some sort of wood that won't float. Gray Shirt says it is a bridge across an under-swamp river. Having survived this and reached the opposite bank, we shortly fell in with a party of men and women, who were taking, they said, a parcel of rubber to Holty's. They told us N'dorko was quite close, and that the plantations we saw before us were its outermost ones, but spoke of a swamp, a bad swamp. We knew it, we said, in the foolishness of our hearts thinking they meant the one we had just forded, and leaving them resting, passed on our way; half-a-mile further on we were wiser and sadder, for then we stood on the rim of one of the biggest swamps I have ever seen south of the Rivers. It stretched away in all directions, a great sheet of filthy water, out of which sprang gorgeous marsh plants, in islands, great banks of screw pine, and coppices of wine palm, with their lovely fronds reflected back by the still, mirror-like water, so that the reflection was as vivid as the reality, and above all remarkable was a plant, {241} new and strange to me, whose pale-green stem came up out of the water and then spread out in a flattened surface, thin, and in a peculiarly graceful curve. This flattened surface had growing out from it leaves, the size, shape and colour of lily of the valley leaves; until I saw this thing I had held the wine palm to be the queen of grace in the vegetable kingdom, but this new beauty quite surpassed her.

Our path went straight into this swamp over the black rocks forming its rim, in an imperative, no alternative, "Come-along-this-way" style. Singlet, who was leading, carrying a good load of bottled fish and a gorilla specimen, went at it like a man, and disappeared before the eyes of us close following him, then and there down through the water. He came up, thanks be, but his load is down there now, worse luck. Then I said we must get the rubber carriers who were coming this way to show us the ford; and so we sat down on the bank a tired, disconsolate, dilapidated-looking row, until they arrived. When they came up they did not plunge in forthwith; but leisurely set about making a most nerve-shaking set of preparations, taking off their clothes, and forming them into bundles, which, to my horror, they put on the tops of their heads. The women carried the rubber on their backs still, but rubber is none the worse for being under water. The men went in first, each holding his gun high above his head. They skirted the bank before they struck out into the swamp, and were followed by the women and by our party, and soon we were all up to our chins.

We were two hours and a quarter passing that swamp. I was one hour and three-quarters; but I made good weather of it, closely following the rubber-carriers, and only going in right over head and all twice. Other members of my band were less fortunate. One and all, we got horribly infested with leeches, having a frill of them round our necks like astrachan collars, and our hands covered with them, when we came out.

We had to pass across the first bit of open country I had seen for a long time—a real patch of grass on the top of a low ridge, which is fringed with swamp on all sides save the one we made our way to, the eastern. Shortly after passing through another plantation, we saw brown huts, and in a few minutes were standing in the middle of a ramshackle village, at the end of which, through a high stockade, with its gateway smeared with blood which hung in gouts, we saw our much longed for Rembwé River. I made for it, taking small notice of the hubbub our arrival occasioned, and passed through the gateway, setting its guarding bell ringing violently; I stood on the steep, black, mud slime bank, surrounded by a noisy crowd. It is a big river, but nothing to the Ogowé, either in breadth or beauty; what beauty it has is of the Niger delta type—black mud-laden water, with a mangrove swamp fringe to it in all directions. I soon turned back into the village and asked for Ugumu's factory. "This is it," said an exceedingly dirty, good-looking, civil-spoken man in perfect English, though as pure blooded an African as ever walked. "This is it, sir," and he pointed to one of the huts on the right-hand side, indistinguishable in squalor from the rest. "Where's the Agent?" said I. "I'm the Agent," he answered. You could have knocked me down with a feather. "Where's John Holt's factory?" said I. "You have passed it; it is up on the hill." This showed Messrs. Holt's local factory to be no bigger than Ugumu's. At this point a big, scraggy, very black man with an irregularly formed face the size of a tea-tray and looking generally as if he had come out of a pantomime on the Arabian Nights, dashed through the crowd, shouting, "I'm for Holty, I'm for Holty." "This is my trade, you go 'way," says Agent number one. Fearing my two Agents would fight and dam-age each other, so that neither would be any good for me, I firmly said, "Have you got any rum?" Agent number one looked crestfallen, Holty's triumphant. "Rum, fur sure," says he; so I gave him a five-franc piece, which he regarded with great pleasure, and putting it in his mouth, he legged it like a lamplighter away to his store on the hill. "Have you any tobacco?" said I to Agent number one. He brightened, "Plenty tobacco, plenty cloth," said he; so I told him to give me out twenty heads. I gave my men two heads apiece. I told them rum was coming, and ordered them to take the loads on to Hatton and Cookson's Agent's hut and then to go and buy chop and make themselves comfortable. They highly approved of this plan, and grunted assent ecstatically; and just as the loads were stowed Holty's anatomy hove in sight with a bottle of rum under each arm, and one in each hand; while behind him came an acolyte, a fat, small boy, panting and puffing and doing his level best to keep up with his long-legged flying master. I gave my men some and put the rest in with my goods, and explained that I belonged to Hatton and Cookson's (it's the proper thing to belong to somebody), and that therefore I must take up my quarters at their Store; but Holty's energetic agent hung about me like a vulture in hopes of getting more five franc-piece pickings. I sent Ngouta off to get me some tea, and had the hut cleared of an excited audience, and shut myself in with Hatton and Cookson's agent, and asked him seriously and anxiously if there was not a big factory of the firm's on the river, because it was self-evident he had not got anything like enough stuff to pay off my men with, and my agreement was to pay off on the Rembwé, hence my horror at the smallness of the firm's N'dorko store. "Besides," I said, "Mr. Glass (I knew the head Rembwé agent of Hatton and Cookson was a Mr. Glass), you have only got cloth and tobacco, and I have promised the Fans to pay off in whatever they choose, and I know for sure they want powder." "I am not Mr. Glass," said my friend; "he is up at Agonjo, I only do small trade for him here." Joy!!!! but where's Agonjo? To make a long story short I found Agonjo was an hour's paddle up the Rembwé and the place we ought to have come out at. There was a botheration again about sending up a message, because of a war palaver; but I got a pencil note, with my letter of introduction from Mr. Cockshut to Sanga Glass, at last delivered to that gentleman; and down he came, in a state of considerable astonishment, not unmixed with alarm, for no white man of any kind had been across from the Ogowé for years, and none had ever come out at N'dorko. Mr. Glass I found an exceedingly neat, well-educated M'pongwe gentleman in irreproachable English garments, and with irreproachable, but slightly floreate, English language. We started talking trade, with my band in the middle of the street; making a patch of uproar in the moonlit surrounding silence. As soon as we thought we had got one gentleman's mind settled as to what goods he would take his pay in, and were proceeding to investigate another gentleman's little fancies, gentleman number one's mind came all to pieces again, and he wanted "to room his bundle," i.e. change articles in it for other articles of an equivalent value, if it must be, but of a higher, if possible. Oh ye shopkeepers in England who grumble at your lady customers, just you come out here and try to serve, and satisfy a set of Fans! Mr. Glass was evidently an expert at the affair, but it was past 11 p.m. before we got the orders written out, and getting my baggage into some canoes, that Mr. Glass had brought down from Agonjo, for N'dorko only had a few very wretched ones, I started off up river with him and all the Ajumba, and Kiva, the Fan, who had been promised a safe conduct. He came to see the bundles for his fellow Fans were made up satisfactorily. The canoes being small there was quite a procession of them. Mr. Glass and I shared one, which was paddled by two small boys; how we ever got up the Rembwé that night I do not know, for although neither of us were fat, the canoe was a one man canoe, and the water lapped over the edge in an alarming way. Had any of us sneezed, or had it been daylight when two or three mangrove flies would have joined the party, we must have foundered; but all went well; and on arriving at Agonjo Mr. Glass most kindly opened his store, and by the light of lamps and lanterns, we picked out the goods from his varied and ample supply, and handed them over to the Ajumba and Kiva, and all, save three of the Ajumba, were satisfied. The three, Gray Shirt, Silence, and Pagan quietly explained to me that they found the Rembwé price so little better than the Lembarene price that they would rather get their pay off Mr. Cockshut, than risk taking it back through the Fan country, so I gave them books on him. I gave all my remaining trade goods, and the rest of the rum to the Fans as a dash, and they were more than satisfied. I must say they never clamoured for dash for top. The Passenger we had brought through with us, who had really made himself very helpful, was quite surprised at getting a bundle of goods from me. My only anxiety was as to whether Fika would get his share all right; but I expect he did, for the Ajumbas are very honest men; and they were going back with my Fan friends. I found out, by the by, the reason of Fika's shyness in coming through to the Rembwé; it was a big wife palaver.

I had a touching farewell with the Fans: and so in peace, good feeling, and prosperity I parted company for the second time with "the terrible M'pongwe," whom I hope to meet with again, for with all their many faults and failings, they are real men. I am faint-hearted enough to hope, that our next journey together, may not be over a country that seems to me to have been laid down as an obstacle race track for Mr. G. F. Watts's Titans, and to have fallen into shocking bad repair.

CHAPTER X

BUSH TRADE AND FAN CUSTOMS

WHEREIN THE VOYAGER, HAVING FALLEN AMONG THE BLACK TRADERS, DISCOURSES ON THESE MEN AND THEIR MANNER OF LIFE; AND THE DIFFICULTIES AND DANGERS ATTENDING THE BARTER THEY CARRY ON WITH THE BUSH SAVAGES; AND ON SOME OF THE REASONS THAT MAKES THIS BARTER SO BELOVED AND FOLLOWED BY BOTH THE BLACK TRADER AND THE SAVAGE. TO WHICH IS ADDED AN ACCOUNT OF THE MANNER OF LIFE OF THE FAN TRIBE; THE STRANGE FORM OF COINAGE USED BY THESE PEOPLE; THEIR MANNER OF HUNTING THE ELEPHANT, WORKING IN IRON; AND SUCH LIKE THINGS.

I SPENT A FEW, LAZY, pleasant days at Agonjo, Mr. Glass doing all he could to make me comfortable, though he had a nasty touch of fever on him just then. His efforts were ably seconded by his good lady, an exceedingly comely Gaboon woman, with pretty manners, and an excellent gift in cookery. The third member of the staff was the store-keeper, a clever fellow: I fancy a Loango from his clean-cut features and spare make, but his tribe I know not for a surety.

One of these black trader factories is an exceedingly interesting place to stay at, for in these factories you are right down on the bed rock of the trade. On the Coast, for the greater part, the white traders are dealing with black traders, middle men, who have procured their trade stuff from the bush natives, who collect and prepare it. Here, in the black trader factory, you see the first stage of the export part of the trade: namely the barter of the collected trade stuff between the collector and the middleman. I will not go into details regarding it. What I saw merely confirmed my opinion that the native is not cheated; no, not even by a fellow African trader; and I will merely here pause to sing a pæan to a very unpopular class—the black middleman as he exists on the South-West Coast.

It is impossible to realise the gloom of the lives of these men in bush factories, unless you have lived in one. It is no use saying "they know nothing better and so don't feel it," for they do know several things better, being very sociable men, fully appreciative of the joys of a Coast town, and their aim, object and end in life is, in almost every case, to get together a fortune that will enable them to live in one, give a dance twice a week, card parties most nights, and dress themselves up so that their fellow Coast townsmen may hate them and their townswomen love them. From their own accounts of the dreadful state of trade; and the awful and unparalleled series of losses they have had, from the upsetting of canoes, the raids and robberies made on them and their goods by "those awful bush savages"; you would, if you were of a trustful disposition, regard the black trader with an admiring awe as the man who has at last solved the great commercial problem of how to keep a shop and live by the loss. Nay, not only live, but build for himself an equivalent to a palatial residence, and keep up, not only it, but half a dozen wives, with a fine taste for dress every one of them. I am not of a trustful disposition and I accept those "losses" with a heavy discount, and know most of the rest of them have come out of my friend the white trader's pockets. Still I can never feel the righteous indignation that I ought to feel, when I see the black trader "down in a seaport town with his Nancy," etc., as Sir W. H. S. Gilbert classically says, because I remember those bush factories.

Mr. Glass, however, was not a trader who made a fortune by losing those of other people; for he had been many years in the employ of the firm. He had risen certainly to the high post and position of charge of the Rembwé, but he was not down giddy-flying at Gaboon. His accounts of his experiences when he had been many years ago away up the still little known Nguni River, in a factory in touch with the lively Bakele, then in a factory among Fans and Igalwa on the Ogowé, and now among Fans and Skekiani on the Rembwé, were fascinating, and told vividly of the joys of first starting a factory in a wild district. The way in which your customers, for the first month or so, enjoyed themselves by trying to frighten you, the trader, out of your wits and goods, and into giving them fancy prices for things you were trading in, and for things of no earthly use to you, or any one else! The trader's existence during this period is marked by every unpleasantness save dulness; from that he is spared by the presence of a mob of noisy, dangerous, thieving savages all over his place all day; invading his cook-house, to put some nastiness into his food as a trade charm; helping themselves to portable property at large; and making themselves at home to the extent of sitting on his dining-table. At night those customers proceed to sleep all over the premises, with a view to being on hand to start shopping in the morning. Woe betide the trader if he gives in to this, and tolerates the invasion, for there is no chance of that house ever being his own again; and in addition to the local flies, etc., on the table-cloth, he will always have several big black gentlemen to share his meals. If he raises prices, to tide over some extra row, he is a lost man; for the Africans can understand prices going up, but never prices coming down; and time being no object, they will hold back their trade. Then the district is ruined, and the trader along with it, for he cannot raise the price he gets for the things he buys.

What that trader has got to do, is to be a "Devil man." They always kindly said they recognised me as one, which is a great compliment. He must betray no weakness, but a character which I should describe as a compound of the best parts of those of Cardinal Richelieu, Brutus, Julius Caesar, Prince Metternich, and Mezzofanti, the latter to carry on the native language part of the business; and he must cast those customers out, not only from his house; but from his yard; and adhere to the "No admittance except on business" principle. This causes a good deal of unpleasantness, and the trader's nights are now cheered by lively war-dances outside his stockade; the accompanying songs advertising that the customers are coming over the stockade to raid the store, and cut up the trader "into bits like a fish." Sometimes they do come—and then—finish; but usually they don't; and gradually settle down, and respect the trader greatly as "a Devil man"; and do business on sound lines during the day. Over the stockade at night, by ones and twos, stealing, they will come to the end of the chapter.

Moonlight nights are fairly restful for the bush trader, but when it is inky black, or pouring with rain, he has got to be very much out and about, and particularly vigilant has he got to be on tornado nights—a most uncomfortable sort of weather to attend to business in, I assure you.

The factory at Agonjo was typical; the house is a fine specimen of the Igalwa style of architecture; mounted on poles above the ground; the space under the house being used as a store for rubber in barrels, and ebony in billets; thereby enabling the trader to hover over these precious possessions, sleeping and waking, like a sitting hen over her eggs. Near to the house are the sleeping places for the beach hands, and the cook-house. In front, in a position commanded by the eye from the verandah, and well withdrawn from the stockade, are great piles of billets of red bar wood. The whole of the clean, sandy yard containing these things, and divers others, is surrounded by a stout stockade, its main face to the river frontage, the water at high tide lapping its base, and at low tide exposing in front of it a shore of black slime. Although I cite this factory as a typical factory of a black trader, it is a specimen of the highest class, for, being in connection with Messrs. Hatton and Cookson it is well kept up and stocked. Firms differ much in this particular. Messrs. Hatton and Cookson, like Messrs. Miller Brothers in the Bights, take every care that lies in their power of the people who serve them, down to the Kruboys working on their beaches, giving ample and good rations and providing good houses. But this is not so with all firms on the Coast. I have seen factories belonging to the Swedish houses beside which this factory at Agonjo is a palace although those factories are white man factories, and the unfortunate white men in them are expected by these firms to live on native chop—an expectation the Agents by no means realise, for they usually die. Black hands, however, do not suffer much at the hands of such firms, for the Swedish Agents are a quiet, gentle-manly set of men, in the best sense of that much misused term, and they do not employ on their beaches such a staff of black helpers as the English houses, so the two or three Kruboys on a starvation beach can fairly well fend for them-selves, for there is always an adjacent village, and in that village there are always chickens, and on the shore crabs, and in the river fish, and for the rest of his diet the Kruboy flirts with the local ladies.

Although, as I have laid down, the bush factory at its best is a place, as Mr. Tracey Tupman would say, more fitted for a wounded heart than for one still able to feast on social joys, it is a luxurious situation for a black trader compared to the other form of trading he deals with—that of travelling among the native villages in the bush. This has one hundred times the danger, and a thousand times the discomfort, and is a thoroughly unhealthy pursuit. The journeys these bush traders make are often remarkable, and they deserve great credit for the courage and enterprise they display. Certainly they run less risk of death from fever than a white man would; but, on the other hand, their colour gives them no protection; and their chance of getting murdered is distinctly greater, the white governmental powers cannot revenge their death, in the way they would the death of a white man, for these murders usually take place away in some forest region, in a district no white man has ever penetrated.

You will naturally ask how it is that so many of these men do survive "to lead a life of sin" as a missionary described to me their Coast town life to be. This question struck me as requiring explanation. The result of my investi-gations, and the answers I have received from the men themselves, show that there is a reason why the natives do not succumb every time to the temptation to kill the trader, and take his goods, and this is twofold: firstly, all trade in West Africa follows definite routes, even in the wildest parts of it; and so a vil-lage far away in the forest, but on the trade route, knows that as a general rule twice a year, a trader will appear to purchase its rubber and ivory. If he does not appear somewhere about the expected time, that village gets uneasy. The ladies are impatient for their new clothes; the gentlemen half wild for want of tobacco; and things coming to a crisis, they make inquiries for the trader down the road, one village to another, and then, if it is found that a village has killed the trader, and stolen all his goods, there is naturally a big palaver, and things are made extremely hot, even for equatorial Africa, for that village by the tobac-coless husbands of the clothesless wives. Herein lies the trader's chief safety, the village not being an atom afraid, or disinclined to kill him, but afraid of their neighbouring villages, and disinclined to be killed by them. But the trader is not yet safe. There is still a hole in his armour, and this is only to be stopped up in one way, namely, by wives; for you see although the village cannot safely kill him, and take all his goods, they can still let him die safely of a disease, and take part of them, passing on sufficient stuff to the other villages to keep them quiet. Now the most prevalent disease in the African bush comes out of the cooking pot, and so to make what goes into the cooking pot—which is the important point, for earthen pots do not in themselves breed poison—safe and whole-some, you have got to have some one who is devoted to your health to attend to the cooking affairs, and who can do this like a wife? So you have a wife—one in each village up the whole of your route. I know myself one gentleman whose wives stretch over 300 miles of country, with a good wife base in a Coast town as well. This system of judiciously conducted alliances, gives the black trader a security nothing else can, because naturally he marries into influential families at each village, and all his wife's relations on the mother's side regard him as one of themselves, and look after him and his interests. That security can lie in women, especially so many women, the so-called civilised man may ironi-cally doubt, but the security is there, and there only, and on a sound basis, for remember the position of a travelling trader's wife in a village is a position that gives the lady prestige, the discreet husband showing little favours to her family and friends, if she asks for them when he is with her; and then she has not got the bother of having a man always about the house, and liable to get all sorts of silly notions into his head if she speaks to another gentleman, and then go and impart these notions to her with a cutlass, or a kassengo, as the more domestic husband, I am assured by black ladies, is prone to.

You may now, I fear, be falling into the other adjacent error—from the wonder why any black trader survives, namely, into the wonder why any black trader gets killed; with all these safeguards, and wives. But there is yet another danger, which no quantity of wives, nor local jealousies avail to guard him through. This danger arises from the nomadic habits of the bush tribes, no-tably the Fan. For when a village has made up its mind to change its district, either from having made the district too hot to hold it, with quarrels with neighbouring villages; or because it has exhausted the trade stuff, i.e. rubber and ivory in reach of its present situation; or because some other village has raided it, and taken away all the stuff it was saving to sell to the black trader; it resolves to give itself a final treat in the old home, and make a commer-cial coup at one fell swoop. Then when the black trader turns up with his boxes of goods, it kills him, has some for supper, smokes the rest, and takes it and the goods, and departs to found new homes in another district.

The bush trade I have above sketched is the bush trade with the Fans. In those districts on the southern banks of the Ogowé the main features of the trade, and the trader's life are the same, but the details are more intricate, for the Igalwa trader from Lembarene, Fernan Vaz, or Njole, deals with another set of trading tribes, not first hand with the collectors. The Fan villages on the trade routes may, however, be regarded as trade depots, for to them filters the trade stuff of the more remote villages, so the difference is really merely technical, and in all villages alike the same sort of thing occurs.

The Igalwa or M'pongwe trader arrives with the goods he has received from the white trader, and there are great rejoicing and much uproar as his chests and bundles and demijohns are brought up from the canoe. And presently, after a great deal of talk, the goods are opened. The chiefs of the village have their pick, and divide this among the principal men of the village, who pay for it in part with their store of collected rubber or ivory, and take the rest on trust, promising to collect enough rubber to pay the balance on the next visit of the trader. Thereby the trader has a quantity of debts outstanding in each village, liable to be bad debts, and herein lies his chief loss. Each chief takes a certain understood value in goods as a commission for himself - nye-no - giving the trader, as a consideration for this, an understood bond to assist him in getting in the trust granted to his village. This nyeno he utilises in buying trade stuff from villages not on the trade route. Among the Fans the men who have got the goods stand by with these to trade for rubber with the general public and bachelors of the village, in a way I will presently explain. In tribes like Ajumbas, Adooma, etc., the men having the goods travel off, as traders, among their various bush tribes, similarly paying their nyeno, and so by the time the goods reach the final producing men, only a small portion of them is left, but their price has necessarily risen. Still it is quite absurd for a casual white traveller, who may have dropped in on the terminus of a trade route, to cry out regarding the small value the collector (who is often erroneously described as the producer) gets for his stuff, compared to the price it fetches in Europe. For before it even reaches the factory of the Coast Settlement, that stuff has got to keep a whole series of traders. It appears at first bad that this should be the case, but the case it is along the west coast of the continent save in the districts commanded by the Royal Niger company, who, with courage and enterprise, have pushed far inland, and got in touch with the great interior trade routes—a performance which has raised in the breasts of the Coast trader tribes who have been supplanted, a keen animosity, which like most animosity in Africa, is not regardful of truth. The tribes that have had the trade of the Bight of Biafra passing through their hands have been accustomed, according to the German Government who are also pressing inland, to make seventy-five per cent. profit on it, and they resent being deprived of this. A good deal is to be said in favour of their views; among other things that the greater part of the seaboard districts of West Africa, I may say every part from Sierra Leone to Cameroon, is structurally incapable of being self-supporting under existing conditions. Below Cameroon, on my beloved South-west coast, which is infinitely richer than the Bight of Benin, rich producing districts come down to the sea in most places until you reach the Congo; but here again the middleman is of great use to the interior tribes, and if they do have to pay him seventy-five per cent, serve them right. They should not go making wife palaver, and blood palaver all over the place to such an extent that the inhabitants of no village, unless they go en masse, dare take a ten mile walk, save at the risk of their lives, in any direction, so no palaver live.

We will now enter into the reason that induces the bush man to collect stuff to sell among the Fans, which is the expensiveness of the ladies in the tribe. A bush Fan is bound to marry into his tribe, because over a great part of the territory occupied by them there is no other tribe handy to marry into; and a Fan residing in villages in touch with other tribes, has but little chance of getting a cheaper lady. For there is, in the Congo Français and the country adjacent to the north of it (Batanga), a regular style of aristocracy which may be summarised firstly thus: All the other tribes look down on the Fans, and the Fans look down on all the other tribes. This aristocracy has sub-divisions, the M'pongwe of Gaboon are the upper circle tribe; next come the Benga of Corisco; then the Bapuka; then the Banaka. This system of aristocracy is kept up by the ladies. Thus a M'pongwe lady would not think of marrying into one of the lower tribes, so she is restricted, with many inner restrictions, to her own tribe. A Benga lady would marry a M'pongwe, or a Benga, but not a Banaka, or Bapuka; and so on with the others; but not one of them would marry a Fan. As for the men, well of course they would marry any lady of any tribe, if she had a pretty face, or a good trading connection, if they were allowed to: that's just man's way. To the south-east the Fans are in touch with the Bakele, a tribe that has much in common with the Fan, but who differ from them in getting on in a very friendly way with the little dwarf people, the Matimbas, or Watwa, or Akoa: people the Fans cannot abide. With these Bakele the Fan can intermarry, but there is not much advantage in so doing, as the price is equally high, but still marry he must.

A young Fan man has to fend for himself, and has a scratchy kind of life of it, aided only by his mother until—if he be an enterprising youth—he is able to steal a runaway wife from a neighbouring village, or if he is a quiet and steady young man, until he has amassed sufficient money to buy a wife. This he does by collecting ebony and rubber and selling it to the men who have been allotted goods by the chief of the village, from the consignment brought up by the black trader. He supports himself meanwhile by, if the situation of his village permits, fishing and selling the fish, and hunting and killing game in the forest. He keeps steadily at it in his way, reserving his roysterings until he is settled in life. A truly careful young man does not go and buy a baby girl cheap, as soon as he has got a little money together; but works and saves on until he has got enough to buy a good, tough widow lady, who, although personally unattractive, is deeply versed in the lore of trade, and who knows exactly how much rubbish you can incorporate in a ball of india rubber, without the white trader, or the black bush factory trader, instantly detecting it. When the Fan young man has married his wife, in a legitimate way on the cash system, he takes her round to his relations, and shows her off; and they make little presents to help the pair set up housekeeping. But the young man cannot yet settle down, for his wife will not allow him to. She is not going to slave herself to death doing all the work of the house, etc., and so he goes on collecting, and she preparing, trade stuff, and he grows rich enough to buy other wives—some of them young children, others widows, no longer necessarily old. But it is not until he is well on in life that he gets sufficient wives, six or seven. For it takes a good time to get enough rubber to buy a lady, and he does not get a grip on the ivory trade until he has got a certain position in the village, and plantations of his own which the elephants can be discovered raiding, in which case a percentage of the ivory taken from the herd is allotted to him. Now and again he may come across a dead elephant, but that is of the nature of a windfall; and on rubber and ebony he has to depend during his early days. These he changes with the rich men of his village for a very peculiar and interesting form of coinage—bikei—little iron imitation axe-heads which are tied up in bundles called ntet, ten going to one bundle, for with bikei must the price of a wife be paid. You do not find bikei close down to Libreville, among the Fans who are there in a semi-civilised state, or more properly speaking in a state of disintegrating culture. You must go for bush. I thought I saw in bikei a certain resemblance in underlying idea with the early Greek coins I have seen at Cambridge, made like the fore-parts of cattle; and I have little doubt that the articles of barter among the Fans before the introduction of the rubber, ebony, and ivory trades, which in their districts are comparatively recent, were iron implements. For the Fans are good workers in iron; and it would be in consonance with well-known instances among other savage races in the matter of stone implements, that these things, important of old, should survive, and be employed in the matter of such an old and important affair as marriage. They thus become ju-ju; and indeed all West African legitimate marriage, although appearing to the casual observer a mere matter of barter, is never solely such, but always has ju-ju in it.

We may as well here follow out the whole of the domestic life of the Fan, now we have got him married. His difficulty does not only consist in getting enough bikei together but in getting a lady he can marry. No amount of bikei can justify a man in marrying his first cousin, or his aunt; and as relationship among the Fans is recognised with both his father and his mother, not as among the Igalwa with the latter's blood relations only, there are an awful quantity of aunts and cousins about from whom he is debarred. But when he has surmounted his many difficulties, and dodged his relations, and married, he is seemingly a better husband than the man of a more cultured tribe. He will turn a hand to anything, that does not necessitate his putting down his gun outside his village gateway. He will help chop firewood, or goat's chop, or he will carry the baby with pleasure, while his good lady does these things; and in bush villages, he always escorts her so as to be on hand in case of leopards, or other local unpleasantnesses. When inside the village he will lay down his gun, within handy reach, and build the house, tease out fibre to make game nets with, and plait baskets, or make pottery with the ladies, cheerily chatting the while.

Fan pottery, although rough and sunbaked, is artistic in form and ornamented, for the Fan ornaments all his work; the articles made in it consist of cooking pots, palm-wine bottles, water bottles and pipes, but not all water bottles, nor all pipes are made of pottery. I wish they were, particularly the former, for they are occasionally made of beautifully plaited fibre coated with a layer of a certain gum with a vile taste, which it imparts to the water in the vessel. They say it does not do this if the vessel is soaked for two days in water, but it does, and I should think contaminates the stream it was soaked in into the bargain. The pipes are sometimes made of iron very neatly. I should imagine they smoked hot, but of this I have no knowledge. One of my Ajumba friends got himself one of these pipes when we were in Efoua, and that pipe was, on and off, a curse to the party. Its owner soon learnt not to hold it by the bowl, but by the wooden stem, when smoking it; the other lessons it had to teach he learnt more slowly. He tucked it, when he had done smoking, into the fold in his cloth, until he had had three serious conflagrations raging round his middle. And to the end of the chapter, after having his last pipe at night with it, he would lay it on the ground, before it was cool. He learnt to lay it out of reach of his own cloth, but his fellow Ajumbas and he himself persisted in always throwing a leg on to it shortly after, and there was another row.

The Fan basket-work is strongly made, but very inferior to the Fjort basket-work. Their nets are, however, the finest I have ever seen. These are made mainly for catching small game, such as the beautiful little gazelles (Ncheri) with dark gray skins on the upper part of the body, white underneath, and satin-like in sleekness all over. Their form is very dainty, the little legs being no thicker than a man's finger, the neck long and the head ornamented with little pointed horns and broad round ears. The nets are tied on to trees in two long lines, which converge to an acute angle, the bottom part of the net lying on the ground. Then a party of men and women accompanied by their trained dogs, which have bells hung round their necks, beat the surrounding bushes, and the frightened small game rush into the nets, and become entangled. The fibre from which these nets are made has a long staple, and is exceedingly strong. I once saw a small bush cow caught in a set of them and unable to break through, and once a leopard; he, however, took his section of the net away with him, and a good deal of vegetation and sticks to boot. In addition to nets, this fibre is made into bags, for carrying things in while in the bush, and into the water bottles already mentioned.

The iron-work of the Fans deserves especial notice for its excellence. The anvil is a big piece of iron which is embedded firmly in the ground. Its upper surface is flat, and pointed at both ends. The hammers are solid cones of iron, the upper part of the cones prolonged so as to give a good grip, and the blows are given directly downwards, like the blows of a pestle. The bellows are of the usual African type, cut out of one piece of solid but soft wood; at the upper end of these bellows there are two chambers hollowed out in the wood and then covered with the skin of some animal, from which the hair has been removed. This is bound firmly round the rim of each chamber with tie-tie, and the bag of it at the top is gathered up, and bound to a small piece of stick, to give a convenient hand hold. The straight cylinder, terminating in the nozzle, has two channels burnt in it which communicate with each of the chambers respectively, and half-way up the cylinder, there are burnt from the outside into the air passages, three series of holes, one series on the upper surface, and a series at each side. This ingenious arrangement gives a constant current of air up from the nozzle when the bellows are worked by a man sitting behind them, and rapidly and alternately pulling up the skin cover over one chamber, while depressing the other. In order to make the affair firm it is lashed to pieces of stick stuck in the ground in a suitable way so as to keep the bellows at an angle with the nozzle directed towards the fire. As wooden bellows like this if stuck into the fire would soon be aflame, the nozzle is put into a cylinder made of clay. This cylinder is made sufficiently large at the end, into which the nozzle of the bellows goes, for the air to have full play round the latter.

The Fan bellows only differ from those of the other iron-working West Coast tribes in having the channels from the two chambers in one piece of wood all the way. His forge is the same as the other forges, a round cavity scooped in the ground; his fuel also is charcoal. His other smith's tool consists of a pointed piece of iron, with which he works out the patterns he puts at the handle-end of his swords, etc.

I must now speak briefly on the most important article with which the Fan deals, namely ivory. His methods of collecting this are several, and many a wild story the handles of your table knives could tell you, if their ivory has passed through Fan hands. For ivory is everywhere an evil thing before which the quest for gold sinks into a parlour game; and when its charms seize such a tribe as the Fans, "conclusions pass their careers." A very common way of collecting a tooth is to kill the person who owns one. Therefore in order to prevent this catastrophe happening to you yourself, when you have one, it is held advisable, unless you are a powerful person in your own village, to bury or sink the said tooth and say nothing about it until the trader comes into your district or you get a chance of smuggling it quietly down to him. Some of these private ivories are kept for years and years before they reach the trader's hands. And quite a third of the ivory you see coming on board a vessel to go to Europe is dark from this keeping: some teeth a lovely brown like a well-coloured meerschaum, others quite black, and gnawed by that strange little creature—much heard of, and abused, yet little known in ivory ports—the ivory rat.

Ivory, however, that is obtained by murder is private ivory. The public ivory trade among the Fans is carried on in a way more in accordance with European ideas of a legitimate trade. The greater part of this ivory is obtained from dead elephants. There are in this region certain places where the elephants are said to go to die. A locality in one district pointed out to me as such a place, was a great swamp in the forest. A swamp that evidently was deep in the middle, for from out its dark waters no swamp plant, or tree grew, and evidently its shores sloped suddenly, for the band of swamp plants round its edge was narrow. It is just possible that during the rainy season when most of the surrounding country would be under water, elephants might stray into this natural trap and get drowned, and on the drying up of the waters be discovered, and the fact being known, be regularly sought for by the natives cognisant of this. I inquired carefully whether these places where the elephants came to die always had water in them, but they said no, and in one district spoke of a valley or round-shaped depression in among the mountains. But natives were naturally disinclined to take a stranger to these ivory mines, and a white person who has caught—as any one who has been in touch must catch—ivory fever, is naturally equally disinclined to give localities.

A certain percentage of ivory collected by the Fans is from live elephants, but I am bound to admit that their method of hunting elephants is disgracefully unsportsmanlike. A herd of elephants is discovered by rubber hunters or by depredations on plantations, and the whole village, men, women, children, babies and dogs turn out into the forest and stalk the monsters into a suitable ravine, taking care not to scare them. When they have gradually edged the elephants on into a suitable place, they fell trees and wreathe them very roughly together with bush rope, all round an immense enclosure, still taking care not to scare the elephants into a rush. This fence is quite inadequate to stop any elephant in itself, but it is made effective by being smeared with certain things, the smell whereof the elephants detest so much that when they wander up to it, they turn back disgusted. I need hardly remark that this preparation is made by the witch doctors and its constituents a secret of theirs, and I was only able to find out some of them. Then poisoned plantains are placed within the enclosure, and the elephants eat these and grow drowsier and drowsier; if the water supply within the enclosure is a pool it is poisoned, but if it is a running stream this cannot be done. During this time the crowd of men and women spend their days round the enclosure, ready to turn back any elephant who may attempt to break out, going to and fro to the village for their food. Their nights they spend in little bough shelters by the enclosure, watching more vigilantly than by day, as the elephants are more active at night, it being their usual feeding time. During the whole time the witch doctor is hard at work making incantations and charms, with a view to finding out the proper time to attack the elephants. In my opinion, his decision fundamentally depends on his knowledge of the state of poisoning the animals are in, but his version is that he gets his information from the forest spirits. When, however, he has settled the day, the best hunters steal into the enclosure and take up safe positions in trees, and the outer crowd set light to the ready-built fires, and make the greatest uproar possible, and fire upon the staggering, terrified elephants as they attempt to break out. The hunters in the trees fire down on them as they rush past, the fatal point at the back of the skull being well exposed to them.

When the animals are nearly exhausted, those men who do not possess guns dash into the enclosure, and the men who do, reload and join them, and the work is then completed. One elephant hunt I chanced upon at the final stage had taken two months' preparation, and although the plan sounds safe enough, there is really a good deal of danger left in it with all the drugging and ju-ju. There were eight elephants killed that day, but three burst through everything, sending energetic spectators flying, and squashing two men and a baby as flat as botanical specimens.

The subsequent proceedings were impressive. The whole of the people gorged themselves on the meat for days, and great chunks of it were smoked over the fires in all directions. A certain portion of the flesh of the hind leg was taken by the witch doctor for ju-ju, and was supposed to be put away by him, with certain suitable incantations in the recesses of the forest; his idea being apparently either to give rise to more elephants, or to induce the forest spirits to bring more elephants into the district.

Dr. Nassau tells me that the manner in which the ivory gained by one of these hunts is divided is as follows:—"The witch doctor, the chiefs, and the family on whose ground the enclosure is built, and especially the household whose women first discovered the animals, decide in council as to the division of the tusks and the share of the flesh to be given to the crowd of outsiders. The next day the tusks are removed and each family represented in the assemblage cuts up and distributes the flesh." In the hunt I saw finished, the elephants had not been discovered, as in the case Dr. Nassau above speaks of, in a plantation by women, but by a party of rubber hunters in the forest some four or five miles from any village, and the ivory that would have been allotted to the plantation holder in the former case, went in this case to the young rubber hunters.

Such are the pursuits, sports and pastimes of my friends the Fans. I have been considerably chaffed both by whites and blacks about my partiality for this tribe, but as I like Africans in my way—not à la Sierra Leone—and these Africans have more of the qualities I like than any other tribe I have met, it is but natural that I should prefer them. They are brave and so you can respect them, which is an essential element in a friendly feeling. They are on the whole a fine race, particularly those in the mountain districts of the Sierra del Cristal, where one continually sees magnificent specimens of human beings, both male and female. Their colour is light bronze, many of the men have beards, and albinoes are rare among them. The average height in the mountain districts is five feet six to five feet eight, the difference in stature between men and women not being great. Their countenances are very bright and expressive, and if once you have been among them, you can never mistake a Fan. But it is in their mental characteristics that their difference from the lethargic, dying-out coast tribes is most marked. The Fan is full of fire, temper, intelligence and go; very teachable, rather difficult to manage, quick to take offence, and utterly indifferent to human life. I ought to say that other people, who should know him better than I, say he is a treacherous, thievish, murderous cannibal. I never found him treacherous; but then I never trusted him, remembering one of the aphorisms of my great teacher Captain Boler of Bonny, "It's not safe to go among bush tribes, but if you are such a fool as to go, you needn't go and be a bigger fool still, you've done enough." And Captain Boler's other great aphorism was: "Never be afraid of a black man." "What if I can't help it?" said I. "Don't show it," said he. To these precepts I humbly add another: "Never lose your head." My most favourite form of literature, I may remark, is accounts of mountaineering exploits, though I have never seen a glacier or a permanent snow mountain in my life. I do not care a row of pins how badly they may be written, and what form of bumble-puppy grammar and composition is employed, as long as the writer will walk along the edge of a precipice with a sheer fall of thousands of feet on one side and a sheer wall on the other; or better still crawl up an arête with a precipice on either. Nothing on earth would persuade me to do either of these things myself, but they remind me of bits of country I have been through where you walk along a narrow line of security with gulfs of murder looming on each side, and where in exactly the same way you are as safe as if you were in your easy chair at home, as long as you get sufficient holding ground: not on rock in the bush village inhabited by murderous cannibals, but on ideas in those men's and women's minds; and these ideas, which I think I may say you will always find, give you safety. It is not advisable to play with them, or to attempt to eradicate them, because you regard them as superstitious; and never, never shoot too soon. I have never had to shoot, and hope never to have to; because in such a situation, one white alone with no troops to back him means a clean finish. But this would not discourage me if I had to start, only it makes me more inclined to walk round the obstacle, than to become a mere blood splotch against it, if this can be done without losing your self-respect, which is the mainspring of your power in West Africa.

As for flourishing about a revolver and threatening to fire, I hold it utter idiocy. I have never tried it, however, so I speak from prejudice which arises from the feeling that there is something cowardly in it. Always have your revolver ready loaded in good order, and have your hand on it when things are getting warm, and in addition have an exceedingly good bowie knife, not a hinge knife, because with a hinge knife you have got to get it open—hard work in a country where all things go rusty in the joints—and hinge knives are liable to close on your own fingers. The best form of knife is the bowie, with a shallow half moon cut out of the back at the point end, and this depression sharpened to a cutting edge. A knife is essential, because after wading neck deep in a swamp your revolver is neither use nor ornament until you have had time to clean it. But the chances are you may go across Africa, or live years in it, and require neither. It is just the case of the gentleman who asked if one required a revolver in Carolina and was answered, "You may be here one year, and you may be here two and never want it; but when you do want it you'll want it very bad."

The cannibalism of the Fans, although a prevalent habit, is no danger, I think, to white people, except as regards the bother it gives one in preventing one's black companions from getting eaten. The Fan is not a cannibal from sacrificial motives like the negro. He does it in his common sense way. Man's flesh, he says, is good to eat, very good, and he wishes you would try it. Oh dear no, he never eats it himself, but the next door town does. He is always very much abused for eating his relations, but he really does not do this. He will eat his next door neighbour's relations and sell his own deceased to his next door neighbour in return; but he does not buy slaves and fatten them up for his table as some of the Middle Congo tribes I know of do. He has no slaves, no prisoners of war, no cemeteries, so you must draw your own conclusions. No, my friend, I will not tell you any cannibal stories. I have heard how good M. du Chaillu fared after telling you some beauties, and now you come away from the Fan village and down the Rembwé river.

CHAPTER XI

DOWN THE REMBWÉ

Setting forth how the Voyager descends the Rembwé River,
with divers excursions and alarms, in the company of a black
trader, and returns safely to the Coast.

Getting away from Agonjo seemed as if it would be nearly as difficult as getting to it, but as the quarters were comfortable and the society fairly good, I was not anxious. I own the local scenery was a little too much of the Niger Delta type for perfect beauty, just the long lines of mangrove, and the muddy river lounging almost imperceptibly to sea, and nothing else in sight. Mr. Glass, however, did not take things so philosophically. I was on his commercial conscience, for I had come in from the bush and there was money in me. Therefore I was a trade product—a new trade stuff that ought to be worked up and developed; and he found himself unable to do this, for although he had secured the first parcel, as it were, and got it successfully stored, yet he could not ship it, and he felt this was a reproach to him.

Many were his lamentations that the firm had not provided him with a large sailing canoe and a suitable crew to deal with this new line of trade. I did my best to comfort him, pointing out that the most enterprising firm could not be expected to provide expensive things like these, on the extremely remote chance of ladies arriving per bush at Agonjo—in fact not until the trade in them was well developed. But he refused to see it in this light and harped upon the subject, wrapped up, poor man, in a great coat and a muffler, because his ague was on him.

I next tried to convince Mr. Glass that any canoe would do for me to go down in. "No," he said, "any canoe will not do;" and he explained that when you got down the Rembwé to 'Como Point you were in a rough, nasty bit of water, the Gaboon, which has a fine confused set of currents from the tidal wash and the streams of the Rembwé and 'Como rivers, in which it would be improbable that a river canoe could live any time worth mentioning. Progress below 'Como Point by means of mere paddling he considered impossible. There was nothing for it but a big sailing canoe, and there was no big sailing canoe to be had. I think Mr. Glass got a ray of comfort out of the fact that Messrs. John Holt's sub-agent was, equally with himself, unable to ship me.

At this point in the affair there entered a highly dramatic figure. He came on to the scene suddenly and with much uproar, in a way that would have made his fortune in a transpontine drama. I shall always regret I have not got that man's portrait, for I cannot do him justice with ink. He dashed up on to the verandah, smote the frail form of Mr. Glass between the shoulders, and flung his own massive one into a chair. His name was Obanjo, but he liked it pronounced Captain Johnson, and his profession was a bush and river trader on his own account. Every movement of the man was theatrical, and he used to look covertly at you every now and then to see if he had produced his impression, which was evidently intended to be that of a reckless, rollicking skipper. There was a Hallo-my-Hearty atmosphere coming off him from the top of his hat to the soles of his feet, like the scent off a flower; but it did not require a genius in judging men to see that behind, and under this was a very different sort of man, and if I should ever want to engage in a wild and awful career up a West African river I shall start on it by engaging Captain Johnson. He struck me as being one of those men, of whom I know five, whom I could rely on, that if one of them and I went into the utter bush together, one of us at least would come out alive and have made something substantial by the venture; which is a great deal more than I could say, for example, of Ngouta, who was still with me, as he desired to see the glories of Gaboon and buy a hanging lamp.

Captain Johnson's attire calls for especial comment and admiration. However disconnected the two sides of his character might be, his clothes bore the impress of both of his natures to perfection. He wore, when first we met, a huge sombrero hat, a spotless singlet, and a suit of clean, well-got-up dungaree, and an uncommonly picturesque, powerful figure he cut in them, with his finely moulded, well-knit form and good-looking face, full of expression always, but always with the keen small eyes in it watching the effect his genial smiles and hearty laugh produced. The eyes were the eyes of Obanjo, the rest of the face the property of Captain Johnson. I do not mean to say that they were the eyes of a bad bold man, but you had not to look twice at them to see they belonged to a man courageous in the African manner, full of energy and resource, keenly intelligent and self-reliant, and all that sort of thing.

I left him and the refined Mr. Glass together to talk over the palaver of shipping me, and they talked it at great length. Finally the price I was to

pay Obanjo was settled and we proceeded to less important details. It seemed
Obanjo, when up the river this time, had set about constructing a new and large
trading canoe at one of his homes, in which he was just thinking of taking his
goods down to Gaboon. Next morning Obanjo with his vessel turned up, and
saying farewell to my kind host, Mr. Sanga Glass, I departed.

She had the makings of a fine vessel in her; though roughly hewn out of an
immense hard-wood tree: her lines were good, and her type was that of the big
sea-canoes of the Bight of Panavia. Very far forward was a pole mast, roughly
made, but European in intention, and carrying a long gaff. Shrouds and stays
it had not, and my impression was that it would be carried away if we dropped
in for half a tornado, until I saw our sail and recognised that that would go to
darning cotton instantly if it fell in with even a breeze. It was a bed quilt that
had evidently been in the family some years, and although it had been in places
carefully patched with pieces of previous sets of the captain's dungarees, in other
places, where it had not, it gave "free passage to the airs of Heaven"; which I
may remark does not make for speed in the boat mounting such canvas. Partly
to this sail, partly to the amount of trading affairs we attended to, do I owe the
credit of having made a record trip down the Rembwé, the slowest white man
time on record.

Fixed across the stern of the canoe there was the usual staging made of bam-
boos, flush with the gunwale. Now this sort of staging is an exceedingly good
idea when it is fully finished. You can stuff no end of things under it; and over
it there is erected a hood of palm-thatch, giving a very comfortable cabin five or
six feet long and about three feet high in the centre, and you can curl yourself
up in it and, if you please, have a mat hung across the opening. But we had not
got so far as that yet on our vessel, only just got the staging fixed in fact; and
I assure you a bamboo staging is but a precarious perch when in this stage of
formation. I made myself a reclining couch on it in the Roman manner with
my various belongings, and was exceeding comfortable until we got nearly out
of the Rembwé into the Gaboon. Then came grand times. Our noble craft had
by this time got a good list on her from our collected cargo—ill stowed. This
made my home, the bamboo staging, about as reposeful a place as the slope of
a writing desk would be if well polished; and the rough and choppy sea gave
our vessel the most peculiar set of motions imaginable. She rolled, which made
it precarious for things on the bamboo staging, but still a legitimate motion,
natural and foreseeable. In addition to this, she had a cataclysmic kick in her—
that I think the heathenish thing meant to be a pitch—which no mortal being
could foresee or provide against, and which projected portable property into the
waters of the Gaboon over the stern and on to the conglomerate collection in
the bottom of the canoe itself, making Obanjo repeat, with ferocity and feeling,

words he had heard years ago, when he was boatswain on a steamboat trading on the Coast. It was fortunate, you will please understand, for my future, that I have usually been on vessels of the British African or the African lines when voyaging about this West African sea-board, as the owners of these vessels prohibit the use of bad language on board, or goodness only knows what words I might not have remembered and used in the Gaboon estuary.

We left Agonjo with as much bustle and shouting and general air of brisk seamanship as Obanjo could impart to the affair, and the hopeful mind might have expected to reach somewhere important by nightfall. I did not expect that; neither, on the other hand, did I expect that after we had gone a mile and only four, as the early ballad would say, that we should pull up and anchor against a small village for the night; but this we did, the captain going ashore to see for cargo, and to get some more crew.

There were grand times ashore that night, and the captain returned on board about 2 A.M. with some rubber and pissava and two new hands whose appearance fitted them to join our vessel; for a more villainous-looking set than our crew I never laid eye on. One enormously powerful fellow looked the incarnation of the horrid negro of buccaneer stories, and I admired Obanjo for the way he kept them in hand. We had now also acquired a small dug-out canoe as tender, and a large fishing-net. About 4 A.M. in the moonlight we started to drop down river on the tail of the land breeze, and as I observed Obanjo wanted to sleep I offered to steer. After putting me through an examination in practical seamanship, and passing me, he gladly accepted my offer, handed over the tiller which stuck out across my bamboo staging, and went and curled himself up, falling sound asleep among the crew in less time than it takes to write. On the other nights we spent on this voyage I had no need to offer to steer; he handed over charge to me as a matter of course, and as I prefer night to day in Africa, I enjoyed it. Indeed, much as I have enjoyed life in Africa, I do not think I ever enjoyed it to the full as I did on those nights dropping down the Rembwé. The great, black, winding river with a pathway in its midst of frosted silver where the moonlight struck it: on each side the ink-black mangrove walls, and above them the band of star and moonlit heavens that the walls of mangrove allowed one to see. Forward rose the form of our sail, idealised from bed-sheetdom to glory; and the little red glow of our cooking fire gave a single note of warm colour to the cold light of the moon. Three or four times during the second night, while I was steering along by the south bank, I found the mangrove wall thinner, and standing up, looked through the network of their roots and stems on to what seemed like plains, acres upon acres in extent, of polished silver—more specimens of those awful slime lagoons, one of which, before we reached Ndorko, had so very nearly collected me. I watched them, as we leisurely stole past, with a sort of fascination. On the second night, towards the dawn, I had the great joy of seeing Mount Okoneto, away to the S.W., first showing moonlit, and then taking the colours of the dawn before they reached us down below. Ah me! give me a West African river and a canoe for sheer good pleasure. Drawbacks, you say? Well, yes, but where are there not drawbacks? The only drawbacks on those Rembwé nights were the series of horrid frights I got by steering on to tree shadows and thinking they were mud banks, or trees themselves, so black and solid did they seem. I never roused the watch fortunately, but got her off the shadow gallantly single-handed every time, and called myself a fool instead of getting called one. My nautical friends carp at me for getting on shadows, but I beg them to consider before they judge me, whether they have ever steered at night down a river quite unknown to them an unhandy canoe, with a bed-sheet sail, by the light of the moon. And what with my having a theory of my own regarding the proper way to take a vessel round a corner, and what with having to keep the wind in the bed-sheet where the bed-sheet would hold it, it's a wonder to me I did not cast that vessel away, or go and damage Africa.

By daylight the Rembwé scenery was certainly not so lovely, and might be slept through without a pang. It had monotony, without having enough of it to amount to grandeur. Every now and again we came to villages, each of which was situated on a heap of clay and sandy soil, presumably the end of a spit of land running out into the mangrove swamp fringing the river. Every village we saw we went alongside and had a chat with, and tried to look up cargo in the proper way. One village in particular did we have a lively time at. Obanjo had a wife and home there, likewise a large herd of goats, some of which he was desirous of taking down with us to sell at Gaboon. It was a pleasant-looking village, with a clean yellow beach which most of the houses faced. But it had ramifications in the interior. I being very lazy, did not go ashore, but watched the pantomime from the bamboo staging. The whole flock of goats enter at right end of stage, and tear violently across the scene, disappearing at left. Two minutes elapse. Obanjo and his gallant crew enter at right hand of stage, leg it like lamplighters across front, and disappear at left. Fearful pow-wow behind the scenes. Five minutes elapse. Enter goats at right as before, followed by Obanjo and company as before, and so on da capo. It was more like a fight I once saw between the armies of Macbeth and Macduff than anything I have seen before or since; only our Rembwé play was better put on, more supers, and noise, and all that sort of thing, you know. It was a spirited performance I assure you and I and the inhabitants of the village, not personally interested in goat-catching, assumed the rôle of audience and cheered it to the echo.

We had another cheerful little incident that afternoon. While we were going along softly, softly as was our wont, in the broiling heat, I wishing I had an umbrella—for sitting on that bamboo stage with no sort of protection from the sun was hot work after the forest shade I had had previously—two small boys in two small canoes shot out from the bank and paddled hard to us and jumped on board. After a few minutes' conversation with Obanjo one of them carefully sank his canoe; the other just turned his adrift and they joined our crew. I saw they were Fans, as indeed nearly all the crew were, but I did not think much of the affair. Our tender, the small canoe, had been sent out as usual with the big black man and another A. B. to fish; it being one of our industries to fish hard all the time with that big net. The fish caught, sometimes a bushel or two at a time, almost all grey mullet, were then brought alongside, split open, and cleaned. We then had all round as many of them for supper as we wanted, the rest we hung on strings over our fire, more or less insufficiently smoking them to prevent decomposition, it being Obanjo's intention to sell them when he made his next trip up the 'Como; for the latter being less rich in fish than the Rembwé they would command a good price there. We always had our eye on things like this, being, I proudly remark, none of your gilded floating hotel of a ferry-boat like those Cunard or White Star liners are, but just a good trader that was not ashamed to pay, and not afraid of work.

Well, just after we had leisurely entered a new reach of the river, round the corner after us, propelled at a phenomenal pace, came our fishing canoe, which we had left behind to haul in the net and then rejoin us. The occupants, particularly the big black A. B., were shouting something in terror stricken accents. "What?" says Obanjo springing to his feet. "The Fan! the Fan!" shouted the canoe men as they shot towards us like agitated chickens making for their hen. In another moment they were alongside and tumbling over our gunwale into the bottom of the vessel still crying "The Fan! The Fan! The Fan!" Obanjo then by means of energetic questioning externally applied, and accompanied by florid language that cast a rose pink glow smelling of sulphur, round us, elicited the information that about 40,000 Fans, armed with knives and guns, were coming down the Rembwé with intent to kill and slay us, and might be expected to arrive within the next half wink. On hearing this, the whole of our gallant crew took up masterly recumbent positions in the bottom of our vessel and turned gray round the lips. But Obanjo rose to the situation like ten lions. "Take the rudder," he shouted to me, "take her into the middle of the stream and keep the sail full." It occurred to me that perhaps a position underneath the bamboo staging might be more healthy than one on the top of it, exposed to every microbe of a bit of old iron and what not and a half that according to native testimony would shortly be frisking through the atmosphere from those Fan guns; and moreover I had not forgotten having been previously shot in a somewhat similar situation, though in better company. However I did not say anything; neither, between ourselves, did I somehow believe in those Fans. So regardless of danger, I grasped the helm, and sent our gallant craft flying before the breeze down the bosom of the great wild river (that's the proper way to put it, but in the interests of science it may be translated into crawling towards the middle). Meanwhile Obanjo performed prodigies of valour all over the place. He triced up the mainsail, stirred up his fainthearted crew, and got out the sweeps, i.e. one old oar and four paddles, and with this assistance we solemnly trudged away from danger at a pace that nothing slower than a Thames dumb barge, going against stream, could possibly overhaul. Still we did not feel safe, and I suggested to Ngouta he should rise up and help; but he declined, stating he was a married man. Obanjo cheering the paddlers with inspiriting words sprang with the agility of a leopard on to the bamboo staging aft, standing there with his gun ready loaded and cocked to face the coming foe, looking like a stat- ue put up to himself at the public expense. The worst of this was, however, that while Obanjo's face was to the coming foe, his back was to the crew, and they forthwith commenced to re-subside into the bottom of the boat, paddles and all. I, as second in command, on seeing this, said a few blood-stirring words to them, and Obanjo sent a few more of great power at them over his shoulder, and so we kept the paddles going.

Presently from round the corner shot a Fan canoe. It contained a lady in the bows, weeping and wringing her hands, while another lady sympathetically howling, paddled it. Obanjo in lurid language requested to be informed why they were following us. The lady in the bows said, "My son! my son!" and in a second more three other canoes shot round the corner full of men with guns. Now this looked like business, so Obanjo and I looked round to urge our crew to greater exertions and saw, to our disgust, that the gallant band had success- fully subsided into the bottom of the boat while we had been eyeing the foe. Obanjo gave me a recipe for getting the sweeps out again. I did not follow it, but got the job done, for Obanjo could not take his eye and gun off the leading canoe and the canoes having crept up to within some twenty yards of us, poured out their simple tale of woe.

It seemed that one of those miscreant boys was a runaway from a Fan vil- lage. He had been desirous, with the usual enterprise of young Fans, of seeing the great world that he knew lay down at the mouth of the river, i.e. Libreville Gaboon. He had pleaded with his parents for leave to go down and engage in work there, but the said parents holding the tenderness of his youth unfitted to combat with Coast Town life and temptation, refused this request, and so the young rascal had run away without leave and with a canoe, and was surmised to have joined the well-known Obanjo. Obanjo owned he had (more armed canoes were coming round the corner), and said if the mother would come and fetch her boy she could have him. He for his part would not have dreamed of taking him if he had known his relations disapproved. Every one seemed much relieved, except the causa belli. The Fans did not ask about two boys and providentially we gave the lady the right one. He went reluctantly. I feel pretty nearly sure he foresaw more kassengo than fatted calf for him on his return home. When the Fan canoes were well back round the corner again, we had a fine hunt for the other boy, and finally unearthed him from under the bamboo staging.

When we got him out he told the same tale. He also was a runaway who wanted to see the world, and taking the opportunity of the majority of the people of his village being away hunting, he had slipped off one night in a canoe, and dropped down river to the village of the boy who had just been reclaimed. The two boys had fraternised, and come on the rest of their way together, lying waiting, hidden up a creek, for Obanjo, who they knew was coming down river; and having successfully got picked up by him, they thought they were safe. But after this affair boy number two judged there was no more safety yet, and that his family would be down after him very shortly; for he said he was a more valuable and important boy than his late companion, but his family were an uncommon savage set. We felt not the least anxiety to make their acquaintance, so clapped heels on our gallant craft and kept the paddles going, and as no more Fans were in sight our crew kept at work bravely. While Obanjo, now in a boisterous state of mind, and flushed with victory, said things to them about the way they had collapsed when those two women in a canoe came round that corner, that must have blistered their feelings, but they never winced. They laughed at the joke against themselves merrily. The other boy's family we never saw and so took him safely to Gaboon, where Obanjo got him a good place.

Really how much danger there was proportionate to the large amount of fear on our boat I cannot tell you. It never struck me there was any, but on the other hand the crew and Obanjo evidently thought it was a bad place; and my white face would have been no protection, for the Fans would not have suspected a white of being on such a canoe and might have fired on us if they had been unduly irritated and not treated by Obanjo with that fine compound of bully and blarney that he is such a master of.

Whatever may have been the true nature of the affair, however, it had one good effect, it got us out of the Rembwé into the Gaboon, and although at the time this seemed a doubtful blessing, it made for progress. I had by this time mastered the main points of incapability in our craft. A. we could not go against the wind. B. we could not go against the tide. While we were in the Rembwé there was a state we will designate as C - the tide coming one way, the wind another. With this state we could progress, backwards if the wind came up against us too strong, but seawards if it did not, and the tide was running

down. If the tide was running up, and the wind was coming down, then we
went seaward, softly, softly alongside the mangrove bank, where the rip of the
tide stream is least. When, however, we got down off 'Como Point, we met
there a state I will designate as D - a fine confused set of marine and fluvial
phenomena. For away to the north the 'Como and Boqué and two other lesser,
but considerable streams, were, with the Rembwé, pouring down their waters
in swirling, intermingling, interclashing currents; and up against them, to make
confusion worse confounded, came the tide, and the tide up the Gaboon is a
swift strong thing, and irregular, and has a rise of eight feet at the springs, two-
and-a-half at the neaps. The wind was lulled too, it being evening time. In this
country it is customary for the wind to blow from the land from 8 P.M. until 8
A.M., from the south-west to the east. Then comes a lull, either an utter dead
hot brooding calm, or light baffling winds and draughts that breathe a few
panting hot breaths into your sails and die. Then comes the sea breeze up from
the south-south-west or north-west, some days early in the forenoon, some days
not till two or three o'clock. This breeze blows till sundown, and then comes
another and a hotter calm.

Fortunately for us we arrived off the head of the Gaboon estuary in this
calm, for had we had wind to deal with we should have come to an end. There
were one or two wandering puffs, about the first one of which sickened our
counterpane of its ambitious career as a marine sail, so it came away from its
gaff and spread itself over the crew, as much as to say, "Here, I've had enough
of this sailing. I'll be a counterpane again." We did a great deal of fine varied,
spirited navigation, details of which, however, I will not dwell upon because
it was successful. We made one or two circles, taking on water the while and
then returned into the south bank backwards. At that bank we wisely stayed
for the night, our meeting with the Gaboon so far having resulted in wrecking
our sail, making Ngouta sea-sick and me exasperate; for from our noble vessel
having during the course of it demonstrated for the first time her cataclysmic
kicking power, I had had a time of it with my belongings on the bamboo stage.
A basket constructed for catching human souls in, given me as a farewell gift
by a valued friend, a witch doctor, and in which I kept the few things in life I
really cared for, i.e. my brush, comb, tooth brush, and pocket handkerchiefs,
went over the stern; while I was recovering this with my fishing line (such was
the excellent nature of the thing, I am glad to say it floated) a black bag with
my blouses and such essentials went away to leeward. Obanjo recovered that,
but meanwhile my little portmanteau containing my papers and trade tobacco
slid off to leeward; and as it also contained geological specimens of the Sierra
del Cristal, a massive range of mountains, it must have hopelessly sunk had it
not been for the big black, who grabbed it. All my bedding, six Equetta cloths,

given me by Mr. Hamilton in Opobo River before I came South, did get away successfully, but were picked up by means of the fishing line, wet but safe. After this I did not attempt any more Roman reclining couch luxuries, but stowed all my loose gear under the bamboo staging, and spent the night on the top of the stage, dozing precariously with my head on my knees.

When the morning broke, looking seaward I saw the welcome forms of König (Dambe) and Perroquet (Mbini) Islands away in the distance, looking, as is their wont, like two lumps of cloud that have dropped on to the broad Gaboon, and I felt that I was at last getting near something worth reaching, i.e. Glass, which though still out of sight, I knew lay away to the west of those islands on the northern shore of the estuary. And if any one had given me the choice of being in Glass within twenty-four hours from the mouth of the Rembwé, or in Paris or London in a week, I would have chosen Glass without a moment's hesitation. Much as I dislike West Coast towns as a general rule, there are exceptions, and of all exceptions, the one I like most is undoubtedly Glass Gaboon; and its charms loomed large on that dank chilly morning after a night spent on a bamboo staging in an unfinished native canoe.

The Rembwé, like the 'Como, is said to rise in the Sierra del Cristal. It is navigable to a place called Isango which is above Agonjo; just above Agonjo it receives an affluent on its southern bank and runs through mountain country, where its course is blocked by rapids for anything but small canoes. Obanjo did not seem to think this mattered, as there was not much trade up there, and therefore no particular reason why any one should want to go higher up. Moreover he said the natives were an exceedingly bad lot; but Obanjo usually thinks badly of the bush natives in these regions. Anyhow they are Fans—and Fans are Fans. He was anxious for me, however, to start on a trading voyage with him up another river, a notorious river, in the neighbouring Spanish territory. The idea was I should buy goods at Glass and we should go together and he would buy ivory with them in the interior. I anxiously inquired where my profits were to come in. Obanjo who had all the time suspected me of having trade motives, artfully said, "What for you come across from Ogowé? You say, see this country. Ah! I say you come with me. I show you plenty country, plenty men, elephants, leopards, gorillas. Oh! plenty thing. Then you say where's my trade?" I disclaimed trade motives in a lordly way. Then says he, "You come with me up there." I said I'd see about it later on, for the present I had seen enough men, elephants, gorillas and leopards, and I preferred to go into wild districts under the French flag to any flag. I am still thinking about taking that voyage, but I'll not march through Coventry with the crew we had down the Rembwé—that's flat, as Sir John Falstaff says. Picture to yourselves, my friends, the charming situation of being up a river surrounded by rapacious savages with a lot of valuable goods in a canoe and with only a crew to defend them possessed of such fighting mettle as our crew had demonstrated themselves to be. Obanjo might be all right, would be I dare say; but suppose he got shot and you had eighteen stone odd of him thrown on your hands in addition to your other little worries. There is little doubt such an excursion would be rich in incident and highly interesting, but I am sure it would be, from a commercial point of view, a failure.

Trade has a fascination for me, and going transversely across the nine-mile-broad rough Gaboon estuary in an unfinished canoe with an inefficient counterpane sail has none; but I return duty bound to this unpleasant subject. We started very early in the morning. We reached the other side entangled in the trailing garments of the night. I was thankful during that broiling hot day of one thing, and that was that if Sister Ann was looking out across the river, as was Sister Ann's invariable way of spending spare moments, Sister Ann would never think I was in a canoe that made such audaciously bad tacks, missed stays, got into irons, and in general behaved in a way that ought to have lost her captain his certificate. Just as the night came down, however, we reached the northern shore of the Grand Gaboon at Dongila, just off the mouth of the 'Como, still some eleven miles east of König Island, and further still from Glass, but on the same side of the river, which seemed good work. The foreshore here is very rocky, so we could not go close alongside but anchored out among the rocks. At this place there is a considerable village and a station of the Roman Catholic Mission. When we arrived a nun was down on the shore with her school children, who were busy catching shell-fish and generally merry-making. Obanjo went ashore in the tender, and the holy sister kindly asked me, by him, to come ashore and spend the night; but I was dead tired and felt quite unfit for polite society after the long broiling hot day and getting soaked by water that had washed on board.

We lay off Dongila all night, because of the tide. I lay off everything, Dongila, canoe and all, a little after midnight. Obanjo and almost all the crew stayed on shore that night, and I rolled myself up in an Equetta cloth and went sound and happily asleep on the bamboo staging, leaving the canoe pitching slightly. About midnight some change in the tide, or original sin in the canoe, caused her to softly swing round a bit, and the next news was that I was in the water. I had long expected this to happen, so was not surprised, but highly disgusted, and climbed on board, needless to say, streaming. So, in the darkness of the night I got my portmanteau from the hold and thoroughly tidied up. The next morning we were off early, coasting along to Glass, and safely arriving there, I attempted to look as unconcerned as possible, and vaguely hoped Mr. Hudson would be down in Libreville; for I was nervous about meeting him, knowing that since he had carefully deposited me in safe hands with Mme. Jacot, with many injunctions to be careful, that there were many incidents in my career that would not meet with his approval. Vain hope! he was on the pier! He did not approve! He had heard of most of my goings on.

This however in no way detracts from my great obligation to Mr. Hudson, but adds another item to the great debt of gratitude I owe him; for had it not been for him I should never have seen the interior of this beautiful region of the Ogowé. I tried to explain to him how much I had enjoyed myself and how I realised I owed it all to him; but he persisted in his opinion that my intentions and ambitions were suicidal, and took me out the ensuing Sunday, as it were on a string.

CHAPTER XII

FETISH

IN WHICH THE VOYAGER ATTEMPTS CAUTIOUSLY TO APPROACH THE SUB-JECT OF FETISH, AND GIVES A CLASSIFICATION OF SPIRITS, AND SOME ACCOUNT OF THE IBET AND ORUNDA.

HAVING GIVEN SOME ACCOUNT of my personal experiences among an African tribe in its original state, i.e. in a state uninfluenced by European ideas and culture, I will make an attempt to give a rough sketch of the African form of thought and the difficulties of studying it, because the study of this thing is my chief motive for going to West Africa. Since 1893 I have been collecting information in its native state regarding Fetish, and I use the usual terms fetish and ju-ju because they have among us a certain fixed value—a conventional value, but a useful one. Neither "fetish" nor "ju-ju" are native words. Fetish comes from the word the old Portuguese explorers used to designate the objects they thought the natives worshipped, and in which they were wise enough to recognise a certain similarity to their own little images and relics of Saints, "Feitiço." Ju-ju, on the other hand, is French, and comes from the word for a toy or doll, {286} so it is not so applicable as the Portuguese name, for the native image is not a doll or toy, and has far more affinity to the image of a saint, inasmuch as it is not venerated for itself, or treasured because of its prettiness, but only because it is the residence, or the occasional haunt, of a spirit.

Stalking the wild West African idea is one of the most charming pursuits in the world. Quite apart from the intellectual, it has a high sporting interest; for its pursuit is as beset with difficulty and danger as grizzly bear hunting, yet the climate in which you carry on this pursuit—vile as it is—is warm, which to me is almost an essential of existence. I beg you to understand that I make no pretension to a thorough knowledge of Fetish ideas; I am only on the threshold.

"Ich weiss nicht all doch viel ist mir bekannt," as Faust said—and, like him after he had said it, I have got a lot to learn.

I do not intend here to weary you with more than a small portion of even my present knowledge, for I have great collections of facts that I keep only to compare with those of other hunters of the wild idea, and which in their present state are valueless to the cabinet ethnologist. Some of these may be rank lies, some of them mere individual mind-freaks, others have underlying them some idea I am not at present in touch with.

The difficulty of gaining a true conception of the savage's real idea is great and varied. In places on the Coast where there is, or has been, much missionary influence the trouble is greatest, for in the first case the natives carefully conceal things they fear will bring them into derision and contempt, although they still keep them in their innermost hearts; and in the second case, you have a set of traditions which are Christian in origin, though frequently altered almost beyond recognition by being kept for years in the atmosphere of the African mind. For example, there is this beautiful story now extant among the Cabindas. God made at first all men black—He always does in the African story—and then He went across a great river and called men to follow Him, and the wisest and the bravest and the best plunged into the great river and crossed it; and the water washed them white, so they are the ancestors of the white men. But the others were afraid too much, and said, "No, we are comfortable here; we have our dances, and our tom-toms, and plenty to eat—we won't risk it, we'll stay here"; and they remained in the old place, and from them come the black men. But to this day the white men come to the bank, on the other side of the river, and call to the black men, saying, "Come, it is better over here." I fear there is little doubt that this story is a modified version of some parable preached to the Cabindas at the time the Capuchins had such influence among them, before they were driven out of the lower Congo regions more than a hundred years ago, for political reasons by the Portuguese.

In the bush—where the people have been little, or not at all, in contact with European ideas—in some ways the investigation is easier; yet another set of difficulties confronts you. The difficulty that seems to occur most easily to people is the difficulty of the language. The West African languages are not difficult to pick up; nevertheless, there are an awful quantity of them and they are at the best most imperfect mediums of communication. No one who has been on the Coast can fail to recognise how inferior the native language is to the native's mind behind it—and the prolixity and repetition he has therefore to employ to make his thoughts understood.

The great comfort is the wide diffusion of that peculiar language, "trade English"; it is not only used as a means of intercommunication between whites and blacks, but between natives using two distinct languages. On the south-west Coast you find individuals in villages far from the sea, or a trading station, who know it, and this is because they have picked it up and employ it in their dealings with the Coast tribes and travelling traders. It is by no means an easy language to pick up—it is not a farrago of bad words and broken phrases, but is a definite structure, has a great peculiarity in its verb forms, and employs no genders. There is no grammar of it out yet; and one of the best ways of learning it is to listen to a seasoned second mate regulating the unloading or loading, of cargo, over the hatch of the hold. No, my Coast friends, I have not forgotten—but though you did not mean it helpfully, this was one of the best hints you ever gave me.

Another good way is the careful study of examples which display the highest style and the most correct diction; so I append the letter given by Mr. Hutchinson as being about the best bit of trade English I know.

"To Daddy nah Tampin Office, -

Ha Daddy, do, yah, nah beg you tell dem people for me; make dem Sally-own pussin know. Do yah. Berrah well.

Ah lib nah Pademba Road—one bwoy lib dah oberside lakah dem two Docter lib overside you Tampin office. Berrah well.

Dah bwoy head big too much—he say nah Militie Ban—he got one long long ting so so brass, someting lib dah go flip flap, dem call am key. Berrah well. Had! Dah bwoy kin blow!—she ah!—na marin, oh!—nah sun time, oh! nah evenin, oh!—nah middle night, oh!—all same—no make pussin sleep. Not ebry bit dat, more lib da! One Boney bwoy lib oberside nah he like blow bugle. When dem two woh-woh bwoy blow dem ting de nize too much too much.

When white man blow dat ting and pussin sleep he kin tap wah make dem bwoy carn do so? Dem bwoy kin blow ebry day eben Sunday dem kin blow. When ah yerry dem blow Sunday ah wish dah bugle kin go down na dem troat or dem kin blow them head-bone inside.

Do nah beg you yah tell all dem people 'bout dah ting wah dem two bwoy dah blow. Till am Amtrang Boboh hab febah bad. Till am titty carn sleep nah night. Dah nize go kill me two pickin, oh!

Plabba done. Good by Daddy.

Crashey Jane."

Now for the elementary student we will consider this letter. The complaint in Crashey Jane's letter is about two boys who are torturing her morning, noon, and night, Sunday and weekday, by blowing some "long long brass ting" as well as a bugle, and the way she dwells on their staying power must bring a sympathetic pang for that black sister into the heart of many a householder in London who lives next to a ladies' school, or a family of musical tastes. "One touch of nature," etc. "Daddy" is not a term of low familiarity but one of esteem and respect, and the "Tampin Office" is a respectful appellation for the Office of the "New Era" in which this letter was once published. "Bwoy head big too much," means that the young man is swelled with conceit because he is connected with "Militie ban." "Woh woh" you will find, among all the natives in the Bights, to mean extremely bad. I think it is native, having some connection with the root Wo—meaning power, etc.; but Mr. Hutchinson may be right, and it may mean "a capacity to bring double woe."

"Amtrang Boboh" is not the name of some uncivilised savage, as the uninitiated may think; far from it. It is Bob Armstrong—upside down, and slightly altered, and refers to the Hon. Robert Armstrong, stipendiary magistrate of Sierra Leone, etc.

"Berrah well" is a phrase used whenever the native thinks he has succeeded in putting his statement well. He sort of turns round and looks at it, says "Berrah well," in admiration of his own art, and then proceeds.

"Pickin" are children.

"Boney bwoy" is not a local living skeleton, but a native from Bonny River.

"Sally own" is Sierra Leone.

"Blow them head-bone inside" means, blow the top off their heads.

I have a collection of trade English letters and documents, for it is a language that I regard as exceedingly charming, and it really requires study, as you will see by reading Crashey Jane's epistle without the aid of a dictionary. It is, moreover, a language that will take you unexpectedly far in Africa, and if you do not understand it, land you in some pretty situations. One important point that you must remember is that the African is logically right in his answer to such a question as "You have not cleaned this lamp?"—he says, "Yes, sah"—which means, "yes, I have not cleaned the lamp." It does not mean a denial to your accusation; he always uses this form, and it is liable to confuse you at first, as are many other of the phrases, such as "I look him, I no see him "; this means "I have been searching for the thing but have not found it"; if he really meant he had looked upon the object but had been unable to get to it, he would say: "I look him, I no catch him," etc.

The difficulty of the language is, however, far less than the whole set of difficulties with your own mind. Unless you can make it pliant enough to follow the African idea step by step, however much care you may take, you will not bag your game. I heard an account the other day of a representative of Her Majesty in Africa who went out for a day's antelope shooting. There were plenty of antelope about, and he stalked them with great care; but always, just before he got within shot of the game, they saw something and bolted. Knowing he and the boy behind him had been making no sound and could not have been seen, he stalked on, but always with the same result; until happening to look round, he saw the boy behind him was supporting the dignity of the Empire at large, and this representative of it in particular, by steadfastly holding aloft the consular flag. Well, if you go hunting the African idea with the flag of your own religion or opinions floating ostentatiously over you, you will similarly get a very poor bag.

A few hints as to your mental outfit when starting on this sport may be useful. Before starting for West Africa, burn all your notions about sun-myths and worship of the elemental forces. My own opinion is you had better also burn the notion, although it is fashionable, that human beings got their first notion of the origin of the soul from dreams.

I went out with my mind full of the deductions of every book on Ethnology, German or English, that I had read during fifteen years—and being a good Cambridge person, I was particularly confident that from Mr. Frazer's book, The Golden Bough, I had got a semi-universal key to the underlying idea of native custom and belief. But I soon found this was very far from being the case. His idea is a true key to a certain quantity of facts, but in West Africa only to a limited quantity.

I do not say, do not read Ethnology—by all means do so; and above all things read, until you know it by heart, Primitive Culture, by Dr. E. B. Tylor, regarding which book I may say that I have never found a fact that flew in the face of the carefully made, broad-minded deductions of this greatest of Ethnologists. In addition you must know your Westermarck on Human Marriage, and your Waitz Anthropologie, and your Topinard—not that you need expect to go measuring people's skulls and chests as this last named authority expects you to do, for no self-respecting person black or white likes that sort of thing from the hands of an utter stranger, and if you attempt it you'll get yourself disliked in West Africa. Add to this the knowledge of all A. B. Ellis's works; Burton's Anatomy of Melancholy; Pliny's Natural History; and as much of Aristotle as possible. If you have a good knowledge of the Greek and Latin classics, I think it would be an immense advantage; an advantage I do not possess, for my classical knowledge is scrappy, and in place of it I have a knowledge of Red Indian dogma: a dogma by the way that seems to me much nearer the African in type than Asiatic forms of dogma.

Armed with these instruments of observation, with a little industry and care you should in the mill of your mind be able to make the varied tangled rag-bag of facts that you will soon become possessed of into a paper. And then I advise you to lay the results of your collection before some great thinker and he will write upon it the opinion that his greater and clearer vision makes him more fit to form.

You may say, Why not bring home these things in their raw state? And bring them home in a raw state you must, for purposes of reference; but in this state they are of little use to a person unacquainted with the conditions which surround them in their native homes. Also very few African stories bear on one subject alone, and they hardly ever stick to a point. Take this Fernando Po legend. Winwood Reade (Savage Africa, p. 62) gives it, and he says he heard it twice. I have heard it, in variants, four times—once on Fernando Po, once in Calabar and twice in Gaboon. So it is evidently an old story: -

"The first man called all people to one place. His name was Raychow. 'Hear this, my people' said he, 'I am going to give a name to every place, I am King in this River.' One day he came with his people to the Hole of Wonga Wonga, which is a deep pit in the ground from which fire comes at night. Men spoke to them from the Hole, but they could not see them. Raychow said to his son, 'Go down into the Hole'—and his son went. The son of the King of the Hole came to him and defied him to a contest of throwing the spear. If he lost he should be killed, if he won he should go back in safety. He won—then the son of the King of the Hole said, 'It is strange you should have won, for I am a spirit. Ask whatever you wish,' and the King's son asked for a remedy for every disease he could remember; and the spirit gave him the medicines, and when he had done so, he said, 'There is one sickness you have forgotten—it is the Krawkraw, and of that you shall die.'

"A tribe named Ndiva was then strong but now none remain (Winwood Reade says four remain). They gave Raychow's son a canoe and forty men, to take him back to his father's town, and when he saw his father he did not speak. His father said, 'My son, if you are hungry eat.' He did not answer, and his father said, 'Do you wish me to kill a goat?' He did not answer; his father said, 'Do you wish me to give you new wives?' He did not answer. Then his father said, 'Do you want me to build you a fetish hut?' Then he answered, 'Yes,' and the hut was built, and the medicines he had brought back from the Hole were put into it.

"'Now,' said the son of King Raychow, 'I go to make Moondah enter the Orongo' (Gaboon); so he went and dug a canal and when this was finished all his men were dead. Then he said, 'I will go and kill river-horse in the Benito.' He killed four, and as he was killing the fifth, the people descended from the mountains against him. So he made fetish on his great war-spear and sang

My spear, go kill these people,

Or these people will kill me;

and the spear went and killed the people, except a few who got into canoes and flew to Fernando Po. Then said their King, 'My people shall never wear cloth till we have conquered the M'pongwe,' and to this day the Fernando Poians go naked and hate with a special hatred the M'pongwe."

Now this is a noble story—there is a lot of fine confused feeding in it, as the Scotchman said of boiled sheep's head.

You learn from it -

A. The name of the first man, and also that he was filled with a desire for topographical nomenclature.

B. You hear of the Hole Wonga Wonga, and this is most interesting because to this day, apart from the story, you are told by the natives of a hole that emits fire, and Dr. Nassau says it is always said to be north of Gaboon; but so far no white man has any knowledge of an active volcano there, although the district is of volcanic origin. The crater of Fernando Po may be referred to in the legend because of the king's son being sent home in a canoe; but I do not think it is, because the Hole is known not to be Fernando Po, and it has got, according to local tradition, a river running from it or close to it.

C. The kraw-kraw is a frightfully prevalent disease; no one has a remedy for it, presumably owing to Raychow's son's forgetfulness.

D. The silence of the son to the questions is remarkable, because you always find people who have been among spirits lose their power of asking for what they want, for a time, and can only answer to the right question.

E. The sudden way in which Raychow's son gets fired with the desire to turn civil engineer just when he has got a magnificent opening in life as a doctor is merely the usual flightiness of young men, who do not see where their true advantages lie—and the conduct of the men in dying, after digging a canal is normal, and modern experiences support it, for men who dig canals down in West Africa die plentifully, be they black, white, or yellow; so you can't help believing in those men, although it is strange a black man should have been so enterprising as to go in for canal digging at all. There is no other case of it extant to my knowledge, and a remarkable fact is, that the Moondah does so nearly connect, by one creek, with the Gaboon estuary that you can drag a boat across the little intervening bit of land.

F. Is a sporting story that turns up a little unexpectedly, certainly; but the Benito is within easy distance north of the Moondah, so the geography is all right.

G. The inhabitants of Fernando Po have still an especial hatred for the M'pongwe, and both they and the M'pongwe have this account of the one tribe driving the other off the mainland. Then the Bubis {295} - as the inhabitants on Fernando Po are called, from a confusion arising in the minds of the sailors calling at Fernando Po, between their stupidity and their word Bâbi = stranger, which they use as a word of greeting—these Bubis are undoubtedly a very early African race. Their culture, though presenting some remarkable points, is on the whole exceedingly low.

They never wear clothes unless compelled to, and their language depends so much on gesture that they cannot talk in it to each other in the dark.

I give this as a sample of African stories. It is far more connected and keeps to the point in a far more business-like way than most of them. They are of great interest when you know the locality and the tribe they come from; but I am sure if you were to bring home a heap of stories like this, and empty them over any distinguished ethnologist's head, without ticketing them with the culture of the tribe they belonged to, the conditions it lives under, and so forth, you would stun him with the seeming inter-contradiction of some, and utter pointlessness of the rest, and he would give up ethnology and hurriedly devote his remaining years to the attempt to collect a million postage stamps, so as to do something definite before he died. Remember, you must always have your original material—carefully noted down at the time of occurrence—with you, so that you may say in answer to his Why? Because of this, and this, and this.

However good may be the outfit for your work that you take with you, you will have, at first, great difficulty in realising that it is possible for the people you are among really to believe things in the way they do. And you cannot associate with them long before you must recognise that these Africans have often a remarkable mental acuteness and a large share of common sense; that there is nothing really "child-like" in their form of mind at all. Observe them further and you will find they are not a flighty-minded, mystical set of people in the least. They are not dreamers, or poets, and you will observe, and I hope observe closely—for to my mind this is the most important difference between their make of mind and our own—that they are notably deficient in all mechanical arts: they have never made, unless under white direction and instruction, a single fourteenth-rate piece of cloth, pottery, a tool or machine, house, road, bridge, picture or statue; that a written language of their own construction they none of them possess. A careful study of the things a man, black or white, fails to do, whether for good or evil, usually gives you a truer knowledge of the man than the things he succeeds in doing. When you fully realise this acuteness on one hand and this mechanical incapacity on the other which exist in the people you are studying, you can go ahead. Only, I beseech you, go ahead carefully. When you have found the easy key that opens the reason underlying a series of facts, as for example, these: a Benga spits on your hand as a greeting; you see a man who has been marching regardless through the broiling sun all the forenoon, with a heavy load, on entering a village and having put down his load, elaborately steal round in the shelter of the houses, instead of crossing the street; you come across a tribe that cuts its dead up into small pieces and scatters them broadcast, and another tribe that thinks a white man's eye-ball is a most desirable thing to be possessed of—do not, when you have found this key, drop your collecting work, and go home with a shriek of "I know all about Fetish," because you don't, for the key to the above facts will not open the reason why it is regarded advisable to kill a person who is making Ikung; or why you should avoid at night a cotton tree that has red earth at its roots; or why combings of hair and paring of nails should be taken care of; or why a speck of blood that may fall from your flesh should be cut out of wood—if it has fallen on that— and destroyed, and if it has fallen on the ground stamped and rubbed into the soil with great care. This set requires another key entirely.

I must warn you also that your own mind requires protection when you send it stalking the savage idea through the tangled forests, the dark caves, the swamps and the fogs of the Ethiopian intellect. The best protection lies in rec- ognising the untrustworthiness of human evidence regarding the unseen, and also the seen, when it is viewed by a person who has in his mind an explanation of the phenomenon before it occurs. The truth is, the study of natural phenom- ena knocks the bottom out of any man's conceit if it is done honestly and not by selecting only those facts that fit in with his preconceived or ingrafted notions. And, to my mind, the wisest way is to get into the state of mind of an old ma- rine engineer who oils and sees that every screw and bolt of his engines is clean and well watched, and who loves them as living things, caressing and scolding them himself, defending them, with stormy language, against the aspersions of the silly, uninformed outside world, which persists in regarding them as mere machines, a thing his superior intelligence and experience knows they are not. Even animistic-minded I got awfully sat upon the other day in Cameroon by a superior but kindred spirit, in the form of a First Engineer. I had thoughtlessly repeated some scandalous gossip against the character of a naphtha launch in the river. "Stuff!" said he furiously; "she's all right, and she'd go from June to January if those blithering fools would let her alone." Of course I apologised.

The religious ideas of the Negroes, i.e. the West Africans in the district from the Gambia to the Cameroon region, say roughly to the Rio del Rey (for the Bakwiri appear to have more of the Bantu form of idea than the negro, although physically they seem nearer the latter), differ very considerably from the religious ideas of the Bantu South-West Coast tribes. The Bantu is vague on religious subjects; he gives one accustomed to the Negro the impression that he once had the same set of ideas, but has forgotten half of them, and those that he possesses have not got that hold on him that the corresponding or super-im- posed Christian ideas have over the true Negro; although he is quite as keen on the subject of witchcraft, and his witchcraft differs far less from the witchcraft of the Negro than his religious ideas do.

The god, in the sense we use the word, is in essence the same in all of the Bantu tribes I have met with on the Coast: a non-interfering and therefore a negligible quantity. He varies his name: Anzambi, Anyambi, Nyambi, Nzambi, Anzam, Nyam, Ukuku, Suku, and Nzam, but a better investigation shows that Nzam of the Fans is practically identical with Suku south of the Congo in the Bihe country, and so on.

They regard their god as the creator of man, plants, animals, and the earth, and they hold that having made them, he takes no further interest in the affair. But not so the crowd of spirits with which the universe is peopled, they take only too much interest and the Bantu wishes they would not and is perpetually saying so in his prayers, a large percentage whereof amounts to "Go away, we don't want you." "Come not into this house, this village, or its plantations." He knows from experience that the spirits pay little heed to these objurgations, and as they are the people who must be attended to, he develops a cult whereby they may be managed, used, and understood. This cult is what we call witchcraft.

As I am not here writing a complete work on Fetish I will leave Nzam on one side, and turn to the inferior spirits. These are almost all malevolent; sometimes they can be coaxed into having creditable feelings, like generosity and gratitude, but you can never trust them. No, not even if you are yourself a well-established medicine man. Indeed they are particularly dangerous to medicine men, just as lions are to lion tamers, and many a professional gentleman in the full bloom of his practice, gets eaten up by his own particular familiar which he has to keep in his own inside whenever he has not sent it off into other people's.

I am indebted to the Reverend Doctor Nassau for a great quantity of valuable information regarding Bantu religious ideas—information which no one is so competent to give as he, for no one else knows the West Coast Bantu tribes with the same thoroughness and sympathy. He has lived among them since 1851, and is perfectly conversant with their languages and culture, and he brings to bear upon the study of them a singularly clear, powerful, and highly-educated intelligence.

I shall therefore carefully ticket the information I have derived from him, so that it may not be mixed with my own. I may be wrong in my deductions, but Dr. Nassau's are above suspicion.

He says the origin of these spirits is vague—some of them come into existence by the authority of Anzam (by which you will understand, please, the same god I have quoted above as having many names), others are self-existent—many are distinctly the souls of departed human beings, "which in the future which is all around them" retain their human wants and feelings, and the Doctor assures me he has heard dying people with their last breath threatening to return as spirits to revenge themselves upon their living enemies. He could not tell me if there was any duration set upon the existence as spirits of these

human souls, but two Congo Français natives, of different tribes, Benga and Igalwa, told me that when a family had quite died out, after a time its spirits died
too. Some, but by no means all, of these spirits of human origin, as is the case
among the Negro Effiks, undergo reincarnation. The Doctor told me he once
knew a man whose plantations were devastated by an elephant. He advised that
the beast should be shot, but the man said he dare not because the spirit of his
dead father had passed into the elephant.

Their number is infinite and their powers as varied as human imagination
can make them; classifying them is therefore a difficult work, but Doctor Nassau thinks this may be done fairly completely into: -

1. Human disembodied spirits - Manu.

2. Vague beings, well described by our word ghosts: Abambo.

3. Beings something like dryads, who resent intrusion into their territory,
on to their rock, past their promontory, or tree. When passing the residence
of one of these beings, the traveller must go by silently, or with some cabalistic
invocation, with bowed or bared head, and deposit some symbol of an offering
or tribute even if it be only a pebble. You occasionally come across great trees
that have fallen across a path that have quite little heaps of pebbles, small shells,
etc., upon them deposited by previous passers-by. This class is called Ombwiri.

4. Beings who are the agents in causing sickness, and either aid or hinder
human plans - Mionde.

5. There seems to be, the Doctor says, another class of spirits somewhat
akin to the ancient Lares and Penates, who especially belong to the household,
and descend by inheritance with the family. In their honour are secretly kept a
bundle of finger, or other bones, nail-clippings, eyes, brains, skulls, particularly
the lower jaws, called in M'pongwe oginga, accumulated from deceased members of successive generations.

Dr. Nassau says "secretly," and he refers to this custom being existent in
non-cannibal tribes. I saw bundles of this character among the cannibal Fans,
and among the non-cannibal Adooma, openly hanging up in the thatch of the
sleeping apartment.

6. He also says there may be a sixth class, which may, however only be a
function of any of the other classes—namely, those that enter into any animal
body, generally a leopard. Sometimes the spirits of living human beings do
this, and the animal is then guided by human intelligence, and will exercise its
strength for the purposes of its temporary human possessor. In other cases it is
a non-human soul that enters into the animal, as in the case of Ukuku.

Spirits are not easily classified by their functions because those of different class may be employed in identical undertakings. Thus one witch doctor
may have, I find, particular influence over one class of spirit and another over

another class; yet they will both engage to do identical work. But in spite of this I do not see how you can classify spirits otherwise than by their functions; you cannot weigh and measure them, and it is only a few that show themselves in corporeal form.

There are characteristics that all the authorities seem agreed on, and one is that individual spirits in the same class vary in power: some are strong of their sort, some weak.

They are all to a certain extent limited in the nature of their power; there is no one spirit that can do all things; their efficiency only runs in certain lines of action and all of them are capable of being influenced, and made subservient to human wishes, by proper incantations. This latter characteristic is of course to human advantage, but it has its disadvantages, for you can never really trust a spirit, even if you have paid a considerable sum to a most distinguished medicine man to get a powerful one put up in a ju-ju, or monde, {301} as it is called in several tribes.

The method of making these charms is much the same among Bantu and Negroes: I have elsewhere described the Gold Coast method, so here confine myself to the Bantu. This similarity of procedure naturally arises from the same underlying idea existing in the two races.

You call in the medicine man, the "oganga," as he is commonly called in Congo Français tribes. After a variety of ceremonies and processes, the spirit is induced to localise itself in some object subject to the will of the possessor. The things most frequently used are antelopes' horns, the large snail-shells, and large nutshells, according to Doctor Nassau. Among the Fan I found the most frequent charm-case was in the shape of a little sausage, made very neatly of pineapple fibre, the contents being the residence of the spirit or power, and the outside coloured red to flatter and please him—for spirits always like red because it is like blood.

The substance put inside charms is all manner of nastiness, usually on the sea coast having a high percentage of fowl dung.

The nature of the substance depends on the spirit it is intended to be attractive to—attractive enough to induce it to leave its present abode and come and reside in the charm.

In addition to this attractive substance I find there are other materials inserted which have relation towards the work the spirit will be wanted to do for its owner. For example, charms made either to influence a person to be well disposed towards the owner, or the still larger class made with intent to work evil on other human beings against whom the owner has a grudge, must have in them some portion of the person to be dealt with—his hair, blood, nail-parings, etc.—or, failing that, his or her most intimate belonging, something that has got his smell in—a piece of his old waist-cloth for example.

This ability to obtain power over people by means of their blood, hair, nails, etc., is universally diffused; you will find it down in Devon, and away in far Cathay, and the Chinese, I am told, have in some parts of their empire little ovens to burn their nail- and hair-clippings in. The fear of these latter belongings falling into the hands of evilly-disposed persons is ever present to the West Africans. The Igalwa and other tribes will allow no one but a trusted friend to do their hair, and bits of nails and hair are carefully burnt or thrown away into a river; and blood, even that from a small cut or a fit of nose-bleeding, is most carefully covered up and stamped out if it has fallen on the earth. The underlying idea regarding blood is of course the old one that the blood is the life.

The life in Africa means a spirit, hence the liberated blood is the liberated spirit, and liberated spirits are always whipping into people who do not want them.

Charms are made for every occupation and desire in life—loving, hating, buying, selling, fishing, planting, travelling, hunting, etc., and although they are usually in the form of things filled with a mixture in which the spirit nestles, yet there are other kinds; for example, a great love charm is made of the water the lover has washed in, and this, mingled with the drink of the loved one, is held to soften the hardest heart.

Some kinds of charms, such as those to prevent your getting drowned, shot, seen by elephants, etc., are worn on a bracelet or necklace. A new-born child starts with a health-knot tied round the wrist, neck, or loins, and throughout the rest of its life its collection of charms goes on increasing. This collection does not, however, attain inconvenient dimensions, owing to the failure of some of the charms to work.

That is the worst of charms and prayers. The thing you wish of them may, and frequently does, happen in a strikingly direct way, but other times it does not. In Africa this is held to arise from the bad character of the spirits; their gross ingratitude and fickleness. You may have taken every care of a spirit for years, given it food and other offerings that you wanted for yourself, wrapped it up in your cloth on chilly nights and gone cold, put it in the only dry spot in the canoe, and so on, and yet after all this, the wretched thing will be capable of being got at by your rival or enemy and lured away, leaving you only the case it once lived in.

Finding, we will say, that you have been upset and half-drowned, and your canoe-load of goods lost three times in a week, that your paddles are always breaking, and the amount of snags in the river and so on is abnormal, you judge that your canoe-charm has stopped. Then you go to the medicine man who supplied you with it and complain. He says it was a perfectly good charm when he sold it you and he never had any complaints before, but he will investigate the affair; when he has done so, he either says the spirit has been lured away from the home he prepared for it by incantations and presents from other people, or that he finds the spirit is dead; it has been killed by a more powerful spirit of its class, which is in the pay of some enemy of yours. In all cases the little thing you kept the spirit in is no use now, and only fit to sell to a white man as "a big curio!" and the sooner you let him have sufficient money to procure you a fresh and still more powerful spirit—necessarily more expensive—the safer it will be for you, particularly as your misfortunes distinctly point to some one being desirous of your death. You of course grumble, but seeing the thing in his light you pay up, and the medicine man goes busily to work with incantations, dances, looking into mirrors or basins of still water, and concoctions of messes to make you a new protecting charm.

Human eye-balls, particularly of white men, I have already said are a great charm. Dr. Nassau says he has known graves rifled for them. This, I fancy, is to secure the "man that lives in your eyes" for the service of the village, and naturally the white man, being regarded as a superior being, would be of high value if enlisted into its service. A similar idea of the possibility of gaining possession of the spirit of a dead man obtains among the Negroes, and the heads of important chiefs in the Calabar districts are usually cut off from the body on burial and kept secretly for fear the head, and thereby the spirit, of the dead chief, should be stolen from the town. If it were stolen it would be not only a great advantage to its new possessor, but a great danger to the chief's old town; because he would know all the peculiar ju-ju relating to it. For each town has a peculiar one, kept exceedingly secret, in addition to the general ju-jus, and this secret one would then be in the hands of the new owners of the spirit. It is for similar reasons that brave General MacCarthy's head was treasured by the Ashantees, and so on.

Charms are not all worn upon the body, some go to the plantations, and are hung there, ensuring an unhappy and swift end for the thief who comes stealing. Some are hung round the bows of the canoe, others over the doorway of the house, to prevent evil spirits from coming in—a sort of tame watch-dog spirits.

The entrances to the long street-shaped villages are frequently closed with a fence of saplings and this sapling fence you will see hung with fetish charms to prevent evil spirits from entering the village and sometimes in addition to charms you will see the fence wreathed with leaves and flowers. Bells are frequently hung on these fences, but I do not fancy ever for fetish reasons. At Ndorko, on the Rembwé, there were many guards against spirit visitors, but the bell, which was carefully hung so that you could not pass through the gateway without ringing it, was a guard against thieves and human enemies only.

Frequently a sapling is tied horizontally near the ground across the entrance. Dr. Nassau could not tell me why, but says it must never be trodden on. When the smallpox, a dire pestilence in these regions, is raging, or when there is war, these gateways are sprinkled with the blood of sacrifices, and for these sacrifices and for the payments of heavy blood fines, etc., goats and sheep are kept. They are rarely eaten for ordinary purposes, and these West Coast Africans have all a perfect horror of the idea of drinking milk, holding this custom to be a filthy habit, and saying so in unmitigated language.

The villagers eat the meat of the sacrifice, that having nothing to do with the sacrifice to the spirits, which is the blood, for the blood is the life. {306}

Beside the few spirits that the Bantu regards himself as having got under control in his charms, he has to worship the uncontrolled army of the air. This he does by sacrifice and incantation.

The sacrifice is the usual killing of something valuable as an offering to the spirits. The value of the offering in these S.W. Coast regions has certainly a regular relationship to the value of the favour required of the spirits. Some favours are worth a dish of plantains, some a fowl, some a goat and some a human being, though human sacrifice is very rare in Congo Français, the killing of people being nine times in ten a witchcraft palaver.

Dr. Nassau, however, says that "the intention of the giver ennobles the gift," the spirit being supposed, in some vague way, to be gratified by the recognition of itself, and even sometimes pleased with the homage of the mere simulacrum of a gift. I believe the only class of spirits that have this convenient idea are the Imbwiri; thus the stones heaped by passers-by on the foot of some great tree, or rock, or the leaf cast from a passing canoe towards a promontory on the river, etc., although intrinsically valueless and useless to the Ombwiri nevertheless gratify him. It is a sort of bow or taking off one's hat to him. Some gifts, the Doctor says, are supposed to be actually utilised by the spirit.

In some part of the long single street of most villages there is built a low hut in which charms are hung, and by which grows a consecrated plant, a lily, a euphorbia, or a fig. In some tribes a rudely carved figure, generally female, is set up as an idol before which offerings are laid. I saw at Egaja two figures about 2 feet 6 inches high, in the house placed at my disposal. They were left in it during my occupation, save that the rolls of cloth (their power) which were round their necks, were removed by the owner chief; of the significance of these rolls I will speak elsewhere.

Incantations may be divided into two classes, supplications analogous to our idea of prayers, and certain cabalistic words and phrases. The supplications are addresses to the higher spirits. Some are made even to Anzam himself, but the spirit of the new moon is that most commonly addressed to keep the lower spirits from molesting.

Dr. Nassau gave me many instances out of the wealth of his knowledge. One night when he was stopping at a village, he saw standing out in the open street a venerable chief who addressed the spirits of the air and begged them, "Come ye not into my town;" he then recounted his good deeds, praising himself as good, just, honest, kind to his neighbours, and so on. I must remark that this man had not been in touch with Europeans, so his ideal of goodness was the native one—which you will find everywhere among the most remote West Coast natives. He urged these things as a reason why no evil should befall him, and closed with an impassioned appeal to the spirits to stay away. At another time, in another village, when a man's son had been wounded and a bleeding artery which the Doctor had closed had broken out again and the hæmorrhage seemed likely to prove fatal, the father rushed out into the street wildly gesticulating towards the sky, saying, "Go away, go away, go away, ye spirits, why do you come to kill my son?" In another case a woman rushed into the street, alternately objurgating and pleading with the spirits, who, she said, were vexing her child which had convulsions. "Observe," said the Doctor in his impressive way, "these were distinctly prayers, appeals for mercy, agonising protests, but there was no praise, no love, no thanks, no confession of sin." I said, considering the underlying idea, I did not see how that could be, thinking of the thing as they did, and the Doctor and I had one of our little disagreements. I shall always feel grateful to him for his great toleration of me, but I am sure this arose from his feeling that I saw there was an underlying idea in the minds of the people he loved well enough to lay down his life for in the hope of benefiting and ennobling them, and that I did not, as many do, set them down as idiotic brutes, glorying in an aimless cruelty that would be a disgrace to a devil.

Regarding the cabalistic words and phrases, things which had long given me great trouble to get any comprehension of, the Doctor gave me great help. He says some of these phrases and words are coined by the person himself, others are archaisms handed down from ancestors and believed to possess an efficacy, though their actual meaning is forgotten. He says they are used at any time as defence from evil, when a person is startled, sneezes, or stumbles. Among these I think I ought to class that peculiar form of friendly farewell or greeting which the Doctor poetically calls a "blown blessing" and the natives Ibata. I thought the three times it was given to me that it was just spitting on the hand. Practically it is so, but the Doctor says the spitting is accidental, a by-product I suppose. The method consists in taking the right hand in both yours, turning it palm upwards, bending your head low over it, and saying with great energy and a violent propulsion of the breath, Ibata.

Idols are comparatively rare in Congo Français, but where they are used the people have the same idea about them as the true Negroes have, namely, that they are things which spirits reside in, or haunt, but not in their corporeal nature adorable. The resident spirit in them and in the charms and plants, which are also regarded as residences of spirits, has to be placated with offerings of food and other sacrifices. You will see in the Fetish huts above mentioned dishes of plantain and fish left till they rot. Dr. Nassau says the life or essence of the food only is eaten by the spirit, the form of the vegetable or flesh being left to be removed when its life is gone out.

In cases of emergency a fowl with its blood is laid at the door of the Fetish hut, or when pestilence is expected, or an attack by enemies, or a great man or woman is very ill, goats and sheep are sacrificed and the blood put in the Fetish hut as well as on the gateways of the village. These sacrifices among the Fan are made with a very peculiar-shaped knife, a fine specimen of which I secured by the kindness of Captain Davies; it is shaped like the head of a hornbill and is quite unlike the knives in common use among the tribes, which are either long, leaf-shaped blades sharpened along both edges, or broad, trowel-shaped, almost triangular daggers. All Fan knives are fine weapons, superior to the knives of all other Coast tribes I have met with, but the sacrifice knife is distinctly peculiar. I found to my great interest the same superstition in Congo Français that I met with first in the Oil Rivers. Its meaning I am unable to fully account for, but I believe it to be a form of sacrifice. In Calabar each individual has a certain forbidden thing or things. These things are either forms of food, or the method of eating. In Calabar this prohibition is called Ibet, and when, in consequence of the influence of white culture, a man gives up his Ibet, he is regarded by good sound ju-juists as leading an irregular and dissipated life, and even the unintentional breaking of the Ibet is regarded as very dangerous. Special days are set apart by each individual; on these days he eats only the smallest quantity and plainest quality of food. No one must eat with him, nor any dog, fowl, etc., feed off the crumbs, nor any one watch him while eating. I suspect on this day the Ibet is eaten, but I have not verified this, only getting, from an untrust-worthy source, a statement that supported it.

Dr. Nassau told me that among Congo Français tribes certain rites are performed for children during infancy or youth, in which a prohibition is laid upon the child as regards the eating of some particular article of food, or the doing of certain acts. "It is difficult," he said, "to get the exact object of the 'Orunda.' Certainly the prohibited article is not in itself evil, for others but the inhibited individual may eat or do with it as they please. Most of the natives blindly follow the custom of their ancestors without being able to give any raison d'être, but again, from those best able to give a reason, you learn the prohibited article is a sacrifice ordained for the child by its parents and the magic doctor as a gift to the governing spirit of its life. The thing prohibited becomes removed from the child's common use, and is made sacred to the spirit. Any use of it by the child or man would therefore be a sin, which would bring down the spirit's wrath in the form of sickness or other evil, which can be atoned for only by expensive ceremonies or gifts to the magic doctor who intercedes for the offender."

Anything may be an Orunda or Ibet provided only that it is connected with food; I have been able to find no definite ground for the selection of it. The Doctor said, for example, that "once when on a boat journey, and camped in the forest for the noon-day meal, the crew of four had no meat. They needed it. I had a chicken but ate only a portion, and gave the rest to the crew. Three men ate it with their manioc meal, the fourth would not touch it. It was his Orunda." "On another journey," said the Doctor, "instead of all my crew leaving me respectfully alone in the canoe to have my lunch and going ashore to have theirs, one of them stayed behind in the canoe, and I found his Orunda was only to eat over water when on a journey by water." "At another place, a chief at whose village we once anchored in a small steamer when a glass of rum was given him, had a piece of cloth held up before his mouth that the people might not see him drink, which was his Orunda."

I know some ethnologists will think this last case should be classed under another head, but I think the Doctor is right. He is well aware of the existence of the other class of prohibitions regarding chiefs and I have seen plenty of chiefs myself up the Rembwé who have no objection to take their drinks coram publico, and I have no doubt this was only an individual Orunda of this particular Rembwé chief.

Great care is requisite in these matters, because a man may do or abstain from doing one and the same thing for divers reasons.

CHAPTER XIII

FETISH—(continued)

IN WHICH THE VOYAGER DISCOURSES ON DEATHS AND WITCHCRAFT, AND, WITH NO INTENTIONAL SLUR ON THE MEDICAL PROFESSION, ON MEDICAL METHODS AND BURIAL CUSTOMS, CONCLUDING WITH SUNDRY OBSERVATIONS ON TWINS.

IT IS EXCEEDINGLY INTERESTING TO COMPARE the ideas of the Negroes with those of the Bantu. The mental condition of the lower forms of both races seems very near the other great border-line that separates man from the anthropoid apes, and I believe that if we had the material, or rather if we could understand it, we should find little or no gap existing in mental evolution in this old, undisturbed continent of Africa.

Let, however, these things be as they may, one thing about Negro and Bantu races is very certain, and that is that their lives are dominated by a profound belief in witchcraft and its effects.

Among both alike the rule is that death is regarded as a direct consequence of the witchcraft of some malevolent human being, acting by means of spirits, over which he has, by some means or another, obtained control.

To all rules there are exceptions. Among the Calabar negroes, who are definite in their opinions, I found two classes of exceptions. The first arises from their belief in a bush-soul. They believe every man has four souls: a, the soul that survives death; b, the shadow on the path; c, the dream-soul; d, the bush-soul.

This bush-soul is always in the form of an animal in the forest—never of a plant. Sometimes when a man sickens it is because his bush-soul is angry at being neglected, and a witch-doctor is called in, who, having diagnosed this as being the cause of the complaint, advises the administration of some kind of offering to the offended one. When you wander about in the forests of the Calabar region, you will frequently see little dwarf huts with these offerings in them. You must not confuse these huts with those of similar construction you are continually seeing in plantations, or near roads, which refer to quite other affairs. These offerings, in the little huts in the forest, are placed where your bush-soul was last seen. Unfortunately, you are compelled to call in a doctor, which is an expense, but you cannot see your own bush-soul, unless you are an Ebumtup, a sort of second-sighter.

But to return to the bush-soul of an ordinary person. If the offering in the hut works well on the bush-soul, the patient recovers, but if it does not he dies. Diseases arising from derangements in the temper of the bush-soul however, even when treated by the most eminent practitioners, are very apt to be intractable, because it never realises that by injuring you it endangers its own existence. For when its human owner dies, the bush-soul can no longer find a good place, and goes mad, rushing to and fro—if it sees a fire it rushes into it; if it sees a lot of people it rushes among them, until it is killed, and when it is killed it is "finish" for it, as M. Pichault would say, for it is not an immortal soul.

The bush-souls of a family are usually the same for a man and for his sons, for a mother and for her daughters. Sometimes, however, I am told all the children take the mother's, sometimes all take the father's. They may be almost any kind of animal, sometimes they are leopards, sometimes fish, or tortoises, and so on.

There is another peculiarity about the bush-soul, and that is that it is on its account that old people are held in such esteem among the Calabar tribes. For, however bad these old people's personal record may have been, the fact of their longevity demonstrates the possession of powerful and astute bush-souls. On the other hand, a man may be a quiet, respectable citizen, devoted to peace and a whole skin, and yet he may have a sadly flighty disreputable bush-soul which will get itself killed or damaged and cause him death or continual ill-health.

There is another way by which a man dies apart from the action of bush-souls or witchcraft; he may have had a bad illness from some cause in his previous life and, when reincarnated, part of this disease may get reincarnated with him and then he will ultimately die of it. There is no medicine of any avail against these reincarnated diseases.

The idea of reincarnation is very strong in the Niger Delta tribes. It exists, as far as I have been able to find out, throughout all Africa, but usually only in scattered cases, as it were; but in the Delta, most—I think I may say all—human souls of the "surviving soul" class are regarded as returning to the earth again, and undergoing a reincarnation shortly after the due burial of the soul.

These two exceptions from the rule of all deaths and sickness being caused by witchcraft are, however, of minor importance, for infinitely the larger proportion of death and sickness is held to arise from witchcraft itself, more particularly among the Bantu.

Witchcraft acts in two ways, namely, witching something out of a man, or witching something into him. The former method is used by both Negro and Bantu, but is decidedly more common among the Negroes, where the witches are continually setting traps to catch the soul that wanders from the body when a man is sleeping; and when they have caught this soul, they tie it up over the canoe fire and its owner sickens as the soul shrivels.

This is merely a regular line of business, and not an affair of individual hate or revenge. The witch does not care whose dream-soul gets into the trap, and will restore it on payment. Also witch-doctors, men of unblemished professional reputation, will keep asylums for lost souls, i.e. souls who have been out wandering and found on their return to their body that their place has been filled up by a Sisa, a low class soul I will speak of later. These doctors keep souls and administer them to patients who are short of the article.

But there are other witches, either wicked on their own account, or hired by people who are moved by some hatred to individuals, and then the trap is carefully set and baited for the soul of the particular man they wish to injure, and concealed in the bait at the bottom of the pot are knives and sharp hooks which tear and damage the soul, either killing it outright, or mauling it so that it causes its owner sickness on its return to him. I knew the case of a Kruman who for several nights had smelt in his dreams the savoury smell of smoked crawfish seasoned with red peppers. He became anxious, and the headman decided some witch had set a trap baited with this dainty for his dream-soul, with intent to do him grievous bodily harm, and great trouble was taken for the next few nights to prevent this soul of his from straying abroad.

The witching of things into a man is far the most frequent method among the Bantu, hence the prevalence among them of the post-mortem examination,—a practice I never found among the Negroes.

The belief in witchcraft is the cause of more African deaths than anything else. It has killed and still kills more men and women than the slave-trade. Its only rival is perhaps the smallpox, the Grand Kraw-Kraw, as the Krumen graphically call it.

At almost every death a suspicion of witchcraft arises. The witch-doctor is called in, and proceeds to find out the guilty person. Then woe to the unpopular men, the weak women, and the slaves; for on some of them will fall the accusation that means ordeal by poison, or fire, followed, if these point to guilt, as from their nature they usually do, by a terrible death: slow roasting alive—mutilation by degrees before the throat is mercifully cut—tying to stakes at low tide that the high tide may come and drown—and any other death human ingenuity and hate can devise.

The terror in which witchcraft is held is interesting in spite of all its horror. I have seen mild, gentle men and women turned by it, in a moment, to incarnate fiends, ready to rend and destroy those who a second before were nearest and dearest to them. Terrible is the fear that falls like a spell upon a village when a big man, or big woman is just known to be dead. The very men catch their breaths, and grow grey round the lips, and then every one, particularly those belonging to the household of the deceased, goes in for the most demonstrative exhibition of grief. Long, low howls creep up out of the first silence— those blood-curdling, infinitely melancholy, wailing howls—once heard, never to be forgotten.

The men tear off their clothes and wear only the most filthy rags; women, particularly the widows, take off ornaments and almost all dress; their faces are painted white with chalk, their heads are shaven, and they sit crouched on the earth in the house, in the attitude of abasement, the hands resting on the shoulders, palm downwards, not crossed across the breast, unless they are going into the street.

Meanwhile the witch-doctor has been sent for, if he is not already present, and he sets to work in different ways to find out who are the persons guilty of causing the death.

Whether the methods vary with the tribe, or with the individual witch-doctor, I cannot absolutely say, but I think largely with the latter.

Among the Benga I saw a witch-doctor going round a village ringing a small bell which was to stop ringing outside the hut of the guilty. Among the Cabindas (Fjort) I saw, at different times, two witch-doctors trying to find witches, one by means of taking on and off the lid of a small basket while he repeated the names of all the people in the village. When the lid refused to come off at the name of a person, that person was doomed. The other Cabinda doctor first tried throwing nuts upon the ground, also repeating names. That method apparently failed. Then he resorted to another, rubbing the flattened palms of his hands against each other. When the palms refused to meet at a name, and his hands flew about wildly, he had got his man.

The accused person, if he denies the guilt, and does not claim the ordeal, is tortured until he not only acknowledges his guilt but names his accomplices in the murder, for remember this witchcraft is murder in the African eyes.

If he claims the ordeal, as he usually does, he usually has to take a poison drink. Among all the Bantu tribes I know this is made from Sass wood (sass = bad; sass water = rough water; sass surf = bad surf, etc.), and is a decoction of the freshly pulled bark of a great hard wood forest tree, which has a tall unbranched stem, terminating in a crown of branches bearing small leaves. Among the Calabar tribes the ordeal drink is of two kinds: one made from the Calabar bean, the other, the great ju-ju drink Mbiam, which is used also in taking oaths.

In both the sass-wood and Calabar bean drink the only chance for the accused lies in squaring the witch-doctor, so that in the case of the sass-wood drink it is allowed to settle before administration, and in the bean that you get a very heavy dose, both arrangements tending to produce the immediate emetic effect indicative of innocence. If this effect does not come on quickly you die a miserable death from the effects of the poison interrupted by the means taken to kill you as soon as it is decided from the absence of violent sickness that you are guilty.

The Mbiam is not poisonous, nor is its use confined, as the use of the bean is, entirely to witch palaver; but it is the most respected and dreaded of all oaths, and from its decision there is but one appeal, the appeal open to all condemned persons, but rarely made—the appeal to Long ju-ju. This Long ju-ju means almost certain death, and before it a severe frightening that is worse to a negro mind than mere physical torture.

The Mbiam oath formula I was able to secure in the upper districts of the Calabar. One form of it runs thus, and it is recited before swallowing the drink made of filth and blood: -

"If I have been guilty of this crime,
"If I have gone and sought the sick one's hurt,
"If I have sent another to seek the sick one's hurt,
"If I have employed any one to make charms or to cook bush,
"Or to put anything in the road,
"Or to touch his cloth,
"Or to touch his yams,
"Or to touch his goats,
"Or to touch his fowl,
"Or to touch his children,
"If I have prayed for his hurt,
"If I have thought to hurt him in my heart,
"If I have any intention to hurt him,
"If I ever, at any time, do any of these things (recite in full),
"Or employ others to do these things (recite in full),
"Then, Mbiam! Thou deal with me."

This form I give was for use when a man was sick, and things were generally going badly with him, for it is not customary in cases of disease to wait until death occurs before making an accusation of witchcraft. In the case of

Mbiam being administered after a death this long and complicated oath would be worded to meet the case most carefully, the future intention clauses being omitted. In all cases, whenever it is used, the greatest care is taken that the oath be recited in full, oath-takers being sadly prone to kiss their thumb, as it were, particularly ladies who are taking Mbiam for accusations of adultery, in conjunction with the boiling oil ordeal. Indeed, so unreliable is this class of offenders, or let us rather say this class of suspected persons, that some one usually says the oath for them.

From the penalty and inconveniences of these accusations of witchcraft there is but one escape, namely flight to a sanctuary. There are several sanctuaries in Congo Français. The great one in the Calabar district is at Omon. Thither mothers of twins, widows, thieves, and slaves fly, and if they reach it are safe. But an attempt at flight is a confession of guilt; no one is quite certain the accusation will fall on him, or her, and hopes for the best until it is generally too late. Moreover, flying anywhere beyond a day's march, is difficult work in West Africa. So the killing goes on and it is no uncommon thing for ten or more people to be destroyed for one man's sickness or death; and thus over immense tracts of country the death-rate exceeds the birth-rate. Indeed some of the smaller tribes have thus been almost wiped out. In the Calabar district I have heard of an entire village taking the bean voluntarily because another village had accused it en bloc of witchcraft. Miss Slessor has frequently told me how, during a quarrel, one person has accused another of witchcraft, and the accused has bolted off in a towering rage and swallowed the bean.

The witch-doctor is not always the cause of people being subjected to the ordeal or torture. In Calabar and the Okÿon districts all the widows of a dead man are subjected to ordeal.

They have to go the next night after the death, before an assemblage of chiefs and the general surrounding crowd, to a cleared space where there is a fire burning. A fowl is tied to the right hand of each widow, and should that fowl fail to cluck at the sight of the fire the woman is held guilty of having bewitched her dead husband and is dealt with accordingly.

Among the Bantu, although the killing among the wives from the accusation of witchcraft is high, some of them being almost certain to fall victims, yet there is not the wholesale slaughter of women and slaves sent down with the soul of the dead that there is among the Negroes.

In doubtful cases of death, i.e. in all cases not arising from actual violence, when blood shows in the killing, the Bantu of the S.W. Coast make post-mortem examinations. Notably common is this practice among the Cameroons and Batanga region tribes. The body is cut open to find in the entrails some sign of the path of the injected witch.

I am informed that it is the lung that is most usually eaten by the spirit. If the deceased is a witch-doctor it is thought, as I have mentioned before, that his familiar spirit has eaten him internally, and he is opened with a view of securing and destroying his witch. In 1893 I saw in a village in Kacongo five unpleasant-looking objects stuck on sticks. They were the livers and lungs, and in fact the plucks, of witch-doctors, and the inhabitants informed me they were the witches that had been found in them on post-mortems and then been secured.

Mrs. Grenfell, of the Upper Congo, told me in the same year, when I had the pleasure of travelling with her from Victoria to Matadi, that a similar practice was in vogue among several of the Upper Congo tribes.

Again in 1893 I came across another instance of the post-mortem practice. A woman had dropped down dead on a factory beach at Corisco Bay. The natives could not make it out at all. They were irritated about her conduct: "She no sick, she no complain, she no nothing, and then she go die one time."

The post-mortem showed a burst aneurism. The native verdict was "She done witch herself," i.e. she was a witch eaten by her own familiar.

The general opinion held by people living near a river is that the spirit of a witch can take the form of a crocodile to do its work in; those who live away from large rivers or in districts like Congo Français, where crocodiles are not very savage, hold that the witch takes on the form of a leopard. Still the crocodile spirit form is believed in in Congo Français, and to a greater extent in Kacongo, because here the crocodiles of the Congo are very ferocious and numerous, taking as heavy a toll in human life as they do in the delta of the Niger and the estuaries of the Sierra Leone and Sherboro' Rivers.

One witch-doctor I know in Kacongo had a strange professional method. When, by means of his hand rubbings, etc., he had got hold of a witch or a be-witched one, he always gave the unfortunate an emetic and always found several lively young crocodiles in the consequence, and the stories of the natives in this region abound in accounts of people who have been carried off by witch croc-odiles, and kept in places underground for years. I often wonder whether this idea may not have arisen from the well-known habit of the crocodile of burying its prey on the bank. Sometimes it will take off a limb of its victim at once, but frequently it buries the body whole for a few days before eating it. The body is always buried if it is left to the crocodile.

I have a most profound respect for the whole medical profession, but I am bound to confess that the African representatives of it are a little empirical in their methods of treatment. The African doctor is not always a witch-doctor in the bargain, but he is usually. Lady doctors abound. They are a bit dangerous in pharmacy, but they do not often venture on surgery, so on the whole they are safer, for African surgery is heroic. Dr. Nassau cited the worst case of it I know of. A man had been accidentally shot in the chest by another man with a gun on the Ogowé. The native doctor who was called in made a perpendicular incision into the man's chest, extending down to the last rib; he then cut diagonally across, and actually lifted the wall of the chest, and groped about among the vitals for the bullet which he successfully extracted. Patient died. No anæsthetic was employed.

I came across a minor operation. A man had broken the ulna of the left arm. The native doctor got a piece—a very nice piece—of bamboo, drove it in through the muscles and integuments from the wrist to the elbow, then encased the limb in plantain leaves, and bound it round, tightly and neatly, needless to say with tie-tie. The arm and hand when I saw it, some six or seven months after the operation, was quite useless, and was withering away.

Many of their methods, however, are better. The Dualla medicos are truly great on poultices for extracting foreign substances, such as bits of iron cooking-pot—a very frequent form of foreign substance in a man out here, owing to their being generally used as bullets. Almost incredible stories are told by black and white of the efficacy of these poultices; one case I heard from a reliable source of a man who had been shot with fragments of iron pot in the thigh. The white doctor extracted several pieces and said he had got all out, but the man still went on suffering, and could not walk, so, at his request, a native doctor was called in, and he applied his poultice. In a few minutes he removed it, and on its face were two pieces of jagged iron pot. Probably they had been in the poultice when it was applied, anyhow the patient recovered rapidly.

Baths accompanied by massage are much esteemed. The baths are sometimes of hot water with a few herbs thrown in, sometimes they are made by digging a hole in the earth and putting into it a quantity of herbs, and bruised cardamoms, and peppers. Boiling water is then plentifully poured over these and the patient is placed in the bath and is covered over with the parboiled green stuff; a coating of clay is then placed over all, leaving just the head sticking out. The patient remains in this bath for a period of a few hours, up to a day and a half, and when taken out is well rubbed and kneaded. This form of bath I saw used by the M'pongwe and Igalwas, and it is undoubtedly good for many diseases, notably for that curse of the Coast, rheumatism, which afflicts black and white alike. Rubbing and kneading and hot baths are, I think, the best native remedies, and the plaster of grains-of-paradise pounded up, and mixed with clay, and applied to the forehead as a remedy for malarial headache, or brow ague, is often very useful, but apart from these, I have never seen, in any of these herbal remedies, any trace of a really valuable drug.

The Calabar natives are notably behindhand in their medical methods, depending more on ju-ju than the Bantus. In a case of rheumatism, for example, instead of ordering the hot bath, the local practitioner will "woka" his patient and extract from the painful part, even when it has not been wounded, pieces of iron pot, millipedes, etc., and, in cases of dysentery, bundles of shred-up palm-leaves. These things, he asserts, have been by witchcraft inserted into the patient. His conduct can hardly be regarded as professional; and moreover as he goes on to diagnose who has witched these things into the patient's anatomy, it is highly dangerous to the patient's friends, relations, and neighbours into the bargain.

With no intentional slur on the medical profession, after this discussion on their methods I will pass on to the question of dying.

Dying in West Africa particularly in the Niger Delta, is made very unpleasant for the native by his friends and relations.

When a person is insensible, violent means are taken to recall the spirit to the body. Pepper is forced up the nose and into the eyes. The mouth is propped open with a stick. The shredded fibres of the outside of the oil-nut are set alight and held under the nose and the whole crowd of friends and relations with whom the stifling hot hut is tightly packed yell the dying man's name at the top of their voices, in a way that makes them hoarse for days, just as if they were calling to a person lost in the bush or to a person struggling and being torn or lured away from them. "Hi, hi, don't you hear? come back, come back. See here. This is your place," etc.

This custom holds good among both Negroes and Bantus; but the funeral ceremonies vary immensely, in fact with every tribe, and form a subject the details of which I will reserve for a separate work on Fetish.

Among the Okÿon tribes especial care is taken in the case of a woman dying and leaving a child over six months old. The underlying idea is that the spirit of the mother is sure to come back and fetch the child, and in order to pacify her and prevent the child dying, it is brought in and held just in front of the dead body of the mother and then gradually carried away behind her where she cannot see it, and the person holding the child makes it cry out and says, "See, your child is here, you are going to have it with you all right." Then the child is hastily smuggled out of the hut, while a bunch of plantains is put in with the body of the woman and bound up with the funeral binding clothes.

Very young children they do not attempt to keep, but throw them away in the bush alive, as all children are thrown who have not arrived in this world in the way considered orthodox, or who cut their teeth in an improper way. Twins are killed among all the Niger Delta tribes, and in districts out of English control the mother is killed too, except in Omon, where the sanctuary is.

There twin mothers and their children are exiled to an island in the Cross River. They have to remain on the island and if any man goes across and marries one of them he has to remain on the island too. This twin-killing is a widely diffused custom among the Negro tribes.

There is always a sense of there being something uncanny regarding twins in West Africa, and in those tribes where they are not killed they are regarded as requiring great care to prevent them from dying on their own account. I remember once among the Tschwi {324} trying to amuse a sickly child with an image which was near it and which I thought was its doll. The child regarded me with its great melancholy eyes pityingly, as much as to say, "A pretty fool you are making of yourself," and so I was, for I found out that the image was not a doll at all but an image of the child's dead twin which was being kept near it as a habitation for the deceased twin's soul, so that it might not have to wander about, and, feeling lonely, call its companion after it.

The terror with which twins are regarded in the Niger Delta is exceedingly strange and real. When I had the honour of being with Miss Slessor at Okÿon, the first twins in that district were saved with their mother from immolation owing entirely to Miss Slessor's great influence with the natives and her own unbounded courage and energy. The mother in this case was a slave woman— an Eboe, the most expensive and valuable of slaves. She was the property of a big woman who had always treated her—as indeed most slaves are treated in Calabar—with great kindness and consideration, but when these two children arrived all was changed; immediately she was subjected to torrents of virulent abuse, her things were torn from her, her English china basins, possessions she valued most highly, were smashed, her clothes were torn, and she was driven out as an unclean thing. Had it not been for the fear of incurring Miss Slessor's anger, she would, at this point, have been killed with her children, and the bodies thrown into the bush.

As it was, she was hounded out of the village. The rest of her possessions were jammed into an empty gin case and cast to her. No one would touch her, as they might not touch to kill. Miss Slessor had heard of the twins' arrival and had started off, barefooted and bareheaded, at that pace she can go down a bush path. By the time she had gone four miles she met the procession, the woman coming to her and all the rest of the village yelling and howling behind her. On the top of her head was the gin-case, into which the children had been stuffed, on the top of them the woman's big brass skillet, and on the top of that her two market calabashes. Needless to say, on arriving Miss Slessor took charge of affairs, relieving the unfortunate, weak, staggering woman from her load and carrying it herself, for no one else would touch it, or anything belonging to those awful twin things, and they started back together to Miss Slessor's house in the forest-clearing, saved by that tact which, coupled with her courage, has given Miss Slessor an influence and a power among the negroes unmatched in its way by that of any other white.

She did not take the twins and their mother down the village path to her own house, for though had she done so the people of Okÿon would not have prevented her, yet so polluted would the path have been, and so dangerous to pass down, that they would have been compelled to cut another, no light task in that bit of forest, I assure you. So Miss Slessor stood waiting in the broiling sun, in the hot season's height, while a path was being cut to enable her just to get through to her own grounds. The natives worked away hard, knowing that it saved the polluting of a long stretch of market road, and when it was finished Miss Slessor went to her own house by it and attended with all kindness, promptness, and skill, to the woman and children. I arrived in the middle of this affair for my first meeting with Miss Slessor, and things at Okÿon were rather crowded, one way and another, that afternoon. All the attention one of the children wanted—the boy, for there was a boy and a girl—was burying, for the people who had crammed them into the box had utterly smashed the child's head. The other child was alive, and is still a member of that household of rescued children all of whom owe their lives to Miss Slessor. There are among them twins from other districts, and delicate children who must have died had they been left in their villages, and a very wonderful young lady, very plump and very pretty, aged about four. Her mother died a few days after her birth, so the child was taken and thrown into the bush, by the side of the road that led to the market. This was done one market-day some distance from the Okÿon town. This particular market is held every ninth day, and on the succeeding market-day some women from the village by the side of Miss Slessor's house happened to pass along the path and heard the child feebly crying: they came into Miss Slessor's yard in the evening, and sat chatting over the day's shopping, etc., and casually mentioned in the way of conversation that they had heard the child crying, and that it was rather remarkable it should be still alive. Needless to say, Miss Slessor was off, and had that waif home. It was truly in an awful state, but just alive. In a marvellous way it had been left by leopards and snakes, with which this bit of forest abounds, and, more marvellous still, the driver ants had not scented it. Other ants had considerably eaten into it one way and another; nose, eyes, etc., were swarming with them and flies; the cartilage of the nose and part of the upper lip had been absolutely eaten into, but in spite of this she is now one of the prettiest black children I have ever seen, which is saying a good deal, for negro children are very pretty with their round faces, their large mouths not yet coarsened by heavy lips, their beautifully shaped flat little ears, and their immense melancholy deer-like eyes, and above these charms they possess that of being fairly quiet. This child is not an object of terror, like the twin children; it was just thrown away because no one would be bothered to rear it, but when Miss Slessor had had all the trouble of it the natives had no objection to pet and play with it, calling it "the child of wonder," because of its survival.

With the twin baby it was very different. They would not touch it and only approached it after some days, and then only when it was held by Miss Slessor or me. If either of us wanted to do or get something, and we handed over the bundle to one of the house children to hold, there was a stampede of men and women off the verandah, out of the yard, and over the fence, if need be, that was exceedingly comic, but most convincing as to the reality of the terror and horror in which they held the thing. Even its own mother could not be trusted with the child; she would have killed it. She never betrayed the slightest desire to have it with her, and after a few days' nursing and feeding up she was anxious to go back to her mistress, who, being an enlightened woman, was willing to have her if she came without the child.

The main horror is undoubtedly of the child, the mother being killed more as a punishment for having been so intimately mixed up in bringing the curse, danger, and horror into the village than for anything else.

The woman went back by the road that had been cut for her coming, and would have to live for the rest of her life an outcast, and for a long time in a state of isolation, in a hut of her own into which no one would enter, neither would any one eat or drink with her, nor partake of the food or water she had cooked or fetched. She would lead the life of a leper, working in the plantation by day, and going into her lonely hut at night, shunned and cursed. I tried to find out whether there was any set period for this quarantine, and all I could arrive at was that if—and a very considerable if—a man were to marry her and she were subsequently to present to Society an acceptable infant, she would be to a certain extent socially rehabilitated, but she would always be a woman with a past—a thing the African, to his credit be it said, has no taste for.

The woman's own lamentations were pathetic. She would sit for hours singing or rather mourning out a kind of dirge over herself: "Yesterday I was a woman, now I am a horror, a thing all people run from. Yesterday they would eat with me, now they spit on me. Yesterday they would talk to me with a sweet mouth, now they greet me only with curses and execrations. They have smashed my basin, they have torn my clothes," and so on, and so on. There was no complaint against the people for doing these things, only a bitter sense of injury against some superhuman power that had sent this withering curse of twins down on her. She knew not why; she sang "I have not done this, I have not done that"—and highly interesting information regarding the moral stand-point a good deal of it was. I have tried to find out the reason of this widely diffused custom which is the cause of such a pitiful waste of life; for in addition to the mother and children being killed it often leads to other people, totally unconcerned in the affair, being killed by the relatives of the sufferer on the suspicion of having caused the calamity by witchcraft, and until one gets hold of the underlying idea, and can destroy that, the custom will be hard to stamp out in a district like the great Niger Delta. But I have never been able to hunt it down, though I am sure it is there, and a very quaint idea it undoubtedly is. The usual answer is, "It was the custom of our fathers," but that always and only means, "We don't intend to tell."

Funeral customs vary considerably between the Negro and Bantu, and I never yet found among the Bantu those unpleasant death charms which are in vogue in the Niger Delta.

The Calabar people, when the Consular eye is off them, bury under the house. In the case of a great chief the head is cut off and buried with great secrecy somewhere else, for reasons I have already stated. The body is buried a few days after death, but the really important part of the funeral is the burying of the spirit, and this is the thing that causes all the West Africans, Negro and Bantu alike, great worry, trouble, and expense. For the spirit, no matter what its late owner may have been, is malevolent—all native-made spirits are. The family have to get together a considerable amount of wealth to carry out this burial of the spirit, so between the body-burying and the spirit-burying a considerable time usually elapses; maybe a year, maybe more. The custom of keeping the affair open until the big funeral can be made obtains also in Cabinda and Loango, but there, instead of burying the body in the meantime, {329} it is placed upon a platform of wood, and slow fires kept going underneath to dry it, a mat roof being usually erected over it to keep off rain. When sufficiently dried, it is wrapped in clothes and put into a coffin, until the money to finish the affair is ready. The Duallas are more tied down; their death-dances must be celebrated, I am informed, on the third, seventh, and ninth day after death. On these days the spirit is supposed to be particularly present in its old home. In all the other cases, I should remark, the spirit does not leave the home until its devil is made and if this is delayed too long he naturally becomes fractious.

Among the Congo Français tribes there are many different kinds of burial—as the cannibalistic of the Fan. I may remark, however, that they tell me themselves that it is considered decent to bury a relative, even if you subsequently dig him up and dispose of the body to the neighbours. Then there is the earth-burial of the Igalwas and M'pongwe, and the beating into unrecognisable pulp of the body which, I am told on good native authority, is the method of several Upper Ogowé tribes, including the Adoomas. I had no opportunity of making quiet researches on burial customs when I was above Njoli, because I was so busy trying to avoid qualifying for a burial myself; so I am not quite sure whether this method is the general one among these little-known tribes, as I am told by native traders, who have it among them that it is—or whether it is reserved for the bodies of people believed to have been possessed of dangerous souls.

Destroying the body by beating up, or by cutting up, is a widely diffused custom in West Africa in the case of dangerous souls, and is universally followed with those that have contained wanderer-souls, i.e. those souls which keep turning up in the successive infants of a family. A child dies, then another child comes to the same father or mother, and that dies, after giving the usual trouble and expense. A third arrives and if that dies, the worm—the father, I mean—turns, and if he is still desirous of more children, he just breaks one of the legs of the body before throwing it in the bush.

This he thinks will act as a warning to the wanderer-soul and give it to understand that if it will persist in coming into his family, it must settle down there and give up its flighty ways. If a fourth child arrives in the family, "it usually limps," and if it dies, the justly irritated parent cuts its body up carefully into very small pieces, and scatters them, doing away with the soul altogether.

The Kama country people of the lower Ogowé are more superstitious and full of observances than the upper river tribes.

Particularly rich in Fetish are the Ncomi, a Fernan Vaz tribe. I once saw a funeral where they had been called in to do the honours, and M. Jacot told me of an almost precisely similar occurrence that he had met with in one of his many evangelising expeditions from Lembarene. I will give his version because of his very superior knowledge of the language.

He was staying in a Fan town where one of the chiefs had just died. The other chief (there are usually two in a Fan town) decided that his deceased confrère should have due honour paid him, and resolved to do the thing handsomely.

The Fans openly own to not understanding thoroughly about death and life and the immortality of the soul, and things of that sort, and so the chief called in the Ncomi, who are specialists in these subjects, to make the funeral customs.

M. Jacot said the chief made a speech to the effect that the Fans did not know about these things, but their neighbours, the Ncomi, were known to be well versed in them and the proper things to do, so he had called them in to pay honour to the dead chief. Then the Ncomi started and carried on their weird, complicated death-dance.

The Fans sat and stood round watching them in a ring for a long time, but to a rational, common-sense, shrewd, unimaginative set of people like the Fans, just standing hour after hour gazing on a dance you do not understand, and which consists of a wriggle and a stamp, a wriggle and a stamp, in a solemn walk, or prance, round and round, to the accompaniment of a monotonous phrase thumped on a tom-tom and a monotonous, melancholy chant, uttered in a minor key interspersed every few minutes with an emphatic howl, produces a feeling of boredom, therefore the Fans softly stole away and went to bed, which disgusted the Ncomi, and there was a row. In the dance I saw the same thing happened, only when the Ncomi saw the audience getting thin they complained and said that they were doing this dance in honour of the Fans' chief, in a neighbourly way, and the very least the Fans could do, as they couldn't dance themselves, was to sit still and admire people who could. The Fan chief in my village quite saw it, and went and had the Fans who had gone home early turned up and made them come and see the performance some more; this they did for a time, and then stole off again, or slept in their seats, and the Ncomi were highly disgusted at those brutes of Fans, whom they regarded, they said in their way, as Philistines of an utterly obtuse and degraded type.

The Ncomi themselves put the body into coffins. A barrel is the usual one, but gun-cases or two trade boxes, the ends knocked out and the cases fitted together, is another frequent form of coffin used by them. These coffins are not buried, but are put into special places in the forest.

Along the bank of the Ogowé you will notice here and there long stretches of uninhabited bush. These are not all mere stretches of swamp forest. If you land on some of these and go in a little way you will find the forest full of mounds—or rather heaps, because they have no mould over them—made of branches of trees and leaves; underneath each of these heaps there are the remains of a body. One very evil-looking place so used I found when I was on the Karkola river. Dr. Nassau tells me they are the usual burying grounds (Abe) of the Ajumbas.

CHAPTER XIV

FETISH—(continued)

IN WHICH THE VOYAGER DISCOURSES ON THE LEGAL METHODS OF NA-
TIVES OF THIS COUNTRY, THE IDEAS GOVERNING FORMS OF BURIAL, OF
THEIR MANNER OF MOURNING FOR THEIR DEAD, AND THE CONDITION
OF THE AFRICAN SOUL IN THE UNDER-WORLD.

GREAT AS ARE THE INCIDENTAL MISERIES and dangers surrounding death
to all the people in the village in which a death occurs, undoubtedly
those who suffer most are the widows of a chief or free man.

The uniform custom among both Negroes and Bantus is that those who
escape execution on the charge of having witched the husband to death, shall
remain in a state of filth and abasement, not even removing vermin from themselves, until after the soul-burial is complete—the soul of the dead man being
regarded as hanging about them and liable to be injured. Therefore, also to the
end of preventing his soul from getting damaged, they are confined to their
huts; this latter restriction is not rigidly enforced, but it is held theoretically to
be the correct thing.

They maintain the attitude of grief and abasement, sitting on the ground,
eating but little food, and that of a coarse kind. In Calabar their legal rights
over property, such as slaves, are meanwhile considerably in abeyance, and they
are put to great expense during the time the spirit is awaiting burial. They have
to keep watch, two at a time, in the hut, where the body is buried, keeping
lights burning, and they have to pay out of their separate estate for the entertainment of all the friends of the deceased who come to pay him compliment;
and if he has been an important man, a big man, the whole district will come,
not in a squadron, but just when it suits them, exactly as if they were calling
on a live friend. Thus it often happens that even a big woman is bankrupt by

the expense. I will not go into the legal bearings of the case here, for they are intricate, and, to a great extent, only interesting to a student of Negro law.

The Bantu women occupy a far inferior position in regard to the rights of property to that held by the Negro women.

The disposal of wives after the death of the husband among the M'pongwe and Igalwa is a subject full of interest; but it is, like most of their law, very complicated. The brothers of the deceased are supposed to take them—the younger brother may not marry the elder brother's widows, but the elder brothers may marry those of the younger brother. Should any of the women object to the arrangement, they may "leave the family."

I own that the ground principle of African law practically is "the simple plan that they should take who have the power, and they should keep who can," and this tells particularly against women and children who have not got living, powerful relations of their own. Unless the children of a man are grown up and sufficiently powerful on their own account, they have little chance of sharing in the distribution of his estate; but in spite of this abuse of power there is among Negroes and Bantus a definite and acknowledged Law, to which an appeal can be made by persons of all classes, provided they have the wherewithal to set the machinery of it in motion. The difficulty the children and widows have in sharing in the distribution of the estate of the father and husband arises, I fancy, in the principle of the husband's brothers being the true heir, which has sunk into a fossilised state near the trading stations in the face of the white culture. The reason for this inheritance of goods passing from the man to his brother by the same mother has no doubt for one of its origins the recognition of the fact that the brother by the same mother must be a near relation, whereas, in spite of the strict laws against adultery, the relationship to you of the children born of your wives is not so certain. Nevertheless this is one of the obvious and easy explanations for things it is well to exercise great care before accepting, for you must always remember that the African's mind does not run on identical lines with the European—what may be self-evident to you is not so to him, and vice versa. I have frequently heard African metaphysicians complain that white men make great jumps in their thought-course, and do not follow an idea step by step. You soon become conscious of the careful way a Negro follows his idea. Certain customs of his you can, by the exercise of great patience, trace back in a perfectly smooth line from their source in some natural phenomenon. Others, of course, you cannot, the traces of the intervening steps of the idea having been lost, owing partly to the veneration in which old customs are held, which causes them to regard the fact that their fathers had this fashion as reason enough for their having it, and above all to the total absence of all but oral tradition. But so great a faith have I in the lack of inventive power in the African, that I feel sure all their customs, had we the material that has slipped down into the great swamp of time, could be traced back either, as I have said, to some natural phenomenon, or to the thing being advisable, for reasons of utility.

The uncertainty in the parentage of offspring may seem to be such a utilitarian underlying principle, but, on the other hand, it does not sufficiently explain the varied forms of the law of inheritance, for in some tribes the eldest or most influential son does succeed to his father's wealth; in other places you have the peculiar custom of the chief slave inheriting. I think, from these things, that the underlying idea in inheritance of property is the desire to keep the wealth of "the house," i.e. estate, together, and if it were allowed to pass into the hands of weak people, like women and young children, this would not be done. Another strong argument against the theory that it arises from the doubtful relationship of the son, is that certain ju-ju always go to the son of the chief wife, if he is old enough, at the time of the father's death, even in those tribes where the wealth goes elsewhere.

Certain tribes acknowledge the right of the women and children to share in the dead man's wealth, given that these are legally married wives, or the children of legally married wives; it is so in Cameroons, for example. An esteemed friend of mine who helps to manage things for the Fatherland down there was trying a palaver the other day with a patience peculiar to him, and that intelligent and elaborate care I should think only a mind trained on the methods of German metaphysicians could impart into that most wearisome of proceedings, wherein every one says the same thing over fourteen different times at least, with a similar voice and gesture, the only variation being in the statements regarding the important points, and the facts of the case, these varying with each individual. This palaver was made by a son claiming to inherit part of his father's property; at last, to the astonishment, and, of course, the horror, of the learned judge, the defendant, the wicked uncle, pleaded through the interpreter, "This man cannot inherit his father's property, because his parents married for love." There is no encouragement to foolishness of this kind in Cameroon, where legal marriage consists in purchase.

In Bonny River and in Opobo the inheritance of "the house" is settled primarily by a vote of the free men of the house; when the chief dies, their choice has to be ratified by the other chiefs of houses; but in Bonny and Opobo the white traders have had immense influence for a long time, so one cannot now find out how far this custom is purely native in idea.

Among the Fans the uncle is, as I have before said, an important person although the father has more rights than among the Igalwa, and here I came across a peculiar custom regarding widows. M. Jacot cited to me a similar case or so, one of which I must remark was in an Ajumba town. The widows were inside the dead husband's hut, as usual; the Fan huts are stoutly built of sheets of flattened bark, firmly secured together with bark rope, and thatched—they never build them in any other way except when they are in the bush rubber-collecting or elephant-hunting, when they make them of the branches of trees. Well, round the bark hut, with the widows inside, there was erected a hut made of branches, and when this was nearly completed, the Fans commenced pulling down the inner bark hut, and finally cleared it right out, thatch and all, and the materials of which it had been made were burnt. I was struck with the performance because the Fans, though surrounded by intensely superstitious tribes, are remarkably free from superstition {338} themselves, taking little or no interest in speculative matters, except to get charms to make them invisible to elephants, to keep their feet in the path, to enable them to see things in the forest, and practical things of that sort, and these charms they frequently gave me to assist and guard me in my wanderings.

The M'pongwe and Igalwa have a peculiar funeral custom, but it is not confined in its operation to widows, all the near relatives sharing in it. The mourning relations are seated on the floor of the house, and some friend—Dr. Nassau told me he was called in in this capacity—comes in and "lifts them up," bringing to them a small present, a factor of which is always a piece of soap. This custom is now getting into the survival form in Libreville and Glass. Nowadays the relatives do not thus sit, unwashed and unkempt, keenly requiring the soap. Among the bush Igalwa, I am told, the soap is much wanted.

It is not only the widows that remain, either theoretically or practically unwashed; all the mourners do. The Ibibios seem to me to wear the deepest crape in the form of accumulated dirt, and all the African tribes I have met have peculiar forms of hair cutting—shaving the entire head, not shaving it at all, shaving half of it, etc.—when in mourning. The period of the duration of wearing mourning is, I believe, in all West Coast tribes that which elapses between the death and the burial of the soul. I believe a more thorough knowledge would show us that there is among the Bantu also a fixed time for the lingering of the soul on earth after death, but we have not got sufficient evidence on the point yet. The only thing we know is that it is not proper for the widow to re-marry while her husband's soul is still in her vicinity.

Among the Calabar tribes the burial of his spirit liberates the woman. Among the Tschwi she requires special ceremonies on her own account. In Togoland, among the Ewe people, I know the period is between five and six weeks, during which time the widow remains in the hut, armed with a good stout stick, as a precaution against the ghost of her husband, so as to ward off attacks should he be ill-tempered. After these six weeks the widow can come out of the hut, but as his ghost has not permanently gone hence, and is apt to revisit the neighbourhood for the next six months, she has to be taken care of during this period. Then, after certain ceremonies, she is free to marry again. So I conclude the period of mourning, in all tribes, is that period during which the soul remains round its old possessions, whether these tribes have a definite soul-burial or devil-making or not.

The ideas connected with the under-world to which the ghost goes are exceedingly interesting. The Negroes and Bantus are at one on these subjects in one particular only, and that is that no marriages take place there. The Tschwis say that this under-world, Srahmandazi, is just the same as this world in all other particulars, save that it is dimmer, a veritable shadow-land where men have not the joys of life, but only the shadow of the joy. Hence, says the Tschwi proverb, "One day in this world is worth a year in Srahmandazi." The Tschwis, with their usual definiteness in this sort of detail, know all about their Srahmandazi. Its entrance is just east of the middle Volta, and the way down is difficult to follow, and when the sun sets on this world it rises on Srahmandazi. The Bantus are vague on this important and interesting point. The Benga, for example, although holding the absence of marriage there, do not take steps to meet the case as the Tschwis do, and kill a supply of wives to take down with them. This reason for killing wives at a funeral is another instance that, however strange and cruel a custom may be here in West Africa, however much it may at first appear to be the flower of a rootless superstition, you will find on close investigation that it has some root in a religious idea, and a common-sense element. The common-sense element in the killing of wives and slaves among both the Tschwi and the Calabar tribes consists in the fact that it discourages poisoning. A Calabar chief elaborately explained to me that the rigorous putting down of killing at funerals that was being carried on by the Government not only landed a man in the next world as a wretched pauper, but added an additional chance to his going there prematurely, for his wives and slaves, no longer restrained by the prospect of being killed at his death and sent off with him would, on very slight aggravation, put "bush in his chop." It is sad to think of this thorn being added to the rose-leaves of a West Coast chief's life, as there are 99.9 per cent. of thorns in it already.

I came across a similar case on the Gold Coast, when a chief complained to me of the way the Government were preserving vermin, in the shape of witches, in the districts under its surveillance. You were no longer allowed to destroy them as of old, and therefore the vermin were destroying the game; for, said he, the witches here live almost entirely on the blood they suck from children at night. They used, in old days, to do this furtively, and do so now where native custom is unchecked; but in districts where the Government says that witchcraft is utter nonsense, and killing its proficients utter murder which will be dealt with accordingly, the witch flourishes exceedingly, and blackmails the fathers and mothers of families, threatening that if they are not bought off they will have their child's blood; and if they are not paid, the child dies away gradually—poison again, most likely.

I often think it must be the common-sense element in fetish customs that enables them to survive, in the strange way they do, in the minds of Africans who have been long under European influence and education. In witching, for example, every intelligent native knows there is a lot of poison in the affair, but the explanation he gives you will not usually display this knowledge, and it was not until I found the wide diffusion of the idea of the advisability of administering an emetic to the bewitched person, that I began to suspect my black friends of sound judgment.

The good ju-juist will tell you all things act by means of their life, which means their power, their spirit. Dr. Nassau tells me the efficacy of drugs is held to depend on their benevolent spirits, which, on being put into the body, drive away the malevolent disease-causing spirits—a leucocytes-versus-pathogenic-bacteria sort of influence, I suppose. On this same idea also depends the custom of the appeal to ordeal, the working of which is supposed to be spiritual. Nevertheless, the intelligent native, believing all the time in this factor, squares the commonsense factor by bribing the witch-doctor who makes the ordeal drink.

The feeling regarding the importance of funeral observances is quite Greek in its intensity. Given a duly educated African, I am sure that he would grasp the true inwardness of the Antigone far and away better than any European now living can. A pathetic story which bears on this feeling was told me some time ago by Miss Slessor when she was stationed at Creek Town. An old blind slave woman was found in the bush, and brought into the mission. She was in a deplorable state, utterly neglected and starving, her feet torn by thorns and full of jiggers, and so on. Every care was taken of her and she soon revived and began to crawl about, but her whole mind was set on one thing with a passion that had made her alike indifferent to her past sufferings and to her present advantages. What she wanted was a bit, only a little bit, of white cloth. Now, I may remark, white cloth is anathema to the Missions, for it is used for ju-ju offerings, and a rule has to be made against its being given to the unconverted, or the missionary becomes an accessory before the fact to pagan practices, so white cloth the old woman was told she could not have, she had been given plenty of garments for her own use and that was enough. The old woman, however, kept on pleading and saying the spirit of her dead mistress kept coming to her asking and crying for white cloth, and white cloth she must get for her, and so at last, finding it was not to be got at the Mission station, she stole away one day, unobserved, and wandered off into the bush, from which she never again reappeared, doubtless falling a victim to the many leopards that haunted hereabouts.

To provide a proper burial for the dead relation is the great duty of a negro's life, its only rival in his mind is the desire to avoid having a burial of his own. But, in a good negro, this passion will go under before the other, and he will risk his very life to do it. He may know, surely and well, that killing slaves and women at a dead brother's grave means hanging for him when their Big Consul knows of it, but in the Delta he will do it. On the Coast, Leeward and Windward, he will spend every penny he possesses and, on top, if need be, go and pawn himself, his wives, or his children into slavery to give a deceased relation a proper funeral.

This killing at funerals I used to think would be more easily done away with in the Delta than among the Tschwi tribes, but a little more knowledge of the Delta's idea about the future life showed me I was wrong.

Among the Tschwi the slaves and women killed are to form for the dead a retinue, and riches wherewith to start life in Srahmandazi (Yboniadse of the Oji), where there are markets and towns and all things as on this earth, and so the Tschwi would have little difficulty in replacing human beings at funerals with gold-dust, cloth, and other forms of riches, and this is already done in districts under white influence. But in the Delta there is no under-world to live in, the souls shortly after reaching the under-world being forwarded back to this, in new babies, and the wealth that is sent down with a man serves as an indication as to what class of baby the soul is to be repacked and sent up in. As wealth in the Delta consists of women and slaves I do not believe the under-world gods of the Niger would understand the status of a chief who arrived before them, let us say, with ten puncheons of palm oil, and four hundred yards of crimson figured velvet; they would say, "Oh! very good as far as it goes, but where is your real estate? The chances are you are only a trade slave boy and have stolen these things"; and in consequence of this, killing at funerals will be a custom exceedingly difficult to stamp out in these regions. Try and imagine yourself how abhorrent it must be to send down a dear and honoured relative to the danger of his being returned to this world shortly as a slave. There is no doubt a certain idea among the Negroes that some souls may get a rise in status on their next incarnation. You often hear a woman saying she will be a man next time, a slave he will be a freeman, and so on, but how or why some souls obtain promotion I have not yet sufficient evidence to show. I think a little more investigation will place this important point in my possession. I once said to a Calabar man, "But surely it would be easy for a man's friends to cheat; they could send down a chief's outfit with a man, though he was only a small man here?"

"No," said he, "the other souls would tell on him, and then he would get sent up as a dog or some beast as a punishment."

My first conception of the prevalence of the incarnation idea was also gained from a Delta negro. I said, "Why in the world do you throw away in the bush the bodies of your dead slaves? Where I have been they tie a string to the leg of a dead slave and when they bury him bring the string to the top and fix it to a peg, with the owner's name on, and then when the owner dies he has that slave again down below."

"They be fool men," said he, and he went on to explain that the ghost of that slave would be almost immediately back on earth again growing up ready to work for some one else, and would not wait for its last owner's soul down below, and out of the luxuriant jungle of information that followed I gathered that no man's soul dallies below long, and also that a soul returning to a family, a thing ensured by certain ju-jus, was identified. The new babies as they arrive in the family are shown a selection of small articles belonging to deceased members whose souls are still absent; the thing the child catches hold of identifies him. "Why he's Uncle John, see! he knows his own pipe;" or "That's cousin Emma, see! she knows her market calabash," and so on.

I remember discoursing with a very charming French official on the difficulty of eradicating fetish customs.

"Why not take the native in the rear, Mademoiselle," said he, "and convert the native gods?"

I explained that his ingenious plan was not feasible, because you cannot convert gods. Even educating gods is hopeless work. All races of men through countless ages, have been attempting to make their peculiar deities understand how they are wanted to work, and what they are wanted to do, and the result is anything but encouraging.

As I have dwelt on the repellent view of Negro funeral custom, I must in justice to them cite their better view. There is a custom that I missed much on going south of Calabar, for it is a pretty one. Outside the villages in the Calabar districts, by the sides of the most frequented roads, you will see erections of boughs. I do not think these are intended for huts, but for beds, for they are very like the Calabar type of bed, only made in wood instead of clay. Over them a roof of mats is put, to furnish a protection against rain.

These shelters—graves or fetish huts they are wrongly called by Europeans—are made by driving four longish stout poles into the ground while at the height of about three feet or so four more poles are tied so as to make a skeleton platform which is filled in with withies and made flat. Another set of five poles is tied above, and to these the roof is affixed. On the platform, is placed the bedding belonging to the deceased, the undercloth, counterpane, etc., and at the head are laid the pillows, bolster-shaped and stuffed with cotton-tree fluff, or shredded palm-leaves, and covered with some gaily-coloured cotton cloth. In every case I have seen—and they amount to hundreds, for you cannot take an hour's walk even from Duke Town without coming upon a dozen or so of these erections—the pillows are placed so that the person lying on the bed would look towards the village.

On the roof and on the bed, and underneath it on the ground, are placed the household utensils that belonged to the deceased; the calabashes, the basins, the spoons cut out of wood, and the boughten iron ones, as we should say in Devon, and on the stakes are hung the other little possessions; there is one I know of made for the ghost of a poor girl who died, on to the stakes of which are hung the dolls and the little pincushions, etc., given her by a kind missionary.

Food is set out at these places and spirit poured over them from time to time, and sometimes, though not often, pieces of new cloth are laid on them. Most of the things are deliberately damaged before they are put on the home for the spirit; I do not think this is to prevent them from being stolen, because all are not damaged sufficiently to make them useless. There was a beautifully made spoon with a burnt-in pattern on one of these places when I left Calabar to go South, and on my return, some six months after, it was still there. On another there was a very handsome pair of market calabashes, also much decorated, that were only just chipped and in better repair than many in use in Calabar markets, and I make no doubt the spoon and they are still lying rotting among the débris of the pillows, etc. These places are only attended to during the time the spirit is awaiting burial, as they are regarded merely as a resting-place for it while it is awaiting this ceremony. The body is not buried near them, I may remark.

In spite, however, of the care that is taken to bury spirits, a considerable percentage from various causes—poverty of the relations, the deceased being a stranger in the land, accidental death in some unknown part of the forest or the surf—remain unburied, and hang about to the common danger of the village they may choose to haunt. Many devices are resorted to, to purify the villages from these spirits. One which was in use in Creek Town, Calabar, to within a few years ago, and which I am informed is still customary in some interior villages, was very ingenious, and believed to work well by those who employed it.

In the houses were set up Nbakim,—large, grotesque images carved of wood and hung about with cloth strips and gew-gaws. Every November in Creek Town (I was told by some authorities it was every second November) there was a sort of festival held. Offerings of food and spirits were placed before these images; a band of people accompanied by the rest of the population used to make a thorough round of the town, up and down each street and round every house, dancing, singing, screaming and tom-toming, in fact making all the noise they knew how to—and a Calabar Effik is very gifted in the power of making noise. After this had been done for what was regarded as a sufficient time, the images were taken out of the houses, the crowd still making a terrific row and were then thrown into the river, and the town was regarded as being cleared of spirits.

The rationale of the affair is this. The wandering spirits are attracted by the images, and take shelter among their rags, like earwigs or something of that kind. The charivari is to drive any of the spirits who might be away from their shelters back into them. The shouting of the mob is to keep the spirits from venturing out again while they are being carried to the river. The throwing of the images, rags and all, into the river, is to destroy the spirits or at least send them elsewhere. They did not go and pour boiling water on their earwig-traps, as wicked white men do, but they meant the same thing, and when this was over they made and set up new images for fresh spirits who might come into the town, and these were kept and tended as before, until the next N'dok ceremony came round.

It is owing to the spiritual view which the African takes of existence at large that ceremonial observances form the greater part of even his common-law procedure.

There is, both among the Negro and Bantu, a recognised code of law, founded on principles of true but merciless justice. It is not often employed, because of the difficulty and the danger to the individual who appeals to it, should that individual be unbacked by power, but nevertheless the code exists.

The African is particularly hard on theft; he by no means "compounds for sins he is inclined to by damning those he has no mind to," for theft is a thing he revels in.

Persons are tried for theft on circumstantial evidence, direct testimony, and ordeal. Laws relating to mortgage are practically the same among Negroes and Bantu and Europeans. Torts are not recognised; unless the following case from Cameroon points to a vague realisation of them. A. let his canoe out to B., in good order, so that B. could go up river, and fetch down some trade. B. did not go himself, but let C., who was not his slave, but another free man who also wanted to go up for trade, have the canoe on the understanding that in payment for the loan of the said canoe C. should bring down B's. trade.

A. was not told about this arrangement at all. B. says A. was, only A. was so blind drunk at the time he did not understand. Well, up river C. goes in the canoe, and fetches up on a floating stump in the river, and staves a hole you could put your head in, in the bow of the said canoe. C. returns it to B. in this condition. B. returns it to A. in this condition. A. sues B. before native chief, saying he lent his canoe to B. on the understanding, always implied in African loans, that it was to be returned in the same state as when lent, fair wear and tear alone excepted. B. tries first to get C. to pay for the canoe, and for the rent of the canoe on top, as a compensation for the delay in bringing down his, B's., trade. C. calls B. the illegitimate offspring of a greenhouse-lizard, and pleads further that the floating log was a force majeure - an act of God, and denies liability on all counts. B. then pleads this as his own defence in the case of A. and B. (authorities cited in support of this view); he also pleads he is not liable, because C. is a free man, and not his slave.

The case went on for a week; the judge was drunk for five days in his attempt to get his head clear. The decision finally was that B. was to pay A. full compensation. B. v. C. is still pending.

The laws against adultery are, theoretically, exceedingly severe. The punishment is death, and this is sometimes carried out. The other day King Bell in Cameroon flogged one of his wives to death, and the German Government have deposed and deported him, for you cannot do that sort of thing with impunity within a stone's throw of a Government head-quarters. But as a general rule all along the Coast the death penalty for murder or adultery is commuted to a fine, or you can send a substitute to be killed for you, if you are rich. This is frequently done, because it is cheaper, if you have a seedy slave, to give him to be killed in your stead than to pay a fine which is often enormous.

The adultery itself is often only a matter of laying your hand, even in self-defence from a virago, on a woman—or brushing against her in the path. These accusations of adultery are, next to witchcraft, the great social danger to the West Coast native, and they are often made merely from motives of extortion or spite, and without an atom of truth in them.

It is customary for a chief to put his wives frequently to ordeal on this point, and this is almost always done after there has been a big devil-making, or a dance, which his family have been gracing with their presence. The usual method of applying the ordeal is by boiling palm-oil—a pot is nearly filled with the oil, which is brought to the boil over a fire; when it is seething, the woman to be tried is brought out in front of it. She first dips her hands into water, and then has administered to her the M'biam oath saying or having said for her that long elaborate formula, in a form adjusted to meet the case. Then she plunges her hand into the boiling oil for an instant, and shakes the oil off with all possible rapidity, and the next woman comes forward and goes through the same performance, and so on. Next day, the hands of the women are examined, and those found blistered are adjudged guilty, and punished. In order to escape heavy punishment the woman will accuse some man of having hustled against her, or sat down on a bench beside her, and so on, and the accused man has to pay up. If he does not, in the Calabar district, Egbo will come and "eat the adultery," and there won't be much of that man's earthly goods left. Sometimes the accusation is volunteered by the woman, and frequently the husband and wife conspire together and cook up a case against a man for the sake of getting the damages. There is nothing that ensures a man an unblemished character in West Africa, save the possession of sufficient power to make it risky work for people to cast slurs on it.

The ownership of children is a great source of palaver. The law among Negroes and Bantus is that the children of a free woman belong to her. In the case of tribes believing in the high importance of uncles considerable powers are vested in that relative, while in other tribes certain powers are vested in the father.

The children of slave wives are the only children the father has absolute power over if he is the legal owner of the slave woman. If, as is frequently the case, a free man marries a slave woman who belongs to another man, all her children are the absolute property of her owner, not her husband; and the owner of the woman can take them and sell them, or do whatsoever he chooses with them, unless the free man father redeems them, as he usually does, although the woman may still remain the absolute property of the owner, recallable by him at any time.

This law is the cause of the most brain-spraining palavers that come before the white authorities. There is naturally no statute of limitations in West Africa, because the African does not care a row of pins about time. The wily A. will let his slave woman live with B. without claiming the redemption fees as they become due—letting them stand over, as it were, at compound interest. All the male as well as the female children of the first generation are A.'s property, and all the female children of these children are his property even unto the second and third generation and away into eternity. A. may die before he puts in his claim, in which case the ownership passes on into the hands of his heir or assignees, who may foreclose at once, on entering into their heritage, or may again let things accumulate for their heirs. Anyhow, sooner or later the foreclosure comes and then there is trouble. X., Y., Z., etc., free men, have married some of the original A.'s slave woman's descendants. They have either bought them right out, or kept on conscientiously redeeming children of theirs as they arrived. Of course A., or his heirs, contend that X., Y., Z., etc. have been wasting time and money by so doing, because the people X., Y., Z. have paid the money to had no legal title to the women. Of course X., Y., Z. contend that their particular woman, or her ancestress, was duly redeemed from the legal owner.

Remember there is no documentary evidence available, and squads of equally reliable and oldest inhabitants are swearing hard—all both ways. Just realise this, and that your Government says that whenever native law is not blood-stained it must be supported, and you may be able to realise the giddy mazes of a native palaver, which if you conscientiously attempt to follow with the determination that justice shall be duly administered, will for certain lay you low with an attack of fever.

The law of ownership is not all in favour of the owner, masters being responsible for damage done by their slaves, and this law falls very heavily and expensively on the owner of a bad slave. Indeed, when one lives out here and sees the surrounding conditions of this state of culture, the conviction grows on you that, morally speaking, the African is far from being the brutal fiend he is often painted, a creature that loves cruelty and blood for their own sake. The African does not; and though his culture does not contain our institutions, lunatic asylums, prisons, workhouses, hospitals, etc., he has to deal with the same classes of people who require these things. So with them he deals by means of his equivalent institutions, slavery, the lash, and death. You have just as much right, my logical friend, to call the West Coast Chief hard names for his habit of using brass bars, heads of tobacco, and so on, in place of sixpenny pieces, as you have to abuse him for clubbing an inveterate thief. It's deplorably low of him, I own, but by what alternative plan of government his can be replaced I do not quite see, under existing conditions. In religious affairs, the affairs which lead him into the majority of his iniquities, his real sin consists in believing too much. In his witchcraft, the sin is the same. Toleration means indifference, I believe, among all men. The African is not indifferent on the subject of witchcraft, and I do not see how one can expect him to be. Put yourself in his place and imagine you have got hold of a man or woman who has been placing a live crocodile or a catawumpus of some kind into your own or a valued relative's, or fellow-townsman's inside, so that it may eat up valuable viscera, and cause you or your friend suffering and death. How would you feel? A little like lynching your captive, I fancy.

I confess that the more I know of the West Coast Africans the more I like them. I own I think them fools of the first water for their power of believing in things; but I fancy I have analogous feelings towards even my fellow-countrymen when they go and violently believe in something that I cannot quite swallow.

CHAPTER XV

FETISH—(continued)

HOWEVER MUCH SOME of the African's mental attributes get under-rated, I am sure there are others of them for which he gets more credit than he deserves. One of these is his imagination. It strikes the new-comer with awe, and frequently fills him with rage, when he first meets it; but as he matures and gets used to the African, he sees the string. For the African fancy is not the "aërial fancy flying free," mentioned by our poets, but merely the aërial of the theatre suspended by a wire or cord. The wire that supports the African's fancy may be a very thin, small fact indeed, or in some cases merely his incapacity to distinguish between animate and inanimate objects, which give rise to his idea that everything is possessed of a soul. Everything has a soul to him, and to make confusion worse confounded, he usually believes in the existence of matter apart from its soul. But there is little he won't believe in, if it comes to that; and I have a feeling of thankfulness that Buddhism, Theosophy, and above all Atheism, which chases its tail and proves that nothing can be proved, have not yet been given the African to believe in.

The African's want of making it clear in his language whether he is referring to an animate or inanimate thing, has landed me in many a dilemma, and his foolishness in not having a male and female gender in his languages amounts to a nuisance. For example, I am a most ladylike old person and yet get constantly called "Sir." The other day, circumstances having got beyond my control during the afternoon, I arrived in the evening in a saturated condition at a white settlement, and wishing to get accommodation for myself and my men, I made my way to the factory of a firm from whose representatives I have always received great and most courteous help. The agent in charge was not at home, and his steward-boy said, "Massa live for Mr. B.'s house." "Go tell him I live for come from," etc., said I, and "I fit for want place for my men." I had nothing to write on, or with, and I thought the steward-boy could carry this little message to its destination without dropping any of it, as Mr. B.'s house was close by; but I was wrong. Off he went, and soon returned with the note I here give a copy of: —

"DEAR OLD MAN,

"You must be in a deuce of a mess after the tornado. Just help yourself to a set of my dry things. The shirts are in the bottom drawer, the trousers are in the box under the bed, and then come over here to the sing-song. My leg is dickey or I'd come across.—Yours," etc.

Had there been any smelling salts or sal volatile in this subdivision of the Ethiopian region, I should have forthwith fainted on reading this, but I well knew there was not, so I blushed until the steam from my soaking clothes (for I truly was "in a deuce of a mess") went up in a cloud and then, just as I was, I went "across" and appeared before the author of that awful note. When he came round, he said it had taken seven years' growth out of him, and was intensely apologetic. I remarked it had very nearly taken thirty years' growth out of me, and he said the steward-boy had merely informed him that "White man live for come from X," a place where he knew there was another factory belonging to his firm, and he naturally thought it was the agent from X who had come across.

You rarely, indeed I believe never, find an African with a gift for picturesque descriptions of scenery. The nearest approach to it I ever got was from my cook when we were on Mungo mah Lobeh. He proudly boasted he had been on a mountain, up Cameroon River, with a German officer, and on that mountain, "If you fall down one side you die, if you fall down other side you die."

Graphic and vivid descriptions of incidents you often get, but it is not Art. The effect is produced entirely by a bald brutality of statement, the African having no artistic reticence whatsoever. One fine touch, however, which does not come in under this class was told me by my lamented friend Mr. Harris of Calabar. Some years ago he had out a consignment of Dutch clocks with hanging weights, as is natural to the Dutch clock. They were immensely popular among the chiefs, and were soon disposed of save one, which had seen trouble on the voyage out and lost one of its weights. Mr. Harris, who was a man of great energy and resource, melted up some metal spoons and made a new weight and hung it on the clock. The day he finished this a chief came in, anxious for a Dutch clock, and Mr. Harris forthwith sold him the repaired one.

About a week elapsed, and then the chief turned up at the factory again with a rueful countenance, followed by a boy carrying something swathed in a cloth. It was the clock.

"You do me bad too much, Mr. Harris," said the chief. Mr. Harris denied this on the spot with the vehemence of injured innocence. The chief shook his head and spat profusely and sorrowfully.

"You no sabe him clock you done sell me?" said he. "When I look him clock it no be to-day, it be to-morrow." Mr. Harris took the clock back, to see what was the cause of this strange state of affairs. Of course it arose from his having been too liberal in the amount of spoon in the weight, and this being altered, the chief was not hurried onward to his grave at such a rattling pace; "but," said Mr. Harris, "that clock was a flyer to the last."

But I will not go into the subject of African languages here, but only remark of them that although they are elaborate enough to produce, for their users, nearly every shade of erroneous statement, they are not, save perhaps M'pon-gwe, elaborate enough to enable a native to state his exact thought. Some of them are very dependent on gesture. When I was with the Fans they frequently said, "We will go to the fire so that we can see what they say," when any question had to be decided after dark, and the inhabitants of Fernando Po, the Bubis, are quite unable to converse with each other unless they have sufficient light to see the accompanying gestures of the conversation. In all cases I feel sure the African's intelligence is far ahead of his language.

The African is usually great at dreams, and has them very noisily; but he does not seem to me to attach immense importance to them, certainly not so much as the Red Indian does. I doubt whether there is much real ground for supposing that from dreams came man's first conception of the spirit world, and I think the origin of man's religious belief lies in man's misfortunes.

There can be little doubt that the very earliest human beings found, as their descendants still find, their plans frustrated, let them plan ever so wisely and carefully; they must have seen their companions overtaken by death and disaster, arising both from things they could see and from things they could not see. The distinction between these two classes of phenomena is not so definitely recognised by savages or animals as it is by the more cultured races of humanity. I doubt whether a savage depends on his five senses alone to teach him what the world is made of, any more than a Fellow of the Royal Society does. From this method of viewing nature I feel sure that the general idea arose—which you find in all early cultures—that death was always the consequence of the action of some malignant spirit, and that there is no accidental or natural death, as we call it; and death is, after all, the most impressive attribute of life.

If a man were knocked on the head with a club, or shot with an arrow, the cause of death is clearly the malignancy of the person using these weapons; and so it is easy to think that a man killed by a fallen tree, or by the upsetting of a canoe in the surf, or in an eddy in the river, is also the victim of some being using these things as weapons.

A man having thus gained a belief that there are more than human actors in life's tragedy, the idea that disease is also a manifestation of some invisible being's wrath and power seems to me natural and easy; and he knows you can get another man for a consideration to kill or harm a third party, and so he thinks that, for a consideration, you can also get one of these superhuman beings, which we call gods or devils, but which the African regards in another light, to do so.

A certain set of men and women then specialise off to study how these spirits can be managed, and so arises a priesthood; and the priests, or medicine men as they are called in their earliest forms, gradually, for their own ends, elaborate and wrap round their profession with ritual and mystery.

The savage is also conscious of another great set of phenomena which, he soon learns, take no interest in human affairs. The sun which rises and sets, the moon which changes, the tides which come and go:—what do they care? Nothing; and what is more, sacrifice to them what you may, you cannot get them to care about you and your affairs, and so the savage turns his attention to those other spirits that do take only too much interest, as is proved by those unexpected catastrophes; and, as their actions show, these spirits are all malignant, so he deals with them just as he would deal with a bad man whom he was desirous of managing. He flatters and fees them, he deprives himself of riches to give to them as sacrifices, believing they will relish it all the more because it gives him pain of some sort to give it to them. He holds that they think it will be advisable for them to encourage him to continue the giving by occasionally doing what he asks them. Naturally he never feels sure of them; he sees that you may sacrifice to a god for years, you may wrap him up—or more properly speaking, the object in which he resides—in your only cloth on chilly nights while you shiver yourself; you and your children, and your mother, and your sister and her children, may go hungry that food may rot upon his shrine; and yet, in some hour of dire necessity, the power will not come and save you—because he has been lured away by some richer gifts than yours.

You white men will say, "Why go on believing in him then?" but that is an idea that does not enter the African mind. I might just as well say "Why do you go on believing in the existence of hansom cabs," because one hansom cab driver malignantly fails to take you where you want to go, or fails to arrive in time to catch a train you wished to catch.

The African fully knows the liability of his fetish to fail, but he equally fully knows its power. One, to me, grandly tragic instance of this I learnt at Opobo. There was a very great Fetish doctor there, universally admired and trusted, who lived out on the land at the mouth of the Great River. One day he himself fell sick, and he made ju-ju against the sickness; but it held on, and he grew worse. He made more ju-ju of greater power, but again in vain, and then he made the greatest ju-ju man can make, and it availed nought, and he knew he was dying; and so, with his remaining strength, he broke up and dishonoured and destroyed all the Fetishes in which the spirits lived, and cast them out into the surf and died like a man.

Then horror came upon the people when they knew he had done this, and they burnt his house and all things belonging to him, and cried upon the spirits not to forsake them, not to lay this one man's deadly sin at their doors.

In connection with the gods of West Africa I may remark that in almost all the series of native tradition there, you will find accounts of a time when there was direct intercourse between the gods or spirits that live in the sky, and men. That intercourse is always said to have been cut off by some human error; for example, the Fernando Po people say that once upon a time there was no trouble or serious disturbance upon earth because there was a ladder, made like the one you get palm-nuts with, "only long, long;" and this ladder reached from earth to heaven so the gods could go up and down it and attend personally to mundane affairs. But one day a cripple boy started to go up the ladder, and he had got a long way up when his mother saw him, and went up in pursuit. The gods, horrified at the prospect of having boys and women invading heaven, threw down the ladder, and have since left humanity severely alone. The Timneh people, north-east of Sierra Leone, say that in old times God was very friendly with men, and when He thought a man had lived long enough on earth, He sent a messenger to him telling him to come up into the sky, and stay with Him; but once there was a man who, when the messenger of God came, did not want to leave his wives, his slaves, and his riches, and so the messenger had to go back without him; and God was very cross and sent another messenger for him, who was called Disease, but the man would not come for him either, and so Disease sent back word to God that he must have help to bring the man; and so God sent another messenger whose name was Death; and Disease and Death together got hold of the man, and took him to God; and God said in future He would always send these messengers to fetch men.

The Fernando Po legend may be taken as fairly pure African, but the Timneh, I expect, is a transmogrified Arabic story—though I do not know of anything like it among Arabic stories; but they are infinite in quantity, and there is a certain ring about it I recognise, and these Timnehs are much in contact with the Mohammedan, Mandingoes, etc. In none of the African stories is there given anything like the importance to dreams that there is given to attempts to account for accidents and death; and surely it must have been more impressive and important to a man to have got his leg or arm snapped off by a crocodile in the river, or by a shark in the surf, or to have got half killed, or have seen a friend killed by a falling tree in the forest in the day time, than to have experienced the most wonderful of dreams. He sees that however terrific his dream-experiences may have been, he was not much the worse for them. Not so in the other case, a limb gone or a life gone is more impressive, and more necessary to account for.

No trace of sun-worship have I ever found. The firmament is, I believe, always the great indifferent and neglected god, the Nyan Kupon of the Tschwi, and the Anzambe, Nzam, etc., of the Bantu races. The African thinks this god has great power if he would only exert it, and when things go very badly with him, when the river rises higher than usual and sweeps away his home and his plantations; when the smallpox stalks through the land, and day and night the corpses float down the river past him, and he finds them jammed among his canoes that are tied to the beach, and choking up his fish traps; and then when at last the death-wail over its victims goes up night and day from his own village, he will rise up and call upon this great god in a terror maddened by despair, that he may hear and restrain the evil workings of these lesser devils; but he evidently finds, as Peer Gynt says, "Nein, er hört nicht. Er ist taub wie gewöhnlich" for there is no organised cult for Anzam.

Accounts of apparitions abound in all the West Coast districts, and although the African holds them all in high horror and terror, he does not see anything supernatural in his "Duppy." It is a horrid thing to happen on, but there is nothing strange about it, and he is ten thousand times more frightened than puzzled over the affair. He does not want to "investigate" to see whether there is anything in it. He wants to get clear away, and make ju-ju against it, "one time."

These apparitions have a great variety of form, for, firstly, there are all the true spirits, nature spirits; secondly, the spirits of human beings—these human spirits are held to exist before as well as during and after bodily life; thirdly, the spirits of things. Probably the most horrid of class one is the Tschwi's Sasabonsum. Whether Sasabonsum is an individual or a class is not quite clear, but I believe he is a class of spirits, each individual of which has the same characteristics, the same manner of showing anger, the same personal appearance, and the same kind of residence. I am a devoted student of his cult and I am always coming across equivalent forms of him in other tribes as well as the Tschwi, and I think he is very early. As the Tschwi have got their religious notions in a most tidy and definite state, we will take their version of Sasabonsum.

He lives in the forest, in or under those great silk-cotton trees around the roots of which the earth is red. This coloured earth identifies a silk-cotton tree as being the residence of a Sasabonsum, as its colour is held to arise from the blood it whips off him as he goes down to his under-world home after a night's carnage. All silk-cotton trees are suspected because they are held to be the roosts for Duppies. But the red earth ones are feared with a great fear, and no one makes a path by them, or a camp near them at night.

Sasabonsum is a friend of witches. He is of enormous size, and of a red colour. He wears his hair straight and he waylays unprotected wayfarers in the forest at night, and in all districts except that of Apollonia he eats them. Round Apollonia he only sucks their blood. Natives of this district after meeting him have crawled home and given an account of his appearance, and then expired.

Ellis says he is believed to be implacable, and when angered can never be mollified or propitiated, but it is certain that human victims are constantly sacrificed to him in districts beyond white control; in districts under it, the equivalent value of a human sacrifice in sheep and goats is offered to him. In Ashantee he has priests, and of course human sacrifice. Away among the Da-homeyan tribes—where he has kept his habits but got another name, and seems to have crystallised from a class into an individual—the usual way in which a god develops—he has priests and priestesses, and they are holy terrors; but among the Tschwi, Sasabonsum is mainly dealt with by witches, and people desirous of possessing the power of becoming witches. They derive their power from him in a remarkable way. I put myself to great personal inconvenience (fever risk, mosquito certainty, high leopard and snake palaver probability, and grave personal alarm and apprehension) to verify Colonel Ellis's account of the methods witches employ in this case, to obtain ehsuhman and I find his account correct. {363}

The chief use of a suhman is the power it gives its owner to procure the death of other people, not necessarily his own enemies, for he will sell charms made by the agency of his suhman to another person whose nerves have not been equal to facing Sasabonsum on his own account. He can also provide by its agency other charms, such as those that protect houses from fire, and things and individuals from accidents on the road, or in canoes, and the home circle from good-looking but unprincipled young men, and so on.

As a rule the person who has a suhman keeps the fact pretty quiet, for the possession of such an article would lead half the catastrophes in his district, from the decease of pigs, fowls, and babies, to fires, etc., to be accredited to him, which would lead to his neighbours making "witch palaver" over him, and he would have to undergo poison-ordeal and other unpleasantness to clear his character. He, however, always keeps a special day in his suhman's honour, and should he be powerful, as a king or big chief, he will keep this day openly. King Kwoffi Karri Kari, whom we fought with in 1874, used to make a big day for his suhman, which was kept in a box covered with gold plates, and he sacrificed a human victim to it every Tuesday, with general festivities and dances in its honour.

I should remark that Sasabonsum is married. His wife, or more properly speaking his female form, is called Shamantin. She is far less malignant than the male form. Her name comes from Srahman—ghost or spirit; the termination "tin" is an abbreviation of sintstin - tall. She is of immense height, and white; perhaps this idea is derived from the white stem of the silk-cotton trees wherein she invariably abides. Her method of dealing with the solitary wayfarer is no doubt inconvenient to him, but it is kinder than her husband's ways, for she does not kill and eat him, as Sasabonsum does, but merely detains him some months while she teaches him all about the forest: what herbs are good to eat, or to cure disease; where the game come to drink, and what they say to each other, and so forth. I often wish I knew this lady, for the grim, grand African forests are like a great library, in which, so far, I can do little more than look at the pictures, although I am now busily learning the alphabet of their language, so that I may some day read what these pictures mean.

Do not go away with the idea, I beg, that goddesses as a general rule, are better than gods. They are not. There are stories about them which I could—I mean I could not—tell you. There is one belonging also to the Tschwi. She lives at Moree, a village five miles from Cape Coast. She is, as is usual with deities, human in shape and colossal in size, and as is not usual with deities, she is covered with hair from head to foot,—short white hair like a goat. Her abode is on the path to surf-cursed Anamabu near the sea-beach, and her name is Aynfwa; a worshipper of hers has only got to mention the name of a person he wishes dead when passing her abode and Aynfwa does the rest. She is the goddess of all albinoes, who are said to be more frequent in occurrence round Moree than elsewhere. Ellis says that in 1886, when he was there, they were 1 per cent. of the entire population. These albinoes are, ipso facto, her priests and priestesses, and in old days an albino had only to name anywhere a person Aynfwa wished for, and that person was forthwith killed.

I think I may safely say that every dangerous place in West Africa is regarded as the residence of a god—rocks and whirlpools in the rivers—swamps "no man fit to pass"—and naturally, the surf. Along the Gold Coast, at every place where you have to land through the surf, it fairly swarms with gods. A little experience with the said surf inclines you to think, as the dabblers in spiritualism say "that there is something in it." I will back this West Coast surf—"the Calemma," as we call it down South, against any other malevolent abomination, barring only the English climate. Its ways of dealing with human beings are cunning and deceitful. In its most ferocious moods it seizes a boat, straightway swamps it, and feeds its pet sharks with the boat's occupants. If the surf is merely sky-lark-ing it lets your boat's nose just smell the sand, and then says "Thought you were all right this time, did you though," and drags the boat back again under the incoming wave, or catches it under the stern and gaily throws it upside down over you and yours on the beach. Variety, they say, is charming. Let those who say it, and those who believe it, just do a course of surf-work, and I'll warrant they will change their minds.

There is one thing about the surf that I do not understand, and that is why witches always walk stark naked along the beach by it at night, and eat sea crabs the while. That such is a confirmed habit of theirs is certain; and they tell me that while doing this the witches emit a bright light, and also that there is a certain medicine, which, if you have it with you, you can throw over the witch, and then he, or she, will remain blazing until morning time, running to and fro, crying out wildly, in front of the white, breaking, thundering surf wall, and when the dawn comes the fire burns the witch right up, leaving only a grey ash—and palaver set in this world and the next for that witch.

A highly-esteemed native minister told me when I was at Cape Coast last, that a fortnight before, he had been away in the Apollonia district on mission work. One evening he and a friend were walking along the beach and the night was dark, so that you could see only the surf. It is never too dark to see that, it seems to have light in itself. They saw a flame coming towards them, and after a moment's doubt they knew it was a witch, and feeling frightened, hid them-selves among the bushes that edge the sandy shore. As they watched, it came straight on and passed them, and they saw it disappear in the distance. My informant laughed at himself, and very wisely said, "One has not got to believe those things here, one has in Apollonia."

To the surf and its spirits the sea-board-dwelling Tschwis bring women who have had children and widows, both after a period of eight days from the birth of the child, or the death of the husband.

A widow remains in the house until this period has elapsed, neglecting her person, eating little food, and sitting on the bare floor in the attitude of mourn-ing. On the Gold Coast they bury very quickly, as they are always telling you, usually on the day after death, rarely later than the third day, even among the natives; and the spirit, or Srah, of the dead man is supposed to hang about his wives and his house until the ceremony of purification is carried out. This is done, needless to say, with uproar. The relations of each wife go to her house with musical instruments—I mean tom-toms and that sort of thing—and they take a quantity of mint, which grows wild in this country, with them. This mint they burn, some of it in the house, the rest they place upon pans of live coals and carry round the widow as she goes in their midst down to the surf, her relatives singing aloud to the Srah of the departed husband, telling him that now he is dead and has done with the lady he must leave her. This singing serves to warn all the women who are not relations to get out of the way, which of course they always carefully do, because if they were to see the widow their own husbands would die within the year.

When the party has arrived at the shore, they strip every rag off the widow, and throw it into the surf; and a thoughtful female relative having brought a suit of dark blue baft with her for the occasion, the widow is clothed in this and returns home, where a suitable festival is held, after which she may marry again; but if she were to marry before this ceremony, the Srah of the husband would play the mischief with husband number two or three, and so on, as the case might be.

In the inland Gold Coast districts the widows remain in a state of mourning for several months, and a selection of them, a quantity of slaves, and one or two free men are killed to escort the dead man to Srahmandazi; and as well as these, and in order to provide him with merchandise to keep up his house and state in the under-world, quantities of gold dust, rolls of rich velvets, silks, satins, etc., are thrown into the grave.

Among the dwellers in Cameroon, when you are across the Bantu border-line, velvets, etc., are buried with a big man or woman; but I am told it is only done for the glorification of his living relatives, so that the world may say, "So and so must be rich, look what a lot of trade he threw away at that funeral of his wife," or his father, or his son, as the case may be; but I doubt whether this is the true explanation. If it is, I should recommend my German friends, if they wish to intervene, to introduce the income tax into Cameroon—that would eliminate this custom.

The Tschwis hold that there is a definite earthly existence belonging to each soul of a human kind. Let us say, for example, a soul has a thirty years' bodily existence belonging to it. Well, suppose that soul's body gets killed off at twenty-five, its remaining five years it has to spend, if it is left alone, in knocking about its old haunts, homes, and wives. In this state it is called a Sisa, and is a nuisance. It will cause sickness. It will throw stones. It will pull off roofs, and it will play the very mischief with its wives' subsequent husbands, all because, not having reached its full term of life, it has not learnt its way down the dark and difficult path to Srahmandazi, the entrance to which is across the Volta River to the N.E. This knowledge of the path to Srahmandazi is a thing that grows gradually on a man's immortal soul (the other three souls are not immortal), and naturally not having been allowed to complete his life, his knowledge is imperfect. A man's soul, however, can be taught the way, if necessary, in the funeral "custom" made by his relatives and the priests; but in a case of an in-completelifeonearthsoul, as a German would say, when it does arrive in the land of Insrah (pl.) it is in a weak and feeble state from the difficulties of its journey, whereas a soul that has lived out its allotted span of life goes straightway off to Srahmandazi as soon as its "custom" or "devil" is made and gives its surviving relatives no further trouble. Still there is great difference of opinion among all the Tschwis and Ga men I have come across on this point, and Ellis likewise remarks on this difference of opinion. Some informants say that a soul that has been sent hence before its time, although it is exhausted by the hardships it has suffered on its journey down, yet recovers health in a month or so; while a soul that has run its allotted span on earth is as feeble as a new-born babe on arriving in Srahmandazi, and takes years to pull round. Other informants say they have no knowledge of these details, and state that all the difference they know of be-tween the souls of men who have been killed and the men who have died, is that the former can always come back, and that really the safest way of disposing of this class of soul is, by suitable spells and incantations, to get it to enter into the body of a new-born baby, where it can live out the remainder of its life.

Before closing these observations on Srahmandazi I will give the best ac-count of that land that I am at present able to. Some day perhaps I may share the fate of the Oxford Professor in In the Wrong Paradise and go there myself, but so far my information is second-hand.

It is like this world. There are towns and villages, rivers, mountains, bush, plantations, and markets. When the sun rises here it sets in Srahmandazi. It has its pleasures and its pains, not necessarily retributive or rewarding, but dim. All souls in it grow forward or backward into the prime of life and remain there, some informants say; others say that each inhabitant remains there at the same age as he was when he quitted the world above. This latter view is most like the South West one. The former is possibly only an attempt to make Srahmandazi into a heaven in conformation with Christian teaching, which it is not, any more than it is a hell.

I have much curious information regarding its flora and fauna. A great deal of both is seemingly indigenous, and then there are the souls of great human beings, the Asrahmanfw, and the souls of all the human beings, animals, and things sent down with them. The ghosts do not seem to leave off their interest in mundane affairs, for they not only have local palavers, but try palavers left over from their earthly existence; and when there is an outbreak of sickness in a Fantee town or village, and several inhabitants die off, the opinion is often held that there is a big palaver going on down in Srahmandazi and that the spirits are sending up on earth for witnesses, subpoenaing them as it were. Medicine men or priests are called in to find out what particular earthly grievance can be the subject of the ghost palaver, and when they have ascertained this, they take the evidence of every one in the town on this affair, as it were on commission, and transmit the information to the court sitting in Srahmandazi. This prevents the living being incommoded by personal journeys down below, and although the priests have their fee, it is cheaper in the end, because the witnesses' funeral expenses would fall heavier still.

Although far more elaborated and thought out than any other African underworld I have ever come across, the Tschwi Srahmandazi may be taken as a type of all the African underworlds. The Bantu's idea of a future life is a life spent in much such a place. As far as I can make out there is no definite idea of eternity. I have even come across cases in which doubt was thrown on the present existence of the Creating God, but I think this has arisen from attempts having been made to introduce concise conceptions into the African mind, conceptions that are quite foreign to its true nature and which alarm and worry it. You never get the strange idea of the difference between time and eternity—the idea I mean, that they are different things—in the African that one frequently gets in cultured Europeans; and as for the human soul, the African always believes "that still the spirit is whole, and life and death but shadows of the soul."

CHAPTER XVI

FETISH—(concluded)

<small>IN WHICH THE DISCOURSE ON APPARITIONS IS CONTINUED, WITH SOME OBSERVATIONS ON SECRET SOCIETIES, BOTH TRIBAL AND MURDER, AND THE KINDRED SUBJECT OF LEOPARDS.</small>

APPARITIONS ARE BY NO MEANS ALWAYS of human soul origin. All the Tschwi and the Ewe gods, for example, have the habit of appearing pretty regularly to their priests, and occasionally to the laity, like Sasabonsum; but it is only to priests that these appearances are harmless or beneficial. The effect of Sasabonsum's appearance to the layman I have cited above, and I could give many other examples of the bad effects of those of other gods, but will only now mention Tando, the Hater, the chief god of the Northern Tschwi, the Ashantees, etc. He is terribly malicious, human in shape, and though not quite white, is decidedly lighter in complexion than the chief god of the Southern Tschwi, Bobowissi. His hair is lank, and he carries a native sword and wears a long robe. His well-selected messengers are those awful driver ants (Inkran) which it is not orthodox to molest in Tando's territories. He uses as his weapons lightning, tempest, and disease, but the last is the most favourite one.

There is absolutely no trick too mean or venomous for Tando. For example, he has a way of appearing near a village he has a grudge against in the form of a male child, and wanders about crying bitterly, until some kind-hearted, unsuspecting villager comes and takes him in and feeds him. Then he develops a contagious disease that clears that village out.

This form of appearance and subsequent conduct is, unhappily, not rigidly confined to Tando, but is used by many spirits as a method of collecting arrears in taxes in the way of sacrifices. I have found traces of it among Bantu gods or spirits, and it gives rise to a general hesitation in West Africa to take care of waifs and strays of unexplained origin.

Other things beside gods and human spirits have the habit of becoming incarnate. Once I had to sit waiting a long time at an apparently perfectly clear bush path, because in front of us a spear's ghost used to fly across the path about that time in the afternoon, and if any one was struck by it they died. A certain spring I know of is haunted by the ghost of a pitcher. Many ladies when they have gone alone to fill their pitchers in the evening time at this forest spring have noticed a very fine pitcher standing there ready filled, and thinking exchange is no robbery, or at any rate they would risk it if it were, have left their own pitcher and taken the better looking one; but always as soon as they have come within sight of the village huts, the new pitcher has crumbled into dust, and the water in it been spilt on the ground; and the worst of it is, when they have returned to fetch their own discarded pitcher, they find it also shattered into pieces.

There is also another class of apparition, of which I have met with two instances, one among pure Negroes (Okÿon); the other among pure Bantu (Kangwe). I will give the Bantu version of the affair, because at Okÿon the incident had happened a good time before the details were told me, and in the Bantu case they had happened the previous evening. But there was very little difference in the main facts of the case, and it was an important thing because in both cases the underlying idea was sacrificial.

The woman who told me was an exceedingly intelligent, shrewd, reliable person. She had been to the factory with some trade, and had got a good price for it, and so was in a good temper on her return home in the evening. She got out of her canoe and leaving her slave boy to bring up the things, walked to her house, which was the ordinary house of a prosperous Igalwa native, having two distinct rooms in it, and a separate cook-house close by in a clean, sandy yard. She trod on some nastiness in the yard, and going into the cook-house found the slave girls round a very small and inefficient fire, trying to cook the evening meal. She blew them up for not having a proper fire; they said the wood was wet, and would not burn. She said they lied, and she would see to them later, and she went into the chamber she used for a sleeping apartment, and trod on something more on the floor in the dark; those good-for-nothing hussies of slaves had not lit her palm-oil lamp, and mentally forming the opinion that they had been out flirting during her absence, and resolving to teach them well the iniquity of such conduct, she sat down on her bed into a lot of messy stuff of a clammy, damp nature. Now this fairly roused her, for she is a notable housewife, who keeps her house and slaves in exceedingly good order. So dismissing from her mind the commercial consideration she had intended to gloat over when she came into her room, she called Ingremina and others in a tone that brought those young ladies on the spot. She asked them how they dared forget to light her lamp; they said they had not, but the lamp in the room must have gone out like the other lamps had, after burning dim and spluttering. They further said they had not been out, but had been sitting round the fire trying to make it burn properly. She duly whacked and pulled the ears of all within reach. I say within reach for she is not very active, weighing, I am sure, upwards of eighteen stone. Then she went back into her room and got out her beautiful English paraffin lamp, which she keeps in a box, and taking it into the cook-house, picked up a bit of wood from the hissing, spluttering fire, and lit it. When she picked up the wood she noticed that it was covered with the same sticky abomination she had met before that evening, and it smelt of the same faint smell she had noticed as soon as she had reached her house, and by now the whole air seemed oppressive with it.

As soon as the lamp was alight she saw what the stuff was, namely, blood. Blood was everywhere, the rest of the sticks in the fire had it on them, it sizzled at the burning ends, and ran off the other in rills. There were pools of it about her clean, sandy yard. Her own room was reeking, the bed, the stools, the floor; it trickled down the door-post; coagulated on the lintel. She herself was smeared with it from the things she had come in contact with in the dark, and the slaves seemed to have been sitting in pools of it. The things she picked up off the table and shelf left rims of it behind them; there was more in the skillets, and the oil in the open palm-oil lamps had a film of it floating on the oil. Investigation showed that the whole of the rest of her house was in a similar mess. The good lady gave a complete catalogue of the household furniture and its condition, which I need not give here. The slave girls when the light came were terrified at what they saw, and she called in the aristocracy of the village, and asked them their opinion on the blood palaver. They said they could make nothing of it at first, but subsequently formed the opinion that it meant something was going to happen, and suggested with the kind, helpful cheerfulness of relatives and friends, that they should not wonder if it were a prophecy of her own death. This view irritated the already tried lady, and she sent them about their business, and started the slaves on house-cleaning. The blood cleaned up all right when you were about it, but kept on turning up in other places, and in the one you had just cleaned as soon as you left off and went elsewhere; and the morning came and found things in much the same state until "before suntime," say about 10 o'clock, when it faded away.

I cautiously tried to get my stately, touchy dowager duchess to explain how it was that there was such a lot of blood, and how it was it got into the house. She just said "it had to go somewhere," and refused to give rational explanations as Chambers's Journal does after telling a good ghost story. I found afterwards that it was quite decided it was a case of "blood come before," and at Okÿon, Miss Slessor told me, in regard to the similar case there, that this was the opinion held regarding the phenomenon. It is always held uncanny in Africa if a person dies without shedding blood. You see, the blood is the life, and if you see it come out, you know the going of the thing, as it were. If you do not, it is mysterious. At Okÿon, a few days after the blood appeared, a nephew of the person whose house it came into was killed while felling a tree in the forest; a bough struck him and broke his neck, without shedding a drop of blood, and this bore out the theory, for the blood having "to go somewhere" came before. In the Bantu case I did not hear of such a supporting incident happening.

Certain African ideas about blood puzzle me. I was told by a Batanga friend, a resident white trader, that a short time previously a man was convicted of theft by the natives of a village close to him. The hands and feet of the criminal were tied together, and he was flung into the river. He got himself free, and swam to the other bank, and went for bush. He was recaptured, and a stone tied to his neck, and in again he was thrown. The second time he got free and ashore, and was recaptured, and the chief then, most regretfully, ordered that he was to be knocked on the head before being thrown in for a third time. This time palaver set, but the chief knew that he would die himself, by spitting the blood he had spilt, from his own lungs, before the year was out. I inquired about the chief when I passed this place, more than eighteen months after, and learnt from a native that the chief was dead, and that he had died in this way. The objection thus was not to shedding blood in a general way, but to the shedding in the course of judicial execution. There may be some idea of this kind underlying the ingenious and awful ways the negroes have of killing thieves, by tying them to stakes in the rivers, or down on to paths for the driver ants to kill and eat, but this is only conjecture; I have not had a chance yet to work this subject up; and getting reliable information about underlying ideas is very difficult in Africa. The natives will say "Yes" to any mortal thing, if they think you want them to; and the variety of their languages is another great hindrance. Were it not for the prevalence of Kru English or trade English, investigation would be almost impossible; but, fortunately, this quaint language is prevalent, and the natives of different tribes communicate with each other in it, and so round a fire, in the evening, if you listen to the gossip, you can pick up all sorts of strange information, and gain strange and often awful lights on your absent white friends' characters, and your present companions' religion. For example, the other day I had a set of porters composed of four Bassa boys, two Wei Weis, one Dualla, and two Yorubas. None of their languages fitted, so they talked trade English, and pretty lively talk some of it was, but of that anon.

I cannot close this brief notice of native ideas without mentioning the secret societies; but to go fully into this branch of the subject would require volumes, for every tribe has its secret society. The Poorah of Sierra Leone, the Oru of Lagos, the Egbo of Calabar, the Isyogo of the Igalwa, the Ukuku of the Benga, the Okukwe of the M'pongwe, the Ikun of the Bakele, and the Lukuku of the Bachilangi Baluba, are some of the most powerful secret societies on the West African Coast.

These secret societies are not essentially religious, their action is mainly judicial, and their particularly presiding spirit is not a god or devil in our sense of the word. The ritual differs for each in its detail, but there are broad lines of agreement between them. There are societies both for men and for women, but mixed societies for both sexes are rare. Those that I have mentioned above are all male, except the Lukuku, and women are utterly forbidden to participate in the rites or become acquainted with their secrets, for one of the chief duties of these societies is to keep the women in order; and besides it is undoubtedly held that women are bad for certain forms of ju-ju, even when these forms are not directly connected, as far as I can find out, with the secret society. For example, the other day a chief up the Mungo River deliberately destroyed his ju-ju by showing it to his women. It was a great ju-ju, but expensive to keep up, requiring sacrifices of slaves and goats, so what with trade being bad, fall in the price of oil and ivory and so on, he felt he could not afford that ju-ju, and so destroyed its power, so as to prevent its harming him when he neglected it.

The general rule with these secret societies is to admit the young free people at an age of about eight to ten years, the boys entering the male, the girls the female society. Both societies are rigidly kept apart. A man who attempts to penetrate the female mysteries would be as surely killed as a woman who might attempt to investigate the male mysteries; still I came, in 1893, across an amusing case which demonstrates the inextinguishable thirst for knowledge, so long as that knowledge is forbidden, which characterises our sex.

It was in the district just south of Big Batanga. The male society had been very hard on the ladies for some time, and one day one star-like intellect among the latter told her next-door neighbour, in strict confidence, that she did not believe Ikun was a spirit at all, but only old So-and-so dressed up in leaves. This rank heresy spread rapidly, in strict confidence, among the ladies at large, and they used to assemble together in the house of the foundress of the theory, secretly of course, because husbands down there are hasty with the cutlass and the kassengo, and they talked the matter over. Somehow or other, this came to the ears of the men. Whether the ladies got too emancipated and winked when Ikun was mentioned, or asked how Mr. So-and-so was this morning, in a pointed way, after an Ikun manifestation, I do not know; some people told me this was so, but others, who, I fear, were right, considering the acknowledged slowness of men in putting two and two together, and the treachery of women towards each other, said that a woman had told a man that she had heard some of the other women were going on in this heretical way. Anyhow, the men knew, and were much alarmed; scepticism had spread by now to such an extent that nothing short of burning or drowning all the women could stamp it out and reintroduce the proper sense of awe into the female side of Society, and after a good deal of consideration the men saw, for men are undoubtedly more gifted in foresight than our sex, that it was no particular use reintroducing this awe if there was no female half of Society to be impressed by it. It was a brain-spraining problem for the men all round, for it is clear Society cannot be kept together without some superhuman aid to help to keep the feminine portion of it within bounds.

Grave councils were held, and it was decided that the woman at whose house these treasonable meetings were held should be sent away early one morning on a trading mission to the nearest factory, a job she readily undertook; and while the other women were away in the plantation or at the spring, certain men entered her house secretly and dug a big chamber out in the floor of the hut, and one of them, dressed as Ikun, and provided with refreshments for the day, got into this chamber, and the whole affair was covered over carefully and the floor re-sanded. That afternoon there was a big manifestation of Ikun. He came in the most terrible form, his howls were awful, and he finally went dancing away into the bush as the night came down. The ladies had just taken the common-sense precaution of removing all goats, sheep, fowls, etc., into enclosed premises, for, like all his kind, he seizes and holds any property he may come across in the street, but there was evidently no emotional thrill in the female mind regarding him, and when the leading lady returned home in the evening the other ladies strolled into their leader's hut to hear about what new cotton prints, beads, and things Mr.--- had got at his factory by the last steamer from Europe, and interesting kindred subjects bearing on Mr.---. When they had threshed these matters out, the conversation turned on to religion, and what fools those men had been making of themselves all the afternoon with their Ikun. No sooner was his name uttered than a venomous howl, terminating in squeals of rage and impatience, came from the ground beneath them. They stared at each other for one second, and then, feeling that something was tearing its way up through the floor, they left for the interior of Africa with one accord. Ikun gave chase as soon as he got free, but what with being half-stifled and a bit cramped in the legs, and much encumbered with his vegetable decorations, the ladies got clear away and no arrests were made—but Society was saved. Scepticism became in the twinkling of an eye a thing of the past; and, although no names were taken, the men observed that certain ladies were particularly anxious, and regardless of expense, in buying immunity from Ikun, and they fancied that these ladies were probably in that hut on that particular evening, but they took no further action against them, save making Ikun particularly expensive. There ought to be a moral to an improving tale of this order, I know, but the only one I can think of just now is that it takes a priest to get round a woman; and I always feel inclined to jump on to the table myself when I think of those poor dear creatures sitting on the floor and feeling that awful thing clapper-clawing its way up right under them.

Tattooing on the West Coast is comparatively rare, and I think I may say never used with decorative intent only. The skin decorations are either paint or cicatrices—in the former case the pattern is not kept always the same by the individual. A peculiar form of it you find in the Rivers, where a pattern is painted on the skin, and then when the paint is dry, a wash is applied which makes the unpainted skin rise up in between the painted pattern. The cicatrices are sometimes tribal marks, but sometimes decorative. They are made by cutting the skin and then placing in the wound the fluff of the silk cotton tree.

The great point of agreement between all these West African secret societies lies in the methods of initiation.

The boy, if he belongs to a tribe that goes in for tattooing, is tattooed, and is handed over to instructors in the societies' secrets and formula. He lives, with the other boys of his tribe undergoing initiation, usually under the rule of several instructors, and for the space of one year. He lives always in the forest, and is naked and smeared with clay.

The boys are exercised so as to become inured to hardship; in some districts, they make raids so as to perfect themselves in this useful accomplishment. They always take a new name, and are supposed by the initiation process to become new beings in the magic wood, and on their return to their village at the end of their course, they pretend to have entirely forgotten their life before they entered the wood; but this pretence is not kept up beyond the period of festivities given to welcome them home. They all learn, to a certain extent, a new language, a secret language only understood by the initiated.

The same removal from home and instruction from initiated members is also observed with the girls. However, in their case, it is not always a forest-grove they are secluded in, sometimes it is done in huts. Among the Grain Coast tribes however, the girls go into a magic wood until they are married. Should they have to leave the wood for any temporary reason, they must smear themselves with white clay. A similar custom holds good in Okÿon, Calabar district, where, should a girl have to leave the fattening-house, she must be covered with white clay. I believe this fattening-house custom in Calabar is not only for fattening up the women to improve their appearance, but an initiatory custom as well, although the main intention is now, undoubtedly, fattening, and the girl is constantly fed with fat-producing foods, such as fou-fou soaked in palm oil. I am told, but I think wrongly, that the white clay with which a Calabar girl is kept covered while in the fattening-house, putting on an extra coating of it should she come outside, is to assist in the fattening process by preventing perspiration.

The duration of the period of seclusion varies somewhat. San Salvador boys are six months in the wood. Cameroon boys are twelve months. In most districts the girls are betrothed in infancy, and they go into the wood or initiatory hut for a few months before marriage. In this case the time seems to vary with the circumstances of the individual; not so with the boys, for whom each tribal society has a duly appointed course terminating at a duly appointed time; but sometimes, as among some of the Yoruba tribes, the boy has to remain under the rule of the presiding elders of the society, painted white, and wearing only a bit of grass cloth, if he wears anything, until he has killed a man. Then he is held to have attained man's estate by having demonstrated his courage and also by having secured for himself the soul of the man he has killed as a spirit slave.

The initiation of boys into a few of the elementary dogmas of the secret society by no means composes the entire work of the society. All of them are judicial, and taken on the whole they do an immense amount of good. The methods are frequently a little quaint. Rushing about the streets disguised under masks and drapery, with an imitation tail swinging behind you, while you lash out at every one you meet with a whip or cutlass, is not a European way of keeping the peace, or perhaps I should say maintaining the dignity of the Law. But discipline must be maintained, and this is the West African way of doing it.

The Egbo of Calabar is a fine type of the secret society. It is exceedingly well developed in its details, not sketchy like Isyogo, nor so red-handed as Poorah. Unfortunately, however, I cannot speak with the same amount of knowledge of Egbo as I could of Poorah.

Egbo has the most grades of initiation, except perhaps Poorah, and it exercises jurisdiction over all classes of crime except witchcraft. Any Effik man who desires to become an influential person in the tribe must buy himself into as high a grade of Egbo as he can afford, and these grades are expensive, £1,500 or £1,000 English being required for the higher steps, I am informed. But it is worth it to a great trader, as an influential Effik necessarily is, for he can call out his own class of Egbo and send it against those of his debtors who may be of lower grades, and as the Egbo methods of delivering its orders to pay up consist in placing Egbo at a man's doorway, and until it removes itself from that doorway the man dare not venture outside his house, it is most successful.

Of course the higher a man is in Egbo rank, the greater his power and security, for lower grades cannot proceed against higher ones. Indeed, when a man meets the paraphernalia of a higher grade of Egbo than that to which he belongs, he has to act as if he were lame, and limp along past it humbly, as if the sight of it had taken all the strength out of him, and, needless to remark, higher grade debtors flip their fingers at lower grade creditors.

After talking so much about the secret society spirits, it may be as well to say what they are. They are, one and all, a kind of a sort of a something that usually (the exception is Ikun) lives in the bush. Last February I was making my way back toward Duke Town—late, as usual; I was just by a town on the Qwa River. As I was hurrying onward I heard a terrific uproar accompanied by drums in the thick bush into which, after a brief interval of open ground, the path turned. I became cautious and alarmed, and hid in some dense bush as the men making the noise approached. I saw it was some ju-ju affair. They had a sort of box which they carried on poles, and their dresses were peculiar, and abnormally ample over the upper part of their body. They were prancing about in an ecstatic way round the box, which had one end open, beating their drums and shouting. They were fairly close to me, but fortunately turned their attention to another bit of undergrowth, or that evening they would have land-ed another kind of thing to what they were after. The bushes they selected they surrounded and evidently did their best to induce something to come out of them and go into their box arrangement. I was every bit as anxious as they were that they should succeed, and succeed rapidly, for you know there are a nasty lot of snakes and things in general, not to mention driver ants, about that Cal-abar bush, that do not make it at all pleasant to go sitting about in. However, presently they got this something into their box and rejoiced exceedingly, and departed staggering under the weight. I gave them a good start, and then made the best of my way home; and all that night Duke Town howled, and sang, and thumped its tom-toms unceasingly; for I was told Egbo had come into the town. Egbo is very coy, even for a secret society spirit, and seems to loathe pub-licity; but when he is ensconced in this ark he utters sententious observations on the subject of current politics, and his word is law. The voice that comes out of the ark is very strange, and unlike a human voice. I heard it shortly after Egbo had been secured. I expect, from what I saw, that there was some person in that ark all the time, but I do not know. It is more than I can do to understand my ju-ju details at present, let alone explain them on rational lines. I hear that there is a tribe on the slave coast who have been proved to keep a small child in the drum that is the residence of their chief spirit, and that when the child grows too large to go in it is killed, and another one that has in the meantime been trained by the priests takes the place of the dead one, until it, in its turn, grows too big and is killed, and so on. I expect this killing of the children is not sacrificial, but arises entirely from the fact that as ex-kings are dangerous to the body politic, therefore still more dangerous would ex-gods be.

Very little is known by outsiders regarding Egbo compared to what there must be to be known, owing to a want of interest or to a sense of inability on the part of most white people to make head or tail out of what seems to them a horrid pagan practice or a farrago of nonsense.

It is still a great power, although its officials in Duke or Creek Town are no longer allowed to go chopping and whipping promiscuous-like, because the Consul-General has a prejudice against this sort of thing, and the Effik is learning that it is nearly as unhealthy to go against his Consul-General as against his ju-ju. So I do not believe you will ever get the truth about it in Duke Town, or Creek Town. If you want to get hold of the underlying idea of these societies you must go round out-of-the-way corners where the natives are not yet afraid of being laughed at or punished.

Of the South-West Coast secret societies the Ukuku seems the most powerful. The Isyogo belonging to those indolent Igalwas, and M'pongwe is now little more than a play. You pretty frequently come upon Isyogo dances just round Libreville. You will see stretched across the little street in a cluster of houses, a line from which branches are suspended, making a sort of screen. The women and children keep one side of this screen, the men dancing on the other side to the peculiar monotonous Isyogo tune. Poorah I have spoken of elsewhere.

I believe that these secret societies are always distinct from the leopard societies. I have pretty nearly enough evidence to prove that it is so in some districts, but not in all. So far my evidence only goes to prove the distinction of the two among the Negroes, not among the Bantu, and in all cases you will find some men belonging to both. Some men, in fact, go in for all the societies in their district, but not all the men; and in all districts, if you look close, you will find several societies apart from the regular youth-initiating one.

These other societies are practically murder societies, and their practices usually include cannibalism, which is not an essential part of the rites of the great tribal societies, Isyogo or Egbo. In the Calabar district I was informed by natives that there was a society of which the last entered member has to provide, for the entertainment of the other members, the body of a relative of his own, and sacrificial cannibalism is always breaking out, or perhaps I should say being discovered, by the white authorities in the Niger Delta. There was the great outburst of it at Brass, in 1895, and the one chronicled in the Liverpool Mercury for August 13th, 1895, as occurring at Sierra Leone. This account is worth quoting. It describes the hanging by the Authorities of three murderers, and states the incidents, which took place in the Imperi country behind Free Town.

One of the chief murderers was a man named Jowe, who had formerly been a Sunday-school teacher in Sierra Leone. He pleaded in extenuation of his offence that he had been compelled to join the society. The others said they committed the murders in order to obtain certain parts of the body for ju-ju purposes, the leg, the hand, the heart, etc. The Mercury goes on to give the statement of the Reverend Father Bomy of the Roman Catholic Mission. "He said he was at Bromtu, where the St. Joseph Mission has a station, when a man was brought down from the Imperi country in a boat. The poor fellow was in a dreadful state, and was brought to the station for medical treatment. He said he was working on his farm, when he was suddenly pounced upon from behind. A number of sharp instruments were driven into the back of his neck. He presented a fearful sight, having wounds all over his body supposed to have been inflicted by the claws of the leopard, but in reality they were stabs from sharp-pointed knives. The native, who was a powerfully-built man, called out, and his cries attracting the attention of his relations, the leopards made off. The poor fellow died at Bromtu from the injuries. It was only his splendid physique that kept him alive until his arrival at the Mission." The Mercury goes on to quote from the Pall Mall, and I too go on quoting to show that these things are known and acknowledged to have taken place in a colony like Sierra Leone, which has had unequalled opportunities of becoming christianised for more than one hundred years, and now has more than one hundred and thirty places of Christian worship in it. "Some twenty years ago there was a war between this tribe Taima and the Paramas. The Paramas sent some of their war boys to be ambushed in the intervening country, the Imperi, but the Imperi delivered these war boys to the enemy. In revenge, the Paramas sent the Fetish Boofima into the Imperi country. This Fetish had up to that time been kept active and working by the sacrifice of goats, but the medicine men of the Paramas who introduced it into the Imperi country decreed at the same time that human sacrifices would be required to keep it alive, thereby working their vengeance on the Imperi by leading them to exterminate themselves in sacrifice to the Fetish. The country for years has been terrorised by this secret worship of Boofima and at one time the Imperi started the Tonga dances, at which the medicine men pointed out the supposed worshippers of Boofima—the so-called Human Leopards, because when seizing their victims for sacrifice they covered themselves with leopard skins, and imitating the roars of the leopard, they sprang upon their victim, plunging at the same time two three-pronged forks into each side of the throat. The Government some years ago forbade the Tonga dances, and are now striving to suppress the human leopards. There are also human alligators who, disguised as alligators, swim in the creeks upon the canoes and carry off the crew. Some of them have been brought for trial but no complete case has been made out against them!" In comment upon this account, which is evidently written by some one well versed in the affair, I will only remark that sometimes, instead of the three-pronged forks, there are fixed in the paws of the leopard skin sharp-pointed cutting knives, the skin being made into a sort of glove into which the hand of the human leopard fits. In one skin I saw down south this was most ingeniously done. The knives were shaped like the leopard's claws, curved, sharp-pointed, and with cutting edges underneath, and I am told the American Mendi Mission, which works in the Sierra Leone districts, have got a similar skin in their possession.

The human alligator mentioned, is our old friend the witch crocodile—the spirit of the man in the crocodile. I never myself came across a case of a man in his corporeal body swimming about in a crocodile skin, and I doubt whether any native would chance himself inside a crocodile skin and swim about in the river among the genuine articles for fear of their penetrating his disguise mentally and physically.

In Calabar witch crocodiles are still flourishing. There is an immense old brute that sporting Vice-Consuls periodically go after, which is known to contain the spirit of a Duke Town chief who shall be nameless, because they are getting on at such a pace just round Duke Town that haply I might be had up for libel. When I was in Calabar once, a peculiarly energetic officer had hit that crocodile and the chief was forthwith laid up by a wound in his leg. He said a dog had bit him. They, the chief and the crocodile, are quite well again now, and I will say this in favour of that chief, that nothing on earth would persuade me to believe that he went fooling about in the Calabar River in his corporeal body, either in his own skin or a crocodile's.

The introduction of the Fetish Boofima into the country of the Imperi is an interesting point as it shows that these different tribes have the same big ju-ju. Similarly, Calabar Egbo can go into Okÿon, and will be respected in some of the New Calabar districts, but not at Brass, where the secret society is a distinct cult. Often a neighbouring district will send into Calabar, or Brass, where the big ju-ju is, and ask to have one sent up into their district to keep order, but Egbo will occasionally be sent into a district without that district in the least wanting it; but, as in the Imperi case, when it is there it is supreme. But say, for example, you were to send Egbo round from Calabar to Cameroon. Cameroon might be barely civil to it, but would pay it no homage, for Cameroon has got no end of a ju-ju of its own. It can rise up as high as the Peak, 13,760 feet. I never saw the Cameroon ju-ju do this, but I saw it start up from four feet to quite twelve feet in the twinkling of an eye, and I was assured that it was only modest reticence on its part that made it leave the other 13,748 feet out of the performance.

Doctor Nassau seems to think that the tribal society of the Corisco regions is identical with the leopard societies. He has had considerable experience of the workings of the Ukuku, particularly when he was pioneering in the Benito regions, when it came very near killing him. He says the name signifies a departed spirit. "It is a secret society into which all the males are initiated at puberty, whose procedure may not be seen by females, nor its laws disobeyed by any one under pain of death, a penalty which is sometimes commuted to a fine, a heavy fine. Its discussions are uttered as an oracle from any secluded spot by some man appointed for the purpose.

"On trivial occasions any initiated man may personate Ukuku or issue commands for the family. On other occasions, as in Shiku, to raise prices, the society lays its commands on foreign traders."

Some cases of Ukuku proceedings against white traders have come under my own observation. A friend of mine, a trader in the Batanga district, in some way incurred the animosity of the society's local branch. He had, as is usual in the South-West Coast trade several sub-factories in the bush. He found himself boycotted; no native came in to his yard to buy or sell at the store, not even to sell food. He took no notice and awaited developments. One evening when he was sitting on his verandah, smoking and reading, he thought he heard some one singing softly under the house, this, like most European buildings hereabouts, being elevated just above the earth. He was attracted to the song and listened: it was evidently one of the natives singing, not one of his own Kruboys, and so, knowing the language, and having nothing else particular to do, he attended to the affair.

It was the same thing sung softly over and over again, so softly that he could hardly make out the words. But at last, catching his native name among them, he listened more intently than ever, down at a knot-hole in the wooden floor. The song was—"They are going to attack your factory at . . . to-morrow. They are going to attack your factory at . . . to-morrow," over and over again, until it ceased; and then he thought he saw something darker than the darkness round it creep across the yard and disappear in the bush. Very early in the morning he, with his Kruboys and some guns, went and established themselves in that threatened factory in force. The Ukuku Society turned up in the evening, and reconnoitred the situation, and finding there was more in it than they had expected, withdrew.

In the course of the next twenty-four hours he succeeded in talking the palaver successfully with them. He never knew who his singing friend was, but suspected it was a man whom he had known to be grateful for some kindness he had done him. Indeed there were, and are, many natives who have cause to be grateful to him, for he is deservedly popular among his local tribes, but the man who sang to him that night deserves much honour, for he did it at a terrific risk.

Sometimes representatives of the Ukuku fraternity from several tribes meet together and discuss intertribal difficulties, thereby avoiding war.

Dr. Nassau distinctly says that the Bantu region leopard society is identical with the Ukuku, and he says that although the leopards are not very numerous here they are very daring, made so by immunity from punishment by man. "The superstition is that on any man who kills a leopard will fall a curse or evil disease, curable only by ruinously expensive process of three weeks' duration under the direction of Ukuku. So the natives allow the greatest depredations and ravages until their sheep, goats, and dogs are swept away, and are roused to self-defence only when a human being becomes the victim of the daring beast. With this superstition is united another similar to the werewolf of Germany, viz., a belief in the power of human metamorphosis into a leopard. A person so metamorphosed is called 'Uvengwa.' At one time in Benito an intense excitement prevailed in the community. Doors and shutters were rattled at the dead of night, marks of leopard claws were scratched on door-posts. Then tracks lay on every path. Women and children in lonely places saw their flitting forms, or in the dusk were knocked down by their spring, or heard their growl in the thickets. It is difficult to decide in many of these reports whether it is a real leopard or only an Uvengwa—to native fears they are practically the same,—we were certain this time the Uvengwa was the thief disguised in leopard's skin, as theft is always heard of about such times."

When I was in Gaboon in September, 1895, there was great Uvengwa excitement in a district just across the other side of the estuary, mainly at a village that enjoyed the spacious and resounding name of Rumpochembo, from a celebrated chief, and all these phenomena were rife there. Again, when I was in a village up the Calabar there were fourteen goats and five slaves killed in eight days by leopards, the genuine things, I am sure, in this case; but here, as down South, there was a strong objection to proceed against the leopard, and no action was being taken save making the goat-houses stronger. In Okÿon, when a leopard is killed, its body is treated with great respect and brought into the killer's village. Messages are then sent to the neighbouring villages, and they send representatives to the village and the gall-bladder is most carefully removed from the leopard and burnt coram publico, each person whipping their hands down their arms to disavow any guilt in the affair. This burning of the gall, however, is not ju-ju, it is done merely to destroy it, and to demonstrate to all men that it is destroyed, because it is believed to be a deadly poison, and if any is found in a man's possession the punishment is death, unless he is a great chief—a few of these are allowed to keep leopards' gall in their possession. John Bailey tells me that if a great chief commits a great crime, and is adjudged by a conclave of his fellow chiefs to die, it is not considered right he should die in a common way, and he is given leopards' gall. A precisely similar idea regarding the poisonous quality of crocodiles' gall holds good down South.

The ju-ju parts of the leopard are the whiskers. You cannot get a skin from a native with them on, and gay, reckless young hunters wear them stuck in their hair and swagger tremendously while the Elders shake their heads and keep a keen eye on their subsequent conduct.

I must say the African leopard is an audacious animal, although it is un-grateful of me to say a word against him, after the way he has let me off person-ally, and I will speak of his extreme beauty as compensation for my ingratitude. I really think, taken as a whole, he is the most lovely animal I have ever seen; only seeing him, in the one way you can gain a full idea of his beauty, namely in his native forest, is not an unmixed joy to a person, like myself, of a nervous disposition. I may remark that my nervousness regarding the big game of Af-rica is of a rather peculiar kind. I can confidently say I am not afraid of any wild animal—until I see it—and then—well I will yield to nobody in terror; fortunately as I say my terror is a special variety; fortunately, because no one can manage their own terror. You can suppress alarm, excitement, fear, fright, and all those small-fry emotions, but the real terror is as dependent on the inner make of you as the colour of your eyes, or the shape of your nose; and when terror ascends its throne in my mind I become preternaturally artful, and intelligent to an extent utterly foreign to my true nature, and save, in the case of close quarters with bad big animals, a feeling of rage against some unknown person that such things as leopards, elephants, crocodiles, etc., should be al-lowed out loose in that disgracefully dangerous way, I do not think much about it at the time. Whenever I have come across an awful animal in the forest and I know it has seen me I take Jerome's advice, and instead of relying on the power of the human eye rely upon that of the human leg, and effect a masterly retreat in the face of the enemy. If I know it has not seen me I sink in my tracks and keep an eye on it, hoping that it will go away soon. Thus I once came upon a leopard. I had got caught in a tornado in a dense forest. The massive, mighty trees were waving like a wheat-field in an autumn gale in England, and I dare say a field mouse in a wheat-field in a gale would have heard much the same up-roar. The tornado shrieked like ten thousand vengeful demons. The great trees creaked and groaned and strained against it and their bush-rope cables groaned and smacked like whips, and ever and anon a thundering crash with snaps like pistol shots told that they and their mighty tree had strained and struggled in vain. The fierce rain came in a roar, tearing to shreds the leaves and blossoms and deluging everything. I was making bad weather of it, and climbing up over a lot of rocks out of a gully bottom where I had been half drowned in a stream, and on getting my head to the level of a block of rock I observed right in front of my eyes, broadside on, maybe a yard off, certainly not more, a big leopard. He was crouching on the ground, with his magnificent head thrown back and his eyes shut. His fore-paws were spread out in front of him and he lashed the ground with his tail, and I grieve to say, in face of that awful danger—I don't mean me, but the tornado—that depraved creature swore, softly, but repeatedly and profoundly. I did not get all these facts up in one glance, for no sooner did I see him than I ducked under the rocks, and remembered thankfully that leopards are said to have no power of smell. But I heard his observation on the weather, and the flip-flap of his tail on the ground. Every now and then I cautiously took a look at him with one eye round a rock-edge, and he remained in the same position. My feelings tell me he remained there twelve months, but my calmer judgment puts the time down at twenty minutes; and at last, on taking another cautious peep, I saw he was gone. At the time I wished I knew exactly where, but I do not care about that detail now, for I saw no more of him. He had moved off in one of those weird lulls which you get in a tornado, when for a few seconds the wild herd of hurrying winds seem to have lost themselves, and wander round crying and wailing like lost souls, until their common rage seizes them again and they rush back to their work of destruction. It was an immense pleasure to have seen the great creature like that. He was so evidently enraged and baffled by the uproar and dazzled by the floods of lightning that swept down into the deepest recesses of the forest, showing at one second every detail of twig, leaf, branch, and stone round you, and then leaving you in a sort of swirling dark until the next flash came; this, and the great conglomerate roar of the wind, rain and thunder, was enough to bewilder any living thing.

I have never hurt a leopard intentionally; I am habitually kind to animals, and besides I do not think it is ladylike to go shooting things with a gun. Twice, however, I have been in collision with them. On one occasion a big leopard had attacked a dog, who, with her family, was occupying a broken-down hut next to mine. The dog was a half-bred boarhound, and a savage brute on her own account. I, being roused by the uproar, rushed out into the feeble moon-light, thinking she was having one of her habitual turns-up with other dogs, and I saw a whirling mass of animal matter within a yard of me. I fired two mushroom-shaped native stools in rapid succession into the brown of it, and the meeting broke up into a leopard and a dog. The leopard crouched, I think to spring on me. I can see its great, beautiful, lambent eyes still, and I seized an earthen water-cooler and flung it straight at them. It was a noble shot; it burst on the leopard's head like a shell and the leopard went for bush one time. Twenty minutes after people began to drop in cautiously and inquire if anything was the matter, and I civilly asked them to go and ask the leopard in the bush, but they firmly refused. We found the dog had got her shoulder slit open as if by a blow from a cutlass, and the leopard had evidently seized the dog by the scruff of her neck, but owing to the loose folds of skin no bones were broken and she got round all right after much ointment from me, which she paid me for with several bites. Do not mistake this for a sporting adventure. I no more thought it was a leopard than that it was a lotus when I joined the fight. My other leopard was also after a dog. Leopards always come after dogs, because once upon a time the leopard and the dog were great friends, and the leopard went out one day and left her whelps in charge of the dog, and the dog went out flirting, and a snake came and killed the whelps, so there is ill-feeling to this day between the two. For the benefit of sporting readers whose interest may have been excited by the mention of big game, I may remark that the largest leopard skin I ever measured myself was, tail included, 9 feet 7 inches. It was a dried skin, and every man who saw it said, "It was the largest skin he had ever seen, except one that he had seen somewhere else."

The largest crocodile I ever measured was 22 feet 3 inches, the largest gorilla 5 feet 7 inches. I am assured by the missionaries in Calabar, that there was a python brought into Creek Town in the Rev. Mr. Goldie's time, that extended the whole length of the Creek Town mission-house verandah and to spare. This python must have been over 40 feet. I have not a shadow of doubt it was. Stay-at-home people will always discredit great measurements, but experienced bushmen do not, and after all, if it amuses the stay-at-homes to do so, by all means let them; they have dull lives of it and it don't hurt you, for you know how exceedingly difficult it is to preserve really big things to bring home, and how, half the time, they fall into the hands of people who would not bother their heads to preserve them in a rotting climate like West Africa.

The largest python skin I ever measured was a damaged one, which was 26 feet. There is an immense one hung in front of a house in San Paul de Loanda which you can go and measure yourself with comparative safety any day, and which is, I think, over 20 feet. I never measured this one. The common run of pythons is 10-15 feet, or rather I should say this is about the sized one you find with painful frequency in your chicken-house.

Of the Lubuku secret society I can speak with no personal knowledge. I had a great deal of curious information regarding it from a Bakele woman, who had her information second-hand, but it bears out what Captain Latrobe Bateman says about it in his most excellent book The First Ascent of the Kasai (George Phillip, 1889), and to his account in Note J of the Appendix, I beg to refer the ethnologist. My information also went to show what he calls "a dark inference as to its true nature," a nature not universally common by any means to the African tribal secret society.

In addition to the secret society and the leopard society, there are in the Delta some ju-jus held only by a few great chiefs. The one in Bonny has a complete language to itself, and there is one in Duke Town so powerful that should you desire the death of any person you have only to go and name him before it. "These jujus are very swift and sure." I would rather drink than fight with any of them—yes, far.

CHAPTER XVII

ASCENT OF THE GREAT PEAK OF CAMEROONS

Setting forth how the Voyager is minded to ascend the mountain called Mungo Mah Lobeh, or the Throne of Thunder, and in due course reaches Buea, situate thereon.

After returning from Corisco I remained a few weeks in Gaboon, and then left on the Niger, commanded by Captain Davies. My regrets, I should say, arose from leaving the charms and interests of Congo Français, and had nothing whatever to do with taking passage on one of the most comfortable ships of all those which call on the Coast.

The Niger was homeward-bound when I joined her, and in due course arrived in Cameroon River, and I was once again under the dominion of Germany. It would be a very interesting thing to compare the various forms of European government in Africa—English, French, German, Portuguese, and Spanish; but to do so with any justice would occupy more space than I have at my disposal, for the subject is extremely intricate. Each of these forms of government have their good points and their bad. Each of them are dealing with bits of Africa differing from each other—in the nature of their inhabitants and their formation, and so on—so I will not enter into any comparison of them here.

From the deck of the Niger I found myself again confronted with my great temptation—the magnificent Mungo Mah Lobeh—the Throne of Thunder. Now it is none of my business to go up mountains. There's next to no fish on them in West Africa, and precious little good rank fetish, as the population on them is sparse—the African, like myself, abhorring cool air. Nevertheless, I feel quite sure that no white man has ever looked on the great Peak of Cameroon without a desire arising in his mind to ascend it and know in detail the highest point on the western side of the continent, and indeed one of the highest points in all Africa.

So great is the majesty and charm of this mountain that the temptation of it is as great to me to-day as it was on the first day I saw it, when I was feeling my way down the West Coast of Africa on the S.S. Lagos in 1893, and it revealed itself by good chance from its surf-washed plinth to its skyscraping summit. Certainly it is most striking when you see it first, as I first saw it, after coasting for weeks along the low shores and mangrove-fringed rivers of the Niger Delta. Suddenly, right up out of the sea, rises the great mountain to its 13,760 feet, while close at hand, to westward, towers the lovely island mass of Fernando Po to 10,190 feet. But every time you pass it by its beauty grows on you with greater and greater force, though it is never twice the same. Sometimes it is wreathed with indigo-black tornado clouds, sometimes crested with snow, sometimes softly gorgeous with gold, green, and rose-coloured vapours tinted by the setting sun, sometimes completely swathed in dense cloud so that you cannot see it at all; but when you once know it is there it is all the same, and you bow down and worship.

There are only two distinct peaks to this glorious thing that geologists brutally call the volcanic intrusive mass of the Cameroon Mountains, viz., Big Cameroon and Little Cameroon. The latter, Mungo Mah Etindeh, has not yet been scaled, although it is only 5,820 feet. One reason for this is doubtless that the few people in fever-stricken, over-worked West Africa who are able to go up mountains, naturally try for the adjacent Big Cameroon; the other reason is that Mungo Mah Etindeh, to which Burton refers as "the awful form of Little Cameroon," is mostly sheer cliff, and is from foot to summit clothed in an almost impenetrable forest. Behind these two mountains of volcanic origin, which cover an area on an isolated base of between 700 and 800 square miles in extent, there are distinctly visible from the coast two chains of mountains, or I should think one chain deflected, the so-called Rumby and Omon ranges. These are no relations of Mungo, being of very different structure and conformation; the geological specimens I have brought from them and from the Cameroons being identified by geologists as respectively schistose grit and vesicular lava.

After spending a few pleasant days in Cameroon River in the society of Frau Plehn, my poor friend Mrs. Duggan having, I regret to say, departed for England on the death of her husband, I went round to Victoria, Ambas Bay, on the Niger, and in spite of being advised solemnly by Captain Davies to "chuck it as it was not a picnic," I started to attempt the Peak of Cameroons as follows.

September 20th, 1895.—Left Victoria at 7.30, weather fine. Herr von Lucke, though sadly convinced, by a series of experiments he has been carrying on ever since I landed, and I expect before, that you cannot be in three places at one time, is still trying to do so; or more properly speaking he starts an

experiment series for four places, man-like, instead of getting ill as I should under the circumstances, and he kindly comes with me as far as the bridge across
the lovely cascading Lukole River, and then goes back at about seven miles an
hour to look after Victoria and his sick subordinates in detail.

I, with my crew, keep on up the grand new road the Government is making, which when finished is to go from Ambas Bay to Buea, 3,000 feet up on
the mountain's side. This road is quite the most magnificent of roads, as regards
breadth and general intention, that I have seen anywhere in West Africa, and
it runs through a superbly beautiful country. It is, I should say, as broad as
Oxford Street; on either side of it are deep drains to carry off the surface waters,
with banks of varied beautiful tropical shrubs and ferns, behind which rise, 100
to 200 feet high, walls of grand forest, the column-like tree-stems either hung
with flowering, climbing plants and ferns, or showing soft red and soft grey
shafts sixty to seventy feet high without an interrupting branch. Behind this
again rise the lovely foot hills of Mungo, high up against the sky, coloured the
most perfect soft dark blue.

The whole scheme of colour is indescribably rich and full in tone. The very
earth is a velvety red brown, and the butterflies—which abound—show themselves off in the sunlight, in their canary-coloured, crimson, and peacock-blue
liveries, to perfection. After five minutes' experience of the road I envy those
butterflies. I do not believe there is a more lovely road in this world, and besides, it's a noble and enterprising thing of a Government to go and make it,
considering the climate and the country; but to get any genuine pleasure out of
it, it is requisite to hover in a bird- or butterfly-like way, for of all the truly awful
things to walk on, that road, when I was on it, was the worst.

Of course this arose from its not being finished, not having its top on in fact:
the bit that was finished, and had got its top on, for half a mile beyond the bridge,
you could go over in a Bath chair. The rest of it made you fit for one for the rest
of your natural life, for it was one mass of broken lava rock, and here and there
leviathan tree-stumps that had been partially blown up with gunpowder.

When we near the forest end of the road, it comes on to rain heavily, and
I see a little house on the left-hand side, and a European engineer superintending a group of very cheerful natives felling timber. He most kindly invites
me to take shelter, saying it cannot rain as heavily as this for long. My men
also announce a desire for water, and so I sit down and chat with the engineer
under the shelter of his verandah, while the men go to the water-hole, some
twenty minutes off.

After learning much about the Congo Free State and other matters, I presently see one of my men sitting right in the middle of the road on a rock, totally
unsheltered, and a feeling of shame comes over me in the face of this black

man's aquatic courage. Into the rain I go, and off we start. I conscientiously attempt to keep dry, by holding up an umbrella, knowing that though hopeless it is the proper thing to do.

We leave the road about fifty yards above the hut, turning into the unbroken forest on the right-hand side, and following a narrow, slippery, muddy, root-beset bush-path that was a comfort after the road. Presently we come to a lovely mountain torrent flying down over red-brown rocks in white foam; exquisitely lovely, and only a shade damper than the rest of things. Seeing this I solemnly fold up my umbrella and give it to Kefalla. I then take charge of Fate and wade.

This particular stream, too, requires careful wading, the rocks over which it flows being arranged in picturesque, but perilous confusion; however all goes well, and getting to the other side I decide to "chuck it," as Captain Davies would say, as to keeping dry, for the rain comes down heavier than ever.

Now we are evidently dealing with a foot-hillside, but the rain is too thick for one to see two yards in any direction, and we seem to be in a ghost-land forest, for the great palms and red-woods rise up in the mist before us, and fade out in the mist behind, as we pass on. The rocks which edge and strew the path at our feet are covered with exquisite ferns and mosses—all the most delicate shades of green imaginable, and here and there of absolute gold colour, looking as if some ray of sunshine had lingered too long playing on the earth, and had got shut off from heaven by the mist, and so lay nestling among the rocks until it might rejoin the sun.

The path now becomes an absolute torrent, with mud-thickened water, which cascades round one's ankles in a sportive way, and round one's knees in the hollows in the path. On we go, the path underneath the water seems a pretty equal mixture of rock and mud, but they are not evenly distributed. Plantations full of weeds show up on either side of us, and we are evidently now on the top of a foot-hill. I suspect a fine view of the sea could be obtained from here, if you have an atmosphere that is less than 99¾ per cent. of water. As it is, a white sheet—or more properly speaking, considering its soft, stuffy woolliness, a white blanket—is stretched across the landscape to the south-west, where the sea would show.

We go down-hill now, the water rushing into the back of my shoes for a change. The path is fringed by high, sugar-cane-like grass which hangs across it in a lackadaisical way, swishing you in the face and cutting like a knife whenever you catch its edge, and pouring continually insidious rills of water down one's neck. It does not matter. The whole Atlantic could not get more water on to me than I have already got. Ever and again I stop and wring out some of it from my skirts, for it is weighty. One would not imagine that anything could come down in the way of water thicker than the rain, but it can. When one is on the top of the hills, a cold breeze comes through the mist chilling one to the bone, and bending the heads of the palm trees, sends down from them water by the bucketful with a slap; hitting or missing you as the case may be.

Both myself and my men are by now getting anxious for our "chop," and they tell me, "We look them big hut soon." Soon we do look them big hut, but with faces of undisguised horror, for the big hut consists of a few charred roof-mats, etc., lying on the ground. There has been a fire in that simple savage home. Our path here is cut by one that goes east and west, and after a consultation between my men and the Bakwiri, we take the path going east, down a steep slope between weedy plantations, and shortly on the left shows a steep little hillside with a long low hut on the top. We go up to it and I find it is the habitation of a Basel Mission black Bible-reader. He comes out and speaks English well, and I tell him I want a house for myself and my men, and he says we had better come and stay in this one. It is divided into two chambers, one in which the children who attend the mission-school stay, and wherein there is a fire, and one evidently the abode of the teacher. I thank the Bible-reader and say that I will pay him for the house, and I and the men go in streaming, and my teeth chatter with cold as the breeze chills my saturated garment while I give out the rations of beef, rum, blankets, and tobacco to the men. Then I clear my apartment out and attempt to get dry, operations which are interrupted by Kefalla coming for tobacco to buy firewood off the mission teacher to cook our food by.

Presently my excellent little cook brings in my food, and in with it come two mission teachers—our first acquaintance, the one with a white jacket, and another with a blue. They lounge about and spit in all directions, and then chiefs commence to arrive with their families complete, and they sidle into the apartment and ostentatiously ogle the demijohn of rum.

They are, as usual, a nuisance, sitting about on everything. No sooner have I taken an unclean-looking chief off the wood sofa, than I observe another one has silently seated himself in the middle of my open portmanteau. Removing him and shutting it up, I see another one has settled on the men's beef and rice sack.

It is now about three o'clock and I am still chilled to the bone in spite of tea. The weather is as bad as ever. The men say that the rest of the road to Buea is far worse than that which we have so far come along, and that we should never get there before dark, and "for sure" should not get there afterwards, because by the time the dark came down we should be in "bad place too much." Therefore, to their great relief, I say I will stay at this place—Buana—for the night, and go on in the morning time up to Buea; and just for the present I think I will wrap myself up in a blanket and try and get the chill out of me, so I give the chiefs a glass of rum each, plenty of head tobacco, and my best thanks for their kind call, and then turn them all out. I have not been lying down five minutes on the plank that serves for a sofa by day and a bed by night, when Charles comes knocking at the door. He wants tobacco. "Missionary man no fit to let we have firewood unless we buy em." Give Charles a head and shut him out again, and drop off to sleep again for a quarter of an hour, then am aroused by some enterprising sightseers pushing open the window-shutters; when I look round there are a mass of black heads sticking through the window-hole. I tell them respectfully that the circus is closed for repairs, and fasten up the shutters, but sleep is impossible, so I turn out and go and see what those men of mine are after. They are comfortable enough round their fire, with their clothes suspended on strings in the smoke above them, and I envy them that fire. I then stroll round to see if there is anything to be seen, but the scenery is much like that you would enjoy if you were inside a blanc-mange. So as it is now growing dark I return to my room and light candles, and read Dr. Günther on Fishes. Room becomes full of blacks. Unless you watch the door, you do not see how it is done. You look at a corner one minute and it is empty, and the next time you look that way it is full of rows of white teeth and watching eyes. The two mission teachers come in and make a show of teaching a child to read the Bible. After again clearing out the rank and fashion of Buana, I prepare to try and get a sleep; not an elaborate affair, I assure you, for I only want to wrap myself round in a blanket and lie on that plank, but the rain has got into the blankets and horror! there is no pillow. The mission men have cleared their bed paraphernalia right out. Now you can do without a good many things, but not without a pillow, so hunt round to find something to make one with; find the Bible in English, the Bible in German, and two hymn-books, and a candle-stick. These seem all the small articles in the room—no, there is a parcel behind the books—mission teachers' Sunday trousers—make delightful arrangement of books bound round with trousers and the whole affair wrapped in one of my towels. Never saw till now advantage of Africans having trousers. Civilisation has its points after all. But it is no use trying to get any sleep until those men are quieter. The partition which separates my apartment from theirs is a bamboo and mat affair, straight at the top so leaving under the roof a triangular space above common to both rooms. Also common to both rooms are the smoke of the fire and the conversation. Kefalla is holding forth in a dogmatic way, and some of the others are snoring. There is a new idea in decoration along the separating wall. Mr. Morris might have made something out of it for a dado. It is composed of an arrangement in line of stretched out singlets. Vaseline the revolver. Wish those men would leave off chattering. Kefalla seems to know the worst about most of the people, black and white, down in

Ambas Bay, but I do not believe those last two stories. Evidently great jokes in next room now; Kefalla has thrown himself, still talking, in the dark, on to the top of one of the mission teachers. The women of the village outside have been keeping up, this hour and more, a most melancholy coo-ooing. Those foolish creatures are evidently worrying about their husbands who have gone down to market in Ambas Bay, and who, they think, are lost in the bush. I have not a shadow of a doubt that those husbands who are not home by now are safely drunk in town, or reposing on the grand new road the kindly Government have provided for them, either in one of the side drains, or tucked in among the lava rock.

September 21st.—Coo-ooing went on all night. I was aroused about 9.30 P.M., by uproar in adjacent hut: one husband had returned in a bellicose condition and whacked his wives, and their squarks and squalls, instead of acting as a warning to the other ladies, stimulate the silly things to go on coo-ooing louder and more entreatingly than ever, so that their husbands might come home and whack them too, I suppose, and whenever the unmitigated hardness of my plank rouses me I hear them still coo-ooing.

No watchman is required to wake you in the morning on the top of a Cameroon foot-hill by 5.30, because about 4 A.M. the dank chill that comes before the dawn does so most effectively. One old chief turned up early out of the mist and dashed me a bottle of palm wine; he says he wants to dash me a fowl, but I decline, and accept two eggs, and give him four heads of tobacco.

The whole place is swathed in thick white mist through which my audience arrive. But I am firm with them, and shut up the doors and windows and disregard their bangings on them while I am dressing, or rather re-dressing. The mission teachers get in with my tea, and sit and smoke and spit while I have my breakfast. Give me cannibal Fans!

It is pouring with rain again now, and we go down the steep hillock to the path we came along yesterday, keep it until we come to where the old path cuts it, and then turn up to the right following the old path's course and leave Buana without a pang of regret. Our road goes N.E. Oh, the mud of it! Not the clearish cascades of yesterday but sticky, slippery mud, intensely sticky, and intensely slippery. The narrow path which is filled by this, is V-shaped underneath from wear, and I soon find the safest way is right through the deepest mud in the middle.

The white mist shuts off all details beyond ten yards in any direction. All we can see, as we first turn up the path, is a patch of kokos of tremendous size on our right. After this comes weedy plantation, and stretches of sword grass hanging across the road. The country is even more unlevel than that we came over yesterday. On we go, patiently doing our mud pulling through the valleys;

toiling up a hillside among lumps of rock and stretches of forest, for we are now beyond Buana's plantations; and skirting the summit of the hill only to descend into another valley. Evidently this is a succession of foot-hills of the great mountain and we are not on its true face yet. As we go on they become more and more abrupt in form, the valleys mere narrow ravines. In the wet season (this is only the tornado season) each of these valleys is occupied by a raging torrent from the look of the confused water-worn boulders. Now among the rocks there are only isolated pools, for the weather for a fortnight before I left Victoria had been fairly dry, and this rich porous soil soaks up an immense amount of water. It strikes me as strange that when we are either going up or down the hills, the ground is less muddy than when we are skirting their summits, but it must be because on the inclines the rush of water clears the soil away down to the bed rock. There is an outcrop of clay down by Buana, but though that was slippery, it is nothing to the slipperiness of this fine, soft, red-brown earth that is the soil higher up, and also round Ambas Bay. This gets churned up into a sort of batter where there is enough water lying on it, and, when there is not, an ice slide is an infant to it.

My men and I flounder about; thrice one of them, load and all, goes down with a squidge and a crash into the side grass, and says "damn!" with quite the European accent; as a rule, however, we go on in single file, my shoes giving out a mellifluous squidge, and their naked feet a squish, squash. The men take it very good temperedly, and sing in between accidents; I do not feel much like singing myself, particularly at one awful spot, which was the exception to the rule that ground at acute angles forms the best going. This exception was a long slippery slide down into a ravine with a long, perfectly glassy slope up out of it.

After this we have a stretch of rocky forest, and pass by a widening in the path which I am told is a place where men blow, i.e. rest, and then pass through another a little further on, which is Buea's bush market. Then through an opening in the great war-hedge of Buea, a growing stockade some fifteen feet high, the lower part of it wattled.

At the sides of the path here grow banks of bergamot and balsam, returning good for evil and smiling sweetly as we crush them. Thank goodness we are in forest now, and we seem to have done with the sword-grass. The rocks are covered with moss and ferns, and the mist curling and wandering about among the stems is very lovely.

In our next ravine there is a succession of pools, part of a mountain torrent of greater magnitude evidently than those we have passed, and in these pools there are things swimming. Spend more time catching them, with the assistance of Bum. I do not value Kefalla's advice, ample though it is, as being of any real value in the affair. Bag some water-spiders and two small fish. The heat is less oppressive than yesterday. All yesterday one was being alternately smothered in the valley and chilled on the hill-tops. To-day it is a more level temperature, about 70°, I fancy.

The soil up here, about 2,500 feet above sea-level, though rock-laden is exceedingly rich, and the higher we go there is more bergamot, native indigo, with its underleaf dark blue, and lovely coleuses with red markings on their upper leaves, and crimson linings. I, as an ichthyologist, am in the wrong paradise. What a region this would be for a botanist!

The country is gloriously lovely if one could only see it for the rain and mist; but one only gets dim hints of its beauty when some cold draughts of wind come down from the great mountains and seem to push open the mist-veil as with spirit hands, and then in a minute let it fall together again. I do not expect to reach Buea within regulation time, but at 11.30 my men say "we close in," and then, coming along a forested hill and down a ravine, we find ourselves facing a rushing river, wherein a squad of black soldiers are washing clothes, with the assistance of a squad of black ladies, with much uproar and sky-larking. I too think it best to wash here, standing in the river and swishing the mud out of my skirts; and then wading across to the other bank, I wring out my skirts. The ground on the further side of the river is cleared of bush, and only bears a heavy crop of balsam; a few steps onwards bring me in view of a corrugated iron-roofed, plank-sided house, in front of which, towards the great mountain which now towers up into the mist, is a low clearing with a quadrangle of native huts—the barracks.

I receive a most kindly welcome from a fair, grey-eyed German gentleman, only unfortunately I see my efforts to appear before him clean and tidy have been quite unavailing, for he views my appearance with unmixed horror, and suggests an instant hot bath. I decline. Men can be trying! How in the world is any one going to take a bath in a house with no doors, and only very sketchy wooden window-shutters?

The German officer is building the house quickly, as Ollendorff would say, but he has not yet got to such luxuries as doors, and so uses army blankets strung across the doorway; and he has got up temporary wooden shutters to keep the worst of the rain out, and across his own room's window he has a frame covered with greased paper. Thank goodness he has made a table, and a bench, and a washhand-stand out of planks for his spare room, which he kindly places at my disposal; and the Fatherland has evidently stood him an iron bedstead and a mattress for it. But the Fatherland is not spoiling or cosseting this man to an extent that will enervate him in the least.

The mist clears off in the evening about five, and the surrounding scenery is at last visible. Fronting the house there is the cleared quadrangle, facing which on the other three sides are the lines of very dilapidated huts, and behind these the ground rises steeply, the great S.E. face of Mungo Mah Lobeh. It looks awfully steep when you know you have got to go up it. This station at Buea is 3,000 feet above sea-level, which explains the hills we have had to come up. The mountain wall when viewed from Buea is very grand, although it lacks snowcap or glacier, and the highest summits of Mungo are not visible because we are too close under them, but its enormous bulk and its isolation make it highly impressive. The forest runs up it in a great band above Buea, then sends up great tongues into the grass belt above. But what may be above this grass belt I know not yet, for our view ends at the top of the wall of the great S.E. crater. My men say there are devils and gold up beyond, but the German authorities do not support this view. Those Germans are so sceptical. This station is evidently on a ledge, for behind it the ground falls steeply, and you get an uninterrupted panoramic view of the Cameroon estuary and the great stretches of low swamp lands with the Mungo and the Bimbia rivers, and their many creeks and channels, and far away east the strange abrupt forms of the Rumby Mountains. Herr Liebert says you can see Cameroon Government buildings from here, if only the day is clear, though they are some forty miles away. This view of them is, save a missionary of the Basel mission, the only white society available at Buea.

I hear more details about the death of poor Freiherr von Gravenreuth, whose fine monument of a seated lion I saw in the Government House grounds in Cameroons the other day. Bush fighting in these West African forests is dreadfully dangerous work. Hemmed in by bush, in a narrow path along which you must pass slowly in single file, you are a target for all and any natives invisibly hidden in the undergrowth; and the war-hedge of Buea must have made an additional danger and difficulty here for the attacking party. The lieutenant and his small band of black soldiers had, after a stiff fight, succeeded in forcing the entrance to this, when their ammunition gave out, and they had to fall back. The Bueans, regarding this as their victory, rallied, and a chance shot killed the lieutenant instantly. A further expedition was promptly sent up from Victoria and it wiped the error out of the Buean mind and several Bueans with it. But it was a very necessary expedition. These natives were a constant source of danger to the more peaceful trading tribes, whom they would not permit to traverse their territory. The Bueans have been dealt with mercifully by the Germans, for their big villages, like Sapa, are still standing, and a continual stream of natives come into the barrack-yard, selling produce, or carrying it on down to Victoria markets, in a perfectly content and cheerful way. I met this morning a big burly chief with his insignia of office—a great stick. He, I am told, is the chief or Sapa whom Herr von Lucke has called to talk some palaver with down in Victoria.

At last I leave Herr Liebert, because everything I say to him causes him to
hop, flying somewhere to show me something, and I am sure it is bad for his
foot. I go and see that my men are safely quartered. Kefalla is laying down
the law in a most didactic way to the soldiers. Herr Liebert has christened him
"the Professor," and I adopt the name for him, but I fear "Windbag" would fit
him better.

At 7.30 a heavy tornado comes rolling down upon us. Masses of indigo
cloud with livid lightning flashing in the van, roll out from over the wall of the
great crater above; then with that malevolence peculiar to the tornado it sees
all the soldiers and their wives and children sitting happily in the barrack yard,
howling in a minor key and beating their beloved tom-toms, so it comes and
sits flump down on them with deluges of water, and sends its lightning running
over the ground in livid streams of living death. Oh, they are nice things are
tornadoes! I wonder what they will be like when we are up in their home; up
atop of that precious wall? I had no idea Mungo was so steep. If I had—well,
I am in for it now!

CHAPTER XVIII

ASCENT OF THE GREAT PEAK OF CAMEROONS—(continued)

WHEREIN IS RECOUNTED HOW THE VOYAGER SETS OUT FROM BUEA, AND
GOES UP THROUGH THE FOREST BELT TO THE TOP OF THE S.E. CRATER
OF MUNGO MAH LOBEH, WITH MANY DILEMMAS AND DISASTERS THAT
BEFELL ON THE WAY.

SEPTEMBER 22ND.—Wake at 5. Fine morning. Fine view towards Cameroon River. The broad stretch of forest below, and the water-eaten mangrove swamps below that, are all a glorious indigo flushed with rose colour from "the death of the night," as Kiva used to call the dawn. No one stirring till six, when people come out of the huts, and stretch themselves and proceed to begin the day, in the African's usual perfunctory, listless way.

My crew are worse than the rest. I go and hunt cook out. He props open one eye, with difficulty, and yawns a yawn that nearly cuts his head in two. I wake him up with a shock, by saying I mean to go on up to-day, and want my chop, and to start one time. He goes off and announces my horrible intention to the others. Kefalla soon arrives upon the scene full of argument, "You no sabe this be Sunday, Ma?" says he in a tone that tells he considers this settles the matter. I "sabe" unconcernedly; Kefalla scratches his head for other argument, but he has opened with his heavy artillery; which being repulsed throws his rear lines into confusion. Bum, the head man, then turns up, sound asleep inside, but quite ready to come. Bum, I find, is always ready to do what he is told, but has no more original ideas in his head than there are in a chair leg. Kefalla, however, by scratching other parts of his anatomy diligently, has now another argument ready, the two Bakwiris are sick with abdominal trouble, that requires rum and rest, and one of the other boys has hot foot.

Herr Liebert now appears upon the scene, and says I can have some of his labourers, who are now more or less idle, because he cannot get about much with his bad foot to direct them, so I give the Bakwiris and the two hot foot cases "books" to take down to Herr von Lucke who will pay them off for me, and seeing that they have each a good day's rations of rice, beef, etc., eliminate them from the party.

In addition to the labourers, I am to have as a guide Sasu, a black sergeant, who went up the Peak with the officers of the Hyæna, and I get my breakfast, and then hang about watching my men getting ready very slowly to start. Off we get about 8, and start with all good wishes, and grim prophecies, from Herr Liebert.

Led by Sasu, and accompanied by "To-morrow," a man who has come to Buea from some interior unknown district, and who speaks no known language, and whose business it is to help to cut a way through the bush, we go down the path we came and cross the river again. This river seems to separate the final mass of the mountain from the foot-hills on this side. Immediately after crossing it we turn up into the forest on the right hand side, and "To-morrow" cuts through an over-grown track for about half-an-hour, and then leaves us.

Everything is reeking wet, and we swish through thick undergrowth and then enter a darker forest where the earth is rocky and richly decorated with ferns and moss. For the first time in my life I see tree-ferns growing wild in luxuriant profusion. What glorious creations they are! Then we get out into the middle of a koko plantation. Next to sweet-potatoes, the premier abomination to walk through, give me kokos for good all-round tryingness, particularly when they are wet, as is very much the case now. Getting through these we meet the war hedge again, and after a conscientious struggle with various forms of vegetation in a muddled, tangled state, Sasu says, "No good, path done got stopped up," so we turn and retrace our steps all the way, cross the river, and horrify Herr Liebert by invading his house again. We explain the situation. Grave headshaking between him and Sasu about the practicability of any other route, because there is no other path. I do not like to say "so much the better," because it would have sounded ungrateful, but I knew from my Ogowé experiences that a forest that looks from afar a dense black mat is all right underneath, and there is a short path recently cut by Herr Liebert that goes straight up towards the forest above us. It had been made to go to a clearing, where ambitious agricultural operations were being inaugurated, when Herr Liebert hurt his foot. Up this we go, it is semi-vertical while it lasts, and it ends in a scrubby patch that is to be a plantation; this crossed we are in the Urwald, and it is more exquisite than words can describe, but not good going, particularly at one spot where a gigantic tree has fallen down across a little rocky ravine, and has to be crawled under. It occurs to me that this is a highly likely place for snakes and an absolutely sure find for scorpions, and when we have passed it three of these latter interesting creatures are observed on the load of blankets which is fastened on to the back of Kefalla. We inform Kefalla of the fact on the spot. A volcanic eruption of entreaty, advice, and admonition results, but we still hesitate. However, the gallant cook tackles them in a sort of tip-cat way with a stick, and we proceed into a patch of long grass, beyond which there is a reach of amomums. The winged amomum I see here in Africa for the first time. Horrid slippery things amomum sticks to walk on, when they are lying on the ground; and there is a lot of my old enemy the calamus about.

On each side are deep forested dells and ravines, and rocks show up through the ground in every direction, and things in general are slippery, and I wonder now and again, as I assume with unnecessary violence a recumbent position, why I came to Africa; but patches of satin-leaved begonias and clumps of lovely tree-ferns reconcile me to my lot. Cook does not feel these forest charms, and gives me notice after an hour's experience of mountain forest-belt work; what cook would not?

As we get higher we have to edge and squeeze every few minutes through the aërial roots of some tremendous kind of tree, plentiful hereabouts. One of them we passed through I am sure would have run any Indian banyan hard for extent of ground covered, if it were measured. In the region where these trees are frequent, the undergrowth is less dense than it is lower down.

Imagine a vast, seemingly limitless cathedral with its countless columns covered, nay, composed of the most exquisite dark-green, large-fronded moss, with here and there a delicate fern embedded in it as an extra decoration. The white, gauze-like mist comes down from the upper mountain towards us: creeping, twining round, and streaming through the moss-covered tree columns— long bands of it reaching along sinuous, but evenly, for fifty and sixty feet or more, and then ending in a puff like the smoke of a gun. Soon, however, all the mist-streams coalesce and make the atmosphere all their own, wrapping us round in a clammy, chill embrace; it is not that wool-blanket, smothering affair that we were wrapped in down by Buana, but exquisitely delicate. The difference it makes to the beauty of the forest is just the same difference you would get if you put a delicate veil over a pretty woman's face or a sack over her head. In fact, the mist here was exceedingly becoming to the forest's beauty. Now and again growls of thunder roll out from, and quiver in the earth beneath our feet. Mungo is making a big tornado, and is stirring and simmering it softly so as to make it strong. I only hope he will not overdo it, as he does six times in seven, and make it too heavy to get out on to the Atlantic, where all tornadoes ought to go. If he does the thing will go and burst on us in this forest to-night.

294

MARY KINGSLEY

The forest now grows less luxuriant though still close—we have left the begonias and the tree-ferns, and are in another zone. The trees now, instead of being clothed in rich, dark-green moss, are heavily festooned with long, green-ish-white lichen. It pours with rain.

At last we reach the place where the sergeant says we ought to camp for the night. I have been feeling the time for camping was very ripe for the past hour, and Kefalla openly said as much an hour and a half ago, but he got such scathing things said to him about civilians' legs by the sergeant that I did not air my own opinion.

We are now right at the very edge of the timber belt. My head man and three boys are done to a turn. If I had had a bull behind me or Mr. Fildes in front, I might have done another five or seven miles, but not more.

The rain comes down with extra virulence as soon as we set to work to start the fire and open the loads. I and Peter have great times getting out the military camp-bed from its tight, bolster-like case, while Kefalla gives advice, until, being irritated by the bed's behaviour, I blow up Kefalla and send him to chop firewood. However, we get the thing out and put up after cutting a place clear to set it on; owing to the world being on a stiff slant hereabouts, it takes time to make it stand straight. I get four stakes cut, and drive them in at the four corners of the bed, and then stretch over it Herr von Lucke's waterproof ground-sheet, guy the ends out to pegs with string, feel profoundly grateful to both Herr Liebert for the bed and Herr von Lucke for the sheet, and place the baggage under the protection of the German Government's two belongings. Then I find the boys have not got a fire with all their fuss, and I have to demon-strate to them the lessons I have learnt among the Fans regarding fire-making. We build a fire-house and then all goes well. I notice they do not make a fire Fan fashion, but build it in a circle.

Evidently one of the labourers from Buea, named Xenia, is a good man. Equally evidently some of my other men are only fit to carry sandwich-boards for Day and Martin's blacking. I dine luxuriously off tinned fat pork and hot tea, and then feeling still hungry go on to tinned herring. Excellent thing tinned herring, but I have to hurry because I know I must go up through the edge of the forest on to the grass land, and see how the country is made during the brief period of clearness that almost always comes just before nightfall. So leaving my boys comfortably seated round the fire having their evening chop, I pass up through the heavily lichen-tasselled fringe of the forest-belt into deep jungle grass, and up a steep and slippery mound.

In front the mountain-face rises like a wall from behind a set of hillocks, similar to the one I am at present on. The face of the wall to the right and left has two dark clefts in it. The peak itself is not visible from where I am; it rises behind and beyond the wall. I stay taking compass bearings and look for an easy way up for to-morrow. My men, by now, have missed their "ma" and are yelling for her dismally, and the night comes down with great rapidity for we are in the shadow of the great mountain mass, so I go back into camp. Alas! how vain are often our most energetic efforts to remove our fellow creatures from temptation. I knew a Sunday down among the soldiers would be bad for my men, and so came up here, and now, if you please, these men have been at the rum, because Bum, the head man, has been too done up to do anything but lie in his blanket and feed. Kefalla is laying down the law with great detail and unction. Cook who has been very low in his mind all day, is now weirdly cheerful, and sings incoherently. The other boys, who want to go to sleep, threaten to "burst him" if he "no finish." It's no good—cook carols on, and soon succumbing to the irresistible charm of music, the other men have to join in the choruses. The performance goes on for an hour, growing woollier and woollier in tone, and then dying out in sleep.

I write by the light of an insect-haunted lantern, sitting on the bed, which is tucked in among the trees some twenty yards away from the boys' fire. There is a bird whistling in a deep rich note that I have never heard before.

September 23rd.—Morning gloriously fine. Rout the boys out, and start at seven, with Sasu, Head man, Xenia, Black boy, Kefalla and Cook.

The great south-east wall of the mountain in front of us is quite un-flecked by cloud, and in the forest are thousands of bees. We notice that the tongues of forest go up the mountain in some places a hundred yards or more above the true line of the belt. These tongues of forest get more and more heavily hung with lichen, and the trees thinner and more stunted, towards their ends. I think that these tongues are always in places where the wind does not get full play. All those near our camping place on this south-east face are so. It is evidently not a matter of soil, for there is ample soil on this side above where the trees are, and then again on the western side of the mountain—the side facing the sea—the timber line is far higher up than on this. Nor, again, is it a matter of angle that makes the timber line here so low, for those forests on the Sierra del Cristal were growing luxuriantly over far steeper grades. There is some peculiar local condition just here evidently, or the forest would be up to the bottom of the wall of the crater. I am not unreasonable enough to expect it to grow on that, but its conduct in staying where it does requires explanation.

We clamber up into the long jungle grass region and go on our way across a series of steep-sided, rounded grass hillocks, each of which is separated from the others by dry, rocky watercourses. The effects produced by the seed-ears of the long grass round us are very beautiful; they look a golden brown, and each ear and leaf is gemmed with dewdrops, and those of the grass on the sides of the hillocks at a little distance off show a soft brown-pink.

After half an hour's climb, when we are close at the base of the wall, I observe the men ahead halting, and coming up with them find Monrovia Boy down a hole; a little deep blow-hole, in which, I am informed, water is supposed to be. But Monrovia soon reports "No live."

I now find we have not a drop of water, either with us or in camp, and now this hole has proved dry. There is, says the sergeant, no chance of getting any more water on this side of the mountain, save down at the river at Buea.

This means failure unless tackled, and it is evidently a trick played on me by the boys, who intentionally failed to let me know of this want of water before leaving Buea, where it seems they have all learnt it. I express my opinion of them in four words and send Monrovia Boy, who I know is to be trusted, back to Buea with a scribbled note to Herr Liebert asking him to send me up two demijohns of water. I send cook with him as far as the camp in the forest we have just left with orders to bring up three bottles of soda water I have left there, and to instruct the men there that as soon as the water arrives from Buea they are to bring it on up to the camp I mean to make at the top of the wall.

The men are sulky, and Sasu, Peter, Kefalla, and Head man say they will wait and come on as soon as cook brings the soda water, and I go on, and presently see Xenia and Black boy are following me. We get on to the intervening hillocks and commence to ascend the face of the wall.

The angle of this wall is great, and its appearance from below is impressive from its enormous breadth, and its abrupt rise without bend or droop for a good 2,000 feet into the air. It is covered with short, yellowish grass through which the burnt-up, scoriaceous lava rock protrudes in rough masses.

I got on up the wall, which when you are on it is not so perpendicular as it looks from below, my desire being to see what sort of country there was on the top of it, between it and the final peak. Sasu had reported to Herr Liebert that it was a wilderness of rock, in which it would be impossible to fix a tent, and spoke vaguely of caves. Here and there on the way up I come to holes, similar to the one my men had been down for water. I suppose these holes have been caused by gases from an under hot layer of lava bursting up through the upper cool layer. As I get higher, the grass becomes shorter and more sparse, and the rocks more ostentatiously displayed. Here and there among them are sadly tried bushes, bearing a beautiful yellow flower, like a large yellow wild rose, only scentless. It is not a rose at all, I may remark. The ground, where there is any basin made by the rocks, grows a great sedum, with a grand head of whity-pink flower, also a tall herb, with soft downy leaves silver grey in colour, and having a very pleasant aromatic scent, and here and there patches of good honest parsley.

Bright blue, flannelly-looking flowers stud the grass in sheltered places and a very pretty large green orchid is plentiful. Above us is a bright blue sky with white cloud rushing hurriedly across it to the N.E. and a fierce sun. When I am about half-way up, I think of those boys, and, wanting rest, sit down by an inviting-looking rock grotto, with a patch of the yellow flowered shrub growing on its top. Inside it grow little ferns and mosses, all damp; but alas! no water pool, and very badly I want water by this time.

Below me a belt of white cloud had now formed, so that I could see neither the foot-hillocks nor the forest, and presently out of this mist came Xenia toiling up, carrying my black bag. "Where them Black boy live?" said I. "Black boy say him foot be tire too much," said Xenia, as he threw himself down in the little shade the rock could give. I took a cupful of sour claret out of the bottle in the bag, and told Xenia to come on up as soon as he was rested, and meanwhile to yell to the others down below and tell them to come on. Xenia did, but sadly observed, "softly softly still hurts the snail," and I left him and went on up the mountain.

When I had got to the top of the rock under which I had sheltered from the blazing sun, the mist opened a little, and I saw my men looking like so many little dolls. They were still sitting on the hillock where I had left them. Buea showed from this elevation well. The guard house and the mission house, like little houses in a picture, and the make of the ground on which Buea station stands, came out distinctly as a ledge or terrace, extending for miles N.N.E. and S.S.W. This ledge is a strange-looking piece of country, covered with low bush, out of which rise great, isolated, white-stemmed cotton trees. Below, and beyond this is a denser band of high forest, and again below this stretches the vast mangrove-swamp fringing the estuary of the Cameroons, Mungo, and Bimbia rivers. It is a very noble view, giving one an example of the peculiar beauty one oft-times gets in this West African scenery, namely colossal sweeps of colour. The mangrove-swamps looked to-day like a vast damson-coloured carpet threaded with silver where the waterways ran. It reminded me of a scene I saw once near Cabinda, when on climbing to the top of a hill I suddenly found myself looking down on a sheet of violet pink more than a mile long and half a mile wide. This was caused by a climbing plant having taken possession of a valley full of trees, whose tops it had reached and then spread and interlaced itself over them, to burst into profuse glorious laburnum-shaped bunches of flowers.

After taking some careful compass bearings for future use regarding the Rumby and Omon range of mountains, which were clearly visible and which look fascinatingly like my beloved Sierra del Cristal, I turned my face to the wall of Mungo, and continued the ascent. The sun, which was blazing, was reflected back from the rocks in scorching rays. But it was more bearable now, because its heat was tempered by a bitter wind.

The slope becoming steeper, I gradually made my way towards the left until I came to a great lane, as neatly walled with rock as if it had been made with human hands. It runs down the mountain face, nearly vertically in places and at stiff angles always, but it was easier going up this lane than on the outside rough rock, because the rocks in it had been smoothed by mountain torrents during thousands of wet seasons, and the walls protected one from the biting wind, a wind that went through me, for I had been stewing for nine months and more in tropic and equatorial swamps.

Up this lane I went to the very top of the mountain wall, and then, to my surprise, found myself facing a great, hillocky, rock-encumbered plain, across the other side of which rose the mass of the peak itself, not as a single cone, but as a wall surmounted by several, three being evidently the highest among them.

I started along the ridge of my wall, and went to its highest part, that to the S.W., intending to see what I could of the view towards the sea, and then to choose a place for camping in for the night.

When I reached the S.W. end, looking westwards I saw the South Atlantic down below, like a plain of frosted silver. Out of it, barely twenty miles away, rose Fernando Po to its 10,190 feet with that majestic grace peculiar to a volcanic island. Immediately below me, some 10,000 feet or so, lay Victoria with the forested foot-hills of Mungo Mah Lobeh encircling it as a diadem, and Ambas Bay gemmed with rocky islands lying before it. On my left away S.E. was the glorious stretch of the Cameroon estuary, with a line of white cloud lying very neatly along the course of Cameroon River.

In one of the chasms of the mountain wall that I had come up—in the one furthest to the north—there was a thunderstorm brewing, seemingly hanging on to, or streaming out of the mountain side, a soft billowy mass of dense cream-coloured cloud, with flashes of golden lightnings playing about in it with soft growls of thunder. Surely Mungo Mah Lobeh himself, of all the thousands he annually turns out, never made one more lovely than this. Soon the white mists rose from the mangrove-swamp, and grew rose-colour in the light of the setting sun, as they swept upwards over the now purple high forests. In the heavens, to the north, there was a rainbow, vivid in colour, one arch of it going behind the peak, the other sinking into the mist sea below, and this mist sea rose and rose towards me, turning from pale rose-colour to lavender, and where the shadow of Mungo lay across it, to a dull leaden grey. It was soon at my feet, blotting the under-world out, and soon came flowing over the wall top at its lowest parts, stretching in great spreading rivers over the crater plain, and then these coalescing everything was shut out save the two summits: that of Cameroon close to me, and that of Clarence away on Fernando Po. These two stood out alone, like great island masses made of iron rising from a formless, silken sea.

The space around seemed boundless, and there was in it neither sound nor colour, nor anything with form, save those two terrific things. It was like a vision, and it held me spell-bound, as I stood shivering on the rocks with the white mist round my knees until into my wool-gathering mind came the memory of those anything but sublime men of mine; and I turned and scuttled off along the rocks like an agitated ant left alone in a dead Universe.

I soon found the place where I had come up into the crater plain and went down over the wall, descending with twice the rapidity, but ten times the scratches and grazes, of the ascent.

I picked up the place where I had left Xenia, but no Xenia was there, nor came there any answer to my bush call for him, so on I went down towards the place where, hours ago, I had left the men. The mist was denser down below, but to my joy it was warmer than on the summit of the wind-swept wall.

I had nearly reached the foot of this wall and made my mind up to turn in for the night under a rock, when I heard a melancholy croak away in the mist to the left. I went towards it and found Xenia lost on his own account, and distinctly quaint in manner, and then I recollected that I had been warned Xenia is slightly crazy. Nice situation this: a madman on a mountain in the mist. Xenia, I found, had no longer got my black bag, but in its place a lid of a saucepan and an empty lantern. To put it mildly, this is not the sort of outfit the R.G.S. Hints to Travellers would recommend for African exploration. Xenia reported that he gave the bag to Black boy, who shortly afterwards disappeared, and that he had neither seen him nor any of the others since, and didn't expect to this side of Srahmandazi. In a homicidal state of mind, I made tracks for the missing ones followed by Xenia. I thought mayhap they had grown on to the rocks they had sat upon so long, but presently, just before it became quite dark, we picked up the place we had left them in and found there only an empty soda-water bottle. Xenia poured out a muddled mass of observations to the effect that "they got fright too much about them water palaver."

I did not linger to raise a monument to them, but I said I wished they were in a condition to require one, and we went on over our hillocks with more confidence now that we knew we had stuck well to our unmarked track.

"The moving Moon went up the sky,
And nowhere did abide:
Softly she was going up,
And a star or two beside."

Only she was a young and inefficient moon, and although we were below the thickest of the mist band, it was dark. Finding our own particular hole in the forest wall was about as easy as finding "one particular rabbit hole in an unknown hay-field in the dark," and the attempt to do so afforded us a great deal of varied exercise. I am obliged to be guarded in my language, because my feelings now are only down to one degree below boiling point. The rain now began to fall, thank goodness, and I drew the thick ears of grass through my parched lips as I stumbled along over the rugged lumps of rock hidden under the now waist-high jungle grass.

Our camp hole was pretty easily distinguishable by daylight, for it was on the left-hand side of one of the forest tongues, the grass land running down like a lane between two tongues here, and just over the entrance three conspicuously high trees showed. But we could not see these "picking-up" points in the darkness, so I had to keep getting Xenia to strike matches, and hold them in his hat while I looked at the compass. Presently we came full tilt up against a belt of trees which I knew from these compass observations was our tongue of forest belt, and I fired a couple of revolver shots into it, whereabouts I judged our camp to be.

This was instantly answered by a yell from human voices in chorus, and towards that yell in a slightly amiable—a very slightly amiable—state of mind I went.

I will draw a veil over the scene, particularly over my observations to those men. They did not attempt to deny their desertion, but they attempted to explain it, each one saying that it was not he but the other boy who "got fright too much."

I closed the palaver promptly with a brief but lurid sketch of my opinion on the situation, and ordered food, for not having had a thing save that cup of sour claret since 6.30 A.M., and it being now 11 P.M., I felt sinkings. Then arose another beautiful situation before me. It seems when Cook and Monrovia got back into camp this morning Master Cook was seized with one of those attacks of a desire to manage things that produce such awful results in the African servant, and sent all the beef and rice down to Buea to be cooked, because there was no water here to cook it. Therefore the men have got nothing to eat. I had a few tins of my own food and so gave them some, and they became as happy as kings in a few minutes, listening and shouting over the terrible adventures of Xenia, who is posing as the Hero of the Great Cameroon. I get some soda-water from the two bottles left and some tinned herring, and then write out two notes to Herr Liebert asking him to send me three more demijohns of water, and some beef and rice from the store, promising faithfully to pay for them on my return.

I would not prevent those men of mine from going up that peak above me after their touching conduct to-day. Oh! no; not for worlds, dear things.

CHAPTER XIX

THE GREAT PEAK OF CAMEROONS—(continued)

SETTING FORTH HOW THE VOYAGER FOR A SECOND TIME REACHES THE
S.E. CRATER, WITH SOME ACCOUNT OF THE PLEASURES INCIDENTAL TO
CAMPING OUT IN THE SAID CRATER.

SEPTEMBER 24TH.—Lovely morning, the grey-white mist in the forest makes it like a dream of Fairyland, each moss-grown tree stem heavily gemmed with dewdrops. At 5.30 I stir the boys, for Sasu, the sergeant, says he must go back to his military duties. The men think we are all going back with him as he is our only guide, but I send three of them down with orders to go back to Victoria—two being of the original set I started with. They are surprised and disgusted at being sent home, but they have got "hot foot," and something wrong in the usual seat of African internal disturbances, their "tummicks," and I am not thinking of starting a sanatorium for abdominally-afflicted Africans in that crater plain above. Black boy is the other boy returned, I do not want another of his attacks.

They go, and this leaves me in the forest camp with Kefalla, Xenia, and Cook, and we start expecting the water sent for by Monrovia boy yesterday forenoon. There are an abominable lot of bees about; they do not give one a moment's peace, getting beneath the waterproof sheets over the bed. The ground, bestrewn with leaves and dried wood, is a mass of large flies rather like our common house-fly, but both butterflies and beetles seem scarce; and I confess I do not feel up to hunting much after yesterday's work, and deem it advisable to rest. My face and particularly my lips are a misery to me, having been blistered all over by yesterday's sun, and last night I inadvertently whipped the skin all off one cheek with the blanket, and it keeps on bleeding, and, horror of horrors, there is no tea until that water comes. I wish I had got the mountaineering spirit, for then I could say, "I'll never come to this sort of place again, for you can get all you want in the Alps." I have been told this by my mountaineering friends—I have never been there—and that you can go and do all sorts of stupendous things all day, and come back in the evening to table d'hôte at an hotel; but as I have not got the mountaineering spirit, I suppose I shall come fooling into some such place as this as soon as I get the next chance.

About 8.30, to our delight, the gallant Monrovia boy comes through the bush with a demijohn of water, and I get my tea, and give the men the only half-pound of rice I have and a tin of meat, and they eat, become merry, and chat over their absent companions in a scornful, scandalous way. Who cares for hotels now? When one is in a delightful place like this, one must work, so off I go to the north into the forest, after giving the rest of the demijohn of water into the Monrovia boy's charge with strict orders it is not to be opened till my return. Quantities of beetles.

A little after two o'clock I return to camp, after having wandered about in the forest and found three very deep holes, down which I heaved rocks and in no case heard a splash. In one I did not hear the rocks strike, owing to the great depth. I hate holes, and especially do I hate these African ones, for I am frequently falling, more or less, into them, and they will be my end.

The other demijohns of water have not arrived yet, and we are getting anxious again because the men's food has not come up, and they have been so exceedingly thirsty that they have drunk most of the water—not, however, since it has been in Monrovia's charge; but at 3.15 another boy comes through the bush with another demijohn of water. We receive him gladly, and ask him about the chop. He knows nothing about it. At 3.45 another boy comes through the bush with another demijohn of water; we receive him kindly; he does not know anything about the chop. At 4.10 another boy comes through the bush with another demijohn of water, and knowing nothing about the chop, we are civil to him, and that's all.

A terrific tornado which has been lurking growling about then sits down in the forest and bursts, wrapping us up in a lively kind of fog, with its thunder, lightning, and rain. It was impossible to hear, or make one's self heard at the distance of even a few paces, because of the shrill squeal of the wind, the roar of the thunder, and the rush of the rain on the trees round us. It was not like having a storm burst over you in the least; you felt you were in the middle of its engine-room when it had broken down badly. After half an hour or so the thunder seemed to lift itself off the ground, and the lightning came in sheets, instead of in great forks that flew like flights of spears among the forest trees. The thunder, however, had not settled things amicably with the mountain; it roared its rage at Mungo, and Mungo answered back, quivering with a rage as great, under our feet. One feels here as if one were constantly dropping, unasked and unregarded, among painful and violent discussions between the elemental powers of the Universe. Mungo growls and swears in thunder at the sky, and sulks in white mist all the morning, and then the sky answers back, hurling down lightnings and rivers of water, with total disregard of Mungo's visitors. The way the water rushes down from the mountain wall through the watercourses in the jungle just above, and then at the edge of the forest spreads out into a sheet of water that is an inch deep, and that flies on past us in miniature cascades, trying the while to put out our fire and so on, is—quite interesting. (I exhausted my vocabulary on those boys yesterday.)

As soon as we saw what we were in for, we had thrown dry wood on to the fire, and it blazed just as the rain came down, so with our assistance it fought a good fight with its fellow elements, spitting and hissing like a wild cat. It could have managed the water fairly well, but the wind came, very nearly putting an end to it by carrying away its protecting bough house, which settled on "Professor" Kefalla, who burst out in a lecture on the foolishness of mountaineering and the quantity of devils in this region. Just in the midst of these joys another boy came through the bush with another demijohn of water. We did not receive him even civilly; I burst out laughing, and the boys went off in a roar, and we shouted at him, "Where them chop?" "He live for come," said the boy, and we then gave him a hearty welcome and a tot of rum, and an hour afterwards two more boys appear, one carrying a sack of rice and beef for the men, and the other a box for me from Herr Liebert, containing a luxurious supply of biscuits, candles, tinned meats, and a bottle of wine and one of beer.

We are now all happy, though exceeding damp, and the boys sit round the fire, with their big iron pot full of beef and rice, busy cooking while they talk. Wonderful accounts of our prodigies of valour I hear given by Xenia, and terrible accounts of what they have lived through from the others, and the men who have brought up the demijohns and the chop recount the last news from Buea. James's wife has run away again.

I have taken possession of two demijohns of water and the rum demijohn, arranging them round the head of my bed. The worst of it is those tiresome bees, as soon as the rain is over, come in hundreds after the rum, and frighten me continually. The worthless wretches get intoxicated on what they can suck from round the cork, and then they stagger about on the ground buzzing malevolently. When the boys have had the chop and a good smoke, we turn to and make up the loads for to-morrow's start up the mountain, and then, after more hot tea, I turn in on my camp bed—listening to the soft sweet murmur of the trees and the pleasant, laughing chatter of the men.

September 25th.—Rolled off the bed twice last night into the bush. The rain has washed the ground away from under its off legs, so that it tilts; and there were quantities of large longicorn beetles about during the night—the sort with spiny backs; they kept on getting themselves hitched on to my blankets and when I wanted civilly to remove them they made a horrid fizzing noise and showed fight—cocking their horns in a defiant way. I awake finally about 5 A.M. soaked through to the skin. The waterproof sheet has had a label sewn to it, so is not waterproof, and it has been raining softly but amply for hours.

About seven we are off again, with Xenia, Head man, Cook, Monrovia boy and a labourer from Buea—the water-carriers have gone home after having had their morning chop.

We make for the face of the wall by a route to the left of that I took on Monday, and when we are clambering up it, some 600 feet above the hillocks, swish comes a terrific rain-storm at us accompanied by a squealing, bitter cold wind. We can hear the roar of the rain on the forest below, and hoping to get above it we keep on; hoping, however, is vain. The dense mist that comes with it prevents our seeing more than two yards in front, and we get too far to the left. I am behind the band to-day, severely bringing up the rear, and about 1 o'clock I hear shouts from the vanguard and when I get up to them I find them sitting on the edge of one of the clefts or scars in the mountain face.

I do not know how these quarry-like chasms have been formed. They both look alike from below—the mountain wall comes down vertically into them—and the bottom of this one slopes forward, so that if we had had the misfortune when a little lower down to have gone a little further to the left, we should have got on to the bottom of it, and should have found ourselves walled in on three sides, and had to retrace our steps; as it is we have just struck its right-hand edge. And fortunately, the mist, thick as it is, has not been sufficiently thick to lead the men to walk over it; for had they done so they would have got killed, as the cliff arches in under so that we look straight into the bottom of the scar some 200 or 300 feet below, when there is a split in the mist. The sides and bottom are made of, and strewn with, white, moss-grown masses of volcanic cinder rock, and sparsely shrubbed with gnarled trees which have evidently been under fire—one of my boys tells me from the burning of this face of the mountain by "the Major from Calabar" during the previous dry season.

We keep on up a steep grass-covered slope, and finally reach the top of the wall. The immense old crater floor before us is to-day the site of a seething storm, and the peak itself quite invisible. My boys are quite demoralised by the cold. I find most of them have sold the blankets I gave them out at Buana; and those who have not sold them have left them behind at Buea, from laziness perhaps, but more possibly from a confidence in their powers to prevent us getting so far.

I believe if I had collapsed too—the cold tempted me to do so as nothing else can—they would have lain down and died in the cold sleety rain.

I sight a clump of gnarled sparsely-foliaged trees bedraped heavily with lichen, growing in a hollow among the rocks; thither I urge the men for shelter and they go like storm-bewildered sheep. My bones are shaking in my skin and my teeth in my head, for after the experience I had had of the heat here on Monday I dared not clothe myself heavily.

The men stand helpless under the trees, and I hastily take the load of blankets Herr Liebert lent us off a boy's back and undo it, throwing one blanket round each man, and opening my umbrella and spreading it over the other blankets. Then I give them a tot of rum apiece, as they sit huddled in their blankets, and tear up a lot of the brittle, rotten wood from the trees and shrubs, getting horrid thorns into my hands the while, and set to work getting a fire with it and the driest of the moss from beneath the rocks. By the aid of it and Xenia, who soon revived, and a carefully scraped up candle and a box of matches, the fire soon blazes, Xenia holding a blanket to shelter it, while I, with a cutlass, chop stakes to fix the blankets on, so as to make a fire tent.

The other boys now revive, and I hustle them about to make more fires, no easy work in the drenching rain, but work that has got to be done. We soon get three well alight, and then I clutch a blanket—a wringing wet blanket, but a comfort—and wrapping myself round in it, issue orders for wood to be gathered and stored round each fire to dry, and then stand over Cook while he makes the men's already cooked chop hot over our first fire, when this is done getting him to make me tea, or as it more truly should be called, soup, for it contains bits of rice and beef, and the general taste of the affair is wood smoke.

Kefalla by this time is in lecturing form again, so my mind is relieved about him, although he says, "Oh, ma! It be cold, cold too much. Too much cold kill we black man, all same for one as too much sun kill you white man. Oh, ma!. . .," etc. I tell him they have only got themselves to blame; if they had come up with me on Monday we should have been hot enough, and missed this storm of rain.

When the boys have had their chop, and are curling themselves up comfortably round their now blazing fires Xenia must needs start a theory that there is a better place than this to camp in; he saw it when he was with an unsuccessful expedition that got as far as this. Kefalla is fool enough to go off with him to find this place; but they soon return, chilled through again, and unsuccessful in their quest. I gather that they have been to find caves. I wish they had found caves, for I am not thinking of taking out a patent for our present camp site.

The bitter wind and swishing rain keep on. We are to a certain extent sheltered from the former, but the latter is of that insinuating sort that nothing but a granite wall would keep off.

Just at sundown, however, as is usual in this country, the rain ceases for a while, and I take this opportunity to get out my seaman's jersey. When I have fought my way into it, I turn to survey our position, and find I have been carrying on my battle on the brink of an abysmal hole whose mouth is concealed among the rocks and scraggly shrubs just above our camp. I heave rocks down it, as we in Fanland would offer rocks to an Ombwiri, and hear them go "knickity-knock, like a pebble in Carisbrook well." I think I detect a far away splash, but it was an awesome way down. This mountain seems set with these man-traps, and "some day some gentleman's nigger" will get killed down one.

The mist has now cleared away from the peak, but lies all over the lower world, and I take bearings of the three highest cones or peaks carefully. Then I go away over the rocky ground southwards, and as I stand looking round, the mist sea below is cleft in twain for a few minutes by some fierce down-draught of wind from the peak, and I get a strange, clear, sudden view right down to Ambas Bay. It is just like looking down from one world into another. I think how Odin hung and looked down into Nifelheim, and then of how hot, how deliciously hot, it was away down there, and then the mist closes over it. I shiver and go back to camp, for night is coming on, and I know my men will require intellectual support in the matter of procuring firewood.

The men are now quite happy; over each fire they have made a tent with four sticks with a blanket on, a blanket that is too wet to burn, though I have to make them brace the blankets to windward for fear of their scorching.

The wood from the shrubs here is of an aromatic and a resinous nature, which sounds nice, but it isn't; for the volumes of smoke it gives off when burning are suffocating, and the boys, who sit almost on the fire, are every few moments scrambling to their feet and going apart to cough out smoke, like so many novices in training for the profession of fire-eaters. However, they soon find that if they roll themselves in their blankets, and lie on the ground to windward they escape most of the smoke. They have divided up into three parties: Kefalla and Xenia, who have struck up a great friendship, take the lower, the most exposed fire. Head man, Cook, and Monrovia Boy have the upper fire, and the labourer has the middle one—he being an outcast for medical reasons. They are all steaming away and smoking comfortably.

I form the noble resolution to keep awake, and rouse up any gentleman who may catch on fire during the night, and see to wood being put on the fires, so elaborately settle myself on my wooden chop-box, wherein I have got all the lucifers which are not in the soap-box. Owing to there not being a piece of ground the size of a sixpenny piece level in this place, the arrangement of my box camp takes time, but at last it is done to my complete satisfaction, close to a tree trunk, and I think, as I wrap myself up in my two wet blankets and lean against my tree, what a good thing it is to know how to make one's self comfortable in a place like this. This tree stem is perfection, just the right angle to be restful to one's back, and one can rely all the time on Nature hereabouts not to let one get thoroughly effete from luxurious comfort, so I lazily watch and listen to Xenia and Kefalla at their fire hard by.

They begin talking to each other on their different tribal societies; Kefalla is a Vey, Xenia a Liberian, so in the interests of Science I give them two heads of tobacco to stimulate their conversation. They receive them with tragic grief, having no pipe, so in the interests of Science I undo my blankets and give them two out of my portmanteau; then do myself up again and pretend to be asleep. I am rewarded by getting some interesting details, and form the opinion that both these worthies, in their pursuit of their particular ju-jus, have come into contact with white prejudices, and are now fugitives from religious persecution. I also observe they have both their own ideas of happiness. Kefalla holds it lies in a warm shirt, Xenia that it abides in warm trousers; and every half-hour the former takes his shirt off, and holds it in the fire smoke, and then puts it hastily on; and Xenia, who is the one and only trouser wearer in our band, spends fifty per cent. of the night on one leg struggling to get the other in or out of these garments, when they are either coming off to be warmed, or going on after warming.

There seem but few insects here. I have only got two moths to-night—one pretty one with white wings with little red spots on, like an old-fashioned petticoat such as an early Victorian-age lady would have worn—the other a sweet thing in silver.

(Later, i.e., 2.15 A.M.). I have been asleep against that abominable vegetable of a tree. It had its trunk covered with a soft cushion of moss, and pretended to be a comfort—a right angle to lean against, and a softly padded protection to the spine from wind, and all that sort of thing; whereas the whole mortal time it was nothing in this wretched world but a water-pipe, to conduct an extra supply of water down my back. The water has simply streamed down it, and formed a nice little pool in a rocky hollow where I keep my feet, and I am chilled to the innermost bone, so have to scramble up and drag my box to the side of Kefalla and Xenia's fire, feeling sure I have contracted a fatal chill this time. I scrape the ashes out of the fire into a heap, and put my sodden boots into them, and they hiss merrily, and I resolve not to go to sleep again. 5 A.M.—Have been to sleep twice, and have fallen off my box bodily into the fire in my wet blankets, and should for sure have put it out like a bucket of cold water had not Xenia and Kefalla been roused up by the smother I occasioned and rescued me—or the fire. It is not raining now, but it is bitter cold and Cook is getting my tea. I give the boys a lot of hot tea with a big handful of sugar in, and they then get their own food hot.

CHAPTER XX

THE GREAT PEAK OF CAMEROONS—(continued)

SETTING FORTH HOW THE VOYAGER ATTAINS THE SUMMIT OF MUNGO
MAH LOBEH, AND DESCENDS THEREFROM TO VICTORIA, TO WHICH IS
ADDED SOME REMARKS ON THE NATURAL HISTORY OF THE WEST COAST
PORTER, AND THE NATIVE METHODS OF MAKING FIRE.

SEPTEMBER 26TH.—The weather is undecided and so am I, for I feel doubtful about going on in this weather, but I do not like to give up the peak
after going through so much for it. The boys being dry and warm with
the fires have forgotten their troubles. However, I settle in my mind to keep on,
and ask for volunteers to come with me, and Bum, the head man, and Xenia
announce their willingness. I put two tins of meat and a bottle of Herr Liebert's
beer into the little wooden box, and insist on both men taking a blanket apiece,
much to their disgust, and before six o'clock we are off over the crater plain.
It is a broken bit of country with rock mounds sparsely overgrown with tufts
of grass, and here and there are patches of boggy land, not real bog, but damp
places where grow little clumps of rushes, and here and there among the rocks
sorely-afflicted shrubs of broom, and the yellow-flowered shrub I have mentioned before, and quantities of very sticky heather, feeling when you catch hold
of it as if it had been covered with syrup. One might fancy the entire race of
shrubs was dying out; for one you see partially alive there are twenty skeletons
which fall to pieces as you brush past them.

It is downhill the first part of the way, that is to say, the trend of the land is
downhill, for be it down or up, the details of it are rugged mounds and masses
of burnt-out lava rock. It is evil going, but perhaps not quite so evil as the lower
hillocks of the great wall where the rocks are hidden beneath long slippery grass.
We wind our way in between the mounds, or clamber over them, or scramble

along their sides impartially. The general level is then flat, and then comes a rise towards the peak wall, so we steer N.N.E. until we strike the face of the peak, and then commence a stiff rough climb.

We keep as straight as we can, but get driven at an angle by the strange ribs of rock which come straight down. These are most tiresome to deal with, getting worse the higher we go, and so rotten and weather-eaten are they that they crumble into dust and fragments under our feet. Head man gets half a dozen falls, and when we are about three parts of the way up Xenia gives in. The cold and the climbing are too much for him, so I make him wrap himself up in his blanket, which he is glad enough of now, and shelter in a depression under one of the many rock ridges, and Head man and I go on. When we are some 600 feet higher the iron-grey mist comes curling and waving round the rocks above us, like some savage monster defending them from intruders, and I again debate whether I was justified in risking the men, for it is a risk for them at this low temperature, with the evil weather I know, and they do not know, is coming on. But still we have food and blankets with us enough for them, and the camp in the plain below they can reach all right, if the worst comes to the worst; and for myself—well—that's my own affair, and no one will be a ha'porth the worse if I am dead in an hour. So I hitch myself on to the rocks, and take bearings, particularly bearings of Xenia's position, who, I should say, has got a tin of meat and a flask of rum with him, and then turn and face the threatening mist. It rises and falls, and sends out arm-like streams towards us, and then Bum, the head man, decides to fail for the third time to reach the peak, and I leave him wrapped in his blanket with the bag of provisions, and go on alone into the wild, grey, shifting, whirling mist above, and soon find myself at the head of a rock ridge in a narrowish depression, walled by massive black walls which show fitfully but firmly through the mist.

I can see three distinctly high cones before me, and then the mist, finding it cannot drive me back easily, proceeds to desperate methods, and lashes out with a burst of bitter wind, and a sheet of blinding, stinging rain. I make my way up through it towards a peak which I soon see through a tear in the mist is not the highest, so I angle off and go up the one to the left, and after a desperate fight reach the cairn—only, alas! to find a hurricane raging and a fog in full possession, and not a ten yards' view to be had in any direction. Near the cairn on the ground are several bottles, some of which the energetic German officers, I suppose, had emptied in honour of their achievement, an achievement I bow down before, for their pluck and strength had taken them here in a shorter time by far than mine. I do not meddle with anything, save to take a few specimens and to put a few more rocks on the cairn, and to put in among them my card, merely as a civility to Mungo, a civility his Majesty will soon turn into pulp. Not that it matters—what is done is done.

The weather grows worse every minute, and no sign of any clearing shows in the indigo sky or the wind-reft mist. The rain lashes so fiercely I cannot turn my face to it and breathe, the wind is all I can do to stand up against.

Verily I am no mountaineer, for there is in me no exultation, but only a deep disgust because the weather has robbed me of my main object in coming here, namely to get a good view and an idea of the way the unexplored mountain range behind Calabar trends. I took my chance and it failed, so there's nothing to complain about.

Comforting myself with these reflections, I start down to find Bum, and do so neatly, and then together we scramble down carefully among the rotten black rocks, intent on finding Xenia. The scene is very grand. At one minute we can see nothing save the black rocks and cinders under foot; the next the wind-torn mist separates now in one direction, now in another, showing us always the same wild scene of great black cliffs, rising in jagged peaks and walls around and above us. I think this walled cauldron we had just left is really the highest crater on Mungo. {439}

We soon become anxious about Xenia, for this is a fearfully easy place to lose a man in such weather, but just as we get below the thickest part of the pall of mist, I observe a doll-sized figure, standing on one leg taking on or off its trousers—our lost Xenia, beyond a shadow of a doubt, and we go down direct to him.

When we reach him we halt, and I give the two men one of the tins of meat, and take another and the bottle of beer myself, and then make a hasty sketch of the great crater plain below us. At the further edge of the plain a great white cloud is coming up from below, which argues badly for our trip down the great wall to the forest camp, which I am anxious to reach before nightfall after our experience of the accommodation afforded by our camp in the crater plain last night.

While I am sitting waiting for the men to finish their meal, I feel a chill at my back, as if some cold thing had settled there, and turning round, see the mist from the summit above coming in a wall down towards us. These mists up here, as far as my experience goes, are always preceded by a strange breath of ice-cold air—not necessarily a wind.

Bum then draws my attention to a strange funnel-shaped thing coming down from the clouds to the north. A big waterspout, I presume: it seems to be moving rapidly N.E., and I profoundly hope it will hold that course, for we have quite as much as we can manage with the ordinary rain-water supply on this mountain, without having waterspouts to deal with.

We start off down the mountain as rapidly as we can. Xenia is very done up, and Head man comes perilously near breaking his neck by frequent falls among the rocks; my unlucky boots are cut through and through by the latter. When we get down towards the big crater plain, it is a race between us and the pursuing mist as to who shall reach the camp first, and the mist wins, but we have just time to make out the camp's exact position before it closes round us, so we reach it without any real difficulty. When we get there, about one o'clock, I find the men have kept the fires alight and Cook is asleep before one of them with another conflagration smouldering in his hair. I get him to make me tea, while the others pack up as quickly as possible, and by two we are all off on our way down to the forest camp.

The boys are nervous in their way of going down over the mountain wall. The misadventures of Cook alone would fill volumes. Monrovia boy is out and away the best man at this work. Just as we reach the high jungle grass, down comes the rain and up comes the mist, and we have the worst time we have had during our whole trip, in our endeavours to find the hole in the forest that leads to our old camp.

Unfortunately, I must needs go in for acrobatic performances on the top of one of the highest, rockiest hillocks. Poising myself on one leg I take a rapid slide sideways, ending in a very showy leap backwards which lands me on the top of the lantern I am carrying to-day, among miscellaneous rocks. There being fifteen feet or so of jungle grass above me, all the dash and beauty of my performance are as much thrown away as I am, for my boys are too busy on their own accounts in the mist to miss me. After resting some little time as I fell, and making and unmaking the idea in my mind that I am killed, I get up, clamber elaborately to the top of the next hillock, and shout for the boys, and "Ma," "ma," comes back from my flock from various points out of the fog. I find Bum and Monrovia boy, and learn that during my absence Xenia, who always fancies himself as a path-finder, has taken the lead, and gone off some- where with the rest. We shout and the others answer, and we join them, and it soon becomes evident to the meanest intelligence that Xenia had better have spent his time attending to those things of his instead of going in for guiding, for we are now right off the track we made through the grass on our up journey, and we proceed to have a cheerful hour or so in the wet jungle, ploughing hither and thither, trying to find our way.

At last we pick up the top of a tongue of forest that we all feel is ours, but we—that is to say, Xenia and I, for the others go like lambs to the slaughter wherever they are led—disagree as to the path. He wants to go down one side of the tongue, I to go down the other, and I have my way, and we wade along, skirting the bushes that fringe it, trying to find our hole. I own I soon begin to feel shaky about having been right in the affair, but soon Xenia, who is lead- ing, shouts he has got it, and we limp in, our feet sore with rugged rocks, and everything we have on, or in the loads, wringing wet, save the matches, which providentially I had put into my soap-box.

Anything more dismal than the look of that desired camp when we reach it, I never saw. Pools of water everywhere. The fire-house a limp ruin, the camp bed I have been thinking fondly of for the past hour a water cistern. I tilt the water out of it, and say a few words to it regarding its hide-bound idiocy in obeying its military instructions to be waterproof; and then, while the others are putting up the fire-house, Head man and I get out the hidden demijohn of rum, and the beef and rice, and I serve out a tot of rum each to the boys, who are shivering dreadfully, waiting for Cook to get the fire. He soon does this, and then I have my hot tea and the men their hot food, for now we have returned to the luxury of two cooking pots.

Their education in bush is evidently progressing, for they make themselves a big screen with boughs and spare blankets, between the wind and the fire-house, and I get Xenia to cut some branches, and place them on the top of my waterproof sheet shelter, and we are fairly comfortable again, and the boys quite merry and very well satisfied with themselves.

Unfortunately the subject of their nightly debating society is human conduct, a subject ever fraught with dangerous elements of differences of opinion. They are busy discussing, with their mouths full of rice and beef, the conduct of an absent friend, who it seems is generally regarded by them as a spendthrift. "He gets plenty money, but he no have none no time." "He go frow it away—on woman, and drink." "He no buy clothes." This last is evidently a very heavy accusation, but Kefalla says, "What can a man buy with money better than them thing he like best?"

There is a very peculiar look on the rotten wood on the ground round here; to-night it has patches and flecks of iridescence like one sees on herrings or mackerel that have been kept too long. The appearance of this strange eerie light in among the bush is very weird and charming. I have seen it before in dark forests at night, but never so much of it.

September 27th.—Fine morning. It's a blessing my Pappenheimers have not recognised what this means for the afternoon. We take things very leisurely. I know it's no good hurrying, we are dead sure of getting a ducking before we reach Buea anyhow, so we may as well enjoy ourselves while we can.

I ask my boys how they would "make fire suppose no matches live." Not one of them thinks it possible to do so, "it pass man to do them thing suppose he no got live stick or matches." They are coast boys, all of them, and therefore used to luxury, but it is really remarkable how widely diffused matches are inland, and how very dependent on them these natives are. When I have been away in districts where they have not penetrated, it is exceedingly rarely that the making of fire has to be resorted to. I think I may say that in most African villages it has not had to be done for years and years, because when a woman's fire has gone out, owing to her having been out at work all day, she just runs into some neighbour's hut where there is a fire burning, and gives compliments, and picks up a burning stick from the fire and runs home. From this comes the compliment, equivalent to our "Oh! don't go away yet," of "You come to fetch fire." This will be said to you all the way from Sierra Leone to Loanda, as far as I know, if you have been making yourself agreeable in an African home, even if the process may have extended over a day or so. The hunters, like the Fans, have to make fire, and do it now with a flint and steel; but in districts where their tutor in this method—the flint-lock gun—is not available, they will do it with two sticks, not always like the American Indians' fire-sticks. One stick is placed horizontally on the ground and the other twirled rapidly between the palms of the hands, but sometimes two bits of palm stick are worked in a hole in a bigger bit of wood, the hole stuffed round with the pith of a tree or with silk cotton fluff, and the two sticks rotated vigorously. Again, on one occasion I saw a Bakele woman make fire by means of a slip of rafia palm drawn very rapidly, to and fro, across a notch in another piece of rafia wood. In most domesticated tribes, like the Effiks or the Igalwa, if they are going out to their plantation, they will enclose a live stick in a hollow piece of a certain sort of wood, which has a lining of its interior pith left in it, and they will carry this "fire box" with them. Or if they are going on a long canoe journey, there is always the fire in the bow of the canoe put into a calabash full of sand, or failing that, into a bed of clay with a sand rim round it.

By 10 o'clock we are off down to Buea. At 10.15 it pours as it can here; by 10.17 we are all in our normal condition of bedraggled saturation, and plodding down carefully and cheerfully among the rocks and roots of the forest, following the path we have beaten and cut for ourselves on our way up. It is dangerously slippery, particularly that part of it through the amomums, and stumps of the cut amomums are very likely to spike your legs badly—and, my friend, never, never, step on one of the amomum stems lying straight in front of you, particularly when they are soaking wet. Ice slides are nothing to them, and when you fall, as you inevitably must, because all the things you grab hold of are either rotten, or as brittle as Salviati glass-ware vases, you hurt yourself in no end of places, on those aforesaid cut amomum stumps. I am speaking from sad experiences of my own, amplified by observations on the experiences of my men.

The path, when we get down again into the tree-fern region, is inches deep in mud and water, and several places where we have a drop of five feet or so over lumps of rock are worse work going down than we found them going up, especially when we have to drop down on to amomum stems. One abominable place, a V-shaped hollow, mud-lined, and with an immense tree right across it—a tree one of our tornadoes has thrown down since we passed—bothers the men badly, as they slip and scramble down, and then crawl under the tree and slip and scramble up with their loads. I say nothing about myself. I just take a flying slide of twenty feet or so and shoot flump under the tree on my back, and then deliberate whether it is worth while getting up again to go on with such a world; but vanity forbids my dying like a dog in a ditch, and I scramble up, rejoining the others where they are standing on a cross-path: our path going S.E. by E., the other S.S.W. Two men have already gone down the S.W. one, which I feel sure is the upper end of the path Sasu had led us to and wasted time on our first day's march; the middle regions of which were, as we had found from its lower end, impassable with vegetation. So after futile attempts to call the other two back, we go on down the S.E. one, and get shortly into a plantation of giant kokos mid-leg deep in most excellent fine mould—the sort of stuff you pay 6 shillings a load for in England to start a conservatory bed with. Upon my word, the quantities of things there are left loose in Africa, that ought to be kept in menageries and greenhouses and not let go wild about the country, are enough to try a Saint.

We then pass through a clump of those lovely great tree-ferns. The way their young fronds come up with a graceful curl, like the top of a bishop's staff, is a poem; but being at present fractious, I will observe that they are covered with horrid spines, as most young vegetables are in Africa. But talking about spines, I should remark that nothing save that precious climbing palm—I never like to say what I feel about climbing palms, because one once saved my life—equals the strong bush rope which abounds here. It is covered with short, strong, curved thorns. It creeps along concealed by decorative vegetation, and you get your legs twined in it, and of course injured. It festoons itself from tree to tree, and when your mind is set on other things, catches you under the chin, and gives you the appearance of having made a determined but ineffectual attempt to cut your throat with a saw. It whisks your hat off and grabs your clothes, and commits other iniquities too numerous to catalogue here. Years and years that bush rope will wait for a man's blood, and when he comes within reach it will have it.

We are well down now among the tree-stems grown over with rich soft green moss and delicate filmy-ferns. I should think that for a botanist these south-eastern slopes of Mungo Mah Lobeh would be the happiest hunting grounds in all West Africa.

The vegetation here is at the point of its supreme luxuriance, owing to the richness of the soil; the leaves of trees and plants I recognise as having seen elsewhere are here far larger, and the undergrowth particularly is more rich and varied, far and away. Ferns seem to find here a veritable paradise. Everything, in fact, is growing at its best.

We come to another fallen tree over another hole; this tree we recognise as an old acquaintance near Buea, and I feel disgusted, for I had put on a clean blouse, and washed my hands in a tea-cupful of water in a cooking pot before leaving the forest camp, so as to look presentable on reaching Buea, and not give Herr Liebert the same trouble he had to recognise the white from the black members of the party that he said he had with the members of the first expedition to the peak; and all I have got to show for my exertion that is clean or anything like dry is one cuff over which I have been carrying a shawl.

We double round a corner by the stockade of the station's plantation, and are at the top of the mud glissade—the new Government path, I should say—that leads down into the barrack-yard.

Our arrival brings Herr Liebert promptly on the scene, as kindly helpful and energetic as ever, and again anxious for me to have a bath. The men bring our saturated loads into my room, and after giving them their food and plenty of tobacco, I get my hot tea and change into the clothes I had left behind at Buea, and feeling once more fit for polite society, go out and find his Imperial and Royal Majesty's representative making a door, tightening the boards up with wedges in a very artful and professional way. We discourse on things in general and the mountain in particular. The great south-east face is now showing clear before us, the clearness that usually comes before night-fall. It looks again a vast wall, and I wish I were going up it again to-morrow. When "the Calabar major" set it on fire in the dry season it must have been a noble sight.

The north-eastern edge of the slope of the mountain seems to me unbroken up to the peak. The great crater we went and camped in must be a very early one in the history of the mountain, and out of it the present summit seems to have been thrown up. From the sea face, the western, I am told the slope is continuous on the whole, although there are several craters on that side; seventy craters all told are so far known on Mungo.

The last reported eruption was in 1852, when signs of volcanic activity were observed by a captain who was passing at sea. The lava from this eruption must have gone down the western side, for I have come across no fresh lava beds in my wanderings on the other face. Herr Liebert has no confidence in the mountain whatsoever, and announces his intention of leaving Buea with the army on the first symptom of renewed volcanic activity. I attempt to discourage him from this energetic plan, pointing out to him the beauty of that Roman soldier at Pompeii who was found, centuries after that eruption, still at his post; and if he regards that as merely mechanical virtue, why not pursue the plan of the elder Pliny? Herr Liebert planes away at his door, and says it's not in his orders to make scientific observations on volcanoes in a state of eruption. When it is he'll do so—until it is, he most decidedly will not. He adds Pliny was an admiral and sailors are always as curious as cats.

Buea seems a sporting place for weather even without volcanic eruptions, during the whole tornado season (there are two a year), over-charged tornadoes burst in the barrack yard. From the 14th of June till the 27th of August you never see the sun, because of the terrific and continuous wet season downpour. At the beginning and end of this cheerful period occurs a month's tornado season, and the rest of the year is dry, hot by day and cold by night.

They are talking of making Buea into a sanatorium for the fever-stricken. I do not fancy somehow that it's a suitable place for a man who has got all the skin off his nerves with fever and quinine, and is very liable to chill; but all Governments on the Coast, English, German, or French, are stark mad on the subject of sanatoriums in high places, though the experience they have had of them has clearly pointed out that they are valueless in West Africa, and a man's one chance is to get out to sea on a ship that will take him outside the three-mile-deep fever-belt of the coast.

Herr Liebert gives me some interesting details about the first establishment of the station here and a bother he had with the plantations. Only a short time ago the soldiers brought him in some black wood spikes, which they had found with their feet, set into the path leading to the station's koko plantations, to the end of laming the men. On further investigation there were also found pits, carefully concealed with sticks and leaves, and the bottoms lined with bad thorns, also with malicious intent. The local Bakwiri chiefs were called in and asked to explain these phenomena existing in a country where peace had been concluded, and the chiefs said it was quite a mistake, those things had not been put there to kill soldiers, but only to attract their attention, to kill and injure their own fellow-tribesmen who had been stealing from plantations latterly. That's the West African's way entirely all along the Coast; the "child-like" native will turn out and shoot you with a gun to attract your attention to the fact that a tribe you never heard of has been and stolen one of his ladies, whom you never saw. It's the sweet infant's way of "rousing up popular opinion," but I do not admire or approve of it. If I am to be shot for a crime, for goodness sake let me commit the crime first.

September 28th.—Down to Victoria in one day, having no desire to renew and amplify my acquaintance with the mission station at Buana. It poured torrentially all the day through. The old chief at Buana was very nice to-day when we were coming through his territory. He came out to meet us with some of his wives. Both men and women among these Bakwiri are tattooed, and also painted, on the body, face and arms, but as far as I have seen not on the legs. The patterns are handsome, and more elaborate than any such that I have seen. One man who came with the party had two figures of men tattooed on the region where his waistcoat should have been. I gave the chief some tobacco though he never begged for anything. He accepted it thankfully, and handing it to his wives preceded us on our path for about a mile and a half and then having reached the end of his district, we shook hands and parted.

After all the rain we have had, the road was of course worse than ever, and as we were going through the forest towards the war hedge, I noticed a strange sound, a dull roar which made the light friable earth quiver under our feet, and I remembered with alarm the accounts Herr Liebert has given me of the strange ways of rivers on this mountain; how by Buea, about 200 metres below where you cross it, the river goes bodily down a hole. How there is a waterfall on the south face of the mountain that falls right into another hole, and is never seen again, any more than the Buea River is. How there are in certain places under-ground rivers, which though never seen can be heard roaring, and felt in the quivering earth under foot in the wet season, and so on. So I judged our present roar arose from some such phenomenon, and with feminine nervousness began to fear that the rotten water-logged earth we were on might give way, and engulf the whole of us, and we should never be seen again. But when we got down into our next ravine, the one where I got the fish and water-spiders on our way up, things explained themselves. The bed of this ravine was occupied by a raging torrent of great beauty, but alarming appearance to a person desirous of getting across to the other side of it. On our right hand was a waterfall of tons of water thirty feet high or so. The brown water wreathed with foam dashed down into the swirling pool we faced, and at the other edge of the pool, striking a ridge of higher rock, it flew up in a lovely flange some twelve feet or so high, before making another and a deeper spring to form a second waterfall. My men shouted to me above the roar that it was "a bad place." They never give me half the credit I deserve for seeing danger, and they said, "Water all go for hole down there, we fit to go too suppose we fall." "Don't fall," I yelled which was the only good advice I could think of to give them just then.

Each small load had to be carried across by two men along a submerged ridge in the pool, where the water was only breast high. I had all I could do to get through it, though assisted by my invaluable Bakwiri staff. But no harm befell. Indeed we were all the better for it, or at all events cleaner. We met five torrents that had to be waded during the day; none so bad as the first but all superbly beautiful.

When we turned our faces westwards just above the wood we had to pass through before getting into the great road, the view of Victoria, among its hills, and fronted by its bay, was divinely lovely and glorious with colour. I left the boys here, as they wanted to rest, and to hunt up water, etc., among the little cluster of huts that are here on the right-hand side of the path, and I went on alone down through the wood, and out on to the road, where I found my friend, the Alsatian engineer, still flourishing and busy with his cheery gang of woodcutters. I made a brief halt here, getting some soda water. I was not anxious to reach Victoria before nightfall, but yet to reach it before dinner, and while I was chatting, my boys came through the wood and the engineer most kindly gave them a tot of brandy apiece, to which I owe their arrival in Victoria. I left them again resting, fearing I had overdone my arrangements for arriving just after nightfall and went on down that road which was more terrible than ever now to my bruised, weary feet, but even more lovely than ever in the dying light of the crimson sunset, with all its dark shadows among the trees begemmed with countless fire-flies—and so safe into Victoria—sneaking up the Government House hill by the private path through the Botanical Gardens.

Idabea, the steward, turned up, and I asked him to let me have some tea and bread and butter, for I was dreadfully hungry. He rushed off, and I heard tremendous operations going on in the room above. In a few seconds water poured freely down through the dining-room ceiling. It was bath palaver again. The excellent Idabea evidently thought it was severely wanted, more wanted than such vanities as tea. Fortunately, Herr von Lucke was away down in town, looking after duty as usual, so I was tidy before he returned to dinner. When he returned he had the satisfaction a prophet should feel. I had got half-drowned, and I had got an awful cold, the most awful cold in the head of modern times, I believe, but he was not artistically exultant over my afflictions.

My men having all reported themselves safe I went to my comfortable rooms, but could not turn in, so fascinating was the warmth and beauty down here; and as I sat on the verandah overlooking Victoria and the sea, in the dim soft light of the stars, with the fire-flies round me, and the lights of Victoria away below, and heard the soft rush of the Lukola River, and the sound of the sea-surf on the rocks, and the tom-tomming and singing of the natives, all matching and mingling together, "Why did I come to Africa?" thought I. Why! who would not come to its twin brother hell itself for all the beauty and the charm of it!

CHAPTER XXI

TRADE AND LABOUR IN WEST AFRICA

A S I AM UNDER THE IMPRESSION that the trade of the West African Coast is its most important attribute, I hope I may be pardoned for entering into this subject. My chief excuse for so doing lies in the fact that independent travellers are rare in the Bights. The last one I remember hearing of was that unfortunate gentleman who went to the Coast for pleasure and lost a leg on Lagos Bar. Now I have not lost any portion of my anatomy anywhere on the Coast, and therefore have no personal prejudice against the place. I hold a brief for no party, and I beg the more experienced old coaster to remember that "a looker on sees the most of the game."

First of all it should be remembered that Africa does not possess ready-made riches to the extent it is in many quarters regarded as possessing. It is not an India filled with the accumulated riches of ages, waiting for the adventurer to enter and shake the pagoda tree. The pagoda tree in Africa only grows over stores of buried ivory, and even then it is a stunted specimen to that which grew over the treasure-houses of Delhi, Seringapatam, and hundreds of others as rich as they in gems and gold. Africa has lots of stuff in it; structurally more than any other continent in the world, but it is very much in the structure, and it requires hard work to get it out, particularly out of one of its richest regions, the West Coast, where the gold, silver, copper, lead, and petroleum lie protected against the miner by African fever in its deadliest form, and the produce prepared by the natives for the trader is equally fever-guarded, and requires white men of a particular type to work and export it successfully—men endowed with great luck, pluck, patience, and tact.

The first things to be considered are the natural resources of the country. This subject may be divided into two sub-sections—(1) The means of working these resources as they at present stand; (2) The question of the possibility of increasing them by introducing new materials of trade-value in the shape of tea, coffee, cocoa, etc.

With regard to the first sub-division the most cheerful things that there are to say on the West Coast trade can be said; the means of transport being ahead of the trade in all districts save the Gold Coast. I know this is heresy, so I will attempt to explain the matter. First, as regards communication to Europe by sea, the West Coast is extremely well off, the two English lines of steamers managed by Messrs. Elder Dempster, the British African, and the Royal African, are most enterprisingly conducted, and their devotion to trade is absolutely pathetic. Let there be but the least vague rumour (sometimes I have thought they have not waited for the rumour, but "gone in" as an experiment) of a puncheon of oil, or a log of timber waiting for shipment at an out-of-the-world, one house port, one of these vessels will bear down on that port, and have that cargo. In addition to the English lines there is the Woermann line, equally devoted to cargo, I may almost say even more so, for it is currently reported that Woermann liners will lie off and wait for the stuff to grow. This I will not vouch for, but I know the time allowed to a Woermann captain by his owners between Cameroons and Big Batanga just round the corner is eight days.

These English and German lines, having come to a friendly understanding regarding freights, work the Bights of Benin, Biafra, and Panavia, without any rivals, save now and again the vessels chartered by the African Association to bring out a big cargo, and the four sailing vessels belonging to the Association which give an eighteenth-century look to the Rivers, and have great adventures on the bars of Opobo and Bonny. {455} The Bristol ships on the Half Jack Coast are not rivals, but a sort of floating factories, shipping their stuff home and getting it out by the regular lines of steamers. The English and German liners therefore carry the bulk of the trade from the whole Coast. Their services are complicated and frequent, but perfectly simple when you have grasped the fact that the English lines may be divided into two sub-divisions—Liverpool boats and Hamburg boats, either of which are liable when occasion demands to call at Havre. The Liverpool line is the mail line to the more important ports, the Hamburg line being almost entirely composed of cargo vessels calling at the smaller ports as well as the larger.

There is another classification that must be grasped. The English boats being divided into, firstly, a line having its terminus at Sierra Leone and calling at the Isles do Los; secondly, a line having its terminus at Akassa; thirdly, a line having its terminus at Old Calabar; fourthly, a line having its terminus at San Paul de Loanda, and in addition, a direct line from Antwerp to the Congo, chartered by the Congo Free State Government. Division 4, the South-westers, are the quickest vessels as far as Lagos, for they only call at the Canaries, Sierra Leone, off the Kru Coast, at Accra, and off Lagos; then they run straight from Lagos into Cameroons, without touching the Rivers, reaching Cameroons in twenty-seven days from Liverpool. After Cameroons they cross to Fernando Po and run into Victoria, and then work their way steadily down coast to their destination. Thence up again, doing all they know to extract cargo, but never succeeding as they would wish, and so being hungry in the hold when they get back to the Bight of Benin, they are liable to smell cargo and go in after it, and therefore are not necessarily the quickest boats home.

Two French companies run to the French possessions, subsidised by their Government (as the German line is, and as our lines are not)—the Chargeurs Réunis and the Fraissinet. The South-west Coast liners of these companies run to Gaboon and then to Koutonu, up near Lagos, then back to Gaboon, and down as far as Loango, calling on their way home at the other ports in Congo Français. They are mainly carriers of import goods, because they run to time, and on the South-west Coast unless Time has an ameliorating touch of Eternity in it you cannot get export goods off.

Below the Congo the rivals of the English and German lines are the vessels of the Portuguese line, Empreza Naçional. These run from Lisbon to the Cape Verde Islands, thence to San Thomé and Principe, then to the ports of Angola (Loanda, Benguella, Mossamedes, Ambrizette, etc.), and they carry the bulk of the Angola trade at present, because of the preferential dues on goods shipped in Portuguese bottoms.

The service of English vessels to the West Coast is weekly; to the Rivers fortnightly; to the South-west Coast monthly; and it is the chief thing in West Coast trade enterprise that England has to be proud of.

Any one of the English boats will go anywhere that mortal boat can go; and their captains' local knowledge is a thing England at large should be proud of and the rest of the civilised world regard with awe-stricken admiration. That they leave no room for further development of ocean carriage has been several times demonstrated by the collapse of lines that have attempted to rival them— the Prince line and more recently the General Steam Navigation.

But although the West Coast trader has at his disposal these vessels, he has by no means an easy time, or cheap methods, of getting his stuff on board, save at Sierra Leone and in the Oil Rivers. Of the Gold Coast surf, and Lagos bar I have already spoken, and the Calemma as we call the South-west Coast surf is nearly, if not quite as bad as that on the Gold Coast. Indeed I hold it is worse, but then I have had more experience of it, and it has frequently to be worked in native dugouts, and not in the well-made surf boats used on the Gold Coast. But although these surf-boats are more safe they are also more expensive than canoes, as a fine £40 or £60 surf-boat's average duration of life is only two years in the Gold Coast surf, so there is little to choose from a commercial standpoint between the two surfs when all is done.

As regards interior transport, the difficulty is greater, but in the majority of the West Coast possessions of European powers there exist great facilities for transport in the network of waterways near the coast and the great rivers running far into the interior.

These waterways are utilised by the natives, being virtually roads; in many districts practically the only roads existing for the transport of goods in bulk, or in the present state of the trade required to exist. But there is room for more white enterprise in the matter of river navigation; and my own opinion is that if English capital were to be employed in the direction of small suitably-built river steamers, it would be found more repaying than lines of railway. Waterways that might be developed in this manner exist in the Cross River, the Volta, and the Ancobra. I do not say that there will be any immediate dividend on these river steamboat lines, but I do not think that there will be any dividend, immediate or remote, on railways in West Africa. This question of transport is at present regarded as a burning one throughout the Continent; and for the well-being of certain parts of the West Coast railways are essential, such as at Lagos, and on the Gold Coast. Of Lagos I do not pretend to speak. I have never been ashore there. Of the Gold Coast I have seen a little, and heard a great deal more, and I think I may safely say that railway making would not be difficult on it, for it is good hard land, not stretches of rotten swamp. The great difficulty in making railroads here will consist in landing the material through the surf. This difficulty cannot be got over, except at enormous expense, by making piers, but it might be surmounted by sending the plant ashore on small bar boats that could get up the Volta or Ancobra. When up the Volta it may be said, "it would be nowhere when any one wanted it," but the cast-iron idea that goods must go ashore at places where there are Government headquarters like Accra and Cape Coast, places where the surf is about at its worst, seems to me an erroneous one. The landing place at Cape Coast might be made safe and easy by the expenditure of a few thousands in "developing" that rock which at present gives shelter when you get round the lee side of it, but this would only make things safer for surf-boats. No other craft could work this bit of beach; and there is plenty of room for developing the Volta, as it is a waterway which a vessel drawing six feet can ascend fifty miles from July till November, and thirty miles during the rest of the year. The worst point about the Volta is the badness of its bar—a great semicircular sweep with heavy breakers—too bad a bar for boats to cross; but a steamer on the Lagos bar boat plan might manage it, as the Bull Frog reported in 1884 nineteen to twenty-one feet on it, one hour before high water. The absence of this bar boat, and the impossibility of sending goods out in surf-boats across the bar, causes the goods from Adda (Riverside), the chief town on the Volta, situated about six miles up the river from its mouth, to be carried across the spit of land to Beach Town, and then brought out through the shore surf—the worst bit of surf on the whole Gold Coast. The Ancobra is a river which penetrates the interior, through a district very rich in gold and timber and more than suspected of containing petroleum. It is from eighty to one hundred yards wide up as far as Akanko, and during the rains carries three and a half to four and a half fathoms, and boats are taken up to Tomento about forty miles from its mouth with goods to the Wassaw gold mines. But the bar of the Ancobra is shallow, only giving six feet, although it is firm and settled, not like that of the Volta and Lagos; and the Portuguese, in the sixteenth century, used to get up this river, and work the country to a better profit than we do nowadays.

The other chief Gold Coast river, the Bosum Prah, that enters the sea at Chama, is no use for navigation from the sea, being obstructed with rock and rapids, and its bar only carrying two feet; but whether these rivers are used or not for the landing of railroad plant, it is certain that that plant must be landed, and the railways made, for if ever a district required them the Gold Coast does. It is to be hoped it will soon enter into the phase of construction, for it is a return to the trade (from which it draws its entire revenue) that the local government owes, and owes heavily; and if our new acquisition of Ashantee is to be developed, it must have a railway bringing it in touch with the Coast trade, not necessarily running into Coomassie, but near enough to Coomassie to enable goods to be sold there but a small advance on Coast prices.

It is an error, easily fallen into, to imagine that the natives in the interior are willing to give much higher prices than the sea-coast natives for goods. Be it granted that they are compelled now to give say on an average seventy-five per cent. higher prices to the sea-coast natives who at present act as middlemen between them and the white trader, but if the white trader goes into the interior, he has to face, first, the difficulty of getting his goods there safely; secondly, the opposition of the native traders who can, and will drive him out of the market, unless he is backed by easy and cheap means of transport. Take the case of Coomassie now. A merchant, let us say, wants to take up from the Coast to Coomassie £3,000 worth of goods to trade with. To transport this he has to employ 1,300 carriers at one shilling and three pence per day a head. The time taken is eight days there, and eight days back, = sixteen days, which figures out at £1,300, without allowing for loss and damage. In order to buy produce with these goods that will cover this, and all shipping expenses, etc., he would have to sell at a far higher figure in Coomassie than he would on the sea-coast, and the native traders would easily oust him from the market. Moreover so long as a district is in the hands of native traders there is no advance made, and no development goes forward; and it would be a grave error to allow this to take place at Coomassie, now that we have at last done what we should have done in 1874 and taken actual possession, for Coomassie is a grand position that, if properly managed for a few years, will become a great interior market, attracting to itself the routes of interior trade. It is not now a great centre; because of the oppression and usury which the Kings of Ashantee have inflicted on all in their power, and which have caused Coomassie mainly to attract one form of trade, viz., slaves; who were used in their constant human sacrifices, and for whom a higher price was procurable here than from the Mohammedan tribes to the north under French sway. And as for the other trade stuffs, they have naturally for years drained into the markets of the French Soudan; instead of through such a country as Ashantee, into the markets of the English Gold Coast; and so unless we run a railroad up to encourage the white traders to go inland, and make a market that will attract these trade routes into Coomassie, we shall be a few years hence singing out "What's the good of Ashantee?" and so forth, as is our foolish wont, never realising that the West Coast is not good unless it is made so by white effort.

The new régime on the Gold Coast is undoubtedly more active than the old—more alive to the importance of pushing inland and so forth—and a road is going to be made twenty-five feet wide all the way to Coomassie, and then beyond it, which is an excellent thing in its way. But it will not do much for trade, because the pacification of the country, and the greater security of personal property to the native, which our rule will afford will aid him in bringing his goods to the coast, but not so greatly aid our taking our goods inland, for the carriers will require just as much for carrying goods along a road, as they do for carrying goods along a bush path, and rightly too, for it is quite as heavy work for them, and heavier, as I know from my experience of the governmental road in Cameroon. In such a country as West Africa there can be no doubt that a soft bush path with a thick coating of moss and leaves on it, and shaded from the sun above by the interlacing branches, is far and away better going than a hard, sunny wide road. This road will be valuable for military expeditions possibly, but military expeditions are not everyday affairs on the Gold Coast; and it cannot be of use for draught animals, because of the horse-sickness and tsetse fly which occur as soon as you get into the forest behind the littoral region: so it must not be regarded as an equivalent for steam transport, as it will only serve to bring down the little trickle of native trade, and possibly not increase that trickle much.

The question of transport of course is not confined to the Gold Coast. Below Lagos there is the great river system, towards which the trade slowly drains through native hands to the white man's factories on the river banks, but this trade being in the hands of native traders is not a fraction of what it would become in the hands of white men; and any mineral wealth there may be in the heavily-forested stretches of country remains unworked and unknown. The difficulty of transport here greatly hampers the exploitation of the timber wealth, it being utterly useless for the natives to fell even a fine tree, unless it is so close to a waterway that it can be floated down to the factory. This it is which causes the ebony, bar, and cam wood to be cut up by them into small billets which a man can carry. The French and Germans are both now follow-ing the plan of getting as far as possible into the interior by the waterways, and then constructing railways. The construction of these railways is fairly easy, as regards gradients, and absence of dense forest, when your waterway takes you up to the great park-like plateau lands which extend, as a general rule, behind the forest belt, and the inevitable mountain range. The most important of these railways will be that of M. de Brazza up the Sanga valley in the direction of the Chad. When this railway is constructed, it will be the death of the Cameroon and Oil River trade, more particularly of the latter, for in the Cameroons the Germans have broken down the monopoly of the coast tribes, which we in our possessions under the Niger Coast Protectorate have not. The Niger Company has broken through, and taken full possession of a great interior, doing a bit of work of which every Englishman should feel proud, for it is the only thing in West Africa that places us on a level with the French and Germans in courage and enterprise in penetrating the interior, and fortunately the regions taken over by the Company are rich and not like the Senegal "made of sand and sav-age savages." Where in West Africa outside the Company will you find men worthy as explorers to be named in the same breath with de Brazza, Captain Binger, and Zintgraff?

Some day, I fear when it will be too late, we shall realise the foolishness of sticking down on the sea coast, tidying up our settlements, establishing schools, and drains, and we shall find our possessions in the Rivers and along the Gold Coast valueless, particularly in the Rivers, for the trade will surely drain towards the markets along the line of the French railroad behind them, for the middlemen tribe that we foster exact a toll of seventy-five per cent. on the trade that comes through their hands, and the English Government is showing great signs of an inclination to impose such duties on the only stuff the native cares much for—alcohol—that he will take his goods to the market where he can get his alcohol; even if he pays a toll to these markets of fifty per cent. But of this I will speak later, and we will return to the question of trans-port. Mr. Scott Elliot, {463} speaking on this subject as regarding East African regions, has given us a most interesting contribution based on his personal experience, and official figures. As many of his observations and figures are equally applicable to the West Coast, I hope I may be forgiven for quoting him. His criticism is in favour of the utilisation of every mile of waterway available. He says, regarding the Victoria Nyanza, that "it is possible to place on it a steamer at the cost of £12,677. Taking the cost of maintenance, fuel and working expenses at £1,200 a year (a large estimate) a capital expenditure of £53,000, (£13,000 for the steamer and £40,000 to yield three per cent. interest) would enable this steamer to convey, say thirty tons at the rate of five to ten miles an hour for £1,600 a year. This makes it possible to convey a ton at the rate of a halfpenny a mile, while it would require about £53,000 to build a railway only eighteen miles long."

The Congo Free State railway I am informed, has cost, at a rate per mile, something like eight times this. Further on Mr. Elliot says: "In America the surplus population of Europe, and the markets in the Eastern States have made railway development profitable on the whole, but in Africa, until pioneer work has been done, and the prospects of colonisation and plantation are sufficiently definite and settled to induce colonists to go out in considerable numbers, it will be ruinous to build a long railway line."

I do not quote these figures to discourage the West Coaster from his railway, but only to induce him to get his Government to make it in the proper direction, namely, into the interior, where further development of trade is possible. Judging from other things in English colonies, I should expect, if left to the spirit of English (West Coast) enterprise, it would run in a line that would enable the engine drivers to keep an eye on the Atlantic Ocean instead of the direction in which it is high time our eyes should be turned. I confess I am not an enthusiast on civilising the African. My idea is that the French method of dealing with Africa is the best at present. Get as much of the continent as possible down on the map as yours, make your flag wherever you go a sacred thing to the native—a thing he dare not attack. Then, when you have done this, you may abandon the French plan, and gradually develop the trade in an English manner, but not in the English manner à la Sierra Leone. But do your pioneer work first. There is a very excellent substratum for English pioneer work on our Coasts in the trading community, for trade is the great key to the African's heart, and everywhere the English trader and his goods stand high in West African esteem. This pioneer work must be undertaken, or subsidised by the Government as it has been in the French possessions, for the West Coast does not offer those inducements to the ordinary traveller that, let us say, East Africa with its magnificent herds of big game, or the northern frontier of India, with its mountains and its interesting forms, relics, and monuments of a high culture, offer. Travel in West Africa is very hard work, and very unhealthy. There are many men who would not hesitate for a moment to go there, were the dangers of the native savagery the chief drawback; but they hesitate before a trip which means, in all probability, month after month of tramping through wet gloomy forests with a swamp here and there for a change, {465} and which will, the chances are 100 to 1, end in their dying ignominiously of fever in some wretched squalid village.

Reckless expenditure of money in attempts to open up the country is to be deprecated, for this hampers its future terribly, even if attended with partial success, the mortgage being too heavy for the estate, as the Congo Free State finances show; and if it is attended with failure it discourages further efforts. What we want at present in West Africa are three or four Bingers and Zintgraffs to extend our possessions northwards, eastwards, and south-eastwards, until they command the interior trade routes. And there is no reason that these men should enter from the West Coast, getting themselves killed, or half killed, with fever, before they reach their work. Uganda, if half one hears of it is true, would be a very suitable base for them to start from, and then travelling west they might come down to the present limit of our West Coast possessions. This belt of territory across the continent would give us control of, and place us in touch with, the whole of the interior trade. A belt from north to south in Africa— thanks to our supineness and folly—we can now never have.

I will now briefly deal with the second sub-division I spoke of some pages back—the possibility of introducing new trade exports by means of cultivating plantations. The soil of West Africa is extremely rich in places, but by no means so in all, for vast tracts of it are mangrove swamps, and other vast tracts of it are miserably poor, sour, sandy clay. It is impossible in the space at my disposal to enter into a full description of the localities where these unprofitable districts occur, but you will find them here and there all along the Coast after leaving Sierra Leone. The sour clay seems to be new soil recently promoted into the mainland from dried-up mangrove swamps, and a good rough rule is, do not start a plantation on soil that is not growing hard-wood forest. Considerable areas on the Gold Coast, even though the soil is good, are now useless for culti-vation, on account of their having been deforested by the natives' wasteful way of making their farms, coupled with the harmattan and the long dry season.

The regions of richest soil are not in our possessions, but in those of Germa-ny, France, Spain, and Portugal, namely, the Cameroons and its volcanic island series, Fernando Po, Principe, and San Thomé.

The rich volcanic earths of these places will enable them to compete in the matter of plantations with any part of the known world. Cameroons is undoubtedly the best of these, because of its superior river supply, and al-though not in the region of the double seasons it is just on the northern limit of them, and the height of the Peak—13,760 feet—condenses the water-laden air from its surrounding swamps and the Atlantic, so that rain is pretty frequent throughout the year. When within the region of the double seasons just south of Cameroons you have a rainfall no heavier than that of the Rivers, yet better distributed, an essential point for the prosperity of such plantations as those of tea and tobacco, which require showers once a month. To the north of Cameroons there is no prospect of either of these well-paying articles being produced in a quantity, or quality, that would compete with South America, India, or the Malayan regions, and they will have to depend in the matter of plantations on coffee and cacao. Below Cameroons, Congo Français possesses the richest soil and an excellently arranged climate. The lower Congo soil is bad and poor close to the river. Kacongo, the bit of Portuguese territory to the north of the Congo banks, and that part of Angola as far as the River Bingo, are pretty much the same make of country as Congo Français, only less heavily forested. The whole of Angola is an immensely rich region, save just round Loanda where the land is sand-logged for about fifty square miles, and those regions to the extreme south and south-east, which are in the Kalahari desert regions.

Coffee grows wild throughout Angola in those districts removed from the dry coast-lands—in the districts of Golongo Alto and Cassengo in great profusion, and you can go through utterly uncultivated stretches of it, thirty miles of it at a time. The natives, now the merchants have taught them its value, are collecting this wild berry and bringing it in in quantities, and in addition the English firm of Newton and Carnegie have started plantations up at Cassengo. The greater part of these plantations consist of clearing and taking care of the wild coffee, but in addition regularly planting and cultivating young trees, as it is found that the yield per tree is immensely increased by cultivation.

Six hundred to eight hundred bags a month were shipped from Ambrizette alone when I was there in 1893, and the amount has since increased and will still further increase when that leisurely, but very worthy little railroad line, which proudly calls itself the Royal Trans-African, shall have got its sections made up into the coffee district. It was about thirty miles off at Ambaca when I was in Angola, but by now it may have got further. However, I do not think it is very likely to have gone far, and I have a persuasion that that railroad will not become trans-African in my day; still it has an "immediate future" compared with that which any other West Coast railway can expect; for besides the coffee, Angola is rich in malachite and gum of high quality, and its superior government will attract the rubber from the Kassai region of the Congo Free State.

In our own possessions the making of plantations is being carried on with much energy by Messrs. Miller Brothers on the Gold Coast, {468} by several private capitalists, including Mr. A. L. Jones of Liverpool, at Lagos; by the Royal Niger Company in their territory, and by several head Agents in the Niger Coast Protectorate. Sir Claude MacDonald offered every inducement to this trade development, and gave great material help by founding a botanical station at Old Calabar, where plants could be obtained. He did his utmost to try and get the natives to embark on plantation-making, ably seconded by Mr. Billington, the botanist in charge of the botanical station, who wrote an essay in Effik on coffee growing and cultivation at large for their special help and guidance. A few chiefs, to oblige, took coffee plants, but they are not enthusiastic, for the slaves that would be required to tend coffee and keep it clean, in this vigorous forest region, are more profitably employed now in preparing palm oil.

Of the coffee plantation at Man o' War Bay I have already spoken, and of those in Congo Français, which, although not at present shipping like the German plantation, will soon be doing so. In addition to coffee and cacao attempts are being made in Congo Français to introduce the Para rubber tree, a large plantation of which I frequently visited near Libreville, and found to be doing well. This would be an excellent tree to plant in among coffee, for it is very clean and tidy, and seems as if it would take to West Africa like a duck to water, but it is not a quick cropper, and I am informed must be left at least three or four years before it is tapped at all, so, as the gardening books would say, it should be planted early.

It is very possible many other trees producing tropical products valuable in commerce might be introduced successfully into West Africa. The cultivation of cloves and nutmegs would repay here well, for allied species of trees and shrubs are indigenous, but the first of these trees takes a long time before coming into bearing and the cultivation of the second is a speculative affair. Allspice I have found growing wild in several districts, but in no large quantity. Cotton with a fine long staple grows wild in quantities wherever there is open ground, but it is not cultivated by the natives; and when attempts have been made to get them to collect it they do so, but bring it in very dirty, and the traders having no machinery to compress it like that used in America, it does not pay to ship. Indigo is common everywhere along the Coast and used by the natives for dyeing, as is also a teazle, which gives a very fine permanent maroon; and besides these there are many other dyes and drugs used by them—colocynth, datura soap bark, cardamom, ginger, peppers, strophanthus, nux vomica, etc., etc., but the difficulty of getting these things brought in to the traders in sufficient quantities prevents their being exported to any considerable extent. Tea has not been tried, and is barely worth trying, though there is little doubt it would grow in Cameroons and Congo Français where it would have an excellent climate and pretty nearly any elevation it liked. But I believe tea has of late years been discovered to be like coffee, not such a stickler for elevation as it used to be thought, merely requiring not to have its roots in standing water.

Vanilla grows with great luxuriance in Cameroons. In Victoria a grove of gigantic cacao trees is heavily overgrown with this lovely orchid in a most perfect way. It does not seem to injure the cacaos in the least, and there are other kinds of trees it will take equally well to. I saw it growing happily and luxuriantly under the direction of the Roman Catholic Mission at Landana; but it requires a continuously damp climate. Vanilla when once started gives little or no trouble, and its pods do not require any very careful manipulation before sending to Europe, and this is a very important point, for a great hindrance - the great hindrance to plantation enterprise on the Coast—is the difficulty of getting neat-handed labourers. I had once the pleasure of meeting a Dutch gentleman—a plantation expert, who had been sent down the West Coast by a firm trading there, and also in the Malay Archipelago—prospecting, at a heavy fee, to see whether it would pay the firm to open up plantations there better than in Malaysia. I believe his final judgment was adverse to the West African plan, because of the difficulty of getting skilful natives to tend young plants, and prepare the products. Tea he regarded as quite hopeless from this difficulty, and he said he did not think you would ever get Africans at as cheap a rate, or so deftly fingered to roll tea, as you can get Asiatics. No one knows until they have tried it the trouble it is to get an African to do things carefully; but it is a trouble, not an impossibility. If you don't go off with fever from sheer worry and vexation the thing can be done, but in the meantime he is maddening. I have had many a day's work on plantations instructing cheerful, willing, apparently intelligent Ethiopians of various sexes and sizes on the mortal crime of hoeing up young coffee plants. They have quite seen it. "Oh, Lor! massa, I no fit to do dem thing." Aren't they! You go along to-morrow morning, and you'll find your most promising pupils laying around them with their hoes, talking about the disgraceful way their dearest friends go on, and destroying young coffee right and left. They are just as bad, if not slightly worse, particularly the ladies, when it comes to picking coffee. As soon as your eye is off them, the bough is off the tree. I know one planter who leads the life of the Surprise Captain in W. H. S. Gilbert's ballad, lurking among his groves, and suddenly appearing among his pickers. This, he says, has given them a feeling of uncertainty as to when and where he may appear, kassengo and all, that has done much to preserve his plantation; but it is a wearying life, not what he expected from his book on coffee-plantations, which had a frontispiece depicting a planter seated in his verandah, with a tumblerful of something cool at his right hand, and a pipe in his mouth, contemplating a large plantation full of industrious natives picking berries into baskets on all sides.

LABOUR

THE LABOUR PROBLEM is one that must be studied and solved before West Africa can advance much further than its present culture condition, because the climate is such that the country cannot be worked by white labourers; and that this state of affairs will remain as it is until some true specific is discovered for malaria, something important happens to the angle of the earth's axis, or some radical change takes place in the nature of the sun, is the opinion of all acquainted with the region. The West African climate shows no signs of improving whatsoever. If it shows any sign of alteration it is for the worse, for of late years two extremely deadly forms of fever have come into notice here, malarial typhoid and blackwater. The malarial typhoid seems confined to districts where a good deal of European attention has been given to drainage systems, which is in itself discouraging.

The labour problem has been imported with European civilisation. The civilisation has not got on to any considerable extent, but the labour problem has; for, being a malignant nuisance, it has taken to West Africa as a duck to water, and it is now flourishing. It has not yet, however, attained its zenith; it is just waiting for the abolition of domestic slavery for that—and then! Meanwhile it grows with the demand for hands to carry on plantation work, and public works. On the West Coast—that is to say, from Sierra Leone to Cameroon—it is worse than on the South West Coast from Cameroon to Benguella.

The Kruman, the Accra, and the Sierra Leonian are at present on the West Coast the only solution available. The first is as fine a ship-and-beach-man as you could reasonably wish for, but no good for plantation work. The second is, thanks to the practical training he has received from the Basel Mission, a very fair artisan, cook, or clerk, but also no good for plantation work, except as an overseer. The third is a poor artisan, an excellent clerk, or subordinate official, but so unreliable in the matter of honesty as to be nearly reliable to swindle any employer. Lagos turns out a large quantity of educated natives, but owing to the growing prosperity of the colony, these are nearly all engaged in Lagos itself.

An important but somewhat neglected factor in the problem is the nature of the West African native, and as I think a calm and unbiassed study of this factor would give us the satisfactory solution to the problem, I venture to give my own observations on it.

The Kruboys, as the natives of the Grain Coast are called, irrespective of the age of the individual, by the white men—the Menekussi as the Effiks call them—are the most important people of West Africa; for without their help the working of the Coast would cost more lives than it already does, and would be in fact practically impossible. Ever since vessels have regularly frequented the Bights, the Kruman has had the helpful habit of shipping himself off on board, and doing all the heavy work. Their first tutors were the slavers, who initiated them into the habit, and instructed them in ship's work, that they might have the benefit of their services in working their vessels along the Slave Coast. And in order to prevent any Kruboy being carried off as a slave by mistake, which would have prejudiced these useful allies, the slavers persuaded them always to tattoo a band of basket-work pattern down their foreheads and out on to the tip of their broad noses: this is the most extensive bit of real tattoo that I know of in West Africa, and the Kruboys still keep the fashion. Their next tutors were the traders, who have taught and still teach them beach work; how to handle cargo, try oil, and make themselves generally useful in a factory,—"learn sense," as the Kruboy himself puts it. To religious teaching the Kruboy seems for an African singularly impervious, but the two lessons he has learnt—ship and shore work—are the best that the white has so far taught the black, because unattended with the evil consequences that have followed the other lessons. Unfortunately, the Kruman of the Grain Coast and the Cabinda of the South West Coast, are the only two tribes that have had the benefit of this kind of education, but there are many other tribes who, had circumstances led the trader and the slaver to turn their attention to them, would have done their tutors quite as much credit. But circumstances did not, and so nowadays, just as a hundred years ago, you must get the Kruboy to help you if you are going to do any work, missionary or mercantile, from Sierra Leone to Cameroon. Below Cameroon the Kruboy does not like to go, except to the beach of an English or German house, for he has suffered much from the Congo Free State, and from Spaniards and Portuguese, who have not respected his feelings in the matter of wanting to return every year, or every two years at the most, to his own country, and his rooted aversion to agricultural work and carrying loads about the bush.

The pay of the Kruboy averages £1 a month. There are modifications in the way in which this sum is reached; for example, some missionaries pay each man £20 a year, but then he has to find his own chop. Some South-West Coast traders pay £8 a year, but they find their boys entirely, and well, in food, and give them a cloth a week. English men-of-war on the West African Station have, like other vessels to take them on to save the white crew, and they pay the Kruboys the same as they pay the white men, i.e., £4.10s. a month with rations. Needless to say, men-of-war are popular, although service on board them cuts our friend off from almost every chance of stealing chickens and other things of which I may not speak, as Herodotus would say. I do not know the manner in which men-of-war pay off the Kruboy, but I think in hard cash. In the circles of society I most mix with on the Coast—the mercantile marine and the trading—he is always paid in goods, in cloth, gin, guns, tobacco, gunpowder, etc., with little concessions to his individual fancy in the matter, for each of these articles has a known value, and just as one of our coins can be changed, so you can get here change for a gun or any other trade article.

The Kruboy much prefers being paid off in goods. I well remember an exquisite scene between Captain --- and King Koffee of the Kru Coast when the subject of engaging boys was being shouted over one voyage out. The Captain at that time thought I was a W.W.T.A.A. and ostentatiously wanted Koffee to let him pay off the boys he was engaging to work the ship in money, and not in gin and gunpowder. King Koffee's face was a study. If Captain ---, whom he knew of old, had stood on his head and turned bright blue all over with yellow spots, before his eyes, it would not have been anything like such a shock to his Majesty. "What for good him ting, Cappy?" he said, interrogation and astonishment ringing in every word. "What for good him ting for We country, Cappy? I suppose you gib gin, tobacco, gun he be fit for trade, but money—" Here his Majesty's feelings flew ahead of the Royal command of language, great as that was, and he expectorated with profound feeling and expression. Captain ---'s expressive countenance was the battle ground of despair and grief at being thus forced to have anything to do with a traffic unpopular in missionary circles. He however controlled his feelings sufficiently to carefully arrange the due amount of each article to be paid, and the affair was settled.

The somewhat cumbrous wage the Kruboy gets at the end of his term of service, minus those things he has had on account and plus those things he has "found," is certainly a source of great worry to our friend. He obtains a box from the carpenter of the factory, or buys a tin one, and puts therein his tobacco and small things, and then he buys a padlock and locks his box of treasure up, hanging the key with his other ju-jus round his neck, and then he has peace regarding this section of his belongings. Peace at present, for the day must some time dawn when an experimental genius shall arise among his fellow countrymen, who will try and see if one key will not open two locks. When this possibility becomes known I can foresee nothing for the Kruboy but nervous breakdown; for even now, with his mind at rest regarding the things in his box, he lives in a state of constant anxiety about those out of it, which have to lie on the deck during the return voyage to his home. He has to keep a vigilant eye on them by day, and sleep spread out over them by night, for fear of his companions stealing them. Why he should take all this trouble about his things on his voyage home I can't make out, if what is currently reported is true, that all the wages earned by the working boys become the property of the Elders of his tribe when he returns to them. I myself rather doubt if this is the case, but expect there is a very heavy tax levied on them, for your Kruboy is very much a married man, and the Elders of his tribe have to support and protect his wives and families when he is away at work, and I should not wonder if the law was that these said wives and families "revert to the State" if the boy fails to return within something like his appointed time. There must be something besides nostalgia to account for the dreadful worry and apprehension shown by a detained Kruboy. I am sure the tax is heavily taken in cloth, for the boys told me that if it were made up into garments for themselves they did not have to part with it on their return. Needless to say, this makes our friend turn his attention to needlework during his return voyage and many a time I have seen the main deck looking as if it had been taken possession of by a demoniacal Dorcas working party.

Strangely little is known of the laws and language of these Krumen, considering how close the association is between them and the whites. This arises, I think, not from the difficulty of learning their language, but from the ease and fluency with which they speak their version of our own—Kru-English, or "trade English," as it is called, and it is therefore unnecessary for a hot and wearied white man to learn "Kru mouth." What particularly makes me think this is the case is, that I have picked up a little of it, and I found that I could make a Kruman understand what I was driving at with this and my small stock of Bassa mouth and Timneh, on occasions when I wished to say something to him I did not want generally understood. But the main points regarding Krumen are well enough known by old Coasters—their willingness to work if well fed, and their habit of engaging for twelve-month terms of work and then returning to "We country." A trader who is satisfied with a boy gives him, when he leaves, a bit of paper telling the captain of any vessel that he will pay the boy's passage to his factory again, when he is willing to come. The period that a boy remains in his beloved "We country" seems to be until his allowance of his own earnings is expended. One can picture to one's self some sad partings in that far-away dark land. "My loves," says the Kruboy to his families, his voice heavy with tears, "I must go. There is no more cloth, I have nothing between me and an easily shocked world but this decayed filament of cotton." And then his families weep with him, or, what is more likely, but not so literary, expectorate with emotion, and he tears himself away from them and comes on board the passing steamer in the uniform of Gunga Din—"nothing much before and rather less than half of that behind," and goes down Coast on the strength of the little bit of paper from his white master which he has carefully treasured, and works like a nigger in the good sense of the term for another spell, to earn more goods for his home-folk.

Those boys who are first starting on travelling to work, and those without books, have no difficulty in getting passages on the steamers, for a captain is glad to get as many on board as he can, being sure to get their passage money and a premium for them, so great is the demand for Kru labour. But even this help to working the West Coast has been much interfered with of late years by the action of the French Government in imposing a tax per head on all labourers leaving their ports on the Ivory Coast. This tax, I believe, is now removed or much reduced; but as for the Liberian Republic, it simply gets its revenue in an utterly unjustifiable way out of taxing the Krumen who ship as labourers. The Krumen are no property of theirs, and they dare not interfere with them on shore; but owing to that little transaction in the celebrated Rubber Monopoly, the Liberians became possessed of some ready cash, which, with great foresight, they invested in two little gun-boats which enabled them to enforce their tax on the Krumen in their small canoes. I do not feel so sympathetic with the Krumen or their employers in this matter as I should, for the Krumen are silly hens not to go and wipe out Liberia on shore, and the white men are silly hens not to—but I had better leave that opinion unexpressed.

The power of managing Kruboys is a great accomplishment for any one working the West Coast. One man will get 20 per cent. more work out of his staff, and always have them cheerful, fit, and ready; while another will get very little out of the same set of men except vexation to himself, and accidents to his goods; but this very necessary and important factor in trade is not to be taught with ink. Some men fall into the proper way of managing the boys very quickly, others may have years of experience and yet fail to learn it. The rule is, make them respect you, and make them like you, and then the thing is done; but first dealing with the Kruboy, with all his good points, is very trying work, and they give the new hand an awful time of it while they are experimenting on him to see how far they can do him. They do this very cleverly, but shortsightedly, more Africano, for they spoil the tempers of half the white men whom they have to deal with. It is not necessary to treat them brutally, in fact it does not pay to do so, but it is necessary to treat them severely, to keep a steady hand over them. Never let them become familiar, never let them see you have made a mistake. When you make a mistake in giving them an order let it be understood that that way of doing a thing is a peculiarly artful dodge of your own, and if it fails, that it is their fault. They will quite realise this if it is properly managed. I speak from experience; for example, once, owing to the superior sex being on its back with fever and sending its temperature up with worrying about getting some ebony logs off to a bothering wretch of a river steamer that must needs come yelling along for cargo just then, I said, "You leave it to me, I'll get it shipped all right," and proceeded, with the help of three Kruboys, to raft that ebony off. I saw as soon as I had embarked on the affair, from the Kruboys' manner, I was down the wrong path, but how, or why, I did not see until a neat arrangement of ebony billets tied together with tie-tie was in the water. Then I saw that I had constructed an excellent sounding apparatus for finding out the depth of water in the river; and that ebony had an affinity for the bottom of water, not for the top. The situation was a trying one and the way the captain of the vessel kept dancing about his deck saying things in a foreign tongue, but quite comprehensible, was distracting; but I did not devote myself to giving him the information he asked for, as to what particular kind of idiot I was, because he was neither a mad doctor nor an ethnologist and had no right to the information; but I put a raft on the line of a very light wood we had a big store of, and this held up the ebony, and the current carried it down to the steamer all right. Then we hauled the line home and sent him some more on the patent plan, but, just to hurry up, you understand, and not delay the ship, a deadly crime, some of that ebony went off in a canoe and all ended happily, and the Kruboys regarded themselves as having been the spectators of another manifestation of white intelligence. In defence of the captain's observations, I must say he could not see me because I was deploying behind a woodstack; nevertheless, I do not mean to say this method of shipping ebony is a good one. I shall not try it again in a hurry, and the situation cannot be pulled through unless you have, as Allah gave me, a very swift current; and although, when the thing went well, I did say things from behind the woodstack to the captain, I did not feel justified in accepting his apologetic invitation to come on board and have a drink.

My experiences with Kruboys would, if written in full, make an excellent manual for a new-comer, but they are too lengthy for this chapter. My first experience with them on a small bush journey aged me very much; and ever since I have shirked chaperoning Kruboys about the West African bush among ticklish-tempered native gentlemen and their forward hussies of wives.

I have always admired men for their strength, their courage, their enterprise, their unceasing struggle for the beyond—the something else, but not until I had to deal with Krumen did I realise the vastness to which this latter characteristic of theirs could attain. One might have been excused for thinking that a man without rates and taxes, without pockets, and without the manifold, want-creating culture of modern European civilisation and education would necessarily have been bounded, to some extent, in his desires. But one would have been wrong, profoundly wrong, in so thinking, for the Kruman yearns after, and duns for, as many things for his body as the lamented Faustus did for his soul, and away among the apes this interesting creature would have to go, at once, if the wanting of little were a crucial test for the determination of the family termed by the scientific world the Hominidæ. Later, when I got to know the Krumen well, I learnt that they desired not only the vast majority of the articles that they saw, but did more—obtained them—at all events some of them, without asking me for them; such commodities, for example, as fowls, palm wine, old tins and bottles, and other gentlemen's wives were never safe. One of that first gang of boys showed self-help to such a remarkable degree that I christened him Smiles. His name—You-be-d--d—being both protracted and improper, called for change of some sort, but even this brought no comfort to one still hampered with conventional ideas regarding property, and frequent roll-calls were found necessary, so that the crimes of my friend Smiles and his fellows might not accumulate to an unmanageable extent.

This used to be the sort of thing—"Where them Nettlerash lib?" "He lib for drunk, Massa." "Where them Smiles?" "He lib for town, for steal, Massa." "Where them Black Man Misery?" But I draw a veil over the confessional, for there is simply no artistic reticence about your Kruman when he is telling the truth, or otherwise, regarding a fellow creature.

After accumulating with this gang enough experience to fill a hat (remembering always "one of the worst things you can do in West Africa is to worry yourself") I bethought me of the advice I had received from my cousin Rose Kingsley, who had successfully ridden through Mexico when Mexico was having a rather worse revolution than usual, "to always preserve a firm manner." I thought I would try this on those Kruboys and said "NO" in place of "I wish you would not do that, please." I can't say it was an immediate success. During this period we came across a trader's lonely store wherein he had a consignment of red parasols. After these appalling objects the souls of my Krumen hungered with a great desire. "NO," said I, in my severest tone, and after buying other things, we passed on. Imagine my horror, therefore, hours afterwards and miles away, to find my precious crew had got a red parasol apiece. Previous experience quite justified me in thinking that these had been stolen; and I pictured to myself my Portuguese friends, whose territory I was then in, commenting upon the incident, and reviling me as another instance of how the brutal English go looting through the land. I found, however, I was wrong, for the parasols had been "dashed" my rapacious rascals "for top," and the last one connected with the affair who deserved pity was the trader from whom I had believed them stolen. It was I, not he, who suffered, for it was the wet season in West Africa and those red parasols ran. To this day my scientific soul has never been able to account for the vast body of crimson dye those miserable cotton things poured out, plentifully drenching myself and their owners, the Kruboys, and everything we associated with that day. I am quite prepared to hear that some subsequent wanderer has found a red trail in Africa itself like that one so often sees upon the maps. When they do, I hereby claim that real red trail as mine.

I confess I like the African on the whole, a thing I never expected to do when I went to the Coast with the idea that he was a degraded, savage, cruel brute; but that is a trifling error you soon get rid of when you know him. The Kruboy is decidedly the most likeable of all Africans that I know. Wherein his charm lies is difficult to describe, and you certainly want the patience of Job, and a conscience made of stretching leather to deal with the Kruboy in the African climate, and live. In his better manifestations he reminds me of that charming personality, the Irish peasant, for though he lacks the sparkle, he is full of humour, and is the laziest and the most industrious of mankind. He lies and tells the truth in such a hopelessly uncertain manner that you cannot rely on him for either. He is ungrateful and faithful to the death, honest and thievish, all in one and the same specimen of him.

Ingratitude is a crime laid very frequently to the score of all Africans, but I think unfairly; certainly I have never had to complain of it, and the Krumen often show gratitude for good treatment in a grand way. The way those Kruboys of gallant Captain Lane helped him work Lagos Bar and save lives by the dozen from the stranded ships on it and hauled their "Massa" out from among the sharkey foam every time he went into it, on the lifeboat upsetting, would have done credit to Deal or Norfolk lifeboat men, but the secret of their devotion is their personal attachment. They do not save people out of surf on abstract moral principles. The African at large is not an enthusiast on moral principles, and one and all they'll let nature take its course if they don't feel keen on a man surviving.

Half the African's ingratitude, although it may look very bad on paper, is really not so very bad; for half the time you have been asking him to be grateful to you for doing to, or giving him things he does not care a row of pins about. I have quite his feelings, for example, for half the things in civilised countries I am expected to be glad to get. "Oh, how nice it must be to be able to get about in cars, omnibuses and railway trains again!" Is it? Well I don't think so, and I do not feel glad over it. Similarly, we will take an African case of ingratitude. A white friend of mine put himself to an awful lot of trouble to save the life of one of his sub-traders who had had an accident, and succeeded. It had been the custom of the man's wife to bring the trader little presents of fowls, etc., from time to time, and some time after the accident he met the lady and told her he had noticed a falling off in her offerings and he thought her very ungrateful after what he had done for her husband. She grunted and the next morning she brings in as a present the most forlorn, skinny, one-and-a-half-feathered chicken you ever laid eye on, and in answer to the trader's comments she said: "Massa, fo sure them der chicken no be 'ticularly good chicken, but fo sure dem der man no be 'ticularly good man. They go" (they match each other).

I have referred at great length to the Krumen because of their importance, and also because they are the natives the white men have more to do with as servants than any other; but methods of getting on with them are not necessarily applicable to dealing with other forms of African labourers, such as plantation hands in the Congo Français, Angola, and Cameroon. In Cameroon the Germans are now using largely the Batanga natives on the plantations; the Duallas, the great trading tribe in Cameroon River, being too lazy to do any heavy work; and they have also tried to import labourers from Togo Land, but this attempt was not a success, ending in the revolt of 1894, which lost several white lives. The public work is carried on, as it is in our own colonies, by the criminals in the chain-gang. The Germans have had many accusations hurled against them by people of their own nationality, but on the whole these "atrocities" have been much exaggerated and only half understood; and certainly have not amounted to anything like the things that have gone on in the "philanthropic" Congo Free State. The food given out by the German Government is the best Government rations given on the whole West Coast. When they have allowed me to have some of their native employés, as when I was up Cameroon Mountain, for example, I bought rations from the Government stores for them, and was much struck by the soundness and good quality of both rice and beef, and the rations they gave out to those Dahomeyans or Togolanders who revolted was so much more than they could, or cared to eat, that they used to sell much of it to the Duallas in Bell Town. This is not open to the criticism that the stuff was too bad for the Togolanders to eat, as was once said to me by a philanthropic German who had never been to the Coast, because the Duallas are a rich tribe, perfectly free traders in the matter, able to go to the river factories and buy provisions there had they wished to, and so would not have bought the Government rations unless they were worth having. The great point that has brought the Germans into disrepute with the natives employed by them is their military spirit, which gives rise to a desire to regulate everything; and that other attribute of the military spirit, nagging. You should never nag an African, it only makes him bothered and then sulky, and when he's sulky he'll lie down and die to spite you. But in spite of the Germans being over-given to this unpleasant habit of military regularity and so on, the natives from the Kru Coast and from Bassa and the

French Ivory Coast return to them time after time for spells of work, so there must be grave exaggeration regarding their bad treatment, for these natives are perfectly free in the matter.

The French use Loango boys for factory hands, and these people are very bright and intelligent, but as a M'pongwe, who knew them well, said: "They are much too likely to be devils to be good too much" and are undoubtedly given to poisoning, which is an unpleasant habit in a house servant. Their military force are composed of Senegalese Laptot, very fine, fierce fellows, superior, I believe, as fighting men to our Hausas, and very devoted to, and well treated by, their French officers.

That the Frenchman does not know how to push trade in his possessions, the trade returns, with the balance all on the wrong side, clearly show; still he does know how to get possession of Africa better than we do, and this means he knows how to deal with the natives. The building up of Congo Français, for example, has not cost one-third of the human lives, black or white, that an equivalent quantity of Congo Belge has, nor one-third of the expense of Uganda or Sierra Leone. It is customary in England to dwell on the commercial failure, and deduce from it the erroneous conclusion that France will soon leave it off when she finds it does not pay. This is an error, because commercial success—the making the thing pay—is not the French ideal in the affair. It is our own, and I am the last person to say our ideal is wrong; but it is not the French ideal, and I am the last person to say France is wrong either. There may exist half a hundred or more right reasons for doing anything, and the reasons France has for her energetic policy in Africa are sound ones; for they are the employment of her martial spirits where their activity will not endanger the State, the stowing of these spirits in Paris having been found to be about as advisable as stowing over-proof spirits and gunpowder in a living-room with plenty of lighted lucifers blazing round; and her other reason is the opportunity African enterprise affords for sound military training. You will often hear in England regarding French annexation in Africa, "Oh! let her have the deadly hole, and much good may it do her." France knows very well what good it will do her, and she will cheerfully take all she is allowed to get quietly, as a sop for her quietness regarding Egypt, and she will cheerfully fight you for the rest—small blame to her. She knows Africa is a superb training ground for her officers. Sham fights and autumn manoeuvres have a certain value in the formation of a fighting army, but the whole of these parlour-games, put together in a ten-year lump, are not to be compared to one month's work at real war, to fit an army for its real work, and France knows well the real work will come again some day—not far off—for her army. How soon it comes she little cares, for she has no ideal of Peace before her, never has had, never will have, and the next time she tries conclusions with one of us Teutonic nations, she will be armed with men who have learned their trade well on the burning sands of Senegal, and they will take a lot of beating. We do not require Africa as a training ground for our army; India is as magnificent a military academy as any nation requires; but we do require all the Africa we can get, West, East, and South, for a market, and it is here we clash with France; for France not only does not develop the trade of her colonies for her own profit, but stamps trade at large out by her preferential tariffs, etc.; so that we cannot go into her colonies and trade freely as she and Germany can come into ours. We can go into her colonies and do business with French goods, and this is done; but French goods are not so suitable, from their make, nor capable of being sold at a sufficient profit to make a big trade. But France throws few obstacles, if any, in the matter of plantation enterprise. Still this enterprise being so hampered by the dearth of good labour is not at the present time highly remunerative in Africa.

FOREIGN LABOUR

S EVERAL IMPORTANT AUTHORITIES have advocated the importation of foreign labour into Africa. This seems to me to be a fatal error, for several reasons. For one thing, experience has by now fully demonstrated that the West Coast climate is bad for men not native to it, whether those men be white, black, or yellow. The United Presbyterian Mission who work in Old Calabar was founded with the intention of inaugurating a mission which, after the white men had established it, was to be carried on by educated Christian blacks from Jamaica, where this mission had long been established and flourished. But it was found that these men, although primarily Africans, had by their deportation from Africa in the course, in some cases, of only one generation, lost the power of resistance to the deadly malarial climate their forefathers possessed, and so the mission is now carried on by whites; not that these good people have a greater resistance to the fever than the Jamaica Christians, but because they are more devoted to the evangelisation of the African; and what black assistance they receive comes, with the exception of Mrs. Fuller, from a few educated Effiks of Calabar.

The Congo Free State have imported as labourers both West Indian negroes—principally Barbadians—and Chinamen. In both cases the mortality has been terrible—more than the white mortality, which competent authorities put down for the Congo at 77 per cent., and the experiment has therefore failed. It may be said that much of this mortality has arisen from the way in which these labourers have been treated in the Free State, but that this is not entirely the case is demonstrated by the case of the Annamese in Congo Français, who are well treated. These Annamese are the political prisoners arising from the French occupation of Tong-kin; and the mortality among one gang of 100 of them who were employed to make the path through swampy ground from Glass to Libreville—a distance of two and a half miles—was seventy, and this although the swamp was nothing particularly bad as swamps go, and was swept by sea-air the whole way.

Even had the experiment of imported labour been successful for the time being, I hold it would be a grave error to import labour into Africa. For this reason, that Africa possesses in herself the most magnificent mass of labour material in the whole world, and surely if her children could build up, as they have, the prosperity and trade of the Americas, she should, under proper guidance and good management, be able to build up her own. But good guidance and proper management are the things that are wanted—and are wanting. It is impossible to go into this complicated question fully here, and I will merely ask unprejudiced people who do not agree with me, whether they do not think that as so much has been done with one African tribe, the Krumen—a tribe possessing no material difference in make of mind or body from hundreds of other tribes, but which have merely been trained by white men in a different way from other tribes—that there is room for great hope in the native labour supply? And would not a very hopeful outlook for West Africa regarding the labour question be possible, if a régime of common sense were substituted for our present one?

This is of course the missionary question—a question which I feel it is hopeless to attempt to speak of without being gravely misunderstood, and which I therefore would willingly shirk mentioning, but I am convinced that the future of Africa is not to be dissociated from the future of its natives by the importation of yellow races or Hindoos; and the missionary question is not to be dissociated from the future of the African natives; and so the subject must be touched on; and I preface my remarks by stating that I have a profound personal esteem for several missionaries, naturally, for it is impossible to know such men and women as Mr. and Mrs. Dennis Kemp, of the Gold Coast, Mme. and M. Jacot, and Mme. and M. Forget, and M. Gacon, and Dr. Nassau, of Gaboon, and many others without recognising at once the beauty of their natures, and the nobility of their intentions. Indeed, taken as a whole, the missionaries must be regarded as superbly brave, noble-minded men who go and risk their own lives, and often those of their wives and children, and definitely sacrifice their personal comfort and safety to do what, from their point of view, is their simple duty; but it is their methods of working that have produced in West Africa the results which all truly interested in West Africa must deplore; and one is bound to make an admission that goes against one's insular prejudice—that the Protestant English missionaries have had most to do with rendering the African useless.

The bad effects that have arisen from their teaching have come primarily from the failure of the missionary to recognise the difference between the African and themselves as being a difference not of degree but of kind. I am aware that they are supported in this idea by several eminent ethnologists; but still there are a large number of anatomical facts that point the other way, and a far larger number still relating to mental attributes, and I feel certain that a black man is no more an undeveloped white man than a rabbit is an undeveloped hare; and the mental difference between the two races is very similar to that between men and women among ourselves. A great woman, either mentally or physically, will excel an indifferent man, but no woman ever equals a really great man. The missionary to the African has done what my father found them doing to the Polynesians—"regarding the native minds as so many jugs only requiring to be emptied of the stuff which is in them and refilled with the particular form of dogma he is engaged in teaching, in order to make them the equals of the white races." This form of procedure works in very various ways. It eliminates those parts of the native fetish that were a wholesome restraint on the African. The children in the mission school are, be it granted, better than the children outside it in some ways; they display great aptitude for learning anything that comes in their way—but there is a great difference between white and black children. The black child is a very solemn thing. It comes into the world in large quantities and looks upon it with its great sad eyes as if it were weighing carefully the question whether or no it is a fit place for a respectable soul to abide in. Four times in ten it decides that it is not, and dies. If, however, it decides to stay, it passes between two and three years in a grim and profound study—occasionally emitting howls which end suddenly in a sob—whine it never does. At the end of this period it takes to spoon food, walks about and makes itself handy to its mother or goes into the mission school. If it remains in the native state it has no toys of a frivolous nature, a little hoe or a little calabash are considered better training; if it goes into the school, it picks up, with astonishing rapidity, the lessons taught it there—giving rise to hopes for its future which are only too frequently disappointed in a few years' time. It is not until he reaches years of indiscretion that the African becomes joyful; but, when he attains this age he always does cheer up considerably, and then, whatever his previous training may have been, he takes to what Mr. Kipling calls "boot" with great avidity—and of this he consumes an enormous quantity. For the next sixteen years, barring accidents, he "rips"; he rips carefully, terrified by his many fetish restrictions, if he is a pagan; but if he is in that partially converted state you usually find him in when trouble has been taken with his soul—then he rips unrestrained.

It is most unfair to describe Africans in this state as "converted," either in missionary reports or in attacks on them. They are not converted in the least. A really converted African is a very beautiful form of Christian; but those Africans who are the chief mainstay of missionary reports and who afford such material for the scoffer thereat, have merely had the restraint of fear removed from their minds in the mission schools without the greater restraint of love being put in its place.

The missionary-made man is the curse of the Coast, and you find him in European clothes and without, all the way down from Sierra Leone to Loanda. The pagans despise him, the whites hate him, still he thinks enough of himself to keep him comfortable. His conceit is marvellous, nothing equals it except perhaps that of the individual rife among us which the Saturday Review once aptly described as "the suburban agnostic"; and the "missionary man" is very much like the suburban agnostic in his religious method. After a period of mission-school life he returns to his country-fashion, and deals with the fetish connected with it very much in the same way as the suburban agnostic deals with his religion, i.e. he removes from it all the inconvenient portions. "Shouldn't wonder if there might be something in the idea of the immortality of the soul, and a future Heaven, you know—but as for Hell, my dear sir, that's rank superstition, no one believes in it now, and as for Sabbath-keeping and food-restrictions—what utter rubbish for enlightened people!" So the backsliding African deals with his country-fashion ideas: he eliminates from them the idea of immediate retribution, etc., and keeps the polygamy and the dances, and all the lazy, hazy-minded native ways. The education he has received at the mission school in reading and writing fits him for a commercial career, and as every African is a born trader he embarks on it, and there are pretty goings on! On the West Coast he frequently sets up in business for himself; on the South-West Coast he usually becomes a sub-trader to one of the great English, French, or German firms. On both Coasts he gets himself disliked, and brings down opprobrium on all black traders, expressed in language more powerful than select. This wholesale denunciation of black traders is unfair, because there are many perfectly straight trading natives; still the majority are recruited from missionary school failures, and are utterly bad.

"Post hoc non propter hoc" is an excellent maxim, but one that never seems to enter the missionary head down here. Highly disgusted and pained at his pupils' goings-on, but absolutely convinced of the excellence of his own methods of instruction, and the spiritual equality, irrespective of colour, of Christians; the missionary rises up, and says things one can understand him saying about the bad influence of the white traders; stating that they lure the pupils from the fold to destruction. These things are nevertheless not true. Then the white trader hears them, and gets his back up and says things about the effect of missionary training on the African, which are true, but harsh, because it is not the missionaries' intent to turn out skilful forgers, and unmitigated liars, although they practically do so. My share when I drop in on this state of mutual recrimination is to get myself into hot water with both parties. The missionary thinks me misguided for regarding the African's goings-on as part of the make of the man, and the trader regards me as a soft-headed idiot when I state that it is not the missionary's individual blame that a lamb recently acquired from the fold has gone down the primrose path with the trust, or the rum. Shade of Sir John Falstaff! what a life this is!

The two things to which the missionary himself ascribes his want of success are polygamy and the liquor traffic. Now polygamy is, like most other subjects, a difficult thing to form a just opinion on, if before forming the opinion you make a careful study of the facts bearing on the case. It is therefore advisable, if you wish to produce an opinion generally acceptable in civilised circles, to follow the usual recipe for making opinions—just take a prejudice of your own, and fix it up with the so-called opinion of that class of people who go in for that sort of prejudice too. I have got myself so entangled with facts that I cannot follow this plan, and therefore am compelled to think polygamy for the African is not an unmixed evil; and that at the present culture-level of the African it is not to be eradicated. This arises from two reasons; the first is that it is perfectly impossible for one African woman to do the work of the house, prepare the food, fetch water, cultivate the plantations, and look after the children attributive to one man. She might do it if she had the work in her of an English or Irish charwoman, but she has not, and a whole villageful of African women do not do the work in a week that one of these will do in a day. Then, too, the African lady is quite indifferent as to what extent her good man may flirt with other ladies so long only as he does not go and give them more cloth and beads than he gives her; and the second reason for polygamy lies in the custom well-known to ethnologists, and so widely diffused that one might say it was constant throughout all African tribes, only there are so many of them whose domestic relationships have not been carefully observed.

As regards the drink traffic—no one seems inclined to speak the truth about it in West Africa; and what I say I must be understood to say only about West Africa, because I do not like to form opinions without having had opportunities for personal observation, and the only part of Africa I have had these opportunities in has been from Sierra Leone to Angola; and the reports from South Africa show that an entirely different, and a most unhealthy state of affairs exists there from its invasion by mixed European nationalities, with individuals of a low type, greedy for wealth. West African conditions are no more like South African conditions than they are like Indian. The missionary party on the whole have gravely exaggerated both the evil and the extent of the liquor traffic in West Africa. I make an exception in favour of the late superintendent of the Wesleyan mission on the Gold Coast, the Rev. Dennis Kemp, who had enough courage and truth in him to stand up at a public meeting in Liverpool, on July 2nd, 1896, and record it as his opinion that, "the natives of the Gold Coast were remarkably abstemious; but spirits were, 'he believed,' of no benefit to the natives, and they would be better without them." I have quoted the whole of the remark, as it is never fair to quote half a man says on any subject, but I do not agree with the latter half of it, and the Gold Coast natives are not any more abstemious, if so much so, as other tribes on the Coast. I have elsewhere {493} attempted to show that the drink-traffic is by no means the most important factor in the mission failure on the West Coast, but that it has been used in an unjustifiable way by the missionary party, because they know the cry against alcohol is at present a popular one in England, and it has also the advantage of making the subscribers at home regard the African as an innocent creature who is led away by bad white men, and therefore still more interesting and more worthy, and in more need of subscriptions than ever. I should rather like to see the African lady or gentleman who could be "led away"—all the leading away I have seen on the Coast has been the other way about.

I do not say every missionary on the West Coast who makes untrue statements on this subject is an original liar; he is usually only following his leaders and repeating their observations without going into the evidence around him; and the missionary public in England and Scotland are largely to blame for their perpetual thirst for thrilling details of the amount of Baptisms and Experiences among the people they pay other people to risk their lives to convert, or for thrilling details of the difficulties these said emissaries have to contend with. As for the general public who swallow the statements, I think they are prone, from the evidence of the evils they see round them directly arising from drink, to accept as true—without bothering themselves with calm investigation—statements of a like effect regarding other people. I have no hesitation in saying that in the whole of West Africa, in one week, there is not one-quarter the amount of drunkenness you can see any Saturday night you choose in a couple of hours in the Vauxhall Road; and you will not find in a whole year's investigation on the Coast, one-seventieth part of the evil, degradation, and premature decay you can see any afternoon you choose to take a walk in the more densely-populated parts of any of our own towns. I own the whole affair is no business of mine; for I have no financial interest in the liquor traffic whatsoever. But I hate the preying upon emotional sympathy by misrepresentation, and I grieve to see thousands of pounds wasted that are bitterly needed by our own cold, starving poor. I do not regard the money as wasted because it goes to the African, but because such an immense percentage of it does no good and much harm to him.

It is customary to refer to the spirit sent out to West Africa as "poisonous" and as raw alcohol. It is neither. I give an analysis of a bottle of Van Hoytima's trade-gin, which I obtained to satisfy my own curiosity on the point.

"ANALYSIS OF SAMPLE OF TRADE-GIN.

"With reference to the bottle of the above I have the honour to report as follows:—

It contains...Per cent.
Absolute alcohol 39.35
Acidity expressed as acetic acid 0.0068
Ethers expressed as acetic acid 0.021
Aldehydes .... Present in small quantity.
Furfural .... Ditto ditto
Higher alcohols............................. Ditto ditto

"The only alcohol that can be estimated quantitatively is Ethyl Alcohol.

"There is no methyl, and the higher alcohols, as shown by Savalie's method, only exist in traces. The spirit is flavoured by more than one essential oil, and apparently oil of juniper is one of these oils.

"The liquid contains no sugar, and leaves but a small extract. In my opinion the liquid essentially consists of a pure distilled spirit flavoured with essential oils.

"Of course no attempt to identify these oils in the quantity sent, viz., 632 c.c. (one bottle) was made. The ethers are returned as ethyl acetate, but from fractional distillation amyl acetate was found to be present.

"I have the honour to be, etc.,
(Signed) "G. H. ROBERTSON.
"Fellow of the Chemical Society,
"Associate of the Institute of Chemistry."

In a subsequent letter Mr. Robertson observed that he had been "assisted in making the above analysis by an expert in the chemistry of alcohols, who said that the present sample differed in no material particulars from, and was neither more nor less deleterious to health than, gin purchased in different parts of London and submitted to analysis."

In addition to this analysis I have also one of Messrs. Peters' gin, equally satisfactory, and as Van Hoytima and Peters are the two great suppliers of the gin that goes to West Africa, I think the above is an answer to the "poison" statements, and should be sufficient evidence against it for all people who are not themselves absolute teetotalers. Absolute teetotalers are definite-minded people, and one respects them more than one does those who do not hold with teetotalism for themselves, but think it a good thing for other people, and moreover it is of no use arguing with them because they say all alcohol is poison, and won't appreciate any evidence to the contrary, so "palaver done set"; but a large majority of those who attack, or believe in the rectitude of the attack on, the African liquor traffic are not teetotalers and so should be capable of forming a just opinion.

My personal knowledge of the district where most of the liquor goes in— the Oil Rivers—has been gained in Duke Town, Old Calabar. I have been there four separate times, and last year stayed there continuously for some months during a period in which if Duke Town had felt inclined to go on the bust, it certainly could have done so; for the police and most of the Government officials were away at Brass in consequence of the Akassa palaver, and those few who were left behind and the white traders were down with an epidemic of malarial typhoid. But Duke Town did nothing of the kind. I used to be down in the heart of the town, at Eyambas market by Prince Archebongs's house, night after night alone, watching the devil-makings that were going on there, and the amount of drunkenness I saw was exceedingly small. I did the same thing at the adjacent town of Qwa. My knowledge of Bonny, Bell, and Akkwa towns, Libreville, Lembarene, Kabinda, Boma, Banana, Nkoi, Loanda, etc., is extensive and peculiar, and I have spent hours in them when the whole of the missionary and Government people have been safe in their distant houses; so had the evils of the liquor traffic been anything like half what it is made out to be I must have come across it in appalling forms, and I have not.

The figures of the case I will not here quote because they are easily obtainable from Government reports by any one interested in the matter. I regard their value as being small unless combined with a knowledge of the West Coast trade. The liquor goes in at a few ports on the West Coast, and into the hands of those tribes who act as middlemen between the white trader and the interior trade-stuff-producing tribes; and is thereby diffused over an enormous extent of thickly inhabited country. We English are directly in touch with none of the interior trade—save in the territory of the Royal Niger Company, and the Delta tribes with whom we deal in the Oil Rivers subsist on this trade between the interior and the Coast, and they prefer to use spirits as a buying medium because they get the highest percentage of profit from it, and the lowest percentage of loss by damage when dealing with it. It does not get spoilt by damp, like tobacco and cloth do; indeed, in addition to the amount of moisture supplied by their reeking climate, they superadd a large quantity of river water to the spirit before it leaves their hands, while with the other articles of trade it is one perpetual grind to keep them free from moisture and mildew. In their Coast towns there are immense stores of gin in cases, which they would as soon think of drinking themselves as we, if we were butchers, would think of eating up the stock in the shop. A certain percentage of spirit is consumed in the Delta, and if spirits are wanted anywhere they are wanted in the Niger Delta region; and about one-eighth part of that used here is used for fetish-worship, poured out on the ground and mixed with other things to hang in bottles over fish-traps, and so on to make residences for guardian spirits who are expected to come and take up their abode in them. Spirits to the spirits, on the sweets to the sweet principle is universal in West Africa; and those photographs you are often shown of dead chiefs' graves with bottles on them merely demonstrate that the deceased was taking down with him a little liquor for his own use in the under-world—which he holds to be possessed of a chilly and damp climate—and a little over to give a propitiatory peg to one of the ruling authorities there—or any old friend he may come across in the Elysian fields. This is possibly a misguided heathen thing of him to do, and it is generally held in European circles that the under-world such an individual as he will go to is neither damp, nor chilly. But granting this, no one can contest but that the world he spends his life here in is damp, and that the natives of the Niger Delta live in a saturated forest swamp region that reeks with malaria. Their damp mud-walled houses frequently flooded, they themselves spend the greater part of their time dabbling about in the stinking mangrove swamps, and then, for five months in the year, they are wrapped in the almost continuous torrential downpour of the West African wet season, followed in the Delta by the so-called "dry" season, with its thick morning and evening mists, and the air rarely above dew-point. Then their food is of poor quality and insufficient quantity, and in districts near the coast noticeably deficient in meat of any kind. I think the desire for spirits and tobacco, given these conditions, is quite reasonable, and that when they are taken in moderation, as they usually are, they are anything but deleterious. The African himself has not a shadow of a doubt on the point, and some form of alcohol he will have. When he cannot get white man's spirit - min makara, as he calls it in Calabar—he takes black man's spirit min effik. This is palm wine, and although it has escaped the abuse heaped on rum and gin, it is worse for the native than either of the others, for he has to drink a disgusting quantity of it, because from the palm wine he does not get the stimulating effect quickly as from gin or rum, and the enormous quantity consumed at one sitting will distribute its effects over a week. You can always tell whether a native has had a glass too much rum, or half a gallon or so too much palm wine; the first he soon recovers from, while the palm wine keeps him a disgusting nuisance for days, and the constitutional effects of it are worse, for it produces a definite type of renal disease which, if it does not cut short the life of the sufferer in a paroxysm, kills him gradually with dropsy. There is another native drink which works a bitter woe on the African in the form of intoxication combined with a brilliant bilious attack. It is made from honey flavoured with the bark of a certain tree, and as it is very popular I had better not spread it further by giving the recipe.

The imported gin keeps the African off these abominations which he has to derange his internal works with before he gets the stimulus that enables him to resist this vile climate; particularly will it keep him from his worst intoxicant lhiamba (Cannabis sativa), a plant which grows wild on the South-West Coast and on the West for all I know, as well as the African or bowstring hemp (Sanseviera guiniensis). The plant that produces the lhiamba is a nettle-like plant growing six to ten feet high, and the natives collect the tops of the stems, with the seed on, in little bundles and dry them. It is evidently the seeds which are regarded by them as being the important part, although they do not collect these separately; but you hear great rows among them when buying and selling a little bundle, on the point of the seeds being shaken out, "Chi! Chi! Chi!" says A., "this is worthless, there are no seeds." "Ai, Ai," says B., "never were there so many seeds in a bunch of lhiamba," etc. It is used smoked, like the ganja of India, not like the preparation bhang, and the way the Africans in the Congo used it was a very quaint one. They would hollow out a little hole in the ground, making a little dome over it; then in went a few hemp-tops; and on to them a few stones made red hot in a fire. Then the dome was closed up and a reed stuck through it. Then one man after another would go and draw up into his lungs as much smoke as he could with one prolonged deep inspiration; and then go apart and cough in a hard, hacking distressing way for ten minutes at a time, and then back to the reed for another pull. In addition to the worry of hearing their coughs, the lhiamba gives you trouble with the men, for it spoils their tempers, making them moody and fractious, and prone to quarrel with each other; and when they get an excessive dose of it their society is more terrifying than tolerable. I once came across three men who had got into this state and a fourth man who had not, but was of the party. They fought with him, and broke his head, and then we proceeded on our way, one gentleman taking flying leaps at some places, climbing up trees now and again, and embedding himself in the bush alongside the path "because of the pools of moving blood on it." ("If they had not kept moving," he said as he sat where he fell—"he could have managed it")—the others having grand times with various creatures, which, judging from their description of them, I was truly thankful were not there. The men's state of mind, however, soon cleared; and I must say this was the only time I came across this lhiamba giving such strong effects; usually the men just cough with that racking cough that lets you know what they have been up to, and quarrel for a short time. When, however, a whiff of lhiamba is taken by them in the morning before starting on a march, the effect seems to be good, enabling them to get over the ground easily and to endure a long march without being exhausted. But a small tot of rum is better for them by far. Many other intoxicants made from bush are known to and used by the witch doctors.

You may say:—Well! if it is not the polygamy and not the drink that makes the West African as useless as he now is as a developer, or a means of developing the country, what is it? In my opinion, it is the sort of instruction he has received, not that this instruction is necessarily bad in itself, but bad from being unsuited to the sort of man to whom it has been given. It has the tendency to develop his emotionalism, his sloth, and his vanity, and it has no tendency to develop those parts of his character which are in a rudimentary state and much want it; thereby throwing the whole character of the man out of gear.

The great inferiority of the African to the European lies in the matter of mechanical idea. I own I regard not only the African, but all coloured races, as inferior—inferior in kind not in degree—to the white races, although I know it is unscientific to lump all Africans together and then generalise over them, because the difference between various tribes is very great. But nevertheless there are certain constant quantities in their character, let the tribe be what it may, that enable us to do this for practical purposes, making merely the distinction between Negroes and Bantu, and on the subject of this division I may remark that the Negro is superior to the Bantu. He is both physically and intellectually the more powerful man, and although he does not christianise well, he does often civilise well. The native officials cited by Mr. Hodgson in his letter to the Times of January 4, 1895, as having satisfactorily carried on all the postal and the governmental printing work of the Gold Coast Colony, as well as all the subordinate custom-house officials in the Niger Coast Protectorate—in fact I may say all of them in the whole of the British possessions on the West Coast— are educated Negroes. I am aware that all sea-captains regard this latter class as poisonous nuisances, but then every properly constituted sea-captain regards custom-house officials, let their colour be what it may, as poisonous nuisances anywhere. In addition to these, you will find, notably in Lagos, excellent pure-blooded Negroes in European clothes, and with European culture. The best men among these are lawyers, doctors, and merchants, and I have known many ladies of Africa who have risen to an equal culture level with their lords. On the West African seaboard you do not find the Bantu equally advanced, except among the M'pongwe, and I am persuaded that this tribe is not pure Bantu but of Negro origin. The educated blacks that are not M'pongwe on the Bantu coast (from Cameroons to Benguela), you will find are Negroes, who have gone down there to make money, but this class of African is the clerk class, and we are now concerned with the labourer. The African's own way of doing anything mechanical is the simplest way, not the easiest, certainly not the quickest: he has all the chuckle-headedness of that overrated creature the ant, for his head never saves his heels. Watch a gang of boat-boys getting a surf boat down a sandy beach. They turn it broadside on to the direction in which they wish it to go, and then turn it bodily over and over, with structure-straining bumps to the boat, and any amount of advice and recriminatory observations to each other. Unless under white direction they will not make a slip, nor will they put rollers under her. Watch again a gang of natives trying to get a log of timber down into the river from the bank, and you will see the same sort of thing—no idea of a lever, or any thing of that sort—and remember that, unless under white direction, the African has never made an even fourteenth-rate piece of cloth or pottery, or a machine, tool, picture, sculpture, and that he has never even risen to the level of picture-writing. I am aware of his ingenious devices for transmitting messages, such as the cowrie shells, strung diversely on strings, in use among the Yoruba, but even these do not equal the picture-writing of the South American Indians, nor the picture the Red Indian does on a raw elk hide; they are far and away inferior to the graphic sporting sketches left us of mammoth hunts by the prehistoric cave men.

This absence of mechanical aptitude is very interesting, though it most likely has the very simple underlying reason that the conditions under which the African has been living have been such as to make no call for a higher mechanical culture. In his native state he does not want to get heavy surf-boats into the sea; his own light dug-out is easily slid down, he does not want to cut down heavy timber trees, and get them into the river, and so on; but this state is now getting disturbed by the influx of white enterprise, and not only disturbed, but destroyed, and so he must alter his ways or there will be grave trouble; but it is encouraging to remark that the African is almost as teachable and as willing to learn handicrafts as he is to assimilate other things, provided his mind has not been poisoned by fallacious ideas, and the results already obtained from the Krumen and the Accras are good. The Accras are not such good workmen as they might be, because they are to a certain extent spoilt by getting, owing to the dearth of labour, higher wages and more toleration for indifferent bits of work than they deserve, or their work is worth; but they have not yet fallen under that deadly spell worked by so many of the white men on so many of the black—the idea that it is the correct and proper thing not to work with your own hands but to get some underling to do all that sort of thing for you, while you read and write. This false ideal formed by the native from his empirical observations of some of the white men around him, has been the cause of great mischief. He sees the white man is his ruling man, rich, powerful, and honoured, and so he imitates him, and goes to the mission-school classes to read and write, and as soon as an African learns to read and write he turns into a clerk. Now there is no immediate use for clerks in Africa, certainly no room for further development in this line of goods. What Africa wants at present, and will want for the next 200 years at least, are workers, planters, plantation hands, miners, and seamen;

and there are no schools in Africa to teach these things or the doctrine of the nobility of labour save the technical mission-schools. Almost every mission on the Coast has now a technical school just started or having collections made at home to start one; but in the majority of these crafts such as bookbinding, printing, tailoring, etc., are being taught which are not at present wanted. Still any technical school is better than none, and apart from lay considerations, is of great religious value to the mission indirectly, for there are many instances in mission annals of a missionary receiving great encouragement from the natives when he first starts in a district. At first the converts flock in, get baptised in batches, go to church, attend school, and adopt European clothes with an alacrity and enthusiasm that frequently turns their devoted pastor's head, but after the lapse of a few months their conduct is enough to break his heart. Dressing up in European clothes amuses the ladies and some of the young men for a long time, in some cases permanently, but the older men and the bolder youths soon get bored, and when an African is bored—and he easily is so—he goes utterly to the bad. It is in these places that an industrial mission would be so valuable to the spiritual cause, for by employing and amusing the largely preponderating lower faculties of the African's mind, it would give the higher faculties time to develop. I have frequently been told when advocating technical instruction, that there are objections against it from spiritual standpoints, which, as my own views do not enable me to understand them, I will not enter into. Also several authorities, not mission authorities alone, state with ethnologists that the African is incapable of learning, except during the period of childhood.

Prof A. H. Keane says—"their inherent mental inferiority, almost more marked than their physical characters, depends on physiological causes by which the intellectual faculties seem to be arrested before attaining their normal development"; and further on, "We must necessarily infer that the development of the negro and white proceeds on different lines. While with the latter the volume of the brain grows with the expansion of the brain-pan; in the former the growth of the brain is on the contrary arrested by the premature closing of the cranial sutures, and lateral pressure of the frontal bone." {504} You will frequently meet with the statement that the negro child is as intelligent, or more so, than the white child, but that as soon as it passes beyond childhood it makes no further mental advance. Burton says: "His mental development is arrested, and thenceforth he grows backwards instead of forwards." Now it is nervous work contradicting these statements, but with all due respect to the makers of them I must do so, and I have the comfort of knowing that many men with a larger personal experience of the African than these authorities have, agree with me, although at the same time we utterly disclaim holding the opinion that the African is a man and a brother. A man he is, but not of the same species; and his cranial sutures do, I agree, close early; indeed I have seen them almost obliterated in skulls of men who have died quite young; but I think most anthropologists are nowadays beginning to see that the immense value they a few years since set upon skull measurements and cranial capacity, etc., has been excessive and not to have so great a bearing on the intelligence as they thought. There has been an enormous amount of material carefully collected, mainly by Frenchmen, on craniology, which is exceedingly interesting, but full of difficulty, and giving very diverse indications. Take the weights of brain given by Topinard: -

1 Annamite	1233 grammes
7 African negroes	1238 "
8 African negroes	1289 "
1 Hottentot	1417 "

and I think you will see for practical purposes such considerations as weight of brain, or closure of sutures, etc., are negligible, and so we need not get paralysed with respect for "physiological causes." Moreover I may remark that the top-weight, the Hottentot, was a lady, and that M. Broca weighed one negro's brain which scaled 1,500 grammes, while 105 English and Scotchmen only gave an average of 1,427.

So I think we may make our minds easy on the safety of sticking to outside facts, and say that after all it does not much affect the question of capacity for industrial training in the African if he does choose to close up the top of his head early, and that the whole attempt to make out that the African is a child-form, "an arrested development," is—well, not supported by facts. The very comparison between white and black children's intelligence to the disadvantage of the former is all wrong. The white child is not his inferior; he is not so quick in picking up parlour tricks; but then where are either of the children at that alongside a French poodle? What happens to the African from my observations is just what happens to the European, namely, when he passes out of childhood, he goes into a period of hobbledehoyhood. During this period, his skull might just as well be filled inside with wool as covered outside with it. But after a time, during which he has succeeded in distracting and discouraging the white men who hoped so much of him when he was a child, his mind clears up again and goes ahead all right. It is utter rubbish to say "You cannot teach an adult African," and that "he grows backwards"; for even without white interference he gets more and more cunning as the time goes on. Does any one who knows them feel inclined to tell me that those old palm-oil chiefs have not learnt a thing or two during their lives? or that a well-matured bush trader has not? Go down to West Africa yourself, if you doubt this, and carry on a series of experiments with them in subjects they know of—trade subjects—try and get the best

of a whole series of matured adults, male or female, and I can promise you you will return a wiser and a poorer man, but with a joyful heart regarding the capacity of the African to grow up. Whether he does this by adding convolutions or piling on his gray matter we will leave for the present. All that I wish to urge regarding the African at large is that he has been mismanaged of late years by the white races. The study of this question is a very interesting one, but I have no space to enter into it here in detail. In my opinion—I say my own, I beg you to remark, only when I am uttering heresy—this mismanagement has been a by-product of the wave of hysterical emotionalism that has run through white culture and for which I have an instinctive hatred.

I have briefly pointed out the evil worked by misdirected missionary effort on the native mind, but it is not the missionary alone that is doing harm. The Government does nearly as much. Whether it does this because of the fear of Exeter Hall as representing a big voting interest, or whether just from the tendency to get everything into the hands of a Council, or an Office, to be everlastingly nagging and legislating and inspecting, matters little; the result is bad, and it fills me with the greatest admiration for my country to see how in spite of this she keeps the lead. That she will always keep it I believe, because I believe that it is impossible that this phase of emotionalism—no, it is not hypocrisy, my French friends, it is only a sort of fit—will last, and we shall soon be back in our clear senses again and say to the world, "We do this thing because we think it is right; because we think it is best for those we do it to and for ourselves, not because of the wickedness of war, the brotherhood of man, or any other notion bred of fear."

The way in which the present ideas acting through the Government do harm in Africa are many. English Government officials have very little and very poor encouragement given them if they push inland and attempt to enlarge the sphere of influence, which their knowledge of local conditions teaches them requires enlarging, because the authorities at home are afraid other nations will say we are rapacious landgrabbers. Well, we always have been, and they will say it anyhow; and where after all is the harm in it? We have acted in unison with the nations who for good sound reasons of their own have cut down Portuguese possessions in Africa because we were afraid of being thought to support a nation who went in for slavery. I always admire a good move in a game or a brilliant bit of strategy, and that was a beauty; and on our head now lie the affairs of the Congo Free State, while France and Germany smile sweetly, knowing that these affairs will soon be such that they will be able to step in and divide that territory up between themselves without a stain on their character—in the interests of humanity—the whole of that rich region, which by the name of Livingstone, Speke, Grant, Burton, and Cameron, should now be ours.

Then again in commercial competition our attitude seems to me very lacking in dignity. We are now just beginning to know it is a fight, and this commercial war has been going on since 1880—since, in fact, France and Germany have recovered from their war of 1870.

And if we are to carry on this commercial war with any hope of success, we must abandon our "Oh! that's not fair; I won't play" attitude—and above all we must have no more Government restrictions on our foreign trade. In West Africa governmental restriction settles, like dew in autumn, on the liquor traffic. It is a case of give a dog a bad name and hang him. Moreover, raising the import dues on liquor may bring into the Government a good revenue; but it is a short-sighted policy—for the liquor is the thing there is the best market for in West Africa. The natives have no enthusiasm about cotton-goods, as they seem from some accounts to have in East Central, and the supply of them they now get, and get cheap and good, is as much as they require. And if the question of the abstract morality of introducing clothes, or introducing liquor, to native races, were fairly gone into, the results would be interesting—for clothing native races in European clothes works badly for them and kills them off. Indeed the whole of this question of trade with the lower races is full of curious and unexpected points. Speaking at large, the introduction of European culture—governmental, religious, or mercantile—has a destructive action on all the lower races; many of them the governmental and religious sections have stamped right out; but trade has never stamped a race out when dissociated from the other two, and it certainly has had no bad effect in tropical Africa. With regard to the liquor traffic, try and put yourself in the West African's place. Imagine, for example, that you want a pair of boots. You go into a shop, prepared to pay for them, but the man who keeps the shop says, "My good friend, you must not have boots, they are immoral. You can have a tin of sardines, or a pocket-handkerchief, they are much better for you." Would you take the sardines or the pocket-handkerchiefs? more particularly would you feel inclined to take them instead of your desired boots if you knew there was a shop in a neighbouring street where boots are to be had? And there is a neighbouring shop-street to all our West Coast possessions which is in the hands of either France or Germany.

I do not for a moment deny that the liquor traffic requires regulation, but it requires more regulation in Europe than it does in Africa, because Europe is more given to intoxication. In Africa all that is wanted is that the spirit sent in should be wholesome, and not sold at a strength over 45° below proof. These requirements are fairly well fulfilled already on the West Coast, and I can see no reason for any further restriction or additional impost. If further restrictions in the sale of it are wanted, it is not for interior trade where the natives are not given to excess, but in the larger Coast towns, where there is a body of natives who are the débris of the disintegrating process of white culture. But even in those towns like Sierra Leone and Lagos these men are a very small percentage of the population. {508} If things are even made no worse for him than they are at present, the English trader may be trusted to hold the greater part of the trade of West Africa for the benefit of the English manufacturers; if he is more heavily hampered, the English trade will die out, the English trader remain, because he is the best trader with the natives; but it will be small profit to the English manufacturers because the trader will be dealing in foreign-made stuff, as he is now in the possessions of France and Germany. English manufacturers, I may remark, have succeeded in turning out the cloth goods best suited for the African markets, but there has of late years been an increase in the quantity of other goods made by foreigners used in the West Coast trade. The imports from France and Germany and the United States to the Gold Coast for 1894 (published 1896) were £217,388 0s. 1d., the exports £212,320 1s. 3d.; and the Consular Report (158) for the Gold Coast says that while the trade with the United Kingdom has increased from £1,054,336 17s. 6d. in 1893 to £1,190,532 1s. 3d in 1894, or roughly 13 per cent., the trade with foreign countries has increased upwards of 22 per cent., namely, from £350,387 3s. 5d to £429,708 1s. 4d. In the Lagos Consular Report (No. 150) similar comparative statistics are not given, but the increase at that place is probably greater than on the Gold Coast, as a heavy percentage of the Lagos trade goes through the hands of two German firms; but this increase in foreign trade in our colonies seems to be even greater in other parts of Africa, for in a Foreign Office Report from Mozambique it is stated, regarding Cape Colony, that "while British imports show an otherwise satisfactory increase, German trade has more than trebled." {509}

There is a certain school of philanthropists in Europe who say that it is not advisable to spread white trade in Africa, that the native is provided by the Bountiful Earth with all that he really requires, and that therefore he should be allowed to live his simple life, and not be compelled or urged to work for the white man's gain. I have a sneaking sympathy with these good people, because I like the African in his bush state best; and one can understand any truly human being being horrified at the extinction of native races in the Polynesian, Melanesian, and American regions. But still their view is full of error as regards Africa, for one thing I am glad to say the African does not die off as do those weaker races under white control, but increases; and herein lies the impossibility of accepting this plan as within the sphere of practical politics, most certainly in regard to all districts under white control, for the Bountiful Earth does not amount to much in Africa with native methods of agriculture. It sufficed when a percentage of the population were shipped to America as slaves; now it suffices only to help to keep the natives in their low state of culture—a state that is only kept up even to its present level by trade. The condition of the African native will be a very dreadful one if this trade is not maintained; indeed, I may say if it is not increased proportionately to the increase of white Government control— for this governmental control does many things that are good in themselves, and glorious on paper. It prevents the export slave trade; it suppresses human sacrifice; it stops internecine war among the natives—in short, it does everything save suppress the terrible infant mortality (why it does not do this I need not discuss) to increase the native population, without in itself doing anything to increase the means of supporting this population; nay, it even wants to decrease these by importing Asiatics to do its work, in making roads, etc.

It may be said there is no fear of the trade, which keeps the native, disappearing from the West Coast, but it is well to remember that the stuff that this trade is dependent on, the stuff brought into the traders' factory by the native, is mainly—indeed, save for the South-West Coast coffee and cacao, we may say, entirely—bush stuff, uncultivated, merely collected and roughly prepared, and it is so wastefully collected by the native that it cannot last indefinitely. Take rubber, for example, one of the main exports. Owing to the wasteful methods employed in its collection it gets stamped out of districts. The trade in it starts on a bit of coast; for some years so rich is the supply, that it can be collected almost at the native's back door, but owing to his cutting down the vine, he clears it off, and every year he has to go further and further afield for a load. But his ability to go further than a certain point is prevented by the savage interior tribes not under white control; and also on its paying him to go on these long journeys, for the price at home takes little notice of his difficulties because of the more carefully collected supply of rubber sent into the home markets by South America and India; therefore the native loses, and when he has cleared the districts reachable by him, the trade is finished there, and he has no longer the wherewithal to buy those things which in the days of his prosperity he has acquired a taste for. The Oil Rivers, which send out the greatest quantity of trade on the West Coast possessions, subsist entirely on palm oil for it. Were anything to happen to the oil palms in the way of blight, or were a cheap substitute to be found for palm oil at home, the population of the Oil Rivers, even at its present density, would starve. The development of trade is a necessary condition for the existence of the natives, and the discovery of products in the forests that will be marketable in Europe, and the making of plantations whose products will help to take the place of those he so recklessly now destroys, will give him a safer future than can any amount of abolitions of domestic slavery, or institutions of trial by jury, etc. If white control advances and plantations are not made and trade with the interior is not expanded, the condition of the West African will be a very wretched one, far worse than it was before the export slave-trade was suppressed. In the more healthy districts the population will in-crease to a state of congestion and will starve. The Coast region's malaria will al-ways keep the black, as well as the white, population thinned down, but if desert-ed by the trader, and left to the Government official and the missionary, without any longer the incentive of trade to make the native exert himself, or the resulting comforts which assist him in resisting the climate, which the trade now enables him to procure, the Coast native will sink, viâ vice and degradation, to extinction, and most likely have this process made all the more rapid and unpleasant for him by incursions of the wild tribes from the congested interior.

I do not cite this as an immediate future for the West African, but "a little more and how much it is, a little less and how far away." Remember human beings are under the same rule as other creatures; if you destroy the things that prey on them, they are liable to overswarm the food-producing power of their locality. It may be said this is not the case; look at the Polynesians, the South American Indians, and so on. You may look at them as much as you choose, but what you see there will not enable you to judge the African. The African does not fade away like a flower before the white man—not in the least. Look at the increase of the native in the Cape territory; look at what he has stood on the West Coast. Christopher Columbus visited him before he discovered the American Indians. Whaling captains, and seamen of all sorts and nationali-ties have dropped in on him "frequent and free." He has absorbed all sorts of doctrine from religious sects; cotton goods, patent medicines, foreign spirits, and—as the man who draws up the Lagos Annual Colonial Report poetically observes—twine, whisky, wine, and woollen goods. Yet the West Coast African is here with us by the million—playing on his tom-tom, paddling his dug-out canoe, living in his palm leaf or mud hut, ready and able to stand more "white man stuff." Save for an occasional habit of going raving or melancholy mad when educated for the ministry, and dying when he, and more particularly she, is shut up in the broiling hot, corrugated-iron school-room with too many clothes on, and too much headwork to do, he survives in a way which I think you will own is interesting, and which commands my admiration and respect. But there is nowadays a new factor in his relationship with the white races—the factor of domestic control. I do not think the African will survive this and flourish, if it is to be of the nature that the present white ideas aim to make it. But, on the other hand, I do not believe that he will be called upon to try, for under the present conditions white control will not become very thorough; and in the event of an European war, governmental attention will be distracted from West Africa, and the African will then do what he has done several times before when the white eye has been off him for a decade or so,—sink back to his old level as he has in Congo after the Jesuits tidied him up, and as he must have done after his intercourse with the Phoenicians and Egyptians. The travellers of a remote future will find him, I think, still with his tom-tom and his dug-out canoe—just as willing to sell as "big curios" the débris of our importations to his ancestors at a high price. Exactly how much he will ask for a Devos patent paraffin oil tin or a Morton's tin, I cannot imagine, but it will be something stiff—such as he asks nowadays for the Phoenician "Aggry" beads. There will be then as there is now, and as there was in the past, individual Africans who will rise to a high level of culture, but that will be all for a very long period. To say that the African race will never advance beyond its present culture-level, is saying too much, in spite of the mass of evidence supporting this view, but I am certain they will never advance above it in the line of European culture. The country he lives in is unfitted for it, and the nature of the man himself is all against it—the truth is the West Coast mind has got a great deal too much superstition about it, and too little of anything else. Our own methods of instruction have not been of any real help to the African, because what he wants teaching is how to work. Bishop Ingram would have been able to write a more cheerful and hopeful book than his Sierra Leone after 100 Years, if the Sierra Leonians had had a thorough grounding in technical culture, suited to the requirements of their country, instead of the ruinous instruction they have been given, at the cost of millions of money, and hundreds of good, if ill-advised, white men's lives. For it is possible for a West African native to be made by European culture into a very good sort of man, not the same sort of man that a white man is, but a man a white man can shake hands with and associate with without any loss of self-respect. It is by no means necessary, however, that the African should have any white culture at all to become a decent member of society at large. Quite the other way about, for the percentage of honourable and reliable men among the bushmen is higher than among the educated men. I do not believe that the white race will ever drag the black up to their own particular summit in the mountain range of civilisation. Both polygamy and slavery {514} are, for divers reasons, essential to the well-being of Africa—at any rate for those vast regions of it which are agricultural, and these two institutions will necessitate the African having a summit to himself. Only—alas! for the energetic reformer—the African is not keen on mountaineering in the civilisation range. He prefers remaining down below and being comfortable. He is not conceited about this; he admires the higher culture very much, and the people who inconvenience themselves by going in for it—but do it himself? NO. And if he is dragged up into the higher regions of a self-abnegatory religion, six times in ten he falls back damaged, a morally maimed man, into his old swampy country fashion valley.

CHAPTER XXII

DISEASE IN WEST AFRICA

G REAT AS IS THE DELAY AND DIFFICULTY placed in the way of the development of the immense natural resources of West Africa by the labour problem, there is another cause of delay to this development greater and more terrible by far—namely, the deadliness of the climate. "Nothing hinders a man, Miss Kingsley, half so much as dying," a friend said to me the other day, after nearly putting his opinion to a practical test. Other parts of the world have more sensational outbreaks of death from epidemics of yellow fever and cholera, but there is no other region in the world that can match West Africa for the steady kill, kill, kill that its malaria works on the white men who come under its influence.

Malaria you will hear glibly talked of; but what malaria means and consists of you will find few men ready to attempt to tell you, and these few by no means of a tale. It is very strange that this terrible form of disease has not attracted more scientific investigators, considering the enormous mortality it causes throughout the tropics and sub-tropics. A few years since, when the peculiar microbes of everything from measles to miracles were being "isolated," several bacteriologists isolated the malarial microbe, only unfortunately they did not all isolate the same one. A résuméof the various claims of these microbes is impossible here, and whether one of them was the true cause, or whether they all have an equal claim to this position, is not yet clear; for malaria, as far as I have seen or read of it seems to be not so much one distinct form of fever as a group of fevers—a genus, not a species. Many things point to this being the case; particularly the different forms so called malarial poisoning takes in different localities. This subject may be also subdivided and complicated by going into the controversy as to whether yellow fever is endemic on the West Coast or not. That it has occurred there from time to time there can be no

362

question: at Fernando Po in 1862 and 1866, in Senegal pretty frequently; and at least one epidemic at Bonny was true yellow fever. But in the case of each of these outbreaks it is said to have been imported from South America, into Fernando Po, by ships from Havana, and into Bonny by a ship which had on her previous run been down the South American ports with a cargo of mules. The litter belonging to this mule cargo was not cleared out of her until she got into Bonny, when it was thrown overside into the river, and then the yellow fever broke out. But, on the other hand, South America taxes West Africa—the Guinea Coast—with having first sent out yellow fever in the cargoes of slaves. This certainly is a strange statement, because the African native rarely has malarial fever severely—he has it, and you are often informed So-and-so has got yellow fever, but he does not often die of it, merely is truly wretched and sick for a day or so, and then recovers.

Regarding the hæmaturia there is also controversy. A very experienced and excellent authority doubts whether this is entirely a malarial fever, or whether it is not, in some cases at any rate, brought on by over-doses of quinine, and Dr. Plehn asserts, and his assertions are heavily backed up by his great success in treating this fever, that quinine has a very bad influence when the characteristic symptoms have declared themselves, and that it should not be given. I hesitate to advise this, because I fear to induce any one to abandon quinine, which is the great weapon against malaria, and not from any want of faith in Dr. Plehn, for he has studied malarial fevers in Cameroon with the greatest energy and devotion, bringing to bear on the subject a sound German mind trained in a German way, and than this, for such subjects, no better thing exists. His brother, also a doctor, was stationed in Cameroon before him, and is now in the German East African possessions, similarly working hard, and when these two shall publish the result of their conjoint investigations, we shall have the most important contribution to our knowledge of malaria that has ever appeared. It is impossible to over-rate the importance of such work as this to West Africa, for the man who will make West Africa pay will be the scientific man who gives us something more powerful against malaria than quinine. It is too much to hope that medical men out at work on the Coast, doctoring day and night, and not only obliged to doctor, but to nurse their white patients, with the balance of their time taken up by giving bills of health to steamers, wrestling with the varied and awful sanitary problems presented by the native town, etc., can have sufficient time or life left in them to carry on series of experiments and of cultures; but they can and do supply to the man in the laboratory at home grand material for him to carry the thing through; meanwhile we wait for that man and do the best we can.

The net results of laboratory investigation, according to the French doctors, is that the mycetozoic malarial bacillus, the microbe of paludism, is amœboid in its movements, acting on the red corpuscles, leaving nothing of them but the dark pigment found in the skin and organs of malarial subjects. The German doctors make a practice of making microscopic examinations of the blood of a patient, saying that the microbes appear at the commencement of an attack of fever, increase in quantity as the fever increases, and decrease as it decreases, and from these investigations they are able to judge fairly accurately how many remissions may be expected; in fact to judge of the severity of the case which, taken with the knowledge that quinine only affects malarial microbes at a certain stage of their existence, is helpful in treatment.

There is, I may remark, a very peculiar point regarding hæmaturic disease, the most deadly form of West Coast fever. This disease, so far as we know, has always been present on the South-West Coast, at Loando, the Lower Congo and Gaboon, but it is said not to have appeared in the Rivers until 1881, and then to have spread along the West Coast. My learned friend, Dr. Plehn, doubts this, and says people were less observant in those days, but the symptoms of this fever are so distinct, that I must think it also totally impossible for it not to have been differentiated from the usual remittent or intermittent by the old West Coasters if it had occurred there in former times with anything like the frequency it does now; but we will leave these theoretical and technical consid-erations and turn to the practical side of the question.

You will always find lots of people ready to give advice on fever, particularly how to avoid getting it, and you will find the most dogmatic of these are people who have been singularly unlucky in the matter, or people who know nothing of local conditions. These latter are the most trying of all to deal with. They tell you, truly enough no doubt, that the malaria is in the air, in the exhalations from the ground, which are greatest about sunrise and sunset, and in the drink-ing water, and that you must avoid chill, excessive mental and bodily exertion, that you must never get anxious, or excited, or lose your temper. Now there is only one—the drinking water—of this list that you can avoid, for, owing to the great variety and rapid growth of bacteria encouraged by the tropical tempera-ture, and the aqueous saturation of the atmosphere from the heavy rainfall, and the great extent of swamp, etc., it is practically impossible to destroy them in the air to a satisfactory extent. I was presented by scientific friends, when I first went to the West Coast, with two devices supposed to do this. One was a lamp which you burnt some chemical in; it certainly made a smell that nothing could live with—but then I am not nothing, and there are enough smells on the Coast now. I gave it up after the first half-hour. The other device was a muzzle, a res-pirator, I should say. Well! all I have got to say about that is that you need be a better-looking person than I am to wear a thing like that without causing panic in a district. Then orders to avoid the night air are still more difficult to obey—may I ask how you are to do without air from 6.30 P.M. to 6.30 A.M.? or what other air there is but night air, heavy with malarious exhalations, available then?

The drinking water you have a better chance with, as I will presently state; chill you cannot avoid. When you are at work on the Coast, even with the greatest care, the sudden fall of temperature that occurs after a tornado coming at the end of a stewing-hot day, is sure to tell on any one, and as for the orders regarding temper neither the natives, nor the country, nor the trade, help you in the least. But still you must remember that although it is impossible to fully carry out these orders, you can do a good deal towards doing so, and preventive measures are the great thing, for it is better to escape fever altogether, or to get off with a light touch of it, than to make a sensational recovery from Yellow Jack himself.

There is little doubt that a certain make of man has the best chance of surviving the Coast climate—an energetic, spare, nervous but light-hearted creature, capable of enjoying whatever there may be to enjoy, and incapable of dwelling on discomforts or worries. It is quite possible for a person of this sort to live, and work hard on the Coast for a considerable period, possibly with better health than he would have in England. The full-blooded, corpulent and vigorous should avoid West Africa like the plague. One after another, men and women, who looked, as the saying goes, as if you could take a lease of their lives, I have seen come out and die, and it gives one a sense of horror when they arrive at your West Coast station, for you feel a sort of accessory before the fact to murder, but what can you do except get yourself laughed at as a croaker, and attend the funeral?

The best ways of avoiding the danger of the night air are—to have your evening meal about 6.30 or 7,—8 is too late; sleep under a mosquito curtain whether there are mosquitoes in your district or not, and have a meal before starting out in the morning, a good hot cup of tea or coffee and bread and butter, if you can get it, if not, something left from last night's supper or even aguma. Regarding meals, of course we come to the vexed question of stimulants—all the evidence is in favour of alcohol, of a proper sort, taken at proper times, and in proper quantities, being extremely valuable. Take the case of the missionaries, who are almost all teetotalers, they are young men and women who have to pass a medical examination before coming out, and whose lives on the Coast are far easier than those of other classes of white men, yet the mortality among them is far heavier than in any other class.

Mr. Stanley says that wine is the best form of stimulant, but that it should not be taken before the evening meal. Certainly on the South-West Coast, where a heavy, but sound, red wine imported from Portugal is the common drink, the mortality is less than on the West Coast. Beer has had what one might call a thorough trial in Cameroon since the German occupation and is held by authorities to be the cause in part of the number of cases of hæmaturic fever in that river being greater than in other districts. But this subject requires scientific comparative observation on various parts of the Coast, for Cameroons is at the beginning of the South-West Coast, whereon the percentage of cases of hæmaturic to those of intermittent and remittent fevers is far higher than on the West Coast.

A comparative study of the diseases of the western division of the continent would, I should say, repay a scientific doctor, if he survived. The material he would have to deal with would be enormous, and in addition to the history of hæmaturic he would be confronted with the problem of the form of fever which seems to be a recent addition to West African afflictions, the so-called typhoid malaria, which of late years has come into the Rivers, and apparently come to stay. This fever is, I may remark, practically unknown at present in the South-West Coast regions where the "sun for garbage" plan is adhered to. At present the treatment of all white man's diseases on the Coast practically consists in the treatment of malaria, because whatever disease a person gets hold of takes on a malarial type which masks its true nature. Why, I knew a gentleman who had as fine an attack of the smallpox as any one would not wish to have, and who for days behaved as if he had remittent, and then burst out into the characteristic eruption; and only got all his earthly possessions burnt, and no end of carbolic acid dressings for his pains.

I do not suppose this does much harm, as the malaria is the main thing that wants curing; unless Dr. Plehn is right and quinine is bad in hæmaturia. His success in dealing with this fever seems to support his opinion; and the French doctors on the Coast, who dose it heavily with quinine, have certainly a very heavy percentage of mortality among their patients with the hæmaturic, although in the other forms of malarial fever they very rarely lose a patient.

But to return to those preventive measures, and having done what we can with the air, we will turn our attention to the drinking water, for in addition to malarial microbes the drinking and washing water of West Africa is liable to contain dermazoic and entozoic organisms, and if you don't take care you will get from it into your anatomy Tinea versicolor, Tinea decalvans, Tinea circinata, Tinea sycosis, Tinea favosa, or some other member of that wretched family, let alone being nearly certain to import Trichocephalus dispar, Ascaris lumbricoides, Oxyuris vermicularis, and eight varieties of nematodes, each of them with an awful name of its own, and unpleasant consequences to you, and, lastly, a peculiar abomination, a Filaria. This is not, what its euphonious name may lead you to suppose, a fern, but it is a worm which gets into the white of the eye and leads there a lively existence, causing distressing itching, throbbing and pricking sensations, not affecting the sight until it happens to set up inflammation. I have seen the eyes of natives simply swarming with these Filariæ. A curious thing about the disease is that it usually commences in one eye, and when that becomes over-populated an emigration society sets out for the other eye, travelling thither under the skin of the bridge of the nose, looking while in transit like the bridge of a pair of spectacles. A similar, but not identical, worm is fairly common on the Ogowé, and is liable to get under the epidermis of any part of the body. Like the one affecting the eye it is very active in its movements, passing rapidly about under the skin and producing terrible pricking and itching, but very trifling inflammation in those cases which I have seen. The treatment consists of getting the thing out, and the thing to be careful of is to get it out whole, for if any part of it is left in, suppuration sets in, so even if you are personally convinced you have got it out successfully it is just as well to wash out the wound with carbolic or Condy's fluid. The most frequent sufferers from these Filariæ are the natives, but white people do get them.

Do not confuse this Filaria with the Guinea worm, Filaria medinensis, which runs up to ten and twelve feet in length, and whose habits are different. It is more sedentary, but it is in the drinking water inside small crustacea (cyclops). It appears commonly in its human host's leg, and rapidly grows, curled round and round like a watch-spring, showing raised under the skin. The native treatment of this pest is very cautiously to open the skin over the head of the worm and secure it between a little cleft bit of bamboo and then gradually wind the rest of the affair out. Only a small portion can be wound out at a time, as the wound is very liable to inflame, and should the worm break, it is certain to inflame badly, and a terrible wound will result. You cannot wind it out by the tail because you are then, so to speak, turning its fur the wrong way, and it catches in the wound.

I should, I may remark, strongly advise any one who likes to start early on a canoe journey to see that no native member of the party has a Filaria medinensis on hand; for winding it up is always reserved for a morning job and as many other jobs are similarly reserved it makes for delay.

I know, my friends, that you one and all say that the drinking water at your particular place is of singular beauty and purity, and that you always tell the boys to filter it; but I am convinced that that water is no more to be trusted than the boys, and I am lost in amazement at people of your intelligence trusting the trio of water, boys, and filter, in the way you do. One favourite haunt of mine gets its drinking water from a cemented hole in the back yard into which drains a very strong-smelling black little swamp, which is surrounded by a ridge of sandy ground, on which are situated several groups of native houses, whose inhabitants enhance their fortunes and their drainage by taking in washing. At Fernando Po the other day I was assured as usual that the water was perfection, "beautiful spring coming down from the mountain," etc. In the course of the afternoon affairs took me up the mountain to Basile, for the first part of the way along the course of the said stream. The first objects of interest I observed in the drinking-water supply were four natives washing themselves and their clothes; the next was the bloated body of a dead goat reposing in a pellucid pool. The path then left the course of the stream, but on arriving in the region of its source I found an interesting little colony of Spanish families which had been import-ed out whole, children and all, by the Government. They had a nice, neat little cemetery attached, which his excellency the doctor told me was "stocked mostly with children, who were always dying off from worms." Good, so far, for the drinking water! and as to what that beautiful stream was soaking up when it was round corners—I did not see it, so I do not know—but I will be bound it was some abomination or another. But it's no use talking, it's the same all along, Sierra Leone, Grain Coast, Ivory Coast, Gold Coast, Lagos, Rivers, Cameroon, Congo Français, Kacongo, Congo Belge, and Angola. When you ask your white friends how they can be so reckless about the water, which, as they know, is a decoction of the malarious earth, exposed night and day to the malarious air, they all up and say they are not; they have "got an awfully good filter, and they tell the boys," etc., and that they themselves often put wine or spirit in the water to kill the microbes. Vanity, vanity! At each and every place I know, "men have died and worms have eaten them." The safest way of dealing with water I know is to boil it hard for ten minutes at least, and then instantly pour it into a jar with a narrow neck, which plug up with a wad of fresh cotton-wool—not a cork; and should you object to the flat taste of boiled water, plunge into it a bit of red-hot iron, which will make it more agreeable in taste. Before boiling the water you can carefully filter it if you like. A good filter is a very fine thing for clearing drinking water of hippopotami, crocodiles, water snakes, catfish, etc., and I daresay it will stop back sixty per cent. of the live or dead African natives that may be in it; but if you think it is going to stop back the microbe of marsh fever—my good sir, you are mistaken. And remember that you must give up cold water, boiled or unboiled, altogether; for if you take the boiled or filtered water and put it into one of those water-coolers, and leave it hanging exposed to night air or day on the verandah, you might just as well save yourself the trouble of boiling it at all.

Next in danger to the diseases come the remedies for them. Let the new-comer remember, in dealing with quinine, calomel, arsenic, and spirits, that they are not castor sugar nor he a glass bottle, but let him use them all—the two first fairly frequently—not waiting for an attack of fever and then ladling them into himself with a spoon. The third, arsenic—a drug much thought of by the French, who hold that if you establish an arsenic cachexia you do not get a malarial one—should not be taken except under a doctor's orders. Spirit is undoubtedly extremely valuable when, from causes beyond your control, you have got a chill. Remember always your life hangs on quinine, and that it is most important to keep the system sensitive to it, which you do not do if you keep on pouring in heavy doses of it for nothing and you make yourself deaf into the bargain. I have known people take sixty grains of quinine in a day for a bilious attack and turn it into a disease they only got through by the skin of their teeth; but the prophylactic action of quinine is its great one, as it only has power over malarial microbes at a certain state of their development,—the fully matured microbe it does not affect to any great degree—and therefore by taking it when in a malarious district, say, in a dose of five grams a day, you keep down the malaria which you are bound, even with every care, to get into your system. When you have got very chilled or over-tired, take an extra five grains with a little wine or spirit at any time, and when you know, by reason of aching head and limbs and a sensation of a stream of cold water down your back and an awful temper, that you are in for a fever, send for a doctor if you can. If, as generally happens, there is no doctor near to send for, take a compound calomel and colocynth pill, fifteen grains of quinine and a grain of opium, and go to bed wrapped up in the best blanket available. When safely there take lashings of hot tea or, what is better, a hot drink made from fresh lime-juice, strong and without sugar—fresh limes are almost always to be had—if not, bottled lime-juice does well. Then, in the hot stage, don't go fanning about, nor in the perspiring stage, for if you get a chill then you may turn a mild dose of fever into a fatal one. If, however, you keep conscientiously rolled in your blanket until the perspiring stage is well over, and stay in bed till the next morning, the chances are you will be all right, though a little shaky about the legs. You should continue the quinine, taking it in five-grain doses, up to fifteen to twenty grains a day for a week after any attack of fever, but you must omit the opium pill. The great thing in West Africa is to keep up your health to a good level, that will enable you to resist fever, and it is exceedingly difficult for most people to do this, because of the difficulty of getting exercise and good food. But do what you may it is almost certain you will get fever during a residence of more than six months on the Coast, and the chances are two to one on the Gold Coast that you will die of it. But, without precautions, you will probably have it within a fortnight of first landing, and your chances of surviving are almost nil. With precautions, in the Rivers and on the S.W. Coast your touch of fever may be a thing inferior in danger and discomfort to a bad cold in England.

Yet remember, before you elect to cast your lot in with the West Coasters, that 85 per cent. of them die of fever or return home with their health permanently wrecked. Also remember that there is no getting acclimatised to the Coast. There are, it is true, a few men out there who, although they have been resident in West Africa for years, have never had fever, but you can count them up on the fingers of one hand. There is another class who have been out for twelve months at a time, and have not had a touch of fever; these you want the fingers of your two hands to count, but no more. By far the largest class is the third, which is made up of those who have a slight dose of fever once a fortnight, and some day, apparently for no extra reason, get a heavy dose and die of it. A very considerable class is the fourth—those who die within a fortnight to a month of going ashore.

The fate of a man depends solely on his power of resisting the so-called malaria, not in his system becoming inured to it. The first class of men that I have cited have some unknown element in their constitutions that renders them immune. With the second class the power of resistance is great, and can be renewed from time to time by a spell home in a European climate. In the third class the state is that of cumulative poisoning; in the fourth of acute poisoning.

Let the new-comer who goes to the Coast take the most cheerful view of these statements and let him regard himself as preordained to be one of the two most favoured classes. Let him take every care short of getting frightened, which is as deadly as taking no care at all, and he may—I sincerely hope he will—survive; for a man who has got the grit in him to go and fight in West Africa for those things worth fighting for—duty, honour and gold—is a man whose death is a dead loss to his country.

The cargoes from West Africa truly may "wives and mithers maist despairing ca' them lives o' men." Yet grievous as is the price England pays for her West African possessions, to us who know the men who risk their lives and die for them, England gets a good equivalent value for it; for she is the greatest manufacturing country in the world, and as such requires markets. Nowadays she requires them more than new colonies. A colony drains annually thousands of the most enterprising and energetic of her children from her, leaving behind them their aged and incapable relations. Moreover, a colony gradually becomes a rival manufacturing centre to the mother country, whereas West Africa will remain for hundreds of years a region that will supply the manufacturer with his raw material, and take in exchange for it his manufactured articles, giving him a good margin of profit. And the holding of our West African markets drains annually a few score of men only—only too often for ever—but the trade they carry on and develop there—a trade, according to Sir George Baden-Powell, of the annual value of nine millions sterling—enables thousands of men, women and children to remain safely in England, in comfort and pleasure, owing to the wages and profits arising from the manufacture and export of the articles used in that trade.

So I trust that those at home in England will give all honour to the men still working in West Africa, or rotting in the weed-grown, snake-infested cemeteries and the forest swamps—men whose battles have been fought out on lonely beaches far away from home and friends and often from another white man's help, sometimes with savages, but more often with a more deadly foe, with none of the anodyne to death and danger given by the companionship of hundreds of fellow soldiers in a fight with a foe you can see, but with a foe you can see only incarnate in the dreams of your delirium, which runs as a poison in burning veins and aching brain—the dread West Coast fever. And may England never again dream of forfeiting, or playing with, the conquests won for her by those heroes of commerce, the West Coast traders; for of them, as well as of such men as Sir Gerald Portal, truly it may be said—of such is the Kingdom of England.

APPENDIX

THE INVENTION OF THE CLOTH LOOM

This story is taken down from an Eboe, but practically the same story can be found among all the cloth-making tribes in West Africa.

In the old times there was a man who was a great hunter; but he had a bad wife, and when he made medicine to put on his spear, she made medicine against his spear, but he knew nothing of this thing and went out after bush cow.

By and by he found a big bush cow, and threw his spear at it, but the bush cow came on, and drove its horns through his thigh, so the man crept home, and lay in his house very sick, and the witch doctor found out which of his wives had witched the spear, and they killed her, and for many days the man could not go out hunting. But he was a great hunter, and his liver grew hot in him for the bush, so he dragged himself to the bush, and lay there every day. One day, as he lay, he saw a big spider making a net on a bush and he watched him. By and by he saw how the spider caught his game, and that the spider was a great hunter, and the man said "If I had hunted as this spider hunts, if I had made a trap like that and put it in the bush and then gone aside and let the game get into it and weary itself to death quickly,—quicker and safer than they do in pit-falls—that bush cow would not have gored me." And so after a time he tried to make a net like the spider's, out of bush rope, and he did this thing and put his net into the forest, and caught bush deer (gazelles) and earthpig (pangolins) and porcupines, and he made more nets, and every net he made was better, and he grew well, and became a greater hunter than before. One day he made a very fine net, and his wife said "This is a cloth, it is better than our cloth (bark cloth) because when the rain gets to it, it does not shrivel. Make me a cloth like this and then I will beat it with the mallet and wear it." And the man tried to do this thing, but he could not get it a good shape and he said, "Yet the spider gets a shape in his cloth. I will go and ask him again this thing." And he went to the spider, and took him another offering, and said: "Oh, my lord, teach me more things." And he sat and watched him for many days. By and by he saw more (his eyes were opened) and he saw the spider made his net on sticks, and so he went home and got fine bush rope that he had collected, and taken there, to make his game nets with, and he brought them to the bush near the spider, and fixing the strings on to the bush he made a new net and he got shape into it, and he made more nets this way, and every net he made was better. And his wife was pleased and gave him sons, and by and by the man saw that he did not want all the sticks of a bush to make his net on, only some of them; and so he took these home and put them up in his house, and made his nets there, and after a time his wife said: "Why do you make the stuff for me with that bush rope? Why do you not make it with something finer?" And he went into the bush and took offerings to the spider and said: "Oh, my lord, teach me more things!" And he sat and watched the spider, but the spider only went on making stuff out of his belly. And the man said: "Oh, my lord, you pass me. I cannot do this thing." And as he went home he thought and saw that there are trees, and there are bush ropes, thick bush rope and thin bush rope, and then there is grass which was thinner still, and he took the grass, and tried to make a net with it, and did this thing and made more nets and every net he made was better. And his wife was pleased and said "This is good cloth." And the man lived to be very old and was a great chief and a great hunter. For it is good for a man to be a great hunter, and it is good for a man to please women. This is the origin of the cloth loom.

It was in the old time, and men have got now thread on spools from the white man, for the white man is a great spider; but this is how the black man learnt to make cloth.

NOTES

{14} Sierra Leone has been known since the voyage of Hanno of Carthage in the sixth century B.C., but it has not got into general literature to any great extent since Pliny. The only later classic who has noticed it is Milton, who in a very suitable portion of Paradise Lost says of Notus and Afer, "black with thunderous clouds from Sierra Lona." Our occupation of it dates from 1787.

{15} Lagos also likes to bear this flattering appellation, and has now-a-days more right to the title.

{28} Along the Coast, and in other parts of Africa, the coarser, flat-sided kinds of banana are usually called plantains, the name banana being reserved for the finer sorts, such as the little "silver banana."

{37} From Point Limbok, the seaward extremity of Cameroons Mountain, to Cape Horatio, the most eastern extremity of Fernando Po, the soundings are, from the continent, 13, 17, 20, 23, 27, 29, 30, 34 fathoms; close on to the island, 35 and 29 fathoms.

{44} I am informed that the allowance made to these priests exceeds by some pounds the revenues Spain obtains from the Island. In Spanish possessions alone is a supporting allowance made to missionaries though in all the other colonies they obtain a government grant.

{47} Ten Years' Wanderings among the Ethiopians, T. J. Hutchinson.

{48a} There is difference of opinion among authorities as to whether Fernando Po was discovered by Fernando Po or by Lopez Gonsalves.

{48b} From April 1777 till the end of 1782, 370 men out of the 547 died of fever.

{51} Porto is the Bubi name for black men who are not Bubis, these were in old days Portuguese slaves, "Porto" being evidently a corruption of "Portuguese," but it is used alike by the Bubi to designate Sierra Leonian and Accras, in fact, all the outer barbarian blacks. The name for white men, Mandara, used by the Bubis, has a sort of resemblance to the Effik name for whites, Makara, i.e., the ruling one, but I do not know whether these two words have any connection.

{55} I am glad to find that my own observations on the drink question entirely agree with those of Dr. Oscar Baumann, because he is an unprejudiced scientific observer, who has had great experience both in the Congo and Cameroon regions before he came to Fernando Po. In support of my statement I may quote his own words:—"Die Bube trinken nämlich sehr gerne Rum; Gin verschmähen sie vollständig, aber ausser Tabak und Salz gehört Rum zu den gesuchtesten europäischen Artikeln für sie. Wie bekannt hat sich in Europa ein heftiges Geschrei gegen die Vergiftung der Neger durch Alcohol erhoben. Wenn dasselbe schon für die meisten Stämme Westafrikas der Berechtigung fast vollständig entbehrt und in die Categorie verweisen worden muss die man mit dem nicht sehr schönen aber treffenden Ausdrücke 'Humanitätsduselei' bezeichnet, so ist es den Bube gegenüber wohl mehr als zwecklos. Es mag ja vorkommen dass ein Bube wenn er sein Palmöl verkauft hat, sich ein oder zweimal im Jahre mit Rum ein Räuschlein antrinkt. Deshalb aber gleich von Alkohol-Vergiftung zu sprechen wäre mindestens lächerlich. Ich bin überzeugt dass mancher jener Herren die in Wort und Schrift so heftig gegen die Alkolismus der Neger zetern in ihren Studenten-jahren allein mehr geistige Getränke genossen haben als zehn Bube während ihres ganzen Lebens. Der Handelsrum welcher wie ich mich öfters überzeugt zwar recht verwässert aber keineswegs abstossend schlecht schmeckt, ist den Bube gewöhnlich nur eine Delikatesse welche mit Andacht schluckweise genossen wird. Wenn ein Arbeiter bei uns einen Schluck Branntwein oder ein Glas Bier geniesst um sich zu stärken, so findet das Jeder in der Ordnung; der Bube jedoch, welcher splitternackt tagelang in feuchten Bergwäldern umher klettern muss, soll beliebe nichts als Wasser trinken!" Eine Africanische Tropen. insel Fernando Póo, Dr. Oscar Baumann, Edward Hölzer, Wien, 1888.

{56} "Beiträge zur Kenntniss der Bubisprache auf Fernando Póo," O. Baumann, Zeitschrift für afrikanische Sprachen. Berlin, 1888.

{61} Ten Years' Wanderings among the Ethiopians. T. J. Hutchinson.

{80} The Sierra del Cristal and the Pallaballa range are, by some geographers, held to be identical; but I have reason to doubt this, for the specimens of rock brought home by me have been identified by the Geological Survey, those of the Pallaballa range as mica schist and quartz; those of the Sierra del Cristal as "probably schistose grit, but not definitely determinable by inspection," and "quartz rock." The quantity of mica in the sands of the Ogowé, I think, come into it from its affluents from the Congo region because you do not get these mica sands in rivers which are entirely from the Sierra del Cristal, such as the Muni. The Rumby and Omon ranges are probably identical with the Sierra del Cristal, for in them as in the Sierra you do not get the glistening dove-coloured rock with a sparse vegetation growing on it, as you do in the Pallaballa region.

{96} The villages of the Fans and Bakele are built in the form of a street. When in the forest there are two lines of huts, the one facing the other, and each end closed by a guard house. When facing a river there is one line of huts facing the river frontage.

{167} The M'pongwe speaking tribes are the M'pongwe, Orungu, Nkâmi, Ajumba, Inlenga and the Igalwa.

{170} These four Ajumba had been engaged, through the instrumentality of M. Jacot, to accompany me to the Rembwé River. The Ajumba are one of the noble tribes and are the parent stem of the M'pongwe; their district is the western side of Lake Ayzingo.

{181} As this river is not mentioned on maps, and as I was the first white traveller on it, I give my own phonetic spelling; but I expect it would be spelt by modern geographers "Kâkola."

{185} A common African sensation among natives when alarmed, somewhat akin to our feeling some one walk over our graves.

{189} Since my return I think the French gentleman may have been M. F. Tenaille d'Estais, who is down on the latest map (French) as having visited a lake in this region in 1882, which is set down as Lac Ebouko. He seems to have come from and returned to Lake Ayzingo—on map Lac Azingo—but on the other hand "Ebouko" was not known on the lake, Ajumba and Fans alike calling it Ncovi.

{200} Diospyros and Copaifua mopane.

{205} Vipera nasicornis; M'pongwe, Ompenle.

{208} I have no hesitation in saying that the gorilla is the most horrible wild animal I have seen. I have seen at close quarters specimens of the most important big game of Central Africa, and, with the exception of snakes, I have run away from all of them; but although elephants, leopards, and pythons give you a feeling of alarm, they do not give that feeling of horrible disgust that an old gorilla gives on account of its hideousness of appearance.

{223} An European coat or its equivalent value is one of the constant quantities in an ivory bundle.

{241} Specimen placed in Herbarium at Kew.

{286} It is held by some authorities to come from gru-gru, a Mandingo word for charm, but I respectfully question whether gru-gru has not come from ju-ju, the native approximation to the French joujou.

{295} The proper way to spell this name is booby, i.e. silly, but as Bubi is the accepted spelling, I bow to authority.

{301} This article has different names in different tribes; thus it is called a bian among the Fan, a tarwiz, gree-gree, etc., on other parts of the Coast.

{306} Care must be taken not to confuse with sacrifices (propitiations of spirits) the killing of men and animals as offerings to the souls of deceased persons.

{324} Pronounced Tchwee.

{329} Among the Fjort the body cannot be buried until all the deceased's debts are paid.

{338} In speaking of native ideas I should prefer to use the good Yorkshire term of "overthrowing" in place of "superstition," but as the latter is the accepted word for such matters I feel bound to employ it.

{363} "Tshi-speaking People," Colonel Sir H. B. Ellis.

{439} Since my return to England I have read Sir Richard Burton's account of his first successful attempt to reach the summit of the Great Cameroons in 1862. His companions were Herr Mann, the botanist, and Señor Calvo. Herr Mann claimed to have ascended the summit a few days before the two others joined him, but Burton seems to doubt this. The account he himself gives of the summit is: "Victoria mountain now proved to be a shell of a huge double crater opening to the south-eastward, where a tremendous torrent of fire had broken down the weaker wall, the whole interior and its accessible breach now lay before me plunging down in vertical cliff. The depth of the bowl may be 360 feet. The total diameter of the two, which are separated by a rough partition of lava, 1,000 feet. . . Not a blade of grass, not a thread of moss, breaks the gloom of this Plutonic pit, which is as black as Erebus, except where the fire has painted it red or yellow." This ascent was made from the west face. I got into the "Plutonic pit" through the S.E. break in its wall, and was said to be the first English person to reach it from the S.E., and the twenty-eighth ascender, according to my well-informed German friends.

{455} The African Association now own two steamers. Alexander Miller Brothers and Co. also charter steamers.

{463} A Naturalist in Mid Africa, 1896.

{465} The accounts given by the various members of the Stanley Emin Relief Expedition well describe the usual sort of West African hinterland work, but the forests of the Congo are less relieved by open park-like country than those of the rivers to the north or south. Still the Congo, in spite of this disadvantage, has greater facilities for transport in the way of waterways than is found east of the Cross or Cameroon.

{468} Export of coffee from the Gold Coast, 1894, given in the Colonial Report on that year published in 1896, was of the value of £1,265 3s. 4d.; cocoa, £546 17s. 4d. The greater part of this coffee goes to Germany.

Export of coffee from Lagos, given in Colonial Report for 1892, published in 1893, was of the value of £12. No figures on this subject are given in the 1894 report, published in 1896, but I cite these figures to show the delay in publishing these reports by the Colonial Office and the difficulty of getting reliable statistics on West African trade.

{493} "The Development of Dodos." National Review, March, 1896.

{504} Ethnology, p. 266. A. H. Keane, Cambridge, 1896.

{508} Lagos Annual Consular Report (150, p.6), 1894: "There were only three cases of drunkenness. Considering that in the Island of Lagos alone the population is over 33,300, this clearly proves that drunkenness in this part of Africa is uncommon, and that there is insufficient evidence for the contention which is advanced that the native is being ruined by what is so often spoken of as the heinous gin traffic; it is a well-known fact by those in a position best able to judge by long residence that the inhabitants of this country have a natural repugnance to intemperance."

{509} Board of Trade Journal, August 1896.

{514} By slavery, I mean the quasi-feudal system you find existing among the true negroes. I do not mean either the form of domestic slavery of Egypt, or the system of labour existing in the Congo Free State; although I am of opinion that the suppression of his export slave trade to the Americas was a grave mistake. It has been fraught with untold suffering to the African, which would have been avoided by altering the slave trade into a coolie system.

{516} Bilious Hæmoglobinuric, black water fever.

{517} See also Klebs and Tommasi Crudeli, Arch. f. exp. Path., xi.; Ceci, ibid., xv.; Tommasi Crudeli, La Malaria de Rome, Paris, 1881; Nuovi Studj sulla Natura della Malaria, Rome, 1881; "Malaria and the Ancient Drainage of the Roman Hills," Practitioner, ii., 1881; Instituzioni de anat. Path., vol. i., Turin, 1882; Marchiafava e Cuboni, Nuovi Studj sulla Natura della Malaria, Acad. dei Lincei, Jan. 2, 1881; Marchand, Virch. Arch., vol. lxxxviii.; Laveran, Nature parasitaire des Accidents d'Impaludisme, Paris, 1881; Richard, Comptes Rendus, 1881; Steinberg, Rep. Nat. Board of Health (U.S.), 1881. Malaria-krankheiten, K. Schwalbe; Berlin, 1890; Parkes, On the Issue of a Spirit Ration in the Ashantee Campaign, Churchill, 1875; Zumsden, Cyclopædia of Medicine; Ague, Dr. M. D. O'Connell, Calcutta, 1885; Roman Fever, North, Appendix I. British Central Africa, Sir H. H. Johnstone.

BIOGRAPHY OF ISABELLA BIRD

Isabella Bird was born on October 15, 1831 in Yorkshire, England to Dora Lawson and Reverend Edward Bird. Her family moved several times throughout her childhood to accommodate her father's inclination towards controversial sermons, namely his condemnation of labor on Sundays—he relocated his curacy whenever his congregation began to dwindle.

Frail and sickly as a child, Bird's doctors recommended travel and outdoor activity to alleviate her pain; she learned to ride and row at a young age. She had an operation to remove a spinal tumor at the age of nineteen, but it was only partially successful, leaving her with residual physical pain in addition to insomnia and depression. This diagnosis was as much a result of her physical ailments as a psychological reaction to the stifling nature of domestic life for a woman in a Victorian middle-class household. When travelling, her health improved dramatically, only to falter when she spent time at home. She acknowledges this in her work *A Lady's Life in the Rocky Mountains,* writing:

> I am well as long as I live on horseback, go to bed at eight, sleep out-of-doors, or in a log cabin, and lead in all respects a completely unconventional life. But each time that for a few days at Honolulu or San Francisco I have civilised, I have found myself rapidly going down again.

With a doctor's prescription for a long sea voyage, Bird's father gave her 100 pounds to travel wherever she wanted. Bird's first expedition was to North America, where she spent several months in eastern Canada and the United States. This trip inspired her first book of twenty-two, *The Englishwoman in America.* Upon arriving home, she met publisher John Murray, who helped her to establish a rhythm of travel, write, publish, and use the profits to plan another trip.

After her father's death in 1858, Bird moved to Edinburgh, Scotland with her mother and sister. From there, she traveled back and forth to North America three times, and went once to the Mediterranean. Her mother passed away in

1866 and her sister in 1880, leaving Bird with increasingly fewer ties to home. Between 1872 and 1873, she spent a total of eighteen months away from home on voyages to Australia, Hawaii, and through the Colorado Rocky Mountains. These travels fueled her 1875 and 1879 works *Six Months in the Sandwich Islands* and *A Lady's Life in the Rocky Mountains*, in which she chronicled the pleasures of visiting places untouched even by locals during her 3,000-mile horseback ride, living among native people, and adventures like riding alone through a blizzard with her eyes frozen shut and a courtship with one-eyed outlaw and poet Jim Nugent, also known as Rocky Mountain Jim.

In Hawaii, she began riding astride rather than sidesaddle, which cured her backaches from constant riding and gave her even more mobility, allowing her to climb to the peaks of Hawaii's volcanic mountains like Mauna Kea and Mauna Loa. Unlike Kingsley, she dressed more practically for her adventures in a sturdy jacket and long skirt over trousers, though she threatened to sue the *Times* for saying she dressed like a man in addition to riding like one.

Shortly thereafter, Bird made Japan her next destination, hiring an eighteen-year-old guide and translator. Together, they traveled north to Hokkaido to stay with the Ainu tribe, early non-Japanese inhabitants of the country. She made her way back home through China, Vietnam, and Singapore, staying for five weeks on the Malayan Peninsula. Upon arriving home, she began writing about her travels through Japan and enjoyed considerable renown for her popular books on Hawaii and the Rocky Mountains. She published *Unbeaten Tracks in Japan* in 1880.

Bird married Dr. John Bishop in 1881, having met him while he treated her sister's illness. She continued to travel in her married life, although she wrote about feeling guilty for leaving her husband. In 1886, he fell ill, and she returned home to care for him devotedly until his death that year. Widowed at fifty-nine with no remaining family, Bird began her expeditions to Persia, where she dedicated her time to medical and missionary pursuits. In 1887, she took a medicine course at St. Mary's Hospital in London, which set the foundation for her 1888 establishment of the Henrietta Bird Hospital in Amritsar and the John Bishop Memorial Hospital in Srinagar, India.

Her travels through northern India towards Tibet were some of her most difficult—in one incident, her horse lost its footing in a river and drowned, leaving her with two broken ribs. On her return to India from Tibet, she crossed paths with Major Herbert Sawyer of the Indian Army on his way to Persia to conduct a geographical military survey, and the pair braved the desert in the dead of winter and arrived in Tehran in the early spring of 1890, having barely survived the journey. In the same year, she became the first woman to be awarded the Honorary Fellowship of the Royal Scottish Geographical Society. During her time in Persia, she had access to aspects of Persian family life and society that her male colleagues were barred from; she kept company with diplomats and their wives without having to conform to their strict protocols.

Returning to England once again for a short time, Bird became the first female member of the Royal Geographical Society in 1892. While home, she met with Prime Minister William Gladstone to address the atrocities committed against Armenians in the Middle East, but despite her political activism she soon grew restless again. In 1894, she left to spend more time in Asia, touring China, Korea, and Japan, and traveled home via a route through the Tibetan Mountains, arriving back home in 1897. Three years later, she published *The Yangtze Valley and Beyond* before making what would be her final trip to Morocco in 1901. She passed away on October 7, 1904, at the age of 73, in the midst of planning for another trip.

AMONG THE
TIBETANS

BY

Isabella Bird

CHAPTER I

THE START

THE VALE OF KASHMIR IS TOO WELL KNOWN to require description. It is the 'happy hunting-ground' of the Anglo-Indian sportsman and tourist, the resort of artists and invalids, the home of pashm shawls and exquisitely embroidered fabrics, and the land of Lalla Rookh. Its inhabitants, chiefly Moslems, infamously governed by Hindus, are a feeble race, attracting little interest, valuable to travellers as 'coolies' or porters, and repulsive to them from the mingled cunning and obsequiousness which have been fostered by ages of oppression. But even for them there is the dawn of hope, for the Church Missionary Society has a strong medical and educational mission at the capital, a hospital and dispensary under the charge of a lady M.D. have been opened for women, and a capable and upright 'settlement officer,' lent by the Indian Government, is investigating the iniquitous land arrangements with a view to a just settlement.

I left the Panjab railroad system at Rawul Pindi, bought my camp equipage, and travelled through the grand ravines which lead to Kashmir or the Jhelum Valley by hill-cart, on horseback, and by house-boat, reaching Srinagar at the end of April, when the velvet lawns were at their greenest, and the foliage was at its freshest, and the deodar-skirted mountains which enclose this fairest gem of the Himalayas still wore their winter mantle of unsullied snow. Making Srinagar my headquarters, I spent two months in travelling in Kashmir, half the time in a native house-boat on the Jhelum and Pohru rivers, and the other half on horseback, camping wherever the scenery was most attractive.

By the middle of June mosquitos were rampant, the grass was tawny, a brown dust haze hung over the valley, the camp-fires of a multitude glared through the hot nights and misty moonlight of the Munshibagh, English tents dotted the landscape, there was no mountain, valley, or plateau, however remote, free from the clatter of English voices and the trained servility of Hindu servants, and even Sonamarg, at an altitude of 8,000 feet and rough of access, had capitulated to lawn- tennis. To a traveller this Anglo-Indian hubbub was intolerable, and I left Srinagar and many kind friends on June 20 for the uplifted plateaux of Lesser Tibet. My party consisted of myself, a thoroughly competent servant and passable interpreter, Hassan Khan, a Panjabi; a seis, of whom the less that is said the better; and Mando, a Kashmiri lad, a common coolie, who, under Hassan Khan's training, developed into an efficient travelling servant, and later into a smart khitmatgar.

Gyalpo, my horse, must not be forgotten—indeed, he cannot be, for he left the marks of his heels or teeth on every one. He was a beautiful creature, Badak-shani bred, of Arab blood, a silver-grey, as light as a greyhound and as strong as a cart-horse. He was higher in the scale of intellect than any horse of my acquaintance. His cleverness at times suggested reasoning power, and his mischievousness a sense of humour. He walked five miles an hour, jumped like a deer, climbed like a yak, was strong and steady in perilous fords, tireless, hardy, hungry, frolicked along ledges of precipices and over crevassed glaciers, was absolutely fearless, and his slender legs and the use he made of them were the marvel of all. He was an enigma to the end. He was quite untamable, rejected all dainties with indignation, swung his heels into people's faces when they went near him, ran at them with his teeth, seized unwary passers-by by their kamar bands, and shook them as a dog shakes a rat, would let no one go near him but Mando, for whom he formed at first sight a most singular attachment, but kicked and struck with his forefeet, his eyes all the time dancing with fun, so that one could never decide whether his ceaseless pranks were play or vice. He was always tethered in front of my tent with a rope twenty feet long, which left him practically free; he was as good as a watch-dog, and his antics and enigmatical savagery were the life and terror of the camp. I was never weary of watching him, the curves of his form were so exquisite, his movements so lithe and rapid, his small head and restless little ears so full of life and expression, the variations in his manner so frequent, one moment savagely attacking some unwary stranger with a scream of rage, the next laying his lovely head against Mando's cheek with a soft cooing sound and a childlike gentleness. When he was attacking anybody or frolicking, his movements and beauty can only be described by a phrase of the Apostle James, 'the grace of the fashion of it.' Colonel Durand, of Gilgit celebrity, to whom I am indebted for many other kindnesses, gave him to me in exchange for a cowardly, heavy Yarkand horse, and had previously vainly tried to tame him. His wild eyes were like those of a seagull. He had no kinship with humanity.

In addition, I had as escort an Afghan or Pathan, a soldier of the Maha-rajah's irregular force of foreign mercenaries, who had been sent to meet me when I entered Kashmir. This man, Usman Shah, was a stage ruffian in appearance. He wore a turban of prodigious height ornamented with poppies or birds' feathers, loved fantastic colours and ceaseless change of raiment, walked in front of me carrying a big sword over his shoulder, plundered and beat the people, terrified the women, and was eventually recognised at Leh as a murderer, and as great a ruffian in reality as he was in appearance. An attendant of this kind is a mistake. The brutality and rapacity he exercises naturally make the people cowardly or surly, and disinclined to trust a traveller so accompanied.

Finally, I had a Cabul tent, 7 ft. 6 in. by 8 ft. 6 in., weighing, with poles and iron pins, 75 lbs., a trestle bed and cork mattress, a folding table and chair, and an Indian dhurrie as a carpet.

My servants had a tent 5 ft. 6 in. square, weighing only 10 lbs., which served as a shelter tent for me during the noonday halt. A kettle, copper pot, and frying pan, a few enamelled iron table equipments, bedding, clothing, working and sketching materials, completed my outfit. The servants carried wadded quilts for beds and bedding, and their own cooking utensils, unwillingness to use those belonging to a Christian being nearly the last rag of religion which they retained. The only stores I carried were tea, a quantity of Edwards' desiccated soup, and a little saccharin. The 'house,' furniture, clothing, &c., were a light load for three mules, engaged at a shilling a day each, including the muleteer. Sheep, coarse flour, milk, and barley were procurable at very moderate prices on the road.

Leh, the capital of Ladakh or Lesser Tibet, is nineteen marches from Srinagar, but I occupied twenty-six days on the journey, and made the first 'march' by water, taking my house-boat to Ganderbal, a few hours from Srinagar, via the Mar Nullah and Anchar Lake. Never had this Venice of the Himalayas, with a broad rushing river for its high street and winding canals for its back streets, looked so entrancingly beautiful as in the slant sunshine of the late June afternoon. The light fell brightly on the river at the Residency stairs where I embarked, on perindas and state barges, with their painted arabesques, gay canopies, and 'banks' of thirty and forty crimson-clad, blue-turbaned, paddling men; on the gay facade and gold-domed temple of the Maharajah's Palace, on the massive deodar bridges which for centuries have defied decay and the fierce flood of the Jhelum, and on the quaintly picturesque wooden architecture and carved brown lattice fronts of the houses along the swirling waterway, and glanced mirthfully through the dense leafage of the superb planes which overhang the dark-green water. But the mercury was 92 degrees in the shade and the sun-blaze terrific, and it was a relief when the boat swung round a corner, and left the stir of the broad, rapid Jhelum for a still, narrow, and sharply winding canal, which intersects a part of Srinagar lying between the Jhelum

and the hill-crowning fort of Hari Parbat. There the shadows were deep, and
chance lights alone fell on the red dresses of the women at the ghats, and on
the shaven, shiny heads of hundreds of amphibious boys who were swimming
and aquatically romping in the canal, which is at once the sewer and the water
supply of the district.

Several hours were spent in a slow and tortuous progress through scenes
of indescribable picturesqueness—a narrow waterway spanned by sharp-angled
stone bridges, some of them with houses on the top, or by old brown wooden
bridges festooned with vines, hemmed in by lofty stone embankments into
which sculptured stones from ancient temples are wrought, on the top of which
are houses of rich men, fancifully built, with windows of fretwork of wood,
or gardens with kiosks, and lower embankments sustaining many-balconied
dwellings, rich in colour and fantastic in design, their upper fronts projecting
over the water and supported on piles. There were gigantic poplars wreathed
with vines, great mulberry trees hanging their tempting fruit just out of reach,
huge planes overarching the water, their dense leafage scraping the mat roof of
the boat; filthy ghats thronged with white- robed Moslems performing their
scanty religious ablutions; great grain boats heavily thatched, containing not
only families, but their sheep and poultry; and all the other sights of a crowded Srinagar waterway, the houses being characteristically distorted and out of
repair. This canal gradually widens into the Anchar Lake, a reedy mere of in-
definite boundaries, the breeding-ground of legions of mosquitos; and after the
tawny twilight darkened into a stifling night we made fast to a reed bed, not
reaching Ganderbal till late the next morning, where my horse and caravan
awaited me under a splendid plane-tree.

For the next five days we marched up the Sind Valley, one of the most beautiful in Kashmir from its grandeur and variety. Beginning among quiet rice-fields
and brown agricultural villages at an altitude of 5,000 feet, the track, usually
bad and sometimes steep and perilous, passes through flower-gemmed alpine
meadows, along dark gorges above the booming and rushing Sind, through
woods matted with the sweet white jasmine, the lower hem of the pine and
deodar forests which ascend the mountains to a considerable altitude, past rifts
giving glimpses of dazzling snow-peaks, over grassy slopes dotted with villages,
houses, and shrines embosomed in walnut groves, in sight of the frowning crags
of Haramuk, through wooded lanes and park-like country over which farms are
thinly scattered, over unrailed and shaky bridges, and across avalanche slopes,
till it reaches Gagangair, a dream of lonely beauty, with a camping-ground of
velvety sward under noble plane-trees. Above this place the valley closes in between walls of precipices and crags, which rise almost abruptly from the Sind
to heights of 8,000 and 10,000 feet. The road in many places is only a series

of steep and shelving ledges above the raging river, natural rock smoothed and polished into riskiness by the passage for centuries of the trade into Central Asia from Western India, Kashmir, and Afghanistan. Its precariousness for animals was emphasised to me by five serious accidents which occurred in the week of my journey, one of them involving the loss of the money, clothing, and sporting kit of an English officer bound for Ladakh for three months. Above this tremendous gorge the mountains open out, and after crossing to the left bank of the Sind a sharp ascent brought me to the beautiful alpine meadow of Sonamarg, bright with spring flowers, gleaming with crystal streams, and fringed on all sides by deciduous and coniferous trees, above and among which are great glaciers and the snowy peaks of Tilail. Fashion has deserted Sonamarg, rough of access, for Gulmarg, a caprice indicated by the ruins of several huts and of a church. The pure bracing air, magnificent views, the proximity and accessibility of glaciers, and the presence of a kind friend who was 'hutted' there for the summer, made Sonamarg a very pleasant halt before entering upon the supposed seventies of the journey to Lesser Tibet.

The five days' march, though propitious and full of the charm of magnificent scenery, had opened my eyes to certain unpleasantnesses. I found that Usman Shah maltreated the villagers, and not only robbed them of their best fowls, but requisitioned all manner of things in my name, though I scrupulously and personally paid for everything, beating the people with his scabbarded sword if they showed any intention of standing upon their rights. Then I found that my clever factotum, not content with the legitimate 'squeeze' of ten per cent., was charging me double price for everything and paying the sellers only half the actual price, this legerdemain being perpetrated in my presence. He also by threats got back from the coolies half their day's wages after I had paid them, received money for barley for Gyalpo, and never bought it, a fact brought to light by the growing feebleness of the horse, and cheated in all sorts of mean and plausible ways, though I paid him exceptionally high wages, and was prepared to 'wink' at a moderate amount of dishonesty, so long as it affected only myself. It has a lowering influence upon one to live in a fog of lies and fraud, and the attempt to checkmate a fraudulent Asiatic ends in extreme discomfiture.

I left Sonamarg late on a lovely afternoon for a short march through forest-skirted alpine meadows to Baltal, the last camping-ground in Kashmir, a grassy valley at the foot of the Zoji La, the first of three gigantic steps by which the lofty plateaux of Central Asia are attained. On the road a large affluent of the Sind, which tumbles down a pine-hung gorge in broad sheets of foam, has to be crossed. My seis, a rogue, was either half-witted or pretended to be so, and, in spite of orders to the contrary, led Gyalpo upon a bridge at a considerable height, formed of two poles with flat pieces of stone laid loosely over them not more than a foot broad. As the horse reached the middle, the structure gave a sort of turn, there was a vision of hoofs in air and a gleam of scarlet, and Gyalpo, the hope of the next four months, after rolling over more than once, vanished among rocks and surges of the wildest description. He kept his presence of mind, however, recovered himself, and by a desperate effort got ashore lower down, with legs scratched and bleeding and one horn of the saddle incurably bent.

Mr. Maconochie of the Panjab Civil Service, and Dr. E. Neve of the C. M. S. Medical Mission in Kashmir, accompanied me from Sonamarg over the pass, and that night Mr. M. talked seriously to Usman Shah on the subject of his misconduct, and with such singular results that thereafter I had little cause for complaint. He came to me and said, 'The Commissioner Sahib thinks I give Mem Sahib a great deal of trouble;' to which I replied in a cold tone, 'Take care you don't give me any more.' The gist of the Sahib's words was the very pertinent suggestion that it would eventually be more to his interest to serve me honestly and faithfully than to cheat me.

Baltal lies at the feet of a precipitous range, the peaks of which exceed Mont Blanc in height. Two gorges unite there. There is not a hut within ten miles. Big camp-fires blazed. A few shepherds lay under the shelter of a mat screen. The silence and solitude were most impressive under the frosty stars and the great Central Asian barrier. Sunrise the following morning saw us on the way up a huge gorge with nearly perpendicular sides, and filled to a great depth with snow. Then came the Zoji La, which, with the Namika La and the Fotu La, respectively 11,300, 13,000, and 13,500 feet, are the three great steps from Kashmir to the Tibetan heights. The two latter passes present no difficulties. The Zoji La is a thoroughly severe pass, the worst, with the exception perhaps of the Sasir, on the Yarkand caravan route. The track, cut, broken, and worn on the side of a wall of rock nearly 2,000 feet in abrupt elevation, is a series of rough narrow zigzags, rarely, if ever, wide enough for laden animals to pass each other, composed of broken ledges often nearly breast high, and shelving surfaces of abraded rock, up which animals have to leap and scramble as best they may.

Trees and trailers drooped over the path, ferns and lilies bloomed in moist recesses, and among myriads of flowers a large blue and cream columbine was conspicuous by its beauty and exquisite odour. The charm of the detail tempted one to linger at every turn, and all the more so because I knew that I should see nothing more of the grace and bounteousness of Nature till my projected descent into Kulu in the late autumn. The snow-filled gorge on whose abrupt side the path hangs, the Zoji La (Pass), is geographically remarkable as being the lowest depression in the great Himalayan range for 300 miles; and by it, in spite of infamous bits of road on the Sind and Suru rivers, and consequent losses of goods and animals, all the traffic of Kashmir, Afghanistan, and the Western Panjab finds its way into Central Asia. It was too early in the season, however, for more than a few enterprising caravans to be on the road.

The last look upon Kashmir was a lingering one. Below, in shadow, lay the Baltal camping-ground, a lonely deodar-belted flowery meadow, noisy with the dash of icy torrents tumbling down from the snowfields and glaciers upborne by the gigantic mountain range into which we had penetrated by the Zoji Pass. The valley, lying in shadow at their base, was a dream of beauty, green as an English lawn, starred with white lilies, and dotted with clumps of trees which were festooned with red and white roses, clematis, and white jasmine. Above the hardier deciduous trees appeared the Pinus excelsa, the silver fir, and the spruce; higher yet the stately grace of the deodar clothed the hillsides; and above the forests rose the snow mountains of Tilail, pink in the sunrise. High above the Zoji, itself 11,500 feet in altitude, a mass of grey and red mountains, snow-slashed and snow- capped, rose in the dewy rose-flushed atmosphere in peaks, walls, pinnacles, and jagged ridges, above which towered yet loftier summits, bearing into the heavenly blue sky fields of unsullied snow alone. The descent on the Tibetan side is slight and gradual. The character of the scenery undergoes an abrupt change. There are no more trees, and the large shrubs which for a time take their place degenerate into thorny bushes, and then disappear. There were mountains thinly clothed with grass here and there, mountains of bare gravel and red rock, grey crags, stretches of green turf, sunlit peaks with their snows, a deep, snow-filled ravine, eastwards and beyond a long valley filled with a snowfield fringed with pink primulas; and that was CENTRAL ASIA.

We halted for breakfast, iced our cold tea in the snow, Mr. M. gave a final charge to the Afghan, who swore by his Prophet to be faithful, and I parted from my kind escorts with much reluctance, and started on my Tibetan jour-ney, with but a slender stock of Hindustani, and two men who spoke not a word of English. On that day's march of fourteen miles there is not a single hut. The snowfield extended for five miles, from ten to seventy feet deep, much crevassed, and encumbered with avalanches. In it the Dras, truly 'snow-born,' appeared, issuing from a chasm under a blue arch of ice and snow, afterwards to rage down the valley, to be forded many times or crossed on snow bridges. After walking for some time, and getting a bad fall down an avalanche slope, I mounted Gyalpo, and the clever, plucky fellow frolicked over the snow, smelt and leapt crevasses which were too wide to be stepped over, put his forelegs together and slid down slopes like a Swiss mule, and, though carried off his feet in a ford by the fierce surges of the Dras, struggled gamely to shore. Steep grassy hills, and peaks with gorges cleft by the thundering Dras, and stretches of rolling grass succeeded each other. Then came a wide valley mostly covered with stones brought down by torrents, a few plots of miserable barley grown by irrigation, and among them two buildings of round stones and mud, about six feet high, with flat mud roofs, one of which might be called the village, and the other the caravanserai. On the village roof were stacks of twigs and of the dried dung of animals, which is used for fuel, and the whole female population, adult and juvenile, engaged in picking wool. The people of this village of Matayan are Kashmiris. As I had an hour to wait for my tent, the women descended and sat in a circle round me with a concentrated stare. They asked if I were dumb, and why I wore no earrings or necklace, their own persons being loaded with heavy ornaments. They brought children afflicted with skin- diseases, and asked for ointment, and on hearing that I was hurt by a fall, seized on my limbs and shampooed them energetically but not undexterously. I prefer their sociability to the usual chilling aloofness of the people of Kashmir.

The Serai consisted of several dark and dirty cells, built round a blazing piece of sloping dust, the only camping-ground, and under the entrance two platforms of animated earth, on which my servants cooked and slept. The next day was Sunday, sacred to a halt; but there was no fodder for the animals, and we were obliged to march to Dras, following, where possible, the course of the river of that name, which passes among highly-coloured and snow-slashed mountains, except in places where it suddenly finds itself pent between walls of flame- coloured or black rock, not ten feet apart, through which it boils and rages, forming gigantic pot-holes. With every mile the surroundings became more markedly of the Central Asian type. All day long a white, scintillating sun blazes out of a deep blue, rainless, cloudless sky. The air is exhilarating. The traveller is conscious of daily-increasing energy and vitality. There are no trees, and deep crimson roses along torrent beds are the only shrubs. But for a brief fortnight in June, which chanced to occur during my journey, the valleys and lower slopes present a wonderful aspect of beauty and joyousness. Rose and pale pink primulas fringe the margin of the snow, the dainty Pedicularis tubiflora covers moist spots with its mantle of gold; great yellow and white, and small purple and white anemones, pink and white dianthus, a very large myosotis, bringing the intense blue of heaven down to earth, purple orchids by the water, borage staining whole tracts deep blue, martagon lilies, pale green lilies veined and spotted with brown, yellow, orange, and purple vetches, painter's brush, dwarf dandelions, white clover, filling the air with fragrance, pink and cream asters, chrysanthemums, lychnis, irises, gentian, artemisia, and a hundred others, form the undergrowth of millions of tall Umbelliferae and Compositae, many of them peach-scented and mostly yellow. The wind is always strong, and the millions of bright corollas, drinking in the sun-blaze which perfects all too soon their brief but passionate existence, rippled in broad waves of colour with an almost kaleidoscopic effect. About the eleventh march from Srinagar, at Kargil, a change for the worse occurs, and the remaining marches to the capital of La-dakh are over blazing gravel or surfaces of denuded rock, the singular Caprifolia horrida, with its dark-green mass of wavy ovate leaves on trailing stems, and its fair, white, anemone- like blossom, and the graceful Clematis orientalis, the only vegetation.

Crossing a raging affluent of the Dras by a bridge which swayed and shiv-ered, the top of a steep hill offered a view of a great valley with branches sloping up into the ravines of a complexity of mountain ranges, from 18,000 to 21,000 feet in altitude, with glaciers at times descending as low as 11,000 feet in their hollows. In consequence of such possibilities of irrigation, the valley is green with irrigated grass and barley, and villages with flat roofs scattered among the crops, or perched on the spurs of flame-coloured mountains, give it a wild cheerfulness. These Dras villages are inhabited by hardy Dards and Baltis, short, jolly-looking, darker, and far less handsome than the Kashmiris; but, unlike them, they showed so much friendliness, as well as interest and curiosity, that I remained with them for two days, visiting their villages and seeing the 'sights' they had to show me, chiefly a great Sikh fort, a yak bull, the zho, a hybrid, the interiors of their houses, a magnificent view from a hilltop, and a Dard dance to the music of Dard reed pipes. In return I sketched them individually and collectively as far as time allowed, presenting them with the results, truthful and ugly. I bought a sheep for 2s. 3d., and regaled the camp upon it, the three which were brought for my inspection being ridden by boys astride.

The evenings in the Dras valley were exquisite. As soon as the sun went behind the higher mountains, peak above peak, red and snow- slashed, flamed against a lemon sky, the strong wind moderated into a pure stiff breeze, bring-ing up to camp the thunder of the Dras, and the musical tinkle of streams sparkling in absolute purity. There was no more need for boiling and filtering. Icy water could be drunk in safety from every crystal torrent.

Leaving behind the Dras villages and their fertility, the narrow road passes through a flaming valley above the Dras, walled in by bare, riven, snow-patched peaks, with steep declivities of stones, huge boulders, decaying avalanches, walls and spires of rock, some vermilion, others pink, a few intense orange, some black, and many plum-coloured, with a vitrified look, only to be represent-ed by purple madder. Huge red chasms with glacier-fed torrents, occasional snowfields, intense solar heat radiating from dry and verdureless rock, a ravine so steep .and narrow that for miles together there is not space to pitch a five-foot tent, the deafening roar of a river gathering volume and fury as it goes, rare openings, where willows are planted with lucerne in their irrigated shade, among which the traveller camps at night, and over all a sky of pure, intense blue purpling into starry night, were the features of the next three marches, noteworthy chiefly for the exchange of the thundering Dras for the thundering Suru, and for some bad bridges and infamous bits of road before reaching Kargil, where the mountains swing apart, giving space to several villages. Miles of alluvium are under irrigation there, poplars, willows, and apricots abound, and on some damp sward under their shade at a great height I halted for two days to enjoy the magnificence of the scenery and the refreshment of the greenery. These Kargil villages are the capital of the small State of Purik, under the Governorship of Baltistan or Little Tibet, and are chiefly inhabited by Ladakhis who have become converts to Islam. Racial characteristics, dress, and manners are everywhere effaced or toned down by Mohammedanism, and the chilling aloofness and haughty bearing of Islam were very pronounced among these converts.

The daily routine of the journey was as follows: By six a.m. I sent on a coolie carrying the small tent and lunch basket to await me half-way. Before seven I started myself, with Usman Shah in front of me, leaving the servants to follow with the caravan. On reaching the shelter tent I halted for two hours, or till the caravan had got a good start after passing me. At the end of the march I usually found the tent pitched on irrigated ground, near a hamlet, the headman of which provided milk, fuel, fodder, and other necessaries at fixed prices. 'Afternoon tea' was speedily prepared, and dinner, consisting of roast meat and boiled rice, was ready two hours later. After dinner I usually conversed with the headman on local interests, and was in bed soon after eight. The servants and muleteers fed and talked till nine, when the sound of their 'hubble-bubbles' indicated that they were going to sleep, like most Orientals, with their heads closely covered with their wadded quilts. Before starting each morning the account was made out, and I paid the headman personally.

The vagaries of the Afghan soldier, when they were not a cause of annoyance, were a constant amusement, though his ceaseless changes of finery and the daily growth of his baggage awakened grave suspicions. The swashbuckler marched four miles an hour in front of me with a swinging military stride, a large scimitar in a heavily ornamented scabbard over his shoulder. Tanned socks and sandals, black or white leggings wound round from ankle to knee with broad bands of orange or scarlet serge, white cambric knickerbockers, a white cambric shirt, with a short white muslin frock with hanging sleeves and a leather girdle over it, a red-peaked cap with a dark-blue pagri wound round it, with one end hanging over his back, earrings, a necklace, bracelets, and a profusion of rings, were his ordinary costume; and in his girdle he wore a dirk and a revolver, and suspended from it a long tobacco pouch made of the furry skin of some animal, a large leather purse, and etceteras. As the days went on he blossomed into blue and white muslin with a scarlet sash, wore a gold embroidered peak and a huge white muslin turban, with much change of ornaments, and appeared frequently with a great bunch of poppies or a cluster of crimson roses surmounting all. His headgear was colossal. It and the head together must have been fully a third of his total height. He was a most fantastic object, and very observant and skilful in his attentions to me; but if I had known what I after-wards knew, I should have hesitated about taking these long lonely marches with him for my sole attendant. Between Hassan Khan and this Afghan violent hatred and jealousy existed.

I have mentioned roads, and my road as the great caravan route from Western India into Central Asia. This is a fitting time for an explanation. The traveller who aspires to reach the highlands of Tibet from Kashmir cannot be borne along in a carriage or hill-cart. For much of the way he is limited to a foot pace, and if he has regard to his horse he walks down all rugged and steep descents, which are many, and dismounts at most bridges. By 'roads' must be understood bridle-paths, worn by traffic alone across the gravelly valleys, but elsewhere constructed with great toil and expense, as Nature compels, the road-maker to follow her lead, and carry his track along the narrow valleys, ravines, gorges, and chasms which she has marked out for him. For miles at a time this road has been blasted out of precipices from 1,000 feet to 3,000 feet in depth, and is merely a ledge above a raging torrent, the worst parts, chiefly those round rocky projections, being 'scaffolded,' i.e. poles are lodged horizontally among the crevices of the cliff, and the roadway of slabs, planks, and brushwood, or branches and sods, is laid loosely upon them. This track is always amply wide enough for a loaded beast, but in many places, when two caravans meet, the animals of one must give way and scramble up the moun-tain-side, where foothold is often perilous, and always difficult. In passing a caravan near Kargil my servant's horse was pushed over the precipice by a loaded mule and drowned in the Suru, and at another time my Afghan caused the loss of a baggage mule of a Leh caravan by driving it off the track. To scat-ter a caravan so as to allow me to pass in solitary dignity he regarded as one of his functions, and on one occasion, on a very dangerous part of the road, as he was driving heavily laden mules up the steep rocks above, to their im-minent peril and the distraction of their drivers, I was obliged to strike up his sword with my alpenstock to emphasise my abhorrence of his violence. The bridges are unrailed, and many of them are made by placing two or more logs across the stream, laying twigs across, and covering these with sods, but often so scantily that the wild rush of the water is seen below. Primitive as these bridges are, they involve great expense and difficulty in the bringing of long poplar logs for great distances along narrow mountain tracks by coolie labour, fifty men being required for the average log. The Ladakhi roads are admirable

as compared with those of Kashmir, and are being constantly improved under
the supervision of H. B. M.'s Joint Commissioner in Leh.

Up to Kargil the scenery, though growing more Tibetan with every march,
had exhibited at intervals some traces of natural verdure; but beyond, after leaving the Suru, there is not a green thing, and on the next march the road crosses
a lofty, sandy plateau, on which the heat was terrible—blazing gravel and a blazing heaven, then fiery cliffs and scorched hillsides, then a deep ravine and the
large village of Paskim (dominated by a fort-crowned rock), and some planted
and irrigated acres; then a narrow ravine and magnificent scenery flaming with
colour, which opens out after some miles on a burning chaos of rocks and sand,
mountain-girdled, and on some remarkable dwellings on a steep slope, with
religious buildings singularly painted. This is Shergol, the first village of Buddhists, and there I was 'among the Tibetans.'

CHAPTER II

SHERGOL AND LEH

THE CHAOS OF ROCKS AND SAND, walled in by vermilion and orange mountains, on which the village of Shergol stands, offered no facilities for camping; but somehow the men managed to pitch my tent on a steep slope, where I had to place my trestle bed astride an irrigation channel, down which the water bubbled noisily, on its way to keep alive some miserable patches of barley. At Shergol and elsewhere fodder is so scarce that the grain is not cut, but pulled up by the roots.

The intensely human interest of the journey began at that point. Not greater is the contrast between the grassy slopes and deodar-clothed mountains of Kashmir and the flaming aridity of Lesser Tibet, than between the tall, dark, handsome natives of the one, with their statuesque and shrinking women, and the ugly, short, squat, yellow- skinned, flat-nosed, oblique-eyed, uncouth-looking people of the other. The Kashmiris are false, cringing, and suspicious; the Tibetans truthful, independent, and friendly, one of the pleasantest of peoples. I 'took' to them at once at Shergol, and terribly faulty though their morals are in some respects, I found no reason to change my good opinion of them in the succeeding four months.

The headman or go-pa came to see me, introduced me to the objects of interest, which are a gonpo, or monastery, built into the rock, with a brightly coloured front, and three chod-tens, or relic-holders, painted blue, red, and yellow, and daubed with coarse arabesques and representations of deities, one having a striking resemblance to Mr. Gladstone. The houses are of mud, with flat roofs; but, being summer, many of them were roofless, the poplar rods which support the mud having been used for fuel. Conical stacks of the dried excreta of animals, the chief fuel of the country, adorned the roofs, but the general aspect was ruinous and poor. The people all invited me into their dark and dirty rooms, inhabited also by goats, offered tea and cheese, and felt my clothes. They looked the wildest of savages, but they are not. No house was so poor as not to have its 'family altar,' its shelf of wooden gods, and table of offerings. A religious atmosphere pervades Tibet, and gives it a singular sense of novelty. Not only were there chod-tens and a gonpo in this poor place, and family altars, but prayer-wheels, i.e. wooden cylinders filled with rolls of paper inscribed with prayers, revolving on sticks, to be turned by passers-by, inscribed cotton bannerets on poles planted in cairns, and on the roofs long sticks, to which strips of cotton bearing the universal prayer, Aum mani padne hun (O jewel of the lotus-flower), are attached. As these wave in the wind the occupants of the house gain the merit of repeating this sentence.

The remaining marches to Leh, the capital of Lesser Tibet, were full of fascination and novelty. Everywhere the Tibetans were friendly and cordial. In each village I was invited to the headman's house, and taken by him to visit the chief inhabitants; every traveller, lay and clerical, passed by with the cheerful salutation Tzu, asked me where I came from and whither I was going, wished me a good journey, admired Gyalpo, and when he scaled rock ladders and scrambled gamely through difficult torrents, cheered him like English-men, the general jollity and cordiality of manners contrasting cheerily with the chilling aloofness of Moslems.

The irredeemable ugliness of the Tibetans produced a deeper impression daily. It is grotesque, and is heightened, not modified, by their costume and ornament. They have high cheekbones, broad flat noses without visible bridges, small, dark, oblique eyes, with heavy lids and imperceptible eyebrows, wide mouths, full lips, thick, big, projecting ears, deformed by great hoops, straight black hair nearly as coarse as horsehair, and short, square, ungainly figures. The faces of the men are smooth. The women seldom exceed five feet in height, and a man is tall at five feet four.

The male costume is a long, loose, woollen coat with a girdle, trousers, un-der-garments, woollen leggings, and a cap with a turned- up point over each ear. The girdle is the depository of many things dear to a Tibetan—his purse, rude knife, heavy tinder-box, tobacco pouch, pipe, distaff, and sundry charms and amulets. In the capacious breast of his coat he carries wool for spinning—for he spins as he walks—balls of cold barley dough, and much besides. He wears his hair in a pigtail. The women wear short, big-sleeved jackets, shortish, full-plait-ed skirts, tight trousers a yard too long, the superfluous length forming folds above the ankle, a sheepskin with the fur outside hangs over the back, and on gala occasions a sort of drapery is worn over the usual dress. Felt or straw shoes and many heavy ornaments are worn by both sexes. Great ears of brocade, lined and edged with fur and attached to the hair, are worn by the women. Their hair is dressed once a month in many much-greased plaits, fastened together at the back by a long tassel. The head-dress is a strip of cloth or leather, sewn over with large turquoises, carbuncles, and silver ornaments. This hangs in a point over the brow, broadens over the top of the head, and tapers as it reaches the waist behind. The ambition of every Tibetan girl is centred in this singular headgear. Hoops in the ears, necklaces, amulets, clasps, bangles of brass or silver, and various implements stuck in the girdle and depending from it, complete a costume pre- eminent in ugliness. The Tibetans are dirty. They wash once a year, and, except for festivals, seldom change their clothes till they begin to drop off. They are healthy and hardy, even the women can carry weights of sixty pounds over the passes; they attain extreme old age; their voices are harsh and loud, and their laughter is noisy and hearty.

After leaving Shergol the signs of Buddhism were universal and imposing, and the same may be said of the whole of the inhabited part of Lesser Tibet. Colossal figures of Shakya Thubba (Buddha) are carved on faces of rock, or in wood, stone, or gilded copper sit on lotus thrones in endless calm near villages of votaries. Chod-tens from twenty to a hundred feet in height, dedicated to 'holy' men, are scattered over elevated ground, or in imposing avenues line the approaches to hamlets and gonpos. There are also countless manis, dykes of stone from six to sixteen feet in width and from twenty feet to a fourth of a mile in length, roofed with flattish stones, inscribed by the lamas (monks) with the phrase Aum, &c., and purchased and deposited by those who wish to obtain any special benefit from the gods, such as a safe journey. Then there are prayer-mills, sometimes 150 in a row, which revolve easily by being brushed by the hand of the passer-by, larger prayer-cylinders which are turned by pulling ropes, and others larger still by water-power. The finest of the latter was in a temple overarching a perennial torrent, and was said to contain 20,000 repetitions of the mystic phrase, the fee to the worshipper for each revolution of the cylinder being from 1d. to 1s. 4d., according to his means or urgency.

The glory and pride of Ladak and Nubra are the gonpos, of which the illustrations give a slight idea. Their picturesqueness is absolutely enchanting. They are vast irregular piles of fantastic buildings, almost invariably crowning lofty isolated rocks or mountain spurs, reached by steep, rude rock staircases, chod-tens below and battlemented towers above, with temples, domes, bridges over chasms, spires, and scaffolded projections gleaming with gold, looking, as at Lamayuru, the outgrowth of the rock itself. The outer walls are usually whitewashed, and red, yellow, and brown wooden buildings, broad bands of red and blue on the whitewash, tridents, prayer-mills, yaks' tails, and flags on poles give colour and movement, while the jangle of cymbals, the ringing of bells, the incessant beating of big drums and gongs, and the

braying at intervals of six-foot silver horns, attest the ritualistic activities of
the communities within. The gonpos contain from two up to three hundred
lamas. These are not cloistered, and their duties take them freely among the
people, with whom they are closely linked, a younger son in every family being a monk. Every act in trade, agriculture, and social life needs the sanction
of sacerdotalism, whatever exists of wealth is in the gonpos, which also have a
monopoly of learning, and 11,000 monks, linked with the people, yet ruling
all affairs of life and death and beyond death, are connected closely by education, tradition, and authority with Lhassa.

Passing along faces of precipices and over waterless plateaux of blazing red
gravel—'waste places,' truly—the journey was cheered by the meeting of red
and yellow lamas in companies, each lama twirling his prayer-cylinder, abbots,
and skushoks (the latter believed to be incarnations of Buddha) with many re-
tainers, or gay groups of priestly students, intoning in harsh and high-pitched
monotones, Aum mani padne hun. And so past fascinating monastic buildings,
through crystal torrents rushing over red rock, through flaming ravines, on rock
ledges by scaffolded paths, camping in the afternoons near friendly villages on
oases of irrigated alluvium, and down the Wanla water by the steepest and
narrowest cleft ever used for traffic, I reached the Indus, crossed it by a wooden
bridge where its broad, fierce current is narrowed by rocks to a width of six-
ty-five feet, and entered Ladak proper. A picturesque fort guards the bridge, and
there travellers inscribe their names and are reported to Leh. I camped at Khalsi,
a mile higher, but returned to the bridge in the evening to sketch, if I could,
the grim nudity and repulsive horror of the surrounding mountains, attended
only by Usman Shah. A few months earlier, this ruffian was sent down from Leh
with six other soldiers and an officer to guard the fort, where they became the
terror of all who crossed the bridge by their outrageous levies of blackmail. My
swashbuckler quarrelled with the officer over a disreputable affair, and one night
stabbed him mortally, induced his six comrades to plunge their knives into the
body, sewed it up in a blanket, and threw it into the Indus, which disgorged it
a little lower down. The men were all arrested and marched to Srinagar, where
Usman turned 'king's evidence.'

The remaining marches were alongside of the tremendous granite ranges
which divide the Indus from its great tributary, the Shayok. Colossal scenery,
desperate aridity, tremendous solar heat, and an atmosphere highly rarefied and
of nearly intolerable dryness, were the chief characteristics. At these Tibetan
altitudes, where the valleys exceed 11,000 feet, the sun's rays are even more
powerful than on the 'burning plains of India.' The day wind, rising at 9 a.m.,
and only falling near sunset, blows with great heat and force. The solar heat at
noon was from 120 degrees to 130 degrees, and at night the mercury frequently

fell below the freezing point. I did not suffer from the climate, but in the case of most Europeans the air passages become irritated, the skin cracks, and after a time the action of the heart is affected. The hair when released stands out from the head, leather shrivels and splits, horn combs break to pieces, food dries up, rapid evaporation renders water-colour sketching nearly impossible, and tea made with water from fifteen to twenty below the boiling-point of 212 degrees, is flavourless and flat.

After a delightful journey of twenty-five days I camped at Spitak, among the chod-tens and manis which cluster round the base of a lofty and isolated rock, crowned with one of the most striking monasteries in Ladak, and very early the next morning, under a sun of terrific fierceness, rode up a five-mile slope of blazing gravel to the goal of my long march. Even at a short distance off, the Tibetan capital can scarcely be distinguished from the bare, ribbed, scored, jagged, vermilion and rose-red mountains which nearly surround it, were it not for the palace of the former kings or Gyalpos of Ladak, a huge building attaining ten storeys in height, with massive walls sloping inwards, while long balconies and galleries, carved projections of brown wood, and prominent windows, give it a singular picturesqueness. It can be seen for many miles, and dwarfs the little Central Asian town which clusters round its base.

Long lines of chod-tens and manis mark the approach to Leh. Then come barley fields and poplar and willow plantations, bright streams are crossed, and a small gateway, within which is a colony of very poor Baltis, gives access to the city. In consequence of 'the vigilance of the guard at the bridge of Khalsi,' I was expected, and was met at the gate by the wazir's jemadar, or head of police, in artistic attire, with spahis in apricot turbans, violet chogas, and green leggings, who cleared the way with spears, Gyalpo frolicking as merrily and as ready to bite, and the Afghan striding in front as firmly, as though they had not marched for twenty-five days through the rugged passes of the Himalayas. In such wise I was escorted to a shady bungalow of three rooms, in the grounds of H. B. M.'s Joint Commissioner, who lives at Leh during the four months of the 'caravan season,' to assist in regulating the traffic and to guard the interests of the numerous British subjects who pass through Leh with merchandise. For their benefit also, the Indian Government aids in the support of a small hospital, open, however, to all, which, with a largely attended dispensary, is under the charge of a Moravian medical missionary.

Just outside the Commissioner's grounds are two very humble whitewashed dwellings, with small gardens brilliant with European flowers; and in these the two Moravian missionaries, the only permanent European residents in Leh, were living, Mr. Redslob and Dr. Karl Marx, with their wives. Dr. Marx was at his gate to welcome me.

To these two men, especially the former, I owe a debt of gratitude which in no shape, not even by the hearty acknowledgment of it, can ever be repaid, for they died within a few days of each other, of an epidemic, last year, Dr. Marx and a new-born son being buried in one grave. For twenty-five years Mr. Redslob, a man of noble physique and intellect, a scholar and linguist, an expert botanist and an admirable artist, devoted himself to the welfare of the Tibetans, and though his great aim was to Christianize them, he gained their confidence so thoroughly by his virtues, kindness, profound Tibetan scholarship, and manliness, that he was loved and welcomed everywhere, and is now mourned for as the best and truest friend the people ever had.

I had scarcely finished breakfast when he called; a man of great height and strong voice, with a cheery manner, a face beaming with kindness, and speaking excellent English. Leh was the goal of my journey, but Mr. Redslob came with a proposal to escort me over the great passes to the northward for a three weeks' journey to Nubra, a district formed of the combined valleys of the Shayok and Nubra rivers, tributaries of the Indus, and abounding in interest. Of course I at once accepted an offer so full of advantages, and the performance was better even than the promise.

Two days were occupied in making preparations, but afterwards I spent a fortnight in my tent at Leh, a city by no means to be passed over without remark, for, though it and the region of which it is the capital are very remote from the thoughts of most readers, it is one of the centres of Central Asian commerce. There all traders from India, Kashmir, and Afghanistan must halt for animals and supplies on their way to Yarkand and Khotan, and there also merchants from the mysterious city of Lhassa do a great business in brick tea and in Lhassa wares, chiefly ecclesiastical.

The situation of Leh is a grand one, the great Kailas range, with its glaciers and snowfields, rising just behind it to the north, its passes alone reaching an altitude of nearly 18,000 feet; while to the south, across a gravelly descent and the Indus Valley, rise great red ranges dominated by snow-peaks exceeding 21,000 feet in altitude. The centre of Leh is a wide bazaar, where much polo is played in the afternoons; and above this the irregular, flat-roofed, many-balconied houses of the town cluster round the palace and a gigantic chod-ten alongside it. The rugged crest of the rock on a spur of which the palace stands is crowned by the fantastic buildings of an ancient gonpo. Beyond the crops and plantations which surround the town lies a flaming desert of gravel or rock. The architectural features of Leh, except of the palace, are mean. A new mosque glaring with vulgar colour, a treasury and court of justice, the wazir's bungalow, a Moslem cemetery, and Buddhist cremation grounds, in which each family has its separate burning place, are all that is noteworthy. The narrow alleys, which would be abominably dirty if dirt were possible in a climate of such intense dryness, house a very mixed population, in which the Moslem element is always increasing, partly owing to the renewal of that proselytising energy which is making itself felt throughout Asia, and partly to the marriages of Moslem traders with Ladaki women, who embrace the faith of their husbands and bring up their families in the same.

On my arrival few of the shops in the great place, or bazaar, were open, and there was no business; but a few weeks later the little desert capital nearly doubled its population, and during August the din and stir of trade and amusements ceased not by day or night, and the shifting scenes were as gay in colouring and as full of variety as could be desired.

Great caravans en route for Khotan, Yarkand, and even Chinese Tibet arrived daily from Kashmir, the Panjab, and Afghanistan, and stacked their bales of goods in the place; the Lhassa traders opened shops in which the specialties were brick tea and instruments of worship; merchants from Amritsar, Cabul, Bokhara, and Yarkand, stately in costume and gait, thronged the bazaar and opened bales of costly goods in tantalising fashion; mules, asses, horses, and yaks kicked, squealed, and bellowed; the dissonance of bargaining tongues rose high; there were mendicant monks, Indian fakirs, Moslem dervishes, Mecca pilgrims, itinerant musicians, and Buddhist ballad howlers; bold-faced women with creels on their backs brought in lucerne; Ladakis, Baltis, and Lahulis tended the beasts, and the wazir's jemadar and gay spahis moved about among the throngs. In the midst of this picturesque confusion, the short, square-built, Lhassa traders, who face the blazing sun in heavy winter clothing, exchange their expensive tea for Nubra and Baltistan dried apricots, Kashmir saffron, and rich stuffs from India; and merchants from Yarkand on big Turkestan horses offer hemp, which is smoked as opium, and Russian trifles and dress goods, under cloudless skies. With the huge Kailas range as a background, this great rendezvous of Central Asian traffic has a great fascination, even though moral shadows of the darkest kind abound.

On the second morning, while I was taking the sketch of Usman Shah which appears as the frontispiece, he was recognised both by the Joint Commissioner and the chief of police as a mutineer and murderer, and was marched out of Leh. I was asked to look over my baggage, but did not. I had trusted him, he had been faithful in his way, and later I found that nothing was missing. He was a brutal ruffian, one of a band of irregulars sent by the Maharajah of Kashmir to garrison the fort at Leh. From it they used to descend on the town, plunder the bazaar, insult the women, take all they wanted without payment, and when one of their number was being tried for some offence, they dragged the judge out of court and beat him! After holding Leh in terror for some time the British Commissioner obtained their removal. It was, however, at the fort at the Indus bridge, as related before, that the crime of murder was committed. Still there was something almost grand in the defiant attitude of the fantastic swash buckler, as, standing outside the bungalow, he faced the British Commissioner, to him the embodiment of all earthly power, and the chief of police, and defied them. Not an inch would he stir till the wazir gave him a coolie to carry his baggage. He had been acquitted of the murder, he said, 'and though I killed the man, it was according to the custom of my country—he gave me an insult which could only be wiped out in blood!' The guard dared not touch him, and he went to the wazir, demanded a coolie, and got one!

Our party left Leh early on a glorious morning, travelling light, Mr. Redslob, a very learned Lhassa monk, named Gergan, Mr. R.'s servant, my three, and four baggage horses, with two drivers engaged for the journey. The great Kailas range was to be crossed, and the first day's march up long, barren, stony valleys, without interest, took us to a piece of level ground, with a small semi-subterranean refuge on which there was barely room for two tents, at the altitude of the summit of Mont Blanc. For two hours before we reached it the men and animals showed great distress. Gyalpo stopped every few yards, gasping, with blood trickling from his nostrils, and turned his head so as to look at me, with the question in his eyes, What does this mean? Hassan Khan was reeling from vertigo, but would not give in; the seis, a creature without pluck, was carried in a blanket slung on my tent poles, and even the Tibetans suffered. I felt no inconvenience, but as I unsaddled Gyalpo I was glad that there was no more work to do! This 'mountain-sickness,' called by the natives ladug, or 'pass-poison,' is supposed by them to be the result of the odour or pollen of certain plants which grow on the passes. Horses and mules are unable to carry their loads, and men suffer from vertigo, vomiting, violent headache and bleeding from the nose, mouth, and ears, as well as prostration of strength, sometimes complete, and occasionally ending fatally.

After a bitterly cold night I was awakened at dawn by novel sounds, gruntings, and low, resonant bellowing round my tent, and the grey light revealed several yaks (the Bos grunniens, the Tibetan ox), the pride of the Tibetan highlands. This magnificent animal, though not exceeding an English shorthorn cow in height, looks gigantic, with his thick curved horns, his wild eyes glaring from under a mass of curls, his long thick hair hanging to his fetlocks, and his huge bushy tail. He is usually black or tawny, but the tail is often white, and is the length of his long hair. The nose is fine and has a look of breeding as well as power. He only flourishes at altitudes exceeding 12,000 feet. Even after generations of semi-domestication he is very wild, and can only be managed by being led with a rope attached to a ring in the nostrils. He disdains the plough, but condescends to carry burdens, and numbers of the Ladak and Nubra people get their living by carrying goods for the traders on his broad back over the great passes. His legs are very short, and he has a sensible way of measuring distance with his eyes and planting his feet, which enables him to carry loads where it might be supposed that only a goat could climb. He picks up a living anyhow, in that respect resembling the camel.

He has an uncertain temper, and is not favourably disposed towards his rider. Indeed, my experience was that just as one was about to mount him he usually made a lunge at one with his horns. Some of my yak steeds shied, plunged, kicked, executed fantastic movements on the ledges of precipices, knocked down their leaders, bellowed defiance, and rushed madly down mountain sides, leaping from boulder to boulder, till they landed me among their fellows. The rush of a herd of bellowing yaks at a wild gallop, waving their huge tails, is a grand sight.

My first yak was fairly quiet, and looked a noble steed, with my Mexican saddle and gay blanket among rather than upon his thick black locks. His back seemed as broad as that of an elephant, and with his slow, sure, resolute step, he was like a mountain in motion. We took five hours for the ascent of the Digar Pass, our loads and some of us on yaks, some walking, and those who suffered most from the 'pass- poison' and could not sit on yaks were carried. A number of Tibetans went up with us. It was a new thing for a European lady to travel in Nubra, and they took a friendly interest in my getting through all right. The dreary stretches of the ascent, though at first white with edelweiss, of which the people make their tinder, are surmounted for the most part by steep, short zigzags of broken stone. The heavens were dark with snow-showers, the wind was high and the cold severe, and gasping horses, and men prostrate on their faces unable to move, suggested a considerable amount of suffering; but all safely reached the summit, 17,930 feet, where in a snowstorm the guides huzzaed, praised their gods, and tucked rag streamers into a cairn.

The loads were replaced on the horses, and over wastes of ice, across snowfields margined by broad splashes of rose-red primulas, down desert valleys and along irrigated hillsides, we descended 3,700 feet to the village of Digar in Nubra, where under a cloudless sky the mercury stood at 90 degrees!

Upper and Lower Nubra consist of the valleys of the Nubra and Shayok rivers. These are deep, fierce, variable streams, which have buried the lower levels under great stretches of shingle, patched with jungles of hippophae and tamarisk, affording cover for innumerable wolves. Great lateral torrents descend to these rivers, and on alluvial ridges formed at the junctions are the villages with their pleasant surroundings of barley, lucerne, wheat, with poplar and fruit trees, and their picturesque gonpos crowning spurs of rock above them. The first view of Nubra is not beautiful. Yellow, absolutely barren mountains, cleft by yellow gorges, and apparently formed of yellow gravel, the huge rifts in their sides alone showing their substructure of rock, look as if they had never been finished, or had been finished so long that they had returned to chaos. These hem in a valley of grey sand and shingle, threaded by a greyish stream. From the second view point mountains are seen descending on a pleasanter part of the Shayok valley in grey, yellow, or vermilion masses of naked rock, 7,000 and 8,000 feet in height, above which rise snow capped peaks sending out fantastic spurs and buttresses, while the colossal walls of rock are cleft by rifts as colossal. The central ridge between the Nubra and Upper Shayok valleys is 20,000 feet in altitude, and on this are superimposed five peaks of rock, ascertained by survey to be from 24,000 to 25,000 feet in height, while at one point the eye takes in a nearly vertical height of 14,000 feet from the level of the Shayok River! The Shayok and Nubra valleys are only five and four miles in width respectively at their widest parts. The early winter traffic chiefly follows along river beds, then nearly dry, while summer caravans have to labour along difficult tracks at great heights, where mud and snow avalanches are common, to climb dangerous rock ladders, and to cross glaciers and the risky fords of the Shayok. Nubra is similar in character to Ladak, but it is hotter and more fertile, the mountains are loftier, the gonpos are more numerous, and the people are simpler, more religious, and more purely Tibetan. Mr. Redslob loved Nubra, and as love begets love he received a hearty welcome at Digar and everywhere else.

The descent to the Shayok River gave us a most severe day of twelve hours. The river had covered the usual track, and we had to take to torrent beds and precipice ledges, I on one yak, and my tent on another. In years of travel I have never seen such difficulties. Eventually at dusk Mr. Redslob, Gergan, the servants, and I descended on a broad shingle bed by the rushing Shayok; but it was not till dawn on the following day that, by means of our two yaks and the muleteers, our baggage and food arrived, the baggage horses being brought down unloaded, with men holding the head and tail of each. Our saddle horses, which we led with us, were much cut by falls. Gyalpo fell fully twenty feet, and got his side laid open. The baggage horses, according to their owners, had all gone over one precipice, which delayed them five hours.

Below us lay two leaky scows, and eight men from Sati, on the other side of the Shayok, are pledged to the Government to ferry travellers; but no amount of shouting and yelling, or burning of brushwood, or even firing, brought them to the rescue, though their pleasant lights were only a mile off. Snow fell, the wind was strong and keen, and our tent-pegs were only kept down by heavy stones. Blankets in abundance were laid down, yet failed to soften the 'paving stones' on which I slept that night! We had tea and rice, but our men, whose baggage was astray on the mountains, were without food for twenty-two hours, positively refusing to eat our food or cook fresh rice in our cooking pots! To such an extent has Hindu caste-feeling infected Moslems!

The disasters of that day's march, besides various breakages, were, two servants helpless from 'pass-poison' and bruises; a Ladaki, who had rolled over a precipice, with a broken arm, and Gergan bleeding from an ugly scalp wound, also from a fall.

By eight o'clock the next morning the sun was high and brilliant, the snows of the ravines under its fierce heat were melting fast, and the river, roaring hoarsely, was a mad rush of grey rapids and grey foam; but three weeks later in the season, lower down, its many branches are only two feet deep. This Shayok, which cannot in any way be circumvented, is the great obstacle on this Yarkand trade route. Travellers and their goods make the perilous passage in the scow, but their animals swim, and are often paralysed by the ice-cold water and drowned. My Moslem servants, white-lipped and trembling, committed themselves to Allah on the river bank, and the Buddhists worshipped their sleeve idols. The gopa, or headman of Sati, a splendid fellow, who accompanied us through Nubra, and eight wild-looking, half-naked satellites, were the Charons of that Styx. They poled and paddled with yells of excitement; the rapids seized the scow, and carried her broadside down into hissing and raging surges; then there was a plash, a leap of maddened water half filling the boat, a struggle, a whirl, violent efforts, and a united yell, and far down the torrent we were in smooth water on the opposite shore. The ferrymen recrossed, pulled our saddle horses by ropes into the river, the gopa held them; again the scow and her frantic crew, poling, paddling, and yelling, were hurried broadside down, and as they swept past there were glimpses above and among the foam-crested surges of the wild- looking heads and drifting forelocks of two grey horses swimming desperately for their lives,—a splendid sight. They landed safely, but of the baggage animals one was sucked under the boat and drowned, and as the others refused to face the rapids, we had to obtain other transport. A few days later the scow, which was brought up in pieces from Kashmir on coolies' backs at a cost of four hundred rupees, was dashed to pieces!

A halt for Sunday in an apricot grove in the pleasant village of Sati refreshed us all for the long marches which followed, by which we crossed the Sasir Pass, full of difficulties from snow and glaciers, which extend for many miles, to the Dipsang Plain, the bleakest and dreariest of Central Asian wastes, from which the gentle ascent of the Karakorum Pass rises, and returned, varying our route slightly, to the pleasant villages of the Nubra valley. Everywhere Mr. Redslob's Tibetan scholarship, his old-world courtesy, his kindness and adaptability, and his medical skill, ensured us a welcome the heartiness of which I cannot describe. The headmen and elders of the villages came to meet us when we arrived, and escorted us when we left; the monasteries and houses with the best they contained were thrown open to us; the men sat round our camp-fires at night, telling stories and local gossip, and asking questions, everything being translated to me by my kind guide, and so we actually lived 'among the Tibetans.'

CHAPTER III

NUBRA

I N ORDER TO VISIT LOWER NUBRA and return to Leh we were obliged to cross the great fords of the Shayok at the most dangerous season of the year. This transit had been the bugbear of the journey ever since news reached us of the destruction of the Sati scow. Mr. Redslob questioned every man we met on the subject, solemn and noisy conclaves were held upon it round the camp-fires, it was said that the 'European woman' and her 'spider-legged horse' could never get across, and for days before we reached the stream, the chupas, or government water-guides, made nightly reports to the village headmen of the state of the waters, which were steadily rising, the final verdict being that they were only just practicable for strong horses. To delay till the waters fell was impossible. Mr. Redslob had engagements in Leh, and I was already somewhat late for the passage of the lofty passes between Tibet and British India before the winter, so we decided on crossing with every precaution which experience could suggest.

At Lagshung, the evening before, the Tibetans made prayers and offerings for a day cloudy enough to keep the water down, but in the morning from a cloudless sky a scintillating sun blazed down like a magnesium light, and every glacier and snowfield sent its tribute torrent to the Shayok. In crossing a stretch of white sand the solar heat was so fierce that our European skins were blistered through our clothing. We halted at Lagshung, at the house of a friendly zemindar, who pressed upon me the loan of a big Yarkand horse for the ford, a kindness which nearly proved fatal; and then by shingle paths through lacerating thickets of the horrid Hippophae rhamnoides, we reached a chod-ten on the shingly bank of the river, where the Tibetans renewed their prayers and offerings, and the final orders for the crossing were issued. We had twelve horses, carrying only quarter loads each, all led; the servants were mounted, 'water-guides' with ten-foot poles sounded the river ahead, one led Mr. Redslob's horse (the rider being bare-legged) in front of mine with a long rope, and two more led mine, while the gopas of three villages and the zemindar steadied my horse against the stream. The water- guides only wore girdles, and with elf-locks and pig-tails streaming from their heads, and their uncouth yells and wild gesticulations, they looked true river-demons.

The Shayok presented an expanse of eight branches and a main stream, divided by shallows and shingle banks, the whole a mile and a half in width. On the brink the chupas made us all drink good draughts of the turbid river water, 'to prevent giddiness,' they said, and they added that I must not think them rude if they dashed water at my face frequently with the same object. Hassan Khan, and Mando, who was livid with fright, wore dark-green goggles, that they might not see the rapids. In the second branch the water reached the horses' bodies, and my animal tottered and swerved. There were bursts of wild laughter, not merriment but excitement, accompanied by yells as the streams grew fiercer, a loud chorus of Kabadar! Sharbaz! ('Caution!' 'Well done!') was yelled to encourage the horses, and the boom and hiss of the Shayok made a wild accompaniment. Gyalpo, for whose legs of steel I longed, frolicked as usual, making mirthful lunges at his leader when the pair halted. Hassan Khan, in the deepest branch, shakily said to me, 'I not afraid, Mem Sahib.' During the hour spent in crossing the eight branches, I thought that the risk had been exaggerated, and that giddiness was the chief peril.

But when we halted, cold and dripping, on the shingle bank of the main stream I changed my mind. A deep, fierce, swirling rapid, with a calmer depth below its farther bank, and fully a quarter of a mile wide, was yet to be crossed. The business was serious. All the chupas went up and down, sounding, long before they found a possible passage. All loads were raised higher, the men roped their soaked clothing on their shoulders, water was dashed repeatedly at our faces, girths were tightened, and then, with shouts and yells, the whole caravan plunged into deep water, strong, and almost ice-cold. Half an hour was spent in that devious ford, without any apparent progress, for in the dizzy swirl the horses simply seemed treading the water backwards. Louder grew the yells as the torrent raged more hoarsely, the chorus of kabadar grew frantic, the water was up to the men's armpits and the seat of my saddle, my horse tottered and swerved several times, the nearing shore presented an abrupt bank underscooped by the stream. There was a deeper plunge, an encouraging shout, and Mr. Redslob's strong horse leapt the bank. The gopas encouraged mine; he made a desperate effort, but fell short and rolled over backwards into the Shayok with his rider under him. A struggle, a moment of suffocation, and I was extricated by strong arms, to be knocked down again by the rush of the water, to be again dragged up and hauled and hoisted up the crumbling bank. I escaped with a broken rib and some severe bruises, but the horse was drowned. Mr. Redslob, who had thought that my life could not be saved, and the Tibetans were so distressed by the accident that I made very light of it, and only took one day of rest. The following morning some men and animals were carried away, and afterwards the ford was impassable for a fortnight. Such risks are among the amenities of the great trade route from India into Central Asia!

The Lower Nubra valley is wilder and narrower than the Upper, its apricot orchards more luxuriant, its wolf-haunted hippophae and tamarisk thickets more dense. Its villages are always close to ravines, the mouths of which are filled with chod-tens, manis, prayer-wheels, and religious buildings. Access to them is usually up the stony beds of streams over-arched by apricots. The camping-grounds are apricot orchards. The apricot foliage is rich, and the fruit small but delicious. The largest fruit tree I saw measured nine feet six inches in girth six feet from the ground. Strangers are welcome to eat as much of the fruit as they please, provided that they return the stones to the proprietor. It is true that Nubra exports dried apricots, and the women were splitting and drying the fruit on every house roof, but the special raison d'etre of the tree is the clear, white, fragrant, and highly illuminating oil made from the kernels by the simple process of crushing them between two stones. In every gonpo temple a silver bowl holding from four to six gallons is replenished annually with this almond-scented oil for the ever-burning light before the shrine of Buddha. It is used for lamps, and very largely in cookery. Children, instead of being washed, are rubbed daily with it, and on being weaned at the age of four or five, are fed for some time, or rather crammed, with balls of barley-meal made into a paste with it.

At Hundar, a superbly situated village, which we visited twice, we were received at the house of Gergan the monk, who had accompanied us throughout. He is a zemindar, and the large house in which he made us welcome stands in his own patrimony. Everything was prepared for us. The mud floors were swept, cotton quilts were laid down on the balconies, blue cornflowers and marigolds, cultivated for religious ornament, were in all the rooms, and the women were in gala dress and loaded with coarse jewellery. Right hearty was the welcome. Mr. Redslob loved, and therefore was loved. The Tibetans to him were not 'natives,' but brothers. He drew the best out of them. Their superstitions and beliefs were not to him 'rubbish,' but subjects for minute investigation and study. His courtesy to all was frank and dignified. In his dealings he was scrupulously just. He was intensely interested in their interests. His Tibetan scholarship and knowledge of Tibetan sacred literature gave him almost the standing of an abbot among them, and his medical skill and knowledge, joyfully used for their benefit on former occasions, had won their regard. So at Hundar, as everywhere else, the elders came out to meet us and cut the apricot branches away on our road, and the silver horns of the gonpo above brayed a dissonant welcome. Along the Indus valley the servants of Englishmen beat the Tibetans, in the Shayok and Nubra valleys the Yarkand traders beat and cheat them, and the women are shy with strangers, but at Hundar they were frank and friendly with me, saying, as many others had said, 'We will trust any one who comes with the missionary.'

Gergan's home was typical of the dwellings of the richer cultivators and landholders. It was a large, rambling, three-storeyed house, the lower part of stone, the upper of huge sun-dried bricks. It was adorned with projecting windows and brown wooden balconies. Fuel— the dried exereta of animals—is too scarce to be used for any but cooking purposes, and on these balconies in the severe cold of winter the people sit to imbibe the warm sunshine. The rooms were large, ceiled with peeled poplar rods, and floored with split white pebbles set in clay. There was a temple on the roof, and in it, on a platform, were life-size images of Buddha, seated in eternal calm, with his downcast eyes and mild Hindu face, the thousand-armed Chan- ra-zigs (the great Mercy), Jam-pal-yangs (the Wisdom), and Chag-na- dorje (the Justice). In front on a table or altar were seven small lamps, burning apricot oil, and twenty small brass cups, containing minute offerings of rice and other things, changed daily. There were prayer-wheels, cymbals, horns and drums, and a prayer-cylinder six feet high, which it took the strength of two men to turn. On a shelf immediately below the idols were the brazen sceptre, bell, and thunderbolt, a brass lotus blossom, and the spouted brass flagon decorated with peacocks' feathers, which is used at baptisms, and for pouring holy water upon the hands at festivals. In houses in which there is not a roof temple the best room is set apart for religious use and for these divinities, which are always surrounded with musical instruments and symbols of power, and receive worship and offerings daily, Tibetan Buddhism being a religion of the family and household. In his family temple Gergan offered gifts and thanks for the deliverances of the journey. He had been assisting Mr. Redslob for two years in the translation of the New Testament, and had wept over the love and sufferings of our Lord Jesus Christ. He had even desired that his son should receive baptism and be brought up as a Christian, but for himself he 'could not break with custom and his ancestral creed.'

In the usual living-room of the family a platform, raised only a few inches, ran partly round the wall. In the middle of the floor there was a clay fireplace, with a prayer-wheel and some clay and brass cooking pots upon it. A few shelves, fire-bars for roasting barley, a wooden churn, and some spinning arrangements were the furniture. A number of small dark rooms used for sleeping and storage opened from this, and above were the balconies and reception rooms. Wooden posts supported the roofs, and these were wreathed with lucerne, the firstfruits of the field. Narrow, steep staircases in all Tibetan houses lead to the family rooms. In winter the people live below, alongside of the animals and fodder. In summer they sleep in loosely built booths of poplar branches on the roof. Gergan's roof was covered, like others at the time, to the depth of two feet, with hay, i.e. grass and lucerne, which are wound into long ropes, experience having taught the Tibetans that their scarce fodder is best preserved thus from breakage and waste. I bought hay by the yard for Gyalpo.

Our food in this hospitable house was simple: apricots, fresh, or dried and stewed with honey; zho's milk, curds and cheese, sour cream, peas, beans, balls of barley dough, barley porridge, and 'broth of abominable things.' Chang, a dirty-looking beer made from barley, was offered with each meal, and tea frequently, but I took my own 'on the sly.' I have mentioned a churn as part of the 'plenishings' of the living-room. In Tibet the churn is used for making tea! I give the recipe. 'For six persons. Boil a teacupful of tea in three pints of water for ten minutes with a heaped dessert- spoonful of soda. Put the infusion into the churn with one pound of butter and a small tablespoonful of salt. Churn until as thick as cream.' Tea made after this fashion holds the second place to chang in Tibetan affections. The butter according to our thinking is always rancid, the mode of making it is uncleanly, and it always has a rank flavour from the goatskin in which it was kept. Its value is enhanced by age. I saw skins of it forty, fifty, and even sixty years old, which were very highly prized, and would only be opened at some special family festival or funeral.

During the three days of our visits to Hundar both men and women wore their festival dresses, and apparently abandoned most of their ordinary occupations in our honour. The men were very anxious that I should be 'amused,' and made many grotesque suggestions on the subject. 'Why is the European woman always writing or sewing?' they asked. 'Is she very poor, or has she made a vow?' Visits to some of the neighbouring monasteries were eventually proposed, and turned out most interesting.

The monastery of Deskyid, to which we made a three days' expedition, is from its size and picturesque situation the most imposing in Nubra. Built on a majestic spur of rock rising on one side 2,000 feet perpendicularly from a torrent, the spur itself having an altitude of 11,000 feet, with red peaks, snow-capped, rising to a height of over 20,000 feet behind the vast irregular pile of red, white, and yellow temples, towers, storehouses, cloisters, galleries, and balconies, rising for 300 feet one above another, hanging over chasms, built out on wooden buttresses, and surmounted with flags, tridents, and yaks' tails, a central tower or keep dominating the whole, it is perhaps the most picturesque object I have ever seen, well worth the crossing of the Shayok fords, my painful accident, and much besides. It looks inaccessible, but in fact can be attained by rude zigzags of a thousand steps of rock, some natural, others roughly hewn,

getting worse and worse as they rise higher, till the later zigzags suggest the difficulties of the ascent of the Great Pyramid. The day was fearfully hot, 99 degrees
in the shade, and the naked, shining surfaces of purple rock with a metallic lus-
tre radiated heat. My 'gallant grey' took me up half-way—a great feat— and the
Tibetans cheered and shouted 'Sharbaz!' ('Well done!') as he pluckily leapt up
the great slippery rock ledges. After I dismounted, any number of willing hands
hauled and helped me up the remaining horrible ascent, the rugged rudeness
of which is quite indescribable. The inner entrance is a gateway decorated with
a yak's head and many Buddhist emblems. High above, on a rude gallery, fifty
monks were gathered with their musical instruments. As soon as the Kan-po or
abbot, Punt-sog-sogman (the most perfect Merit), received us at the gate, the
monkish orchestra broke forth in a tornado of sound of a most tremendous
and thrilling quality, which was all but overwhelming, as the mountain echoes
took up and prolonged the sound of fearful blasts on six-foot silver horns, the
bellowing thunder of six-foot drums, the clash of cymbals, and the dissonance
of a number of monster gongs. It was not music, but it was sublime. The blasts
on the horns are to welcome a great personage, and such to the monks who
despised his teaching was the devout and learned German missionary. Mr. Redslob explained that I had seen much of Buddhism in Ceylon and Japan, and
wished to see their temples. So with our train of gopas, zemindar, peasants, and
muleteers, we mounted to a corridor full of lamas in ragged red dresses, yellow
girdles and yellow caps, where we were presented with plates of apricots, and
the door of the lowest of the seven temples heavily grated backwards.

   The first view, and indeed the whole view of this temple of Wrath or Justice, was suggestive of a frightful Inferno, with its rows of demon gods, hideous beyond Western conception, engaged in torturing writhing and bleeding
specimens of humanity. Demon masks of ancient lacquer hung from the pillars, naked swords gleamed in motionless hands, and in a deep recess whose
'darkness' was rendered 'visible' by one lamp, was that indescribable horror the
executioner of the Lord of Hell, his many brandished arms holding instruments
of torture, and before him the bell, the thunderbolt and sceptre, the holy water,
and the baptismal flagon. Our joss-sticks fumed on the still air, monks waved
censers, and blasts of dissonant music woke the semi-subterranean echoes. In
this temple of Justice the younger lamas spend some hours daily in the supposed
contemplation of the torments reserved for the unholy. In the highest temple,
that of Peace, the summer sunshine fell on Shakya Thubba and the Buddhist
triad seated in endless serenity. The walls were covered with frescoes of great
lamas, and a series of alcoves, each with an image representing an incarnation of
Buddha, ran round the temple. In a chapel full of monstrous images and piles
of medallions made of the ashes of 'holy' men, the sub-abbot was discoursing to

the acolytes on the religious classics. In the chapel of meditations, among lighted incense sticks, monks seated before images were telling their beads with the object of working themselves into a state of ecstatic contemplation (somewhat resembling a certain hypnotic trance), for there are undoubtedly devout lamas, though the majority are idle and unholy. It must be understood that all Tibetan literature is 'sacred,' though some of the volumes of exquisite calligraphy on parchment, which for our benefit were divested of their silken and brocaded wrappings, contain nothing better than fairy tales and stories of doubtful morality, which are recited by the lamas to the accompaniment of incessant cups of chang, as a religious duty when they visit their 'flocks' in the winter.

The Deskyid gonpo contains 150 lamas, all of whom have been educated at Lhassa. A younger son in every household becomes a monk, and occasionally enters upon his vocation as an acolyte pupil as soon as weaned. At the age of thirteen these acolytes are sent to study at Lhassa for five or seven years, their departure being made the occasion of a great village feast, with several days of religious observances. The close connection with Lhassa, especially in the case of the yellow lamas, gives Nubra Buddhism a singular interest. All the larger gonpos have their prototype in Lhassa, all ceremonial has originated in Lhassa, every instrument of worship has been consecrated in Lhassa, and every lama is educated in the learning only to be obtained at Lhassa. Buddhism is indeed the most salient feature of Nubra. There are gonpos everywhere, the roads are lined by miles of chod-tens, manis, and prayer-mills, and flags inscribed with sacred words in Sanskrit flutter from every roof. There are processions of red and yellow lamas; every act in trade, agriculture, and social life needs the sanction of sacerdotalism; whatever exists of wealth is in the gonpos, which also have a monopoly of learning, and 11,000 monks closely linked with the laity, yet ruling all affairs of life and death and beyond death, are all connected by education, tradition, and authority with Lhassa.

We remained long on the blazing roof of the highest tower of the gonpo, while good Mr. Redslob disputed with the abbot 'concerning the things pertaining to the kingdom of God.' The monks standing round laughed sneeringly. They had shown a little interest, Mr. R. said, on his earlier visits. The abbot accepted a copy of the Gospel of St. John. 'St. Matthew,' he observed, 'is very laughable reading.' Blasts of wild music and the braying of colossal horns honoured our departure, and our difficult descent to the apricot groves of Deskyid. On our return to Hundar the grain was ripe on Gergan's fields. The first ripe ears were cut off, offered to the family divinity, and were then bound to the pillars of the house. In the comparatively fertile Nubra valley the wheat and barley are cut, not rooted up. While they cut the grain the men chant, 'May it increase, We will give to the poor, we will give to the lamas,' with every stroke.

They believe that it can be made to multiply both under the sickle and in the threshing, and perform many religious rites for its increase while it is in sheaves. After eight days the corn is trodden out by oxen on a threshing-floor renewed every year. After winnowing with wooden forks, they make the grain into a pyramid, insert a sacred symbol, and pile upon it the threshing instruments and sacks, erecting an axe on the apex with its blade turned to the west, as that is the quarter from which demons are supposed to come. In the afternoon they feast round it, always giving a portion to the axe, saying, 'It is yours, it belongs not to me.' At dusk they pour it into the sacks again, chanting, 'May it increase.' But these are not removed to the granary until late at night, at an hour when the hands of the demons are too much benumbed by the nightly frost to diminish the store. At the beginning of every one of these operations the presence of lamas is essential, to announce the auspicious moment, and conduct religious ceremonies. They receive fees, and are regaled with abundant chang and the fat of the land.

In Hundar, as elsewhere, we were made very welcome in all the houses. I have described the dwelling of Gergan. The poorer peasants occupy similar houses, but roughly built, and only two-storeyed, and the floors are merely clay. In them also the very numerous lower rooms are used for cattle and fodder only, while the upper part consists of an inner or winter room, an outer or supper room, a verandah room, and a family temple. Among their rude plenishings are large stone corn chests like sarcophagi, stone bowls from Baltistan, cauldrons, cooking pots, a tripod, wooden bowls, spoons, and dishes, earthen pots, and yaks' and sheep's packsaddles. The garments of the household are kept in long wooden boxes.

Family life presents some curious features. In the disposal in marriage of a girl, her eldest brother has more 'say' than the parents. The eldest son brings home the bride to his father's house, but at a given age the old people are 'shelved,' i.e. they retire to a small house, which may be termed a 'jointure house,' and the eldest son assumes the patrimony and the rule of affairs. I have not met with a similar custom anywhere in the East. It is difficult to speak of Tibetan life, with all its affection and jollity, as 'family life,' for Buddhism, which enjoins monastic life, and usually celibacy along with it, on eleven thousand out of a total population of a hundred and twenty thousand, farther restrains the increase of population within the limits of sustenance by inculcating and rigidly upholding the system of polyandry, permitting marriage only to the eldest son, the heir of the land, while the bride accepts all his brothers as inferior or subordinate husbands, thus attaching the whole family to the soil and family roof-tree, the children being regarded legally as the property of the eldest son, who is addressed by them as 'Big Father,' his brothers receiving the title of 'Little

Father.' The resolute determination, on economic as well as religious grounds, not to abandon this ancient custom, is the most formidable obstacle in the way of the reception of Christianity by the Tibetans. The women cling to it. They say, 'We have three or four men to help us instead of one,' and sneer at the dulness and monotony of European monogamous life! A woman said to me, 'If I had only one husband, and he died, I should be a widow; if I have two or three I am never a widow!' The word 'widow' is with them a term of reproach, and is applied abusively to animals and men. Children are brought up to be very obedient to fathers and mother, and to take great care of little ones and cattle. Parental affection is strong. Husbands and wives beat each other, but separation usually follows a violent outbreak of this kind. It is the custom for the men and women of a village to assemble when a bride enters the house of her husbands, each of them presenting her with three rupees. The Tibetan wife, far from spending these gifts on personal adornment, looks ahead, contemplating possible contingencies, and immediately hires a field, the produce of which is her own, and which accumulates year after year in a separate granary, so that she may not be portionless in case she leaves her husband!

It was impossible not to become attached to the Nubra people, we lived so completely among them, and met with such unbounded goodwill. Feasts were given in our honour, every gonpo was open to us, monkish blasts on colossal horns brayed out welcomes, and while nothing could exceed the helpfulness and alacrity of kindness shown by all, there was not a thought or suggestion of backsheesh. The men of the villages always sat by our camp-fires at night, friendly and jolly, but never obtrusive, telling stories, discussing local news and the oppressions exercised by the Kashmiri officials, the designs of Russia, the advance of the Central Asian Railway, and what they consider as the weakness of the Indian Government in not annexing the provinces of the northern frontier. Many of their ideas and feelings are akin to ours, and a mutual understanding is not only possible, but inevitable. {1}

Industry in Nubra is the condition of existence, and both sexes work hard enough to give a great zest to the holidays on religious festival days. Whether in the house or journeying the men are never seen without the distaff. They weave also, and make the clothes of the women and children! The people are all cultivators, and make money also by undertaking the transit of the goods of the Yarkand traders over the lofty passes. The men plough with the zho, or hybrid yak, and the women break the clods and share in all other agricultural operations. The soil, destitute of manure, which is dried and hoarded for fuel, rarely produces more than tenfold. The 'three acres and a cow' is with them four acres of alluvial soil to a family on an average, with 'runs' for yaks and sheep on the mountains. The farms, planted with apricot and other fruit trees, a prolific

loose-grained barley, wheat, peas, and lucerne, are oases in the surrounding deserts. The people export apricot oil, dried apricots, sheep's wool, heavy undyed
woollens, a coarse cloth made from yaks' hair, and pashm, the under fleece of
the shawl goat. They complained, and I think with good reason, of the merciless
exactions of the Kashmiri officials, but there were no evidences of severe poverty, and not one beggar was seen.

It was not an easy matter to get back to Leh. The rise of the Shayok made it
impossible to reach and return by the Digar Pass, and the alternative route over
the Kharzong glacier continued for some time impracticable—that is, it was
perfectly smooth ice. At length the news came that a fall of snow had rough-
ened its surface. A number of men worked for two days at scaffolding a path,
and with great difficulty, and the loss of one yak from a falling rock, a fruitful
source of fatalities in Tibet, we reached Khalsar, where with great regret we
parted with Tse-ring-don-drub (Life's purpose fulfilled), the gopa of Sati, whose
friendship had been a real pleasure, and to whose courage and promptitude,
in Mr. Redslob's opinion, I owed my rescue from drowning. Two days of very
severe marching and long and steep ascents brought us to the wretched hamlet
of Kharzong Lar-sa, in a snowstorm, at an altitude higher than the summit
of Mont Blanc. The servants were all ill of 'pass-poison,' and crept into a cave
along with a number of big Tibetan mastiffs, where they enjoyed the comfort of
semi-suffocation till the next morning, Mr. R. and I, with some willing Tibetan
helpers, pitching our own tents. The wind was strong and keen, and with the
mercury down at 15 degrees Fahrenheit it was impossible to do anything but
to go to bed in the early afternoon, and stay there till the next day. Mr. Redslob
took a severe chill, which produced an alarming attack of pleurisy, from the
effects of which he never fully recovered.

We started on a grim snowy morning, with six yaks carrying our baggage
or ridden by ourselves, four led horses, and a number of Tibetans, several more
having been sent on in advance to cut steps in the glacier and roughen them
with gravel. Within certain limits the ground grows greener as one ascends,
and we passed upwards among primulas, asters, a large blue myosotis, gentians,
potentillas, and great sheets of edelweiss. At the glacier foot we skirted a deep
green lake on snow with a glorious view of the Kharzong glacier and the pass, a
nearly perpendicular wall of rock, bearing up a steep glacier and a snowfield of
great width and depth, above which tower pinnacles of naked rock. It presented
to all appearance an impassable barrier rising 2,500 feet above the lake, grand
and awful in the dazzling whiteness of the new-fallen snow. Thanks to the ice
steps our yaks took us over in four hours without a false step, and from the
summit, a sharp ridge 17,500 feet in altitude, we looked our last on grimness,
blackness, and snow, and southward for many a weary mile to the Indus valley

lying in sunshine and summer. Fully two dozen caresses of horses newly dead lay in cavities of the glacier. Our animals were ill of 'pass-poison,' and nearly blind, and I was obliged to ride my yak into Leh, a severe march of thirteen hours, down miles of crumbling zigzags, and then among villages of irrigated terraces, till the grand view of the Gyalpo's palace, with its air- hung gonpo and clustering chod-tens, and of the desert city itself, burst suddenly upon us, and our benumbed and stiffened limbs thawed in the hot sunshine. I pitched my tent in a poplar grove for a fortnight, near the Moravian compounds and close to the travellers' bungalow, in which is a British Postal Agency, with a Tibetan postmaster who speaks English, a Christian, much trusted and respected, named Joldan, in whose intelligence, kindness, and friendship I found both interest and pleasure.

CHAPTER IV

MANNERS AND CUSTOMS

JOLDAN, THE TIBETAN BRITISH POSTMASTER in Leh, is a Christian of spotless reputation. Every one places unlimited confidence in his integrity and truthfulness, and his religious sincerity has been attested by many sacrifices. He is a Ladaki, and the family property was at Stok, a few miles from Leh. He was baptized in Lahul at twenty-three, his father having been a Christian. He learned Urdu, and was for ten years mission schoolmaster in Kylang, but returned to Leh a few years ago as postmaster. His 'ancestral dwelling' at Stok was destroyed by order of the wazir, and his property confiscated, after many unsuccessful efforts had been made to win him back to Buddhism. Afterwards he was detained by the wazir, and compelled to serve as a sepoy, till Mr. Heyde went to the council and obtained his release. His house in Leh has been more than once burned by incendiaries. But he pursues a quiet, even course, brings up his family after the best Christian traditions, refuses Buddhist suitors for his daughters, unobtrusively but capably helps the Moravian missionaries, supports his family by steady industry, although of noble birth, and asks nothing of any one. His 'good morning' and 'good night,' as he daily passed my tent with clockwork regularity, were full of cheery friendliness; he gave much useful information about Tibetan customs, and his ready helpfulness greatly facilitated the difficult arrangements for my farther journey.

The Leh, which I had left so dull and quiet, was full of strangers, traffic, and noise. The neat little Moravian church was filled by a motley crowd each Sunday, in which the few Christians were distinguishable by their clean faces and clothes and their devout air; and the Medical Mission Hospital and Dispensary, which in winter have an average attendance of only a hundred patients a month, were daily thronged with natives of India and Kashmir, Baltis, Yarkandis, Dards, and Tibetans. In my visits with Dr. Marx I observed, what was confirmed by four months' experience of the Tibetan villagers, that rheumatism, inflamed eyes and eyelids, and old age are the chief Tibetan maladies. Some of the Dards and Baltis were lepers, and the natives of India brought malarial fever, dysentery, and other serious diseases. The hospital, which is supported by the Indian Government, is most comfortable, a haven of rest for those who fall sick by the way. The hospital assistants are intelligent, thoroughly kind- hearted young Tibetans, who, by dint of careful drilling and an affectionate desire to please 'the teacher with the medicine box,' have become fairly trustworthy. They are not Christians.

In the neat dispensary at 9 a.m. a gong summons the patients to the operating room for a short religious service. Usually about fifty were present, and a number more, who had some curiosity about 'the way,' but did not care to be seen at Christian worship, hung about the doorways. Dr. Marx read a few verses from the Gospels, explaining them in a homely manner, and concluded with the Lord's Prayer. Then the out-patients were carefully and gently treated, leprous limbs were bathed and anointed, the wards were visited at noon and again at sunset, and in the afternoons operations were performed with the most careful antiseptic precautions, which are supposed to be used for the purpose of keeping away evil spirits from the wounds! The Tibetans, in practice, are very simple in their applications of medical remedies. Rubbing with butter is their great panacea. They have a dread of small-pox, and instead of burning its victims they throw them into their rapid torrents. If an isolated case occur, the sufferer is carried to a mountain-top, where he is left to recover or die. If a small-pox epidemic is in the province, the people of the villages in which it has not yet appeared place thorns on their bridges and boundaries, to scare away the evil spirits which are supposed to carry the disease. In ordinary illnesses, if butter taken internally as well as rubbed into the skin does not cure the patient, the lamas are summoned to the rescue. They make a mitsap, a half life-size figure of the sick person, dress it in his or her clothes and ornaments, and place it in the courtyard, where they sit round it, reading passages from the sacred classics fitted for the occasion. After a time, all rise except the superior lama, who continues reading, and taking small drums in their left hands, they recite incantations, and dance wildly round the mitsap, believing, or at least leading the people to believe, that by this ceremony the malady, supposed to be the work of a demon, will be transferred to the image. Afterwards the clothes and ornaments are presented to them, and the figure is carried in procession out of the yard and village and is burned. If the patient becomes worse, the friends are apt to resort to the medical skill of the missionaries. If he dies they are blamed, and if he recovers the lamas take the credit.

At some little distance outside Leh are the cremation grounds—desert places, destitute of any other vegetation than the Caprifolia horrida. Each family

has its furnace kept in good repair. The place is doleful, and a funeral scene on
the only sunless day I experienced in Ladak was indescribably dismal. After
death no one touches the corpse but the lamas, who assemble in numbers in
the case of a rich man. The senior lama offers the first prayers, and lifts the lock
which all Tibetans wear at the back of the head, in order to liberate the soul if it
is still clinging to the body. At the same time he touches the region of the heart
with a dagger. The people believe that a drop of blood on the head marks the
spot where the soul has made its exit. Any good clothing in which the person
has died is then removed. The blacksmith beats a drum, and the corpse, covered
with a white sheet next the dress and a coloured one above, is carried out of the
house to be worshipped by the relatives, who walk seven times round it. The
women then retire to the house, and the chief lama recites liturgical passages
from the formularies. Afterwards, the relatives retire, and the corpse is carried
to the burning-ground by men who have the same tutelar deity as the deceased.
The leading lama walks first, then come men with flags, followed by the blacksmith with the drum, and next the corpse, with another man beating a drum
behind it. Meanwhile, the lamas are praying for the repose and quieting of the
soul, which is hovering about, desiring to return. The attendant friends, each
of whom has carried a piece of wood to the burning-ground, arrange the fuel
with butter on the furnace, the corpse wrapped in the white sheet is put in,
and fire is applied. The process of destruction in a rich man's case takes about
an hour. During the burning the lamas read in high, hoarse monotones, and
the blacksmiths beat their drums. The lamas depart first, and the blacksmiths,
after worshipping the ashes, shout, 'Have nothing to do with us now,' and run
rapidly away. At dawn the following day, a man whose business it is searches
among the ashes for the footprints of animals, and according to the footprints
found, so it is believed will be the re-birth of the soul.

Some of the ashes are taken to the gonpos, where the lamas mix them with
clay, put them into oval or circular moulds, and stamp them with the image
of Buddha. These are preserved in chod-tens, and in the house of the nearest
relative of the deceased; but in the case of 'holy' men, they are retained in the
gonpos, where they can be purchased by the devout. After a cremation much
chang is consumed by the friends, who make presents to the bereaved family.
The value of each is carefully entered in a book, so that a precise return may
be made when a similar occasion occurs. Until the fourth day after death it is
believed to be impossible to quiet the soul. On that day a piece of paper is inscribed with prayers and requests to the soul to be quiet, and this is burned by
the lamas with suitable ceremonies; and rites of a more or less elaborate kind are
afterwards performed for the repose of the soul, accompanied with prayers that
it may get 'a good path' for its re-birth, and food is placed in conspicuous places

about the house, that it may understand that its relatives are willing to support it. The mourners for some time wear wretched clothes, and neither dress their hair nor wash their faces. Every year the lamas sell by auction the clothing and ornaments, which are their perquisites at funerals. {2}

The Moravian missionaries have opened a school in Leh, and the wazir, finding that the Leh people are the worst educated in the country, ordered that one child at least in each family should be sent to it. This awakened grave suspicions, and the people hunted for reasons for it. 'The boys are to be trained as porters, and made to carry burdens over the mountains,' said some. 'Nay,' said others, 'they are to be sent to England and made Christians of.' [All foreigners, no matter what their nationality is, are supposed to be English.] Others again said, 'They are to be kidnapped,' and so the decree was ignored, till Mr. Redslob and Dr. Marx went among the parents and explained matters, and a large attendance was the result; for the Tibetans of the trade route have come to look upon the acquisition of 'foreign learning' as the stepping-stone to Government appointments at ten rupees per month. Attendance on religious instruction was left optional, but after a time sixty pupils were regularly present at the daily reading and explanation of the Gospels. Tibetan fathers teach their sons to write, to read the sacred classics, and to calculate with a frame of balls on wires. If farther instruction is thought desirable, the boys are sent to the lamas, and even to the schools at Lhassa. The Tibetans willingly receive and read translations of our Christian books, and some go so far as to think that their teachings are 'stronger' than those of their own, indicating their opinions by tearing pages out of the Gospels and rolling them up into pills, which are swallowed in the belief that they are an effective charm. Sorcery is largely used in the treatment of the sick. The books which instruct in the black art are known as 'black books.' Those which treat of medicine are termed 'blue books.' Medical knowledge is handed down from father to son. The doctors know the virtues of in any of the plants of the country, quantities of which they mix up together while reciting magical formulas.

I was heartily sorry to leave Leh, with its dazzling skies and abounding colour and movement, its stirring topics of talk, and the culture and exceeding kindness of the Moravian missionaries. Helpfulness was the rule. Gergan came over the Kharzong glacier on purpose to bring me a prayer-wheel; Lob-sang and Tse-ring-don-drub, the hospital assistants, made me a tent carpet of yak's hair cloth, singing as they sewed; and Joldan helped to secure transport for the twenty-two days' journey to Kylang. Leh has few of what Europeans regard as travelling necessaries. The brick tea which I purchased from a Lhassa trader was disgusting. I afterwards understood that blood is used in making up the blocks. The flour was gritty, and a leg of mutton turned out to be a limb of a goat of much experience. There were no straps, or leather to make them of, in the bazaar, and no buckles; and when the latter were provided by Mr. Redslob, the old man who came to sew them upon a warm rug which I had made for Gyalpo out of pieces of carpet and hair-cloth put them on wrongly three times, saying after each failure, 'I'm very foolish. Foreign ways are so wonderful!' At times the Tibetans say, 'We're as stupid as oxen,' and I was inclined to think so, as I stood for two hours instructing the blacksmith about making shoes for Gyalpo, which kept turning out either too small for a mule or too big for a dray-horse.

I obtained two Lahul muleteers with four horses, quiet, obliging men, and two superb yaks, which were loaded with twelve days' hay and barley for my horse. Provisions for the whole party for the same time had to be carried, for the route is over an uninhabited and arid desert. Not the least important part of my outfit was a letter from Mr. Redslob to the headman or chief of the Chang-pas or Champas, the nomadic tribes of Rupchu, to whose encampment I purposed to make a detour. These nomads had on two occasions borrowed money from the Moravian missionaries for the payment of the Kashmiri tribute, and had repaid it before it was due, showing much gratitude for the loans.

Dr. Marx accompanied me for the three first days. The few native Christians in Leh assembled in the gay garden plot of the lowly mission-house to shake hands and wish me a good journey, and not a few who were not Christians, some of them walking for the first hour beside our horses. The road from Leh descends to a rude wooden bridge over the Indus, a mighty stream even there, over blazing slopes of gravel dignified by colossal manis and chod-tens in long lines, built by the former kings of Ladak. On the other side of the river gravel slopes ascend towards red mountains 20,000 feet in height. Then comes a rocky spur crowned by the imposing castle of the Gyalpo, the son of the dethroned king of Ladak, surmounted by a forest of poles from which flutter yaks' tails and long streamers inscribed with prayers. Others bear aloft the trident, the emblem of Siva. Carefully hewn zigzags, entered through a much-decorated and colossal chod-ten, lead to the castle. The village of Stok, the prettiest and most prosperous in Ladak, fills up the mouth of a gorge with its large farm-houses among poplar, apricot, and willow plantations, and irrigated terraces of barley; and is imposing as well as pretty, for the two roads by which it is approached are avenues of lofty chod-tens and broad manis, all in excellent repair. Knolls, and deeply coloured spurs of naked rock, most picturesquely crowded with chod-tens, rise above the greenery, breaking the purple gloom of the gorge which cuts deeply into the mountains, and supplies from its rushing glacier torrent the living waters which create this delightful oasis.

The gopa came forth to meet us, bearing apricots and cheeses as the Gyalpo's greeting, and conducted us to the camping-ground, a sloping lawn in a willow-wood, with many a natural bower of the graceful Clematis orientalis. The tents were pitched, afternoon tea was on a table outside, a clear, swift stream made fitting music, the dissonance of the ceaseless beating of gongs and drums in the castle temple was softened by distance, the air was cool, a lemon light bathed the foreground, and to the north, across the Indus, the great mountains of the Leh range, with every cleft defined in purple or blue, lifted their vermilion peaks into a rosy sky. It was the poetry and luxury of travel.

At Leh I was obliged to dismiss the seis for prolonged misconduct and cruelty to Gyalpo, and Mando undertook to take care of him. The animal had always been held by two men while the seis groomed him with difficulty, but at Stok, when Mando rubbed him down, he quietly went on feeding and laid his lovely head on the lad's shoulder with a soft cooing sound. From that moment Mando could do anything with him, and a singular attachment grew up between man and horse.

Towards sunset we were received by the Gyalpo. The castle loses nothing of its picturesqueness on a nearer view, and everything about it is trim and in good order, it is a substantial mass of stone building on a lofty rock, the irregularities of which have been taken most artistic advantage of in order to give picturesque irregularity to the edifice, which, while six storeys high in some places, is only three in others. As in the palace of Leh, the walls slope inwards from the base, where they are ten feet thick, and projecting balconies of brown wood and grey stone relieve their monotony. We were received at the entrance by a number of red lamas, who took us up five flights of rude stairs to the reception room, where we were introduced to the Gyalpo, who was in the midst of a crowd of monks, and, except that his hair was not shorn, and that he wore a silver brocade cap and large gold earrings and bracelets, was dressed in red like them. Throneless and childless, the Gyalpo has given himself up to religion. He has covered the castle roof with Buddhist emblems (not represented in the sketch). From a pole, forty feet long, on the terrace floats a broad streamer of equal length, completely covered with Aum mani padne hun, and he has surrounded himself with lamas, who conduct nearly ceaseless services in the sanctuary. The attainment of merit, as his creed leads him to understand it, is his one aim in life. He loves the seclusion of Stok, and rarely visits the palace in Leh, except at the time of the winter games, when the whole population assembles in cheery, orderly crowds, to witness races, polo and archery matches, and a species of hockey. He interests himself in the prosperity of Stok, plants poplars, willows, and fruit trees, and keeps the castle maims and chod-tens in admirable repair.

Stok Castle is as massive as any of our mediaeval buildings, but is far lighter and roomier. It is most interesting to see a style of architecture and civilisation which bears not a solitary trace of European influence, not even in Manchester cottons or Russian gimcracks. The Gyalpo's room was only roofed for six feet within the walls, where it was supported by red pillars. Above, the deep blue Tibetan sky was flushing with the red of sunset, and from a noble window with a covered stone balcony there was an enchanting prospect of red ranges passing into translucent amethyst. The partial ceiling is painted in arabesques, and at one end of the room is an alcove, much enriched with bold wood carving.

The Gyalpo was seated on a carpet on the floor, a smooth-faced, rather stupid-looking man of twenty-eight. He placed us on a carpet beside him, and coffee, honey, and apricots were brought in, but the conversation flagged. He neither suggested anything nor took up Dr. Marx's suggestions. Fortunately, we had brought our sketch-books, and the views of several places were recognised, and were found interesting. The lamas and servants, who had remained respectfully standing, sat down on the floor, and even the Gyalpo became animated. So our visit ended successfully.

There is a doorway from the reception room into the sanctuary, and after a time fully thirty lamas passed in and began service, but the Gyalpo only stood on his carpet. There is only a half light in this temple, which is further obscured by scores of smoked and dusty bannerets of gold and silver brocade hanging from the roof. In addition to the usual Buddhist emblems there are musical instruments, exquisitely inlaid, or enriched with niello work of gold and silver of great antiquity, and bows of singular strength, requiring two men to bend them, which are made of small pieces of horn cleverly joined. Lamas gabbled liturgies at railroad speed, beating drums and clashing cymbals as an accompaniment, while others blew occasional blasts on the colossal silver horns or trumpets, which probably resemble those with which Jericho was encompassed. The music, the discordant and high-pitched monotones, and the revolting odours of stale smoke of juniper chips, of rancid butter, and of unwashed woollen clothes which drifted through the doorway, were over-powering. Attempted fights among the horses woke me often during the night, and the sound of worship was always borne over the still air.

Dr. Marx left on the third day, after we had visited the monastery of Hemis, the richest in Ladak, holding large landed property and possessing much metallic wealth, including a chod-ten of silver and gold, thirty feet high, in one of its many halls, approached by gold- plated silver steps and incrusted with precious stones; there is also much fine work in brass and bronze. Hemis abounds in decorated buildings most picturesquely placed, it has three hundred lamas, and is regarded as 'the sight' of Ladak.

At Upschi, after a day's march over blazing gravel, I left the rushing olive-green Indus, which I had followed from the bridge of Khalsi, where a turbulent torrent, the Upshi water, joins it, descending through a gorge so narrow that the track, which at all times is blasted on the face of the precipice, is occasionally scaffolded. A very extensive rock-slip had carried away the path and rendered several fords necessary, and before I reached it rumour was busy with the peril. It was true that the day before several mules had been carried away and drowned, that many loads had been sacrificed, and that one native traveller had lost his life. So I started my caravan at daybreak, to get the water at its lowest, and ascended the gorge, which is an absolutely verdureless rift in mountains of most brilliant and fantastic stratification. At the first ford Mando was carried down the river for a short distance. The second was deep and strong, and a caravan of valuable goods had been there for two days, afraid to risk the crossing. My Lahulis, who always showed a great lack of stamina, sat down, sobbing and beating their breasts. Their sole wealth, they said, was in their baggage animals, and the river was 'wicked,' and 'a demon' lived in it who paralysed the horses' legs. Much experience of Orientals and of travel has taught me to surmount difficulties in my own way, so, beckoning to two men from the opposite side, who came over shakily with linked arms, I took the two strong ropes which I always carry on my saddle, and roped these men together and to Gyalpo's halter with one, and lashed Mando and the guide together with the other, giving them the stout thongs behind the saddle to hold on to, and in this compact mass we stood the strong rush of the river safely, the paralysing chill of its icy waters being a far more obvious peril. All the baggage animals were brought over in the same way, and the Lahulis praised their gods.

At Gya, a wild hamlet, the last in Ladak proper, I met a working naturalist whom I had seen twice before, and 'forgathered' with him much of the way. Eleven days of solitary desert succeeded. The reader has probably understood that no part of the Indus, Shayok, and Nubra valleys, which make up most of the province of Ladak, is less than 9,500 feet in altitude, and that the remainder is composed of precipitous mountains with glaciers and snowfields, ranging from 18,000 to 25,000 feet, and that the villages are built mainly on alluvial soil where possibilities of irrigation exist. But Rupchu has peculiarities of its own.

Between Gya and Darcha, the first hamlet in Lahul, are three huge passes, the Toglang, 18,150 feet in altitude, the Lachalang, 17,500, and the Baralacha, 16,000,—all easy, except for the difficulties arising from the highly rarefied air. The mountains of the region, which are from 20,000 to 23,000 feet in altitude, are seldom precipitous or picturesque, except the huge red needles which guard the Lachalang Pass, but are rather 'monstrous protuberances,' with arid surfaces of disintegrated rock. Among these are remarkable plateaux, which are taken advantage of by caravans, and which have elevations of from 14,000 to 15,000 feet. There are few permanent rivers or streams, the lakes are salt, beside the springs, and on the plateaux there is scanty vegetation, chiefly aromatic herbs;

but on the whole Rupchu is a desert of arid gravel. Its only inhabitants are 500 nomads, and on the ten marches of the trade route, the bridle paths, on which in some places labour has been spent, the tracks, not always very legible, made by the passage of caravans, and rude dykes, behind which travellers may shelter themselves from the wind, are the only traces of man. Herds of the kyang, the wild horse of some naturalists, and the wild ass of others, graceful and beautiful creatures, graze within gunshot of the track without alarm, I had thought Ladak windy, but Rupchu is the home of the winds, and the marches must be arranged for the quietest time of the day. Happily the gales blow with clockwork regularity, the day wind from the south and south-west rising punctually at 9 a.m. and attaining its maximum at 2.30, while the night wind from the north and north-east rises about 9 p.m. and ceases about 5 a.m. Perfect silence is rare. The highly rarefied air, rushing at great speed, when at its worst deprives the traveller of breath, skins his face and hands, and paralyses the baggage animals. In fact, neither man nor beast can face it. The horses 'turn tail' and crowd together, and the men build up the baggage into a wall and crouch in the lee of it. The heat of the solar rays is at the same time fearful. At Lachalang, at a height of over 15,000 feet, I noted a solar temperature of 152 degrees, only 35 degrees below the boiling point of water in the same region, which is about 187 degrees. To make up for this, the mercury falls below the freezing point every night of the year, even in August the difference of temperature in twelve hours often exceeding 120 degrees! The Rupchu nomads, however, delight in this climate of extremes, and regard Leh as a place only to be visited in winter, and Kulu and Kashmir as if they were the malarial swamps of the Congo!

We crossed the Toglang Pass, at a height of 18,150 feet, with less suffering from ladug than on either the Digar or Kharzong Passes. Indeed Gyalpo carried me over it stopping to take breath every few yards. It was then a long dreary march to the camping-ground of Tsala, where the Chang-pas spend the four summer months; the guides and baggage animals lost the way and did not appear until the next day, and in consequence the servants slept unsheltered in the snow. News travels as if by magic in desert places. Towards evening, while riding by a stream up a long and tedious valley, I saw a number of moving specks on the crest of a hill, and down came a surge of horsemen riding furiously. Just as they threatened to sweep Gyalpo away, they threw their horses on their haunches, in one moment were on the ground, which they touched with their foreheads, presented me with a plate of apricots, and the next vaulted into their saddles, and dashing up the valley were soon out of sight. In another half- hour there was a second wild rush of horsemen, the headman dismounted, threw himself on his face, kissed my hand, vaulted into the saddle, and then led a swirl of his tribesmen at a gallop in ever-narrowing circles round me till they subsided into the decorum of an escort. An elevated plateau with some vegetation on it, a row of forty tents, 'black' but not 'comely,' a bright rapid river, wild hills, long lines of white sheep converging towards the camp, yaks rampaging down the hillsides, men running to meet us, and women and children in the distance were singularly idealised in the golden glow of a cool, moist evening.

Two men took my bridle, and two more proceeded to put their hands on my stirrups; but Gyalpo kicked them to the right and left amidst shrieks of laughter, after which, with frantic gesticulations and yells of 'Kabardar!', I was led through the river in triumph and hauled off my horse. The tribesmen were much excited. Some dashed about, performing feats of horsemanship; others brought apricots and dough-balls made with apricot oil, or rushed to the tents, returning with rugs; some cleared the camping-ground of stones and raised a stone platform, and a flock of goats, exquisitely white from the daily swims across the river, were brought to be milked. Gradually and shrinkingly the women and children drew near; but Mr. -'s Bengali servant threatened them with a whip, when there was a general stampede, the women running like hares. I had trained my servants to treat the natives courteously, and addressed some rather strong language to the offender, and afterwards succeeded in enticing all the fugitives back by showing my sketches, which gave boundless pleasure and led to very numerous requests for portraits! The gopa, though he had the oblique Mongolian eyes, was a handsome young man, with a good nose and mouth. He was dressed like the others in a girdled chaga of coarse serge, but wore a red cap turned up over the ears with fine fur, a silver inkhorn, and a Yarkand knife in a chased silver sheath in his girdle, and canary-coloured leather shoes with turned-up points. The people prepared one of their own tents for me, and laying down a number of rugs of their own dyeing and weaving, assured me of an unbounded welcome as a friend of their 'benefactor,' Mr. Redslob, and then proposed that I should visit their tents accompanied by all the elders of the tribe.

CHAPTER V

CLIMATE AND NATURAL FEATURES

THE LAST CHAPTER LEFT ME with the chief and elders of the Chang-pas starting on 'a round of visits,' and it was not till nightfall that the solemn ceremony was concluded. Each of the fifty tents was visited: at every one a huge, savage Tibetan mastiff made an attempt to fly at me, and was pounced upon and held down by a woman little bigger than himself, and in each cheese and milk were offered and refused. In all I received a hearty welcome for the sake of the 'great father,' Mr. Redslob, who designated these people as 'the simplest and kindliest people on earth.'

This Chang-pa tribe, numbering five hundred souls, makes four moves in the year, dividing in summer, and uniting in a valley very free from snow in the winter. They are an exclusively pastoral people, and possess large herds of yaks and ponies and immense flocks of sheep and goats, the latter almost entirely the beautiful 'shawl goat,' from the undergrowth at the base of the long hair of which the fine Kashmir shawls are made. This pashm is a provision which Nature makes against the intense cold of these altitudes, and grows on yaks, sheep, and dogs, as well as on most of the wild animals. The sheep is the big, hornless, flop-eared huniya. The yaks and sheep are the load carriers of Rupchu. Small or easily divided merchandise is carried by sheep, and bulkier goods by yaks, and the Chang-pas make a great deal of money by carrying for the Lahul, Central Ladak, and Rudok merchants, their sheep travelling as far as Gar in Chinese Tibet. They are paid in grain as well as coin, their own country producing no farinaceous food. They have only two uses for silver money. With part of their gains they pay the tribute to Kashmir, and they melt the rest, and work it into rude personal ornaments. According to an old arrangement between Lhassa and Leh, they carry brick tea free for the Lhassa merchants. They are Buddhists, and practise polyandry, but their young men do not become lamas, and owing to the scarcity of fuel, instead of burning their dead, they expose them with religious rites face upwards in desolate places, to be made away with by the birds of the air. All their tents have a god-shelf, on which are placed small images and sacred emblems. They dress as the Ladakis, except that the men wear shoes with very high turned-up points, and that the women, in addition to the perak, the usual ornament, place on the top of the head a large silver coronet with three tassels. In physiognomy they resemble the Ladakis, but the Mongolian type is purer, the eyes are more oblique, and the eyelids have a greater droop, the chins project more, and the mouths are handsomer. Many of the men, including the headman, were quite good-looking, but the upper lips of the women were apt to be 'tucked up,' displaying very square teeth, as we have shown in the preceding chapter.

The roofs of the Tsala tents are nearly flat, and the middle has an opening six inches wide along its whole length. An excavation from twelve to twenty-four inches deep is made in the soil, and a rude wall of stones, about one foot high, is built round it, over which the tent cloth, made in narrow widths of yak's or goat's hair, is extended by ropes led over forked sticks. There is no ridge pole, and the centre is supported on short poles, to the projecting tops of which prayer flags and yaks' tails are attached. The interior, though dark, is not too dark for weaving, and each tent has its loom, for the Chang-pas not only weave their coarse woollen clothing and hair cloth for saddlebags and tents, but rugs of wool dyed in rich colours made from native roots. The largest tent was twenty feet by fifteen, but the majority measured only fourteen feet by eight and ten feet. The height in no case exceeded six feet. In these much ventilated and scarcely warmed shelters these hardy nomads brave the tremendous winds and winter rigours of their climate at altitudes varying from 13,000 to 14,500 feet. Water freezes every night of the year, and continually there are differences in temperature of 100 degrees between noon and midnight. In addition to the fifty dwelling tents there was one considerably larger, in which the people store their wool and goat's hair till the time arrives for taking them to market. The floor of several of the tents was covered with rugs, and besides looms and confused heaps of what looked like rubbish, there were tea-churns, goatskin churns, sheep and goat skins, children's bows and arrows, cooking pots, and heaps of the furze root, which is used as fuel.

They expended much of this scarce commodity upon me in their hospitality, and kept up a bonfire all night. They mounted their wiry ponies and performed feats of horsemanship, in one of which all the animals threw themselves on their hind legs in a circle when a man in the centre clapped his hands; and they crowded my tent to see my sketches, and were not satisfied till I executed some daubs professing to represent some of the elders. The excitement of their first visit from a European woman lasted late into the night, and when they at last retired they persisted in placing a guard of honour round my tent.

In the morning there was ice on the pools, and the snow lay three inches deep. Savage life had returned to its usual monotony, and the care of flocks and herds. In the early afternoon the chief and many of the men accompanied us across the ford, and we parted with mutual expressions of good will. The march was through broad gravelly valleys, among 'monstrous protuberances' of red and yellow gravel, elevated by their height alone to the dignity of mountains. Hail came on, and Gyalpo showed his high breeding by facing it when the other animals 'turned tail' and huddled together, and a storm of heavy sleet of some hours' duration burst upon us just as we reached the dismal camping-ground of Rukchen, guarded by mountain giants which now and then showed glimpses of their white skirts through the dark driving mists. That was the only 'weather' in four months.

A large caravan from the heat and sunshine of Amritsar was there. The goods were stacked under goat's hair shelters, the mules were huddled together without food, and their shivering Panjabi drivers, muffled in blankets which only left one eye exposed, were grubbing up furze roots wherewith to make smoky fires. My baggage, which had arrived previously, was lying soaking in the sleet, while the wretched servants were trying to pitch the tent in the high wind. They had slept out in the snow the night before, and were mentally as well as physically benumbed. Their misery had a comic side to it, and as the temperature made me feel specially well, I enjoyed bestirring myself and terrified Mando, who was feebly 'fadding' with a rag, by giving Gyalpo a vigorous rub-down with a bath-towel. Hassan Khan, with chattering teeth and severe neuralgia, muffled in my 'fisherman's hood' under his turban, was trying to do his work with his unfailing pluck. Mando was shedding futile tears over wet furze which would not light, the small wet corrie was dotted over with the Amritsar men sheltering under rocks and nursing hopeless fires, and fifty mules and horses, with dejected heads and dripping tails, and their backs to the merciless wind, were attempting to pick some food from scanty herbage already nibbled to the root. My tent was a picture of grotesque discomfort. The big stones had not been picked out from the gravel, the bed stood in puddles, the thick horse blanket was draining over the one chair, the servant's spare clothing and stores were on the table, the yaks' loads of wet hay and the soaked grain sack filled up most of the space; a wet candle sputtered and went out, wet clothes dripped from the tent hook, and every now and then Hassan Khan looked in with one eye, gasping out, 'Mem Sahib, I can no light the fire!' Perseverance succeeds eventually, and cups of a strong stimulant made of Burroughes and Wellcome's vigorous 'valoid' tincture of ginger and hot water, revived the men all round.

Such was its good but innocent effect, that early the next morning Hassan came into my tent with two eyes, and convulsed with laughter. 'The pony men' and Mando, he said, were crying, and the coolie from Leh, who before the storm had wanted to go the whole way to Simla, after refusing his supper had sobbed all night under the 'flys' of my tent, while I was sleeping soundly. Afterwards I harangued them, and told them I would let them go, and help them back; I could not take such poor-spirited miserable creatures with me, and I would keep the Tartars who had accompanied me from Tsala. On this they protested, and said, with a significant gesture, I might cut their throats if they cried any more, and begged me to try them again; and as we had no more bad weather, there was no more trouble.

The marches which followed were along valleys, plains, and mountain-sides of gravel, destitute of herbage, except a shrivelled artemisia, and on one occasion the baggage animals were forty hours without food. Fresh water was usually very scarce, and on the Lingti plains was only obtainable by scooping it up from the holes left by the feet of animals. Insect life was rare, and except grey doves, the 'dove of the valleys,' which often flew before us for miles down the ravines, no birds were to be seen. On the other hand, there were numerous herds of kyang, which in the early mornings came to drink of the water by which the camps were pitched. By looking through a crevice of my tent I saw them distinctly, without alarming them. In one herd I counted forty.

They kept together in families, sire, dam, and foal. The animal certainly is under fourteen hands, and resembles a mule rather than a horse or ass. The noise, which I had several opportunities of hearing, is more like a neigh than a bray, but lacks completeness. The creature is light brown, almost fawn colour, fading into white under his body, and he has a dark stripe on his back, but not a cross. His ears are long, and his tail is like that of a mule. He trots and gallops, and when alarmed gallops fast, but as he is not worth hunting, he has not a great dread of humanity, and families of kyang frequently grazed within two hundred and fifty yards of us. He is about as untamable as the zebra, and with his family affectionateness leads apparently a very happy life.

On the Kwangchu plateau, at an elevation of 15,000 feet, I met with a form of life which has a great interest of its own, sheep caravans, numbering among them 7,000 sheep, each animal with its wool on, and equipped with a neat packsaddle and two leather or hair-cloth bags, and loaded with from twenty-five to thirty-two pounds of salt or borax. These, and many more which we passed, were carrying their loads to Patseo, a mountain valley in Lahul, where they are met by traders from Northern British India. The sheep are shorn, and the wool and loads are exchanged for wheat and a few other commodities, with which they return to Tibet, the whole journey taking from nine months to a year. As the sheep live by grazing the scanty herbage on the march, they never accomplish more than ten miles a day, and as they often become footsore, halts of several days are frequently required. Sheep, dead or dying, with the birds of prey picking out their eyes, were often met with. Ordinarily these caravans are led by a man, followed by a large goat much bedecked and wearing a large bell. Each driver has charge of one hundred sheep. These men, of small stature but very thickset, with their wide smooth faces, loose clothing of sheepskin with the wool outside, with their long coarse hair flying in the wind, and their uncouth shouts in a barbarous tongue, are much like savages. They sing wild chants as they picket their sheep in long double lines at night, and with their savage mastiffs sleep unsheltered under the frosty skies under the lee of their piled-up saddlebags. On three nights I camped beside their caravans, and walked round their orderly lines of sheep and their neat walls of saddlebags; and, far from showing any discourtesy or rude curiosity, they held down their fierce dogs and exhibited their ingenious mode of tethering their animals, and not one of the many articles which my servants were in the habit of leaving outside the tents was on any occasion abstracted. The dogs, however, were less honest than their masters, and on one night ran away with half a sheep, and I should have fared poorly had not Mr. — shot some grey doves.

Marches across sandy and gravelly valleys, and along arid mountain- sides spotted with a creeping furze and cushions of a yellow-green moss which seems able to exist without moisture, fords of the Sumgyal and Tserap rivers, and the crossing of the Lachalang Pass at an altitude of 17,500 feet in severe frost, occupied several uneventful days. Of the three lofty passes on this route, the To-glang, which is higher, and the Baralacha, which is lower, are featureless billows of gravel, over which a carriage might easily be driven. Not so is the Lachalang, though its well-made zigzags are easy for laden animals. The approach to it is fantastic, among precipitous mountains of red sandstone, and red rocks weath-ered into pillars, men's heads, and numerous groups of gossipy old women from thirty to fifty feet high, in flat hats and long circular cloaks! Entering by red gates of rock into a region of gigantic mountains, and following up a crystal torrent, the valley narrowing to a gorge, and the gorge to a chasm guarded by nearly perpendicular needles of rock flaming in the westering sun, we forded the river at the chasm's throat, and camped on a velvety green lawn just large enough for a few tents, absolutely walled in by abrupt mountains 18,000 and 19,000 feet in height. Long after the twilight settled down on us, the pinna-cles above glowed in warm sunshine, and the following morning, when it was only dawn below, and the still river pools were frozen and the grass was white with hoar-frost, the morning sun reddened the snow-peaks and kindled into vermilion the red needles of Lachalang. That camping-ground under such conditions is the grandest and most romantic spot of the whole journey.

Verdureless and waterless stretches, in crossing which our poor animals were two nights without food, brought us to the glacier-blue waters of the Serchu, tumbling along in a deep broad gash, and farther on to a lateral torrent which is the boundary between Rupchu, tributary to Kashmir, and Lahul or British Tibet, under the rule of the Empress of India. The tents were ready pitched in a grassy hollow by the river; horses, cows, and goats were grazing near them, and a number of men were preparing food. A Tibetan approached me, accompanied by a creature in a nondescript dress speaking Hindustani volubly. On a band across his breast were the British crown, and a plate with the words 'Commissioner's chaprassie, Kulu district.' I never felt so extinguished. Liberty seemed lost, and the romance of the desert to have died out in one moment! At the camping-ground I found rows of salaaming Lahulis drawn up, and Hassan Khan in a state which was a compound of pomposity and jubilant excitement. The tahsildar (really the Tibetan honorary magistrate), he said, had received instructions from the Lieutenant-Governor of the Panjab that I was on the way to Kylang, and was to 'want for nothing.' So twenty-four men, nine horses, a flock of goats, and two cows had been waiting for me for three days in the Serchu valley. I wrote a polite note to the magistrate, and sent all back except the chaprassie, the cows, and the cowherd, my servants looking much crestfallen.

We crossed the Baralacha Pass in wind and snow showers into a climate in which moisture began to be obvious. At short distances along the pass, which extends for many miles, there are rude semicircular walls, three feet high, all turned in one direction, in the shelter of which travellers crouch to escape from the strong cutting wind. My men suffered far more than on the two higher passes, and it was difficult to dislodge them from these shelters, where they lay groaning, gasping, and suffering from vertigo and nose-bleeding. The cold was so severe that I walked over the loftiest part of the pass, and for the first time felt slight effects of the ladug. At a height of 15,000 feet, in the midst of general desolation, grew, in the shelter of rocks, poppies (Mecanopsis aculeata), blue as the Tibetan skies, their centres filled with a cluster of golden-yellow stamens,- -a most charming sight. Ten or twelve of these exquisite blossoms grow on one stalk, and stalk, leaf, and seed-vessels are guarded by very stiff thorns. Lower down flowers abounded, and at the camping- ground of Patseo (12,000 feet), where the Tibetan sheep caravans exchange their wool, salt, and borax for grain, the ground was covered with soft greensward, and real rain fell. Seen from the Baralacha Pass are vast snowfields, glaciers, and avalanche slopes. This barrier, and the Rotang, farther south, close this trade route practically for seven months of the year, for they catch the monsoon rains, which at that altitude are snows from fifteen to thirty feet deep; while on the other side of the Baralacha and throughout Rupchu and Ladak the snowfall is insignificant. So late as August, when I crossed, there were four perfect snow bridges over the Bhaga, and snowfields thirty-six feet deep along its margin. At Patseo the tahsildar, with a retinue and animals laden with fodder, came to pay his respects to me, and invited me to his house, three days' journey. These were the first human beings we had seen for three days.

A few miles south of the Baralacha Pass some birch trees appeared on a slope, the first natural growth of timber that I had seen since crossing the Zoji La. Lower down there were a few more, then stunted specimens of the pencil cedar, and the mountains began to show a shade of green on their lower slopes. Butterflies appeared also, and a vulture, a grand bird on the wing, hovered ominously over us for some miles, and was succeeded by an equally ominous raven. On the excellent bridle-track cut on the face of the precipices which overhang the Bhaga, there is in nine miles only one spot in which it is possible to pitch a five-foot tent, and at Darcha, the first hamlet in Lahul, the only camping-ground is on the house roofs. There the Chang-pas and their yaks and horses who had served me pleasantly and faithfully from Tsala left me, and returned to the freedom of their desert life. At Kolang, the next hamlet, where the thunder of the Bhaga was almost intolerable, Hara Chang, the magistrate, one of the thakurs or feudal proprietors of Lahul, with his son and nephew and a large retinue, called on me; and the next morning Mr. — and I went by invitation to visit him in his castle, a magnificently situated building on a rocky spur 1,000 feet above the camping-ground, attained by a difficult climb, and nearly on a level with the glittering glaciers and ice-falls on the other side of the Bhaga. It only differs from Leh and Stok castles in having blue glass in some of the smaller windows. In the family temple, in addition to the usual life-size images of Buddha and the Triad, there was a female divinity, carved at Jallandhur in India, copied from a statue representing Queen Victoria in her younger days—a very fitting possession for the highest government official in Lahul. The thakur, Hara Chang, is wealthy and a rigid Buddhist, and uses his very considerable influence against the work of the Moravian missionaries in the valley. The rude path down to the bridle-road, through fields of barley and buckwheat, is bordered by roses, gooseberries, and masses of wild flowers.

The later marches after reaching Darcha are grand beyond all description. The track, scaffolded or blasted out of the rock at a height of from 1,000 to 3,000 feet above the thundering Bhaga, is scarcely a rifle-shot from the mountain mass dividing it from the Chandra, a mass covered with nearly unbroken ice and snowfields, out of which rise pinnacles of naked rock 21,000 and 22,000 feet in altitude. The region is the 'abode of snow,' and glaciers of great size fill up every depression. Humidity, vegetation, and beauty reappear together, wild flowers and ferns abound, and pencil cedars in clumps rise above the artificial plantations of the valley. Wheat ripens at an altitude of 12,000 feet. Picturesque villages, surrounded by orchards, adorn the mountain spurs; chod-tens and gonpos, with white walls and fluttering flags, brighten the scene; feudal castles crown the heights, and where the mountains are loftiest, the snowfields and glaciers most imposing, and the greenery densest, the village of Kylang, the most important in Lahul as the centre of trade, government, and Christian missions, hangs on ledges of the mountain-side 1,000 feet above Bhaga, whose furious course can be traced far down the valley by flashes of sunlit foam.

The Lahul valley, which is a part of British Tibet, has an altitude of 10,000 feet. It prospers under British rule, its population has increased, Hindu merchants have settled in Kylang, the route through Lahul to Central Asia is finding increasing favour with the Panjabi traders, and the Moravian missionaries, by a bolder system of irrigation and the provision of storage for water, have largely increased the quantity of arable land. The Lahulis are chiefly Tibetans, but Hinduism is largely mixed up with Buddhism in the lower villages. All the gonpos, however, have been restored and enlarged during the last twenty years. In winter the snow lies fifteen feet deep, and for four or five months, owing to the perils of the Rotang Pass, the valley rarely has any communication with the outer world.

At the foot of the village of Kylang, which is built in tier above tier of houses up the steep side of a mountain with a height of 21,000 feet, are the Moravian mission buildings, long, low, whitewashed erections, of the simplest possible construction, the design and much of the actual erection being the work of these capable Germans. The large building, which has a deep verandah, the only place in which exercise can be taken in the winter, contains the native church, three rooms for each missionary, and two guest-rooms. Round the garden are the printing rooms, the medicine and store room (stores arriving once in two years), and another guest-room. Round an adjacent enclosure are the houses occupied in winter by the Christians when they come down with their sheep and cattle from the hill farms. All is absolutely plain, and as absolutely clean and trim. The guest-rooms and one or two of the Tibetan rooms are papered with engravings from the Illustrated London News, but the rooms of the missionaries are only whitewashed, and by their extreme bareness reminded me of those of very poor pastors in the Fatherland. A garden, brilliant with zinnias, dianthus, and petunias, all of immense size, and planted with European trees, is an oasis, and in it I camped for some weeks under a willow tree, covered, as many are, with a sweet secretion so abundant as to drop on the roof of the tent, and which the people collect and use as honey.

The mission party consisted of Mr. and Mrs. Shreve, lately arrived, and now in a distant exile at Poo, and Mr. and Mrs. Heyde, who had been in Tibet for nearly forty years, chiefly spent at Kylang, without going home. 'Plain living and high thinking' were the rule. Books and periodicals were numerous, and were read and assimilated. The culture was simply wonderful, and the acquaintance with the latest ideas in theology and natural science, the latest political and social developments, and the latest conceptions in European art, would have led me to suppose that these admirable people had only just left Europe. Mrs. Heyde had no servant, and in the long winters, when household and mission work are over for the day, and there are no mails to write for, she pursues her tailoring and other needlework, while her husband reads aloud till midnight. At the time of my visit (September) busy preparations for the winter were being made. Every day the wood piles grew. Hay, cut with sickles on the steep hillsides, was carried on human backs into the farmyard, apples were cored and dried in the sun, cucumbers were pickled, vinegar was made, potatoes were stored, and meat was killed and salted.

It is in winter, when the Christians have come down from the mountain, that most of the mission work is done. Mrs. Heyde has a school of forty girls, mostly Buddhists. The teaching is simple and practical, and includes the knitting of socks, of which from four to five hundred pairs are turned out each winter, and find a ready sale. The converts meet for instruction and discussion twice daily, and there is daily worship. The mission press is kept actively employed in printing the parts of the Bible which have been translated during the summer, as well as simple tracts written or translated by Mr. Heyde. No converts are better instructed, and like those of Leh they seem of good quality, and are industrious and self-supporting. Winter work is severe, as ponies, cattle, and sheep must always be hand-fed, and often hand-watered. Mr. Heyde has great repute as a doctor, and in summer people travel long distances for his advice and medicine. He is universally respected, and his judgment in worldly affairs is highly thought of; but if one were to judge merely by apparent results, the devoted labour of nearly forty years and complete self-sacrifice for the good of Kylang must be pronounced unsuccessful. Christianity has been most strongly opposed by men of influence, and converts have been exposed to persecution and loss. The abbot of the Kylang monastery lately said to Mr. Heyde, 'Your Christian teaching has given Buddhism a resurrection.' The actual words used were, 'When you came here people were quite indifferent about their religion, but since it has been attacked they have become zealous, and now they KNOW.' It is only by sharing their circumstances of isolation, and by getting glimpses of their everyday-life and work, that one can realise at all what the heroic perseverance and self-sacrificing toil of these forty years have been, and what is the weighty influence on the people and on the standard of morals, even though the number of converts is so small. All honour to these noble German missionaries, learned, genial, cultured, radiant, who, whether teaching, preaching, farming, gardening, printing, or doctoring, are always and everywhere 'living epistles of Christ, known and read of all men!' Close by the mission house, in a green spot under shady trees, is God's Acre, where many children of the mission families sleep, and a few adults.

As the winter is the busiest season in mission work, so it is the great time in which the lamas make house-to-house peregrinations and attend at festivals. Then also there is much spinning and weaving by both sexes, and tobogganing and other games, and much drinking of chang by priests and people. The cattle remain out till nearly Christmas, and are then taken into the houses. At the time of the variable new year, the lamas and nuns retire to the monasteries, and dulness reigns in the valleys. At the end of a month they emerge, life and noise begin, and all men to whom sons have been born during the previous year give chang freely. During the festival which follows, all these jubilant fathers go out of the village as a gaudily dressed procession, and form a circle round a picture of a yak, painted by the lamas, which is used as a target to be shot at with bows and arrows, and it is believed that the man who hits it in the centre will be blessed with a son in the coming year. After this, all the Kylang men and women collect in one house by annual rotation, and sing and drink immense quantities of chang till 10 p.m.

The religious festivals begin soon after. One, the worshipping of the lamas by the laity, occurs in every village, and lasts from two to three days. It consists chiefly of music and dancing, while the lamas sit in rows, swilling chang and arrack. At another, which is celebrated annually in every house, the lamas assemble, and in front of certain gods prepare a number of mystical figures made of dough, which are hung up and are worshipped by the family. Afterwards the lamas make little balls which are worshipped, and one of the family mounts the roof and invites the neighbours, who receive the balls from the lamas' hands and drink moderately of chang. Next, the figures are thrown to the demons as a propitiatory offering, amidst 'hellish whistlings' and the firing of guns. These ceremonies are called ise drup (a full life), and it is believed that if they were neglected life would be cut short.

One of the most important of the winter religious duties of the lamas is the reading of the sacred classics under the roof of each householder. By this means the family accumulate merit, and the longer the reading is protracted the greater is the accumulation. A twelve-volume book is taken in the houses of the richer householders, each one of the twelve or fifteen lamas taking a page, all reading at an immense pace in a loud chant at the same time. The reading of these volumes, which consist of Buddhist metaphysics and philosophy, takes five days, and while reading each lama has his chang cup constantly replenished. In the poorer households a classic of but one volume is taken, to lessen the expense of feeding the lamas. Festivals and ceremonies follow each other closely until March, when archery practice begins, and in April and May the people prepare for the operations of husbandry.

The weather in Kylang breaks in the middle of September, but so fascinating were the beauties and sublimity of Nature, and the virtues and culture of my Moravian friends, that, shutting my eyes to the possible perils of the Rotang, I remained until the harvest was brought home with joy and revelry, and the flush of autumn faded, and the first snows of winter gave an added majesty to the glorious valley. Then, reluctantly folding my tent, and taking the same faithful fellows who brought my baggage from Leh, I spent five weeks on the descent to the Panjab, journeying through the paradise of Upper Kulu and the interesting native states of Mandi, Sukket, Bilaspur, and Bhaghat, and early in November reached the amenities and restraints of the civilisation of Simla.

Footnotes:

{1} Mr. Redslob said that when on different occasions he was smitten by heavy sorrows, he felt no difference between the Tibetan feeling and expression of sympathy and that of Europeans. A stronger testimony to the effect produced by his twenty-five years of loving service could scarcely be given than our welcome in Nubra. During the dangerous illness which followed, anxious faces thronged his humble doorway as early as break of day, and the stream of friendly inquiries never ceased till sunset, and when he died the people of Ladak and Nubra wept and 'made a great mourning for him,' as for their truest friend.

{2} For these and other curious details concerning Tibetan customs I am indebted to the kindness and careful investigations of the late Rev. W. Redslob, of Leh, and the Rev. A. Heyde, of Kylang.

BIOGRAPHY OF LADY FLORENCE DIXIE

LADY FLORENCE CAROLINE DOUGLAS and her twin brother were born in Scotland on May 24, 1855, into an upper-class family with four other children. Her father, Arhcibald William, Marquis of Queensbury, died of apparent suicide in 1860 while cleaning a gun. After her father's death, her mother Caroline Margaret Douglas moved her children to England and converted to Catholicism, nearly losing custody of her own children in the process. One year later, one of Douglas's older brothers died in a mountain climbing accident on the Matterhorn, thus causing Douglas's childhood to be fraught with instability.

Douglas's early exposure to foreign travel (and its dangers), women's lack of legal rights, and time spent outside learning to ride and hunt formed the basis for her writing. She began writing poetry at age ten under the pseudonym "Darling," and although her efforts were not stylistically impressive, she established her pro-women's rights views in writing early on and showed an inclination to rebel against the conventions of her time by casting a critical eye on her society.

At the age of nineteen, Lady Florence Douglas married Sir Alexander Beaumont Churchill Dixie, nicknamed Sir A.B.C.D., and gave birth to two sons within their first three years of marriage. Although this gives the appearance of domesticity, Dixie unquestionably ruled her husband. They shared a love of hunting and other outdoor pursuits along with a love of liquor, earning them the title "Sir Always and Lady Sometimes Tipsy."

Two months after her second son was born, Dixie left him at home and set out with her husband and brothers for South America. From her experiences there, she created *Across Patagonia*, which is written in a style that depicts her as a heroine, easily keeping up with and sometimes outwitting her male companions. As the narrator, she is the focus of the story, often referring to her companions only as "my husband" or "my brothers." She writes about her 600-mile trek across the continent on horseback, drinking alcohol, hunting for sport and for food, and sleeping outside. The experience of freedom from her domestic tasks awakened the desire for social reform in Dixie in addition to an intense appreciation for the aesthetic of the landscape through which she traveled.

While in South America, she was attacked by jaguars and fled up a tree to escape. She shot the mother in self-defense, but saved one of the cubs and took him home as a pet. Affums, as Dixie named him, lived in London with her for years until he began hunting deer in Windsor Great Park and had to be sent to London Zoo. Her encounter with jaguars is one of several descriptions in Across Patagonia in which she details the characteristics and habits of exotic species, even corresponding via letters with Charles Darwin regarding her discoveries.

After her return home, Dixie began to question the morality of her love for hunting and eventually came to terms on the side of her conscience, joining the Humanitarian League and publishing a pamphlet called *The Horror of Sport* that detailed the barbarity of inflicting pain on animals.

In 1880, Dixie once again began to feel stifled by home life, leaving for South Africa to help with Boer War relief efforts. The Morning Post employed her as perhaps the first female war correspondent. Although the war had officially ended at the time of her arrival there, she wrote about ongoing conflicts in the region, which were later compiled in her second travel narrative, *In the Land of Misfortune* (1882). While it retained some of the adventurous spirit from her first narrative, this work acted as a political manifesto condemning Britain's destruction of the Zulu nation and other damage caused by colonization. She opened and closed this work with interviews she conducted with the deposed Zulu king, Cetshwayo, during his imprisonment to frame the story in a political lens.

Upon returning home from South Africa, Dixie turned her attention to political activism in the areas of women's suffrage, animal rights, the reinstatement of the Zulu king, and Irish Home Rule. She also adjusted her style of writing from the travel narrative to the novel, writing strong female protagonists fighting for egalitarian societies. In her work *Gloriana; or, the Revolution of 1900*, Dixie depicts a utopian society as one led by a female parliament. Her protagonist, Gloriana, disguises herself as a man to become the Prime Minister of England. Echoing her own experiences with the stifling nature of Victorian domesticity, Dixie called limiting women's education and rights and forcing them to rear children "arbitrary and cruel, and false to Nature."

In line with her political views on women, Dixie was a member of the Rational Dress Club, promoting comfortable and practical clothing for both men and women. She worked to establish a women's football league, and in 1895 became president of the British Ladies' Football Club.

Dixie's forays into Irish politics made her unpopular with some factions, and she received death threats in such numbers that her husband bought her a

Saint Bernard to protect her. In 1883, she was allegedly attacked by two men dressed as women. In her report to a newspaper, she claimed that one held her by the neck and tried to stab her, but the knife was deflected by the whalebone in her corset. She shouted at his second attempt to kill her, which alerted her dog, Hubert, to fight off the intruders. Dixie gained further infamy from this story as it was never proven to be true. Despite the crime scene's visibility and high traffic, no one nearby saw or heard anything to support Dixie's story, nor did she show any physical signs of having been thrown to the ground or hurt. Some blamed this episode on hallucinations due to her drinking habit, but no decisive conclusions can be made either way.

In November of 1905, Dixie died from a sudden bout of diphtheria. Before her death, she had been working on a series of children's stories with heroines based loosely on herself and her childhood experiences. *The Story of Ijain, or The Evolution of a Mind and Izra: A Child of Solitude*, her final book, was published posthumously.

ACROSS PATAGONIA

BY

Lady Florence Dixie

WITH ILLUSTRATIONS
FROM SKETCHES BY JULIUS BEERBOHM
ENGRAVED BY WHYMPER AND PEARSON

CROSSING THE CABEZA DEL MARE

PUCHO

LONDON:
RICHARD BENTLEY AND SON

Publishers in Ordinary to Her Majesty the Queen
1880

TO
HIS ROYAL HIGHNESS,
ALBERT EDWARD, PRINCE OF WALES,

THIS WORK
DESCRIPTIVE OF

SIX MONTHS' WANDERINGS OVER UNEXPLORED
AND UNTRODDEN GROUND,
IS BY KIND PERMISSION RESPECTFULLY DEDICATED

BY HIS ROYAL HIGHNESS'S
OBLIGED AND OBEDIENT SERVANT,

THE AUTHOR.

CONTENTS

Chapter I

Why Patagonia? —Good-Bye—The Start—Dirty Weather—Lisbon—
The Island of Palma—Pernambuco 456

Chapter II

Bahia—Rio De Janeiro—Rio Harbour—The Town—An Upset—Tijuca—A Tropical Night—More Upsets—Safety at Last.......
....461

Chapter III

Beauties of Rio—Monte Video—Straits of Magellan—Tierra Del
Fuego—Arrival at Sandy Point—Preparations for the Start—Our
Outfit—Our Guides...467

Chapter IV

The Start for Cape Negro—Riding Along the Straits—Cape Ne-
gro—The First Night Under Canvas—Unexpected Arrivals—Our
Guests—A Novel Picnic—Rough-Riding—There Was a Sound of
Revelry by Night..471

Chapter V

Departure of our Guests—The Start for the Pampas—An Untoward
Accident—A Day's Sport—Unpleasant Effects of the Wind—Off
Cape Gregorio 478

Chapter VI

Visit to the Indian Camp—A Patagonian—Indian Curiosity—Physique—Costume—Women—Prominent Characteristics—An Indian
Incroyable—Superstitiousness.......................................485

Chapter VII

The Prairie Fire 492

Chapter VIII

Unpleasant Visitors— "Speed the Parting Guest"—Off Again—An Ostrich Egg—I'Aria Misleads Us—Striking Oil—Preparations for the Chase—Wind and Hail—A Guanaco at Last—An Exciting Run—The Death—Home—Hungry as Hunters— "Fat-Behind-The-Eye" 495

Chapter IX

Elastic Leagues—The Laguna Blanca—An Earthquake—Ostrich-Hunting 505

Chapter X

Departure from Laguna Blanca—A Wild-Cat—Ibis Soup—A Fertile Canadon—Indian Law and Equity—Our First Puma—Cowardice of the Puma—Discomforts of a Wet Night—A Mysterious Dish—A Good Run 513

Chapter XI

A Numerous Guanaco Herd—A Pampa Hermit—I'Aria Again Loses the Way—Chorlitos—A New Emotion—A Moon Rainbow—Weather Wisdom—Optimist and Pessimist—Wild Fowl Abundant 519

Chapter XII

A Monotonous Ride—A Dreary Landscape—Short Fuel Rations—The Cordilleras—Features of Patagonian Scenery—Heat and Gnats—A Puma Again— "The Rain is Never Weary"—Dampness, Hunger, Gloom—I'Aria to the Rescue—His Ingenuity 524

Chapter XIII

A Surprise—A Strange Scene—Califate Berries—Guanaco Stalking—A Dilemma—Mosquitoes—A Good Shot—Mosquitoes ..532

Chapter XIV

An Unknown Country—Passing the Barrier—Cleopatra's Needles—Foxes—A Good Run—Our Forest Sanctuary—Roughing It—A Bath—A Varied Menu 537

Chapter XV

Excursions into the Mountains—Mysteries of the Cordilleras—Wild Horse Tracks—Deer—Man the Destroyer 547

Chapter XVI

An Alarm—The Wild-Horses—An Equine Combat—The Wild Stallion Victorious—The Struggle Renewed—Retreat of the Wild Horses 554

Chapter XVII

Excursion to the Cleopatra Needles—A Bog—A Winding River—Difficult Travelling—A Strange Phenomenon—A Fairy Haunt—Wild Horses Again—Their Agility—The Blue Lake—The Cleopatra Peaks—The Promised Land 557

Chapter XVIII

We Think of Returning—Good-Bye to the Cordilleras—The Last of the Wild Horses—Mosquitoes—A Stormy Night—A Calamity—The Last of our Buscuit—Utility of Fire-Signals 564

Chapter XIX

Isidoro—An Unsavoury Meal—Expensive Loaves—Guanaco Scarce—Disappointment—Night Suprises Us—Supperless—Continued Fasting—No Meat in the Camp 570

Chapter XX

The Horses Lost!—Unpleasant Prospects—Found—Short Rations—A Strange Hunt—A Stern Chase—The Mystery Solved—The Cabeza Del Mar—Safely Across—A Damp Night—Cabo Negro Again 575

Chapter XXI

Cabo Negro—Home News—Civilisation Again—Our Disreputable Appearance—Pucho Missing—The Coming of Pucho—Pucho's Characteristics 582

LIST OF ILLUSTRATIONS

Pucho...449

Crossing the Cabeza del Mar.............................448

A Guanaco on the Look-Out.............................455

The Straits of Magellan......................................472

"Collecting the 'Tropilla' —Saddling Up"............481

Indian Camp..487

Guanacos 502

The Last Double...511

The Puma's Death-Spring 529

Ravine Entrance to the Cordilleras 538

The "Cleopatra Needles" 541

Encampment in the Cordilleras..........................543

"The Wild-Horse Glen".....................................550

"We Were the First Who Ever Burst on to that Silent Sea"...562

CHAPTER I

WHY PATAGONIA?—GOOD-BYE—THE START—DIRTY WEATHER—LISBON—THE ISLAND OF PALMA—PERNAMBUCO

"PATAGONIA! WHO WOULD EVER THINK OF GOING TO SUCH A PLACE?" "Why, you will be eaten up by cannibals!" "What on earth makes you choose such an outlandish part of the world to go to?" "What can be the attraction?" "Why, it is thousands of miles away, and no one has ever been there before, except Captain Musters, and one or two other adventurous madmen!"

These, and similar questions and exclamations I heard from the lips of my friends and acquaintances, when I told them of my intended trip to Patagonia, the land of the Giants, the land of the fabled Golden City of Manoa. What was the attraction in going to an outlandish place so many miles away? The answer to the question was contained in its own words. Precisely because it was an outlandish place and so far away, I chose it. Palled for the moment with civilisation and its surroundings, I wanted to escape somewhere, where I might be as far removed from them as possible. Many of my readers have doubtless felt the dissatisfaction with oneself, and everybody else, that comes over one at times in the midst of the pleasures of life; when one wearies of the shallow artificiality of modern existence; when what was once excitement has become so no longer, and a longing grows up within one to taste a more vigorous emotion than that afforded by the monotonous round of society's so-called "pleasures."

Well, it was in this state of mind that I cast round for some country which should possess the qualities necessary to satisfy my requirements, and finally I decided upon Patagonia as the most suitable. Without doubt there are wild countries more favoured by Nature in many ways. But nowhere else are you so completely alone. Nowhere else is there an area of 100,000 square miles which you may gallop over, and where, whilst enjoying a healthy, bracing climate, you are safe from the persecutions of fevers, friends, savage tribes, obnoxious animals, telegrams, letters, and every other nuisance you are elsewhere liable to be exposed to. To these attractions was added the thought, always alluring to an active mind, that there too I should be able to penetrate into vast wilds, virgin as yet to the foot of man. Scenes of infinite beauty and grandeur might be lying hidden in the silent solitude of the mountains which bound the barren plains of the Pampas, into whose mysterious recesses no one as yet had ever ventured. And I was to be the first to behold them!—an egotistical pleasure, it is true; but the idea had a great charm for me, as it has had for many others. Thus, under the combined influence of the above considerations, it was decided that Patagonia was to be the chosen field of my new experiences.

My party consisted of Lord Queensberry and Lord James Douglas, my two brothers, my husband, and myself, and a friend, Mr. J. Beerbohm, whose book, Wanderings in Patagonia, had just been published when we left England. We only took one servant with us, knowing that English servants inevitably prove a nuisance and hindrance in expeditions of the kind, when a great deal of "roughing it" has to be gone through, as they have an unpleasant knack of falling ill at inopportune moments.

Our outfit was soon completed, and shipped, together with our other luggage, on board the good ship "Britannia," which sailed from Liverpool on the 11th December 1878. We ourselves were going overland to join her at Bordeaux, as we thereby had a day longer in England. Then came an unpleasant duty, taking leave of our friends. I hate saying good-bye. On the eve of a long journey one cannot help thinking of the uncertainty of everything in this world. The voice that bids you God-speed may, before you return, perhaps be silent for ever. The face of each friend who grasps your hand vividly recalls some scene of pleasant memory. Now it reminds you of some hot August day among the purple hills of Scotland, when a good bag, before an excellent lunch, had been followed by some more than usually exciting sport. The Highlands had never looked so beautiful, so merry a party had never clambered down the moors homeward, so successful a day had never been followed by so jolly an evening; and then, with a sigh, as your friend leaves you, you ask yourself, "Shall I ever climb the moors again?" Now it is to Leicestershire that your memory reverts. The merry blast of the huntsman's horn resounds, the view-halloa rings out cheerily on the bright crisp air of a fine hunting morning; the fox is "gone away," you have got a good start, and your friend has too. "Come on," he shouts, "let us see this run together!" Side by side you fly the first fence, take your horse in hand, and settle down to ride over the broad grass country. How distinctly you remember that run, how easily you recall each fence you flew together, each timber-rail you topped, and that untempting bottom you both got so luckily and safely over, and above all, the old farm-yard, where the gallant fox yielded up his life. Meanwhile, with a forced smile and a common-place remark, you part; and together, perhaps, you may never hear the huntsman's horn, never charge the ox-fence, never strive to be foremost in the chase again!

With these thoughts passing through my mind I began to wonder why I wanted to leave England. I remembered for the moment only the pleasant features of the past, and remembering them, forgot the feelings and circumstances which had prompted me to embark on my present enterprise. The stern sex will possibly reprehend this exhibition of female fickleness of purpose. May I urge in its palliation that my weakness scarcely lasted longer than it has taken me to write this?

14th December.—On a cold, rainy afternoon we steamed down from Bordeaux in a little tender to join the "Britannia," which was anchored off Pauillac. We were soon alongside, and were welcomed on board by Captain Brough, under whose guidance we inspected, with a good deal of interest, the fine ship which was to be our home for some time. It would be superfluous for me to describe the excellent internal arrangements on board; few of my readers, I imagine, but are acquainted, either from experience or description, with the sumptuous and comfortable fittings-up of an Ocean passenger-steamer.

Soon the anchor was up—the propeller was in motion, and our nerves had hardly recovered from the shock inflicted by the report of the gun which fired the parting salute, ere Pauillac was scarcely distinguishable in the mist and rain astern. By the time dinner was over we were altogether out of sight of land, the rain was still falling heavily, and prognostications of dirty weather were being indulged in by the sailors. Giving a last look at the night, I turned into the captain's cosy deck-house, where I found my companions deep in the intricacies and wranglings of a rubber at whist, in which I, too, presently took a hand. As time went on, indications that it was getting rather rough were not wanting, in the swaying of the ship and the noise of the wind; but so comfortable were we in our little cabin, with the curtains drawn and lamps lit, that we were quite astonished when the captain paid us a visit at about nine o'clock, and told us that it was blowing a regular gale.

The words were hardly out of his mouth when the ship heeled suddenly over under a tremendous shock, which was followed by a mighty rush of water along the decks. We ran out, thinking we must have struck a rock. The night was as black as pitch, and the roaring of the wind, the shouts of the sailors, and the wash of the water along the decks, heightened with their deafening noise, the anxiety of the moment. Fortunately the shock we had experienced had no worse cause than an enormous sea, which had struck the ship forward, and swept right aft, smashing whatever opposed its destructive course, and bending thick iron stanchions as if they had been mere wires.

As soon as the hubbub attendant on this incident had somewhat subsided, thankful that it had been no worse, we returned to our game at whist, which occupied us till eleven o'clock, at which hour, "all lights out" being the order of the ship, we turned into our cabins to sleep the first night of many on board the "Britannia."

The next day was fine and sunny, and so the weather continued till we reached Lisbon, three days after leaving Bordeaux, when it grew rather rough again. At Lisbon we remained a day, taking in coal and fresh provisions—and then once more weighed anchor, not to drop it again till the shores of the New World should have been reached.

Just as it was beginning to dawn on the morning of the second day after leaving Lisbon, I was awakened by the speed of the vessel being reduced to half its usual ratio, for so accustomed does one become in a short time to the vibration of the screw, that any change from its ordinary force immediately disturbs one's sleep. Looking out of my cabin-window I could see that we were close to land, so, dressing hurriedly, I went on deck. We seemed to be but a stone's-throw from an island, whose bold rugged heights rose up darkly against the pale light that shone in the morning sky. At one point of the shore the revolving light of a beacon flashed redly at intervals, growing fainter and fainter each time, as day slowly broke, and a golden haze began to flood the eastern horizon. In the darkness the island looked like a huge bare rock, but daylight showed it clothed in tolerably luxuriant vegetation. The presence of man was indicated by the little white houses, which could be distinguished nestling in crannies of its apparently steep green slopes. This was the island of Palma, one of the Canary group, and small though it looked, it numbers a good many inhabitants, and furnishes a fair contingent of emigrants to the River Plate, where "Canarios," as they are called, are favourably looked upon, being a skilful, industrious race.

The days slipped quickly by, and soon, as we neared the equator, it began to grow intensely hot. Christmas Day spent in the tropics did not rightly appear as such, though we kept it in the orthodox manner, the head-steward preparing quite a banquet, at which much merriment reigned, and many speeches were spoken.

We arrived at Pernambuco on the 28th December, but did not go on shore, as we were only stopping in the port a couple of hours, and were told, moreover, that there is nothing to be seen when one is there. We amused ourselves watching the arrival of some fresh Brazilian passengers, who were going with us to Rio. The extensiveness of their get-up might have vied with that of Solomon "in all his glory"—but tall hats, white trousers, and frock-coats seemed ludicrously out of place on board ship. Not less funny was the effusiveness of their affectionate leave-takings. At parting they clasped their friends to their breasts, interchanging kisses in the most pathetic manner, and evincing an absence of mauvaise honte in the presence of us bystanders, which was at once edifying and refreshing. Autres pays, autres mœurs.

Some boatmen came alongside, bringing baskets of the celebrated Pernambuco white pineapples. We bought some of this fruit, which we thought delicious: it is the only tropical fruit which, in my opinion, can vie with European kinds. "Luscious tropical fruit" sounds very well, as does "the flashing Southern Cross;" but nearer acquaintance with both proves very disappointing, and dispels any of the illusions one may have acquired respecting them, from the over-enthusiastic descriptions of imaginative travellers. Very soon the captain came off shore again, with the mails, etc. A bell was rung, the fruit-vendors were bundled over the side of the ship, chattering and vociferating,—last kisses were interchanged by the Brazilian passengers and their friends, up went the anchor, round went the screw, bang! went our parting salute, and, thank God, we are off again, with a slight breeze stealing coolingly over us, doubly grateful after the stifling heat which oppressed us while at anchor.

CHAPTER II

BAHIA—RIO DE JANEIRO—RIO HARBOUR—THE TOWN—
AN UPSET—TIJUCA—A TROPICAL NIGHT—MORE UP-
SETS—SAFETY AT LAST

A DAY AFTER LEAVING PERNAMBUCO we dropped anchor again; this time in the magnificent "Bahia de todos los Santos," the ample dimensions of which make its name a not inapposite one. Bahia itself is built on a high ridge of land, which runs out into the sea, and forms a point at the entrance of the harbour. The town is half hidden among huge banana trees and cocoanut palms, and seen from on board looks picturesque enough. After breakfast our party went on shore, accompanied by the captain, and for an hour or so we walked about the streets and markets of the lower town, which stands at the base of the ridge above mentioned. We found it as dirty and ugly as could well be, and our sense of smell had no little violence done to it by the disagreeable odours which pervaded the air. There was a great deal of movement going on everywhere, and the streets swarmed with black slaves, male and female, carrying heavy loads of salt meat, sacks of rice, and other merchandise to and from the warehouses which lined the quays. They all seemed to be very happy, to judge by their incessant chatter and laughter, and not overworked either, I should think, for they were most of them plump enough, the women especially being many of them almost inconveniently fat. Finding little to detain us in the lower town, we had ourselves transported to the upper in an hydraulic lift, which makes journeys up and down every five minutes.

Then we got into a mule-tramway, which bowled us along the narrow streets at a famous pace. Soon getting clear of the dirty town, we drove along a pleasant high-road, on either side of which stood pretty little villas, shaded by palms and banana-trees, and encircled by trim well-kept gardens, bright with a profusion of tropical flowers. Now and then we could catch a glimpse of the sea too, and as we went along we found the tram was taking us out to the extreme point of the ridge mentioned above. Before we reached it we had to change our conveyance once or twice, as occasionally we came to a descent so steep that carriages worked up and down by hydraulic machinery had been established to ply in conjunction with the ordinary mule-trams. At last we were set down close to the seashore, near a lighthouse which stands in a commanding position on the point. The view which was now before us was a splendid one; the immense bay lay at our feet, and beyond spread the ocean, dotted with the tiny white sails of numberless catamarans, as the queer native fishing-boats are called, which looked like white gulls resting on its blue waters. But the heat in the open was so overpowering that we soon had to take refuge in a little café close by, where we had some luncheon, after which we went back to Bahia the way we had come, by no means sorry to get on board the cool, clean ship again. Half an hour after our arrival the anchor was weighed, and we steamed off, en route for Rio de Janeiro.

New Year's Day, like Christmas Day, was passed at sea, and we celebrated it with much festivity. Altogether our life on board was a most agreeable one, thanks to the kindness and attentions of the captain and his officers, and the days flew by with surprising rapidity. Four days after leaving Bahia we sighted land off Rio, at an early hour of the morning. Anxious to lose nothing of the scenery, I had risen at about four o'clock, and certainly I had no reason to repent of my eagerness. We had passed Cape Frio, and were steaming along a line of coast which runs from the cape up to the opening of the bay. Thick mists hung over the high peaks and hills, shrouding their outlines, and along the shore the surf broke with a sullen roar against the base of the cliffs which fell abruptly down to the sea. As yet all was grey and indistinct. But presently the sun, which for a long time had been struggling with the mists, shone victoriously forth; the fog disappeared as if by magic, disclosing, bathed in the glow of sunrise, a grand scene of palm-covered cliffs and mountains, which rose, range beyond range, as far as the eye could reach. In front of us lay Rio Harbour, with the huge Paõ de Agucar, or Sugar Loaf Mountain, standing like a gigantic sentry at its entrance. In shape it is exactly like the article of grocery from which it takes its name, and rises abruptly, a solid mass of smooth rock, to a height of 1270 feet. Its summit, long considered inaccessible, was reached by some English middies a few years ago. Much to the anger and disgust of the inhabitants of Rio, these adventurous youngsters planted the Union Jack on the highest point of the Loaf, and there it floated, no one daring to go up to take it down, till a patriotic breeze swept it away. Directly opposite is the Fort Santa Cruz, which, with its 120 guns, forms the principal defence of the harbour. Soon we were gliding past it, and threading our way through the numerous craft which studded the bay, we presently dropped anchor in front of Rio, and found ourselves at leisure to examine the harbour, one of the finest and largest in the world. Covering a space of sixteen miles in a north and south direction, it gradually widens from about three-quarters of a mile at its entrance to fifteen miles at its head. The town stands on the western side of the bay, at about two miles from its entrance. It is backed by a high range of mountains, and, as seen from the bay, nestling amidst oceans of green, presents a most pleasing appearance. The harbour is dotted with little islands, and all along its shores are scattered villages, country seats, and plantations.

As soon as the captain had got through his duties we took our places in his boat, and started off for the shore. On landing at a slippery, dirty, stone cause-way, we were surrounded by a crowd of negroes, who jabbered and grinned and gesticulated like so many monkeys. Making our way through their midst, we passed by the market-place, and then, threading a number of hot, dirty, little streets, we at last got into the main street of the town, which was rather broad, and shaded on either side by a row of trees.

The public buildings at Rio are all distinguished by their peculiar ugliness. They are mostly painted yellow, a hue which seems to prevail everywhere here, possibly in order to harmonise with the complexion of the inhabitants. The cathedral forms no exception to the general rule. We entered it for a moment, thinking that we might possibly see some good pictures from the time of the Portuguese dominion. But we found everything covered up in brown holland. Nossa Senhora da Francisca, or whatever virgin saint the church is dedicated to, was evidently in curl-papers, and we could see nothing, though we could smell a great deal more than was agreeable. Truly I did not envy the saints their odour of sanctity. To my mundane nostrils this same odour smacked strongly of garlic and other abominations. We soon got tired of wandering aimlessly about, and feeling little desire to stop in the town any longer, we hired a carriage and started off for a little place called Tijuca, which lies high up among the hills behind Rio.

Our coach was drawn by four fine mules, who galloped along the streets at a rattling and—inasmuch as the driver was evidently an unskilful one—an undesirable pace. We remonstrated with him, but were told that it was the custom of the country to drive at that rate. So, in deference to the "custom of the country," on we went at full gallop, shaving lamp-posts, twisting round sharp corners, frightening foot-passengers, and narrowly missing upsetting, or being upset by, other vehicles which came in the way.

I was quite thankful when we at last got safely clear of the town. The road lay amongst the most beautiful scenery, and the heat, though considerable, was not oppressive enough to interfere with my enjoyment of it. After a couple of hours' driving we halted to give the mules a rest near a little brook, which came rippling out from the shady mass of vegetation which lined the road. I sat down under a banana tree, letting my eyes wander in lazy admiration over the scene at our feet. We had gradually got to a good height above Rio, and through a frame of leaves and flowers I could see the town, the blue bay studded with tiny green islands, and beyond, the rugged mountains, with a light mist hanging like a silver veil over their purple slopes.

When the mules were sufficiently rested we got into the carriage, and starting at a brisk trot, it was not long before we got to the summit of a hill, at the foot of which, in a little valley, lies Tijuca. Before reaching it a rather stiff incline had to be descended, and one of the wheelers, either blown or obstinate, refused to hold the carriage back. The driver insisted that the animal was only showing temper, and commenced to flog it. Foreseeing the result, we all got out of the carriage, and left the man to his own devices. He persisted in whipping the recalcitrant mule, and, as might have been expected, he presently started the other animals off at full gallop, leaving their comrade the option of following suit or falling. It chose the latter course, and after a good deal of slipping and sliding, went down with a tremendous crash. The other three, taking fright, immediately bolted, and we soon lost sight of carriage and driver in a cloud of dust. We followed on down the hill as fast as we could, rather anxious for the safety of the driver. Here and there, as we hurried along, we came across a piece of broken harness, and presently, on turning a sharp corner, we suddenly came upon the overturned carriage, the mules struggling and kicking in a confused heap, and the driver, unhurt but frightened, sitting in the grass by the side of the road. Assistance having been procured from Tijuca, which was close at hand, the mules were freed, and the carriage raised off the dragged mule, which we expected to find killed. To our surprise, however, no sooner were its limbs at liberty than it sprang up and began to crop the grass in utter unconcern as to the numerous wounds all over its body. A horse in such a state would have been completely cowed, and would probably never have been of any use again.

Leaving the driver to make the best of his position, we walked down to the Hotel Whyte, which lies snugly ensconced among palms and orange-groves at Tijuca. The building, with its clean cool rooms, shaded by verandahs, looked particularly inviting after the establishments we had been in at Rio, and it was pleasant too, to be waited on by Englishmen—the proprietor and his staff being of that nationality. A little stream runs past the hotel, feeding a basin which has been hewn out of the rock, where visitors can refresh themselves with a plunge, a privilege of which the gentlemen of our party were not slow to profit.

After I had rested a little I strolled away among the woods, feasting my eyes on the beauty and novelty of the vegetation, and on the delightful glimpses of scenery I occasionally stumbled across, to attempt to describe which would only be doing them an injustice. But that even this paradise had its drawbacks I was not long in discovering. I was about to throw myself on a soft green bank, fringed with gold and silver ferns and scarlet begonias, that stretched along a sparkling rivulet, when suddenly my little terrier darted at something that was lying on the bank, and pursued it for a second, till my call brought her back. The "something" was a snake of the Cross, whose bite is almost instantaneously fatal, and as I quickly retraced my steps to safer ground I thanked my stars that I had been spared a closer acquaintance with this deadly reptile. When I got back I had a swim in the rocky basin above mentioned, which refreshed me wonderfully. Soon afterwards we sat down to dinner, winding up the day by a cheery musical evening.

Before going to bed, enticed by the beauty of the night, I strolled for an hour or more among the woods at the back of the hotel, and gradually, attracted by the noise of falling waters, I made my way to a little cataract, which, coming from some rocky heights above, dashed foaming into a broad basin, and swirling and bubbling over a stony bed, disappeared below in the shadows of a lonely glen. The moon, which was now shining brightly, cast a pale gleam over its waters, and myriads of fireflies flashed around like showers of sparks. Not a sound was heard save the roar of the water, and hardly a breath of wind stirred the giant foliage of the sleeping forests. For a long time I sat giving myself up to the softening influences of my surroundings, and thinking, amidst the splendour of that warm tropical night, of the dear old country far away, now, no doubt, covered with ice and snow.

As we had to be on board the steamer by twelve o'clock the next morning, the carriages were ordered for eight o'clock, by which time we were up and had breakfasted. The captain, my husband, brother, and myself, took our seats in a carriage drawn by two mules, Queensberry and Mr. B. following in a Victoria. Having said good-bye to Mr. Whyte, we told our driver to start, cautioning him, as he was the same Jehu who had driven us so recklessly the day before, to be more careful. But again, for some unaccountable reason, he cracked his whip and started off at full gallop. Again the mules bolted, and like lightning we went down a little incline which leads from the hotel to the road. Then a sharp turn had to be made, seeing which we held on like grim death to the carriage, an upset being now palpably inevitable. On we went—the carriage heeled over, balanced itself for a moment on its two left wheels, and then, catching the corner of a stone bridge, over it went with a crash, burying us four luckless occupants beneath it, and hurling the driver into the brook below. Happily the shock had thrown the mules as well, for had they galloped on, huddled as we were pell-mell among the wheels of the carriage, the accident must have ended in some disaster. As it was, we had a most miraculous escape. The driver, who meanwhile had picked himself, drenched and crestfallen, out of the brook, came in for a shower of imprecations, which his stupidity and recklessness had well earned for him. He made some feeble attempts at an explanation, but no one understood him, and he only aggravated the virulence of our righteous wrath.

However, something had to be done, and quickly, if we were to reach the steamer by twelve o'clock. The Victoria was now the only conveyance left, and we could not all get into it. As luck would have it, whilst we were debating, a diligence was seen coming along the road, and, as it proved, there were sufficient vacant seats to accommodate all our party,—Queensberry, Mr. B. and myself going in the Victoria. The driver having assured us that the mules were perfectly quiet, and he himself appearing a steadier sort of man than the other unfortunate creature, we felt more at ease, and certainly at first start all went smoothly enough. But, strange to say, we were doomed to incur a third upset. When we came to a steep descent, instead of driving slowly, our coachman, for some inexplicable reason, actually urged his animals into a gallop. We called to him to stop, but that was already beyond his power, the mules having again bolted, and, to make matters still more desperate, one of the reins broke, leaving us completely at the mercy of accidents. The road wound down the side of a steep hill, and each time the swaying carriage swung round one of the sharp curves we were in imminent danger of being dashed over the roadside, down a precipice three hundred feet in depth. The peril of this eventuality increased with our momentum, and, as the lesser of two evils, we had to choose jumping out of the carriage. This we did at a convenient spot, and fortunately, though we were all severely cut and bruised, no bones were broken. In another second the coach and driver would have disappeared over the precipice had not one of the mules suddenly fallen, and, acting as a drag on the coach, enabled the driver to check the other mule just in the nick of time.

To meet with three accidents in twenty-four hours was rather too much of a good thing, and vowing that we had had enough of Brazilian coachmanship to last us all our lives, we completed the rest of the way on foot, arriving two hours after the appointed time, on board the old "Britannia." We presented a very strange appearance, our clothes torn and dust-stained, and our faces covered with cuts and bruises; but a bath and a little court-plaster soon put us all right, and we were on deck again in time to have a last look at Rio as we steamed away.

CHAPTER III

BEAUTIES OF RIO—MONTE VIDEO—STRAITS OF MAGELLAN—TIERRA DEL FUEGO—ARRIVAL AT SANDY POINT—PREPARATIONS FOR THE START—OUR OUTFIT— OUR GUIDES

I COULD NOT REPRESS A PANG OF REGRET as we steamed slowly out of Rio Harbour. There may be scenes more impressively sublime; there are, without doubt, landscapes fashioned on a more gigantic scale; by the side of the Himalayas or the Alps, the mountains around Rio are insignificant enough, and one need not go out of England in search for charming and romantic scenery. But nowhere have the rugged and the tender, the wild and the soft, been blended into such exquisite union as at Rio, and it is this quality of unrivalled contrasts, that, to my mind, gives to that scenery its charm of unsurpassed loveliness. Nowhere else is there such audacity, such fierceness even of outline, coupled with such multiform splendour of colour, such fairy-like delicacy of detail. As a precious jewel is encrusted by the coarse rock, the smiling bay lies encircled by frowning mountains of colossal proportions and the most capricious shapes. In the production of this work the most opposite powers of nature have been laid under contribution. The awful work of the volcano; the immense boulders of rock which lie piled up to the clouds in irregular masses, have been clothed in a brilliant web of tropical vegetation, spun from sunshine and mist. Here nature revels in manifold creation, life multiplies itself a million fold, the soil bursts with exuberance of fertility, and the profusion of vegetable and animal life beggars description. Every tree is clothed with a thousand luxuriant creepers, purple and scarlet-blossomed; they in their turn support myriads of lichens and other verdant parasites. The plants shoot up with marvellous rapidity, and glitter with flowers of the rarest hues and shapes, or bear quantities of luscious fruit, pleasant to the eye and sweet to the taste.

The air resounds with the hum of insect-life; through the bright green leaves of the banana skim the sparkling humming-birds, and gorgeous butterflies of enormous size float, glowing with every colour of the rainbow on the flower-scented breezes. But over all this beauty, over the luxuriance of vegetation, over the softness of the tropical air, over the splendour of the sunshine, over the perfume of the flowers, Pestilence has cast her fatal miasmas, and, like the sword of Damocles, the yellow fever hangs threateningly over the head of those who dwell among these lovely scenes. Nature, however, is not to be blamed for this drawback to one of her most charming creations. With better drainage and cleanlier habits amongst its population, there is no reason why Rio should not be a perfectly healthy place. To exorcise the demon who annually scourges its people, no acquaintance with the black art is necessary. The scrubbing-brush and Windsor soap—»this only is the witchcraft need be used.» Four days after leaving Rio we arrived at Monte Video, but as we came from an infected port we were put into quarantine, much to our disgust, and were of course unable to go on shore. After we had discharged what cargo we carried for Monte Video, we proceeded to a little island, where we were to land the quarantine passengers, amongst whom was my brother Queensberry, who wanted to stop in Monte Video for a fortnight, following us by the next steamer. The quarantine island, which was a bare rocky little place, did not look at all inviting, and I certainly did not envy my brother his three-days› stay on it. He told me afterwards that he had never passed such a miserable time in all his life, the internal domestic arrangements being most primitive.

The days after leaving Monte Video passed swiftly enough, as it had got comparatively cool, and we were able to have all kinds of games on deck. After seven days at sea, early one morning we sighted Cape Virgins, which commands the north-eastern entrance to the Straits of Magellan. The south-eastern point is called Cape Espiritu Santo; the distance between the two capes being about twenty-two miles. Whilst we were threading the intricate passage of the First Narrows, which are not more than two miles broad, I scanned with interest the land I had come so many thousand miles to see—Patagonia at last! Desolate and dreary enough it looked, a succession of bare plateaus, not a tree nor a shrub visible anywhere; a grey, shadowy country, which seemed hardly of this world; such a landscape, in fact, as one might expect to find on reaching some other planet. Much as I had been astonished by the glow and exuberance of tropical life at Rio, the impression it had made on my mind had to yield in intensity to the vague feelings of awe and wonder produced by the sight of the huge barren solitudes now before me.

After passing the Second Narrows, Elizabeth Island, so named by Sir Francis Drake, came in sight. Its shores were covered with wild fowl and sea-birds, chiefly shag. Flocks of these birds kept flying round the ship, and the water itself, through which we passed, literally teemed with gulls and every imaginable kind of sea-fowl. We were soon abreast of Cape Negro, about fourteen miles from Sandy Point. Here the character of the country suddenly changes, for Cape Negro is the point of the last southerly spur of the Cordilleras, which runs along the coast, joining the main ridge beyond Sandy Point. All these spurs, like the Cordilleras themselves, are clothed with beech forests and thick underwood of the magnolia species, a vegetation, however, which ends as abruptly as the spurs, from the thickly-wooded sides of which, to the completely bare plains, there is no graduation whatever.

As we went along we passed a couple of canoes containing Fuegians, the inhabitants of the Tierra del Fuego, but they were too far off to enable me to judge of their appearance, though I should have liked to have had a good look at them. They are reputed to be cannibals, and no doubt justly so. I have even been told that in winter, when other food is scarce, they kill off their own old men and women, though of course they prefer a white man if obtainable.

At one o'clock we cast anchor off Sandy Point. This settlement is called officially by the Chileans, to whom it belongs, "La Colonia de Magellanes." It was formerly only a penal colony, but in consequence of the great increase of traffic through the Straits, the attention of the Chilian Government was drawn to the importance the place might ultimately assume, and, accordingly, grants of land and other inducements were offered to emigrants. But the colony up to the present has never flourished as was expected, and during a mutiny which took place there in 1877, many of the houses were burned down, and a great deal of property destroyed. As the steamer was to leave in two hours, we began preparations for landing, but meantime the breeze, which had sprung up shortly after our arrival, freshened into a gale, and the sea grew so rough that it was impossible to lower a boat, and the lighters that had come off shore to fetch away cargo dared not go back. The gale lasted all day and the greater part of the night, calming down a little towards three o'clock in the morning. Every effort was accordingly made to get us on shore, the alternative being that we should have to go on with the steamer to Valparaiso, the Company's regulations not allowing more than a certain length of time to be spent at Sandy Point. As may be imagined, we by no means liked the idea of such a possible consummation, and the weather was eagerly scanned, whilst our luggage and traps were being hurried over the sides, as a fresh increase in the strength of the wind would have been fatal.

At last all was ready; we said good-bye to the captain and officers, to whose kindness during the voyage we were so much indebted for our enjoyment of our trip on board the "Britannia"—and climbing down the gangway took our seats in the boat which was to carry us ashore. I felt quite sad as we rowed away, leaving behind us the good ship which we had come to look upon as a home, and for which I at least felt almost a personal affection.

CHAPTER IV

THE START FOR CAPE NEGRO—RIDING ALONG THE STRAITS—CAPE NEGRO—THE FIRST NIGHT UNDER CANVAS—UNEXPECTED ARRIVALS—OUR GUESTS—A NOVEL PICNIC—ROUGH-RIDING—THERE WAS A SOUND OF REVELRY BY NIGHT

EARLY IN THE MORNING THE HORSES WERE DRIVEN up and saddled, some trouble being experienced with the pack-mules, who were slightly restive, taking rather unkindly to their loads at first.

As our guides were busy hunting up the requisite number of horses, and finishing their preparations for the journey, we took another man with us for the time that we should have to remain at Cabo Negro, as well as a little boy, a son of Gregorio's, to help to drive the horses along. After a hurried breakfast we got into the saddle; the pack-horses were driven together, not without a great deal of trouble, for they were as yet strangers to each other, and every now and then one or two would bolt off, a signal to the whole troop to disperse all over the place, so that nearly an hour had elapsed before we had got well clear of the colony, and found ourselves riding over an undulating grassy stretch, en route for the pampas.

Our way lay over this plain for about an hour, and then, having forded a small stream, we entered the outskirts of the beechwood forests that line the Straits. The foliage of the trees was fresh and green, the sky clear and blue, the air sun-lit and buoyant, and everything seeming to augur favourably for the success of our trip, we were all in the best of spirits.

Our road presently brought us down to the Straits of Magellan, along whose narrow strip of beach, in some places barely three yards broad, we had now to ride in single file. Along the coast the land terminates abruptly, and the trees and bushes form an impenetrable thicket, which comes down almost to the water's edge. Point after point shoots out into the sea, each bearing a monotonous resemblance to the other, though, as we advanced, the vegetation that covered them grew more and more stunted and scanty, till at last the trees and bushes disappeared altogether, and after a three hours' ride we found ourselves journeying along under the shadow of some steep bluffs, on which the only vegetation was a profusion of long coarse grass. Innumerable species of gulls and albatrosses were disporting themselves on the blue water, and seemed little alarmed at our approach, lazily rising from the water a moment as we went past them, to resume almost immediately their fishing operations. All along the beach, carried there by the sea from the opposite side, I noticed great quantities of the cooked shells of crayfish, the remains of many a Fuegian-Indian meal. The Tierra del Fuego itself was distinctly visible opposite, and at different points we could see tall columns of smoke rising up into the still air, denoting the presence of native encampments, just as Magellan had seen them four hundred years before, giving to the island, on that account, the name it still bears.

At Cabo Negro we stopped for a moment at a little farmhouse, and partook of some maté, which was hospitably offered us by the farmer's wife, and then mounting again, we galloped over a broad grassy plain where some sheep and cattle were grazing, till we came to a steep, wooded hill. On its crest, under some spreading beeches, we resolved to pitch our camp, water being near at hand, and the position otherwise favourable. In a short time the pack-horses were relieved of their loads, and neighing joyfully, they galloped away to graze in the plain we had just crossed. Our tents were pitched, and having made up our beds in them, so as to have everything ready by night-time, we began to set about preparing dinner. Wood being abundant, a roaring fire was soon blazing away cheerily, some meat we had brought from Sandy Point was put into the iron pot, together with some rice, onions, etc., and then we lay down round the fire, not a little fatigued by our day's exertions; but inhaling the grateful odours arising from the pot, with the expectant avidity of appetites which the keen Patagonian air had stimulated to an unusual extent.

By the time dinner was over night had set in. The moon had risen, and the clear star-lit sky gave assuring promises of a continuance of fine weather. A slight breeze stirred the branches overhead, and in the distance we could hear the lowing of the cattle on the plains, and the faint tinkling of the bells of the brood-mares. The strange novelty of the scene seemed to influence us all, and the men smoked their pipes in silence. Before going to bed I went for a short stroll to the shores of a broad lagoon which lay at the foot of the hill on which our camp was pitched. Its waters glittered brightly in the moonlight, but the woods which surrounded it were sombre and dark. Occasionally the sad plaintive cry of a grebe broke the silence, startling me not a little the first time I heard it, for it sounds exactly like the wail of a human being in pain. Going back to the camp I found my companions preparing to go to bed, an example I was not slow to follow, and soon, wrapt up in our guanaco-fur robes, with our saddles for pillows, we were all fast asleep.

It had been agreed that the next morning one of our party should go back to Sandy Point, to see how the guides were getting on, and Mr. B. having volunteered to perform that task, I rose at an early hour to get him his breakfast and see him off on his journey. Then, whilst my brother and husband went out with their guns to shoot wild-duck, I busied myself writing a few last letters to friends at home. This done, I rode down to the Straits, and had a plunge into the water, but it was so cold that I got quite numbed, and with difficulty managed to dry and dress myself. Late in the afternoon the sportsmen returned, bringing an excellent bag with them, and we speedily set about plucking a few birds, and making other preparations for dinner. Just as, that meal being over, we had settled ourselves comfortably round the fire, prepared lazily to enjoy the lovely evening, our camp-servant, who had been on the look-out for the return of Mr. B., reported that a troop of about ten horsemen were coming our way. As Indian traders do not go out to the pampas in such large parties, he was quite at a loss to imagine who the people could be who were riding out so late at night, especially as they had no pack-horses with them. We all got up and went to have a look at these mysterious horsemen. As they approached the foot of our hill we could see that they were all armed with guns and rifles, a circumstance which began to suggest unpleasant recollections of the last Sandy Point mutiny. Could it be that another outbreak had occurred, and that these men were escaping to the pampas? If so, they might possibly make a descent on us in passing, and supply any deficiencies in their own outfit from ours. This was a rather startling state of affairs, and we were hurriedly holding counsel as to what was the best course to take under the circumstances, when our dogs suddenly started up, and began barking furiously. Then came the sound of horses' hoofs, and brushing through the tall furze, two horsemen galloped straight towards our camp, followed, as the sound of voices told us, by the rest of the party. In another second the two foremost ones reined up in front of us, turning out to be, not bloodthirsty mutineers, but Mr. Dunsmuir and Mr. Beerbohm. A few words explained all. The party was composed of some officers of the "Prinz Adalbert," a German man-of-war, which had anchored at Sandy Point that morning, Mr. B. having gone on board and invited them out to our camp for a day's shooting. Delighted at this solution of the situation, we hurried to welcome our new guests, who now arrived tired and hungry after their long ride. Among their number were H.I.H. Prince Henry of Prussia, who was on a cruise in the "Prinz Adalbert," and her commander, Captain Maclean.

Fresh logs were added to the blazing fire, meat was set to roast, soup put on to cook, and every preparation made for a good supper—an easy task, as the officers had brought plentiful supplies of all kinds of provisions with them. We then lay round the fire, the new-comers evidently quite charmed by our cosy sylvan quarters, and by the novelty of the strange picnic, which they had little anticipated making in Patagonia, of all places in the world.

I was much amused at Mr. B.'s account of how the expedition had been initiated. He had got into Sandy Point at about nine o'clock, and at ten the "Prinz Adalbert" was signalled in the offing.

As soon as she had cast anchor he went on board, having been previously acquainted with the captain, and at breakfast explained his presence in such an out-of-the-way part of the world as Sandy Point, by an account of our intended trip, and finally asked the captain and the officers to come out to our camp and try for themselves what open-air life in Patagonia was like. He had little difficulty in persuading them to accept his offer, and whilst the officers made their preparations, he went on shore to hunt up ten horses, the number required. This was an easy matter; but it was another thing to find as many saddles, for, though many people in Sandy Point own numbers of horses, few have more than one saddle, and such being the case, they are loth to lend what at any moment may be of pressing necessity for themselves. However, by dint of ingenious combinations, some kind of an apology for a saddle was fitted to each horse, and the whole party at last set off on their trip in high spirits, and very well pleased with everything. Each officer carried a blanket or rug with him, and, as some shooting was expected, a gun and some ammunition. For the first two hours all went well, the air was warm and sunny, the scenery novel and interesting, and a zest was given to the expedition by its unconventional character and the suddenness with which it had been improvised.

But after a time the hard action of the horses and the roughness of some of the saddles began to have their effect, especially as many of the officers were little accustomed to riding. Occasionally Mr. B. would be asked, at first in tones of implied cheerful unconcern, "How far is it to the camp?" To this question he would reply by a wave of the hand in the direction of one of the many points which shoot out along the Straits, saying, "A little beyond that point." Then, as point after point was passed, and the answer to inquiries still continued, as before, "A little beyond that point," gradually the laughter and chat which had enlivened the outset of the trip grew more constrained, occasional lapses of complete silence intervening. Now and then one of the riders would move uneasily in the saddle and sigh—and on the faces of many (especially of those who rode stirrupless saddles) fell in time an expression of fixed resignation to suffering, which was not unheroic. Mr. B. observed all this, and his conscience began to smite him. At starting, in an amiable endeavour to put everything in a rosy light, he had slightly understated the distance to our camp, and now the terrible consequences of his rashness were already visiting him. The quasi-martyrs whom he was leading, it was but too evident, were only bearing up against suffering by the comforting consciousness that they must be close to the camp. He could not undeceive them; he felt himself woefully wanting in courage enough to break the truth; and yet the only alternative was to go on repeating the now to him, as to everybody else, hateful formula, "A little beyond that point." His victims could only imagine one thing—that he had lost the way, though in fact he knew the road and its length only too well. Never, as he said, had it been so palpably brought before him that the way to hell is paved with good intentions; and his intentions, when mystifying the party as to the length of the road, had been of the best.

However, all things come to an end, and at last, with a feeling of deep relief, he was able to point out our hill to the weary saddle-worn band, whose advent, as possible mutineers, had thrown us into such a panic.

By the time Mr. B. had finished his story supper was ready, and that important fact having been duly announced, our hungry guests fell to, and made a hearty meal. The strain which their number put on the capabilities of our batterie de cuisine was fortunately relieved by a profusion of tinned provisions of all kinds which they had wisely brought with them, and under those Patagonian beeches, together with the native mutton, were discussed asperges en jus, which had attained their delicate flavour under the mild fostering of a Dutch summer, patés elaborated far away among the blue Alsatian mountains, and substantial, though withal subtly flavoured, sausages from the fatherland itself. After supper pipes were lit, and the wine-cup went round freely, the woods resounding with laughter and song till nearly midnight, by which time most of the party were beginning to feel the effects of their day's exertions, and to long for bed. In one of our tents we managed to make up four couches, on which the

Prince, the Captain, Count Seckendorff, and another officer respectively laid their weary limbs, and went to sleep as best they might. The Captain, a strong stout man, had suffered more than any one from the ride, and it must have been a moot question in his secret heart whether the day's enjoyment had not been somewhat dearly purchased.

The others kept up the ball still later, and it must have been quite two o'clock before the last convive rolled himself up in his blanket by the fire, and silence fell over our camp. At about that hour I peered out of my tent at the scene. Round a huge heap of smouldering logs, in various attitudes, suggestive of deep repose, lay the forms of the sleepers whom chance had thus strangely thrown together for one night. Our dogs had risen from their sleep, and in their turn were making merry over whatever bones or other fragments of the feast they managed to ferret out. A few moonbeams struggled through the canopy of leaves and branches overhead, throwing strange lights and shadows over the camp, and the weird effect of the whole scene was heightened by the mysterious wail of the grebe, which at intervals came floating up in the air from the lake below, like the voice of an unquiet spirit.

CHAPTER V

DEPARTURE OF OUR GUESTS—THE START FOR THE PAMPAS—AN UNTOWARD ACCIDENT—A DAY'S SPORT—UNPLEASANT EFFECTS OF THE WIND—OFF CAPE GREGORIO.

THE SUN HAD HARDLY RISEN THE NEXT MORNING ere our little camp was again astir. Making a hasty toilet I stepped out and found that our guests had all risen, and were busy in getting their guns and shooting accoutrements ready for the coming sport. As soon as they had partaken of some coffee, the whole party started off to the plains below, and for an hour or so, till their return, the repeated reports of their guns seemed to indicate that they were having good sport. Towards breakfast-time they came back, fairly satisfied with their morning's work, though I am inclined to attribute this satisfaction to their evident desire to look at everything connected with their picnic from an optimist point of view, as their bag was in reality a very small one, consisting only of a few brace of snipe and wild-duck. We then set to work to get a good breakfast ready, at which employment Prince Henry lent an intelligent hand, turning out some poached eggs in excellent style. We had a very pleasant meal, the officers expressing great regret that they were unable to prolong their stay in our beechwood quarters, the steamer being obliged to continue her journey that evening. Whilst they smoked a last pipe, the horses were driven up and saddled, and at about eight o'clock, Mr. B. and myself accompanying them as guides, they mounted and set out on the road homeward.

The stiffness consequent on their exertions of the previous day must have made the sensations they experienced on returning to the saddle anything but pleasant ones, and at the start a decidedly uncheerful spirit seemed to prevail among them; but as we cantered along, and they warmed to their work, this uneasiness disappeared, and soon all were as merry as possible. The day was lovely, and the scenery looked to the best advantage, the only drawback to our enjoyment of the ride being that the sun was rather too hot.

After we had gone several miles we got off our horses to rest under the shade of some trees, by the side of a little stream which came bubbling out of the cool depths of the forest, emptying itself into the adjacent Straits. Here an incident occurred which might have been attended with inconvenient consequences. One of the officer's horses suddenly took it into its head to trot off, and, before any one could stop it, disappeared round a point in the direction of Sandy Point. Mr. B. got on his horse and started in pursuit, and in the meanwhile a time of some suspense ensued, for, in the event of his being unsuccessful, some unfortunate would have had to make the best of his way on foot. However, this unpleasant contingency was happily avoided; Mr. B. soon reappeared, having managed to catch the runaway, not indeed without a great deal of trouble.

We reached Sandy Point late in the afternoon, and very glad the whole party must have been to get there, for they were most of them completely done up, and, considering the length of the ride, their rough horses and rougher saddles, this was no wonder.

After having said good-bye to the officers, with many expressions of thanks on their part for the unexpected diversion our presence in that outlandish part of the world had afforded them, Mr. B. and I immediately set out to return to the camp, which we managed to reach just as it was getting dark.

Everything was now ready for our journey, and it was resolved that we should make a start the next morning. We were therefore up early, in order to help the guides as much as possible with the packing, which was quite a formidable undertaking. It took fully three hours to get our miscellaneous goods and chattels stowed away on the pack-horses, whose number was thirteen. At last, however, all was ready; we got into the saddle, and with a last glance at the beechwood camp, which had grown quite familiar and home-like to us, we rode off, now fairly started on our journey into the unknown land that lay before us. We soon had our hands full to help the guides to keep the horses together, a rather difficult task. The mules in particular gave great trouble, and were continually leading the horses into mischief. At one time, as if by preconcerted signal, the whole troop dispersed in different directions into the wood, and there, brushing through the thick underwood, many of the pack-horses upset their packs, and trampled on the contents, whilst some of the others turned tail, and coolly trotted back to the pasture-ground they had just left at Cabo Negro.

All this was very provoking, but, with a little patience and a good deal of swearing on the part of the guides, the refractory pack-horses were re-saddled, the troop was got together again, and by dint of careful driving we at last got safely out of the wooded country, and emerged on the rolling pampa, where there was for some distance a beaten Indian track, along which the horses travelled with greater ease, till, gradually understanding what was required of them, they jogged on in front of us with tolerable steadiness and sobriety, which was only occasionally disturbed by such slight ebullitions as a free fight between two of the stallions, or an abortive attempt on the part of some hungry animal to make a dash for some particularly inviting-looking knoll of green grass at a distance off the line of our march.

COLLECTING THE 'TROPILLA'— SADDLING UP

The country we were now crossing was of a totally different character to that we had left behind us. Not a tree or a shrub was to be seen anywhere, and while to the left of us lay the rugged range of the Cordilleras, in front and to the right an immense plain stretched away to the horizon, rising and falling occasionally in slight undulations, but otherwise completely and monotonously level. The ground, which was rather swampy, was covered with an abundance of coarse green grass, amongst which we could see flocks of wild geese grazing in great numbers. We passed several freshwater lakes, covered with wild-fowl, who flew up very wild at our approach. A hawk or two would occasionally hover over our heads, and once the dogs started off in pursuit of a little grey fox that had incautiously shown itself; but except these, there was no sign of animal life on the silent, seemingly interminable plain before us.

After we had ridden for several hours, we turned off to the left, facing the Cordilleras again, and soon the plain came to a sudden end, a broken country now appearing, over which we rode till nightfall, when we came in sight of the "Despuntadero," the extremity of Peckett's Harbour, an arm of the sea which runs for some distance inland. Here we were to camp for the night, and as we were all rather tired and hungry after our long ride, we urged on our horses to cover the distance that still lay between us and our camping-place as quickly as possible. But to "hasten slowly" would have been a wiser course in this case, as in most others. The rapid trot at which we now advanced disturbed the equilibrium of one of the packs, the cords holding which had already become slack, and down came the whole pack, iron pot, tin plates, and all, with an awful clatter, whilst the mare who carried it, terrified out of her wits, dashed off at a gallop, spurring with her heels her late encumbrances, and followed by the whole troop of her equally frightened companions.

The pampa was strewn with broken bags; and rice, biscuits, and other precious stores lay scattered in all directions. When we had picked up what we could, and replaced the pack on the mare, who in the meantime had been caught again, we were further agreeably surprised by the sight of another pack-less animal galloping over the brow of a distant hill, followed at some distance by Gregorio, who was trying to lasso it, whilst I'Aria was descried in another direction, endeavouring to collect together another scattered section of our troop. Off we scampered to aid him, turning on the way to drive up one of the mares, whom we accidentally found grazing with her foal in a secluded valley, "the guides forgetting, by the guides forgot."

By the time we got up to I'Aria, the obstinacy and speed of the refractory animals had evidently proved too much for him, inasmuch as we found him sitting under a bush philosophically smoking a pipe. In answer to our query as to what had become of the horses, he waved his hand vaguely in the direction of a distant line of hills, and we were just setting off on what we feared would prove a rather arduous quest when a welcome tinkle suddenly struck our ears, and the troop reappeared from the depths of a ravine, driven up by Francisco, who had providentially come across them in time to intercept their further flight.

It was quite dark as we rode down and pitched our camp by the shore of the inlet above mentioned, under the lee of a tall bluff, not far from a little pool of fresh water. After the tents had been set up some of the men went to look for firewood, but there was a scarcity of that necessary in the region we were now in, and the little they could collect was half green. However, we managed to make a very fair fire with it, and our dinner was soon cooked and eaten, whereupon we retired to rest.

The next morning was fine, and we resolved to stop a day at our present encampment and have some shooting,—game, as Gregorio informed us, being plentiful in that region. After a light breakfast we took our guns and started off in the direction of a group of freshwater lakes which lay beyond a range of hills behind our camp. We were rewarded for our arduous climb by some excellent sport, wild geese, duck, etc., being very plentiful, and on our way back we crossed some marshy ground where there were some snipe, several brace of which we bagged. In the afternoon, it being rather hot and sultry, we refreshed ourselves with a bath in the sea, and then came dinner-time, and by half-past seven we were in bed and asleep.

The following day we continued our journey northward. A long day's ride brought us to some springs, called "Pozos de la Reina," where we camped for the night. After we had rested for a short time round the fire, and had leisure to look at one another, we became aware of a most disagreeable metamorphosis that had taken place in our faces. They were swollen to an almost unrecognisable extent, and had assumed a deep purple hue, the phenomenon being accompanied by a sharp itching. The boisterous wind which we had encountered during the day, and which is the standing drawback to the otherwise agreeable climate of Patagonia, was no doubt the cause of this annoyance, combined possibly with our salt-water bath of the day previous.

After a few days the skin of our faces peeled off completely, but the swelling did not go down for some time. I would advise any person who may make the same journey to provide themselves with masks; by taking this precaution they will save themselves a great deal of the discomfort we suffered from the winds.

The following day we left "Pozos de la Reina," and pushed forward as quickly as possible, as we had no meat left, and had not yet arrived in the country of the guanacos and ostriches. The Indians had very recently passed over all the ground we were now crossing, and, as usual, had swept away any game there might have been there.

The range where guanaco really become plentiful is about eighty miles away from Sandy Point. Still we kept a good look-out, and any ostrich or guanaco that might have had the misfortune to show itself would have stood a poor chance of escape with some eight or nine hungry dogs and a number of not less keen horsemen at its heels.

But the day wore on, and we arrived at our destination empty-handed. The spot we camped at lay directly in front of Cape Gregorio, which was hazily visible in the distance. There was an abundance of wood in the locality, and the Indian camp being not far off, we were conveniently situated in every respect, as we intended paying these interesting people a visit before continuing our journey.

CHAPTER VI

VISIT TO THE INDIAN CAMP—A PATAGONIAN—INDIAN CURIOSITY—PHYSIQUE—COSTUME—WOMEN—PROMINENT CHARACTERISTICS—AN INDIAN INCROYABLE—SUPERSTITIOUSNESS

SINCE WE LEFT SANDY POINT our dogs had had no regular meal, and had subsisted chiefly on rice and biscuits, a kind of food which, being accustomed to meat only, was most uncongenial to their tastes and unprofitable to their bodies. For their sakes, therefore, as well as for our own, we looked forward to our visit to the Indian camp, apart from other motives of interest, in the hopes of obtaining a sufficient supply of meat to last for all of us, until we should arrive in the promised land of game.

After breakfast the horses were saddled, and taking some sugar, tobacco, and other articles for bartering purposes, we set out for the Indian camp, accompanied by Gregorio and Guillaume. I'Aria and Storer were left in charge of our camp, and Francisco went off with the dogs towards Cape Gregorio, in the hope of falling in with some stray ostrich or guanaco. The weather was fine, and for once we were able to rejoice in the absence of the rough winds which were our daily annoyance. We had not gone far when we saw a rider coming slowly towards us, and in a few minutes we found ourselves in the presence of a real Patagonian Indian. We reined in our horses when he got close to us, to have a good look at him, and he doing the same, for a few minutes we stared at him to our hearts' content, receiving in return as minute and careful a scrutiny from him. Whatever he may have thought of us, we thought him a singularly unprepossessing object, and, for the sake of his race, we hoped an unfavourable specimen of it. His dirty brown face, of which the principal feature was a pair of sharp black eyes, was half-hidden by tangled masses of unkempt hair, held together by a handkerchief tied over his forehead, and his burly body was enveloped in a greasy guanaco-capa, considerably the worse for wear. His feet were bare, but one of his heels was armed with a little wooden spur, of curious and ingenious handiwork. Having completed his survey of our persons, and exchanged a few guttural grunts with Gregorio, of which the purport was that he had lost some horses and was on their search, he galloped away, and, glad to find some virtue in him, we were able to admire the easy grace with which he sat his well-bred looking little horse, which, though considerably below his weight, was doubtless able to do its master good service.

Continuing our way we presently observed several mounted Indians, sitting motionless on their horses, like sentries, on the summit of a tall ridge ahead of us, evidently watching our movements. At our approach they disappeared over the ridge, on the other side of which lay their camping-ground. Cantering forward we soon came in sight of the entire Indian camp, which was pitched in a broad valley-plain, flanked on either side by steep bluffs, and with a little stream flowing down its centre. There were about a dozen big hide tents, in front of which stood crowds of men and women, watching our approach with lazy curiosity. Numbers of little children were disporting themselves in the stream, which we had to ford in order to get to the tents. Two Indians, more inquisitive than their brethren, came out to meet us, both mounted on the same horse, and saluted us with much grinning and jabbering. On our arrival in the camp we were soon encircled by a curious crowd, some of whose number gazed at us with stolid gravity, whilst others laughed and gesticulated as they discussed our appearance in their harsh guttural language, with a vivacious manner which was quite at variance with the received traditions of the solemn bent of the Indian mind. Our accoutrements and clothes seemed to excite great interest, my riding-boots in particular being objects of attentive examination, and apparently of much serious speculation. At first they were content to observe them from a distance, but presently a little boy was delegated by the elders, to advance and give them a closer inspection. This he proceeded to do, coming towards me with great caution, and when near enough, he stretched out his hand and touched the boots gently with the tips of his fingers. This exploit was greeted with roars of laughter and ejaculations, and emboldened by its success, many now ventured to follow his example, some enterprising spirits extending their researches to the texture of my ulster, and one even going so far as to take my hand in his, whilst subjecting a little bracelet I wore to a profound and exhaustive scrutiny.

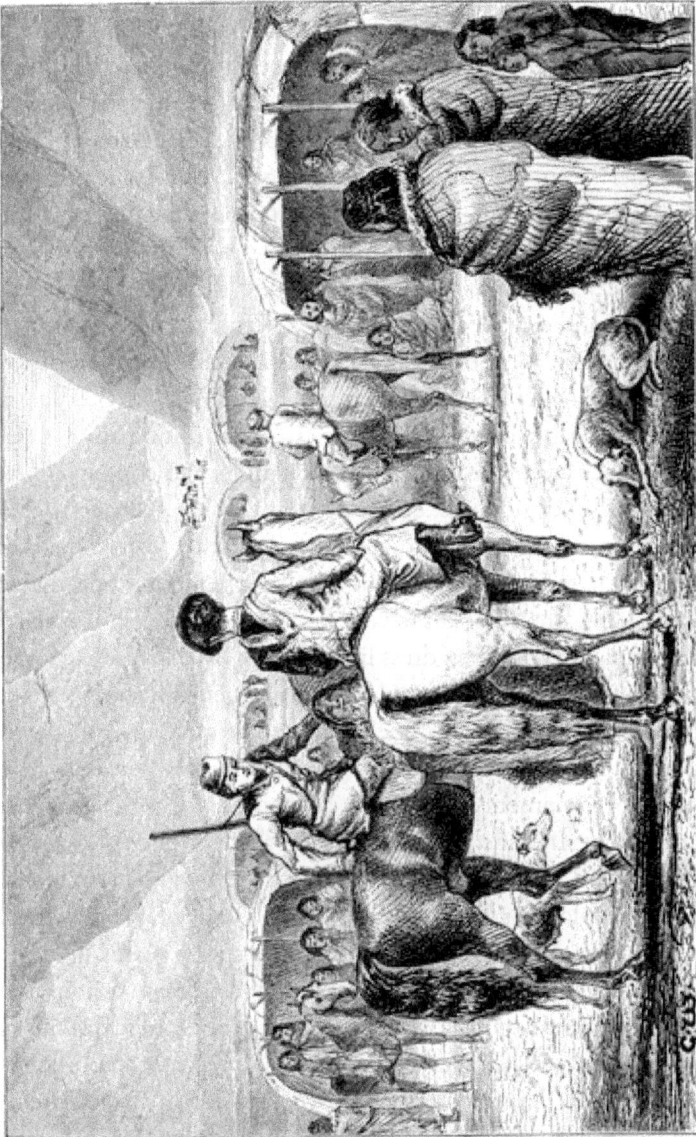

Whilst they were thus occupied I had leisure to observe their general appearance. I was not struck so much by their height as by their extraordinary development of chest and muscle. As regards their stature, I do not think the average height of the men exceeded six feet, and as my husband stands six feet two inches I had a favourable opportunity for forming an accurate estimate. One or two there were, certainly, who towered far above him, but these were exceptions. The women were mostly of the ordinary height, though I noticed one who must have been quite six feet, if not more. The features of the pure-bred Tehuelche are extremely regular, and by no means unpleasant to look at. The nose is generally aquiline, the mouth well shaped and beautified by the whitest of teeth, the expression of the eye is intelligent, and the form of the whole head affords a favourable index to their mental capabilities. These remarks do not apply to the Tehuelches in whose veins there is a mixture of Araucanian or Fuegian blood. The flat noses, oblique eyes, and badly proportioned figures of the latter make them most repulsive objects, and they are as different from a pure-bred Tehuelche in every respect as "Wheel-of-Fortune" from an ordinary carthorse. Their hair is long and coarse, and is worn parted in the middle, being prevented from falling over their faces by means of a handkerchief, or fillet of some kind, tied round the forehead. They have naturally little hair on the face, and such growth as may appear is carefully eradicated, a painful operation, which many extend even to their eyebrows. Their dress is simple, and consists of a "chiripá," a piece of cloth round the loins, and the indispensable guanaco capa, which is hung loosely over the shoulders and held round the body by the hand, though it would obviously seem more convenient to have it secured round the waist with a belt of some kind. Their horse-hide boots are only worn, for reasons of economy, when hunting. The women dress like the men except as regards the chiripá, instead of which they wear a loose kind of gown beneath the capa, which they fasten at the neck with a silver brooch or pin. The children are allowed to run about naked till they are five or six years old, and are then dressed like their elders. Partly for ornament, partly also as a means of protection against the wind, a great many Indians paint their faces, their favourite colour, as far as I could see, being red, though one or two I observed had given the preference to a mixture of that colour with black, a very diabolical appearance being the result of this combination.

The Tehuelches are a race that is fast approaching extinction, and even at present it scarcely numbers eight hundred souls. They lead a rambling nomadic existence, shifting their camping places from one region to another, whenever the game in their vicinity gets shy or scarce. It is fortunate for them that the immense numbers of guanaco and ostriches makes it an easy matter for them to find subsistence, as they are extremely lazy, and, plentiful as game is around them, often pass two or three days without food rather than incur the very slight exertion attendant on a day's hunting.

But it is only the men who are cursed or blessed with this indolent spirit. The women are indefatigably industrious. All the work of Tehuelche existence is done by them except hunting. When not employed in ordinary household work they busy themselves in making guanaco capas, weaving gay-coloured garters and fillets for the hair, working silver ornaments, and so forth. Not one of their least arduous tasks is that of collecting firewood, which, always a scarce article, becomes doubly hard to find, except by going great distances, when they camp long in one place.

But though treated thus unfairly as regards the division of labour, the women can by no means complain of want of devotion to them on the part of the men. Marriages are matters of great solemnity with them, and the tie is strictly kept. Husband and wife show great affection for one another, and both agree in extravagant love of their offspring, which they pet and spoil to their hearts' content.

The most prominent characteristic of the Tehuelche is his easy-going good humour, for whereas most aboriginal races incline to silence and saturnine gravity, he is all smiles and chatter. The other good qualities of the race are fast disappearing under the influence of "aquadiente," to the use of which they are getting more and more addicted, and soon, it is to be feared, they will become nothing more than a pack of impoverished, dirty, thieving ragamuffins.

After having sat for some time on horseback, in the centre of the numerous circle above referred to, we dismounted, the act causing fresh animation and merriment in our interviewers, whose interest in us, after a thorough examination, had begun to flag somewhat. An object which greatly excited their feelings was a rifle belonging to my brother, and their delight knew no bounds when he dismounted and fired it off for their edification once or twice at a distant mark. At each discharge they set up a lusty howl of satisfaction, and nothing would do for them but for each to be allowed to handle the weapon and inspect its mechanism. There was a trader in the camp who had arrived about the same time as we did, and amongst other wares he had brought a rusty carbine with him for sale. He was called upon by the Indians to produce it and fire it off to compare its qualities with those of my brother's rifle. This he proceeded to do, but seven times in succession the cartridges missed fire. Each time this happened he was greeted with shouts of derisive laughter, and it was evident that both he and his weapon were the objects of most disparaging remarks on the part of the Tehuelches. One of them, a man of some humour, brought out a small piece of ostrich meat and offered it to the trader in exchange for his carbine, saying in broken Spanish, "Your gun never kill piece of meat as big as this. Your gun good to kill dead guanaco." At which witticism there was renewed and prolonged applause, as the newspapers say.

But excitement reached its height when I produced the bag of sugar we had brought, and began to distribute small handfuls of its contents among the children. Everybody pressed round me—men and women, hustling and pushing in their eagerness to get some of the coveted dainty. I was obliged to be careful in my bounty, however, or we should not have enough left to obtain any meat in exchange, and a great many sweet-toothed Tehuelches had to remain disappointed in consequence. As it was, we found considerable difficulty in obtaining any meat. The Indians had not been out hunting for three days, and there was hardly anything but pemmican in the camp,—a greasy concoction, with which we by no means cared to experiment on our stomachs. With difficulty we at last succeeded in obtaining the leg and breast of an ostrich, and a small piece of half sun-dried guanaco meat, which looked extremely untempting. This transaction having been accomplished, we wandered leisurely about the camp, glancing at the different objects of interest that came in our way, pestered not a little as we moved along by swarms of yelping curs, which barked and snapped viciously at us, and could only be kept at a respectful distance by a free use of stones and whips. At one of the tents we saw two remarkably clean and pretty girls, who were engaged on some kind of sewing work; and beside them—probably making love to one (or both)—stood an equally good-looking youth, who struck me by the peculiar neatness of his dress, and his general "tiré à quatre epingles" appearance. His hair was brushed and combed, and carefully parted,—a bright red silk handkerchief keeping its glossy locks in due subjection. His handsome guanaco capa was new, and brilliantly painted on the outside, and being half opened, displayed a clean white chiripá, fastened at the waist by a silver belt of curious workmanship. A pair of neatly fitting horse-hide boots encased his feet, reaching up to the knees, where they were secured by a pair of gay-coloured garters, possibly the gift of one of the fair maidens at his side.

Struck by his graceful bearing and well-bred looking face, I begged Mr. B., who had brought a sketch-book with him, to make a sketch of this handsome son of the pampa. During the process the young Indian never moved, and preserved a perfectly indifferent demeanour; but when the picture was finished, and given to him for inspection, his forehead contracted with anger, an expression of fear came in his eyes; he gave vent to some angry sounding gutturals, and finally, much to our annoyance, tore the portrait to pieces. He was under the impression that the object of making the sketch was to throw some evil spell over him, and that a misfortune would happen if it were not destroyed. Being relieved of this danger, his feelings regained their natural calm, and he grinned contentedly at our evident wrath at his high-handed proceeding.

The Indians were about to make their annual visit to Sandy Point, where they go to obtain the rations of sugar, tobacco, etc., allowed to them by the Chilian Government, and to barter with the inhabitants for the luxuries of civilisation, in exchange for furs and ostrich feathers, at which transactions, as they are seldom sober during their stay outside the colony, they generally get worsted by the cunning white man. Our curiosity regarding the Indians being satisfied, and having obtained all the meat we could from them, we now turned homewards.

CHAPTER VII

THE PRAIRIE FIRE

A S WE RODE ALONG, our attention was attracted by a faint smell of burning, and presently thick clouds of smoke came rolling towards us. We pressed wonderingly on, anxious to discover the whereabouts of the fire, which we trusted lay somewhere far from our camp. Reaching a slight eminence, we were able to command a view of the country ahead. A cry of dismay escaped our lips as we looked around, and drawing rein, we stared blankly at one another. A fearful sight lay before us. To our left, right in front, and gradually wreathing the hills to our right, a huge prairie fire came rushing rapidly along. Dense masses of smoke curled aloft, and entirely obscured the sky; the flames, which shot fiercely up, cast a strange yellow glare over everything. Even whilst we watched, a strong gust of wind swept the fire with incredible swiftness towards us, and in a second we were enveloped in such a dense cloud of smoke that we were unable to see one another. The situation had now become critical, and not a moment was to be lost. Half choked, and bewildered by the suddenness with which the danger had come upon us, we scarcely knew what course to take. Already our horses were snorting with fear, as the crackling of the burning grass and bushes came nearer and nearer. To run away from the coming fire was useless; the alternative was to face it at a gallop, and get through it if possible. To throw our guanaco mantles over our heads, and draw them as tightly round us as we could, was the work of a second, and then digging our spurs into our horses, we dashed forward, every one for himself. The moments that followed seemed an eternity. As I urged my unwilling horse forward, the sense of suffocation grew terrible, I could scarcely draw breath, and the panting animal seemed to stagger beneath me. The horrible crackling came nearer and nearer; I became conscious of the most intolerable heat, and my head began to swim round. My horse gave two or three furious plunges, and then burst madly forward. Almost choked, come what might, I could bear the mantle over my head no longer, and tore it off me. The sudden sense of relief that came over me as I did so, I shall never forget. I looked up, the air was comparatively clear, and the fire behind me. By some miracle I had passed through it unhurt! I looked for my companions, and, to my inexpressible joy, saw them emerge one by one from the black mass of smoke, which was now rapidly receding into the distance. Congratulations and exclamations over, we retraced our steps to try and discover how we had managed to escape so luckily. The reason was soon apparent. By a piece of fortune we had happened to ride over a narrow pebbly tract of ground, where the grass was extremely sparse, and where there were but few bushes; had chance led us over any other track, where the grass was thick and tall, we could scarcely ever have got through the danger. Our poor horses had suffered a good deal as it was, their feet and legs being scorched and singed severely.

Our thoughts now flew to our camp, and to Storer and I'Aria, whom we had left behind there. That they had escaped we had little doubt, but for our tents and chattels we felt there was no hope. The landscape seemed completely changed by the fire, all around, as far as we could see, stretched black smoking plains, and the outlines of the hills had become quite unfamiliar to us.

With rather heavy hearts we pushed forward, eagerly scanning the country for some indication which might guide us to the quarter where our camp had stood. If, as we had every reason to believe, our things were burnt, our Patagonian trip was at an end, for the present, at all events. Fortunately things did not turn out so badly. Presently my husband, who was riding in advance of the others, gave a shout, and made signals for us to come on. I need hardly say that we did not lose a moment in joining him, and a welcome sight, as we got up to him, met our eyes. Some two or three hundred yards below the hill on which we were, we perceived our little white tents standing safe and unharmed on a narrow green tract of land, which looked like a smiling island in the midst of the vast black plain. Storer and I'Aria, too, we could see moving about, and, overjoyed, we galloped down towards them, they running out to meet us, having suffered no little anxiety, on their parts, as to what might have happened to us. We pressed question after question to I'Aria and Storer as to how they had managed to save the camp. Storer was unable to give any intelligible account, so entirely upset was he by fright, but I'Aria's natural philosophical calm had not deserted him, even on this occasion, and from him we heard all particulars. The fire, he informed us, had been caused by the Indian we had met in the morning on the look-out for strayed horses. This man had amused himself by setting fire to the long dry grass in various places, and, fanned by a strong wind, the flames spread, and soon assumed enormous proportions.

Quick to perceive the possible danger our camp was in, the Indian at once galloped up, and with the assistance of I'Aria and Storer, set about making a "contra-fuego" or counter fire, that is to say, they gradually set fire to the grass all round the camp, letting it burn a considerable tract, but always keeping it well in subjection, beating it out with bushes and trampling it under foot, so that it could not get beyond their control. This precautionary measure was fortunately completed by the time the big fire came on, and although, for a minute or two, they were half suffocated by the smoke, the fire passed harmlessly by the camp itself, the burnt belt around it proving an effectual safeguard.

Our horses were all safe, as they had been grazing on the far side of a stream in an adjacent valley. The camp was in great disorder; the tents were blackened by the smoke, the provision-bags and other chattels lay scattered in confusion. Our furs and rugs had been used to cover the cartridges with, for, whilst the fire raged around it, the camp was deluged with showers of sparks, and an explosion might easily have occurred, had this precaution not been taken. For some time we were busy putting things straight, and in the meanwhile François arrived from his hunting excursion. It had proved unsuccessful; and as we had obtained but very little meat from the Indians, for the sake of our dogs, who had been on very short rations for some time, it became a matter of great urgency that we should get as soon as possible into regions where guanaco and ostrich were plentiful, and accordingly we decided to start on the following day. Dinner over, my companions were not long before they went to sleep, but feeling little inclination to follow their example, I strolled out, and wandered round the camp, watching with interest the strange changes that came over the landscape as day waned and night came slowly on. The black hills behind the camp loomed like shadowy phantoms against the sky; far and wide slept the silent pampa, its undulating surface illumined by the rays of a lovely moon. The faint glow which tinged the horizon, and the strange noises which a puff of wind occasionally brought to my ears, showed that the mighty fire was still burning in the distance with unbated fury, perhaps not to stop in its devastating course till it reached the sea-coast.

For a long time I stood immersed in the contemplation of this weird desolate scene, giving myself up to the mysterious feelings and the many vague and fanciful thoughts it suggested, till, overcome with the excitement and exertions of the day, I had at last to give way to drowsiness and seek my couch.

CHAPTER VIII

UNPLEASANT VISITORS—"SPEED THE PARTING GUEST"—
OFF AGAIN—AN OSTRICH EGG—I'ARIA MISLEADS
US—STRIKING OIL—PREPARATIONS FOR THE CHASE—
WIND AND HAIL—A GUANACO AT LAST—AN EXCITING
RUN—THE DEATH—HOME—HUNGRY AS HUNTERS—
"FAT-BEHIND-THE-EYE."

THE NEXT MORNING we were up betimes, as we were going to continue our journey. Whilst we were engaged in the tedious operation of packing up, an Indian woman walked suddenly into the ring of bushes which surrounded our encampment, and seated herself silently by the fire. Gregorio elicited from her that on the previous night the Indians had been drinking heavily, and that she had had a quarrel with her husband whilst both were inebriated, in consequence of which she had left his tent, and was now on her way to Sandy Point. She had walked the whole distance from the Indian camp barefoot, but did not seem in the least tired. I suppose she counted on her husband's regretting his behaviour, and coming after her to fetch her back, for she could hardly have seriously entertained the idea of walking all the way to Sandy Point. I offered her some biscuits and a stick of chocolate, which she accepted readily enough, but without even so much as a grunt by way of thanks. Presently she told Gregorio that the Indians were breaking up their camp, and that some were going to march on to Sandy Point. This piece of information made us hurry on with our work, as we dreaded being surprised by a party of Indians, with all our effects scattered about, offering tempting facilities for abstraction, which the Tehuelche heart was sure not to be able to resist. To such a visit we were moreover extremely liable, as our camp was unfortunately close to the trail to Sandy Point.

Our fears were realised only too soon, for about a quarter of an hour after the arrival of the squaw two Indians came crashing unceremoniously through the bushes; and wheeling their horses about the camp, careless of our crockery, after a short examination they dismounted, and coolly sat down by our fire, answering our angry looks with imperturbed stares of stolid indifference. Five minutes later another party arrived, followed shortly by a further batch, and presently we were quite inundated by a swarm of these unbidden guests. Of course our work was stopped, all our attention being required to look after our goods and chattels. Over these we kept guard in no very good humour, breathing fervent prayers the while for speedy relief from our friends, who on their part evinced no particular hurry to go away. They had made themselves comfortable at our fire, and were passing round the social pipe in evident good humour with themselves and their present quarters. To complete the irony of the situation, one of their number who could speak Spanish came and asked me for a little coffee, which he purposed to cook in our kettle, which was still simmering conveniently on the fire. As may be imagined, he met with an indignant refusal; however, it only appeared to amuse him and his friends, and by no means influenced them in hastening their departure.

Meanwhile time went on, and some expedient for getting rid of them had to be devised unless we wished to lose a whole day. It occurred to us that they might possibly be bribed to go away by means of a small offering of whisky; and through Gregorio we accordingly intimated to them that if they would leave us they should be rewarded for their kindness with a glass of that spirit. To our relief they accepted this offer, and we presently had the satisfaction of seeing them ride leisurely away. To do them justice, I must say that, contrary to our fears, they did not steal any of our effects, though possibly the strict watch we kept over them may have had something to do with this unusual display of honesty.

The moment they had gone we redoubled our efforts, and succeeded in getting all our horses saddled and packed without further molestation. The three mules still remained to be packed, but these we left to the care of Gregorio and Guillaume who were to follow us, we, meanwhile, starting off under the guidance of old l'Aria. Francisco went off alone, by another route, in order to forage for meat, be it ostrich or guanaco, of which both ourselves and the dogs stood very much in need, the small supply we had got from the Indians being quite exhausted.

Just as we were leaving an Indian galloped up, who turned out to be the husband of the pedestrian squaw, who, after the departure of the other Indians, still remained in our camp. The reconciliation scene was a very short one, and did not go beyond a few inexpressive grunts on either side, after which the squaw got up on horseback behind her husband, and off they rode towards Sandy Point.

We now struck northwards, leaving Cape Gregorio, which lay directly opposite our late encampment, at our backs. l'Aria having to keep the troop together singlehanded we had plenty to do to help him, and in galloping after refractory horses, urging on the lazy ones, and occasionally stopping to adjust packs, the time passed quickly enough. We occasionally crossed tracts of land covered with a plant bearing a profusion of red berries of the cranberry species. They were quite ripe now, and we found them pleasant and refreshing. The weather was, as usual, sunny and bracing; and except that as yet we had not seen a guanaco or given chase to a single ostrich, we had nothing to grumble about. I'Aria told us that we were certain to meet with guanaco on that day's march, so, with this assurance, we comforted ourselves and kept a sharp look-out, eagerly scanning the horizon of each successive plain, and woe betide the unfortunate animal that might appear within our ken. The day passed, however, and a dark patch of beeches, which stood near the spot where we were to camp that night, appeared in view without our having seen either an ostrich or a guanaco. Somebody found an ostrich egg though, and it was carefully kept against dinner-time, for although it must have been laid two or perhaps three months, there was still a possibility of its being tolerably good, as these eggs occasionally keep till the month of April, six months after laying time.

Towards sunset we arrived at a broad valley scattered over with picturesque clumps of beeches, and bordered on its far side by a thick wood of the same tree. I'Aria pointed out a spot to us where he said there were some springs, by the side of which we were to camp, and thither we accordingly rode. But when we got there no springs were to be seen, and I'Aria said he must have mistaken the place. He suddenly remembered, however, that a conspicuous clump of beeches, some way up the valley, marked the right spot, so we turned in that direction. But again was I'Aria mistaken, and when—following various of his sudden inspirations—we had wandered about the valley in all directions for a considerable time without coming across these problematic springs, we began to think ourselves justified in presuming that I'Aria had lost his way, and in charging him with the same. He denied the accusation, however, with a calm and steady assurance, which, considering that all the time he was leading us about in aimless helplessness, would have had something rather humorous about it had our situation been a less serious one. If we did not succeed in finding the springs, besides having to endure the torture of thirst ourselves we should have to stop up all night to look after the horses, who would be certain to go off in search of water and get lost. It was rapidly getting dark too, and there were no signs of the arrival of any of the other guides, whose absence was a further confirmation that we could not be on the right track. As a last resource we resolved to separate, and each go in a different direction in search of water, though I must say we had little hopes of success, it being known to us that beyond the springs in question there was no other water in that part of the country for a considerable distance. Hurling bitter but useless anathemas at I'Aria, who was now confidently pointing out a new spot as the "really" right one, we accordingly broke up, and having arranged to fire a shot as a signal, should any one of us find water, dispersed over the valley in all directions.

I had hardly skirted the beechwood for more than a minute or so when my horse suddenly neighed joyfully, and in an opening among the trees I saw two or three small pools of spring water. Overjoyed, I lost no time in firing off my gun, the report of which soon brought up all the others, who had not gone far. In justice to I'Aria it must be said that for the last hour he had been wandering about close to where the springs lay, and his persistent denial of having lost his way was so far justified. Besides, as there was no trail of any description across the pampa over which we had that day ridden, it was really no easy matter to hit on the right spot immediately.

We had just set up the tents and made the fire when Gregorio and Guillaume, at whose prolonged absence, now that we were at the springs ourselves, we had become rather uneasy, appeared with the mules. They had been delayed on the road by the packs getting undone. Francisco too soon came up, and though he had been unsuccessful in the chase, he arrived in time to cook an excellent omelette for our dinners with the ostrich egg, which turned out to be perfectly sound and palatable.

The next day was to be devoted to guanaco-hunting, the want of meat having become quite a serious matter; our dogs were getting weak, and our stores, on which we had to rely solely for food, were disappearing in an alarmingly quick manner.

It is marvellous how the ordinary excitement of hunting is increased when, as in our case, one's dinner depends on one's success; and it was with feelings almost of solemnity, that early in the morning we selected and saddled our best horses, sharpened our hunting-knives, slung our rifles, and, followed by the dogs, who knew perfectly well that real earnest sport was meant, threaded the beechwood and rode up on to the plateau, where, according to the unanimous assurance of the guides, we could not fail to meet with guanaco.

I'Aria and Storer having been left behind to look after the camp, our hunting-party numbered seven. In order to cover as much ground as possible we spread out in a line, extending over about two miles, and in this order we cantered northward from the valley, carefully scanning the plain, which stretched flat away for a good distance, but apparently as bare of guanaco as it was of grass. The weather, unlike that of the preceding day, was very cold, and a bitterly sharp wind blew right into our faces, making those of our number who had neglected to bring their greatcoats or furs very uncomfortable. This, however, was a trifling matter, if only those good guanacos would obligingly make their appearance! But evidently nothing was farther from their minds, and we rode over the plain, mile after mile, with hopes which, like the thermometer, were gradually sinking towards zero. As time went on, the haze which bound the plateau at our approach solidified itself into an escarpment. In due time this was reached, and I rode up it, expecting to find another plain on its summit as usual. Instead, however, a broken, hilly country appeared in view, crossed in all directions by ravines. I looked eagerly about, but still no guanaco. Our line of advance, meantime, lost its order, owing to the changed nature of the ground, and frequently I lost sight of all my companions, as I descended into a ravine, or rode round the base of some tall hillock; but it was never long before I caught a glimpse of one or other of them again.

The wind got colder and colder, a white cloud crept up on the horizon, and grew and grew, sweeping swiftly towards me, till I suddenly found myself enveloped in a furious hail-storm. I came to a stand-still, and covered up my head to protect myself from the hailstones, which were very large. The squall did not last long, but when I looked up again I found the whole country was whitened over, an atmospheric freak having created a dreary winter landscape in the middle of summer. Suddenly I started; close to me stood, perfectly motionless, and staring me full in the face, a tall guanaco. I was so startled and surprised that for the space of a minute I sat quietly returning his stare. A movement of my horse broke the spell. The guanaco darted up the side of a hill like lightning, and pausing a moment on its summit, disappeared. I meanwhile had unslung my rifle, and was off in pursuit of him. Instead of climbing the hill, I rode quickly round its base, and on the other side, as I had expected, I discovered my friend looking upward, no doubt thinking I should appear by the same road he had come. I had the selfishness, though I am sure sportsmen will excuse it, to wish to kill the first guanaco myself, and I was therefore by no means displeased to find that my companions had not as yet perceived us. With a beating heart I dismounted and walked slowly towards the guanaco, who, though he saw me coming, still remained quietly standing. My weapon was a light rook-rifle, but though an excellent arm, it did not carry more than 150 yards with precision, and I was now something over 180 yards from my prey. He allowed me to advance till within the required distance, but then, to my disgust, just as I was preparing to fire, leisurely walked on another thirty or forty yards before he stopped again, watching me the while, as it seemed with an amused look of impertinence, which aggravated me considerably. I slowly followed him, vowing to fire the moment I was within range, whether he moved or not. This time I was more successful. The guanaco allowed me to come within about the necessary 150 yards. "Poor fellow!" I murmured generously, as I brought my rifle up to my shoulder and took aim just behind his. Only one step forward to make quite certain. Alas! I took it, and down I went into a hole, which in my eagerness I had not noticed, falling rather heavily on my face. In a second I was up again, just in time to see the guanaco bounding up a far escarpment, taking with him my chance of becoming the heroine of the day. There was nothing for it but to walk back to where I had left my horse, and see what had become of my companions.

I took the same road the guanaco had taken, on the remote possibility of falling in with him again. Riding up the escarpment above referred to, I came on to a broad plain, and there an exciting chase was going on, in which, as it appeared, I was condemned to take the part of a spectator only. At some distance, and going across my line of sight, was a guanaco running at full speed, closely followed by a pack of dogs, in whose track, but some way behind, galloped three horsemen, whom I made out to be my husband, and brother, and Gregorio. The guanaco at first seemed to be losing ground, but it was only for an instant; in another he bounded away with ease, and it was apparent that as yet he was only playing with his pursuers. The pace soon began to tell on the dogs; the less speedy were already beginning to tail off, one of them, probably Gregorio's swift Pié-de-Plata, being far in advance of its comrades, and by no means to be shaken off by the guanaco, who had now given up any playful demonstrations of superiority, and had settled down to run in good earnest.

On, on they go—quarry, dogs, horsemen, will soon be out of sight. But what's this? The guanaco has stopped! Only for a moment, though. But he has swerved to the left, and behind him a new dog and horseman have appeared on the scene, emerging, as if by magic, from the bowels of the earth. The chase is now better under my view. If some lucky chance would only bring the guanaco my way! The fresh dog is evidently discomforting him, and his having had to swerve has brought all the other dogs a good bit nearer to his heels. But on he goes, running bravely, and making for the escarpment, for in the hilly country below he knows he is at an advantage The dogs seem to be aware of this too, for they redouble their efforts, a splendid race ensuing. Suddenly another horseman appears on the plateau, and the unfortunate guanaco must again swerve to the left, a movement which, hurrah! brings him almost facing towards where I am standing. That is to say, he must cross the escarpment at some point on a line between myself and the new-comer, the other horsemen, from the manner the race had been run, forming a circle in his rear, which debarred his escape in any other direction. Seeing this, wild with excitement, I dug my spurs into my horse, and flew along the edge of the escarpment, the horseman on the other side doing the same, in order to shut out the guanaco and throw him back on his foes behind. Seeing his last chance about to be cut off, he redoubled his efforts to get through between us. On, on we strain. Nearer and nearer he gets to the edge of the plain, and already, with despair,

I see that I shall be too late. But faster even than the swift guanaco, a gallant blackhound has crept up, and in another instant, though the former dashes past me within a yard of my horse's nose and disappears over the side of the escarpment, the good dog has already made its spring, and, clinging like grim death to the guanaco's haunch, vanishes with him.

After them, in another instant, swept the whole quarry of dogs, and by the time I reined in, and got my horse down the steep ravine-side, they had thrown the guanaco, which Pié-de-Plata had brought to a standstill below; and Francisco, the horseman who had last appeared on the plateau, and at so opportune a moment, had already given the coup-de-grace with his knife.

One after another the other hunters gradually arrived, their horses more or less blown; and whilst pipes were lit and flasks produced, we had leisure to examine this, our first guanaco. Looking at his frame, his long, powerful legs, his deep chest, and body as fine-drawn almost as a greyhound's, we no longer wondered that guanacos run as swiftly as they do. Indeed, this one would have laughed at us, had he not been closed in as he was. The fur of the full-grown guanaco is of a woolly texture, and in colour of a reddish brown on the back, the neck, and the quarters; being whitish on the belly and the inner sides of the legs. The head closely resembles that of a camel; the eyes, which have a strange look on account of the peculiar shape of the eye bones, are very large and beautiful. A fair-sized guanaco weighs from 180 to 200 pounds.

Meantime, Gregorio having begun to cut up the guanaco, to our chagrin it was discovered to be mangy—a disease very common among these animals, probably on account of the brackishness of the water; and the meat being consequently unfit for food, we abandoned it to the dogs, who now made the first good meal they had had since we left Sandy Point. They were soon gorged to such an extent that they became useless for hunting purposes, and we had therefore to ride on, now relying solely on our rifles.

Gregorio had seen a herd of guanacos at the far end of the plain over which the chase had taken place, and thither we accordingly rode. After half an hour's galloping, we reached its limit, finding below a broad valley broken up into various depressions and hillocks. At the base of one of the latter we saw a small herd of guanaco, within range of which, by dint of careful stalking, we presently managed to come. Two fortunate shots brought a couple of their number down, and luckily both turned out to be quite healthy. Under the skilful manipulation of Gregorio and Francisco, in a marvellously short space of time they were cut up, and the meat having been distributed among our various saddles, heavily laden, we turned homewards.

The way back seemed terribly long, now that we had no longer the excitement of hunting to shorten the time; and it seemed quite incredible that we had gone the distance we had been, when, towards sunset, after a cold and weary ride, we at last stood on the edge of the plain which overlooked the valley where lay our home for the nonce.

The evening had turned out fine, the boisterous wind which had annoyed us so much in the daytime had died away, and the sky was now bright and clear. Through the branches of the beech trees I could catch a glimpse of our camp, with its white tents just peeping over the green bushes, and a thin column of blue smoke rising up into the air, pleasantly suggestive of warm tea and other comforts awaiting us. Farther on, in the long green grass of the valley, which was now glowing under the last rays of the sun, were our horses, some grazing, others lying stretched out, lazily enjoying their day's respite from work, whilst the colts and fillies, as is their wont at sundown, were frisking about and kicking up their heels in all the exuberance of youth, unconscious as yet of heavy packs and sharp spurs. Whatever special character the peaceful scene might otherwise want was fully supplied by the picturesquely wild appearance of my companions, as, eschewing contemplation, and anticipating dinner, they rode quickly ahead towards the camp on their shaggy, sturdy horses, their bodies muffled in the graceful guanaco robe, and huge pieces of red raw meat dangling on either side of their saddles, followed by the blood-stained hounds, who seemed thoroughly tired after their hard day's work.

But whatever country one is in, whatever scenes one may be among—in one's own cosy snuggery in England, or in the bleak steppes of Patagonia— there is a peculiar sameness in the feeling that comes over one towards the hours of evening, and which inevitably calls up the thought, It must be getting near dinner-time. Yielding to this admonition, which to-day was by no means less plain than usual, I quitted my eyrie and rode down to the camp.

When I got there I found preparations for an ample meal in full swing. Ingeniously spitted on a wooden stave, the whole side of a guanaco was roasting before a blazing fire, and in the pot a head of the same animal was yielding its substance towards the production of what I was assured would turn out an excellent soup. At dinner-time I was able practically to confirm this assurance; a better broth cannot be concocted than that obtained from such a guanaco head, with the addition of rice, dried vegetables, chilis, etc. But, at the risk of incurring the charge of digressing too much on the subject of eating, I must pay a tribute to the delicacy of a peculiar morsel in the guanaco, which we called "Fat-behind-the-Eye," and which is, in fact, a piece of fat situated as indicated by its name. The tongue and the brain are rare tit-bits, but they must yield in subtle savouriness to the aforesaid bonne-bouche. Having once tasted it, till the end of our trip guanaco head formed a standing item in our daily messes, and whatever other culinary novelties we discussed, and they were as numerous as strange, "Fat-behind-the-eye" always retained its supremacy in our affections as the *ne plus ultra* of pampa delicacies.

CHAPTER IX

ELASTIC LEAGUES—THE LAGUNA BLANCA—AN EARTH-
QUAKE—OSTRICH-HUNTING

W E SHOULD LIKE TO HAVE LINGERED on in the beechwood valley, but the necessity of pushing forward as quickly as possible was too urgent to allow of our indulging in our lazy desires, and daybreak saw our party once more in the saddle.

The country over which we rode this day was more rugged and hilly than any we had crossed previously; the sun shone down upon us in all the intensity of its summer heat, and the glare of the hot dry ground affected our eyes painfully as we rode along.

"How far have we still to go?" was a question which was often on our lips, though, from experience, we might have known that, whatever answer we got from the guides, we should be no wiser than before. They would reply glibly enough, four or five leagues, as the case might be, but we had found that their ideas of a league were most elastic, appearing to vary daily, and to an extent which made it impossible for us to form any mean average even, to guide us to an approximate estimation of the value of their assertions. Thus, a league might mean ten miles to-day, and to-morrow possibly only one.

At length, as the sun was beginning to sink, a shout from one of the guides made us glance wearily up. We found ourselves on the brow of an escarpment, at the foot of which extended a far-stretching plain, in the midst of which, shimmering like a sheet of silver, lay a broad lake, called "Laguna Blanca," or the White Lake.

This welcome sight at once revived our drooping spirits, and for the next hour we rode merrily forward, following Gregorio, who was seeking for a little ravine, where there was a small freshwater stream which flowed down towards the lake. We soon came upon it, and lost no time in jumping out of the saddle and setting to work with a will, at the erection of our tents and the preparation of our evening meal. The latter having been discussed, we went to bed.

The sun was rather high in the heavens when I opened my eyes the next morning, and, pulling aside the flap of the tent, looked out upon the scene. All our camp was still wrapt in sleep save I'Aria, who was sitting over the fire smoking his pipe, whilst he watched the kettle boiling, in placid expectation of his morning coffee. The plains below were silent; but the air was noisy with the cries of the flocks of geese and wild-duck, who were winging their flight from the lake towards the rich fields of cranberries farther inland. The sharp quack of the ibis would occasionally startle me, as a bevy of these birds passed seemingly just over my head, but, in reality, far up in the air.

From the contemplation of this scene I was suddenly and rudely awakened. A loud rumbling sound rose on the air; and, before I had time to wonder what it could mean, a heaving of the ground, resembling a sea-swell, sent me flying on my back, and, as by magic, the silent camp became alive with shouts of fear and wonder, as everybody rushed out of the tents in dismay. The shocks occurred again and again, but each time weaker, and in about five minutes they had ceased altogether, but it was some time before we recovered our equanimity. This was the first time I had ever experienced an earthquake, and such a sickly sensation of helplessness as comes over one during the heaving up and down of the earth would, I should think, be hard to equal. Our guides told us that none of them had ever felt an earthquake in Patagonia before, nor had they ever heard of one having taken place.

Later on, on our return to Sandy Point, we learnt that the earthquake had caused a good deal of disaster in the colony. All the bottles and stores in Pedro's shop were thrown from their shelves and broken, and there were few inhabitants in the colony who did not sustain some similar loss.

As may be imagined, the earthquake provided us with matter for conversation for some time, and in that respect, at least, was a not unwelcome occurrence.

Breakfast over, it was agreed that we should separate into two parties, one for the purpose of ostrich-hunting, whilst the other should devote its energies to the pursuit of the guanaco. My husband and Mr. B. preferring the latter chase, rode off with their rifles, together with Gregorio and Guillaume, towards the hilly country we had crossed the day before.

As soon as they were gone my brother and I, with François, started off along a ridge of hills which exactly faced our camp, and which sloped down into the plains below. We were followed by four ostrich hounds, and were mounted on the best and fleetest horses we could select out of our tropilla. The little animal that I bestrode could not have exceeded fifteen hands. He was a high-spirited little bay with a white blaze down his face, and three white legs. He would clamber up precipitous places where the stones and rocks crumbled and gave way beneath his feet, or canter down a steep decline, and jump the wide gullies with the greatest ease. As we galloped along the smoother ground which intervened between the hills, and which was deeply undermined by hundreds of holes of the "tuca-tuca" (prairie rat), his activity in avoiding a fall astonished me. My brother was equally well mounted on a long, low, clever black, who had the reputation of great speed; while François rode a well-shaped brown, with handsome arching neck and tiny head.

As we rode silently along, with our eyes well about us, in the hopes of sighting an ostrich, my horse suddenly shied at something white lying on the ground at a few paces distant. Throwing the reins over his head, I dismounted and walked towards the spot. Amongst some long grass I discovered a deserted nest of an ostrich containing ten or eleven eggs, and calling François to examine them, was greatly chagrined to find that none of them were fresh. With the superstition of an ostrich-hunter François picked up a feather lying close at hand, and sticking it in his cap, assured us that this was a good sign, and that it would not be long before we came across one of these birds.

His prediction was speedily verified, for on reaching the summit of a little hill, up which we had slowly and stealthily proceeded, two small gray objects suddenly struck my eye. I signed to François and my brother, who where riding some twenty yards behind me, and putting spurs to my horse, galloped down the hill towards the two gray objects I had perceived in the distance. "Choo! choo!" shouted François, a cry by which the ostrich-hunters cheer their dogs on, and intimate to them the proximity of game. Past me like lightning the four eager animals rushed, bent on securing the prey which their quick sight had already detected.

The ostriches turned one look on their pursuers, and the next moment they wheeled round, and making for the plain, scudded over the ground at a tremendous pace.

And now, for the first time, I began to experience all the glorious excitement of an ostrich-hunt. My little horse, keen as his rider, took the bit between his teeth, and away we went up and down the hills at a terrific pace. On and on flew the ostriches, closer and closer crept up "Leona," a small, red, half-bred Scotch deerhound, with "Loca," a wiry black lurcher at her heels, who in turn was closely followed by "Apiscuña" and "Sultan." In another moment the little red dog would be alongside the ostriches. Suddenly, however, they twisted right and left respectively, scudding away in opposite directions over the plain, a feint which of course gave them a great advantage, as the dogs in their eagerness shot forward a long way before they were able to stop themselves. By the time they had done so the ostriches had got such a start that, seeing pursuit was useless, we called the dogs back. We were very much disappointed at our failure, and in no very pleasant frame of mind turned our horses' heads in the direction of our camp.

As we rode along we were surprised by the sudden appearance of a man on horseback, galloping towards us. He was dressed in a guanaco robe, and his long black hair floating on the wind, gave him a very wild look. "An Indian!" I exclaimed. But François shook his head, and we rode up to meet the stranger. When he got up to us he shook hands with François, whom he seemed to know, and, without evincing any sign of curiosity as regarded ourselves, turned his horse round, and prepared to accompany us. I observed that although his face, legs, and hands were almost as copper-coloured as those of an Indian, his features were those of a white man. François presently told me that he was a Chilian convict, who had deserted from Sandy Point a good many years ago, and that since then he had lived among the Indians, adopting their dress and customs, till he had now become quite one of them. In reply to my questions it appeared that he was camping with some Indians on the other side of the lake. They had been out hunting, and he was just returning home when he saw us, and having nothing better to do, thought he might as well pay a visit to our camp.

We were a good deal chaffed when we got home on the score of our non-success, my husband and Mr. B. having had a good day's sport, bringing plenty of guanaco meat back with them. Over pipes and coffee that night a serious council of war was held by the whole of our party, as regards ostrich-hunting for the morrow.

The Chilian suggested the forming of a circle, and professed himself willing, in return for our hospitality, to remain another day and join in the affair. Forming a circle is the method by which the Indians nearly always obtain game. It is formed by lighting fires round a large area of ground into which the different hunters ride from all sides. A complete circle of blazing fires is thus obtained, and any game found therein is pretty sure to become the prey of the dogs, as no ostrich or guanaco will face a fire. Wherever they turn they see before them a column of smoke, or are met by dogs and horsemen. Escape becomes almost impossible, and it is not long before they grow bewildered and are captured. In anticipation of a hard day's work on the morrow, we hereupon broke up our council of war, and turned in at an earlier hour than usual.

Next morning, the horses being all ready, we lost no time in springing into the saddle, leaving Storer to take charge of the camp, much to his alarm, and in spite of his earnest remonstrance. The poor man vainly protested that, were the Indians to discover our retreat, he would be perfectly powerless to prevent their pillaging the whole camp, especially as his ignorance of their "jargon," as he scornfully termed the Tehuelche language, would place him in a most helpless position. Regardless of his arguments and imploring looks we rode away, determining to risk the improbable intrusion of the Indians, whose camp lay at least twenty miles distant from our own. For about half an hour we followed Gregorio and the Chilian along a line of broken hillocks, after which, calling a halt, we sent forward Guillaume and l'Aria to commence the first and most distant proceedings of the circle. They departed at a brisk canter, and it was not long before several rising columns of smoke testified that they were already busily engaged. The next to compose the centre circle were my husband, François, and Mr. B., shortly after supported on the right by the Chilian and my brother. Immediately on their left Gregorio and myself commenced operations, and soon a distinct circle of fires might be seen springing quickly up from all points. I could not help being greatly impressed with the novel sight now before me. From the high plain we were on I could look over miles and miles of untrodden desert land, where countless herds of guanaco were roaming in peaceful lazy ease. In the distance towered the peaks of the Andes, wrapped in their cloak of mystery, lonely and unexplored. The huge columns of smoke and the lurid flames of the circle-fires lent a wild appearance to the thrilling scene, to which the frightened knots of guanacos, which were hurrying to escape from the circle and the eager galloping horsemen, lent additional active animation.

For some time Gregorio and I rode slowly and silently on our way, when a sudden unexpected bound which my horse gave all but unseated me. "Avestruz! Avestruz!" shouted Gregorio, and turned his horse with a quick movement. "Choo! choo! Plata!" I cry to the dog who followed at my horse's heels, as a fine male ostrich scudded away towards the hills we had just left with the speed of lightning. Plata has sighted him, and is straining every limb to reach the terrified bird. He is a plucky dog and a fleet one, but it will take him all his time to come alongside that great raking ostrich as he strides away in all the conscious pride of his strength and speed. "We shall lose him!" I cry, half mad with excitement, spurring my horse, who is beginning to gasp and falter as the hill up which we are struggling grows steeper and steeper. But the ostrich suddenly doubles to the left, and commences a hurried descent. The cause is soon explained, for in the direction towards which he has been making a great cloud of smoke rises menacingly in his path, and, baulked of the refuge he had hoped to find amidst the hills, the great bird is forced to alter his course, and make swiftly for the plains below. But swiftly as he flies along, so does Plata, who finds a down-hill race much more suited to his splendid shoulders and rare stride. Foot by foot he lessens the distance that separates him from his prey, and gets nearer and nearer to the fast sinking, fast tiring bird. Away we go, helter-skelter down the hill, unchecked and undefeated by the numerous obstacles that obstruct the way. Plata is alongside the ostrich, and gathers himself for a spring at the bird's throat. "He has him, he has him!" I shout to Gregorio, who does not reply, but urges his horse on with whip and spur. "Has he got him, though?" Yes—no—the ostrich with a rapid twist has shot some thirty yards ahead of his enemy, and whirling round, makes for the hills once more. And now begins the struggle for victory. The ostrich has decidedly the best of it, for Plata, though he struggles gamely, does not like the uphill work, and at every stride loses ground. There is another fire on the hill above, but it lies too much to the left to attract the bird's attention, who has evidently a safe line of escape in view in that direction. On, on we press; on, on flies the ostrich; bravely and gamely struggles in its wake poor Plata. "Can he stay?" I cry to Gregorio, who smiles and nods his head. He is right, the dog can stay, for hardly have the words left my lips when, with a tremendous effort, he puts on a spurt, and races up alongside the ostrich. Once more the bird points for the plain; he is beginning to falter, but he is great and strong, and is not beaten yet. It will take all Plata's time and cunning to pull that magnificent bird to the ground, and it will be a long fierce struggle ere the gallant creature yields up his life. Unconscious of anything but the exciting chase before me, I am suddenly disagreeably reminded that there is such a thing as caution, and necessity to look where you are going to, for, putting his foot in an unusually deep tuca-tuca hole, my little horse comes with a crash upon his head, and turns completely over on his back, burying me beneath him in a hopeless muddle. Fortunately, beyond a shaking, I am unhurt, and remounting, endeavour to rejoin the now somewhat distant chase. The ostrich, Gregorio, and the dog have reached the plain, and as I gallop quickly down the hill I can see that the bird has begun doubling. This is a sure sign of fatigue, and shows that the ostrich›s strength is beginning to fail him. Nevertheless it is a matter of no small difficulty for one dog to secure his prey, even at this juncture, as he cannot turn and twist about as rapidly as the ostrich. At each double the bird shoots far ahead of his pursuer, and gains a considerable advantage. Away across the plain the two animals fly, whilst I and Gregorio press eagerly in their wake. The excitement grows every moment more intense, and I watch the close struggle going on with the keenest interest. Suddenly the stride of the bird grows slower, his doubles become more frequent, showers of feathers fly in every direction as Plata seizes him by the tail, which comes away in his mouth. In another moment the dog has him by the throat, and for a few minutes nothing can be distinguished but a gray struggling heap. Then Gregorio dashes forward and throws himself off his horse, breaks the bird's neck, and when I arrive upon the scene the struggle is over. The run had lasted for twenty-five minutes.

Our dogs and horses were in a most pitiable state. Poor Plata lay stretched on the ground with his tongue, hot and fiery, lolling out of his mouth, and his sides going at a hundred miles an hour. The horses, with their heads drooped till they almost touched the ground, and their bodies streaming with perspiration, presented a most pitiable sight, and while Gregorio disembowelled and fastened the ostrich together, I loosened their girths, and led them to a pool hard by to drink. At length they became more comfortable, and as soon as they seemed in a fit state to go on, Gregorio and I lifted the huge bird on to his horse, and tied it across the animal's withers. Encumbered thus, Gregorio turned to depart in the direction of the camp, followed by Plata, while I went in an opposite direction in search of my companions down in the plain. It was not long before I distinguished in the far distance an ostrich coming straight towards me, closely followed by a dog and two horsemen. Galloping to meet them, I was the means of turning the bird into "Peaché's" jaws, for such was the name of I'Aria's dog. The two horsemen turned out to be the old fellow in question and my brother, who arrived, hot and full of excitement, on the scene just as I was throwing myself from my horse to prevent Peaché from tearing the bird to pieces. Leaving I'Aria to complete the hunter's work, my brother and I rode slowly back towards our camp, discussing the merits of our horses, dogs, and the stamina of the two ostriches we had slain. So engrossed were we that we could hardly believe our eyes when we came suddenly in full view of our snug little retreat, but, nevertheless, we were very glad to dismount and refresh ourselves with the hot coffee which we found old Storer had ready waiting.

One by one the other hunters dropped in. They had all been successful, with the exception of Guillaume; and as we stood grouped round the five large ostriches lying on the ground, we congratulated ourselves on our good fortune, and on the excellent sport we had had. At dinner we passed judgment on ostrich-meat, which we now really tasted for the first time, for what we had obtained from the Indian camp had been dry and unpalatable. We thought it excellent; the breast and wings are particularly good; the latter much resemble pheasant.

CHAPTER X

DEPARTURE FROM LAGUNA BLANCA—A WILD-CAT—IBIS
SOUP—A FERTILE CAÑADON—INDIAN LAW AND EQUI-
TY—OUR FIRST PUMA—COWARDICE OF THE PUMA—DIS-
COMFORTS OF A WET NIGHT—A MYSTERIOUS DISH—A
GOOD RUN

A FTER A FOUR DAYS' STAY at Laguna Blanca, our horses being sufficiently
rested, we resolved to continue our journey. I had got to feel quite at
home in the little ravine where our camp had been pitched, and notwithstanding my anxiety to push forward and get over the monotony of the
plains as soon as possible, in leaving it felt just a slight touch of regret. Each
bush I passed recalled some trivial incident of our stay, and came in for a share
of the good-bye I inwardly vouchsafed to all my late surroundings.

Whilst we were trotting along I noticed that one of the brood-mares was
continually looking anxiously back, and on counting the foals I found that one
was missing. I'Aria, whose attention I drew to this fact, immediately returned
to our camp to look for the lost animal, which he thought had probably been
left behind in a ravine where the horses had been in the habit of grazing. In the
meantime we rode on, presently passing the site of the camp of the Indians, the
smoke of whose fires we had noticed from the Laguna Blanca. They themselves
had left it the day before, and were now on the march southwards, as indicated
by several columns of smoke which we could see on the distant skyline, it being
their habit, when on the march, to light fires at intervals.

Shortly after passing the Indian camp we were startled by a series of howls,
given vent to by Guillaume's dog, "Negro," whom we descried struggling with
some animal in the long grass. In a second he was joined by the other dogs, and
by the time we got up we found them all engaged in mortal combat with a huge
wild-cat, which had already punished Negro most severely, and was defending

itself fiercely against the united onslaught of its enemies. Two revolver shots were fired at it without effect, but presently Gregorio managed to kill it with a blow from the "bolas." Up to its last gasp it spat and clawed with undaunted fury, and nearly all the dogs were more or less badly wounded; poor "Negro" in particular, being severely gashed and torn. Whilst we washed the dogs in a pool of water hard by, Gregorio skinned the wild-cat, and then made a search for its companion, which during the fray some one had observed making good its retreat. However, his search was fruitless, and we rode forward again, the incident just related furnishing us with a topic for conversation wherewith to beguile the next hour or so. I'Aria meanwhile rejoined us, but although he had thoroughly searched all the country in the vicinity of our late camp, he had been unable to find any traces of the missing foal, which had doubtless fallen a prey to some puma.

Towards evening we arrived at a large freshwater lake called Laguna Larga, by the shores of which we set up our tents. My husband, going out with his gun, managed to kill an ibis, the first any of us had shot, although we had often tried to do so whilst at Laguna Blanca, being aware that this bird makes excellent soup. This one was put in the pot, and though its meat proved rather tough, the broth it gave was all that could be desired. Laguna Larga, like nearly all the lakes we saw in Patagonia, swarmed with wild-fowl, and amongst other birds we observed two flamingoes, whose gorgeous red plumage excited our covetousness, and an elaborate stalking-party was organised with the object of securing one of them. However, they never gave us a chance, and sailed majestically away at the first approach of danger.

Our road the next day lay for the most part along a fertile valley, down the middle of which flowed a narrow but exceedingly deep stream. The breadth of this "cañadon" was about five miles, and we followed its windings for about twenty miles. Its whole length, for it doubtless stretched down to the sea-coast, must have been about 150 miles. The grass was tall and green, in many places reaching up to our horses' bellies. As equally fertile valleys are to be found intersecting the barren plains in all directions, an enormous number of cattle and sheep might be reared in this country were it not for the heavy snows in winter and the floods in spring, which latter immerse all these valleys for a considerable period, during which the animals would have to seek sustenance on the plains, where, it is needless to say, they would not find it.

As we emerged from the valley on to the plains, an animal was descried on the sky-line, which at first we took for a gigantic guanaco, but which presently resolved itself into a horse. Gregorio having seen it first had become ipso facto, in accordance with the unwritten law of the pampas, its owner, that is to say, should it be caught; so, taking I'Aria with him, he rode off to the left, with the intention of getting behind his prospective property and driving it towards our troop. This he accomplished without difficulty. The horse stood staring at our advancing cavalcade for some time, and then came galloping towards us with loud neighs of greeting, spreading consternation among our troop, who neighed and snorted in return, apparently by no means pleased at the sight of the new-comer. Matters were peaceably arranged, however, and after some further slight demonstrations, he was admitted into the troop, evidently much pleased to find himself among his own kind again. According to Gregorio, he had belonged to some Indian, who had probably lost him on the march. I asked Gregorio whether the owner might claim the horse again, and he told me that the law among Indians is that the finder receives about one-third of the value of the object found from the owner. Some difficulty generally arises in these cases as to the value of the find, as the parties naturally over-estimate and depreciate it as suits their respective interests; this being especially the case when the bargain is debated between an Indian and a white man. Amongst themselves the Indians are remarkably fair in their dealings, but as they know that the traders cheat them whenever they can, they recognise quite another standard of morality in their dealings with the latter.

As we were approaching the spot where we intended camping, one of the mules, which was heading the troop, suddenly turned and dashed away, and in another instant the whole troop broke up and dispersed, galloping in all directions. What was the cause of this stampede? We pressed quickly forward, but nothing stirred in the long grass, though we scoured everywhere. We were baffled for a minute. "It's a puma somewhere," said Gregorio. The words were hardly out of his mouth when a loud view-holloa rent the air. "There he goes—there he goes!" shouted two or three of our party in chorus, and sure enough, there he was going—a mighty yellow puma—slouching swiftly away at some distance to our left, with my brother following close on his track. For us all to gallop after and come up within ten yards of the puma was the work of a moment, but to get nearer than ten yards or so was quite another matter, as our horses were quivering with fright, and with difficulty were kept from turning tail and bolting from the dread presence of their mortal enemy. Meanwhile the puma, finding himself surrounded, lay sullenly down, eyeing us with dogged hate, and scarcely seeming to heed the presence of the dogs, who were growling furiously at him at a respectful distance from his claws. Finding it useless to try to approach on horseback, my brother dismounted, and a rifle being at hand, took steady aim at the crouching animal and fired. Simultaneous with the report, with outstretched paws and a deep growl, the puma sprang forward, and then fell heavily to the ground, whilst our horses, becoming wholly unmanageable, reared up and fairly bolted. When we again got control of them, nothing would induce them to return to the spot where the now lifeless body of the puma lay, and we had to dismount and walk there. Very fierce and dangerous it looked; and at the sight of its ponderous paws with their sharp talons and its cruel white teeth, we wondered whether, if it knew its own powers, the puma would be such a cowardly animal as it is. They scarcely ever attack man, even when brought to bay, but lie down and doggedly meet their fate, though they can kill a full-grown guanaco with one blow of the paw, and pull down a horse with similar ease. The Indians affirm that the puma only bears young ones in two years, but whether this be true or not I do not know. They certainly seem very scarce, comparatively, a circumstance which may be due to this peculiarity, coupled with the fact that the Indians and traders destroy a good number annually.

The excitement attendant on the puma's demise being over, and our horses having been driven together again, we made for our intended camping place. We lodged that night in the valley I have described above, and here, for the first time since we reached the plains, the night was wet. It is by no means agreeable to hear rain pattering down on the canvas of one's tent, especially when one has doubts as to the waterproof capabilities of the canvas, and as yet we had had no opportunity of testing ours. Fortunately, on this occasion the rain did not last long, and, excepting a general sense of dampness, we experienced no further inconvenience. Continuing our journey, on the following day we reached the River Gallegos, which we forded at a spot called "Paso de los Morros;" these Morros being two conically shaped hills of equal height, which form a striking landmark, being conspicuous at a considerable distance. The river at the time was very low; but owing to the inequality of its bed and the rapidity of the current, some care had to be taken in crossing the ford for fear any of the packhorses should come to grief. We passed without any accident, however, and pitched our camp near the bank, under shelter of a snug little clump of beech trees. We liked the place so much that we resolved to pass a couple of days there, especially as the packhorses required a rest after the long march from Laguna Blanca.

The first day we dawdled pleasantly away in all kinds of useful occupations, such as cleaning guns, writing up journals, etc., though I am bound to say that the best part of the time was given up to cooking experiments, my brother and Mr. B. both being anxious to prove their respective superiority in the culinary department. Much amusement was afforded us by a mysterious dish which my brother passed the whole afternoon in elaborating, and which, if his own glowing anticipations had been verified, would certainly have proved a triumph of skill. The care he devoted to the preparation of his dish, and the impressive secrecy with which he conducted his operations, led us into the firm belief that a most agreeable surprise was in store for us. But when dinner-time came, and soup and joint had been hurriedly got through in order to enable us to do all the more justice to his effort, the surprise—for surprise it was—turned out to be a very unpleasant one; the "plat" on which so much care had been bestowed proving to be a homely though curious concoction of rice, preserved milk, and brown sugar, with a decided taste of burn; and after swallowing a few spoonfuls, even its concoctor had to avow, with a grimace, that his exertions had resulted in a failure. My brother having thus signally proved his incapacity for occupying the high office of cook, we for the future left the kitchen department to Francisco's supervision, and very well we fared at his hands.

The next day was spent in ostrich-hunting. We made two or three circles, but game seemed very scarce, and we were unable to entrap a single ostrich. We were going home towards evening, rather disconsolately, when some one observed an ostrich running straight towards us, apparently with the express intention of obliging us, by allowing himself to be killed. But as we started into a gallop to meet him half-way, he changed his mind, and darted off sideways, our whole party following. The dogs unfortunately, as often happens when they are wanted, had fallen behind, and a depression in the plain hid us from their view. It seemed rather a forlorn chase, therefore, as our tired horses were no match for the ostrich, who drew away at every stride. To our surprise, however, he suddenly began to "double," and we saw that he was being hard pressed by one of Guillaume's dogs, from which he had evidently been escaping when he met us. With fresh zest we pushed forward, spreading out in a semicircle, so as to be able to turn the ostrich back to the dog should he double round our way. An exciting chase ensued. The dog, a clever brute, did its utmost to make the ostrich double towards us, but without success, and the speed at which they were both going prevented us from getting any nearer. The dog was tiring, but he held out stoutly, double after double slowly exhausting him. At last, overshooting himself in an attempt to stop short, he turned a complete somersault, and the ostrich, profiting by the moment's respite, literally set all sail and skimmed away, with a strong wind in his favour. "He is lost!" shouted Francisco, reining in. "No, no—the river, the river!" cried Gregorio, spurring the harder, and away we went after him, and right enough, there was the river glittering before us, with the ostrich not fifty yards from the bank, and, hurrah! our whole pack of dogs close on his heels. He must take the water, or he is ours. In another second he reaches the bank, and pauses. He is in! No—his heart has failed him, and with an ominous droop of his wings, but with a tremendous spurt he has darted off again, with not five yards between him and the straining dogs. On, on we go. The ostrich gains ground; ah, that treacherous bend of the river! It forces him to swerve round, and in a second he is met by Gregorio. A dexterous double rids him of his new enemy, and with a last effort he shoots forward again. But the circle closes, the shouts of the horsemen on all sides bewilder him, he hesitates a second, but in that second the dogs are upon him, and the next he lies a struggling, quivering mass of feathers. Horses, dogs, and men—we are all panting and breathless. The dogs, so hot had been the pace, were too blown to move; and even when Francisco began to cut up the bird, this proceeding, usually of such interest to them on account of the savoury perquisites which fell to their share, scarcely excited their languid attention.

We were rather tired when we got home, and after dinner, the run having been most minutely discussed in all its bearings, we were all glad to get to bed.

CHAPTER XI

A NUMEROUS GUANACO HERD—A PAMPA HER-
MIT—I'ARIA AGAIN LOSES THE WAY—CHORLITOS—A
NEW EMOTION—A MOON RAINBOW—WEATHER
WISDOM—OPTIMIST AND PESSIMIST—WILD-FOWL
ABUNDANT—BAD LUCK

T HE NEXT DAY FOUND US ONCE MORE IN THE SADDLE, jogging along over the plains with the hopes of a speedy arrival at the Cordilleras to cheer us, under the depression of spirits which the dreary monotony of the country could not fail to produce. The character of the landscape was what we had been accustomed to since leaving Cabo Negro, being in this region, if anything, possibly more barren than usual.

This day's ride was memorable for the immense number of guanacos which covered the plains in all directions. On arriving at a broad depression we were surprised by the sight of a herd of these animals, which could not have numbered less than five thousand. This enormous living mass defiled past us up the side and over the brow of an escarpment which bound the depression referred to, occupying a space of time of about ten minutes—although they were going at a very quick pace—and once or twice before the day was over we met an equally numerous herd. How such an extraordinary number of animals can find subsistence on the barren plains, which they even seem to prefer to the grassy ravines, is a matter difficult of explanation. Certain it is that the withered pampa grass must contain great nourishing properties, as the guanacos thrive and grow very fat on it. Although they are generally rather shy, we passed one herd composed of some unusually tame animals. As we approached them, instead of running away, the whole herd came slowly trotting towards us, staring at us with naïve unconcern, which showed that they were innocent of the chase. As it chanced, we had plenty of meat, so we left them unmolested. It was not often that we found them so tame, especially when we happened to be short of meat; in such cases, with the usual perverseness of things, they would scarcely allow one to approach within rifle-range.

As we went on we observed a column of smoke to the westward, which Gregorio judged to proceed from some fire near the Cordilleras; and from his account it marked the camp of an eccentric Englishman, named Greenwood, who, it appears, particularly affects that region, and who scrupulously avoids contact with his fellow-creatures, scarcely ever coming down to Sandy Point. In fact, according to Gregorio, he seemed to live the life of a hermit. He had renounced the world and its vanities, even to the extent of disdaining the ordinary rough comforts of the other inhabitants of the pampa. Clothed in the most primitive fashion, he roams along the slopes of the Cordilleras, and rather than make a trip to the colony to lay in a store of provisions, passes a whole year on a diet of ostrich and guanaco meat, pure and simple.

I was rather interested in this species of Wild Man of the Woods, and kept a sharp look out as we journeyed through that region in the hopes of seeing him. But, if near us at any time—and of course our fires, had he chosen to come, gave sufficient indication of our whereabouts—he did not relax his rule of exclusiveness in our favour, and I, consequently, never had an opportunity of making his acquaintance.

During the march we started up a male ostrich, which had about forty young ones under its care. Though we called our dogs back, nothing could restrain them, and they gave chase, killing one of the small ostriches before we could get up to them; the male bird and the others escaped. The flesh of the young ostrich is not very palatable, so we left the bird, taking only its legs, which make very nice handles for umbrellas and whips. On this day I'Aria again distinguished himself by losing the way, he having been entrusted by the other guides with the leadership on this occasion, as he was supposed to be better acquainted than any one with this particular region.

For quite two hours we followed him in all directions through an extensive beechwood thicket, in search of the springs we were to camp by that night; and when they were at last found, it was by Gregorio, and in quite another direction than the one in which I'Aria, with his usual pertinacious confidence, was taking us. He came in for a good deal of abuse from his colleagues, and a fair share of black looks from us, all of which he bore with the cheerful indifference which characterised him under all circumstances.

The present was to be our last camp among beeches, as we had now to strike across a perfectly woodless region, on our way to the point at which we intended entering the Cordilleras. These occasional patches of beeches are only to be found in the vicinity of the mountains; in the plains that stretch down to the coast nothing is to be met with in the way of fuel but "berberis" and a few other scrubby kinds of bushes. We therefore made the most of our present abundance of wood, and revelled in huge fires, in order to lay in a store of warm memories at least to carry with us into the bleak region we were about to enter. At dinner this day we tasted a novelty in the way of fowl, of such excellence that I cannot let the occasion pass without expatiating for a moment on its merits. In the daytime we had met with large flights of a bird which the natives call "chorlito," or "batatu," in species something between a golden plover and a woodcock. These birds come down to Patagonia in incredible numbers at this season, to feast on the ripe cranberries which grow everywhere in profusion, and on which the ostriches, ibis, and wild geese all feed and thrive. We had shot some of these "chorlitos," and they had been roasted for dinner on the spit, along with some snipe and wild duck we had brought with us from Gallegos. At dinner, however, they were at first rather neglected, as we had got rather tired of birds, having had so much of them at Laguna Blanca. Presently, however, dinner being finished, some one of our party, in a spirit of careless curiosity rather than from any desire to satisfy an already satiated appetite, pulled one of these chorlitos off the spit, and with a half-deprecating air took a bite of it. But when he had done so, the sudden alteration in his bearing from apathy to activity was a sight to see. The expression on his face, till then one of weary indifference, gave way to a look of intense astonishment, which finally became one of placid delight, as bit by bit the chorlito disappeared down his throat. Though he did not speak, his silent action spoke volumes of eloquent recommendation, and, as may be imagined, we were soon all engaged in eating chorlitos; for a time no sound being heard but the smacking of lips, the crunching of bones, and occasionally such exclamations as "Stunning!" "By Jove!" "Delicious!" etc. etc. The fact is, we had discovered what some Persian king offered half his kingdom for—a new emotion—for so seductively succulent, so exquisitely flavoured, so far beyond anything the gourmet might dream of in the sublimest flight of his imagination, is the flesh of the cranberry-fed chorlito, that the sensation it produces on the palate when tasted for the first time may, without hyperbole, be described as rising to the dignity of an emotion.

Unfortunately, as we travelled northward we seemed to leave the region of these birds, and only on this and two other occasions were we able to feast upon them.

We witnessed a phenomenon that night in the shape of a moon rainbow, and many were the conjectures as to whether it presaged good or bad weather. Rain is the one thing above all others calculated to make an open-air life unpleasant, and a fear of it being constantly present to our minds, nearly every evening meteorological speculations formed a staple topic of conversation for the whole camp. A great amount of weather wisdom was developed among us, and very soon a party spirit was imported into the question, our camp splitting into two sections—Optimists and Pessimists. Just before bedtime the sky would be conned, and the various weather indications eagerly discussed, often with some heat; and it was amusing to see how frequently the optimists would enlist as arguments in favour of their prophecies of fine weather, the very same phenomena of cloud or temperature on which, on the other hand, the pessimists grounded their equally confident prognostications of rain. On occasions when these discussions had been carried on with more than usual earnestness, shouldthe rain suddenly begin to patter down on the tents in the middle of the night, one might often hear conversations like the following:—

Pessimist (in tone of triumph, evidently pleased that it was raining, as his antagonist was thereby confounded). "Well! who was right about the rain? I told you it was sure to come!"

Optimist (cheerily, and half implying that he believes it isn't raining at all). Pessimist (fervently praying that it may rain cats and dogs for the next twelve hours). "You will think it›s something though, when you are swamped. (Confidently) It's bound to rain till morning."

Optimist (scornfully). "Rain till morning! Stuff! Why, it never rains long with a full moon" (or no moon, as may suit the case).

Pessimist (derisively). "That's exactly when it does rain. Didn't you know that?"

Optimist (pertinaciously). "Why, only yesterday you said yourself that one might be certain it would not rain long with a full moon, so there!"

Pessimist (conveniently forgetful). "I'm sure I never said anything of the kind."

Optimist gives vent to a sleepy but uncomplimentary ejaculation against people generally who don't know what they are talking about.

Pessimist retorts with drowsy ditto, whereupon follows silence, or silence broken by snores.

On this particular evening the halo was naturally a strong feature in the discussion, and much ingenious special pleading was employed on both sides to prove that its presence was an infallible indication of rain or no rain. This time the optimists gained a signal victory, as the night was fine throughout.

The next day was spent in shooting wild-fowl down by a big lake which lay about a couple of miles distant from the camp. I shot a great many lovely specimens of water-fowl, the like of which I had never seen before, and loaded my horse with a great quantity of geese, duck, and plover. Riding home quietly after my day's sport I started up a big ostrich, who rose from the ground not more than a couple of yards distant. How I longed for one of the greyhounds, and shouted loudly to François, whom I could descry in camp idly doing nothing, but he could not or would not hear. Galloping towards him, I hastily explained in which direction the ostrich had disappeared, and mounting his horse he went off in pursuit. An hour later he returned empty-handed. He had come across the ostrich and given chase, but the bird, taking to the beech woods, had disappeared therein, closely followed by the dogs. After a long and fruitless search for both, he had been obliged to return without his dogs to the camp. Doubtless, as he observed, they had managed to kill their prey, and were even then indulging in a heavy feed. His words were verified when, later on, the animals returned, presenting an undeniable appearance of having partaken of a large repast. Gregorio had been absent all day in search of guanaco, but as he had gone on foot and taken no dogs with him, he had been unable to secure the one or two which he had managed to wound. So, altogether, our attempts in the chase did not on this occasion flourish.

CHAPTER XII

A MONOTONOUS RIDE—A DREARY LANDSCAPE—SHORT
FUEL RATIONS—THE CORDILLERAS—FEATURES OF
PATAGONIAN SCENERY—HEAT AND GNATS—A PUMA
AGAIN—"THE RAIN IS NEVER WEARY"—DAMPNESS, HUN-
GER, GLOOM—I'ARIA TO THE RESCUE—HIS INGENUITY

AFTER ANOTHER DAY'S SOJOURN at this encampment we resumed our journey. We took a good supply of fuel with us, as we were now entering on the barren, woodless region, during our transit over which we should have to rely solely on the provision we now made.

Leaving the beechwood behind us we rode up on to a plain, on whose edge we could distinguish what appeared to be a little black cloud. In reality it was a peak, or rather clump of peaks of the Cordilleras, at the foot of which we were one day to camp, and towards which for the next few days we directed our horses' heads.

This day's ride, and it was a long one, was by far more monotonous and dreary than any of the preceding ones. The immense plateau over which we rode for six or seven hours was remarkable for its gloom and barrenness, even in a region where all is sterility and dreariness. There was no sun, and the sky, lowering and dark, formed a fit counterpart to the plain, which stretched flatly away to the indistinct horizon, gray, mournful, and silent.

We could not help being affected by the aspect of the scenery around us, and I do not remember ever to have felt anything to equal the depression of spirits to which I, in common with all our party, fell a prey, and to whose influence even the guides succumbed.

For once they drove the troop along without enlivening their work with the customary cheery cries of "Iegua! Iegua! Mula! Mula!" etc., and the very bells of the Madrinas seemed to have a muffled, solemn sound, very unlike their usual lively jingle.

A single incident occurred during that day's march. A little guanaco, which had lost its mother somehow, seeing us coming, instead of running away, trotted trustingly towards us. Unfortunately our bloodthirsty dogs dashed out and threw it before we could get up to stop them. The poor thing got up again, however, and at first did not seem much hurt. It was the sweetest little creature imaginable, with soft silky fur, and bright, gentle eyes, and it thrust its nose against my cheek in a caressing manner, without the least sign of fear. I determined to carry it with me, in hopes that as it got bigger it would learn to keep with our troop, especially as the mare who had lost her filly at Laguna Blanca would have made an excellent foster-mother for it. But I hardly formed the idea when the little guanaco began to stagger about, and it became evident that it must have received some bite from the dogs which we had not noticed. On examining it this proved to be the case; indeed, in a few minutes its eyes glazed, and to my grief in a very short time it died, apparently without suffering. I would have given anything that it could have lived, as I am sure it would have become attached to me, and finally have found its way to England with us. Tame guanacos are often kept at Sandy Point, and their gentle ways and amiable dispositions make them charming pets.

We were thoroughly tired of our dull march when we at last arrived at a ravine where there were a few pools of water, and where we camped for the night. As we were on short fuel rations, the fire was allowed to go out directly after dinner, and we went to bed, now the only warm place.

Off again the next day, the clump of peaks mentioned above growing more distinct, but still terribly far, and no wood to be got till we reached them. Plains as usual studded with guanacos, but having no time to go out with our rifles, we had to confine ourselves to ostrich meat. Of these birds there was an abundance, and many an exciting run we had pursuing them. Wild-fowl were numerous too, but having eaten every imaginable species—geese, duck, teal, widgeon, snipe, Barbary duck, we were quite tired of them.

After another long march we camped in an open shelterless ravine, and then again pushed hurriedly on, our stock of fuel getting ominously low, towards the tantalising clump of peaks, which at the end of a long day's ride scarcely seemed to come any nearer. They were now beginning to disappear, as we descended into an immense basin which lay between us and them, and whose farther end was bound by a succession of plateaus, rising abruptly one over the other as it appeared to us, though, when we ultimately came up to them, we found the graduating ascent almost imperceptible.

After camping one night in a most disagreeable sandy region, where our food and clothes and furs all got impregnated with grit and dust, and where we burned our last stick, we again pushed on, with the unpleasant knowledge that

that night we should possibly have to camp without a fire to warm ourselves and cook our food. The basin we were now crossing seemed interminable. We were to camp that night at the foot of the escarpment which bound its farther end, whence to the mountains was only one day's march. We were now out of sight of the latter again, but we were cheered by the comforting consciousness that each step was bringing us nearer to them.

Just as it was getting dark, after a weary day's ride, we reached a brawling mountain-stream, which swept along the base of an escarpment, and which we hailed as the first sign that we were at last approaching the Cordilleras. Fording it we pitched our camp in the long green grass, just under shelter of the escarpment. But before unsaddling, eager to see how near we had come to the clump of peaks which had so long been before our eyes, we rode up the escarpment, from the top of which we hoped to get a good view of the country westward.

Our expectations were not disappointed. There, seemingly not a mile away, rose up, compact and dark, not the huddled clump of peaks we had seen two days ago, but a mighty mountain chain, which lost itself westward in the gathering dusk of evening—standing like a mysterious barrier between the strange country we had just crossed and a possibly still stranger country beyond. The sun had long set, and the base of the mountains was wrapped in darkness, but their jagged fantastically-shaped crests stood clearly defined against the light which still glimmered in the sky, and here and there a snow-covered peak, higher than its comrades, still retained a faint roseate glow, which contrasted strangely with the gray gloom of all below.

For a long time after complete darkness had fallen over everything, I stood alone, giving myself up to the influence of the emotions the scene described awoke in me, and endeavouring, though vainly, to analyse the feeling which the majestic loneliness of Patagonian scenery always produced in my mind—a feeling which I can only compare—for it would be impossible for me to seize on any definite feature of the many vague sensations which compose it—to those called up by one of Beethoven's grand, severe, yet mysteriously soft sonatas.

I was awakened from my reverie by Francisco, who was wandering about trying to gather a few dry sticks for the fire. Fortunately he managed to collect enough to enable us to cook a tolerable dinner with; having eaten which, as usual, when we were fireless, we sought our couches as speedily as possible.

The morning broke with every sign of bad weather. The air was heavy and sultry, a hot dry wind blew over the plains, whirling up clouds of fine dust, and the mountain-chain was half-hidden by dark masses of clouds of threatening aspect. We saddled and packed up as hurriedly as possible, fervently hoping that the rain, which sooner or later we saw must come, would kindly hold over till we had reached our destination.

As we journeyed on, the sultriness grew more and more oppressive, and we were vexed by innumerable swarms of minute gnats, which got into our eyes and mouths, buzzed about us in a hopelessly persistent manner, and by no means allayed the state of irritation the combined influence of dust and heat had brought us into. A slight diversion presently occurred by the appearance of an animal whose claims to our polite and immediate attention were not to be denied. This was an enormous puma, who suddenly sprang up from the midst of our cavalcade, sending the mules and luggage horses stampeding away in all directions. True to its cowardly nature, the animal slouched hurriedly off, and disappeared down the side of a ravine. Quick as thought we pursued it, but fast as we galloped, not a trace of it was to be seen. At a short distance from where we stood eagerly searching for the vanished animal, I perceived a small bush growing, the only one for miles round, and to this I pointed as the probable place where the brute had sought a hiding-place. We lost no time in galloping towards the spot, and the terrified snorting of our horses when we drew near, assured us of the correctness of my surmise, and put us on our guard.

We caught sight of him, as he crouched with angry glowing eyes and an expression on his face which, on discovering that none of us carried a rifle, was the reverse of reassuring, especially as we knew from our guides that, for some reason or other, these Cordillera pumas are fiercer than their kindred of the plains, and often attack their assailants,—a piece of temerity the latter have never been known to be capable of.

Fortunately, at this moment, my husband came up with a gun, though indeed it was only loaded with small shot. Dismounting hastily he approached within eight or nine yards of the growling animal. Bang! bang! went his gun, and through the cloud of smoke we saw the puma jump up in the air and fall backwards on the bush. For a moment or two it rolled about in the throes of death, and then, with a last growl stretched itself slowly out, and lay still. Gregorio, who arrived at this moment, set to work at once, to remove its skin. The guides all declared it to be the biggest puma they had ever seen. The skin, which adorns the floor of the room where I am at present writing, measures exactly nine feet from the tip of the tail to the point of the nose. We then hurried on again, anxiously scanning the weather, which meanwhile had grown more and more threatening. The sultriness had increased so as to have become almost unbearable, and the swarms of gnats above alluded to had grown numerous in proportion. Before long a fearful thunderstorm burst over our heads, and for a short time the rain came down in sheets. Then a shift of the wind changed the temperature again. It became quite chilly, and the heavy rain resolved itself into a thick drizzling mist, which soon wetted us to the skin. For hours we rode in this comfortless plight,—wet, cold, and tired, and by no means cheered by the aspect of the country, the little we could see of which—most of it being hidden by the mist aforesaid—looking blacker and sadder than ever.

THE PUMA'S DEATH-SPRING

We were in hopes that at least before evening it would clear up, as the prospect of having to pitch our camp in the drizzling sleet was far from pleasant, but as it grew darker the fog increased in thickness, and soon we could hardly see fifty paces ahead of our horses' noses. How Gregorio managed to find the way, I don't know. At last it being, as near as I could judge, about sunset, we descended a very steep declivity, and came on to what appeared to be a ravine of the ordinary kind, where grass and underwood were apparently abundant. We halted at a semicircle of tall bushes, and set disconsolately to work to get up the tents. This by no means easy task being accomplished, we collected the provisions and cartridges together, and got them under shelter into the smaller of the two tents. Our rugs, furs, and coverings were wet through, so we carried them into the other tent and proceeded to wring them and lay them out to dry. This being done, we turned our attention towards making a fire, but the guides and everybody declared the attempt impossible, and indeed so it seemed, for there was not a dry twig or blade of grass to be found anywhere. Back we all crept into our damp tents, and prepared to dine as genially as we could off sardines and dry biscuit. But though we might choose to resign ourselves thus supinely to discomfort, old I'Aria, for his part, was by no means inclined to do so. Whilst the discussion as to the possibility of making a fire had been carried on, after listening a minute or two to the arguments which were being urged proving conclusively that nothing could be done towards it, he silently withdrew, and busied himself in setting up his own little tent,—a rather dilapidated one by the way, as, whenever he required something wherewith to patch up a rent in his curious garments, he was in the habit of supplying his want by cutting out a piece of the canvas of his "casa" (house) as he called it—an ingenious method of robbing Peter to pay Paul.

Meanwhile we had retired to our tents, and were beginning to arrange our furs preparatory to going to bed, when I heard some conversation going on between I'Aria, my husband, and Mr. B., the latter an inveterate maté drinker, and who, I must say, had been the only one at the council who had expressed himself hopefully as regarded the possibility of making a fire. Looking out of the tent I saw them all crouched under a bush, dripping wet, but earnestly engaged in some elaborate preparations for conquering damp and getting soaked wood to burn.

Finding they disregarded my friendly advice to save themselves the trouble of doing what could only be termed useless, I withdrew into my tent again. Half an hour later I could still hear them bravely battling against the inevitable, but presently Mr. B. went past my tent with a kettle in his hand. "The fire is burning, is it?" I called out ironically to him. "No, but it will very soon," he replied. "Meanwhile I am going to fill the kettle; would you like tea or coffee?" I answered something sarcastic, but sighed. I certainly would have given anything for a cup of hot tea. The hopeful expression of Mr. B.'s face had struck me, so, covering myself up in a cloak, I went up to where I'Aria was busy at work, to see if really there was any hope of his succeeding. I found he had stuck four little stakes in the ground, over which a cloth was drawn, under whose shelter he had built an elaborate structure of wooden matches, laid crosswise one over the other, so as to be handy when required; over these lay a small heap of fine twigs, as dry as could be procured, as well as some stout sticks, and finally several logs, which he informed me would soon be merrily blazing. Everything being ready, he applied a light to the matches, and as soon as they began to blaze, added the twigs, which in their turn, after a little doubtful spluttering, took fire, and presently—this was the critical moment—the sticks were laid on. For a time my worst fears seemed about to be realised, the sticks only smoked viciously, the matches had long burned away, and the twigs now began to glow doubtfully. But old I'Aria did not give in without a struggle. Kneeling down he tried gently to fan the fading glow with his breath. At times, as we anxiously watched it, it seemed to gain strength, at others it became reduced to a single spark. But patience conquered at last; the glow spread, the sticks began to blaze, and before long there was a good blazing fire, which brought every one from his tent, especially as, meantime, the rain had ceased, though a thick mist still hung over everything, making the darkness of the night still more intense. Kettles were put on to boil, maté, tea, coffee, imbibed, and Francisco prepared an excellent ostrich-fry, à la minute, discussing which, blessings were invoked on I'Aria's head,—to his perseverance these comforts being due. Supper over, we groped our way back to our tents, and, enveloped in a dense damp mist, went to sleep, not at all satisfied with the inhospitable greeting the Cordilleras had vouchsafed us.

CHAPTER XIII

A SURPRISE—A STRANGE SCENE—AN IDLE DAY—
CALIFATÉ BERRIES—GUANACO-STALKING—A DILEM-
MA—MOSQUITOES—A GOOD SHOT

THE NEXT MORNING I WAS PLEASANTLY AWAKENED by a bright ray of sunshine, which forced its way through the opening in my tent, leaving me
little inclination to sleep any longer. I lost no time in getting up, and
stepped out, anxious to see what kind of country we had got into under cover
of the fog of the previous day.

For a moment I was quite bewildered by the contrast of the scene now
before me and the dreary impression the unfavourable weather conditions had
lent to the country on our arrival. I found we were camped in a broad valley,
which looked bright and smiling beneath a clear blue sky and a warm sun. A
slight breeze swept over the long green grass, which was studded here and there
with clumps of califaté bushes, and an enlivening colour variety was given to
the verdant carpet by occasional tracts of white and yellow flowers. One end
of the valley was bound by some tall hills, covered with dark patches of beech
trees, and beyond these again, ridge above ridge, range above range, the snow
and glacier covered Cordilleras of the Andes towered majestically to the sky. The
air was marvellously clear; looking long westward, I could gradually distinguish,
in the haze of the distance, over the mountains which first met my gaze, white
snowy ranges, of such height that they seemed to float in mid-air, and only after
my vision had acquired sharpness from long concentration, could I trace their
outlines basewards. But it was the sight at the near end of the valley which most
claimed my attention. From behind the green hills that bound it rose a tall chain
of heights, whose jagged peaks were cleft in the most fantastic fashion, and fret-
ted and worn by the action of the air and moisture into forms, some bearing the
semblance of delicate Gothic spires, others imitating with surprising closeness

the bolder outlines of battlemented buttresses and lofty towers. The bare rock which formed them was red porphyry, and the morning sun glittering on it, lent it a variety of bright tints, purple and golden, which were thrown into striking relief by the blue background of the sky and the white masses of snow, which, in parts, clung to the peaks. The abrupt flanks of these tall heights were scored with deep gullies and ravines, and strewn with detached boulders of rock; but nowhere was there any trace of vegetation, either bush or grass.

The suddenness with which this novel scenery burst upon me considerably heightened its effect. But yesterday we had stood on the plains, with their eternal monotony of colour and outline; last night we had gone to bed, as we thought, in a similar dreary waste; and now, as if by magic, from the bowels of the earth, a grand and glorious landscape had sprung up around us, as totally different, in its diversity of outline and colour, from that which only a few hours ago had depressed and wearied us, as could well be imagined.

It was amusing to hear the exclamations of surprise with which my companions greeted the scene, as one by one they came out of their tents and gazed on the pleasant metamorphosis which had taken place during our slumbers. We had grumbled a good deal the day before about the country, and had anathematised it with many ill-tempered expletives; but all that was now forgotten, and as we looked around us we felt that our trouble had not been unrewarded.

Taking advantage of the fine weather, we spread our damp furs on the bushes, and, thanks to the wind and sun, they were soon dry. Breakfast over, my brother started off with his rifle to explore the peaks at the end of the valley, whilst we others stretched ourselves on our furs under the shade of some tall bushes, and with the help of books and pipes, a little desultory conversation, and the lazy contemplation of the fair scenery before us, we managed to pass away the hot hours of noon pleasantly enough.

When it got cooler, and we had drank our fill of idleness, we found plenty to occupy ourselves with. There were guns to be cleaned. I had my journal to write up; and, although I am no good hand with the needle, the rough usage my apparel had lately received made some attempts at sewing and patching imperative. The guides busied themselves in repairing saddle-gear, making reins or lassos from guanaco hide, and similar work. Our English servant Storer, who had somehow created for himself the reputation of one expert in the stuffing of birds and the curing of skins, was busy with several unsavoury smelling specimens of the latter, which he had been carrying about him for some days, having to-day, for the first time, leisure to operate upon them. Mr. B. went 1off to make a sketch of our camp and its picturesque surroundings, and in searching for a suitable site came across a califaté bush, the blue berries on which were almost ripe. He brought back a capful, and though we found them rather acid, mashed up with plenty of sugar they made a very nice refreshing dish, which was especially welcome to us after our late uniform diet. In the long grass near the stream that flowed down the valley we found some wild celery, which, put in the soup, was a decided improvement on the dried "Julienne" we had brought with us, and of which by this time we had but little left. Just as we were getting rather anxious about him, as it was already near sunset, my brother came back from his excursion to the Porphyry Peaks. Arriving at their base much later than he expected, having been deceived in the distance, he had only had time to climb about half-way up them, but even at that height had got a splendid view of the country beyond, his accounts of which made us eager to penetrate into it as soon as possible. But as our packhorses required rest, this had to be deferred for a couple of days yet.

The next day a hunting-party was organised. Neither our guides nor ourselves knowing whether any game was to be found in the country we were about to enter, it was necessary that we should take a good supply of meat with us. We made a circle in the usual manner, and were successful, as far as ostriches were concerned, inasmuch as, after some good runs, we managed to kill three.

Having observed a herd of guanaco grazing in a valley at some distance, those of us whose horses were still tolerably fresh then set out to try and get one, the meat of three ostriches not being sufficient to last ourselves and dogs for more than two days. The dogs were all too tired with their previous exertions to be of any use to us, so we had to rely solely on our rifles. This being the case, it was necessary to stalk the herd with great precautions, and this we proceeded to do, choosing our ground carefully, so as to keep out of their sight. But we had not gone far when we heard a shrill neigh close by, and looking round, we saw a guanaco standing on the crest of a hill overlooking the valley. He had scarcely uttered his cry when it was repeated at a little distance off by another watchful sentinel, and then they both slowly cantered off, looking back at us as they went along, and neighing loudly at intervals. The herd, meanwhile, warned of the approach of danger, leisurely trotted up the escarpment on the other side of the valley, and as leisurely disappeared over the plain. My husband took a vindictive pot-shot at one of the retreating sentinels, but missed him; and we had to make the best of our disappointment, and search for some less watchful herd. In this we had considerable difficulty, the guanacos on this particular day appearing to be shyer than we had ever known them. At last, after a great deal of fruitless stalking, my husband got a shot at a little knot of four or five, who were standing together, almost out of range. One fell, and the others took to their heels. With a cry of triumph we galloped up to the wounded one, but to our dismay, at our approach, he sprang to his feet and started off full speed after his companions, to all appearance unhurt. Spurring our horses, we followed closely in his wake, down steep ravines, up hills, over the plains, at times losing him altogether, but always catching sight of him again, going as fresh as ever, till at last we began to despair of ever running him down. One by one my companions dropped off, till presently only my husband, Mr. B., and myself, were left in the chase. Had he not been so palpably hit, we should have desisted too; but it seemed a pity, having gone so far, to give in, so we kept on, hoping to tire out our prey by sheer persistence. But gradually, and no wonder, our jaded horses began to show signs of exhaustion; we had run them almost to a standstill, and, reflecting on the distance we had to ride back to the camp, we were just going to rein in, when the guanaco suddenly stopped and lay down. Sure now of getting him, we pushed on towards him. But when we had got to within about six yards of him, up he got, and galloped off again, distancing us at every stride. Hesitating what to do, we kept in his wake, though all the time we were wishing we had never started after him. Slower and slower our panting horses struggled towards a ravine, down the side of which the guanaco had disappeared. We came to its edge and looked down. The guanaco was nowhere to be seen. We were at a loss to imagine what could have become of him. He had not climbed the other side, or we should have seen him emerge on the plain, nor could he have gone along the ravine, either to the right or the left, as we commanded a view of it in both directions for a long distance. In this dilemma we were staring open-mouthed with astonishment about us, when something moved in the long grass below, and directing our steps thither we came upon our guanaco lying stretched out in a pool of blood. The movement that had drawn our attention to him had evidently been his last effort, for he was now quite dead. Examining him, we found the bullet had entered his side, and passing through the lungs and lights, had lodged near the spine; and yet, thus severely wounded, he had gone quite ten miles at a cracking pace! Later on we experienced still more extraordinary instances of the toughness and tenacity of life of these animals, in comparison with whom the cat with its nine lives is absolutely nowhere. Having cut up the guanaco, and distributed its meat on the saddles of our horses, we turned back towards our camp; and a long ride we had before we got there. I'Aria, we found, had also killed a guanaco, and we had therefore plenty of meat to last us, should we have difficulty in getting game in the Cordilleras.

The next day was passed in idleness. It was extremely hot, scarcely a breath of wind stirring, and in the evening we were rather bothered by mosquitoes, this being the first acquaintance we made with them in Patagonia. During the day a bird was seen hovering over the camp at an immense height, which we were told was a 1condor. It was so high up that it looked scarcely bigger than an ordinary hawk. Taking advantage of a moment when it hung perfectly motionless, my husband had a shot at it, and, by a marvellous fluke, the ball took effect, and down the creature came, growing bigger and bigger as it fell, till at last, reaching the earth with a loud thud, there it was, the most gigantic bird I had ever seen. We found it measured twelve feet from wing to wing. The most distinctive feature of the condor is the white down ruff which encircles the neck two or three inches below the head, which latter is completely bare of feathers and repulsively ugly. In the female bird the colour of this ruff is black.

This night the mosquitoes became a positive nuisance. I tried all kinds of stratagems to protect myself from them—such as tying my handkerchief over my face, or burying myself under my furs, but between being smothered and bitten, I preferred the latter evil. Similarly, the plan we adopted of lighting some damp grass in the tent, so as to smoke our trying enemies out, had ultimately to be abandoned in favour of passive endurance of the inevitable. I quite envied old I'Aria. Throughout the night, whilst from all sides exclamations and expletives of varying irritability and force were continually to be heard, the placid snore which floated from his tent showed that, thanks to his parchment skin, he was enabled to bear the sting of the outrageous mosquito with serene indifference.

CHAPTER XIV

AN UNKNOWN COUNTRY—PASSING THE BARRIER—
CLEOPATRA'S NEEDLES—FOXES—A GOOD RUN—OUR
FOREST SANCTUARY—ROUGHING IT—A BATH—A
VARIED MENU

WE WERE UP EARLY THE NEXT MORNING, for we had perhaps a long journey before us, the country we were about to penetrate being as unknown to our guides as to ourselves; and no one could say when and where we might find a suitable place for camping that night. All helped to drive up and saddle the horses; their long rest and the rich grass in the valley had done them good, and they were in very fair condition, which was fortunate, as we might have some arduous climbs to face, and pasture lands might be scarce among the mountains.

The day before, the guides had been on a reconnoitring expedition, with the object of finding the most practicable route towards the interior, and having discovered a ravine, which appeared to wind in the direction of the mountains, and which, at the same time, afforded easy going for our horses, we resolved to make it our highway. Accordingly, all being ready, we said good-bye to the plains, and, fording the stream which flowed down the valley, we entered on the winding ravine, full of curiosity as to what kind of country we were now to break in upon.

The ravine was in itself a fit preparation for something strange and grand. Its steep slopes towered up on either side of us to an immense height; and the sunlight being thus partially excluded, a mysterious gloom reigned below, which, combined with the intense, almost painful silence of the spot, made the scene inexpressibly strange and impressive. Its effect was intensified by the knowledge that since these gigantic solitudes had been fashioned by nature, no human eye had ever beheld them, nor had any human voice ever raised the echoes, which, awakening now for the first time, repeated in sonorous chorus the profane shouts of "Iegua! Iegua!" with which our guides drove the horses along.

We hurried on, anxious to reach the mouth of the ravine, and behold the promised land as soon as possible, but several hours elapsed before we at last reached its farther end, and emerged from its comparative gloom into the sunshine of the open. A glance showed us that we were in a new country. Before us stretched a picturesque plain, covered with soft green turf, and dotted here and there with clumps of beeches, and crossed in all directions by rippling streams. The background was formed by thickly-wooded hills, behind which again towered the Cordilleras,—three tall peaks of a reddish hue, and in shape exact facsimiles of Cleopatra's Needle, being a conspicuous feature in the landscape. The califaté bushes here were of a size we had never met on the plains, and were covered with ripe berries, on which hosts of small birds were greedily feasting. The very air seemed balmier and softer than that we had been accustomed to, and instead of the rough winds we had hitherto encountered there was a gentle breeze of just sufficient strength agreeably to temper the heat of the sun. Here and there guanaco were grazing under the shade of a spreading beech tree, and by the indolent manner in which they walked away as we approached, it was easy to see that they had never known what it was to have a dozen fierce dogs and shouting horsemen at their heels. But soon we all dismounted round a huge califaté bush, and there we ate our fill of its sweet juicy berries, taking a supply with us to be eaten after dinner, mashed up with sugar, as dessert. Then we gaily cantered on towards the hills, passing many a pleasant-looking nook, and enjoying many a charming glimpse of landscape, doubly delightful after the ugliness of the plains.

Numerous small lagoons, covered with wild-fowl of strange and novel appearance, frequently came in our way, and by their shores basked hundreds of the lovely white swans whose species I have already mentioned. Unlike their comrades of the plains they appeared perfectly tame, merely waddling into the water when we approached close up alongside them, and never once attempting to fly away. I was greatly struck by the thousands of ducks and geese that covered these lakes.

Crossing a broad mountain-stream which ran down from the hills on our left, and disappeared into a mighty gorge stretching away into those on our right, we still directed our march along the grassy plain which led direct towards the three huge Cleopatra peaks rising from out of the snow glaciers far ahead of us. The thickly-wooded slopes which we could perceive in the distance filled us with eager longing to reach them, as it was many a day since we had last seen trees of any kind. In the vast forests which lay before us we promised ourselves a goodly supply of fuel and many a roaring fire around the camp. On the way we occasionally gave chase to the foxes which started up at our approach. There are a great many of these animals in Patagonia, and one has to be careful to put all leather articles in some safe place at night, or else in the morning one is apt to find them gnawed to pieces by these sly marauders. Their fur is very soft, and silver gray in colour. I resolved to make a collection of their skins, and carry them back to England to be made up into rugs and other useful articles. It is very rarely that a dog can catch one of these foxes by himself: our best ostrich hound, "La Plata," after an exciting chase of half an hour, found himself outpaced and outstayed. So quickly can they twist, turn, and double, that it is out of the power of one dog to equal them.

THE "CLEOPATRA NEEDLES"

Whilst we were slowly jogging along, my horse, with a snort of terror suddenly swerved violently on one side. Close to him there rose up a magnificent ostrich, who, after one astonished gaze at our party, turned and fled in the direction by which we had just come. With a merry shout François was after him, followed by my brother and myself. Loca and Leona, who had caught sight of the ostrich in a moment, lost no time in straining every limb to come alongside the fast-fleeting bird, who scudded away at a tremendous pace over the rough uneven ground. Our progress on horseback was also by no means an easy task, as the line taken by the ostrich presented many obstacles, such as high thick bushes, sharp-pointed, half-hidden rocks, and broad, deep chasms. These latter obstacles could only be negotiated at certain places, as their sides were jagged and rotten; and woe betide the horse who should fall into one of these deep, untempting-looking bottoms. But when his blood is up, and the excitement of the chase at its highest pitch, what keen sportsman cares to crane or wonder what danger lies on the other side of the obstacle that confronts him? His only thought is to get forward and keep a front rank in the merry chase that goes gaily sweeping along. And so on we pressed as fast as we could, and urged our horses to do their utmost. Fully entering into the excitement of the moment, the game little beasts answered willingly to our call, and in spite of the rough, difficult going, we managed to keep the dogs and ostrich in sight.

"They'll soon have him now," calls out my brother to me, as a cloud of feathers float away in the still air, torn from the bird's tail by La Leona, who shakes her head to get rid of those that cling round her mouth and clog her tongue and throat. The bird has begun to double, but finds his match in the two clever little ladies at his side, and before long succumbs an easy prey to them both.

This little incident lent a pleasant variety to the winding up of a long tiring day; and full of triumph in the success of our hunt, we trotted towards the camping-place our companions had chosen.

ENCAMPMENT IN THE CORDILLERAS

On our arrival we found active preparations going on in the culinary department, and every one very busily engaged. Three huge fires blazed merrily in
front of my tent, and a little farther off a succession of smaller ones indicated
the spot where the cooks were employed in preparing dinner. Over one of
these hung a pot of soup, carefully superintended by my husband; at another
Storer was watching and turning the roasting ribs of a guanaco, while at a third
Gregorio occupied himself in frying a rich steak of ostrich, and roasting three
or four of their wings as a bonne bouche, which was to succeed the roast. Nor
were Guillaume or l'Aria idle, as the goodly pile of firewood that lay stacked
up near each fire spoke volumes for their activity and energy. After we had
unsaddled our horses and turned them loose to join their companions hard by,
we refreshed ourselves with maté, and then proceeded to take part in the general work and arrangement of the camp. Mysteriously promising us something
extra good in the shape of a new dish, François retired into his tent, dragging
after him the ostrich which we had just killed. The result of his efforts, he
assured us, would produce a pleasant surprise, and an agreeable change in the
monotony of our daily diet. Though full of curiosity as to what that result
might prove, we judged it best to leave him alone, remembering the proverb
that "Too many cooks spoil a dish." Collecting the rows of pack-saddles and
articles of riding gear, I proceeded to arrange them tidily, together with the
numerous sacks and baggage, in a corner of Storer's tent, and then gathering up
a roll of guanaco furs, turned my attention to the making up of our beds. On
the pampa it had always been a matter of some difficulty to discover ground
smooth enough whereon to lay out the beds, on account of the rough, uneven
nature of the plains; but on this occasion I had no cause to grumble, for beneath the lofty spreading beech trees the smooth, velvety, mossy turf afforded the softest and most luxurious of feather beds in the world. Our couches
were simple enough, as doubtless the reader imagines. The ground supplied
the want of a bedstead or mattress, a single blanket occupied the place of a
sheet, and our guanaco capas served as covering, being remarkable for their
great warmth. With our saddles for our pillows, a complete and final touch was
given to the whole arrangement, and on these hard beds, tired with our day's
exertions, we would sleep as soundly and comfortably as though they were the
most luxurious spring mattresses imaginable.

The beds arranged to my satisfaction, I next proceeded to go the round of
the camp to see if everything was in order, on finding which to be the case, with a
sigh of relief I felt that my work was over for the day, and the time for rest arrived.

Roughing it may be all very well in theory, but it is not so easy in practice.
After a long tiring march, when you have been in the saddle twelve or thirteen
hours under a hot sun, it is by no means a light task, on the arrival at your

journey's end, to have to unload your horses, pitch your tents, cook your dinner, clean your saddles and bridles, unpack and remove the baggage, and place everything in order and neatness, while it occupies a long and weary time. In England, on your return every day from hunting, you come home tired and weary, no doubt, but it is to a cosy hunting-box, where a warm room, a blazing fire, an easy arm-chair await you, with servants in plenty to attend to your wants, a refreshing hot bath, and the luxury of a clean change of clothes. But all this is not forthcoming on the pampa, and before you can rest, the whole business I have mentioned has to be gone through, everybody, no matter who it is, taking his or her share of work, while the thought of fatigue must be banished, and every one must put his shoulder to the wheel, and undertake and accomplish his separate task cheerfully and willingly. Only by so doing can things be kept going in the brisk orderly manner they should.

Our camp had been pitched close to the bank of a lovely little mountain stream, which made its appearance from out the thick woods that rose to a great height behind us. The sound of its splashing waters filled me with an irresistible longing for a plunge. Accordingly, armed with a rough towel, I proceeded to follow its winding course upwards, and through the dense foliage of the beech trees I could make out its silver stream descending like a white streak from an immense height. Presently I arrived at a spot where, fed by a small cascade, a clear cool pool of water presented a most convenient and inviting appearance for a bath. I lost no time in undressing and indulging in the luxury of a plunge, which greatly refreshed and invigorated me after the long tiring day I had undergone.

On my return to the camp I found that dinner was quite ready. Nine hungry human beings, and nine still hungrier dogs, require a good substantial meal. Our menu that night was neither mean nor small. As it may interest my readers, I append it:—

Soup.—Guanaco Head, slices of Ostrich, and rice.—Roast ribs of Guanaco.

Fried Ostrich Picane. (Back of the ostrich, resembling a very rich Rumpsteak).

Roast Goose and Ducks.

Ostrich Wings.

Ostrich Liver and fat (consisting of square pieces of ostrich liver and fat, toasted on a stick).

Blood Pudding.

Dessert.—Califatés, Coffee, Maté, Tea, Biscuits.

The blood-pudding proved to be the dish about which François had observed so much secrecy and mystery. It was certainly exceedingly good, and we were loud in praise of its merits. The ostrich liver and fat, a new dish also, was most acceptable, and that night we drank the health of François in a glass of whisky and water all round. Dinner over, we replenished the numerous fires that burned in a semicircle in front of our camp; and then, tired and weary, we sought our couches, and, canopied o'erhead by the rustling trees, with the bright moonlight shining down upon us, slept as sound and contented a sleep as the fatigues we had undergone entitled us to.

CHAPTER XV

EXCURSIONS INTO THE MOUNTAINS—MYSTERIES OF THE CORDILLERAS—WILD-HORSE TRACKS—DEER— MAN THE DESTROYER

THE FIRST FEW DAYS OF OUR SOJOURN in the mountains were spent in making short excursions into the different gorges that stretched away inwards for miles and miles—far as the eye could reach. We were full of curiosity to penetrate and fathom their hidden mysteries; but this was out of the question, owing to the limited supply of provisions which we were able to carry with us. In these solitary wanderings we came across no sign or vestige of the haunts of human beings, and few and far between were the animals that crossed our path. Occasionally, from some jagged plateau or rugged height, we would catch a glimpse of small deer or guanaco, and now and again a wild horse would peer at us suspiciously from behind a huge rock, and then, with a neigh of astonishment rather than fright, dash hurriedly off, its beautiful mane and tail flowing in the breeze, giving it a grand, wild, and picturesque appearance.

Musters tells us in his Narrative of Patagonia, that the Indians fully believe in the existence of an unknown tribe, or of an enchanted or hidden city, which, they superstitiously aver, lies concealed somewhere in the recesses of these mountains.

Farther north the Araucanian Indians profess to having discovered in their vicinity a settlement of white people who spoke an unknown tongue. Numerous legends and stories are current amongst the Patagonians, who all behold with awe and superstition the distant wooded slopes and far-stretching glaciers of the Cordilleras, into whose shades they never attempt to penetrate.

The Chilotes declare that in the western forests of the Cordillera, an animal exists bearing the form of a wild man covered all over with coarse shaggy hair. Tranco is the appellation by which it goes. It is difficult to bring oneself to believe that amidst these immense solitudes a species of human being does not exist. Imaginative minds may conjure up all sorts of extraordinary fancies, and people unknown regions with strange and fantastic figures; and it is hard to prevent oneself from giving a kind of credence to these vague stories which are told with so much confidence and belief by the inhabitants of the country.

The hilly, undulating country which stretched away in the direction of the three Cleopatra peaks filled us with an eager desire to explore its unknown territory; and accordingly, accompanied by Gregorio and François, we all set off on horseback early one morning, soon after daybreak. The air was keen and invigorating, and we trotted along for some time, following and skirting the line of forest which extended on our right and in front of us as far as we could distinguish. Away on our left stretched a bright green valley, gay with many-coloured flowers, and watered by innumerable streams and water-courses, whilst beyond rose high hills, covered with vegetation, and crowned in the distance by thick impenetrable woods. Califaté bushes, loaded with ripe berries of a great and unusual size, frequently brought us to a halt, as it was impossible to resist their tempting and refreshing aspect.

About midday, when the sun was at its height, and we began to feel the effects of its hot, scorching rays, the valley through which we had been pursuing our way suddenly came to an abrupt termination. Breasting the hill which confined its limits, we halted on the summit to give the horses a few moments' rest, and to contemplate in silence and delight the lovely scene that lay stretched at our feet.

Of a totally different aspect was this new country on which we were entering from that we had just quitted, for the woods closed in on all sides, and huge masses of rocks rose from out their leafy tops, giving the appearance of ruined strongholds to those who beheld them for the first time. Sunny glades, carpeted by rich green grass, opened out here and there, as though they had been cleared and fashioned by the hand of man, while a lovely little stream, which made its appearance from out of the woods on our right, continued its course towards a deep ravine, which we could distinguish in the distance. Away to our left, and surrounded by thick woods, glittered the clear sparkling waters of an immense lake, which we judged to be about two miles distant, and beyond all rose up like a huge frowning barrier, the lofty snow-clad peaks of the Cordillera. Not a sound disturbed the deathlike stillness which reigned over everything; no animal life was stirring, and the impression conveyed to an eye-witness who beheld this scene for the first time was a sense of utter loneliness and desolation.

Descending the hill on which we had halted to breathe the horses, we entered upon the woodland scene I have just described, and following the course of the little brook that flowed towards the great ravine, were not long in arriving at the edge of its steep perpendicular descent. It proved to be a ravine of no ordinary size, for many hundreds of feet below, its base was formed by what appeared to be a tiny winding stream, but which a later expedition, of which I have yet to speak, proved in reality to be a broad though shallow river. Far away below us, to our right, roared an enormous cataract, which, half hidden in the trees, left scarcely any part of itself visible, and were it not for the clouds of spray that rose to a great height, an eye-witness could not have distinguished its real position amidst its leafy hiding-place.

We were not long in ascertaining that it would be impossible to get horses down the steep precipitous sides of this great ravine, and therefore reluctantly abandoned any hope of being able that day to make any farther progress towards the three great peaks which still towered in front of us. Directing our horses to the left, we entered a long stretch of narrow woodland, which appeared to lead in the direction of the lake we had distinguished a little time back. It was not long before we struck upon a wild horse track, and concluding that it was formed by these animals on their way to drink at the lake, we followed its tortuous and many winding ways for some time.

Frequently the brushwood became so dense, the trees so close together, that we had to dismount and creep through the openings made by our horses, having previously driven them through. Now and then the path we were following would suddenly cease, and it would be some time before we came upon its track again. At last we emerged from some thick underwood into a broad clearing, and eagerly pushed forward.

Proceeding at a quicker rate than my companions, I was soon far ahead of them; and in fear of being lost, and anxious to avoid such an unpleasant contretemps, I drew rein, and dismounting, sat down to await their arrival. Presently a cracking sound as of sticks breaking close to me attracted my attention. Looking in the direction whence the sound proceeded, I espied a species of deer, of a dark golden colour, eyeing me with extreme astonishment. He was a fine buck, with beautiful branching antlers, and large dark languishing eyes. Close behind him cautiously peered two does, and a little farther off I could make out several other animals of the same kind.

How I longed for a rifle, but of this firearm I knew we had not brought one with us, and though I had a gun, it was not at hand, and was being carried by Storer. Crawling away from the spot as quietly as I could, I placed a good hundred yards between myself and the place from which I had first caught sight of these animals, and then springing to my feet, ran as hard as I could in the direction I judged my companions were coming. As soon as they came in sight I endeavoured by signs to get them to halt. They quickly perceived me, and guessing what I wanted, immediately drew rein and waited for me to come up. I lost no time in informing them of the discovery I had made, and taking my gun, proceeded to regain as quietly and stealthily as possible the spot I had lately quitted. The rest of my companions remained stationary, waiting for the report of my gun, which was to bring them all up.

Yes, there he was, a beautiful animal, still in the same attitude of inquiring curiosity in which I had left him. Anxious to avoid spoiling the head, I took aim behind the shoulder, and fired. The report was followed by a crashing sound in the direction in which I had fired. Into the glade some half-dozen deer bounded, and like lightning disappeared into the opposite wood. When the smoke cleared away I perceived the one at which I had fired on his knees, evidently unable to proceed. Full of anxiety to place the poor beast out of his agony I fired a second barrel at him, which had the effect of knocking him over. Springing up immediately, however, he walked slowly away, seemingly unconcerned and unhurt. I could not make out what was the matter with myself and my gun. He had evidently been hit both times, and yet seemed to be perfectly unconcerned at the whole thing. I could not bring myself to fire again, but Gregorio did with his revolver, and broke the unfortunate animals leg. Limping away on three, he went and lay down under an overhanging rock, appearing more stupefied than in pain. Disgusted at such butchery, I begged one of my companions, all of whom had come up, to despatch the unfortunate beast, and my husband, going close up to him, placed his revolver within a foot of the deer's forehead and fired. Slowly it sank forward, stunned and apparently lifeless, but when we came alongside it, it was still breathing, and there was no mark to show that the bullet had penetrated the skull. Here François came to our aid, and with the help of his hunting-knife, the poor creature was put out of his misery.

As I wished to keep the skin, the coat of which was very thick and long, Gregorio set to work to remove it. The process occupied some time, and proved most difficult and tedious to accomplish. During our stay in the Cordilleras we frequently came across these deer; but our experience of their tameness, the great difficulty of killing them, and the utter absence of sport which lay therein, prevented us from ever again attempting to bring another down. The flesh was decidedly good, and much to be appreciated after the monotonous diet of ostrich and guanaco meat; but even with this inducement at hand, the golden deer of the Cordilleras remained unmolested and sacred in our eyes for the rest of the time we remained in their hitherto undisturbed and peaceful solitudes. If regret could atone for that death, of which I unfortunately was the cause, then it has long ago been forgiven; for, for many a day I was haunted by a sad remorse for the loss of that innocent and trusting life, which had hitherto remained in ignorance of the annihilating propensities of man—that man who, directly he sees something beautiful and rare, becomes filled with the desire to destroy.

The shoulders, ribs, and head were packed on to the horses of Storer, François, and Gregorio, the remainder being left as food for the dogs and condors. Some dozen of the latter, having scented blood, were already hovering high above our heads, and as soon as we were out of sight would doubtless swoop down and make greedy feast on the remains left by the dogs. Five minutes' riding brought us to the shores of the great lagoon towards which we had been directing our steps. Here we dismounted, and tethering our horses, left them to browse on the long rich grass which grew luxuriantly and thickly all round. A couple of hours were quickly and happily whiled away duck shooting. It was not till late that night that we reached our camp in safety, tired and hungry, but having thoroughly enjoyed our day.

CHAPTER XVI

AN ALARM—THE WILD-HORSES—AN EQUINE COMBAT—
THE WILD STALLION VICTORIOUS—THE STRUGGLE
RENEWED—RETREAT OF THE WILD HORSES

ONE EVENING, AFTER DINNER, we were all sitting round the camp-fire, discussing coffee, when I'Aria, who had gone to have a last look at the horses before turning in, came running back, and announced that he could see the Indians coming down the valley in great numbers. We immediately jumped up and hurried out to inspect the new arrivals, not a little annoyed at the prospect of our privacy being intruded upon by these unwelcome guests.

Looking up the valley, we saw a dark mass moving slowly towards us. Presently it came nearer, and Gregorio, looking at it closely for a moment, said excitedly, "That's not the Indians, but a herd of wild horses; we had better look out for our own!" An extraordinary commotion was indeed visible among our animals. They were running to and fro, evidently in a state of great perturbation, now collecting together in a knot, now dispersing at a gallop over the valley, neighing and whinnying shrilly.

As Gregorio spoke, one of the wild horses detached itself from the main troop and galloped at full speed towards our horses. "Quick! quick! your rifles, or we shall lose our tropilla," shouted Gregorio, in evident alarm; and though we did not quite understand the full extent of our danger, we ran for our rifles, and started off as quick as we could, to get between the wild horses and our own, Gregorio explaining as we ran along, that the wild stallion, if we did not stop him, would drive off our troop, and leave us in the most perilous plight. Of course nothing more was needed to urge us on to our utmost speed, to avert the threatening danger. But the stallion flew like the wind towards our horses, who were now all huddled together in a corner of the valley, and we could scarcely hope to be in time to save them. Suddenly he staggered and fell; he had got into a bog. In the few seconds he lost in extricating himself we had time to get within range. Bang! bang! bang! went our rifles, but unscathed he sped on, and was soon within twenty yards of our terrified animals, and far in front of us. "We are lost!" cried the guides simultaneously; and filled with dismay, we all stood still, perfectly paralysed at the thought of the position we should be in without horses, three hundred miles away from Sandy Point.

But at this moment Gregorio's big bay stallion, the master of the troop, rushed out to meet the enemy, both halting when they met, and fronting one another. Thankful for this diversion in our favour, we again ran forward, in hopes of being able to get up before Gregorio's stallion should have been compelled to fly, as the superior size of his adversary left no doubt he would ultimately have to do. In the meantime the two animals, after pawing the air for a second or two, made a dash at one another, and engaged in a fierce combat, carried on chiefly with their teeth, though occasionally they would rise on their hind legs and fight with their fore feet. Our horses, not daring to stir, watched them on one side, and the wild herd, which had meanwhile trotted up close to the field of battle, looked on from the other side, apparently deeply interested in the issue of the struggle.

We hurried along as quick as we could, though, unfortunately, we could make but slow progress, encumbered as we were with our rifles, and retarded by the long grass. Meanwhile—another misfortune—we discovered that beyond three bullets my husband happened to have had in his pocket when we started, and which we had fired off in the first volley, no one had brought any ammunition, this essential having been overlooked in the hurry and excitement of the moment. Hoping we should be able to cope with the stallion, should we get up in time, with our revolvers, we pressed on, our eyes fixed on the two combatants, the endurance of our champion being now our only chance. He was evidently already worsted, and any second might turn tail and fly. Still he fought on, and still we drew nearer and nearer.

Suddenly my brother, who was a little in front of us, seemed to fall. Running to him we found him up to the waist in a bog, which stretched up the valley between us and the horses. It was impossible to cross it; indeed, we had some difficulty in pulling him out. We had to run a good distance before we could get on to firmer ground; and in the meantime the battle went against our stallion, who suddenly turned tail and fled. After giving him a parting kick, the wild horse rushed at our troop, and began to drive them at a gallop towards his own, punishing with vicious bites and kicks any animal that showed signs of becoming refractory, or that did not go quick enough. The moment was critical. We strained every nerve to get between the two troops, as, if they once joined, our chances were hopeless. But for another unexpected diversion in our favour,

our efforts would have been defeated. This diversion was the sudden reappearance on the scene of our stallion, who, at the sight of his retreating wives, had evidently once more screwed up his courage to the fighting point.

The combat that now ensued was fiercer even than the last one. Profiting by it, we got up to our horses, who had stood still again, and hurriedly drove them in front of us towards our camp. We had gone some distance when the wild stallion, having again proved victor, came swooping after us, neighing proudly, and evidently meaning mischief. We began to shout and wave our hands as he approached, in the hopes of driving him off. When within forty yards of us, he stopped, but continued to circle round us, stamping and pawing, and neighing angrily. Our object was to drive the horses up to the camp and get to our rifle ammunition, it being evident that the only way to relieve ourselves of this troublesome Don Juan was by despatching him altogether. We soon got near to the camp, and shouted to I'Aria to bring us some bullets. At the report of the first shot the stallion fled in dismay, and with such rapidity that the two or three bangs we had at him missed their mark. He made straight for his own troop, who, during the whole performance, had stood in watchful expectation. The moment he reached them they all started off at a gallop, and, in the twinkling of an eye, swept up the steep escarpment on the far side of the valley and disappeared. Our horses were so frightened and bewildered by the day's events, that they seemed to have little desire to graze, but stood quite quiet together for upwards of an hour near the camp. We were in some apprehension lest the stallion should return in the night, but Gregorio said that he thought there was no danger of such an occurrence taking place, and we accordingly turned in and went to sleep, and were glad to see our troop grazing tranquilly next morning as usual.

CHAPTER XVII

EXCURSION TO THE CLEOPATRA NEEDLES—A BOG—A WINDING RIVER—DIFFICULT TRAVELLING—A STRANGE PHENOMENON—A FAIRY HAUNT—WILD HORSES AGAIN—THEIR AGILITY—THE BLUE LAKE—THE CLEOP-ATRA PEAKS—THE PROMISED LAND

IT WAS ARRANGED THAT NIGHT that Mr. B. and my brother and myself should make an expedition with Gregorio, towards the three strange peaks already mentioned. In order to spare our horses, no cumbersome articles were to be taken, a kettle, some biscuits, coffee, and meat, being all we contemplated carrying with us, except, of course, our guanaco furs and guns.

Thus equipped, we started the next morning shortly after sunrise. Our trip began badly. We had not gone far before my brother got into a morass, out of which he had no little difficulty in extricating himself; and as for his horse, at one time we thought the poor brute would never get out again, so deep had it sunk into the trembling, boggy ground. However, we managed to get it out at last, and, though both well plastered with mud, neither its rider nor itself were any the worse for this little contretemps. Proceeding on our journey, we followed Gregorio at a merry trot towards the great ravine, through which flowed that broad and rapid mountain stream, which it was necessary for us to ford.

The ravine side was so steep that we had to dismount and lead our horses down by a narrow track made by the wild horses. This pathway seemed to fall almost perpendicularly down to the river, which roared along, two or three hundred feet below us, and a slip or stumble might have sent us pell mell, one over the other, into it. No such mishap occurred, however, and, safely reaching the bottom, we proceeded to ford the river. It was not so deep as we had expected, but it ran with great force, and its bed being composed of shifting pebbles and large boulders of rock, our horses floundered and splashed about in a distressing

way, and we all got more or less drenched by the time we got through it. This
being the summer season the water was comparatively low, and we were able
to follow the windings of the ravine, riding over the dry strip of river-bed for
a good distance. But then the river began to dart about capriciously from one
side of the ravine to the other, the consequence being that we were continually
finding ourselves obliged to ford it again; and the ravine sides were now so steep
and thickly wooded that we had no option but to follow the river. After two
hours of splashing, and many a narrow escape from complete duckings, the river made a sudden turn southward, and in order to keep on our road towards the
peaks we had to say farewell to our convenient ravine, and make our way as best
we could through the beechwood forest. This was an arduous task. At times we
would get into a thicket which made progress impossible, forcing us to retrace
our steps, and try some other route, often to meet only the same difficulty as
before. Then a good broad clearing would turn out to be equally impracticable,
on account of a belt of bog stretching across it, or a little ravine, which favoured
our journey for a time, would resolve itself into an impasse, and again we would
have to turn back. Fortunately the weather was fine and sunny, and we made
light of our difficulties, occasionally resting for a while to admire some of the
many lovely bits of landscape chance presented to our eyes, or to feast on some
bush, heavy laden with wild red currants, which were now ripe and sweet. A
peculiar phenomenon, suggestive of some great fire in bygone ages, struck me
in these forests. Everywhere, among the younger trees, stood huge dead giants,
gray and leafless, and partially charred, as if a sudden sea of fire had swept over
them, drying up their sap and destroying their vital powers, being quenched,
however, by some sudden agency before it had time to destroy their branches and trunks completely. These gray skeletons of a bygone age looked weird
and ghastly, standing amid the fresh green trees around them, and the wind,
sweeping through their branches, produced a dry harsh rattle, which contrasted
strangely with the melodious rustle of the leafy crests of their comrades.

For three or four hours we worked our way through the forest, and I never
was more astonished at the marvellous powers of endurance of our horses than
on this occasion, to say nothing of their extraordinary cleverness in scrambling
over the trunks of fallen trees, and in picking their way through boggy ground,
where a wrong step to the right or left would have been disastrous. At last we
reached the outskirts of the wood, all more or less scratched and bruised, and
thoroughly tired with our exertions.

But the peaks were still far off, and the sun was getting low, and soon
another strip of forest loomed ominously in front of us. We resolved, therefore, to go no farther that day, and accordingly cast about for some suitable
camping-place.

We were not long in finding a little nook which was admirably adapted to our purpose. Sheltered by a cluster of moss and grass-covered boulders, and well fenced in by a circle of shrubs and trees, we found a fairy circle of soft, velvety greensward, jewelled here and there with knots of scarlet verbenas and wild violets. Bubbling from out among the rocks a silver clear little stream flowed down its centre, giving just the slight touch of life and movement required to make this sylvan retreat as cheerful as it was cosy, not to speak of its convenience as regards the kettle.

We soon had our horses unsaddled, and then Gregorio and Mr. B. set to work to light a fire, whilst my brother went out with his gun, and I gathered a capful of red currants, which I mashed up with sugar, with a view to dessert. By the time my brother came back, bringing with him a brace of wood-pigeons and parrots, which were soon plucked and spitted, the rib of guanaco Gregorio had set to roast was done to a nicety, and we all fell to and made a hearty meal, finishing with the red currants aforesaid.

Then the men lit their pipes, and the social maté-bowl went round, whilst we lay watching the sun setting over the mountains, gilding their peaks with ever varying tints, and making their snowy glaciers glow warm and golden under its magic touch. Far below, at our feet, lay the ravine, with the river we had so often crossed that day, looking like a winding silver thread in the distance. Around us reigned perfect peace; the chattering flocks of parrots, which had made the woods noisy during day-time, had gone to their leafy roosts, and not a breath of wind stirred the silent trees. A few little birds, who no doubt had their homes in the chinks of the boulders which formed the background of our camp, hovered around us anxiously for some time, till, finding they had nothing to fear from their strange visitors, they took heart, and hopped from stone to stone into their respective lodgings, and, after chirping a note or two, were silent for the night.

We were not long in following their example, and rolling myself up in my guanaco robe, with my head on my saddle, I slept as sound and sweet a sleep "under the greenwood tree" as ever blessed a weary mortal. Neither Puck nor Ariel played any pranks with me; though, for ought I know, Titania and Oberon, and their fairy following, flying from the sceptical modern spirit which ignores them, may well have made these secluded sylvan haunts their own.

We were in the saddle early the next morning, and, plunging into the woods, pursued our way through the same difficulties which had hampered our progress the day before. After a time, however, we came to a region evidently much frequented by wild horses, and eventually we hit on a path worn by them right through the woods, and following this, we jogged along at a very fair pace. Soon our horses began to neigh and prick up their ears as we advanced towards a clearing. Their cries were answered from somewhere beyond us, and pushing forward into the open, we came upon a herd of wild horses, who, hearing our advance, had stopped grazing, and now they stood collected in a knot together, snorting and stamping, and staring at us in evident amazement. One of their number came boldly trotting out to meet us, and evidently with no pacific intentions; his wicked eye, and his white teeth, which he had bared fiercely, looked by no means reassuring. But suddenly he stopped short, looked at us for a moment, and then, with a wild snort, dashed madly away, followed by the whole herd. They disappeared like lightning over the brow of a deep ravine, to emerge again on our view after a couple of seconds, scampering like goats up its opposite side, which rose almost perpendicular to a height of six or seven hundred feet. They reached its crest at full gallop in the twinkling of an eye, and without pausing an instant disappeared again, leaving us wondering and amazed at their marvellous agility. I had often seen their paths leading up hill-sides which a man could scarcely climb, but till now that I had witnessed a specimen of their powers with my own eyes, I had scarcely been able to believe them possessed of a nimbleness and cleverness of foot which would not discredit a chamois.

From the open space on which we were now standing we could see a broad lake lying at the base of some very high hills, behind which lay the mighty mountain which culminated in the three peaks we were desirous of reaching, and as a ravine appeared to wind in that direction from the head of the lake, we now pushed forward towards the latter, occasionally profiting by numerous wild horse paths to expedite our advance. After a weary scramble of several hours' duration, we threaded a last belt of forest, blundered and floundered through a last bog, and after a short ride over a grassy plain studded with bushes, which were literally blue with a profusion of califaté-berries, found ourselves on the shores of a splendid sheet of water. The sight well repaid us for our trouble. The lake, which was two or three miles broad, lay encircled by tall hills, covered with thick vegetation, which grew close down to the water's edge. Beyond the hills rose the three red peaks and the Cordilleras. Their white glaciers, with the white clouds resting on them, were all mirrored to marvellous perfection in the motionless lake, whose crystal waters were of the most extraordinarily brilliant blue I have ever beheld. Round the lake ran a narrow strip of white sand, and exactly in its centre stood a little green island with a clump of beeches growing on it. Each colour—the white, the green, the blue—was so brilliant; the scene—the wooded hills, the glaciers rising into the blue above, and sinking mirrored into the blue below—was so unique, the spirit of silence and solitude which lay over all so impressive, that for a long time we stood as if spellbound, none of us uttering a word. Suddenly we were startled by a rushing sound behind us, and in another instant, making the air shake as it went, and almost touching me with the tip of its mighty wing, a condor swept past us, rising with rapid flight up, up, up into the air, we following him with our eyes, till he became a mere speck on the sky, and finally disappeared, thousands of feet up in the air. This incident seemed to break the charm that held us silent, and we broke into a chorus of exclamations of praise and wonder as every second some new beauty in the scene before us struck our admiring gaze. Resuming our journey, we rode along the narrow strip of beach towards the head of the lake. Occasionally we were forced into the water, as at some spots there was no beach at all; but at any rate we got on much quicker here than we had up to the present, and in a comparatively short space of time found ourselves at the head of the lake. We were close to the three peaks, which we could now see were parts of the crater of an extinct volcano—the other portions of which had fallen in, a prey to the action of the weather. We camped by the side of a little stream which flowed into the lake. All night long we could hear the thunder of avalanches, or what, perhaps, might have been the rumbling of some distant volcano; and I found myself nervously expecting a repetition of the earthquake which had surprised us so disagreeably at the Laguna Blanca.

"WE WERE THE FIRST WHO EVER BURST ON TO THAT
SILENT SEA"

In the morning we rode up a tall hill, from which we could get a good view of the interior. At the same time we were able to assure ourselves that it would be useless, slightly provisioned as we were, to attempt to penetrate any farther, the country before us being still more thickly wooded than that we had already traversed.

For some distance we could catch glimpses among the hills of bright green valleys, with whose excellent pastures our nimble friends the wild horses were doubtless well acquainted; and farther on rose a forest of white peaks, one towering above the other, till the tallest faded, hazy and indistinct, into the skies. I would fain have dived into their farthest mystery, but it was not to be; so, with a sigh of regret, we turned our horses' heads in a homeward direction. We got back to the camp late in the evening, having taxed our horses' powers to the utmost to accomplish our return trip in one day. Our account of the wonderful blue lake and the strange country beyond excited the envy of those who had remained behind, and led to a discussion as to the practicability of our entering the mountains, bag and baggage. But the difficulties in our way were too many and formidable, and reluctantly we were compelled to abandon this seductive plan.

CHAPTER XVIII

WE THINK OF RETURNING—GOOD-BYE TO THE COR-
DILLERAS—THE LAST OF THE WILD HORSES—MOSQUI-
TOES—A STORMY NIGHT—A CALAMITY—THE LAST OF
OUR BISCUIT—THE UTILITY OF FIRE-SIGNALS

A FEW MORE DAYS SPENT IN THE CORDILLERAS brought us near the time
when it was necessary to begin to think of returning to Sandy Point.
Our provisions were beginning to sink rapidly; tea and coffee and sugar
we still had plenty of, but the biscuit bags were getting ominously low, and all
our other dainties had already been consumed; and many of our camps were
painfully remembered in connection with this or that article of food, which
had been partaken of there for the last time. Thus, near "Los Bargnales" we had
finished our last tin of butter; "Los Morros" witnessed the broaching of our
last tin of preserved milk; and here, in the Cordilleras, we ruefully swallowed
our last dish of porridge. Guanaco meat is good, so is ostrich meat; good, too,
is an open-air, gipsy life in a bright climate, with lots of sport and pleasant
companionship; but the goodness of all these things is materially enhanced by
the accompaniment of good cheer, and materially depreciated by the lack of it.
Thus, when our daily menu began to consist of a series of ingenious changes
on the monotonous theme of ostrich and guanaco meat, varied only by baked
biscuits, our thoughts somehow began to run in the groove of home; and we
often found ourselves talking of «dear old England» and its roast beef in a strain
of affectionate longing. Somehow the air of Patagonia did not seem so bracing
and inspiriting as at first; we began to grow sceptical on the subject of guanaco
and ostrich hunting; we discovered that the wild duck were too tame to give
real good sport, and that snipe-shooting in a country where these birds get up
in flocks, is simply a matter of loading and pulling the trigger. Discomforts
and hardships, of which we once made light, we now began to take as serious

matters, and our tempers, once so sweet and accommodating, had begun to grow acrid and touchy. We all felt more inclined to dwell on the weight of our individual opinions, and less disposed to value those of our companions. Once we had avoided discussions, as liable to disturb the harmony which reigned among us; now we welcomed them as pleasant irritants, and even went out of our way to provoke them. The result was that one day, on somebody's suggesting that perhaps we had better think of returning; after a little opposition, as a matter of course (for in our then mood it was quite sufficient for anybody to propose a plan for everybody else to immediately gainsay it), we unanimously agreed that, considering that we had seen a good deal of Patagonia, considering, too, that our provisions were nearly exhausted, and that our horses were very stale, it was better to start at once.

So one morning the packhorses were driven up, and the familiar occupation of loading them gone through. It had now become a much simpler matter than formerly, and we were enabled to comfort ourselves with the reflection that the loss in our larder was a gain as regards the time economised every day in packing up.

Before leaving our pretty camp we carved our names on one of the trees, and erected a cairn, on the top of which we left a bottle—the only emblem of civilisation we could spare. Then, mounting, we turned our backs on the Cordilleras, and set out towards the ravine we had entered by, whose name, among the traders, is "The Wild Horse Ravine." As we were riding along, a solitary horse suddenly appeared on the crest of a hill, and, after eyeing us for a moment, came tearing down towards us at a frantic gallop, with a loud neigh, and perhaps dangerous intentions. Our troop of horses scattered in all directions; Gregorio and I'Aria got out their "bolas," prepared for emergencies, and we curiously awaited the sequel of the incident. Nearer and nearer came the untamed steed, without abating his speed one jot, and evidently determined to charge right at us. We began to feel uncomfortable, but put our trust in Gregorio's deftness, though it was perhaps well it was not put to the test. When within about ten yards of us the wild horse suddenly stopped, stood still for one second, and then turned, and, with two sets of "bolas" whizzing harmlessly round his ears, went bounding away as fast as he had come, never stopping till he reached the top of the hill he had first appeared on. This was the last we saw of the "Bagnales."

Late in the afternoon we crossed the ravine where we had camped before entering the Cordilleras. Here we were assailed by a thick cloud of mosquitoes, who annoyed us and our poor horses horribly, buzzing round us, and biting viciously wherever they could settle. For a time nothing was to be heard but angry exclamations and objurgations, mingled with occasional cries of fiendish joy as one of us succeeded in destroying half a dozen of our thirsty tormentors with one slap of the hand. But from the fury of their numbers there was no refuge, opposition only increased their virulence, and those who were fiercest and most energetic in driving them off were always surrounded by the thickest cloud. Relief only came when we got out of the ravine into the plain, and there one puff of wind swept our enemy clean away in a second, not one mosquito remaining to curse at or to kill.

Thankful for our release from this annoyance, we were not disposed to grumble very much at the oppressive heat to which we were exposed during the whole of the day, though the sun beat down on us from a cloudless sky with overpowering force, and our burnt and blistered faces smarted painfully under its fiery rays. We camped that night near a broad lagoon, and for the next few days continued our journey over the plains, without anything of note occurring. Hitherto we had been pretty fortunate as regards the weather, and the nights especially, with hardly an exception, had been calm and fine. But one march before reaching Coy-Inlet River we camped in a broad valley, where our experience of Patagonian nights was unpleasantly varied. Shortly after we had gone to bed, the misgivings which the threatening aspect of the sky had called up, as we took a last glance at the weather before turning in, were more than realised. The wind began to pipe ominously through the grass, and before long it was blowing a regular gale. A sudden squall carried our tents clean out of their pickets, and sent them whirling through the air. A scene of the most uncomfortable confusion ensued. It was pouring with rain, pitch dark, and the wind was blowing with such force that it was hard to keep one's legs. Rugs, and clothes, and smouldering embers were being blown in all directions; everybody was blundering about in the darkness, tripping up over something, or falling against some one else; and the howling of the wind, the rush of the river, the chorus of loud imprecations in various languages, and the unearthly moaning and whimpering of the dogs, made up as wild a scene of noisy confusion as could possibly be imagined.

Several vain attempts were made to set up the tents, but the wind was too strong; and at last, perfectly drenched through, we had to give up the attempt, and crawl into whatever furs first came to hand, to wait till the storm should pass over. This it did not do till about four o'clock in the morning, just as it was getting light. It was too late or early to go to bed again then, so we crept out, sleepy, and damp, and miserable, and drank hot coffee round a smoking fire, till the sun got up and warmed us thoroughly.

We were to camp that evening by the Coy-Inlet River, and as it was a good way off we set out soon after breakfast. We passed several herds of guanaco, and also a herd of about eighty or a hundred ostriches. I had never seen so many together before. We gave chase to them, but the dogs got so excited, running first after one ostrich and then after another, that at last they all got away. A calamity happened to us that afternoon. The mare who carried the two little bags with all that remained of our greatest treasure—our biscuits, suddenly took fright at something, and galloped wildly away. We followed her course with anxious eyes and beating hearts, not daring to go after her, lest it should aggravate her fears. For a time the pack sat firmly, and we began to breathe, but even while we watched, oh, horror! it began to incline towards one side, and then gradually slid over. The moment the mare felt it underneath her she began to kick out, and galloping quicker and quicker, in a very few seconds she was packless and pacified. Then only did we gallop forward to know the worst, and the worst was bad indeed. A long trail of broken biscuits, sown in the grass, marked the course the unfortunate mare had taken, and when we got to the bags only a few small handfuls remained. We tried to gather together what we could, but the biscuit, by long travel, had broken into fine dust, and it was quite impossible to pick much out of the long grass it had fallen into. Our last kettle had also severely suffered in the fracâs, a big hole appearing in its side when, after a long search, it was at last found. Guillaume talked hopefully of being able to mend it, but failing this desirable consummation, farewell the cheering cup of maté; farewell the morning bowl of grateful coffee; farewell content—the camp-life's chiefest comfort gone! Slowly and mournfully we tied up what was left of the biscuits in a small canvas bag, which Gregorio secured to his saddle, and then, after having devoted a quarter of an hour to grazing on all fours on such fragments as could be found among the grass, we continued our journey, reflecting on the vanity of all things.

We arrived at Coy-Inlet River that evening, and fording it, camped near the bank. It rained again during the night, but as there was little or no wind, it did not matter much, and excepting a pervading sense of dampness, we suffered no great discomfort. Continuing our march that day over the plains that lay between Coy-Inlet River and the Gallegos, we saw the smoke of numerous fires in the distance; but there was no response to the fires we lit in answer, and so we concluded that they were only old fires, which were still smouldering. The next day one of our party had an opportunity of practically testing the value of fires as a means of signalling one's whereabouts in the pampa. He had got up early in the morning, and had gone out on foot at about five o'clock with his rifle, to try and stalk a guanaco. At ten o'clock he had not returned. As we had only a short march to make that day, it did not matter if we started a little later than usual, so we lay about, waiting for his return. Eleven, twelve o'clock came, but still no signs of him. He had now been away more than seven hours, and I began to think that something must have happened to him. We therefore rode up on the plains to look for him, lighting fires at intervals, to show the position of the camp, and anxiously scanning the horizon to see whether he had also made a fire. But though we rode about for a long time nothing was to be seen, and we went back to the camp, wondering what could have happened. Just as we were in the middle of a perplexed discussion as to what steps to take in the matter, to our relief he suddenly came into the camp, blood-stained and tired, and carrying the head and ribs of a guanaco on his back. Shortly after leaving the camp he had wounded a guanaco, which went off, however, and led him a long dance for two or three hours, without his being able to come within range of it again. In despair, he at last fired a couple of shots at it from a long range, but, as it seemed, without reaching his mark. These shots exhausted his ammunition, our supply of ball-cartridges being very low, and he having only allowed himself three rounds. Loath to abandon the wounded animal, he had followed it pertinaciously over ravines and hills, always vowing to himself that beyond a certain point he would follow no farther, but always being lured on by the signs of exhaustion the guanaco was showing, to go just a little farther. At last he had the satisfaction of seeing it lie down, and with a shout of triumph ran forward to despatch it with his hunting-knife. But at his approach the guanaco jumped up again, and slowly as it ran, it was enabled to outdistance its relentless pursuer, who was already thoroughly done up with his exertions; but feeling that with patience he must conquer at last, he felt less inclined than ever to abandon his prey. Already numerous hawks and condors were circling over the doomed guanaco, and the thought that the fruit of his labours would only go to provide a feast for these hateful marauders was an additional incentive to persevere. At last success rewarded his efforts. Waiting till the guanaco lay down once more, he approached it by degrees, and then, when within twenty yards or so of it, made a dash towards it. It stumbled in trying to get up, and he had just time to rush up and catch it by the ear, and with a happy stroke of his long hunting-knife end its sufferings. It was only when he had cut it up, and laden himself with the best parts, that he began to reflect that in the excitement of the chase he had quite forgotten in which direction the camp lay. He had followed the guanaco now to the right, now to the left, often having to run to keep it in view, and all he knew was that several hours must have elapsed since he started in its pursuit. He lit several fires, but he only had a few matches, and the fires unfortunately soon went out, so that he had no means of showing us his own whereabouts. However, he struck out in a direction in which he imagined the camp must lie, and kept wearily trudging on under his load, which, tired as he was, he was naturally loath to part from. After he had gone a good distance he looked around, and then the skyline behind him appeared to be singularly like that he remembered having seen on leaving the camp. But then the skyline to the left, somehow, had the same look too. Which was the right one? He was just revolving this puzzling question in his mind, in no very pleasant humour, when he caught a glimpse of the smoke of the fires we had lit, and happily not far off, in the direction he had instinctively chosen from the first as the right one. The sight gave him new vigour, and though he had still a good distance to go, he managed to reach the camp at last, without having to throw away the meat which had cost him such a hard day's work.

CHAPTER XIX

ISIDORO—AN UNSAVOURY MEAL—EXPENSIVE LOAVES—
GUANACO SCARCE—DISAPPOINTMENT—NIGHT SUR-
PRISES US—SUPPERLESS—CONTINUED FASTING—NO
MEAT IN THE CAMP

WE RODE DOWN A BROAD VALLEY, which led to the Gallegos River, where we were to camp for the night. On reaching its farther end we were suddenly surprised by the sight of an Indian camp, composed of three tents, which were pitched on the other side of the river. Having little curiosity to make the acquaintance of their inmates, we continued our journey along the river towards our intended camp, but Gregorio and Mr. B. rode over to see them. They rejoined us an hour afterwards; Mr. B. had found an old friend, an Argentine Gaucho, named Isidoro, who had accompanied him on a former trip, and whom, curiously enough, he had parted from a year before, on exactly the same spot where he now met him. I was glad to hear that Isidoro was going to pay us a visit the next day, as I had heard a great deal about him, and was anxious to make his acquaintance. We camped near the river, seven or eight miles away from the Indian camp, and consequently, we hoped, rather too far to attract a call from these people, the disagreeable experience of their visit whilst we were at Cape Gregorio being still fresh in my mind.

Early in the morning we saw a man riding in the direction of the camp, who, I was told, was Isidoro. He presently appeared among us, and, except for his moustache and beard, and the superior cleanliness of his dress, he might have been taken for an Indian. He was warmly welcomed by the guides, amongst whom his unequalled proficiency in all that pertains to the pampa craft, and his personal character, had gained him great prestige. Isidoro did not stop long, as he was going to hunt with the Indians that day; so, after

570

having taken a few cups of maté, and smoked a pipe or two in silence, he said good-bye, and took his departure.

As he rode away, I could not help admiring his manly bearing and his perfect seat on a splendid, well-bred looking horse, which seemed not unworthy of its master. He wore his guanaco capa with a certain foppish grace that one might have looked in vain for in Gregorio or any of the others, and every article of his accoutrements, from his carefully coiled lasso to the bright-coloured garters round his new potro-boots, was perfectly finished and natty.

After he had gone, my husband and myself started off guanaco-hunting. We soon killed a guanaco, and were busily engaged in the laborious operation of cutting it up, when we heard a grunt, and looking up, saw an Indian behind us on horseback. He watched our clumsy efforts for some time in silence, occasionally breaking out into loud laughter, and then dismounting, took out his own knife, and with a few adroit and easy cuts, did the whole trick in no time. He rewarded himself for his labours by cutting out the kidneys and the heart, and eating them raw and bloody, there and then! This disgusting repast over, he smacked his lips, mounted his horse, and rode away, grinning eloquently, and leaving us wondering and horrified.

The evening after our halt at Gallegos we camped in a stony, rocky region, where there was very little grass, but plenty of quail, several of which we shot, though we found them to be very dry and unpalatable. It poured all the next day, so we were compelled to remain where we were, much against our will. To have to lie all day in a little tent, with a dreary bit of gray landscape to look out upon, while the rain patters on the canvas in a remorseless, dispiriting monotone, is one of the most severe trials one's patience can be put to, and ours came very badly out of the ordeal, Patagonia being by no means complimentarily alluded to in the course of these weary hours. However, towards sundown, it cleared up, and we were able to have a turn and stretch our limbs in the open air before it got dark.

Two days after leaving this camp we struck the Indian trail to Sandy Point, and on the third we camped opposite Cape Gregorio, not far from the place whence we had made our visit to the Indians. Here we intended halting for a couple of days to take in a good supply of meat before starting for Sandy Point, as neither guanaco nor ostriches were to be met with, except by a mere chance, any farther south, and all our other provisions being exhausted, we had now to rely solely upon the product of the chase for our food.

In the morning two traders passed through our camp, and we were delighted to find that they had a small bag of bread, which they were taking to the Indians. They sold us twenty small loaves, each about the size of a penny roll, for five pounds; and I think they got the best of the bargain, for the bread was half mildewed and scarcely eatable, and so heavy, that even the stomach of an ostrich could scarcely have compassed its digestion with impunity. Famished as we were, we preferred to give it to the dogs, who showed their good sense by turning up their noses at it; and unless the foxes rashly experimented upon it after our departure, for aught I know these expensive loaves may still be lying in a fossil state on the Patagonian pampas!

We all went out guanaco-hunting that day, but were not very successful. I'Aria managed to run down a young one with his dog, and Mr. B. shot one; but as he killed it some twenty miles away from our camp he could only bring the head and the two sides, not daring to load his dead-beat horse with more.

But meat had to be procured somehow, so next day, whilst the others went on along the trail with the packhorses, my husband, Mr. B., myself, and Gregorio, went out hunting again, intending to catch up the others before the evening. We rode for several hours towards Cape Gregorio, but although we saw several ostriches, they got up very wild, and pursuit of them was always out of the question. Guanaco, there were none to be seen. This was very dispiriting; if we did not manage to kill anything here it was still more unlikely that we should be able to do so farther on. Our companions were relying on our efforts, and to have to join them empty-handed would have been in itself vexatious enough from a sportsman's point of view, apart from the serious and practical consideration that we could scarcely go on to Sandy Point, which was quite three days' march away, without food. So we kept riding on towards Cape Gregorio, in the hopes of still being able to find something. We presently sighted some guanacos grazing at the base of a ridge of hills, and whilst Gregorio went after an ostrich, which sprang up at that moment, we three spurred our horses, and separating, so as to attract as little attention as possible, rode towards them.

I soon lost sight of my companions, who disappeared down some of the many gulches that led to the valley where the guanaco were grazing. Fervently praying that one of us might be successful, I hurried on. When I got into the valley, to my chagrin I saw that the guanaco, already aware of danger, were moving slowly up the valley, not at a great distance from where I was, but still a good way beyond rifle-range. Mr. B., who was a long way to the left, was much nearer to them, and my husband was in a similar position to the right. As we approached, the guanaco trotted up among the hills and disappeared. We had no option but to follow them, entering on the range of hills at different points, as the herd would probably scatter as soon as we came close upon them.

I came upon them of a sudden, and, as I had surmised, they all broke into different directions. I took a flying shot at one, but missed, and presently a report on each side of me showed that the others had had a shot too. I was soon joined by my husband, who had also been unsuccessful, but Mr. B. did not turn up, and we began to hope that he might have killed something. We presently saw him galloping full speed up a distant hill after a guanaco, which was no doubt wounded, but which seemed to be going too gamely to admit of our being very sanguine as to his chance of ultimately getting at it. We waited for some time, but he did not reappear, and so we went down into the valley to look for Gregorio. He soon came in sight, and, unfortunately, as empty-handed as we ourselves were. Matters were now getting serious. The day was far gone, and to catch up our companions on our jaded horses would have been a hard task, unless we started at once. We were therefore obliged to relinquish all hope of getting any guanaco ourselves that day, our only consolation being that Mr. B.'s prolonged absence boded that he at least had been successful.

We waited for him a little, but as he did not come, knowing that he could find the way to the place where the others were to camp, we rode on, lighting fires at intervals, to show our whereabouts. Our horses were so tired that we could scarcely get them into a trot, and to our dismay we suddenly found it was getting dark. The sky had been clouded all day, and we had had no sun to judge the time by, the result being that we were two or three hours out in our calculations. It is very easy to guess the time within half an hour or so, under ordinary circumstances, but the excitement of our various runs after guanacos and ostriches had so absorbed us that the hours had slipped by unperceived. We thus found ourselves face to face with the uncomfortable knowledge that, it being quite impossible to catch up the others, we should have to go to bed in the open, and unless Mr. B. had killed his guanaco, supperless. The unpleasantness of this at any time disagreeable contingency was increased on this occasion by the prospect of our getting wet through into the bargain, for the aspect of the sky was very threatening, and it was only in keeping with our day's luck that there should be a downpour of rain during the night. But there was absolutely nothing to be done but give in to the inevitable as cheerfully as we could, so we dismounted and unsaddled our horses, carefully tethering them to some bushes, lest they should stray away in the night, and then we sat down to await Mr. B's coming, the numerous fires we had lit on the way making us quite sure he would be able to find us. But it grew darker and darker, the tooth of hunger got fiercer and fiercer, and still he did not come. What could have happened? Surely he must have run down the guanaco, or given up the chase hours ago. Perhaps he has met with some accident! That's impossible! With these and other reflections we beguiled the anxious moments, hoping against hope that before long a goodly rib of guanaco would be roasting at the blazing fire we had prepared in rash anticipation of its advent. But time went on; already we could scarcely distinguish the bushes in the distance, the hills faded away altogether into the darkness, and our missing companion did not come. Having strained our eyes blind, peering into the gloom, we now sat silently, straining our ears to catch the slightest sign of an approaching footstep; but our hopes grew gradually fainter and fainter, and at last we were obliged to give them up altogether. Gregorio fortunately found a small piece of guanaco meat in one of his saddle-bags, which we cooked and ate, a small mouthful being all each of us got. Mingled with our regrets for our enforced fast were speculations as to what Mr. B. was doing at that moment. Had he killed his guanaco, and (horrible thought!) was he at that very moment perhaps roasting its head in the ashes? or was he in a worse plight than ourselves,—supperless as well as companionless? Our thoughts reverted to the other party too, who no doubt were in some anxiety as to what could have become of us. I did not sleep very sound that night, nor did my companions, as may be imagined. Just as day broke the dogs gave tongue; there was a crashing among the bushes, and Mr. B. rode up, with an eager, hungry look on his face, which boded no good. "Have you got anything to eat?" were his first words, to which our despairing answer was, "Good gracious! haven't you?" And our faces grew longer and more disconsolate than ever, as the hopes of a good breakfast, which had hitherto sustained us, were remorselessly shattered on both sides.

There was nothing to be done but immediately saddle and ride off to join our companions. On the way Mr. B. told us how he had followed the wounded guanaco till he had run his horse to a complete standstill, and like us, having been overtaken by darkness, had been obliged to stop where he was till morning.

After several hours' ride we got to the place where the others were camped, and found them very much alarmed at our protracted absence, though they had naturally supposed that we had been taken a long distance out of our way by the chase. We lost no time in making a hearty meal on what remained of the guanaco meat, which being finished, there was no food of any kind in the camp.

CHAPTER XX

THE HORSES LOST—UNPLEASANT PROSPECTS—
FOUND—SHORT RATIONS—A STRANGE HUNT—A STERN
CHASE—THE MYSTERY SOLVED—THE CABEZA DEL
MAR—SAFELY ACROSS—A DAMP NIGHT—CABO NEGRO
AGAIN

WE HAD A SHORT MARCH TO MAKE NEXT DAY, and it was nearly noon, therefore, when l'Aria started off on his usual morning task of driving up the horses.

In the evening, as one may rely on their not straying very far, the horses are turned loose, after being unsaddled. In fact, no other method would be practicable, for if they were kept picketed during the night they would not be able to graze, and would soon become useless. As they all follow the bell-mare, one is always sure of finding them together, even should they stray three or four miles in the night, which, although it does occasionally occur, is quite exceptional. That, however, this necessity of leaving the horses at liberty may give rise to considerable inconvenience, and possibly bring one into the most serious dilemmas, we had an opportunity of discovering at the cost of some anxiety and a day's hard labour.

After l'Aria had been gone about an hour we began to wonder at his prolonged absence; but as there had been a strong breeze during the night, it was very probable, as Gregorio suggested, that the horses had wandered some distance in search of a sheltered valley. But another hour elapsed, and still l'Aria did not appear. Guillaume and François then went off in different directions to continue the search, agreeing to light a fire should either of them sight the horses.

We in the meantime were left a prey to very disagreeable reflections, though as yet we had no strong grounds for fearing the worst. We kept an anxious watch for the first signs of smoke, especially in the direction l'Aria had taken, as he must have covered five or six miles by the time he had been gone. To our dismay he presently turned up, however, very tired and footsore, without having seen a trace of the horses anywhere. Matters now began to look really serious, but we still comforted ourselves with the hope that François or Guillaume would be more successful. But they too, after a time, came back, bringing the same dismal story. The situation looked gloomy; a hundred suppositions were hazarded as to what could have become of the horses. I'Aria said he had "cut the trail" on the side he had taken without success, and Guillaume and François having done the same, it was clear that the only direction in which the horses could have gone was over the plain at the back of our camp, though what could have induced them to leave the pasturage of the valley for the barren upland it was hard to understand. Meanwhile there was nothing to be done but immediately make search for them in that direction, though our prospects of finding them seemed small indeed. Should we not do so we should have to accomplish the rest of our journey to Sandy Point on foot. We had eaten our last round of guanaco meat that morning, so that a four days' walk on empty stomachs, apart from being an unpleasant undertaking, was one which it was a question whether our powers were equal to compassing. We might, it is true, opportunely meet some trader on the way, from whom we might obtain provisions; but, on the other hand, we might not be so fortunate; and, on the principle that it never rains but it pours, we were justified in considering the latter contingency as the probable one. We commenced our task, therefore, with feelings the reverse of cheerful. Leaving Storer in the camp, we all went on to the plain, and started off in different directions towards the distant hills that bound it. A fire, should any of us be successful, was to immediately communicate the news to the others.

With my eyes bent on the ground, eagerly scanning it for any trace of a hoof mark, I walked slowly along, occasionally giving a glance over the plain, in the hopes of seeing the welcome column of smoke rise up into the air. But time went on, and my hopes of success grew fainter and fainter. Gregorio had expressed a fear that the horses had got on to the Indian trail to Sandy Point; and taking to it, had gone off at a trot towards Cabo Negro, on whose pastures they were "at home," or "aquerenciado," as the natives say. The possibility of their having done so assumed more and more the feature of a probability, as hour after hour passed, and I was still only half-way across the plain, and no traces of the objects of my search as yet forthcoming. In fact, it seemed useless to continue plodding on farther, and instinctively I broke off, and turned to the left, observing that there the plain ended in a hilly country, where, although I'Aria had assured us he had searched in that direction, it certainly seemed more likely that the horses would be, supposing they had not gone to Sandy Point.

It was a happy inspiration of mine; I had not gone half a dozen yards down a grassy ravine before, turning a sharp bend, I suddenly came upon the whole troop, quietly grazing at their ease, in supreme indifference as to the trouble and anxiety they had caused half a dozen human beings for the last five or six hours. My first step was to throw a few lighted matches into the long dry grass, which I left to do their work, and then, by dint of some patience and cunning, I managed to persuade one of the tamest horses to allow me to get my arm round its neck and effect its capture. Improvising a kind of bridle from my scarf, I mounted, and driving the horses together, conveyed them towards the camp, not a little proud and elated at my achievement, which was due rather to good fortune than judgment, for, had I followed out the plan of search we had agreed upon, who knows what the upshot would have been? Meanwhile, the matches had had due effect; fanned by the breeze, the fire spread quickly, and soon the ravine was ablaze across its whole breadth, a mighty column of smoke being whirled high into the air, carrying, doubtless, intense relief into the hearts of my companions, who were still toiling over the plains.

I soon got to the camp with my charges, and was thankful to be able to lie down and rest after my exertions. One by one the others dropped in, and, as may be imagined, we were all equally elated at so fortunate an issue of a contretemps, which might have had the most serious consequences,—just on the eve too, of the conclusion of a trip otherwise particularly free from dangerous mishaps.

It was too late to set out that afternoon, so we passed the remainder of the day in trying to shoot some duck for supper. In the pleasure of finding our horses again, we were not disposed to grumble at minor hardships, and cheerfully, therefore, we endeavoured to make as good a supper off a brace of small duck, which was all we could kill, as eight hungry people might be expected to do.

After a cup of coffee next morning we drew our belts a little tighter, and set out, keeping a sharp look-out, on the forlorn chance of an ostrich coming within coursing distance. But during the whole of that day's march neither beast nor fowl, save a fox or two, showed itself, and as our appetites, which we had kept in tolerable subjection during daytime, began loudly to assert themselves towards sundown, the spirit which reigned among us was by no means a cheerful one. We were just discussing the faint probability that existed of our meeting an Indian trader before reaching the Colony, when suddenly we descried a man riding along the trail towards us, and driving two horses before him. With a unanimous shout of delight we all galloped forward to meet this welcome stranger, on whose provisions we meant to make a friendly but extensive raid. But, to our astonishment, on perceiving us, he suddenly drew up his horse, hesitated for a moment, and then dashed away over the pampa. Without stopping to inquire what could be the motive of such extraordinary behaviour, and seeing only that our chance of supper was vanishing as fast as four legs could carry it, we all clapped spurs to our steeds, and galloped after him with as much alacrity as he had shown. The harder we went, the more he urged his horse along, occasionally looking back in a state of evident terror. For five minutes or so this strange man-chase continued, neither pursued nor pursuers gaining any ground on one another, but then we gradually drew nearer to our quarry, whose horse was already beginning to show signs of distress. We were soon within earshot, and called loudly on him to stop, saying that we were friends. Whether he heard us or not I don't know, but the effect of our shouting was that he redoubled his efforts, and for a time the chase again became doubtful.

But we were not to be beat; curiosity to know this man's motives for running away from us as if we were wild beasts, combined with an equally strong desire to obtain some provisions from the amply filled saddle-bags which were gliding along in front of us, kept us to our work, and we felt that till our horses dropped this queer quarry must be followed. The spurt he had put on soon died away, and then we crept up to him again, wild with excitement, and giving vent to some sounding "view-holloas," which, now I come to think of it, may have possibly increased the terrors of the poor man's situation. But everything comes to an end, even a stern chase, and soon Gregorio was within ten or twelve yards of the unknown. "Párase amigo, soy Gregorio," he called out several times, and at last, feeling G.'s hand on his shoulder, the man did stop. In a second or two we were all up, more or less breathless with the run. The man, with whom Gregorio was now rapidly conversing in Spanish, looked very pale and frightened at first, but gradually the expression on his face brightened as he listened to Gregorio's explanations, and eventually he even began to smile. We, meanwhile, eager to know the solution of the mystery, pressed Gregorio to solve it. It appeared that this man was a convict, who had escaped from Sandy Point two days before, and having "requisitioned" two Government horses, was now on his way to the Santa Cruz river, on the other side of which he would be free from pursuit. When he saw us coming towards him at a gallop, he had been seized with a sudden panic, thinking we might want to capture him, and had galloped off, with the results known.

Of course we could not ask for any of his provisions as he would require them much more than we should; so, after exchanging a few words with him, we left him, and proceeded to rejoin Storer, who had remained behind with the horses whilst we had been engaged on our novel hunt.

The incident furnished us with matter for conversation for a time, but it was not long before we came back to the more important topic of food, for we were now all of us really faint with hunger, and our prospects of getting anything for the next thirty-six hours were faint indeed.

Our goal that evening was the "Cabeza del Mar," an arm of the sea which runs for some distance inland, and which, at a certain point, is fordable at low water if the wind is not blowing strongly from an unfavourable direction. As we rode along we caught a glimpse of the sea itself—a welcome sight, and forgetting our hunger for a moment we gave a loud cheer.

At about seven o'clock, just as it was getting dark, we arrived at the "Cabeza del Mar." We found that we should not be able to ford it for four or five hours; and as we were anxious to get to Cabo Negro as soon as possible, in order to break our prolonged fast, we decided on passing that night, rather than wait till next morning. Having relieved the packhorses of their loads we sat down by the fire and brewed some coffee with the last spoonfuls that remained to us of that comfort, and having drunk it, nothing remained for us but to wait and dream of the meal we meant to devour on the first opportunity.

We tried to snatch a nap, but few of us succeeded in doing so, as hunger kept us awake, and so the hours dragged their slow length wearily along, whilst we sat and waited for the tide to serve. To add to the discomforts of our plight, the sky covered over and the rain began to fall, and the night got so dark that we almost thought we should not be able to cross over. However, the time came when we thought the tide ought to serve, and we rode down to the water to inspect matters. Occasionally a moonbeam breaking through the thick rain-clouds allowed us to get a glimpse of the rocks in the middle of the water; and our guides were thus able to judge the right moment for making the attempt. There was, as they said, just the possibility of the water not being quite low enough to enable us to cross without more or less of a ducking, and besides, in the darkness, the leader might mistake the way, and a false step would land us into a rocky bottom, where we might flounder hopelessly about, and in all probability get unhorsed, and God knows what besides.

These considerations served to make us feel rather uncomfortable when the moment arrived for us to commit ourselves to the chances that might be awaiting us in the dark mass of water which swept eddying swiftly past us, and but for the acute pangs of hunger we should certainly have deferred the experiment until daytime. But no time was to be lost, so, ranging in single file behind I'Aria, who was acting as guide, we started—the other horses, with Guillaume and Gregorio driving them, following. For a few seconds there was a great deal of splashing and shouting, incidental on the objections shown by the packhorses to take the water; but soon they were all in and fairly on their way. Then came a few seconds' silence, as we drew into deep water, every one cautiously following his leader, so as to be able to rein in in time should the latter come to grief. Suddenly I'Aria gave a cry, and through the darkness we could dimly see him floundering about, his horse having evidently lost footing. After splashing about for some seconds, however, he got all right again, and calling out to us to keep more to the left, he moved on. The water was now up to our knees, and at each step it got deeper, but fortunately our horses still kept their footing, and soon the worst was over, and the bank was reached without any mishap having occurred.

All the dogs had remained on the other side, crying and yelling in a gloomy concert, as they saw us leaving them behind; but as soon as they saw us ride up on to the plain, they plunged into the water, and swam over in no time.

After having counted the horses and examined their packs, which had all got well drenched, as we ourselves had, we continued our ride, with the intention of marching the whole night, so as to arrive at Cabo Negro in the morning, for we were now positively frantic with hunger. For a time, notwithstanding the intense darkness, we managed to get along pretty well, but presently we found that we had got off the trail somehow, and we had to stop, whilst the guides blundered about in the darkness, searching for it. Then, after we had got on to it once more, the horses shied at a big white stone lying on the road, and bolted in all directions, and of course had to be got together again—a task which involved nearly an hour's delay.

Apart from these mishaps, our progress was necessarily so slow, owing to the darkness, that we at last came to the conclusion that after all it would be better to halt where we were, and proceed at daybreak. Acting on this determination, we immediately unsaddled, and, too tired to put up the tents, rolled ourselves up in our furs, and slept, or tried to sleep, till morning. I think this was the unpleasantest night of the whole trip. Faint with hunger, drenched and cold, I could not get repose, although I felt as tired and jaded as could possibly be. The ground too, where we were camped, was stony and hillocky; and when, at the first sign of dawn, I crept out of my furs, my bones were so stiff that I could with difficulty move, my companions being all in an equally bad plight. But we were in good spirits for all that. Four hours' riding would bring us to the wood of Cabo Negro, and there we should get food in abundance. Never had the horses been so quickly saddled and packed as on that morning; within half an hour from commencing operations we were already cantering along the trail.

Scaling the brow of a steep hill we came in view of the familiar landscape—the Straits and the Cordilleras, and not far off the black patches of beechwood round Cabo Negro; and, nestling amid them, the little farm-house on whose stores we projected a determined raid.

My brother and Mr. B. now rode ahead in order to have something ready against our arrival. After two or three hours' sharp riding they reached the farm-house, and without speaking a word rushed off to the kitchen, and laid their hands on and utterly devoured what was to have been the breakfast of the farmer and his family. The farmer appeared on the scene just as they had swallowed the last mouthful, and it appears being no doubt used to such strange visits, seemed less surprised than one would have imagined to see two dirty wild-looking men sitting uninvited in his kitchen, who between them had calmly demolished the morning meal of a whole household.

Having thus satisfied their own immediate wants they applied themselves to catering for ours; and to such good purpose that, by the time we reached our old camp under the beeches of Cabo Negro, we found a good fire already blazing, half a sheep hanging on a tree, ready for roasting, and such stores of bread, eggs, and other provisions as made our eyes glisten and our mouths water. How we feasted need not be told. I think very little of that half sheep remained to be warmed up for supper, and most of the other provisions shared a similar speedy fate.

CHAPTER XXI

CABO NEGRO—HOME NEWS—CIVILISATION AGAIN—
OUR DISREPUTABLE APPEARANCE—PUCHO MISSING—
THE COMING OF PUCHO—PUCHO'S CHARACTERISTICS

WE HAD STILL THREE DAYS TO WAIT till the date for the arrival of the steamer, and as we by no means liked the idea of having to pass them in Sandy Point, we resolved to remain at Cabo Negro for a couple of days more, and only get into the colony in time to settle with our guides, and make ourselves look a little civilised against going on board.

But as we were naturally most anxious to get our correspondence, my brother rode into Sandy Point to fetch it. He returned, bringing a bagful of letters and newspapers, and we devoted a whole afternoon to their perusal, and to discussing their contents. These letters seemed to bring us back to the world again, to the world and its almost forgotten responsibilities, pains, and pleasures, which but the day before had seemed as remote to us as if we had quitted the earth altogether, and were living in some other planet. How many things seemed to have happened since we had been away, and how the interest in these events was magnified, hearing of them as we did, thousands of miles away from home, after so long an absence! Occurrences which, in the bustle and noise of ordinary existence, would hardly have excited more than few exclamations of surprise, or scarcely a passing thought, now seemed to assume the most important proportions, and were discussed at inordinate length, and with the keenest interest. There was a letter from the gamekeeper, telling with interminable prosiness how cleverly he had surprised, in flagrante delicto, the man whom he had long and so wisely suspected of poaching; how, notwithstanding every care on his part, the severe winter had proved too much for a favourite old setter; and, thanks to his efforts, how extraordinary a number of pheasants there was in the copses, etc. Another from the head stable-man, with intelligence of a similar nature from his department; lengthy documents from the agent, telling how one tenant couldn't pay his rent, how another wouldn't though he could, how one lot of cottages required repairing, and how advantageous to the property, if a fresh lot were built; the peculiarity of all these epistles being the predominance of the bad over the good news. Then were letters telling how A. had married, and "the very last woman one would have thought, too;" how B. had got a divorce, "and no wonder, one might have seen that all along;" how C. had gone off to shoot big game in the Rocky Mountains; and how D. had merely gone and shot himself—and so forth, and so forth; every trivial item affording us a goodly space for lengthy gossip, a luxury which, since our departure for the plains, had so signally failed us. It is only when unable to indulge in it that we find what an important factor the tittle-tattle and small talk of ordinary life is, in general conversation.

There were several papers too in our budget, and we devoured their three-months' old intelligence with no less avidity and eagerness than that with which we had perused our letters.

That day passed, and the next, and then the hour came for us to saddle up once more, and ride in to Sandy Point. As may be imagined, this time we did not jog along behind the pack-horses. Leaving these to the care of the guides, to come on at their leisure, we cantered merrily on alone—along the familiar path by the shore of the Straits. As the huts of Sandy Point came in sight, we began to realise that at last we were getting back to civilisation, and prospectively to England, and already plans of what we were to do on arriving home were formed and discussed. There was only one night more to pass before setting foot on board the steamer which was to take us back to the world; but so impatient were we, that even that short time seemed all too long, and we wondered if it ever would pass.

Soon we were trotting along the streets of Sandy Point; and, reaching Pedro's house, dismounted, and found ourselves under a roof once more! Pedro, advised of our coming, had prepared breakfast for us, and, without more ado, we sat down to it. We handled our knives and forks very awkwardly at first; it required almost an effort to eat in a civilised manner, and, accustomed of late to take our meals in a recumbent position, we by no means felt very comfortable in our chairs. And now, for the first time, the scales fell from our eyes, and the sight of the clean table-cloth and neat room caused us to become aware of our own personal appearance, and the enviable "giftie" was ours, of seeing ourselves as others saw us. The sight was certainly not a delectable one. Our looks and garments were not out of keeping with our late life in the pampas, but, surrounded by cleanliness and civilisation, they were decidedly out of place. We had performed our ablutions as often and as thoroughly as circumstances would permit, but they had not permitted much. The men of our party, particularly, were unpleasant to look at. Their hair had grown long and elfin; their faces were tanned to a dark red-brown, which the dust, and the smoke from the camp-fires had deepened into—well—black; and their unshaven chins were disfigured by a profuse growth of coarse stubble. Our clothes did not bear close inspection, the blood of many a guanaco, the grease of many an ostrich-dinner, the thorn of many a califaté bush, had left their marks; and, altogether, a more ruffianly, disreputable lot than we looked it would be hard to imagine. But hot water, soap, and razors, and a change of raiment, did wonders; and when, after several hours' hard work, we met again we were scarcely able to recognise one another.

We passed the day in settling with the guides, and in packing up our few traps in anticipation of the arrival of the steamer early next morning.

Feeling tired, I went to sleep early, but the comfort I expected from lying between sheets again was by no means vouchsafed me, and the soft mattress and cool sheets, instead of inviting slumber, seemed to frighten it away. I felt half inclined to get up and go to sleep on the floor. However, my eyes closed at last; and from a dream, in which I was once more chasing the ostrich in sight of the memorable Cleopatra Peaks, I was awakened by Mr. Dunsmuir banging at my door, telling me that the steamer had arrived and that it was time to be off. I jumped up and dressed hurriedly, and found all the others ready to go on board. The luggage had already been put into a boat, and there was nothing further to be done but to say good-bye to our guides and walk down to the jetty to embark.

I had only one regret on leaving Sandy Point. The day we arrived at Cabo Negro one of our dogs, called "Pucho," who was rather a favourite of mine, and whom I wished to take with me to England, was suddenly missing. Pucho, a peculiar dog, had joined us under peculiar circumstances at our camp at Laguna Larga. We were quietly sitting round the camp-fire after dinner, when suddenly the dogs jumped up and began to bark furiously at some unseen enemy. We got up and peered out into the dusk, but could see nothing, though it was evident that something there was, for the growls of our dogs increased in earnestness and fury every instant. "A puma!" suggested somebody, but our horses were grazing quietly, so it could not be a puma. "An Indian, or some trader, perhaps!" was another equally unfounded surmise. What could it be? Here, as if to settle the mystery at once, the dogs all rushed out of one accord, and for a few moments we could hear a terrible snarling and growling going on in the distance. It came nearer and nearer, and then the cause of the commotion was explained. Surrounded by our dogs, who were giving it a by no means friendly welcome, a strange dog walked slowly towards the camp-fire. It bore its tail between its legs, seeming half-humbly, half-defiantly, to crave admission into our circle. Its humble demeanour, however, only bore reference to us, for the defiant manner in which it occasionally bared its white teeth, and turned on our dogs whenever they came too near, showed that it cared little for them. We called out in friendly tones, and this settled its bearing for once and for all. It turned round, made one savage dash at one or two of its tormentors, and then calmly made its way towards the fire, looked out for the most comfortable spot, stretched itself leisurely, and lay down with its head resting on its crossed paws, seemingly as much at home as if it had known us all its life. I ventured to stroke it, but my advances were received in a most unfriendly, and, considering its position of alien outcast, audaciously impertinent manner, for it snapped viciously at me. But from the first "Pucho," as we called him, made it a point of distinctly refusing to be patronised. He joined us, he gave us to understand, not on sufferance, not as a suppliant for our favours, not as a guest even, but as an equal; and this status he claimed as regards us only, for as to our dogs, he ignored them completely, though willing, as subsequently appeared, to make use of their good services. He looked sleek and fat, a circumstance which led us to think highly of his powers of speed, as it is by no means easy for a dog to run down a guanaco singly, and most dogs who lose their master, as this dog had evidently done, soon die of starvation. We therefore congratulated ourselves on his arrival, as we hoped he would be able to afford our own dogs help in the chase. But we had grievously reckoned without our host. The next day, on the march, a guanaco was sighted close to us. Now was the time. "Choo! choo! Pucho!" we shouted, expecting to see him speed out like an arrow after the guanaco. But nothing could have been further from his thoughts. He looked first at us and then at the guanaco for a moment, not without interest, perhaps, but certainly without showing the slightest inclination to hostile demonstration. Then, with another look at us, which said as plainly as words could, "Well, that's a guanaco, no doubt, but what then?" he quietly trotted on. We were very angry at seeing our hopes deceived, besides being surprised at his extraordinary demeanour; but Gregorio, giving the dog the benefit of the doubt, said that perhaps it had only been trained to run ostriches, as Indians frequently teach their dogs to do. This seemed plausible enough, and our confidence in Pucho was momentarily restored. Presently an ostrich started up. Now then: "Choo! choo! Pucho!" was the excited cry again. All the other dogs flew out like the wind after the bird, and Pucho followed them. But only at a trot, and apparently merely to judge how the other dogs behaved, for he soon stopped, and contented himself with watching the chase till it disappeared from view, and then he leisurely came back to his usual post at my horse's heels. Everybody was enraged with him; Francisco suggested that being a "bouche inutile," Pucho should be knocked on the head with the bolas; but I could not hear of this, and Pucho's life was spared. And so he remained with us, and I had ample opportunities for studying his peculiar character. As on the first day, so he continued. Although generally there or thereabouts when a distribution of the spoils took place, he never once helped the dogs in the chase. That this did not arise from inability or want of speed, but rather from a sense of his own superior dignity, was shown by the fact of his once having been seen to pursue and catch a fox, a feat none of our other dogs were capable of. Amongst other peculiarities he had a way of mysteriously disappearing if the day's march was too long. "Where is Pucho?" was a frequent cry, and "Thank God, he's gone at last!" was an ejaculation often heard on these occasions. But so sure as the guanaco-rib for dinner was done to a turn, the soup ready, and the fire blazing comfortably, so sure would Pucho suddenly appear on the scene, look out for the most cosy spot near the fire, and cheerfully await his supper, as if nothing had happened.

When, therefore, he was missing at Cabo Negro, I took little notice, thinking he would be sure to turn up. But dinner-time came, and no Pucho; nor did he appear again, even when we went on to Sandy Point.

This was the thought that was troubling me as I walked down to the pier, for I had taken a liking to this dog, or I had better say I held him in reverential awe; for I think he would object himself to the term "like," as savouring of patronage. Half absently, therefore, before going down the ladder into the boat, I turned round to take a last look for Pucho. Surely that is a dog coming down the street, I thought, as I looked up; and right enough it was a dog, and what is more, Pucho himself! There was no mistaking the calm mien, the leisurely trot. He picked his way along the battered pier, half wagged his tail as he saw me—a great condescension, and then, without a moment's hesitation, led the way down the ladder into the boat, much to the surprise of my companions, who had thought and hoped that they had really seen the last of him.

I took him, or rather he came to England with me, and as I write this he is sitting in the cosiest corner by my fire, a privilege he allows my pet terrier to share with him, an act very foreign to his usual nature, and one for which I have never been able to account.

So here we are on board at last. We say good-bye to Mr. Dunsmuir, the anchor is weighed, the screw goes round, and we are off. Sandy Point disappears from view; one by one Cape Negro and Cape Gregorio are passed, and before I know it—so engrossed am I in the thoughts that crowd into my mind at the sight of these well-known points—we are abreast of Cape Virgins. It fades again astern, there is no land on either side, and Patagonia, bleak and silent and solemn, with the days we spent on its mysterious shores, is behind us.

As I write, these days come vividly to my mind again, and in fancy I once more behold that distant desert land,—the land of the lonely plains, where the guanaco and the ostrich and the Red Indians roam far from the ken of mankind, and where I spent a careless, happy time, which I can never forget. I remember the days when, after a long and weary ride, I slept, pillowed on my saddle, the open sky above me, a sounder and sweeter sleep than I had ever slept before; I remember those grand mountain-scenes, where we traced the wild horse to his home, through beechwood glens, by lonely lakes, by mountain torrents, where no mortal foot had ever trod before me. I remember many an exciting chase and many a pleasant evening spent round the cheery camp-fire. I remember, too, many a discomfort—the earthquake, the drenching rains, the scorching sun, the pitiless mosquitoes, and the terrible blasting winds. But from the pleasure with which I look back on my wild life in Patagonia, these unpleasant memories can detract but little. Taking it all in all, it was a very happy time, and a time on whose like I would gladly look again.

THE END.

Printed by R. & R. Clark, Edinburgh.

A SUPPLEMENT TO MESSRS
RICHARD BENTLEY & SON'S
CATALOGUE OF NEW
AND
STANDARD WORKS
OCTOBER 1880
A LIST OF FORTHCOMING WORKS
FOR THE NEW SEASON
Spottiswoode & Co., Printers, New-street Square, London

The EDITOR of
TEMPLE BAR
Begs to announce that
A NEW SERIAL
ENTITLED
THE FRERES
BY
MRS. ALEXANDER
(The Author of 'The Wooing o't' &c.)
WILL BE
COMMENCED
IN
THE JANUARY 1881 NUMBER
OF
The Temple Bar Magazine.

'One can never help enjoying TEMPLE BAR.'—Guardian.

BIOGRAPHY OF GERTRUDE BELL

GERTRUDE BELL WAS BORN ON JULY 14, 1868 in County Durham, England, to a prosperous family. The wealth that allowed her to travel as much as she desired stemmed from her grandfather Sir Isaac Lowthian Bell's industrial plants and his prowess in the iron and steel industries. His role in Parliament also allowed her insight into politics that sparked her own proclivity for activism. Bell's mother, Mary Shield, died when her daughter was only three, and Bell remained close with her father thereafter.

With access to more educational opportunities than were standard for a woman of her time, Bell was the first woman to graduate with a First in Modern History from Oxford, a feat which she completed in only two years. Following her graduation in 1888, she traveled to Tehran where her uncle was British Minister.

Following her time in Tehran, Bell developed her interest in mountaineering sparked as a child in climbing the scaffolding of her childhood home, Red Barns. She gained renown for her mountain-climbing prowess in the Alps—one of the Swiss peaks is named after her.

Persia, the source of the work *Safar Nameh, Persian Pictures: A Book of Travel*, was one of her first expeditions. In addition to her early education and travels, by the age of thirty she had taught herself enough of the Farsi language to translate *The Divan of Hafez,* a project that established her reputation as a linguist and Middle Eastern cultural interpreter. She learned to speak Arabic and Persian, working at archaeological sites and traveling through the deserts.

During World War I, Bell's knowledge of the region garnered the interest of Sir Percy Cox and Sir Arnold Wilson, and the two men hired her to work in British Intelligence. By 1915, she had been recruited to the Arab Bureau in Cairo where she worked to mobilize the Arabs against Turkey. She was responsible for helping to place Hashemite ruler Faysal I on the Iraqi throne in 1921.

Despite her successful forays into spywork and politics, Bell's passion remained in archaeology. In the last few years of her life, she was the first to insist on excavated relics staying in their homeland, ensuring that the National Museum of Iraq would be able to house a collection of its own historical artifacts.

Bell's health declined and she grew lonely in her final days, and on July 12, 1926, she took a fatal dose of sleeping pills and passed away in Baghdad.

SAFAR NAMEH

PERSIAN PICTURES

A BOOK OF TRAVEL

BY

Gertrude Bell

LONDON
RICHARD BENTLEY AND SON
Publishers in Ordinary to Her Majesty the Queen
1894

'Warum bin ich vergänglich, O Zeus? so fragte die Schönheit.
Macht ich doch, sagte der Gott, nur das Vergängliche schön.
Und die Liebe, die Blumen, der Tau und die Jugend vernahmens,
Alle gingen sie weg weinend von Jupiters Thron.'

GOETHE

'Now, a traveller is a creature not always looking at sights—he remembers (how often!) the happy land of his birth; he has, too, his moments
of humble enthusiasm about fire and food—about shade and drink.'

KINGLAKE

CONTENTS

An Eastern City 596
The Tower of Silence..602
In Praise of Gardens...605
The King of Merchants 610
The Imam Hussein 613
The Shadow of Death 618
Dwellers in Tents 623
Three Noble Ladies 627
The Treasure of the King...632
Sheikh Hassan 636
A Persian Host...641
A Stage and a Half...645
A Bridle-Path..649
Two Palaces..655
The Month of Fasting 661
Requiescant in Pace 666
The City of King Prusias 671
Shops and Shopkeepers...675
A Murray of the First Century 679
Travelling Companions...684

ERRATUM.
Page 138, line 2, for 'bouches de cheveux' read 'bouches de chevaux.'

AN EASTERN CITY

The modern capital of Persia lies in a plain ringed half-way round by mountains, which on the northern side touch with frozen summits the regions of eternal snow, and on the east sink into low ranges of hills, stretching their naked arms into the desert. It is the chief city of a land of dust and stones—waste and desolate, Persia unfolds her monotonous length, broken only by ridges of hills even more barren than the plain itself, southward from the gates of Tehran. There is a certain fine simplicity in a landscape from which the element of water, with all the varied life it brings in its murmuring train, is entirely absent. The empty world looks like a great room cleared for the reception of some splendid company; presently it will be filled by a vast pageant of men or angels: their lance-heads will flash back the dazzling rays of the sun, their banners will float out many-coloured against the sombre background, the peal of their trumpets will re-echo from mountain to mountain. But no! day after day rises upon the same silence, the same solitude, and at length the watcher turns away impatiently, with the conviction that he has been gazing with futile expectation upon the changeless features of the dead. The pageant has long since swept over the land—swept onward. Mother of human energies, strewn with the ruins of a Titanic past, Persia has slipped out of the vivid world, and the simplicity of her landscape is the fine simplicity of death. 'Alas, poor Yorick!' says Hamlet, yielding, in an exceptionally unpremeditated moment, the natural tribute of pity from the living to the dead. Persia in such an aspect may be pitiful enough, but it is not admirable.

To the north of Tehran, however, the lower slopes of the Shimran range are clothed with gardens and cornfields, as though the dense vegetation which, by a strange freak of nature, stretches its belt of green along the southern shore of the Caspian, between the shifting sands of the Oxus and the black, naphtha-saturated earth of Baku, had sent its roots through the very heart of the mountains and found a foothold for its irrepressible luxuriance even among dust and stones. The capital itself, as you approach it from the west, presents the appearance of a wood rather than of a city—nor minaret, nor tower, nor dome forms a landmark above it, the trees of its gardens conceal its stunted buildings, and it is not until the traveller finds himself under its very walls that he can say, 'Here is Tehran!' It owes its life to the snow mountains, from whence its water flows; the ground between them and the town is undermined by a network of passages, vaulted over with stone, and ventilated by air-holes at intervals of about fifty yards, each hole being protected by a mound of earth. Within, these arteries of the city are the width of a man's shoulders, and scarcely high enough to allow him to walk upright; he stumbles, knee-deep in water, along the uneven bed, bending himself double where the vault drops lower, squeezing past narrow corners cut out of the solid rock. On either side black apertures open into more passages, bringing in tributary streams from right and leftward, and at intervals the darkness is broken by the ray of sunlight which strikes through one of the air-holes, burying itself, like an ill-directed spear, deep into the earth. No other form of irrigation remains, no storage of water, in a country where these arts were probably familiar to the far larger population which dwelt in former ages at the foot of the mountains. The present system is clumsy and laborious. Constant watchfulness is needed to keep the Kanats from falling into disrepair and from becoming blocked by masses of roots, and if this were to be relaxed, Tehran would in a few years cease to exist.

To what merit it owes its position of capital remains a mystery. It is the seat of no native industry; arid deserts and narrow mountain-passes, traversed only by caravans of mules, cut it off from all convenient intercourse with the west. Isfahan is invested with the traditions of a former importance; about Shiraz linger the vestiges of a still mightier antiquity; Casvin lies a hundred miles nearer to the Caspian; Tehran is only a modern seat of government called to importance by the arbitrary will of the present race of sovereigns.

Many gates lead into the city, breaking the level of the mud walls, with their arches and turrets, which are decorated with tiles of faïence set into patterns and pictures and inscriptions. The space enclosed by the walls is a large one, but it is not by any means filled with houses. Passing through one of the western gateways, you will find yourself at first in desolate tracts of sand, stretching between unfinished or ruined buildings; occasionally the open doorway in a long mud wall will reveal to you a luxuriant garden full of tanks and fountains and flower-beds, under whose plane-trees stands the house of some rich man who can afford himself a weekly sufficiency of water to turn the wilderness into fertile pleasure-grounds; further on you will come upon wide streets, very empty and silent, fringed by low, mud-built houses; gradually the streets narrow, the sloping counters of shops present their wares to the passers-by: fruit and vegetables, and the broad thin flaps of Persian bread; here and there a European shop-window, behind which the goods are more miscellaneous than tempting; here and there the frontage of some Government building, with a doorway gaily patterned in coloured bricks. As the streets grow narrower, they become more crowded. A kaleidoscopic world of unfamiliar figures passes to and fro beneath the white mulberry-trees which spring out between the cobble stones of the pavement: grave elders holding their cloaks discreetly round them, dervishes with a loincloth about their waists, and a brilliant scarf bound over their ragged locks, women enveloped from head to foot in loose black garments, a linen veil hanging over their faces, and making them look like the members of some strange religious order, negro slaves and white-robed Arabs, beggars and loiterers, and troops of children pressing in and out between the horsemen and the carriages. Sometimes a beggar will accost you—a woman, perhaps, drawing aside a corner of her veil and imploring alms in a sweet high voice. If you turn a deaf ear to her prayers, she will invoke curses on your head, but a copper coin will purchase you every blessing known to man, including the disappearance of the lady in question, who would otherwise have followed you with unblushing persistence, shouting, 'Pul! pul! pul!'—Money! money! money!—in your ear.

At a street corner a group of soldiers are shaking the branches of a mulberry-tree, and eagerly devouring the sickly fruit which falls into the dust at their feet. Judging from the appearance of the Persian army, a foreigner would be tempted to conclude that it subsisted entirely upon white mulberries, and was reduced to a state of starvation when the summer was over. The hands of paymasters are adhesive in the East: but a small proportion of his earnings reaches the common soldier, and mulberries, flavoured with dust, have at least the merit of furnishing him with an inexpensive meal. His outward man is not calculated to inspire much alarm in the breast of his enemies. His gait is slouching, his uniform torn and discoloured; not infrequently he wears his shirt outside his trousers, and the ragged flounce of brownish-gray linen hanging below his tunic lends him an air anything but martial. His temperament seems to be childlike and peaceable in the extreme. He amuses himself while he is on guard with foolish games, constructing, for instance, a water-mill of tiny wheels, which the stream in front of the palace will set a-turning, and whose movement will delight his eyes as he passes up and down. It is even related (and the tale is scarcely past credence) that on a certain occasion when a person of importance was visiting a southern fortress, he found one of the men who guarded the gateway engaged in knitting stockings, and the other turning an honest penny by the sale of apples. Nevertheless, the Shah is proud of his army. He spends happy hours devising new uniforms for his men—uniforms which are the strangest jumble of European reminiscences and an Oriental love of bright colour.

Bearing towards the north-eastern quarter of the city, you will enter a broad square which is looked upon as the ne plus ultra of municipal magnificence. It is here that the Shah causes his part in the annual Feast of Sacrifice to be performed, and here the inhabitants of Tehran assemble in great numbers to witness the slaughter of a camel by the mollahs, in token that his Majesty has not forgotten, amid the cares of State, how Abraham bound Ishmael upon the altar (for the Mohammedans assert that it was the son of Hagar who was the hero of the legend) in obedience to the command of God. Immediately after the camel has fallen he is cut up by the knives of the mollahs, and the nearest bystanders, pouncing upon some portion of the victim, make off with it at full speed to the palace, where the first comer receives a large reward.

It must be confessed that, in spite of its size, the square makes no favourable impression upon the mind of the sophisticated European. The gates leading into it are adorned with ugly modern tiles, the buildings round it lack all trace of architectural merit. Their stucco face is questionably embellished by a fresco of lions, exceedingly ill drawn, each animal looking nervously round at the sun disc with its spiked circle of rays, which rises from behind its shoulders. Nor does it contain any press of human activity to atone for its lack of beauty. About the gate which leads into the Ark, where the palace is situated, there are indeed some signs of life—groups of soldiers are diversified by the figures of servants of the palace, clad in brilliant scarlet uniforms, and mounted on horses wearing bits and collars of solid silver, and by the fantastic liveries of the Shah's runners, whose dress closely resembles that which is depicted on a court-card, and whose headgear partakes equally of the nature of a beadle's and of a jester's; but for the rest this square is comparatively empty, and the wind sweeps the dust-clouds round the park of antiquated cannon which stands in its midst.

More narrow, squalid streets bring you to the bazaar, where, though little really beautiful or precious is to be found, the thronging Oriental life is in itself an endless source of delight. Ride through it on a summer morning, when its vaulted coolness will offer you a grateful shelter from the sun, and before its activity has been hushed by the heat of mid-day. In the shadow of the entrance there stands a small merchant, posted on the doorstep like an emblem of Oriental commerce—a solemn, long-robed child, so little that his mother's heart must have ached when she trusted the dear turbaned head out of her sight. This morsel of humanity has brought some bunches of flowers to sell, and has spread them out on a large stone in front of him. In his improvised shop he stands, motionless and imperturbable, watching the comers and goers, and waiting in dignified patience till one of them shall pause and buy. Wish him good luck under your breath (for he would resent the blessings of unbelievers), and pass on beneath the dark arches of the bazaar.

Here, at any rate, is bustle enough; trains of laden mules and donkeys shoulder your horse into the gutter, paying small heed to your cries of 'Avardah!'—Make room!—skilful housewives block the narrow way, driving hard bargains under the protection of their veils; groups of hungry men cluster round the roasters of kabobs, anxiously awaiting a breakfast. The shopkeepers alone are unmoved by the universal haste, but sit cross-legged among their wares, smoking the morning kalyan. On either side of the street arched doorways lead into caravanseries and high market-places. In one of them the sellers of cotton goods have established themselves, their counters laden with piles of cheap printed stuffs, bearing the Manchester stamp in one corner; next door is the booksellers' court, and a certain air of scholastic leisure pervades it; here are a row of fruit-shops, where the blue earthenware bowls of curds stand among heaped-up grapes and melons; there you may buy narrow-necked bottles of rosewater; further on you find yourself in a street of metal-workers, where the bright mule-bells hang in festoons over the counters; round the next corner the fires of smithies gleam on half-naked figures, labouring with strained muscles at their anvils. The whole bazaar resounds with talk, with the cries of the mule-drivers, the tinkling bells of the caravans, and the blows of the smiths' hammers. The air is permeated with the curious smell, half musty, half aromatic, of fruits and frying meats, merchandise and crowded humanity. The light comes from the top through a round hole in each of the countless tiny domes of the roof; through each hole falls a shaft of brilliant sunshine, cutting the surrounding darkness like a sword, and striking the hurrying multitude in successive flashes, white turban and bright-coloured robe gleaming—fading, gleaming—fading, in an endless sequence of sun and shadow, as their wearers pass to and fro.

So you may ride through street after narrow crooked street till your ears are full of sound, and your eyes of colour, and your mind of restless life, and before you have had time to recover your composure, you will find yourself in the sunny square, filled with stacks of hay, and tenanted by disbanded armies of mules, which lies within the Meshed Gate. Here, too, the town is afoot. Like a swarm of bees the people jostle one another through the archway. Peasants are driving in their donkeys laden with roped bundles of grass from the meadows of Shah Abdul Azim, strings of camels file through the gate, bringing in the produce of the great cities of the south and east, busy officials are hurrying Tehranwards in the early morning about their affairs, sellers of salted nuts have established themselves under the trees, beggars are lying by the roadside, pilgrims returning from Meshed hasten their step as the homeward goal comes into sight.

With the impression of the deserted western roads still fresh in your memory, the appearance of the bazaars and of this eastern gate will fill you with surprise. Tehran, which from the west looked almost like a city of the dead, cut off from intercourse with the outer world, is alive after all and in eager relationship with a world of its own. Here in the dust and the sunshine is an epitome of the living East, and standing unnoticed in such a doorway, you will admit that you have not travelled in vain. But as the wonderful procession of people files past you, too intent upon their own affairs to give you more than a contemptuous glance, you will realize what a gulf lies between you. The East looks to itself; it knows nothing of the greater world, of which you are a citizen, asks nothing of you and of your civilization.

THE TOWER OF SILENCE

HUNDREDS OF YEARS AGO, when the Persian race first issued from unknown Bactria and the grim Hyrcanian forests, passing through the Caspian Gates, they came upon a fertile land lying to the north-east of the country, which was subsequently named Media. There on the edge of the province known to-day as Khorasan they founded a city, which with the rolling centuries gathered greatness and riches and power; the Greeks (for her fame had penetrated to the limits of the civilized world) called her Rages. Key to Hyrcania and Parthia, the geographical position of the Median city lent her considerable importance. The Jews knew her well: in Rages dwelt that Gabelus to whom the pious Tobit entrusted his ten talents of silver in the days of the Captivity; there Tobias was journeying when the angel Raphael met him and instructed him in the healing properties of fishes; there, relates the author of the Book of Judith, reigned Phraortes whom Nebuchadnezzar smote through with his darts and utterly destroyed.

Rages, the Ancient of Days, passed through many vicissitudes of fortune in the course of her long-drawn life. Under her walls fled the last Darius when Alexander's army chased him, vanquished at Arbela, over the wide plains of Khorasan—fled to the mountains of the Caspian to seek a luckless fate at the hands of the cruel Bactrian satrap. At Rages, perhaps, the generous Alexander mourned the untimely death of his rival, from her palaces hurled his vengeance against Bessus, and saw the satrap dragged a captive to execution. Twice the city was destroyed, by earthquake and by Parthian invaders, twice to rise up afresh under new names. At length, in the twelfth century, an enemy more devastating than the Parthian hordes, more vindictive than the earthquake, swept over pleasant Khorasan and turned the fertile province into the wilderness it is to this day. Tartars from the uttermost ends of the earth left no stone of Rages standing, and the great Median city vanished from the history of men. A few miles to the north-east Tehran has sprung up to be the capital of modern Persia—a Persia to whom the glorious traditions of the past are as forgotten as the strength of Phraortes' walls. 'The Lion and the Lizard keep the courts where Jemshyd gloried and drank deep,' but the foundations of Rages, the mother of Persian cities, can be traced only by conjecture.

Through waste and solitary places we rode one morning to the city and the citadel of the dead. It was still so early that the sun had not overtopped the range of eastern mountains. We rode out of sleeping Tehran, and took our way along the deserted track that skirts its walls; to our left lay the wilderness, wrapped in transparent shadow, and sloping gradually upwards to the barren foot-hills over which winds the road to Meshed. Before we had gone far, with a flash and a sudden glitter, the sun leapt up above the snow-peaks, and day rushed across the plain—day, crude and garish, revealing not the bounteous plenty of the cornfields and pastures which encircled Rages, but dust and stones and desert scrub, and the naked, forbidding mountains, wrinkled by many winters.

To us, with the headlong flight of Darius and the triumph of the conqueror surging before our eyes, the broken ground round the site of the ancient stronghold piled itself into ruined turret and rampart, sank into half-obliterated fosse and ditch. Where we imagined the walls to have been, we discovered a solid piece of masonry, and our minds reeled at the thought that it was wildly possible Alexander's eyes might have rested on this even brickwork. Time has made gates in the battlements, but the desert has not even yet established unquestioned rule within them. At the foot of the wall we came upon a living pool lying under the shadow of a plane-tree. Round such a pool the sick men of Bethsaida gathered and waited for the stirring of the waters, but in Rages all was solitude, 'and the desired angel came no more.'

Towards the east two parallel lines of hills rear themselves out of the desert, dividing it from the wider stretch of desert that reaches southward to Isfahan. Between the hills lies a stony valley, up which we turned our steps, and which led us to the heart of desolation and the end of all things. Half-way up the hillside stands a tower, whose whitewashed wall is a landmark to all the country round. Even from the far distant peaks of the opposite mountains, the Tower of Silence is visible, a mocking gleam reminding the living of the vanity of their eager days. For the tower is the first stage in the weary journey of the dead; here they come to throw off the mantle of the flesh before their bones may rest in the earth without fear of defiling the holy element, before their souls, passing through the seven gates of the planets, may reach the sacred fire of the sun.

The tower is roofless; within, ten or twelve feet below the upper surface of its wall, is a chalky platform on which the dead bodies lie till sun and vultures have devoured them. This grim turret-room was untenanted. Zoroaster's religion has faded from that Media where once it reigned, and few and humble now are the worshippers who raise prayers to Ormuzd under the open heaven, and whose bodies are borne up the stony valley and cast into the Tower of Silence.

We dismounted from our horses and sat down on the hillside. The plain stretched below us like a monotonous ocean which had billowed up against the mountain flanks and had been fixed there for ever; we could see the feet of the mountains themselves planted firmly in the waves of dust, and their glistening peaks towering into the cloudless sky; the very bones of the naked earth were exposed before us, and the fashion of its making was revealed.

With the silence of an extinct world still heavy upon us, we made our way to the upper end of the valley, but at the gates of the plain Life came surging to meet us. A wild hollyhock stood sentinel among the stones; it had spread some of its yellow petals for banner, and on its uplifted spears the buds were fat and creamy with coming bloom. Rain had fallen in the night, and had called the wilderness itself to life, clothing its thorns with a purple garment of tiny flowers; the delicious sun struck upon our shoulders; a joyful little wind blew the damp, sweet smell of the reviving earth in gusts towards us; our horses sniffed the air and, catching the infection of the moment, tugged at the bit and set off at racing speed across the rain-softened ground. And we, too, passed out of the silence and remembered that we lived. Life seized us and inspired us with a mad sense of revelry. The humming wind and the teeming earth shouted 'Life! life!' as we rode. Life! life! the bountiful, the magnificent! Age was far from us—death far; we had left him enthroned in his barren mountains, with ghostly cities and out-worn faiths to bear him company. For us the wide plain and the limitless world, for us the beauty and the freshness of the morning, for us youth and the joy of living!

IN PRAISE OF GARDENS

THERE IS A COUPLET IN AN ELIZABETHAN BOOK of airs which might serve as a motto for Eastern life: 'Thy love is not thy love,' says the author of the songs in the 'Muses' Garden of Delights' (and the pretty stilted title suits the somewhat antiquated ring of the lines):

'Thy love is not thy love if not thine own,
And so it is not, if it once be known.'

If it once be known! Ah yes! the whole charm of possession vanishes before the gaze of curious eyes, and for them, too, charm is driven away by familiarity. It takes the mystery of a Sphinx to keep the world gazing for thirty centuries. The East is full of secrets—no one understands their value better than the Oriental; and because she is full of secrets she is full of entrancing surprises. Many fine things there are upon the surface: brilliance of colour, splendour of light, solemn loneliness, clamorous activity; these are only the patterns upon the curtain which floats for ever before the recesses of Eastern life, its essential charm is of more subtle quality. As it listeth, it comes and goes; it flashes upon you through the open doorway of some blank, windowless house you pass in the street, from under the lifted veil of the beggar woman who lays her hand on your bridle, from the dark, contemptuous eyes of a child; then the East sweeps aside her curtains, flashes a facet of her jewels into your dazzled eyes, and disappears again with a mocking little laugh at your bewilderment; then for a moment it seems to you that you are looking her in the face, but while you are wondering whether she be angel or devil, she is gone.

She will not stay—she prefers the unexpected; she will keep her secrets and her tantalizing charm with them, and when you think you have caught at last some of her illusive grace, she will send you back to shrouded figures and blank house-fronts.

You must be content to wait, and perhaps some day, when you find her walking in her gardens in the cool of the evening, she will take a whim to stop and speak to you, and you will go away fascinated by her courteous words and her exquisite hospitality.

For it is in her gardens that she is most herself—they share her charm, they are as unexpected as she. Conceive on every side such a landscape as the dead world will exhibit when it whirls naked and deserted through the starry interspace—a gray and featureless plain, over which the dust-clouds rise and fall, build themselves into mighty columns, and sink back again among the stones at the bidding of hot and fitful winds; prickly low-growing plants for all vegetation, leafless, with a foliage of thorns; white patches of salt, on which the sunlight glitters; a fringe of barren mountains on the horizon.... Yet in this desolation lurks the mocking beauty of the East. A little water and the desert breaks into flower, bowers of cool shade spring up in the midst of dust and glare, radiant stretches of soft colour gleam in that gray expanse. Your heart leaps as you pass through the gateway in the mud wall; so sharp is the contrast, that you may stand with one foot in an arid wilderness and the other in a shadowy, flowery paradise. Under the broad thick leaves of the plane-trees tiny streams murmur, fountains splash with a sweet fresh sound, white-rose bushes drop their fragrant petals into tanks, lying deep and still like patches of concentrated shadow. The indescribable charm of a Persian garden is keenly present to the Persians themselves—the 'strip of herbage strown, which just divides the desert from the sown,' an endlessly beautiful parable. Their poets sing the praise of gardens in exquisite verses, and call their books by their names. I fear the Muses have wandered more often in Sa'di's Garden of Roses than in the somewhat pretentious pleasure-ground which our Elizabethan writer prepared for them.

The desert about Tehran is renowned for the beauty of its gardens. The Shah possesses several, others belong to his sons, others to powerful ministers and wealthy merchants. Sometimes across the gateways a chain is drawn, denoting that the garden is Bast—sanctuary—and into these the European may not go; but places of refuge for the hunted criminal are, fortunately, few, and generally the garden is open to all comers.

Perhaps the most beautiful of all is one which belongs to the Shah, and which lies under a rocky hillock crowned with the walls and towers of a palace. We found ourselves at its gate one evening, after an aimless canter across the desert, and determined to enter. The loiterers in the gateway let us pass through unchallenged. We crossed the little entrance-court and came into a long dark avenue, fountains down the middle of it, and flower-beds, in which the plants were pale and meagre for want of light; roses, the pink flowers which scent the rosewater, and briars, a froth of white and yellow bloom, growing along its edges in spite of the deep shade of the plane-trees. Every tiny rill of water was fringed with violet leaves—you can imagine how in the spring the scent of the violets greets you out in the desert when you are still far away, like a hospitable friend coming open-armed down his steps to welcome you. We wandered along intersecting avenues, until we came to one broader than the rest, at the end of which stood a little house. Tiny streams flowed round and about it, flowed under its walls and into its rooms; fountains splashed ceaselessly in front of it, a soft light wind swayed the heavy folds of the patterned curtains hanging half-way down across its deep balconies. The little dwelling looked like a fairy palace, jewelled with coloured tiles, unreal and fantastic, built half out of the ripple of water, and half out of the shadowy floating of its great curtains. Two or three steps and a narrow passage, and we were in the central room—such a room to lie and dream in through the hot summer days!—tiled with blue, in the middle an overflowing fountain, windows on either side opening down to the ground, the vaulted ceiling and the alcoved walls set with a mosaic of looking-glass, in whose diamonds and crescents the blue of the tiles and the spray of the tossing waters were reflected.

As we sat on the deep step of the windowsill, a door opened softly, and a long-robed Persian entered. He carried in his hand a twanging stringed instrument, with which he established himself at the further side of the fountain, and began to play weird, tuneless melodies on its feeble strings—an endless, wailing minor. Evening fell, and the dusk gathered in the glittering room, the fountain bubbled lower and sank into silence, the wind blew the sweet smell of roses in to us where we sat—and still the Persian played, while in the garden the nightingales called to one another with soft thrilling notes.

A week or two later we came back to Doshan Tepe. This time we found it peopled by a party of Persians. They were sitting round the edge of one of the tanks at the end of the avenue, men and little children, and in their green and yellow robes they looked to us as we entered like a patch of brilliant water-plants, whose vivid colours were not to be dimmed by the shade of the plane leaves. But the musician did not reappear; he was too wise a magician to weave his spells 'save to the span of heaven and few ears.'

There was a deserted garden at the foot of the mountains which had a curious history. It belonged to the Zil es Sultan, the Shah's eldest son, who had inherited it from his mother, that Schöne Müllerin whose beauty captivated the King of Kings in the days of his youth. The Zil (his title, being interpreted, signifies 'The shadow of the King') has fallen into disgrace. The Shah casts his shadow far, and in order that it may never grow less, the Zil is not allowed to move from Isfahan; his Shimran garden therefore is empty, and his house is falling into disrepair. It stands on the edge of a rushing mountain torrent, which, we will hope, turned the mill-wheels in old days (though some men assert that the girl was not a miller's daughter, after all), and it boasts some magnificent plane-trees, under which we picnicked one evening, hanging Persian lanterns from the boughs. The night had brought tall yellow evening primroses into flower, and their delicious smell mingled with that of the jessamine, which covered the decaying walls. The light of our lanterns shone on the smooth tree trunks, between the leaves glimmered a waning moon, and behind us the mountain-sides lay in sheets of light. We did not envy the Zil his palaces in Isfahan.

Once in another garden we found the owner at home. It was early in the morning; he was standing on his doorstep, judging between the differences of two people of his village, a man and a veiled woman, who had come to seek his arbitration. They were both talking loudly, she with shrill exclamations and calls upon God to witness, in her eagerness forgetting the laws of modesty, and throwing aside her thick linen veil, that she might plead with eyes and expression, as well as voice—or perhaps it was policy, for she had a beautiful face, dark-eyed and pale, round which the folds of black cloak and white linen fell like the drapery round the head of a Madonna. When our unknown host saw us, he dismissed his clamorous petitioners, and greeted us with the courtesy which is the heirloom of the Persian race. Seats were brought for us, tea and coffee served to us, a blue cotton-clothed multitude of gardeners offered us baskets of unripe plums, dishes of lettuce, and bunches of stiffly-arranged flowers. We sat and conversed, with no undue animation, here and there an occasional remark, but the intervals were rendered sociable by the bubbling of kalyans. At length we rose to go, and as we walked down the garden-paths many compliments passed between us and our host. At the gate he assured us that our slave had been honoured by our acceptance of his hospitality, and with low bows we mounted our horses and rode away.

We had not in reality trenched upon his privacy. There was, indeed, a part of his domains where even his hospitality would not have bidden us enter. Behind the house in which we were received lay the women's dwelling, a long, low, verandaed building standing round a deep tank, on whose edge solemn children carry on their dignified games, and veiled women flit backwards and forwards. Shaded by trees, somewhat desolate and uncared-for in appearance, washed up at the further end of the garden beyond the reach of flowers, the sight of the andarun and of its inhabitants knocks at the heart with a weary sense of discontent, of purposeless, vapid lives—a wailing, endless minor.

So in the wilderness, between high walls, the secret, mysterious life of the East flows on—a life into which no European can penetrate, whose standards, whose canons, are so different from his own that the whole existence they rule seems to him misty and unreal, incomprehensible, at any rate unfathomable; a life so monotonous, so unvaried from age to age, that it does not present any feature marked enough to create an impression other than that of vague picturesqueness, of dulness inexpressible, of repose which has turned to lethargy, and tranquillity carried beyond the point of virtue.

And these gardens, also with their tall trees and peaceful tanks, are subject to the unexpected vicissitudes of Eastern fortune. The minister falls into disgrace, the rich merchant is ruined by the exactions of his sovereign; the stream is turned off, the water ceases to flow into the tanks and to leap in the fountains, the trees die, the flowers wither, the walls crumble into unheeded decay, and in a few years the tiny paradise has been swept forgotten from the face of the earth, and the conquering desert spreads its dust and ashes once more over it all.

THE KING OF MERCHANTS

QUITE EARLY IN THE MORNING we rode out to his garden. We had left Tehran, and moved up to one of the villages lying eight miles nearer the mountains on the edge of the belt of fertile country which stretches along their lower slopes. Our road that morning led us still further upwards through a green land full of wild-flowers, which seemed to us inexpressibly lovely after the bare and arid deserts about the town. The air was still fresh with the delicious freshness of the dawn; dew there was none, but a light, brisk wind, the sun's forerunner, had shaken the leaves and grass by the roadside and swept the dust from them, and dying, it had left some of its cool fragrance to linger till mid-day in shadowy places. We rode along dark winding paths, under sweet-smelling walnut-trees, between the high mud walls of gardens, splashing through the tiny precious streams which came down to water fields, where, although it was only June, the high corn was already mellowing amidst a glory of purple vetch. The world was awake—it wakes early in the East. Laden donkeys passed us on their way to the town, veiled women riding astride on gaily-caparisoned mules, white-turbaned priests, and cantering horsemen sitting loosely in their padded saddles. Ragged beggars and half-naked dervishes were encamped by the roadside, and as we passed implored alms or hurled imprecations, as their necessity or their fanaticism indicated.

At the foot of the mountains we stopped before a long wall, less ruinous than most—a bare mud wall, straight and uncompromising, with an arched doorway in the midst of it. At our knock the double panels of the door were flung open, disclosing a flight of steps. Up these we climbed, and stood at the top amazed by the unexpected beauty which greeted us. The garden ran straight up the hillside; so steep it was that the parallel lines of paths were little but flights of high narrow stairs—short flights broken by terraces on which flower-beds were laid out, gay with roses and nasturtiums and petunias. Between the two staircases, from the top of the hill to the bottom, ran a slope of smooth blue tiles, over which flowed cascades, broadening out on the terraces into tiny tanks and fountains where the water rose and fell all day long with a cool, refreshing sound, and a soft splashing of spray. We toiled up the stairs till we came to the topmost terrace, wider than the rest. Here the many-coloured carpet of flowers gave place to a noble grove of white lilies, which stood in full bloom under the hot sunlight, and the more the sun blazed the cooler and whiter shone the lilies, the sweeter and heavier grew their fragrance. Those gardens round Tehran to which we were accustomed had been so thickly planted with trees that no ray of light had reached the flower-beds, but here in the hills, where the heat was tempered by cool winds, there was light and air in abundance. On the further side of this radiant bodyguard was a pleasure-house—not a house of walls, but of windows and of shutters, which were all flung open, a house through which all the winds of heaven might pass unchallenged. There was a splashing fountain in the midst of it, and on all four sides deep recesses arched away to the wide window-frames. We entered, and flinging ourselves down on the cushions of one of these recesses, gazed out on the scene below us. First in the landscape came the glitter of the little garden; lower down the hillside the clustered walnuts and poplars which shaded the villages through which we had ridden; then the brown, vacant plain, with no atmosphere but the mist of dust, with no features but the serpentining lines of mounds which marked the underground course of a stream, bounded far away by a barren line of hills, verdureless and torrent-scored, and beyond them more brown plains, fainter lines of barren hills to the edge of the far horizon. Midway across the first desert lay a wide patch of trees sheltering the gardens of Tehran. Down there in the town how the sun blazed! The air was a haze of heat and dust, and a perspiring humanity toiled, hurrying hither and thither, under the dark arches of the bazaar; but in the garden of the King of Merchants all day long cool winds blew from the gates of the hills, all day long the refreshing water rippled and sparkled, all day long the white lilies at our feet lay like a reflection of the snow-capped mountains above us.

We sat idly gazing while we sipped our glasses of milkless tea much sugared, nibbled sweetmeats from the heaped-up dishes on the ground beside us, handed round the gurgling kalyans, and held out our hands to be filled with stalkless jessamine blossoms deliciously scented. At noon we rose, and were conducted yet deeper into the domains of the royally hospitable merchant—up more flights of steps, past a big tank at the further side of which stood the andarun, the women's lodging, where thinly-clad and shrouded forms stepped silently behind the shutters at our approach, down long shady paths till we came to another guest-house standing at the top of another series of cascades and fountains. Here an excellent repast was served to us—piles of variously flavoured rice mixed with meat and fruits and sauces, roasted kabobs, minces wrapped in vine-leaves, ices, fruits, and the fragrant wine of Shiraz.

Towards the cool of the evening the King of Merchants appeared on the threshold of his breeze-swept dwelling, a man somewhat past the prime of life, with a tall and powerful figure wrapped in the long brown cloak, opening over the coloured under-robe and spotless linen, which is the dress of rich and poor alike. He was of a pleasing countenance, straight-browed, red-lipped, with a black beard and an olive complexion, and his merry dark eyes had a somewhat unexpected twinkle under his high, white-turbaned forehead. A hospitable friend and a cheerful host is he, the ready quip, the apt story, the appreciative laugh, for ever on his lips; a man on whom the world has smiled, and who smiles back at that Persian world of his which he has made so pleasant for himself, strewing it with soft cushions and glowing carpets, and planting it round with flowers. Every evening the hot summer through, he is to be found in his airy garden at the foot of the mountains; every evening strings of guests knock at his hospitable gates, nor do they knock in vain. At the top of his many staircases he greets them, smiling, prosperous—those stairs of his need never be wearisome for alien feet to climb. He takes the new-comers by the hand, and leads them into one of his guest-houses; there, by the edge of a fountain, he spreads carpets on which they may repose themselves; there, as the night draws on, a banquet of rice and roasted meats and fruits is laid before them, tall pitchers of water, curiously flavoured sherbets, silver kalyans; and while they eat the King of Merchants sits with them and entertains them with stories garnished with many a cheerful jest, many a seasonable quotation from the poets. At length he leaves them to sleep till dawn, when they arise, and, having drunk a parting glass of weak golden tea, repair to the nearest bath, and so away from the cool mountain valley and back to the heat and labour of the day. He himself spends the night in his andarun, or lying wrapped in a blanket on the roof of his gate-house, from whence he can watch the day break over the wide plain below.

We took our share in his welcome, listened to his anecdotes, and played backgammon with him, nor did we bid him farewell until the ring of lighted lamps on the mosque close at hand warned us that unless we intended to spend the night on his house-top it was time to be gone.

THE IMAM HUSSEIN

Towards the middle of July the month of Muharram began—the month of mourning for the Imam Hussein. Such heat must have weighed upon the Plain of Kerbela when the grandson of the Prophet, with his sixty or seventy followers, dug the trenches of their camp not far from the Euphrates stream. The armies of Yezid enclosed them, cutting them off from the river and from all retreat; hope of succour there was none; on all sides nothing but the pitiless vengeance of the Khalif—the light of the watch-fires flickered upon the tents of his armies, and day revealed only the barren plain of Kerbela behind them—the Plain of Sorrow and Vexation.

In memory of the sufferings and death of that forlorn band and of their sainted leader, all Persia broke into lamentation. He, the holy one, hungered and thirsted; the intercessor with God could gain no mercy from men; he saw his children fall under the spears of his enemies, and when he died his body was trampled into the dust, and his head borne in triumph to the Khalif. The pitiful story has taken hold of the imagination of half the Mohammedan world. Many centuries, bringing with them their own dole of tragedy and sorrow, have not dimmed it, nor lessened the feeling which its recital creates, partly, no doubt, because of the fresh breeze of religious controversy which has swept the dust of time perpetually from off it, but partly, too, because of its own poignant simplicity. The splendid courage which shines through it justifies its long existence. Even Hussein's enemies were moved to pity by his patient endurance, by the devotion of his followers, and by the passionate affection of the women who were with him. The recorded episodes of that terrible tenth of Muharram are full of the pure human pathos which moves and which touches generation after generation. It is not necessary to share the religious convictions of the Shiahs to take a side in the hopeless battle under the burning sun, or realize the tragic picture of the Imam sitting before his tent-door with the dead child in his arms, or lifting the tiny measure of water to lips pierced through by an arrow-shot—a draught almost as bitter as the sponge of vinegar and hyssop.

'Men travel by night,' says Hussein in the miracle play, 'and their destinies travel towards them.' It was a destiny of immortal memory that he was journeying to meet on that march by night through the wilderness, side by side with El Hurr and the Khalifs army.

Shortly after we landed in Persia we came unexpectedly upon the story of the martyrdom. In the main street of Kasvin, up which we were strolling while our horses were being changed (for we were on our way to Tehran), we found a crowd assembled under the plane-trees. We craned over the shoulders of Persian peasants, and saw in the centre of the circle a group of players, some in armour, some robed in long black garments, who were acting a passion play, of which Hussein was the hero. One was mounted on a horse which, at his entries and exits, he was obliged to force through the lines of people which were the only wings of his theatre; but except for the occasional scuffle he caused among the audience, there was little action in the piece—or, at least, in the part of it which we witnessed—for the players confined themselves to passing silently in and out, pausing for a moment in the empty space which represented the stage, while a mollah, mounted in a sort of pulpit, read aloud the incidents they were supposed to be enacting.

But with the beginning of Muharram the latent religious excitement of the East broke loose. Every evening at dusk the wailing cries of the mourners filled the stillness, rising and falling with melancholy persistence all through the night, until dawn sent sorrow-stricken believers to bed, and caused sleepless unbelievers to turn with a sigh of relief upon their pillows. At last the tenth day of Muharram came—a day of deep significance to all Mohammedans, since it witnessed the creation of Adam and Eve, of heaven and hell, of life and death; but to the Shiahs of tenfold deeper moment, for on it Hussein's martyrdom was accomplished.

Early in the afternoon sounds of mourning rose from the village. The inhabitants formed themselves into procession, and passed up the shady outlying avenues, and along the strip of desert which led back into the principal street—a wild and savage band whose grief was a strange tribute to the chivalrous hero whose bones have been resting for twelve centuries in the Plain of Kerbela. But tribute of a kind it was. Many brave men have probably suffered greater tortures than Hussein's, and borne them with as admirable a fortitude; but he stands among the few to whom that earthly immortality has been awarded which is acknowledged to be the best gift the capricious world holds in her hands. If he shared in the passionate desire to be remembered which assails every man on the threshold of forgetfulness, it was not in vain that he died pierced with a hundred spears; and though his funeral obsequies were brief twelve hundred years ago, the sound of them has echoed down the centuries with eternal reverberation until to-day.

First in the procession came a troop of little boys, naked to the waist, leaping round a green-robed mollah, who was reciting the woes of the Imam as he moved forward in the midst of his disordered crew. The boys jumped and leapt round him, beating their breasts—there was no trace of sorrow on their faces. They might have been performing some savage dance as they came onwards, a compact mass of bobbing heads and naked shoulders—a dance in which they themselves took no kind of interest, but in which they recognised that it was the duty of a Persian boy to take his part. They were followed by men bearing the standards of the village—long poles surmounted by trophies of beads and coloured silks, streamers and curious ornaments; and in the rear came another reciter and another body of men, beating their breasts, from which the garments were torn back, striking their foreheads and repeating the name of the Imam in a monotonous chorus, interspersed with cries and groans.

But it was in the evening that the real ceremony took place. The bazaar in the centre of the village was roofed over with canvas and draped with cheap carpets and gaudy cotton hangings; a low platform was erected at one end, and the little shops were converted into what looked very like the boxes of a theatre. They were hung with bright-coloured stuffs and furnished with chairs, on which the notabilities sat and witnessed the performance, drinking sherbet and smoking kalyans the while. We arrived at about nine o'clock and found the proceedings in full swing. The tent was crowded with peasants, some standing, some sitting on the raised edge of a fountain in the centre. Round this fountain grew a mass of oleander-trees, their delicate leaves and exquisite pink flowers standing out against the coarse blue cotton of the men's clothing, and clustering round the wrinkled, toil-worn peasant faces. On the platform was a mollah, long-robed and white-turbaned, who was reading exhortations and descriptions of the martyrdom with a drawling, chanting intonation. At his feet the ground was covered with women, their black cloaks tucked neatly round them, sitting with shrouded heads and with the long strip of white linen veil hanging over their faces and down into their laps. They looked for all the world like shapeless black and white parcels set in rows across the floor. The mollah read on, detailing the sufferings of the Imam: 'He thirsted, he was an hungered!' the women rocked themselves to and fro in an agony of grief, the men beat their bare breasts, tears streamed over their cheeks, and from time to time they took up the mollah's words in weary, mournful chorus, or broke into his story with a murmured wail, which gathered strength and volume until it had reached the furthest corners of the tent: 'Hussein! Hussein! Hussein!'

It was intensely hot. Cheap European lamps flared and smoked against the canvas walls, casting an uncertain light upon the pink oleander flowers, the black-robed women, and the upturned faces of the men, streaming with

sweat and tears, and all stricken and furrowed with cruel poverty and hunger—their sufferings would have made a longer catalogue than those of the
Imam. The mollah tore his turban from his head and cast it upon the ground,
and still he chanted on, and the people took up the throbbing cry: 'Hussein!
Hussein! Hussein!'

Presently a dervish shouldered his way through the throng. A scanty garment was knotted round his loins, his ragged hair hung over his shoulders,
and about his head was bound a brilliant scarf, whose stripes of scarlet and
yellow fell down his naked back. He had come from far; he held a long staff
in his hands, and the dust of the wilderness was on the shoes which he laid by
the edge of the platform. He stood there, reciting, praying, exhorting—a wild
figure, with eyes in which flashed the madness of religious fanaticism, straining
forward with passionate gestures through the smoky light which shone on his
brilliant headgear and on his glistening face, distorted by suffering and excitement. When he had finished speaking he stepped off the platform, picked up
his shoes and staff, and hurried out into the night to bear his eloquence to
other villages....

There is nothing more difficult to measure than the value of visible emotion. To the Englishman tears are a serious matter; they denote only the deepest and the most ungovernable feelings, they are reserved for great occasions.
Commonplace sensations are, in his opinion, scarcely worth bringing on to the
surface. The facile expression of emotion in a foreigner is surprising to him—he
can scarcely understand the gestures of a nation so little removed from him as
the French, and he is apt to be led astray by what seems to him the visible sign
of great excitement, but which to them is only a natural emphasis of speech.
In the East these difficulties are ten times greater. The gesture itself has often
a totally different significance; the Turk nods his head when he says 'No,' and
shakes it when he wishes to imply assent; and even when this is not the case,
the feeling which underlies it is probably quite incomprehensible—quite apart
from the range of Western emotion—and its depth and duration are ruled by
laws of which we have no knowledge. The first thing which strikes us in the
Oriental is his dignified and impassive tranquillity. When we suddenly come
upon the other side of him, and find him giving way, for no apparent reason,
to uncontrolled excitement, we are ready to believe that only the most violent
feelings could have moved him so far from his habitual calm. So it was that
evening. At first it seemed to us that we were looking upon people plunged
into the blackest depths of grief, but presently it dawned upon us that we were
grossly exaggerating the value of their tears and groans. The Oriental spectators
in the boxes were scarcely moved by an emotion which they were supposed
to be sharing; they sat listening with calm faces, partook of a regular meal of

sweetmeats, ices, and sherbets, and handed round kalyans with polite phrases and affable smiles. Our Persian servants were equally unmoved; they conformed so far to the general attitude as to tap their well-clad chests with inattentive fingers, but they kept the corners of their eyes fixed upon us, and no religious frenzy prevented them from supplying our every want. And on the edges of the crowd below us the people were paying no heed to what was going forward; we watched men whose faces were all wet with tears, whose breasts were red and sore with blows, stepping aside and entering into brisk conversation with their neighbours, sharing an amicable cup of tea, or bargaining for a handful of salted nuts, as though the very name of Hussein were unknown to them. Seeing this, we were tempted to swing back to the opposite extreme, and to conclude that this show of grief was a mere formality, signifying nothing—a view which was probably as erroneous as the other.

But whatever it meant, it meant something which we could not understand, and the whole ceremony excited in our minds feelings not far removed from disgust and weariness. It was forced, it was sordid, and it was ugly. The hangings of the tent looked suspiciously as though they had come from a Manchester loom, and if they had, they did not redound to the credit of Manchester taste; the lamps smelt abominably of oil, the stifling air was loaded with dust, and the grating chant of the mollahs was as tedious as the noise of machinery. How long it all lasted I do not know; we were glad enough to escape from it after about an hour, and as we walked home through the cool village street, we shook a sense of chaotic confusion from our minds, and heard with satisfaction the hoarse sounds fading gradually away into the night air....

After such fashion the Shiahs mourn the death of the Imam Hussein, the Rose in the Garden of Glory; and whether he and his descendants are indeed the only rightful successors of the Prophet is a question which will never be definitely settled until the coming of the twelfth and last Imam, who, they say, has already lived on earth, and who will come again and resume the authority which his deputy, the Shah, holds in his name. 'When you see black ensigns'—so tradition reports Mohammed's words—'black ensigns coming out of Khorasan, then go forth and join them, for the Imam of God will be with those standards, whose name is El Mahdi. He will fill the world with equity and justice.'

THE SHADOW OF DEATH

Slowly, slowly through the early summer the cholera crept nearer. Out of the far East came rumours of death ... the cholera was raging In Samarkand ... it had crossed the Persian frontier ... it is in Meshed! said the telegrams. A perfunctory quarantine was established between Tehran and the infected district, and the streams of pilgrims that flock ceaselessly to Meshed were forbidden to enter the holy city. Then came the daily bulletins of death, the number of the victims increasing with terrible rapidity. Meshed was almost deserted, for all whom the plague had spared had fled to the mountains, and when a week or two later its violence began to abate, flashed the ominous news: 'It is spreading among the villages to the westward.' From day to day it drew ever closer, leaping the quarantine bulwark, hurrying over a strip of desert, showing its sudden face in a distant village, sweeping northwards, and causing sanguine men to shake their heads and murmur: 'Tehran will be spared; it never comes to Tehran'—in a moment seizing upon the road to the Caspian, and ringing the city round like a cunning strategist. Then men held their breath and waited, and almost wished that the suspense were over and the ineluctable day were come. Yet with the cholera knocking at their doors they made no preparations for defence, they organized no hospitals, they planned no system of relief; cartloads of over-ripe fruit were still permitted to be brought daily into the town, and the air was still poisoned by the refuse which was left to rot in the streets. It was the month of Muharram; every evening the people fell into mad transports of religious excitement, crowding together in the Shah's theatre to witness the holy plays and to mourn with tears the death of Hussein. Perhaps a deeper fervour was thrown into the long prayers and a greater intensity into the wailing lamentations, for at the door the grim shadow was standing, and which of the mourners could answer for it that not on his own shoulder the clutching hand would fall as he passed out into the night? The cloud of dust that hung for ever over the desert and the city assumed a more baleful aspect; it hung now like an omen of the deeper cloud which was settling down upon Tehran. And still above it the sun shone pitilessly, and under the whole blue heaven there was no refuge from the hand of God. So the days passed, and the people drank bad water and gorged themselves on rotten fruit, and on a sudden the blow fell—the cholera was in Tehran.

Woe to them that were with child in those days and to them that were sick! One blind impulse seized alike upon rich and poor—flight! flight! All who possessed a field or two in the outlying villages, and all who could shelter themselves under a thin canvas roof in the desert, gathered together their scanty possessions, and, with the bare necessaries of life in their hands, crowded out of the northern gateways. The roads leading to the mountains were blocked by a stream of fugitives, like an endless procession of Holy Families flying before a wrath more terrible than that of Herod: the women mounted on donkeys and holding their babes in front of them wrapped in the folds of their cloaks, the men hurrying on foot by their side. For the vengeance of the Lord is swift; in the East he is still the great and terrible God of the Old Testament; his hand falls upon the just and upon the unjust, and punishes folly as severely as it punishes crime. In vain the desert was dotted over with the little white tents of the fugitives, in vain they sought refuge in the cool mountain villages. Wherever they went they bore the plague in the midst of them; they dropped dead by the roadside, they died in the sand of the wilderness, they spread the fatal infection among the country people.

Oriental fatalism, which sounds fine enough in theory, breaks down woefully in practice. It is mainly based upon the helplessness of a people to whom it has never occurred to take hold of life with vigorous hands. A wise philosophy bids men bear the inevitable evil without complaint, but we of the West are not content until we have discovered how far the coil is inevitable, and how far it may be modified by forethought and by a more complete knowledge of its antecedents. It may be that we turn the channel of immediate fate but little, but with every effort we help forward the future safety of the world. But fatalism can seldom be carried through to its logical conclusions—the attitude of mind which prevented the Persians from laying in medical stores did not save them a fortnight later from headlong flight.

The most degrading of human passions is the fear of death. It tears away the restraints and the conventions which alone make social life possible to man; it reveals the brute in him which underlies them all. In the desperate hand-to-hand struggle for life there is no element of nobility. He who is engaged upon it throws aside honour, he throws aside self-respect, he throws aside all that would make victory worth having—he asks for nothing but bare life. The impalpable danger into whose arms he may at any moment be precipitating himself unawares tells more upon his nerves and upon his imagination than a meeting with the most redoubtable enemy in the open; his courage breaks under the strain.

Such fear laid hold of the people of Tehran.

The Persian doctors, whose duty it was to distribute medicines among the sufferers, shut up their stores, and were among the first to leave the stricken city; masters turned their servants into the streets and the open fields, if they showed symptoms of the disease, and left them to die for want of timely help; women and little children were cast out of the andaruns; the living scarcely dared to bury the bodies of the dead.

One little group of Europeans preserved a bold front in the midst of the universal terror. The American missionaries left their homes in the villages and went down into the town to give what help they could to the sick, and to hearten with the sight of their own courage those whom the cholera had not yet touched. They visited the poorer quarters, they distributed medicines, they started a tiny hospital, in which they nursed those whom they found lying in the streets, giving them, if they recovered, clean and disinfected clothes, and if they died a decent burial. They tried to teach a people who received both their help and their wisdom at the point of the sword, the elementary laws of commonsense, to prevent them from eating masses of fruit, and to put a stop to a fertile cause of fresh infection by persuading them to burn the clothes of the dead instead of selling them for a few pence to the first comer. Sometimes we would meet one of these men riding up from the town in the cool of the evening, when ceaseless labour and much watching had rendered it imperative that he should take at least one night's rest. His face had grown thin and white with the terrible strain of the work, and in his eyes was the expression which the sight of helpless suffering puts into the eyes of a brave man.

'One morning,' related the doctor months afterwards, 'as I was going out early to make my rounds, I found a woman lying on the doorstep. She was half naked, and she had been dead some hours, for her body was quite cold. A child crept round her, moaning for food, and on her breast was a little living baby fast asleep.... It was the most terrible thing I ever saw in my life,' he added after a moment. The missionaries were aided by one or two European volunteers and native pupils from their own schools, who stood shoulder to shoulder with them, and helped them to bear the heat and burden of the day. Their courage and their splendid endurance will remain graven on the minds of those who knew of it long after shameful memories of cowardice have been forgotten.

For it was not only the Persians who were terror-stricken; among the Europeans also there were instances of cowardice. There were men who, in spite of former protestations of indifference, turned sick and white with fear when the moment of trial came; there were those who fled hastily, leaving their servants and their companions to die in their deserted gardens; and there were those who took to their beds and who even went to the length of giving up the ghost, victims to no other malady than sheer terror. The English doctor had his hands full both in the town and in the country; by many a sick bed he brought comfort where his skill could not avail to save, and courage to many who were battling manfully with the disease.

Religious fervour grew apace under the influence of fear. Men to whom travel and intercourse with foreigners had given a semblance of Western civilization, exchanged their acquired garb for a pilgrim's cloak, and set forth on the long journey to Mecca. The air was full of rumours. It was whispered that the mollahs were working upon native fanaticism, and pointing to the presence of Europeans as a primary cause of evil which must be straightway removed. To-day an incredible number of deaths were reported to have taken place in Tehran during the last twenty-four hours, to-morrow the news would run from lip to lip that the Shah himself had succumbed. At the time when the cholera broke out in Tehran, his Majesty was making his summer journey through the country. He at once despatched an order to the effect that the disease was on no account to be permitted to come near his camp, but it was not within his conception of the duties of kingship to take precautions for the safety of any dweller in his realms but himself. He appeared to be considerably alarmed by the approach of an enemy who is no respecter of persons. He dismissed the greater part of his followers, and, making a few nights' halt in a palace in the neighbourhood of his capital, he hurried on into the mountains. Even in those nights forty or fifty people died in his camp, but he was kept in ignorance of this untoward occurrence. Fortunate indeed were those ladies of his andarun who accompanied him on his travels, or who had enough influence to succeed in having themselves transported to one of the numerous country palaces; the others were obliged to continue in the town, no one having time to spare them any attention, and it was not till the fury of the cholera was spent that the poor women were allowed to move into a less dangerous neighbourhood.

Even under the shadow of death there were incidents which were not lacking in a certain grim humour. Such, for example, was the tale of the half-mad and more than half-naked negro who lived in the desert beyond our doors, and who was accustomed to come whining to us for alms when we rode out. He must have possessed a sardonic sense of comedy, and the adventures of the Hunchback cannot have been unfamiliar to him. He had a wife lurking in the village, though we were unconscious of her existence till he came in tears to inform us of her decease, begging that he might be given money wherewith to pay for her burial. A charitable person provided him with the necessary sum, with which (having never, in all probability, seen so much silver in his dirty palm) he

incontinently decamped. But before he left he took the precaution of setting up
the dead body of his wife against the palings of our garden, thereby forcing the
European dogs to bear twice over the expenses of her funeral. Persian beggars
and cripples have more lives than they have limbs. Many good men died in
Tehran, but when we returned there at the end of the season we found precisely
the same group of maimed and ragged loiterers hanging about our doors.

The cholera was not of very long duration. A slight fall of rain reduced
the daily number of deaths by several hundreds; before six weeks were past
the people were returning to the streets they had quitted in precipitate haste;
a fortnight later the surrounding villages also were free of sickness, and had
resumed their accustomed aspect, except for an air of emptiness in the tiny
bazaars, from which in some cases a third of the population had been reft,
and a corresponding number of fresh graves in the burial-grounds. But another
disease follows on the heels of cholera: typhoid fever is the inevitable result of an
absolute disregard of all sanitary laws. The system of burial among the Persians
is beyond expression evil. They think nothing of washing the bodies of the dead
in a stream which subsequently runs through the length of the village, thereby
poisoning water which is to be used for numberless household purposes, and
in their selection of the graveyard they will not hesitate to choose the ground
lying immediately above a kanat which is carrying water to many gardens and
drinking-fountains. Even when they are buried, the bodies are not allowed to
rest in peace. The richer families hold it a point of honour to lay the bones of
their relations in some holy place—Kerbela, where Hussein was slain, or the
sacred shrine of Meshed. They therefore commit them only temporarily to the
earth, laying them in shallow graves, and covering them with an arched roof of
brickwork, which practice accounts for the horrible smell round the graveyards
after an outbreak of cholera. A few months later, and long before time has
killed the germs of disease, these bodies are taken up, wrapped in sackcloth, and
carried, slung across the backs of mules, to their distant resting-place, sowing
not improbably the seeds of a fresh outbreak as they go. The wonder is, not
that the cholera should prove fatal to so many, but that so large a proportion of
the population should survive in a land where Ignorance is for ever preparing a
smooth highway for the feet of Death.

DWELLERS IN TENTS

EVERY MAN, SAYS A PHILOSOPHER, is a wanderer at heart. Alas! I fear the axiom would be truer if he had confined himself to stating that every man loves to fancy himself a wanderer, for when it comes to the point there is not one in a thousand who can throw off the ties of civilized existence—the ties and the comforts of habits which have become easy to him by long use, of the life whose security is ample compensation for its monotony. Yet there are moments when the cabined spirit longs for liberty. A man stands a-tiptoe on the verge of the unknown world which lures him with its vague promises; the peaceful years behind lose all their value in his dazzled eyes; like him, 'qui n'a pas du ciel que ce qui brille par le trou du volet,' he pines to stand in the great free sunlight, the great wide world which is all too narrow for his adventurous energy. For one brief moment he shakes off the traditions of a lifetime, swept away by the mighty current which silently, darkly, goes watering the roots of his race. He, too, is a wanderer like his remote forefathers; his heart beats time with the hearts long stilled that dwelt in their bosoms, who came sweeping out of the mysterious East, pressing ever resistlessly onward till the grim waste of Atlantic waters bade them stay. He remembers the look of the boundless plain stretching before him, the nights when the dome of the sky was his ceiling, when he was awakened by the cold kisses of the wind that flies before the dawn. He cries for space to fling out his fighting arm; he burns to measure himself unfettered with the forces of God.

Many hundreds of miles away, to the southward of the Caspian Sea, lies a country still untraversed by highroad or railway line. Here rise mountains clothed in the spring with a gay mantle of crocuses and wild tulips, but on whose scorched sides the burning summer sun leaves nothing but a low growth of thorns; here are steep valleys, where the shadows fall early and rise late, strewn with rocks, crowned with fantastic crags, scarred with deep watercourses; here the hawks hover, the eagle passes with mournful cry, and the prisoned wind dashes madly through the gorge. Here lie reaches of plain bounded on all sides by the mountain wall, plateau after thorny plateau—a rolling wilderness over which the headlands stand out as over a sea. Through the middle of the plain flows a river, its stony bed cut deep into the earth; silver trout leap in its pools, strips of grass border it—stretches of pastureland in the midst of the desert—flocks of goats feed along its banks, and from some convenient hollow rises the smoke of a nomad camp.

For beautiful as it is in its majestic loneliness, this country is not one where men are tempted to seek an abiding dwelling. In the spring, when the fresh grass clothes the bottom of the valleys, in the summer, when the cool winds sweep the plain, they are content to pitch their tents here; but with the first nip of autumn cold they strike camp, and are off to warmer levels, leaving the high snow-carpeted regions empty of all inhabitants but the wild goats and the eagles. To-day, perhaps, the gloomiest depth of a narrow gorge, which looks as though from the time of its creation no living thing had disturbed its solitude, is strewn with black tents, flocks of horses and camels crop the grass by the edge of the stream, the air is full of the barking of dogs and the cries of women and children; but to-morrow no sign of life remains—the nomads have moved onward, silence has spread itself like a mantle from mountain to mountain, and who can tell what sound will next strike against their walls?

The sight fills you at first with a delightful sense of irresponsibility. Go where you will, the rocks will retain no impress of your footsteps; dwell where you please, the mountains are your only witnesses, and they gaze with equal indifference on your presence and on your absence. But the fitfulness of human habitation among them, the absence of any effort to civilize them, to make them shelter man and minister to his wants, gives them an air of stubborn hopeless sterility, very imposing, very repelling. Gradually the loneliness will strike into your heart with a feeling almost akin to horror. We are not accustomed to finding ourselves face to face with nature. Even the most trivial evidences of the lordship of man afford a certain sense of protection—the little path leading you along the easiest slope, the green bench selecting for you the best view, the wooden finger-post with 'Zum Wasserfall' written up upon it in large letters telling you what other men have thought worth seeing. Other men have been there before—they have smoothed out the way for you—you will find them waiting at the end, and ready to provide you with shelter and with food.... But here there is nothing—nothing but vast and pathless loneliness, silent and desolate.

For the nomads can no more give you a sense of companionship than the wild goats; they are equally unconscious of the desolation which surrounds them. All day long the men lie before the low doors of their tents lazily watching the grazing herds; towards evening, perhaps, they will stroll along the banks of the river with a bent stick for fishing-rod, dropping a skilful line into the pools where lie the guileless trout of those waters. Meantime the women sit weaving the coarse black roofs which shelter them, or twisting the yellow reeds into matting for walls, working so deftly that in an incredibly short time a new dwelling has grown under their fingers. In the clear sunlight the encampment looks sordid enough; night, which with sudden fingers sweeps away the sun, revealing the great depths of heaven and the patined stars, reveals also the mysterious picturesqueness of camp-life. The red light of the fires flickers between the tents; the crouching figures of men and women preparing the evening meal seem to be whispering incantations into the hot ashes. They rise, dim and gigantic, with faces gleaming in the uncertain starlight; they flit like demons backwards and forwards between the glowing rays of the fires and the darkness beyond. You find yourself transplanted into a circle of the Inferno, of which the shaggy dogs that leap out barking to meet you are no less vigilant guardians than Cerberus himself A woman with neck and breast uncovered catches you by the sleeve, and offers to sell you a bowl of clotted cream or a vociferous fowl; her dark eyes glisten through the dusk as she tosses the matted hair from her forehead; perhaps if you stayed to eat at the bidding of this Queen of Dis you would be kept eternally a prisoner in her mournful domains. With the dawn the mystery vanishes—the place through which you passed last night is only a dull little camp, after all—and this woman clothed in dirty rags, is it possible that she can be the regal figure of last night?

But daylight will not bring you into closer fellowship with the nomads; even if you fall into speech with one of them, there are few common topics on which you can converse. He will question you as to your nationality. Are you a Russian? he inquires, naming probably the only European nation he knows. You try to explain that you are English, and come from far across the seas; and he listens attentively, though you know that your words throw no light on his boundless ignorance. Presently he will change the conversation to matters more within his understanding. What news is there of the Shah? Is he coming this summer to his camp at Siah Palas? Has the sickness struck him? The sickness! So with terrible significance he speaks of the cholera which is ravaging the country, and goes on to tell you that he and his family are flying before it. 'From over there they have come,' pointing to distant valleys. 'The sickness fell on them; eleven of their men died, and since they moved down here two more have been carried off.' A sudden picture of grim fear flashes up before you at his simple words. With what shapeless terror does the plague fill the feeble little camp! With what awful solemnity must the dead body invest the frail, small hut! What wailing cries take the place of all the cheerful sounds, and with what hurried dread is the corpse committed to an unremembered grave! Many processions of villages on the march pass you now, flying from the terror of death—a little herd of goats and horses driven by the children, a few camels carrying the rolled-up bundles of reed-dwellings, on the top of which sit the men of the family, women on foot following in the rear, a convoy of yellow dogs barking round the tiny caravan into whose narrow compass all the worldly goods of so many human beings are compressed.

But the nomads are not the only inhabitants of the valley; there are one or two more luxurious encampments. An Indian prince has pitched his camp there, and greets you as you pass, fishing-rod in hand, with an amicable 'Good-evenin', sar.' His scanty English, confined though it be to this one salutation, somewhat destroys the local colour of the scene. Noble Persians fly in the summer to this cool retreat, pitching elaborate tents of French or Indian manufacture by the edge of the river, stabling thirty or forty horses in the open air, riding through the country attended by an army of servants whom they carry with them even on their fishing expeditions, and who follow close behind their masters when they venture waist-high into the stream in the enthusiasm of sport. The grandees bring their women with them; white canvas walls enclose the tents of wives and daughters whom captivity holds even in these free solitudes, and their negro attendants are familiar figures by the river sallows, where their shrouded forms hover sadly. They understand camp life, these Persian noblemen; they are as much at home among the mountains as in their gardens and palaces. Their lavish magnificence is not out of keeping with the splendours of nature.... But you are only playing at nomads, after all, and when the moonlight strikes the wall of rock behind your camp, you try to banish from your mind the recollection of painted theatre scenes which it involuntarily suggests, and which makes it all seem so unreal to you.

Unreal—unreal! 'The fancy cannot cheat so well as she is famed to do.' In vain you try to imagine yourself akin to these tented races, in vain you watch and imitate their comings and goings; the whole life is too strange, too far away. It is half vision and half nightmare; nor have you any place among dwellers in tents. Like the empty bottles and greased papers with which a troop of Bank-holiday Philistines sullies the purity of a purple moor, your presence is a blot on the wild surroundings, a hint of desecration.

Return to your cities, to your smooth paths and ordered lives; these are not of your kindred. The irretrievable centuries lie between, and the stream of civilization has carried you away from the eternal loneliness of the mountains.

THREE NOBLE LADIES

WHEN THE SHAH TAKES A GIRL into his andarun it is said to be a matter for universal rejoicing among her family, not so much because of the honour he has done her, as because her relatives look to using her influence as a means of gaining for themselves many an envied favour. For aught I know to the contrary, the girl, too, may think herself a fortunate creature, and the important position of the one man she may possibly govern may console her for the monotony of her kingdom; but however delightful as a place of abode the royal andarun may be, in one respect it must fall short of the delights of the kingdom of heaven—there cannot fail to be endless talk of marrying and giving in marriage within its walls. The number of the Shah's wives is great, and he is blessed with a proportionately large family; it must therefore be difficult to find a sufficiency of high-born suitors with whom to match his daughters. Moreover, there may be a trace of reluctance in the attitude of the suitors themselves, for the privilege of being the Shah's son-in-law is not without its disadvantages. If the nobleman selected happen to be wealthy, the Shah will make their close relationship an excuse for demanding from him large gifts; if at any subsequent period he should have a mind to take another wife, the etiquette of the Court will stand in his way; and still worse, if he be already married, he will find himself obliged to seek a divorce from his wife that he may obey the Shah's command. The negotiations preceding the match must be complicated in the extreme, and great must be the excitement in the andarun before they are concluded.

With one such household we were acquainted. The husband, whose title may be translated as the Assayer of Provinces, was a charming person, who had spent much of his youth (much also of his fortune) in Paris. He was a cultivated man and an enthusiast for sports; a lover of dogs, which for most Persians are unclean animals, and a devotee to the art of fishing. He had suffered not a little at the hands of his royal father-in-law, and had withdrawn in indignation from all public life, spending his days in hunting and shooting, in improving his breed of horses, and in looking after his estates. His residence abroad had made him more liberal-minded than most of his countrymen. He paid special attention to the education of his daughters, refused to allow them to be married before they had reached a reasonable age, and gave them such freedom as was consistent with their rank. They were two in number; we made their acquaintance, and that of the Princess their mother, one afternoon in Tehran.

Now, an afternoon call in Persia is not to be lightly regarded; it is a matter of much ceremony, and it lasts two hours. When we arrived at the house where the three ladies lived, we were conducted through a couple of courts and a long passage, and shown into a room whose windows opened into a vine-wreathed veranda. There was nothing Oriental in its aspect: a modern French carpet, with a pattern of big red roses on a white ground, covered the floor; photographs and looking-glasses hung upon the walls; the mantelpiece was adorned with elaborate vases under glass shades, and on some brackets stood plaster casts of statues. We might have imagined ourselves in a French château, but for the appearance of the châtelaine.

The Princess was a woman of middle age, very fat and very dark; her black eyebrows met together across her forehead; on her lips there was more than the suspicion of a moustache; the lower part of her face was heavy, and its outline lost itself in her neck. The indoor costume of a Persian lady is not becoming. She wears very full skirts, reaching barely to the knee, and standing out round her like those of a ballet-dancer; her legs are clothed in white cotton stockings, and on her feet are satin slippers. These details are partly concealed by an outer robe, unfastened in front, which the wearer clutches awkwardly over her bulging skirts, and which opens as she walks, revealing a length of white cotton ankles. In the case of the Princess this garment was of pale blue brocade. She wore her hair loose, and a white muslin veil was bound low upon her forehead, falling down over the hair behind. She was too civilized a woman to have recourse to the cosmetics which are customary in the East; the orange-stain of henna was absent from her finger-nails, and in the course of conversation she expressed much disapproval of the habit of painting the eyes, and great astonishment when we informed her that such barbarism was not unknown even in England.

It must not be imagined that the conversation was of an animated nature. In spite of all our efforts and of those of the French lady who acted as interpreter, it languished woefully from time to time. Our hostess could speak some French, but she was too shy to exhibit this accomplishment, and not all the persuasions of her companion could induce her to venture upon more than an occasional word. She received our remarks with a nervous giggle, turning aside her head and burying her face in her pocket-handkerchief, while the Frenchwoman replied for her, 'Her Royal Highness thinks so and so.' When the interview had lasted for about half an hour, cups of tea were brought in and set on a round table in the midst of us; shortly afterwards the two daughters entered, sweeping over the floor towards us in green and pink satin garments, and taking their places at the table. The younger girl was about sixteen, an attractive and demure little person, whose muslin veil encircled a very round and childish face; the other was two years older, dark, like her mother, though her complexion was of a more transparent olive, and in her curly hair there were lights which were almost brown. Her lips were, perhaps, a little too thick, though they were charmingly curved, and her eyes were big and brown and almond-shaped, with long lashes and a limpid, pathetic expression—just such an expression as you see in the trustful eyes of a dog when he pushes his nose into your hand in token of friendship. Nor did her confiding air belie her: she took our hands in her little brown ones and told us shyly about her studies, her Arabic, and her music, and the French newspapers over which she puzzled her pretty head, speaking in a very low, sweet voice, casting down her black eyelashes when we questioned her, and answering in her soft guttural speech: 'Baleh Khanum'—'Yes, madam,' or with a little laugh and a slow, surprised 'Naghai-ai-r!' when she wished to negative some proposition which was out of the range of her small experience.

During the course of the next hour we were regaled on lemon ices, and after we had eaten them it was proposed that we should be taken into the garden. So we wandered out hand-in-hand, stopping to speak to an unfriendly monkey who was chained under the oleanders, and who turned a deaf ear to all our blandishments. In the garden there was a large pond, on the banks of which lay a canoe—an inconvenient vessel, one would imagine, for ladies attired in stiff and voluminous petticoats! Tents were pitched on the lawn, for our hostesses were on the eve of departure for their summer camp in the mountains, and had been examining the condition of their future lodgings. The garden, with its tents and its water, was like some fantastic opera stage, and the women, in their strange bright garments, the masqueraders, who would begin to dance a pas de trois before us as soon as the orchestra should strike up. But the play was unaccountably delayed, and while we sat under the trees servants appeared bringing coffee, a signal that the appointed time of our visit had come to an end, and that we might be permitted to take our leave. The girls accompanied us into the outer court, and watched us through the half-open doors till we drove away, wishing, perhaps, that they too might drive out into the world with such unfettered liberty, or perhaps wondering at our unveiled shamelessness.

We went to see the three ladies again when we were in the mountains. Their camp was pitched about a mile lower down the river than ours, on a grassy plateau, from which they had a magnificent view down the long bare valley and across mountains crowned by the white peak of Demavend. No sooner had we forded the river in front of our tents than a storm of wind and rain and hail broke upon us, but we continued dauntlessly on our way, for the day of our visit had been fixed some time before, and it was almost pleasant after the summer's drought to feel the rain beating on our faces. When we reached the Persian camp we dismounted before a canvas wall which surrounded the women's tents, a curtain was drawn aside for us by a negro slave, and we were taken into a large tent, where the Princess was sitting on a rolled-up bed for sofa. We greeted her with chattering teeth and sat down on some wooden chairs round her, carrying on a laboured conversation in the French tongue, while our wet clothes grew ever colder upon us. We remembered the steaming cups of tea of our former visit, and prayed that they might speedily make their appearance, but, alas! on this occasion they were omitted, and lemon ices alone were offered to us. It is not to be denied that lemon ices have their merit on a hot summer afternoon, but the Persian's one idea of hospitality is to give you lemon ices—lemon ices in hail storms, lemon ices when you are drenched with rain, lemon ices when a biting wind is blowing through the tent door—it was more than the best regulated constitution could stand. We politely refused them.

An important event had taken place in the household during the last two months: a marriage had been arranged between the eldest daughter and a young Persian nobleman, whose wealth and influence matched themselves satisfactorily with her rank. He, too, was spending the summer in the mountains; his camp lay a little beyond ours, and we were therefore able to observe the daily visits which took place between him and his future father-in-law, when they rode, attended by troops of mounted servants, backwards and forwards along the stony bridle-path on the opposite bank. Doubtless great discussions of the approaching marriage and of the art of fly-fishing took place in those August days. We stood in the centre of this Oriental romance, and felt as though we were lending a friendly hand to the negotiations. Certainly, if good wishes could help them, we did much for the young couple.

The Assayer of Provinces spent most of his time trout-fishing. He used to make us presents of gaudy flies manufactured by his negro slave (himself a most successful fisherman), and we found that these attracted the trout of the Lar considerably more than our March browns and palmers. The eldest daughter shared her father's taste. When she and her sister joined us in her mother's tent that thundery afternoon, we fell into a lively discussion of the joys and the disappointments of the sport, comparing the number of fish we had killed and the size of our largest victim. The Persian girls had never gone far afield—they contented themselves with the pools and streams near their tents—but that they should fish at all spoke volumes for their energy. To throw a well-considered fly is a difficult art at best, but to throw it when you are enveloped from head to foot in sweeping robes must be well-nigh impossible.

This second visit passed more cheerfully than the first. The fresh mountain wind had blown away the mists of ceremony, there was no interpreter between us, and we had a common interest on which to exchange our opinions. That is the secret of agreeable conversation. It is not originality which charms; even wit ceases in the end to provoke a smile. The true pleasure is to recount your own doings to your fellow-man, and if by a lucky chance you find that he has been doing precisely the same thing, and is therefore able to listen and reply with understanding, no further bond is needed for perfect friendship. Unfortunately, this tie was lacking between us and the monkey, who was also in villeggiatura by the banks of the Lar, and in consequence we got no further forward with him than before. Our presence seemed, indeed, to exasperate him more than ever. He spent the time of our visit making spiteful dashes at us, in the vain hope that the gods might in the end reward his perseverance and lengthen his chain sufficiently to allow him to bite us but once before we left.

But the gods have eternity in their hand, and we must hasten, for our time is short; long ere the monkey's prayer was answered we had risen and taken leave of the three ladies. We left them gazing after us from behind their canvas walls. Their prisoned existence seemed to us a poor mockery of life as we cantered homewards up the damp valley, the mountain air sending a cheerful warmth through our veins. The thunderstorm was past, the sun dropped in clear splendour behind the mountains, leaving a red glory to linger on the slopes of Demavend, and bearing the fulness of his light to the Western world—to our own world.

THE TREASURE OF THE KING

CHOLERA HAD SWEPT THROUGH TEHRAN since last we set foot in its streets, and they seemed to us more than usually empty and deserted in the vacant sunshine that autumn morning. But the Ark, the centre and heart of the city, was crowded still. Though many of the tiny shops had been closed by owners whose own account had been closed summarily and for ever, the people who remained went about their business as cheerfully as before, gesticulated over their bargains, drew their long robes round them in dignified disgust as we passed, and sipped their glasses of tea with unimpaired enjoyment. The motley crowd was yet further diversified by the scarlet coats of the Shah's farrashes, the many-coloured garments and fantastic headgear of the servants of the palace, and the ragged uniforms of the soldiers who hung about the street corners—an army scarcely more efficient, I should imagine, than its rudely-painted counterpart upon the walls. These rough drawings satisfy the eye and tickle the artistic taste of the King of Kings. He is not difficult to please. Take a wooden soldier for model (carefully omitting his little green stand), magnify him to the size of life, put the brightest colours into his uniform and his cheeks, and you will be furnished with a design which is considered worthy of decorating not only the principal gateways of Tehran, but all the streets leading to the palace.

In Eastern life there are no modulations. As the day leaps suddenly into night with no warning time of twilight, so, to adapt the words of Omar the Tent-Maker, between the house of riches and of penury there is but a breath. We were accustomed to strange contrasts, yet it scarcely seemed possible that this gaudy squalor could be the setting of the priceless Treasure of the King. The stories we had heard of its magnificence must be due to the fecundity of the Oriental imagination. The East is the birthplace of wonders; there the oft-repeated tale gains a semblance of veracity which ends by deceiving not only credulous listeners, but him also who invented it. We should have received it like other fairy stories, sedulously nursing the happy faith which flies all opportunity of proving itself a superstition.

632

We stopped before an unregal gateway, and were conducted with much ceremony into the palace. The palace was expectedly beautiful, after all. Crossing a narrow strip of garden, we found ourselves in its first court—a court of Government offices, we were told, though the word office conveys no impression of the graceful buildings, from the upper galleries of which curtains floated, fanning the air within to coolness. Our guides led us beneath more archways, through high, dark passages, and out into the sunlight of the central garden. It was built round with an irregular architecture. Here the walls were radiant with faïence, there a row of arches stood back from the sun-beaten pavement— delicate arches which might have graced some quiet Italian cloister—beyond them stood the much-decorated building where the Shah sits in state on the day of the New Year, and which was separated from the garden in front only by the folds of an immense curtain, which, when it is drawn back, discloses the carved throne set in a grove of columns. Still further on we reached the palace itself, two-storied and many-windowed, from whose steps stretched the dainty pleasure-grounds, with their paved paths and smooth, fresh grass, their trees and gay flower-beds, between which fountains leapt joyfully, and streams meandered over their blue-tiled beds. They were bounded by the impenetrable and forbidding walls of the andarun.

Mounting the marble staircase, we found ourselves before a big wooden doorway, the seal on whose lock had to be broken ere it could be thrown open to us. We stood expectantly while the Minister, our guide, fumbled at the lock. Perhaps he was really some powerful efreet whom, after long captivity, our presence had released from the bottle in which Solomon had prisoned him. We were half prepared for the fairy treasures he had come forth to reveal to us.

Prepared? Ah, no, indeed! For what sober mortal could be prepared for the sight that burst upon us?

A great vaulted room with polished floor and painted walls, with deep alcoves through whose long narrow windows splashes of sunlight fell—and everywhere jewels! Jewels on all the shelves of the alcoves, thick-sown jewels on the carpets which hung against the walls, jewels coruscating from the throne at the top of the room, jewels in glass cases down the middle, flashing and sparkling in the sunlight, gleaming through dark corners, irradiating the whole hall with their scintillant brightness. With dazzled eyes we turned to one of the alcoves, and fell to examining the contents of the shelves. Here were swords sheathed in rubies; here were wands and sceptres set from end to end with spirals of turquoise and sapphire; diamond crowns, worthy to throw a halo of light round the head of an emperor; breastplates and epaulets, from whose encrusted emeralds the spear of the enemy would glance aside, shields whose bewildering splendour would blind his eyes. Here were rings and bracelets and marvellous necklaces, stars and orders and undreamt-of ornaments, and, as though the ingenuity of the goldsmiths had been exhausted before they had reached the end of their task, rows and rows of tiny glasses filled with unset stones—diamonds, sapphires, topazes, amethysts—the nectar of an Olympian god frozen in the cup. Under glass cases lay the diadems of former kings, high, closed helmets ablaze with precious stones; masses of unstrung pearls; costly and hideous toys, remarkable only for their extraordinary value—a globe, for instance, supported by an unbroken column of diamonds, whose seas were made of great flat emeralds, and whose continents of rubies and sapphires; and scattered with lavish profusion among the cases, festoons of turquoise rings and broad gold pieces which have long passed out of use, but in which regal currency, it is related, an immense subsidy was once paid to the Czar. On the other side of the room the treasures were scarcely less valuable and even more beautiful, for cupboard after cupboard was filled with delicate enamel, bowls and flagons, and the stems of kalyans all decorated with exquisite patterns in the soft blended colours whose freshness is immortal. These lay far beyond the criticism of captious connoisseurs, who would not have failed to point out to us that the jewels were tinselbacked, after all, and that most of the enormous rose diamonds were flawed and discoloured.

Taking an honoured place among the jewels and the enamel there were some objects which raised a ripple of laughter in the midst of our admiration. The royal owner of the treasure-house, doubtless anxious to show that he considered no less the well-being of the inward than the adornment of the outward man, had filled some of his upper shelves with little bottles of——what could those silvery globules be? we wondered, gazing curiously upwards. Not white enough for pearls, and yet they could not be, though they looked suspiciously like—yes, they were!—they were pills! Yes, indeed they were pills—quack remedies which the Shah had collected on his Western travels, had brought home and placed among his treasures. After this discovery we were not surprised to find bottles of cheap scents and of tooth-powder among the diamonds, nor to observe that some of the priceless cloisonné bowls were filled with toothbrushes; nor was it even a disillusion when we were solemnly told that the wooden cases placed at intervals down the room, each on its small table, were only musical boxes, which it is the delight of the Protector of the Universe to set a-playing all at once when he comes to inspect his treasures. Heaven knows by what fortunate combination of circumstances he finds those treasures still intact, for they seemed to us very insufficiently guarded, unless the tutelary efreet watches over them. There is, indeed, a locked door, of which the King and the Prime Minister alone possess a key; but a thief is not usually deterred by the necessity of forcing a lock, and if a scrupulous sense of honour prevented him from breaking the royal seal, with a little ingenuity he might contrive an entrance through one of the many windows, or even through the roof, were he of an enterprising disposition; and once within, nothing but the glass cupboard-doors would separate him from riches so vast that he might carry away a fortune without fear of detection.

We were next taken to see the world-famous Peacock Throne, which is reported to have been brought from Delhi by a conquering Shah. A scarlet carpet sewn with pearls covered its floor, on which the King sits cross-legged in Eastern fashion, surrounded by a blaze of enamel and precious stones. A year ago this throne had been the centre of a hideous story of cupidity and palace intrigue—who can tell what forgotten crimes have invested its jewels with their cruel, tempting glitter? We passed on into a long succession of charming rooms with low, painted ceilings, walls covered with a mosaic of looking-glass, and windows facing the smiling garden. Execrable copies of the very worst European pictures adorned them; one was hung with framed photographs—groups taken on the Shah's travels, in which his shabby figure occupied a prominent place, and all wearing that inane vacuity of expression which is characteristic of photographic groups, whether they be of royal personages or of charity school children. Here and there a wonderful carpet lent its soft glow to the rooms, but for the most part the floors were covered with coarse productions of European looms—those flaming roses, and vulgar, staring patterns, which exercise an unfortunate attraction over the debased Oriental taste of to-day.

With a feeling of hopeless bewilderment, we at length quitted the palace where we had been dazzled by inconceivable wealth and moved to ridicule by childish folly. Wealth and childishness seemed to us equally absurd as we rode home in silence along the dusty roads.

Before our garden gates there dwelt a holy dervish. He, too, was a king—in the realms of poverty—and over the narrow strip of wilderness he bore undisputed sway. He levied pious alms for taxes, his palace was a roof of boughs, four bare poles were the columns of his throne, and the stones of the desert his crown jewels. His days were spent in a manner which differed little from that of his neighbour and brother sovereign. The whole long summer through he had collected the surrounding stones and piled them into regular heaps. His futile religious exercise was almost completed, he was putting the finishing touches to a work which winter winds and snows would as surely destroy as the winter of ill-fortune will scatter the other's wealth. But the dervish was untroubled by thoughts of the future; he laboured to the glory of God in his own strange fashion, and though his jewels needed neither locks nor seals nor men-at-arms to guard them, their human interest lent them a value unattained by the Treasure of the King.

SHEIKH HASSAN

I USED TO WATCH HIM COMING round the curve of the avenue, his quick step somewhat impeded by the long robes he wore, holding his cloak round him with one hand, his head bent down, and his eyes fixed on the ground. As he drew near he would glance up, wrinkling his eyebrows in the effort to pierce the darkness of the great tent under which I was sitting. The plane-trees grew straight and tall on each side of the road; overhead their branches touched one another, arching together and roofing it with leaves fresh and green, as only plane-leaves can be all through the hot summer. Between the broad leaves fell tiny circles of sunshine, which flickered on his white turban and on the linen vest about his throat as he came. He looked like a very part of his surroundings, for his woollen cloak was of a faded gray, the colour of Persian dust, and his under-robe was as green as the plane-leaves, and his turban gleamed like the sunshine; but his face was his own, brown and keen, with dark eyes, deep-set under the well-marked brows, and his thin brown hands were his own too, and instinct with character. If you had only seen the hands, you might fairly have hazarded a guess at the sort of man he was, for they were thoughtful hands, delicate and nervous, with thin wrists, on which the veins stood out, and long fingers, rather blunt at the tips; and the skin, which was a shade darker than the sun can tan, would have told you he was an Oriental. I believe he came up from Tehran on a mule on the days appointed for our lesson, and reached our village at some incredibly early hour in order to avoid the morning heat; but the six-mile journey must have been disagreeable at best, for the roads were ankle-deep in dust, and the sun blazed fiercely almost as soon as it was above the horizon. The cool shaded garden and the dark tent, with an overflowing tank in the midst of it, and a stream of fresh water running over the blue tiles in front, was a welcome refuge after the close heat of the town and the dusty ride.

'Peace be with you!' he would say with a low bow. 'Is the health of your Excellency good?' 'Thanks be to God, it is very good,' I would answer. 'Thanks be to God!' he would return piously, with another bow. Then he would draw up a chair and sit down in front of me, folding his hands under his wide sleeves, crossing his white-stockinged feet, and gazing round him with his bright quick eyes. He made use of no gestures while he talked, his hands remained folded and his feet crossed, and only his keen, restless glances and the sudden movements round the corners of his lips told when he was interested. He never laughed, though he smiled often, and his smile was enigmatical, and betokened not so much amusement as indulgent surprise at the curious views of Europeans. I often wondered what thoughts there were, lurking in his brain, that brought that odd curl round the corners of his mouth, but I never arrived at any certainty as to what was passing through his mind, except that sometimes he was indubitably bored, and was longing that the lesson were over, and that he might be permitted to go and sleep through the hot hours. On these occasions he expressed his feelings by yawns, very long and very frequent—it certainly was hot! I was often sleepy too, for I had been up and out riding quite as early as he.

Our intercourse was somewhat restricted by the fact that we had no satisfactory medium through which to convey our thoughts to each other. He spoke French—such French as is to be acquired at Tehran! and I—ah well! I fear my Persian never carried me very far. Nevertheless, we were accustomed to embark recklessly on the widest discussions. He was a bit of a reformer was Sheikh Hassan; indeed, he had got himself into trouble with the Government on more occasions than one by a too open expression of his opinions, and the modern equivalent for the bow-string had perhaps flicked nearer his shoulders than he quite liked; a free-thinker too, and a sceptic to the tips of his brown fingers. A quatrain of Omar Khayyam's would plunge us into the deepest waters of philosophic uncertainty, with not even the poor raft of a common tongue to float us over, from whence we would emerge, gasping and coughing, with a mutual respect for each other's linguistic efforts, but small knowledge of what they were intended to convey. Pity that such a gulf lay between us, though I dare say it came to much the same in the end, for, as Hafiz has remarked in another metaphor, 'To no man's wisdom those grim gates stand open, or will ever stand!'

The Sheikh had an unlimited contempt for Persian politics. 'It is all rotten!' he would say—'rotten! rotten! What would you have?' (with a lifting of the eyebrows). 'We are all corrupt, and the Shah is our lord. You would have to begin by sweeping away everything that exists.' But his disbelief in the efficacy of European civilization was equally profound, and his pessimism struck me as being further sighted than the careless optimism of those who seek to pile one edifice upon another, a Western upon an Eastern world, and never pause to consider whether, if it stands at all, the newer will only stand by crushing the older out of all existence. Sheikh Hassan, at all events, was not very hopeful. 'Triste pays!'

he would say at the end of such a conversation. 'Ah, triste pays!' and though I knew he had his own views as to the possible future of his country, he was far too discreet a man to confide them to frivolous ears.

Concerning his private life I never liked to question him, though I would have given much to know what his own household was like. He had a wife and children down in Tehran. The good lady looked with unmitigated disapproval upon infidel foreigners, and her husband was obliged to conceal from her how many hours of the day he spent with them. Judging by an anecdote I heard of her during the cholera time, she must have ruled the establishment with a hand of iron. The Sheikh, being much concerned over the risk his family was running in the plague-stricken town, had taken the precaution of laying in six bottles of brandy, the most convenient medicine he could obtain, and hearing at the same time that a good bargain offered itself in the matter of olive-oil, he, as a prudent man, had also purchased six bottles of oil and stored them too in his cellar. But on one luckless morning, when his wife happened to enter there, she espied the brandy lurking in a dark corner. Being a lady of marked religious convictions, she at once called to mind the words which the Prophet has pronounced against alcoholic liquors, and without more ado opened the bottles and poured out their contents upon the floor. On further search her eldest daughter discovered the oil in another corner. Having observed the conduct of her mother, she concluded that she could not do better than imitate it, and accordingly the innocent liquid also streamed out over the cellar floor, libation to an unheeding god. The unfortunate Sheikh found on his return that his foresight and his skill in bargaining had alike been brought to nought by the misguided fervour of the female members of his family. To none of them did the cholera prove fatal, though the wife suffered from a slight attack; but Sheikh Hassan spent anxious weeks until the danger was over. 'For thirty-seven nights,' he told me pathetically, 'I lay awake and considered what could be done for my children's safety.' With true Oriental fatalism, he did not seem to have taken any active steps in the matter, and at the end of his thirty-seven nights of thought he was as far from any conclusion as ever. Happily, the extreme fury of the cholera had by that time abated.

The mysteries of Eastern education were no less unfathomable to me. Though he was a man of middle age, Sheikh Hassan had only recently quitted the Madrasseh, a sort of religious college, of which he had been a student. There he had been taught Arabic, geography and astronomy; he had read some philosophy too, for he was acquainted, in a translation, with the works of Aristotle, and he had learnt much concerning the doctrines of religion, which study had profited him little, since he heartily disbelieved in them all. He wrote a beautiful hand, and was very proud of the accomplishment. He would sharpen a reed pen and sit for half an hour writing out quatrains with elaborate care and the most exquisite flourishes, and he evinced such delight over the performance that I could not find it in my heart to interrupt him. He was very anxious that I, too, should acquire this art. I asked him how much time I should have to devote to it. 'Well,' he replied reflectively, 'if for five or six years you were to spend three hours of every day in writing, you might at the end be tolerably proficient.' He did not appear to consider that the achievement was in any way incommensurate with the labour he proposed that I should undergo, and I abstained from all criticism that might hurt his feelings. I wrote him long letters in Persian characters. 'Duste azize man,' they began—'Dear friend of mine.' He would read them during the lesson, and answer them in terms of the most elaborate politeness—'My slave was honoured by my commands,' and so forth; and my crude and uncertain lines became abhorrent to me when I saw him covering his paper with a lovely decorative design of courteous phrases. He was not without dreams of literary fame. One day he laid before me a vast scheme of collaboration: we were to compile a Persian grammar together; it would be such a grammar as the world had never seen (in which statement I fancy he came nearer the truth than he well knew!); he would write the Persian, and I should translate it into French. I agreed to all, being well assured that we should never bring our courage to the sticking point. We never did—the grammar of the Persian language is still to be written.

The one really useful piece of knowledge he possessed had not been taught him at the Madrasseh—he had picked up French by himself, he told me. I could have wished that he had picked it up in a somewhat less fragmentary condition, for his translations did but little to define the meaning of the original Persian. We read some of Hafiz together, but the Sheikh had only one gender at his disposal, and the poet's impassioned descriptions of his mistresses were always conveyed to me in the masculine. 'Boucles de cheveux' seemed at first a strange beauty in a lady, but custom, the leveller of sensations, brought me to accept without question even this Gorgon-like adornment. The Sheikh took a particular pleasure in the more philosophical verses. Over these I would puzzle for long hours, and in all innocence arrive at the conclusion that some anecdote of angels, or what not, appertaining, doubtless, to the Mohammedan religion, was related in them. The Sheikh would then proceed to annotate them in halting French, pointing out that a pun was contained in every rhyme, that half the words bore at the smallest computation two or three different meanings, and that therefore the lines might be done into several English versions, each with an entirely different significance, and each an equally truthful rendering of the Persian. At this my brain would begin to whirl. I was unable to deal with the confusion of difficulties among which the Sheikh Hassan was delightedly battling; it was enough for me if I could seize some of the beauty which lay like a sheath about the poems, the delicate, exquisite rhythm of the love-songs, the recurrent music of the rhyme, and the noble swing of the refrains. I received and admired their proud stoicism as it stood written: women were women and wine red wine for me, the cup-bearer was the person whose advent was most eagerly to be greeted; roses and nightingales, soft winds and blooming gardens, were all part of a beautiful imaginative world, and fit setting for a poet's dreams.

But this was wilful stupidity. If I had listened to the wisdom of Sheikh Hassan, I should have realized that we were in the midst of sublime abstractions, and that the most rigid morality and the strictest abstinence were inculcated by those glowing lines. In practice, however, I had the poets themselves on my side; the days of Hafiz sped merrily, if tradition has not belied him, and the last prayer of the Tent-Maker was that he might be buried in a rose-garden, where the scented petals would fall softly upon his head and remind him after his death of the joys he had loved on earth.

Were these things also abstractions?

For lighter reading we had the Shah's Diary, a work whose childlike simplicity admitted of but one interpretation. I never got through very much of it, but I read far enough to see that the royal author did not consider himself bound by the ordinary rules of literary production. He was accustomed in particular to pass from one subject to another with a rapidity which was almost breathless. The book began somewhat after this fashion: 'In the month of Sha'ban, God looked with extraordinary clemency upon the world; the crops stood high in the fields, and plenty was showered upon his fortunate people by the hand of Allah. I mounted my horse and proceeded to the review....'

At last the day of parting came; with much regret I told the Sheikh I was about to leave Persia. 'Ah, well,' he replied, 'I'm very glad you are going. Healthy people should not stay here; it's not the place for healthy people.' We fell to making many plans for a meeting in England, a country he had often expressed a desire to visit, I as often assuring him that an enthusiastic reception should be his. I fear these also will never be brought to fulfilment, but if he should ever come, it would be interesting to find what peculiarities in us and in our ways would attract the notice of his bright, observant eyes. I confess it would give me no small pleasure to meet him walking along Piccadilly in his white turban and flowing robes, and to hear once more the familiar salutation: 'The health of your Excellency is good? Thanks be to God!'

A PERSIAN HOST

W<small>E WERE RIDING</small>. We had left Tehran the previous evening in a storm of rain and hail, which had covered the mountain-tops with their first sheet of winter snow. We had slept at a tiny post-house, sixteen miles from the city gates—an unquiet lodging it had proved, for travellers came clattering in all through the early hours of the night, and towards morning the post dashed past, changing horses and speeding forward on its way to Tabriz. The beauty of the night compensated in a measure for wakeful hours; the moon—our last Persian moon—shone out of a clear heaven, its beams glittered on the fields of freshly-fallen snow far away on the mountains, and touched with mysterious light the sleeping forms of Persian travellers stretched in rows on the ground in the veranda of the post-house. We were up before the autumn dawn, and started on our road just as the sun shot over the mountains. Ali Akbar led the way—Ali Akbar, the swiftest rider on the road to Resht, he with the surest judgment as to the merits of a post-horse, the richest store of curses for delinquent post-boys, the deftest hand in the confection of a pillau, the brightest twinkle of humour darting from under shaggy brows—friend, counsellor, protector, and incidentally our servant. He had wound a scarlet turban round his head, he made it a practice not to wash on a journey, and his usually shaven beard had begun to assume alarming proportions before we reached the Caspian. His saddle-bags and his huge pockets bulged with miscellaneous objects—a cake, a pot of marmalade, a crossed Foreign Office bag, a saucepan, a pair of embroidered slippers which he had produced in the rain and presented to us a mile or two from Tehran, with a view, I imagine, to establishing the friendliest relations between us. We followed; in the rear came two baggage-horses carrying our scanty luggage, and driven by a mounted post-boy, generally deficient. These three, the baggage-horses and the post-boy, were our weak point—a veritable heel of Achilles; they represented to us 'black Care,' which is said to follow behind every horseman. What a genius those horses had for tumbling over stones! What a limitless capacity for sleep was possessed by those post-boys! How easily could the Gordian knot have been unloosed if its ropes had shared in the smallest measure that feeling for simplicity which animated those which bound our baggage!

The first stage that morning was pleasant enough; then came the heat and the dust with it. Sunshine—sunshine! tedious, changeless, monotonous! Not that discreet English sunshine which varies its charm with clouds, with rainbows, with golden mist, as an attractive woman varies her dress and the fashion of her hair—'ever afresh and ever anew,' as the Persian poet has it—here the sun has long ceased trying to please so venerable a world. The long straight road lay ahead; the desolate plain stretched southwards, mile after uninterrupted mile; the bare mountain barrier shut out the north; and for sound, the thud of our horses' feet as we rode, the heavy, tired thud of cantering feet, and the gasp of the indrawn breath, for as the stage drew to its close the weary beasts cantered on more and more sullenly through dust and heat.

At last far away, where the road dipped and turned, stood the longed-for clump of trees, clustered round the great caravanserai and the glittering blue-tiled dome of the little mosque. This was not an ordinary post-house, but a stately pile, four-square, built by some pious person in the reign of Shah Abbas, and the mosque was the shrine and tomb of a saint, a descendant of the Prophet. Behind it lay a huge mound of earth, a solid watch-tower heaped up in turbulent times. From its summit the anxious inhabitants of the caravanserai could see far and wide over the plain, and shut their gates betimes before an on-coming foe.... War has passed away round the shrine of the Yengi Imam, yet it is not security, but indifference, that is high-priest under the blue dome, and though the shadows of the old watchers gazing from the earth-heap would see no sturdy band of Persian robbers rushing down on them from the mountains, they may tremble some day before a white-capped Russian army, marching resistless along the dusty road.

The clatter of the post-horses over the stones broke the noon-day silence. Yengi Imam looked very desolate and uncared-for as we rode through the mud-heaps before its hospitable doors. Half the blue tiles had fallen from the dome, unnoticed and unreplaced, meagre poplars shivered in the sun, stunted pomegranate bushes carpeted the ground with yellow autumn leaves, their heavy dark-red fruit a poor exchange for the spring glory of crimson flower. Persians love pomegranates, and on a journey prize them above all other fruits, and even to the foreigner their pink fleshy pips, thick set like jewels, are not without charm. But it is mainly the charm of the imagination and of memories of Arabian Night stories in which disguised princes ate preserved pomegranate seeds, and found them delicious. Do not attempt to follow their example, for when you have tasted the essence of steel knife with which a pomegranate is flavoured, you will lose all confidence in the judgment of princes, even in disguise. And it is a pity to destroy illusions. But for beauty give me pomegranate bushes in the spring, with dark, dark green leaves and glowing flowers, thick and pulpy like a fruit, and winged with delicate petals, red as flame.

Through the low door of the caravanserai we entered the cool vault of the stable which ran all round the garden court. A lordly stable it was, lighted by shafts of sunshine falling from the glass balls with which each tiny dome was studded—vault beyond vault, dusty light and shadowy darkness following each other in endless succession till the eye lost itself in the flickering sunshine of a corner dome. Here stood weary post-horses, sore-backed and broken-kneed; here lay piles of sweet-smelling hay and heaped-up store of grain. At one corner was a minute bazaar, where we could buy thin flaps of bread if we had a mind to eat flour mixed in equal parts with sand and fashioned into the semblance of brown paper; raisins also, and dried figs, bunches of black grapes, sweet and good, and tiny glasses of weak hot tea, much sugared, which pale amber-coloured beverage is more comforting to the traveller on burning Persian roads than the choicest of the forbidden juices of the grape. The great stable enclosed a square plot of garden—orchard, rather, for it was all planted with fruit-trees—which, after the manner of Eastern gardens, was elaborately watered by a network of rivulets flowing into a large central tank, roofed over to protect it from the sun. He did his work well, the pious founder of the caravanserai, but he thought more of the comfort of beasts than of men. One or two bare rooms opening into the garden, a few windowless, airless holes in the inner wall, a row of dark niches above the mangers—that was what he judged to be good enough for such as he; the high, cool domes were for weary horses and tinkling caravans of mules.

We were well content to stretch ourselves in the mules' palace with a heap of their hay for bed. Thirty-two miles of road lay behind us, thirty-two miles in front—an hour's rest at mid-day did not come amiss.

As we lay we saw in the garden a Persian, dressed in the pleated frock-coat and the tall brimless astrakhan hat which are the customary clothes of a gentleman. Round his hat was wrapped a red scarf to protect it from the dust of travelling; the rest of his attire was as spotless as though dust were an unknown quantity to him. He watched us attentively for some minutes, and then beckoned us to his room opposite. We rose, still stiff from the saddle, and walked slowly round the court. He greeted us with the calm dignity of bearing that sits as easily on the Oriental as his flowing robes. Manner and robe would be alike impossible in the busy breathless life of the West, where, if you pause for a moment even to gird your loins, half your competitors have passed you before you look up. The Oriental holds aloof, nor are the folds of his garments disturbed by any unseemly activity. He stands and waits the end; his day is past.

There is much virtue in immobility if you take the attitude like a philosopher, yet to fade away gracefully is a difficult task for men or nations—the mortal coil is apt to entangle departing feet and compromise the dignity of the exit.

'Salaam uleikum!' said our new friend—'Peace be with you!' and, taking us by the hand, he led us into his room, which was furnished with a mat and a couple of wooden bedsteads. On one of these he made us sit, and set out before us on a sheet of bread a roast chicken, an onion, some salt, a round ball of cheese, and some bunches of grapes; then, seeing that we hesitated as to the proper mode of attacking the chicken, he took it in his fingers, delicately pulled apart wings, legs and breast, and motioned us again to eat. He himself was provided with another, to which he at once turned his attention, and thus encouraged, we also fell to. Never did roast chicken taste so delicious! I judge from other experiences that he was probably tough; he was, alas! small, but, for all that, we look back to him with gratitude as having furnished the most excellent luncheon we ever ate. In ten minutes his bones, the onion, and a pile of grape skins were the only traces left of our repast, and we got up feeling that two more stages on tired post-horses were as nothing in the length of a September afternoon.

We said farewell to our unknown host, stammering broken phrases of polite Persian. 'Out of his great kindness we had eaten an excellent breakfast; the clemency of his nobility was excessive; we hoped that he might carry himself safely to Tehran, and that God would be with him.' But though our Persian was poor, gratitude shone from our faces. He bowed and smiled, and assured us that our servant was honoured by our having partaken of his chicken, but he would not shake hands with us because he had not yet washed his fingers, which, as he had used them as knives and forks both for himself and for us, were somewhat sticky.

So we mounted our horses, and rode away towards our crude Western world, and he mounted his and passed eastward into his own cities. Who he is, and what his calling, we shall never know—nor would we. He remains to us a type, a charming memory, of the hospitality, the courtesy, of the East. Whether he be prince or soldier or simple traveller, God be with him! Khuda hafez— God be his Protector!

A STAGE AND A HALF

'AS MUSIC AT THE CLOSE IS SWEETEST LAST,' says Shakespeare. We cling regretfully to the close, but the beginning is what is worth having—the beginning, with all its freshness, all its enthusiasm, all its unexpected charm, Hercules for strength, Atalanta for speed, Gabriel for fair promise. Say what you will, the end is sad. Do not linger over the possibilities to which (all unfulfilled) it sets a term, but remember the glorious energy which spurred you forward at first, and which lies ready to spring forth anew.

When we were riding post, we had occasion to study the philosophy of beginnings. 'Ah, if we could only have gone on like that!' we sighed when, finding ourselves at the end of a weary day only thirty miles removed from our starting-point, we remembered the sixty flashing miles that had passed beneath our horses' feet the day before. The long road to the sea seemed an eternity of space not to be measured by our creeping, tired steps. Yet with the dawn our views had changed. However weary, however stiff you may be when in the dusk you reach the last half-farsakh of the last half-stage, the night's rest will send you on with as keen a pleasure as if you had been lying idle for a week before. The clear day, the low cool sun, the delicious cup of tea flavoured with the morning, the fresh horse, the long straight road in front of you—away! away! A careful jog, a steady canter, who does not feel that he could put a girdle round the earth at the beginning of the first stage? And then the sun creeps higher, shadows and mists vanish, the dust dances in the hot road, your horse jogs on more slowly— how large the world is, how long four farsakhs! And beyond them lie another four, and yet another; better not to think of them—Inshallah, we shall sleep somewhere to-night!

Through all these vicissitudes of mood we were destined to pass on the second day of our riding. The sun was already high when we reached the city which lay at the end of our first stage, and passed under its tiled gateway into a wide street, a good half of whose mud houses were so ruinous that they can have fulfilled none of the objects for which houses are erected. As we penetrated further into the city, the streets narrowed and became more populous—thronged, indeed, with long-robed men and shrouded women, buying and selling, eating fruit, chatting before the barbers' shops, scowling at us as they moved out of our way. We rode down a wide tree-planted avenue, bordered by houses gaily patterned with coloured bricks, past the hammam where the coarse blue towels were stretched in line against the wall to dry, past the beautiful gateway of the Prince's palace, under whose arch of blue and green and yellow faïence we could see the cool garden set with trees and fountains. Presently we were lying in a little alcove under the archway of a tiny tumble-down post-house, vainly demanding fresh horses. Stray Persians sat round in the street, eating grapes and bread, drinking water out of earthen pitchers, watching us with grave, observant faces, quite unmoved by our expostulations and entreaties. There was a mythical mail in front of us which had swept away an incredible number of horses—seventeen or eighteen, the owner of the post-house assured us; indeed, he had none left. We had heard of this mail before—all our difficulties and discomforts were in turn attributed to it. No one could explain what made the bags so unusually heavy, but I fancy such an obstacle is not infrequent on Persian roads. At any rate, the postmaster was not mistaken when he foretold our disbelief of his statements.

At length we were off again at the very hottest moment of the day. At the town gate the baggage-horses turned homesick, and refused to move any further from their ruined stalls; in despair we left Ali Akbar to deal with them and rode on alone. On and on slowly through endless vineyards, past an evil-smelling cemetery where the cholera had dug many rows of fresh graves; on and on till the signs of habitation that encircled the town had disappeared, and we found ourselves in a bare, flat, desolate land. A keen wind rose, and blew from the mountains wreaths of storm-cloud which eclipsed the sun, and still there was no sign of the little town which marked the next half-stage. We looked round us in complete ignorance of our whereabouts, and espied in the distance a village walled round with crenellated mud, in front of whose gates some children were playing. Riding up to them, we inquired whether we were on the right road. Alas! we were not. Unperceived, it had trended away northwards, and heaven knows to what dim cities we were diligently riding! So we turned northwards, directed by a barely defined track through the wilderness.

Just as the storm began to break we met a blue-robed pedlar with a merry face, who assured us that we had only half an hour further to go. He, too, was making for Agababa; he had seen our nobilities lying in the post-house at Kasvin—yes, it was only a thin farsakh more now. At length, through wind and rain, we reached the vineyards and gardens of Agababa, and passed under the shelter of its big gate-house. Here we determined to lodge, deciding that on such a night further progress was out of the question. We turned to the people who were gathered under the archway, talking and smoking kalyans, and asked them whose house this was. It belonged to Hadgi Abdullah, the Shah's farrash. We intimated that we wished to lodge here—where was Hadgi Abdullah? He was in Tehran, they replied, but offered no suggestion as to the course we should pursue. We left them to smoke their kalyans in peace, and, taking the matter into our own hands, we dismounted, ordered tea and fire, and climbed the steep staircase that led into the balakhaneh. It consisted of three rooms: a large one in the centre, with a long low window of tiny panes set in delicate but broken woodwork, and opening on to a balcony; on either side two smaller rooms, one of which was furnished with a carpet and inhabited by two Persians, while the other was completely empty except for some walnuts spread out to dry in one corner. Here we established ourselves, to the entire unconcern of the Persians, who treated the sudden invasion of their quarters by two damp and muddy travellers as a matter not worthy of remark. Half an hour later Ali Akbar joined us. We interrogated him as to the probable fate of the baggage. He replied, laying his head upon his clasped hands, that the horses were most likely asleep, which seemed so reasonable an explanation from what we had seen of their disposition that it did not occur to us to inquire why no steps had been taken to have them awakened. But the valiant Ali Akbar was not to be daunted by the unpromising aspect of things. Borrowing a brazier, he began to cook us a meal, a process which we impeded by vainly attempting to dry our clothes over the glowing charcoal, for our own fire smoked so abominably that it was not possible to stay in the same room with it, and in self-defence we were obliged to let it go out. It was a glad moment when our supper was set before us, for since the cake and tea of the early morning we had eaten nothing, and the chicken, the eggs, and the boiled rice (which had been filched from the evening meal of some inhabitant of Agababa) looked most appetising. Moreover, the same obliging person—he was a ragged muleteer, whose feet had been developed to an abnormal size either by much travelling or by the necessity of kicking his mules to drive them onward—had provided us with a large dish of delicious grapes.

The servants of the palace are not, unfortunately, numbered among our friends, and it seems improbable that we shall ever make the acquaintance of Hadgi Abdullah, but we remain eternally his debtors for the night's shelter his roof afforded us. His hospitality went no further than a roof—we spread our own cloaks for beds, our own saddles served us for pillows, and for our dinner we went a-foraging—but though his floor was hard, though his fire smoked, though his walnuts stained our elbows when we leant on them, though the bond of bread and salt is not between us, still that unknown pilgrim was a benefactor to us pilgrims of a more distant land than holy Mecca. How does he spend his days, I wonder, in that Agababa gate-house of his, where for one stormy autumn night we rested? Does he fly to his peaceful, mud-walled village from time to time when the service of the palace has become hateful to him? Does he sit at sunset on the balcony overlooking his laden fruit-trees, smoking a kalyan, and watching the village folk as they drive home the flocks of goats under his archway—as they stagger through it loaded with wood bundles? And when the sun has set behind the sweeping curve of mountains, what peaceful thoughts of the future, of restful age, of projects accomplished, come to him with the sweet smell of wood fires and of savoury evening meals?

Ah, simple pleasures, so familiar in a land so far removed! Not in great towns, not in palaces, had we felt the tie of humanity which binds East and West, but in that distant roadside village, lying on the floor of the Shah's farrash, we claimed kinship with the toilers of an alien soil. For one night we, too, were taking our share in their lives, with one flash of insight the common link of joy and sorrow was revealed to us—to us of a different civilization and a different world.

So we lay and listened to the wind, and slept a little; but a waterproof is not the best of mattresses, and our beds were passing hard. Moreover, the good pilgrim had neglected the sweeping of his floors for some time previously, and there were many strange inhabitants of the dust besides ourselves. In the middle of the night news was brought that our baggage had passed us and gone on to the end of the stage; an hour or two later we rose and followed it, with the keen storm-wind still blowing in our faces. A late waning moon shone brilliantly over our heads, and behind the house of Hadgi Abdullah lay the first white streaks of the day.

A BRIDLE-PATH

WHEN WE SAW THE POST-HOUSE OF MAZREH, where we rejoined our missing baggage, we rejoiced that not under its roof, but under the hospitable roof of Hadgi Abdullah, we had taken shelter through the windy night. It was more than common dirty: the mud floors were littered with eggshells and with nameless horrors, which spoke of a yet more uneasy lodging than that of the previous evening. It stood some little way from the village of Mazreh, which lay on the lower slopes of the mountains, and beyond it our path turned upwards and was lost in the mist that hid the top of the pass.

In a year or two this bridle-path across the hills will have joined the long roll of things that were; no more will travellers entering Persia climb the narrow track which was the Shah's highway; no more will their horses' feet slip among pools of mud and ring out against the solid rock; the Russian Government have taken the highroad to Tehran into their hands, and are even now constructing a broad carriage-way from the Caspian to join the Persian road at Kasvin. But the bridle-path, which had served generations of travellers before us, had a charm of its own, too—the charm of all such tracks which lead you, as it were, through the very heart of a country as uncivilized as when the waters first retreated from the hill-tops. A foot on either side of you the mountains rise in steep slopes and walls of rock, or fall into deep valleys and precipices. The narrow way seems to vanish into wilderness as you pass over it, but when you look ahead you see it running between Scylla and Charybdis, clear and secure.

The post-horses of Mazreh matched the accommodation it offered. We spent an hour listening to Ali Akbar condemning the father of the postmaster to eternal fire, and at the end found ourselves provided with sorry beasts, the merest apologies for horses, to which animals they bore but a blurred resemblance. A few hundred yards up the hill, however, we met a man driving some laden beasts, and cajoled him so successfully that he consented to exchange baggage-horses with us, whereupon we went gaily onwards, leaving him to his fate. In all probability he is still toiling towards Kasvin, with his own goods and the skins of our horses upon his shoulders.

Our path breasted the hillside boldly, and we were presently buried in a cold mist, which seemed to us all the colder after the dust and heat of the last two days in the plain. The mist lay thickly round us at the top of the pass; we pushed on at a good pace until we caught sight of a solitary tree which grows just above the hollow, where, somewhat sheltered from winter winds and snows, lies the village of Kharzan, a tiny citadel girt round with mud walls. Only half the stage was done, but we stopped at the caravanserai to breathe our horses after the long pull.

The gateway of a caravanserai is lined within on either side by a narrow platform, on which you can sit enjoying rest and shelter, smoking your kalyan and drinking your cup of tea. At Kharzan a wood-fire was burning merrily upon the bricks of one of these platforms; various Persians who were cooking and warming themselves over it made room for us when they saw us approaching, and gave us steaming glasses of tea, which we drank gratefully. There was a good deal of coming and going through the archway: laden donkeys and men wrapped in coats of sheepskin over their blue cotton garments appeared suddenly out of the mist and disappeared as suddenly into it; the crackling sticks sent bright jets of firelight flickering over wild faces and the rough coats of men and animals.

Leaving Kharzan, we turned down the pass between mountain sides bare now after the summer's scorching, but where in the spring we had seen masses of scarlet tulips in full bloom. The lower slopes in spring and autumn are covered with the black tent roofs and yellow reed walls of nomads driving their flocks from lowland pastures up to mountain-tops when the snow melts, and back to the valleys when the winter returns. But the season was well advanced when we passed, and the mountains were already deserted.

As we descended, slipping down steep places and stumbling over shelving rocks, the sun began to play that old game of his by which he loves to prove himself superior to wind and storms. We loosened and finally stripped off waterproofs, coats and cloaks, and fastened them behind our saddles; but nothing would satisfy him—he blazed more and more furiously upon the narrow, open path and upon the walls of rock and upon us, until we regretted the chill mist which still lay upon the Kharzan Pass behind us. At length we reached the bottom of the hill and crossed a stony river-bed, overgrown with tamarisk bushes, at the further side of which stood a post-house, with some fig-trees in front of it. The post-house of Paichenar is not an agreeable resting-place. It is a 'murmurous haunt of flies' even on late autumn afternoons: flies are served up with your roast chicken, flies flavour your pillau, flies swim in your wine, they buzz through the tiny rooms, and creep up the whitewashed walls, regardless of the caustic references to their presence which are written up in all languages by travellers whose patience they have tried beyond endurance. Flies are so illiterate; not one of those many tongues appeals to them.

We ate our mid-day meal in their company, and set off again towards Menjil, following the course of the river—a long stage through burning afternoon sun and the cold chill of dusk, before we reached the Valley of the White River. Menjil has an unhonoured name among Persian villages; it is reputed to be the windiest place in all the Iranian Empire. Morning, noon and night the wind whistles round its mud-houses—that they stand at all must be due only to the constant interposition of Providence in their favour, and even so they stand in a most dilapidated condition. It blows the branches of the olive-trees all to one side, making them look like stunted people breasting the elements, with their hair streaming out behind them; it lashes the swift current of the Sefid Rud until its waters seem to turn backward and beat in waves against the lower side of the bridge piers. By the time we caught sight of the twinkling lights of the village, we felt as though we had traversed every climate the world has to offer, beginning with the frigid zone in the morning, and crossing the equator in the afternoon, to say nothing of a long evening ride through the second circle of the Inferno and the 'Bufera infernal che mai non resta.'

It was dark as we plashed through the stream which runs between the low houses as you approach Menjil, almost too dark to avoid trampling on the children who were playing along it, and the homeward plodding goats which stepped suddenly out of the night. We knew our way, however, and turned up from the water (not without a curious sensation of surprise at our own intimacy with that small and remote Persian village) into the main street, where the post-house and the telegraph-office stand. The post-house, where we had slept before on our outward journey, was comfortable enough as post-houses go—it was even furnished with some luxury, for it boasted a wooden table and some chairs. There was a Russian family in possession when we arrived, father, mother, and a troop of children, who were making their way down to Enzeli; but they did not discommode us, as they appeared to be content with one room, and resigned the other two to us. They had left Tehran some days before us, but had travelled very slowly, the women and children going at a foot-pace, either slung in covered panniers across the backs of mules, or carried in a box-shaped litter, which, as it crossed hills and valleys, jolted them first on to their feet and then on to their heads in a manner which must have been disturbing to the most equable of temperaments.

We went to the telegraph-office, where we sent and received messages, profiting by the opportunity of being once more in touch with the world of men. The telegraph clerk was an agreeable Persian, who entertained us with cups of tea while we delivered our messages. His office was hung round with curtains, behind which we could hear much chattering and laughing going forward in subdued tones, and between the folds we caught from time to time glimpses of the inquisitive, laughing faces of his womenkind. What with the tea and the laughing women and the conversation of the clerk, the sending of telegrams becomes an amusing pastime in Menjil.

Next day, when we descended into the street, we found our servant engaged in heaping objurgations upon the head of a European who was sullenly watching the saddling of our fresh mounts. We inquired as to the cause of difference between them, and were informed by Ali Akbar that the man—he was an Austrian merchant—had attempted to suborn the people of the post-house, and to purloin our horses while we slept.

'And when you would have reached the parakhod (steamer),' said Ali Akbar, 'Allah alone knows, for there are no other horses fit for your Excellencies to ride!'

The stables must have been passing ill supplied, for our Excellencies had not been accustomed to show a very critical spirit in the matter of horseflesh.

'Does he also wish to reach the parakhod?' we asked in sympathetic tones.

'He is the son of a dog!' Ali Akbar replied laconically, upon which we felt that the subject might fitly be brought to a close.

The Austrian did not appear on the steamer, from which we argued that he had not succeeded in securing post-horses, after having been baffled in his attempt to ride away on ours.

We rode all the morning along a rocky little path, following the downward course of the Sefid Rud. The river where the bridge of Menjil crosses it presents an aspect extraordinarily wild and beautiful. The deep, bare valley below the bridge opens out above it into wider ground, bordered by rugged mountains, and narrowing away upwards to where heavy clouds rest upon blue peaks. The wind races through the desolate valley, and finding nothing to resist it but the bridge, whose strong piers stand firmly in the foaming water, it wreaks its vengeance on the storm-clouds, which it collects and scatters at its pleasure, tearing them apart and driving them headlong in front of it, till the valley is flecked with their dark shadows, and with glints of brilliant sunshine between.

We rode through the tiny village of Rudbar, embedded in a wealth of olives, down by the water's edge. Some inhabitant, with a tasteful eye for decoration, had covered the houses with a continuous pattern of red lines and rows of rudely-drawn hands, with the five fingers outstretched, intended to represent the Prophet's hands, and to serve not only as an adornment, but as a charm against evil. We had great difficulty in persuading our baggage-mules to pass by open doors and narrow side streets without satisfying their curiosity as to what lay beyond; they developed all the qualities of ardent explorers, and whenever we were not looking, turned into courtyards and disappeared up slums, Ali Akbar pursuing them with cries and curses, waving his Turkoman lash over his head and dealing blows to right and left. The villagers were gathering in the olive harvest; we shouted to them to throw us some of the fruit, but on experience we came to the conclusion that olives au naturel are not good eating.

Towards mid-day we reached the post-house of Rustemabad, standing half-way up the hillside, and from the platform in front of it we looked across the valley and saw the opposite mountains covered with—forest! Damp, delicious, green forest, trees and trees set thickly over the uneven ground—such a joy to the eye as never was after long months of arid desert, dust and stones! We lunched and changed horses (with some regret, for wisdom had been justified in Ali Akbar, and the Menjil mounts had proved to be excellent, full of spirit and go—a delightful break in the usual monotony of stumbling three-legged brutes), and then we hurried down into the fertile province of Ghilan. Oh, the pleasant forest track all overgrown with moss and maidenhair fern, and the damp, sweet smell of leaves, and the shafts of tempered sunlight between interlacing boughs, and the sound of splashing water! We lifted our eyes only to see the wide Sefid Rud foaming down over his stones, and beyond him more woods, and more and more.

At the bottom of the hill we rested for a few minutes, and drank tea at the caravanserai of the Imam Zadeh Hashem. Here our friendly bridle-path came to an end, and a muddy road lay before us, leading to Resht and the Caspian. We set off with renewed spirits, and traversed the four or five miles between us and our last post-house at a gentle canter. On either side of the road rose a wall of densest vegetation, with here and there a marshy pond covered with rushes, and here and there a tiny clearing, from which the encroaching jungle was with difficulty held back. A luxuriant plant-life covered every stem and every log of wood with moss and ferns, the very huts were half hidden under gourds, which climbed up the walls and laid their fruit and broad leaves across the thatching of the roofs. Charming indeed are the wooden cottages of Ghilan, standing with their backs set into the forest, which has been forced to yield them a foot or two of ground, with verandas supported by columns of rudely-dressed tree-trunks, and with the glow of the firelight (as when we passed that evening) shining through doors and chinks and crevices, while the pleasant smell of wood-smoke rises round them; but the damp climate has set its seal of disease upon the people—they are white and hollow-cheeked, the dark eyes look enormous in the thin faces and glow with the light of fever. They die young, these people, whose meagre bodies are consumed by malaria and shaken by agues.

The post-house of Kudum stands in a small clearing, with ponds round it, the abode of frogs. We found it tolerably comfortable; the swallows which had been nesting in the rafters when we had passed in the spring, and which had disturbed us in the very early hours of the morning with twitterings and flutterings, had fled now, taking their fledged little ones with them; but one of the rooms which was offered to us seemed to belong to someone more important than swallows. His bed was all prepared in it, and on a table were strewn his writing materials, reed pens and inkpots and sheets of paper. We inquired whose was the room of which we had thus summarily entered into possession. 'Oh,' said the people of the post-house indifferently, 'it is only the room of the Naïb.' Now, Naïb means deputy, it is also the title of the Shah's third son, the Commander-in-Chief—who this particular Naïb was we failed to ascertain, but we had visions of a trampling ragged army surrounding our beds late at night, while the Naïb-es-Sultan, with the portrait of the Shah blazing in diamonds upon his breast, commanded us in indignant tones to quit the rooms which had been prepared for him, or of waking to find some humbler deputy seated at the table and writing busily with his reed pens complaints of our insolence to his Government. We were undisturbed, however, except by frogs, who croaked unsoothing lullabies in our ears, and by the bells of a caravan of camels which passed at dead of night—an endless train, with silent, ghostly steps, looming out like shadows through the mists, and passing like shadows into the mists again.

Next morning we woke to feel with relief that our ride was over; for the last time we saw our luggage strapped on to the backs of pack-horses, and mounting ourselves into a battered shay, we jolted down the road to the red roofs and the civilization of Resht.

TWO PALACES

MANY, MANY YEARS HAVE PASSED since the ingenious Shahrazad beguiled the sleepless hours of the Sultan Shahriyar with her deftly-woven stories, and still for us they are as entrancing, as delightful, as they were for him when they first flowed from her lips. Still those exciting volumes keep generations of English children on wakeful pillows, still they throw the first glamour of mystery and wonder over the unknown East. By the light of our earliest readings we look upon that other world as upon a fairy region full of wild and magical possibilities; imprisoned efreets and obedient djinns, luckless princesses and fortunate fishermen, fall into their appointed places as naturally as policemen and engine-drivers, female orators and members of the Stock Exchange with us; flying carpets await them instead of railway trains, and the one-eyed Kalender seeks a night's shelter as readily in the palace of the three beautiful ladies as he would hie him to the Crown Hotel at home. Yet though one may be prepared in theory for the unexpected, some feeling of bewilderment is excusable when one finds one's self actually in the midst of it, for even in these soberer days the East remembers enough of her former arts as to know that surprise lies at the root of all witchcraft. The supply of bottled magicians seems, indeed, to be exhausted, and the carpets have, for the most part, lost their migratory qualities—travellers must look nowadays to more commonplace modes of progression, but they will be hard put to it from time to time if they do not consent to resign themselves so far to the traditions of their childhood as to seek refuge under a palace roof. It may be that the modern dispensation is as yet incompletely understood, or perhaps civilization marches slowly along Persian roads—at any rate, you will search in vain for the welcoming sign which hangs in English cottage windows, and if the village of mud huts be but a little removed from the track beaten by the feet of post horses, not even the most comfortless lodging will offer itself to you. Fortunately palaces are many in this land where inns are few, and if the hospitality of a king will satisfy you, you may still be tolerably at ease. But luxury will not be yours. The palaces, too, have changed since the fairy-tale days; they are empty now, unfurnished, neglected, the rose-gardens have run wild, the plaster is dropping from the walls, and the Shah himself, when he visits them, is obliged to carry the necessaries of life with him. Take, therefore, your own chicken if you would dine, and your own bed if you have a mind to sleep, and send your servants before you to sweep out the dusty rooms.

It was to the palace of Afcheh, twenty miles to the north-east of Tehran, that we were riding one hot evening. Our road led us across a sun-scorched plain and over a pass, at the top of which we found ourselves looking down on to a long upland valley. A river ran through it, giving life to a belt of trees and cornfields, and on each side rose the bare mountains which are the Shah's favourite hunting grounds. Down on the river bank stood a tea-house with an inviting veranda, roofed over with green boughs, under which a group of Persians were sitting, listening with inattentive ears to an excited story-teller while he wove some tale of adventure in the sleepy warmth of the twilight. The veranda was screened from the road by clumps of oleanders, whose pink flowers made an exquisite Japanese setting to the cluster of blue-robed peasants. Beyond the tea-house the river was spanned by a bridge, the arches of which were so skilfully fitted into the opposite hill that a carriage—if ever carriage comes—driving down the steep and crooked path must almost inevitably fall headlong into the water below. Night fell as we made our way along the valley; the moon rose, turning the mountain-sides into gleaming sheets of light, filling the gorges with deepest, most mysterious shadow, and after an hour or two of foot-pace riding, we reached the village of Afcheh, our destination.

In the courtyard of the palace preparations for the night were already afoot. In one corner glowed a charcoal brazier, over which the cook was busily concocting a dinner, a table was spread in the middle, and at the further end, protected from the brilliant moonlight by the shadow of a wall, stood a row of camp-beds, for though numberless empty rooms were at our disposal, we had been warned that they were infested by insects, and had chosen the more prudent course of sleeping in the open air. Fortunately, the night was hot and fine, and the court was amply large enough to serve as kitchen, dining-room, and bedroom.

We retired, therefore, to rest, but an Eastern night is not meant for sleep. The animals of the village shared this conviction to the full. The horses, our near neighbours, moved to and fro, and tugged impatiently against their tethering ropes; a traveller riding down the stony streets was saluted by a mad outcry of dogs, who felt it incumbent upon them to keep up a fitful barking long after the sound of his footsteps had died away; and stealthy cats crept round our beds, and considered (not without envy) the softness of our blankets. It was too light for sleep. The moon flooded high heaven, and where the shadow of the wall ended, the intense brightness beat even through closed eyelids. The world was too lovely for sleep. It summoned you forth to watch and to wonder, to listen to the soft rush of mountain streams and the whispering of poplar leaves, to loiter through the vacant palace rooms where the moonbeams fell in patches from the latticed windows, to gaze down the terraced gardens bathed in the deceptive light which seemed to lay everything bare, and yet hid neglect and decay, to strain your eyes towards the shimmering mud roofs on which the villagers snatched a broken rest, turning over with a sigh and a muttered prayer or rising to seek a smoother bed; and yet away towards the dim ranges of mountains that stretched southwards. All the witchery of an Eastern night lay upon Afcheh—surely, if Shahrazad had but once conducted her lord to his open window, she might have spared her fertile imagination many an effort.

In the early hours of the morning the moon set, and darkness fell upon the world, for though the sky was alive with newly revealed stars, their rays were lost in the depths of heaven, and left night to reign on the earth. A little wind shivered through the poplars in the garden, warning us it was time to continue on our way if we would reach the top of the next pass before the heat of day fell upon us, and we drank an early cup of tea in the dark, and waited under the clump of trees that served for stables while the mules were loaded and the horses saddled.

As we waited, suddenly the daystar flashed up over the mountains, a brilliant herald summoning the world to wake. The people on the house-tops lifted their heads, and saw that the night was past. As we rode down the village street they were rising and rolling up their beds, and by the time we reached the valley they were breakfasting on their doorsteps, and the glory of the star had faded in the white dawn. In some meadows watered by the mountain streams a family of nomads had already struck camp, and were starting out on their day's journey; the narrow path over the hills—at best little more than a steep staircase of rock—was blocked by trains of mules laden with coal (black stone, explained our servants); the air rang with the cries of the mule-drivers, and as we rode upwards in cold shadow, the sun struck the mountain-tops, and turned them into solid gold. Day is swift-footed in the East, and man early abroad. Half-way up the pass we paused to look back at our last night's resting-place, but a shoulder of rock hid the palace, and we carried away with us only an impression of the mysterious beauty of its moonlit courts and gardens.

Autumn had come and had almost passed before we found ourselves a second time the guests of the Shah, and under his roof we spent our last two nights in Persia—the one willingly, the other unwillingly.

This other palace stood in the midst of a grove of orange-trees; the waters of the Caspian lapped round its walls, and before its balconies stretched the densely-wooded hills of Ghilan. The Russian steamer which was to take us to

Baku (for no Persian flag may float on the inland sea) touched at Enzeli early in
the morning to pick up passengers, and we had been advised to pass the night
there, so that we might be ready betimes. Accordingly, we had driven through
the damp flat country, a tangled mass of vegetation, that lies between Resht
and the sea, we had been rowed by half-naked sailors up the long canal and
across the lagoons, and in the evening we had reached the peninsula on which
the village stands. We were conducted at once to the palace, and, passing down
moss-grown garden paths, bordered by zinnias and some belated China roses,
we came upon a two-storied house, with deep verandas, and a red-tiled roof rising above the orange-trees. At the top of the staircase we found ourselves in an
endless succession of rooms, most of them quite tiny, with windows opening on
to the veranda—all unpeopled, all desolate. We chose our suite of apartments,
and proceeded to establish ourselves by setting up our beds and dragging a
wooden table into our dining-room. Next door to us Ali Akbar had organized
his kitchen, and we sat hungrily waiting while he roasted a chicken and heated
some boiled rice for our supper. Presently a shadow darkened our doorway, and
from the veranda there entered a Persian general dressed in shabby uniform,
with some inferior order on his breast, and the badge of the Lion and the Sun
fastened into his kolah. He bowed, and politely claimed acquaintance with us,
and after a moment of hesitation we recognised in him a fasting official who
had come to meet us on our arrival in Persia. The month of Ramazan was then
just over, and, in instant expectation of the appearance of the new moon, he had
neglected to make a good meal just before dawn. For some reason unknown to
us the moon had not been seen that night, and mid-day had found him still
compelled to fast. He had sat for full two hours in suffering silence while we
crossed the lagoons, but as we paused by the banks of the canal someone had
shouted to him that the moon had, in fact, been signalled, and in jubilant haste
he had jumped out of our boat, and had rushed away to enjoy his long-deferred
breakfast, from which he returned to us smiling, contented, and, I trust, replete.
This gentleman it was who now stood upon our palatial threshold; we brought
some wooden chairs from one of the numberless untenanted rooms, and invited him and the friend he had with him to enter. They sat down opposite
to us and folded their hands, and we sat down, too, and looked at them, and
wondered how they expected to be entertained. After an interval of silence we
ventured upon a few remarks touching the weather and similar topics, to which
they replied with a polite assent that did not seem to contain the promise of
many conversational possibilities.

We questioned them as to the condition of Enzeli—what the people did
there, how they lived, and, finally, how many inhabitants the peninsula contained. At this our military friend fell into deep thought, so prolonged that we

argued from it that he was about to give us the most recent and accurate statistics. At length he looked up with a satisfied air, as though he had succeeded in recalling the exact figures to mind, and replied, 'Kheli!'—'A great many!' No wonder the question had puzzled him. The matter-of-fact European mode of arriving at the size of a village had never before been presented to his Persian brain. How many people? Why, enough to catch fish for him, to make caviare, to sell in the bazaars and tend the orange-gardens—Kheli, therefore, a great many. The interview came to a close when our servant appeared with steaming dishes. Our two guests rose, and, saying they would leave us to the rest and refreshment we must surely need, bowed themselves out.

A curious savour of mingled East and West hung about the little palace. We slept in bare Persian rooms, the loaded orange boughs touched our verandas, and the soft air of the Eastern night rustled through the reed curtains that hung over them; but the brisk, fresh smell of the sea mixed itself with the heavy Oriental atmosphere, beyond the garden walls the moon shone on the broad Caspian, highway to many lands, and the silence of the night was broken by the whistling of steamers, as though Enzeli itself were one of those greater ports on busier seas to which we were speeding.

Speeding? Alas! we had forgotten that we were still in Persia. Next morning the steamer had not come in; we went down to the quay and questioned the officials as to the possible time of its arrival. They, however, shrugged their shoulders in mute surprise at our impatience. How could they know when it might please Allah to send the steamer? We strolled idly through the orange-grove and into a larger pleasure-ground, laid out with turf and empty flower-beds, as though some Elizabethan gardener had designed it—and had left it to be completed by Orientals. The pleasant melancholy of autumn lay upon it all, but of an autumn unlike those to which we were accustomed, for it had brought renewed freshness to the grass, scorched by the summer sun, and a second lease of life to the roses. It was almost with surprise that we noticed the masses of fruit hanging on the green orange boughs which 'never lose their leaves nor ever bid the spring adieu.' In the inner garden stood a tower into whose looking-glass rooms we climbed, and from its balconies searched the Caspian for some sign of our ship. But none was to be seen. In despair we sallied forth into the bazaar, and purchased fish and fowls, honey and dried figs, on which we made an excellent breakfast.

All day long we waited, and how the 'many' inhabitants of Enzeli contrive to pass the time remains a mystery to us. As a watering-place, it is not to be recommended, for the tideless sea leaves all the refuse of the village to rot in the sand; sleep may prove a resource to them, as it did to us, for the greater part of the afternoon and evening; but their lot in the narrow peninsula did not seem to us an enviable one as we hurried through the orange-grove in the dawn, summoned by the whistling of the long-expected boat.

So we steamed away across the Caspian, and the sleepy little place vanished behind the mists that hung over its lagoons and enveloped its guardian mountains—faded and faded from our eyes till the Shah's palace was no longer visible; faded and faded from our minds, and sank back into the mist of vague memories and fugitive sensations.

THE MONTH OF FASTING

O F THE POWERS WHICH COME by prayer and fasting, every Mohammedan should have a large share. It is impossible, of course, for the uninitiated to judge how far the inward grace tallies with the outward form, but he can at least bear witness that the forms of the Mohammedan religion are stricter, and that they appear to be more accurately obeyed, than those of the Christian. Religious observances call upon a man with a rougher and a louder voice, and at the same time they are more intimately connected with his everyday life—before the remembrance of the things which are not of this world can have faded from his mind, the muezzin summons him again to turn the eye of faith towards Mecca. The mosques of Constantinople wear a friendly and a homelike air which is absent from Western churches; even those frequented shrines in some small chapel of one of our cathedrals, hung about with pictures and votive offerings, and lighted with wax tapers by pious fingers, do not suggest a more constant devotion than is to be found in the stern and beautiful simplicity of Mohammedan places of worship. At every hour of the day you may see grave men lifting the heavy curtain which hangs across the doorway, and, with their shoes in their hand, treading softly over the carpeted floor, establishing themselves against one of the pillars which support a dome bright with coloured tiles, reading under their breath from the open Koran before them, meditating, perhaps, or praying, if they be of the poorer sort which meditates little, but, however poor they may be, their rags unabashed by glowing carpets and bright-hued tiles. As you pass, slipping over the floor in your large outer shoes, they will look up for a moment, and immediately return to devotions which are too serious to be disturbed by the presence of unbelievers.

To the stranger, religious ceremonies are often enough the one visible expression of a nation's life. In his churches you meet a man on familiar ground, for, prince or beggar, Western or Oriental, all have this in common—that they must pray. We had seen the beggars, we were also to see the Sultan on his way to mosque in Stamboul. He crosses the Golden Horn for this purpose only twice in the year, and even when these appointed times come round, he is so fearful of assassination that he does his best to back out of the disagreeable duty—small wonder, when you think of the examples he has behind him! When he finally decides to venture forth, no one knows until the last moment what route he will take; all the streets and bridges are lined with rows of soldiers, through which, when he comes, his carriage drives swiftly, followed by innumerable carriage-loads of the women of his harem, dressed in pink and blue and green satin, their faces very incompletely concealed by muslin veils—wrappings which are extremely becoming to dark-eyed beauties.

Every Friday Abdul Hamed goes to mid-day prayers in a small mosque near his palace of Yildiz Kiosk. We stood one sunny morning on the balconies of a house opposite the mosque waiting for his coming; the roads were again lined with soldiers—those tall lean Turks whose grim faces danger and hardship are powerless to disturb—the bands played waltz tunes, the muezzin appeared upon the platform of the minaret, and the Sultan's horses came prancing through the crowds of spectators. Just as he turned into the enclosure of the mosque, a man broke through the crowd and rushed, shouting and waving a roll of paper above his head, towards the carriage window. He pushed his way through two lines of soldiers, with such impetuous force he came, but the third turned him back, still struggling and waving his petition above his head. The waltz tunes drowned his cries, the Sultan disappeared into the mosque, and the petitioner, having been shoved and buffeted from hand to hand, having lost his paper and the better part of his garments in the scuffle, was sent homeward sadly and in rags. When the Sultan came out half an hour later and drove his white horses back through the serried lines of people, the soldiers were again standing with imperturbable faces, and peace had been restored to the Ottoman Empire.

In Constantinople religious observances go far to paralyze the conduct of mundane affairs. Three days of the week are dies non: on Friday the Turks are making holiday, Saturday is the Jewish Sabbath, and on Sunday the Christians do no work. Moreover, as far as the Mohammedans are concerned, there is one month of the year when all business is at a standstill. During the twenty-eight days of Ramazan they are ordered by the Prophet to fast from an hour before sunrise until sunset. The Prophet is not always obeyed; the richer classes rarely keep the fast; those whose position does not lift them entirely beyond the pressure of public opinion, soften the harshness of his command by sleeping during the day and carousing during the night—a part of the bazaars, for instance, is not opened until mid-day in Ramazan, at which hour sleepy merchants may be seen spreading out their wares upon the counters with a tribute of many yawns to last night's wakefulness; but the common people still keep to the letter of the law, and to all Ramazan is a good excuse for postponing any disagreeable business.

Such a fast as that enjoined by Mohammed would fill the most ascetic Christian of to-day with indignant horror. Not only is every true believer forbidden to eat during the prescribed hours, but nothing of any kind may pass his lips: he may drink nothing, he may not smoke. These rules, which are to be kept by all except travellers and the sick, fall heavily upon the poorer classes, who alone preserve them faithfully. Porters carrying immense loads up and down the steep streets of Pera and Galata, caïquejis rowing backwards and forwards under the hot sun across the Golden Horn and the swift current of the Bosphorus, owners of small shops standing in narrow, stuffy streets and surrounded by smells which would take the heart out of any man—all these not one drop of water, not one whiff of tobacco, refreshes or comforts during the weary hours of daylight. As the sun sinks lower behind the hill of Stamboul, the tables in front of the coffee-shops are set out with bottles of lemon-water and of syrups, and with rows and rows of water-pipes, and round them cluster groups of men, thirstily awaiting the end of the fast. The moments pass slowly, slowly—even the European grows athirst as he watches the faces about him—the sun still lingers on the edge of the horizon. On a sudden the watchman sees him take his plunge into another hemisphere, and the sunset-gun booms out over the town, shaking minarets and towers as the sound rushes from hill to hill, shaking the patient, silent people into life. At once the smoke of tobacco rises like an incense into the evening air, the narghilehs begin to gurgle merrily, the smoke of cigarettes floats over every group at the street corners, the very hamal pauses under his load as he passes down the hills and lights the little roll of tobacco which he carries all ready in the rags about his waist. Iced water and syrups come later; still later tongues will be loosened over the convivial evening meal; but for the moment what more can a man want than the elusive joy of tobacco-smoke?

From that hour until dawn time passes gaily in Constantinople, and especially in Stamboul, the Turkish quarter. The inhabitants are afoot, the mosques are crowded with worshippers, the coffee-shops are full of men eating, drinking, smoking, and listening to songs and to the tales of story-tellers. The whole city is bright with twinkling lamps; the carved platforms round the minarets, which are like the capitals of pillars supporting the great dome of the sky, are hung about with lights, and, slung on wires between them, sentences from the Koran blaze out in tiny lamps against the blackness of the night. As you look across the Golden Horn the slender towers of the minarets are lost in the darkness, rings of fire hang in mid-air over Stamboul, the word of God flames forth in high heaven, and is reflected back from the waters beneath. Towards morning the lamps fade and burn out, but at dusk the city again decks herself in her jewels, and casts a glittering reflection into her many waters.

On the twenty-fourth night the holy month reaches its culminating point. It is the Night of Predestination; God in heaven lays down His decrees for the coming year, and gives them to His angels to carry to the earth in due season. No good Mohammedan thinks of sleep; the streets are as bright as day, and from every mosque rise the prayers of thousands of worshippers. The great ceremony takes place in the mosque of St. Sophia. Under that vast dome, which the most ancient temples have been ransacked to adorn, until from Heliopolis, from Ephesus, from Athens, and from Baalbec, the dead gods have rendered up their treasures of porphyry and marble—under the dome which was the glory of Christendom is celebrated the festival of the Mohammedan faith. By daylight St. Sophia is still the Christian church, the place of memories. The splendours of Justinian linger in it; the marbles glow with soft colour as though they had caught and held the shadow of that angel's wings who was its architect; the doves which flit through the space of the dome are not less emblems of Christianity than the carved dove of stone over the doorway; the four great painted angels lift their mutilated faces in silent protest against the desecration of the church they guard. Only the bareness, the vast emptiness, which keeps the beauty of St. Sophia unspoilt by flaring altars and tawdry decorations, reminds you that it is a mosque in which you are standing, and the shields hung high up above the capitals, whose twisted golden letters proclaim the names of the Prophet and his companions. Long shafts of dusty sunlight counterchange the darkness, weaving peaceful patterns on the carpeted pavement which was once washed with the blood of fugitives from Turkish scimitars.

But on the Night of Power Christian memories are swept aside, and the stern God of Mohammed fills with His presence the noblest mosque in all the world. As you look down between the pillars of the vast gallery your eyes are blinded by a mist of light—thousands of lamps form a solid roof of brightness between you and the praying people on the floor of the mosque. Gradually the light breaks and disparts, and between the lamps you see the long lines of worshippers below—long, even lines, set all awry across the pavement that the people may turn their eyes not to the East, but further south, where the Ka'bah stands in holy Mecca. From the pulpit the words of the preacher echo round the mosque, and every time that he pronounces the name of God the people fall upon their faces with a great sound, which is like the sound of all nations falling prostrate before their Creator. For a moment the silence of adoration weighs upon the air, then they rise to their feet, and the preacher's voice rolls out again through arches and galleries and domes. 'God is the Light of Heaven and Earth!' say the golden letters overhead. 'He is the Light!' answer the thousands of lamps beneath. 'God Is the Light!' reads the preacher. 'God is the Light!' repeats a praying nation, and falls with a sound like thunder, prostrate before His name.

With the Night of Predestination Ramazan is drawing to a close. On the fifth succeeding evening all the Mohammedan world will be agog to catch the first glimpse of the crescent moon, whose rays announce the end of the fast. Woe to true believers if clouds hang over the horizon! The heaven-sent sign alone may set a term to the penance imposed by heavenly decree, and not until the pale herald has ushered in the month of Shawwal may men return to the common comforts of every day.

REQUIESCANT IN PACE

I T IS A FRIENDLY ORDERING OF THE WORLD that the episodes of each man's life come to him with so vivid a freshness that his own experience (which is nothing but the experience of all his fellows) might be unique in the history of the race. Providence is but an unskilful strategist, and having contrived one scheme to fill the three-score years and ten, she keeps a man to it, regardless of his disposition and of his desires. Sometimes, indeed, he forces her hand, wresting from her here a little more of power, there a sweeter burst of romance, making her blow a louder peal of warrior trumpets to herald him, and beat a longer roll of drums when he departs; sometimes he outwits her, dying before he has completed the task she set him, or disturbing her calculations by his obstinate vitality. But for the most part he is content to obey, and the familiar story takes its course until death abruptly closes the chapter, and sends the little universe of his deeds to roll unevenly down the centuries, balanced or unbalanced as he left it, with no hand more to modify its course. Familiar and yet never monotonous—though wherever you turn the air is full of memories everywhere the same, though the page of every historian repeats the same tale, though every poet sighs over it, and every human being on the earth lives it over again in his own person. A man will not complain of the want of originality; he is more likely to be cheered when he looks round him and sees his fellows suffering and rejoicing in like manner with himself, when he looks back and sees his predecessors absorbed by the same cares, urged forward by the same hopes. The experience of those who have passed before him along the well-trodden road will not hold him back or turn him aside; to each newcomer the way is new and still to be enjoyed—new and exciting the dangers and the difficulties, new the pleasant sensation of rest by the fountain at mid-day, new and terrible the hunger and the foot-soreness, new, with a grim unexpectedness, the forbidding aspect of that last caravanserai where he lays himself down to sleep out the eternal night. Yes, Death is newest of all and least considered in the counsels of men—Death, who comes silent-footed at all moments, who brushes us with his sleeve as he passes us by, who plucks us warningly by the cloak lest we should forget his presence—he, too, will surprise us at the last.

And if it were not so, small pleasure would be reaped from life. If the past were to stand for ever holding a mirror of the future before his eyes, many a man would refuse to venture forward—it is upon the unknown that he lays his trust—and if the universal presence of death had but once found a lodging in his mind, the whole world would seem to him to be but one vast graveyard, the cheerful fields but a covering for dead men's bones, and the works of their hands but as tombstones under which the dead hands lie.

Yet at times they are good and quiet company, the dead; they will not interrupt your musings, but when they speak, whether they be Jews or Turks or heathens, they will speak in a tongue all can understand. There are even countries where the moving, breathing people are less intelligible, dwell in a world further apart from you, than that silent population under the earth. You may watch the medley of folk hurrying into Stamboul across the Galata Bridge—that causeway between East and West—and the Dervishes washing their feet under the arches of a mosque, and the eager bartering in the bazaars, without one feeling of fellowship with these men and women who look at you askance as you go by; you may pass between long rows of crumbling, closely-latticed houses without venturing to hazard the widest solution of the life within—without even knowing whether there be life at all, so inhospitable they seem, so undomestic. But, once beyond the walls, you have done with distinctions of race. From the high towers of Yedi Kuli on the topmost hill down to the glittering waters of the Golden Horn are scattered countless graves—on the one hand, the triple line of Constantine's city wall, rent and torn, with cracking bastions and dismantled towers, in its hopeless decrepitude still presenting a noble front to all comers, save where the great breach tells of the inrush of the Turkish conquerors Judas-trees drop their purple flowers over the spot where Constantine Palæologus fell, red rose-bushes spring from the crevices, a timid army of lizards garrisons the useless forts. On the other hand, the great city of the dead—acre upon acre of closely-packed graves, regiment upon regiment of headstones, some with a rude turban carved atop, some (and these mark where women lie) unadorned, and all pushed awry by time and storms and the encroaching roots and stems of cypress-trees, all neglected, all desolate. Constantinople, the dying city, is girt about with graves—not more forgotten the names of those that rest there than her own glory on the lips of men. So they speak to you, these dead warriors, dead statesmen, dear dead women, and to the spiritual ear they speak in tragic tones.

The cypresses cast their shadows over this page of Turkish history, springing upwards in black and solemn luxuriance, nourished by dead bodies. The

cypress-trees are like mutes, who follow the funeral procession clothed in mourning garments, but with sleek and well-fed faces. They rear their dark heads into
the blue sky and beckon to their fellows in Scutari across the Bosphorus.

From the Scutari hill-top the eye is greeted by one of the most enchanting
prospects the world has to show—the blue waters of Marmora traversed by
greener Bosphorus currents, light mists resting along the foot of the hill-bound
coast of Asia, a group of islands floating on the surface of the water, the Gold-
en Horn glimmering away northwards, with the marble walls of the Seraglio
stretching a long white finger between it and the sea, Stamboul crowned with
minarets and domes. Flocks of gray birds flit aimlessly across the water—the
restless souls of women, says Turkish legend—the waves lap round the tower
of Leander, the light wind comes whispering down between the exquisite
Bosphorus shores, bringing the breath of Russian steppes to shake the plane-
leaves in Scutari streets. Constantinople the Magnificent gathers her rags round
her, throws over her shoulders her imperial robe of sunshine, and sits in peaceful
state with her kingdom of blue waters at her feet.... But all around you the dead
speak and command your ears. The ground is thick with the graves of men who
died fighting, who died of cold and hunger in bleak Crimea; under your feet are
great pits filled with unhonoured bones, and the white stones which strew the
grass cry aloud the story of struggle and fight into the quiet air. Beyond them
the dark canopy of cypresses shadows countless thousands of Turkish graves;
the surface of the ground is broken and heaped up as though the dead men had
not been content to sleep, but had turned and twisted in their shallow covering
of earth, knocking over their tombstones in the effort to force a way out of
the cold and the dark into the beautiful world a foot or two above their heads.
'Remember us—remember us!' they cried, as we passed under the cypress-trees.
But no one remembered them, and their forgotten sorrows could only send a
thrill of vague pity through our hearts.

Not less pitiful in their magnificence are the tombs of the Sultans in Stamboul itself. Here under marble domes, adorned with priceless tiles and hung
round with inlaid armour, you may sit upon the ground and tell sad stories of
the death of kings, and as you tell of poison and of dagger, of unfaithful wives
and treacherous sons, each splendid sarcophagus will serve as illustration to
your words. The graves of the dead Sultans are strewn with costly hangings,
and set about with railings of mother-of-pearl and precious woods; plumed
and jewelled turbans stand over their heads, their wives lie round them like a
bodyguard, but gold and pearl and precious stones all serve to blazon forth the
tragic histories of those men who lie buried in such mournful state.

With the glitter of this vain pomp before our eyes, we idled on a windy
Friday through one of the poorer quarters of the town. A bazaar was being held

in Kassim Pasha; women were bargaining over their weekly purchases of dried fruits and grains and household goods; copper pots lay in shining rows among the coarse crockery and the flowers and cheap luxuries of the poor; the sun shone upon veils and turbans and bronzed faces. It was the hour of mid-day prayer, the little mosque at the end of the street was full to overflowing, the people were kneeling all down the sunny outer steps, rising and falling, bowing their heads upon the stone at the name of God. We paused a moment, and went on round the mosque. In the shadow of a neglected corner behind it, supported on a couple of trestles, lay something swathed in coarse blue linen, with a stick planted into the ground at its head, and surmounted by a discoloured fez. It was the corpse of a man which lay waiting there until the mid-day prayers should be concluded, and his relations could find time for his burial. The wind flapped the corners of his blue cotton coverings to and fro, and shook the worn-out fez, but the dead man waited patiently upon the pleasure of the living—perhaps he knew that he was already forgotten and was content.

In Turkish cities the graves are scattered up and down and anywhere; the stone lattice-work of a saint's tomb breaks the line of houses in every street of Stamboul; wherever there is a little patch of disused ground, there spring a couple of cypresses under which half a dozen tombstones lean awry, and solemn Turkish children play in and out among the graves. We, too, scrambled down the slopes between the half-obliterated mounds, and stood under the shadow of their guardian trees, until the nodding stone turbans wore to us as familiar an aspect as the turbaned heads before the coffee shop in the street.

From time to time, indeed, we remembered the strangeness of this companionship with the generations behind us. One April afternoon, as we were walking down the steep streets of Trebizond, looking round us with curious eyes, there fell upon our ears a continuous tinkling of bells. We listened: there was no sound of feet, but the bells came nearer and nearer, and at last from one of the narrow streets emerged a camel, and behind him more camels and more, marching on with noiseless padded tread, with impassive Oriental faces and outstretched necks, round which the rows of tiny bells swung backwards and forwards with every step. By their side trudged their drivers, noiselessly, too, in sandalled feet, their faces half hidden by huge caps of long-haired fur, and wearing an expression less human than that of the beasts over which they cracked their whips. 'Look,' said our guide; 'it is a caravan from Tabriz,' and he pushed us back out of the road, for camels have an evil reputation, and are apt to enliven the way by a fretful biting at any person they may happen to encounter. So we stood, without noticing where we had retreated, and watched the long caravan as it passed us with even, measured tread—so slowly that we fell to wondering how many hundred hundred thousand of those deliberate steps had marked the dust and crunched upon the stones across the mountains and valleys and deserts between Trebizond and Tabriz. And though their caravanserai was in sight, the camels never mended their pace, and though they had come so many hundred miles, they did not seem weary with their journey or glad to reach their goal; but as they passed they turned their heads and looked us in the eyes, and we knew that they were thinking that we were only Westerns, and could not understand their placid Oriental ways. When they had passed we glanced down, and found that we were standing upon a grave mound; behind us sprang cypress-trees, and the stone upon which we were leaning bore the dead man's turban carved upon it. There he lay upon the edge of the great road which he too, perhaps, had trodden from end to end in his day—lay now at rest with the cypresses to shade his head, and the caravans moving ceaseless past him, away and away into the far East. May he rest in peace, the dead man by the living road!

To such charming Turkish sepulchres we looked back as to hallowed resting-places when we had come to know the Persian graveyards. The stretch of dusty stony earth outside the mud walls of the town, the vacant space in the heart of the village where the gravestones were hardly to be distinguished from the natural rockiness of the earth, the home of evil smells, untrodden by living feet, though it lay in the centre of the village life—those shallow graves seemed to us ill-suited to eternal rest. From many of them, indeed, the occupants were to suffer a premature resurrection. After a few months' sleep they would be rudely awakened, wrapped in cloths, and carried on the backs of mules to the holy places. Men who have met these caravans of the dead winding across the desert say that their hearts stood still as that strange and mournful band of wayfarers passed them silently by.

But the pang of sorrow is only for the living. Though we find it hard enough to dissociate sensation from the forms which have once felt like ourselves, the happy dead people are no longer concerned with the fate of the outer vestments they have cast off. They fear no more the heat of the sun, nor the furious winter's rages; the weary journey to Kerbela is nothing to them, nor whether they lie under cypresses, whose silent fingers point to heaven, or under marble domes, of out in the bare desert. Wherever they rest, they rest in peace.

THE CITY OF KING PRUSIAS

AT THE FOOT OF THE BITHYNIAN OLYMPUS lies a city founded, says tradition, by Cyrus. Philip, the son of Demetrius, gave it to Prusias, King of Bithynia, the friend of Hannibal; Prusias rebuilt it, calling it after himself, and for over two hundred years it was the capital of the Bithynian kingdom. In the first century after Christ it fell into the hands of the Romans; Roman governors took up their abode in Brusa, the younger Pliny described to Trajan the agora, the library, the baths of sulphur, which gave it an honoured place in the civilization of Rome. During the ensuing centuries many men fought and fell for its possession; the cry of battle raged perpetually about its walls. Turks and Christians contended for Brusa, Theodore Lascaris, the Roumanian despot, held it, Orkan ravished it from the Greeks, Timur overwhelmed it with his shepherd warriors from distant Tartary; finally the Turks reconquered it and turned the capital of King Prusias into the capital of the Ottoman Empire.

The soaring minarets, the white domes of mosques and baths, lie amid cypresses and plane-trees at the foot of the mountain. The streams of Olympus, many-fountained like its neighbour Ida, water the town and the surrounding country with such profusion that every inch of ground yields fruit and flowers in tenfold abundance; the hot steam of the sulphur springs diffuses a drowsy warmth through the atmosphere; the city is full of the sound of tinkling fountains and murmuring plane-leaves, and of the voices of black-eyed Turkish children—no wonder if the eagerness of men for its possession drove peace for so many hundred years from its vineyards and olive-groves.

It is said that of the Romans no trace remains. If this be so, the spirit of the Roman builders must have lingered on among Byzantine masons. There is a gateway at the southern side of the town from which part of the stone casing has fallen away, revealing that exquisite brickwork whose secret was known to the Romans only—an entablature of long, narrow bricks, set into arches of complicated pattern, with the sure eye and the even hand that ennoble the commonest materials, and make Roman bricks and plain Roman stonework as beautiful in their way as frieze, or fresco, or marble-casing. Pliny's baths, how-ever, are gone; the present buildings are of Turkish origin. They lie a little to the east of the town, in fields which vine and olive share with irises and great scarlet poppies. You enter, and find yourself under the dome of a large hall, round the walls of which are railed off compartments where, upon piles of cushions, the bathers rest after the exertion of the bath, smoking a narghileh and drinking a cup of coffee. Beyond this is another and smaller hall, with a fountain of clear cold water in the midst of it, and through various chambers of different tem-peratures you reach the farthest and hottest of all. The air is thick and heavy with the steam which rises from the blue-tiled basin, where, when the process of washing is over, the Turkish youths swim in the hot water of the sulphur springs, while through the mist the sunlight glimmers down on them from the windows in the dome.

The mosques share the indescribable charm of Brusa—a charm in which the luxuriant fertility of the land and the accumulated arts of many nations bear an equal part. The tomb of Orkan the Conqueror owes its beauty to the Byzantines, for it lies in the church they reared and dedicated to the prophet Elijah. Before the Green Mosque is a fountain, one of those exquisite fountains of Olympus, shaded by huge plane-trees, and protected by a pointed roof rising on delicate columns, and arches with the Moorish curve in them; and on the mosque itself, the colour of leaves with the sun shining through them is rivalled by the brilliant green of the tiles which encase the dome, and the tracery of laden branches against the sky by the carving round the doorway, until you cannot tell which is the most successful decorator, man or nature. Sultan Mahmud employed Christian workmen in the mosque he built; its architecture wears a curious likeness to that of the West, and the Christian vines and fig-trees are wreathed round the capitals of the Mohammedan shafts. In the big mosque in the centre of the town the builders seem to have recognised that the beauty of curving roofs and the splendour of coloured tiles could go no further—they have called in Heaven to their aid. The entrance, indeed, is vaulted over, the floor is strewn with carpets, and the walls glow with colour; but the central court is open to the sky, and a fountain plashes under the blaze of light and sunshine which falls through the opening. Round the edge of the basin beggars sit washing their feet, grave elders dip their hands and bathe their faces in the cool water; in the columned darkness beyond, bands of Turkish children play at hide-and-seek between the pillars, so noiselessly that they do not disturb the quiet worshippers and the groups of men chatting in undertones, or drown the delicious sound of water and the whispering of the outer airs which fill the building.

Above the town Olympus rears his lofty head: his feet are planted in groves of plane-trees, among the soaring dark spires of cypresses and the white spires of the minarets, beech thickets cover his flanks, and on his shoulders lies a mantle of snow, which narrows and narrows as the summer climbs upwards, but which never entirely disappears.

As we ascended the mountain on our lean ponies, we felt as though we were gradually leaving Turkey behind us, and climbing up into Greece. The snow still lay low enough (for it was in the early summer) to prevent our reaching the summit, yet we could see over the shoulders of the hills the spurs of the beautiful range of Ida, and where the plain of Troy might be on clearer days, with Lake Aphnitis, the furthest boundary of the Troad, gleaming on its edge—'Aphneian Trojans,' says Homer in his catalogue of warriors, 'who inhabit Zeleia at the furthest extremity of Ida, and drink the dark waters of Æsepus.' We could see, too, the long stretch of Marmora and the peninsula of Cyzicus, whose king met with such dire ill-fortune at the hands of Jason, and though this was not that Olympus which was crowned with the halls of Zeus, we comforted ourselves by imagining that Homer may have had the slopes of the Bithynian mountain in the eye of his mind when he wandered singing through the Troad. The beech coppices whispered graceful legends in our ears, the glades, thickset with flowers, seemed to us to be marked with the impress of divine feet—it was the Huntress and her train who had stirred the fritillary bells, Pan's pregnant footing had called the golden crocuses to life, the voices of the nymphs who charmed away Hylas the Argonaut still floated on the air, and through the undergrowth what glimpse was that of flying robe and unloosed shining locks?... We rode upward beyond the region of sheltered, flower-strewn glades, beyond the pines, until we came to rough, stony ground, sprinkled with juniper-bushes—and to the very edge of the snow. The mountain-top was all bare and silent; no clash of battle rises now above the plain of Troy; in the blue peaks of Ida, Œnone's cries are hushed; Paris is dead, of Helen's beauty there is nothing but the name; Zeus no longer watches the tide of war from the summit of the Bithynian Olympus, and the nymphs have fled....

The day was nearly over when we descended, the cypresses of Brusa cast long shadows between the white domes—it was the magic moment when the sun, like a second Midas, turns all he touches into gold. The western sky was a sheet of pure gold, the broad plane-leaves hung in golden patterns upon the boughs, the low light lay in a carpet of gold upon the grass, the very air breathed incantations, and on the lowest slope of the mountain we found Ganymede awaiting us. There he sat under a tree by the roadside; he had clothed himself in the semblance of an old Turkish beggar, and hidden his yellow curls beneath a scarlet fez, and the nectar he offered us was only Turkish coffee; but we knew him, in spite of his disguise, when he put one of the tiny cups into our hands, for no coffee brewed by mortal could have tasted so ambrosial or mingled so divine a fragrance with the sweet flowery smell of evening. We sat down on the grass round the primitive brazier—a mere dishful of charcoal set on a shaky iron tripod. The heavenly cup-bearer was well versed in the arts of coffee-making; he kept half a dozen of his little copper pots a-boiling on the tray of charcoal, which he blew to a red glow round them, and when the coffee frothed up over the edges, he poured it in the nick of time into the cups which we held out to him. The sun flooded our Olympian hall of plane-trees with soft light; we lay in grateful silence upon our couch of grass while the coffee bubbled up over the charcoal fire and frothed steaming into our cups. At length we rose, handed our Ganymede some Turkish coins, at which he must have chuckled in his Greek heart, and rode away in the twilight through the streets of Brusa.

SHOPS AND SHOPKEEPERS

'WE LIVED TOGETHER for the space of a month,' related the second of the three ladies of Baghdad to Haroun al Rashid, Ja'far the Wezir, and Mesroor the Executioner, 'after which I begged my husband that he would allow me to go to the bazaar to purchase some stuffs for dress.' She went, accompanied by the inevitable old woman, to the house of a young merchant whose father had recently died, leaving him great wealth. 'He produced all we wanted, and we handed him the money, but he refused to take it, saying: "It is an offer of hospitality for your visit." I said: "If he will not take themoney, I will return to him the stuffs." But he would not receive it again, and exclaimed: "By Allah! I will take nothing from you; all this is a present from me for a single kiss, which I will value more than the contents of my whole shop."' The Khalifeh, when the story was concluded—it went on through many and surprising adventures—expressed no astonishment at the young man's generosity. Such an exaggerated view of hospitality seemed to him quite natural on the part of a shopkeeper, nor did he pause to inquire whether the inflammable young man found that the wealth which his father had left him increased with any rapidity through his transactions with pretty ladies.

So reckless a disposition is no longer to be found among Eastern merchants; shopping is now conducted purely on business principles, though it is not without a charm which is absent from Western counters. Instead of the sleek young man, indistinguishable from his fellows, you have the turbaned Turk, bundled up in multitudinous baggy garments, which he holds round him with one hand, while he takes down his goods with the other; or the keen-featured Persian, from whom you need hope to make no large profit, wrapped in closely-hanging robes, his white linen shirt buttoned neatly across his brown chest; or the specious Armenian in his red fez, cunning and voluble, an easy liar, asking impossible prices for worthless objects, and hoping to ingratiate you by murmuring with a leer that he remembers seeing your face in Spitalfields last time he was there. Shopping with these merchants is not merely the going through of certain forms for the acquisition of necessary commodities—it is an end in itself, an art which combines many social arts, an amusement which will not pall, though many hours be devoted to it, a study in character and national characteristics.

It was in Brusa that we went out to purchase some 'stuffs for dress'—not that we contemplated making for ourselves ten robes each to the value of a thousand golden pieces, like the lady of Baghdad, but that we had heard rumours of certain of the Brusa silks which were suited to less extravagant requirements. It was a hot, steaming afternoon; we hired diminutive donkeys and rode down Brusa streets and under the many domes of the bazaar. The quick, short steps of the donkeys clicked over the cobble stones; we looked round us as they went at the rows and rows of shop-counters, the high vaults which arched away to right and left ward, the courtyards open to the sky, set round with shops, grown over with vines, gleaming with sunshine at the end of some dark narrow passage, the people standing about in leisurely attitudes, and the donkeys, which walked diligently up and down, carrying now a veiled woman sitting astride on her padded saddle, now a turbaned Turk, and now a bale of merchandise. At length we came to the street of the silk merchants, and dismounted before the shop of an old Turk who was sitting cross-legged within.

He rose, and with many polite salaams begged us to enter, and set chairs for us round the low enamelled table. We might have been paying a morning call: we talked—those of us who could speak Turkish—of Sa'di and the musical glasses, we sipped our cups of delicious coffee, we puffed our narghilehs—those of us who could derive any other pleasure from a narghileh than that of a strong taste of charcoal flavoured with painted wood. Presently the subject of silks was broached, and set aside again as unworthy of discussion; after a few more minutes our—host, shall I say?—laid before us a bundle of embroideries, which we examined politely, complimenting him upon his possessions. At length, as if the idea had just struck him, though he knew perfectly well the object of our visit, he pulled a roll of silk from a corner of the shop and laid it before us. We asked tentatively whether he would not permit us to see more, and the business of the afternoon began. The stuffs were certainly charming. There were the usual stripes of silk and cotton, there were muslins woven with tinsel lines, coarse Syrian cottons, and the brocades for which Brusa is famous, mixtures of cotton and silk woven in small patterns something like a Persian pattern, yellow on white, gold on blue, orange on yellow. No doubt we paid more for our purchases than they were worth, but not more than the pleasure of a delightful afternoon spent in the old Turk's company was worth to us.

On our way home we stopped before a confectioner's shop and invited him to let us taste of his preserves. He did not, like the confectioner in the Arabian

Nights, prepare for us a delicious dish of pomegranate-seeds, but he gave us Rahat Lakoum, and slices of sugared oranges, and a jelly of rose-leaves (for which cold cream is a good European substitute), and many other delicacies, ending with some round white objects, which I take to have been sugared onions, floating in syrup—after we had tasted them we had small desire to continue our experimental repast.

The bazaars in Constantinople are not so attractive: the crowds jostle you, the shopkeepers, throwing aside Oriental dignity, run after you and catch you by the sleeve, offering to show you Manchester cottons and coarse embroidered muslins. A fragrant savour, indeed, of fried meats and garlic hangs about the eating-shops, on whose counters appetizing mixtures of meat and rice are displayed, and bowls of a white substance like curds, into which a convenient spoon is sticking for the common use of all hungry passers-by, and under the high vaults of the carpet bazaar solemn merchants sit in state among their woven treasures, their silver, and their jewels.

We spent a morning among Persian and Circassian shopmen in Tiflis. There the better part of the bazaar is not roofed over, and the shops open on to a street inches deep in dust or in mud, according to the weather, as is the manner of the streets of Tiflis. They were full of lovely silver ornaments, and especially we noted the heavy silver belts which were hanging in every window and round the waist of every Circassian merchant. We fixed upon one which was being thus informally exhibited round a waist, and, in spite of the many protestations of its wearer, we succeeded in buying it from him. It had belonged to his father, he said, and I think that it was with some reluctance that he pocketed our gold pieces and saw us carrying off his family heirloom.

In Persia the usual order of shopping is reversed: you buy not when you stand in need, but when the merchants choose to come to you. Moreover, the process is very deliberative, and a single bargain may stretch out over months. The counters are the backs of mules, which animals are driven into your garden whenever their owners happen to be passing by. As you sit under the shadow of your plane-trees you become conscious of bowing figures before you, leading laden mules by the bridle; you signify to them that they may spread out their goods, and presently your garden-paths are covered with crisp Persian silks and pieces of minute stitching, with Turkoman tent-hangings, embroideries from Bokhara, and carpets from Yezd and Kerman, and the sunlight flickers down through the plane-leaves into the extemporary shop. There is a personal note about these charming materials which lends them an interest other than that which could be claimed by bright colours and soft textures alone. They speak of individual labour and individual taste. Those tiny squares of Persian work have formed part of a woman's dress—in some andarun, years of a woman's life were spent stitching the close intricate pattern in blended colours from corner to corner; those strips of linen on which the design of red flowers and green leaves is not quite completed, come from the fingers of a girl of Bokhara, who, when she married, threw aside her embroidery-needle and left her fancy-work thus unfinished.

The bargaining begins: you turn over the stuffs with careless fingers—this one is very dirty, that very coarse; you lift a corner of the carpets, and, examining the wrong side with what air of knowledge you can summon to your aid, you mutter that they are only partially silken, after all. Finally you make your offer, which is received with indignant horror on the part of the merchant. He sweeps his wares aside, and draws from the folds of his garments a box of turquoises, which he displays to you with many expressions of admiration, and which you return to him with contemptuous politeness: 'Mal-e shuma!'—'They are your possession!' He packs up his bundles and retires. In a week or two he will return with reduced demands; you will raise your offer a toman or two, and after a few months of coming and going and of mutual concessions, the disputed carpet will be handed over to you at perhaps half the price that the owner originally asked; or perhaps the merchant will return in triumph and inform you that he has sold it to someone less grasping than you.

Urbane Persian phrases are confusing at first to the brusque European; it was not until we had made several mistakes that we grew accustomed to them.

As we were coming through the garden in the dusk one evening a somewhat ragged stranger accosted us and handed us a long-haired kitten. 'Mal-e shuma!' he said. We were surprised, but since we had been making inquiries for long-haired kittens, we thought that some kind acquaintance had heard of our wants and taken this opportunity of making us a present—presents from casual acquaintances being not uncommon in the East. We thanked the man and passed on with our mewing acquisition. But the Persian did not seem satisfied; he followed us with dogged persistence, and at length the thought struck us that it might not be a gift, after all. We turned and asked:

'What is the cost?'

'Out of your great kindness,' he replied, 'the cost of the cat is three tomans' (about thirty shillings).

'By Allah!' we said, 'in that case it is your possession still;' and we gave the kitten back to him.

When you buy, you might think from the words that pass that you had gained, together with your purchase, a friend for life; and even when you refuse to buy, you veil the terms of your refusal in such a manner that the uninitiated would conclude that you were making a handsome present to your vagrant shopkeeper.

A MURRAY OF THE FIRST CENTURY

THERE ARE FEW MORE CURIOUS SUBJECTS for observation than the continuity of human life in a given place. Generations of men will go on living on the same spot, though it does not offer them any particular advantages—even though, living there, they must be content with poverty, with insignificance, with a station outside the great swing of the world. 'Some little town by river or sea-shore' is all their universe—not theirs only, but their children's and their children's children's from century to century. You are tempted to believe that these anchored people, who cling like limpets to the rock on which they find themselves, are no more conscious of their own vitality than the limpets their counterparts; rather, it is the town which knows that it exists; with living eyes it watches the coming and going of races, the ebb and flow of the tide of history, trusting in its own immortality, and careless whether Greek or Barbarian, washed up to it on the wave of a folk wandering, fill its walls.

The truth is that man is a stationary animal, and that which seems a backwater of life is the stagnant mid-ocean, after all—that is the first lesson which the East writes in her big wise book, which you may read and read and never reach the last chapter. For the most part, he is unenterprising; he prefers to remain with the evils he knows rather than risk worse fortune in the hope of better, and unless he be driven forth by hunger or by the sword, he will not seek fresh woods and pastures new. It has been said before, and repeated until it should be familiar, that the swift current of Western life is an exception to the general rule, and not the rule itself—said and repeated, and yet when you are brought face to face with tiny towns and remote fishing villages, for whose birth there seems to be no reason but caprice, for whose continuance even caprice can scarcely be alleged, and which may yet boast two thousand years of life, you will stand aghast at such hoar conservative antiquity. Where is progress? Where is the march of civilization? Where the evolution of the race?... You have passed beyond the little patch of the globe where these laws bear sway; they are not eternal, still less are they universal, the great mass of mankind is untouched by them, and if you must generalize, you will come nearer the truth in saying that man is stationary than that he is progressive.

On the southern shores of the Black Sea, where the mountains of Anatolia drop their wooded flanks into the water, cluster villages to which the name of progress is unknown; the Greek colonists laid their foundation stones—wanderers they, a seafaring folk of unexampled activity. In those steep valleys and on the open stretches of beach two thousand five hundred years have slipped past almost unnoticed. The Greek names, indeed, have been mutilated by barbarian tongues, and other gods are worshipped on those coasts; the temples of Amisus are buried among brushwood, Mars finds no honour in the island of Aretias, nor does the most adventurous of travellers follow in the steps of Hercules through the mouth of the Acherusian cavern; the slender columns of minarets shoot upwards over the flat white roofs, and the Turk is master in the Bithynian waters. For the rest, what difference? Still from sheltered beaches the rude fishing-boats put forth; still the hard oaks are felled in the mountains and sold in the Byzantium of to-day; still the people till their fields of millet, and gather the wild fruits on the fertile lower slopes; still the harbour of Sinope is filled with the sound of the building of ships, as it was when the Milesian navy anchored behind Cape Syrias. Nay, more—you may journey here with the latest guide-book in one hand and Strabo in the other, and the Murray of the first century will furnish you with more minute information than he of the nineteenth.

For Strabo knew this country well; it was the land of his birth. 'Amaseia, my native place,' lay not far away on the banks of the river Iris, which the Turks call Jeschil Irmak. He praises its fertility, he unfolds its riches, he enumerates every village it contains. He is much occupied, too, with its past history, and to his elaborate researches there is little to be added even to-day, save here and there the story of a Genoese and a Venetian settlement, or of a Byzantine church, and of the final invasion of the Turkish conquerors. He collects much conflicting evidence concerning the origin of divers tribes along the coast—a question which it would puzzle the most learned ethnologist to decide with the materials that lay to Strabo's hand; he notes the boundary of the dominions of Mithridates, and the manner in which the Roman emperors divided the kingdom of Pontus in later times; he sketches the history of Heracleia, the Eregli of to-day, and the birth of the colony of Amastris, which the Turks call Sesamyos, and which was formed by Queen Amastris, niece of Darius and wife of Dionysius the Tyrant, out of four cities—Sesamus, Cytorum (whose green box groves have been famous since the days of Homer), Cromna, and Tieum, the Turkish Tilijos. Above all, he catches at any allusion in the Homeric poems: from these mountains, sings the poet, the warriors marched forth to the defence of Troy; 'From Cromna and Ægialus and the lofty Erythini' they came, they left their country where the wild mules breed, they left the banks of the Sangarius and of that Parthenius stream whose name was tribute to its virgin beauty. I fear the wild mules breed no longer by the river Sakaria, but Ægialus is still to be found under the name of Kara Agatsch, and the lofty Erythini still lift their rocky heads out of the sea.

Some of the places which Strabo mentions were sufficiently unimportant even in his day to have escaped all observation less accurate than his own. Concerning Ak Liman, an anchoring place to the west of Sinope, he quotes a joking proverb: 'He who had nothing to do built a wall about Armene.' Some have fallen from a higher estate, as Sinope itself, which was a naval power of repute in the first century, and the Colchian coast at the eastern end of the Black Sea, which, as he justly remarks, must have been celebrated in the earliest antiquity, as is shown by the story of Jason's voyage thither in search of the Golden Fleece. He explains the legend of the Golden Fleece, by the way, quite in the modern spirit: the torrents of the Caucasus, he says, bring down gold; the Barbarians collect their waters in troughs pierced with holes and lined with the fleeces of sheep, which catch and hold the dust.

Such memories were our travelling companions as we coasted along the wooded shores towards the latter end of the spring. They came rushing in upon us one evening when our ship stopped at a tiny port built at the bottom of a valley sloping down to the water. Intercourse with the outer world is limited to such passing visits of steamers; the inhabitants of the Black Sea villages grow nearly all the necessaries of life in their fertile valleys, and content themselves with a small exchange of wood and dried fruits for cloth and sugar and a few of the luxuries of civilization, amongst which, oddly enough, tombstones are an important item. As we watched the wide Turkish boats, rising high out of the water at stem and stern, which came dancing out towards us over the swell of the waves and poised round us like great sea-birds while the tombstones and the bundles of goods were dropped into them, we fell to wondering, while the evening light faded from land and sea, what the meagre history of Ineboli could be—so remote it seemed, so forgotten—and it presently occurred to us to consult the learned Strabo. There in his book it was duly mentioned: 'Abonteichos, a small city,' 'the modern Ineboli,' added a commentator, and we gazed with different eyes at the small city which was backed by such a long line of experiences.

Next day we reached Samsoun, Strabo's 'Amisus, which Mithridates adorned with temples.' A number of Turks, who were passengers on our ship, disembarked there, for what reason Heaven only knows—Mithridates' pomp has been long since forgotten, and one would think that a man must be hard pressed for occupation before he would seek it in Samsoun. The town lies on sloping ground, rising gently upwards; on the hill behind it we could see the broad road which leads to Diabekir and the people walking in it; the sound of Armenian church bells came to us across the water, and from hour to hour a clock tolled out Turkish time, though no one seemed to heed it. Some Armenian women came on board to examine the ship, and ran up and down the companion ladders, looking at everything with curious eyes and much loud laughter. They were dressed in very bright colours and unveiled, which struck us as indecent in a woman.

Very early on the following morning we woke to find ourselves outside Kerasounde, the Greek Pharnacia—'a small fortified city,' says Strabo. It was a charming little place, just waking under the misty morning sunshine. Its irregular streets dropped down to the water's edge, and even beyond, for some of the wide-roofed houses were planted out on stakes in the shallow bay. The mountain-side against which it nestled was white with blossoming fruit-trees, and behind it the higher peaks were still white with snow. As for the fortifications, they seem to have disappeared, and, indeed, what foe would turn his arms against Kerasounde?

Towards mid-day we reached Trebizond, and greeted it with almost as much enthusiasm as Xenophon must have displayed when he and his Ten Thousand saw it lying at their feet with the blue sea beyond, and knew that an end was set at last to their weary march. Greek and Roman and Genoese merchant have successively borne sway in Trebizond; fortress walls, churches and monasteries tell of their rule. The Turk has encamped himself now within the fortified limits of the old town, but a large Armenian suburb, half hidden under plane-trees, holds to the religion which he displaced.

It happened that on that day the foundations of an Armenian church were being laid, and the Christian town wore a festive air. We watched the ceremony, standing among a crowd of men dressed in their shabby European best, and of women wrapped in white feridgis, with beautiful caps of coins upon their heads. It was not very attractive. A priest was reading prayers before a gaudy picture of the Virgin, a troop of little boys droned Gregorian chants, their discordant voices led by an old man in a fez and blue spectacles, and with no ear for music, who was apparently the choirmaster. Higher up, on the top of the hill overlooking the town, we came upon an interesting and beautiful Byzantine monastery, walled about like a fort—though the walls were in ruins—and with a chapel cut into the solid rock. The chapel walls were covered with frescoes, the half-effaced portraits of saints and of Greek emperors—those banished Comneni who ruled in Trebizond; a pleasant smell of incense hung about the courtyard, round which were built the cells of the monks—rather dilapidated indeed, but still charming under their roofs of red tiles; blue starch hyacinths lifted their prim heads beneath the apple trees which stood in full flower in the rocky gardens on the hillside, and from the summit of the peaceful walls we could see far inland towards the valleys where the Amazons dwelt, and where, says Strabo, quoting Homer, were the silver mines. Silver is still to be found there, but the Amazons are gone; they might have troubled the good monks in their lodging on the hill-top.

So with regret we returned to our ship, and quitted the cypresses and the plane trees of Trebizond, taking our way 'to Phasis, where ships end their course,' as Strabo quotes (or very near it), thence to pursue our journey by means other than those which the primitive Murray recommends, and through countries which he knew only by hearsay.

TRAVELLING COMPANIONS

ALL THE EARTH IS SEAMED WITH ROADS, and all the sea is furrowed with the tracks of ships, and over all the roads and all the waters a continuous stream of people passes up and down—travelling, as they say, for their pleasure. What is it, I wonder, that they go out for to see? Some, it is very certain, are hunting the whole world over for the best hotels; they will mention with enthusiasm their recent journey through Russia, but when you come to question them, you will find that they have nothing to tell except that in Moscow they were really as comfortable as if they had been at home, and even more luxurious, for they had three varieties of game at the table of their host. Some have an eye fixed on the peculiarities of foreign modes of life, that they may gratify their patriotic hearts by condemning them when they differ (as they not infrequently do) from the English customs which they have left, and to which their thoughts turn regretfully; as I have heard the whole French nation summarily dismissed from the pale of civilization because they failed to perceive that boiled potatoes were an essential complement to the roast. To some travelling is merely the traversing of so many hundred miles; no matter whether not an inch of country, not an object of interest, remains in the eye of the mind—they have crossed a continent, they are travellers. These bring back with them only the names of the places they have visited, but are much concerned that the list should be a long one. They will cross over to Scutari that they may conscientiously say they have been in Asia, and traverse India from end to end that they may announce that they have visited all the tombs. They are full of expedients to lighten the hardships of a road whose varied pleasures have no charm for them. They will exhibit with pride their bulky luncheon-baskets, and cast withering glances at that humble flask of yours which has seen so many adventures over the edge of your coat-pocket. 'Ah,' they will say, 'when you have travelled a little you will begin to learn how to make yourself comfortable.' And you will hold your peace, and hug your flask and your adventures the closer to your heart.

All these, and more also, are not travellers in the true sense of the word; they might as well have stayed at home and read a geography-book, or turned over a volume of photographs, and engaged a succession of cooks of different nationalities; but the real travellers, what pleasures are they seeking in fresh lands and strange cities? Reeds shaken in the wind are a picturesque foreground, but scarcely worth a day's journey into the wilderness; men clothed in soft raiment are not often to be met with in hotel or caravanserai, and as for prophets, there are as many at home, maybe, as in other places.

Well, every man carries a different pair of eyes with him, and no two people would answer the question in the same fashion. For myself, I am sometimes tempted to believe that the true pleasure of travel is to be derived from travelling companions. Such curious beings as you fall in with, and in such unexpected places! Although your acquaintance may be short in hours, it is long in experience; and when you part you feel as intimate as if you had shared the same slice of bread-and-butter in your nursery, and the same bottle of claret in your college hall. The vicissitudes of the road have a wonderful talent for bringing out the fine flavour of character. One day may show a man in as many different aspects as it would take ten years of the customary life to exhibit. Moreover, time goes slowly on a ship or in a railway train, and a man is apt to better its pace by relating the incidents of his career to a sympathetic listener. In this manner the doors of palaces and of secret chambers in remote corners of the world fly open to you, and though you may have crossed no more unfamiliar waters than those of the North Sea, you pass through Petersburg and Bokhara, Poland and Algeria, on your way to Antwerp. English people are not so communicative, even abroad, and what they have to tell is of less interest if you are athirst for unknown conditions; their tales lack the charm of those which fall from the lips of men coming, as it were, out of a dream-world, crossing but once the glow of solid reality which lights your own path, and vanishing as suddenly as they came into space. Like packmen, we unfasten our wares, open our little bundle of experiences, spread them out and finger them over: the ship touches at the port, the silks and tinsel are gathered up and strapped upon our backs and carried—God knows where!

The man who carried the most amusing wares we ever examined was a Russian officer, and he spread them out for our inspection as we steamed round the eastern and northern coasts of the Black Sea. He was a magnificent creature, fair-haired, blue-eyed, broad-shouldered, and tall; he must have stood six feet four in those shining top boots of his. His beard was cut into a point, and his face was like that of some handsome, courteous seventeenth-century nobleman smiling out of a canvas of Vandyke's. He was a mighty hunter, so he told us; he lived with his wife and daughters out in Transcaspia, where he governed a province, and hunted the lions and the wolves (and perhaps the Turkomans also) with packs of dogs and regiments of mounted huntsmen. He was writing a book about Transcaspia; there would be much, he said, of hunt in its pages. He spoke English, and hastened to inform us that every Russian of good family learnt English from his youth up. I trust that the number of his quarterings was in direct proportion to the number of grammatical errors he perpetrated in our tongue, for if so our friend must have been as well connected as he said he was. He told wonderful stories of the wealth and splendour of his family; all the great Slav houses and all their most ancient names seemed to be united in his person. His mother was Princess This, his wife was Princess That, his father had been a governor of such and such a province; he himself, until a few years back, was the most brilliant of the officers In the Czar's guards— indeed, he had only left Petersburg because, with a growing family, he could no longer afford to spend £40,000 a year (or some such sum—I remember it seemed to us enormous). 'And you know,' he added, 'under £40,000 a year you cannot live in Petersburg—not as I am accustomed to live.' So he had retired to economize among the lions and the Turkomans until his fortunes should retrieve themselves, which there was every prospect of their doing, since his wife was to inherit one of the largest properties in Russia, and he himself would come into the second largest on the death of his mother. Of that lady he spoke with a gentle sorrow: 'She is very miser,' he would say whenever he alluded to her. 'She send me her blessing, but no pence!' We murmured words of sympathy, but he was not to be comforted—her avarice rankled. 'Ah, yes,' he sighed, when her name came up again in the course of conversation, 'she is very miser!'

It may be that our agreeable companion did not consider himself to be bound by those strict rules of accuracy which tied in a measure our own tongues; his velvets may have been cotton-backed, and his diamonds paste, for all their glitter. We had the opportunity of testing only one of his statements, and I must confess that we were lamentably disappointed. One evening at dinner he was telling us of the prodigies of strength he had accomplished, how he had lifted men with one finger, thrown stupendous weights, and grappled with wild beasts of monstrous size. He even descended into further details. 'In the house of my mother,' he said, 'I took a napkin and bent him twenty times and tore him across!' We were interested, and, to beguile the monotony of the evening, we begged him to perform the same feat on the captain's linen; he acceded, and after dinner we assembled on deck full of expectation. The napkin was produced and folded three or four times; he tore and tore—not a thread gave way! Again he pulled and wrenched until he was red in the face with pulling (and we with shame), and still the napkin was as united as ever. At length we offered some effete excuses—in the house of his mother, even though she was so very miser, the linen was probably of finer quality; no one could be expected to tear one of the ship's napkins, which was as coarse as sackcloth! He accepted the explanation, but nothing is so disconcerting as to be convicted of exaggeration, and though we were heartily sorry for our indiscretion, our acquaintance never again touched those planes of intimacy which it had reached before. Next morning we arrived at Odessa, and parted company with distant bows, nor will he ever, I fear me, send us the promised volume containing some description of Transcaspia and much of hunt.

There is a curious reservation in the communicativeness of a Russian. He will tell you all you wish to know (and more) of himself and of his family, but once touch upon his country or his Government and he is dumb. We noticed this trait in another casual travelling acquaintance, who talked so freely of his own doings, and even of more general topics, such as the novels of Tolstoi, that we were encouraged to question him concerning the condition of the peasantry. 'What of the famine?' we asked. 'Famine!' he said, and a blank expression came over his face. 'I have heard of no famine—there is no famine in Russia!' And yet credible witnesses had informed us that the people were dying by thousands in the southern provinces, not so far removed from Batoum, where our friend occupied a high official position. Doubtless, if we had asked of the Jews, he would have replied with the same imperturbable face—'Jews! I have heard of no Jews in Russia!'

The charm of such friendships lies in their transient character. Before you have time to tire of the new acquaintances they are gone, and in all probability the discussion, which was beginning to grow a little tedious, will never be renewed. You meet them as you meet strangers at a dinner-table, but with less likelihood that the chances of fortune will throw you again together, and less within the trammels of social conventions. Ah, but for those conventions how often might one not sit beside the human being instead of beside the suit of evening clothes! People put on their indistinctive company manners with their indistinctive white shirt-fronts, and only once can I remember to have seen the man pierce through the dress. The transgressor was a Turkish secretary of legation. He was standing gloomily before a supper-table, eyeing the dishes with a hungry glance, when someone came up and asked him why he would not sup. 'Ah,' he sighed, 'ma ceinture! Elle est tellement serrée que je ne puis rien manger!' There was a touch of human nature for you! The suffering Turk said nothing memorable for the rest of the evening, but his own remark brands itself upon the mind, and will not be easily forgotten. I have often wondered at what compromise he and his waistband have arrived during the elapsing years, which must, in spite of all his care, have added certain inches to his circumference.

Not with such fugitive acquaintanceships alone may your fellow-travellers beguile the way: there are many whom you never come to know, and who yet afford a delightful field for observation. In the East a man may travel with his whole family, and yet scarcely interrupt the common flow of everyday life, and by watching them you will learn much concerning Oriental habits which would never otherwise have penetrated through the harem walls. A Turk will arrive on board a ship with half a dozen of his womenkind and as many misshapen bundles, scarcely to be distinguished in form from the beveiled and becloaked ladies themselves. In the course of the next half-hour you will discover that these bundles contain the beds of the family, their food, and all the necessaries of life for the three or four days of the voyage. They will proceed presently to camp out on some portion of the deck roped off for their protection, spreading out their mattresses and their blankets under the open sky, performing what summary toilet they may under their feridgis, eating, sleeping, praying, conversing together, or playing with the pet birds they have brought with them, all in full view of the other passengers, but with as little heed to them as if the rope barrier were really the harem wall it simulates. Meantime, the grave lord of this troop of women paces the deck with dignified tread, and from time to time stops beside his wife and daughters and throws them a word of encouragement.

These family parties may prove of no small inconvenience to other passengers, as once when we were crossing the Sea of Marmora we found the whole of the upper deck cut off from us by an awning and canvas walls, and occupied by chattering women. We remonstrated, and were told that it was unavoidable; the women were great ladies, the family of the Governor of Brousa, with their attendants; they were going to Constantinople, there to celebrate the marriage of one of his daughters with the son of a wealthy pasha. Hence all the laughter and the subdued clatter of tongues, and the air of festive expectation which penetrated through cloaks and veils and canvas walls. But we, who had not the good fortune to be related to pashas, were obliged to content ourselves with the stairs which led on to the deck, on which we seated ourselves with the bad grace of Europeans who feel that they have been cheated of their rights.

Such comparative comfort is enjoyed only by the richer sort; for the poor a sea-voyage is a matter of considerable hardship. They, too, sleep on deck; down on the lower deck they spread their ragged mattresses among ropes and casks and all the miscellaneous detritus of a ship, with the smell and the rattle of the engines in the midst of them, and their rest disturbed by the coming and going of sailors and the bustle of lading and unlading. They cook their own food, for they will not touch that which is prepared by Christian hands, and on chilly nights they seek what shelter they may under the warm funnels. We used to watch these fellow-travellers of ours upon the Caspian boat, setting forth their evening meal as the dusk closed in—it needed little preparation, but they devoured their onions and cheese and coarse sandy cakes of bread with no less relish, and scooped out the pink flesh of their water-melons until nothing but the thinnest paring of rind remained. And as we watched the strange dinner-party of rags and tatters, we fancied that we realized what the feelings of that hasty personage in the Bible must have been after he had gathered in the people from the highways and the byways to partake of his feast, and we congratulated ourselves that we were not called upon to sit as host among them.

Pilgrims from Mecca form a large proportion of the Oriental travellers on the Black Sea. There were two such men on our boat. They were Persians; they wore long Persian robes of dark hues, and on their heads the Persian hat of astrakhan; but you might have guessed their nationality by their faces—the pale, clear-cut Persian faces, with high, narrow foreheads, deep-set eyes and arching brows. They were always together, and held little or no converse with the other passengers, than whom they were clearly of a much higher social status. They stood in the ship's bow gazing eastward, as though they were already looking for the walls of their own Meshed on the far horizon, and perhaps they pondered over the accomplishment of the holy journey, and over the aspect of the sacred places which they, too, had seen at last, but I think their minds were occupied with the prospect of rejoining wife and children and Heimat out there in Meshed, and that was why their silent gaze was turned persistently eastward.

We tried to picture what miseries these people must undergo when storms sweep the crowded deck, and the wind blows through the tattered blankets, and the snow is bedfellow on the hard mattresses; but for us the pleasant summer weather lies for ever on those inland seas, sun and clear starlight bathe coasts beautiful and desolate, sloping down to green water, the playing-ground of porpoises, the evening meals are eaten under the clear skies we knew, and morning breaks fresh and cool through the soft mists to light mysterious lands and wonderful.

THE END

BILLING AND SONS, PRINTERS, GUILDFORD.
J. D. & Co.

BIOGRAPHY OF HELEN CADDICK

HELEN CADDICK WAS BORN IN 1845 in Edgbaston, one of four daughters of lawyer Elisha Caddick. Her first trip outside of Europe took place beginning in 1889, and she traveled alone on all her adventures, hiring guides as needed. After her first expedition on a tour through the Middle East, the extensive list of places she visited includes several countries in Africa, the United States, Mexico, the Caribbean, New Zealand, Panama, Peru, Argentina, Cambodia, China, Korea, Burma, and the Philippines. On her travels, she kept thorough diaries of her experiences, which she would later publish in volumes like *A White Woman in Central Africa*.

Caddick's reasons for traveling—curiosity and the desire to see the world—made her a relatively impartial observor. She had no obligation to further any causes or adjust her political stance for anyone's benefit, and no reason to censor her voice to avoid offending any sponsors. With no husband, she had access to women's spaces within African culture that men were barred from. In her work, she comments on the hypocrisy of English "civilization" in Africa, wherein English missionaries preached peace but shot animals carelessly for sport, leaving them to die slowly and suffer where they fell. Likewise, the English condemned the "primitive" practice of Africans burning forests without considering their own felling of huge sections of trees to burn on their new steamships. She reflects that, "In Africa we always appear to consider the country ours and the natives the intruders." Although Caddick was not a critic of colonialism, her sharp observations and criticisms of the damage it did to African culture are prevalent in her work.

Several of the souvenirs she collected in her travels—objects she bought or traded for rather than excavated and stole—accumulated as a collection that Caddick organized into the Oak House Museum that she founded in 1898. Other travelers donated their own artifacts to the museum, filling it with other cultures' relics. Today, her collection belongs to the Sandwell Museum Service.

In addition to her travels, Caddick was a lifelong advocate for women's education, becoming the first female member of the West Bromwich Education

Committee. She was one of the first governors of Birmingham University, and in the last years of her life taught classes at Lodge Road Chapel in West Bromwich. Caddick passed away in 1927 at the age of eighty-two, and upon her death most of her collection of objects from her travels went to the Oak House Museum.

A WHITE WOMAN

IN CENTRAL AFRICA

BY

Helen Caddick

PREFACE

D URING THE LAST FEW YEARS, Africa has been very much in the minds
of people everywhere; especially has it been in the minds of the British
people, therefore I hope it will be thought that no apology is necessary
for my writing this brief account of a lady's journey from the mouth of the
Zambesi to the great Lake Tanganyika, which divides German East Africa from
the Congo Free State. The journey was full of interest to me, and, having been
undertaken through love of travel, and for the purposes of observation only,
has presented to me aspects and incidents of native life in British Central Africa
which, I hope, will interest and amuse those who have neither time nor inclination to travel so far. Also, I should like them to know how kind and attentive
the natives, who are spoken of in England as 'savages,' can be to a lady travelling
absolutely alone with them.

LIST OF ILLUSTRATIONS

Huts in Angoniland 711
Native Grain Stores 715
A Machila 702
Pounding and Sifting Corn 733
Unloading 'Domira' at Karonga 743
Men Sewing 761
Ant Hill 762
Stockade 764
Sausage Tree 777
Wnkonde Hut 778
Bamboo Bridge 784
Descending Bamboo Bridge 786
Goats going to Bed 787
Store at Kondowe 792
African Face on the Rock 795

CONTENTS

CHAPTER I

Up the Zambesi—Chinde —The 'Pious Paddler' —The Zambesi Sport on the River—Mrs Livingstone's Grave —The Baobab Tree 703

CHAPTER II

On the Shire River— 'Wooding' Stations—Excursions to Native Villages—The Shire River—The Native Camps— British Central Africa—Port Herald—Chiromo..710

CHAPTER III

Overland—The Shire to Blantyre—Katunga—The Murchison Falls and Rapids—Natives Carriers—My First Experience of a Machila—The Sclater Road—Arrival at Blantyre—Blantyre 719

CHAPTER IV

Blantyre to Liwonde—My Carriers—Journey to Zomba— Society in Zomba—Zomba Mountain—Domasi—Native Fashions round Domasi—Songani—Native Paths on the Way to Liwonde—The Grass Fire—Sifting Corn 726

CHAPTER V

Voyage on the 'Livingstone' and the 'Domira' —Lake Pa-Mlombe—Fort Johnston—The 'Domira' —Lake Nyasa— Religious Beliefs and Customs—Kota-Kota—Universities' Mission— Bandawe—Kungo Fly—Natives at their Toilet —Karonga...735

CHAPTER VI

From Karonga across the Plateau to Fife—Karonga— Natives—Preparations for Journey to Tanganyika—My English-speaking Boy—Bark Cloth—Musical Instruments —Camp at Mpata—Visit to the Cook—

Games with the Children—Native Food—My Carriers—Fort Hill—
Mwenzo —Fife..745

CHAPTER VII

From Fife to Lake Tanganyika—Start with Fresh Carriers —Interview with
a Chief—Camp by One of the Sources of the Congo—Mambwe French
Fathers—Division of Work among Natives—Birds—Kawimbe—Amusing
Re ception at the Mission Station—Mbala—Kituta......754

CHAPTER VIII

Return Journey from Lake Tanganyika to Karonga— Kituta—The 'Good
News' —Day on the Lake—Crowd from the Native Village—Copper Wire
Drawing—Native Dance—Disagreement among my Men—Kawimbe—
Native Games—Rats—Plagues of Africa—Chiefs Stool—Funny Scene:
Natives' love of Pombe—Karonga................................763

CHAPTER IX

Karonga again—Lion Story—Start for German Kondeland —Crossing
the Songwe —The Kabira River—Ipiana—Salt Making—Rutenganyo—
Weaving—Basket Work—Rungwe —Native Dance—Makarere—Bamboo Bridge over Lufirio River—Manow—Legend of a Lake—Native
Counting— Ipiana—'Ngerenge—Karonga for the Third Time
....772

CHAPTER X

Leave Karonga with a Poor Team—Encounter with a Chief— Native Style
of Ironing Clothes —Pottery—Climb to Kondowe—Kondowe Mission—
Lion Tale—Cave Dwell ings—Mount Chiombi—Descent to Lake Nya-
sa—' Dorhirae' again—Fort Johnston—The 'Guendolen'—Matope-—
Run away again—Blantyre—Mlanje—Adventures of a Horse —No
Luggage—Ruo Falls—Chiromo—Chinde—Home by Zanzibar and the
Suez Canal..785

A MACHILA

CHAPTER I

UP THE ZAMBESI

I LEFT ENGLAND FOR CAPETOWN early in January 1898, and after arranging some personal affairs there, I travelled to Pretoria, Johannesburg, Kimberley, Bulawayo, the ruins of Zimbabwe, and thence to Beira. I had intended going home to England from Beira, but was persuaded to visit the region of the Great Lakes. The warning with which every account of the journey concluded, namely, that I must not go alone, made me the more desirous to set out. While thinking about it, I learned that the steamer 'Matabele' was going from Beira to Quilimane, a place some way north of the Zambesi, and on her return would call at Chinde, which is the starting-point for the Great Lakes. I at once took passage for Chinde, and, after a pleasant sea trip, arrived there at the beginning of June.

Chinde is a small place built on a low sandbank at one of the four mouths of the Zambesi. The Portuguese, I was told, had granted to the British, a concession of a certain area of land on this sandbank, on which to build the houses and warehouses necessary in connection with the steamboat traffic on the Zambesi, and its tributary, the Shire. Only nine people are allowed to live on the concession; two belonging to each steamer's company, and one belonging to the missionary boat. Everything is admitted duty free, if landed direct from the steamers; but nothing can be taken outside the gates of the concession into Portuguese territory without paying a certain tax. The land is being rapidly washed away by the river, and several 'stores' have had to be moved back to the extreme limit. The original area granted was about five acres in extent, and the Portuguese administration have now decided to make good, by a grant of additional land, that part which has been carried away by the river.

The British Consul lives on what is called the 'Outer Concession,' where he has a pleasant house with a delightfully wide, cool-looking verandah. For me, one of the most interesting attractions of the place was a splendid fish eagle that lived in a large cage close by the entrance gate. It was amusing to watch the bird throw back its head and utter piercing cries the moment a stranger entered. It was an excellent watch, and gave good warning of the approach of a visitor.

Anchored in the middle of the river, opposite Chinde, was an old hulk on which a family lived. They had made a very pretty and comfortable home of it, and appeared to be very happy there. It always seems to me as if there were something uncanny about such a residence. I suppose one gets an impression that it is derelict and may go under any moment.

I just missed the African Lakes steamer that goes up the Zambesi from Chinde to Katunga, and had to wait in Chinde for nearly three days for the missionary boat, which was the next to go up the river. It was rather a weary wait, as there was absolutely nothing to do. The sand on which Chinde is built is so soft and deep that walking is almost impossible; and yet it is necessary, as there is no other means of getting about. To reach the seashore involves a great struggle, but when one has got there the difficulty is at an end. Here you find good hard sand on which you can walk for miles, or bicycle, if you are the fortunate possessor of a machine. The heat during my stay was great, and as I had little to do but think about it, I suffered all the more on that account. Therefore I was very glad when the steamer was ready to start. This boat was named the 'Henry Henderson,' but as it was the only paddle boat on the river, and belonged to the missionaries, it was generally called the 'Pious Paddler.' The other boats were all stern wheelers.

When I got on board I felt repaid for the time I had spent in waiting, for I found it was very comfortable, and I was told, and I have no doubt correctly, that it was the most comfortable of the river boats, and that it provided the cleanest accommodation and the best food. At first I thought it very insecure, as there was no taffrail or protection of any kind round it, and I felt certain I should step out of my cabin into the river, or roll off from the little upper deck where we sat under an awning. But, of course, being in the river, the boat was perfectly steady, and did not roll and pitch as a steamer does in the open sea, and after a little while the feeling of insecurity passed away.

During part of the voyage we had on each side of our boat a large barge full of cargo. These added to our sense of security, as there are crocodiles in the river, but they were detrimental both to our speed and appearance. Also, they made the navigation more difficult, as we were going up at a time when the river was getting very low, and the channels were constantly altering and were not very easy to find. Naturally, in many places where the steamer could have got through alone, one or other of the barges was sure to bump on the sand.

When this happened there was great fun and excitement; in an instant the whole crew of natives jumped over into the water, shouting and yelling to each other to haul and shove the boat off the sand, while the captain, a white man, danced up and down shouting directions and inciting them to greater exertions. Thanks to the vigorous measures that were immediately taken, we never had a really bad 'stick,' neither were those we had as bad as they might have been, as boys were always at each side of the boat with long poles trying the depth of the water, and there was an excellent pilot in charge of the wheel.

This pilot was a native, and a very funny-looking fellow. His ordinary dress was the customary loin-cloth of white calico, called a 'Nsaru,' beads and wire ornaments on his wrists and ankles, a comb stuck in his hair, and an old black frock coat, of which he was intensely proud, feeling, I am sure, that it added greatly to his dignity and importance. In his spare moments he occupied himself in combing his hair and frizzing it out, making a thick mass of it, and greatly increasing the apparent size of his head. His hair, like that of many of the natives, grew in tight little separate curls all over his head, showing the skin between, and reminding me of the South African Karroo, with its tufts of little bushes.

The natives take great interest and pride in their hair, and their ways of dressing it are many and wonderful. It was always an intense amusement to me, when I came in contact with a fresh set of men, to study the new fashions. Some shaved one side of the head completely, leaving the other, a thick bush; sometimes both sides were shaved, leaving only a thick ridge like the crest of a helmet. Another very charming style was a sort of garden arrangement, in which little pathways were shaved, winding in and out in all directions among and around beds of hair. When the whole head was shaved, a tiny bunch of hair was always left just on the top. Mohammedans are said to leave a tuft for Mahomet to pull them up to heaven by; the reason why these natives leave one I could not discover. Probably they have borrowed the idea from Mohammedans whom they have seen, or it may be that they have simply devised it for the sake of variety. I was told that when the whole head was shaved it was a sign of mourning; but though that may be so among some tribes, I do not think it is in the case of all, as many of the men I afterwards employed shaved their heads just when the fancy seized them.

With the exception of myself (English), the captain, his wife, the engineer, and my one fellow-passenger, all of whom were Scotch, the rest on board were natives. The work of the boat seemed to be done easily and well, and without more noise than is usual on a steamer. The cooking was excellent, but that was, I believe, the result of the supervision of the captain's wife, for, when later I was left to the mercy of the native cook, I did not experience the same satisfaction in eating my meals.

There were on the boat four little cabins, each with two bunks, for the passengers, and a large cabin for the captain, and as there were only two passengers, we travelled in a most comfortable manner. We had our meals at a table set across the stern of the boat. Generally speaking, we spent the day on the upper deck, which was really the roof of the boat and was covered with an awning, and furnished with comfortable lounging basket chairs. From this point of vantage we could see well over the banks, and had a good view of the surrounding country.

For some distance above Chinde the river is not very wide, and its windings are numerous, while the banks are thickly wooded to the water's edge. This made the navigation difficult, and the steering, in consequence of the sharp bends, was most interesting to watch. The scenery, though it can hardly be called picturesque, is certainly pretty.

A few hours' journey from Chinde brought us into the Zambesi proper. Here the river widened out considerably, often to a width of three to four miles, though it never looked so wide, owing to the number of channels into which it was broken up by the numerous islands. The banks in this part were usually flat and low, and were covered with quite a jungle of grass and reeds from eight to ten feet high. Here and there were patches of a kind of waving Pampas grass mixed with papyrus, the appearance of which was very charming. In striking contrast to these were the gloomy-looking mangrove swamps which we came upon at intervals.

Not a day passed without our seeing numbers of hippos, great, unwieldy monsters, thrusting their huge heads out of the water to see what was coming to disturb their peace. Sometimes there were several on the sand-banks; and a most amusing sight it was to see them 'galumping' along to get into the water out of our way. 'Galumping' seems the only word that in the least expresses their ponderous mode of progression, which was too clumsy by far to be called 'bounding.' They are marvellous creatures, with an ugliness that impresses and fascinates as long as you are safely out of the way. To meet them would be extremely awkward and uncomfortable, if you were in a little native boat, as they have a way of popping up unexpectedly, and should they choose to come up under your boat, you would get a sudden shock, an upset, and a bath. Of steamers they seem to have a wholesome dread. They kept out of our way very cleverly, ducking to escape the shots that were fired off at them as soon as they were seen. Sometimes they would give a great yawn, displaying a huge cavern that looked as if they might easily have swallowed us, boat and all.

Another curious, and in a sense fascinating, creature to look out for and to watch was the crocodile—and crocodiles abounded. They were all sizes and colours. We often saw a number of them lying on a bank in a heap together fast asleep, or at all events not taking the least notice of us until a shot came and sent them tumbling into the water, one confused mass of heads, feet and tails. Even when not shot at, the least alarm will send them off wriggling and scuttling into the water with incredible swiftness. Some of the crocodiles had handsome skins, green with spots, others were difficult to distinguish, as they looked like logs of old wood lying on the banks; but we never had much chance of observing them, as the boys were much quicker at seeing them than we were; and the moment they shouted 'Crocs,' and pointed to where they were lying, guns were instantly fired and the crocodiles disappeared.

The crocodiles were, of course, fair game; but I most strongly objected to the way the birds were fired at. The reeds on both sides of the river were full of birds of every sort, size and colour. King fishers, reedmartins, and tiny birds of rose, green and scarlet colours. Of larger birds there were fish eagles, African cuckoos, black and white ibis, divers, herons, saddle-billed storks, egrets, and quantities of duck and guinea-fowl. When I remonstrated with the men for shooting at the birds, I was laughed at for not liking 'sport.' Where the 'sport' of the proceeding lay I could not discover, for there was nothing of skill about the shooting. It was just like firing into a poultry yard, and when a bird was killed, it could not be picked up, as the steamer did not stop. Often a number of wounded and helpless birds were left to die. One of the men who took part in the 'sport' belonged to the 'Society for the Prevention of Cruelty to Animals' at home, and was, moreover, proud of his active work for the society.

One day another man wounded a heron. As it flew off with its broken leg dangling, the natives shrieked with laughter and began to imitate it; upon this, the man, boiling over with righteous indignation, came up to me and said he could not stand the cruelty of the natives. 'The way they enjoyed seeing any-thing in pain,' etc., etc. When he had finished, I told him I thought the man who shot the bird for his own amusement was infinitely more cruel than the natives, at which he looked much astonished. I discussed the subject with the captain, who seemed to think the wounding of birds and animals of very little consequence where there were so many, and it was not until I told him I should leave the boat at the next station that he promised to have the shooting stopped. He kept his word, and during that journey, at least, the birds had a peaceful time. So had I in watching them, for the boat was often quite close to the banks, giving me a good chance to see them and their nests.

Among the many practices of white men out here which tend to retard the civilising of the natives, this is a prominent one. The missionaries endeavour to impress them with a sense of the gentleness and tenderness of Christianity, and yet they see professing Christians indulge in wanton cruelty of this nature. Birds and animals of all kinds are shot at, wounded, and left to die in great pain.

In many parts of Africa the native fauna are fast disappearing, owing to the 'sporting' proclivities of the white man. The tendency is to pass laws for their protection, when there is no longer any to protect.

Life on the boat was never in the least monotonous. The villages we passed always offered something curious to interest and amuse us. It was delightfully comfortable to lie lazily on a long cane chair on the upper deck and watch the way the steamer crossed from side to side of the river, in order to follow the current and dodge the sandbanks. The river was falling very fast, the channels were constantly altering, and a very sharp look-out had to be kept.

We had two goats on board, which supplied us with exceptionally good milk. This, for me, was a great treat, as I had had none for some time. The goats were well fed with grass, which the boys cut from the banks of the river as we went along. One or other of the barges sometimes got among the reeds, and then there was great excitement, while they all cut and pulled as much green stuff as possible without stopping the boat.

If in their excitement any of the boys tumbled into the water, they did not mind in the least, and were soon on the boat again. One afternoon we had a great fright; suddenly we heard the anchor chain running out, the engineer rushed down and stopped the boat, and then it was discovered that one of the boys had tumbled off the deck, and in falling had clutched at the chain and pulled the anchor over. Fortunately, in dropping over, it did not fall on him, and he escaped with a good scare, followed by a scolding.

As we approached Shipanga, the country became more thickly wooded, and we saw one large forest which was said to extend to Beira. Judging by what we could see of it from the boat, it appeared to be very dense. At Shipanga itself we saw Mrs Livingstone's grave, and the house, or rather the remains of the house, where she died. A huge baobab tree marks the spot, and can be seen in going up and down the river.

As this was the first time I had come across one of these trees, I was much struck by its remarkable appearance. It is indeed a curious and wonderful kind of tree, and looks as if it belonged to the days before the Flood. It appears as strange on the land as the hippo does in the water. One of these trees often measures seventy feet or more in circumference. The thick trunk gradually ta-pers towards the top. It has no waving branches covered with foliage, but at intervals thick boughs project from the main trunk, and are covered with little twigs and leaves. These branches are exact fac-similes of the trunk. The fruit is large, that is to say, about the size of a shaddock, with a hard but velvety green shell, full of small nuts of cream-of-tartar. The natives make a hole in the shell, fill it with water, and use it as a drinking cup, the cream-of-tartar giving the water a pleasant flavour. They fill it again and again with water till all the taste of cream-of-tartar is gone, then they throw it away and get a fresh one. These trees are found chiefly on the plains; I do not remember to have seen any growing on the high lands.

CHAPTER II

ON THE SHIRE RIVER

URING THE VOYAGE we stopped pretty often at 'wooding' stations—places where the supply of wood for fuel for the steamers was stacked ready to be put on board; a large supply is needed to keep them all going.

One is constantly hearing about the way the natives spoil the timber, and of their wasteful method of cutting it down to make their fires and to clear the ground for their gardens. Both charges are true; but nothing is ever said about the immense amount of timber we have felled for burning on our steamers. In Africa we always appear to consider the country ours and the natives the intruders.

While stopping at the stations, I was always glad to go on shore and have a look round the native villages, and in these little tours I found plenty of amusement, and saw many new and curious things.

At one village the Portuguese collector was having a new house built. The ground had been marked out and the floor was being made first. Its preparation was a very curious, not to say amusing, proceeding. A number of women, with babies tied on their backs, were down on their knees smearing mud on the floor with their hands. The mud used is made from the old ant-hills, and is of a peculiar hardness, and therefore suitable for floors. The hardness appears to be owing to some kind of excretion which the ants mix with the mould of which they make their hills. The clay of the ant-hills is pounded up and sprinkled on the ground, then the women dip their hands in water and smooth it over. The process certainly looked nasty, but the effect produced was good.

When the floor was finished, another mixture, in which cow-dung is an ingredient, was smeared over in the same way, in order to keep off the insects. The ants in Africa cannot be overlooked, they are a wonderful power for good and evil. They are splendid scavengers, but they are also destructive. In a house it is most difficult to keep eatables out of their reach. If the food is on a table,

its legs must stand on glasses or in bowls of water, and it must be well away from a wall, or anything else that the ants can climb up. They are very clever at finding a bridge to help them across to the food, and once found, the table is soon swarming with them. Sometimes, when you wake in the morning, you will find an ant-heap one or two feet high by the side of your bed. I heard of one unfortunate man, who, on going to put on his shoes in the morning, found the tops come off in his hand. The ants had eaten all round them in the night.

At another village I watched the natives making a large 'dug-out,' or native canoe. It was made from the trunk of a large tree, with the inside burnt out. The trunk was chopped into shape with their small axes. The axes were much smaller and lighter than those our people use at home, but they seemed to do the work as quickly and as well.

Close to the place where they were working at the boat was a wonderful blacksmith's forge. The bellows were made of a goat's skin. The head of the goat had been cut off, and into the neck there had been fixed a clay pipe which went into the furnace. Round this pipe the skin was firmly fastened. The wide end of the goat skin was cut across, and to each side was fixed a bamboo stick. A native sat on the ground, and taking these sticks in his hands, drew the sides of the skin apart until it was filled with air. Then placing the sticks together, so as to close the aperture, he pressed the skin downwards, and thus forced the air through the pipe into the fire. The contrivance was crude, but produced good results.

Some of the villages were very pretty. They consisted of round huts made of bamboo and thatched with grass. They were beautifully made with deep over-hanging eaves, and had a sort of outer wall of grass and bamboo to enclose the hut and yard. Most of the villages were fairly clean; but all had a very peculiar smell, arising from the native corn, of which the villagers cook so much, and the bhang they smoke. Bhang is supposed to have a soothing effect, but it makes those who smoke it extremely silly. I could always tell when they had been smoking it, for after sneezing loudly they continued to make foolish, idiotic noises until, to my intense joy, they fell asleep.

Three days' journey from Chinde we came in sight of the Morambala Mountain; and on the fourth day we turned out of the Zambesi into the Shiré River, which is much narrower and has higher banks. The scenery became more interesting, and we had lovely views of the mountains in the Shiré Highlands.

The river winds a good deal, and for one whole day we were going round Morambala. It is a beautiful mountain, covered with bush to the top; but the marsh all round, through which the river runs, is a most unhealthy spot, and swarms with mosquitoes and insects of many kinds. Consequently, we did not much enjoy the time we had to spend there. During the night we heard noises made by various wild animals, and the splash of crocodiles in the water; but fortunately no animal paid us a visit on the boat.

The steamer was always tied up to the bank for the night soon after sunset, about six-thirty or seven o'clock, and we started again in the morning about five or six.

Directly the work of tying up the boat was completed, there was an exodus of all the natives. They infinitely preferred sleeping on the bank to remaining on the boat; and they set to work at once to make large fires, at which to cook their evening meal, and round which to gather for a good chat. Soon numbers of other natives joined them, and a curiously weird and picturesque sight it was to see them all squatting round their big fires, chattering as only natives can. Their voices never ceased all night, at least, whenever I woke up, I always heard them. At these festive gatherings the indispensable pipe played, of course, a great part. Men of all races and colour seem to derive great joy and comfort from smoking. These natives, evidently thinking they could not have too much of a good thing, carried a huge pipe with them, which, whenever we stopped, and they had time to thoroughly enjoy it, was always passed round, each taking a few whiffs. The stem of the pipe, and the bowl to hold water, were made of one of the curiously-shaped and long-stalked gourds, which they grow and use for so many purposes. A hole is made in the top part of the bowl and a small piece of bamboo firmly inserted, then a large clay bowl for the tobacco is fixed on to the bamboo. The tobacco is lighted with a bit of wood from the fire, and then they suck up the smoke through the water and the long stem. It is in fact a kind of 'hubble-bubble;' many of the clay bowls are well ornamented, and curious patterns are drawn on the stem and bowl of the gourd. I have one pipe whose clay bowl is five and a half inches in diameter and nineteen inches long. The stem measures twenty inches in length, while the bowl for water measures eighteen inches in circumference. It was the largest I saw in use, and I had considerable difficulty in persuading its owners to part with it, and even more difficulty in packing and bringing it safely home. It has adorned the wall of my room for more than six months, and it is more than twelve months since it has been used; but the odour of the tobacco still clings to it, and indeed pervades the room if it is shut up for a time.

We had been travelling for six days after leaving Chinde, going all the time through Portuguese territory, when one morning we spied a large notice board erected on the river bank, like a warning that 'trespassers will be prosecuted.' But this was not the sort of notice we found. We could make out the words painted in large letters upon it— 'Here commences B. C. A. territory and reaches to' … we could not make out the rest, as the letters were worn or rubbed off. It was presumably thought unnecessary or imprudent at present to paint them in again, and to say how far British territory extends.

About there the land was very fairly cultivated. The natives had planted quantities of bananas and large patches of mealies and native corn near their villages. These villages were larger and more frequent than those we had hitherto seen; and, in addition to the huts for living in, there were always a number of huts for storing grain. These last were round in shape, and were built on piles to keep the corn safe from the rats, with which the country abounds.

The first British station that we came to was called Port Herald. Behind it is a fine range of mountains, on which there are said to be some large coffee plantations, which are doing extremely well. Port Herald itself is a well-laid-out place. Its straight roads have been planted on each side with trees, which cast a pleasant shade; and there are two or three neat-looking houses with well-thatched roofs and wide verandahs. Here the Europeans live; but most of the inhabitants of the place are Banyans, as the Indian traders are called. It seems to me a great pity to encourage so many of them to come and settle in B. C. A., as they are filling up the places wanted for our own surplus population. The Banyans can work for less money, and can live on considerably less than the ordinary white man. They have even fewer scruples as to correct weights and measures, and consequently can get on and flourish where a European would starve. The Banyans have already become a great difficulty in Durban, just as the Chinese have become in America; and surely, when we have so many difficulties to contend with in Africa, it is, to say the least, unwise to introduce another.

Two or three hours further up the river is Chiromo—a delightful station. The former consul took great pride in the place and laid it out exceedingly well. Of course, the roads were made perfectly straight and crossed each other at right angles. All had trees planted on each side for shade. A fine old baobab tree stands just at the end of the principal road, and is a very picturesque object. There are a good many houses for Europeans, and all stand well back from the roads and are surrounded by good gardens.

The consulate is a very pretty residence, with a charming view from the verandah overlooking the river Ruo, which runs into the Shiré at Chiromo. It

was a very lively house, as there were three or four British officials living there together. Indeed, all the inhabitants of Chiromo seemed to get on extremely well together, and to have a very good time. Many people might think there was a great drawback to their happiness on hearing that there was not a European lady in the place. Although deprived of the charm of their fellow-country-women's society, they were, they assured me, extremely happy. Still, they did not appear to object to a visit from a lady, just for a change, and they kindly asked me up to dinner, an invitation which I was very pleased to accept.

When I arrived at the consulate and was crossing the verandah, I was met by a cat flying for its life. Then I heard shouts of laughter. It seemed that I was the first European woman the cat had seen, and that she was terrified at the sight. But before I left we became good friends. I learnt from the consul that though a good many missionary ladies, both German and English, go up the river, I was the first lady who had been to call; indeed, I was the first Planet Pilgrim to travel that way. Somebody called me the 'first vagrant,' as I had no business to do and no connection with any work in that part. Of course, during dinner, I heard a number of lion tales; and the very night I arrived at Chiromo, a man was brought in having been terribly mauled by a lion, but owing to the good care the doctor took of him he recovered. The consul's immediate predecessor had had a delightful adventure. One evening he was walking home from the river in the dusk, when he saw something coming slowly along the path towards him. He politely stepped aside to allow it to pass, and as it did so he saw that it was a lion. For a moment he was too frightened to move. Then it occurred to him that he had better 'make tracks' for home, as the probability was that, after the lion had quenched his thirst at the river; he would wish for something to eat.

My hosts were much horrified at the idea of my going alone to Lake Tanganyika, and many and terrible were the consequences they foretold. They also made many kind and wonderful suggestions for the preservation of my health, and for keeping off the much-dreaded attacks of fever. Probably my immunity from fever was due to the fact that I did not adopt any of the suggestions. During my journey I was frequently asked, 'How many grains of quinine do you take daily?' and my questioners were much astonished to hear that I took no more than I should do at home, but followed the advice once given me by an old traveller, only to take quinine when I felt 'cheap.' Twice I thought I really was going to have an experience of fever, but on these occasions it was only that I was overfatigued or suffering from a chill caused by the sudden change of temperature experienced in passing from the lake to the high land, for I was all right again next day.

I was in B. C. Africa from June until November, and I never once was stopped by illness, or had to give up any expedition I had planned. Of course, it was the healthiest time of the year, but a good many people were ill with fever during that time. From what I heard and saw, I feel sure there would be a great deal less fever if those whose lot it is to live out there would learn to be more careful of their health. They do things that would make them ill in any country, and then put it down to the climate. Of course, working so much in the sun causes fever, and also working in houses with those detestable corrugated iron roofs. Some of these have nothing under the roof to keep out the heat; but surely it is not right to expose yourself in either way.

Directors of companies at home might give more care and thought to the comfort and health of their agents and clerks out there; but their chief care seems to be about the dividends. I certainly did long to see a few directors of the luxurious sort popped down in one of the offices at Chiromo, when the thermometer was 116° in the shade, the sun pouring down on the iron roof, striking on the heads of those within, and making the chairs so hot that one could hardly sit on them. On the verandah, too, you had to sit with your sun-shade up, or a wet cloth on your head, as that also had an iron roof. Imagine having to do brain work in such a heat. How soon the directors would have all this put right and made comfortable, even at the risk of having no dividend at all for a year or two, if they had to work under such conditions.

Another terrible bane is whisky drinking. Everyone knows what an immense amount of harm it does and how much fever it causes, yet nothing is done to stop it; while endless trouble and expense is incurred to find out other causes of fever.

My stay at Chiromo had been so interesting, and I had met with so much kindness, and had found so much amusement, that I was quite sorry when the 'Pious Paddler' was ready to continue her journey up the river; but I had the pleasure of thinking I should probably call there again on my way down, and in my turn have plenty of adventures to relate.

After leaving Chiromo, the river was still very winding, and the views of the mountains in the Shiré Highlands were lovely. The sandbanks were getting more frequent, and, of course, we stuck many times, but never badly. I think we should have felt that the day was too monotonous if we had not had the excitement of striking on a sandbank. These incidents gave rise to very amusing scenes, and were always sufficiently varied to excite interest. Besides, there was always the possibility of getting firmly fixed.

At one of the villages near a place where we tied up for the night, the captain bought a quantity of fowl and Muscovy duck. I went with him to buy them, and was highly amused at the bargaining. Of course, it was a long business, as it always is in the East, and it resulted in his getting the fowls for twopence each and the ducks for fivepence. This seemed wonderfully cheap, but I found that it was quite a good price as markets go there, and the natives were glad to part with them for the price mentioned.

From Chiromo to Katunga was only two days' journey, and here the river part of the expedition ended.

CHAPTER III

OVERLAND—THE SHIRE—TO BLANTYRE

KATUNGA IS SO CALLED AFTER THE CHIEF to whom that part of the country which surrounds the station belonged. Indeed, most places are named after chiefs, and many of the names have a very musical sound, and serve to recall some fact in the history of the country. Therefore it seems a pity that so many English and Scotch names are now being substituted when they have no meaning out there, and do not commemorate any special deed, either religious, civil or military.

Katunga is a curious and, in some ways, an interesting place. There is one large store with the buildings belonging to it, and all around, at the time of my visit, there was a confused mass of goods of every description, piled up just as they were left when unloaded from the river steamers—huge iron plates, parts of steamers, boilers, railway and telegraph stuff, and cases of every shape and size were all waiting to be carried off by the natives either up to Blantyre, a distance of about thirty miles, or to another station on the river at a place called Matope, some sixty miles off.

The Murchison Falls and Rapids are but a little way above Katunga, and of course they make it impossible for boats to go further. The river Shiré has here a drop of about twelve hundred feet in some thirty-five miles. Were it not for these rapids, the journey up from the coast to Lake Nyasa would be extremely simple, but not nearly so interesting.

It was almost dark when we arrived at Katunga, and I did not go on shore until next morning. I was not sorry to find I should have to stay until the following day, because all the natives about the station were employed in carrying loads, and, in order to have me and my luggage conveyed to Blantyre, others had to be sent for from the villages near.

Around Katunga there was plenty to see that was amusing and interesting.

719

For a long time I sat and watched the natives going off with their loads. A man sometimes carried as much as sixty pounds, though fifty-six pounds was the usual weight of a load for a single carrier. When the package was heavier, bamboo poles were fastened to it, and two or more men carried it. I was astonished to see how well they contrived to carry even very unwieldy things across the mountain. A good many of their loads consisted of the iron plates for the new gunboat, the 'Guendolen,' which was being built at Fort Johnston when I was there. These things were not only heavy, but they were also, owing to their shape, extremely difficult to carry. The angles of the plates were sharp and rough, and must have been exceedingly irksome when borne on bare shoulders. Yet they were wonderfully quiet and patient in going off with these awkward loads; but it was not a pleasant sight, and I was always glad when a load was such that they could put it on their heads, for, so placed, it seemed quite easy for them to manage it, and they always walked off with it quite cheerfully.

Here I saw several new styles of dressing the hair. One, which was very much in favour, was to have the tufts of hair twisted with wire or cotton, so that they stuck up in hard points all over the head. Some of the women had beads twisted in their hair, producing the effect of a bead fringe to a mat, which flopped and jingled as they ran.

On the following morning I was able to engage some men, and by eleven o'clock I was ready to start. The start was a most exciting and interesting performance, though just at first I was rather appalled at the array of wild-looking men. There were fourteen of them, twelve to carry me and two to carry my luggage, which weighed just sixty pounds, so that it was an easy load for two. I was to be carried in a machila, which is really a hammock made of strong sailcloth and slung on a bamboo pole. It was carried by two men, one at each end. Sometimes there is a cover all along the top of the pole, to make a shade, but as I found it interfered with the view, I only had curtains at the head, that I could draw or push back as I wished. A very important item in the make-up of the machila is the pillows. These, when well arranged, add greatly to the traveller's comfort. Much, too, depends on having them the right size and shape. I was miserably uncomfortable at first, but after a time I learnt how to ride with perfect ease; and next, after a Japanese jinrikisha, I consider machila travelling the most delightful mode of progression in a hot country.

Having inspected my conveyance, I proceeded to get in, but as I was not used to a hammock, when I got in on one side I promptly rolled out on the other. The boys shrieked with laughter and rushed to pick me up. Then when I tried again to get in, they formed up in a row on the off-side to prevent the possibility of a repetition of the accident. This time I succeeded in getting in, but my cushions were most uncomfortable, and I was afraid of moving much lest I should again roll out. Then, as the carriers got warm, the 'Bouquet d'Afrique' became almost unbearable, and when we came to the foot of the mountain I was thankful to get out and walk.

The men, when carrying the machila, go at a kind of trot, and travel at the rate of about four miles an hour. There is a wonderful difference in the way different men carry you. Some contrive to jolt most miserably, but, as a rule, they go very easily and change without stopping. In lifting the pole over their heads, just to change shoulders, they often give their heads an awful knock, but it does not trouble them, their skulls seem too thick for them to mind such a trifling blow.

The men who were carrying me were a happy lot, and sang and shouted at the top of their voices. The words of their songs were generally improvised about the 'Ulendo' (the journey), and the person they were carrying, and all the extraordinary things he or she had done or said. One man led off, a few more joined in, and they all ended up with a powerful chorus. Then, at intervals, without any provocation, they clapped the machila pole violently with their hands and uttered piercing shrieks and yells.

The men whose turn it was next to carry the machila would run by the side, and when the time came for them to take their part, they just slipped their shoulders under the pole and the others retired to the back to rest and walk quietly.

The road to Blantyre is called the Sclater road, after the man who made it, and it is a wonderfully good one. The first part out from Katunga was planted on both sides with limes, lemons and oranges. There was a good deal of fruit on some of the trees, and the scent was delicious. I often wished they had been continued further along the road. For some distance the way was very level and kept to the plain. By-and-by we came to the foot of the mountain, and there I got out and walked, as the ascent was very steep. The road went up in long zig-zags, while the native paths took short cuts, and as they were more in the shade of the trees, I preferred going up them, stopping often to enjoy the lovely view over the plain, along which we could see the river Shiré winding for a great distance. In this way it took us nearly an hour to reach the top of the Pass. Then, as the men wanted to go more quickly, I got into the machila again; but before we got to a kind of rest-house at 'Mbami, half-way to Blantyre, I had another hour's walk and climb. It was half-past two o'clock when I arrived at 'Mbami. At this rest-house I found a native who could speak a few words of English, and what was even a greater joy, he knew how to make tea, and had a tin of nice biscuits. The men were glad of a rest, and we remained about an hour before we set off again.

We journeyed on and on, the sun set, and I began to feel rather anxious. I was getting tired, and of course could not speak to the men to find out how much further we had to go, so I had to cultivate patience, and trust we should soon get to the end of our journey. Fortunately there was a lovely moon to light us, and the men relieved the monotony of the journey by their singing, shouting and funny antics.

At last, about half-past seven, we stopped. All that I could discern were some high gates, a wall and a round tower. The men made signs for me to get out of the machila, which I did, though very much puzzled as to the place, which seemed to me to be a prison. After some hammering at the doors, a native inside came and unlocked and unbarred them, had a long confabulation with my men, and finally let us all in. We found ourselves in a large open space with buildings all round. I discovered at last that we had reached Blantyre, and that this place belonged to the African Lakes Company. Their stores and offices were built round this large square in order to afford protection and defence against the natives in case of a rising, and also to serve as a laager for the Europeans of the neighbourhood.

The manager's house was at one end, and there I received a very kind welcome, and an invitation to stay. The house was a grand one, for that part of the world; it was two storeys high, which is most unusual, and it had a splendid verandah all round. It is called 'Mandala,' the native word for glasses. The builder and first occupier of the house wore glasses, and of course it was named after him, as the natives have their own names, taken from some peculiarity, for all Europeans and for European things.

When I went up to my room I found a large white owl in possession. The natives, who are very superstitious, were horrified, as they consider them very unlucky. Fortunately, they have a firm belief that owls cannot be killed, so they do not attempt to destroy them. A curious thing happened once to confirm that belief. A European raised his gun and aimed at an owl, the natives said they were certain he could not shoot it, and sure enough something had happened to the gun and it declined to go off. Of course, before it could be put right, the owl had quietly flown away.

I was told here, that another creature of which the natives have a great horror is the chameleon, but of those they kill all they can find. They say the chameleon and the lizard were sent into the world as messengers of life and death. The lizard went off at a great rate, but the chameleon loitered on the way, and when he arrived he found the lizard had been on the earth for some time and had instituted Death, and therefore, because of his laziness, the natives destroy all the chameleons they come across.

Blantyre is cool, and should be healthy. It is three thousand feet above the sea, and the air was quite bracing after the heat of the plains. The scenery round is good, and there are some lovely mountains, which are four to five thousand feet in height, as well as numerous hills of less altitude. It is a curiously-arranged place, and each hill seems to have its own settlement. Mandala is on one, the mission station on another, the civil Boma, with the post and telegraph offices, on a third. 'Boma' is the native word for stockade, and as there is always one round the collector's house, the 'seat of government' has acquired the name of 'Boma.' On yet another hill is the hospital, which did not appear to be much used, despite its many comforts and lovely situation. The reason for this seems to be, that people prefer being nursed in their own homes whenever that is possible. Certainly the advent of trained nurses in that part of the world has been an immense blessing, and now that several have been sent out by the missions and the government, who are at liberty to go to the homes of the patients, there are many more recoveries from bad attacks of fever than formerly. In old days there was very little chance of recovery for anyone down with fever, who was left only to the care of the natives. These, though anxious to do their best, knew very little of the wants of Europeans. Doctors, too, were fewer in number, and were extremely difficult to get at. They often arrived too late to be of use, as the distances are so great.

It was Livingstone's idea to found a Scotch colony in the Shiré Highlands, and after his death this was done, and it has been named Blantyre, after his birthplace. The inhabitants, apart from the natives, are almost entirely Scotch; and, indeed, the whole way from Chinde to Lake Tanganyika, you meet Scotchmen, and nearly every one's name begins with 'Mac.' All kinds of things seem to flourish about Blantyre, roses and many other home flowers, wheat, maize, rice, potatoes, sugar-cane, tobacco, and, of course, coffee. There are many large coffee plantations doing extremely well. The first plant was brought over from the Edinburgh Botanical Gardens, and was planted in the Blantyre Mission garden, where it flourished for many years, and is the parent of all the plantations. Nyasaland coffee commands the best price in the London market, and is certainly most excellent in flavour; but, unfortunately, I seldom had the pleasure of tasting it in Nyasaland, owing to the trouble of roasting and grinding it. Tea is so much more easily made, that you get a great deal more of it.

The coffee plantations were very interesting to go through, and they were a very pretty sight, for when I was there, at the end of July, the bushes were loaded with the bright red fruit, and the natives were all busy picking it into baskets. After seeing the picking, we followed the berries to the pulpers and saw the soft outer covering taken off, and then watched all the various processes, till finally we saw some of the coffee put in sacks ready to be shipped off to England. Certainly it appeared to me to be the finest coffee I had ever seen, and I have seen coffee growing in many countries.

Another day I went to see a tobacco plantation. There is, of course, plenty of tobacco used in B. C. Africa, and as the plant seems to flourish well, the growing of it ought to be a paying industry. I was astonished to see the number of processes the leaf has to go through before it is ready for smoking.

A visit to the mission took up another and a most interesting day, as there were so many kinds of work going on. Of course, it is quite an old settlement. Having been started, I believe, in 1875, everything is well established, and the work goes on regularly and well. The church is a wonderful building. It would attract attention and admiration anywhere, but seen in a part of the world that at home we consider far away from all civilisation, it excites amazement. It took about three years to build, and is entirely native work. The missionary was the architect, the natives made and laid the bricks, and did all the wood-carving and ornamentation. The design of the church is most elaborate; it has towers and domes, and a circular east end with good stained glass. In the nave there are two stained windows. The glass, of course, has come from home. The pulpit is of native wood well carved, and there is a good deal of carving about the doors. The church stands in a large, open square, and there is a beautiful avenue of eucalyptus trees, nearly a mile long, leading up to it. The trees are from sixty to a hundred feet high, and were planted in 1879.

Near the church are good schools. In addition to the ordinary school instruction, carpentering, printing, gardening, etc., are taught to the boys, and needlework, laundry, dairy and housework to the girls. All this instruction makes them very useful servants for us; but I sometimes wondered how much is for ourselves and how much is honestly and solely for the good of the natives. We are certainly creating in the native a desire, and even greed, for money, and with that a wish for finery and clothing such as they had not before, and that certainly is not for their good. They look far better and are healthier with only their nsaru, or loin cloth, made of native cloth, or even of the poor calico we send out to them, than when wearing old soldiers' coats, and the shabby things they are tempted to buy at the stores—clumsy boots that deform their feet and make them walk badly, and horrid old hats stuck on their heads. They never wore hats formerly, and the sun is no hotter now, so that they cannot be necessary, and are certainly dirty and untidy. Moreover, if we are teaching them many of our own industries, they are forgetting their own. The native iron and copper work was excellent, and their axes, hoes, spears and knives were all beautifully made and ornamented. All the things they use were carved, or had brass, copper or iron wire tastefully twisted round them. The gourds for drinking were adorned with all kinds of quaint designs, and their ntangas, or baskets for holding their possessions, were much prettier than the ugly boxes in which we keep ours. They had decidedly an idea of making their things tasteful as well as useful, and of course had plenty of time to spend on decoration. The native weaving and the bead-work, too, is dying out as, now money is earned, all these things can be obtained more cheaply at the stores. Architecturally, we are not improving the look of the country. Red brick houses are certainly not pretty; while the Wankonde huts at the north end of Lake Nyasa are most picturesque and beautifully clean and neat. They have a framework of bamboo, then clay pressed into different shapes is placed in patterns between the bamboo, or sometimes the bamboo is plaited in patterns and the clay is plastered on inside. Then with a good thatch, and provided with well overhanging eaves, they have a delightfully cool house and a very pretty one. If the difficulty is that the huts are not roomy enough, surely it cannot be difficult to teach the natives to make them larger and with better accommodation. It seems a pity we cannot develop and improve all the good in the natives without having to teach them all our own fads and customs, many of which have certainly not proved entirely satisfactory at home. We English are an odd mixture, we send out large sums for missions, and then permit and encourage such a show in London as 'Savage Africa,' which must thoroughly demoralise the natives, and undo years of patient work. It would be curious to know what the natives think of a nation that goes in crowds to see a representation of such a terribly sad incident as 'Wilson's last stand,' in which possibly some of the very same natives who took part in the slaughter are being employed to act it over again, just for the amusement of Wilson's countrymen. It surely will be counted one of the disgraces of the nineteenth century that such a show was permitted and supported. It is most earnestly to be hoped that no more shows of the same kind will ever be allowed. The great hold we have over the natives in Africa is on account of the respect, and almost awe, they have for the white man, and their belief in his superiority; but such shows must lessen their respect for us, and do incalculable harm.

CHAPTER IV

BLANTYRE TO LIWONDE

AFTER SPENDING SOME DAYS IN BLANTYRE, I started off in my machila, with seventeen boys, to see something of the surrounding country. I had again two boys for my baggage, but this time I took fourteen to carry the machila, as I was going longer distances. Of course, there was a 'capitao,' as the head man is called, to look after the others. He generally walked along in a most dignified manner, carrying a quite useless gun. Each of the others carried a spear, a small axe and a knobkerry—a stick with a heavy knob at the end, which is useful in helping to support the load on their shoulder. It is also used as a weapon, and with it the native can give a deadly blow. They were a picturesque-looking crew, with their cat-skin bags filled with food and slung on their arms, and looking like stuffed animals.

The skins of some wild cats are very handsome. When they have killed the cat, the natives just cut off the head, and then literally 'let the cat out of the bag.' The inside of the skin is then rubbed with stones to get it clean, and is afterwards dried in the sun. It is next turned with the fur outside again, and it makes a perfect bag, never having been cut anywhere, except at the neck. The legs make useful and separate pockets for snuff, of which the natives take a great deal, and for tobacco, etc.

The men's clothing consisted of a loin cloth, and plenty of necklaces, armlets, and anklets, made of beads and twisted copper and brass wire. Their hair was trimmed, of course, in all sorts of amusing fashions; and their bodies were well rubbed with oil, which shone in the sun, and polished up the colour of their skins, which is a dark chocolate. They were happy and noisy, just like a lot of children, and seemed to be as easily amused.

My destination that day was Zomba, which was forty-two miles off; too far to travel comfortably in one day. As I did not want to camp on the way, a relay of men had been sent on the night before to relieve the others when we got about half-way, and enable them to return home. I started about seven a.m., and did not reach Zomba till nearly seven p.m. Of course, we often stopped for a rest, and I did a good deal of walking, which is not such a quick way of getting on as being carried; but I got so tired of riding in the machila, that I was glad to get out and walk occasionally, by way of a change. It was rather disconcerting to be unable to speak to my carriers, but they were uncommonly clever at making themselves understood by signs, and as no difficulties arose on the way, there was no real necessity to talk to them.

The only mishap was the loss of my mid-day meal. I was to have stopped at a coffee planter's on the way, but I could not discover where he lived. Either the boys did not know, or they did not wish to stop there, and I arrived at Zomba very hungry and tired. One is made wise by experience, and after that day I always carried a small stock of biscuits, and a bottle of tea, in the machila with me. The road was a very good one all the way from Blantyre to Zomba, though it was rather hilly; but a bicycle could easily go along it. There was a great deal of the usual scrubby kind of forest; the trees, of course, looked worse at that time of the year, as many had no leaves on them.

At last I reached Zomba, and was surprised to find it such a remarkably civilised place. I had known that it was the Seat of Government, but at home one thinks of everyone in B. C. Africa as struggling with hardships, so that I was quite unprepared to find so much of comfort, and almost luxury, as I did here.

It is prettily situated at the foot of a high mountain of the same name, which overlooks a big plain, with Lake Shirwa in the middle, and the mountains of Mlanje in the distance. The residency is a fine building, and has beautifully laid-out grounds; but the interior of the house had a rather forlorn appearance. The place is not considered very healthy, and a new residency is to be built in a better situation. The Government and post and telegraph offices are close by; and, dotted about among the trees on the hillside, are pretty one-storied houses occupied by the European residents. There is a good store belonging to the A. L. C., where all ordinary wants can be supplied, a large tennis ground, that seems to be well used, and a military station, where about three hundred natives were, at this time, being drilled.

When I was at Zomba, there were only four ladies living there, two married ladies and the two Government nurses. They were all made much of, and seemed to be having a thoroughly good time, indeed the whole settlement struck me as being a very happy one. It was amusing to hear of the fuss that was made over the 'Zomba baby,' the first white child born in that part of the world. It was just a year old, and, a few days before I arrived there, had held a grand reception on its birthday. Everyone called on it, and the amount of cake eaten on that occasion was considered responsible for all the illness for some time after.

Zomba mountain is a lovely place, and puts thoughts of picnics into one's mind. The plateau on the top ought to be a grand 'health resort' for the people living on the plains, when the heat there becomes too intense. It is about four thousand feet high, and we found the ascent long and steep. The views obtained on the way up were glorious; and as the friends who went with me up the mountain had arranged to start early, there was plenty of time to enjoy the climb and the prospect before the heat became too great. From the top, you look over a large, well-wooded plain, with Lake Shirwa in the centre, the Mlanje mountains opposite, and Mount Chiradzulu on one side.

July is not the best month for the flowers, but we found a great variety, and some of very brilliant colours. The ferns, too, were splendid, especially those near the streams. The top of the mountain is charming country, where one can walk for miles, up and down hills, across streams and up mountains almost as high as Zomba itself. In one place we came upon a lovely waterfall, where the water dashed over great ledges of granite, and here we found large patches of osmunda, maidenhair, and other varieties of fern. Many of the trees were flat-topped—the kind one sees so often in Central and South-East Africa. Game seemed abundant. We saw a good many bok in the distance, and the boys showed us the spoor of wild cats, leopards, etc. We boiled our kettle and had tea by a lovely stream, and felt very loath to leave the plateau and go down again to the plain. In descending the mountain the views were even more lovely, as a slight haze made the light softer and the colouring more beautiful.

When I left Zomba I went on to Domasi, another Scotch mission station, only two hours and a half distant. My boys left the road and took me by native paths, going round to the other side of Mount Zomba, which is totally different, and very much finer—a precipice of grey rock.

The first view of Domasi is very pretty. The mission buildings are all thatched, the church has a deep red roof, and the wooded mountains and grey rocks at the back formed a charming picture. Here again I received a most kindly welcome, and much enjoyed a stay of a day or two; though the manse is, without exception, the most draughty place I ever was in. The rooms are large and lofty, no door or window fits, and there are brick floors. This all sounds as if it ought to be delightful in British Central Africa. But Domasi stands high, and it happened to be very cold weather, 'exceptionally cold,' of course. I had just come up from the heat of the plains, and most heartily wished I had brought warmer clothing with me. The natives seemed to feel the cold very much too, and went about in the early morning well wrapped up in their arms, which is their method of keeping themselves warm. They cross their arms in front, and clutch their shoulders with their hands.

There was a funny little native boy about the manse. He was only four years old, and was found two years ago by Colonel Manning during some fighting up country. He was the only living creature left in a native village, and he had two bad wounds, one of them on his head. The child was brought to the manse, to be taken care of, and of course has been made a great pet, and is becoming a sharp, amusing little lad.

Many of the native women round Domasi wear 'Peleles' in their upper lip, making it stick out like a pig's snout. The largest one I saw there was of solid ivory, two inches long, and three and a half inches in circumference. A slit is cut in the upper lip, just under the nose, and a piece of wood or ivory is inserted to prevent it healing, then gradually larger and larger pieces are put in till they reach the fashionable size. Further up country I got a very large and queer one; it was of tin, hollow like a dish, and was five inches in circumference and rather more than one inch deep. It was quite the most ugly 'ornament' I have ever seen. It puzzled me to understand how the women talked and ate with such decorations in their lips, but apparently use was second nature, for it was only when the 'Pelele' was taken out that they experienced a difficulty in talking. The two women whom I persuaded, by liberal offers of beads and salt, to let me have the very large ones they were wearing, had to get thick pieces of wood to put in at once when they took the others out. The younger women are not following this fashion, but as they must have some ornament, they put a thick piece of lead or ivory in one side of the nose. In the lobe of each ear they wear large discs, the size of a five-shilling piece, made of ivory or wood ornamented with brass nails. Sometimes, in addition, the whole ear is studded round with brass or ivory. The men, too, do not disdain to wear large and solid pieces of ivory or wood in the lobes of their ears, and sometimes the large hole thus made is found useful to carry other things, such as snuff boxes, or trifles of that sort.

The faces and bodies of both men and women are often tattooed in wonderful patterns, and they always have a tribal mark. The tattooing in B. C. A. is done quite differently from the way it is done in Japan, and from the way our sailors do it. The patterns are formed by means of raised lumps. These are made on the skin by cutting it, and rubbing something in to raise it up. This is done on the face or any part of the body, in all sorts of patterns, and sometimes in rows of wonderfully straight parallel lines.

I noticed, too, that there were many fashions in teeth. Teeth do not seem to lend themselves to fashion's caprices, but the natives have discovered the possibility of considerably altering their appearance. Some have all of them filed to points, looking like the teeth of a saw; others have the upper front teeth notched, and some have the two front teeth taken out. Of course, all this may have been the result of other motives than a desire to become 'advantageously varied,' but I could not discover them.

Many of the women adorned themselves wonderfully, and looked very gay and picturesque. Round their heads they wore a band of beadwork, beautifully made, loads of bead necklaces adorned their necks, bead arrangements swathed their waists, and on arms and ankles they wore a number of copper, iron and brass bangles. I much admired the colour of their skin. It is a rich chocolate, and, when well kept, has a beautifully clear, smooth look, almost like satin. Out in Africa it looks infinitely handsomer than the yellowish white skin of the Europeans; for out there, a really lovely English complexion is not to be found, and 'white' people are usually either red, yellow or brown; shades which certainly do not harmonise as well with the surroundings as does the native colour.

The making of these bead ornaments was an interesting process to watch; it was almost as intricate as lace-making. The women make the cotton they use as thread. They have no needles, but make a fine point to the cotton and thread each bead separately; most of the patterns they invent themselves, but they are delighted to be shown new ones.

From Domasi I went to see a coffee plantation at Songani. It seemed to me a rather amusing proceeding to take my machila and my seventeen men about with me wherever I went. At first I was troubled as to what would become of them when I stayed a few days at a station; but I found it was the custom, and no one objected to my arriving with that number of men, and the men themselves were perfectly content and happy. They always took themselves off to the nearest native village, and waited with the most absolute indifference just as long as I wished. It was perfectly delightful to meet with beings who had so much spare time.

As we approached Songani, the men gave ample warning of our arrival, and, for fully a quarter of an hour before reaching the house, they began to sing at the top of their voices, then they gave vent to yells, shrieks and every imaginable sort of noise. I tried to make them be quiet. I saw it was a nice house we were coming to, and I felt terribly ashamed to arrive in such a fashion with such a horde of lunatics, but my efforts to make them quieter were, I think, construed into approval of the noise, and only incited them to greater exertions. When my hostess came out to welcome me, I immediately poured forth my apologies, but she only laughed, and said that it was the custom, and they rather liked it, as it let them know that friends were coming, and also showed that the men were happy and getting on well.

I thoroughly enjoyed my visit to Songani. The house was extremely picturesque. Its broad verandah, with its tempting lounging chairs and pleasant shade, gave it an air of comfort. The garden was bright with flowers, and beyond was the steep granite side of Mount Zomba. The road up to the house led through a large nursery of young coffee plants, all looking strong and healthy, and the ground was so beautifully kept, that there was not a weed to be seen. When, after a rest, I went round the estate, I found the large coffee plantations equally well cared for; and, indeed, the whole place was so wonderfully neat, that it was difficult to believe one was in Africa.

During my stay there we went for a walk through two of the adjacent native villages, and watched the women pounding corn in tall mortars made of wood. They use a long, heavy pole, about six feet long and four inches thick, to pound with. Two women pound at the same time, and they lift the poles with such regularity that, though the mortar is very narrow, they seldom clash. When the pounding is done, they crush the corn quite fine, by rubbing it between two stones, one small stone over another big flat one. This sometimes makes the flour very gritty, as the stones are often not very hard, and a good deal gets rubbed off into the flour.

While I was at Songani, the natives came in with balls of rubber for sale. They collect it from a kind of vine that grows wild in Nyasaland; they cut the rind of the vine in places, and as the juice oozes out, they smear it over their hands, arms and bodies. Then, on their way home, when it has set a little, they roll it off into balls.

From Songani I started off to reach the river again at Liwonde. There was, I believe, a good road most of the way, but the natives preferred the paths, and I was very pleased when they turned off the road. Then the way became much more interesting, though at times it was terribly rough. I had constantly to get out and walk; and many times when I was riding I found why it was necessary to have the hammock made of strong sail cloth instead of netting, for the machila caught on the tops of thorn bushes, stumps roughly chopped off, and sharp rocks sticking up by the pathways. A native path is said to go as direct as possible from one village to another, but the windings and turnings, to avoid a stone or a fallen tree, are endless, and I am sure increase the distance at least one mile in four. Still, I thought it pleasanter and more amusing than going straight on, and time was no object to me or my boys.

The path through the high grass and thorn bushes was only wide enough for a native, and while traversing it, I had to take great care to avoid a creeping-plant called the 'Cowitch,' the proper name of which is, I believe, the macuna bean. It has bunches of pods, which look like lovely old-gold plush, but the 'plush' consists of tiny spines, which, if you touch them, cause a terrible irritation, that drives you nearly frantic with pain. The only relief seems to come from getting into water, and that is not always at hand. The thorns, too, were very bad, many of them being from four to four and a half inches long, and the grass was higher than my head.

We crossed several streams, sometimes on queer bridges made of bamboo, but more often on a pole thrown across, and much more suited to an acrobat than to me. The boys seemed thoroughly to enjoy the fun of getting me over, and never once let me tumble.

As we went along, I had noticed a good deal of smoke, which I knew came from a big grass fire. I rather wondered if we should get caught in it, but the boys went on, so I supposed it was all right. Presently, however, I heard the curious crackling sound of the fire, and a sudden turn brought us into full view of it. On both sides of the path the flames were blazing up as high as the trees, and coming towards us. The boys ran back with me to where the path was wider, and the grass not so high, then they each got a stick, and we waited till the fire came nearer and there seemed a good chance of getting through. As we waited we saw hares flying for their lives, and poor beetles and frogs scurrying along in hope of escape. Then four of the boys seized the machila and simply flew through the burning grass, while the others on each side beat the flames back as well as they could. How they escaped getting badly burned was a marvel. I was very thankful when we were through, for the heat and smoke were stifling, and I was well covered with bits of burnt grass. For a long distance the heat from the smouldering wood was very great.

As we got nearer to the river, we saw again a great many of the large, strange-looking baobab trees, then the river came in sight, and, to my astonishment, I found the station was on the other side. I was wondering how the crossing would be accomplished, when the 'Collector' caught sight of me, and most kindly came across in his canoe to fetch me. The boys and the machila went over in native 'dug-outs.' Then, as I intended going further up the river to Lake Nyasa, I had to part with my cheery team of boys, and they went off, rejoicing greatly over the few yards of calico which I gave them in addition to their pay.

I had timed my arrival at Liwonde on the day on which I had been told the river steamer, the 'Livingstone,' would be waiting for me, but there was no sign of it, and it did not arrive until two days later. Things are, of course, very casual in that part of the world, and the only possible way to have any happiness is just to take things as they come, and forget such evil habits as keeping appointments, or fixing times for anything.

While waiting I always found plenty of amusement in strolling about a village and watching the women employed at their beadwork, or in sifting corn— work which they do with great quickness and much grace of movement. They shake the corn in an open basket, and as the coarse grains come to the top, they

send them out with a little toss on the mat below. It looked such an easy process, that, to their great amusement, I had a try, but of course I could not manage it at all. However, before I left Africa, I was able, after repeated trials, to do it after a fashion.

CHAPTER V

VOYAGE ON THE 'LIVINGSTONE' AND 'DOMIRA'

WHEN AT LAST THE 'LIVINGSTONE' arrived at Liwonde, it had on board so many people who were going up to various stations, that I was thankful I had not to spend a night on the steamer. We started from Liwonde at seven a.m., and at eight p.m. we reached Fort Johnston, which is within a few miles of the point where the river leaves the lake. The journey had been a very pleasant one. All our meals were served on the upper deck, and there was the usual excitement of seeing hippos and crocs, of stoppages at 'wooding' stations, and of visits to native villages. It was the season for gathering the castor-oil berries, and many of the natives were busy drying and crushing them, in order to extract the oil, which they appear to make use of in a great variety of ways. They apply it both externally and internally. It puts a splendid gloss on their skin, but it has a decidedly unpleasant odour.

We crossed Lake Pa-Mlombe, which is supposed to have been formerly part of Lake Nyasa, and to have been divided from it by the silting-up of the sand, which has in this manner formed a separate lake. Lake Pa-Mlombe has nothing of the picturesque about it; it is about twelve or fifteen miles long and ten to twelve broad. The water is of a dirty colour, and carried a great deal of mud and sand in solution; while the navigation appeared to be very difficult, owing to its shallowness.

As it was quite dark when we got to Fort Johnston, I could see nothing of the place that evening. Next morning, however, I had a good look round, and was astonished to see what a large and well-arranged station it was. The whole place has only quite lately been planned and laid out. The old Fort Johnston was nearer the lake, in a low-lying spot. The ground round it was very swampy, and in consequence of its unhealthiness, arising from this fact, had to be abandoned, and a site for a new station selected in a more sanitary locality. Accordingly the new station is in a much better position, which is raised above the river, and commands a lovely view of the wooded mountains opposite. It made the place look quite gay and pretty when several of the lake and river steamers and the gunboats happened to be anchored opposite the station at the same time. The new gun boat for Lake Nyasa, the 'Guendolen,' was being built while I was there. She was the first boat to be built on a proper 'slip,' and the noise made by the workmen hammering on the iron plates reminded one of the Clyde.

There are people who say it was a serious mistake to build Fort Johnston in its present position. They say it should have been built on the lake instead of nearly five miles down the river, because, in the dry season, the bar is often impassable for the lake steamers. The consequence of this is, that, in dry seasons, the cargo has to be sent up and down in barges, with the result that unnecessary expense, trouble and delay is caused. Also, they complain that it is not on the line of the proposed railway; and their last, but most important objection is, that it is unhealthy. Poor Fort Johnston! If all these complaints are well founded, there is probably another move in prospect for it.

There are a number of government officials living at Fort Johnston, and the commander was lucky enough to have his wife out with him. This made a wonderful difference to the social life of the place. If others would follow his example, and bring their wives out too, it would certainly make an immense and much-to-be-desired social improvement; though, possibly, it might not be the happy lot of everyone to have a wife who would so thoroughly enjoy the life out there, and manage everything so well as the commander's wife. I was sorry when, having spent nine delightful days, the lake steamer, 'Domira,' arrived, and bore me off. But I was made happy by the thought that I should have to call there again on my return to the coast.

The 'Domira' was a curious little steamer of about eighty tons. Its highest part was the middle, and it looked very much like an old 'Noah's Ark.' Down below was a tiny cabin with two bunks. It was just like a cupboard with two shelves. This cabin was allotted to me, and, of course, I called it my 'State Room.' The rest of the space below was intended for a saloon, but part of it was curtained off to make extra separate sleeping places when wanted; and when the boat was full, mattresses were laid on the rest of the floor. We had our meals on the upper deck. The first two days it was impossible to move about on deck, as there were ten passengers, and we could hardly find room for our chairs in addition to the table. This state of things, however, only lasted two days; the rest of the way there were only two passengers besides myself. The lower deck for'ard, where the engines, the galley and the crew were, was covered with steel, and was so hot and slippery, that I wondered there were no accidents to the men when going backwards and forwards, and sometimes carrying awkward loads.

The 'Domira' turned out to be a much better boat than she looked, and she was uncommonly plucky in a storm. She had an excellent captain, a kind and amusing man, who contributed a great deal to my entertainment. He told me much about the natives and their ways, and, what was very useful to me afterwards, he taught me many of their words.

On our way up Lake Nyasa we saw the old 'Ilala' lying up for repairs. She is a tiny little steamer, no bigger than a steam-launch, and was the first European steam-boat that was ever on Lake Nyasa. She was brought out from England in pieces, and put together there, and the natives were intensely astonished to see her go along without rowers. They could not understand how such a thing was possible; but they have now become quite accustomed to the sight of steamers, and they very much enjoy going on one. Just after we had crossed the bar, and got into the lake, a large barge came alongside with about a hundred natives, who wanted to be taken on board. They had been down to the south end of the lake to do some work, in order to earn money to pay their hut tax, and they were now going back home. The 'Domira' reminded me still more of Noah's Ark when the natives were all climbing up the side and packing themselves in.

I had a great shock the first night, when, on taking possession of my 'state room,' I found that I would have to share it with an enormous number of cock-roaches. They were the largest I had ever seen, and the most voracious. Some of them greedily ate all the kid off my shoes, while others, who were not so engaged, ran races over my bunk and nibbled my hair. The next night I had a mosquito curtain put up and tucked well in. It kept me safe from the cock-roaches, but it made the bunk very hot and stuffy. It was a choice of evils, and the heat was the lesser one.

The day after we left Fort Johnston we stopped at Monkey Bay, a lovely 'wooding' station, with splendid granite rocks coming down on either side to the water, and behind them wooded mountains inhabited by numbers of monkeys. We made a stay of two or three hours here, while the crew were engaged in taking wood on board, and this gave me an opportunity of having a good walk round.

The captain had told me of a curious native burial ground a little distance away from the bay, and after some searching I found it. There were small grass huts put up near to the graves, on which were baskets and pots of food, and several broken pots and gourds. I was told afterwards by someone who had lived for some time in Nyasaland, that the little grass huts were for the spirits of the deceased, and that they might be consulted there, and would receive gifts. The natives have a kind of ancestor worship, and always offer food and presents to the spirits of their dead relatives who, they believe, can help them on special occasions. They also believe in many spirits, good and evil, which they imagine inhabit air, earth and water. These they propitiate from time to time with offerings of food and drink. When anyone dies, all his cooking utensils, water-pots and calabashes are put in or on the grave after having been broken, or 'killed,' as they call it. An official once asked a native why he put such offerings of food and drink on the grave, adding, 'You know the dead cannot eat or see these things.' The native gave the excellent answer, 'Of course, we know they do not eat them, but even you don't know that they cannot see them, and are not pleased at finding that we still think of them.'

I was in the country too short a time to learn much for myself of their religious customs and observances; but, of course, I heard a great deal about the witch doctors and the 'Mfiti,' which last seems to be an evil spirit that takes possession of some man in a village or tribe, and makes him work all kinds of evil. When trouble arises in a village, it is the witch doctor's business to discover the man who has caused it. Generally two people are accused, and they have to go through the ordeal of drinking poisonous Mwavi. If the poison acts as an emetic they are innocent, but if either dies there is great rejoicing, because they think the evil spirit has been discovered and driven away. In some cases fowls are chosen to represent the suspected people, and the Mwavi is administered to them instead. If a native has only a headache, he thinks one of his ancestors is angry with him for something that he has done. Accordingly he makes an offering. But he does not confide only in their assistance. He resorts to the very human and primitive plan of tightly binding his aching head with a piece of cloth or rag.

Domira Bay was our next stopping-place, and there seven of the passengers landed. The shore here was very flat and swampy, and all of them had to be carried by natives from the boats to the dry land. This method of landing resulted in a rather amusing procession, in which, after a time, I had to take part. The natives always carried me on their shoulders, and I found it by no means easy to keep my balance, with nothing to hold on to, while my bearer floundered about through the water on very uneven ground. While on the 'Domira,' a splendidly big, strong fellow carried me, and brought me safely to the shore and boat each time I landed, but I often 'had my doubts' on the way. The natives always carried the male passengers 'pick-a-back,' which was a much easier and more secure way of crossing the water, but was not as dignified as riding on the shoulder.

We reached Kota-Kota at dusk, and I did not go on shore till the next morning. When I did land, I had a very enjoyable time. The shore is low and uninteresting, but this is compensated for by the large number of trees, and the beautifully green appearance which their foliage gives to the place. The collector is very particular about the trees, and does not allow them to be cut down or destroyed. Formerly Kota-Kota used to be a great stronghold of the

Arabs, and had an enormous population. Though the population has greatly diminished, a sort of census that has lately been taken shows that it still numbers 8700. Jumbe used to be the great chief of that part, and his widow still lives there. She is delighted to receive a call from any visitor, and is a fine-looking woman, with brilliant eyes and beautifully white teeth. I asked the collector, who kindly went with me to visit her, to tell her how much I admired them. She was greatly pleased at the expression of my admiration, and replied that, as regards the teeth, the English, even at her age, would have quite as beautiful ones if they would not eat their food so hot. She showed me all her silver and ivory ornaments, some of which were very handsome. She wore a good many of them on her neck, wrists and ankles. She had several women in attendance, and they, too, wore many ornaments, and had their ears studded all round with ivory. When I left, she and her women accompanied me as far as the gate of the stockade which surrounded the compound, in which was her own spacious hut, and the huts of her attendants.

At Kota-Kota the Universities' Mission has a station. Having an impression that a university mission must show signs of its superiority, I was much disappointed at seeing the uncomfortable and untidy way in which the missionaries live there. The house looked wretched, and its want of neatness could not be a good example to the natives. The health of the missionaries must, I am sure, suffer from living under such depressing conditions. The church, on the other hand, was very prettily built in native style. It had a thatched roof, and its rafters were made of the ribs of the palm. Its walls were of mud and wattle, with a dado of mud inlaid with bits of quartz, which looked like bright mosaic, and the floor was spread with mats for the natives to squat on. New schools are being built, and when they are finished a new mission-house will probably be erected, and a chance given to the missionaries of taking better care of their health.

At Bandawe—another mission station on the lake—the inhabitants were greatly puzzled when they saw a lady coming ashore, and wondered to what mission I belonged. Then when I had landed, and they heard that I did not belong to any mission, but was only travelling for pleasure, they seemed to look upon me as a lunatic, and were thankful I was harmless.

Bandawe is a very pretty place, but is said to be very unhealthy. It has a long stretch of sandy beach, and, in one place, a rocky point juts out into the lake; also, there are rocky islands near the shore. It took me about ten minutes to walk from the landing-place up to the station. The dispensary was the first building I came to. This has, in addition to the dispensing room, three rooms for native patients. A little further on was the house of one of the missionaries, then the doctor's house, and, last in the row, the house of the head missionary. All were good houses, with well-thatched roofs and wide verandahs. Their front view is on to lovely mountains, which stretch beyond the forest far into the distance, and their back and side views are towards the lake, which looked just like the sea. Its water was a deep blue, almost indigo in colour, and it had waves which came splashing on to the rocks and sandy beach. It was very lovely, and looked such a paradise, that it was difficult to believe that fever or any other ill ever came there. Yet of one of the lesser disagreeables to which it was subject, I had already seen something. Just before reaching Bandawe, we had noticed tiny flies rising in great clouds out of the lake. The captain had kept the steamer out of their way as well as he could, as he knew by experience how suffocating these clouds of flies were. As they rise the wind blows them on shore, where they completely smother the shrubs and trees. Then the women come out with baskets or mats, into which they shake them off the trees. Having collected them, they mix them with native flour, and bake it into cakes, which are said to be delicious, and to taste of fish. I had a cake given me, but I never could make up my mind to taste it; the smell and the sight of the flies at Bandawe were sufficient for me. Everything was covered with them, and had a horribly nasty fishy smell. These fly-cakes are made round and thick, and are very dark in colour. I still possess mine, and consider it a most interesting relic. It is quite safe to leave it about, for I do not think anyone would dare to touch it. The fly is called 'Kungo,' and just at the season at which I visited Bandawe, great clouds of them were constantly rising up out of the water.

There had lately been rather a scare at Bandawe, about some leopards that were said to have killed a number of goats. Accordingly two white men, accompanied by some natives, set off to hunt them. Presently they found a place in the long grass where, it was evident, one of them had recently lain, as the ground was still warm. The boys formed a ring round it, and the men got their guns ready. After a little while the leopard emerged from the long grass, and was fired at and wounded, but not fatally. With a great bound he sprang on one of the white men, bringing him to the ground. Holding his victim he turned and growled savagely at the others. The boys gave a wild yell of fear, and then like a shot the leopard sprang away. He had not been the least frightened by the guns, but was terrified at the yell. The man attacked by the leopard was ill for a long time, and finally had to go home to England, as one of his eyes was badly injured.

After leaving Bandawe, the scenery became very lovely, high mountains and well-wooded hills coming right down to the water. Between the hills were deep, dark-looking ravines, whose dark shadows were here and there relieved by bright silver lines, which marked the course of tumbling cascades. Now and then we came upon a beautiful little bay, with a white beach studded with native huts. We called at one of these, Ntaka Bay, where there is an administration and a telegraph station, and also at Florence Bay, the station for Kondowe. Here is Dr Law's Mission, which is already well up on its way to heaven, for it takes three hours' hard climbing to reach it, situated, as it is, on the top of the mountain. The pleasure of a visit there was deferred until my return journey. Near to Florence Bay is Mount Chiombi, or, as it is now called, Mount Waller, which is nearly 6000 feet high, and of a formation that is different from any mountain we had hitherto seen. It rises in four distinct terraces, and has a long flat top.

From the steamer we could catch glimpses of the telegraph line, and I realised the difficulties that must have been encountered in making it. Many of the places that had to be crossed were so steep, that the men had to be let down by ropes in order to fix the line.

Whenever we stopped to take in wood, or for any other purpose, I went on shore for a good walk, and hunted for shells and strange plants. I did not succeed in finding many varieties of shells. Either I was not lucky, or there are not many to be found by the lake-side. But I got some queer beans, and found the lovely jacquerity growing in greater perfection than I had ever seen it before. It was climbing all over the bushes and brambles, and the bunches of pods had burst open and showed the brilliant little scarlet seeds with their black heads. I was almost afraid of gathering them lest the seeds should fall out, and their beauty be lost, but I ventured, and succeeded in getting several bunches, which I brought home, where they still delight my eyes, and recall the lovely scene in the midst of which I gathered them. The day on which I collected these was a glorious one, and just perfect in the shade. Numbers of fish eagles could be seen in the trees looking out for their food, and uttering their extraordinary cry. They live well, for there is plenty of fish in Lake Nyasa, and that is one reason why the lake crocodiles are not so much feared by the people who live on its shores, for they say that where the crocodiles get plenty of fish they seldom attack man.

On the verandah of a trader's house near the lake I saw the lufah growing. This, too, is a creeper, and the ripe pods hang down just like large brown cucumbers, and when a bit of the brown outer covering is chipped off, the well-known network of the lufah appears. The Kaffir orange that grows so plentifully in Matabele and Mashonaland grows here too. The fruit is smooth and of a dark green colour, which turns rather yellow when ripe. It is about the size of a large orange, but has a hard shell instead of a rind. The natives like the fruit and find it refreshing, but I did not care for it; indeed, there is very little native fruit for which Europeans do care.

There was another lovely bean, of which I do not know the proper name, but out there it goes by the name of the 'Mahogany Bean.' The tree is large and spreading, and the pod is of a deep mahogany colour, and in size about five inches long and three broad. Inside it has a row of lovely beans, shaped like acorns, bright black with brilliant scarlet cups. I do not know if they are edible; I never heard of anyone eating them, and I did not try them.

As we approached Karonga, it was great fun to watch the natives making preparations for landing. Their bundles were unpacked and the most wonderful finery was produced. Some of them had worked at Blantyre two or three months, and having received their pay, had bought and brought back most extraordinary garments, in order to excite the envy and admiration of their friends. Two had selected old scarlet coats belonging to a Highland regiment. Very proud, but fearfully hot they looked in them when, with great difficulty, they had discovered the way to put them on. Of course, besides the coat, they only wore their Nsaru and plenty of beads and copper wire. The girls had bought brilliantly-coloured calico, in which they swathed themselves. Having accomplished their toilet so far, both men and girls proceeded to dress their hair. Concerning this, a great many consultations were held in order to determine the exact width and direction of the little path that had to be shaved, and the height of the forehead; for some of them wore their hair shaved quite a long way back, while others were content to leave it as it had grown. In shaving they used no soap, the native head supplying sufficient grease.

During the whole voyage it had been of great interest to me to watch the natives, especially the women with their tiny babies. The washing of the babies was a very simple process. The mother just dipped her hand in water and drew it over the child, but occasionally she poured a gourd full of water over it, and this always brought piercing screams from the infant. Then followed massage, I don't mean smacking, but really good gentle massage, which must have been splendid for the children. The feeding was the most remarkable proceeding. In addition to their natural food, the babies, from the time they are a day or two old, have one meal a day of native corn ground very fine and mixed with water in the form of gruel. This the mother stuffs into the baby's mouth, and no matter how it struggles and cries, a certain amount has to be swallowed. Curiously enough the babies seem to thrive on this treatment; and indeed, when a white baby dies, the natives say that the mother wished it to die, because she gave it nothing but milk.

The natives were as much interested in me as I was in them, and they especially enjoyed watching me knit. They had never seen any knitting before, and it quite took their fancy. Sometimes I used to sit on the step just above their deck, and then two or three of them would creep along as close as they dared and squat down and watch me. I tried hard to make one or two of the girls do a bit of knitting just for fun. But they would not attempt it while so many were watching, and I had not a second set of pins with me to let them

UNLOADING THE "DOMIRA" AT KARONGA

try by themselves. Some of the natives were busy making ornaments for their wrists of beautifully fine drawn copper wire. Of these they gave me several; and the captain persuaded one of them to make me a bangle of elephant's hair; an ornament which they are very fond of wearing, as it is supposed to give them strength. It had a wonderful fastening, which had to be made while it was on the arm, and very much I wished someone had had a kodak at hand to take a picture of me and the native while he was doing it.

The voyage up Lake Nyasa was drawing to a close. From Fort Johnston to Karonga it takes eight days, as the stoppages for wood are frequent, and the steamer is often delayed by rough water caused by head winds. Livingstone called Nyasa the 'lake of storms,' and very bad the storms often are, especially in September and October, which are the roughest months. It is a big lake, three hundred and sixty miles long, and varying from fifteen to fifty miles in width. It is very deep, but in many places the sand stretches out such a long distance, that it is difficult for the steamer to anchor near the shore. The water is quite sweet and good for drinking. On the voyage we saw several large waterspouts; one, just like the trunk of a huge palm tree, straight and thick, until it ended in a feathery mass in the clouds.

The day before we reached Karonga the country became flatter, and the hills more distant. The lake was very rough, and I felt glad the voyage was coming to an end. When, finally, we did arrive, it was quite too rough to allow of the unloading of the cargo. To put out the cargo, the 'Domira' had to go round to a little bay about two miles from Karonga; but first the passengers were put off into a large canoe which came out to fetch them. When this canoe reached the boat, the pilot ladder was put over the side, and down that we had to scramble as well as we could while the steamer rolled and the canoe bobbed up and down in the most annoying and alarming manner. The A. L. C. agent had come out to fetch us, and I am sure he must have suffered terribly, as I know I crashed down upon him in anything but a fairy-like manner. He hid his sufferings valiantly, and to my joy he did not have to be invalided home. Of course, the canoe could not get quite up to the shore, so the natives had to carry us off. I was mounted on the shoulder of a native, as usual, and when the man started I was not properly balanced. Perhaps on this account, or on account of the waves, which were very strong and rolled in with great force, we went along very unsteadily, and but that another native came to our assistance, we should both have had a tumble into the water. Fortunately, with his help, I was safely landed, none the worse for my perilous ride.

CHAPTER VI

FROM KARONGA ACROSS THE PLATEAU TO FIFE

KARONGA IS A FLAT AND VERY SANDY PLACE; and the sand which lies between the shore and the large 'Boma,' belonging to the A. L. C, is so loose and disagreeable to walk through, that I was glad the distance was not great. The 'Boma' looks a most imposing place. A high brick wall is built all round, with gun-holes in it, and a wide moat surrounds it. It is therefore well protected, and I believe that, some time back, the protection was much needed. The house is large, and has a beautifully wide verandah, and there are several stores and out-buildings, all, of course, inside the protecting wall.

The administration 'Boma,' with the post and the new telegraph office, is just a mile distant from the company's station, and the mission station is about as far on the other side. The agent was much amused and surprised to hear that a 'tourist' had arrived, and he was somewhat appalled when he heard that I wanted men and an outfit to go alone to Lake Tanganyika. He kindly arranged to put me up for two or three days, as I wanted to re-pack and get various things at the store; also, I wanted to talk over my journey, and to have a little rest. There was no need for hurry, and the natives and their villages in that part being considerably different from those I had seen in other places, I was able to spend some time pleasantly in visiting them. They were a much wilder-looking set, tall and very strongly made, and wore nothing much save their ornaments and the skins of wild cats. They had belts made of copper wire twisted round hair, which were made to fit them very tightly. Often they wore five of these 'Manyetas,' as they were called. The brightly-polished copper contrasted well with their dark skins and looked quite handsome. The manyetas are very difficult to buy, and I was much puzzled as to why the natives objected to parting with them. After a time, I came to understand that the belts, being so small, were extremely difficult to get off; and the reason I had not been able to get one was, that at first I was always in too great a hurry. The poor men required time, and were obliged to use a good deal of oil before they could wriggle out of them. When they found I was staying some days at Karonga, they promised to bring me some, and before I left I became the happy possessor of four. They are very heavy, and the weight and size greatly astonished me, as natives usually seem to dislike wearing anything tight or heavy. But it seems that, for the sake of fashion, here, as elsewhere, almost anything will be endured. The women wear thick brass wire, coiled round and round their arms, till it forms a long cuff reaching nearly to their elbows, and in the same way round their necks, till it forms a deep collar, which must be heavy and uncomfortable, but in the brilliant sunshine looks bright and attractive. In the lobes of their ears they wear stoppers as large as draughtmen, and similar in shape.

A large cloud of flies, like those we had seen at Bandawe, had been blown on shore just before we arrived, and the air and trees were full of them, but, fortunately, the natives and the birds soon cleared them off.

I found great amusement in making the preparations necessary for my further journey. I was anxious to get a new hat, as the one I had, had become very dilapidated, and did not give me sufficient protection from the sun. I hunted the store over and could only find one that was at all suitable, and that was a large hat of grey felt, very like a cowboy's. It was hideous, of course; but that I did not mind: what I did mind was that it was too large for my head and tumbled too easily down over my eyes. At last I found a small brown felt hat that fitted my head and went inside the other most comfortably. The two together formed an excellent protection from the sun.

Then I had to find a boy who could speak a little English, as they told me it was absolutely necessary that I should take one with me, in case of any difficulty arising with the carriers. I only knew at the very most about a dozen words of their language. So a boy was engaged for me, who had been brought up at a mission station, and was supposed to speak English. On the journey I discovered that his English was distinctly limited in quantity and peculiar in quality, and the boy himself was seldom to be found when specially wanted. Still he was of some little use, and his English, which he had chiefly learnt from the Bible, was often extremely amusing and quaint. One morning, soon after we set off, I called him several times without any result; at last I heard a scratching on my tent and a voice, 'It is I; behold I am come.' At other times he would use the words 'verily' and 'lo' in a droll way.

After securing a boy, I had to get a cook, and then to select the food I wished to take with me. I took a small stock of tinned meat in case of need, but never used it, as I object to all tinned things, and in such heat I did not care for meat at all. Native fowls can be had nearly everywhere; they are small, but if well-cooked are good eating, and are certainly not expensive. One yard of calico, worth about threepence, purchases two. I took Californian pears, apricots and peaches, even though they were in tins, and thoroughly enjoyed them. I also took a good supply of rice, marmalade and jam, many tins of biscuits, some cocoa, and, of course, plenty of tea. I took for barter calico, both blue and white, beads in great variety, and salt, for money is not used or wanted. Then my cooking utensils had to be selected, but they were very simple. A kettle was the most necessary possession, as all the water for drinking had to be boiled. In addition to a few articles of crockery, besides the kettle, one or two saucepans were, I think, all. Everything was packed in baskets and made up into loads of about fifty pounds.

One morning there came the excitement of choosing the men who were to go with me. The doors leading into the 'Boma' had been opened, as they were every morning, to let in men in want of work. These squatted on the ground, patiently waiting till something was found for them to do. A number of them were called up, and ten men were chosen to carry my machila: they were selected in pairs about the same height and build, and their names were all taken down. Then the 'tenga-tenga,' as the load-carriers are called, were picked out, each was given his load, and his name and the weight of his load were written down. I had to take eleven men to carry the luggage, two for my own personal baggage, and the rest to carry the tent, camp-bed, bedding, food and cooking utensils, etc. In addition to these, I had my boy, cook and sukambali (washer-up), and a capitao over all, making in all twenty-five men. When the selection of the men, and the apportioning of the loads had been satisfactorily concluded, each man had 'posho,' that is, one yard of cloth, given to him to provide him with food for a week. This they took to the native village where they made their purchases, and in about an hour returned ready to start. Nearly all of them came armed with a spear and a small axe, some had a knobkerry as well, and their food was slung on their arms in the skins of wild cats and other animals. The 'tenga-tenga' had been chosen as much as possible from different tribes, as that made it less likely that they would all put down their loads at once and go off and leave me.

All this had, of course, taken a considerable time, and as I did not get fairly started till nearly twelve o'clock, we did not go far the first day. It was tremendously hot, so we went along very quietly and often stopped to rest under any shade-trees we came to. We soon reached a river that was rather deep, and had very steep banks, which were difficult to get down without tumbling into the water, but the boys were used to taking loads across and managed uncommonly well. After crossing the river, the country, which had been very flat, became more hilly and wooded, and the scenery more interesting. Then we crossed another stream, and about four o'clock came to our stopping place at Mpata. There we camped for the night. It was a pretty village, but my tent was surrounded by bananas, and the mosquitoes were terrible. My mosquito net had not been well put up, and the wretched insects kept getting inside the net and worrying me.

While my tent was being put up I wandered round the village to have a look at the natives. I heard the old 'tap, tap,' that one hears so much of in the South Sea Islands, and I found the women busy at the same kind of work they do there—hammering out bark to make cloth for wearing or for wrapping things up in. This bark is the inner bark of the hibiscus and other trees; they soak it for some time in water, then lay it on a piece of wood, or the trunk of a fallen tree, and beat it with a small hammer made of horn, and usually notched in a pattern at the flat end. They hammer it out to about double the original width, then do the same to another strip and, after more soaking, hammer the two edges together, and so on till they get it the desired width and thickness. Then they dye it in patterns according to fancy, with different coloured dyes made from bark.

The boys in the village had several kinds of musical instruments entirely of native make. Indeed, all natives seem fond of music. On the 'sansi,' or native hand piano, they play really sweet tunes. These pianos are made of an oblong piece of wood, and the one I have is about eight inches long and six wide. A narrow bar of iron is fastened across the top of the wood to hold in place the strips of iron, which are of different lengths and form the keys. Across the lower end of the wood is a piece of thin iron or tin to which are fastened pieces of shell, which make a jingling and buzzing sound when the keys are being played. The 'sansi' is held in both hands, the fingers being underneath and the thumbs being used to press the tips of the iron notes, which vary in number from sixteen to thirty, or, as I have been told, even more. Many different kinds of instruments are made with gourds cut in two. The gourd acts as a sounding board, and to it is attached a piece of wood, to which are fastened from one to four strings. These are played either with the fingers or a bit of bamboo. They also have drums of every conceivable size and shape, and queer sorts of rattles. I was never short of music the whole way, but the 'sansi' was decidedly the pleasantest to listen to. I often play on my own when I am alone, and like it quite as well as many pianos I hear; but then I am not musical.

When night fell and the moon rose, there was a fine noise in Mpata village, made by the drums and the singers. It was really a very lovely and picturesque scene; the brilliant moonlight, the huts dotted about and half-hidden in a grove of bananas, the natives squatting round their fires, chattering and smoking their large pipes, the mountains, looking more imposing in the moonlight, and the shining river flowing peacefully on; and my enjoyment of it all was added to considerably by the fun of being alone there.

Next morning I started off in good time, a little before six o'clock, having had a cup of cocoa and some biscuits, while the boys were packing up the tent and all the things we had used. This they did with wonderful quickness. As it was much pleasanter to travel in the morning while it was cool, we all started very briskly. We crossed the river again twice, and for some distance found the way rather rough. It lay along the stony bed of an old river-course. Then we began to go up hill and had a long, stiff climb, for which we were rewarded by an extensive view from the top. All day the road went up and down, frequently crossing streams and the dry beds of rivers, and nearly always through forest, where the trees were mostly stunted and scrubby, for the only fine ones grew in the hollows or near the water. Many of the trees had leaves which reminded me of the fronds of the common polypody, and there were acacias, fig trees of various kinds, and a quantity of bamboo.

About ten o'clock we came to a stream, and there I rested for an hour or more, and had my breakfast. The water was very muddy-looking, but as it was the best we could get, I ventured to use it for making tea. Then we went on again till about two o'clock, when, having found a good place in the forest not far from a stream, where we could camp for the night, we made a halt.

This division of the day suited me, and seemed to suit the men. I much preferred going on quietly till the day's journey was ended, and then having plenty of time to visit a village or to search for curiosities, to resting in the middle of the day and going on again in the afternoon. We generally came to a good place for our camp about two or three o'clock, and when once my tent was put up, work for the day was over for everybody, except the cook. His work was almost too trivial to be so called.

Getting the camp in order was done with remarkable quickness, and with a total absence of confusion, for each boy had his special work to do. Some pitched the tent, some fetched water, and others made the fires, while the arrangement of my personal baggage was allotted to my English-speaking boy. Before starting, it had been suggested to me that I might like to superintend the cook a little, and instruct him in the art of making such nice dishes as might be managed with our limited means. Accordingly, on the second day of our journey, I boldly ventured into the improvised kitchen, but I soon came away somewhat horrified at the state of things I found there. The cook held a plucked fowl in one hand, and was beating it with the other—black, I feared, in both senses—to make it tender. As I wished to be able to eat my dinner, I never went on a tour of inspection again. As far as possible throughout the journey, I ate everything with my fingers, being doubtful of the knives, as I once saw the sukambali cleaning them in the manner in which an unsophisticated school-child will clean his slate. I do not suppose for a moment my cook was worse than many of the native cooks, but I do not think visits to the kitchen are a wise proceeding on the part of those who want to enjoy their meals.

My ten o'clock meal was one which invariably provided me with considerable amusement. I had it, of course, picnic fashion, on the ground, and though, as a rule, when we made our halt, there was not a human being outside our own party to be seen, yet before the breakfast was ready I never failed to find myself the centre of an admiring crowd of natives, men, women and children, who had gathered from all points of the compass, and who squatted on the ground at a respectful distance, and watched me with the most vigilant and curious attention. After a time this persistent scrutiny became embarrassing, and I made an attempt to produce a diversion by starting a game to amuse the children. This was a matter of considerable difficulty, for it was not easy to make the children understand what I wanted them to do, and if I moved the least bit towards them, they screamed with fright and ran off as fast as they could. At last I got them to stand in rows, and hold out their hands to catch the bits of gingerbread and biscuits I threw to them. They were very much frightened and very shy at first, but soon they entered into the fun and were delighted whenever there was a good catch, and I clapped my hands as a mark of approbation. The men thoroughly enjoyed it too, and helped me to start them in races, etc. I was pleased, and not a little surprised, to find that the children were not in the least greedy. Those who were successful saved their biscuits, and at the end divided them with those who had been less fortunate. A game with the children became a regular adjunct to the morning meal, for, to my amusement, I found that my boys at each morning halt initiated the children into the mysteries of the proceedings, and I found them quite ready for a game. Dinner was a more solemn meal, which I generally had at dusk. Sometimes I had to have it by candle-light, though the light of my candles was considerably dimmed by the cloud of mosquitoes, moths and other insects, which circled round the flame until they fell a singed mass into the tallow. My attendants, meanwhile, were usually busy in preparing their own meals, and their friends were interested in watching them.

The natives, as a rule, only eat one big meal a day, but then they devour a perfect mountain of food. They make a sort of thick porridge of native corn, which they boil until it is very stodgy. This done, they cut a large piece of bark from a tree to serve as a dish, turn the stuff out of the pot on to it, and then they all sit round, taking pinches off the heap, with which they stuff themselves, until they attain to the proportions of an alderman. They are very fond, too, of roasting Indian corn, making pop-corn of it. Then they have several kinds of beans, sweet potatoes, pumpkins, cucumbers, ground-nuts, and rice. They are fond of meat when they can get it, but a big meal of freshly-killed meat makes them almost as intoxicated as if they had had too much to drink. During the day they satisfy themselves with smoking their big pipe, which is passed round for each to take a whiff, with nibbling at Indian corn, or perhaps a handful of stodge left from the night before, and with constant drinks of water. Their native-made drink is called pombé. It is made from native corn, and it is said to be intoxicating if drunk in large quantities. I do not think my men ever got hold of any; at all events they were always sober and well behaved.

As we got higher on to the plateau, the nights and mornings became much cooler, in fact, the early mornings were quite cold. And when we started a little before sunrise, about six o'clock, I was quite glad of a good sharp walk with a cape over my shoulders. At this early hour the boys, too, would walk quickly, and they always went along with their arms crossed in front, and a hand on each shoulder. They were very quiet, and had not a bit of cheeriness or fun in them until the sun was well up. Then they would sign for me to get into the machila and off they went, singing and ready for all sorts of games. They were a happy set of boys, just like a lot of children, and I often wished I could talk more to them. But, perhaps, had I been able to do so, I should not have liked them so well. The natives have any amount of patient endurance, and also a keen sense of humour—two very excellent qualities on a journey. I invariably found them perfectly honest, and I am certain white men would not have been more careful of me, or have behaved better, while they certainly would not have been so entertaining. The boys were very good, too, at calling my attention to game, of which, in the early morning, we often saw a great quantity. At times we saw large flocks of guinea-fowl.

On one occasion they were most anxious for me to see some game which was a good distance off. I got out my field-glasses, and after I had had a good look, I offered them to the boys. A funnier sight I have seldom seen. Each in turn took the glasses, screwed up first one eye and then the other, stood on one leg and danced about for joy, before passing on the glasses to the next one. Whether they really saw anything, or only pretended, I do not know, but they were always anxious to look through whenever I used them. Their own sight is marvellously good, and they can see and recognise objects and people far more quickly than a European.

Another day, when I was walking, we came on a long procession of ants crossing the path and each carrying its load. I stopped a while to watch them, and then pointing to the ants I said to the boys, 'tenga-tenga,' load-carriers. They saw at once what I meant, and enjoyed the joke hugely, repeating it to the others behind. On the third day of our journey from Karonga, we came to a painfully well-made road; all the green growth had been cleared off, and ditches had been cut on each side in a way that made it horribly monotonous, it was like a turnpike road, and, from the glare of the white ground, almost unendurable in such bright sun light. I think the boys disliked it as much as I did, for whenever there was a chance of taking a native path they did so.

That evening we came to Fort Hill, an imposing-looking place. The house was large, had a good verandah, and round it was a big stockade and ditch. A sentry was at the gate, but no one appeared to be living there. Accordingly, I had my tent pitched just inside the stockade. Two large hornbills were walking about and making the most melancholy noise. When I gave them food they took it with apparently no enjoyment, and in just the manner one takes pills. Altogether it was a wofully depressing place, and I was glad to move on next morning. I was told afterwards that a white man had been stationed there, but had died, at which I did not wonder. Now a native is the occupant.

Next morning we passed Nyala, another deserted station, where two white men had died, one rather recently, I should imagine, as there were several un-opened cases with his name on, standing in one of the rooms. From this place, too, I hurried away without regret, as it only filled me with sad thoughts, and made me wonder painfully about the occupants to whom death had come in this lonely place, so far from friends and home.

After Nyala, the road was not so distressingly good, and we had a lovely journey over a pass, the name of which, unfortunately, I did not hear. The road was rough for walking, and we had to make many sharp ascents and descents before reaching the top of the pass, but once there, I had an extensive view over endless forest, hill-tops and plains. On the way we had crossed several streams, many almost dry; but whenever there was a little water to be found my boys stopped for a wash and a bath. These lake natives and those on the Tanganyika plateau are much cleaner in their habits than those about Blantyre and Zomba; and on the journey from Karonga, I did not suffer nearly so much from the 'Bouquet d'Afrique.' I may, of course, have got a little more used to it, but at the same time I am quite sure it was not nearly so bad.

On the fifth day out from Karonga we reached the Collector's house at Ikawa, where I saw the first white people since leaving Karonga. The Collector himself was away, but had left most hospitable orders with his native servants. They had been told that anyone who arrived was to be made welcome. I was very thankful for a rest here, for I had had rather a long day, and had been walking too much in the hot sun. As a consequence, I did not feel very well. Instead of being able to talk to the Europeans who, like myself, were availing themselves of the Collector's hospitality, I went off to my room, taking with me some papers and magazines, of which there was a splendid supply, but I was too tired even to enjoy these. Next morning, not wishing again to travel in the heat of the sun, I started off early before anyone was about, in order to reach the mission station at Mwenzo while it was fairly cool.

At Mwenzo I had a very kindly welcome from the missionary and his wife. I thoroughly enjoyed seeing a lady again, and having a 'real good talk,' as for nearly a week I had not had an opportunity of communicating my thoughts to anyone. The house was a perfect picture; everything was so prettily arranged and so bright and clean, that it became in Central Africa evident at a glance that there was a lady at the head of it. I spent a delightful day there, stayed the night, and went on early the next morning, feeling refreshed and fit for anything.

It took only about an hour to go from Mwenzo to Fife, as the African Lakes Station is called, and I arrived there about eight o'clock in the morning, after an easy journey over a good road, running through rather uninteresting country, covered with scrubby forest most of the way.

CHAPTER VII

FROM FIFE TO LAKE TANGANYIKA

WHEN I ARRIVED AT FIFE, THE A. L. C. AGENT advised my going on at once to Lake Tanganyika, as he thought it possible I might just catch the little steamer, the 'Good News,' before she left Kituta.

My boys had only been engaged to go as far as Fife; and though some of them wanted to go on the whole way, it was considered better to take others, who belonged to the country we had to traverse, and I was quite sorry to have to say good-bye to the old hands, they had been so cheery and attentive to me, and had carried me so well. After the business of paying them off had been completed, I had to look over my provisions and belongings, to re-pack them, and then to choose a fresh lot of twenty-two boys. My own boy, the cook and sukambali, all went on with me. I always found the engaging of the boys a very interesting proceeding, and on this occasion I derived as much amusement as before from watching the natives as they were called up by the agent and his head boy, who selected those who were considered suitable for the machila and load carrying. When the list of names was given me, I found it hard work to pronounce them, though, when spoken by the natives, the names all had a musical sound.

By twelve o'clock the same day all was ready for a fresh start, and I set off once more. This was, of course, the hottest part of the day; but it seemed better to start then than to wait until next morning, as probably even then, owing to having the new set of men, there would have been some delay which would have prevented our starting at the usual early hour. We were not under the necessity of going very far that day, and, indeed, we only went on until four o'clock and then camped for the night.

Very soon after leaving Fife I came upon some tents pitched near the road; I found that they belonged to the English members of the British and German Boundary Commission. I stayed long enough to have a most interesting chat with two of them, and then I went on my way feeling that I had suddenly come into quite civilised regions, as during the last two days I had been constantly meeting Europeans.

My new lot of men were even madder than the last ones; they sang and danced most of the time, but were quiet directly they thought I had had enough noise; and when one day I fell asleep in my machila, they walked along as quietly as mice till they saw I was awake again. The capitao was a tall, well-made man, with much better features than most of the natives, and he kept all the boys in excellent order.

The day after leaving Fife I passed another empty house, which had been in habited by a white man; but I think the owner was only away on a journey. I stayed there for my breakfast, and had some delicious fresh milk, the first I had had for some time; for usually, when the chief of a village sent me milk as a present, it was quite sour; I think the natives prefer sour milk.

The interviews I had with the chiefs were always very comical. At each halting place the chief of the adjacent village would arrive after my tent was pitched, and when, having had all my things comfortably arranged, I was sitting in my camp-chair in the shadiest spot I could find, watching my boys and waiting until the kettle boiled for tea. Sometimes, as soon as he made his appearance, the natives who had collected to watch us, and were squatting on the ground near our camp, clapped their hands in a solemn manner, continuing to do so until he had taken his seat. As this was not always done, possibly it had something to do with the rank of the chief, or was only a custom of particular parts. The chief seated himself opposite to me, and we gazed solemnly at each other, until the women folk arrived with gourds containing milk which, to my disappointment, I always found was sour, and presents of eggs, which certainly were not new-laid. In one village, indeed, I saw a woman take some eggs from under a sitting hen and then she offered them to me. These choice gifts I received and passed on to my boy, and in return presented the woman with a few beads and a little salt, which is a great luxury to the natives. They were made wildly happy if, in addition to these, I gave them an empty biscuit tin or a few matches in a box. When this exchange of gifts was completed the chief took his departure; but the other natives waited to watch me have my tea, and were greatly interested to see me pour it out and drink it from a cup with a handle. One day, for fun, I poured some tea into an enamelled tin cup, and when it was cool enough sent it by the boy for the natives to taste. It had neither milk nor sugar in it, but was just as I was drinking it myself. They tasted it eagerly, then made horrid faces and spat it out again. I gave them some more with a lot of sugar in, but though that seemed to please them better, they evidently did not think much of my beverage.

That night I had the prettiest camping place I had had so far. It was in the forest, and had big grey rocks all round, and near it was a narrow, deep ravine, down which was running a lovely stream of pure water, one of the many sources of the Congo. The colours of the trees were very varied. They were putting forth their new leaves, and these showed every variety of tint, brown, pale red, pink, and a fresh light green. One was a perfect glory of scarlet leaves, and many that flowered before the leaves appeared were brilliant with blossoms of white, scarlet and yellow. I went for a good scramble among the rocks and came on the source of the stream where the water bubbled up from under the rocks. It was a great treat to have a good drink of fresh water, after the boiled water to which I had of late been limited.

I was wandering on, thoroughly enjoying myself, when I saw some of the boys coming to fetch me back. I could not understand why, until my English-speaking boy told me they had seen the spoor of a lion, and that it was not safe to wander far away. This, and watching the preparations for making fires all round my tent, was very exciting, though I began to feel a little alarmed lest, in their desire to protect me from the lion, they should set the tent on fire. In the night I got up several times to look out of my tent. It was a very picturesque sight to see the fires blazing away and the groups of men squatting and lying by them. They seemed to be awake and talking the whole night; but I am told that they usually take turns to watch and keep up the fires when lions are about. I heard lots of jackals that night, and all sorts of noises of other beasts, but did not hear the roar of a lion.

In the early morning, when I was up and ready to start, I was again impressed with the loveliness of the place, as the morning light added a fresh beauty to the colouring. All the way from there to Mambwe, one of the B. C. A. stations, the road was very hilly and pretty. Mambwe used to belong to the French Fathers, but after the making of the Stevenson Road, as the road we were on was called, they determined to move to a place less easy of access, and accordingly sold the station. They had made a beautiful garden, as they do at all their settlements, and had planted it with orange and lemon trees, papaws and bananas, strawberries, tomatoes, and various kinds of fruits and vegetables, of which the official now living there, and who bestows considerable pains on keeping up the garden, reaps the benefit. The French Fathers seem to be a fine set of men, clever at adapting themselves to the country, and at making the very best of it. Our people are at last becoming more alive to the benefits which arise from a good garden, and the improvement to their health which comes from having plenty of vegetables and fruit, instead of having to eat so many 'tinned' horrors. In several places when I asked about the garden, the answer was that there had not been time to make one, or that it was too difficult to manage. Yet what the French Fathers have done at all their stations, we ought to be able to do too.

That night I camped at a place called Mpanga, where again there was an empty house. It was quite a large one, with a high stockade all round. The poles of the stockade were adorned at the tops with queer and very roughly-carved birds and animals, and, after a native fight, the heads of the vanquished were doubtless stuck up there in addition.

I visited the large native village near. It was also surrounded by a stockade, and both it and the inhabitants were interesting. The women were wearing more than usually enormous stoppers in the lobes of their ears, some carved, and others covered with tin and ornamented with brass nails. They and the men wore round their necks a great deal of the hair from the elephant's tail, which they suppose gives them strength; and most of them wore also the little horn from a small bok, given them as a charm or cure for illness by the 'medicine man.' At one place an old chief gave me one to wear, 'to give me a good heart'; but whether he meant a kind or a strong one, I could not discover. In all the villages the people seemed busily occupied with their work; the ground was kept swept round the huts, and they were cleaner and less malodorous than our courts and alleys at home. The women's work is to grind and sift the corn, pick the beans, etc., for food, collect the firewood, fetch the water, cook, hoe the ground, and gather in the crops. They also do all the bead-work, and in the parts where pottery is made, that is also their work. The men do all the sewing and mending of what little clothing they have, and they repair the gourds used for household purposes. They clear the ground for planting—a process in the course of which they cut off all the branches from the trees and place them round the trunks, where they leave them till quite dry. Then they set fire to the whole, and, with the wood-ashes that remain, they fertilise the ground. The men also do all the weaving and basket-making. They get iron and smelt it, and make all their implements, spears, arrows, knives, etc. They build the huts, leaving only the floors to be made by the women. Then, of course, they do all the hunting, fighting, and most of the talking.

In some parts of the country the native marriage laws are rather amusing. Separations are very easily obtained. If either speak disrespectfully of the other's friends, or if the husband neglects to mend anything belonging to his wife, or if the wife does not hoe, cook, or do her work diligently, the marriage can be dissolved. The price paid for a wife seemed to vary in different parts; usually the price is so many cows, or hoes, or so much cloth of native weaving.

A short distance from Mpanga, I had a splendid view from the top of a hill over a big plain. There were very few trees, most of the long grass was burnt, and the ground was covered with enormous ant-hills. Some of the old ones were so large, that they had trees and bush growing on them. Most of them were from eight to ten feet high, and some of them were more. The outside of these was extremely hard, owing to a secretion the ants use in preparing the earth for their hills. These were of different shapes, mostly conical, while some had additions in the shape of extra spires or towers. Where the ant-hills are smaller and rounder, the disused ones can be utilised as ovens when hollowed out, and they serve splendidly for boiling a kettle over, assuming that they are properly hollowed out, so that a good fire can be lighted inside.

On descending into the valley, which lay in front of me, I found I had to cross a very long bridge, built of sticks and mud, which stretched for quite a quarter of a mile over a marsh and a river. The bridge was terribly broken and rotten, as it had not been repaired since the last rains. I had to get out of the machila and walk over, not a very easy matter, as in places there were great gaps wider than I dare jump. However, the men were quite equal to the occasion, and scrambled down into the mud and water and lifted me safely over.

Kasanvu, a village close to which we stopped for breakfast, was very picturesque. It stood on the side of a hill, with a good view across the valley to the ridge opposite, which was covered with boulders, great square blocks of rock, with bush growing round and about them. I had to do a good deal of walking, as the road was very steep, and went over rocks and loose stones; but the views were good, and I preferred walking, as I could see so much more, and could stop at will to examine anything curious.

I saw and heard many more birds than I expected. Most of them had very brilliant plumage, some had crimson wings, and there were lovely grass-green birds with crests and red beaks and cheeks. The gaily-coloured birds generally had loud, shrill cries, but often in the early morning, and also about sunset time, I heard very sweet notes, and imagined their owners were much plainer in appearance, as they were difficult to catch sight of. One quite small bird was decorated with a very long feather in each wing. I picked up several of these, and they measure twenty-six inches in length.

That day, as we passed a native village, which, as usual, had a high stockade all round it, my boys began to sing vigorously, and marched along on each side of my machila. The men from the village all came out and sang too, and followed us, singing and shouting, to the top of the next hill. It was most exciting and amusing, and I longed to know why they did it. I was anxious to find out whether the inhabitants of the village were special friends of any of my boys, or if it was just their way of greeting a European traveller.

At length I arrived at Kawimbe, a London Mission Station, and on our arrival my men shouted and yelled their loudest. On hearing the noise, the missionary came out and greeted me most warmly. He said that they had been expecting me for some time, and that my room was all ready for me. I was much astonished, and replied, that I was sure it was not for me, as they could not have heard I was coming. Just then his wife came out and greeted me in the same kind and hearty way. I again protested, but was assured that they had heard I was coming, and wondered why I had been so long on the way. Then came the question, 'But where is your husband?' I replied, 'I have not the least idea.' But where did you leave him?' I assured them I had never done anything so unkind as to leave him. Seeing that they in their turn were quite puzzled, I asked them to tell me who they took me for. Then they told me that they had been expecting some new missionaries. I at once cleared up their misgivings by informing them that these missionaries were still at Fife, resting on account of fever, and that they hoped to come on in a few days. Of course, they had not heard of me, and they were greatly amused and interested to meet someone who had come merely to see the land and the people, and they gave me the kindest possible welcome, although I was not the expected visitor. After my return home I discovered that we had many mutual friends, of whom we should have enjoyed talking, had we only known at the time.

Close to the mission house is a large native village, and the land round it is wonderfully well cultivated. Wheat is grown, and excellent flour made for sale as they have hand-mills for grinding the corn, a great improvement on the old way of crushing and rubbing the corn between stones, which method makes the flour so very gritty. There was a splendid garden belonging to the mission station, where they grew most excellent potatoes, tomatoes, peas, beans, cabbages, onions; in fact, nearly everything that is to be found in an English garden. Also, there was a large farm-yard with quite a number of cows, and we had delicious fresh milk and butter—a rare and delightful luxury in these parts. Here, again, I saw and appreciated the advantage of having a lady to superintend the household.

Roaming about the place were three lovely crested cranes, charmingly dainty-looking birds, which I found most fascinating to watch. These birds are easily tamed and are very intelligent and useful in a garden, as they live chiefly on insects and grubs. They do not seem to wander far away, when once they have settled in a place. I tried hard to get a young one to bring home with me, but could not find one; all I saw were too old and large to take away.

The village by the mission station was a particularly pretty one, especially in the evening light at sunset. Then the colours of the thatch on the huts grew beautiful, showing every shade of brown, and making one long to be able to paint such a picture of it as would convey its beauty to the eyes of friends at home. Photographs, though very delightful, and splendid reminders to those who have seen the places, convey but a poor idea of the beauty of scenery—the chief charm of which lies in the colouring—to those who have not seen it. The huts of this village were as usual round, and the doors were so low that I had to crawl in almost on my hands and knees. In the middle of the hut is a semi-circular screen made of mud and wattle, behind which the natives sleep, and where they can have a fire when required. In the space between this screen and the wall of the hut they have a fire at which they do their cooking. The wide overhanging thatch, which is supported on poles, forms an excellent verandah, which shades them from the sun or rain while they work, talk, or take their mid-day siesta. It is the colouring of the smoke from the fires that gives the thatch such lovely shades. In the village I saw a native being cupped for fever. On each temple was put a horn, the end of which was stopped with bee's-wax, the blood that is drawn out is thrown on the ground, and that gets rid of the disease.

About three hours from Kawimbe is the B. S. A. Station of Mbala, or Abercorn, as it is now called. Just before reaching Mbala, we passed a lovely little lake, Lake Kilwa, which the Collector told me was dry ground only a few years ago. He had many times walked over the part where the lake is now.

I only stayed at Mbala for the men to have a rest, and then, as they were willing, and indeed anxious, to get to Kituta that night, we set off for our journey of five hours. On the way we went up and down several steep rocky hills, and then, for the last hour before reaching Kituta, the road went steadily down, making a descent of three thousand feet. Parts of the way were very rocky and parts very sandy. From many points along it I had lovely peeps of Lake Tanganyika.

As soon as the boys caught sight of the lake, they began to sing and dance most excitedly. They had been very amusing and very mad most of the time. One favourite game of theirs seemed to be to pretend that enemies were hiding in the bush; they would creep and crouch about in the most stealthy manner, then spring out with wild shouts. Once they all vanished, except the two who were carrying me; then suddenly they came yelling and springing from either side of the path, brandishing their spears and axes at me. I clapped my hands and called out their native word for 'good,' at which they were delighted; but, at the same time, I confess, it had been a little alarming, and I was glad to find that it was only pretence and done for my amusement. They were a capital lot of boys, very good-tempered and very happy, and I was sincerely sorry to have to part with them at Kituta. The journey from Karonga to Kituta had only taken me eleven days. The usual time allowed is a fortnight, but the boys had carried me well, and we had not been hindered by illness, as so many people are.

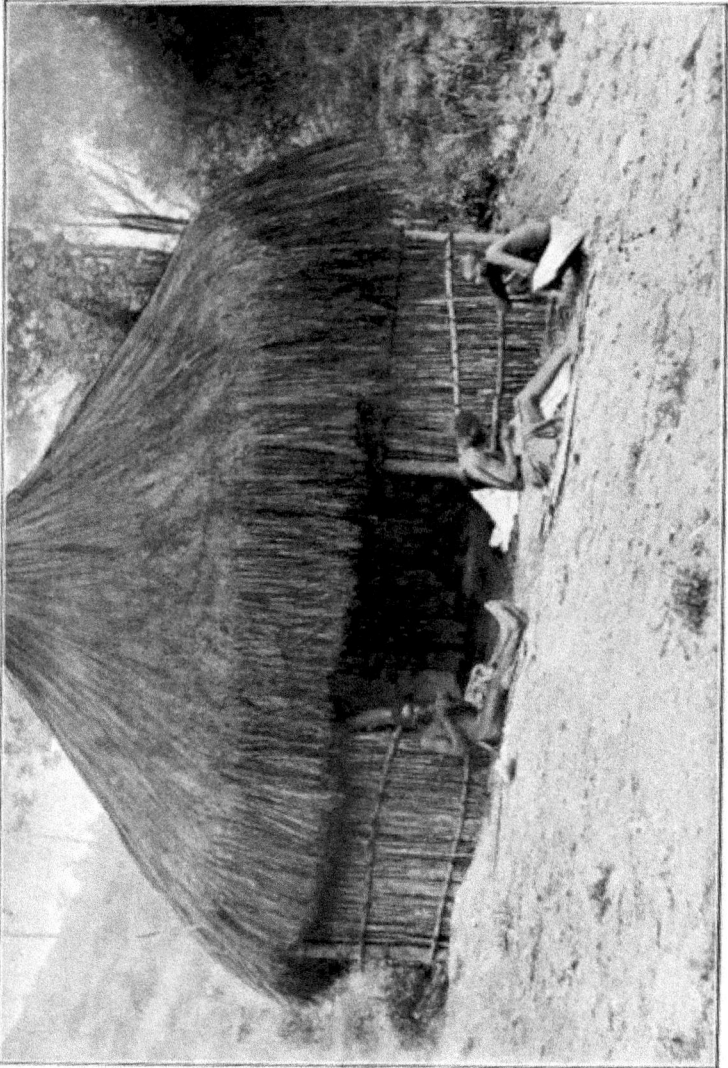

ANT HILL

CHAPTER VIII

RETURN JOURNEY FROM LAKE TANGANYIKA TO KARONGA

MY ARRIVAL AT THE AFRICAN LAKES STATION at Kituta caused great excitement. The agent there had not heard I was coming, and such an event as the arrival of a lady travelling alone, and for pleasure, had never been known in those parts before.

Kituta was quite the best A. L. C. Station I had seen. The house is a long one, with one storey, a good wide verandah, and a well-thatched roof. It stands on a raised piece of ground, with steps up to it, and has a lovely view down on to the lake. The various stores are all in separate buildings, and the whole is surrounded by a high, strong stockade. Along the front of the house is a tall row of cotton trees, the forest at the back, beautifully wooded, mountains on each side, and the lovely lake in front. It was an ideal place, viewed externally, but the inside was dreadfully comfortless, and I felt heartily sorry for the agent stationed there. He had sole charge of the place, and was the only white man in it, save on those occasions when the 'Good News' was at that end of the lake, and then the captain stayed with him. It did not seem right to place a man by himself in such a remote spot. When he had attacks of fever, it must have been miserable for him to have only natives round him, and to be burdened with the anxiety he would naturally feel on such occasions about the large quantity of ivory, cloth and goods of all descriptions for which he was responsible. The house was wretchedly fitted up, and there was scarcely a book about the place. It seemed hard that a company which stationed a man so far away from his fellows did not keep him supplied with papers and literature from home. I had only a few magazines with me, and for these the agent was most thankful.

The garden was a little distance away from the house, and near to a stream, so that it was easily watered. It was not a very good time to see it, as it was looking very bare; but they told me that a great variety of fruit and vegetables grow there.

STOCKADE

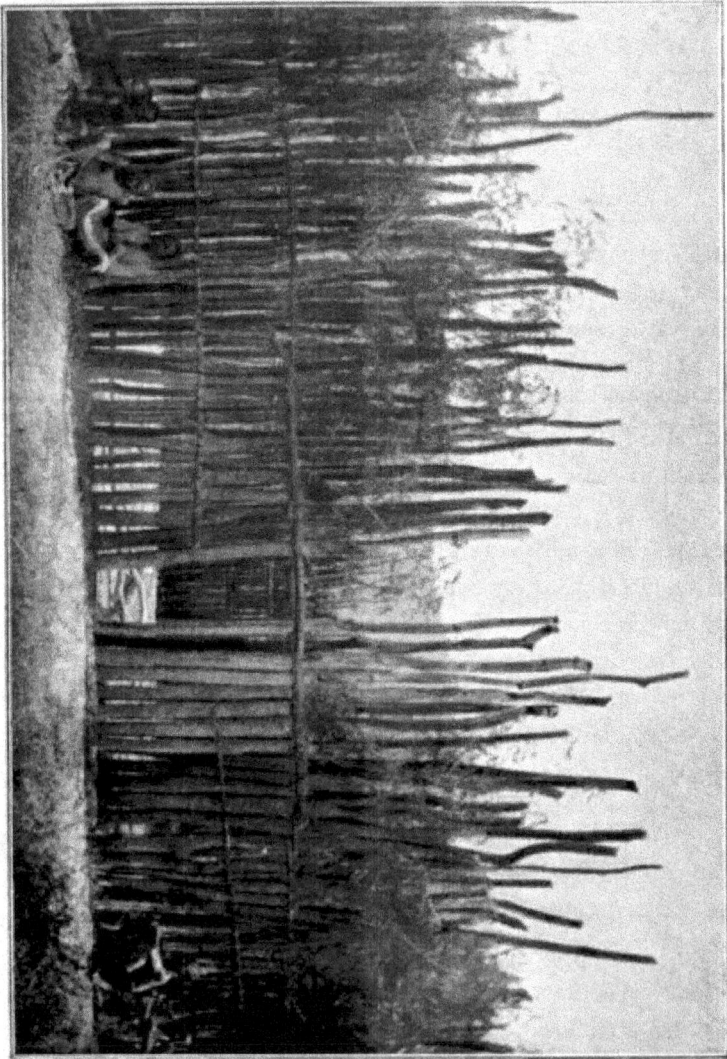

We had a very exciting time the night that I arrived. The native watchman fired off his gun twice, and everyone rushed out; but it was only a hyena, which, of course, escaped uninjured.

Before arriving at Kituta, I had seen that the little steamer was on the lake, and I was in a state of great joy, thinking I had come just at the right time. But, alas! a sad disappointment was in store for me; the 'Good News' certainly was there, but the fire-bars were burnt out, and until fresh ones came, she could not be used for a long journey. As there was no chance of getting to the north end of the lake on the steamer, I enquired about a dhow on which I could perhaps have gone to Ujiji. But there was not one to be had, and the agent absolutely refused to let me have a native boat, as there had just been a very sad accident with one on the lake. Two members of the Belgium Commission, who thought that they could get themselves and their loads more quickly to the other side of the lake by water than by land, had engaged two large canoes, with some thoroughly experienced native rowers; but, unfortunately, they had insisted on rounding a headland, against the wishes of the capitao and the natives, who, of course, understood both the canoe and the lake best, had been struck by a heavy sea and overturned. Though they were all good swimmers, the surf dashing against the stones was too much for them, and the two Europeans, together with the five natives, were drowned. It was a terribly sad affair, and the agent rightly refused to give any assistance to Europeans afterwards who wanted to cross the lake in a native boat. The lake is very treacherous, sudden and bad storms often come on. It is the longest fresh-water lake in the world, being four hundred miles long. The width varies from thirty to sixty miles; the depth is, I believe, unknown.

When the captain of the 'Good News' found how terribly disappointed I was at not being able to go on the lake, he spent a whole day in patching up the fire-bars, and doing all he could to get the steamer into working order, and on the following morning he got up steam and took me out to the widest part of the lake, so that I could get a good view of the south end, which is said to be the most beautiful. Kituta lies at the end of a long narrow bay; and once you get beyond that, the lake widens considerably, until it attains a breadth of sixty miles. In the rainy season it is possible to see both sides, but when I was there in September, the weather was too hazy; there had been no rain since April. Directly the rain begins, usually in November, the whole appearance of the country changes; the smoke-like haze goes, and the air becomes so clear that you can see for very great distances. The mountains round the south end of the lake were high and thickly wooded. One of them was in shape very like Mount Chiombi, on Lake Nyasa, and had terraces up to the top.

While on the lake we saw a great number of hippos and crocodiles, which, of course, are much less disturbed there than on the Shiré River. It afforded me the greatest satisfaction to be on the lake, and I was very sorry when we had to turn back; but it had been hard work all the time to keep the steam up, and it was quite impossible to go on any longer. The captain, in trying to console me for the disappointment I felt at not being able to go the whole length of the lake, told me that there were only four other ladies living who had been on Tanganyika. That, I fear, instead of consoling me, only made me feel more vexed that, having got so far, I could not go farther still. At one time I had thoughts of waiting until the boat was repaired, but that meant staying until the rainy season had begun. I have since heard that the 'Good News' was not got into working order till the December following, so that, as things turned out, I was lucky in deciding to return at once.

There was a very large native village close by the A. L. C. Station, and the inhabitants appeared to have found me extremely interesting; more so, in fact, than was quite agreeable to me, for I could scarcely go for a walk without being followed by a large crowd of women and children, who watched and imitated all that I did. I was anxious to find some shells, and every time I picked one up, all rushed to do the same and brought them to me in handfuls. Though rather annoying, it was not a little amusing to be pursued by such a crowd, all of them whispering and giggling. The children kept running on in front, and then turning round and coming back, in order to get a good look at me. I tried hard not to mind them, for I knew how queer I must seem to them; and I thought of how we Britishers, in much the same way, mob any special hero or heroine. But, notwithstanding my efforts not to feel disconcerted, the annoyance gained on me, and at last I put on a very grave look, and turning round slowly, almost solemnly, faced them, raised my hand, and pointing towards their village, said quietly, but with emphasis, 'Go!' The effect was magical. They did not stop to 'go,' they simply fled, tumbling over one another in their wild haste to get away. Then, for a time, I had a little peace, and a thoroughly happy hunt for shells along the shore.

The mountains and lake looked very beautiful in the afternoon sunshine, and as I sat on an old boat taking in the scenery around me, I revelled in the thought of being there by myself, such an immense distance from home, and abandoned myself to peaceful reverie. But this peaceful meditation was not to last long. Presently I heard a subdued murmuring, as of human voices, and looking round I saw that the curiosity of the crowd had overcome their fears, and that they had returned to watch me. This time, as I could not find it in my heart to send them away again, I made the girls come and show me all their wonderful bangles and ornaments. Their copper-wire bangles were beautifully made from native copper, which they manufacture themselves. They draw it out into the finest possible wire, which they twist on hair. The drawing of the wire is cleverly done. The men cut a hole through a tree, into which they put a piece of iron with a small hole in it. The strip of copper is tapered to a point and put through the hole in the iron. The natives catch hold of the end with a kind of pincers, then a good number of them hang on to it and pull it through. This process is repeated through smaller holes in the iron again and again till the wire is fine enough. Each of six girls gave me one of these bangles, another gave me one of copper and brass finely twisted, and another, one of copper and iron. They are all beautifully made, and the wire is extremely fine and flexible. Of course, when I got back to the house, I gave the girls beads in exchange.

There happened to be a full moon while I was at Kituta, and that is always the time for a grand native dance. When we heard the drums beginning, off we went to look on. The men had coloured themselves with red, white and yellow powder, and looked hideous. They formed a large circle, and danced, shouted and waved axes, spears and knobkerries; while four men stood in the centre, wildly beating two large drums with their hands. In their dance they jumped up in the air every now and then and came down with a tremendous thud on the ground; and all of them moved their muscles in a wonderful way and went through marvellous contortions. They were dancing a very exciting war dance, and how they managed to escape injuring each other severely was a puzzle to me. The excitement became greater as the dance went on, and long after we left them we heard the noise of the drums and the shouting; indeed, it lasted far into the night.

I stayed four or five days at Kituta, and enjoyed the rest, and some lovely expeditions into the surrounding country. When I set off on my return journey I was attended for quite a distance by the girls and women of the village, who ran by the side of the machila, laughing and chattering in the friendliest manner.

All the carriers had been engaged the night previous to my departure, and their loads apportioned, and for once I was able to make an early start. I was anxious to do so, on account of the long, steep climb up from the lake, which would have been very trying to do later in the day. Accordingly, we set off soon after seven; but I did not much like the look of some of the machila boys or of the 'tenga-tenga;' and before I had gone very far, I heard a great row going on. The capitao came up to me gesticulating violently, and dancing about in great excitement. But his excitement was such that I could not in the least understand what was the matter. I thought that possibly he wanted me to do something, and I tried various things without success. As I could not discover the cause of the disturbance, and as my boy was nowhere to be seen, I walked on in despair and left them to settle the matter as best they could. It was not until I reached the mission station that night that I discovered that two of the men had put down their loads and run away, and the capitao had had to make the other men carry their loads in addition to their own. I made it all right with those who had carried the extra loads, and I got two more men; but they were all rather tiresome, and not nearly so amusing as my former men had been. I was not sorry to get to Mwenzo again and to change them.

This time I stayed for a few days at Kawimbe, and was much interested in the natives and their work. They find a quantity of ironstone, and smelt it in curious little erections that I thought were made for storing grain. They are small, round buildings like wide chimneys, about six feet high and two to three feet in diameter, made of fire-hardened clay. The ground inside is hollowed out and lined with clay, and the iron is put in it. The fires, which are made of charcoal, are blown up by air from the goatskin bellows, to which are attached clay tubes through which the air passes into the furnace. All the spears, hoes, axes and knives are their own make, and very strong and well-made they are, and possess good edges.

While I was staying at Kawimbe, on September 15, the first rain fell. We had heard distant thunder for several days, and the clouds had looked very threatening. At last we had two very heavy showers. As I went on my journey afterwards, I was astonished at the difference that a little rain had made to the look of the country; flowers seemed to be springing up all about, and the rain had brought out the brilliant tints of the young leaves.

At Kawimbe I had a good opportunity of seeing the natives play a curious game, which is a favourite pastime in Nyasaland. I could not make it out at all, though I often watched them play. They make two rows of holes in the ground, about sixteen holes in each row, then they chuck pieces of stone into the holes, and pick them out again, till, finally, one boy grabs them all. Only two boys play at it at once. Another favourite game that I saw them playing was, spinning very tiny tops, about the size of acorns. They made a smooth, square place with a low rim round it, and the game seemed to consist in throwing in a spinning-top in such a way that it knocked the opponent's out. It seemed to be a very exciting game, and there were always plenty of onlookers, and much shouting and noise over it.

At Kawimbe the rats in the house were terrible at night. They raced about my room and scampered over my bed in a thoroughly happy manner. I could not sleep at first, but at last I got used to them, and dropped off only to wake up and find a rat with his foot in my ear. One night, at another station, something larger than a rat dropped from the rafters on my bed and awoke me. I lighted the candle, and saw it was a lemur. They are lovely little animals, and are covered with thick fur like chinchilla, and have beautiful, large, round eyes. It looked most fascinating; but not being sure what it would do next, I thought I would try to send it out. I opened the door which led on to the verandah, and proceeded gently to drive it out, but, alas! it objected to going, and sprang straight on to my shoulder, gripping my arm with its sharp little teeth, and refusing to let go, till I well pinched its tail. As it turned round to bite my hand, I tossed it out on to the verandah, and shut the door. I had fewer animals in my tent than in a house; but even in my tent I was apt to wake up and find all sorts of creepy, crawly things about my pillow.

Africa, indeed, seems as full of plagues now as it was in the time of Moses. The jigger, or matakynia, is horrible. It is a small flea, that, instead of biting, bores a hole, usually under the toe nail, and lays its eggs there. If not discovered and taken out quickly, it causes ulcers, and all sorts of trouble. The natives, who get plenty of practice, are very clever at taking them out, and do it without causing pain; whereas, if you try to do it yourself, you often make a large hole and a very sore place. For a long time I escaped the pest, but at last fell a victim like everyone else. The Arabs are supposed to have brought the matakynia across from the west coast, and it has gradually spread to Chinde, and, indeed, all over B. C. Africa. Then there is a sort of bluebottle fly that penetrates through your clothes, and kindly lays its egg in your back; the egg soon becomes a grub, and I saw quite a large one taken out of a child's back. There is, too, a particularly nasty, fat, lightcoloured fly, that is said to be blind, and it comes against you with a great flop, and holds on so firmly with its feet that it is difficult to get rid of it.

On my return journey from Mambwe to Mwenzo, I found the road had been altered in two places by the Boundary Commissioners, and I had to go by a longer and much prettier route. The new road was being made, and, indeed, was nearly finished. Making a road is not a very arduous task, when once it has been marked out, as it is only necessary to cut away the scrub and the trees for a certain width. Natives were stationed at each end of the old road where it had been altered, with a note from the Collector, headed, 'To all whom it may concern.' Following these words were orders that on no account were you to go along the old road.

On the way I passed a native wearing as a hat the skin of a zebra's head. I tried to buy it from him, but for some time could not persuade him to part with it. However, while we were camping, he came up again, and the sight of beads and calico proved too much for him, and I became the happy possessor of the skin, which is a very good one.

I always enjoyed the fun of bartering, it is so much more amusing than giving a fixed price in money. At Ikomba I bought a splendid stool belonging to a chief. It was chopped out of a solid piece of wood, and was beautifully polished by use. The owner was sitting on it, and the first thing to be done was to persuade him to rise. Then I picked up the stool and offered him calico; at which he shook his head, and took hold of a leg of the stool. I held on to the other, and made my boy unroll more calico, till at last he gave in. The chief greatly enjoyed the joke, as, of course, I gave him a good deal more than the stool was worth; but I wanted it, as it was quite the best one I had seen. We were mutually happy and satisfied. It will take the old fellow some time to get another stool up to such a high state of polish.

At Mwenzo I stayed two days and made a short excursion in the machila, to look at the new boundary which is marked only about three-quarters of an hour from the A. L. C. Station. This was marked by a beacon with a tall pole, which was well fixed in, and from it I could see three or four other beacons on distant hills. In travelling along the road between Karonga and Kituta, it is interesting to notice how many boys you meet carrying letters. They carry them in a split bamboo stick, and offer them to any European they meet, in case the letter should be for him. The boys run along very quickly with the letters; and no one thinks anything of sending a boy off with a letter or parcel thirty miles or more.

The day I left Ikawa it was intensely hot, and towards afternoon, when my boys were getting tired, we passed six or eight natives walking along without any loads. They began to chaff my boys and jeer and laugh at them. Suddenly, two of them made a rush at the machila pole, pushed my boys away, and ran off with me as fast as they could, up and down steep 'dongas,' so steep, that I should have had to walk down them with the greatest care. The rest of them came alongside, shouted and sang all the time, and, without stopping, a fresh pair took the machila pole, changing as they ran. They kept up this pace for more than an hour, until we came to a stream where there was shelter from the sun. Then they popped me down, and truly thankful I was, for what with the shaking and the laughing, which their conduct had provoked, I was nearly as tired as they were. It was the funniest sight to see my boys running their hardest to keep up, and all streaming with perspiration, but thoroughly enjoying the fun. Of course, this helped us over the ground splendidly, and after a rest we went on more calmly, leaving our lively crew behind.

I tried hard to get someone to show me another way back to Karonga, but I do not think my carriers approved of the idea, for, at each village, they told me no one knew such a way; and, finally, I gave up trying, for it was too hot to worry, and I did not want to spoil the pleasure of my journey.

One day I witnessed another delightfully entertaining scene. We met some native women carrying huge calabashes on their heads, full of pombé, the native beer. My boys stopped one of the girls, and after much talking, she consented to let him put his hand in the jar and take out all he could. It was in the early stages of making, and was thick and rather solid; accordingly he plunged his hand in and drew it out full. His arm, nearly up to the elbow was thickly covered with pombe, and when the others saw it, they rushed at him and began to lick his arm, while he ate what he had in his hand. It was the queerest sight I had ever seen, and they most thoroughly enjoyed it, laughing and shouting all the time.

The last day we journeyed by a different route to the one I had taken on my way up. It lay through Mlosi's village, where, quite recently, there had been a good deal of fighting. The skulls and bones of the killed had all been thrown into an enclosed piece of ground, which the natives are now afraid to go near, because they believe there are spooks there. The old village had been completely burnt, but already a good many new huts had been put up.

When, at last, I reached Karonga again, I had a most hearty and kindly welcome, and all were interested in hearing of my adventures. I was astonished to find so many Englishmen there, and then I was told that the telegraph line had just reached Karonga, and that they were getting it into working order. While I was there the first message was sent off.

CHAPTER IX

FROM KARONGA THROUGH GERMAN KONDELAND

As I was going into the house at Karonga, I was horrified to hear most melancholy groans. I was told, in answer to enquiries, that the night before an Indian servant had been brought in after having been terribly mauled by a lion. One of the B. S. A. officials, who was camping in the hills some distance from Karonga, had been told that there were lions about, and had ordered good fires to be kept blazing, and the men to be on the lookout. The men were sitting in a circle round the fire, and this Indian, whose groans I had heard, was sitting inside the circle close to the fire, when the lion suddenly sprang over the men, seized him and sprang back again. He yelled terrifically, and when the officer, on hearing the screams, rushed out of his tent, he saw the lion standing with the man in his mouth, looking actually scared at the noise the Indian was making. They all charged the lion with burning sticks, and he dropped his prey and fled. The Indian was carried down to the A. L. C. Station, and was cared for with the greatest kindness by the agent. It requires more than ordinary skill and kindness to attend properly anyone who has been bitten by a lion, as the wounds are terribly disagreeable and nasty to dress. The poor man used to scream with fright when he fell asleep, and his illness was long and tedious, but ultimately he got quite well again.

As I had been disappointed in my journey to the north of Lake Tanganyika, and had, consequently, returned sooner than I intended, I decided to spend a fortnight or three weeks at the north of Lake Nyasa, in German Kondeland, which part of the country, I was told, was very lovely and very little visited. This I found to be quite true, and during the whole time I was there I never saw any European except the missionaries. At present no traders go there, and the missionaries are very thankful to be left so much alone.

In preparation for going to Kondeland, I had to get a fresh lot of carriers and provisions. All being ready, I set out on September 30th. I started soon after eight a.m., and was told I should reach Ipiana that evening. The distance was really too great to get over comfortably in one day, and I had one or two battles on the way with my boys. Accordingly, I did not arrive until six p.m., and I was much amused to find that our first stop was at a place where there were a number of German sausage trees—clearly a sign we were approaching German territory. The fruit is curiously like a German sausage; it is very thick, eighteen inches or more in length, and hangs from the branch by it a thin stalk quite three feet in length. The fruits are very heavy, and the only use that I saw them put to was as seats and pillows for the natives. I broke one open, but found only a sort of white pith inside and some unripe seeds. It was useless to attempt to bring it home, which was disappointing, as I should have liked to show it to my friends. I was told afterwards that the natives sometimes cook and eat the seeds when ripe; but I do not think they cared much for them. The flower was fairly handsome, of a deep maroon colour, and somewhat like the hibiscus in shape.

For several hours our way took us close to the edge of the lake, and most of the time the boys preferred walking in the water, as the sand there was firmer, and, of course, it was cooler to their feet. Also, it was pleasanter for me in my machila, and the splashing of the water made by the feet of my carriers sounded delightfully refreshing. The colour of the lake was lovely—a bright deep blue. A good deal of the sand at the north end was quite black and sparkled in the sunshine; and there was a quantity of pumice lying about— remains of once active volcanoes, of which there are several in that part of the country. A little before two o'clock we came to the Songwe River. This appeared to be difficult to cross, as there was a great deal of water in it, and the banks were very steep. My boy came up to me and said we must camp where we were for the night. I asked if it were 'Ipiana,' to which he replied, 'Oh, no; that is much too far.' However, I had been told we ought to get there, and I insisted that they must take me on. After a good deal of talk among the natives, preparations were made to cross the river. Some of the boys got down into the water and held the machila, while I scrambled down the bank and got in, not a very easy matter. Then I had to cling to the pole with my hands and feet, so as to raise myself as high above the water as possible. Then the boys hoisted the pole on to their heads, instead of carrying it on their shoulders, and the rest held up the hammock part of the machila well under me to keep it out of the water. This was up to the men's waists, and the stream was fairly strong. It was not a very easy matter to get me across, but they managed it splendidly. I felt very thankful at the time that no one was about with a kodak to take a snap shot, though now I should rather like to have one as a memento.

At the next village we came to, the boys made another attempt to stop; but as I persisted that we were to go to Ipiana, and refused to get out of the machila, they went on again. For a time they were very cross, and bumped and banged me against every tree stump and rock that we had to pass. I said nothing, but waited till they seemed in a happier frame of mind, and then got out and walked a good distance to give them a rest.

After crossing the Songwe, it was one succession of villages, banana groves, and cultivated patches all the way to Ipiana. The villages were the nicest I had seen. The huts were beautifully built, well thatched, neat and well kept; they were almost hidden in banana groves, and in each village grew tall trees with dark leaves that made a splendid shade. The natives of that part, the Wnkonde, are the least warlike of any of the tribes, and are more given to agriculture. Also, they are very fond of decorative art.

At last we came to another river, the Kabira, and for some time could not find any place where we could cross. We were just opposite the mission station at Ipiana, and presently the people there heard my boys shouting, and came out to tell us where to find the ford. We had to go a long way up the river to it, and then had to repeat the performance at the Songwe. Both rivers are full of crocodiles, and the natives do not care to go in, unless there are a good many of them together; then they make so much noise and splashing, that there is no danger at all from the 'crocs.'

About six p.m. we reached Ipiana, and again I had a very kind and hearty reception from the missionaries, who were full of astonishment at my travelling alone. Two married missionaries and their wives were living there; indeed, it seems to be the rule among the Germans (and a good one too) always to have two married couples on a station, as they consider it too lonely for one. To save the boys the trouble of putting up my tent, as they had had a long day, my bed was put into an empty room. This had a door which opened in two halves, above and below, like a village shop door. I fastened it as firmly as I could and was soon sound asleep. I had not been asleep long when I was awakened by a noise. Looking up, I saw that the upper half of the door was open, and sitting on the under half, in the moonlight, which streamed in, was an awful-looking animal, seemingly just ready to jump into the room. I yelled and threw a pillow at it, but before the pillow reached the door the animal had vanished. I do not suppose it was anything more than a wild cat; but waking up suddenly and seeing it in the moonlight, it had all the horror of the unknown. I did not feel very happy about going to sleep again; but while I was arranging to keep awake, I dozed off, and did not open my eyes again until my boy came in the morning, to bring me a delicious cup of tea with milk in it.

I spent the morning in strolling about the village and watching the people. Many of their implements and ornaments were very different from those I had seen before. The women wore a curious head-band, made of a piece of dried banana leaf, dyed in patterns, and tied round their heads with the bow in front.

One of the German missionaries was a naturalist, and a most interesting man. He was collecting specimens for the Berlin Museum, and I spent a delightful evening looking over his beetles, butterflies, and snakes. They were most admirably prepared, and very neatly put up. Each label gave the name of the species, and when and where it had been found. I spent two very happy days at Ipiana, and heard a great deal that was full of interest for me, about the country and the natives I was going to visit. My carriers, meantime, had had a good rest; and when I wanted to start, they were quite cheerful and ready to go forward. We had to cross the Kabira River again in the same style as before, we reached our camping place in Mwantipura about two-thirty p.m. The carriers with the loads had gone on first, and, to my delight, on arriving, I found the tent up and the kettle boiling, ready for tea. The boys were always intensely amused at the pleasure I displayed when I found that tea was ready. It puzzled them very much to know why I liked it, for when they tasted it, it gave them no pleasure at all. While camping here I noticed that the fashionable head-dress for the young natives of this part was made of bunches of brown cock-feathers, tied on to a sharp-pointed piece of wood and stuck in the hair. I had a delightful capitao with this lot of boys, and he was very good at getting me queer ornaments, and anything that took my fancy.

The Kabira winds so much, that next day we had to cross it again, so that we got quite used to the performance. Soon after crossing it for the last time, we came to a large swamp, crusted all round with salt. It was amusing to see the eagerness with which they collected as much salt as they could, and licked their hands so as not to lose a grain.

The process of extracting the salt from the earth, which is employed by the natives, is interesting. They take the earth from the dried bed of a lake or stream, and put it into curious funnels, shaped like a tun-dish, which are made of bamboo or closely-woven grass rope. Then they pour water over the salt earth and stir it up. The water drains through the funnels into the pots below, and is then boiled or evaporated in the sun until only cakes of salt are left. They also extract salt from plants as well as from the earth. Salt is an article which all the natives value highly. My boys often used to come in the evening to beg a little salt to put in their food.

Most of the morning, after passing the swamp, we went through forest, broken by stretches of tall grass twelve to fourteen feet high, of a bright yellow colour, and looking very much like huge fields of ripe wheat when seen from a distance.

Occasionally we came on sudden and unexpected gullies full of lovely ferns. I had to walk most of the way until breakfast time, about ten-thirty, as it was difficult to get the machila through the tall grass and bushes with me in it; and after breakfast there was still less chance of riding, as the path went up and down over very rough stony hills all the time. From twelve until two o'clock the heat was very great, and we had to go slowly, and take good long rests in the shade or by the water. The views were very lovely; and one peep that we had of a river reminded me very much of a Swiss stream as it rushed along over rocks and stones, with a delightful suggestion of coolness. Just where we came down to it, there was a huge rock in the middle of the stream, that, at a distance, looked like a square-shaped native hut. One piece of the rock overhung and looked exactly like the thatch. The natives have many legends about it, and it is quite a land mark. The boys plunged into the water in an instant, to have a good wash and bathe. Then we set off again with a big climb before us, for the hills seemed never ending, and when we reached the top of one ridge, it was only to find that we had to go down and then climb another still higher. All the way the views were beautiful, and when, finally, we reached the highest point, there was compensation for our exertions in the glorious view that we obtained. We could see the river winding along among wooded hills and valleys, and, in the far distance, was the glisten of Lake Nyasa.

The boys always seemed pleased when I enjoyed the view; and they always pointed out what they thought interesting. At one place they drew my attention to a curious natural stone bridge, that looked like masonry—smooth and well built on one side, but very rough on the other. The natives say the people who live on the smooth side are good workmen, the others are bad. They had many more tales about it, but my English-speaking boy could not understand much of their language, as they came from a different part of the country; moreover, he was not equal to much translations, as he only knew the most ordinary English words and sentences.

We had not seen a village all the day after leaving Mwantipura quite early, and when at last we reached one we were glad to camp and rest, as we had had a hard, though a very enjoyable, journey. This village, like most of them in Kondeland, was surrounded by banana plantations, and I was able to get plenty of the fruit, which, either cooked or raw, made a pleasant change in my rather monotonous bill of fare.

We did not start very early next morning, but before mid-day we reached Rutenganyo, another mission station. Again there were two married couples, and I had the usual kind reception. They were very much puzzled about the way I had come. We had clearly taken a different route from the one the missionaries knew; but if longer, it had probably been much more lovely, and I came to the conclusion that, though my boys had a great knack of always choosing the

SAUSAGE TREE

WNKONDE HUT

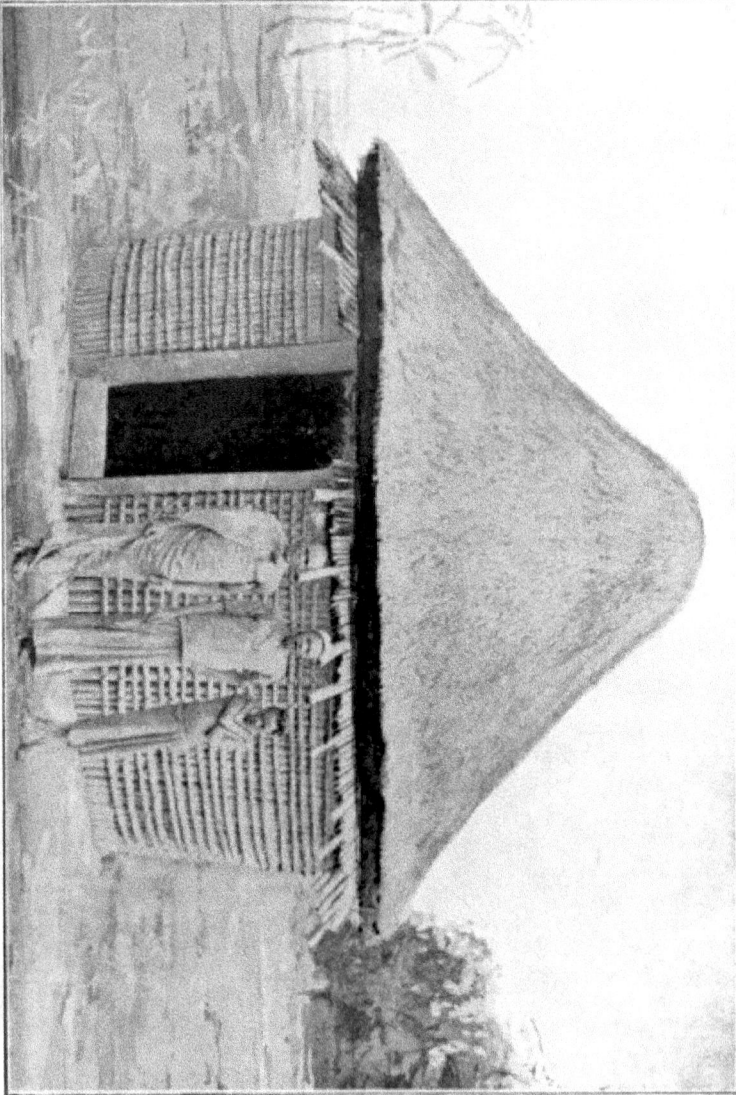

wrong path, they had an eye for fine scenery. From each village a number of paths diverge. Whenever we came to a place where the road divided, the boys, as soon as they had decided which road to take, drew a line, or put the branch of a tree across the other, in order to show the carriers who were following which way we had gone.

The further we got north the cleverer the natives seemed to be. At Otengule, the big chief, 'Merere,' used to have a quantity of good linen work done by the women of his tribe; but, unfortunately, Merere could not get on with the Germans, and he and his people left that part of the country. At present there is no more of this useful work being done, and it is difficult to get good specimens. I have one that is an excellent sample of their weaving. They used to make their own looms in a very primitive fashion, sticking pieces of wood in the ground, fastening the thread to them, working a roughly-made shuttle backwards and forwards. They grew the cotton, and made their own thread, the patterns and the dyes. Basket-work, too, they were very clever at, and it was so firmly done, that milk or water could be carried in the baskets without a drop being lost. Many of the natives, for carrying milk, use bamboo, ornamented with painting or carving. Some of their patterns are very effective, and well done. Over the top they stretch a piece of banana leaf, like a piece of bladder, to keep out flies and other insects.

Another station that I came to was 'Rungwe.' It is in a very volcanic part of the country, just at the foot of the Rungwe Mountain, an extinct volcano, which must have been extremely active once, for it is quite easy to trace where the streams of lava ran down. Some of the lava tracks are over grown with grass, while, in other places, the black lava is plainly visible above the ground. A cutting shows the dark volcanic dust at the top, and ashes and pumice below. The ground, owing to its volcanic origin, was of course very dry and dusty, and a thorough system of irrigation had to be constructed in the garden at the mission station, in order to get good crops. By this means they contrived to grow most of the home vegetables, and plenty of strawberries, which were small, but good.

A short distance away from Rungwe, I had an extremely pretty view of the station, with its church, its schoolhouse and outbuildings. The whole journey that day was delightful; up and down steep gullies and across noisy rushing streams, the banks of which were covered with maidenhair and other ferns. There was hardly a level piece of ground all the way. We crossed one stream where the water tasted just like 'Selters Wasser.' I walked most of the way, as it was very steep, and much too interesting to ride through in a machila.

At the village near to which I camped for the night, there was a great beating of drums and a general uproar. After I had had my tea, I went on a tour of inspection, and found a very grand dance going on—a larger one than I had yet seen—and the natives were most wonderfully dressed up. About one hundred men were dancing, holding in their hands their well-polished spears and axes, and having splendidly bright copper manyetas round their waists. Their bodies had been well rubbed with oil, and most of them had tufts of feathers in their hair. Two had very high plumes of black cock's feathers standing up quite two feet above their heads; another had a fringe of cow's teeth plaited into his hair; others, again, had their faces, backs and legs coloured red, grey, yellow and white. The children, too, were similarly decorated. It was a wonderful dance. They pranced about on their toes, and wriggled after the usual fashion, then, while some were dancing, surprise parties crept out of the banana grove and sprang on them, producing a general scrimmage; and while this was going forward others, again, stole away and came springing back with wild yells and shrieks. As time went on the dance got wilder, and fresh parties joined in the festivity from time to time. How it was that nobody was hurt, seeing that they all carried their spears, is more than I can tell. The singing was wonderful, sometimes very wild, sometimes very musical, and occasionally reminded me of some of Wagner's choruses. Long after I was in my tent the noise continued, and I was beginning to think, with horror, that it would last all night, when suddenly the singing and shrieking and howling rose with a violent crescendo, and the next moment ceased altogether. It was the last flourish—the finale— and in the silence that followed I could hear the patter of their feet as they instantly turned and flew off homewards.

The next day the way was even more difficult, and I wondered much how the boys with the loads managed to get up and down some of the declivities. The machila carriers had awkward work in taking me across the streams; the stones were exceedingly slippery, and the water rushed with considerable force. But, except in crossing streams, they did not have much work to do for me, as I preferred walking and stopping to look about me.

The views of the Livingstone range were very fine. The station I was going to, Makarere, was at the foot of the mountains, and from a distance had a most picturesque appearance. From the valley below Makarere to the top of the range is one succession of peaks, mountain after mountain; and at sunset, and in the early morning, the lights and shadows on the mountains are very lovely. Around Makarere the flowers were coming out fast, and the 'Kaffir Boom' trees were one blaze of scarlet. About here I saw a large tree with dark green leaves that bore a fruit in shape like a pine-apple. This fruit, however, was very sour, though refreshing; and each little division in it had a stone. I stayed at Makarere—one of the most beautiful places I have seen— two whole days, in order to give my boys a good rest and to enjoy the place myself. I engaged another lot of machila boys during the time I was there, for local excursions, and went with them on some lovely expeditions. These boys were used to the hills, and rushed me up and down them at break-neck speed. One charming picnic I had in company with the missionaries was at a deep gorge, through which the Lufirio River rushes, winding between high-wooded mountains. There was a wonderful old bamboo bridge across this river, and I did not much enjoy going over it, as I had to cross alone. It shakes too much if two are on it at the same time. As an inducement to cross, they promised me breakfast on the other side, so, with fear and trembling, I got across, and then we sat in a cool, shady spot, and during our meal watched enormous eagles hovering overhead. They are said to carry off sheep and small children, and they looked to me quite equal to doing it. In the trees were very handsome, but very savage-looking, monkeys, with long black hair, a white ruff round their necks, and very long tails with white tips.

On another day we went to some lovely waterfalls on the Lufirio and the Matesi; two rivers make almost an island of the station. Had I had time, I might have made any number of beautiful excursions among the mountains, but, unfortunately, I could not gratify my wishes in this respect. About Makarere there are a great many bees. The natives put boxes in the trees for them, and in that way get plenty of honey. Of this they are very fond; and they make what is considered a very delicious kind of beer from honey and water fermented. Cows were plentiful, too, so that this part of Africa might truly be called 'a land flowing with milk and honey.' The cows have a hump like the Indian cattle, and they are made to carry bells roughly made of native iron. The sound, as the animals moved about, reminded me of the 'ranz des vaches' in a Swiss valley. The cows are brought up and stalled for the night in long grass huts. There were also numbers of goats and sheep, the latter having broad, fat tails, which sometimes weigh as much as nine and even twelve pounds.

At the mission station there was one little white boy, the son of the missionary. He was about four years old, and it was the prettiest sight possible to see him marching along attended by five or six little black boys, his most devoted admirers, who patiently followed him wherever he went, and were only too delighted when he permitted them to do anything for him.

The only new thing I noticed in use among the natives here was a curious stick which the women use in walking. It has a top like a shepherd's crook and is only used by women. It was so beautiful at Makarere, that I was very much disinclined to leave. It was with many regrets, but with many pleasant memories, that I at length resumed my journey. The Livingstone Mountains are not volcanic; but soon after leaving them I began to get into volcanic country again, and I passed some very deep sulphur pits, all overgrown with lovely ferns. At one of these the boys stopped for me to get out of my machila, and listen to 'the noise the devil was making down there;' that was how my boy translated their statement. Soon after that we crossed a very dreary-looking black lava field. The lava had come down from Kiedyo, an extinct volcano near to Mano, where I stayed.

The country all round Mano was in marked contrast with the well-wooded district round the Livingstone Mountains. At Mano there are good views, but they are over mountains that are quite bare. At a little distance from the mission station there is a large lake in a deep hollow among the bare-looking hills. The lake is nearly square, and is very deep. The natives say that the fish in it have hair on their heads. Unfortunately, they did not seem willing to try to catch any while I waited, though they knew that I should very much have liked to see some. The legend about the lake is, that one of the gods came and asked for water at a village, but the people said they could not be bothered, and that he must get it himself. But a widow and her son brought him some, and then, sending them off to a safe place, he told the others that as they said they had a difficulty in finding water, they should now have plenty. Upon this the water rushed in from all sides, swamped the village, and formed the lake Kyungulalu. The legend sounds like a version of the story of the Flood.

At the place where I stopped for breakfast, I was told there was a wonderful dancer. I requested him to give me a performance, and a very funny one it was. He crept along almost like a serpent, stepped about on the tips of his toes, wriggled and waved his spear most curiously. The natives have marvellously lithe bodies, and seem able to twist themselves about in any shape or way.

When I started on again a crowd of at least fifty women and children escorted me for quite a long distance, running by the side of the machila laughing and talking all the time. I learnt a very curious thing here, namely, that if you beckon to a native in the way we do, he will run away instead of coming to you. The native way of beckoning is to point your fingers towards the earth and to pull them towards you. In counting, a native puts his finger to his lips for one, and again for two. He holds up three fingers for three, and for four, two fingers of each hand. Five, is the hand closed with the thumb poking out between the second and third fingers, and ten is the two closed fists on the top of each other.

The natives tell the time, of course, by the sun. If I asked them when I should arrive at a camping place, they pointed to the position the sun would be in at that time, and they were always wonderfully correct. One day, for a joke, I pointed to where I thought the sun would be, a performance which they hailed with shouts of laughter, as I had inadvertently pointed to the wrong side, i.e., the east, instead of to the west—a mistake no native would ever be guilty of making.

On our journey, we came upon three more lakes, some distance apart, and all hidden away in the forest. They were very deep down, with high banks all round. One afternoon we had to cross a pool and then a swamp, where the water was very black. There were dark trees all round, and the ground had been trampled by large animals, hippos or rhinos. The jungle was very nasty to get through, there was so much bamboo grass and prickly stuff, all dripping wet, as if there had been rain, or very heavy dew. It was the first time I had been wet through, and I did not like it. I was obliged to walk, as they could not possibly get the machila through with me in it. The carriers had to turn and twist it about in many ways in order to get through. We next came to the Mbaka River, which winds so much that we had to cross it three times. Its banks were very steep, but I was getting well used to scrambling down and getting into the machila, while it hung over the water.

At last, after a fortnight's wandering, I got back to Ipiana, and stayed two nights, in order to give my boys a rest, pack a few curios, and relate my adventures to the missionaries. Then I set off for Karonga, taking on my way back a different route, which led by 'Ngerenge. It was a longer and a more tiring way for the boys than that by which we had come, as it lay for a considerable distance through soft sand. But though I twice suggested that we should camp for the night, if they were tired, they declared they could quite easily get back to Karonga, and wished to do so. Of course, they were in much better practice at walking and carrying than they had been at the beginning of the fortnight, and there was a difference going from home and returning to it, which difference was in their favour. They got me to Karonga about half past six o'clock, running, shouting and singing during the last part of the journey as if they had only just started.

It seemed like home to get back to Karonga, as it was my third visit there, and the natives and Britishers had got quite used to seeing me about, and almost considered me as belonging to the place. I received a present there of some crocodile eggs, and was told a lovely tale about them. One day one of the telegraph men met a native with a fine lot of eggs that looked clean and fresh and were unusually cheap. So he had them sent to his tent, and told his boy to cook them. The boy usually cooked eggs extremely well, but these came to table looking rather disagreeable. However, the English man and his friend ate away and enjoyed them, though they thought the eggs had a peculiar flavour. Next day the boy was reproved for cooking them so badly, and was told to do the remainder better. The boy said he could not, and when asked why, replied that 'those eggs were croc's, not hen's eggs, and will never look nice when cooked.' The horror of the poor men who had eaten them was great, and the boy was not required to try his skill on the remainder.

I had a busy time for some days in packing all my treasures, which I was sending by steamer down the lake. Then I finally took leave of Karonga, and all who had been so kind to me there, and with another team I set off for Kondowe, Dr Laws's Mission Station.

BAMBOO BRIDGE

CHAPTER X

KARONGA TO KONDOWE

WHEN I LEFT KARONGA ON THIS OCCASION, I had a very poor set of carriers, Wnkonde boys. There were very few to be had, as a great many had been taken for the telegraph works, the Boundary Commission, and other expeditions. The Wnkonde are bad machila carriers, but I had to be satisfied and thankful that I could get any at all to take me. I did not wish to wait longer at Karonga, as I feared I might miss seeing Dr Laws, who was thought to be going on an expedition into the country just about that time.

I started early in the morning, but the boys dragged along very slowly through the soft sand, and when we stopped for a mid-day rest one of them put down his load and departed. I got another boy to replace him quite easily, but they all went very badly, and seemed to find it such hard work that, when we camped for the night, I determined to get two more to help. Accordingly, I told the capitao to ask the chief of a neighbouring village to let me have two boys to go on with me next morning. He did so, but returned from the village saying that the chief would not let me have any. I told him that was nonsense. I must have them and of course was willing to pay for them. However, he returned again, saying that the chief quite refused to send any. I told him to show me the chief and I would speak to him myself. My boy wished to come with me, saying, 'I could not make the chief understand, as he did not know my language;' but I told him to stay where he was, and off I marched alone to try the effect of a little English. Arrived at the village, I walked very solemnly up to the chief, held up two fingers, and told him he must get me two boys at once. To my joy and amazement he went off promptly and brought back two capital boys, who helped well all the rest of the way. I gave the old chief some salt as a present, and we parted excellent friends. My boy was much astonished at my success, and

GOATS GOING TO BED

wanted to know how I managed it, as 'behold the chief, he speak not English.' I preserved a discreet silence, and did not divulge the secret. Indeed, I could not have told it had I wished.

The road was better next day, there was not so much heavy sand, and the boys were happier, and things went more cheerfully and well. I travelled for some distance along the road, which had been cut for the telegraph line, and met one of the telegraph men bringing back to Karonga the last party of natives who had been working on the line. They were carrying all their ladders, implements, etc. He was much amused at meeting me, and said I was the first white woman he had seen for an age, and he could hardly remember when he had last seen a starched collar. I was greatly delighted at that being noticed, as it was the last one I possessed, and my general appearance was now so forlorn-looking, that that morning I had felt obliged to put on my last outward and visible sign of respectability—a clean collar. My boy had done all my washing, and cotton blouses did not look too beautiful after his way of ironing. He spread a mat on the ground, smoothed out the clothes as well as he could on it, then spread a towel or something large over them, and slid his feet up and down till he thought the smoothing process was complete. He then hung the clothes in the sun to dry, and when dry they were ready to put on. It was a very simple process, and quite enough for most things; but I had not as suitable an outfit as I could have wished for. I had, of course, no idea, even when I left Chinde, that I should be so long in the wilds.

In one of the villages we passed through, the women were busy making pottery. They pound the dark red bark of a tree, mix it with hot water and spread it over the baked pottery while hot. When the pot is cold it has a good red brown glaze outside. Round the neck of the pot they make a very pretty border, the pattern of which is marked out with a piece of stick. The inside usually has a good black glaze.

On our way we saw a good many baobab trees. One of them was enormous. As it was on the line of the telegraph, the branches had all been cut off, but the trunk, on account of its size, was left standing. There was a quantity of the fruit lying about, which my boys were glad to pick up, and when we got down to the lake again, we had nice refreshing drinks of water flavoured with the cream-of-tartar acid of the fruit.

The road we traversed on the day before reaching Kondowe was very hilly, and finally became tremendously steep. I felt as if they were taking me up the side of a house—not a pleasant feeling when you are lying in a hammock with your head down hill. The first chance I had I got out and walked the rest of the way. In the heat the climb was somewhat trying, and I was glad to hold one end of a stick and let a native do a bit of pulling at the other end. It was a good help up the steepest places. Of course, I stopped frequently to admire the view over the lake, which really was very beautiful. The plateau at the top of this ascent was very varied, and on it were hills, some of which might be called mountains.

It is only four years since Dr Laws received permission to settle on this station, yet it is wonderful to observe what he has accomplished in the time. But of course there is much still to be done before it is all that he has planned, and wishes it to be. He and his wife have been in B. C. A. for twenty-five years. He understands the natives, and they thoroughly respect and trust him—which is what the natives should always be able to do to the white man. But there are obstacles in the way, and besides other evils there is often too much 'diplomacy' in our dealings with them. They are led to believe one thing when another is meant, a thing which, when found out, destroys their faith in us.

Dr Laws is a doctor of medicine as well as a missionary — a combination which always seems to have good results. At Kondowe there were two excellent trained nurses, and when I arrived they were greatly excited, as they had just had a most delightful adventure with a lion. They had been nursing a case some distance off, and, on their return journey, started one morning very early from their camp. When they had gone some distance, one of the nurses, who was in front, was stopped by the natives who were with her, saying, 'Lion! lion!' And sure enough the growl of a lion was heard not very far away.

One of the missionaries, who had gone out to meet them and bring them home, quickly got his gun ready, and together with the nurse and some of the natives, who were armed with spears and sticks, went in search of the lion. They followed the growling sound for some time, but when that ceased, they could not tell whereabouts in the long grass the lion was, and they decided to give up the search and turn back. The lion had evidently been watching them, for the moment they turned, out he came with a great bound. At first they took to their heels, but when he was about thirty yards off they turned and faced him, which brought him to a standstill. Quick as thought the man with the gun shot him, and over he went into the long grass. As they could not tell if he were killed or only wounded, the nurse, at the suggestion of the natives, climbed into a tree, while the men went cautiously in search of the wounded beast. Presently they found his spoor. He was evidently badly wounded, as he was dragging himself along. But on hearing the roar of another lion, or, more probably, the lioness, they thought discretion the better part of valour, and returned to the lady up the tree and the rest of their party. The other nurse they found standing with her back to a tree and surrounded by a score or so of natives; she had heard the roars, but had missed the excitement of seeing the lion. They all got back safely to the mission station, and the nurses thoroughly enjoyed telling their story, considering themselves very lucky to have been the heroines of such a thrilling adventure when they had been less than a year in the country.

While I stayed at Kondowe, the nurses took me some beautiful walks, one to a lovely waterfall, where the water pours over a projecting rock, under which you can walk or sit, and have your tea, as we did. In the same ravine there were a number of cave dwellings, old huts and kraals, hidden away down among the rocks and on the sides, where the natives were living when Dr Laws came to that part. They used to be afraid of the Angoni tribe, who came down and raided them; but now that things are quiet and more orderly, they are living up on the plateau. The remains of the stockade across the narrow entrance to the ravine, and a quaint ladder of monkey ropes twisted about for the natives to climb up and keep a look-out, are still to be seen. The whole ravine was very wild and lovely; glorious maidenhair and other ferns grew all about the rocks, and near the waterfall, by which we had tea, was a second, equally beautiful, for each of the two rivers, which join in the valley below, takes a splendid leap over the rocks here.

Another day, the two nurses and I had a delightful expedition to Mount Chiombi. It was about a two hours' ride in a machila to the foot of the mountain, and then we had to climb about three-quarters of an hour in order to reach the top, where we got a lovely view over the lake and the country round. Here there is a large plateau, and we had quite a long walk to the other end of it to see the sphinx—a rock with a perfect resemblance to an African face—looking out east over the lake. I hoped at first it was looking towards the sphinx in Egypt, but, unfortunately, the direction is wrong. The grass on the plateau was very long and dry, so, before coming down, we set it on fire. It burned grandly, and as it became dark there was a glorious blaze, lighting up the whole of the top of the mountain, and making little rivers of fire down the sides. It was the right time of the year for burning the grass, and it caused the new grass to come up beautifully fresh and green afterwards.

One day, much sooner than I could have wished, a messenger came up from the lake to say that the 'Domira' had arrived. There was so much at Kondowe that was interesting to see and hear, and so many delightful walks and expeditions to make, that I was loath to leave; but the steamer was there, and I had to go on board next morning.

On my way to the lake I set off in a machila to the top of the descent, and then had to walk the rest of the way down. It was very rough and steep, and there was so much loose rock and stone, that it was hard to get a foothold, and I soon had an unpleasant tumble. After this I held on to a native. With their bare feet, the natives walk firmly and well. We got down to the lake safely about mid-day, almost melted by the great heat. The sun had been shining directly on me the whole way down, and there was not the least bit of shade.

The captain of the 'Domira' had been watching our descent, and had very kindly provided a good supply of tea for us—a service which I highly appreciated. It was pleasant to be back on the old 'Domira' again, and there was a homelike feeling about it too, though, alas! the cockroaches, as well as my 'state room,' were ready for me.

We had rough weather going down the lake. While we were anchored at Kota-Kota, the wind got up so strongly, that all the awnings had to be taken down, and the steamer dragged her anchors three times, the last time landing so firmly on the sand, that it was a difficult business to get her off. On our way we met the A. L. C. steamer, the 'Queen Victoria,' on her first trip. She looked a fine boat, with good passenger accommodation, and was going along at a good pace on her way to Karonga. It will make a wonderful difference to have another and a larger steamer on the lake. There is now so much large and heavy cargo to be taken up for the telegraph, besides, of course, an increase in goods and personal belongings for the residents, that a second steamer was much needed.

I was glad to reach Fort Johnston again, and I was much struck by the wonderful additions and improvements that had been made during the few months I had been away. The new house and store for the A. L. C. were finished, and appeared quite fine from the river. Their roofs were painted red—a colour which looks well—and is said to resist the heat very well. Several other houses had just been finished, and the whole place looked neat and well laid out. Excellent roads were being made and trees planted. At first there was an idea of having verandahs only in the front of the houses, but, happily, that idea was abandoned, and all have good verandahs which run completely round. The houses are like most European houses, not at all picturesque; but they would have been positively ugly with a verandah only in front, and the poor inhabitants would have had hot, uncomfortable homes.

The 'Guendolen' was making splendid progress, and I much regretted not being able to stay for the launching; but the rainy season was coming on, and I had only about eighteen days left in which to catch the steamer at Chinde, if I would reach home in time for Christmas. The water, too, was getting very low; we just grazed on the two bars as we came out of the lake into the river, and I had to allow time for a chance 'stick' in going down the river to Matope.

It was very hot at Fort Johnston, 106° in the shade, and the mosquitoes were very tiresome, too; but, in spite of all, I was sorry to leave and to say good-bye to the kind and hospitable friends there. I was the only passenger on the 'Monteith' going down the river. It is a comfortable boat, with good cabins, and I much enjoyed my journey down, and had a peaceful view of all the birds, duck and wildfowl, and a last look at the hippos and crocodiles. We tied up for the night at Liwonde, starting next morning at three a.m., and as that part of the river was new to me, I dressed and went on deck. The moonlight was brilliant, and I could see everything clearly. The river winds a great deal, and some of the

STORE AT KONDOWE

turns are so sharp, we had to run into the bank and swing round so as to keep in the channel. The banks are high in some places, and full of the holes of a reed martin, a lovely bird, red and bluish grey in colour. The trees, too, were full of baboons, springing from branch to branch and making their queer noises.

We reached Matope before ten a.m., and, with the kind help of the captain and the A. L. C. agent, I got a machila team and boys to carry my luggage, which had of late much increased in weight, and by eleven o'clock I was off again on my way to Blantyre. But the heat! It was almost unbearable. It was something to have made a start, but, at the first water and shade we came to, we stopped and had a good rest. Matope lies very low and flat, and all the heat in the country seems to concentrate there. When I was in the machila, I seemed to be between two fires, the sun shining down, and the heat striking up from the ground. I found it cooler to get out and walk. My shoes protected my feet, but, to the bare feet of the men, the heat was terrible. I tried it with my hand.

We passed on the way numbers of baobab and German sausage trees, and some very tall trees with trunks of a yellowish green, almost sulphur colour. None of the trees had many leaves on, so we got very little shade, except near to water.

We were crawling along very quietly, without any singing or shouting, when the same thing happened that I had experienced once before. My boys were Angoni, and not very good carriers, and when we came on eight Yao boys going along without loads, the latter began to laugh at them and tease them. At last, with derisive yells of 'Angoni, Angoni,' the Yaos seized the machila and tore off with me at a furious pace, laughing and shouting all the time, till they came to another stream, and there they popped me down in the shade, and went off for a good wash and a smoke. It had been a splendid help, and the Yao boys seemed perfectly happy, and apparently considered it a great joke. When my boys came up I was able to give them some salt as a present, and this pleased them greatly.

By this time it was getting cooler, but had begun to thunder heavily. The lightning was very brilliant, and fear of a storm made my boys trot on as fast as they could. I quite thought that at last I should be caught in a bad storm, but though there was plenty of noise and lightning, very little rain fell. After the sun set, it was very dark till the moon came out of the clouds; I had been wondering how we should get on, as the men stumbled so much over stumps and rocks in the path. However, they pluckily kept going forward, and, just before ten p.m., we reached the mission station at Blantyre. Lights were still in the windows, and I was received with the kindest and heartiest welcome. It had been a long day, as I had been up since three a.m. I was fairly tired, and glad to get a good night's rest.

At Blantyre I had again the delightful feeling of being among old friends, and had much to hear and relate. While staying there we had some heavy storms. One was very curious, it thundered heavily, then down came a furious hail-storm. The stones were enormous, not rounded, but simply rough pieces of ice, and while they were falling the thermometer was 98° in the shade.

I had plenty to do and see during a three days' stay which I made at Blantyre, and had to settle up for my journey and pack all my luggage, which I sent to Chinde by river, while I went round by Mlanje and the Ruo Falls to join the river at Chiromo. This turned out a very beautiful expedition, but a terrible experience. Everything hitherto had gone so well, that I suppose I was careless, and did not make sufficient enquiries and proper arrangements. Altogether, I had trusted too much to luck. It was a long day's journey from Blantyre to Mlanje, and I understood it had been arranged for me to stay at the latter mission station for the night. I started with one team of machila men, and another had been sent on to wait for me halfway, and carry me to Mlanje.

I set off very early, and got on all right until I met my new lot of men. As I could not see any signs of men carrying bedding or cooking utensils, I concluded that they had gone on, as I should not be likely to want them until the next day. It seemed an interminable journey, and it was not till six-thirty that we arrived at a house. I asked if it were the mission station, but the gentleman who came out looked greatly amused, and said we had come nine miles beyond the mission, and that I had arrived at the house of Mr Moir. He added, also, that he was the manager of the estate, and that Mr and Mrs Moir were away staying up in the mountain. I was in despair. Where my luggage had gone I could not imagine, most probably to the mission station, and it was too far to go back there that night. There was nothing for it but to wait for the things to turn up, and I gladly accepted the manager's hospitable invitation to stay there for the night. The boy, with my own personal belongings, arrived about nine o'clock; but all declared there was no more luggage on the road. Rather puzzled as to how I should manage the rest of the journey to Chiromo, I went to my room and was soon asleep.

The journey all day had been across the plain, through pretty country, with lots of bracken and wild asparagus, and we had a grand view of the Mlanje Mountains, which looked lovely in the evening light as we got nearer to them. Mr Moir's house is in a charming situation, just at the foot of the mountain, which is an extinct volcano. The crater is very fine; two peaks, rather like the Matterhorn, form a sort of gateway through which the lava formerly poured, and down which a strong stream of water now rushes.

Mr and Mrs Moir kindly sent to ask me to come and stay with them, in order to enjoy the lovely scenery up the mountain, but as it took a whole day to get to their place, and as I did not want to risk missing my steamer, I had reluctantly to decline their invitation. The Mlanje Mountains are about ten thousand feet high, and on the plateau are again other mountains two or

three thousand feet high. It is a most splendid health resort, and will in time become much more valued and used.

The coffee plantations on Mr Moir's estate were beautiful. The plants were in full bloom, the flowers at a distance looked like snow against the dark leaves. The scent, too, was delicious.

I saw a horse there that had had an interesting adventure. The manager had brought it up from Durban, being the first person who had successfully brought a horse to that part in spite of the Tsetze fly. It was landed all right at Chiromo, then one evening, after they had camped, something frightened the animal and it broke away with the saddle on its back. The boys followed it for some time, but at last lost it, and had to return to the camp and then on to Mlanje. From there natives were sent out to search for the horse; but it was quite a fortnight before a message reached the manager asking him to go and fetch it. When the natives had at last found the animal, it seemed tired out, very hungry and very much frightened. Its saddle was still on, but was turned underneath it. They dared not touch it, for it was the first animal of the kind they had seen; but as it seemed hungry, they gave it a great heap of native corn, and while it was eating that, they put a fence round it, then made a sort of roof to shade it from the sun, and sent off for the owner to come quickly. The horse was a long time before it got over the fright and fatigue, and the sore places caused by the saddle; but when I saw it, it was looking very well and fit.

I arranged to start early the next morning, the manager kindly offering to lend me a camp bed if I would send the boys back with it the next day, which I gladly promised to do. He said I should find a sort of rest-house half-way to Chiromo, where I could stay; so, with a fowl and some tea, by way of provisions, I set off, trusting I should manage all right.

The journey was rather pretty, especially where we stopped for the mid-day rest, at the junction of the Ruo and the Luchirio Rivers. The 'rest-house' was reached soon after five o'clock, and turned out to be a corrugated iron shanty, the floor inches thick with dust and wood ashes, and full of natives with their loads. Of course, when I arrived, they all turned out, and while they swept the place and the dust was settling down, I went off to the river and ate sparingly of my chicken. I was very hungry, but the chicken was all I had to eat during the next day. I saved some also, but was so thirsty that, before I could go to sleep, I was tempted to finish it. Having dined, my thoughts turned towards a wash, and then I realised the horrible fact that I had nothing to wash in. I could therefore only paddle about in a rather muddy place in the stream, and wash my face and hands after a fashion. On the whole, I succeeded in making myself more wet than clean. The mosquitoes were more pleased to have me there than I was to stay; so I wandered back to my uncomfortable home.

I woke up pretty early next morning, had the bedding packed, and sent it back with a grateful message. I should indeed have been miserable without it. Then having had another apology for a wash, I thought about having my breakfast. I unwrapped the chicken carefully, and 'behold,' as my boy used to say, it was black with ants. I tossed it to the boys, who thought that I only wanted the ants removed. Accordingly, after much blowing and shaking they brought it back to me. But I generously presented it to them! Hungry as I was, I could not bring myself to eat that piece of chicken, and I was left to regret the economy I had practised in saving it from my meal the night before. I was now without anything to eat, nor could I get anything to drink, as I was afraid to drink the water in the stream without having first boiled it.

The whole of our journey that day was through very pretty country; up and down hill, through bush, and often near the river. But, of course, there was not much shade, the leaves not being fully out yet. By half-past ten the ground was so hot that the boys could not go on any longer, and we had to stop. Where we stopped there was an old grass hut, and I lay outside in what shade there was, the boys bringing me calabashes of water from the river to cool my head and wrists. They, lucky mortals! went and sat in the river, and thoroughly enjoyed themselves. We stayed there until about four o'clock, and then set off again. The Ruo Falls were not far from the grass hut, and were very fine and well worth a visit. A journey from Chiromo to see them makes a very pleasant excursion.

We reached Chiromo about six o'clock, and when I got to the A. L. C. house, I felt exceedingly tired, and could hardly speak. The heat had been intense all day, and I had not had anything to drink; however, a bath and innumerable cups of tea soon put me right again. The A. L. C. house at Chiromo was intensely hot even at night, the beds and pillows felt as if they had been run over with an old-fashioned warming-pan. The place was full, no less than fifteen passengers were waiting for the steamers, some of them having been there for a week or longer.

At last two steamers arrived. The first to leave was, of course, packed, and was so uncomfortable, that I thought I would risk my chance of catching the ocean steamer at Chinde, and go down a day later on the second boat. At last, after three days' boiling and baking, the other steamer started, and a very comfortable trip I had down the river. On the way I amused myself by counting up the number of miles I had been in a machila, and found it was well over a thousand miles. During the whole journey I had only one fall, and certainly the natives took the greatest possible care of me.

I was fortunate enough to catch the 'Peters' at Chinde; I had only just time to get my luggage and myself on board, as the vessel started off as soon as possible after the river steamer had arrived. At Mozambique I changed on to a larger

German steamer and came home by Zanzibar, Mombasa, and the Suez Canal. The voyage is an extremely interesting one; but the German line is certainly not to be recommended, if the vessel I came home on is typical. I was glad to leave the boat at Marseilles, from which place, travelling overland. I reached home a few days before Christmas, feeling that I had had a glorious time, and had gone through most interesting experiences.

THE END

BIOGRAPHY OF HARRIET MARTINEAU

HARRIET MARTINEAU WAS BORN ON JUNE 12, 1802 to a middle-class family in Norwich, England. From childhood, various illnesses characterized the ways in which she interacted with the world. She was prone to digestive issues, anxiety attacks, and worsening hearing that left her deaf by age thirty. Martineau could have allowed her poor health to confine her to the cloistered life of the delicate Victorian woman, but instead she used her experience to write candidly about the hardships she faced. In her mid-thirties, doctors diagnosed her with uterine tumors and a prolapsed uterus for which there was no cure. She spent five years bed-ridden before undertaking a course of mesmerism, which she believed led to a full recovery.

Her works about her illnesses, "Letter to the Deaf" (1834), *Life in the Sick-Room* (1844), *Letters on Mesmerism* (1845), and *Autobiography* (1877), address readers as potential fellow invalids, sharing details of her maladies and the ways she dealt with them in a candid, unflinching voice. In an era where patients' (and especially female patients') voices were eliminated from medical literature, her contributions to and advocacy for education on women's health are considered some of her most important works. In her posthumously-published *Autobiography*, she writes about the mindset that allowed her to separate herself from her pain by minimizing her sense of individual self-importance: "I feel no reluctance whatever to pass into nothingness, leaving my place in the universe to be filled by another. The very conception of self and other is, in truth, merely human, and when the self ceases to be, the distinction expires."

In *Eastern Life*, she writes about her ear trumpet and draws similarities between the way people speak to her and the way English people speak to Africans—loudly and slowly, as though a difference in the way a person perceived language indicated a lesser intellect. However, for most of the work, she separates her personal experience from her professional focus, detailing climbs up desert sand dunes and taking every opportunity for physically difficult exploration.

Martineau's work anthologized in this volume shows a much greater interest in and sympathy towards history over the present inhabitants of the countries she visited. She argued for the preservation and respect of ancient Egyptian monuments and art, condemning both locals and European tourists' habit of defacing ancient sites with graffiti and campfire smoke. Despite her concern for maintaining Egypt's history, her relationship with the living Egyptians she interacted with lacked the same depth and care. In Eastern Life, she claims to have treated the Egyptians "like children," endorsing this behavior as the best way to establish a rapport with guides and hosts there.

Even during periods of illness, Martineau gained recognition for her series of stories on classical economics published from 1832-1834. During her two-year visit to the United States, she broadened her writing topics to include incisive sociological perspectives on the abolitionist movement. Although slavery was abolished in England in 1833, it was still widely practiced in the United States. Martineau's novel *The Hour and the Man* (1841) use the conventions of historical romance to represent Toussaint L'Ouverture, the leader of the Haitian rebellion, as a tragic hero who loved his family and led with courage and charisma, overwhelmed in the end by the sheer number of French soldiers. Her writing affirmed to Northern abolitionists the necessity of revolution in ending slavery and offered an early example an intelligent, capable, and valiant black hero from a white author.

In addition to her writing for social reform, Martineau also helped to create and popularize the genre of the school story with her book *The Crofton Boys* in 1841. Shortly thereafter, she wrote a series of articles about England's Lake District in a style that advocated for appreciation of nature in the industrial era.

During a trip to the Middle East in 1846, Martineau looked with increasing sharpness at her own religious beliefs and the structure of religion and faith. Her 1851 publication of *Letters on the Laws of Man's Nature and Development*, in which she wrote about her transition from liberal Utilitarianism to atheism, shocked readers. Her own beliefs and experiences notwithstanding, Martineau remained a historical authority, as evidenced by her thorough account in *Eastern Life*, by her popular *The History of the Thirty Years' Peace 1816-1846*, and by her over 1,600 Daily News articles.

In 1876, Martineau died of bronchitis at the age of seventy-four.

EASTERN LIFE,

PRESENT AND PAST.

BY

Harriet Martineau

"Joyful to receive the impression thereof, as the eye joyeth to receive light; and not only delighted in beholding the variety of things, and vicissitude of times, but raised also to find out and discern the ordinances and decrees, which, throughout all these changes, are infallibly observed."

— Bacon, *Advancement of Learning,* I.

COMFLETE IN ONE VOLUME:

PHILADELPHIA: LEA AND BLANCHARD

1848

PREFACE

IN THE AUTUMN OF 1846, I left home for, as I supposed, a few weeks, to visit some of my family and friends. At Liverpool, I was invited by my friends, Mr. and Mrs. Richard V. Yates, to accompany them in their proposed travels in the East. By the zeal and kindness of those who saw what a privilege this journey would be, all obstacles in the shape of business and engagements were cleared away; and in a month, I was ready to set out with my kind friends. — At Malta, we fell in with Mr. Joseph C. Ewart, who presently joined our party, and remained with us till we reached Malta on our return. There is nothing that I do not owe to my companions for their unceasing care and indulgence: but one act of kindness I felt particularly. They permitted me to read to them my Egyptian journal, (there was no time for the others,) that I might have the satisfaction of knowing whether they agreed in my impressions of the facts which came under our observation. About these facts there is an entire agreement between them and me. —For the opinions expressed in this book, no one is answerable but myself.

It is by permission of my companions that I have thus named them here, and spoken of them in my book as occasion required. I am truly obliged to them for granting me this freedom, by which I am spared much trouble of concealment and circumlocution which, in their opinion and mine, the personal affairs of travel are not important enough to require and justify. —Not having asked a similar permission from our comrades in our Arabian journey, I have said as little as possible about them, and suppressed their names. I shall be glad if they find anything in my narrative to remind them pleasantly of that remarkable season of our lives, —our five weeks abode in the Desert.

Sir G. Wilkinson must be almost tired of the testimonies and thanks of grateful travelers: but I must just say that he was, by his books, a daily benefactor to us in Egypt. It is really cheering to find that any one can be so accurate, and on so large a scale, as his works prove him to be. Such almost faultless correctness requires a union of intellectual and moral powers and training, which it is encouraging for those who are interested in the results of travel to contemplate. After making the fullest use of his "Modern Egypt and Thebes," we find only about half-a-dozen points in which we differ from him.

In regard to that difficult matter, —difficult to those who do not understand Arabic, —the spelling of the names of places and persons in Egypt and Arabia, —I have done what every one will allow to be the safest thing; —I have followed the authority of Mr. Lane wherever I could. If any English reader complains of me for altering the look of familiar Egyptian names, it is enough to reply that Mr. Lane knows better than anyone, and that I copy from him. If I have departed from his method anywhere, it is merely because I had not his authority before me in those particular instances.

H.M.

AMBLESIDE, *25th March*, 1848.

CONTENTS

PART I
EGYPT AND ITS FAITH

CHAPTER I
First sight of Africa—First sights in Africa—Alexandria 809
CHAPTER II
From Alexandria to Cairo—First sight of the Pyramids—Preparations for Nile Voyage.. 817
CHAPTER III
Nile incidents—Crew—Birds—Face of the country—The heavens—Towns and shores, between Cairo and Asyoot.. 826
CHAPTER IV
Asyoot—Old sites—Some elements of Egyptian thought—First crocodiles— Soohadj—Girgeh—Kenneh 837
CHAPTER V
Walks ashore—First sight of Thebes—Adfoo—Christmas Day........ 853
CHAPTER VI
Aswán—Slaves—First ride in the Desert—Quarries—Elephantine—River scenery—Preparations for Nubia—First sight of Philœ 862
CHAPTER VII
Ascent of the Cataract 875
CHAPTER VIII
Nubia—The Second Cataract... 879
CHAPTER IX
Historical Sketch, from Menes to the Roman occupation of Egypt.. 891
CHAPTER X
Aboo-Simbil—Egyptian conceptions of the gods 918
CHAPTER XI
Ibreem—Dirr—Subooa—Dakkeh—Garf Hoseyn 927

CHAPTER XII

Dendoor—Kalàb-sheh—Biggeh—Philœ—Leaving Nubia.............. 938

CHAPTER XIII

Kóm Umboo—Quarries of Silsileh—Adfoo—Eilethyia—Old Egyptian Life—
Isna—Arment 956

CHAPTER XIV

Thebes—European travelers and native Arabs—The Pair—The Ramaséum—
El-Kurneh 969

CHAPTER XV

Thebes—Old Egyptian views of Death and Hereafter—The Priests—Interments Tomb of Osirei.. 978

CHAPTER XVI

Thebes—Tombs—Mummies—Medeenet Haboo—Dayr el Bahree—El Kar-
nac 999

CHAPTER XVII

Manufactures at Kenneh—Manners of the crew—Excursion to Abydusx......
.... 1011

CHAPTER XVIII

Benee Hasan—Masgoon—Pyramids of Dashoor and Sakkára—Memphis—
Mummy pits—Consecration of brutes 1018

CHAPTER XIX

Visit to the Pyramids—Ascent of the Great Pyramid—Interior—Traditions
and history about the Pyramids—The Sphinx—Farewell to Ancient Egypt ...
.... 1034

CHAPTER XX

Inundation of the Nile—Famine in Egypt.................................... 1049

CHAPTER XXI

Cairo—Streets and bazaars—Mosques—Citadel—Fete of the Birth of the
Prophet—Entrance of the Mahhmil—The Magician—Society in Cairo—Mr.
Lane 1064

CHAPTER XXII

The Hareem 1082

CHAPTER XXIII

Present condition of Egypt 1094

CHAPTER XXIV

Gardens of Roda and Shoobra—Heliopolis—Petrified forest—Tombs of the
Memlook kings—The Nilometer—Leaving Cairo.......................... 1101

Note: Parts II and III of this work are not included in this volume
due to constraints of book length, but they are public domain material and available online.

PART I

EGYPT AND ITS FAITH

"They are extremely religious, and surpass all men in the worship they render to the gods."

Herodotus, II. 37.

"Wherefore they were highly celebrated by Apollo's oracle (recorded by Porphyrius), and preferred before all other nations for teaching rightly 'that hard and difficult way, that leadeth to God and happiness.'"

Cudworth. Intellectual System, Book I. 4.

"For, as for the uttermost antiquity, which is like Fame that muffles her head, and tells tales, I cannot presume much of it; for I would not willingly imitate the manner of those that describe maps, which, when they come to some far countries, whereof they have no knowledge, set down how there be great wastes and deserts there; so I am not apt to affirm that they knew little, because what they knew is little known to us."

Bacon. Interpretation of Nature, ch. V.

EGYPT AND ITS FAITH

CHAPTER I

FIRST SIGHT OF AFRICA—FIRST SIGHTS IN AFRICA—ALEXANDRIA

MY FIRST SIGHT OF AFRICA was on a somewhat lurid November evening, when the descending sun marked out by its red light a group of purple Tocks to the westward, which had not been visible till then, and which presently became again invisible when the sun had gone down behind them, and the glow of the sky had melted away. What we saw was the island of Zembra, and the neighboring coast of Tunis. Nothing in Africa struck me more than this its first phantom appearance amidst the chill and gathering dusk of evening, and with a vast expanse of sea heaving red between us and it.

My next sight of Africa was when I came on deck early on the morning of the 20th of November. A Lybian headland was looming to the south-east. Bit by bit, more land appeared, low and gray; then the fragments united, and we had before us a continuous line of coast, level, sandy and white, with an Arab tower on a single eminence. Twice more during the day we saw such a tower, on just such an eminence. The sea was now of a milky blue, and lustrous, as if it were one flowing and heaving opal. Presently it became of the lightest shade of green. When a tower and a ruined building were seen together, every one called out "Alexandria!" and we expected to arrive by noon: but we passed the tower and ruins, and saw only a further stretch of low and sandy coast. It was three o'clock before we were in harbor. —When we came on deck after dinner, we found that we were waiting for a pilot; and that we ought to be growing impatient, as there was only an hour of daylight left, and the harbor could not be entered after dark. There was no response from a pilot-boat which we hailed;

and one of our boats was sent off to require the attendance of the pilot, who evidently thought he could finish another piece of business before he attended to ours. He was compelled to come; and it was but just in time. The stars were out, and the last brilliant lights had faded from the waters, before we anchored. As we entered the harbor, there was to the south-west, the crowd of windmills which are so strange an object in an African port: before us was the town, with Pompey's Pillar rising behind the roofs: further north, the Pasha's palace and hareem, with their gardens and rows of palms coming down to the margin of the sea: further round, the lighthouse; and to the east, at the point of the land, a battery. The Pasha's men-of-war, which do not bear well a noon-day examination, looked imposing amidst the brilliant lights and deep shadows of evening, their red flag, with its crescent and single star, floating and falling in the breeze and lull. But for the gorgeous light, there would have been nothing beautiful in the scene, except the flag (the most beautiful in the world) and the figure of our pilot as he stood robed, turbaned and gesticulating on the paddle-box; —a perfect feast to western eyes: but the light shed over the flat and dreary prospect a beauty as home-felt as it does over the gray rain-cloud when it brings out the bow. As we were turning and winding into the harbor, a large French steamer was turning and winding out—setting forth homewards—her passengers on deck, and lights gleaming from her ports. Before we came to anchor, she was aground; and sorry we were to see her lying there when we went ashore.

Before our anchor was down, we had a crowd of boats about us, containing a few European gentlemen and a multitude of screaming Arabs. I know no din to be compared to it but that of a frog concert in a Carolina swamp. We had before wondered how our landing was to be accomplished; and the spectacle of the departure of some of our shipmates did not relieve our doubts. We could not pretend to lay about us with stout sticks, as we saw some amiable gentlemen do, purely from the strength of their philosophical conviction that this is the only way to deal with Arabs. Mr. E. had gone ashore among the first, to secure rooms for us: and what we three should have done with ourselves and our luggage without help, there is no saying. But we had help. An English merchant of Alexandria kindly took charge of us; put our luggage into one boat and ourselves into another, and accompanied us ashore. The silence of our little passage from the ship to the quay was a welcome respite: but on the quay we found ourselves among a crowd of men in a variety of odd dresses, and boys pushing their little donkeys in among us, and carts pulled hither and thither—everybody vociferating and hustling in the starlight. Our luggage was piled upon a long cart, and we followed it on foot: but there was an immediate stoppage about some custom-house difficulty— got over we know not how. Then the horse ran away, broke his girths, and scattered some of our goods. At last, however, we achieved the walk to our hotel—a walk through streets not narrow for an eastern city. All the way we had glimpses of smoking householders in their dim interiors, turbaned artisans, and yellow lamplight behind latticed windows. The heat was oppressive to us, after our cool days at sea. The rest of the evening was fatiguing enough.

The crowd of Bombay passengers hurrying over their preparations, their letter-writing and their tea, in order to start for Cairo at nine o'clock; the growling and snarling of the camels, loading in the Square; the flare of the cressets; —the heat, light, noise and hurry were overpowering after the monotony of sea life. I sought repose in letter-writing, and had nearly forgotten our actual position when I was spoken to by a departing ship-mate, and, looking up, saw a Greek standing at my elbow, an Arab filling up the door-way, and a Nubian nursemaid coming in for a crying child. —Before ten o'clock, all was comparatively quiet—the Square clear of omnibuses, camels, and the glare of torches, and our hotel no longer a scene of crowding and confusion. There was nothing to prevent our having a good night, in preparation for our first day of African sight-seeing.

When I looked out of my window early the next morning, I saw, at the moment, nothing peculiarly African. The Frank Square is spacious, and the houses large; but they would be considered shabby and ugly anywhere else. The consular flag-staves on the roofs strike the eye; and the flood of brilliant sunlight from behind the minaret made the morning as little like England in November as could well be. Presently, however, a string of camels passed through the square, pacing noiselessly along. I thought them then, as I think them now, after a long acquaintance with them, the least agreeable brutes I know. Nothing can be uglier, unless it be the ostrich; which is ludicrously like the camel, in form, gait and expression of face. The patience of the camel, so celebrated in books, is what I never had the pleasure of seeing. So impatient a beast I do not know—growling, groaning and fretting whenever asked to do or bear anything—looking on such occasions as if it longed to bite, if only it dared. Its malignant expression of face is lost in pictures: but it may be seen whenever one looks for it. The mingled expression of spite, fear and hopelessness in the face of the camel always gave me the impression of its being, or feeling itself, a damned animal. I wonder some of the old painters of hell did not put a camel into their foreground, and make a traditional emblem of it. It is true, the Arab loves his own camel, kisses its lips, hugs its neck, calls it his darling and his jewel, and declares he loves it exactly as he loves his eldest son: but it does not appear that any man's affection extends beyond his own particular camel, which is truly, for its services, an inestimable treasure to him. He is moved to kick and curse at any but the domestic member of the species, as he would be by the perverseness and spite of any other ill-tempered creature. The one virtue of the camel is its ability to work without water; but, out of the desert, I hardly think that any rider would exchange the willing, intelligent and proud service of the horse for that of the camel, which objects to everything, and will do no service but under the compulsion of its own fears.

When the camels had passed, some women entered the square from different openings. I was surprised to see their faces hardly covered. They pulled their bit of blue rag over, or half over, their faces when any one approached them, as a matter of form; but in Alexandria, at least, we could generally get a sight of any face we had a mind to see; excepting, of course, those of mounted ladies. As we went up the country, we found the women more and more closely veiled, to the borders of Nubia, where we were again favored with a sight of the female countenance.

The next sight in the square was a hareem, going out for a ride—a procession of ladies on asses—each lady enveloped in a sort of balloon of black silk, and astride on her ass—her feet displaying a pair of bright yellow morocco boots. Each ass was attended by a running footman; and the officer of the hareem brought up the rear.

By this time, my friends were ready for a cup of coffee and a walk before breakfast: and we went forth to see what we could see. After leaving the square, we made our way through heaps of rubbish and hillocks of dust to the new fortifications, passing Arab huts more sordid and desolate-looking than I remember to have seen in other parts of the country. We met fewer blind and diseased persons than we expected; and I must say that I was agreeably surprised, both this morning and throughout my travels in Egypt, by the appearance of the people. About the dirt there can be no doubt—the dirt of both dwellings and persons—and the diseases which proceed from want of cleanliness; but the people appeared to us, there and throughout the country, sleek, well-fed and cheerful. I am not sure that I saw an ill-fed person in all Egypt. There is hardship enough of other kinds—abundance of misery to sadden the heart of the traveler—but not that, as far as we saw, of want of food. I am told, and no doubt truly, that this is partly owing to the law of the Kurán by which every man is bound to share what he has, to the last mouthful, with his brother in need; but there must be enough, or nearly enough food for all, whatever be the law of distribution. Of the progressive depopulation of Egypt for many years past, I am fully convinced; but I am confident that a deficiency of food is not the cause, nor, as yet, a consequence. While I believe that Egypt might again, as formerly, support four times its present population, I see no reason to suppose, amidst all the misgovernment and oppression that the people suffer, that they do not still raise food enough to support life and health. I have seen more emaciated, and stunted, and depressed men, women and children in a single walk in England, than I observed from end to end of the land of Egypt. So much for the mere food question. No one will suppose that in Egypt a sufficiency of food implies, as with us, a sufficiency of some other things scarcely less important to welfare than food.

We saw this morning a sakia[1] for the first time—little thinking how familiar and interesting an object the sakia would become to us in the course of three months, nor how its name would for ever after call up associations of the flowing Nile, and broad green fields, and thickets of sugar-canes, and the melancholy music of the waterwheel, and the picturesque figures of peasant children, driving the oxen in the shady circuit of the weed-grown shed. This, the first we saw, was a most primitive affair, placed among sand hillocks foul with dirt, and its wooden cogwheels in a ruinous state. We presently saw a better one in the garden of the German Consul. It was on a platform, under a trellice of vines. The wheel, which was turned by a blind folded ox, had rude earthen jars bound on its vanes, its revolutions emptying these jars into a trough, from which the water was conducted to irrigate the garden.

In this garden, as in every field and garden in Egypt, the ground was divided off into compartments, which are surrounded by little ridges, in order to retain whatever water they receive. Where there is artificial irrigation, the water is led along and through these ridges, and distributed thus to every part. I found here the first training of the eye to that angularity which is the main characteristic of form in Egypt. It seems to have been a decree of the old gods of Egypt that angularity should be a prime law of beauty—and the decree appears to have been undisputed to this day—and one of the most surprising things to a stranger is to feel himself immediately falling into sympathy with this taste, so that he finds in his new sense and ideas of beauty a fitting avenue to the glories of the temples of the Nile.

The gardens of Alexandria looked rude to our European eyes; but we saw few so good afterwards. In the damp plots grew herbs, and especially a kind of mallow, much in use for soups: and cabbages, put in among African fruits. Among great flowering oleanders, marvel of Peru, figs and oranges, were some familiar plants, cherished, I thought, with peculiar care under the windows of the consular houses; —monthly roses, chrysanthemums, love-lies-bleeding, geraniums, rosemary, and, of course, the African marigold. Many of these plots are overshadowed by palms, —and they form, in fact, the ground of the palm-orchards, as we used to call them. Large clusters of dates were hanging from under the fronds of the palms; and these were usually the most valuable product of the garden. The consular gardens are not, of course, the most

1   Waterwheel

oriental in aspect. We do not see in them, as in those belonging to Arabs, the reservoir for Mohammedan ablution, nor the householder on the margin winding on his turban after his bath, or prostrating himself at his prayers.

The contrast is great between these gardens and the sites of Cleopatra's Needle and Pompey's Pillar, —curiosities which need not be described, as every one has seen them in engravings. The needle stands on the burning sands, close to the new fortification wall, whose embankment is eighty feet high, and now rapidly inclosing the town. The companion obelisk, which was offered to England, but not considered worth bringing away, is now buried in this embankment. There it will not decay; for there is no such preservative as the sand of Egypt. When, and under what circumstances, will it again see the light? In a time when it may be recognized as an object known now? or in an age so distant as that the process of verification must be gone over again? Everyone now knows that these obelisks are of the time of the early Pharaohs, some of whose names they bear inscribed; that they stood originally at Heliopolis, and were transported to Alexandria by the Caesars.

The pillar stands in a yet more desolate place. We reached it through the dreariest of cemeteries, where all was of one dust-color, — even to the aloe which was fixed upon every grave. The graves were covered with mortar, much of which was broken and torn away. A Christian informant told us that this was done by foxes and dogs; but a Mohammedan declared that such ravage was prevented by careful watching. There is a rare old book which happily throws light on what this pillar was. In the twelfth century, while the Crusaders were ravaging Syria, a learned physician of Bagdad, named Abdallatif, visited Egypt, and dwelt a considerable time there. He afterwards wrote an admirable account of whatever he himself saw in the country; and his work has been translated by some Arabic scholars. The best translation is by De Sacy (Paris, 1810). —Abdallatif tells us that the column (now called by us Pompey's Pillar) which is so finely seen from the sea, was called by the Arabs "the pillar of the colonnades;" that he had himself seen the remains of above four hundred columns of the same material, lying on the margin of the sea: and he tells us how they came there. He declared that the governor of Alexandria, the officer put in charge of the city by Saladeen, had overthrown and broken these columns to make a breakwater! "This," observes Abdallatif, "was the act of a child, or of a man who does not know good from evil. He continues, "I have seen also, round the pillar of the colonnades, considerable remains of these columns; some entire, others broken. It was evident from these remains that the columns had been covered by a roof which they supported. Above the pillar is a cupola supported by it. I believe that this was the portico where Aristotle taught, and his disciples after him; and that this was the academy which Alexander erected when he built the city, and where the library was placed which Amrou burned by the permission of Omar."[2] De Sacy reminds us that the alleged destruction of this portico must have taken place, if at all, at most thirty years before the visit of Abdallatif; so that as "all the inhabitants of Alexander, without exception," assured that traveler of the fact, it would be unreasonable to doubt it[3]. He decides that here we have the far-famed Serapéum. —From the base of the pillar the view was curious to novices. The fortifications were rising in long lines, where groups of Arabs were at work in the crumbling, whitish, hot soil; and files of soldiers were keeping watch over them. To the south-east, we had a fine view of Lake Mareotis, whose slender line of shore seemed liable to be broken through by the first ripple of its waters. The space between it and the sea was one expanse of desolation. A strip of vegetation, —some marsh, some field, and some grove, —looked well near the lake; and so did a little settlement on the canal, and a latteen sail, gliding among the trees.

We had a better view than this, one morning, from the fort on Mont Cretin. I believe it is the best point for a survey of the whole district; and our thinking so seemed to give some alarm to the Arabs, who ceased their work to peep at us from behind the ridges, and watch what we did with telescope, map and compass. The whole prospect was bounded by water, —by the sea and Lake Mareotis, —except a little space to the north-east; and that was hidden by an intervening minaret and cluster of houses. Except where some palms arose between us and Lake Mareotis to the south, and where the clustered houses of the town stood up white and clear against the morning sky, there was nothing around us but a hillocky waste, more dreary than the desert, because the dreariness here is not natural but induced. —If we could have stood on this spot no longer ago than the times of the Ptolemies (a date which we soon learned to consider somewhat modern) it would have been more difficult to conceive of the present desolation of the scene than it now is to imagine the city in the days of its grandeur. On the one hand, we should have seen, between us and the lake, the circus, with the multitude going to and fro; and on the other, the peopled gymnasia. Where Pompey's Pillar now stands alone, we should have seen the long lines of the colonnades of the magnificent Serapeum. On the margin of the Old Port, we should then have seen the towers of the noble causeway, the Heptastadium, which connected the island of the Pharos with the mainland. The Great Harbor, now called the New Port, lay afar this day, without a ship or boat within its circuit; and there was nothing but hillocks of bare sand round that bay where there was once a throng of buildings and of people. Thereabouts stood the temple of Arsinoë, and the theatre, and the inner palaces; and there

2   Abdallatif, Relation de l'Egypte. Livre I. ch. 4

3   Appendix A.

was the market. But now, look where we would, we saw no sign of life but the Arabs at work on the fortifications, and a figure or two in a cemetery near. The work of fortification itself seems absurd, judging by the eye; for there appears nothing to take, and therefore nothing to defend. Except in the direction of the small and poor-looking town, the area within the new walls appears to contain little but dusty spaces and heaps of rubbish, with a few lines of sordid huts, and clumps of palms set down in the midst; and a hot cemetery or two, with its crumbling tombs. I have seen many desolate-looking places, in one country or another; but there is nothing like Alexandria, as seen from a height, for utter dreariness. Our friends there told us they were glad we staid a few days, to see whatever was worth seeing, and be amused with some African novelties; for this was the inhabitants' only chance of inspiring any interest. Nobody comes back to Alexandria that can help it, after having seen the beauty of Cairo, and enjoyed the antiquities of Upper Egypt. The only wonder would be if any one came back to Alexandria who could leave the country in any other way.

Before we quitted Mont Cretin this morning, we looked into a hollow where laborers were digging, and saw them uncover a pillar of red granite, — shining and unblemished. Some were picking away at the massive old Roman walls, for the sake of the brick. It is in such places that the traveler detects himself planning wild schemes for the removal of the dust, and the laying bare of buried cities all along the valley of the Nile.

During the four days of our stay at Alexandria, we saw the usual sights; —the Pasha's palace; the naval arsenal; and the garden of the Greek merchant where the Pasha goes often to breakfast; and we enjoyed the hospitality of several European residents. We also heard a good deal of politics; not a word of which do I mean to write down. There is so much mutual jealousy among the Europeans resident in Egypt, and, under the influence of this jealousy, there is so little hope of a fair understanding and interpretation of the events of the day, that the only chance a stranger has of doing no mischief is by reporting nothing. I have my own impressions, of course, about the political prospects of Egypt, and the character of its alliance with various European powers; but while every word said by anybody is caught up and made food for jealousy, and a plea for speculation on the future, the interests of peace and good-will require silence from the passing traveler, whose opinions could hardly, at the best, be worth the rancor which would be excited by the expression of them.

CHAPTER II

FROM ALEXANDRIA TO CAIRO—FIRST SIGHT OF THE PYRAMIDS — PREPARATIONS FOR NILE VOYAGE

O N THE 25TH OF NOVEMBER, we left Alexandria, rising by candle-light at six, and seeing the glorious morning break by the time we were dressed. Our days were now nearly eleven hours long: at the shortest, they would be ten. We were not struck, as we expected to be, by the shortness of the twilight. Instead of the immediate settling down of darkness, after the disappearance of the sun, I found that I could read small print for half an hour after sunset, in our most southerly latitude.

I do not remember to have read of one great atmospheric beauty of Egypt; —the after-glow, as we used to call it. I watched this nightly for ten weeks on the Nile, and often afterwards in the desert, and was continually more impressed with the peculiarity, as well as the beauty, of this appearance. That the sunset in Egypt is gorgeous, everybody knows; but I, for one, was not aware that there is a renewal of beauty, some time after the sun has departed and left all gray. This discharge of color is here much what it is among the Alps, where the flame colored peaks become gray and ghastly as the last sunbeam leaves them. But here, everything begins to brighten again in twenty minutes; —the hills are again purple or golden, —the sands orange, —the palms verdant, —the moonlight on the water, a pale green ripple on a lilac surface: and this after-glow continues for ten minutes, when it slowly fades away.

Mr. E. had brought with him his noble dog Pierre, which created a far greater sensation in Alexandria than we did. European men and women are seen every day there; but so large a dog had probably never been known in that region. Women and children, and even men, fled into their houses, or behind walls, at Pierre's approach, every morning during our walks. Pierre was not safe. Between the jealousy of the native dogs, the fears of the Arabs, and the perils of the desert, Pierre had little chance of secure traveling; and so his master sent him home. We left Alexandria without Pierre: but we had a much better servant in the dragoman engaged there by Mr. E., —Alee Mustafa, —who traveled with us till we reached Alexandria again, the next May, and did his duty by us admirably. He is a native Egyptian, young and strong, able and experienced in his work, and faithful and correct in his money transactions. We met with other traveling parties as content with their dragomen as we were with ours: and I at present remember only one which was cursed with a bad attendant. When we consider what qualifications are requisite in the office, we must see that the dragomen must be a superior class of people. It was one of my amusements to study all whom I met; and when I saw what their knowledge of languages was, —what their efficiency in daily business, their zeal in traveling, and their familiarity with the objects en route wherever we went, their temper in times of hurry and disaster, their power of command co-existing with their diligence and kindliness in service, I felt that some of us might look very small in our vocations, in comparison with our dragomen.

We proceeded in an omnibus to the Mahmoudieh Canal, where we went on board the boat which was to carry us to Atfeh, at the junction of the canal with the Nile. The boat was taken in tow by a smaller steamer, named by a wag "the little Asthmatic." We heard a good deal of her ailments, —the cracks in her boiler, and so forth; so that we hardly expected to reach Atfeh in due course. —The villas in the neighborhood of Alexandria are pleasantly surrounded with gardens, and fenced by hedges or palings hung with the most luxuriant creepers; but the houses are of glaring white, and look dreadfully hot. —The villages on the banks are wretched-looking beyond description; the mud huts square, or in bee-hive form; so low and clustered and earthy, that they suggest the idea of settlements of ants or beavers, rather than of human beings. Yet we were every few minutes meeting boats coming down from the country with produce, —various kinds of grain and roots, in heavy cargoes. Some of these boats were plastered with mud, like the houses; and so thickly that grass grew abundantly on their sides. —On the heaps of grain were squatted muffled women and naked children; naked men towed the boats, —now on the bank, and now wading in the mud; and muffled women came out of the villages to stare. To-day there seemed to be no medium between wrapping up and nakedness; but it became common, up the country, to see women and girls covering their faces with great anxiety, while they had scarcely any clothing elsewhere.

We saw the other extreme of dress in a passenger on board our boat; —the chief eunuch of the royal hareem at Cairo. Neither his beautiful dress, —of the finest cloth, amply embroidered, —nor his attendants and appliances could impress me with the slightest sense of dignity in the case of this extraordinary-looking being. He was quiet in his manners, conversed with apparent ease, said his prayers and made his prostrations duly on the top of the kitchen, telling his beads with his long and skinny fingers; but his emaciation and ugliness baffled all the usual associations with the outward signs of rank. I could not think of him as an official of high station.

This is the canal which, as everybody knows, cost the lives of above twenty thousand people, from the pasha's hurry to have it finished, and the want of due preparation for such a work in such a country. Without tools and sufficient food, the poor creatures brought here by compulsion to work died off rapidly under fatigue and famine. Before the improvements of the pasha are vaunted in European periodicals as putting European enterprises to shame, it might be as well to ascertain their cost, —in other things as well as money; —the taxes of pain and death, as well as of piastres, which are levied to pay for the pasha's public works. There must be some ground for the horror which impels a whole population to such practices as are every day seen in Egypt, to keep out of the reach and the ken of government: —practices such as putting out an eye, pulling out the teeth necessary for biting cartridges, and cutting off a forefinger, to incapacitate men for army service. The fear of every other sort of conscription, besides that for the supply of the army, is no less urgent; and it is a common practice for parents to incapacitate their children for reading and writing by putting out an eye, and cutting off the forefinger of the right hand. Any misfortune is to be encountered rather than that of entering the pasha's army, the pasha's manufactories, the pasha's schools. This can hardly be all baseless folly on the part of the people. If questioned, they could at least point to the twenty-three thousand deaths which took place in six months, in the making of the Mahmoudieh Canal.

The pasha is proud of this canal, as men usually are of achievements for which they have paid extravagantly. And he still brings his despotic will to bear upon it, in defiance of nature and circumstance. I was told to-day of his transmission of Lord Hardinge by it, when Lord Hardinge and everybody else believed the canal to be impassable from want of water. This want of water was duly represented to the pasha: but as he still declared that Lord Hardinge should go by that way and no meaner one, Lord Hardinge had only to wait and see how it would be managed. He went on board the steamer at Alexandria, and proceeded some way, when a bar of dry ground appeared extending across the canal. But this little inconvenience was to be no impediment. A thousand soldiers appeared on the banks, who waded to the steamer, and fairly shouldered it, with all its passengers, and carried it over the bar. The same thing happened at the next dry place, and the next: and thus the pasha is able to say that he forwarded Lord Hardinge by his own steamer on his own great canal.

Nothing can be more dreary than the scenery till within a short distance of
Atfeh. The field of Aboukeer was nothing but hillocky desert, with pools in the
hollows: and after that, we saw little but brown mud banks, till we came to the
acacias near Atfeh. It is a pity that other parts of the canal banks are not planted
in the same way. Besides the beauty of the trees, —to-day very pretty, with the
light pods contrasting with the dark foliage, —the shade for man and beast, and
the binding of the soil by vegetation would be valuable.

It was dusk before we reached Atfeh. Some moonlight mingled with the
twilight, and with the yellow gleams which came from sordid windows, seen
through the rigging of a crowd of small vessels. There were prodigious bustle
and vociferation while we were passing through the lock, and getting on board
the steamer which was to carry us to Cairo. But by seven o'clock we were fairly
off on the broad and placid Nile. The moonlight was glorious; and the whole
company of passengers sat or lay on deck, not minding the crowding in their
enjoyment of the scene, till the dews became so heavy as to send down all who
could find room in the cabins. —I have a vivid recollection of that first evening
on the Nile, —an evening full of enjoyment, though perhaps every other evening I spent on it showed me more. I saw little but the wide quiet river, —the
broadest, I believe, that I had ever been on; and a fringe of palms on the banks,
with here and there a Sheikh's tomb[4] hiding among them, or a tall white minaret springing above them.

Two ladies kindly offered me a place in their inner cabin, where I could lie
down and have the benefit of an open window: but the place was too unclean
for rest. At 3 a. m., we went a-ground on a mud bank. I saw the quivering
poles of the Arab crew from my window, and was confounded by the noise
overhead—the luggage being shifted with all possible outcry. We just floated
for a minute, and then stuck fast again. By the cessation of the noise, I presently
found that the matter was given up till daylight; and I slept for above an hour;
—a very desirable thing, as these groundings made it appear uncertain whether
we should reach Cairo before another night.

When I went on deck, before seven, I found we were opposite Saïs. But
there was nothing to be done. No one could go ashore; and the best consolation is that there is nothing to be seen there by those who can only mourn over
the mounds, and not penetrate them. A mob of Arabs was brought down to
our aid; and a curious scene was that of our release. On deck our luggage was
piled without any order; and blankets were stuffed in among trunks and bags.
From these blankets emerged one fellow-passenger after another, till the set of
unshaven and unwashed gentry was complete. In the river was a long line of

4   These Sheikhs' tombs are very like village ovens: square huts, with
each a white cupola rising from the walls.

naked Arabs, tugging and toiling and screaming till the vessel floated. When we were once more steaming towards Cairo, and the deck was cleared, and the wondrous atmosphere assumed all its glory, and the cool wind breathed upon our faces, we presently forgot the discomforts of the night, and were ready for a day of novelty and charm.

Breakfast was served on deck, under an awning; and greatly was it enjoyed by one of the passengers—a catholic lady of rank, who was traveling absolutely alone, and shifting for herself very successfully. She helped herself to an entire chicken, every bone of which she picked. While doing so, she was disturbed by the waiters passing behind her, between the two tables; and she taught them, by vigorous punches, what it was to interfere with her elbows while they were wanted for cutting up her chicken. Immediately after this feat, she went to the cabin, and kneeled down to her prayers, in the face of as many as chose to see. Between this countess and the eunuch, there was more religious demonstration on board than we had been accustomed to see in such places.

Till 3 p. m., there was little variety in the scenery. I was most struck with the singular coloring; —the diversity of browns. There was the turbid river, of vast width, rolling between earthy banks; and on these banks were mud villages, with their conical pigeon-houses. The minarets and Sheikhs' tombs were fawn-colored and white; and the only variety from these shades of the same color was in the scanty herbage, which was so coarse as to be almost of no color at all. But the distinctness of outline, the glow of the brown, and the vividness of light and shade, were truly a feast to the eye. At 3 o'clock, when approaching Werdán, we saw large spreading acacias growing out of the dusty soil; and palms were clustered thickly about the town; and at last we had something beyond the banks to look at; —a sandy ridge which extends from Tunis to the Nile. When we had passed Werdán, about 4 p. m., Mr. E. came to me with a mysterious countenance, and asked me if I should like to be the first to see the Pyramids. We stole past the groups of careless talkers, and went to the bows of the boat, where I was mounted on boxes and coops, and shown where to look. In a minute I saw them, emerging from behind a sand hill. They were very small; for we were still twenty-five miles from Cairo; but there could be no doubt about them for a moment; so sharp and clear were the light and shadow on the two sides we saw. I had been assured that I should be disappointed in the first sight of the Pyramids; and I had main-tained that I could not be disappointed, as of all the wonders of the world, this is the most literal, and, to a dweller among mountains, like myself, the least imposing. I now found both my informant and myself mistaken. So far from being disappointed, I was filled with surprise and awe: and so far was I from having anticipated what I saw, that I felt as if I had never before looked upon any thing so new as those clear and vivid masses, with their sharp blue shadows, standing firm and alone on their expanse of sand. In a few minutes, they appeared to grow wonderfully larger; and they looked lustrous and most imposing in the evening light. This impression of the Pyramids was never fully renewed. I admired them every evening from my window at Cairo; and I took the surest means of convincing myself of their vastness, by going to the top of the largest; but this first view of them was the most moving: and I cannot think of it now without emotion.

Between this time and sunset, the most remarkable thing was the infinity of birds. I saw a few pelicans and many cormorants; but the flocks—I might say the shoals—of wild ducks and geese which peopled the air, gave me a stronger impression of the wildness of the country, and the foreign character of the scenery, than anything I had yet seen. We passed by moonlight the spot where the great experiment of the Barrage is to be tried; and here we could distinguish the point of the Delta, and the junction of the other branch, and knew when we had issued upon the single Nile. Soon after, the groves of Shoobra—the Pasha's country palace—rose against the sky, on the eastern shore. Then there were glimmerings of white houses; and then rows of buildings and lights which told of our approach to Boolák, the port of Cairo. The palace of Ismael Pasha, who was burnt at Sennaar twenty-nine years ago, rose above the bank; and then there was a blaze of cressets, which showed where we were to land. A carriage from the Hotel d'Orient awaited our party; and we were driven, under an avenue of acacias, a mile or two to Cairo. By the way, we saw some truly Arabian dwellings by torchlight, which made us long for the morrow.

In the morning I found that my windows looked out upon the Ezbekeeyeh—the great Square—all trees and shade, this sunny morning; and over the tree tops rose the Pyramids, apparently only a stone's throw off, though in fact more than ten miles distant. A low canal runs round the Square, just under my windows; and on its bank was a striking group—a patriarchal picture; —an Arab leading down his flock of goats to water. The sides of this canal were grass-grown; and the interior of the Square, the area of 400,000 feet within the belt of trees, was green with shrubs, field-crops, and gardens. While I was gazing upon this new scene, and amusing myself with the appearance and gestures of the people who went by on foot, on asses, or on camels, Mr. Y. and Mr. E. were gone to Boolák, to see about a boat which we had heard of as likely to suit us for our voyage up to the First Cataract. At breakfast they brought us the news that they had engaged the boat, with its crew. We afterwards mounted donkeys, and rode off to Boolák to examine this boat, which has the reputation of being the best on the Nile.

As our thoughts and our time were much engaged with the anticipation of our voyage and with preparations for it, so that we did not now see much of

Cairo, or open our minds thoroughly to what we did see, I shall say nothing here of the great Arabian city. With me it stands last in interest, as latest in time, of the sights of Egypt: and any account that I can give of it will be the more truthful for coming in its right place, —after the cities of the ancient world.

We found on board our dahabieh the old American merchant to whom it belongs, —his tawny finger graced by a magnificent diamond ring. The Rais, —the captain of the crew, who is responsible for the safety of the boat, —was in waiting to take directions from us about some additional accommodation. We liked this man from first to last. His countenance struck me this morning as being fine, notwithstanding a slight squint. It had much of the pathetic expression of the Arab countenance, with strong sense, and, on occasion, abundance of fire. His caution about injuring the boat, made him sometimes appear indolent when we wanted to push on; and he, seeming to indulge us, would yet moor within half-an-hour: but he worked well with the crew at times, —taking an oar, and handling the ropes himself. For many an hour of our voyage, he sat on the gunwale, singing to the rowers some mournful song, to which they replied in a chorus yet more mournful. The manners of this man were as full of courtesy and kindness as we almost invariably found the manners of the Arabs to be; and there was even an unusual degree of the oriental dignity in his bearing.

The boat was so clean that there was no occasion for us to wait for the usual process of sinking, —to drown vermin. The few additions and alterations necessary could easily be made while we were buying our stores; and, in fact, we were off in five days. Our deck afforded a walk of twelve paces, when the crew were not rowing: and this spacious deck was covered with an awning. The first cabin was quite a saloon. It had a continuous row of windows, and a deewán along each side; on the broadest of which the gentlemen's beds were made up at night. We had bookshelves put up here; and there was ample closet accommodation, —for medicines, pickles, tools, paper and string, &c. In the inner cabin, the narrow deewáns were widened by a sort of shelf put up to contain the bedding of Mrs. Y. and myself. The floor and ceiling were painted blue, orange and green, and the many windows had Venetian blinds. It was a truly comfortable chamber, which we inhabited with perfect satisfaction for many weeks.

The bargain made, the gentlemen and Alee were much engaged every day in laying in stores. Mattresses and spices, wine and crockery, maccaroni, campstools, biscuits, candles, a table, fruit. sponges, saucepans, soap, cordage, tea and sugar; —here are a few items of the multitude that had to be attended to. Every morning, the gentlemen were off early to the stores; and the time they gave to sightseeing with Mrs. Y. and me was accepted as a great favor. Active as we thought them, it was an amusement to us to see that it was possible to be more active still. A young Scotchman who was at our hotel, with a sister and two friends, was always before us, however early we might be, and obtained the first choice of everything, from the dahabieh herself to the smallest article she carried. And all this activity and shrewdness lay under a pale young face, a quiet voice and languid manner, betokening poor health, if not low spirits. On the night of our arrival at Cairo, we did not go to bed till past midnight; and our gentlemen were out at five to see about the dahabieh, —knowing that the competition for boats was then very keen: but the Scotchman had been out at four, and had seen and declined the dahabieh before my friends reached Boolak. Whenever we bought any article, we found that our Scotch neighbor had had his choice before us. We seldom went into the store where we obtained almost everything but he was sitting there, tasting wines or preserves, or handling utensils, as if he had been a furniture-monger all his life. It was presently apparent that he was bent on getting off before us, —on obtaining a good start up the river; and it is not to be denied that this roused the combativeness of some of our party; and that our preparations were pressed forward with some view to the question whether the English or Scotch party would get the start. The expectation was that the Scotch would sail on Tuesday, December 1st, and an American party on the same day; while we could not get off till the Wednesday morning, though taking up our abode on board our dahabieh on the Tuesday evening. We were advised to do this, that we might not depart unfurnished with some essential but forgotten article, as was the case with a party who set sail with a fair wind, and were carried exulting up the river for twenty miles, when they found they had no candles. To our surprise, the Scotch party appeared at the late dinner on Tuesday; and when we accompanied the ladies to their rooms afterwards, to see the shady bonnets they were making for tropical wear, we found they were waiting for the washerman, who had disappointed them of their clothes. So we left the hotel before them.

It was bright moonlight when we set off for Boolak, —a curious cavalcade. Of course, we were on donkeys; as were such of our goods as had not been removed before. The donkey boys carried— one, my desk, another, the arrow-root, and a third, the chocolate. It was a merry ride, under the acacias, whose flickering shadows were cast across the road by the clear moon. The tea-things were set in the cabin when we arrived. There was less confusion on board than might have been expected; and we had a comfortable night.

Our crew consisted of fourteen, including the Rais. Of these, five were Nubians, and the rest Cairenes. We had besides, our dragoman, Alee, and his assistant, Hasan; and the cook, —a grotesque and amusing personage. The hire of the boat and crew, who provided themselves with food, was 40l. per month. Times are changed since some acquaintance of ours went up to the

Second Cataract, two years since, for 12*l*. Those of our crew who afforded us the most amusement were some of the Cairenes: but we liked best the quiet and peaceable Nubians. When we set off the whole crew messed together, sitting on their haunches in a circle round their pan of lentile or dourrha pottage. But before we returned, the Cairenes had all quarreled; and the five Nubians were eating together, as amicably as ever, while each Cairene was picking his bread by himself.

When I came on deck in the morning, I found that we were not to start till the afternoon, and that we must put up with extraordinary confusion till then. There was abundant employment for us all, however, and after breakfast, the gentlemen went up to the city, to make some more purchases, and Mrs. Y. and I sat on deck, under the awning, making a curtain for the cabin, a table-cover, &c. The doings of the Arabs on shore were amusing and interesting enough. Among others, I saw a blind man bringing, as he would say, his donkey down to drink; but the donkey led the man. The creature went carefully down the steep and rough bank, and the man followed, keeping his hands on its hind quarters, and scarcely making a false step. The Scotch party came down, in the course of the morning, and presently put off, and went full sail up the river. The American boat was, I believe, already gone. Soon after three, Alee announced that the last crate of fowls was on board; the signal was given, and away we went.

CHAPTER III

NILE INCIDENTS—CREW—BIRDS—FACE OF THE COUNTRY—
THE HEAVENS—TOWNS AND SHORES, BETWEEN CAIRO AND
ASYOOT

AS WE SWEPT UP THE BROAD RIVER, we passed some fine houses, sheltered by dark masses of acacias; and presenting, to the river, spacious overhanging balconies, and picturesque water-wheels. My friends said this was very like the Bosphorus. Presently, Cairo arose in the distance, backed by the white citadel and the yellow range of the Mokuttam hills, with their finely broken outline. On the western shore was El Geezeh, with its long, range of hospital buildings, relieved by massy foliage, behind which towered the Pyramids; and further on were more Pyramids, lessening in the distance. We were aground once and again within an hour; and while we were at dinner, we drove upon a shoal with a great shock. This was not the way to overtake the Scotch party, whose boat could not be supposed ever to get aground; and our Rais was informed that if he struck again, he should be bastinadoed. The wind was too fresh to allow of our dining on deck; and the sun was declining behind the palms when we went down to the cabin. When we came up again, the yellow glow remained, while the rich foliage of, the eastern shore was quivering in the moonlight. Jupiter was as lustrous as if there had been no moon. The breeze now fell, now rose; and the crew set up their wild music, —the pipe and drum, with intervals of mournful song.

I do not know whether all the primitive music in the world is in the minor key: but I have been struck by its prevalence among all the savage, or half-civilized, or uneducated people whom I have known. The music of Nature is all in the minor key; —the melodies of the winds, the sea, the waterfall, birds, and the echoes of bleating flocks among the hills: and human song seems to follow this lead, till men are introduced at once into the new world of harmony and the knowledge of music in the major key. Our crew sang always in unison, and had evidently no conception of harmony. I often wished that I could sing loud enough to catch their ear, amidst their clamor, that I might see whether my second would strike them with any sense of harmony: but their overpowering noise made any such attempt hopeless. We are accustomed to find or make the music which we call spirit-stirring in the major key: but their spirit-stirring music, set up to encourage them at the oar, is all of the same pathetic character as the most doleful, and only somewhat louder and more rapid. They kept time so admirably, and were so prone to singing, that we longed to teach them to substitute harmony for noise, and meaning for mere sensation. The nonsense that they sing is provoking. When we had grown sad under the mournful swell their song, and were ready for any wildness of sentiment, it was vexatious to learn from Alee what they were singing about. Once it was "Put the saddle on the horse. Put the saddle on the horse." And this was all. Sometimes it was "Pull harder. Pull harder." This was expanded into a curious piece of Job's comfort, one evening when they had been rowing all day, and must have been very weary. "Pull hard: pull harder. The nearer you come to Alexandria, the harder you will have to pull. God give help!" Another song might be construed by some vigilant people near the court to have a political meaning. "We have seen the Algerine bird singing on the walls of Alexandria." Another was, "The bird in the tree sings better than we do. The bird comes down to the river to wash itself." The concluding song of the voyage was the best, as to meaning, though not as to music, —in which I must say I preferred the pathetic chaunt about the horse and saddle. As we were approaching Cairo on our return, they sang "This is nearly our last day on the river, and we shall soon be at the city. He who is tired of rowing may go ashore, and sit by the sakia in the shade." I may observe that if the dragoman appears unwilling to translate any song, it is as well not to press for it; for it is understood that many of their words are such as it would give European ears no pleasure to hear.

The water-wagtails were very tame, we observed already. They ran about on the deck, close to our feet as we sat, and looked in at our cabin windows in the most friendly manner. Next morning, we began to acquire some notion of the multitude of birds we were to see in Egypt; a notion which, I think, could hardly be obtained anywhere else. On a spit of sand, I saw, when I came forth, a flock of pelicans which defied counting, while a flight, no less large, was hovering above. A heron was standing fishing on another point; clouds of pigeons rose above every group of dwellings and clump of palms, and multitudes of geese occupied the air at various heights—now in strings which extended almost half across the sky, and now furling and unfurling their line like an immeasurable pennon. The birds of Egypt did not appear to us to be in great

variety, or remarkable beauty; but from their multitude, and being seen in all
their wildness, they were everywhere a very interesting feature of the scenery.
The ostrich I never saw, except tame, in a farmyard, though we had ostrich's eggs
in Nubia. We came upon an eagle here and there, and always where we could
most wish to see one. Sometimes, when in the temples, and most interested in
the monuments, I caught myself thinking of home, and traced the association
to the sparrows which were chirping overhead. I found swallows' nests in these
temples, now and then, in a chink of the wall, or a recess of roof or niche. A
devout soul of an old Egyptian, returning from its probation of three thousand
years, would see that "the sparrow had found a house, and the swallow a nest
for herself, where she might lay her young;" even the altars of the Lord God, so
sacred once to the most imposing worship the world ever saw. Vultures are not
uncommon. I used to see them sometimes during my early walk on shore, busy
about the skull of some dead horse or other carcass. The crested wood-pecker
was often a pretty object among the mournful piles of ruins at Thebes or elsewhere, hopping about so spruce and gay! Where the Arabian hills approached
the river, or the shores presented perpendicular rocks, long rows of cormorants
sat perched before their holes, as still and staid as so many hermits in contemplation. On every islet and jutting point were flocks of pelicans, whose plumage
looked snow-white when set off by a foil of black geese; and now and then, a
single bird of this tribe might be seen in the early morning, balancing itself on
the little billows, and turning its head about in the coyest manner, to prevent its
long beak touching the water. The ibis is elegant in form, and most delicate in
plumage, as everyone knows who has stroked its snowy feathers. It looked best
when standing under the banks, or wading among the reeds in a cove. It looked
most strange and out of place when perched on the back of a buffalo, as I occasionally saw it. We once saw five buffalo in one field, with each a delicate white
ibis perched on its back. And from the nose of one of these buffalo two little
birds were at the same time picking insects, or something else that they relished.

As to the birds which have such a mysterious connection with the sleeping
crocodile, I can give no new information about them. I can only say that on
almost every occasion of our seeing a crocodile, two or three of these birds were
standing beside him; and that I never saw them fly away till he had moved. It is
believed in the country that these birds relieve the crocodile of the little leeches
which infest his throat, and that they keep watch while he sleeps on the sand
and give him warning to escape on the approach of danger. What the crocodile
does for the birds in return, we never heard. As for the pigeons, they abound
beyond the conception of any traveler who has not seen the pigeon flights of the
United States. They do not here, as there, darken the air in an occasional process
of migration, breaking down young trees on which they alight, and lying in

heaps under the attack of a party of sportsmen, but they flourish everywhere as the most prolific of birds may do under the especial protection of man. The best idea that a stranger can form of their multitude is by supposing such a bird population as that of the doves of Venice inhabiting the whole land of Egypt! The houses of the villages throughout Egypt are surmounted by a sort of battlements built for the pigeons, and supplied with fringes of boughs, inserted, in several rows to each house, for the birds to rest on. The chief object is the dung, which is required for manure for the garden, and for other purposes; but it is a mistake to say that the inhabitants do not eat them. They are taken for food, but not to such an extent as to interfere with the necessary supply of dung. One of our party occasionally shot a few wild ones, near the villages, and he met with no hinderance. But it was otherwise with our Scotch friend. Though he had asked leave, and believed he had obtained it, to let fly upon the pigeons in a village, the inhabitants rose upon him, and his Rais had some difficulty in securing his safe return to his boat. He did it by a device which his employer was shocked to hear of afterwards. He declared our friend to be the Pasha's dentist! To form a notion of the importance of this functionary, it is necessary to remember that the pasha's having a dentist is one of the most remarkable signs of our times. That a Mohammedan ruler should have permitted his beard to be handled is a token of change more extraordinary than the adoption of the Frank dress in Turkey, or the introduction of wine at Mohammedan dinners; and the man who was permitted by the Pasha to touch his beard must be regarded throughout the country as a person inestimably powerful with his Highness. Such a personage was our Scotch friend compelled to appear for some way up the river, and very reluctant he was to bear the dignity to which his assent had not been asked. A pretty bird, of the kingfisher kind apparently, colored black, gray and tawny, was flitting about on the shore when I took my first walk on shore this morning. And I think I have now mentioned nearly all the birds we observed in the course of our voyage.

Our object, like that of Egyptian travelers generally, was to sail up the river as fast as the wind would carry us, seeing by the way only as much as would not interfere with the progress of the boat. It was the season when the north wind prevailed; and this advantage was not to be trifled with in a voyage of a thousand miles, certain as we were of the help of the current to bring us back. We were therefore to explore no pyramids or temples on our way up; and to see only so much of the country as we could get a glimpse of on occasion of the failure of the wind, or other accidental delays. To this there was no objection in our minds; for we found at once that in going up the Nile in any manner we should meet with as much novelty and interest as we could bear. The face of the country was enough at one time. To have explored its monuments immediately would have been too much. Moreover, there was a great advantage in going up quickly while the river was yet high enough to afford some view of the country. In returning, we found such a change produced by the sinking of the waters only a few feet, that we felt that travelers going up late in the season can hardly be said to have seen the Country from the river. At all times, the view of the interior from the Nile must be very imperfect, and quite insufficient to justify any decision against the beauty of the great valley. This arises from the singular structure of the country. Everywhere else, where a river flows through the centre of a valley, the land either slopes from the base of the hills down to the river, or it is level. In Egypt, on the contrary, the land rises from the mountains up to the banks of the Nile: and where, as usually happens, the banks are higher than the eye of the spectator on the deck of his boat, all view of the interior, as far as the hills, is precluded. He sees nothing but the towns, villages, and palm-groves on the banks, and the mountains on the horizon. My attention had been directed upon this point before I went by the complaints of some readers of Eastern travels that, after all their reading, they knew no more what the Egyptian valley looked like than if it had never been visited. As this failure of description appeared to regard Egypt alone, there must be some peculiar cause for it: and thus we found it. The remedy was, of course, to go ashore as often as possible, and to mount every practicable eminence. I found this so delightful, and every wide view that I obtained included so much that was wonderful and beautiful, that mounting eminences became an earnest pursuit with me. I carried compass and note-book, and noted down what I saw, from eminence to eminence, along the whole valley, from Cairo to the Second Cataract. Sometimes I looked abroad from the top of a pylon; sometimes from a rock on the banks; sometimes from a sandy ridge of the desert; sometimes from a green declivity of the interior; once from a mountain above Thebes, and once from the summit of the Great Pyramid. My conclusion is that I differ entirely from those who complain of the sameness of the aspect of the country. The constituent features of the landscape may be more limited in number than in other tracts of country of a thousand miles: but they are so grand and so beautiful, so strange, and brought together in such endless diversity, that I cannot conceive that any one who has really seen the country can complain of its monotony. Each panoramic survey that I made is now as distinct in my mind as the images I retain of Niagara, Iona, Salisbury Plain, the Valais, and Lake Garda.

Our opportunities of going ashore were not few, even at the beginning of our voyage, when the wind was fair, and we sailed on, almost continuously, for three days. In the early mornings, one of the crew was sent for milk, and he was to be taken up at a point further on. And if, towards night, the Rais feared a rock, or a windy reach ahead, he would moor at sunset; and this allowed us nearly an hour before it was dark enough for us to mind the howling jackals. When the wind ceased to befriend us, the crew had to track almost all day, following the bends of the river; and we could either follow these also, or strike across the fields to some distant point of the bank. And when on board, there was so much to be seen on the ordinary banks that I was rarely in the cabin. Before breakfast, I was walking on the deck. After breakfast, I was sewing, reading, or writing, or idling on deck, under the shade of the awning. After dinner we all came out eagerly, to enjoy the last hour of sun shine, and the glories of the sunset and the after-glow, and the rising of the moon and constellations. And sorry was I every night when it was ten o'clock, and I must go under a lower roof than that of the dazzling heavens. All these hours of our first days had their ample amusement from what we saw on the banks alone, till we could penetrate further.

There were the pranks of the crew, whose oddities were unceasing, and particularly rich in the early morning. Then it was that they mimicked what-ever they saw us do, —sometimes for the joke, but as often with the utmost seriousness. I sometimes thought that they took certain of our practices for religious exercises. The solemnity with which one or another tried to walk the deck rapidly, to dance, and to skip the rope, looked like this. The poor fellow who laid hands on the skipping-rope paid (he probably thought) the penalty of his impiety. At the first attempt, down he came, flat on his face. If Mr. E. looked through his glass, some Ibraheem or Mustafa would snatch up an oar for a telescope, and see marvellous things in the plain. If, in the heat, either of the gentlemen nodded over his book, half the crew would go to sleep instantly, peeping every moment to see the effect. —Then, there were the veiled women coming down to the river to fill their water-pots. Or the men, at prayer-time, performing their ablutions and prostrations. And there was the pretty sight of the preparation of the drying banks for the new crop; —the hoeing with the short, heavy antique hoe. And the harrow, drawn by a camel, would appear on the ridge of the bank. And the working of the Shadoofs[5] was perpetual, and always interesting. Those who know what the shadoof is like, may conceive the picture of its working: —the almost naked Arabs, — usually in pairs, —low-ering and raising their skin buckets by the long lever overhead, and emptying them into the trough beside them, with an observance of time as regular as in their singing. Where the bank is high, there is another pair of shadoofs at work above and behind: and sometimes a third, before the water can be sent flowing in its little channels through the fields. —Then, there were the endless manoeuvres of innumerable birds, about the islets and rocks: and a buffalo, here and there, swimming from bank to bank, and finding it, at last, no easy matter to gain the land. —Then, there was the ferryboat, with its ragged sail,

5   Pole and bucket, for raising water.

and its motley freight of turbaned men, veiled women, naked children, brown sheep, frightened asses, and imperturbable buffalo. —Then, there were the long palisades of sugar-canes edging the banks; or the steep slopes, all soft and bright with the springing wheat or the bristling lupins. Then, there were the villages, with their somewhat pyramidal houses, their clouds of pigeons, and their shelter of palms: or, here and there, a town, with its minarets rising out of its cincture of acacia. And it was not long before we found our sight sharpened to discern holes in the rocks, far or near: —holes so squared at the entrance as to hint of sculpture or painting within. —And then, as the evening drew on, there was the sinking of the sun, and the coming out of the colors which had been discharged by the glare in the middle of the day. The vast and dreary and hazy Arabian desert became yellow, melting into the purple hills; the muddy waters took a lilac hue; and the shadows of the sharp-cut banks were as blue as the central sky. As for the moon, we could, for the first time in our lives, see her the first night; —the slenderest thread of light, of cup-like form, visible for a few minutes after sun set; the old moon being so clearly marked as to be seen by itself after the radiant rim was gone. I have seen it behind a palm, or resting on the ridge of a mountain like a copper ball. And when the fuller moon came up from the east, and I, forgetting the clearness of the sky, have been struck by the sudden dimness, and have looked up to watch her passing behind a cloud, it was delicious to see, instead of any cloud, the fronds of a palm waving upon her disk. One night, I saw an appearance perfectly new to me. No object was perceptible on the high black eastern bank, above and behind which hung the moon: but in her golden track on the dimpled waters were the shadows of palms, single and in clusters, passing over swiftly, — "authentic tidings of in visible things." And then, there was the rising of Orion. I have said that the constellations were less conspicuous than at home, from the universal brilliancy of the sky: but Orion shone forth, night by night, till the punctual and radiant apparition became almost oppressive to the watching sense. I came at last to know his first star as it rose clear out of the bank. He never issued whole from a haze on the horizon, as at home. As each star rose, it dropped a duplicate upon the surface of the still waters: and on a calm night, it was hard to say which Orion was the brightest. —And how different was the wind from our cloud-laden winds in England! Except that it carried us on, I did not like wind in Egypt. The palms, bowed from their graceful height, and bent all one way, are as ugly as trees can be: and the dust flies in clouds, looking like smoke or haze on land, and settling on our faces, even in the middle of the stream. Though called sand, it is, for the most part, mere dust from the limestone ranges, forming mud when moistened. The wind served, however, to show us a sand-pillar now and then, like a column of smoke moving slowly along the ground. On this second day of our voyage, when we were approaching Benisooeef, the wind made ugly what on a calm evening would have been lovely. A solitary house, in the midst of a slip of alluvial land, all blown upon with dust, looked to us the most dreary of dwellings. But the latteen sails on the river were a pretty feature, —one or two at a time, winding in and out, with the bends of the stream. We saw one before us near Benisooeef, this day. It proved to be our Scotch friends. Our boat beat his in a strong wind; and we swept past in good style, —the gentlemen un-capping and bowing; the ladies waving their handkerchiefs. I had no idea that the racing spirit had entered into them, till one of the ladies told me, the next time we met, "We were so mortified when you passed us!"

Benisooeef is about eighty miles from Cairo: a good progress for twen-ty-three hours! —It is the largest town in Upper Egypt: but it does not look very imposing from the river. Two or three minarets rise from it; and there is one rather good-looking house, which the Pasha inhabits when he comes. Its aspect was pretty as we looked back to it from the south.

The wind carried us on towards the rocky region where our careful Rais would retard our progress by night, though we had a glorious lamp in the moon, the whole night through. We had a rocky shore to the east this afternoon, —the Arabian mountains approaching the river: and in the early morning, we passed the precipitous cliffs, on whose flat summit stands the Coptic convent of "Our Lady Mary the Virgin." The forms of these limestone cliffs are most fantastic; and fantastic was the whole scene; —the long rows of cormorants in front of their holes, —a sort of burlesque upon the monks in their cells above; the un-connected flights of steps here and there on the rocks; the women and naked children on the ridge, giving notice to the begging monks of our approach! and the monks themselves, leaping and racing down the precipice, and then, two of them, racing through the water, struggling with the strong current, to board us for baksheesh. The one who succeeded was quite satisfied, in the midst of his panting and exhaustion, with five paras[6] and an empty bottle. He waited a little, till we had gone about a mile, in order to have the help of the current, and then swam off to his convent.

We passed the pretty town of Minyeh about noon; and then entered upon sugar districts so rich as to make one speculate whether this might not be, some day, one of the great sugar-producing regions of the world. The soil is very rich, and irrigated by perpetually recur ring shadoofs: and the crops of canes on the flats between the rocks and the river were very fine, and extending onwards for some days from this time. The tall chimneys of the Rauda sugar manufactory flood up above the wood on a promontory, looking very strange amidst such a scene. —On our return, we visited the sugar manufactory at Hou, and learned

6   Five paras are a farthing and one-fifth.

something of the condition and prospects of the manufacture. The Hou establishment belongs to Ibraheem Pasha, whom we met there at seven in the morning. It is quite new; and a crowd of little children were employed in the unfinished part, carrying mortar in earthen bowls for Id. per day. The engineers are French, and the engine, one hundred-and-twenty horse power, was made at Paris. The managers cannot have here the charcoal they use in France for clarifying the juice. From the scarcity of wood, charcoal is too dear; and burnt bones are employed instead, —answering the purpose very well. We saw the whole process, which seemed cleverly managed; and the gentlemen pronounced the quality of the sugar good. An Englishman employed there said, however, that the canes were inferior to those of the West Indies, for want of rain. There were a hundred people at work in this establishment; their wages being, besides food, a piastre and a quarter (nearly 3d.) per day. If, however, the payment of wages is managed here as I shall have to show it is usually done in Egypt, the receipts of the work-people must be considered much less than this. We heard so much of the complaints of the people at having to buy, under compulsion, coarse and dear sugar, that it is clear that much improvement in management must take place before Egypt can compete with other sugar-producing countries: but still, what we saw of the extensive growth of the cane, and the quality of the produce, under great disadvantages, made us look upon this as one of the great future industrial resources of Egypt.

The next morning, we could still distinguish the tall chimney of Rauda. We had been at anchor under a bank all night, the Rais being in fear of a rock a-head. The minarets of Melawee were on a flat on the western bank, some way before us: and between us and them, lay the caves of Benee Hasan; —those wonderful repositories of monumental records of the old Egyptians, which we were to explore on our return, but must now pass by, as if they were no more than what they looked, —mere apertures in the face of the mountains.

The crew were tracking this morning, for the first time; —stepping along at a funeral pace, and slipping off, one by one, to light a pipe where four or five smokers were puffing in a circle, among the sugarcanes. Our crew never appeared tired with their tracking; but in the mornings they were slow; and the man who was sent for milk moved very lazily, whether the one chosen were the briskest or the quietest of the company. The cook was rather too deliberate about breakfast, and Alee himself was not a good riser. It was their winter; and cold makes the Arabs torpid instead of brisk. Presently, we had to cross to the more level bank; and then we first saw our people row. It was very ridiculous. They sang at the top of their voices, some of them throwing their heads back, shutting their eyes, and shaking their heads at every quaver, most pathetically, —dipping their oars the while as if they were skimming milk, and all out of time with their singing, and with one another, while their musical time was perfectly good. —The wind presently freshened, and we stood away. It was fitful all day, but blew steadily when the moon rose. Just then, however, the Rais took fright about passing the next point at night, and we moored, beside four other boats, in the deep shadow of a palm-grove. On these occasions, two men of the neighborhood and a dog are appointed to guard each boat that moors to the bank. The boat pays three piastres;[7] and if anything is lost, complaint is made to the Governor of the district, whose business it is to recover the property, and punish the guards.

As we approached Manfaloot, we could perceive how strangely old Nile has gone out of his course, as if for the purpose of destroying the town. The bed of the river was once evidently at the base of the hills, — those orange hills with their blue shadows, —where rows of black holes show ancient catacombs. So strong a reflected light shone into one of these caves, that we could see something of its interior. We called it a perfect smuggler's cave, with packages of goods within, and a dog on guard at the entrance. When we looked at it with the glass, however, we were grave in a moment. We saw that the back and roof were sculptured.

Manfaloot is still a large place, sadly washed down, —sliced away— by the encroachment of the river. Many houses were carried away last year; and some which looked as if cut straight through their interior, have probably followed by this time.

The heat was now great in the middle of the day; and the glare oppressive to people who were on the look-out for crocodiles; —as we were after passing Manfaloot. We were glad of awning, goggles, fans, and oranges. But the crew were all alive, —kicking dust over one another on shore, leaping high in the water, to make a splash, and perpetrating all manner of practical jokes. We do not agree with travelers who declare it necessary to treat these people with coldness and severity, —to repel and beat them. We treated them as children; and this answered perfectly well. I do not remember that any one of them was ever punished on our account: certainly never by our desire. They were always manageable by kindness and mirth. They served us with heartiness, and did us no injury whatever. The only point we could not carry was inducing them to sing softly. No threats of refusing baksheesh availed. Mr. E. obtained some success on a single occasion by chucking dry bread into the throats of one or two who were quavering with shut eyes, and wide-open jaws. This joke availed for the moment, more than any threats; but the truth is, they can no more refrain from the full use of their lungs when at work, than from that of eyes and ears.

On the evening of Monday the 7th, we approached Asyoot: and beautiful

7   About 7d.

was the approach. After arriving in bright sunshine, apparently at its very skirts, and counting its fourteen minarets, and admiring its position at the foot of what seemed the last hill of the range, we were carried far away by a bend of the river; —saw boats, and groups of people and cattle, and noble palm and acacia woods on the opposite bank, and did not anchor till starlight under El Hamra, the village which is the port of Asyoot.

We were sorry to lose the advantage of the fair wind which had sprung up: but it was here that the crew had to bake their bread for the remainder of the voyage up. We had no reason to regret our detention, occasioning, as it did, our first real view of the interior of the country—Asyoot is a post town too; and we were glad of this last certain opportunity of writing home before going quite into the wilds.

CHAPTER IV

ASYOOT—OLD SITES—SOME ELE-
MENTS OF EGYPTIAN THOUGHT— FIRST
CROCODILES—SOOHADJ—GIRGEH—KENNEH

IN THE MORNING, OUR CANVAS WAS DOWN, along the landward side of our boats; so that the people on shore could not pry. It was pleasant, however, to play the spy upon them. There were many donkeys, and gay groups of their owners, just above the boat. On the one hand, were a company of men washing clothes in the river under a picturesque old wall: and on the other, boat-builders diligently at work on the shore. The Arab artisans appear to work well. The hammers of these boat-builders were going all day; and the tinman, shoemakers, and others whom I observed in the bazaars, appeared dexterous and industrious.

Asyoot is the residence of the Governor of Upper Egypt. Selim Pasha held this office as we went up the river. While we were coming down, he was deposed; —to the great regret of all whom we heard speak of it. He was so well thought of that there was every hope of his reinstatement. Selim Pasha is he who married his sister, and made the terrible discovery while at supper on his wedding-day, in his first interview with his bride. Both were Circassian slaves; and he had been carried away before the birth of this sister. This adventure happened when the now gray-bearded man was young: but it invests him with interest still, in addition to that inspired by his high character. We passed his garden to-day, and thought it looked well, —the palace being embosomed among palms, acacias, and the yellow-flowering mimosa; which last, when intermixed with other trees, gives a kind of autumnal tinge to masses of dark foliage.

We were much struck by the causeway, which would be considered a vast work in England. It extends from the river bank to the town, and thence on to the Djebel (mountain) with many limbs from this main trunk. In direct extent,

I think it can hardly be less than two miles: but of this I am not sure. Its secondary object is to retain the Nile water after the inundation, —the water flowing in through sluices which can be easily closed. The land is divided by smaller embankments, within this large one, into compartments or basins, where the most vigorous crops of wheat, clover, and millet were flourishing when we rode by. The water stands not more than two feet deep at high Nile in the most elevated of these basins. Inside the causeway was the canal which yielded its earth to its neighbor. In this canal many pools remained; and the seed was only just springing in the dryest parts. In some places I saw shaken piers, and sluices where the unbaked brick seemed to have melted down in the water: but the new walls and bridges appeared to be solidly constructed. — On the banks of the causeway and canal on the south side of the town were flowering mimosas as large, we thought, as oaks of fifty years growth in England. The causeway afforded an admirable road; — high, broad and level. The effect was strange of entering from such a road into such a town.

The streets had, for the most part, blank walls, brown, and rarely perpendicular. Some sloped purposely, and some from the giving way of the mud bricks. Many were cracked from top to bottom. Jars were built in near the top of several of the houses, for the pigeons. The bazaars appeared well stocked, and the business going forward was brisk. I now began to feel the misery which every Frank woman has to endure in the provincial towns of the East, —the being stared at by all eyes. The staring was not rude or offensive; but it was enough to be very disagreeable; at least, to one who knew, as I did, that the appearance of a woman with an uncovered face is an indecency in the eyes of the inhabitants. At Cairo, Jerusalem and Damascus, one feels nothing of this, and the staring is no more than we give to a Turk in the streets of London or Liverpool: but in the provincial towns there is an air of amazement in the people, mingled in some places with true Mohammedan hatred of the Christians, which it is hard to meet with composure. The gentlemen of my party, who did not care for their share as Christians, wondered at my uneasiness, and disapproved of it: but I could not help it: and though I never gave way to it so far as to omit seeing anything on account of it, I never got over it at all, and felt it throughout to be the greatest penalty of my Eastern travel. Yet I would not advise any Englishwoman to alter her dress or ways. She can never, in a mere passage through an Eastern country, make herself look like an Eastern woman; and an unsupported assumption of any native custom will obtain for her no respect, but only make her appear ashamed of her own origin and ways. It is better to appear as she is, at any cost, than to attempt any degree of imposture.

While we were waiting in the street to have our letters addressed in Arabic to the care of our consul at Cairo, I was, for the first time, struck by the number of blind and one-eyed people among those who surrounded us. Several young boys were one-eyed. As every body knows, this is less owing to disease than to dread of the government.

It was strange to see, in the middle of a large town, vultures and other wild birds flying overhead. Among others, we saw an eagle, with a fish in its beak. —On our way to the caves in the Djebel, we met a funeral procession coming from the cemetery which lies between the town and the hills. The women were uttering a funeral howl worthy of Ireland.

Our donkeys took us up a very steep path, nearly to the first range of caves. When we turned to overlook the landscape, what a view was there! Mr. E., who has traveled much, said he had never seen so rich an expanse of country. I felt that I had seen something like it; but I could not, at the moment, remember where. It was certainly not in England: nor was it like the plains of Lombardy; nor yet the unfenced expanse of cultivation that one sees in Germany. At last, it struck me that the resemblance was to an Illinois prairie. The rich green, spreading on either hand to the horizon, was prairie-like: but I never was, in Illinois, on a height which commanded one hundred miles of unbroken fertility, such as I now saw. And even in Illinois, in the finest season, there is never such an atmosphere as here gave positive brilliancy to every feature of the scenery. A perfect level of the most vivid green extended north and south, till it was lost. not in haze, but from the mere inability of the eye to take in more: and through this wound away, from end to end, the full blue river. To the east, facing us, was the varied line of the Arabian hills, of a soft lilac tint. Seventeen villages, overshadowed by dark palms, were set down beside the river, or some little way into the land; and the plain was dotted with Arab husbandmen and their camels, here and there, as far as the eye could reach. Below us lay the town, with its brown, flat-roofed houses, relieved by the palms of its gardens, and two or three white cupolas, and fourteen minarets, of various heights and forms. Between it and us lay the causeway, enlivened by groups of Arabs, with their asses and camels, appearing and disappearing among the thickets of acacia which bordered it. Behind all lay the brilliant Djebel—with its glowing yellow lights and soft blue shadows. The whole scene looked to my eyes as gay as the rainbow, and as soft as the dawn. As I stood before the cave, I thought nothing could be more beautiful: but one section of it looked yet lovelier when seen through the lofty dark portal of an upper cave. But there is no conveying such an impression as that.

The caves are tombs; some of them very ancient: so ancient, that Abraham might have seen them, if he had come so far up the country. One race of those old times remains; —the wolves. They were sacred here (Asyoot being the Lycopolis of the Greek times); their mummies are in many pits of the Djebel; and we saw the tracks of two in the dust of the caves. —The cave called Stabl d'Antar

(Stable of the Architect) is lofty and large; —about seventy-two feet by thirty-six. Its ceiling is covered with patterns which we should call Greek borders
anywhere else: but this ceiling is older than Greek art. The colors were chiefly
blue, light gray and while. The colors of the hieroglyphic sculptures were red
and blue, —the blue predominating. Two large figures flanked the portal; one
much defaced; the other nearly perfect.

I have since seen so much of the old Egyptian monuments, and they have
become so familiarly interesting to me, that I look back with amusement to this
hour of my first introduction to hieroglyphics and burial caves. I can scarcely
believe it was only a few months ago, —so youthful and ignorant seem now the
feelings of mere curiosity and wonder with which I looked upon such painting
and sculpture as afterwards became an intelligible language to me. I do not
mean by this that I made any attempts to learn the old Egyptian language or
its signs, —beyond a few of the commonest symbols. It is a kind of learning
which requires the devotion of years; and it is perhaps the only kind of learning
of which a smattering can be of no use, and may probably be mischievous. —I
remember being extremely surprised at the amount of sculptured inscriptions
here, —little imagining what a mere sprinkling they were compared with what
and I should see in other places.

In the succession of chambers within, we found ranges of holes for the deposit of wolf mummies, and pits for the reception of coffins. The roofs of some
of these caves had been supported by large square pillars, whose capitals remain
attached, while the shafts are gone. This gave us a hint of the architectural adornment of which we were to see so much hereafter in the tombs of Thebes and
Benee Hasan. In the corner of a tomb lay a human skull, the bone of which was
remarkably thick. Many bones and rags of mummy cloth lay scattered about.
On the side of the hill below, we found a leg and foot. The instep was high by
compression, but very long. There was also a skull, wrapped in mummy-cloth;
not fragrant enough now, for all its antique spicery, to bring away.

In the pits of these caves were the mummies lying when Cambyses was busy
at Thebes, overthrowing the Colossus in the plain. And long after, came the
upstart Greeks, relating here their personal adventures in India under their great
Alexander, and calling the place Lycopolis, and putting a wolf on the reverse
of their local coins. And, long after, came the Romans, and called Lycopolis
the ancient name of the place, and laid the ashes of their dead in some of the
caves. And long after, came the Christian anchorites, and lived a hermit life in
these rock abodes. Among them was John of Lycopolis, who was consulted as
an oracle by the Emperor Theodosius, as by many others, from his supposed
knowledge of futurity. A favorite eunuch, Eutropius, was sent hither from Constantinople, to learn from the hermit what would be the event of the civil war. I

once considered the times of the Emperor Theodosius old times. How modern do they appear on the hill-side at Asyoot!

Our Scotch friends came up in the evening. As they were detained for the same reason as ourselves, we left them behind when we started the next afternoon. They gave us bows and waving of handkerchiefs, when the shouts of our crew gave notice of our departure; and they no doubt hoped to see us again speedily.

The next day, I told Mr. E. that a certain area we were coming to on the east bank must be the site of some old town. I judged this from the advantages evident at a glance. The space was nearly semi-circular, —its chord being the river-bank, and the rest curiously surrounded by three ranges of hills, whose extremities overlapped each other. There was thus obtained a river frontage, shelter from the sands of the desert behind, and a free ventilation through the passages of the hills. We referred to our books and map, and found that here stood Antaeopolis. From this time, it was one of my amusements to deter mine, by observation of the site, where to look for ancient towns; and the requisites were so clear, that I seldom found myself deceived.

Diodorus Siculus tells us that Antae (supposed by Wilkinson to be probably the same with Ombte) had charge of the Ethiopian and Lybian parts of the kingdom of Osiris, while Osiris went abroad through the earth to benefit it with his gifts. Antae seems not to have been always in friendship with the house of Osiris, and was killed here by Hercules,[8] on behalf of Osiris; but he was worshiped here, near the spot where the wife and son of Osiris avenged his death on his murderer Typho. The temple sacred to Antae, (or in the Greek, Antaeus,) parts of which were standing thirty years ago, was a rather modern affair, having been built about the time of the destruction of the Colossus of Rhodes. Ptolemy Philopater built it; and he was the Egyptian monarch who sent presents and sympathy to Rhodes, on occasion of the fall of the Colossus. Now nothing remains of the monuments but some heaps of stones: —nothing whatever that can be seen from the river. The traveler can only look upon hamlets of modern Arabs, and speculate on the probability of vast "treasures hid in the sand."

If I were to have the choice of a fairy gift, it should be like none of the many things I fixed upon in my childhood, in readiness for such an occasion. It should be for a great winnowing fan, such as would, without injury to human eyes and lungs, blow away the sand which buries the monuments of Egypt. What a scene would be laid open then! One statue and sarcophagus, brought from Memphis, was buried one hundred and thirty feet below the mound surface. Who knows but that the greater part of old Memphis, and of other glorious cities, lies almost unharmed under the sand! Who can say what armies of

8   Quite a different personage from the Greek Hercules.

sphinxes, what sentinels of colossi, might start up on the banks of the river, or come forth from the hill-sides of the interior, when the cloud of sand had been wafted away! The ruins which we now go to study, might then appear occupying only eminences, while below might be ranges of pylons, miles of colonnade, temples intact, and gods and goddesses safe in their sanctuaries. What quays along the Nile, and the banks of forgotten canals! What terraces, and flights of wide shallow' steps! What architectural stages might we not find for a thousand miles along the river, where now the orange sands lie so smooth and light as to show the track, —the clear foot-print—of every beetle that comes out to bask in the sun! —But it is better as it is. If we could once blow away the sand, to discover the temples and palaces, we should next want to rend the rocks, to lay open the tombs; and heaven knows what this would set us wishing further. It is best as it is; for the time has not come for the full discovery of the treasures of Egypt. It is best as it is. The sand is a fine means of preservation; and the present inhabitants perpetuate enough of the names to serve for guidance when the day for exploration shall come. The minds of scholars are preparing for an intelligent interpretation of what a future age may find: and science, chemical and mechanical, will probably supply such means hereafter as we have not now, for treating and removing the sand, when its conservative office has lasted long enough. We are not worthy yet of this great unveiling: and the inhabitants are not, from their ignorance, trustworthy as spectators. It is better that the world should wait, if only care be taken that the memory of no site now known be lost. True as I feel it to be that we had better wait, I was forever catching myself in a speculation, not only on the buried treasures of the mounds on shore, but on means for managing this obstinate sand.

And yet, vexatious as is its presence in many a daily scene, this sand has a bright side to its character, —like everything else. Besides its great office of preserving unharmed for a future age the records of the oldest times known to man, the sand of the desert has, for many thousand years, shared equally with the Nile the function of determining the character and the destiny of a whole people, who have again operated powerfully on the characters and destiny of other nations. Everywhere, the minds and fortunes of human races are mainly determined by the characteristics of the soil on which they are born and reared. In our own small island, there are, as it were, three tribes of people, whose lives are much determined still, in spite of all modern facilities for intercourse, by the circumstance of their being born and reared on the mineral strip to the west, —the pastoral strip in the middle, —or the eastern agricultural portion. The Welsh and Cornwall miners are as widely different from the Lincolnshire or Kentish husbandmen, and the Leicestershire herdsmen, as Englishmen can be from Englishmen. Not only their physical training is different; their intellectual faculties are differently exercised, and their moral ideas and habits vary accordingly. So it is in every country where there is a diversity of geological formation: and nowhere is the original constitution of their earth so strikingly influential on the character of its inhabitants as in Egypt. There everything depends—life itself, and all that it includes—on the state of the unintermitting conflict between the Nile and the Desert. The world has seen many struggles; but no other so pertinacious, so perdurable, and so sublime as the conflict of these two great powers. The Nile, ever young, because perpetually renewing its youth, appears to the inexperienced eye to have no chance, with its stripling force, against the great old Goliath, the Desert, whose might has never relaxed, from the earliest days till now; but the giant has not conquered yet. Now and then he has prevailed for a season; and the tremblers whose destiny hung on the event, have cried out that all was over: but he has once more been driven back, and Nilus has risen up again, to do what we see him doing in the sculptures, —bind up his water-plants about the throne of Egypt. These fluctuations of superiority have produced extraordinary effects on the people for the time: but these are not the forming and training influences which I am thinking of now. It is true that when Nile gains too great an accession of strength, and runs in destructively upon the Desert, men are in despair at seeing their villages swept away, and that torrents come spouting out from the sacred tombs in the mountain, as the fearful clouds of the sky come down to aid the river of the valley. It is true that in the opposite case, they tremble when the heavens are alive with meteors, and the Nile is too weak to rise and meet the sand columns that come marching on, followed by blinding clouds of the enemy; and that famine is then inevitable, bringing with it the moral curses which attend upon hunger: It is true that at such times strangers have seen (as we know from Abdallatif, himself an eye-witness) how little children are made food of,[9] and even men slaughtered for meat, like cattle. It is true that such have been the violent effects produced on men's conduct by extremity here; —effects much like what are produced by extremity everywhere. It is not of this that I am thinking when regarding the influence on a nation of the incessant struggle between the Nile and the Desert. It is of the formation of their ideas and habits, and the training of their desires.

From the beginning, the people of Egypt have had everything to hope from the river; nothing from the desert: much to fear from the desert; and little from the river. What their Fear may reasonably be, any one may know who looks upon a hillocky expanse of sand, where the little jerboa burrows, and the hyæna prowls at night. Under these hillocks lie temples and palaces, and under the level sands, a whole city. The enemy has come in from behind, and stifled and buried it. What is the Hope of the people from the river, any one may witness

9   Abdallatif, Relation de l'Egypte. Livre II. ch. 2.

who, at the regular season, sees the people grouped on the eminences, watching the advancing waters, and listening for the voice of the crier, or the boom of the cannon which is to tell the prospect or event of the inundation of the year. Who can estimate the effect on a nation's mind and character of a perpetual vigilance against the desert; (see what it is in Holland of a similar vigilance against the sea!) and of an annual mood of Hope in regard to the Nile? Who cannot see what a stimulating and enlivening influence this periodical anxiety and relief must exercise on the character of a nation?—And then, there is the effect on their Ideas. The Nile was naturally deified by the old inhabitants. It was a god to the mass; and at least one of the manifestations of deity to the priestly class. As it was the immediate cause of all they had, and all they hoped for, —the creative power regularly at work before their eyes, usually conquering, though occasionally checked, it was to them the Good Power; and the Desert was the Evil one. Hence came a main part of their faith, embodied in the allegory of the burial of Osiris in the sacred stream, whence he rose, once a year, to scatter blessings over the earth. —Then, the structure of their country originated or modified their ideas of death and life. As to the disposal of their dead; —they could not dream of consigning their dead to the waters, which were too sacred to receive any meaner body than the incorruptible one of Osiris: nor must any other be placed within reach of its waters, or in the way of the pure production of the valley. There were the boundary rocks, with the hints afforded by their caves. These became sacred to the dead. After the accumulation of a few generations of corpses, it became clear how much more extensive was the world of the dead than that of the living: and as the proportion of the living to the dead became, before men's eyes, smaller and smaller, the state of the dead became a subject of proportionate importance to them, till their faith and practice grew into what we see them in the records of the temples and tombs, —engrossed with the idea of death and in preparation for it. The unseen world became all in all to them; and the visible world and present life of little more importance than as the necessary introduction to the higher and greater. The imagery before their eyes perpetually sustained these modes of thought. Everywhere they had in presence the symbols of the worlds of death and life; —the limited scene of production, activity and change; —the valley with its verdure, its floods, and its busy multitudes, who were all incessantly passing away, to be succeeded by their like; while, as a boundary to this scene of life, lay the region of death, to their view unlimited, and everlastingly silent to the human ear. —Their imagery of death was wholly suggested by the scenery of their abode. Our reception of this is much injured by our having been familiarized with it first through the ignorant and vulgarized Greek adoption of it, in their imagery of Charon, Styx, Cerberus and Rhadamanthus: but if we can forget these, and look upon the older records with fresh eyes, it is inexpressibly interesting to contemplate the symbolical representations of death by the oldest of the Egyptians, before Greek or Persian was heard of in the world; the passage of the dead across the river or lake of the valley, attended by the Conductor of souls, the god Anubus; the formidable dog, the guardian of the mansion of Osiris, (or the divine abode;) the balance in which the heart or deeds of the deceased are weighed against the symbol of Integrity; the infant Harpocrates, — the emblem of a new life, seated before the throne of the judge; the range of assessors who are to pronounce on the life of the being come up to judgment; and finally the judge himself, whose suspended sceptre is to give the sign of acceptance or condemnation. Here the deceased has crossed the living valley and river; and in the caves of the death region, where the howl of the wild dog is heard by night, is this process of judgment going forward; and none but those who have seen the contrasts of the region with their own eyes, —none who have received the idea through the borrowed imagery of the Greeks, or the traditions of any other people, —can have any adequate notion how the mortuary ideas of the primitive Egyptians, and, through them, of the civilized world at large, have been originated by the everlasting conflict of the Nile and the Desert.

How the presence of these elements has, in all ages, determined the occupations and habits of the inhabitants, needs only to be pointed out; the fishing, the navigation, and the almost amphibious habits of the people are what they owe to the Nile; and their practice of laborious tillage, to the Desert. A more striking instance of patient industry can nowhere be found than in the method of irrigation practised in all times in this valley. After the subsidence of the Nile, every drop of water needed for tillage, and for all other purposes, for the rest of the year, is hauled up and distributed by human labor—up to the point where the sakia, worked by oxen, supersedes the shadoof, worked by men. Truly the desert is here a hard task-master—or rather a pertinacious enemy, to be incessantly guarded against—but yet a friendly adversary, inasmuch as such natural compulsion to toil is favorable to a nation's character.

One other obligation which the Egyptians owe to the Desert struck me freshly and forcibly, from the beginning of our voyage to the end. It plainly originated their ideas of art. Not those of the present in habitants, which are wholly Saracenic still, but those of the primitive race who appear to have originated art all over the world. The first thing that impressed me in the Nile scenery, above Cairo, was the angularity of almost all forms. The trees appeared almost the only exception. The line of the Arabian hills soon became so even as to give them the appearance of being supports to a vast table-land, while the sand heaped up at their bases was like a row of pyramids. Elsewhere, one's idea of sand-hills is that of all round eminences they are the roundest, but here their form is generally that of truncated pyramids. The entrances of the caverns are square. The masses of sand left by the Nile are square. The river banks are graduated by the action of the water, so that one may see a hundred natural Nilometers in as many miles. Then, again, the forms of the rocks, especially the limestone ranges, are remarkably grotesque. In a few days, I saw, without looking for them, so many colossal figures of men and animals springing from the natural rock, so many sphinxes and strange birds, that I was quite prepared for anything I afterwards met with in the temples. The higher we went up the country, the more pyramidal became the forms of even the mud houses of the modern people; and in Nubia, they were worthy, from their angularity, of old Egypt. It is possible that the people of Abyssinia might, in some obscure age, have derived their ideas of art from Hindostan, and propagated them down the Nile. No one can now positively contradict it. But I did not feel on the spot that any derived art was likely to be in such perfect harmony with its surroundings as that of Egypt certainly is—a harmony so wonderful as to be perhaps the most striking circumstance of all to a European, coming from a country where all art is derived,[10] and its main beauty therefore lost. It is useless to speak of the beauty of Egyptian architecture and sculpture to those who, not going to Egypt, can form no conception of its main condition—its appropriateness. I need not add that I think it worse than useless to adopt Egyptian forms and decoration in countries where there is no Nile and no Desert, and where decorations are not, as in Egypt, fraught with meaning—pictured language—messages to the gazer. But I must speak more of this hereafter. Suffice it now that in the hills, angular at their summits, with angular mounds at their bases, and angular caves in their strata, we could not but at once see the originals of temples, pyramids and tombs. Indeed, the pyramids look like an eternal fixing down of the shifting sand-hills which are here a main feature of the desert. If we consider further what facility the desert has afforded for scientific observation—how it was the field for the meteorological studies of the Egyptians, and how its permanent pyramidal forms served them, whether originally or by derivation, with instruments of measurement and calculation for astronomical purposes—we shall see that, one way or another, the desert has been a great benefactor to the Egyptians of all time, however fairly regarded, in some senses, as an enemy. The sand may, as I said before, have a fair side to its character, if it has taken a leading part in

10   Even as the Gothic spire is believed by those who know best to be an attenuated obelisk; as the obelisk is an attenuated pyramid. Our Gothic aisles are sometimes conjectured to be a symmetrical stone copy of the glades of a forest; but there are pillared aisles at El Karnac and Medeenet Haboo, which were constructed in a country which had no woods, and before the forests of northern Europa are discernible in the dim picture of ancient history.

determining the ideas, the feelings, the worship, the occupation, the habits, and the arts of the people of the Nile valley, for many thousand years.

The hills now, above Antaeopolis, approached the river in strips, which, on arriving at them, we found to be united by a range at the back. Some fine sites for cities were thus afforded, and many of them were no doubt thus occupied in past ages. A little further on rises a lofty rock; a precipice three hundred feet high, which our Rais was afraid to pass at night. I was on deck before sunrise on the morning of the 11th to see it, but I found there was no hurry. A man was sent for milk from this place, so I landed too and walked some way along the bank. On the Lybian side I overlooked a rich, green, clumpy country; on the Arabian side, the hills came down so close to the water as to leave only a narrow path, scarcely passable for camels at high Nile. There were goats among the rocks; and on the other shore, sheep, whose brown wool is spun by distaff, by men in the fields, or traveling along the bank. The unbleached wool makes the brown garments which all the men wear. I often wished that some one would set the fashion of red garments in the brown Nile scenery. We saw more or less good blue every day, but the only red dress I had seen yet was at Asyoot, where it looked so well that one wished for more. The red tarboosh is a treat to the eye, when the sun touches it; or, at night, the lamp on deck—but the crew did not wear the tarboosh, only little white cotton caps, in the absence of the full-dress turban.

This day was remarkable for our seeing the first doum palm (an angular tree!) and the first crocodile. Alee said he had seen a crocodile two days before: but we had not. And now we saw several. The first was not distinguishable, to inexperienced eyes, from the inequalities of the sand. The next I dimly saw slip off into the water. In the afternoon, a family of crocodiles were seen basking on a mud bank which we were to pass. As we drew near, in silence, the whole boat's company being collected at the bows, the largest crocodile slipped into the water, showing its nose at intervals. Another followed, leaving behind the little one, a yellow monster, asleep, with the sunlight full upon it. Mr. E. fired at it, and at the same moment the crew set up a shout. Of course, it awoke, and was off in an instant, but unhurt. We had no ball; and crocodile shooting is hopeless, with nothing better than shot. Our crew seemed to have no fear of these creatures, plunging and wading in the river without hesitation, whenever occasion required. There being no wind, we moored at sunset; and two of us obtained half-an-hour's walk before dark. Even then, the jackals were howling after us the whole time. Our walk was over mud of various degrees of dryness, and among young wheat and little tamarisks, springing from the cracked soil.

On the 13th we fell in with Selim Pasha, without being aware what we were going to see. Our crew having to track, the Rais and Alee went ashore for charcoal, and Mr. E. and I for a walk. Following a path which wound through coarse grass and thorny mimosas, we found ourselves presently approaching the town of Soohadj: and near the arched gate of the town, and everywhere under the palms, were groups and crowds of people, in clean turbans and best clothes. Then appeared, from behind the trees on the margin, three boats at anchor, one being that of Selim Pasha himself; the others for his suite. He had come up the river to receive his dues, and was about to settle accounts now at Soohadj. He had a crew of twenty-three men, and was proceeding day and night. His interpreter accosted us, offered us service, discussed the wind and weather, and invited us to take coffee on board the Governor's boat. I was sorry to be in the way of Mr. E.'s going; but I could not think of such an adventure, in Mrs. Y.'s absence. We saw the Governor leave his boat, supported by the arms, for dignity's sake. He then took his seat under a palm, and received some papers offered him. He looked old, short, and very business-like. A scribe sat on the top of his cabin, with inkhorn and other apparatus; and a man was hurrying about on shore, with a handful of papers covered with Arabic writing. All this, with the turbaned and gazing groups under the tamarisks, the white-robed soldiers before the gate of the barracks, the stretch of town-walls beside us, and the minarets of Eckmim rising out of the palm-groves on the opposite shore, made up a new and striking scene. Mr. and Mrs. Y. saw, from the boat, part of the reverse side: they saw eight men in irons, reserved to be bastinadoed, for the non-payment of their taxes. —As we walked on, we passed a school, where the scholars were moving their bodies to and fro, and jabbering as usual. Then we descended the embankment of the canal which winds in towards the town, and crossed its sluice; and then we came out upon a scene of millet-threshing. Two oxen, muzzled, were treading out the grain: five men were beating the ears, and a sixth was turning over and shaking the husks with a rake. Such are the groups which incessantly delight the eye in Eastern travel. —Next, we found ourselves among a vast quantity of heavy stones, squared for building. They were deeply imbedded, but did not look like the remains of ancient buildings. And now it was time for us to stop, lest there should be difficulty, if we went further, in getting on board. So we sat down in a dusty but shady place, among some fowl-houses, and beside an oven. I never took a more amusingly foreign walk. —A short ramble that evening was as little like home; but more sad than amusing. We entered a beautiful garden, or cultivated palm orchard, which was in course of rapid destruction by the Nile. Whole plots of soil, and a great piece of wall were washed away. Repeatedly we saw signs of this destruction; and we wondered whether an equivalent advantage was given anywhere else. By day we passed towns which, like Manfaloot, were cut away, year by year; and by night the sullen plash caused by the fall of masses of earth, was heard. In countries where security of property is more thought of than it is here, this liability must seriously affect the value of the best portions of the land; those which have a river frontage. Here it appears to be quietly submitted to, as one of the decrees of inevitable fate. The circumstance of the Nile changing its course must also affect some historical and geographical questions: —in the one case as regards the marches of ancient armies, and the sites of old cities; and in the other, the relations of different parts of the country. Many towns, called inland by geographers, are now on the banks of the river. At Manfaloot, it is clear that the divergence from the old course under the rocks is very great: and near Benee Hasan the change is made almost from year to year. When Sir G. Wilkinson visited the caves,[11] the river was so far off as to leave a breadth of two miles between it and the rocks: and Mrs. Burner, who was there the year before us, describes the passage to the caves as something laborious and terrific: whereas, when we visited the caves on our return, we found the river flowing at the base of the acclivity; and we reached the tombs easily in twelve minutes. From the heights, we traced its present and former course, and could plainly see a third bed, in which it had at one time run. We were sorry to see it cut through fine land, where the crops on either bank showed what the destruction must have been. The banks were falling in during the few hours of our stay; and here, as in similar places, we observed that the river was more turbid than usual. These local accidents must largely affect the great question of the rate of rising of the bed of the river, and, in consequence, that of the whole valley; a question which some have attempted to determine by a comparison of the dates of the buildings at Thebes with the depth of the sand accumulated above their bases.

The next place where we went ashore, Girgeh, once stood a quarter of a mile inland: it is now in course of being washed down. It is a miserable place, as might be expected, with such a fate hanging over it. We staid here an hour, for the purchase of bread, fowls, and a sheep. We gave 30 paras (1 ¾ d.) for a fowl; 6s. for a sheep; and a piastre (2 ¼ d.) for 42 eggs. The small bazaars had few people in them at this hour (7 a. m.), and of those few many were blind; and on our return to the boat, we found a row of blind people on the bank, hoping for baksheesh. The millet stalks here measured eleven feet; and of course, the fields are a perfect jungle. We saw occasionally the millet stalks burnt, and strewn over the fields for a top-dressing. At other times we observed that where the millet had been cut, wheat was sown broadcast among the stubble, which was left to rot. The only manuring that we saw, besides this top-dressing, was that of the gardens with pigeons' dung; and the qualifying of the Nile mud with sand from the desert, or dust out of the temples, brought in frail-baskets on the backs of asses.

11   Wilkinson's Modern Egypt and Thebes. II. 45.

Two of our sapient crew having quarreled at mess about which should have a particular morsel of bread, and fought noisily on shore, the Rais administered the bastinado. The first was laid down, and held by the feet and shoulders, while flogged with a boat-pole. He cried out vigorously. The other came forward cheerfully from the file, and laid himself down. The Rais broke the pole over him: but he made no noise, jumped up, spat the dust out of his mouth, and went to work at the tow-rope, as if nothing had happened. They seem to bear no malice, and joke with one another immediately after the bitterest quarrels. One of our Nubians wears his knife in a sheath, strapped about the upper part of his left arm. Another wears an amulet in the same manner. Two who came from Dongola have their faces curiously gashed with three cuts on each cheek, and four on each side of the eye. These cuts are given them by their parents in childhood, for beauty marks.

We now began to meet rafts of pottery coming down from Kenneh, the seat of the manufacture of the water jars which are in general use. Porous earth and burnt grass are the chief materials used. We meet seven or more rafts in a group. First, a layer of palm fronds is put on the raft; and then a layer of jars; then another layer of each. The jars all have their mouths out of the water. They are so porous that their conductors are continually employed in emptying them of water: that is, they are always so employed when we meet them. Not being worth sponges, they dip in and wring out cloths, with strings to them. The oars are mere branches, whose boughs are tied together at the extremity. Though they bend too much, they answer their purpose pretty well: but the whole af-fair looks rude and precarious enough. In curious contrast with their progress was that of the steamer, conveying the Prince of Prussia, which we met to-day, hurrying down from Thebes. We preferred our method of voyaging, though we now advanced only about twelve miles a day, and had been fourteen days making the same distance that we did the first two.

We cannot understand why the country boats are so badly laden as they ap-pear to be. The cargo is placed so forward as to sink the bows to the water; and so many founder in consequence that we can not conceive why the practice is not altered. We have seen several sunk. One was a merchant boat that had gone down in the night, with five people in her. She was a sad spectacle, —her masts and rigging appearing above water, in the middle of the stream.

On the morning of the 19th, on leaving our anchorage near the high rock of Chenoboscion, we found that a wind had sprung up; and we enjoyed the sensation of more rapid progress. We might now hope to see the temple of Dendara in a few hours. The Arabian mountains retreated, and the Lybian chain advanced. Crocodiles plunged into the water as we sailed past the mud banks. The doum palms began to congregate, and from clumps they became woods.

Behind one of these dark woods, I saw a mass of building which immediately fixed my attention; and when a turn of the river brought us to a point where the sunlight was shining into it, I could clearly distinguish the characteristics of the temple of Dendara. I could see the massive portico; — the dark spaces between the pillars, and the line of the architrave. Thus much we could see for two hours from the opposite shore, as Mr. E. had to ride up to Kenneh for letters: but, as the wind was fair, and the temple was two miles off, we left till our return any closer examination of it.

While Mr. E. and Alee were gone to the town, Mr. Y. walked along the shore, in the direction of Selim Pasha's boats; and Mrs. Y. and I were busy about domestic business on board. I was sewing on deck when Mr. Y. returned, and told me he had been invited to an audience of Selim Pasha. When pipes and coffee had been brought, conversation began, through the medium of some Italian gentlemen of the Pasha's suite. On Mr. Y.'s expressing his hope that, by means of commerce, a friendly feeling between the Egyptians and English would always subsist and increase, one of these officers exclaimed, "How should that be, when you have robbed us of Syria?" On Mr. Y.'s pacific observations being again received with an angry recurrence to this sore subject, the Pasha interposed, saying, "These are great and important affairs which are for our superiors to settle, and with which we subordinates have nothing to do. Let us talk of something pleasant." While Mr. Y. was telling me this, an elderly man, with a white beard, hideous teeth, and coarse face altogether, was approaching the boat: and to my dismay, he stepped on board, —or rather, was pushed in by his attendants. Mr. Y. had been sitting with his back to the shore; and now, taken by surprise, seeing the white beard, and having his head full of his late interview, he announced to me "his Excellency, Selim Pasha." Up I jumped, with my lap-full of work, even more disappointed that this should be the hero of that romantic story than dismayed at the visit. And he looked so unlike the old man I saw under the palm at Souhadj! I called up Mrs. Y. from the cabin. Mr. Y. made signs to the cook (for our only interpreter was absent) for pipes and coffee: and we sat down in form and order, and abundant awkwardness. To complete the absurdity of the scene, a line of towels, just out of the wash-tub, were drying on the top of the cabin; and the ironing blanket was on the cabin table. The first relief was Mrs. Y.'s telling me, "It is not Selim Pasha. These are the son and grandson of the English consul at Kenneh."

Then I began to remember certain things of the English consul at Kenneh—what a discreet old Arab he is reported to be—behaving tenderly to European ladies, and pressing parties to go and dine with him; and then, when they are on the way to the town, stepping back to the boat, and laying hands on all the nice provisions he can find, from eggs to Maraschino: so that he extracts a delectable dinner for himself out of his showy hospitality to strangers. While I was reviving all this in my memory, the old man himself was coming down to us. He shook hands with us all round; and, as I expected, kissed the hand of each lady, and pressed us to go up and dine with him. Alee, who had in the meantime returned with Mr. E., and seen from afar that we were holding a levee, had received his instructions to decline decisively all invitations, and convey that we were in a hurry, as the wind was fair for Thebes: so we were let off with a promise that we would dine with the Consul on our return, if we could. But now arrived the Governor of Kenneh, a far superior-looking person, handsomely dressed in fine brown broadcloth. The Consul's elderly son took the opportunity of exploring the cabins, peeping into every corner, and examining Mr. E.'s glass and fowling-piece. We feared a long detention by visitors; but these departed before any others came; and it was still early in the afternoon when we spread our sail, and were off for Thebes.

CHAPTER V

WALKS ASHORE—FIRST SIGHT OF THEBES—ADFOO— CHRISTMAS DAY

THE NEXT MORNING (SUNDAY, DECEMBER 20TH) we found we must still have patience, as we should not see Thebes for another day. The wind had dropped at seven, the evening before, and had brought us only three miles this morning. In the course of the day we were made fully sensible of our happiness in having plenty of time, and in not being pressed to speed by any discomfort on board our boat. We were walking on shore at noon, among men and children busy about their tillage, and sheep and asses and shadoofs, when we saw two boats, bearing the British and American flags, floating down the stream. They wore round, and landed their respective parties, who were Cairo acquaintances of ours. Neither party had been beyond Thebes. How we pitied them when we thought of Philœ and the Cataracts, and the depths of Nubia, which we were on our way to see! The English gentlemen were pressed for time, and were paying their crew to work night and day; by which they did not appear to be gaining much. The American gentleman and his wife were suffering cruelly under the misery of vermin in their boat: a trouble which all travelers in Egypt must endure in a greater or less degree, but which we found much less terrible than we had expected, and reducible to something very trifling by a little housewifely care and management. The terms in which they spoke of Thebes, after even their hasty journey, warmed our hearts and raised our spirits high.

The next day was the shortest day. It was curious to observe how we had lately gained five minutes of sunlight by our progress south wards. Though we cared to-day for nothing but Thebes, we condescended to examine, in our early walk, a strange, dreary-looking place which we were informed was one of the Pasha's schools. It was a large square mud building, crumbling away in desolation. No children were there; but two officers stared at us out of a window. Another, armed to the teeth, entered the enclosure, and spoke to us, we suppose in Arabic, as he passed. The plots of ground were neglected, and the sheds losing their roofs. It is evident that all is over with this establishment, while the people of the district appear in good condition. There were shadoofs at small distances, and so many husbandmen at hand that they relieve each other every two hours at this laborious work, a crier making known along the bank the expiration of the time. We walked through flourishing fields of tobacco and millet: and we gathered, for the first time, the beautiful yellow blossom of the cotton shrub. The castor oil plant began here to be almost as beautiful as the cotton.

Whenever we went for a walk, we were most energetically warned against the dogs of the peasantry: and one of the crew always sprang ashore with a club for our defence, when we were seen running into the great danger of going where we might meet a dog. I suppose the danger is real—so invariably did the peasants rush towards us, on the barking of a dog, to pelt the animal away. I never saw any harm done by a dog, however; and I never could remember to be on my guard; so that one or another of the crew had often to run after me at full speed, when I had forgotten the need of a club bearer, and gone alone.

From breakfast time this day, we were looking over southwestwards, to the Lybian hills which we knew contained the Tombs of the Kings: and before noon, we had seen what we can never forget. On our return, we spent eight days at Thebes; eight days of industrious search, which make us feel familiar with the whole circuit of monuments. But the first impression remains unimpaired and undisturbed. I rather shrink from speaking of it; it is so absolutely incommunicable! The very air and sunshine of the moment, the time of day, the previous mood of mind, have so much share in such a first impression as this, that it can never come alike to any two people. I can but relate what the objects were; and that most meagerly.

The wind was now carrying us on swiftly; and as we, of course, stood as high as we could, on the roof of the cabin, the scene unfolded before us most favorably. Every ridge of hills appeared to turn, and every recess to open, to show us all sides of what we passed. To our left, spread a wide level country— the eastern expanse of the plain of Thebes, backed by peaked mountains, quite unlike the massive Arabian rocks which had hitherto formed that boundary. There was a thick, wood on that bank; and behind that wood Alee pointed out to us the heavy masses of the ruins of El Karnac. Vast and massy, indeed, they looked. But, as yet, the chief interest was on the western shore. The natural features were remarkable enough—the vastness of the expanse, especially, which confounded all anticipation. The modern world obtruded itself before the ancient—the shores dressed in the liveliest green, and busy with Arabs, camels, and buffalo, partially intercepting the view behind. Between these vivid shores, and before and behind the verdant promontories, lay reach after reach of the soft gray, brimming river. Behind this brilliant foreground stretched immeasurable slopes of land, interrupted here and there by ranges of mounds or ridges of tawny rocks, and dotted over with fragments of ruins, and teeming with indications of more. In the rear was the noble guard of mountains which overlooks and protects the plain of Thebes: mountains now nearly colorless— tawny as the expanse below; but their valleys and hollows revealed by the short, sharp shadows of noon. The old name for this scene was running in my head— "the Lybian suburb;" and when I looked for the edifices of this suburb, what did I not see? I could see, even with the naked eye, and perfectly with the glass, traces of the mighty works which once made this, for greatness, the capital of the world. Long rows of square apertures indicated the ranges of burying places. Straggling remains of building wandered down the declivities of sand. And then the Rameséum was revealed, and I could distinguish its colossal statues. And next appeared—and my heart stood still at the sight—the Pair. There they sat together, yet apart, in the midst of the plain, serene and vigilant—still keeping their untired watch over the lapse of ages and the eclipse of Egypt. I can never believe that anything else so majestic as this Pair has been conceived of by the imagination of Art. Nothing even in nature certainly ever affected me so unspeakably; no thunder storm in my childhood, nor any aspect of Niagara, or the great Lakes of America, or the Alps, or the Desert, in my later years. I saw them afterwards, daily, and many times a day, during our stay at Thebes; and the wonder and awe grew from visit to visit. Yet no impression exceeded the first; and none was like it. Happy the traveler who sees them first from afar; that is, who does not arrive at Thebes by night!

We had not thought of stopping at Thebes on our way up the river: but we were delighted to find that the Rais wanted to have his head shaved, and Alee to buy a sheep and some bread. We drew to the El-Uksur (Luxor) shore, and ran up to the ruins. The most conspicuous portion from the river is the fourteen pillars which stand parallel with it, in a double row: but we went first to the great entrance to the temple. I find here in my journal the remark which occurs oftener than any other; that no preconception can be formed of these places. I know that it is useless to repeat it here; for I meet everywhere at home people who think, as I did before I went, that between books, plates, and the stiff and peculiar character of Egyptian architecture and sculpture, Egyptian art may be almost as well known and conceived of in England as on the spot. I can only testify, without hope of being believed, that it is not so; that instead of ugliness, I found beauty; instead of the grotesque, I found the solemn: and where I looked for rudeness, from the primitive character of Art, I found the

sense of the soul more effectually reached than by works which are the result
of centuries of experience and experiment. The mystery of this fact sets one
thinking, laboriously; I may say, painfully. Egypt is not the country to go to
for the recreation of travel. It is too suggestive and too confounding to be met
but in the spirit of study. One's powers of observation sink under the perpetual
exercise of thought: and the lightest-hearted voyager, who sets forth from Cairo
eager for new scenes and days of frolic, comes back an antique, a citizen of the
world of six thousand years ago, kindred with the mummy. Nothing but large
knowledge and sound habits of thought can save him from returning perplexed
and borne down; —unless indeed it be ignorance and levity. A man who goes
to shoot crocodiles and flog Arabs, and eat ostrich's eggs, looks upon the monuments as so many strange old stone-heaps, and comes back "bored to death with
the Nile;" as we were told we should be. He turns back from Thebes, or from
the First Cataract; — perhaps without having even seen the Cataract, when
within a mile of it, as in a case I know; and he pays his crew to work night and
day, to get back to Cairo as fast as possible. He may return gay and unworn:
and so may the true philosopher, to whom no tidings of Man in any age come
amiss; who has no prejudices to be painfully weaned from, and an imagination
too strong to be overwhelmed by mystery, and the rush of a host of new ideas.
But for all between these two extremes of levity and wisdom, a Nile voyage is as
serious a labor as the mind and spirits can be involved in; a trial even to health
and temper such as is little dreamed of on leaving home. The labor and care are
well bestowed, however, for the thoughtful traveler can hardly fail of returning
from Egypt a wiser, and therefore a better man.

There is something very interesting in meeting with a fellow-feeling in ancient travelers so strong as may be found in the following passage from Abdallatif with that of some modern Egyptian voyagers. The passage is almost
the same as some entries in my journal, made when I had never heard of the
Bagdad physician. He speaks of Memphis, as seen in his day, and as, alas! one
fears it will be seen no more. "Notwithstanding the immense extent of this city,
and its high antiquity: notwithstanding all the vicissitudes of the different governments under which it has passed: notwithstanding the efforts that various
nations have made to destroy it in obliterating the minutest traces, effacing its
smallest remains, carrying off the materials, even to the very stones, of which it
was constructed; laying waste its edifices, mutilating the figures which adorned
them; and notwithstanding all that four thousand years and more have been
able to add to such causes of destruction, these ruins yet offer to the eye of
the spectator such a combination of wonders as confounds his understanding,
and as the most eloquent man would vainly attempt to describe. The longer he
contemplates, the more admiration he feels: and each returning glance at these

ruins causes new ecstasy. Scarcely has the spectacle suggested one idea to the mind of the spectator, when it overpowers it by a greater; and when he thinks he has obtained a perfect knowledge of what is before him, he presently learns that his conceptions are still far below the truth."[12] A yet older traveler, Herodotus, says the same thing more briefly: "I shall enlarge upon what concerns Egypt, because it contains more wonders than any other country; and because there is no other country where we may see so many works which are admirable, and beyond all expression.[13]

It is not the vastness of the buildings which strikes one first at El-Uksur, —vast as they are; it is the marvel of the sculptures with which they are covered; —so old, so spirited, and so multitudinous. It is Homer, alive before one's eyes. And what a thought it is, to one standing here, how long this very sculpture has been an image and a thought to great minds placed one far behind another in the stages of human history! Herodotus, who here seems a modern brother-traveler, stood on this spot, and remembered the Iliad as we were now remembering it. He spoke of Homer, his predecessor by four hundred years, as we speak of those who lived in the crusading times. And Homer told of wars which were the same old romance to the people of his time as the crusades are to us. And at the time of these wars, this Thebes was a city of a thousand years; and these battle-pictures now before our eyes were antiquities, as our cathedrals are to us. Here we were standing before one of the "hundred gates" through which Homer says the Theban warriors passed in and out; and on the flanks of this gateway were sculptured the achievements of the ancestors of these warriors. There are the men and horses and chariots, as if in full career, —as full of life as if painted, and painted in a modern time! The stones of the edifice are parting in many places; and these battle-figures extend over the cracks, almost uninjured by the decay. These graven epics will last some time longer, though the stone records will give way before the paper.

The guardian colossi are mighty creatures, with their massive shoulders and serene heads rising out of the ground. A third helmet is visible; and among the Arab huts near, a fourth. We saw here for the first time columns with the lotus-shaped capitals; the capitals being painted, and the blossoms, buds and leaves which filled up the outline being very distinct. One test of the massive character of the work was curious. A huge block of the architrave has fallen from its place, and rests on the rim of the cup of the lotus, without breaking it. We were now introduced to some of the details of Egyptian architecture, and to some of its great separate features: but all unity of impression was obviated by the intrusion of the mud huts which are plastered up against the

12   Relation de l'Egypt. Livre I. ch. 4.
13   Herod. II. 35.

ruins throughout their range. When we came down the river, and had become
familiar with the structure of Egyptian temples, we could make out the plan
of this, and somewhat discharge from view the blemishes which spoiled everything now. But at present, we were not qualified, and we carried away a painful
impression of confusion as well as ruin.

As we sailed away, I obtained another view of the Pair; and I watched them
till I could hardly tell whether it was distance or the dusk which hid them at last.

The wind carried us on well: too well; for a stay of the foremast gave way;
and this hindered our progress. The calm and pathetic-looking Rais rushed
towards us, vociferated, and pulled Mr. E. by the wrist to the forepart, to see
the crack, —of which Mr. E., with all his experience in such matters, thought
little. The Rais, however, is responsible for the condition of the boat, and he
feared that the owner would "cut his neck off" if anything was carried away. So
we moored to the bank, and some little nails were driven in, so as to do no good
whatever; and then it came out that the Rais wanted to stop here for the night.
We so protested against this that he appeared to yield; but at the end of a mile
or so, he drove us decisively into the eastern bank.

As I was walking the deck before tea, I saw two lights moving up under the
opposite bank; and supposed them to be from Selim Pasha's boats. They crossed
the stream, however; and the boats they be longed to drove into the bank so
immediately behind us as to lift our rigging. It was our Scotch friends, and the
American party. The gentlemen immediately exchanged visits; and our own
party brought us some amusement when they returned. Mr. E.'s first exclamation, as he threw down his hat, was, "What a lucky fellow that is! He has shot
a crocodile." "And why not, if he carries ball?" "Ah! I should have brought ball.
He has done it very cleverly, though." And when the Scotchman returned the
call after tea, we found that he had indeed done a difficult and hazardous feat
very well: and he was in possession of the stuffed hide as a trophy.

The next morning, we had an amusement which seemed ridiculous enough
in the Thebaid, but certainly rather exciting; —a boat race. When I came on
deck, the Scotch gentlemen were just mounting the bank, with their fowling
pieces; and their crew and ours were preparing to track. I was about to go ashore
also for a walk, when I observed that our Rais was getting out the sail, though
there was not a breath of wind. It was clear that he expected to fall in with a
wind at the next reach of the river: so I remained on board. Our sail caught the
eye of our Scotch friends. I saw the halt of their red tarbooshes over the bushes
that fringed the bank. They scampered back, and leaped on board their boat;
and in another moment, up went their sail. In another, up went the American's!
Three sails, no wind, and three crews tracking, at a pace scarcely less funereal
than usual! —At the expected point, the sails filled, all at the same instant, and

off we went. For an hour or more, I could not believe that we were gaining ground, though Mr. E. declared we were. When it was becoming clear that we were, he told that, provoking as it was, we must take in sail and yield the race, as we had to take up, in yonder bay, our milk messenger. There he was, accordingly; and quick was the manoeuvre of putting in, and snatching up the poor fellow. Half a dozen hands hauled him in, and helped to spill the milk. Then, what a shout of laughter there was when the Scotchman shortened sail, and took up his milkman too: and after him, the Americans! We could relish the milk now, which we had thought so much in our way before. The race was fairly decided before ten o'clock. We beat, as we ought, from the superiority of our boat: and before noon, our Scotch friends put into Isna (Esneh) where their crew were to bake their bread. This was the last place, north of the Cataract, where they could do so.

Isna looks well from the river; but we could see nothing of the temple, which is lost to view in the town. We left it for our return: and we meant to do the same with that of Adfoo (Edfou). But it came in sight while we were at dinner the next clay, just when there was no wind. We decided that no time would be lost by a run up to the temple: so we sprang ashore, among cotton and castor-oil plants, and walked a mile in dust, through fields and under rows of palms, and among Arab dwellings, to the front of the mighty edifice. No one of the temples of Egypt struck me more with the conviction that these buildings were constructed as fortifications, as much as for purposes of religious celebration. I will not here give any detailed account of this temple; partly because I understood these matters better when I afterwards saw it again: and yet more, because it was now almost buried in dust, much of which was in course of removal on our return, for manuring the land. —It was here, and now, that I was first taken by surprise with the beauty; —the beauty of everything; —the sculptured columns, with their capitals, all of the same proportion and outline, though exhibiting in the same group the lotus, the date palm, the doum palm and the tobacco: —the decorations—each one, with its fullness of meaning—a delicately sculptured message to all generations, through all time: —and, above all, the faces. I had fancied the faces, even the portraits, grotesque: but the type of the old Egyptian face has great beauty, though a beauty little resembling that which later ages have chosen for their type. It resembles, however, some actual modern faces. In the sweet girlish countenances of Isis and Athor, I often observed a likeness to persons—and especially one very pretty one— at home.

The other thing that surprised me most was the profusion of the sculptured inscriptions. I had often read of the whole of the surfaces of these temples being covered with inscriptions: but the fact was never fairly in my mind till now: and the spectacle was as amazing as if I had never heard of it. The amount of labor invested here seems to shame all other human industry. It reminds one more of the labors of the coral insect than of those of men.

After taking a look at the scanty remains of the smaller temple, we returned to the boat, to set foot on land no more, we hoped, till we reached the boundary of Egypt, at the old Syene. My friends at home had promised to drink our healths at the First Cataract on Christmas day: and, when the wind sprang up, on our leaving Adfoo, and we found, on the morning of the 24th, that it had carried us twenty-five miles in the night, we began to believe we should really keep our appointment.

The quarries of Silsilis have a curious aspect from the river; —half way between rocks and buildings: for the stones were quarried out so regularly as to leave buttresses which resemble pillars or colossal statues. Here, where men once swarmed, working that machinery whose secret is lost, and moving those masses of stone which modern men can only gaze at—in this once busy place, there is now only the hyæna and its prey. In the bright daylight, when the wild beast is hidden in its lair, all is as still as when we passed.

We saw, this morning, a man crossing the river, here very wide, on a bundle of millet stalks. His clothes were on his head, like a huge turban, and he paddled himself over with the branch of a tree.

At sunset, the contrasting colors of the limestone and sandstone ranges were striking. The limestone was of a bright pale yellow: the sandstone purplish. By moonlight, we saw the ruins of Kóm Umbos (Kóm Ombos), which looked fine on the summit of their rock on the eastern bank.

Christmas morning was like a July morning in England. We had made good progress during the night, and were now only eleven miles from Aswán (Essouan), the old Syene—the frontier between Egypt and Nubia. When we came within two miles, we left our letter-writing. The excitement was too strong to allow of any employment. At present, we saw nothing of the wildness of the scenery, of which we had read so much. We found that higher up. The river became more and more lake-like; and there was a new feature in the jutting black rocks. The shores were green and tranquil; and palms abounded more than in any place we had passed. Behind these rich woods, however, the Lybian desert rose, yellow with sand drifts. —Our crew became merry in the near prospect of rest. One of them dressed himself very fine, swathing himself with turbans, and began to dance, to the music and clapping of the rest. He danced up to us, with in sinuating cries of "baa" and "baksheesh," as a hint for a present of a sheep. In the midst of this, we ran aground, and the brisk fellows threw down their drum, pipe, and finery, and went to work as usual. We were now making for the shore, in order to land a man who had begged a passage from Cairo.

He was a Rais; and had served at Constantinople and elsewhere for twenty-five years, during which time he had never been home. For many years he had had no tidings of wife or children; and now, when within a mile or two of his home, he showed no signs of perturbation. He made his acknowledgments to us with an easy cheerful grace, put off his bright red slippers, and descended into the mud, and then thrust his muddy feet into his new slippers with an air of entire tranquillity. We watched him as long as we could see him among the palms, and should have been glad to know how he found all at home. The scene around looked far indeed out of the bounds of Christendom, this Christmas-day, till I saw, on a steep, the ruins of the Coptic convent of St. George. Aswán was now peeping over the palms on the eastern shore; and opposite to it was the island of Elephantine—half rubbish, half verdure. We moored to the shore below Aswán just at two o'clock; and thus we kept our appointment, to dine at the First Cataract on Christmas-day. Our dinner included turkey and plum-pudding. Our Arab cook succeeded well with the last-mentioned novelty. We sent a huge cantle of it to the Rais, who ate it all in a trice, and gave it his emphatic approbation.

CHAPTER VI

ASWÁN—SLAVES—FIRST RIDE IN THE DESERT—QUARRIES—
ELE PHANTINE—RIVER SCENERY—PREPARATIONS FOR NUBIA—
FIRST SIGHT OF PHILŒ

AS SOON AS OUR PLANK WAS DOWN, a sort of mob-market was formed on shore. There was a display of stuffed crocodile, spears, ebony clubs, straw-baskets, coins, walking sticks, an ostrich's egg, a conjurer, &c. It was at this place that a girl offered me for sale an English half-penny; and another the glass stopper of a little bottle. Here, as everywhere, my ear trumpet was handled and examined with quick curiosity; and in almost every case, from Nubia to the Lebanon, the immediate conclusion was the same. The inquirers put the small end to their lips, and gave a satisfied nod. It was clearly a pipe, with an enormous bowl! At Aswán, however, we staid long enough for the people to discover what the trumpet was for; and from the moment of the discovery, they did their best to enable me to do without it. As we passed through the lane they made for us, they pressed forwards to shout into my ears "baksheesh! baksheesh," till Alee pushed and flogged them away. I wonder at their perseverance in thus incessantly begging of strangers; for we could not learn that they ever got anything by it. If, as it appeared to me, travelers give only in return for service, or in consideration of some infirmity, the perseverance in begging seems wonderful. I saw at this place parents teaching a little one to speak: and the word they tried it with was "baksheesh." I saw a little fellow just able to carry his father's slippers, —which were almost as big as himself: —his father gave him a careful training in hugging the slippers with one arm, while he held out the other hand to me for baksheesh. The people here were very good looking. They cannot grow provisions enough for their numbers, —the desert encroaching too much to permit the cultivation of more land than the mere river banks: but they import enough for their wants. Their renowned dates are their principal article of exchange; and traffic goes on here in henneh, baskets, senna, charcoal and slaves from Upper Ethiopia and Abyssinia. Of course, it was impossible to learn their numbers. Nobody knows; and if any one knew, he would not tell. A census may be, and has been ordered; but it cannot be executed. The popular dread of the government renders it impossible. The fellahs (peasants) have such a terror of increased taxation and of the conscription, that they abscond on the mention of a census; and some who can afford it bribe the officials to suppress their names, and those of their families. The last thing that can be learned of any Egyptian town or district is its population.

The walls of the streets are blank here; —not a window, or break of any kind, but a low door here and there. The bazaars looked poor; and I believe the traffic is chiefly carried on elsewhere. We saw two slave-bazaars. One was an inclosure on the rising ground above our boat. The slaves here were only five or six, and all children; —all under sixteen years of age. They were intelligent and cheerful-looking; and I recognized, at the first glance, the likeness to the old Egyptian countenance and costume. The girls had their faces uncovered; and their hair in the Ethiopian fashion, —precisely that which we see in the old sculptures and paintings. One little girl was preparing the pottage for their supper, very cleverly and earnestly. She was said to be fifteen; and 15l. was the sum asked for her. The other bazaar was on the outskirts of the town, and near our boat. It contained, when we saw it on our return, a dozen boys, and about fifteen girls. Most of the girls were grinding millet between two stones, or kneading and baking cakes. They were freshly oiled, in good plight, and very intelligent-looking, for the most part. Some of them were really pretty in their way, —in the old Egyptian way. They appeared cheerful, and at home in their business; and there can scarcely be a stronger contrast than between this slave-market and those I had seen in the United States. The contrast is as strong as between the serfdom of the Egyptian, and the freedom of the American in-habitants of the respective countries: and of course, the first aspect of slavery is infinitely less repulsive in Egypt than in America. What I learned, and may have to tell, of the life of the modern Egyptians proves, however, that the institution is no more defensible here than elsewhere.

I saw a little girl on the shore making cord, for tying round the waists of the men; and was extremely surprised to observe that the process is the same as that of bobbin-making with the lyre by English ladies. Instead of an ivory lyre, this child had two crossed sticks; and her cotton thread was very coarse. It was striking to see this little art existing in places so widely apart.

We walked, this afternoon, to the ruins of the old town, and overlooked its desolation from the top of the rock above the river. The translation of the name of this town is "the Opening:" and a great opening this once was, before the

Nile had changed its character in Ethiopia, and when the more ancient races made this rock their watchtower, on the frontier between Egypt and the South.

That the Nile has changed its character, south of the First Cataract, has been made clear by some recent examination of the shores and monuments of Nubia. Dr. Lepsius has discovered watermarks so high on the rocks, and edifices so placed as to compel the conviction, that the bed of the Nile has sunk extraordinarily, by some great natural process, either of convulsion or wear.[14] The apparent exaggerations of some old writers about the Cataracts at Syene, may thus be in some measure accounted for. If there really was once a cataract here, instead of the rapids of the present day, there is some excuse for the reports given from hearsay, by Cicero and Seneca. Cicero says that "the river throws itself headlong from the loftiest mountains, so that those who live nearest are deprived of the sense of hearing, from the greatness of the noise." Seneca's account is, — " When some people were stationed there by the Persians, their ears were so stunned with the constant roar, that it was found necessary to remove them to a more quiet place."—Supposing the Cataract formerly to have been of any height rendered necessary by the discoveries of Dr. Lepsius, it is clear that Syene must have been the station for the transshipment of merchandise passing north or south. The granite quarries, too, whence much of the building material of old Egypt was drawn, must have added to the business of the place. It is clear, accordingly, that this was, in all former times, a station of great importance. There were temples at Elephantine, to guard the interests of the neighborhood, and to attract and gratify strangers. There was a Nilometer, to give tidings of the deposits of the great god Nilus. There was a garrison in the time of the Persians, and again in that of the Greeks: and Roman fortifications stand in ruin on the heights around. The Saracenic remains are obvious enough: and thus we have, on this frontier spot, and visible from the rock on which we stood, evidence of this place having been prized by successive races, as the Opening which its present name declares it to be.

The ruins of the Saracenic town make their site desolate beyond description: —more desolate to my eyes, if possible, than the five acres I saw laid waste by the great New York fire. Two women were sitting under the wall of a roofless house, with no neighbors but a few prowling dogs. They warned me away till they saw the rest of my party coming up the ascent. The Island of Elephantine, opposite, looked as if just laid waste by an earthquake, scarcely one stone being left upon another of all its once grand edifices. On its rocks were hieroglyphic inscriptions, many and deeply carved. In a hollow of the desert behind us lay the great cemetery, where almost every grave has its little stone, with a Cufic inscription. The red granite was cropping up everywhere; and promontories

14   Appendix C.

and islets of black basalt began to show themselves in the river. Behind us, at the entrance of the desert, were the mountainous masses of granite, where we were to-morrow to look for the celebrated quarries, and their deserted obelisk. Before we came down from our point of survey, we saw the American party crossing, in a ferry-boat, to Elephantine. They had arrived after us, and were to set out, on their return, to Cairo the next day!

As we sat on deck under our awning, this evening, the scene was striking; —the brilliant moonlight resting on the quiet groves, but contending on the shore with the yellow glow from the west, which gilded the objects there; and especially the boat-building near the water's edge; —the crews forming picturesque groups, with their singing, clapping and dancing, while close beside them, and almost among them, were the Rais and two other men going through their prayers and prostrations. This boat-building was the last we saw up the river: and a rude affair it was: —the planks not planed, and wide apart, and irregular. A kandjia was here, which had brought a party of Turkish officers. We had the offer of it, to take us to the Second Cataract; our dahabieh being, of course, too large to ascend the Cataract here. Our gentlemen thought it would not do; —that Mrs. Y. and I could not put up with its accommodations, even for a fortnight. We thought we could: but we agreed that the first thing to be done was to go to the head of the Cataract, and see what boats could be had there.

The next morning, therefore, we had breakfast early, and set off on asses for Mahatta, —the village at the head of the Cataract. This, our first ride in the desert, was full of wonder and delight. It was only about three miles: but it might have been thirty, from the amount of novelty in it. Our thick umbrellas, covered with brown holland, were a necessary protection against the heat, which would have been almost intolerable, but for the cool north wind. —I believed before that I had imagined the Desert: but now I felt that nobody could. No one could conceive the confusion of piled and scattered rocks, which, even in a ride of three miles, deprives a stranger of all sense of direction, except by the heavens. These narrow passes among black rocks, all suffocation and glare, without shade or relief, are the very home of despair. The oppression of the sense of sight disturbs the brain, so that the will of the unhappy wanderer cannot keep his nerves in order. I thought of poor Hagar here, and seemed to feel her story for the first time. I thought of Scotch shepherds lost in the snow, and of their mild case in comparison with that of Arab goat-herds lost in the Desert. The difference is of death by lethargy and death by torture. We were afterwards in the depth of Arabia, and lived five weeks in tents, in the Desert: but no Arabian scene impressed me more with the characteristics of the Desert than this ride of three miles from Aswán to Mahatta. The presence of dragon flies in the Desert surprised me; —not only here, but in places afterwards—where there appeared to be no water within a great distance. To those who have been wont to watch the coming forth of the dragon-fly from its sheath on the rush on the margin of a pool, and flitting about the mountain watercourse, or the moist meadows at home, it is strange to see them by dozens glittering in the sunshine of the desert, where there appears to be nothing for them to alight on; —nothing that would not shrivel them up, if they rested for a moment from the wing. The hard dry locust seemed more in its place, and the innumerable beetles, which everywhere left a net-work of delicate tracks on the light sand. Distant figures are striking in the Desert, in the extreme clearness of light and shade. Shadows strike upon the sense here as bright lights do elsewhere. It seems to me that I remember every figure I ever saw in the Desert: —every veiled woman tending her goats, or carrying her water-jar on her head; — every man in blue skirting the hillocks; every man in brown guiding his ass or his camel through the sandy defiles of the black rocks, or on a slope by moonlight, when he casts a long shadow. Every moving thing has a new value to the eye in such a region.

When we came out upon Mahatta, we were in Nubia, and found ourselves at once in the midst of the wildness of which we had read so much in relation to the First Cataract. The Mississippi is wild: and the Indian grounds of Wisconsin, with their wigwam camps, are wild: but their wildness is only that of primitive Nature. This is fantastic, —impish. It is the wildness of Prospero's island. Prospero's island and his company of servitors were never out of my head between Aswán and the next placid reach of the river above Philœ. —The rocks are not sublime: they are too like Titanic heaps of black paving-stones to be imposing otherwise than by their oddity: and they are strewn about the land and river to an excess and with a caprice which takes one's imagination quite out of the ordinary world. Their appearance is made the more strange by the cartouches and other hieroglyphic inscriptions which abound among them; sometimes on a face above the river; sometimes on a mere ordinary block near the path; —sometimes on an unapproachable fragment in the middle of the stream. When we emerged from the Desert upon Mahatta, the scene was somewhat softened by the cultivation behind the village, and the shade of the spreading sycamores and clustered palms. Heaps of dates, like the wheat in our granaries for quantity, lay piled on the shore; and mounds of packages (chiefly dates) ready for export. The river was all divided into streamlets and ponds by the black islets. Where it was overshadowed, it was dark gray or deep blue; but where the light caught it, rushing between a wooded island and the shore, it was of the clearest green. —The people were wild, —especially the boys, who were naked and excessively noisy: but I did not dislike their behavior; which was very harmless, though they had to be flogged out of the path, like a herd of pigs. —We saw two boats, and immediately became eager to secure the one below. I was delighted at this, as we were thus not deprived of the adventure of ascending the Cataract.

On our return, we sent Alee forward to secure the kandjia; and we diverged to the quarries, passing through the great cemetery with its curious gravestones, inscribed in the Cufic character. The marks of the workmen's tools are as distinct as ever on the granite of the quarries. There are the rows of holes for the wooden pegs or wedges which, being wetted, expanded and split the stone. There are the grooves and the notches made, by men who died several thousands of years ago, in preparation for works which were never done. There are the playful or idle scratches made by men of old in a holiday mood. And there, too, is the celebrated obelisk, about which, I must take leave to say, some mistakes are current at this day.

It may look like trifling to spend any words on the actual condition of an obelisk in the quarry: but, if we really wish to know how the ancients set about works which modern men are unable to achieve, we must collect all the facts we can about such works, leaving it for time to show which are important and which are not. We spend many words in wondering what could be the mechanical powers known to the old Egyptians, by which they could detach, lift, carry, and dress such masses of stone as our resources are wholly inadequate to deal with. When we chance to meet with one such mass in a half-finished state, it is surely worth while to examine and report upon its marks and peculiarities, however unaccountable, as one step towards learning hereafter, how they came there.

This obelisk was declared, by a traveler who judged naturally by the eye, to be lying there unfinished because it was broken before it was completely detached from the rock. Other travelers have repeated the tale, —one measuring the mass, and taking for granted that an irregular groove along the upper surface was the "crack,"—the "fissure;" and another, comfortably seated on an ass, not even getting down to touch it at all. Our friend, Mr. E., was not satisfied without looking into things with his own eyes and his own mind: and he not only measured and poked in the sand, but cleared out the sand from the grooves till he had satisfied himself that there is no breakage or crack about the obelisk at all.

The upper surface is (near the centre of its length) about two feet broad: and there is every appearance of the other three sides having the same measurement, —as the guide says they have, —allowing for the inequalities of the undressed stone. There is no evidence that it is not wholly detached from the rock. Of course, we moderns cannot move it; but the guide declares that, when cleared of sand, a stick may be passed under in every part. And it seems improbable that the apex of the obelisk should be reduced to form before the main body is severed from the rock. —As for the supposed "fissure," it is certainly a carefully wrought groove, and no crack. Its sides are as smooth as any tablet; and its breadth appears to be uniform: —about an inch wide at the top. Its depth is about three inches; and it is smooth and sound all along the bottom. Near it is a slight fault in the stone; a skin-deep crack, —little more than a roughness of the surface. Across the upper face were some remarkable holes. Besides those which are usually prepared for wedges or pegs, there were two deep grooves, slanting and not parallel. If they had been straight and parallel, we should have immediately supposed them intended to hold the chains or ropes by which the mass was to be raised: and it is still possible that they were so. But we do not know what to make of the groove which is commonly called the fissure. It is deep; it is longitudinal; and it is devious; not intended, evidently, to bear any relation to the centre of the face, nor to be parallel with either side, nor to be straight in its direction. The only conjecture we could form was that it was in preparation for the dressing of the stone, after the erection of the obelisk: but then its depth appears too great for such a purpose. We observed a considerable bulge on the upper face of this obelisk. We all know that this is necessary, to obviate that optical deception which gives an appearance of concavity to a perfectly correct pyramidal line; and we all know that the old Egyptians so well understood this architectural secret that they might be the teachers of it to all the world. But the knowledge of this does not lessen the surprise, when the proof of it, in so gigantic a form, is under one's hand. —The block was ninety feet long above the sand, when we were there; and the guide said that the sand covered thirty more. Judging of the proportions of the apex from what we saw, it must either require much cutting away in the dressing, or be a little spire. It would doubtless be much reduced by cutting. —We left the quarries, full of speculation about what manner of men they were who cut and carved their granite mountains in this noble style, and by what inconceivable means they carried away their spoils. It would hardly surprise me more to see a company of ants carrying a life-size statue, than it did to measure the building stones and colossi of the East.

In our walk this evening we saw a pretty encampment of Albanian soldiers among the palms. One had to rub one's eyes to be sure that one was not in a theatre. The open tent, with the blue smoke rising, the group of soldiers, in their Greek dress, on the ground, and seen between the palm stems; the arms piled against a tree, and glittering in the last rays of the sun; —all this was like a sublimated opera scene. And there was another, the next morning, when they took their departure southwards, their file of loaded camels winding away from under the shade into the hot light.

We went early, to Elephantine, this morning (the 27th), after seeing the Scotch boat arrive. The remains on Elephantine are not now very interesting; —at least, we did not find them so: and we do not enter into the ordinary romance about this "Island of Flowers." Not only we saw no flowers; but we could perceive no traces of any; and our guide could not be made to understand what flowers were. Conversation was carried on in Italian, of which the man appeared to have no lack. First he said there were many flowers there: then that there were none: and he ended by asking what "fiori" were. He shook his head in despair when we showed him. The northern end of the island is green and fertile: but the southern end is one dreary heap of old stones and broken pottery. The quantity of broken pottery in these places is unaccountable, —incredible.

The quays are gone, and the great flight of steps to the river. The little ancient temple of Kneph is gone; and another, and the upper portion of the Nilometer were pulled down, some years since, to supply building stone for an official's palace at Aswán. We saw, at the Nilometer, sculptured stones built in among rough ones, —some being upside down, —some set on end. And this is all we could make out of this edifice. There is a granite gateway of the time of Alexander; and this is the only erect work of any interest. —There is a statue of red granite, with the Osiride emblems; —a mean and uncouth image, in comparison with most that we saw. Some slender and broken granite pillars lie about, a little to the north of the gateway: and one of them bears a sculptured cross; which shows that they were part of a Christian temple.

The people on the island are Nubians. Many of their faces, as well as their forms, are fine: and they have the same well-fed and healthy appearance as we observe among the people generally, all along the great valley, and especially in the Nubian part of it. Some of the children were naked; some had ragged clothing; and many were dressed in substantial garments, though of the dusty or brown colors which convey an impression of dirt to an English eye. The children's hair was shining, even dripping with the castor-oil which was to meet our senses everywhere in Nubia.

Our Scotch friends called while we were at breakfast, and offered us their small boat for an expedition to Philœ. Much as I longed to see Philœ, I was startled at the idea of going by water in a small boat, as a mere morning trip: and I was sorry to see our saddles put away, as it appeared to me more practicable to go by the shorter way of the desert, taking a boat from Mahatta. If we had known what we soon learned about the water passage, we should not have dreamed of such an adventure. My next uneasiness was at finding that we were going with only Arab rowers, without an interpreter. It certainly was foolish; but the local Rais had arranged the affair; and it was not for us to dispute the wisdom of the man who must know best. I am glad we went; for we obtained admirable views of this extraordinary part of the river, at more leisure, and with more freedom than when ascending the Cataract in our kandjia, amidst the hubbub of a hundred natives.

The wear of the rocks by thousands of annual inundations exhibits singular effects, in holes, unaccountable fissures, grotesque outlines, and gigantic piling up of blocks. The last deposit of soil on the slopes of smooth stones, and in every recess and crevice, reminded me of the odd tillage one sees in Switzerland, where a miniature field is made on the top of a boulder, by confining the deposited earth with a row of stones. And when we were driven to land, in the course of the morning, it was striking to see in what small and parched recesses a few feet of millet and vetches were grown, where the soil would yield anything. The deposit was always graduated, always in layers, however little there might be of it. In some stones in the middle of the current, there were wrought grooves, and holes for wedges; for what purpose, and whether these stones were always in the middle of the current, let those say who can. They looked like a preparation for the erection of colossal statues, which would have a finer effect amidst this frontier cataract than any Madonna del Mare has amidst the lagoons of Venice. The water here was less turbid than we had yet seen it. Its gushings round the rocks were glorious to see, and, in my opinion, to feel, as we made directly towards them, in order to be swirled away by them to some opposite point which we could not otherwise reach. The only time I was really startled was when we bumped tremendously upon a sunken rock. I saw, however, that the rowers were confident and merry; and when this is the case with local residents, in any critical passage of foreign travel, one may always feel secure. Remembering this, I found our hard won passages through sharp little rapids, and the eagerness and hubbub of the rowers delightful. But all did not find it so: and truly there was a harum-scarum appearance about the adventure which justified a pause and reconsideration what we should do.

It was impossible to obtain any information from the Arabs. Pantomime may go a good way with any people in Europe, from a general affinity of ideas, and of their signs, which prevails over a continent where there is nearly uniform civilization. But it avails nothing, and is even misleading, between Europeans and the natives of Oriental countries. Our gentlemen were much given to pantomime, in the absence of an interpreter; and it was amusing to me to see, with the practised eye of a deaf person, how invariably they were misunderstood; and often, when they had no suspicion of this themselves. They naturally employed many conventional signs; and, of course, so did the Arabs: and such confusion arose out of this that I begged my friends never to put down in their journals any information which they believed they had obtained by means of pantomime. It might be that while they were inquiring about a pyramid, the Arabs might be replying about the sun: while they were asking questions about distance, the Arabs might be answering about ploughing: and so on. To-day we could make out nothing: so we offered very intelligible signs that we wished to land. We landed in a cove of a desert region on the eastern shore: and while Mr. E. was drawing maps on the sand, and the rowers were clamoring and gesticulating about him, I made for a lofty pile of rocks, a little way inland, to seek for a panoramic view. It was dreadfully hot: but I obtained a magnificent view of the river, as well as the surrounding country; by far the finest view of the Cataract that offered. —I could see nothing of Philœ, which was in fact hidden behind the eastern promontories: but from the great sweep the river made above us, and the indescribable intricacy of its channels among its thousand scattered rocks, it seemed plain to me that it would take some hours to reach the Sacred Island. I reported accordingly; and Mr. E. thought he had ascertained from the crew that it would take three hours to get to Philœ. As it was by this time one o'clock, we decided to return. It afterwards appeared that the three hours the men spoke of were from our dahabieh to Philœ: but I am sure it would have taken much more.

From my point of observation, I had seen that several weirs were constructed among the rapids, where a few blackies were busy, —some leaning over from the rocks, and others up to their shoulders in the stream. Their dusky figures contrasted finely with the glittering waters; and it was a truly savage African scene. One man came swimming to us, with a log under his breast, bringing a fish half as big as himself. It was like a gigantic perch; we bought it for 7 ½ d., and found it better than Nile fish usually are. —I have often read of the great resource the Egyptians have in the fish of their river. They do not seem to prize it much; and I do not wonder. We thought the Nile fish very poor in quality, and commended the natives for eating in preference the grain and pulse which their valley yields in abundance.

Several people had collected, —there is no saying from whence—in our cove to see us depart: and I was glad they did; for their figures on the rocks were beautiful. One little naked boy placed himself on the top of a great boulder in an attitude of such perfect grace, —partly sitting, partly kneeling, with his hands resting on one foot, —that I longed to petrify him, and take him home, an ebony statue, for the instruction of sculptors. There is no training any English child to imitate him. An attitude of such perfect grace must be natural: but not, I suppose, in our climate, or to any one who has sat on chairs. Our return, with the current, was smooth, pleasant and speedy. We found that the kandjia had been cleaned, sunk, (three drowned rats being the visible result of the process,) raised, and dried; and the stores were now being laid in: and to-morrow we were to go up to the Rapids, to leave the next day clear for the ascent of the Cataract. —This evening was so warm that Mrs. Y. and I walked on the shore for some time without bonnet or shawl; the first and last occasion, no doubt, of our doing so by moonlight on the 27th of December.

The next morning I rose early, to damp and fold linen; and I was ironing till dinner-time, that we might carry our sheets and towels in the best condition to the kandjia. No one would laugh at, or despise this who knew the importance, in hot countries, of the condition of linen; and none who have not tried can judge of the difference in comfort of ironed linen and that which is rough dried. By sparing a few hours per week, Mrs. Y. and I made neat and comfortable the things washed by the crew; and when we saw the plight of other travelers, — gentlemen in rough dried collars, and ladies in gowns which looked as if they had been merely wrung out of the wash-tub, we thought the little trouble our ironing cost us well bestowed. Everybody knows now that to take English servants ruins everything, —destroys all the ease and comfort of the journey; and the Arabs cannot iron. They cannot comprehend what it is for. One boat's crew last year decided, after a long consultation, that it was the English way of killing lice. This was not our crew: but I do not think ours understood to the last the meaning of the weekly ceremony of the flat-iron. The dragoman of another party, being sounded about ironing his employer's white trowsers, positively declined the attempt; saying that he had once tried, and at the first touch had burnt off the right leg. If any lady going up the Nile should be so happy as to be able to iron, I should strongly advise her putting up a pair of flat-irons among her baggage. If she can also starch, it will add much to her comfort and that of her party, at a little cost of time and trouble.

We went on board our kandjia to dinner, at two o'clock, and were off for the entrance of the Cataract. The smallness of our boat, after our grand dahabieh, was the cause of much amusement, both to-day and during the fortnight of our Nubian expedition. In the inner cabin there was only just room for Mrs. Y. and me by laying our beds close together; and our dressing-room was exactly a yard square. The gentlemen's cabin was somewhat larger; but not roomy enough to admit of our having our meals there, —unless a strong cold wind drove us in to tea; —which, I think, happened twice. Our sitting room was a pretty little vestibule, between the cabins and the deck. This exactly held our table and two chairs; the other seats being two lockers, on which were spread gay carpets. When we sat down to our morning employments, we were careful to bring at once all the books, &c., that we were likely to want, as we could not pass in and out without compelling our neighbors to rise to make way. For all this, and though we felt, on our return to our dahabieh, as if we had got from a coaster into a man-of-war, we were never happier than in our little kandjia. There was some amusement in roughing it for a fortnight; and the Nubian part of our voyage was full as interesting as any other.

The Rais of the Cataract was to meet us, the next morning, with his posse, at a point fixed on, above the first rapid, which we were to surmount ourselves.

We appeared to be surmounting it, just at dusk. Half our crew were hauling at our best rope on the rocks, and the other half poling on board; and we were slowly, —almost imperceptibly—making way against the rushing current, and had our bows fairly through the last mass of foam, when the rope snapped. We swirled down and away, —none of us knew whither, unless it were to the bottom of the river. This was almost the most anxious moment of our whole journey; but it was little more than a moment. The boat, in swinging round at the bottom of the rapid, caught by her stern on a sand bank: and our new Rais quickly brought her round, and moored her, in still water, to the bank.

Here we were for the night: and we thought it a pity not to take advantage of the leisure and the moonlight to visit Philœ. So the gen tlemen and I crossed the rapids to the main in a punt, mounted capital asses, and struck across the desert for Mahatta, where we could get a boat for Philœ.

The sun had just set when we left the kandjia; and the Desert looked superb in the after glow. It had the last depth of coloring I have ever seen in pictures, or heard described. The clear forms and ravishing hues make one feel as if gifted with new eyes.

The boat which took us from Mahatta to Philœ was too heavy for her hands, and could hardly stem some of the currents: but at last, about seven o'clock, we set our feet on the Holy Island, and felt one great object of our journey accomplished. What a moment it was, just before, when we first saw Philœ, as we came round the point, — saw the crowd of temples looming in the mellow twilight. And what a moment it was now, when we trod the soil, as sacred to wise old races of men as Mecca now to the Mohammedan, or Jeru-salem to the Christian; the huge propyls, the sculptured walls, the colonnades, the hypæthral[15] temple all standing, in full majesty, under a flood of moon light! The most sacred of ancient oaths was in my mind all the while, as if breathed into me from without; —the awful oath "By Him who sleeps in Philœ." Here, surrounded by the imperishable Nile, sleeping to the everlasting music of its distant Cataract, and watched over by his Isis, whose temple seems made to stand for ever, was the beneficent Osiris believed to lie. There are many Holy Islands scattered about the seas of the world: the very name is sweet to all ears: but no one has been so long and so deeply sacred as this. The waters all round were, this night, very still; and the more suggestive were they of the olden age when they afforded a path for the processions of grateful worshipers, who came from various points of the mainland, with their lamps, and their harps, and their gifts, to return thanks for the harvests which had sprung and ripened at the bidding of the god. One could see them coming in their boats, there where the last western light gleamed on the river: one could see them land at the steps

15   Hypæthral—open to the sky.

at the end of the colonnade: and one could imagine this great group of temples lighted up till the prominent sculpture of the walls looked almost as bright and real as the moving forms of the actual offerers. — But the silence and desertion of the place soon made themselves felt. Our footsteps on the loose stones, and our voices in an occasional question, and the flapping wings of the birds whom we disturbed were the only sounds: and the lantern which was carried before us in the shadowy recesses was a dismal light for such a place. I could not, under the circumstances, make out anything of the disposition of the buildings: and I think that a visit to Philœ by moonlight had better be preceded by a visit to Philœ by daylight: but I am glad to have seen the solemn sight, now that I can look back upon it with the fresh eyes of clear knowledge of the site and its temples.

A kandjia lay under the bank when we arrived. It had brought our Scotch friends from Mahatta; and we found them in the court of the hypæthral temple, sitting on the terrace wall in the moonlight, —the gentlemen with their chibouques, —the ladies with their bonnets in their hands. Their first and last view of Philœ was on this lovely night: and this was our last sight of them. They were to set off down the river the next morning, at the same hour that we were to begin the ascent of the Cataract. Our greetings, our jokes, our little rivalries were all over; and the probability was that we should never meet again. —How sorry we were for them that they were turning back! We not only had Nubia, with its very old temples—and above all, Aboo-Simbil[16] —full in prospect, but a return to this island, to obtain a clear knowledge of it. My heart would have been very heavy to-night if this had been my only view of Philœ; —a view so obscure, so tantalizing, and so oppressive: and I was sorry accordingly for those who were to see it but once, and thus.

Our desert ride in the moonlight was very fine, among such lights and shadows as I never saw by night before. We encountered no hyænas, though our guide carried a musket, in expectation that we should. We crossed the rapids in safety, and reached our boat excessively tired, and the more eager for rest because the next was to be the greatest day of our journey, —unless perhaps that of our passing Thebes.

---

16   Ipsamboul.

CHAPTER VII

ASCENT OF THE CATARACT

UCH AN EVENT AS THE ASCENT OF THE CATARACT can happen but once in one's life; and we would not hear of going ashore on any such plea as that the feat could be better seen from thence. What I wanted was to feel it. I would have gone far to see a stranger's boat pulled up; but I would not refuse the fortune of being on board when I could. We began, however, with going ashore at the Rapid where we failed the evening before. The rope had been proved untrustworthy; and there was no other till we joined the Rais of the Cataract, with his cable and his posse. Our Rais put together three weak ropes, which were by no means equivalent to one strong one: but the attempt succeeded.

It was a curious scene, —the appearing of the dusky natives on all the rocks around; the eager zeal of those who made themselves our guards, holding us by the arms, as if we were going to jail, and scarcely permitting us to set our feet to the ground, lest we should fall; and the daring plunges and divings of man or boy, to obtain our admiration or our baksheesh. A boy would come riding down a slope of roaring water as confidently as I would ride down a sand-hill on my ass. Their arms, in their fighting method of swimming, go round like the spokes of a wheel. Grinning boys poppled in the currents; and little seven-year-old savages must haul at the ropes, or ply their little poles when the kandjia approached a spike of rock, or dive to thrust their shoulders between its keel and any sunken obstacle: and after every such feat, they would pop up their dripping heads, and cry "baksheesh." I felt the great peculiarity of this day to be my seeing, for the first, and probably the only time of my life, the perception of savage faculty: and truly it is an imposing sight. The quickness of movement and apprehension, the strength and suppleness of frame, and the power of experience in all concerned this day, contrasted strangely with images of the bookworm and the professional man at home, who can scarcely use their own limbs and senses, or conceive of any control over external realities. I always thought in America, and I always shall think, that the finest specimens of human development I have seen are in the United States, where every man, however learned and meditative, can ride, drive, keep his own horse, and roof his own dwelling: and every woman, however intellectual, can do, if necessary, all the work of her own house. At home, I had seen one extreme of power, in the meager helpless beings whose prerogative lies wholly in the world of ideas: here I saw the other, where the dominion was wholly over the power of outward nature: and I must say I as heartily wished for the introduction of some good bodily education at home as for intellectual enlightenment here. I have as little hope of the one as of the other; for there is at present no natural necessity for either: and nothing short of natural compulsion will avail. Gymnastic exercises and field sports are matters only of institution and luxury—good as far as they go, but mere conventional trifles in the training of a man or a nation: and, with all our proneness to toil, I see no prospect of any stimulus to wholesome general activity arising out of our civilization. I wish that, in return for our missions to the heathen, the heathens would send missionaries to us, to train us to a grateful use of our noble natural endowments—of our powers of sense and limb, and the functions which are involved in their activity. I am confident that our morals and our intellect would gain inestimably by it. There is no saying how much vicious propensity would be checked, and intellectual activity equalized in us by such a reciprocity with those whose gifts are at the other extreme from our own.

Throughout the four hours of our ascent, I saw incessantly that though much is done by sheer force, —by men enough pulling at a rope strong enough, —some other requisites were quite as essential; — great forecast, great sagacity; much nice management among currents, and hidden and threatening rocks; and much knowledge of the forces and subtilties of wind and water. The men were sometimes plunging, to heave off the boat from a spike or ledge; sometimes swimming to a distant rock, with a rope between their teeth, which they carried round the boulders; —then squatting upon it, and holding the end of the rope with their feet, to leave their hands at liberty for hauling. Sometimes a man dived to free the cable from a catch under water; then he would spring on board, to pole at any critical pass: and then ashore, to join the long file who were pulling at the cable. Then there were their patience and diligence—very remarkable when we went round and round an eddy many times, after all but succeeding, and failing again and again from the malice of the wind. Once this happened for so long, and in such a boisterous eddy, that we began to wonder what was to be the end of it. Complicated as were the currents in this spot, we were four times saved from even grazing the rocks, when, after having nearly got through, we were borne back, and swung round to try again. The fifth time, there came a faint breath of wind, which shook our sail for a moment, and carried us over the ridge of foam. What a shout there was when we turned into still water! The last ascent but one appeared the most wonderful, —the passage was, twice over, so narrow, —barely admitting the kandjia, — the promontory of rock so sharp, and the gush of water so strong; but the big rope, and the mob of haulers on the shore and the islets heaved us up steadily, and as one might say, naturally, —as if the boat took her course advisedly.

Though this passage appeared to us the most dangerous, it was at the last that the Rais of the Cataract interfered to request us to step ashore. We were very unwilling; but we could not undertake the responsibility of opposing the local pilot. He said it was mere force that was wanted here, the difficulty being only from the rush of the waters, and not from any complication of currents. But no man would undertake to say that the rope would hold; and if it did not, destruction was inevitable. The rope held; we saw the boat drawn up steadily and beautifully; and the work was done. Mr. E., who has great experience in nautical affairs, said that nothing could be cleverer than the management of the whole business. He believed that the feat could be achieved nowhere else, as there are no such swimmers elsewhere.

The mob who took charge of us on the rocks were horribly noisy; the granite we trod on was burning hot, shining and slippery: the light, at an hour after noon, was oppressive: and the wildness of the scenery and of the thronging people was bewildering. The clamor was the worst; and for four hours there was no pause. This is, I think, the only thing in the whole affair really trying to a person of good nerves. The cries are like those of rage and fear; and one has to remind one's self incessantly that this is only the people's way: and then the clamor goes for nothing. When they do speak gently, as to us on matters of business, their voices are agreeable enough, and some very sweet. —Most of the throng to-day were quite black: some tawny. One man looked very odd. His complexion was chocolate color, and his breast and top-knot red.

We returned to the boat heated and thirsty, and quite disposed for wine and water. The critical passage of four hours was over; but the Rais of the Cataract did not leave us till we were off Mahatta, there being still much skill and labor required to pass us through the yet troubled waters. Our boat rolled a good deal, having but little ballast as yet: and when we were about to go to dinner, a lurch caused the breakage of some soup plates and other ware: so we put off dinner till we should be at Philœ, where we were to complete our ballast. — Meantime, we had the poor amusement of seeing a fight on shore, — the Rais and his men quarreling about the baksheesh. The pay of the Rais and his men was included in the contract for the kandjia: but of course the Rais asked for baksheesh. He was offered ten piastres, and refused them; then a bottle of wine,

which he put under his arm, demanding the ten piastres too. Then he refused
both, and went off; but returned for the money; and ended by fighting about
the division of it. The amount is small to contend about; but travelers should
remember those who come after them, and the real good of the natives; and not
give way to encroachment, to save a little trouble.

It was four o'clock when we moored at Philœ under what once was the
great landing place of the island, on the east side. The hypæthral temple, vulgarly called Pharaoh's Bed, stood conspicuous on the height above us: and we ran
up to it after sunset, while the last of our ballast was stowing, —glad of every
opportunity of familiarizing our minds with the aspect of the island, before
returning to explore the remains in due order. —We had seen nothing more
beautiful anywhere than what was before us this evening on our departure by
moonlight. The pillars of the open temple first, and then the massive propyla
of the great temple stood up against the soft, clear sky, and palms fringed every
bank, and crowned every little eminence. The wildness of the rocky boundary
was lost by this light. We felt that we had, for the present, done with rapids
and islands: we were fairly in Nubia, and were now passing into the broad full
stream of the Nile, here calmer than ever, from being so near the dam of the
islands. The Lybian range shone distinctly yellow by moonlight. I thought that
I had never heard of color by moonlight before; and I was sure I had never seen
it. Now my eyes feasted on it night by night. The effect of palm clumps standing
up before these yellow back-grounds, which are themselves bounded by a line
of purple hills, with silver stars hanging above them, and mysterious heavenly
lights gushing up from behind all, exceeds in rich softness any coloring that
sunshine can show.

CHAPTER VIII

NUBIA—THE SECOND CATARACT

W E WERE NOT LONG IN FINDING how different Nubia is from the lower part of the Nile valley, both in its aspect and its people. We soon began to admire these poor Berbers, for their industry and thrift, their apparent contentment, and their pleasant countenances. The blue underlip of the women, some tattoo marks here and there, nose rings, and hundreds of tiny braids of hair, all shining and some dripping with castor oil, might seem likely to make these people appear ugly enough to English eyes: but the open good humor of most of their countenances, and the pathetic thoughtfulness of many, rendered them interesting, I may say charming to us; —to say nothing of the likeness we were constantly tracing in them to the most ancient sculptured faces of the temples. The dyed underlip was the greatest drawback; perhaps from its having a look of disease. The women wore silver bracelets almost universally; and a quantity of bead necklaces. They swathed themselves sufficiently in their blue garments without covering their faces. The men wore very little clothing: the children, for the most part, none at all, except that the girls had a sort of leather fringe tied round the loins. Sometimes the people would run away from us, or be on the start to do so, as we were walking on the shore. Sometimes the women would permit us to bid for their necklaces, or would offer matting or baskets for sale. Sometimes we found their huts empty, —left open while the family were out at work: and we were glad of such an opportunity of examining their dwellings, and forming some notion of their household economy.

The first we entered in the absence of the inmates was a neat house, —the walls mud, and narrowing upwards, so as to give the building a slightly pyramidal form. Mud walls, it must be remembered, are in Nubia quite a different affair from what they are in rainy countries. The smooth plastering gives the dwelling a neat appearance, inside and out: and it is so firmly done, and so secure from wet in that climate, as not to crumble away, or, apparently, to give out dust, as it would with us. —The flat roof of this house was neatly made of palm: the stems lying along, and the fronds forming a sort of thatch. A deewán of mud was raised along the whole of both the side walls; and two large jars, not of the same size, were fixed at the end; one, no doubt, to hold water; the other, grain. The large jar for grain is often fixed outside the house, opposite the door: and we were assured that it is never plundered. Some dwellings have partitions, one or two feet high, separating, as we suppose, the sleeping-places of the family. If the peasant has the rare fortune of possessing a cow and calf, or if there is an ox in the establishment, to work the sakia, there is a mud shed, with a flat roof like the house. The fences are of dry millet stalks, which rise from eleven to fourteen feet high. In the garden or field plot is often seen a pillar of stones, whereon stands the slinger, whose business it is to scare away the birds from the crops. The field plot is often no more than a portion of the sloping river bank. At the season of our visit the plots were full of wheat, barley and lupins. The kidney bean, with a purple blossom and very dark leaves, was beautiful: and so were the castor oil and cotton plants.

Behind the dwelling which we visited, the dark stony desert came down to the very path: and among its scattered rocks lay, not at once distinguishable to the eye, the primitive burying ground of the region. The graves were marked out with ovals of stones; and thorns were laid thick on the more recent ones. A dreary place it looked for the dead to lie in: but the view from it was beautiful; and especially of the hedge-like Lybian bank over the river, where the fringe of mimosas was all overgrown and compacted with bindweed of the brightest green.

I do not at present see that much can be done for the Nubians, as there certainly may for the Egyptians. In Egypt, the population once amounted to 8,000,000, or nearly so; while now it is supposed to be not more than 2,500,000: and there seems no reason why it should not, with the knowledge and skill of our own time, rise to what it once was, and exceed it. Everywhere there are tokens, even to the careless eye of a passing traveler, of land let out of cultivation, —yielded up without a struggle to the great old enemy, the Desert; and even to the encroachments of the friendly Nile. There are signs that drainage is as much wanted as irrigation. However much the natural face of the country may be supposed to have changed, there is abundant evidence of wilful and careless lapse. In Nubia it is far otherwise. There, not only are the villages diminutive, —almost too small to be called hamlets, —and the sprinkling of people between them is so scanty as barely to entitle the country to be called inhabited, but this is clearly from the scarcity of cultivable land. That it was always so is hardly conceivable when we think of the number of temples still visible between the first and second cataracts, and the many villages declared by Pliny to have studded both shores: but that it is to be helped now, I do not see how any one can show who has beheld the hopeless yellow desert, with its black volcanic rocks, coming down to the very river. As the people have no raw material for any manufacture, it is not easy to tell how they could prosper by other kinds of industry, if Egypt supplied them ever so plentifully with food. It appeared to us that they were diligent and careful in making the most of what they have. As soon as we crossed their frontier, we saw the piers which they make, —the stone barriers built out into the stream to arrest the mud as it is carried down, and thus obtain new land. There are so many of these as to be mischievous in some parts; as, when these piers are opposite to each other, they alter the currents, and narrow the river. —We saw dusky laborers on the banks, toiling with the hoe, to form the soil into terraces and ledges, so as to make the most of it. From their diligence, it seems as if the Nubians had sufficient security to induce them to work: and their appearance is that of health, cheerfulness and content. What more can be done for them, beyond perhaps improving their simple arts of life, it is difficult to say.

Simple enough, indeed, are their arts. Early one morning, when walking ashore, I came upon a loom which would excite the astonishment of my former fellow-townsmen, the Norwich weavers. A little pit was dug in the earth under a palm; —a pit just big enough to hold the treadles and the feet of the weaver, who sits on the end of the pit. The beam was made of a slender palm stem, fixed into two blocks. The treadles were made of spines of the palm fixed into bits of stick. The shuttle was, I think, a forked twig. The cotton yarn was even, and the fabric good; that is evenly, woven. It was, though coarse, so thin that one might see the light through: but that was intended, and only appropriate to the climate. I might have wondered at such a fabric proceeding from such an apparatus, if I had not remembered the muslins of India, produced in looms as rude as this. It appears too, from the paintings in the tombs, that the old Egyptian looms were of nearly as simple a construction, though the people were celebrated for their exports of fine linen and woolen stuffs. The stout-looking gay checkered sails of the boats, and the diversified dresses of the people represented in the tombs, were no doubt the produce of the rude looms painted up beside them. The baskets made by the Nubians are strong and good. Their mats are neat; but neither so serviceable nor so pretty as those of India: but then these people have not such material as the Hindoos. Their rope making is a pretty sight; —prettier even than an English ropewalk; though that is a treat to the eye. We often saw men thus employed, —one end of their strands being tied to the top of a tall palm, while they stood at the other, throwing the strands round till they would twist no more.

As for the rent paid by the Nubians for their land, —what we learned is this: but it must be observed that it is very difficult, in these countries, to obtain reliable information. In the most civilized parts, there are so few data, and in the more primitive, the people are so little in the habit of communicating with persons who are not familiar with their condition and ways, that it is scarcely possible to find any uniformity of testimony on any matters of custom or arrangement, —even the simplest. When the people tell of their taxes, the English traveler finds them so enormous that he is incredulous, or too indignant to carry away any accurate knowledge of the facts, unless he remembers that taxes in Egypt are not the same thing as taxes in Europe.

As I understand the matter, it is thus, with regard to these Nubians. The Pasha holds the whole land and river of Egypt and Nubia in fee-simple, except as much as he has given away, for its revenues, to favored individuals: and his rents are included in what are called his taxes. In Egypt, the people pay tax on the land. In Nubia, they pay it on the sakias and palms. The palms, when large, pay a piastre and a quarter (about 3d.) each, per annum: when small, three-fourths of a piastre. Each sakia pays a tax of three hundred and fifty piastres, or 3l. 10s.; and the payer may appropriate as much land as the sakia will water. The quantity taken is usually from eight hundred to twelve hundred square yards.

The mode of collecting the taxes is quite another matter. By corruption in the agents, or a bad practice of taking the amount in kind, or on account, the collector fixing the marketable value of the produce, there may be cruel oppression. In Egypt, it is certain this oppression does exist to a dreadful extent. We did not happen to hear of it in Nubia; and I cannot say how it is there. But, be it as it may, it is a different question from the amount of tax.

What the peasant actually pays for is the land, as above mentioned, the water-wheel itself, the excavation in which it works, the shed under which it stands, and the ox or pair of oxen by which it is driven. How far his bargain answers to him must depend on the marketable value of his produce, in a country little affected by variations of seasons. He has not, however, the advantage of an open market. There is nobody at hand to buy, unless by the accident of a trading kandjia coming by; and he has not usually the means of sending far. The tax-collector must therefore commonly be his market; and not such an one as to enable the stranger to estimate his affairs with any accuracy. All we could do was to observe whether he seemed to have enough of his produce left over for the support of his family, and whether his land appeared to be well tilled. I can only repeat that the people we saw in Nubia looked generally healthful and contented; and that they seemed to be making the most of their little belts and corners of cultivable land. It is to be observed, however, that we remarked a great number of ruined villages, and that we could obtain no answer from either dragoman or Rais as to how this happened. They declared they did not know; and, for once, Alee had neither information nor theory to offer. Which was the popular enemy, the desert or the Pasha, I cannot undertake to say.

Our kandjia was hired for twenty-five days, for the sum of 13l. 10s..; this including all the charges of ascending the cataract, and of the crew (eight men) except the steersman. Of these eight men, I think four were from our dahabieh. Our rais and the rest of our crew were left at Aswan, in charge of the boat and such of our property as we did not take with us. Among those whom we carried up were two of our quiet, serviceable Nubians. Among those who remained behind was the buck, as we called him; perhaps the least serviceable of the whole crew, and certainly the least quiet and most troublesome; but he was so extremely amusing with his pranks that we missed him, during this fortnight, more than we should a better lad. Our other buffoon was with us, the cook. An excellent cook he was; but I do not know that he was much else, except a long story-teller and a consummate coxcomb. He was a bad riser in this (to him) winter weather; not a good hand at giving us breakfast early; and we were there-fore not sorry that he declined going through the desert with us afterwards. The manner of declining, however, smacked of his coxcombry. "I!" said he. "I go through the desert to Syria! No, no; it is all very well for these English, whom nobody inquires after, to go and be killed in Syria; but I am a man whose life is of importance to his family. They may go without me." And we went with a better man in his place. During this Nubian voyage, however, he was in his glory— among stranger comrades who would listen to his long stories. As I sat on deck in the evenings, I used to see him at the bows, flattering himself that he was doing his proper work; holding by the wings a poor fluttering turkey about to have his throat cut, and brandishing his great glittering knife, in the energy of his story-telling. How many times have I chafed at the suspense of one poor bird after another, thus held, head downwards, till the magniloquent cook should have finished his anecdote! He fed us well, however, making a variety very honorable to him in the mutton, fowls and eggs which we lived on during the voyage. Beef and veal have been out of the question since the murrain in 1843. Since that time, the cattle have not been enough to work the sakias, and of course there are none for food. Mr. Y. once had the luck to fall in with a piece of beef—at least we were assured it was beef—but the only good we got out of it was a lesson not to look for beef any more. There is great variety to be made out of a sheep, however, as our cook continually proved to us. I have said that he succeeded well in our Christmas plum-pudding. The only fire we had last win-ter was that which he made with a pool of brandy in the middle of our pudding. Almost the only failure he made was with a goose which we got at Thebes. We thought much of this goose, as a change from the everlasting fowls and turkeys;

but the cook boiled it, and it looked anything but tempting. His excuse was that he feared, if he roasted it, that it would be "stiff"—meaning tough.

All the people on board, and we ourselves, found the weather cold in Nubia; that is, in the evenings and mornings, for at noon it was hot enough to make us glad of fans and water-melon. We entered the tropic at three p.m. of December 30th, and from that time till our return, we seemed sentenced to shiver early and late, in cold strong winds, such as we had hardly met with in the more northerly parts of the river. But the mild nights when we were at anchor were delicious— none more so than that of the first day of this year. We sauntered along the camel-track which ran between the shore and the fine overhanging rocks of the Arabian Desert. The brilliant moonlight cast deep shadows on the sand, and showed us what mighty blocks had fallen, and how others were about to fall. These African nights, soft, lustrous and silent, are worth crossing the world to feel. We met a party of three men, a boy and a donkey—one of the men carrying a spear. They returned our greeting courteously, but stopped to look after us in surprise. Their tread and ours was noiseless on the sand, and the only sound within that wide horizon was of a baying dog, far away on the opposite shore.

The next morning we passed Korosko, and saw the surveying flag of M. Arnault, and the tents of his party of soldiers; but we could not learn how his survey and his search for water proceeded, in preparation for his road to the Red Sea. We were passing temples, from stage to stage, all the way up—and very clearly we saw them—each standing on its platform of sand or rock; but we left them all for examination on our return. This return must now be soon; we sighed to think how soon, when we met on the morning of January 3d, the two boats of a party who told us that, if we wished to send letters to England, we must prepare them, as some gentlemen were at Aboo-Simbil, and would presently be passing us. The great temple of Aboo-Simbil, the chief object of our Nubian voyage, and almost at the extremity of it, so near us! It damped our spirits; but we wrote our letters, and before we had done the expected boat came up. We little thought that morning, any of us, that our three parties would join in the desert, and that we should live together in Arabia for five weeks. Yet so it turned out.

I had been watching the winds and the hours in the fear that we should pass Aboo-Simbil in the dark. But when I came on deck, on the morning of the 4th, I found, to my great joy, that we were only a few miles from it, while a fresh breeze was carrying us well on our course. We passed it before breakfast.

The façade is visible from a considerable distance; and as soon as it becomes visible, it fixes the eye by the singularity of such an object as this smoothed recess of the rugged rock. I found it unlike what I expected, and unlike, I thought, all the representations of it that I had seen. The portal looked low in proportion to the colossi; the façade was smaller, or at least narrower, than I had supposed; and the colossi much nearer together. The white-wash which Champollion (it is said) left on the face of the northernmost colossus, has the curious effect of bringing out the expression of countenance, so as to be seen far off. Nothing can be more strange than so extremely distinct a revelation of a face, in every feature, perhaps a mile off. It is stranger than the first apparition of the good-ly profile of the bronze Borromeo, near Lago Maggiore; because not only the outline of the features stands out clear, but every prominence and shadow of the face. The expression of this colossus is very agreeable; it is so tranquil and cheerful. We had not yet experienced the still stranger sensation of seeing a row of statues precisely alike in all respects. We did not feel it now: for one of the faces being white, and another being broken, and many details lost by distance, the resemblance was not complete enough to cause in us that singular emotion.

The smaller temple of "the Lady of Aboshek,"—Athor—beside the large one, is very striking, as seen from the river. The six statues on the facade stand out bold-ly between buttresses; and their reclining backwards against the rock has a curious effect. All about both temples are inscribed tablets, which look like doors opening into the rock. We had now seen, for the first time, a rock temple: and we were glad that it was the noblest that we saw first. In estimating it, we must remember what Ethiopia was to the Egyptians of its time. The inscription "foreign land" is appended to the titles of Athor in the smaller temple: and the establishment of these edifices here is what it would have been to the Romans who, conquering Great Britain, should have carried their most solemn worship to the Orkneys, and enthroned it there in the noblest edifice they could erect. But we could not fully estimate this till we had examined the temple on our return: nor can my readers do so till the time comes for a fuller account of these great works.

The wind was favorable all day, and at night, as we approached Wadee Hal-fa, very strong. It is to be wished that we had some full meteorological reports of these regions, both for the sake of science and the guidance of travelers. Every voyager, I believe, speaks of strong wind, and, in the traveling season, north wind, near Wadee Halfa. Has any one heard of calm weather there? On inquiry, on the spot, we were told that there is almost always a strong wind, and frequent gales: sometimes from the south, but usually from the north. This night we had experience of a Nile gale.

Our sail was rarely tied, any part of the way; and our Nubian Rais had it always held. To-night it was held by a careful personage, who minded his busi-ness. First, our foresail was taken in, as the wind rose. Then we went sounding on, the poles on each side being kept constantly going. Nevertheless, we struck on a sandbank with a great shock, and the main-sail was let fly. Half-a-dozen poor fellows, already shivering with cold, went over the side, and heaved us off. The wind continued to rise; the night was growing dark; and presently we grounded again. The sail was let go; but it would not fly. The wind strengthened; the sail was obstinate, and the men who had sprung aloft to furl it could not get it in. We seemed to be slowly but surely going over: and for several minutes (a long time in such circumstances) it seemed to me that our only chance was in the mudbank on which we had struck being within our depth. But it was a poor chance; for there was deep water and a strong current between us and the shore: and it was in an uninhabited part of the country. Of our own party, no one spoke. Mr. E. was the only one of us who understood these matters; and as he stood on the watch, we would not interrupt him by questions. Indeed, the case was plain enough; and I saw under his calmness that he felt this to be, as he afterwards told me, the most anxious moment of our adventures. Alee flew about giving orders amidst the rush of the wind; and the cook worked at the poling with all his strength. Even at such a moment I could not but be struck with the lights from the kitchen and the cabin shining on the struggling men and restless sail which were descending together to the water, and on the figures of the Rais, Alee and another, as they stood on the gunwale, hauling at a rope which was fastened to the top of the mast. Amidst the many risks of the moment, the chief was that our tackle would not hold: and a crack was heard now and then among other awful noises. By this time, the inclination of the deck was such that it was impossible to stand, and I had to cling with all my strength to the window of the vestibule. For some time, the Rais feared to quit his hold of the rope on the gunwale; but at last he flung it away, threw off his clothes in a single instant, and sprang up the mast like a cat. His strong arms were what was wanted aloft. The sail was got in, and we righted. The standing straight on one's feet was like a strange new sensation after such a peril.

It was still some time before we were afloat again; and our crew were busy in the water till we were quite sorry for them. When we drifted off at last, our sail was spread again, and we went seething on through the opposing currents to find our proper anchorage at Wadee Halfa. And there again we had almost as much difficulty as before in getting in our sail. This is the worst of the latteen sails which look so pretty, and waft one on so well. We were wrenched about, and carried down some way before we could moor.

The next morning was almost as cold as the night: but we preferred this to heat, as our business to-day was to ride through the western desert to the rock of Abooseer—the furthest point of our African travel. Before breakfast, the gentlemen took a short walk on shore, being carried over the intervening mud. They saw a small village, and a school of six scholars. The boys wrote, to the master's dictation, with reed pens, on tablets of wood, smoothed over with some white substance. They wrote readily, and apparently well. The lesson was from the Kurán; and the master delivered it in a chanting tone. Two extremely small asses were brought down, to cross with us to the western bank. We crossed in a ferry-boat, whose sail did not correspond very well with the climate. It was like a lace veil mended with ticking. Our first visit was to the scanty remains of an interesting old temple near the landing-place. On our way to it, we passed some handsome children, and a charming group of women under a large syc-amore. We thought the people we saw here— (the most southerly we should ever see)—open-faced and good-looking. There are large cattle-yards and sheds in this scarcely-inhabited spot, which the Pasha has made a halting-place for his droves of cattle from Dongola. He continues to import largely from thence, to make up his losses from the murrain of 1843. We saw two large droves of as noble beasts as can be seen.

Near the remains of two other unmarked and less interesting buildings stand the columns of the temple begun, if not wholly erected by two of the Theban kings, soon after the expulsion of the Shepherd race. The dates exist in the hieroglyphic inscriptions of the pillars. This temple was built when the great edifices of Thebes were, for the most part, unthought of. El-Karnac was begun—its more humble halls; and El-Uksur might be surveyed, by that time, as a fitting site for a temple to answer to El-Karnac, but the El-Kurneh temple and the Ramaseum were not conceived of; for the sovereigns who built them were not born. The Memnon statues were yet in the quarry. The Pyramids were, it is now thought, about two thousand years old: and about this time Moses was watching the erection of the great obelisk (which we call Cleopatra's Needle) at Heliopolis, where he studied. If learned men are right in saying that the Philis-tines[17] were of the race expelled from Thebes, they had, by the time this temple was built, settled themselves under the Lebanon and along the southern Syrian coasts, whence they were to be driven out when Moses should be in his grave. If, as some poets tell, Egyptus and Cadmus were among the Shepherd intruders driven out from the Thebaid, the fifty nieces of the one had by this time mur-dered his sons, their husbands, and the dragon's teeth of the other had sprung up into armed men. It is worth while to mention such fables as these last under their assigned dates; because we learn thereby to value as we ought the tangible and reliable records we meet in the Egyptian monuments, in contrast with the dim traditions of later born nations. We may also gather useful hints on the

17   Herodotus tells us (II. 128) that the Egyptians so hated the Pharaohs who built the two largest pyramids, that they would not produce their names; but called those edifices "by the name of the shepherd Philitis, who in those times led his flocks to pasture in their neighborhood." Is the slyness of this notices attributable to the priests or the prudential historian?

history and philosophy of art and science, from the mythi and the monuments together. There is writing on this temple: there is writing on the much-older Pyramids: and it was only at the time of the erection of this temple that letters were carried into Greece. Here is a pillar which is believed to have suggested, in a subsequent age, the Doric column; the oldest of Greek pillars. Here it stands, remarkable for its many-sided form. It was to us now the oldest we had ever seen; but we afterwards saw some, more precisely what is called Doric, in the tombs of Benee Hasan. The columns of this temple are little more than bases. They are nearly all of the same height: some like mere heaps of stone; others bearing uninjured inscriptions. They are small remains: but long may they last! They are the ultimate record of their kind on the ordinary route of Nile travelers, and usually the first subject to their examination.

Our ride to the rock of Abooseer occupied an hour and a half. Thanks to the cool north wind, we highly enjoyed it. Our way lay through a complete desert, over sand hills, and among stony tracts, where scarcely a trace of vegetation is to be seen. In such places the coloquintus is a welcome object, with its thick, milky leaves and stalks, and its velvet blossom. The creeping, thorny coloquintida, too, with its bitter apples, is a handsome plant: or it looked so to us, in the absence of others. Here and there amidst the dreary expanse, or half hidden in some sandy dell, lay the bleached skeleton of a camel. The only living things seen were a brood of partridges and a jerboa, — a graceful and most agile little creature, whose long extended tail, with its tufted end, gave it a most distinctive appearance. Some of our people started off in pursuit, and would not give up for a long time, making extreme efforts to keep the little creature in view, and drive it in one another's way; but it baffled them at last, and got back to its hole.

We rode to the foot of the rock of Abooseer, and then ascended it—in rather heavy spirits, knowing that this was to be our last look southwards. The summit was breezy and charming. I looked down the precipice on which I stood, and saw a sheer descent to the Nile of two hundred feet. The waters were gushing past the foot of this almost perpendicular crag: and from holes in its strata flew out flocks of pigeons, blue in the sunshine. The scene all round under that wide heaven was wild beyond description. There was no moving creature visible but ourselves and the pigeons; and no trace of human habitation but the ruins of two mud huts, and of a white building on the Arabian shore. The whole scene was composed of desert, river, and black basaltic rocks. Round to the north, from the south-west, there is actually nothing to be seen but blackish, sand-streaked rocks near at hand, and sandy desert further off. To the north-east, the river winds away, blue and full, between sands. Two white sails were on it at the moment. From the river, a level sand extended to the soft-tinted Arabian hills, whose varied forms and broken lights and shadows were on the horizon nearly from the north round to the south-east. These level sands then give place to a black rugged sur face, which extends to where two summits, —to-day of a bright amethyst hue, —close the circuit of vision. These summits are at a considerable distance on the way to Dongola. The river is hidden among the black rocks to the south, and its course is not traceable till it peeps out, blue and bright, in two or three places, and hides itself again among the islets. It makes a great bend while thus hidden, and reappears much more to the east. It has now reached the part properly called the Second Cataract; and it comes sweeping down towards the rock on which we stood, dashing and driving among its thousand islets, and then gathering its thousand currents into one, to proceed calmly on its course. Its waters were turbid in the rapids, and looked as muddy where, they poured down from shelf or boulder as in the Delta itself; but in all its calm reaches it reflected the sky in a blue so deep as it would not do to paint. The islets were of fantastic forms, —worn by the cataracts of ages: but still, the outlines were angular, and the black ledges were graduated by the action of the waters, as if they had been soft sand. On one or two islands I saw what I at first took for millet-patches: but they were only coarse grass and reeds. A sombre brownish tamarisk, or dwarfed mimosa, put up its melancholy head here and there; and this was all the vegetation apparent within that wide horizon. —I doubt whether a more striking scene than this, to English eyes, can be anywhere found. It is thoroughly African, thoroughly tropical, very beautiful, —most majestic, and most desolate. Something of the impression might be owing to the circumstances of leave-taking under which we looked abroad from our station: but still, if I saw this scene in an unknown land in a dream, I am sure I should be powerfully moved by it. This day, it certainly interested me more than the First Cataract.

I was tempted by the invitation of a sort of cairn on the top of a hill not far inland, to go there; and thence I obtained another glimpse of the Lybian Desert, and saw two more purple peaks rising westwards, soft and clear.

There is a host of names carved on the accessible side of Abooseer. We looked with interest on Belzoni's and some few others. We cut ours with a nail and hammer. Here, and here only, I left my name. On this wild rock, and at the limit of our range of travel, it seemed not only natural, but right to some who may come after us. Our names will not be found in any temple or tomb. If we ever do such a thing, may our names be publicly held up to shame, as I am disposed to publish those of the carvers and scribblers who have forfeited their right to privacy by inscribing their names where they can never be effaced!

The time arrived when we must go. It was with a heavy heart that I quitted the rock, turned my back on the south, and rode away. We found our boat prepared in the usual manner for the descent of the river—the mainmast removed, and laid along overhead, to support the awning; the kitchen shifted and turned; and the planks of the decks taken up to form seats for the rowers, so as sadly to restrict our small space. One of our dishes at dinner was an excellent omelette, made of part of the contents of an ostrich's egg. Two of these eggs were bought for six piastres, (1s. 2d.) The contents were obtained by boring a hole with a gimlet. The contents of this egg were found to be equal to twenty-nine of the small hen's eggs of this part of the country.

We began our return voyage about 6 p.m., floating, sometimes broadside down, and sometimes in towards the bank, when it became the business of the rowers to bring us out again into the middle of the stream. The wind was hostile, cold, and strong enough to be incessantly shoving us aside. Our progress was very slow. The first night we moored at six miles only from Wadee Halfa.

The next evening (January 6th) we were within half an hour of Aboo-Simbil, when duty ordered me to my cabin. When I left the deck, the moon had risen, the rocks were closing in, and the river was like a placid lake.

In the morning we were to enter upon a new kind of life, as travelers. We were to begin our course of study of the Monuments.

CHAPTER IX

HISTORICAL SKETCH, FROM MENES TO THE ROMAN OCCUPATION OF EGYPT.

BEFORE ENTERING UPON THE STUDY OF THE MONUMENTS, it seems necessary to obtain something like an orderly view of the state of the country before and during their erection. At best, our conceptions must be obscure enough; but we can form none unless we arrange in our minds what we know of the history of Egypt, of which these monuments are at once the chief evidence and the eternal illustration.

The early history of Egypt differs from that of every other explored country in the nature of its records. Elsewhere, we derive all our knowledge from popular legends, which embody the main ideas to be preserved in forms which are not, and were never meant to be historically true. It is the business of the philosophical historian to separate the true ideas from their environment of fiction, and to mark the time when the narrative, from being mythical becomes historically true—to classify the two orders of ancient historians—both inestimable in their way—the Poets who perpetuate national Ideas, and the Historians who perpetuate national Facts. With regard to Egypt, we are in possession of as much of this early material as any nation has furnished; and we have the monuments besides.

These monuments consist of buildings or excavations—of the sculptures upon them—and of their inscriptions. From the edifices or caves we may learn much of the condition, mind, and manners of the people who wrought them, and, if their dates can be obtained, in historical order. From their sculptures we may learn much of the personages, divine and human, about whom they thought most; and their inscriptions are of inestimable use in identifying these personages, and in declaring their dates. Being thus in possession of mythical legends, of the writings of historians, and of edifices and excavations covered with sculptures and inscriptions, we are as well supplied with records of the early history of Egypt as we can probably ever be with regard to any ancient people; and better than we yet are with regard to any other of the nations of the old world.

The legends relating to ancient Egypt are preserved in the works of its historians. It is the business of modern inquirers to separate them from the true historical material, and to extract from them, where possible, the essential Ideas which they embody.

The chief historians of Egypt are Hecatæus of Miletus, who was at Thebes about half a century before Herodotus, and some fragments of whose writings have come down to us: —Herodotus, from whom we learn more than from any other: —the writer of the book of Genesis: —Hecatæus of Abdera, from whose narrative extracts may be found in the works of Diodorus Siculus—Manetho, an Egyptian, of whom also we have only extracts in other authors; but who supplies very valuable information—Eratosthenes of Cyrene, whose writings are at once illustrative of those of Manetho and a check upon them; Diodorus Siculus, who traveled in Egypt, and wrote a history of it, rather more than half a century before the Christian era; Strabo, who has left us a full account of what he saw in Egypt, between Alexandria and the First Cataract—and Abdallatif, an Arabian physician, who supplies a valuable report of the state of the Nile Valley and its people when he visited them in the twelfth century. It is the business of modern inquirers to separate what these historians derived from the depositories of the national mythi from what they personally observed; to compare their works with one another, and to apply them as a key (where this can be done), to the monumental records.

As to the use of the monumental records, several precautions are necessary. Modern inquirers must beware of interpreting what they see by their own favorite ideas, —as travelers do who contrive to see Hebrew groups among the Egyptian sculptures: —they must diligently and patiently work out the knowledge of the ancient language and its signs, and beware of straining the little they know of these, to accommodate any historical theory they may carry in their minds: —and they must remember that the edifice and its sculptures are not always of the same date, and that therefore what is true of the one is not necessarily true of the other.

Without going into any detail (which would fill a volume if entered upon at all) about the respective values of these authorities, and their agreements and conflicts, I may give a slight sketch of what competent modern inquirers believe we have learned from them.

For our first glimpse into ancient Egyptian life we must go back upon the track of Time far further than we have been accustomed to suppose that track to extend. People who had believed all their lives that the globe and man were created together, were startled when the new science of geology revealed to them the great fact that man is a comparatively new creation on the earth, whose oceans and swamps and jungles were aforetime inhabited by monsters never seen by human eye but in their fossil remains. People who enter Egypt with the belief that the human race has existed only six thousand years, and that at that date, the world was uninhabited by men, except within a small circuit in Asia, must undergo a somewhat similar revolution of ideas. All new research operates to remove further back the date of the formation of the Egyptian empire. The differences between the dates given by legendary records and by modern research (with the help of contemporary history) are very great: but the one agrees as little as the other with the popular notion that the human race is only six thousand years old.

When Hecatæus of Miletus was at Thebes, about 500 B. C., he spoke, as Herodotus tells us,[18] to the priests of Amun, of his genealogy, declaring himself to be the sixteenth in descent from a god. Upon this, the priest conducted him into a great building of the temple, where they pointed out to him (as afterwards to Herodotus) the statues of their high priests. Each high priest placed a colossal wooden statue of himself in this place during his life; and each was the son of his predecessor. The priests would not admit that any of these was the son of a god. From first to last they were of human origin; and here in direct lineal succession, were 345. Taking the average length of human life, how many thousand years would be occupied by the succession of 345 high priests, in a direct line from father to son! According to the priests, it was nearly 5000 years from the time of Horus. They further informed Herodotus that gods did reign in Egypt before they deputed their power to mortals.[19] They spoke of eight gods who reigned first, —among whom was one answering to Pan of the Greeks; then came twelve of another series: and again, twelve more, the offspring of the second series: and of these Osiris was one; and it was not till after the reign of his son Horus that the first of these 345 high priests came into power. From Osiris to king Amasis, the priests reckoned 15,000 years, declaring that they had exact registers of the successive lives which had filled up the time.[20] Such is the legendary history, as it existed 500 years before Christ. We can gather from it thus much, —that the priests then looked back upon a long reach of time, and believed the art of registering to be of an old date.

Here we have the earliest report of dates offered us. According to the latest researches,[21] we cannot place the formation of the Egyptian empire under

18   Herod. II. 143.
19   Herod. II. 144, 146.
20   Ibid. 145.
21   Bunsen. "Egypt's Place in the World's History."

Menes, nearer to us than 5500 years ago. And the Egyptians were then a civilized people, subject to legislation and executive authority, pursuing trade, and
capable of the arts. A longer or shorter series of centuries must be allotted for
bringing them up to this state, according to the views of the students of social
life: but the shortest must bring us back to the current date of the creation of
man. How these five or six thousand years are filled up, we may see hereafter.

Leaving it to my readers to fix for themselves the point of time for our
survey of the most ancient period of Egyptian history, I may be permitted to
appoint the place. Let us take our stand above the Second Cataract; —on the
rock of Abooseer, perhaps, where I could only look over southwards, and not
go and learn. This is a good station, because it is a sort of barrier between two
chains of monuments: a frontier resting-place, whence one may survey the area
of ancient Egyptian civilization from end to end.

Looking down the river, northwards, beyond the Nubian region (then
Ethiopia) beyond the First Cataract, and far away over the great marsh which
occupied the Nile valley, we see, coming out of the darkness of oblivion, Menes,
the first Egyptian king, turning the river from its course under the Lybian
mountain into a new bed, in the middle of the valley.[22] Thus the priests of Thebes told Herodotus; saying that Menes made the dykes, by which the land was
reclaimed, on which Memphis afterwards stood. It must strike every one that
this period, 5500 years ago, must have been one of an advanced civilization;
such a work as this embankment requiring scientific ideas and methods, apt
tools, and trained men. The priests ascribed to this same king the building of
Memphis, and of the great temple of Phthah (answering to Vulcan) in that city.
They read to Herodotus a long list of sovereigns (three hundred and thirty) who
succeeded Menes; of whom one was an Egyptian woman, and eighteen were
Ethiopian kings.[23] That there should have been a temple of Phthah implies the
establishment of a priesthood. That a woman should have occupied the throne,
seems to imply the establishment of a principle of hereditary succession; or at
least, it tells of the subordination, in this early age, of force to authority. That
there should have been Ethiopian sovereigns among the Egyptian implies a relation between the two countries, whether of warfare or commerce. During all
this time, the plain of Thebes lay bare.

The next sovereignty that was established in the valley was at This, about
sixty miles below Thebes. A succession of monarchs reigned here—some say
sixteen, some more—while the plain of Thebes still lay bare.

While these sovereigns were reigning at This, and before Thebes was heard
of, the kings of Memphis were building the Pyramids of Geezeh. It is certain

22   Herod. II. 99.
23   Ibid. 100.

that the builders of these pyramids were learned men. How much science is requisite for the erection of such edifices need hardly be pointed out; —the mathematical skill and accuracy; the astronomical science shown in the placing of them true to the cardinal points; the command of mechanical powers which are at this day unknown to us; and the arts of writing and decoration shown in the inscriptions which covered their outside in the days of Herodotus:[24] though the casing which contained them is now destroyed. In the neighboring tombs, however, we have evidence, as will be shown here after, of the state of some of the arts at that date: and I may mention here that the sign of the inkstand and reed-pen are among the representations in the tombs. There is no doubt as to who built the Pyramids. Colonel Howard Vyse found the kings' names inscribed in them. When the Pyramids were built, it was a thousand years before Abraham was born, and the plain of Thebes still lay bare.

Now we must turn southwards, and look over as far as Dongola. For a long way above the Second Cataract, there are no monuments. This is probably owing to the river not being navigable there, so that there were no trading stations. There are obvious reasons why temples and other monuments should rise where commerce halts, where men congregate, and desire protection of person and property, and exercise their social passions and affections. So, for the twenty-five days' journey where the river is impracticable, there are no monuments. Then some occur of rather a modern dale: and far beyond them—up in Dongola—we come upon traces of a time when men were trafficking, building, and worshiping, while yet the plain of Thebes lay bare. To this point did the sovereigns of Memphis and of This extend their hand of power; erecting statues as memorials of themselves, and by their subjects, trading in such articles of use and luxury as they derived from the east. While the Ethiopian subjects of these early Pharaohs were building up that character for piety and probity which spread over the world, and found its way into the earliest legends and poems of distant nations, the plain of Thebes still lay wild and bare; —not one stone yet placed upon another.

And now, the time had arrived for the Theban kings to arise, give glory to the close of the Old Monarchy, and preserve the national name and existence during the thousand years of foreign domination which were to follow. In the course of reigns at which we have now arrived, El-Karnac began to show its massive buildings, and the plain of Thebes to present temptation to a foreign conqueror.

We have now arrived at the end of the First great Period of ascertained Egyptian history; —a period supposed, from astronomical calculation and critical research, to comprehend 889 years. A dark and humiliating season was now drawing on.

24   Ibid. 125.

Considering the great wealth and power of the kings now reigning at Memphis and at Thebes, we are obliged to form a high opinion of the strength of the Shepherd Race who presently subdued Egypt. Whence they came, no one seems to know—further than that it was somewhere from the East. Whether they were Assyrians, as some have conjectured, or the Phoenicians who were encroaching upon the Delta at a subsequent time, or some third party, we cannot learn, the Egyptians having always, as is natural, kept silence about them. The pride of the Egyptians was in their agriculture and commerce; and to be conquered by a pastoral people, whose business lay anywhere among the plains of the earth, rather than in the richly-tilled, narrow valley of the Nile, was a hard stroke of adversity for them. So, in their silence, all that we know of their strong enemy is that the Shepherd Race took Memphis, put garrisons in all the strong places of Egypt, made the kings of Memphis and Thebes tributary to them, and held their empire for 929 years: that is, for a time equal to that which extends from the death of our King Alfred to our own; a long season of subjugation, from which it is wonderful that the native Egyptian race should have revived. This dark season, during which the native kings were not absolutely dethroned, but depressed and made tributary, is commonly called the Middle Monarchy. It is supposed to extend from b. c. 2754 to b. c. 1825.

About this time, a visitor arrived in Egypt, and remained a short while, whose travels are interesting to us, and whose appearance affords a welcome rest to the imagination, after its wanderings in the dim regions of these old ages. The richest of the Phoenicians who found themselves restricted for room and pasturage by the numbers of Chaldeans who moved westwards into Syria, found their way, through Arabia, to the abundance of corn which Lower Egypt afforded. Among these was Abraham, a man of such wealth and distinction that he and his followers were entertained as guests at Memphis, and his wife was lodged in the palace of the king. He must have looked up at the Pyramids, and learned some of the particulars which we, following on his traces, long in vain to know: —how they were reared, and for what purpose precisely; and perhaps many details of the progress of the work. It is true, these pyramids had then stood somewhere about 1500 years: the builders, tens of thousands in number, had slept for many centuries in their graves; the kings who had reared them lay embalmed in the stillness of ages, and the glory of a supremacy which had passed away; and these edifices had become so familiar to the eyes of the inhabitants, that they were like natural features of the landscape: but as Abraham walked round those vast bases, and looked up at the smooth pictured surfaces of their sides, he might have had explained to him those secrets of ancient civilization which we seek to pry into in vain.

We now come to the brilliant Third Period.

The Theban kings had been growing in strength for some time; and at length they were able to rise up against the Shepherd Race, and expel them from Memphis, and afterwards from their stronghold, Abaris. On the surrender of this last place, the enemy were permitted to march out of the country in safety, —the number of their men being recorded as 240,000. The period of 1300 years now entered upon was the grandest of Egyptian history, —if, we may add, the Sesostris of old renown was, as some recent students have supposed, the Ramases II. of this Period. Some high authorities, as Lepsius and Bunsen, believe Sesostris to have belonged to the Old Monarchy. However this may be, all agree that the deeds of many heroes are attributed to the one who now bears the name of Sesostris; and the achievements of Ramases the Great are quite enough to glorify his age, whether he had a predecessor like himself or not. Of these achievements I shall say nothing here, as they will come before us quite often enough in our study of the temples. Suffice it that the empire of Egypt was extended by conquest southwards to Abyssinia; westward over Lybia; northwards over Greece; and eastwards beyond the banks of the Ganges. The rock statues and stelæ of Sesostris may yet be seen in countries far apart, but within this range: his Babylonian captives were employed on some of the great edifices we have seen, and were afterwards permitted to build a city for themselves near the point of the Delta: and the tributary kings and chiefs of all the conquered countries were required to come up to Egypt once a year, to pay homage by drawing the conqueror's chariot, in return for which they received gifts and favor. The kings of Lower Egypt appear to have declined about this period; if even they were not tributary to those of Upper Egypt. Of these kings, one was he who received Joseph into favor,[25] and made him his prime minister; and another was he who afterwards "knew not Joseph." Of Joseph's administration of the affairs of Lower Egypt we know more than of the rule of any other minister of the Pharaohs. I have walked upon the mounds which cover the streets of Memphis, through which Joseph rode, on occasion of his investiture, and where the king's servants ran before him, to bid the people bow the knee. And when at Heliopolis, I was on the spot where he married his wife, —the daughter of the priest and governor of On, afterwards Heliopolis.

It was in the early part of this Third Period of the Egyptian Monarchy that Cecrops is supposed (fable being here mingled with history) to have led a colony from Saïs, and to have founded the kingdom of Athens,[26] beginning here the long series of obligations that Greece, and through Greece Rome and the world, have been under to Egypt. It is almost overpowering to the imagination to contemplate the vast antiquity of the Egyptian empire, already above two thousand

25   Supposed about B.C. 1706.
26   B.C. 1556.

years, in the day when Cecrops was training his band of followers, to lead them in search of a place whereon to build Athens; —in a day long preceding that when Ceres was wandering about the earth in search of her daughter.

It was about this time that a still more important event than even the founding of Athens had taken place. We all know how a certain Egyptian lady went out one day to bathe, and what was found by her maidens in a rushy spot on the banks of the Nile. That lady was the daughter of one of the Pharaohs of Memphis, at a time, (as some think,) shortly before the union on one head of the crowns of Upper and Lower Egypt. When she brought home the child found among the rushes, she little thought that that infant head was to become the organ of a wisdom that should eclipse the glory of Sesostris, and mainly determine the spiritual destinies of the human race, for a longer course of centuries than even Egypt had yet seen.

When the Shepherd Kings and their army were driven out of Egypt, many of their people remained as slaves, and were employed on the public works. The Hebrews were also thus employed; —latterly on the fortifications of Thoum and Heliopolis; and the Egyptians confounded the two races of aliens in a common hatred. From the prevalence of leprosy among the Hebrews, and other causes, they were considered an unclean people; and they were sent by the Pharaoh of their day, under the warning of the priests, to live by themselves in the district allotted to them. Whether the Pharaoh who opposed the departure of this army of slaves was Thothmes III., or his son, Amunoph II., or some later king, is undetermined; but it is believed on high authority that it was Thothmes III[27] and that he reigned many years after the Exodus. The date of the Exodus is agreed upon as about B.C. 1491, whoever was the Pharaoh reigning at the time. There is no assertion in the Mosaic narrative, that Pharaoh himself was lost in the Red Sea,[28] nor that the whole of his host perished: nor is there any allusion in the Song of Moses to the death of the sovereign: and some of the Hebrew traditions declare[29] that Pharaoh survived, and extended his conquests afterwards into Assyria. Thus the supposition that the Israelites marched out in the early year of the reign of this monarch is not irreconcilable with his having reigned thirty-nine years, as Egyptian history declares that he did. Manetho mentions their numbers to have been eighty thousand when they were sent to live by themselves: and it is curious on this account, and on some others, to find the number assigned by the Mosaic history so high as six hundred thousand, besides women and children. Even if we suppose a proportion of these to have been their fellow-slaves of the Shepherd Race, who, being confounded with

27   Wilkinson's Ancient Egyptians, I. p. 54.
28   Ibid, I. p. 55.
29   Pictorial History of Palestine, I. p. 186.

the Hebrews by their masters, took this opportunity of leaving the country, it gives us a high idea of the power and population of Egypt in those days that such a body could be abstracted from the working class of the country, and leave behind a sufficient force for the achievement of such wars and arts as we know were prosecuted after their departure.[30]

As our chief interest in Egypt was till lately from its being the scene of the early life of the Hebrew nation, we are apt to look for records of the Hebrews on the monuments wherever we go. I am convinced that none have been found relating to their connection with Egypt: — none relating to them at all, till the long subsequent time when Jerusalem was conquered by Sheshonk (Shishak). In my opinion, it would be more surprising if there had been such records than that there are not. There is nothing in the presence of a body of slaves to require or suggest a monumental record, unless those slaves were made so by conquest, and had previously been a nation. The Hebrews were not a nation, and had no dream of being so till Moses began the mighty work of making them one. When they had a confirmed national existence; when their great King Solomon had married into the line of the Pharaohs, and their national interests came into collision with those of Egypt, we find them, among other nations, in the train of the captives of Sheshonk, on the walls of El-Karnac. Some Hebrew names among those of the Egyptian months,[31] and a sprinkling of Hebrew words in the Coptic language (which might have found their way there afterwards), are, I believe, the only traceable memorials in Egypt of the residence of the Israelites.

According to Pliny, one of the Ramases was on the throne of Egypt when Troy was taken: and within thirty years of that time, King Solomon married a daughter of one of the Pharaohs. —How great Thebes had long been is clear from the mention of Upper Egypt in Homer, who says, perhaps truly enough in one sense, that it was the birthplace of some of the Greek gods; and that its inhabitants were so wise as to be favorites, and even hosts of those gods. It was with these wise Thebans (then one with the Ethiopians) that Jupiter and his family were supposed by the Greeks to be making holiday, when out of reach, as it seemed, of the prayers of the besiegers of Troy. —The Theban family of monarchs, however, was by this lime declining in power; and after a century or two of weakness, they were displaced by stronger men from a higher station up the river; and Egypt was governed by princes from the hitherto

30   It is probable that no one will content for the accuracy of the numbers as they stand in the Mosaic history; for, taking the longest term assigned for the residence of the Hebrews in Egypt, —430 years, — and supposing the most rapid rate of increase known in the world, their numbers could not have amounted to one-third of that assigned.

31   Sharpe's History of Egypt, p. 37.

subordinate province of Ethiopia. In three generations, Thebes ceased to be the capital of Egypt; and the seat of government was removed to Saïs in the Delta. This event happened nearly 700 years B. C. From this time, we have the advantage of certainty of dates, within, at least, the range of a few months. We have come down to the record of Babylonian eclipses, and the skies light up the history of the earth.

It was in this age that the downfall of old Egypt was provided for by the introduction of Greek influences into the Delta, at the time when the seat of sovereignty was there. While the national throne stood at Thebes, the religion, philosophy, learning and language of the ancient race could be little, if at all, affected by what was doing in other parts of the world: but when the Thebaid became a province, and the metropolis was open to visits from the voyagers of the Mediterranean, the exclusively Egyptian character began to give way; and while Egypt furnished, through these foreigners, the religion, philosophy, and art of the whole civilized world, she was beginning to lose the nationality which was her strength. Nechepsus, one of the kings of Saïs, was a learned priest, and wrote on astronomy. His writings were in the Greek language. The kings of Saïs now began to employ Greek mercenaries. Psammitichus I. not only employed as soldiers large numbers of Ionian and Carian immigrants, but, as Herodotus tells us,[32] committed to them the children of the Egyptians, to be taught Greek, and gave them lands and other advantages for settlement in the Delta. Of course, this was displeasing to his native subjects, and the national unity was destroyed. One curious circumstance occurred under this king, which reveals much of the popular temper, and which has left some remarkable traces behind it, —as will be seen in my next chapter. Psammitichus placed three armies of Egyptians on the three frontiers of Egypt.[33] That on the southern frontier, stationed at Elephantine, grew impatient, after a neglect of three years. Finding their petitions for removal unanswered, and their pay not forthcoming, they resolved to emigrate, and away they marched, up the river, as far beyond Meroë as Meroë is beyond Elephantine, —and there lands were given them, where their descendants were found, three centuries afterwards. The king himself pursued and overtook them, and endeavored by promises and prayers, and by appeals to them not to forsake their gods and their homes, to induce them to return. They told him, however, that they would make homes for themselves, and marched on. Their numbers being, as Herodotus tells, two hundred and forty thousand men, it was impossible to constrain them. The king took with him a force of Greek mercenaries, whom he sent some way, as we shall see by and by, after the deserters; but it appears that he did not go higher than Elephantine.

32   Herod. II. 154.

33   Ibid. 30.

While we thus see how Egypt became weakened in preparation for downfall, it is pretty clear, on the other hand, how the process went on by which the rest of the world became enlightened by her knowledge, and ripened by her wisdom.

About thirty years after Saïs became the capital of Egypt, the first of the Wise Men of Greece, Thales, was born. He went to Egypt to improve his knowledge, —and remarkable, indeed, was the knowledge he brought away. He was the first Greek who predicted an eclipse. He forewarned his Ionian countrymen of that celebrated eclipse which, when it happened, suspended the battle between the Medes and Lydians. It was Thales, we are told, who, after his return from Egypt, fixed the sun's orbit, or determined the duration of the year to be 365 days. It was in Egypt that he obtained his knowledge of Geometry: and he it was who imparted, on his return, the great discovery that the angle in a semicircle is always a right angle. In Egypt he ascertained the elevation of the pyramids by observing the shadows of measurable objects in relation to their height. His connection with Egypt gives us a new interest in his theories of creation or existence. He gave the name of Life to every active principle, as we should call it; and in this sense, naturally declared that the universe was "full of gods." At the same time, he is reported by tradition to have said, "The most ancient of things existing is God; for he is uncreated: the most beautiful thing is the universe, for it is God's creation." Men in Greece wondered at him for saying what would not surprise even the common men in Egypt in his day, that Death does not differ from Life.

About the same time came a sober thinking man from Greece to Egypt, to exchange a cargo of olive-oil from Athens for Egyptian corn and luxuries from the east. After this thoughtful man had done his commercial business, he remained to see what he could of the country and people. He conversed much with a company of priests at Saïs, who taught him, as Plato tells us, much history, and some geography, and evidently not a little of law. His countrymen profited on his return by his studies at Saïs; for this oil-merchant was Solon the lawmaker. One of his laws is assigned immediately to an Egyptian origin; that by which every man was required to give an account to the magistrate of his means of livelihood. As for the geography which Solon might learn at Saïs, there is the testimony of Herodotus that King Necho, the predecessor of Psammitichus I., sent a maritime expedition by the Red Sea, which circumnavigated Africa, and returned by the Pillars of Hercules.[34] Plato tells us that one of Solon's priestly friends, Sonchis, told him of some Atlantic isles, beyond the Pillars of Hercules, which were larger than Asia and

34   Herod. IV. 42. A strong indication of the truth of this story is found in the simple remark of Herodotus that he cannot believe the navigators in one of their assertions, —that they had the sun on their right hand.

Africa united. This sets one thinking whether the Egyptians had not some notion of the existence of America.

Within seventy years or so of Solon's visit to Egypt, a truly great man followed on his traces. Pythagoras was unsatisfied with all that could be learned from teachers at home, —from Thales downwards, — and went to Egypt to study philosophy and morals. He was introduced to King Amasis at Saïs by letters from Polycrates. There is no saying how much of the philosophy of Pythagoras is derived, and how much original: nor, of that which is derived, how much he owed to intercourse with the sages of Chaldæa and other countries. But I think no one who has felt an interest in the study of what is known of the Pythagorean philosophy, can fail to be reminded of the philosopher at every step in those chambers of the tombs at Thebes which relate to life and death subjects. Where the paintings treat of the constitution of things, the regions which the soul of man may inhabit, and the states through which it may pass, one feels that Pythagoras might have been the designer of them, if he were not a learner from them. I strongly suspect it would be found, if the truth could be known, that more of the spiritual religion, the abstruse philosophy, and the lofty ethics and political views of the old Egyptians have found their way into the general mind of our race through Pythagoras than by any or all other channels, except perhaps the institutions of Moses, and the speculations of Plato. Some traditions, among the many which exist in relation to this, the first man who assumed the title of philosopher, report him to have lived twenty years in the Nile valley; and then to have been carried off prisoner to Babylon, on the Persian invasion of Egypt.

This brings us near to the close of the great Third Period of Egyptian history. Before the Persians came, however, Hecatæus of Miletus, mentioned before as the earliest historical authority, went up to Thebes. I have spoken already of what he saw and heard there.

Cyrus was meanwhile meditating a renewal of the old wars between Babylon and Egypt, which had formerly been all to the glory of the Pharaohs. Before his death, Cyrus took Cyprus from the Egyptians: and he bequeathed the task of conquering Egypt itself to his son Cambyses. —The wise and fortunate King Amasis died before Cambyses reached Egypt: and with him, the third period of Egyptian history may be said to have expired; for his son Psammenitus could make so little resistance, that he had completed his surrender to the foolish and cruel conqueror before he had been on the throne six months.

We have now reached the mournful close of the great Third Period of Egyptian history; and there is little to dwell on in the succeeding two hundred years, when Egypt was a province of Persia. Upper Egypt never rose again. If there had been any strength or spirit left in her, she might have driven out Cambyses; for his folly left him open to almost any kind or degree of resistance from man or nature. Nature did her utmost to avenge the conquered people: but they could not help themselves. Cambyses set out for Ethiopia with his Persians, leaving his Greek troops to defend the Delta: but he made no provision for his long march southwards; and his soldiers, after exhausting the country, and killing their beasts of burden for food, began to slay one another, casting lots for one victim in ten of their number.[35] The army of fifty thousand men, whom he had raised in the valley, in order to conquer the Desert, —that is, to take the Oases, and burn the temple of the Oracle, —were never heard of more. Whether they perished by thirst, or were overtaken by the sand, was never known. So, all that the conqueror could do was to lay waste Thebes, where it appears there was now no one to stay his hand. He carried off its treasures of gold, silver and ivory, broke open and robbed the Tombs of the Kings, threw down what he could of the temple buildings, and hewed in pieces such of the colossal statues as were not too strong for the brute force of his army. It was then, if Pausanias says true, that the vocal statue, the eastern-most of the pair, was shattered and overthrown from the waist: after which, however, it still gave out its gentle music to the morning sun. On the return of Cambyses to Memphis,[36] he found the people rejoicing in the investiture of a new bull Apis, which had been found qualified to succeed the one which had died. He was angry at any rejoicing while he was baffled and unfortunate; asked how it was that they showed no joy when he was there before, and so much now when he had lost the chief part of his army; put to death the magistrates who informed him of the occasion of the festival; with his own hand stabbed the bull, and ordered the priests to be scourged. [37] Here again he broke open the tombs, and desecrated the temples. Meantime, the valley swarmed with strangers, who came in embassy from every part of the wide Persian dominion, to offer congratulation and magnificent presents, on the conquest of Egypt. —Yet this new province never became an easy possession. One revolt followed another; and the valley was a scene of almost continual conflict during the two hundred years of its nominal subservience to Persia. Its conquest by Cambyses took place in 525 B.C.

It was only during an occasional revolt that any one from Athens could set foot in Egypt: for the great war between the Greeks and Persians was now going on. Anaxagoras was born 500 B.C., and he was therefore ten years old at the time of the battle of Marathon; and nineteen when that of Salamis was fought. But when he was forty years of age, Egypt became accessible for four years, by means of a revolt. During this time, though the Persians were never dislodged

35   Herod. III. 25.
36   Ibid. 27.
37   Ibid. 29.

from Memphis, both Lower and Upper Egypt appeared to have become independent; and many Greeks, bent on the advancement of learning, and Anaxagoras among them, hastened to the Egyptian schools. Anaxagoras's work on the Nile has perished with his other writings: and there is no saying how much of his philosophy he derived from the teachings of the Egyptian priests: but there is a striking accordance between the opinions which he is variously reported to have held, and for which he is believed to have suffered banishment, and those which constituted part of the philosophy of Egypt. Wherever we turn, in tracing the course of ancient philosophy, we meet the priests of Egypt: and it really appears as if the great men of Greece and other countries had little to say on the highest and deepest subjects of human inquiry, till they had studied at Memphis, or Saïs, or Thebes, or Heliopolis. Here was the master of Socrates, (Footnote: Proclus says that Socrates, as well as Plato, learned the doctrine of the Immortality of the Soul from the Egyptians. If so, his great master, Anaxagoras, was probably, —almost certainly, —the channel through which he received it.) the originator of some of his most important opinions, and the great mover of his mind, studying in Egypt; and we shall hereafter find the great pupil of Socrates, and the interpreter of his mind, Plato, dwelling in the same school, for so long a time, it is thought, as to show in what reverence he held it.

Soon after Anaxagoras came Herodotus. We may be thankful that among the Greeks who visited Egypt, there was one whose taste was more for matter-of-fact, than for those high abstract inquiries which are not popularly included under that name: for the scientific and philosophical writings of his countrymen are, for the most part, lost, while the travels of Herodotus remain, as lively and fresh in their interest as ever. We may mourn that the others are gone; but we must rejoice that these are preserved. Here, at least, we obtain what we have longed for in the whole course of our study of the early Egyptian periods; records of the sayings and doings of the priests, and of the destinies of the people; pictures of the appearance of the great Valley and of its inhabitants; and details of their lives, customs, manners, history and opinions. The temptation is strong to present again here, to fill up and illuminate this sketch of the history of old Egypt, some of the material of Herodotus: but his books lie within reach of every hand: and I will use them no further than is necessary to the illustration of what I myself observed in my study of the Monuments.

Within a hundred years of Herodotus, came Plato. It may be questioned whether this visit of Plato to Egypt be not one of the most important events which have occurred in the history of the human mind. The first thing that strikes us, is how much there must have been to be learned in Egypt at this time, since Plato, his friend Eudoxus the astronomer, and Chrysippus the physician, all came— (such men, and from such a distance!) to study in the schools of

Heliopolis. It is related, and was believed in his own age, that Plato lived thirteen years at Heliopolis: and when Strabo was there, 350 years afterwards, he was shown the house where Plato and Eudoxus lived and studied. — Plato had met Socrates, it is believed, at the age of nineteen. After having learned what he could of him, and sustained his death, and been compelled for political reasons to leave Athens, he had gone to Megara, and joined the school of Euclid[38] —also a pupil of Socrates, and one well qualified to cherish what Socrates had sown in the mind of Plato. Though this school was considered one of doubt and denial, its ultimate doctrine was, that the Supreme Good is always the same, and unchangeable. Thus trained and set thinking, Plato came to Egypt, and sat where Moses had sat, at the feet of the priests, gaining, as Moses had gained, an immortal wisdom from their lips. The methods of learning of these two men, and their acquisitions, differed according to the differing characteristics of their minds. Each took from his teachers what he could best appropriate. Moses was spiritualized to a wonderful degree, considering his position and race; but his surpassing eminence was as a redeeming legislator. Plato had deeply-considered views on political matters; but his surpassing eminence was as a spiritual philosopher. Moses redeemed a race of slaves, made men of them, organized them into a society, and constituted them a nation; while Plato did only theoretical work of that kind, —enough to testify to the political philosophy of Egypt, but not to affect the condition of Greece. But Plato taught the Egyptian doctrine (illustrated on the tombs ages before, and, as Proclus declares, derived by Plato from Egypt) of the Immortality of the Soul, and rewards and punishments in an after-life. This was what Plato taught that Moses did not. The great old Egyptian doctrine, extending back, as the Book of Genesis shows us, as far as the Egyptian traditions reached—the great doctrine of a Divine Moral Government, was the soul alike of the practical legislation of Moses and the speculative philosophy of Plato; and this is, as it seems to us now, their great common qualification for bearing such a part as each does in the constitution of the prevalent Christianity. — We shall have to return to this hereafter, when we have seen more of the Egyptian priesthood. Meantime, I may observe, that unless there is other evidence that Plato visited the Jews than the amount of Judaism in his writings, it does not seem necessary to suppose such a visit. If he passed thirteen years beside that fountain of wisdom where Moses dwelt till his manhood, it is not extraordinary that they should have great Ideas in common. The wonder would be if they had not. The intellectual might of Moses seems to show that the lapse of intervening ages had not much changed the character of the schools: and the result on the respective minds of the two students may have been much the same as if they had sat side by side in bodily presence, as

38   Not the geometrician.

they ever will do in the reason of all who faithfully contemplate the operation of the Christian religion on the minds of men, from the beginning till now. —That Plato derived and adopted much from his predecessors among Greek philosophers, is very evident: and from Pythagoras above all. But many of these Greek philosophers had been trained in Egypt; and especially, as we have seen, Pythagoras, whose abstract ideas would appear to be displayed in a course of illustration on the walls of the Theban tombs, if we did not know that these tombs, with all their pictured mysteries, had been closed many centuries before the philosopher was born.

During all our review of the old Egyptians, we have not yet considered who they were. Of this there is little to say. It is useless to call them Copts; because all we can say of the Copts is that we must suppose them to be of the same race originally as the old Egyptians; and this throws no light on the derivation of either. Speaking of the origin of the Colchians, Herodotus says, that the Egyptians believed them to be descended from followers of Sesostris; and that he thought this probable from (among other reasons) their being black, and having curly hair.[39] This blackness was probably only a relative term; for not only do we find the Nubians at this day, with their strong resemblance to the portraits in the tombs, of a dark bronze, but in the tombs there is a clear distinction between the absolute black of negro captives and other dark complexions. On these walls, the color given to figures generally is a dark red. Where there is a bluish black, or neutral tint on the faces, it is distinctive merely of the priestly caste. The women are sometimes painted yellow; and so are certain strangers, supposed to be Asiatic or European. It is a curious circumstance, related by Sir W. Gell, that in the Tarquinian tombs in Etruria, all the men have the dark red complexion found in the Egyptian tombs. This rather tends to confirm the impression that the red color may be symbolical, like the blue for the priests, and the yellow for the women. On the whole, it is thought probable that the old Egyptian complexion was of the dark bronze of the Nubians of the present day. Herodotus says that, except the Lybians, no people were so blessed in point of health and temperament:[40] and he repeatedly records traits of their cleanliness, and nicety with regard to food and habits. It does not appear that they were insensible or reconciled to the plague of indigenous insects, as natives usually are, —and especially Africans; for he tells us of their sleeping under nets to avoid the mosquitoes.[41] Their dress was of linen, with fringes round the legs,[42]—and over this they wore a cloak of white wool, which must be laid aside before they

39   Herod. II. 104.
40   Ibid. 77.
41   Ibid. 95.
42   Ibid. 81.

entered the temples; —or the tomb; for it was not permitted to bury in woolen garments. Every man had but one wife;[43] and the women were clearly in that state of freedom which must be supposed to exist where female sovereignly was a matter of course in its turn. Herodotus tells that the women went into the market, and conducted commerce while the men stayed at home to weave cloth.[44] He speaks of them as a serious-minded and most religious people. "They are very religious," he says, "and surpass all men in the worship they render to the gods."[45] He tells of their great repugnance to the customs of the Greeks and of all other men;[46] and everywhere attests the originality of the Egyptians, and their having given truth, knowledge and customs to others, without having themselves derived from any.

One of the most interesting inquiries to us is about the language of these people. To form any idea of the labors of modern interpreters of the monuments, we must remember that they have not only to read the perfectly singular cipher of these writers on stone, but to find their very language. Of course, the only hope is in the study of the Coptic; and the Coptic became almost a dead language in the twelfth century of our era, and entirely so in the seventeenth, after having been for ages corrupted by the admixture of foreign terms, going on at the same time with the loss of old native ones. Egypt never had any permanent colonies in which her language might be preserved during the ages when one foreign power after another took possession of her valley, and rendered the language of her people compound and corrupt. Without repeating here the long and well-known story of the progress of discovery of the ancient language, it is enough to give the results thus far attained.

The key not only to the cipher but to the language, was afforded by the discovery of the same inscription written, as the inscription itself declared, in three languages, —the Greek, the Enchorial or ordinary Egyptian writing, and the old sacred character. The most ancient was found to bear a close relation to the Coptic, as then known: a relation probably, as has been observed by a recent writer,[47] "similar to that which the Latin does to the Italian, the Zend to the modern Persian, or the Sanscrit to many of the vernacular dialects now spoken in India." This key was applied with wonderful sagacity and ingenuity by Champollion the younger, who proceeded a good deal further than reading the names and titles of the kings and their officers. He ventured upon introducing or deciphering (whichever it may be called) many words not to be found in

43   Ibid. 92.
44   Ibid. 35.
45   Ibid. 37.
46   Ibid. 91.
47   Penny Cyclopedia; Article, Coptic Language.

the later Coptic, except in their supposed roots, nor, of course, anywhere else. The great difficulty is that, the language having, by lapse of ages, lost its original power of grammatical inflexion, a quality which it seems scarcely possible to restore, the relations of ideas in a sentence, which in the more modern Coptic are expressed by auxiliary terms, must be disposed by conjecture, or by doubtful internal comparison and analogy. It is easy to see how thus, while names and titles, and all declaratory terms may be read, when once the alphabet is secured, all beyond must be in a high degree conjectural, at least till the stock of terms is largely increased. The stock is on the increase, however. Champollion made a noble beginning: Dr. Lepsius has corrected him in some important instances; and the Chevalier Bunsen has offered a Lexicon of the old Egyptian language, placing above four hundred words in comparison with the known Coptic. This is a supply which will go a good way in reading the legends on the monuments; by which process, again, we may be helped to more. The very singular nature of the alphabet being once understood, and the beginning of a Lexicon being supplied, there seems reason to hope that the process of discovery may be carried on by the application of one fresh mind after another to the task which all must see to be as important as any which can occupy the human faculties. Or, if all do not see this, it must be from insufficient knowledge of the facts: —insufficient knowledge of the amount of the records, of their antiquity, and of their general nature. When the traveler gazes at vast buildings covered over in every part with writing; every architrave, every abacus, every recess and every projection, all the lines of the cornice, and all the intervals of the sculptures, he is overwhelmed with the sense of the immensity of knowledge locked up from him before his eyes. Let those at home imagine the ecclesiastical history of Christendom written up thus on every inch of the surface of its cathedrals, and the civil history of any country, from its earliest times, thus engraved on all its public buildings and palaces, and he may form some conception of what it would be, in regard to mere amount, to be able to read the inscriptions in Egypt. If he is also aware that the religion, philosophy and science of the world for many thousand years, a religion, philosophy, and science which reveal a greater nobleness, depth, and extent, the more they are explored, are recorded there, under our very eyes and hands, he will see that no nobler task awaits any lover of truth and of his race, than that of enabling mankind to read these earliest volumes of its own history.

And the world has no other resource in regard to this object. There is no doubt about the ancient Egyptians having had an extensive written literature: but it is lost. It was shelved when the Greek language and literature became the fashion in Egypt: and previous circumstances had been unfavorable to the preservation of the rolls of goat and sheep skins, and the subsequent papyri, which contained the best thoughts of the best men of five or six thousand years ago.

We may mourn over this; —we must mourn, for it is certain that they knew things that we are yet ignorant of, and that they could do things which we can only wonder at: —but the records are lost, and no man can help it now. There has been later damage too, clearly traceable. We all know how early Christianity was introduced into Egypt: and all who have been there have seen how indefatigable the early Christians were in destroying everything relating to the ancient people and their faith that they could lay their hands on. Again, the Emperor Severus carefully collected the writings which related to the mysteries of the priests, and buried them in the tomb of Alexander. And again, Diocletian ordered all the Egyptian books on alchemy to be destroyed, lest these makers of gold should become too rich to remain dependent on Rome. Thus scarcely a vestige of the ancient writing on destructible substances remains, and the monumental records are our only resource. While we take to heart the terrible loss, let us take to heart also the value of the resource, and search for the charm which may remove the spell of dumbness from these eloquent old teachers. Perhaps the solemn Memnon may yet respond if touched by the warm bright rays of zeal and intelligence; and the great Valley may take up the echoes from end to end. And this is a case where he who gives his labor quickly gives twice. Time is a more efficient defacer than even the Coptic Christians: and the indefatigable enemy, the Desert, can bury old records on a vaster scale than any Severus. There are rulers bearing sway, too, who are not more enlightened than the mischievous Diocletian.

As for the Egyptian method of recording the language, there were three kinds of writing: the Hieroglyphic, or picture writing; the Hieratic, —an abridged form of the hieroglyphic, used by the priests for their records; and the Enchorial, in popular use, which appears to be a still further abridgment of the hieratic, whose signs have flowed into a running hand. Written language is found among the very earliest memorials of this most ancient people.

As for their social organization, we know more of it than of most particulars concerning them. The most important, however, in the state appears to have been that of the caste of Priests. The monarch must be of that class. If a member of the next (the military) caste was made king, he must first become a priest.[48] —Herodotus says that Egyptian society was composed of seven castes; Plato says six:[49] Diodorus Siculus says five.[50] The classification of Herodotus is so strange that it is clear that he included under his titles some division of employments which we do not understand. He declares[51] the seven classes to

48   Plutarch. de Is. IX.
49   In Timæo.
50   Diod. I. 74.
51   Herod. II. 164.

be the Priests, the Military, the Herdsmen, the Swineherds, the Tradesmen, the Interpreters, and the Pilots and Seamen. The classification of Diodorus will help us better. He gives us the Priests, the Military, the Husbandmen, the Tradesmen and Artificers, and, lowest of all, the Shepherds; and with them the Poulterers, Fishermen and Servants. The division indicates much of the national mind, as I need not point out. We must remember, throughout our study of the monuments, that the priests were not occupied with religion alone. They had possession besides of the departments of politics, law, medicine, science and philosophy. It is curious to speculate on what must have been the division of employments among them, when we read in Herodotus how they partitioned out their art of medicine, —there being among them no general practitioners, as we should say, but physicians of the heart, the lungs, the abdomen; and oculists, dentists, &c.[52] If such a subdivision was followed out through the whole range of study and practice in all professions, the priestly caste must contain within itself a sufficient diversity to preserve its enlightenment and magnanimity better than we, with our modern view of the tendencies of a system of castes, might suppose.

I have perhaps said enough of this ancient people to prepare for an entrance upon the study of their monuments. The other castes, and a multitude of details of personal and social condition and usage, will come before us when we turn to the sculptures and pictures. Before going on to their successors, we may call to mind the grounds which Herodotus assigns for his fullness of detail about the Pharaohs and their people. He says, "I shall enlarge further on what concerns Egypt, because it contains more wonders than any other country; and because there is no region besides where one sees so many works which are admirable and beyond expression."[53]

Beyond expression, indeed, are those great works. And do we not know that wherever men's works have a grandeur or beauty beyond expression, the feeling which suggested and inspired them is yet more beyond expression still. O! how happy should I be if I could arouse in others by this book, as I experienced it myself from the monuments, any sense of the depth and solemnity of the Ideas which were the foundation of the old Egyptian faith! I did not wait till I went to Egypt to remember that the faculty of Reverence is inherent in all men, and that its natural exercise is always to be sympathized with, irrespective of its objects. I did not wait till I went to Egypt to become aware that every permanent reverential observance has some great Idea at the bottom of it, and that it is our business not to deride or be shocked at the method of manifestation, but to endeavor to apprehend the Idea concerned. I vividly remember

52   Ibid. 84.
53   Ibid. 35.

the satisfaction of ascertaining the ideas that lay at the bottom of those most barbarous South Sea island practices of Human Sacrifice and Cannibalism. If some sympathy in conception and feeling is possible in even this lowest case, how far should we be from contempt or levity in studying the illustrations of Egyptian faith and hope which we find blazoned on works "admirable and beyond expression!" With all Men's tendency to praise the olden time—to say that the former times are better than these—we find that it is usually only the wisdom of their own forefathers that they extol—merely a former mode of holding and acting upon their own existing ideas. They have no such praise for the forefathers of another race, who had other ideas, and acted them out differently. Instead of endeavoring to ascertain the ideas, they revile or ridicule the manifestation, which was never meant to meet their conceptions, and can never be interpreted by them. Thus we, as a society, take upon ourselves to abhor and utterly despise the "Idolatry" of the Egyptians, without asking ourselves whether we comprehend anything of the principles of Egyptian theology. The children, on their stools by our firesides, wonder eternally how people so clever could be so silly as to pay homage to crocodiles and cats; and their parents too often agree with them, instead of pointing out that there might be, and certainly were, reasons in the minds of Egyptians which made it a very different thing in them to cherish sacred animals from what it would be in us. Everybody at home talks of the ugly and grotesque character of the Egyptian works of art; and no wonder, if they judge with English mind and English eyes, from broken specimens in the British Museum. One can only ask them to trust something to the word of travelers who have seen such works in their plenitude, in their own locality and proper connection. Probably some people in Greece were talking of the ugly and grotesque character of such Egyptian decorations as they might have heard of, while Herodotus was gazing on them on their native soil, and declaring in his own mind, as he afterwards did to the whole world and to all time, that they were "admirable and beyond expression." I would ask for these considerations to be borne in mind, not only for the sake of justice to the earliest philosophers of the human race (as far as we know), but because it is impossible to appreciate the monuments—I may say impossible to see them—through any other medium than that of a teachable mind, working with a sympathizing heart. If any one hesitates to grant me this much, let me ask him whether he would be willing to have the Christian religion judged of, five thousand years hence, by such an one as himself, when its existing forms shall have been long forgotten, and its eternal principles shall be expanded in some yet unknown mode of manifestation? Supposing oblivion to have been by that time as completely wrapped round Catholic and Protestant ritual as round the ceremonial of Egyptian worship, would a Christian be content to have his faith judged of by a careless traveler of another race, who should thrust a way among the buried pillars of our cathedral aisles, and look for superstition in every recess, and idolatry in every chapel; and who, lighting upon some carved fox and goose or grinning mask, should go home and declare that Christianity was made up of what was idolatrous, unideal and grotesque? If he is aware that in our Christianity there is much that will not appear on our cathedrals five thousand years hence, let him only remember that there may be much that is ideal and holy in other faiths which we have not had the opportunity of appreciating. I believe this to be the case with every faith which, from the first appearance of the human race upon our globe, has met and gratified the faculty of reverence in any considerable number of men. If I did not believe this with regard to the religion and philosophy of the ancient Egyptians, I must have looked at them merely as a wonderful show, and should certainly have visited them in vain.

Here, then, we take leave of the Pharaohs and their times; and, we may say, of their people; for the spirit of the old Egyptians was gone, and only a lifeless body was left, to be used as it pleased their conquerors. We hear of the brilliant reigns of the Ptolemies, who now succeeded to the Egyptian throne; but theirs was a Greek civilization, which, though unquestionably derived from Egypt, many centuries before, was now as essentially different from that of the old Egyptians as were the characteristics of the two nations.

We must ever observe that there was no true fusion of the minds of the two races. The Greeks learned and adopted much from the Egyptians; but the Egyptians, instead of adopting from the Greeks, died out. No new god was ever introduced into Egypt; while the Greeks, after having long before derived many of their gods from Egypt, now accommodated their deities to those of the Egyptians, and in an arbitrary and superficial way, adopted the old symbols. There is every reason to believe that the priests, when employed by the Ptolemies to interpret the monuments, fitted their new and compounded ideas to the old symbols, and thus produced a theology and philosophy which any resuscitated Pharaoh would have disavowed. The Greeks took no pains to learn the Egyptian language, or to enter into the old Egyptian mind; and there is therefore endless confusion in the accounts they have given to the world of the old gods and the old monarchs of the Nile valley. To understand anything of the monuments of the times we are now entering upon, it will be necessary to bear in mind that the Ptolemies and Caesars built upon Pharaonic foundations, and in imitation of Pharaonic edifices; but necessarily with such an admixture of Greek and Roman ideas with their Egyptian conceptions as to cause a complete corruption of ancient art. It is necessary never to forget this, or we shall be perpetually misled. We may admire the temples of the Ptolemies and Caesars as much or as little as we please; but we must remember that they are not Egyptian.

Every country weak enough to need the aid of Greek mercenaries was sure to become, ere long, Greek property. It was so with Persia, and with its province, Egypt. The event was hastened by the desire of the Egyptians to be quit of their Persian masters. Alexander the Great was the conqueror, as everybody knows. He chose his time when the chief part of the Persian forces of Egypt was absent—sent to fight the Greeks in Asia Minor. When once Alexander had set foot in Pelusium, the rest was easy; for the towns opened their gates to him with joy; and he had only to march to Heliopolis and then to Memphis. He gave his countenance as well as he knew how to the old worship, restoring the temples and honoring the symbols of the gods at Memphis, and marching to the Oasis of Amun, to present gifts to the chief deity of the Egyptians, and to claim to be his son. It was on his way there, by the coast, that he saw in passing the harbor where Alexandria now stands, and perceived its capabilities. He ordered the improvement of the harbor, and the building of the city which would have immortalized his name, if he had done nothing else. This visit of Alexander the Great to Egypt took place 332 B.C. He left orders that the country should be governed by its own laws, and that its religion should be absolutely respected. This was wise and humane, and no doubt we owe some of our knowledge of more ancient times to this conservative principle of Alexander's government. But he was not practically sustained by his deputies; and he died eight years after his visit to Egypt. His successor gave the government of Egypt into the hands of Ptolemy, who called himself the son of Lagus, but was commonly believed to be an illegitimate son of Philip of Macedon. In seventeen years he became king; and with him begins the great line of the Ptolemies, of whom sixteen reigned in succession for 275 years, till the witch Cleopatra let the country go into the hands of the Romans, to become a Roman province, in 30 B.C.

It was under the government of the first Ptolemy that Greek visitors again explored the Nile valley as high as Thebes, and higher. Hecatæus of Abdera was one of these travelers, and a great traveler he was; for, if Diodorus Siculus tells us truly, he once stood on Salisbury Plain, and saw there the great temple of the Sun which we call Stonehenge;[54] and he certainly stood on the plain of Thebes, and saw the great temple of the Sun there. The priests had recovered their courage, under the just rule of the Greeks, and had brought out the gold and silver and other treasures of the temples which had been carefully hidden from the Persians. Thebes, however, was almost dead by this time; and its monuments were nearly all which a stranger had to see. We are glad to know that the records of the priests told of forty-seven tombs existing in the valley of Kings' Sepulchres, of which seventeen had at that time been discovered under their concealment of earth, and laid open. Some of these, and some fresh ones,

54   Sharpe's History of Egypt, p. 146.

have been explored in our own days; but it is an animating thing to believe that there were at least forty-seven originally, and that many yet remain untouched since they were closed on the demise of the Pharaohs. Whose will be the honor of laying them open?—not in the Cambyses spirit of rapine, but in all honor and reverence, in search of treasures which neither moth nor rust can corrupt, nor thieves carry away—a treasure of light out of the darkened place, and of knowledge out of that place where usually no device or knowledge is found!

We are grieved now to lose the old Egyptian names, but at this time they naturally become exchanged for Greek. On becomes Heliopolis. This becomes Abydos. Thebes (called in the Bible No Ammen), becomes Diospolis Magna. Pilak becomes Philœ. Petpieh is Aphroditopolis (the city of Athor). Even the country itself, from being called Khem (answering to Ham in the Bible), is henceforth known as Ægyptus.

In the reign of the second Ptolemy lived a writer of uncommon interest and importance to us now—Manetho, the Egyptian priest. We have only fragments of the writings of Manetho, but they are of great and immediate value to us; fragments of the history of Egypt, which he wrote at the command of Ptolemy Philadelphus. He wrote in Greek, of course, deriving his information from the inscriptions in the temples. What would not we give now for his knowledge of the Egyptian language! and what would we not give to have his works complete! His abode was at that great seat of learning where Moses got his lore—Heliopolis. He is the very man we want—to stand on the ridge of time, and tell us who are below, what was doing in the depths of the old ages. He did so stand, and he did fully tell what he saw; but his words are gone to the four winds, and but a few unconnected declarations have reached us. We have a list of old kings from him, and Josephus has, by extracting, preserved some passages of his account of the Hebrews when in Egypt; but Josephus, in his unscrupulous vanity, wishing to make out that his nation were descended from the Shepherd Kings, puts certain words of his own into Manetho's mouth, thus impairing our trust in the poor extracts we have. It appears, and should be remembered, that the Egyptian records make no mention of the Hebrews, and that what Manetho told of them must therefore be derived from other and probably inferior sources. His list of kings is preserved in some early Christian writers; but the difficulty has been how to use it, and how far to trust it. I must not enter here upon the story, however interesting, of the fluctuations of the credit of Manetho. Suffice it that all recent discoveries have directly tended to establish his character as an able and conscientious historian. The names he gives have been found inscribed in temples and tombs, and even, latterly, in the Pyramids; and the numerous and nameless incidental notices which occur in the study of ancient monuments have, in this instance, gone to corroborate the statements of Manetho.

As the monuments are a confirmation of his statements, so are his statements a key to the monuments; and with this intimation of unbounded obligations to Manetho, we must leave him.

One event which happened in the reign of the second Ptolemy we must just refer to, as it is connected with the chronological questions which make up so much of the interest of the history of Egypt. The Jews then in Egypt were emancipated by this Ptolemy; and they employed their influence with him in obtaining, by his countenance, a good Greek translation of their Scriptures. By communication with the High Priest at Jerusalem, there came about an appointment of seventy qualified men who translated the Hebrew Scriptures into Greek, and presented the world with the version called the Septuagint. The chronology of this work differs widely from that given by the Samaritan and Hebrew versions; the Septuagint assigning between Adam and Abraham, nearly 1400 years more than the Hebrew; and so on. For a long course of time, the learned and religious world believed that the discrepancy between the Septuagint and (so-called) Mosaic histories was ascribable to forgery on the part of the Alexandrian Jews. But now that chronological evidence is flowing in from other sources, the judgment of biblical scholars is becoming favorable to the Septuagint computation. Of course, it becomes at the same time more accordant with the recorded history of Egypt.

In the reign of the third Ptolemy lived Eratosthenes, —a truly great scholar and wise man, —called the second Plato, and also the second of the first man in every science. He was a Greek, understanding Egyptian: and he wrote a history of Egypt in correction of that of Manetho. Their statements, their lists of kings, appear at first sight irreconcilable. This is not the place in which to give an account of the difficulty. It is enough to say that the attention of scholars has been employed upon it to good purpose; and that it may be hoped that two men, reasonably believed so trustworthy, will be found, when we can understand them, to have told the same story, and to have supplied us with new knowledge by the very difference in their way of telling it.

One great event must be noticed before we go on from the dominion of the Ptolemies to that of Rome. The Ptolemies degenerated, as royal races are apt to do; and after a few of their reigns, the Egyptians became as heartily tired of their Greek rulers as they had been of the Persian. In the time of the eighth and ninth sovereigns of this line, Thebes rebelled, and maintained a long resistance against the authority and forces of Ptolemy Lathyrus. The temples were stout citadels, in which the besieged could seclude themselves: and they held them long. When Ptolemy Lathyrus prevailed at last, he made dreadful havoc at Thebes. Cambyses had done wonders in the way of destruction: but Lathyrus far exceeded him. As one walks over the plain of Thebes, whose final overthrow dates from this conflict, one's heart sickens among the ruins made by the Persian, the Greek and the Earthquake. To the last of these, one submits quietly, though mournfully, as to a Fate: but those who do not regard men as necessary agents, —agents of an exact necessity in human history, —may find their spirits rising in resentment against the long-buried invaders, as the spirits of the Thebans rose in resentment while they looked out upon their besiegers from the loopholes of their lofty propyla. This greatest and last act of devastation took place 88 B.C.; fifty-eight years before Egypt became a Roman province.

About thirty years before this annexation, Diodorus Siculus was in Egypt. He probably witnessed the beginning of the building of the temple of Dendera. He saw much religious ceremonial, which it is curious to read of, though there is no saying how far it remained true to the old ideas in which it originated. The testimony of Diodorus as to what happened in his own time is of course more valuable than his essays in the ancient history: but the latter are interesting in their way, as showing what were the priestly traditions current in the last days of the Ptolemies.

As our object in this rapid view of Egyptian history is to obtain some clearness of ideas in preparation for looking at the monuments, we need not go into any detail of the times subsequent to the building of Egyptian monuments or of the times of those Romans who erected some temples, but whose history is familiar to everybody. I need only say that, after the death of the last Cleopatra and her son Caesarion, in 30 B. C., Egypt was annexed to the Roman dominions for seven hundred years. At the end of that period, the ruler of Egypt had enough to do to keep off Persian aggression. He bought off the Arabs, —a stronger enemy, —for a time; but the great conqueror Amrou marched in triumph from his capture of Damascus and Jerusalem, and, after some struggle and mischance, took the great cities of Egypt, and sent the libraries of Alexander to heat the baths of that city; for which purpose, it is said that they lasted six months.

One of the first visitors to Egypt after its annexation to Rome was Strabo, who went up the banks of the Nile with the Prefect, as far as Aswan, and has left a full and careful account of what he saw. He enlarges on Alexandria, at that time a most magnificent city, while Thebes was a village, interspersed with colossal ruins. Memphis was still great, ranking next to Alexandria: but Heliopolis was sunk, and almost gone. Its schools were closed; but the memory of them remained, on the spot, as well as afar: for the house was shown where Plato and Eudoxus lived and studied. Would it were there still! At present, there is nothing left visible of Heliopolis but its obelisk, and a circuit of mounds. Strabo thought the place almost deserted in his time: but what a boon it would be to us to see what was before his eyes, within a few years of the Christian era!

Here, then, we stop; at a period which we have been wont to consider ancient, but which, in regard to our object, is so modern as to have no further interest or purpose which need detain us.

We now proceed to the monuments.

CHAPTER X

ABOO-SIMBIL—EGYPTIAN CONCEPTIONS OF THE GODS

T HE TEMPLES OF ABOO-SIMBIL are both of the time of Ramases II.; — in the earlier part of the great Third Period. Nothing more interesting than these temples is to be found beyond the limits of Thebes.

I went up to the smaller temple early in the morning. Of the six statues of the facade, the two in the centre represent Athor, whose calm and gentle face is surmounted by the usual crown, —the moon contained within the cow's horns. On entering the portal in the rock, I found myself in a hall where there was plenty to look at, though the fires lightened by the Arabs have blackened the walls in some places, and the whole is, as I need not say, very old, —nearly 1400 B. C. This entrance hall is supported by six square pillars, all of which bear the head of Athor on the front face of their capitals, the other three faces being occupied with sculptures, once gayly painted, and still showing blue, red and yellow colors. On the walls here were the men of the old military caste, in their defensive armor; —a sort of cuirass of chain armor, —red links on a yellow ground: and their brethren the civilians, in red frocks: and the women in tight yellow garments, with red sashes tied in front. Most of the figures are represented in the act of bringing offerings to the gods: but on either side the door, the hero Ramases is holding by the hair a captive who is on one knee, and looks up, —in the one instance with a complete negro face; in the other, with a face certainly neither Egyptian nor negro, and whose chin ends in a peaked beard. Here we have the conquests of the hero in upper Africa, and probably in Asia. He holds up his falchion, as if about to strike; but the goddess behind him lifts her hand, as if in intercession, while Osiris, in front, holds forth the great knife, as if to command the slaughter. When Osiris carries, as here, the emblems of the crozier and the flagellum or whip, he is present in his function of Judge: and here, accordingly, we see him deciding the fate of the nations conquered by Ramases.

Within this outer hall is a transverse corridor, ending in two rude chambers, where I found nothing but bats. But beyond the corridor lies the sacred chamber, the shrine of the deity. There she is, in the form of the crowned head of a cow, —her emblematic disk being between the horns. In another part, she stands, as a cow, in a boat surrounded by water plants, —the king and queen bringing offerings to this "Lady of Aboshek, the foreign land." We shall meet with Athor frequently as "Lady of the West;" and therefore as the morning star; as the welcomer of the Sun at the end of his course; and as the mild and transient Night, which is quite a different personage from the stern and fixed Night of Chaos. As possessor or guardian of the West, Athor was patroness of the western part of Thebes, — "the Lybian suburb," as it was called of old.[55] Plutarch says that the death of Osiris was believed to have happened in her month; —the third Egyptian month: that her shrines were in that month carried about in procession; at the time when the Pleiades appear and the husbandmen began to sow their corn. The countenance of this goddess was everywhere in the temples so mild and tranquil as to accord well with the imagery of the Summer Night, the Morning Star, and the Seed-time, which are associated, in the Egyptian worship, with her name. I found the figure in the adytum (Holiest Place) much mutilated: but the head and ears were still distinctly visible. Hieroglyphic legends on each side declare her name and titles. This temple extends, from the portal, about ninety feet into the rock. Little as I had yet learned how to look at temples, I found this full of interest. In the course of the morning, we detected some of our own crew making a fire against the sculptures in the hall. Of course, we interfered, with grave faces: but there is no hope that Arabs will not make their fires in such convenient places, whenever they can. A cave at the top of the bank is irresistible to them, whether it be sculptured or not.

I was impatient to get to the Colossi of the large temple, which looked magnificent from our deck. So, after breakfast, I set forth alone, to see what height I could attain, in the examination of the statues. The southernmost is the only complete one. The next to it is terribly shattered: and the other two have lost the top of the helmet. They are much sanded up, though, thanks to Mr. Hay, much less than they were. The sand slopes up from the half-cleared entrance to the chin of the northernmost colossus: and this slope of sand it was my purpose to climb. It was so steep, loose, and hot to the feet, that it was no easy matter to make my way up. The beetles, which tread lightly and seem to like having warm feet, got on very well; and they covered the sand with a network of tracks: but heavier climbers, shod in leather, are worsted in the race with them. But one cannot reach the chin of a colossus every day: and it was worth an effort. And when I had reached the chin, I made a little discovery about it which may

55   Wilkinson's Ancient Egyptians, IV. 387.

be worth recording, and which surprised me a good deal, at the time. I found that a part of the lower jaw, reaching half way up the lower lip, was composed of the mud and straw of which crude bricks are made. There had been evidently a fault in the stone, which was supplied by this material. It was most beautifully moulded. The beauty of the curves of these great faces is surprising in the stone; —the fidelity of the rounding of the muscles, and the grace of the flowing lines of the cheek and jaw: but it was yet more wonderful in such a material as mud and straw. I cannot doubt that this chin and lip were moulded when the material was in a soft state: —a difficult task in the case of a statue seventy feet high, standing up against the face of a rock. I called the gentlemen up, to bear witness to the fact: and it set us looking for more instances. Mr. E. soon found one. Part of the dress of the Second Osiride on the right hand, entering the temple, is composed of this same material, as smoothly curved and nicely wrought as the chin overhead. On examining closely, we found that this layer of mud and straw covered some chiseling within. The artist had been carving the folds of the dress, when he came upon a fault in the stone which stopped his work till he supplied a surface of material which he could mould. The small figures which stand beside the colossi and between their ankles, and which look like dolls, are not, as sometimes said, of human size. The hat of a man of five feet ten inches does not reach their chins by two inches. These small figures are, to my eye, the one blemish of this temple. They do not make the great Ramases look greater, but only look dollish themselves.

On the legs of the shattered colossus are the Greek letters, scrawled as by a Greek clown, composing the inscription of the soldiers sent by Psammitichus in pursuit of the Egyptian deserters whom I mentioned as going up the country from Elephantine, when weary of the neglect in which they were left there. We are much obliged to "Damearchon, the son of Amæbichus, and Pelephus, the son of Udamus," for leaving, in any kind of scrawl, a record of an event so curious. One of the strangest sensations to the traveler in Egypt, is finding such traces as these of persons who were in their day modern travelers seeing the antiquities of the country, but who take their place now among the ancients, and have become subjects of Egyptian history. These rude soldiers, carving their names and errand on the legs of an ancient statue as they went by, passed the spot a century and a half before Cambyses entered the country. One wonders what they thought of Thebes, which they had just seen in all its glory.

As nearly as we could judge by the eye, and by knowing pretty well the dimensions of the colossi, the facade from the base of the thrones to the top of the row of apes, is nearly or quite one hundred feet high. Above rises the untouched rock.

The faces of Ramases outside (precisely alike) are placid and cheerful, —full of moral grace: but the eight Osirides within (precisely alike too) are more. They are full of soul. It is a mistake to suppose that the expression of a face must be injured by its features being colossal. In Egypt it may be seen that a mouth three feet wide may be as delicate, and a nostril which spans a foot as sensitive in expression as any marble bust of our day. It is very wonderful, but quite true. Abdallatif has left us his testimony as follows, —in speaking of the Sphinx. "A little more than a bow-shot from these Pyramids, we see a colossal head and neck appearing above ground…Its countenance is very charming, and its mouth gives an impression of sweetness and beauty. One would say that it smiles benignly. An able man having asked me what I admired most of all that I had seen in Egypt, I told him that it was the truth of the proportions in the head of the Sphinx… It is very astonishing that in a countenance so colossal, the sculptor should have preserved the precise proportions of all the parts, whilst Nature has presented no model of such a colossus, nor of any thing which could he compared to it."[56] I was never tired of gazing at the Osirides, everywhere, and trying to imprint ineffaceably on my memory the characteristics of the old Egyptian face; —the handsome arched nose, with its delicate nostril; the well-opened, though long eye; the placid, innocent mouth, and the smooth-rounded, amiable chin. Innocence is the prevailing expression; and sternness is absent. Thus the stiffest figures, and the most monotonous gesture, convey still only an impression of dispassionateness and benevolence. The dignity of the gods and goddesses is beyond all description, from this union of fixity and benevolence. The difficulty to us now is, not to account for their having been once worshiped, but to help worshiping them still. I cannot doubt their being the most abstract gods that men of old ever adored. Instead of their being engaged in wars or mutual rivalries, or favoritisms, or toils, or sufferings, here they sit, each complete and undisturbed in his function, —every one supreme, — free from all passion, but capable of all mild and serene affections. The Greek and Roman gods appear like wayward children beside them. Herodotus says that the Greek gods were children to these in respect of age:[57] and truly they appear so in respect of wisdom and maturity. Their limitation of powers, and consequent struggles, rivalries and transgressions, their fondness and vindictiveness, their anger, fear and hope are all attributes of childhood, contrasting strikingly with the majestic passive possession of power, and the dispassionate and benignant frame of these ever-young old deities. of Egypt. Vigilant, serene, benign, here they sit, teaching us to inquire reverently into the early powers and conditions of that Human Mind which was capable of such conceptions of abstract

56   Relation de l'Egypte, 1. I. ch. 4.

57   Herod. II. 4, 50, 58, 146.

qualities as are represented in their forms. I can imagine no experience more suggestive to the thoughtful traveler, anywhere from pole to pole, than that of looking with a clear eye and fresh mind on the ecclesiastical sculptures of Egypt, perceiving, as such an one must do, how abstract and how lofty were the first ideas of Deity known to exist in the world. That he should go with clear eyes and a fresh mind is needful: for if he carries a head full of notions about idolatry, obscenity, folly and ignorance, he can no more judge of what is before his eyes, —he can no more see what is before his face, than a proud Mohammedan can apprehend Christianity in a Catholic chapel at Venice, or an arrogant Jew can judge of Quakerism or Quietism. If the traveler be blessed with the clear eye and fresh mind, and be also enriched by comprehensive knowledge of the workings of the human intellect in its various circumstances, he cannot but be impressed and he may be startled, by the evidence before him of the elevation and beauty of the first conceptions formed by men of the Beings of the unseen world. And the more he traces downwards the history and philosophy of religious worship, the more astonished he will be to find to what an extent this early theology originated later systems of belief and adoration, and how long and how far it has transcended some of those which arose out of it. New suggestions will thence arise, that where in the midst of what is solemn and beautiful he meets with what appears to modern eyes puerile and grotesque, such an appearance may deceive, and there may be a meaning contained in it which is neither puerile nor grotesque. He will consider that Cambyses might be more foolish in stabbing the bull Apis, to show that it could bleed, which nobody denied, than the priests in conserving a sacred idea in the form of the bull. He will consider that the Sphinx might be to Egyptian eyes, not a hideous compound animal, as it is when carved by an English stone mason for a park gate, but a sacred symbol of the union of the strongest physical with the highest intellectual power on earth.

The seriousness I plead for comes of itself into the mind of any thoughtful and feeling traveler, at such a moment as that of entering the great temple of Aboo-Simbil. I entered it at an advantageous moment, when the morning sunshine was reflected from the sand outside so as to cast a twilight even into the adytum, —two hundred feet from the entrance. The four tall statues in the adytum, ranged behind the altar, were dimly visible: and I hastened to them, past the eight Osirides, through the next pillared hall, and across the corridor. And then I looked back, and saw beyond the dark halls and shadowy Osirides the golden sand-hill without, a corner of blue sky, and a gay group of the crew in the sunshine. It was like looking out upon life from the grave. When we left the temple, and the sun had shifted its place, we could no longer see the shrine. It is a great advantage to enter the temple first when the sun is rather low in the east.

The eight Osirides are perfectly alike, —all bearing the crosier and flagellum, and standing up against huge square pillars, the other sides of which are sculptured, as are the walls all round. The aisles behind the Osirides are so dark that we could not make out the devices without the help of torches; and the celebrated medallion picture of the siege would have been missed by us entirely, if one of the crew had not hoisted another on his shoulders, to hold a light above the height of their united statures. There we saw the walled town, and the proceedings of the besieged and besiegers, as they might have happened in the middle ages. The north wall is largely occupied by a tablet, bearing the date of the first year of Ramases the Great: and on the other side of the temple, between two of the pillars, is another tablet, bearing the date of the thirty-fifth year of his reign. The battle scenes on the walls are all alive with strong warriors, flying foes, trampled victims, and whole companies of chariots. I observed that the chariot wheels were not mere disks, as we should have expected in so early an age, but had all six spokes. Every chariot wheel I saw in the country had six spokes, however early the date of the sculpture or painting. One figure on the south wall is admirable, —a warrior in red, who is spearing one foe, while he has his foot on the head of another.

There are two groups of chambers, of three each, opening out of this large hall: and two more separate side chambers. The six included in the two groups are very nearly (but not quite) covered with representations of offerings to the gods: very pretty, but with little variety. The offerings are of piles of cakes and fruit, lamps, vases of various and graceful shapes, and flasks. The lotus, in every stage of growth, is frequent. Sometimes it is painted yellow, veined with red.

The boat, that wonderful and favorite symbol which we meet everywhere, is incessantly repeated here, —the seated figure in the convolution at bow and stern, the pavilion in the middle, and the paddle hanging over the side. One of these boats is carried by an admirable procession of priests, as a shrine, which is borne on poles of palm-trunks lashed together. Stone deewáns run round the walls of most of these little chambers. We could find no evidence of there being any means of ventilating these side-rooms; and how they could be used without, we cannot conceive, —enclosed as they are in the solid rock.

The second and smaller hall has four square pillars, sculptured, of course. Next comes the corridor, which has a bare unfinished little chamber at each end, now possessed by bats. The altar in the adytum is broken; and some barbarous wretches have cut their insignificant initials on it. Are there not rocks enough close by the entrance, on which they might carve their memorials of their precious selves, if carve they must? But this profaning of the altar is not the worst. One creature has cut his name on the tip of the nose of the northernmost colossus: others on the breast and limbs of the Osirides; and others over a large extent of the sculptured walls.

One of the four god figures in the adytum is Ra, who also occupies the niche in the facade over the entrance. Ra is the Sun. He is not Amun Ra, the Unnutterable,[58]—the God of gods, —the only god: but a chief, as the term Ra seems to express. Phra, (Ra with the article,) by us miscalled Pharaoh, means a chief or king among men: and Ra is the chief of the visible creation: and here, in this temple, he is the principal deity, the others being Khem, or Egypt, Kneph, Osiris and Isis. As we go on, we shall perhaps be able to attain some notion of the relative offices and dignities of the gods. At the outset, it is necessary to bear in mind chiefly that the leading point of belief of the Egyptians, from the earliest times known to us, was that there was One Supreme, —or, as they said, —one only God, who was to be adored in silence, (as Jamblichus declares from the ancient Hermetic books,) and was not to be named; that most of the other gods were deifications of his attributes; while others, again, as Egypt, the Nile, the Sun, the Moon, the West, of the Egyptian nation depended. We have also to remember that we must check our tendency to suppose Allegory in every part of the Egyptian system of theology. It is difficult to check this tendency to allegorize, bringing as we do the ideas of a long subsequent age to the interpretation of a theological system eminently symbolical to its priests, though not to the people at large: but we must try to conceive of these Egyptian gods as being, to the general Egyptian mind, actual personages, inseparably connected with the facts and appearances in which they were believed to exist. If we make the mistake of supposing them merely the names of such facts and appearances, and proceed to interpret them by the method of allegorical narrative, we shall soon find ourselves perplexed, and at a loss: for our view of the facts and appearances of Nature can never be like those of the Egyptians, whose science, though unquestionably great, lay in a different direction (for the most part) from ours, and whose heavens and earth were hardly like the same that we see and inhabit.

For one instance, —in their theory of the formation of the world, they believed that when the formless void of eternal matter began to part off into realms, the igneous elements ascending and becoming a firmament of fiery bodies, and the heavier portions sinking and becoming compacted into earth and sea, the earth gave out animals, —beasts and reptiles; an idea evidently derived from their annual spectacle of the coming forth of myriads of living creatures from the soil of their valley, on the subsidence of the flood. When we remember that to them the Nile was the sea, and so called by them, and that they had before them the spectacle which is seen nowhere else, of the springing

58   Manetho says that Amun means "concealment."

of the green herb after the separation of the waters from the land, we shall see how different their view of the creation must be from any which we could naturally form. In this particular case, we have adopted their traditions given to us through the mind of Moses; but where we have not the mind of Moses to interpret them to us, we must abstain from reading their meanings by any other light than that which they themselves afford us. As another instance, how should we allegorize for them about the West? What is the West to us? It is the place where the heavenly bodies disappear: and that is the only point we have in common with them. With them, the West was the unseen state. It was a dreary, unknown region beyond the dark river which the dead had to cross. The abodes of the dead were on its verge; and those solemn caves were the entrance of the Amenti, the region of judgment and retribution. Nothing was heard thence but the bark of the wild dog at night; the vigilant guardian, as they believed, of the heavenly abode which the wicked were not to approach.[59] Nothing was seen there but the descent of the sun, faithful to the goddess who was awaiting him behind the hills;[60] and who, hanging above those hills as the brightest of the stars, showed herself the Protectress of the Western Shore. Such elements as these which they themselves give us, we may take and think over; but if we go on to mix up with them modern Greek additions about Apollo, and yet more modern metaphysical conceptions, in order to construct allegories as a key to old Egyptian theology, we cannot but diverge widely from old Egyptian ideas. And what is worse, we shall miss the perception of the indubitable earnestness of their faith. We have every possible evidence of their unsurpassed devoutness: but we shall lose the sense of it if we get into the habit of supposing them to have set up images of abstract qualities (as abstract qualities are to us) instead of dwelling in constant dependence on living divine personages. We may find symbols everywhere in the Egyptian theology; and analogies in abundance: but I do not know that any instances of complete or continuous allegory can be adduced. When we try to construct such, or think we have found them, we presently begin to complain of an intermixture of personages or of offices, such as should show us, not that the Egpytian worship was confused, but that we do not clearly understand the ideas of the worshipers, and must have mixed them with some of our own.

Kneph, known by his Ram's head, is, as I said, in the adytum with Ra; but, though a higher god than Ra, this temple is not dedicated to him, but to Ra, as is shown by the appearance of the latter on the facade. The deeds of the great Ramases, his adorer, are brought as an offering, and presented on the walls. There appears at first something incongruous in the mingling, in these temples,

59   Wilkinson's Ancient Egyptians, V. 435.
60   Ibid. IV. 388.

of the benign serenity of the gods with the fury and cruelty of their warrior worshipers; but one soon remembers that it is an incongruity which remains to this
day, and will doubtless remain till war is abolished. A custom so durable as that
of consecrating warfare to God must have an idea at the bottom of it: and the
idea is plain enough here. We find the same idea in the mind of this Ramases,
and of Moses in his Song of deliverance, and of the Red Indian who shakes the
scalps of his enemies at the end of his spear in his war-dance, and of the Crusaders in their thanksgivings for victory over the Saracens, and of our Cromwell
in Ireland, and in the vindictive stanza of our National Anthem; — the idea
that power to conquer is given from above, and that the results are, therefore,
to the glory of him who gives the power. Such a method of observance, being
natural in certain stages of the human mind, is right in its place; —in a temple
of Ramases, for instance. The wonder is to find it in the jubilations of Christian
armies, in the dispatches of Cromwell,[61] and even in the Prayer-book of the
English Church, in direct connection with an acknowledgment of the Prince of
Peace, whose kingdom was not of this world.

One thing which struck me as strange in this hall of giants was a dwarfish
statue, without a head. It measured two or three inches less in each limb than
our middle-size, and was of course very insignificant among the Osirides. What
it was, and how it came there, we could not learn. When we looked abroad
from the entrance, the view was calm and sweet. A large island is in the midst
of the river, and shows a sandy beach and cultivated interior. The black, peaked
hills of the opposite desert close in to the south, leaving only a narrow passage
for the river. —It was nearly evening before we put off from the bank below
the temple. It had been an animating and delightful day; and I found myself
beginning to understand the pleasure of "temple-haunting;" a pleasure which
so grew upon us, that we felt real grief when it came to an end. I, for one, had
suspected beforehand that this work would soon become one of mere duty or
routine: but we found, even before we left Nubia, that we were hardly satisfied
to sit down to breakfast without having explored a temple.

---

61 Cromwell to Vice-Admiral Goodson at Jamaica—"Make yourselves as
strong as you can to beat the Spaniard, who will doubtless send a good force
into the Indies. I hope, by this time, the Lord may have blessed you to have
light upon some of their vessels, —whether by burning them in their harbors
or otherwise."—Cromwell's Letters and Speeches, vol, III. p. 156.

CHAPTER XI

IBREEM—DIRR—SUBOOA—DAKKEH—GARF HOSEYN

WHILE AT BREAKFAST THE NEXT MORNING (January 8th) we drew to shore under the great rock on which stands Ibreem, the station of Roman and Saracenic garrisons, in times when it was necessary to over-awe Nubia, and protect the passage southwards. It was an important place during the wars of Queen Candace with the Roman occupants of Egypt and Nubia. It appears that the word Candace was probably a title and not a proper name, —it being borne by a series of Ethiopian queens; —a curious circumstance by itself. Of the Queen Candace who marched against Ibreem (Premnis) we are told by Strabo that she was a woman of masculine courage, and had lost an eye.

We saw from our deck some grottoes in the rock, with paintings inside; and longed to get at them: but they were so difficult of access, (only by a rope) that Mr. E. went alone. They are of the time of the great Ramases and three earlier sovereigns of the same period. The painting is still vivid; representing votive offerings. There are some very small statues in high relief at the upper end.

I could not be satisfied without mounting the cliff: and from its summit I obtained a view second only to that above Aysoot. I could now understand something of the feeling which generates songs in praise of Nubia; for many charming spots were visible from this height, —recesses of verdure, —small alluvions, where the cotton shrub was covered with its yellow blossoms, and crops of grain and pulse were springing vigorously. On the Arabian side, all looked dreary; the sandy areas between its groups of black crags being sprinkled with Sheikhs' tombs, and scarcely anything else; and the only green being on a promontory here and there jutting into the river. The fertility was mainly on the Lybian shore; and there it must once have been greater than now. Patches of coarse yellow grass within the verge of the desert, and a shade of gray over the sand in places, seemed to tell of irrigation and drainage now disused. A solitary doum palm rose out of the sand, here and there; and this was the only object in the vast yellow expanse, till the eye rested on the vast amethyst mountains which bounded all to the south and west. Some of these hills advanced and some receded, so as to break the line: and their forms were as strange and capricious as their disposition. Some were like embankments: some like round tumuli: some like colossal tents. The river here was broad and sinuous; and, as far as I could see, on either hand, its course was marked by the richest verdure. The freshness, and vastness, and sublime tranquillity of this scene singularly impressed me.

The chief interest about the town or fortress was in the mixture of relics, —Egyptian, Greek, Roman, Saracenic and Turkish. The winged globe, Greek borders and columns, Roman walls, Mosques and Turkish fortifications, —all these may be seen in half-an-hour's walk, heaped together or scattered about. The modern dwellings appear to be, for the most part, made of rough stones, instead of mud; —the stones lying ready to the hand, I suppose, and the mud having to be brought up the rock. It is a truly desolate place now.

In the afternoon, we saw the capital: —Dirr, the capital of Nubia. On the bank, we met the governor and his suite, with whom we exchanged salutations. We were walking so slowly, and were so ready to be spoken to, that the governor might have declared his wishes to us if he had not been shy. He preferred sending a message through our Rais, whom we met presently after; and to whom he said that he was ashamed to ask us himself, but he should be much obliged to us to give him a bottle of wine. Such was the request of the Mohammedan governor of the capital of Nubia! Our dragoman could not keep his countenance when he delivered the message. We did not see his excellency again, and he never sent for the wine; so he did not sin against his law by our means.

Dirr reminded me, more than any other place, of the African villages which Mungo Park used to set before us. It has two noble sycamores (so-called), one of which is the finest we saw in the country. It had a deewán round it, where the old people might sit and smoke, while the young sing and dance. The governor's house is partly of burnt brick, —quite a token of grandeur here. The other houses were of mud, as usual; —clean and decent. The cemetery shows signs of care, —some low walls, ornamented at the coping, surrounding some of the graves, and pebbles being neatly strewn over others. The roads were ankle-deep in dust. The palm-groves, with the evening light shining in among the stems, were a luxury to the eye. The people looked clean and open-faced. Some of them were very light; and these were. probably descended from Sultan Selim's Bosnians, like many of the fair-complexioned people in the neighborhood of the sultan's garrisons. Many articles were offered for sale, —the people hastening to spread their mats in the dusty road, and the women holding out their necklaces and bracelets. One woman asked five piastres for her necklace; and she would have had them: but seeing this, she suddenly raised her demand to twenty. She is probably wearing that necklace at this moment. The gentlemen bought mats for our tents here, giving nine piastres (1s. 8 ½ d.) apiece for them.

The temple of Dirr interested us much from the novelty of its area and portico being in the open air, when the rest of the temple is in the rock. I may observe too that this was the only temple we saw in Nubia which stood on the eastern bank. —The area once had eight pillars, the bases only of which remain; and of its war pictures nothing is visible but faint traces. I made out only a chariot wheel, and a few struggling combatants. We have here the same subjects, and the same deity, as at Aboo-Simbil. Ramases the Great consecrates his victories to the god Ra, whom he calls his patron, and after whom he is named Ra-mses. —The corridor or portico is faced with four Osiride pillars. Through it, we enter the rock part of the temple, and find ourselves in a hall supported by six square pillars. The walls are sculptured over in "intaglio relevato," as it has been called; —that is, the outlines are cut in a groove, more or less deep, and the relief of the interior rises from the depth of the groove. The walls are now stained and blackened; and they have a mouldering appearance which portends speedy defacement. But the king and his captives, and his lion and his enemies, and his gods and his children, are still traceable. Over the lion, which seems a valuable auxiliary in the battles of Ramases, and which is here seizing a captive, is written an inscription which says, according to Champollion, "the lion, servant of his majesty, tearing his enemies to pieces."—Champollion found here a valuable list of the names of the children of Ramases, placed according to their age and rank. In the small temple at Aboo-Simbil, the king has his son at his feet, and his wife has her daughters, with their names and titles inscribed. At this temple of Dirr, the list is apparently made complete, there being here seven sons and eight daughters, with declarations of their names and titles.

The adytum is small. The four figures which it once contained are gone: but their seat remains, and their marks against the wall. Two dark chambers, containing some imperfect sculptures, are on either hand; and this is all. This temple is twenty feet deeper in the whole than the small one at Aboo-Simbil, but it is inferior in workmanship.

On our return to the dahabieh, we saw a sight very rare to us now; —a cloudy sky. The sky looked angry, with its crimson flushes, and low hanging fiery clouds. We found the people angry too, —upon a subject which makes people elsewhere strangely passionate, —a currency question. The inhabitants of Dirr have only recently learned what money is, having traded by barter till within a very short time. They had this evening some notion in their heads which our dragoman and Rais thought absurd, about a change in the value of

money in the next trading village; and they came down to the bank clamoring
for more money for their mats and necklaces. When all explanation and remonstrance failed to quiet them, Alee snatched up a tub, and threw water over them:
and then arose a din of screams and curses. We asked Alee what the curses were:
they were merely the rational and safe hope that we might all die.

The crimson flushes faded away from the sky, and the angry clouds melted:
but we had now no moon except before breakfast, when we were glad to see her
waste daily.

There was another temple in waiting for us the next morning (Jan. 9th)—
another temple of the Great Ramases; —that of Subooa. The novelty here was a
very interesting one; the Dromos (Course or avenue) and its sphinxes.

The temple is about five hundred yards from the shore; and a few dwellings lie between. The sand was deep and soft, but, for once, delightfully cool
to the feet, at this early morning hour. The sand has been so blown up against
the sphinxes as to leave but little of them visible. There are four on each hand,
as you go up to the propyla: but one is wholly covered; and five others are
more or less hidden. Two are unburied; but their features are nearly gone. The
head of another is almost complete, and very striking in its wise tranquillity
of countenance. Two rude statues stand beside the sphinxes at the entrance of
the dromos; and two colossi lie overthrown and shattered beside their pedestals at the inner end of the dromos, and before the propyla. The cement seems
to have fallen out between the stones of the propyla: but over their mouldering surface are war-sculptures dimly traceable: —the conquests of Ramases
again. Within the gate way is the hall where ten Osirides are ranged, five on
each hand, dividing the hall into three aisles. Here I saw, for the first time,
how these massive temples were roofed. The ten Osirides supported the heavy
architrave, whose blocks joined, of course, over the heads of the colossi. From
this architrave to the outer walls were laid massive blocks of stone, which
formed the roof. We shall see hereafter that when it was desired to light the
interior, the roof over the middle aisle was raised above that of the side aisles;
and the space left open, except for the necessary supporting blocks, or (as at
El-Karnak) a range of stone gratings.

The Osirides here are very rude; composed of stones of various shapes and
sizes, cemented together. I suppose they were once covered with cement; but
now they look, at the first glance, like mere fragments of pillars. A second look,
however, detects the crossed arms, and the crosier and flagellum. —Of the adytum at the extremity nothing was visible but the globe and asps over its door;
and the sand was so drifted into the hall that we could see over the wall at the
upper end. —It will be perceived that this is a rude and ruined temple, with no
interest belonging to it but its antiquity and its array of sphinxes.

That evening, we had the promise of another temple for the next morning's work. We reached Dakkeh, the Pselchê of Strabo, at 10 p.m.: but we could not moor under the western bank, from the strength of the wind, and were obliged to stand across to the other shore.

The morning of the 10th was bright and cool, and we were early ashore, where we saw a good deal besides the temple. A village, small, but not so minute as usual, stands near the bank; and its inhabitants are good-looking and apparently prosperous. I saw from the top of the propylon, a large patch of fertile land lying back on the edge of the Desert, or in it. A canal or ditch carried water from the river to this land, where there were two or more sakias to lift it. At least, I saw a belt of flourishing castor-oil plants and other shrubs extending from the river to where they met the sakias. Further in the Desert, I observed more of those gray expanses which tell of cultivable soil beneath, and of former irrigation. This must have been a flourishing district once; and it is not a distressed one now.

The women were much adorned with beads—blue, black, and white. Some would permit us to examine them: others fled and hid themselves behind huts or walls, on our merely looking in their faces: and of these none was so swift as the best dressed woman of them all. She had looped back, with her blue necklace, the mantle she wore on her head, to leave her hands and eyes free for making her bread. Of all the scamperers she was the swiftest when our party began to look about them. A mother and daughter sat on the ground within a small enclosure, grinding millet with the antique quhern: a pretty sight, and a dexterously-managed, though slow process. Several of the women had brass nose-rings, which to my eyes look about as barbarous and ugly as ear-rings; and no more. When we come to the piercing flesh to insert ornaments, I do not see that it matters much whether the ear or nose is pierced. The insertion is surely the barbarism.

While I was on the top of the propylon of Dakkeh, I saw far off to the northwest, a wide stretch of blue waters, with the reflection of shores and trees. Rather wondering how such a lake or reach of the river could be there, while the Nile seemed to be flowing northeast, and observing that these waters were bluer than those of the river, I asked myself whether this could possibly be the mirage, by which I had promised myself never to be deceived. My first thought was of mirage: but a little further study nearly convinced me that it was a real water—either a lake left by the inundation, or a reach of the river brought there by a sudden bend. I was still sufficiently uncertain to wish my friends to come up and see; though the reflection of the groves and clumps on the banks was as perfect as possible in every line. Just as I was going down to call my party, I saw a man's head and shoulders come up out of the midst of the lake: —a very large head and shoulders—such as a man might have who was near at hand. The sensation was strange, and not very agreeable. The distant blue lake took itself off in flakes. The head and shoulders belonged to a man walking across the sand below: and the groves and clumps and well-cut banks resolved themselves into scrubby bushes, patches of coarse grass, and simple stones. This was the best mirage I have ever seen, for its beauty and the completeness of the deception. I saw many afterwards in the Desert; and a very fine one in the plain of Damascus: but my heart never beat again as it did on the top of the Dakkeh propylon. I had a noble view of the Desert and the Nile from that height: and it was only sixty-nine steps of winding stair that I had to ascend. These propyla were the watch-towers and bulwarks of the temples in the old days when the temples of the Deities were the fortifications of the country. If the inhabitants had known early enough the advantage of citadels and garrisons, perhaps the Shepherd Race might never have possessed the country; or would, at least, have found their conquest of it more difficult than, according to Manetho, they did. "It came to pass," says Manetho (as Josephus cites him), "I know not how, that God was displeased with us: and there came up from the East, in a strange manner, men of an ignoble race, who had the confidence to invade our country, and easily subdued it by their power, without a battle. And when they had our rulers in their hands, they burnt our cities, and demolished the temples of the gods, and inflicted every kind of barbarity upon the inhabitants, slaying some, and reducing the wives and children of others to slavery." It could scarcely have happened that these Shepherds, "of an ignoble race," would have captured the country "without a battle," and laid hands on the rulers, if there had been such citadels as the later built temples, and such watch-towers and bulwarks as these massive propyla. Whenever I went up one of them, and looked out through the loop-holes in the thick walls, I felt that these erections were for military, full as much as religious purposes. Indeed, it is clear that the ideas were scarcely separable, after war had once made havoc in the valley of the Nile. As for the non-military purposes of these propyla; —they gave admission through the portal in the centre to the visitors to the temple, whether they came in the ordinary way, or in the processions which were so imposing in the olden times. It must have been a fine sight, from the loop-holes or parapets of these great flanking towers—the approach or departure of the procession of the day—the banners bearing the symbol of god or hero; the boat-shrine, borne by the shaven and white-robed priests, in whose hands lay most of the power, and in whose heads all the learning, of their age. To see them marching in between the sphinxes of the avenue, followed by the crowd bearing offerings; —the men with oxen, cakes, and fruits, and the women with turtle doves and incense—all this must have been a treat to many a sacerdotal watchman at this height. Such an one had probably charge of the flags which were hoisted on these occasions on the propyla. There are, on many of these towers, wide perpendicular grooves, occupied by what look like ladders of hieroglyphic figures. These grooves held the flag-staves on festival days, when the banners, covered with symbols, were set floating in the air. These propyla were good stations from which to give out news of the rising or sinking of the Nile: and they were probably also used for observatories. They were a great acquisition to the country when introduced or invented; and their introduction earlier might, perhaps, as I have said, have materially changed the destinies of the nation. The instances are not few in which these flanking towers have been added to a pylon of a much earlier date.

The interest of this temple is not in its antiquity. It is of various dates; and none of them older than the times of the Ptolemies. The interest lies in the traces of the different builders and occupants of this temple, and in the history (according to Diodorus) of the Ethiopian king who built the adytum, —the most sacred part of it. This king Ergamun, who lived within half a century before our era, had his doubts about the rectitude and reasonableness of the method by which the length of kings' reigns was settled in Ethiopia. Hitherto, the custom had been for the priests to send word to their brother, the king, when the gods wished him to enter their presence: and every king, thus far, had quietly destroyed himself, on receiving the intimation. Ergamun abolished the custom, —not waiting, as far as appears, for his summons, but going up to "a high place" with his troops, when he slew the priests in their temple, and reformed some of the institutions out the fact[62] that a somewhat resembling custom still remains in a higher region of Ethiopia, where it is thought shocking that a king should die a natural death; that is, like other people. The kings of this tribe, when they believe themselves about to die, send word to their ministers, who immediately cause them to be strangled. This is reported by the expedition sent by the present ruler of Egypt to explore the sources of the White Nile.

Though Ergamun was not willing to take the word of the priests for the will of the gods, he appears to have been forward in the service of his deities, to whom he is seen presenting offerings, and whom he proudly acknowledges as his patrons, guardians, and nourishers. The old adytum, built by him, looks hoary and crumbling; more so than the more ancient temples we have seen: but the sculptures are plainly distinguishable. It is much blackened by fires; but in one corner, where the sculptures are protected by a block of stone which has fallen across, I found a very clear group, —of the king standing between Ra and Thoth, the god of intellect and the arts, concerning whom Socrates relates a curious anecdote in the Phædrus[63] of Plato. The two gods are holding vases

62   Wilkinson's Modern Egypt and Thebes, II. 319.
63   Phædr. Tayl. Trans. p. 364.

aloft, from which they pour each a stream of the emblem of life; —immortalizing "the ever-living Ergamun," as his cartouche calls him. Under the cornice are four decorative borders, on the four sides of the chamber. One gives the emblems of Ra and Thoth, —the hawk and ibis, —squatted face to face in successive pairs: another, the royal cartouches, guarded by hawks with expanded wings: a third the emblem of duration or permanency: while on the one over the door are strips of hieroglyphics. The thrones of gods and kings have a compartment left in the lower corner of the massive seat, to be filled up with devices. Sometimes this is done: sometimes not. In this adytum the compartment is occupied by the device taken from much older monuments, and see now on the pedestals of the pair at Thebes, —the water plants of the god Nilus which are bound up to support the royal throne.

There was enough of color left here to show us how materially the effect of the sculpture was made to depend upon it. The difference in the clearness of the devices is wonderful when they are seen in a mass, and when each compartment or side of a chamber is marked off by broad bands of deep color. The supplying of details, and yet more of perspective, by painting, gives a totally different character to the sculptures; which difference ought to be allowed for where the colors have disappeared. I am not speaking here of the goodness or badness of the taste which united painting and sculpture in the old Egyptian monuments. I am only pointing out that it was the Egyptian method of representation; and that their works cannot therefore be judged of by the mere outlines. The colors remaining in this chamber are a brilliant blue, a pale clear green (which survives everywhere and is beautiful), and a dull red, —deeper for the garments, lighter for the skins.

This chamber is completely cased, except the entrance, with more modern building. It is shut in, roof and all, as if it had been pushed into a box. The old door-way, also the work of Ergamun, is built round by a later devotee. The chambers erected by the Ptolemies have some modern decorations mixed in with the ancient symbols, — such as the olivewreath, a harp of a different make from the old Egyptian, and the Greek caduceus, instead of the native one.

Some yet more modern occupants have sadly spoiled this temple. The Christians might very naturally feel that they could not go to worship till they had shut out from their eyesight the symbols of the old faith: and we therefore should not be hard upon them for plastering over the walls. We should forgive them all the more readily because such plastering is an admirable method of preserving the old sculptures. But the Christians must have their saints all about them: and there they are, dim, but obvious enough, —with huge wry faces, and flaring glories over their heads. Some of the sculptures which have been restored, and some which appear never to have been plastered, look beautiful beside these daubs.

In the portico of this temple we first saw an instance of the more modern, the Greek, way of at once inclosing and lighting the entrance to a temple, — by inter-columnar screens and doorway; called now a portico in antis. I do not remember seeing this in any of the ancient buildings; while it is found at Philœ, Dendara, Isna, and other Ptolemaic erections. It has its beauty and convenience: but it does not seem to suit the primitive Egyptian style, where the walls were relieved of their deadness by sculpture, but, I think, never by breaks.

There are some Greek inscriptions on different parts of this temple; and two certainly which are not Greek. Whether they are Coptic, or the more ancient Egyptian Enchorial writing, it is not for me to say. — The outside of the temple is unfinished: and fragments of substantial stone wall about it appear like work left, rather than demolished. Within one of these walls, I found a passage; a not uncommon discovery among the massive buildings which might thus conveniently communicate by a safe and concealed method.

This was our work before breakfast. —Another temple was ready for us after dinner; —that of the ancient Tutzis, now Garf Hoseyn.

I walked on shore for a few minutes, while dinner was hastened: and saw some agricultural proceedings which were amusing to a stranger. Two or three donkeys were bringing down dust and sand from the Desert, across a pretty wide tract of cultivated land, to qualify the richness of the Nile mud. Their panniers were mere frail-baskets; and when they were emptied, the wind (which was strong) carried away a good proportion of the contents; and the rest looked such a mere sprinkling, that I admired the patience which could procure enough for a whole field. But carts are not known so high up the Nile, nor panniers worthy of the name. We had moored just under a sakia, whose creak was most melancholy. This creak is the sweetest and most heart stirring music in the world to the Nile peasant; just as the Alp-horn is to the Swiss. It tells of provision, property, wonted occupation, home, the beautiful Nile, and beloved oxen. Any song would be charming with such a burden. But to us it was a mere dismal creak; and when it goes on in the night, as happens under a thrifty proprietor, I am told it is like a human wail, or the cry of a tortured animal. So much for the operation of the same sound through different ideas! The shed of this sakia was really pretty; —inhabited by a sleek ox, and a sprightly boy-driver; shaded by a roof of millet-stalks, and hung over with white convolvulus and the purple bean of this region. Our Dongola sailor caught up a little romping boy from among his companions, and brought him on board by force. The terror of the child was as great as if we had been ogres. I could not have conceived anything like it, and should be glad to know what it was that he feared. His worst moment of panic seemed to be when we offered him good things to eat; though his companions on shore were by that time calling out to him to take what we offered.

His captor forced some raisins into his mouth; and his change from terror to doubt, and from doubt to relish when he began to taste his dose, was amusing to see. Raisins were not a bribe to detain him, however; he was off like a shot, the moment he was released. I suppose his adventure will be a family anecdote, for many generations to come.

The first view of the temple from a distance is very striking, —its area pillars standing forth from the rock, like the outworks of the entrance gate of a mountain. This temple is of the time of the great Ramases, and is dedicated to Phthah, —the god of Artisan Intellect and Lord of Truth:[64]—not the god of Truth, which has its own representative deity; but the possessor of truth, by which he did his creative works. He is the efficient creator, working in reality and by fundamental principles, and not by accommodation or artifice. The scarabæus was sacred to him (though not exclusively) and the frog: the latter as signifying the embryo of the human species; the former, as some say, because the beetle prepares a ball of earth, and there deposits its eggs, and thus presents an image of the globe and its preparation for inhabitancy. However this may be, here we have the creative god, the son of Kneph, the ordaining deity, at whose command he framed the universe. It may be remembered that this was the deity to whom, according to tradition, the first temple was raised in Egypt; —when Menes, having redeemed the site of Memphis from the waters, began the city there, and built the great temple of Phthah, renowned for so many ages afterwards. —Memphis and this Garf Hoseyn formerly bore the same name, derived from their deity: —viz., Phthahei or Thyphthah. His temple has been found by some travelers as imposing as any on the Nile. It has been compared even with Aboo-Simbil. This must be owing, I think, to the singular crowding of the colossi within a narrow space; and perhaps also to the hoary, blackened aspect of this antique speos. The impression cannot possibly arise from any beauty of true grandeur in the work, —to which the inspiration of the god seems to have been sadly wanting. We saw nothing ruder than this temple; which yet is grand in its way.

The whole of it is within the rock except the area. The area has four columns in front, and four Osirides. These colossi are round-faced and ugly, and have lost their helmets, and some their heads. One head lies topsy-turvy, the placid expression of the face contrasting strangely with the agony of its position. The colossi do not hold the crosier and flagellum in their crossed hands, as usual; but both in the right hand, while the left arm hangs by the side. On the remnant of the wall of the area are some faint traces of sculpture, and two niches, containing three figures each. —The striking moment to the visitor is that of entering the rock. He finds himself among six Osirides, which look enormous

64   Wilkinson's Ancient Egyptians, IV. 250.

from standing very near each other; —themselves and the square pillars behind them seeming to fill up half the hall. These figures are, after all, only eighteen feet high; and of most clumsy workmanship; —with short thick legs, short ill-shaped feet, and more bulk than grandeur throughout. I observed here, as at Aboo-Simbil, that the wide separation between the great toe and the next seems to tell of the habitual use of sandals.

In the walls of the aisles behind the Osirides, are eight niches, each containing three figures, in high relief. In every niche, the figures are represented, I think, in the same attitude, —with their arms round one another's necks; but they bear different symbols. The middle figure of every group is Ra, as patron of Ramases; and he is invoked as dwelling at Subooa and Dirr, as well as here; the three temples being, as we have seen, of one group or family. Ra is here called the son of Phthah and Athor. The sculptures on the wall are now much blackened by the torches of visitors, and perhaps by Arab fires. But the bright colors, of which traces yet remain, may have much ameliorated the work in its own day. Across the usual corridor, with its usual pair of chambers inhabited by bats, lies the Holy Place. It has an altar in the middle, and a recess with four figures. The goddess Anouké, crowned with her circlet of feathers, and Athor are here.

This temple extends only one hundred and thirty feet into the rock. Its position and external portico are its most striking features. We returned by the village, and certainly should not have found out for ourselves that the people are the savages they are reputed to be. They appeared friendly, cheerful, and well-fed. We looked into some houses, and found the interiors very clean. Many of the graves of their cemetery have jars at the head, which are duly filled with water every Friday, —the Mohammedan Sabbath. The door of a yard which we passed in the village had an iron knocker, of a thoroughly modern appearance. I wonder how it came there.

There was a strong wind this evening; and the boat rolled so much as to allow of neither writing nor reading in comfort. We were not sorry, therefore, to moor below Dendoor, at 10 p. m., and enjoy the prospect of a quiet night, and another temple before breakfast.

CHAPTER XII

DENDOOR—KALÁB-SHEH—BIGGEH—PHILŒ—LEAVING NUBIA

OF THE TEMPLE OF DENDOOR there is little to say, as it is of Roman time, and therefore, only imitative Egyptian. It has a grotto behind, in the rock; and this grotto contains a pit; so I suppose it is a place of burial. The temple is sacred to the great holy family of Egypt, Osiris, Isis, and Horus; and the sacred chamber contains only a tablet, with a sculpture of Isis upon it, and a few hieroglyphic signs. The quantity of stones heaped in and about this little temple is remarkable.

I took a walk over the rising grounds behind till I lost sight of the temple and our boat and people; and never did I see anything wilder than the whole range of the landscape. There was a black craggy ravine on either hand, which must occasionally, I should think, be the passage of torrents. There are rains now and then, however rarely, in this country; and when they do come, they are violent. Some of the tombs at Thebes bear mournful witness of the force with which torrents rush through any channels of the rocks that they can find. Not only were these ravines black, but the whole wide landscape, except a little peep of the Nile, and a bit of purple distance to the north, and two lilac summits to the south, peeping over the dark ridge. Nothing more dreary could well be conceived, unless it be an expanse of polar snow; yet it was exquisitely beautiful in point of color—the shining black of the whole surface, except where the shadows were jet, the bright green margin of the inch of river; the white sheikh's tomb behind the palms on that tiny spot; and the glowing amethyst of the two southern summits—these in combination were soft and brilliant to a degree inconceivable to those who have not been within the tropics. There was a bracing mild wind on this ridge, which, by reviving the bodily sense, seemed to freshen the outward world; and truly sorry I was to return. This was my last gaze upon tropical scenery too. We were to leave the tropic this afternoon, at Kaláb'-sheh.

I suppose even such an out-of-the-way region as this may be enlightened now and then as to foreign customs by the return of wandering traders or voyagers. I saw to-day on the eastern shore a house which might have been built by an European; its front neatly painted red and white; its doors yellow; and its windows of glass. It was placed with its back to the prevailing north wind; and it had a regular approach between buttresses. Two houses near had glass windows also. Some adventurous Nubian has come home a great man, probably, and is astonishing the natives with his outlandish ways.

While we were at dinner off Kaláb'-sheh, the people came down to the shore, and made a market. When their wares were ranged, they were a pretty sight—the baskets of henneh, the spears and daggers, and the curiosities dug out from the temples.

Having happily some idea what to look for here, we hastened to the small speos of Beyt-el-Wellee, a quarter of a mile from the large temple, while we yet had full daylight. The view from the entrance is beautiful, commanding the recess of fertile ground which seems to flow in from the river, and fill the angle between the hills. This recess was clustered with palms which were softly swaying their shadowy heads below us. The opposite shore was of the bright yellow of evening; and to the right, below us, stood the massive temple of Kaláb'-sheh, with its outworks of heaped stones, and its traces of terraces, flights of steps, and quays, all the way down to the river. This little rock-temple of Beyt-el-Wellee is as interesting as anything in Egypt, except the remains of the First Period. It is full of the glory of the great Ramases again. But it is not dedicated to Ra, but to Amunra—not to the Sun of the Universe, but to the Spiritual Sun—the universal centre of Being—the Unknown and Unutterable—the God of Gods. With him is joined Kneph, the ram-headed god, the animating Spirit of the creation, which gives Life to its organized beings—thus working together with Phthah, the creator, or Artisan-Intellect. The third deity of this little temple is the virgin goddess Anouké, the goddess of Purity and Household ties. She appears very frequently in the more ancient temples, and was especially honored in this southern region, where she becomes quite familiar, with her feather crown, her sceptre of lotus in one hand, and the symbol of Life in the other.

The approach to the cave entrance is between quarried rocks covered with sculptures of extraordinary merit; of which I shall have to speak presently. The temple itself consists of only two chambers: —the outer hall and the Holy Place. At first, one's impression is that one can see nothing, except the two elegant polygonal pillars which were supporting this roof ages before they gave the hint of the early Doric. A few hieroglyphic signs on the faces of these pillars engage the eye; which is then led on to distinguish bands of color; and presently to perceive that the walls have been divided into compartments by margins of

color, and rows of hieroglyphic signs. Some dim appearance of large figures, under the films of dust and mould, is next perceived; and in the inner chamber, it
was plain, as Mr. E. pointed out to me, that one figure had been washed. There
were the tricklings of the water, from the feet to the ground; and the figure
was, though dim, so much brighter than everything else, that I felt irresistibly
tempted to try to cleanse a bit of the wall, and restore to sight some of its ancient
paintings. We sent down to the boat—about half a mile, for water, tow, soap,
and one or two of the crew; and while the rest of my party went to explore the
great modern temple, I tucked up my sleeves, mounted on a stone, and began
to scrub the walls, to show the boy Hasan what I wanted him to do. I would let
no one touch the wall, however, till I had convinced myself that no color would
come off. The colors were quite fast. We might rub with all our strength without
injuring them in the least. It was singularly pleasant work, bringing forth to view
these elaborate old paintings. The colors came out bright and deep as on the day
they were laid on—so many thousand years ago! Every moment, the details of
the costume and features showed themselves on the kingly figure I was unveiling; the red and yellow pattern on the crown, and the flagellum: the armlets,
bracelets, belts, and straps; the ends of the sash; the folds of the garment, and its
wrapping over above the knee; the short mantle, the vest, the tippet or necklaces,
and the devices of the throne. It began to grow dusk before we had finished two
figures; and, indeed, I cannot say that we completely finished any; for a slight
filminess spread over the paintings as they dried, which showed that another
rubbing was necessary. I did long to stay a whole day, to clean the entire temple;
but this could not be done. I was careful to give a dry-rubbing to our work before we left it, that no injury might afterwards arise from damp; and I trust our
attempt may yet be so visibly recorded on the walls as to induce some careful
traveler to follow our example, and restore more of these ancient paintings.

The sculptures on the outside, on either hand of the approach, are now
quite destitute of color; and it does not seem to be wanted here, so finished are
the details. —On one side we see Ramases on his throne, receiving a world of
wealth in the shape of tribute from the conquered Ethiopians. The Prince of
Cush and his two children, all captives, are brought up by the eldest son of the
conqueror; the names of all the parties being affixed in hieroglyphic characters.
We see piles of ostrich's eggs, bags of gold, and ornaments; and array of fans, elephants' teeth, leopard skins, and other southern wealth; a troop of Ethiopians
bringing an Oryx (antelope), a lion, oxen and gazelles: and in the lower line of
tribute-bearers, we see apes and a camelopard. These articles are admirable like-
nesses; and the whole procession is a most lively spectacle. But the battle-scene
at the outer end is remarkably interesting, from the representation given of
the wildness of the enemy's country. The foe are flying into the woods; and

a woman cooking under a tree is warned by her little son that the conqueror is coming. A wounded chief (of whom she may be the wife), is carried by his soldiers; and a boy is throwing dust on his head, in token of despair. The king and his two sons are in separate chariots, each with his charioteer: and the king is discharging his arrows as he goes. —Elsewhere on these walls, the king is his own charioteer, having the reins fastened round his waist, that his arms may be left free. The animals are, as usual in these old sculptures, admirably done; the heads of the oxen appearing to my eye as good in their quiet way as the bull of Paul Potter, in his more vehement mood.

The foe on the opposite wall is supposed to be some people in Arabia Petræa; —Eastern at all events. We have the conqueror again, on his throne, with his lion reposing at its base; in his car; in single combat, and in the act of slaying his foes. We have a walled city; and the other accompaniments of these war-pictures: but the Ethiopian tribute, and the woman cooking at her fire in the wood are more interesting to the observer of this day.

I was struck by the extraordinary grace of some of the objects about this temple. The lamp used in the offerings to the deities is beautiful; —a delicate hand holding a cup from which the flame issues; while an orifice at the elbow-end of the lamp is receiving the oil. —In one of the groups in the adytum, I saw the first instance I had met with (except in the rude sculptures of Garf Hoseyn) of a departure from the severity of attitude usually observed. The union of the deities in the reception of homage is marked by the arm of the one hanging over the shoulder of the other. We are told by Sir G. Wilkinson[65] that this temple has been the abode, at some time, of a Mohammedan hermit. Some have supposed that the Christians have been here, obliterating the sculptures. I saw no traces of them; and I think the clouding-over of the paintings is no more than may be accounted for by lapse of years, and, possibly, a less dry situation than that of many of the old monuments. We must remember that this temple is more than three thousand years old.

On leaving the shadowy speos, I found there was still daylight enough for a survey of the renowned great temple of Kaláb'-sheh. I was glad to go over it, and admire its magnificence, and the elegance of many parts; and be amazed at its vastness; but it is too modern to interest us much here. It was founded and carried on—(not quite to completion)—by one after another of the Caesars: and it is therefore not truly Egyptian. The most interesting circumstance to me was that here we could form some judgment of the effect of the Egyptian color-decoration: for here there were two chambers in fine preservation, except where water had poured down from the massive lion-head spouts (Roman) and had washed away the colors. The relief to the eye of these strips of pure sculpture

65   Wilkinson's Modern Egypt and Thebes, II. p. 313.

was very striking. My conclusion certainly was, from the impression given by these two chambers, that, however valuable color may be for bringing out the details, and even the perspective, of sculptured designs, any large aggregate of it has a very barbaric appearance. —Still, we must not judge of the old Egyptian painting by this Roman specimen. The disk of Isis is here painted deep red, — the color of the ordinary complexion. The pale green and brilliant blue of the ancient times are present; and I saw here, and here only, a violet or plum-color.

As for the rest, this temple is a heap of magnificent ruin; magnificent for vastness and richness; but not for taste. One pillar standing among many over-thrown, —rich capitals toppled down among rough stones; and such mounds of fragments as make us wonder what force could have been used to cause such destruction, —these are the interest of this temple. It may be observed, too, that the adytum has no figure at the end, and that it appears never to have been finished. It is a singular spectacle, —the most sacred part unfinished, while the capitals of the outer columns, with their delicate carvings of vine-leaves and ten-drils twining among the leaves of the doum palm, are overthrown and broken!

This temple is believed to have stood on the site of an older one, from some ancient memorials being found on a few of the stones employed: but the existing building was begun in the reign of Augustus, carried on by some of his successors, and never finished. —As it was the largest temple in Nubia, the Christians naturally laid hands on it; and a saint, and several halos look out very strangely from among the less barbarous heathen pictures on the walls of the room within the outer hall.

This evening we descended the rapids of Kaláb'-sheh, and had left the trop-ic: and a cold, blowing evening it was. —Early next morning, the three pylons of the Dabód temple—its distinguishing feature, — stood out clear on their sandy platform. These pylons are almost the only interesting thing about this temple, which is of the time of the early Ptolemies, and carried on by Augustus and Tiberius. It never was finished; and now its massive walls are cracked and bending in all directions. The soil below seems washed or actually grubbed out, so as to endanger the mass above.

There is a mummy-pit in the brow of the hill, a quarter of a mile behind. I went to see what the little clouds of dust meant, and found some men and boys pulling out human legs and arms for our gratification. I was much better pleased with the view I obtained from the next ridge, whence I saw to the south-west the sandstone quarries which furnished the material for the temple. The recesses and projections of the stone looked as sharp cut as ever.

We were now only six miles from Philœ, where we were to remain twen-ty-four hours. After posting up our journals, we had enough to do in admiring the beauty of the scenery, which we had seen before only in the vagueness of moonlight. I think the five miles above Philœ the most beautiful on the Nile, and certainly the most varied, — with the gorges among the rocks, the black basalt contrasting with the springing wheat and the yellow sands, and the dark green palms; — and soon, Philœ opening on the sight, and its hypæthral temple, (built to look beautiful from hence,) setting up its columns against the sky: and all this so shut in by coves and promontories, and the water rendered so smooth by its approach to the dam of the islands, as to make of the whole an unique piece of lake scenery. Two mosques, a convent, and a sheikh's tomb on a pinnacle of the rock, gave character to the scene: and so did a woman on the shore, with her veiled face and water-jar, reminding us that we were re-entering Egypt Proper. I could not bear to miss any part of this approach to Philœ; and I therefore carried my dinner up to the deck, and received all that singular imagery, never to lose it again while I live.

At four o'clock we were close upon Philœ: but the island of Biggeh, also sacred, looked tempting, and we turned towards it, to explore its remains before sunset. The black rocks round show inscriptions in great numbers: and these are full of light and interest. Some are of the Pharaohs of a very early time; actually inscribed by the tributary kings who reigned at Thebes during the dominion of the Shepherds; and others of the great monarchs who drove out the Shepherds, and raised the glory of Egypt to its highest point. Some inscribe merely their names—their cartouches, which catch the eye on every hand. Some append to these the declaration that they came in pilgrimage to the gods of these holy places. Some carve a record of the granite blocks they have taken for their public works; and others leave a declaration of their victories over the Ethiopians. What an inestimable country this is, where the very rocks by the wayside offer indisputable materials of history to you as you pass by!

The other remains on Biggeh are forlorn enough. Two columns exist of a temple of the Ptolemies re-built upon a very old Pharaonic foundation. Fragments of sculpture lie about: and one pictured wall forms the side of a sordid Arab hut. The Christians have broken away parts of two great sculptured blocks to lodge an arch, which looks hideous. Wherever, in these two islands, the intaglios are filled up with mud, and the reliefs and paintings covered with clay, it is the work of the Christians, who took possession of the temples of the region for their worship.

I could not leave the high grounds of this island while the sun lighted the map-like expanse below and around me. The chaotic rocks, the desert, river, and distant settlements would have absorbed me at any other time: but now, to the south, lay the Holy Island, beyond the gold-crowned palms which waved below my feet, and beyond the piled rocks and clear shadowy river which interposed. The plan of its edifices was clear under my eye; and their superb range was fully displayed, as the sunlight was leaving their colonnades, moment by moment, and at last lingering only on the summits of the propyla. When the last ray melted into the glow which succeeds the sunset, we hastened down to the boat, and rowed over to Philœ, to the eastern cove, below the hypæthral temple, where we had moored this day fortnight, on our way up. There was still time, before the twilight was gone, for a run up to the temples. I came down again, amazed at the vastness of the sculptures on the propyla, and oppressed by a sense of the mass and the intricacy of the edifices. I felt, as I had done twice before, lost among them. But this perplexity was dispelled, and the whole arrangement made clear, by the careful study of the next day.

We all rose early on the morning of the 13th of January; and by half-past seven, we were up at the temples, having breakfasted, and sent away our kandjia, to descend the Cataract, and transfer the stores to the dahabieh.

I spent the first two hours quite alone—setting out to learn the plan of the temples, but lingering at almost every step, impressed by the majesty of the appareil of worship, or bewitched by the beauty of the details of the adornments.

The confusion of temples of which travelers complain cannot arise from their number. The remains consist of the great temple of Isis with its accessories: a little chapel to Athor; a western chapel where the god Nilus is much honored; a little chapel, modern, to Esculapius; the hypæthral temple vulgarly called Pharaoh's Bed; and various edifices of approach from the river. This is not so much to learn! The confusion seems to me rather to arise from the absence of symmetry which, remarkable elsewhere in Egypt, is singularly striking here. I ventured upon making a plan, by the eye and a rough measurement, that I might not hereafter disbelieve the extraordinary perverseness of the arrangements. As this plan lies before me, I see that the propyla do not agree with each other; nor with the colonnade in the avenue; nor with those in the area. No two chambers are of the same size. The doorways do not answer to each other, any more than the columns. There is a total want of coherence of parts. This is not only an impediment to understanding the edifices, but it causes incessant vexation to the eye, which is baulked of a view through gateways, and offended by twists and false measurements. This peculiarity once allowed for, I do not think the group of temples difficult to understand.

The first requisite to a fit survey of the Holy Island and its remains, is a knowledge of why the place is so holy. And in order to understand why the place is so holy, it is necessary to be informed of the history and offices of Osiris. I wish I might hope that any of my readers—any who have not traveled in Egypt—could be at all impressed with the seriousness of this subject. To my mind, no subject is so solemn as that of the faith of any race of men—their sustaining and actuating faith—be its objects what they may. And the objects of a sustaining and actuating faith must always be solemn and noble. Whatever their names may be, they have in them a majesty and endearment which place completely in the wrong all who ignorantly abhor or despise them. How ignorant and how guilty we ourselves may have been in our careless contempt of the idolatries of the world, we may come to perceive, when we have learned to do as we would be done by in separating the Ideas of any faith from its outward celebrations—its philosophy from its corruptions; —and when we become wise enough to discern the close relations which we have now reason to believe exist among all the effectual faiths which have ever operated widely upon mankind. How serious a research that is which would discover the attributes and functions of ancient deities, one may partly feel in contrasting the glibness with which the hallowed name of Osiris slips off the modern tongue with the reserve of old Herodotus, who, like other serious-minded men of his time, could not bring himself to name Osiris at all. I am aware of something of the same contrast in myself. Before I went to Egypt, I talked of the deities of that old nation as school children talk of Neptune and Apollo; as once fanciful personages who have become mere poetical images. It is very different now. As I read old Herodotus on the spot, the awe which made him dumb where I most wished him to speak, thrilled through me. There the calm benign gods were no poetical images, but embodied aspirations of the loftiest powers of man. There, the altars were no mere blocks of disenchanted stone, but the still inviolable depositories of the reverence, gratitude, and hope of whole races of thoughtful human beings, who here acknowledged One unutterable Eternal Being, through whose Attributes they lived, and moved, and had their being. We are apt, at home, to suppose that language to us sacred from religious associations, is either exclusively ours, or could not have meant the same to people living before our form of faith arose. But what should we say to such a supposition on the part of a more advanced race succeeding ourselves? Ought not they to admit the sacredness to us of our sacred language? And are we not bound to admit the sacredness to the old Egyptians of the devotional language which we find inscribed in the Holy Chambers of their temples, and which is delivered to us from out of the records of their faith? This is not claiming parity of value for their objects of faith and ours. It has nothing to do with the comparative elevation, purity, and promise of any two faiths. It is merely a claim that the Old Egyptians should be regarded as having a faith; a faith to which they might refer the loftiest ideas of a high order of intellect, and in which they might repose the affections of their common human heart. Without a clear admission of this much, in that spirit of brotherhood which should unite us with the distant in time as truly as with the distant in space, there is no use in inquiring into the history and offices of Osiris, or of any other object of worship.

Different districts of the great valley assigned their higher honors to different gods: but Osiris, Isis, and their son Horus were generally held in the deepest reverence. I believe that, except the Supreme, Osiris was the only deity who was never named. When Herodotus has described the scourgings and lamentings which follow the sacrifices at the feast of Isis, he adds[66] that it is not permitted to him to tell in whose honor they scourge themselves and lament. And again, in describing the images of the dead, prepared for the guidance of the embalming process, Herodotus says[67] that the best represents, as he is told, Him whose name he has an objection to utter. And thus he always speaks of Osiris, by reverent allusion, and never by name. The reason of this peculiar sacredness of Osiris, above all gods but the Supreme, was his office of Judge of the living and the dead. That which made him so universally and eminently adored was his being the representation, or rather the incarnation, of the Goodness of the Supreme. The plurality of deities in Egypt arose from the practice, for popular use, of deifying the attributes of the Supreme God. We have thus seen his creative Spirit or Will embodied in one god; and the creative art, or Artisan Intellect, in another; and we shall meet with more. His primary attribute, his Goodness, was embodied in Osiris,[68] who left his place in the presence of the Supreme, took a human form, (though not becoming a human being),[69] went about the world doing good to men, sank into death in a conflict with the Power of Evil;[70] rose up to spread blessings over the land of Egypt and the world, and was appointed Judge of the Dead[71] and Lord of the heavenly region, while present with his true worshipers on earth, to do them good. Such were the history and functions of Osiris, as devoutly recorded by the Egyptians of several thousand years ago. And here, in Philœ, was his sepulchre, where the faithful came in pilgrimage, from the mighty Pharaoh to the despised goat herd, for a long course of centuries. He was especially adored for other reasons than his benefactions: as being the only manifestation on earth of the Supreme God. This made him superior to the eight great gods, after whom he ranked on other accounts.[72] How the manifestation was made in a human form without an adoption of human nature, was one of the chief Egyptian mysteries;[73] the ideas of which will now, I fear, never be offered to our apprehension. Upon his

66   Herod. II. 61.
67   Ibid. II. 86.
68   Wilkinson's Ancient Egyptians, IV. 189.
69   Ibid. IV. 317.
70   Ibid. IV. 189.
71   Ibid. IV. 314.
72   Wilkinson's Ancient Egyptians, IV. 317.
73   Ibid. IV. 317.

death, he passed into the region of the dead, (borne there, as the sculptures represent, by the four genii of Hades)—and then, having passed through its stages, was raised to the function of Judge.[74]

Among the allusive names of Osiris were those of "Opener of good,"[75] "Manifester of grace," and "Revealer of truth:" and the description of him was, in the ancient words, "full of grace and truth."[76] He obtained the victory after his death over the Evil Principle which had destroyed him:[77] and it was in his name, which they then assumed, that the virtuous, after judgment, entered into the state of blessedness which they shared with him.[78] The departed, men and women alike, were called Osiris: this spiritual name betokening that they were now in that state where sex was abolished, where no marriage existed, but human beings had become pure as the heaven-born inhabitants.[79]

When it is said that Osiris was the only manifestation of the Supreme upon earth, it must be understood that this means the only manifestation by a native heavenly resident. For all animated beings were supposed to be emanations from, the Centre of Life.[80] The great emanation doctrine which has spread so far over the world was certainly a chief point of faith in Egypt at a very early date; and it is believed that Pythagoras, recognizing it in all their observances which were expositions of doctrine, adopted it from them, and thence sent it on through distant countries and future ages. Plutarch ascribes to the belief of this doctrine the peculiar observances with regard to animals in Egypt. The passage is too well known to need citing here: but it is valuable, not only as testifying to this great fact of the Egyptian mind, but as showing that persons comparatively ancient were wiser than too many of ourselves in seeing in their practice of what we call Brute worship something deeper and more serious than we have been taught to look for. Plutarch cites Herodotus as saying that whatever beings have been endowed with life and any measure of reason are to be regarded as effluxes, or portions of the supreme wisdom which governs the universe; so that the Deity is not less strikingly represented in these than in images of any kind made by the hand of man. Porphyry declares "the Egyptians perceived that the Divinity entered not the human body only, and that the Soul dwelt not, while on earth, in man alone, but passed in a measure through all animals." Thus Osiris was

74   Plutarch de Iside, s. 35, cited by Wilkinson, Ancient Egyptians, IV. 320.
75   Plut. de. is. I. s. 42.
76   Wilkinson's Ancient Egyptians, IV. 180.
77   Ibid. IV. 320.
78   Ibid. IV. 320.
79   Ibid. IV. 316.
80   Ibid. IV. 316.

not the only manifestation of the universal Soul: and so far shared the lot of the
humblest worm bred in the mud of the Nile; but he was the only member of
the heavenly society, the only one of the sons of the Supreme, who came upon
earth to make him known: and he thus took rank above them all.

It is impossible not to perceive that Osiris was to the old Egyptians what
the Messiah is to be to the Jews; and what another has been to the Christians.
The nature, character and offices of Osiris, and the sacred language concerning
him are so coincident with those most interesting to Christians as to compel a
very careful attention on the part of inquirers into Egyptian antiquities. Various
solutions of the extraordinary fact have been offered. Some who hold to the
literal historical truth of the book of Genesis suggest, as their conjecture, that
Noah may have foreknown everything relating to the coming of Christ, even to
the language which should be used concerning him by sacred writers: and that
his descendants may have communicated all this to the ancient Egyptians, who
made a God out of the prophecy and its adjuncts.[81] Others have endeavored
to make out such personal intercourse between Pythagoras and some of the
Hebrew prophets on the one hand, and the Egyptian priests on the other, as
might account for the parallelism in question.[82] Others would have us understand it by concluding that the latest Egyptian priests were disciples of Plato,
and put their own Platonising interpretations on the character of Osiris, as the
Platonising Christians did on that of Christ. Others again, who see that ideas
sire the highest subject of human cognizance, the history of ideas the only true
history, and a common holding of ideas the only real relation of human beings
to each other, believe that this great constellation of ideas is one and the same
to all these different peoples; was sacred to them all in turn, and became more
noble and more glorious to men's minds as their minds became strengthened
by the nourishment and exercise of ages. It is a fact which ought to be attended
to while considering the various solutions offered, that the character and offices
of Osiris were certainly the same in the centuries which preceded the birth of
Abraham, —in the very earliest times known to us, —as after the death of Pythagoras and Plato. This is proved by the sculptures in the oldest monuments.
We see in the tombs cotemporary with the Pyramids that Osiris was to men
then living the same benefactor and final judge that he was to the subjects of
the Ptolemies.[83]

As Osiris was the manifestation of the goodness of the Supreme Being, he
was naturally identified with the most obvious benefits for which the old Egyptians desired to be thankful: and to them the greatest of benefits was the Nile.

81   Wilkinson's Ancient Egyptians, IV. 188.
82   Bayle, Art. Pythagoras, Note H.
83   Wilkinson's Ancient Egyptians, IV. 323.

Hence arose one of their most beautiful traditionary fictions; that his body was deposited in the cataract, whence he arose once a year, to spread blessings over the earth. Hence he was called also the author of agriculture, as the inundation maybe well considered. Hence he is made to say, in one of the most ancient inscriptions, that he is the eldest son of time, and cousin to the day; and that there is no place where he has not been, distributing his benefits to all mankind.[84]

It appears that the antagonism of Good and Evil was not very early recognized in Egypt. At first, Typho was called the brother of Osiris; and good and evil were supposed to be nearly related, and both claiming homage, as necessary and therefore worthy of acceptance. When the god of Evil came to be hated, his sacrifices began to be discontinued, and we even find his images carefully obliterated. He then became the murderer of Osiris, and was in league with Antœ, of whom we have before seen something, and who represented the sand of the Desert. This was an old feud, —this that we witness in our day, between the Nile and the Desert! Osiris declares himself, in the old inscription, "cousin to the day;" and Typho was the god of the Eclipse. Thus, as the old Egyptian philosophy declined, and the corruption crept in which is the invariable consequence of polytheism, the brotherhood of the two attributes grew into antagonism, and Typho became the hated and ugly monster that we see him in the sculptures, —the Satan of the Nile valley, with the ravaging hippopotamus for his symbol.

It was in his office of judge of the dead that Osiris was presented to the minds of Egyptian guests at their banquets, in the mode of a mummy, which was carried round, as Herodotus says,[85] after the feast, to remind every one of his mortality. His name might not be uttered; but his idea was to be ever present. The Greeks gave their own turn to this observance, as Anacreon shows us, and used this memento mori as an incentive to the more eager pursuit of transient pleasure. The Egyptians were more serious minded, and at the same time more cheerful in their views of death. Their view seems to have been that which Thales is wondered at for having professed, and which he probably adopted while in Egypt, that there is nothing to choose between life and death. The accounts of the saying uttered during the ceremony vary, —as perhaps the exhortations themselves varied in course of time. According to Herodotus, it was "Look at this man: you will be like him when you are dead. Drink now, and enjoy yourselves." Plutarch gives it more gravely. The guest was told that men ought "to love one another, and avoid those evils which tend to make them consider life too long, when in reality it is too short." Whatever was said, Osiris was offered to the eye, with his insignia of judgment, the crosier and flagellum, in his hands.

84   Wilkinson's Ancient Egyptians, IV. 323.
85   Herod. II. 78.

Osiris was said to have forty-nine titles: Isis ten thousand.[86] We see her now in her temple at Philœ, as the mourning widow of Osiris, and the mother of Horus. She was the daughter of Seb, or Time; and therefore the sister of Osiris: and it is said that the practice, not uncommon among the priests, and far too common among the Ptolemies, of marrying their sisters, arose from the example of this pair; —from its being supposed that such marriages must be fortunate. We sometimes see Isis as the Land of Egypt, when Osiris is rising from the river. She is the Protectress of Osiris, covering his corpse with her wings. This is a beautiful representation of her, and one which I was never tired of meeting. Sometimes she is nursing Horus. But her most important office is that of colleague of Osiris in the judgment of the dead. From her, in this office, the Greeks directly derived their Hecate; her office being not only the same, but her name standing inscribed, at this day, "Isis, the potent Hekte."[87] As the bringer to judgment, she is sometimes called the Giver of Death, and crowned with the asp. Herodotus says that the Egyptians regarded Isis as the greatest of all the divinities.[88] It might be so in his age: and her festivals, as witnessed by him, were no doubt very majestic: but there is no reason to believe that in an older time she was so much honored as the deities who represented a higher Ideal. —The heifer was held sacred to Isis; and no heifer was ever permitted to be slaughtered in Egypt.[89] The young Horus, her infant, was adopted by the Greeks and called Harpocrates, and made the god of silence by his finger being on his lips. The Egyptian "Hor," however, seems to signify childhood, in the sense of entrance or re-entrance upon life; of production or reproduction[90] In Hades, he appears seated on a lotus, before the throne of Osiris, and in front of the candidate for judgment. He is the child, or new life, of the region beyond the tomb. The lotus, on which the child is seated, is reproductive in a singular manner, as Payne Knight tells us,[91] —by new flowers springing from seeds which could not escape from their sheaths. Isis is perpetually seen holding the stem of the lotus: and the lotus pillar, common everywhere in Egypt, abounds especially at Philœ. It is a remarkable fact, told us by Payne Knight, that Isis, with Horus on her lap, is found on a Lapland drum, and also in ancient Muscovite worship: and with a golden heifer for a symbol of worship, or idol.[92] The Lapland goddess Isa or

86   Wilkinson's Ancient Egyptians, IV. 321, 317.
87   Wilkinson's Ancient Egyptians, IV. 367, 369, 384.
88   Herod. II. 40.
89   Larcher. Note on Herod. II. 41.
90   Wilkinson's Ancient Egyptians, IV. 407.
91   Inquiry into the Symbolic Language of Ancient Art and Mythology—Classical Journal.
92   Ibid.

Disa is symbolized also by a pyramid, with the Egyptian emblem of Life (the most sacred of Egyptian symbols) on the apex.[93] How the ancient faiths and their symbols became spread over the world, from the Ganges to Yucatan, is a question too deep and wide for us to enter on here: but if any portion had a better chance than another of diffusion by the intercourses of men, it was such as related to Osiris, Isis and Horus; not only by their congeniality with universal ideas, but by means of the concourse of strangers who for many centuries came in pilgrimage to these holy islands of Biggeh and Philœ at one time the most enlightened spots in the known world.

The most interesting part to me of this beautiful group of temples was a chamber reached from the roof, always retired and somewhat difficult of access, which represents the death and resurrection of Osiris. This chamber is nearly over the western adytum, forming an upper story of the Holy Place. Here is sculptured the mourning of Osiris, and his embalming, funereal transit, reception by the spirits of Hades, and final investiture as Judge of the Dead. —The next most interesting portion is the birth of Horus, —to which subject the western temple is devoted. The Christians have made sad havoc here, with their mud-plastering; but significant portions may be made out; and at the end, sufficient clearance has been effected to bring out the beautiful group of Isis with Horus on her knees, receiving homage on all hands, the guardian hawk overhead being surrounded with a glory of radiating water-plants.

What a symbol is this defacement itself of that action of the infirm human mind which is for ever obliterating, as far as it can, all ideas but its own! How faithless, in fact, as well as ignorant, is that zeal which would extinguish as dangerous all conceptions but those which suit its own transient needs, and which considers as false and doomed to destruction all ideas, and all expressions of them, which are not at the moment present to themselves! And how great is the symbolical encouragement here in the durability of the old representations, and the ineffectual character of the defacement! These Christians flattered themselves that they had buried away for ever those old gods of Egypt, and driven out the whole time-honored group, to make way for their saints. They thought the thing was done when they had put a yellow halo over the lotus-glory; and the dove over the hawk; and St. Peter with his keys of heaven over Phthah with his key of life; and angels with their palm-branches over the Assessors of the dead with their feather-symbols of Integrity: as the Puritans of modern times supposed they had destroyed superstition by burning altar-pieces and stripping cathedrals. But such extinction, being no man's business, is in no man's power. The mud plaster can be cleared away; and the old gods reappear, serene and beautiful, and almost as venerable as ever to those who can discern

93   Ibid.

their ideal through their forms: and it may be that their worship is as lively as ever in the hearts of those who regard them (as their best worshipers always did regard them) as imperishable ideas presented in forms congenial to their times. The Christian saints, with their halos, keys, palms, and books, share the same privilege. No narrow Puritan zeal can abolish them. In as far as they embody spiritual truth, they must share the immortality of truth: —exactly so far, and no farther. Meantime, we who have stood before the plastered walls of Philœ, and the ruins of Catholic churches, cannot escape the admonition they convey; —to accept the truth which comes to us without daring to interfere with what comes (as they believe) to others: to enjoy our brightening dawn, without trying to put out the moon and stars; which would not have existed, if they had not been wanted by some beings beyond our jurisdiction, and in some place beyond our ken.

The order of the edifices at Philœ may be shortly given, and I hope clearly.

Beginning from the southern shore, where there was once a flight of steps from the water, and a quay, we find first, on the left (west) hand, a sandstone pillar, whose fellow was brought to England by Mr. Bankes. This latter is remarkable as bearing inscribed the petition of the priests of Philœ to Ptolemy Physcon, entreating him to lessen the concourse of people of rank and strangers, who lived on the hospitality of the priests while there. The answer of the king, including an order to the government of the Thebaïd not to permit the priests to be thus encroached upon, was painted on the same pedestal. From the remaining pillar a colonnade extends, continuous on the west side, to the great propyla. The thirty pillars of this western corridor are all unlike each other in the sprouting of their capitals, while the outline is symmetrical enough to avoid offence to the eye. All the vegetation represented is indigenous; the different kinds of palms, water-plants, acacia, tobacco, &c., affording a sufficient variety. Some of the shafts bear hieroglyphic inscriptions, and some are plain. The intercolumnar screens, and the walls behind the pillars, are covered with sculptures. As I have mentioned before, this colonnade is so curved as to prevent the landing-place and the portal of the propyla being seen from each other—a great blemish in modern eyes. The eastern colonnade is unfinished, and the part next the river is in ruins; amidst which ruins stands the little temple of Esculapius—of course a modern affair. Its Greek dedication bears the name of the fifth Ptolemy. Of the sixteen pillars standing of the eastern colonnade, few have finished capitals, and their shafts and the wall behind are plain. The avenue between the two rows of columns is cruelly spoiled with the ruins of a mud village, among which lie two headless sphinxes.

We now come to the great propylon, whose massive pyramidal towers are the first object seen in coming up the river. These towers are built upon and beside the ancient gateway of the time of the Pharaohs. Champollion found the name of Nectanebo on this portal, and on a small chapel dedicated to Athor, in the avenue. These are the only ancient remains, the rest of the great old temple having been overthrown by the Persians, who were scandalized at the idea of worship being carried on anywhere but in the open air. The Ptolemies rebuilt the temple, preserving the Egyptian style much more carefully than in most of their edifices. This old gateway looks very venerable, with its antique winged globe on the cornice. A smaller entrance through the great propylon—a portal on the left (west) hand of the ancient one, leads to the temple I mentioned as appropriated to the welcome of Horus. This temple is built separately, surrounded by pillars bearing the head of Isis for their capitals, and merely joined on to the propyla at each extremity by a gateway.

This temple forming the western side of the area within the great propylon, a row of chambers forms the eastern side. These chambers are small—few of them sculptured—and their wall, looking upon the area, rough and unfinished. The ten columns of its corridor answer to the seven of the opposite temple of Horus—such is the want of symmetry here!

Passing through this area, and the gate of the inner and smaller propylon, we enter the court of the ten celebrated colossal columns. These columns are in pairs as to their design, but not in their position! They support the roof which covers half the court, the other half of which is open to the sky. The ceiling is still brightly colored, as are the ten columns. They are completely covered with sculptures, which shine in a variety of blues and reds, and the pale green which is so beautiful everywhere. The walls here, and in all the succeeding chambers, are completely covered with rich painted sculptures, whose compartments are divided by borders which are not merely decorative, but emblematic also. To the uninitiated eye, these decorations are what we commonly call Greek borders—with no more meaning than so many strips of color. But to their beauty they add meanings such as we never think of embodying in decoration, while we have the printing-press and engraving to communicate our ideas by. Here every morsel of decoration is a message or admonition. While by the principle of repetition (the value of which the Egyptians understood so well), the best decorative effect is produced, every element employed speaks its own meaning to the mind—or did to the minds of ancient visitors. Here we have the lotus—alternate bud and leaf stem (from which our common iron palisading is copied)—and there the drooping cup; here the ibis, and there the wild-duck and reeds; here the symbols of purity and stability in alternation, and there those of life and power. These borders run everywhere, and fill up all spaces not required for more special appeals to the worshiping mind.

To this court succeeds a corridor which leads round the corner of the next chamber, to an entrance to some vaults. The entrance is a mere pit, and the gentlemen could not get far in the subterranean chambers for want of light. Beyond the corridor lie two chambers, for once, with doors answering to each other. Instead of one Holy Place, there are two; an unusual circumstance, but not a singular one. We found the same, and also two portals, at Kóm Umboo, where the temple is dedicated to two deities. The western adytum here is very dark, and smaller than the other, and its walls are so plastered over with mud as hardly to leave any indications of the devices. The eastern adytum was in much the same condition; but some happy cleaning has laid open a beautiful group, of Osiris, and Isis nursing Horus, with an attendant behind. The faces of mother and child are fresh and pleasing.

This account will give some idea of the arrangement of the great temple of Isis at Philœ. I have said nothing of several lateral chambers, and erections on the roof, which have no immediate connection with the general plan. I went wherever it was possible to go—on the roof and to the top of both propyla—so that the confusion I had felt so painfully before, disappeared under the study from the heights of the edifice.

As for the external buildings, —there is a little temple on the western bank filled with the pictured feats and honors of the god Nilus, who is there for ever at his favorite work of binding up his water plants. — On the eastern side, there was once a fine portal of approach which is now filled up nearly to the capitals of its columns, and built up between those capitals, and thus made into a wretched Arab hovel. As it was empty, and had sculptures, and the capitals were beautiful, I went in, and was presently surprised by darkness. A man, woman and boy had blocked up the entrance by sitting down outside on the mud heap which nearly occupied the space. They demanded baksheesh in a very different tone from that which they would have employed if our dragoman or the gentlemen had been in view. The woman slipped in, and laid hold of me, trying to wrench my gold pencil-case out of my hand, while the man and boy spread themselves so as still to cover the entrance. I knew, however, at what peril anybody in Egypt robs a stranger, and that I was perfectly safe. I gave these people nothing, and got away safe by insisting on a passage over the mud heap. As I emerged, the trio ran away, and I saw no more of them.

I found my party preparing to lunch on the terrace of the temple called Pharaoh's Bed. This temple was built with a view to its aspect from the river; and truly, the Ptolemies and Cæsars have given a fine object to voyagers who gaze up at Philœ. We who live in an English climate can hardly reconcile our unaccustomed taste to a hypæthral building anywhere; the only building of that kind that we have at home being the village Pound; and walls without roof not answering to our idea of an edifice at all. But I felt here, and at night, how strong is the temptation to abstain from roofing public buildings, when, above the canopy of the clear air, there are the circling stars to light them. When I saw this temple roofed with Orion and Aldebaran, I could ask for nothing better.

I went three times round the whole outside of the temples, so as to obtain some permanent impression of the immense array of gods, offerers, cartouches and legends. —I saw here, for the first time, a front face among the sculptures; —a proof of their not being ancient. It was the middle face in more than one group of captives, whom the conqueror was holding by the hair, preparatory to cutting off their heads. On a plain space of wall is inscribed the Latitude and Longitude of Philœ, as ascertained by the French Commissioners whose names are appended. The same service is much wanted higher up the river. — There are inscriptions in different parts of the temple recording the visits of the expedition sent here by Gregory XVI, and of the French republican army under Dessaix in 1799.

At last, it was time to go; —absolutely necessary to go; for the boat was waiting which was to take us to Mahatta. We returned again and again to verify points on which we were not, on first comparing notes, fully agreed: but this lingering must come to an end. We could yet see Philœ for some time: and how different it looked now when we understood every angle and every recess! At last we rounded the point which intervenes between Philœ and Mahatta; and we saw the Holy Island no more. "By Him who sleeps in Philœ," I vowed never to part with its image from my interior picture-gallery.

At Mahatta we found asses awaiting us, in the care of two of our crew who had remained with the Dahabieh. Of these, the Buck was one; and his glee at seeing us again was uncontrollable. He shook hands with us all at great length; and kept up a most vigorous pantomime all the way to Aswan. He had dressed himself as splendidly as was in his power. Where his blue shirt had been cut to strips by repeated floggings, he had inserted a large square white patch. He wore prodigious yellow slippers, and a clean white turban: and he had dyed his nails with henneh.

We enjoyed our ride through the Desert to Aswan, and our re-entrance there upon the comforts of our spacious dahabieh. We had visitors to receive, and visits to make, this evening; and on the middle of the next day (January 14th) we set off down the river, —with our heads full of Thebes.

CHAPTER XIII

KÓM UMBOO—QUARRIES OF SILSILEH—ADFOO—EILETHYIA—
OLD EGYPTIAN LIFE—ISNA—ARMENT

OUR DAYS AND SEVERAL TEMPLES LAY, however, between us and Thebes. I will hasten over these temples, observing only their distinguishing characteristics; for I am aware that there is all the difference in the world between painfully putting together in the imagination the details of a written description of such objects, and calling up without effort that bright and solemn image of these marvelous old monuments which remains in the minds of those who have visited them.

We arrived off Kóm Umboo at ten at night of the day we left Aswan: and early in the morning we were up at the temples.

The principal temple here was rebuilt by the Ptolemies on the site of an ancient one bearing the date of the Pharaohs of an early part of the Third Period. The only piece of this great antiquity remaining is a gateway dedicated to Savak, the Lord of Umboo. The larger temple is dedicated to him and to Aroeris, the brother of Osiris: and there are two entrances, each with the winged globe on its cornice; and there were two adyta, side by side. They are buried and lost; but the cornices of their portals are just visible above the sand. This son of Time, Aroeris, is the god of Light; and his colleague Savak is a local deity of the Sun, bearing rule over this southern region, but hated by the former inhabitants of the next region to the north, who waged a savage war with his worshipers, on account of him; —in much the same spirit apparently as the Catholics of our middle ages with the Mohammedans, or the Puritans of our later age with the Catholics: that is, with the passion which seems peculiarly to belong to a faith too intense for its comprehensiveness. No wars are so cruel as wars for religion: and this warfare appears to be the only one in old Egypt in which the combatants are charged (whether falsely or not) with having eaten their enemies.

The hawk and the crocodile are the symbols of Aroeris and Savak: and they are found in companionship in every part of the sculptures of this temple. The thick grove of columns here has a very imposing effect; and the mass of overthrown blocks makes one doubt whether any force short of an earthquake could have been the destructive agent here.

One curious architectural device of the Egyptians, which we found almost everywhere by looking for it, is here apparent at a glance, when one stands on the great circuit wall which incloses the whole group of edifices; —their plan of regularly diminishing the size of the inner chambers, so as to give from the entrance, an appearance of a longer perspective than exists. They evidently like an ascending ground, the ascent of which was disguised as much as possible by the use of extremely shallow steps. The roof was made to descend in a greater degree, the descent being concealed inside by the large cornices and deep architraves they employed. The sides were made to draw in; and thus the Holy Place was always small; while to those who looked towards it from the outer chambers, (and it was entered by the priests alone,) it appeared not small, but distant. I had observed this in some of the Nubian temples, when looking at them sideways from a distance; but here it was particularly evident; the roof descending in deep steps from the portico to the pronaos; from the naos to the corridors; and from the corridors to the adyta; which last were level with the sand.

When I was in the portico, looking up at the architraves, I saw into another ancient secret, which I should have been sorry to have overlooked. Some of the paintings were half-finished; and their ground was still covered with the intersecting red lines by which the artists secured their proportions. These guiding lines were meant to have been effaced as soon as the outlines were completed; yet here they are at the end of, at least, two thousand years! No hand, however light, has touched them, through all the intervening generations of men: —no rains have washed them out, during all the changing seasons that have passed over them: —no damp has moulded them: no curiosity has meddled with them. It is as if the artist had lain down for his siesta, with his tools beside his hand, and would be up presently to resume his work: yet that artist has been a mummy, lying somewhere in the heart of the neighboring hills, ever since the time when our island was bristling with forests, and its inhabitants were dressed in skins, and dyed their bodies blue with woad, to look terrible in battle. In another part of this temple, the stone is diced in small squares to receive the hieroglyphic figures.

The other temple was built on an artificial platform, and must have looked nobly from the river, as indeed its remains still do by moonlight. I found among the strewn fragments one capital, and only one, bearing the head of Athor, — the last relic perhaps of a colonnade which here crowned the precipitous bank.

My journal records that we were much impressed by these ruins, —the size of the parts, and the extraordinary character of their wreck. The wading among blocks of sculptured stone, having the eye caught incessantly by some exquisite device or gay bit of painting, is a strange experience. So far from becoming tired of temple-haunting, we found the eagerness grow from day to day.

In the afternoon, we plunged back into the times of the old Pharaohs. —into the early centuries of the Third Period. We went over the quarries at Silsileh, and saw excavations which might almost make us think that the whole human race had come here for building material, from the founding of Babel to the arrival of the lazy Arabs. On the east side I wandered long and far among lanes and areas in the rock, where the sides spring up like the walls of a mine, or retire in sharp cut gradation, to a mountainous height. All the variety I came upon in this silent wilderness of cut stone, was the tracks of a hyæna in the sand, and the marks in the rock of the tools of three or four thousand years ago. Some of these marks were evidently for the purpose of trying tools. These marks remain; but we long in vain to know what the tools were like. Others seem to have been made in sport; perhaps in illustration of some story the workmen were telling and listening to, while eating their lentil pottage. On the western bank we found much more; —grottoes, pillars, tablets, niches, statues, sculptures and paintings, —all of very ancient date. We have the conquering Pharaoh— Horus, successor of Amunoph III., overriding the Ethiopians, receiving the captives, whose arms are tied in all manner of ways, —some with the elbows above their heads; —and holding groups of the foe by the hair, threatening to cut off their heads. We see him borne in a shrine on men's shoulders, with files of soldiers in attendance, and the lion pacing along beside the royal chariot. In another place we have the most solemn representation those old artists knew how to offer; —the king receiving the symbol of Life from the Supreme god.

The historian revels among such memorials as these. The invariable practice here of sculpturing the names and titles of the kings, and often of their chief officers; and the descriptions of the people conquered; and the names of offerers as well as gods, make research here a self-rewarding effort, very unlike the painful and uncertain speculation which is all that can be attempted among the antiquities of more modern countries. To the historian, such places as these are a glorious field: but they are not less interesting to the moralist or the poet. What a proof it is of the sanctity of the work of temple-building that the very quarries were consecrated to the gods! Truly, they were a religious people, these old Egyptians: —receiving their children as from the gods; bringing their children to the temples in bands to make offerings; invoking the Judge of the dead at their banquets; presenting their conquests as sacrifice to the heavenly powers; and consecrating their work of temple-building by first making the very rocks holy which were to furnish the material. There is a great congregation of gods here, receiving offerings from several Pharaohs. Savak is the local deity: and the god Nilus holds a higher rank than usual: some think because the river here narrows between the rocks, and runs with a strong current: and others because much of the stone cut here for distant works, was committed to the charge of Nilus for transport. The tablets bear some inscriptions of great historical value; and particularly a record of Assemblies held in various years of the reign of the Great Ramases. What these Assemblies were, in their object and details, perhaps some future decipherer of Egyptian records will tell us. At present we know only that they were held in the great halls of the temples, and were considered of the utmost importance; so that the title of President of the Assemblies was one of the highest dignity, offered to the king alone on earth, and supposed to be enjoyed by the gods in their own regions.[94]

We set off after breakfast, on the morning of the 16th, to see the great Adfoo temple, walking about a mile through millet patches, stubble and dust. From our deck we had seen what looked like clouds of smoke rising from the town, and partly obscuring the great propyla. When we reached the edifice this appearance was explained in a way which pleased us very much. The people were carrying off the dust from the area of the temple, to qualify the rich mud of the shore; and donkeys were passing in and out under the entrance gate. Men were loading their asses within the area; and we found the place wonder fully improved since our former visit. We could still handle the capitals of the tallest columns by walking on the sand between them; but the western colonnade and area wall were cleared almost to their bases. The external sculptures of the pro-pylon indicate, however, that much remains to be done; for the captive groups, whose heads the victor is threatening, hardly show their noses above ground. The process which was going forward of course covered us with dust; but we rejoiced in it, for the sake of the good done; if only the Arabs do not fill the court with something worse than even this dust—with such mud hovels as are stuck all over the roofs, and ruin the outline of this magnificent temple. The dust was of the less consequence to some of us that we were destined to be at all events half-choked. The temple chambers can be reached only by going down a hole like the entrance to a coal-cellar, and crawling about like crocodiles, on the sand within, there being barely room, in some places, to squeeze one's prostrate body between the dust and the roof, with a huge capital of a pillar on either hand. The having to carry lights, under penalty of one's own extinction in the noisome air and darkness if they go out, much complicates the difficulty; so that a proper visit to the interior of the Adfoo temple is really something of an adventure. I could not, under the circumstances, trace out the disposition of

94   Wilkinson's Ancient Egyptians, V. 288.

the building; but five gentlemen, the dragoman and I, penetrated a considerable way—as far, indeed, as it was possible to go; traversing, it seemed to me, three chambers, and ending in one which, from its oblong form, I should have supposed to be a corridor; but which, having apparently but one door, must, in that case, have been the adytum. The sculptures were clear and clean; but the place was too stifling, with half-a-dozen people and tallow candles in it, and no fresh air for many years, to admit of more than a rapid survey. The sculptures exhibited offerings to the gods; the offerers being Ptolemies. The temples at Adfoo were both erected by successive monarchs of that race; and the interest of this magnificent edifice is, therefore, rather owing to its being, from its durability, a model to us of the plan and structure of an Egyptian temple, and to the richness of its architecture and sculpture, than to any charm of antiquity.

Its extent and massive character are best perceived from the top of the propylon. For the beauty of the view beyond, too, every traveler should go there. The mass of temple buildings below is a fine centre for such a landscape. About this centre is gathered the poor town, whose fields spread to the river. Almost the whole wide circuit with in the blue mountains, or yellow limestone hills on the horizon, is one bright green level. The only interruptions are from the winding river, and some pools among the western fields; pools at present, but canal at the time of the subsidence of the Nile.

As the morning was shady and cool, we returned on foot to the boat, where we shook off our dust, and wrote our journals, in preparation for new enterprises. The winds were now less cold and strong than within the tropics; but we had frequent cloudy skies—as to-day, for a short time. Towards evening, the sky cleared to the west; and the shore at El Kab, where we were mooring, was gorgeously lighted up by a parting gleam. A strange-looking wall tempted us ashore; and we found that this circuit-wall of the vanished city of Eilethyia, whose tombs we were to see to-morrow, was in fact a substantial fortification, containing a hollow-way between two stout masses of crude brick. This wall enclosed an area large enough for an extensive city; and a level stretches behind, from the wall to the mountains, which might, in the days of the prosperous old tillage, when Egypt was the granary of the world, easily support the population of the district.

The morning of the 17th was charming; most favorable for our ride to the tombs in the Desert. Our asses were of the smallest; so small that the gentlemen could help them on by using a walking-stick as they rode. I never before saw such a variety in the size and strength of animals of the same race, in near neighborhood. To-day it was like riding a dog—and in two days more, at Thebes, we were mounted on donkeys almost as large and strong as mules.

The arid plain that we rode over had drifts of stones which seemed to show that vehement torrents sometimes sweep down here from the hills. The recesses of the Desert are very striking—so utterly still and dreary, with nothing but the blue shadows coming and going, from century to century. Here and there we passed to-day shallow pools of salt water; and there were crusts of natron on the soil.

We visited a very small and very ancient temple, about three miles from the river; and two less antique, nearer the old town. But temples must be imposing indeed to obtain much attention here, where we come upon some old tombs for the first time. In the temples we have the worship and the wars of the old Egyptians. In some of the tombs, we have their thoughts of death, judgment and retribution: but in many we have their daily life, their occupations, their festivals and their mirth; and these are interesting beyond description.

The tombs at Eilethyia are grottoes in the rock; vaulted, and with ceilings elaborately painted. Some have a pit before the entrance; some have pits within; and others communicate with holes or low-roofed caverns where the dead might be deposited. The date is known by the names of several kings being inscribed in the most easterly tomb; those kings being of the beginning of the Third Period, immediately after the expulsion of the Shepherds.

The moment of entering these tombs is that of a sudden withdrawing of the clouds which overhang those far distant ages. Hitherto, we have learned something of their devotional conceptions and feelings; something of their philosophy; and much of their arts of war and of building; but thus far we have learned nothing of the every-day life of common people, except that the offerings in the temples prove what they had to eat, drink, wear and use. Now, however, on entering these and other tombs, the dimness that overhangs the Nile valley clears away, and we see the people at work in the fields, and busy on the river, and merry in their houses. It is no dream, —no transient vision, —with clouds driving up to hide it from us again. It is steady before our eyes, and we can take our time in studying it. We can note every article of dress; every instrument of music; and the very dishes preparing for dinner. How wonderful it is! And what a fortunate thing for us that it was the custom in Egypt for the owner of a tomb to paint it all over with pictures of his life, its possessions, its interests and its deeds! —Now let us see what this family are doing; —master, mistress, children and servants.

This is a rich man. With us, he would be a very rich man: and his possessions are such as would make him wealthy in any part of the world. The first we see of him is in the field where his laborers are ploughing and sowing: that is, his chariot is in the field: so he is no doubt overlooking his people. The inundation has of course subsided: and it appears that his land does not lie very low. If it did, he would hardly be setting his people to plough, but merely to sprinkle the seed on the slime; —to cast his bread upon the waters, that he might find it again, after many days. This plough, however, is a very simple affair; and not wanted to go very deep. A mere scratching of the surface is enough, in such a soil as this. If any stiff clods turn up, they are broken with the hoe: but that does not seem to be the case here; for the sower follows the ploughman pretty close-ly. Herodotus thought the Egyptians very enviable in his day for the ease with which their husbandry was managed. There were no people in the world, he says, who obtained their corn with less labor and pains. "They are not obliged to make toilsome furrows with the plough, to break the clods, and to give to their fields the cares which the rest of men bestow; but when the river has of its own accord watered their lands, and the waters have retired, then every one lets in his hogs, and afterwards sows his field. When the sowing is done, the oxen are driven upon the ground; and after these animals hove buried the grain by tram-pling it in, there is only to await quietly the time of harvest."[95] There is nothing said here of the subsequent irrigation which is quite as toilsome a process as any ploughing in Greece could ever have been. What a waste of seed this sower is making, —unless that cataract of seed is a flourish of the artists! He seems to throw more from his hand than any hand can hold, —or even the basket from which he takes his supply. If it has been "a good Nile" this year, here will be corn for export, after every one is well fed at home. —Ah! we shall soon see that: for here, in the second line of paintings, we are carried on to the harvest. The crops seem certainly very vigorous. This tallest growth is millet, of course: the next, barley; the shortest, wheat. They cut the wheat-ears off short with a sickle very like ours: but they pull up the millet by the roots. There is a woman uprooting it now. Probably they use the stalks for fencing, thatching, or bedding the cattle, as the country people do at this day. What is that man doing with the roots of the plucked millet? Is he knocking off the earth from them? That is a neat sheaf that his comrade is tying; and the man who is carrying another seems to find it large and heavy, as indeed it looks. That instrument, with teeth like a comb, seems to work cleverly in stripping off the grain from the stalk.—It is only the millet that is so treated; for here, in the third line, is the threshing-floor, with the oxen treading out the wheat. The driver is singing; and here is actually his song, written up beside his picture: — [96]

"Thresh for yourselves, O oxen! Thresh for yourselves.
Thresh for yourselves, O oxen! Thresh for yourselves.
Measures for yourselves! Measures for your masters.
Measures for yourselves! Measures for your masters."

This is the song this driver was singing while Moses was a child. — The wheat is swept up, and delivered to the winnowers; who are making showers in

95   Herod. II. 14.
96   Champollion. Lettres sur l'Egypte, 11th and 12th letters.

the air with the falling wheat. And here it is carried to the place where the scribe is ready to see it measured and deposited in the granary.

These scribes look like very stiff writers. How formally they hold the tablet, supporting the left arm on the bent knee! and how hard they seem to be bearing on the style, as if it were steel, and they were graving! But this is only a bit of energy put in by the artist; for the style was only a reed pen; and it made its marks with colored inks. — But here are several scribes, taking account of many things besides the grain which is brought home. These bags that they are causing to be weighed before them, are money bags. This must be a very rich man. Here are gold rings too; —the ancient form of currency. —And here is the livestock: cattle, asses, pigs, goats: what an array! —And the gentleman was a sportsman too, I suppose; or, at least, chose to have his table well supplied; for here are game, and geese, and fish. Probably, the Nile left him plenty of fish within his embankments, when the waters retired: or he might keep fish-ponds stocked; as it appears some people did. The old Egyptians must have been very fond of fowling, judging by the number and variety of nets, and the multitude of fluttering birds which we see among the domestic pictures. —Ah! these people have taken more fish and geese than they want at present; and here we see them salting them. From what we saw ourselves just now, there must have been a good deal of salt produced in the neighborhood: and if not enough for everybody, more was brought down the river by the traders from Ethiopia, where we know salt was brought from the east for sale.

Here is a wine-press: —no wonder! for we are coming presently to the picture of a banquet. We know that the kings and the priests were much restricted in the use of wine: but the sculptures and paintings show that there was much wine-bibbing among gentlemen and ladies generally. Every landed proprietor seems to have had his wine press; as far as this kind of evidence goes: and the sick and tipsy guests at banquets are really a scandal to those old times. By the way, those who had wine-presses must have had lands extending backwards to the skirts of the hills; for vines will not grow in the rich Nile mud nor bear being laid under water for months at a time. The great valley must have been skirted with vineyards in those old times. Besides all that they grew, we know that they imported wine largely, as soon as they could get it. One way and another, —as medicine, or with their food, or at their banquets, they certainly disposed of a great deal. And here are a group of servants, treading the grapes very energetically.

What a splendid affair this boat is, with its band of rowers, and its pavilion, with door and two windows; —quite a house! —and the gay sail, all checkered with bright colors! How well these people wove and dyed in those days! This sail is bulging, as if in a strong wind, which implies that it is stout as well as gay.

What is this wheel, on the roof of the pavilion, and under the corner of the sail? For a long time I believed that this was part of the tackle; and I made a drawing of it for future inquiry. From Sir G. Wilkinson I learn[97] that I did not use my eyes well, or I might have seen that this is the wheel of a chariot, which is placed there for conveyance. I might have discovered this by the horses, whose heads appear in my sketch, in front of the pavilion. This other boat, rowing the contrary way, makes all clear. Here the sail and mast are down; and the chariot on the roof is unmistakable; besides that the horses stand on the deck. The rudder is in shape an enormous paddle, swung on a pivot by a little man standing at the stern. How eager the pilot looks, making gestures from his place at the bow! These capacious and handsome boats, — vessels of a higher order than such as are represented among the chattels of ordinary landed proprietors, —make me hope that this is indeed the tomb of the old Egyptian admiral, which Champollion studied so successfully at Eliethyia. His tablet tells that he was "Chef des nautonniers" in the reign of Thothmes I.; that he served in the earlier time of Amosis, and did battle to great purpose while he commanded on the water: and also that he was himself named Amosis.[98] If this be indeed Amosis, he returned from his exploits on the water to a life of great plenty and some merriment on the shore.

Some merriment: for here is a grand banquet. The provision is various: quarters of beef, cakes, fruits, wine flasks, &c. And in the reception room, how decorous is everything! —at least, before dinner! Here are the host and hostess, in a handsome chair, looking towards their guests, who are ranged in front, the gentlemen in one file; the ladies in another. Every lady is smelling at a large water-lily with all her might. To the host's chair a monkey is tied. Perhaps Amosis brought it home after one of his voyages up to the south. There is a row of musicians, playing on the harp and the double-pipe, and some clapping; by way of a little amusement before dinner.

But to all things there comes an end. We see here the day (how far back in the depths of time!) when these merry feasts were all over, —the lilies dead, —the music hushed, —the last of this man's harvests stored, —the last trip enjoyed by boat or chariot. The fish need no more fear him in their pools, nor the fowl among the reeds. Here he is lying under the hands of the embalmers; and next we see him in mummy form on the bier, in the consecrated boat which was to carry him over the dark river, and land him at the gates of the heavenly abode where the Spirits of the dead, and the Judge Osiris were awaiting him, to try his deeds, and pronounce his sentence for eternal good or ill. Here are the life and death of a man who lived so long ago that at the first mention of him, we think of him as one having no kindred with us. But how like ours were his life

97   Wilkinson's Ancient Egyptians, III. 197.

98   Lettres sur l'Egypte.

and death! Compare him with a retired naval officer made country gentleman in our day, and in how much less do they differ than agree!

I was sorry to see carved, —actually cut, —among the sculptures of the easternmost tomb at Eilethyia, among the intrusions of many who knew no better, such names as these of Irby and Mangles, Belzoni, and Madden. If visitors must leave their names, why not do it on the rough rock by the entrance? Can there ever come a day, however far off, when it will not be a sin for strangers to carve their names all over the statuary in Westminster Abbey?

In the afternoon, between Eilethyia and Isna, we passed five boats with European flags; —one of which was Russian, and the rest English. The Russian countess was an English woman, moreover. I could not but hope that these travelers would not pronounce decisively on the scenery of Egypt, as observed from their boats; for they were too late in the season to see much without the effort of going often ashore. The river had sunk so much that we hardly recognized some districts, whose aspect appeared totally altered from what it was a few weeks before. We had missed the birds, while we were up in Nubia. We never saw again such myriads as filled the depths of the heavens when we set out on our voyage: but now we began to note large flights of them, increasing daily as we drew near the plain of Thebes.

I think I had better say little of Isna, whose temple is so universally praised that every one knows all about it. Those have heard of it who are ignorant of almost everything else about Egypt. If it were ancient, I could not refrain from giving my impressions of it: but the only relic of the old edifice supposed to exist is a small red door jamb, bearing date in the time of Thothmes L, mentioned by Champollion. The portico bears the names of the Cæsars: and, however greatly the world is obliged to them for erecting a very majestic and elegant temple, we are not aided by it in our researches into the affairs of the old Egyptians. The Pasha, as is known, cleared out the portico to the very bases of the columns; and a noble hall it now is. The amount of accumulation is shown by the height of the dust-hill we had to descend, from the alley in front of the temple. Our Rais shut out the children who came swarming after us, as usual; so that, for once, we explored a temple at our ease, in coolness and freedom, and without being asked for baksheesh.

If I were to enlarge on anything in regard to this temple, it would be the amount of inscriptions. But it is indescribable, —unrememberable, —incredible anywhere but on the spot. I have already said all that language can say on this point: and I will leave it.

There is a Zodiac here, as every one knows: not ancient. No Zodiac in Egypt is ancient; but one or two offer Egyptian symbols which it is interesting to notice: —the Scarabæus for the Crab: the double-headed Sphinx for the Twins:

a truly Egyptian compound of an animal for the Seagoat: and a Man with the oriental water-skin, —the Goat or Kid-skin—on his shoulder, for Aquarius.

I saw here first the Serpents, human-headed and human-legged, of which we soon met so much more primitive and satisfactory a representation at Thebes. These Serpents and many other nondescripts abound in this temple; so that it looks like an illustration of much of the book of Revelations. —Here, for the first lime, I saw the glorious Egyptian symbol of the Heavens; —the Long Arms of the goddess Pe encircling a whole compartment of the vast ceiling.

This 18th of January was remarkable for bringing us again among the dwellings and resorts of a town population, after our retirement and dreamings in the still southern regions. We visited the Pasha's palace, (bringing away some splendid jessamine from his garden,) and his cotton factory; and his chained prisoners in the guard-house. All wore chains, which glittered in the sun, —for they were new and bright: and of these, seven had a collar round their necks, and their hands confined in a sort of stocks, —much more clumsy than any hand cuffs. These seven were doomed to death; —desperadoes who would be hanged or shot if the Pasha did not reverse their sentence—of which there seemed to be no expectation. They were as lively as the busy passengers in the streets, and cried "baksheesh" as vigorously as any idler in the place. The other prisoners were, we were told, thieves and deserters.

Our stay at Isna for so many hours was for the sake of the crew; that they might bake their bread. This was done before evening; and we proceeded, in order to reach the temple at Arment (the Greek Hermonthis) by the morning. It was a glorious evening; and, after watching the young moon going down just after the sun, there were still some things to be seen on the western bank. Whatever was on the ridge showed black against the orange sky; —a pacing camel; a string of asses; some children at play, and two or three men at prayers. As they faced the east, every gesture of prostration was seen, and every flow of their majestic garments. —In my childhood, I used to wonder why Pharaoh's kine came up out of the water: but now, and often besides, I saw how truly Egyptian this dream was. The cattle often cross the Nile by swimming, —sometimes resting on a shoal in the middle of the river. This evening, a noble buffalo kept us in a state of interest for half an hour by his incessant efforts to land, and the difficulty he had in doing so. Again and again, he put off, swimming slowly about with only his head above water; and then he would struggle in the tenacious mud, and seem to have obtained a footing; and slip back again, and disappear in the shadow of the bank. Then he would come out again into the light; the failing light, which was almost gone before he was safe. We saw the last shine of it on his sides as he paced slowly up to the ridge, evidently trembling and exhausted. All things in Egypt seem to cross their great highway with as little concern as we do ours. As we walk across a road, they pass through the Nile. Whole droves of cattle, and sometimes asses and sheep; and children, whenever the fancy takes them; and men, with a bundle of millet-stalks under them, or with a log to lean their breasts against; their clothes, or their burden of produce, on their heads. We never witnessed any sign of fear of crocodiles, or heard of any disasters by them, as far as I remember.

At five in the morning, we were at the nearest point to the Arment temple; and I walked the mile and half which lay between the shore and it with great pleasure, having grass to tread on for the first time for several weeks. There was an air of civilization about the village which was rather unusual, —the fences being neatly built of millet-stalks, tall and thick, and the place supplied with water from a well-kept pond, fed by a channel from the river. Immediately beyond the village, we entered the Desert, which was all undulating with mounds of broken pottery and other rubbish. The quantity of broken pottery about these places remained a mystery to us to the last. In a hollow among these mounds lie the ruins of the Christian Church, which was itself built, it is thought, from the materials afforded by the larger temple of Hermonthis. These ruins consist of some portions of wall, very massive from the size of the blocks; much strewn stone, and a considerable number of prostrate columns, of red granite. A little further on stand the remaining pillars of Cleopatra's temple; eight altogether, in the area and portico. The remains are miserably obstructed and deformed by the mud partition and huts which have taken shelter under the sculptured walls and painted roofs of the temple: but one is less concerned about it here than in almost any other case; for the edifice is, as I said, of no older time than Cleopatra's. The witch-queen still interests us enough to make us run after every memorial of her. The many who know her only through Shakespeare hunt for her portrait-figure at Philœ before they look for Osiris and Isis: and they come here to see the hundred representations of her, sitting with the little Caesarion on her knees, —(in honor of whose birth this temple was built,)—or presenting the child to the gods. Nothing can be more distinct than the features of the queen, when seen in the full light, on the outer walls; and they are no doubt to be taken as a portrait, as the edifice was her own work. The face is very charming; the features small, and not at all after the Greek type; and the expression girlish and simple, —like that of the ancient Isis and Athor. We obtain here an impression something like that which we derive from the pictures of Mary Queen of Scots: a conviction of the general resemblance, with no recognition of such extraordinary beauty as we read of, but a sense that the charm might be all that we are told when the soul was at work among those features.

We see how the little Cæsarion is committed to the guardianship, even to the nursing of the god of Hermonthis—the Amun Ra of Thebes here presented under the form of the bull Bash, or Basis—which has characteristics distinguishing it at once to the eye from the bull Apis. In one place we see the bull suckling—that is sustaining—the child; and over the principal gate there is a sculpture of the bull bearing Cæsarion between his horns, while a decorative margin is formed by four copies in small of the same group of Cleopatra with the child on her knees. There is a profusion of ornament throughout the building, but it is of a low style of art—about, however, to give place to a lower —for this is, of course, the last work of the Ptolemies, who now gave place to the Romans.

CHAPTER XIV

THEBES—EUROPEAN TRAVELERS AND NATIVE ARABS—THE PAIR—THE RAMASEUM—EL-KURNEH

A T LAST WE WERE AT THEBES—in the afternoon of this Tuesday, the 19th of January. We were very happy, for there was no hurry. On either hand lay the plain of Thebes, and before us there was leisure to explore it. We stayed eight days—giving five to the western bank and three to the eastern. We made, we thought, good use of our time, exploring daily as much as we could without plunging ourselves into too much fatigue and excitement. What the excitement is can be known only to those who have spent successive days in penetrating the recesses of the palaces, and burying themselves in the tombs of the Pharaohs, who lived among the hundred gates of this metropolis of the world before the Hebrew infant was laid among the nests of the Nile water-fowl. Perhaps some hint of what the interest of Thebes is, may be derived from such poor account as I am able to give of what we saw there; but I shall tell only what we saw, and nothing of what we felt. That can be spoken of nowhere but on the spot.

This first evening we attempted nothing beyond a little stroll on the shore at sunset. The first thing we saw was a throng of boats—five English flags and one Russian. Some were just departing, and others went the next day. Thebes is the last place in the world where one wishes for society; so I dare say every party of the whole throng was longing to see all the rest sail away. In the end we enjoyed as much quietness as we could expect, and suffered no real interruption in our expeditions. After the exchange of sundry greetings with our neighbors, the gentlemen and I walked up to the ruins of the El-Uksur temple, and in and out, and round about, till we arrived at some understanding of their arrangement and object. We now found how much we had gained by practice in looking at temples. This was hardly like the same group of ruins we had visited a few weeks before. By the training of the eye in the intermediate time, we saw new beauty in the proportions—and especially of the obelisk—new spirit in the sculptures, and a higher and fresher glory in the colonnades. We were not less but more impressed by the magnitude of the scale of the architecture, and far more impressible by all its other features.

When the moon came up, it was time to be returning to our boat, but as we were turning the corner of the ruins, a man accosted us, with an air of invitation, courteously pointing out a long flight of steps, and saying apparently (but we had no interpreter with us) something about a castle. Mr. E. told me this was, no doubt, the guard-house, and we agreed to go and see it. Instead of governor, garrison, or chained prisoners, however, we found an elderly gentleman on his deewán, enjoying his chibouque. He addressed us in French, ordered coffee and pipes, offered now some information about the ruins, and next his guidance among them during our stay at Thebes. When he permitted us to depart, at the end of half an hour, Mr. E. said to me, "Well, now, who is this that we have been seeing?" "Nay," said I, "that is what I thought you were going to tell me." He was certainly no official personage, and certainly he was a European. He proved to be the Signor Castellare whom we had heard of as having settled himself at Thebes, to discover antiquities, and explain them to those who have faith in his interpretation, and to sell specimens to such as have money enough to pay his very high prices for them. It is only by connivance that he does these things, for the Pasha's pleasure is that none of the antiquities shall leave the country. And the connivance is not likely to last long, for the people of the place naturally dislike that a stranger should take out of their hands the traffic with visitors, which they find much more profitable than their inevitable sales to the Signor. Whenever the Signor does anything to prove to the world his sound knowledge on the subject of Egyptian antiquities, every one will be glad of his offered guidance, and of his help, at any price, in securing specimens. In the meantime, perhaps the works of Champollion, Rosellini and Wilkinson, compared with the old classical writings which relate to Egypt, will be found to give guidance enough, while there is seldom any scarcity of illustrative curiosities on the spot.

At midnight, three more boats arrived; and their owners roused the echoes of the whole region, by firing guns, in honor of the English boats on the river. We found the English here generally quite as well pleased with the behavior of the Arabs as we were. They found their crews, and also the country people, friendly and helpful—even affectionate, in all their intercourses. The crews were always willing and cheerful about their work, and honest in their transactions with the strangers. The drawbacks were the incessant begging of the country people; and the noise and childish quarreling of the crews among themselves.

These were troublesome incidents; but not to be complained of by us strangers as injuries. Among the many who were pleased, however, there was one who was always making grievous complaints. Never man was, by his own account, in such incessant and pressing danger of robbery, piracy, and murder, as this gentleman on the Nile. Never did any man so suffer from the perils in which he hourly saw his wife and children. Every Arab he met wanted to rob him: every group on the bank, and every party in a boat, was congregated to board and pillage his dahabieh, and murder his family. He showed us a loaded six-barreled pistol which he usually carried in his hand, as he declared to us, wherever he went; and which he was, he assured us, obliged very frequently to discharge. It did not seem to strike him as strange that all the other English, who went unarmed, and feared nothing, were content with the Arabs—lost nothing, and met with no alarms. He remained fully convinced of his danger: and this is the reason why I mention his case here. It is the least that European travelers can do in acknowledgment of the security and facilities which the Pasha's government affords them on the Nile, to testify to that security and those facilities; and the testimony is not less due to the kindly Arabs, on whom so much of their comfort has depended: and if one traveler talks of his dangers and wrongs as this gentleman does, it is necessary to justice that the majority should declare their contrary experience. The worst of it is that one man who has desperate adventures to tell of, will make more impression than a dozen whose testimony is that they had no adventures. But this makes it all the more necessary that they should say what they found the state of things. As for myself, I walked much on shore, and was frequently wandering away by myself among the ruins or in the fields: and I had no reason to consider myself imprudent—except indeed about the dogs. I was incessantly forgetting that Egyptian dogs are dangerous—being trained to attack strangers. But as soon as the barking began, I found the owners quick and eager in restraining the animals: and usually there were some one of the crew within hearing, armed with a club. I do not remember that I ever met with any rude pressure or threatening but twice, while in Egypt: and then I had put myself in the power of poor creatures who could not resist the temptation of grasping at the chance of a large baksheesh. One time was at Philœ, as I have related. The other was this evening in a hut at the El-Uksur temple, where some women closed the door behind me, and proved themselves to be very sturdy beggars, till disturbed by one of my party coming to look for me. Two instances of bold begging, in ten weeks of constant opportunities, is not much.

As I took a brisk walk along the shore, to warm myself, the next morning, "the Lybian suburb" was dressed in the most wonderful coloring by the early sun. It was in that direction that our researches were to lie for some days; and as soon as our boat was clear of visitors after breakfast, we crossed the river, and took up our station off the western bank. Alee was particular in his choice of animals for us to ride, that we might be suited at once for the whole time of our stay on the western side. Mrs. Y. had a horse—quieter than my donkey. I was favored with a strong, spirited donkey, whose curator was an active, open-faced, obliging youth, who discovered my wishes and aims with wonderful quickness, and indulged them to the utmost of his power. He presently found out my liking for visiting the Pair: and also for a canter over the plain: and almost every evening, he would point to the Colossi, and nod and smile, and begin a run in that direction, while the rest of the party went straight to the boat. And he ran so well that we generally fell in with my companions before they had dismounted, though I had made a pretty wide circuit. I can never lose the impression of these sunset rides homewards, after the excitements and toils of the day. The Pair, sitting alone amidst the expanse of verdure, with islands of ruins behind them, grew more striking to us every day. To-day, for the first time, we looked up at them from their base. The impression of sublime tranquillity which they convey when seen from distant points, is confirmed by a near approach. There they sit, keeping watch—hands on knees, gazing straight forward, seeming, though so much of the faces is gone, to be looking over to the monumental piles on the other side of the river, which became gorgeous temples after these throne seats were placed here; —the most immovable thrones that have ever been established on this earth. He who is popularly called the Memnon, is sadly shattered. This is the work that Cambyses tried his hand upon overthrowing. With all his efforts, he shattered it only down to the waist. It is built up again; patched up; —a blank rough space only remaining where we would fain see a face. If the faces were of the tranquil, innocent character which marks the old sculptures, and would eminently suit the composure of the attitude, the impression must have been majestic indeed: inviolable to any one but Cambyses. Strabo says that, as he was told, the damage was done by an earthquake. One would like to think that Nature, rather than Man, had done it; and perhaps the inscriptions of ancient visitors, who lay the blame on Cambyses, need not have much weight. But how came the earthquake to leave the mass of the throne and body unhurt, while shattering the shoulders and head? I suppose nobody thinks that the whole was thrown over, and set up again, the fellow colossus remaining uninjured. The inscriptions are wonderfully numerous; most in Latin; some in Greek. On the pedestal—the side of the throne-chair—is old Nilus, once more busy, as in all times, in binding up the throne of the King with his water-plants. The King is Amunoph III. His name is over the tablet bound up by Nilus; and also on the back of the statue.

These statues sit now, as I have said, in the midst of an expanse of verdure, at the season when travelers visit them. At high Nile, they are islands in the midst of a waste of waters. But of old, their pedestals rose from the pavement of the Dromos or course which formed the avenue to the palace-temple of Amunoph, eleven hundred feet behind the colossi. This palace-temple, once superb with its statues, columns, and sphinxes, is now a mere heap of sandstone; —a little roughness in the plain, when seen from the heights behind. The sphinxes are at St. Petersburgh; the columns are broken oil from their bases; the statues peep out in fragments from under the soil. In the days of the glory of Thebes, the Nile did not come here; but the whole avenue, with all its erections, stood on raised ground—a magnificent sight from the river. The Nile itself has risen since those days; and in proportion to the raising of its bed has been its spread over the plain; so that the pavement of the dromos, and the pedestals of the colossi, have been buried deeper and deeper in mud; and must continue to be so. Sand may be dealt with hereafter, for the rescue of the treasures of Egyptian art; but it does not appear that the mud of the Nile can. How strange it is to look forward to the gradual stifling of these giants —sitting patiently there for more thousands of years, to be buried, inch by inch, out of human sight! They now stand about fifty-three feet above the soil; and seven feet below it. But the mention of the total height gives less idea of their magnitude than the measurement of the limbs. From the elbow to the fingers' ends, they measure seventeen feet nine inches; and from the knee to the plant of the foot, nineteen feet eight inches.

To-day we saw, for the first time, an old Egyptian palace; that of Ramases the Great, so many of whose monuments we had visited higher up the river. This palace of the Ramaseum (commonly and erroneously called the Memnonium) is also a temple. The old Pharaohs brought their gods into their palaces, and also had apartments in the temple; so that the great buildings of this metropolis were appropriated to gods and kings jointly. It is melancholy to sit on the piled stones amidst the wreck of this wonderful edifice, where violence inconceivable to us has been used to destroy what art inconceivable to us had erected. What a rebuke to the vanity of succeeding ages is here! What have we been about, to imagine men in those early times childish or barbarous, —to suppose science and civilization reserved for us of these later ages, when here are works, in whose presence it is a task for the imagination to overtake the eyesight!

I went first to the propylon; and it seemed to me, as I clambered about its ruins, that the stones of this outwork alone would build a cathedral. I found an inclined plane and staircase within the propylon, and climbed till I could make my way no further, seeing glimpses between the fallen blocks of the sunny plain and its mountain boundary. Returning, I clambered over the ruins of the mere external face of the propylon; and when I was doubling whether I had ever before performed such a feat of climbing, I found myself, on coming out at the top, still under the portal! What a gateway it must have been! A loosened jamb which slanted over my head made me feel as one might under a falling oak. Looking through, towards the palace, I saw what at once drew my eyes away from the ranges of columns, and perspective of courts and chambers; —the remains of the largest statue that even Egypt ever produced. It is only from a distance that this mass of granite would be perceived to be a statue, so enormous is its bulk. It lies overthrown among the fragments of its limbs; the fragments themselves being masses which it would not be easy to move. The foot looks like a block preparing for a colossal statue. I had the curiosity to measure the second toe, and found its length from the fork to be two feet seven inches. I climbed upon the pile, walking up the inclined plane of its shoulder, and picking my way on the smooth surface of its neck, and the remains of its cheek. Some travelers have obtained a sure footing by setting their feet in the hieroglyphic letters on its back. The features are gone, the greater part of the face being split away for mill stones by the Arabs! How such a mass could be overthrown from the base remains a mystery. Every writer seems to conclude that the Persians or Ptolemy Lathyrus effected this kind of ruin throughout Thebes: but I do not know why we may not suppose an earthquake to be the agent. At El Karnac the devastation is such as to defy the belief that human agency could have been employed. Enormous columns are there overthrown from the base in one fall, —their circular stones lying overlapping each other like a row of cheeses: and this without any traces of mines, or other channel for the application of explosives. The mountains of stones also of the great propyla at El Karnac, show plainly that they fell at once; and there are no means known to us, even now, after all our study of gunpowder, which could cause such an over throw as that at one stroke, and without leaving any traces of the means. But, supposing this mighty Ramases to have been prostrated by an earthquake, the question remains, how he came here from Syene. Whether the working was done here or at Syene, the granite was brought from thence. SirG. Wilkinson gives its weight as somewhere about 887 tons, 5 ½ cwt.[99] How should we now set about quarrying and conveying such a mass some hundreds of miles?

Beyond this statue, which used to sit in the area, beside the entrance to the place, the building looks like a wood in some petrified region outside our world. The unexpanded lotus is still, to my eye, the most beautiful kind of column: but the full-blown cup is more appropriate perhaps to the larger pillars. I like the eighteen smaller pillars of the great hall here better than the twelve larger. The lighting of this hall is beautiful. The roof in the centre was raised some feet above the lateral roofing; so that large oblong spaces were left for a sight of the blue sky; and when they admitted the slanting rays of the rising and setting sun

99   Modern Egypt and Thebes, II, 145.

upon this grove of pillars, and, through them, lighted up the pictured walls, the glory must have been great. Forty-eight pillars supported these roofs; —roofs which were painted starry and blue like the sky. The hall was one hundred feet long. Beyond it extend pillared chambers, in succession and in groups, till we come upon mere traces of their walls and bases of their columns; and at last, out upon the bare rock. Throughout this range of building, the ground rises and the roofs sink, and the walls close in, so that the whole edifice contracts, the door-ways lessening in proportion; and an appearance is given of a longer perspective than exists.

In the sculptures on the walls, the king pays his duty to the gods, and receives privileges from them. The Supreme is here; with the other two who complete the highest triad: and some inferior deities introduce the king into their presence, while the god of letters, Thoth, notes the dates of the royal victories on his palm-branch. Elsewhere, the Supreme presents him with Life and Power: and in the same hall, the Supreme gives him the falchion and sceptres, ordering him, as the inscription tells us, to smite his foreign enemies with the one, and rule Egypt with the other.[100] How he obeyed these orders, other pictures and legends tell us. One captive group, whom he holds by the hair, are declared to be "foreign chiefs:" and there are Asiatic and other distant enemies among the vanquished in the battle-pieces, and the names of towns inscribed among the legends, as well as represented in sculptures of storming and sieges. As for his home affairs, we find a procession of twenty-three of his sons, and a group of three daughters. The names of the sons are all inscribed. Elsewhere there is a procession of priests, bearing the figures of the Theban ancestors of the king.[101] There is an inscription in the great hall, on one of the architraves, describing the valuable and beautiful character of this edifice, and dedicating the sculptures to his father, —the Supreme, who says, "I grant that your edifice shall be as stable as the sky." (Alas! to look round upon it now!) Isis adds, "I grant you long life to govern Egypt."[102] The next chamber seems, as some of the learned think, to have been the library of the palace. The ceiling bears an astronomical subject; and an inscription, declaratory of the value of the building of this apartment, alludes to the "books of Thoth," the god of letters. This primitive Mercury is here attended, as Champollion records, by a figure with an eye on his head, and surmounted by a legend "Sense of Sight;" the goddess Saf being attended in like manner by a figure with an ear on his head, and labelled "Sense of Hearing:"—(Sôlem.) Champollion interprets these figures as indicators or guardians of the library, — "the books of Thoth." On its walls, the priests bear

100   Wilkinson's Modern Egypt and Thebes, II. 154.
101   Ibid. 151.
102   Champollion. Lettres sur l'Egypte.

shrines in procession. But before the king had leisure, and perhaps qualification for thus honoring the gods and himself, he had to gain his fame, add to his dominions, and put down his enemies. On the outer walls, accordingly, we find his adventures, in a wonderful collection of battle sculptures. What we see are a mere remnant of what existed. The greater number lie in fragments under the mounds of fallen stones: but enough are left to teach us much. The battle-scene on the wall of the area exceeds any representation I ever saw for quantity in a given space. It is barbaric, though including tokens of no mean civilization. There is the common barbarism of making the conqueror and his equipage gigantic in comparison with all the other figures. He stands in a fine attitude in his flying chariot, his bow in hand (which he draws behind his head) and the reins tied round his waist. Two quivers crossed are at his right hand; and the exterior one is decorated with an extended lion. The king's real lion is visible in the battle too. The conqueror drives over prostrate and bound captives; and men are falling around him in all manner of desperate attitudes. The siege and river-scenes are very curious; the scaling-ladder, the shields, the bridges, fosses and towers (labeled "the strong town of Watsch or Batsch"), giving us much insight into the civilization of the time. The phalanx of spearmen is capital; their spear-heads being carefully distinguished from the ripple of the little blue river in which such large men are floundering! Then there is the drowned chief whom his people are trying to revive; and the city wall plainly distinguished from the rock on which it is built. The horses are finely given; and so is the king. Here, as in others of the old sculptures, we come upon what looks like an odd stroke of humor now and then, as in the ass staggering and falling under the weight of a bag of spoil, —meant probably to be thus pointed out as gold. But the humor may be merely in our view of the coalescence of the most literal representation with a method of art which we have been accustomed to consider formal and conventional beyond all other.

The most beautiful point of view for this palace was from about a quarter of a mile to the south, where, looking back upon it, its soft-tinted grove of pillars rose behind the copse of dark tamarisks and acacias which intervened. This was happily not our only view of the Ramaseum. It lay in our way from some other objects, and I became quite familiar with it before the week was out.

We visited to-day a very beautiful temple at El-Kurneh; to me the most interesting, on the whole, of any of the edifices at Thebes. It is old. being begun by the father of the great Ramases, in honor of his father, and completed by his son in honor of himself. I will abstain from giving any detailed account of it, and merely mention some of its peculiarities.

There were once sphinxes in the dromos, the remains of which are still traceable. These sphinxes represented King Osirei himself, conveying the favorite boast of great men of an early time—their union of intellectual power and physical strength. Then comes a ruined pylon— once the second—and another dromos which brings us to the beautiful portico; beautiful, though no two pairs of its columns are at the same distance from each other. These ten columns are composed of the stalks of water plants, bound together below the capital, where they expand, and are again gathered in by the abacus. This very ancient Egyptian order gratified me more than any later ones. In a dedication inscription within we find the following declaration of the great Ramases, to whom the Supreme, Amun Ra, here again presents the symbol of Life. "Ramases, the beloved of Amun, has dedicated this work to his father Amun Ra, king of gods, having made additions for him to the temple of his father, the king, son of the Sun, Osirei."[103] The part of the temple which was dedicated by this Osirei to his father, Ramases I., was finished by the illustrious grandson of the latter, who put in the sculptures. Among these sculptures is one where his grandfather stands behind the gods, bearing the insignia of Osiris, and watching the introduction and homage of his grandson to the gods. The legend over him declares him to be "Ramases deceased, esteemed by the great God, &c. &c." Elsewhere in the same apartment, this king and Osirei, as well as the gods, are receiving the pious offerings of the great Ramases. The faces here are astonishingly preserved, and they have a full measure of the simplicity and sweetness of the old Egyptian type of countenance. I think there can be no doubt of the elegance of this temple-palace, in comparison with those of later date.

Some barbarians, called Charles and Jane Tilt, have cut and blacked their names and the date of their visit in large on some of the sacred places of this temple. As they have thought fit to publish their own names and adventure in a mischievous manner, they have no right to object to a republication which may be useful in the way of warning to others.

I was delighted to find here many of the prevalent symbolical forms —here, in this very ancient temple. The boat which we find everywhere had at each end the finest ram's head I had seen. I was pleased to meet with grapes among the offerings. Those which I bad seen at Kaláb'sheh with leaves and tendrils, were modern. But here were bunches of undeniable grapes. I saw also the elegant lamp I mentioned before, and the lion-shaped bier. The globe and asps were on the cornices, and the ceiling of the portal was beautiful—cartouches and stars on a blue ground.

These were our studies during our first day at Thebes. These palaces, built for the busy and illustrious living, were to us like tombs, for there was a spirit of death within and around them all. Not only the inmates had passed away, but the deeds, the modes of life, the objects of reverence, pride and desire. But to-morrow we were to penetrate deeper into the region of the dead. We were to explore some of the wonders of the Death valley of Thebes.

103   Wilkinson's Modern Egypt and Thebes, II. 140.

CHAPTER XV

THEBES—OLD EGYPTIAN VIEWS OF DEATH AND HEREAFTER—
THE PRIESTS—INTERMENTS—TOMB OF OSIREI

THE MOST STRIKING THING AT THEBES is perhaps the evidence on every hand of the importance to the old Egyptian mind of the state of the dead. To the philosopher there is nothing surprising in this; for he knows that it must be so to an infant race, inexperienced in the history of man, and unlearned as to the powers of the human mind, and the relative value of its aims. Everywhere the mind of man is active, unsatisfied, and aspiring; and while he knows so little of the world he lives in, and the companions beside him, and the unseen region of ideas which lies about him as infantine nations do, he is impelled to refer his activity and his desires to the future which he supposes to contain what he at present wants and cannot find. It is with puerile man as it is with the child who is never satisfied with the present, but always stretching forward into the unknown future, —not knowing the value of what is under his hand, but neglecting it in dreams of what he shall have and do in some desirable state by and by. The aspiration is instinctive, and therefore right: but as yet unenlightened and undisciplined. As he grows up, the present becomes more to him, and the future less. In proportion as he becomes truly wise he discovers that in the present scene and moment lies more than his best industry can understand and his best powers achieve. He brings home his faculties; and finds in the present enough to occupy them all, and to fill his life completely full of interest, activity, and advancement. It is only a child, grown or ungrown—an ignorant and undisciplined child—who would weep for more worlds to conquer: and he is the wisest man who knows that he has always many unexplored and ungoverned worlds on his hands which should leave him no leisure for looking forward into a future which he cannot penetrate. It is with races of men as with individuals. Not knowing yet how to employ their aspirations and desires on the unfathomable and inexhaustible universe in which they are placed; not knowing how adequate their existing human powers are, if fully exercised, to their present human work; not knowing how exact is the momentary retribution of fidelity or unfaithfulness to their powers and their work, they are perpetually referring to the future for a wider scene, for new powers, and for arbitrary reward and punishment. There is nothing blameworthy or despicable in this. On the contrary, the tendency comes in happily to lift men over their infantine age of inexperience, as the child is ennobled by the forecast of his hopes before he can be yet more ennobled by the wisdom of his self-knowledge. And every working of instinct, every direction of natural aspiration, is to be revered in its proper place and at its proper time. We truly respect, accordingly, the child's or the peasant's notion of a literal judgment day, when there will be a process of trial, with books of account opened, and a sentence passed in words, and burning inflicted in the one case, and whatever the individual most desires conferred in the other. We truly respect these notions in the child and the peasant, while we know that no enlightened and disciplined man looks forward to any such actual scene. And the enlightened and disciplined man knows that while he continually thinks less of the future, as the inestimable present of life and duty opens before his contemplation and his industry, his hold of that in estimable present will appear weak and careless to a wiser than he who will come after him. Thus must we, who look back some little way, and from some small height, upon the track of ages, regard with serious respect, the engrossing attention that infantine nations gave to death and the state of the dead; the records they have left of their puerile pride, ambition and violence proving that, at the same time, they were but little aware of the value of what they held in the present life, with all its duties, its spiritual powers and privileges. As I said before, the most striking thing at Thebes is the evidence on every hand of the importance to the old Egyptian mind of the state of the dead: and these evidences will be regarded by the philosopher with the solemn reverence which the wise cannot but feel towards every form in which Faith, the noblest of human faculties, manifests itself. The literal truth of the objects of faith, when those objects are the highest that can be conceived, is a small matter; the exercise of the faculty is everything: and though the imagery of the Egyptian tombs is to us only imagery, while to their inmates it was anticipated fact, we may, in our sympathy with their mood of faith, enter those tombs with an awe perhaps as strong as theirs.

When the Pharaohs built their palaces and temples, they had more aims than one to fulfil. They blazoned their own deeds upon them; but they glorified the deeds of their fathers, even more carefully than their own: and they must have had in view the sympathy and edification of other men, living and to live. But their careful choice and elaborate preparation of their tombs, with every

possible resort in the adornment of them, show us that the unseen state was the
most interesting subject, and that of the firmest faith to them. The Pharaohs
were wont to devote the early years of their reigns to royal deeds of rule and
conquest: and they did not begin to build their palaces and temples till they had
achieved deeds with which to glorify them, and brought home captives to do
the work of building them. But it was quite otherwise with their tombs. Every
man who could afford himself a tomb, began its preparation early in life. A
palace or temple could be carried on to completion by a successor; but a tomb
was sealed up when the owner was laid in it. It could not, therefore, under the
uncertainty of life, be too soon begun; and their practice seems to show that it
could not be too long elaborated. Few or none appear to be finished in every
part; and some were in progress through a long course of years.

The most prominent idea presented to us in these tombs is that their makers
considered them to be really and truly an abode; —literally "a long home;" or,
as they called them, "everlasting habitations;" and to be prepared and provided
accordingly. —The way to the long home of the Theban kings is very appropriate and most impressive; a succession of winding defiles between grand but
most desolate rocks, the recesses of which might seem to invite the candidate
for death to come and rest here in the depth of silence, till his thousands of years
of suspense should be fulfilled: —to rest in silence, but not in solitude: not in
the solitude of the wide desert, but in the still congregation of this deep valley.

To the old Egyptians, as to all who are heedless of the unborn human race
in interest for those who have lived, the true congregation of the human race
must always have been looked for beyond the grave—so immeasurably must
the dead ever outnumber existing men. Every man must have felt himself one
of a very small company in comparison with that which he was to join. But the
case of the kings was strong indeed. Each one of them lived solitary; and it was
only when he died that he could enter among his peers. He went from the solitude of that busy, peopled plain to the sanctified society of the Valley of Death.
To him, this was the great event to which, as we see, he was looking forward
during the best years of his life; and he devoted his wealth, his thoughts, and the
most sacred desires of his heart to preparation for his promotion to the society
of kings, and the presence of the gods. There, an abode would be prepared for
him. On the walls of his tomb he attempted to paint the succession of mansions
in the great heavenly house which he was to inhabit at last: but meanwhile, he
was to dwell, for a vast length of time, in the long home in the valley, where his
peers were lying still (whether asleep or vigilant) all round about him.

How fit and impressive is the choice of this site for the metropolis of the
dead, can be conceived of only by contrasting it with that of the metropolis
of the living. Both might be viewed at once from the mountain ridges behind

western Thebes. There is a ridge where strangers are taken now, to overlook the plain; and glorious is the view: but to-day I went much higher still, to a peak whence I could see quite down into the Valley of the Tombs, and over every recess of the vivid green plain, —every nook which lay between the Arabian and Lybian hills. I chose to see it as it once was. I made myself three thousand years old, and saw from my perch what was worth looking at. Great as are the existing marvels of Thebes, they are, from this height, mere indications of the presence of man. Sprinkled over the expanse of verdure, one notices a few heaps of stones, —the temples and palaces; and a pair of sentinels, —the Colossi: and across the blue and brimming river, a little cobweb railing, which is El-Uksur; and a group of massive towers, —which is El-Karnac. This, with all its soft freshness of coloring, all its African brightness, is too sad and dreary to dwell on. It is better to see it with the eyes of three thousand years ago.

There lies the city below, filling up all the plain, except where there is a girdle of fields. It is those gardens and groves among the houses which make it cover so large a space; for there never was, in this world, such a collection of houses as would cover this plain. How the gardens spread, not only round the palaces, but behind the ranges of dwellings which we should call streets! How their ponds gleam on the eye, and their clusters of palms overshadow their lawns, and intervene between the eye and the fiat house-roofs! I can distinguish the children pushing out from among the reeds in this nearer garden, in their little papyrus boat of nautilus shape. —How finely the city ramifies, —with no circuit wall, but temple ranges running out in all directions! That advanced post of temples at intervals is a sufficient defence, if any foe should dare to come. They are perfect fortifications; and the watchmen on the summits of the propy-la command the valley in both directions, as far as the irregular hill boundary admits. What masses these are, —these four which command the plain! El-Kar-nac and El-Uksur over yonder, and the Ramaseum and Medeenet Haboo below me! How they stand, as if each calling to the other! How each stretches out its dromos, and plants its files of sphinxes, or its pair of colossal sentinels, as if to proclaim "here lives a king, or the glory of a king!" Far over yonder, in the ave-nue between El-Karnac and El-Uksur, I see some movement; —surely it is the floating of pennons, and the carrying of standards. If it crosses the river, I may see what it means. Meantime, how gay is the blue winding Nile, with its heavy, slow-moving boats, —the gay checkered sails up, and the row of long oars glancing in the sun! How pretty are those villas scattered about the edge of the desert, each with its plot of garden or field sloping down into the fertile region of the plain; each with its canopy of shady palms; and every palm swaying in the same light breeze which fills the sails on the river, and floats the pennons of that multitude in the avenues of El-Karnac! Here is a multitude below me too.

The women are exchanging their goods in the areas of the streets, —bargaining slowly, it seems, because, having no coin, they have to settle the worth of their valuables before they can agree on that of their produce. And those men, —how they are toiling about that sledge, —advancing it by hair's-breadths under its load of granite; a mass as large as any merchant's house in the city! What a team of harnessed men, straining at the load! By their light complexions, they are Asiatic captives. They are helping to build yonder palace, on whose walls their captivity is to be commemorated. —The wind strengthens, and brings up some sounds which tell what a multitude is stirring below. Through the hum and buzz there comes the shock of the mallet falling on the wedge in the quarry, and the lowing of the cattle on the farm at the edge of the plain below. And was not that a breath of music? Yes: the blast of a distant trumpet, and some shrill pipe tones. Ah! it is from that concourse over the water. How the multitude comes sweeping down to the river's brink! Surely that crowd of boats is going to bring them over. Yes; there is the funereal boat for the transport of the dead; and those others are making a bridge for the passage of the living. What a train they will be, winding through the defiles of that death region on my left hand! How still it is at this moment! Nothing there but the shadows thrown into the hollows! No sound but of the flapping of the wings of yonder eagle; for the wild dog is quiet till night. What a contrast is that parched, silent, desolate valley to this gay and stirring plain; and how complete, to those on either side, is the barrier of these rocky hills which I, from my perch, can overlook! To-day, as yonder funeral train winds through it, the echoes of the valley of death will be awakened, and they will answer to notes of wailing, or shouts of boasting; and its hot mounds will be alive with shadows: but to-morrow, the two regions which are separated but by a partition of rock, will be once more opposed as activity to oblivion, and Life to Death.

As it appeared to me from that pinnacle, it appeared daily when I rode through the Defiles of the Valley of the Tombs of the Kings. I felt that there was never a nobler seat for a metropolis of the living than the plain of Thebes, and never a nobler approach than by these ravines from the city of the living to the kingdom of the dead.

Every Egyptian king was, as I have said, a priest. He might be chosen out of the Second Caste, —the Military: but he must become a priest before he could assume the sovereignty. It was a sufficient reason for this that the king must always thus be an instructed person, and in fellowship with the high class who held all the dignities and privileges of knowledge and sacred office: but there was another reason. The sovereign in Egypt was assisted in his government by a council of priests: and of course it was necessary for him to hold, in common with his advisers, that knowledge and those secrets of Custom by which the nation was governed. Before looking at their most interesting existing work, it may be well to form in our minds some slight picture of this remarkable order of men.

Herodotus gives us information of their personal habits, which were carefully arranged with a view to their perfection as models before the eyes of the people. We all know how much more necessary, and how much more difficult extreme cleanliness is in Egypt than elsewhere. The priests shaved their heads; and their whole bodies were shaved every three days, that, as Herodotus says, there might not, by possibility, be any vermin or soil on those who served the gods.[104] Twice by day, and twice by night, they washed in cold water: and they wore no other clothing than a dress of linen, and shoes of papyrus. They were daily served with the sacred meats of the temples, ready cooked; but from some articles of food, as fish, they abstained; and were compelled to be very moderate in the use of wine. The food they abstained from seems to have been such as tended to produce leprous and other eruptive diseases. They had an extreme and mysterious horror of beans; never permitting them to be sown in Egypt, or touched when found growing wild. Whatever were their reasons were probably those of Pythagoras in warning his disciples against touching beans. Some have supposed (after a hint in Aristotle) that Pythagoras meant to warn his pupils against political action, —the ballot vote being given by a bean: but as the philosopher derived so much else from Egypt, and as we know the strength of the reprobation of beans there, we need only suppose him to have been more aware of the priestly reasons for that reprobation than we are.

It need scarcely be pointed out that much more was included in the class of sacred things among ancient nations (as among modem half-civilized ones) than with us. Legislation, Geometry, Medicine, every science was a sacred study among the Egyptians, and engrossed by the priests; as was the whole of their religious philosophy. They made laws which they enforced without rendering any reason, holding that the people had "nothing to do with the laws but to obey them." They explored many regions of natural science, giving the people the results in the form of divination and magic. They held among themselves the doctrines of the unity of God, and of a divine moral government, and lowered their doctrine to meet the comprehension of the people, by deifying the attributes of God, and making local rulers of them. The testimony of ages has proved the vice of this method of proceeding: but we must remember that the Egyptian priesthood had not this testimony of ages. We must remember how they stood, a little band of observers, among the wonders and mysteries of the universe; and that, as yet, they had to collect the facts of external nature to a great extent before they could look far into causes (so-called); and that

104   Herod. II. 37.

these facts were not regarded by them with the calm eye of knowledge, but the bashful glance of new and awe-struck perception. They could hardly receive such knowledge as they had, otherwise than as a special gift and revelation to themselves, as students of the universe. It was not known then, not dreamed of by any one, that knowledge is the equal birthright of all, and that truth is of the last importance to every human being. We are not, therefore, to reprobate in the Egyptian priesthood what is worthy of reprobation now in any man or body of men; —a distrust of the general understanding, as compared with our own; a keeping back of the knowledge which is the birthright of all; an offer, under veils and disguises, of that truth which every man has an equal right to see in its native purity and nobleness. The Egyptian priesthood tried the experiment of a civil government which was probably the fittest at the time for its purposes—those purposes being, we may hope, centered in the good of the people: —Pythagoras, at least, thus understood the matter. The experiment, which lay within the terms of natural laws, appears to have succeeded; the Egyptian mode of governing society by a council of the wisest and best having lasted longer than perhaps any other government that nations have experienced. The Egyptian priesthood tried another experiment, which failed, because it violated the terms of natural laws. They tried the experiment of making themselves gods to the people in regard to the administration of knowledge and natural benefits. They took upon themselves to measure and to manage the minds of men in regard to matters which in fact they held only in common with all men. They did this, I doubt not, in all sincerity, fidelity, and benevolence; but it was a mistake of ignorance; and it was followed by its natural retribution. Ignorance, whether guilty or unavoidable, is always presumptuous. These priests were ignorant and presumptuous, while most earnestly intent on doing good with such knowledge as they had. They assumed the exclusive possession of that to which all had a right; and they corrupted themselves and their charge together. The philosophy they held languished and nearly died out. Their own order deteriorated in power, knowledge, and character; and the people became idolaters, sinking into that weakness and under that doom which superstition brings on as surely as the pollution of the atmosphere causes lassitude and lingering death. The experiment of spiritual government failed; but we are not to deal with the priests for it as if they had had our thousands of years of added experience.

I never believed during my school days, and I am sure I never shall now, that any order of men ever carried on a wilful and deliberate fraud, from generation to generation, for any purpose whatever. I used to suspect in my school days, as I believe now, that all the heathen priesthoods which were held up for my scorn as bands of impostors, had faith, one way or another, in what they taught. And there seems every reason to believe this now of the Egyptian priesthood, who taught more extraordinary things perhaps than any other. If we do but put ourselves in their places for an instant, we may perhaps see how many things may have been venerable and true to them, which we, with our knowledge and our ignorance, our experience and our prejudices, do not know how to treat seriously at all.

To them, nothing was so wonderful, so mysterious, so important as Life and Organization. Their purity of life and habits—their taking but one wife, and banishing all indecency from their temple rites enlightens us to much that we might reprobate otherwise in the illustrations of some of their festivals, and a few of their doctrines. Perhaps they were wiser than we are in their reverence for natural instincts; and they were certainly not wrong in thinking life and its production the most sacred and the most real, and therefore the most important fact with which the human race can have concern. When they by degrees led the people down into gross brute-worship (if indeed it is true that they did so), they certainly misapplied or ill-conveyed their reverent appreciation of the great fact of life; but the fault was in the misapplication, and not in the philosophy which recognized in life, wherever found, something altogether sacred, before which the human intellect must bow down, as an insoluble mystery. I am sure that we are wrong in the other extreme, in the levity or utter thoughtlessness with which we regard the races of inferior animals, which have shared with ours, for thousands of years, the yet unsolved mystery of sentient existence, without sharing with us anything else than what is necessary for the support of that existence. We know no more of the experience, one may say, the mind, of the cattle, the swallows, the butterflies, and worms about us than if they lived in another planet. They and man have met hourly for all these thousands of years without having found any means of communication; without having done anything to bridge over the gulf which so separates them, that they appear mere phantoms to each other. The old Egyptian priests recognized the difficulty, and made a mistake upon it; —disastrous enough. We, for the most part, commit the other great mistake of not recognizing the mystery. We are not likely ever to embody our consciousness of it in any form of brute worship; but we are hardly qualified to criticise those who fell into that perhaps sublime error in the early days of human speculation.

Then again, about their Oracles, Magic, and Medicine; —it is need less and therefore unjust, to attribute to them any artifice or insincerity. All who have duly inquired into that class of natural facts, know that among human faculties exist those of perception or apprehension of distant and of future events; and some powers of sympathetic operation, whose nature and limits are as yet but little understood. Those powers are as yet but too little inquired into, notwithstanding the example and exhortations of Bacon, Cuvier, Laplace, and other philosophers who were rendered by their philosophy meek enough to learn from nature. Finding, as we do, indisputable proofs that at present the human being is capable of various states of consciousness, and of knowing events which are happening afar, and of foreknowing events which are future —sometimes spontaneously, and sometimes by means of an agency purposely employed; — knowing, on the other hand, that history abounds with records which every-body believes more or less, of prophecy, of preternatural (so-called) knowledge, of witchcraft, unaccountable sympathies, and miraculous cures; we have every reason to suppose that the Egyptian priesthood encountered and held the facts which some of us encounter and hold, and employed them as sincerely and devoutly as they employed other facts in natural philosophy. It is probable that the oracles were true: and we have no right to doubt that the priests believed them true—as earnestly as they believed that they could cure the sick whom they carried into their temples, and on whose heads they religiously laid their hands, with invocations to the gods. The faculties which drew the attention of Bacon and others are found more vigorous, more spontaneous, and more easily excitable among Orientals than among ourselves. If we find, by the half-dozen, merely by opening our minds to the fact, cases of far-seeing, and fore-seeing, and curative power, it is probable that such cases were familiar to the heathen priest hoods of old; and that they sincerely believed that persons so gifted held a revealing commission from the gods. While fully aware of the means necessary for eliciting the faculty, and using those means, the priest might wait on the speech of the oracular somnambule, believing it to proceed from the veritable inspiration of the god. This is not the place for bringing together the evidence that exists about the dealings of the Egyptian priests with the sick and infirm: but it is curious; and it shows no cause for the assumption that they were jug-glers, or in any way insincere in their practice. They probably believed that they should give relief by the "touching with the hands," which, as Solon tells us, "will immediately restore to health," when soothing medicines are of no avail; and by that "stroking with gentle hands" which Æschylus says was to be had on the Nile: [105] and they were probably justified in their belief by the results. Noth-ing but a very large proportion of cures will account for the continued celebrity of any seat of health during a sequence of many centuries.

As to the oracles, there were many in Egypt; and they were famous from the earliest times of which we have any record. The two most celebrated were those of Amun Ra, in the Oasis of Amun; and that of Buto in the city of that name.[106]

105   Prometheus to Io: "There Zeus will render you sane, stroking you with gentle hand and simply touching you." This sanctuary at Canopus was celebrated for the cures wrought by the god.
106   Herod. II. 83.

Herodotus tells a curious story of the establishment of the oracles of Amun Ra and of Dodona.[107] He heard two versions; —one from the priests of Amun at Thebes; the other from the priestesses of the oracle at Dodona. The Greek priestesses told him that two black doves were carried off from Thebes; one of which went into the Lybian Desert, and the other came to Dodona, perched on an oak, and spoke, saying that it was the will of the king of the gods that he should have an oracle there. The dove which flew to the Lybian oasis delivered a similar command there from Amun Ra. The story of the Theban priests to Herodotus was that two wo men, sacred to the god, were carried off from Thebes by the Phoenicians, and set up oracles at the Oasis and at Dodona. They were probably carried off for the sake of that power of provision which had caused their consecration at Thebes, and which they exercised after wards at the two new oracular seats. Herodotus says expressly that there were no priestesses in Egypt:[108] yet it is certain that women of the priestly caste were, in one way or another, employed and consecrated about the temples; and in all purity and honor. They were probably the utterers of the oracle; and might be also the dispensers of health in the sanctuaries. Among so large a body as that of the Egyptian priesthood, it is probable that there was never any want of somnambules, who would be looked upon as chosen by the god of the region to deliver his oracles; and who would do it, while the faculty worked clearly (which we now find to be rarely for any long time); and without any need of jugglery at the time, or occasion to suspect it now. Diodorus Siculus tells us of a daughter of Sesostris who seems to have had the faculty as eminently as Joan of Arc, exercising it with regard to her father's victories as Joan did about her own. Her father, being king, was also High-priest, and must have known how far to trust his daughter's divination: and he planned his proceedings, and prepared for his conquests, under her direction.[109] Herodotus observes that this Theban oracle and that of Dodona are much like each other:[110] that the art of foretelling future events, as practised in the Greek temples, was derived from Egypt: and that it is certain that the Egyptians were the first of the human race who established feasts and public assemblies, processions, and the manner of approaching God and holding intercourse with him: and that the Greeks had borrowed these customs from the Egyptians.

Every god had, as Herodotus tells us, a high-priest and several other priests; each of whom is succeeded on his death by his son.[111] The principle of their

107   Ibid. 54, 55.
108   Herod. II. 35.
109   Wilkinson's Ancient Egyptians, I. 261.
110   Herod. II. 58.
111   Ibid. 37.

sacrifices was to offer to the gods what was hostile or unacceptable to them; so that the sacrifice, while a sign of homage, was so through an act of vindictiveness. The animals offered were usually those in which a wicked soul was, or might be supposed to be, residing at the time. They laid hands on the head of the victim, charged it with maledictions,[112] and then got rid of it as fast as possible. If there were Greeks at market, the head was sold to them: if not, it was thrown into the river. The bull Apis was, as everybody knows, black, with white marks; the star on the forehead being the sign of its being an incarnation of the deity.[113] If The bullocks offered in sacrifice were red, because Typho was supposed to be of that complexion: and if the priests found a single hair on the animal which was not red, they rejected it.[114]

One of the sacred traditions of Egypt was that Isis had given one-third of the land to the priests, on condition of perpetual honors being paid to Osiris after his death. We know how Joseph left the priests' lands in their possession when he bought up all the rest of the land of Egypt: and when, after the famine, he decreed that the king should have a fifth part of the produce, he excepted the lands of the priests from the impost.[115] The personal wants of the priests were all supplied from the temples: and thus they were entirely free from the cares of life. For one item of property they had the Tombs: and their monopoly of a property in such constant request must have been very profitable.

It appears that there was a lake made near every capital city in Egypt,[116] for the transit of the dead; and a sacred boat to bear the hearse; and a boatman whose official name, written in Greek, was Charon.[117] The funeral trains were obliged to pass over this lake on the way to the tomb; but they might return by land. The purpose of the obligatory custom of crossing the lake was that all the dead might pass through the same ordeal before admission to their "eternal habitation," as the priests called the tomb. This ordeal was judgment by the forty-two[118] assessors who, on earth, performed the first stage of the work which was to be completed by the forty-two heavenly assessors, who awaited the dead within the threshold of the unseen world. Notice was given to these judges of the day of the funeral; and they stood in a half circle on the nearer shore of

112   Ibid. 39.

113   Herodotus says (III. 28), "The Egyptians say that a flash of lightning descends from heaven upon her," (the cow-mother of Apis,) "and that from this ray she conceives the god Apis."

114   Herod. II. 38.

115   Genesis, XLVII. 22, 26.

116   Wilkinson's Ancient Egyptians, V. 420.

117   Diodorus, I. 92.

118   According to Champollion.

the lake, awaiting the arrival of the funeral train. Any person might accuse the deceased in their presence of any immoral act. If the accusation was proved, the deceased was not allowed to pass. If the accuser could not substantiate his story, he was severely punished. Even kings[119] have been known to be turned back from the place of embarkation, when acts of injustice have been proved against them: and it appears that the priests had no more exemption than others from this ordeal. Those of the rejected dead who had left a family behind them were carried home, and their mummy-cases set upright against the wall of some chamber; a perpetual spectacle of shame and grief to their families, who suffered acutely from the disgrace of what had happened. Those who were poor and friendless, as well as vicious, were put into the ground where the rejection took place; and this was the shore where their melancholy ghosts wandered, if poets say true, pining for the Elysian fields which lay beyond; those Elysian fields[120] being the beautiful meadows which, in the principal burial-place of the Nile valley, at Memphis, extended beyond the lake of the Dead, all flowery with lotus and blossoming reeds.

Besides persons convicted of criminal acts, debtors were excluded from burial.[121] "Under his reign, as commerce suffered from a scarcity of money, he published the priests say, a law which forbade borrowing except on condition of the body of the borrower's father being given in pledge. It was added to this law that the creditor should also have in his power the burial of the debtor; and that if he refused to pay the debt for which he had deposited a pledge so precious, he could not, after his death, be laid in the tomb of his fathers, nor in any other; and that he could not, after the death of any of his own family, render them this honor." A creditor might possess himself of the mummy till the family had satisfied his claims; and the priests could refuse a tomb till it could be paid for. It became the ambition of the family of a debtor to furnish forth, sooner or later, a grand funeral, which, as the liabilities of the deceased must be first discharged, was in fact a restoration of the family honor. —In some cases of strong conjugal affection, the survivor retained at home the body of the departed, that both might be carried to the tomb together: but in such cases, it was always understood that a respectable funeral was in reserve.

The priests kept a number of tombs always ready, —probably covered with the ordinary kinds of paintings, and finished, except in the blank spaces left for the name and titles and character of the occupant. It is certain that services for

119   Diodorus, I. 72.

120   Ibid. 96.

121   According to Herodotus, (II. 136) this was a very old arrangement, dating from a law of Asychis, who, early in the First Period, built the Brick Pyramid.

the dead and offerings to them were celebrated at times long after the funeral; and it is thought probable that in cases where a new name is put over the
old one, and a different family has clearly come into possession of the place,
there may have been a discontinuance of the payments and offerings given for
services for the deceased, and the priests have let the tomb for a second-hand
place of burial.[122] Kings and wealthy families no doubt purchased the site, or
the excavated chambers, and adorned them according to their own taste; often
beginning the work in early manhood, as I have mentioned before, and carrying
it on till the day of death.

When I speak of the services and offerings to the dead, it does not follow
that these were presented within the tomb. The tomb appears to have been
closed and sealed at once. But small altars, sculptured with offerings, have, in
so many instances, been found before the entrances of tombs,[123] that we may
suppose the rites to have been celebrated there.

After permission to pass on had been given by the judges, an eulogy on
the deceased, and a prayer to the gods for his welfare in Hades, were read by
one of the officiating priests; and Charon proceeded in his ferrying. When the
opposite shore was reached, and the procession landed, the ground was sprinkled before the wheels of the funeral car; and sometimes palm-branches were
strewn in the way.[124] The body was sometimes crowned with amaranth or other
everlastings, or with bay-leaves, or fresh flowers.[125] There was much display of
sorrow. In the paintings of funeral rites, we always see mourners throwing dust
on their heads, beating themselves, and evidently uttering cries. —In ordinary
cases, the body was laid in one of the pits or recesses in the tomb: but in the
case of kings and great men, we know that there was a sarcophagus in a chamber
appropriated to it.

Thus much before the sealing up of the tomb. What afterwards?

As he had passed the external judgment, he was believed by the mourners
without to be assured of re-union, in his immortal essence, with the Supreme,
from whom all being emanates. The family have likened him, in the preparation
of his body, to Osiris, and have painted the emblems of Osiris on his envelop; and
will henceforth call him by that sacred name. The offerings they bring, and will
continue to bring occasionally, are not consecrated to their mortal comrade, but
to the portion of divinity which dwelt in him. —They place behind their altar of
offerings the images of Isis and Nepthys, the First and the Last: and believe that
the First and the Last attend at the head and feet of the body, as long as it remains

122   Wilkinson's Ancient Egyptians, V. 384.
123   Ibid. V. 387.
124   Ibid. V. 421.
125   Ibid. V. 423.

in the tomb.[126] They think of him as finding his way in the untried regions which they yet seem to themselves to know so familiarly. He leaves behind him the eulogy which is inscribed on the entrance wall of his tomb, and is met by Thoth, the Conductor of the dead, by whom he is fetched away, and led on to a more fearful judgment than that man's judgment by the shore of the lake which he has passed with honor. He is announced, according to his legend, thus: "Arrival of a soul in Amenti." His secret faults, and his sins of omission, of which men could be no judges, are now to come under review: and Thoth, whose legend[127] declares him "the Secretary of Justice of the other great gods," is to produce his book, in which he has recorded the whole moral life of the soul come to judgment. —The forty-two heavenly assessors are believed to represent the forty-two sins which the Egyptians believed man to be subject to. Each searched the newly-arrived soul, and declared its condition in respect to the particular sin.[128] Then came the trial of the balance. The symbol of the actions of the candidate are placed in one scale, and the symbol of integrity in the other. Thoth looks on, ready to record. Ilorus holds the hand of the candidate; and the dog[129] watches the process, ready to turn on the condemned if his scale should be "found wanting." If all is well, he advances in front of the balance, and finds the infant Horus seated on his lotus-blossom before the throne; and on the throne is the Judge, prepared to welcome him by raising the end of his sceptre, and to permit him to enter among the gods within. Of the happy state little was revealed, because, as it was declared, "the heart of man could not conceive of it." Almost the only particular declared was that there was a tree of Life,[130] on whose fruit the gods wrote the names of mortals destined to immortality, and whose fruit made those who ate of it to be as gods. His relatives thought of him as wearing on his head, as a mark of his justification, the feather of integrity: and they wrote beside his name, from that time forward, the name of the goddess of Justice; a practice equivalent to that of affixing the epithet "justified" to his name. This goddess of Justice, Thmei, is present during the trial of the soul: and she is identified in the sculptures by her legend "Thmei, who lives in Amenti, where she weighs hearts in the balance; —no sinner escapes her."[131]

126   Wilkinson's Ancient Egyptians, V. 416.
127   Champollion, Lettres sur l'Egypte.
128   Mischief. Blasphemy. Idleness. Stealing divine goods. Lying. Libertinism. Impurity. Skepticism ("head-shaking at the words of truth.") Long-speechifying. Need for remorse. Gluttony. —Here are some of the forty-two sins read off by Champollion from the Legends. Lettres sur l'Egypte.
129   If any one wishes to know the name of the Egyptian Cerberus, I can indulge him with it, —citing Champollion. The name is Teôuôm-enement.
130   The Persea.
131   Champollion, Lettres sur l'Egypte.

The survivors of any one for whom a burial has been obtained, but who might be suspected of unfitness for the heavenly mansions, were enabled to form but too clear an idea of his fate; for the pains of the wicked could be conceived of by human imagination, though the immortal pleasures of the just could not. The purgatory of the Egyptians was in fact described definitely enough: and the representations of it in the tombs give a strange sensation to the gazer before he has become accustomed to them. At the extreme end of a large tomb at Thebes,[132] I saw some marks on the black and stained wall which made me hold my candle nearer, and persevere till I had made out the whole sculpture, which gave me at last the impression of a bad dream. A hopeless-looking pig, with a bristling back, was in a boat, the stern of which was towards the heavenly regions. Two monkeys were with it, one at the bow, and the other whipping or driving the pig. This was a wicked soul, sent back to earth under the conduct of the agents of Thoth. The busy and gleeful look of the monkeys, and the humbled aspect of the pig, were powerfully given. This was the lowest state of the punished soul; but it would have to pass through some very mournful ones, and for a very long time, —to be probably a wolf, a scorpion, or a kite, or some other odious creature, in weary succession, —for a term of from three thousand to ten thousand years. This was called passing through its "orbit of necessity."

We now know enough of the outward state, and of the views and expectations of a Pharaoh, to understand the illustrations of his tomb. He was a priest, and therefore informed of the secret speculations of the wise upon the nature of the Divine Government and the destiny of man. On account of both his civil and his ecclesiastical rank, he was compelled to blazon forth his deeds and his expectations in great pomp. He has been laid in the chambers of the tomb with every funereal observance; and he has left on those walls illustrations of his faith which the vulgar may take literally, or let alone as unintelligible, while to priestly eyes they once told more than we shall now ever understand; and through those of a Pythagoras spread a philosophy through the world, so lofty as to command the praise at once of heathen, Jew and Christian. Here, where the common eye, then as now, could see only a household of gods and nothing higher, Pythagoras could see, through these transparent shows of attributes, that there was, because there must be, some vital centre, from whence they derived their existence. While the vulgar saw only in the fate of the damned "the circle of necessity," he saw it everywhere, believing that the agency of the central unity was operative wholly through numbers, —which are another name for certainty. Where others saw painted the array of the Hours, he perceived between each two the chain of Cause and Effect. Where others saw altar flames, he recognized the aspirations of the intellect. Where others shrank from pictures

132   Bruce's, or the Harper's.

of torture and dismemberment, he calmly studied the conflicts of the intellect and soul. Where Others saw a range of mummy closets with folding doors, he gained ideas of that succession of spheres through which the aspiring spirit has to pass, before attaining the vital centre from which it came forth, and to which it may, when worthy, return. Where the vulgar saw—what the priests told them to see— "an eternal abode," to which the dead king had come from "the inn" of his own palace,[133] —he knew that here the dust would, sooner or later, return to dust, while the spirit had returned to Him who had given it forth. Josephus says that Pythagoras was the most eminent of the heathens for wisdom and piety; and believes that he would have spoken more wisely still on the highest matters, if he had been safe from the malice of the ignorant. —The testimony of Herodotus is this:[134] "These people," the Egyptians, " are the first who have advanced the doctrine that the soul of man is immortal: that, when the body is dead, the soul enters always into that of some ani mal; and that, having thus passed successively into all kinds of terrestrial, aquatic and aerial creatures, it returns into a human body, during its act of birth: and that these different transmigrations take place in the space of three thousand years. I know that some Greeks have adopted this opinion, —some sooner, and some later; and that they have made use of it as they thought proper. Their names are not unknown to me; but I preserve silence upon them."

If this old traveler, at once so reserved and so garrulous, had spoken out here, the first name doubtless, which he would have uttered, would have been Pythagoras.

Among the many tombs open to us, we may choose one for a regular, however brief, examination. And the most attractive, without question, to any reader whose interest in the subject has carried him through this chapter, will be that discovered by Belzoni, about a quarter of a century ago, whose occupant was Osirei, father of Ramases the Great.

The neighboring peasants observed, about the beginning of the present century, a sinking of the soil in one of the hill sides in the Valley of the Tombs. They pointed this out to successive travelers; and Belzoni happily looked into the matter. He found a tomb extending 320 feet into the hill; and how much more, there is no saying, as the earth had fallen, and barred further progress. Its depth is great, as it descends the whole way, sometimes by inclined planes, and sometimes by staircases.

The first thing we had to do was to plunge down a flight of ruined steps, to a perpendicular depth of 24 feet. This entrance was closed up by masonry when Belzoni was brought to the spot. This staircase landed us in a passage where

133   Diodorus, I. 51.
134   Herod. II. 123.

the walls were covered with inscriptions about Osirei; probably a copy of the eulogy and prayers read at his funeral; as such a record was often inscribed near the entrance of a tomb. —Next comes another staircase, on the walls of which are painted figures of genii which cannot be the Assessors, because they are not forty-two; but thirty-seven on the one wall, and thirty-nine on the other. They are very grotesque; and one longs to know what they mean. It is strange, and exceedingly agreeable, to feel that this longing has more hope in it as the centuries pass. It appeared, a while ago, to all eyes as it appears now to many, that Time buries the sources of our knowledge as he goes, choking them up with his inexhaustible sands, and making a dreary desert of the past. But what do we see next? Here comes Speculation, on her tentative march, her divining rod in hand, indicating to her follower, laborious Science, where and how to work; and lo! out oozes the stream again, —scanty and thick enough at first, but sure to run fuller and clearer every day. See how improved our prospects of Egyptian knowledge are since the days when our Cœur de Lion was besieging Acre! At that time, about 1190, the learned physician of Bagdad, Abdallatif, was lecturing at Cairo. In the excellent account of the Egypt of his day which he has left us, he says, speaking of the Pyramids and other monuments which were be-fore his eyes, "these blocks are completely covered with writing in that ancient character, the import of which is wholly unknown at this day. I have not met with any person, in all Egypt, who could say that he knew, even by hearsay, of any one who understood this character." "Near these Pyramids, the remains of gigantic old edifices, and a great number of solidly constructed tombs are to be seen; and it is rare to meet with any portion of these ruins which is not covered with inscriptions in that ancient character which is wholly unknown at this day."[135] How delightful it must be to any Champollion, Rosellini, Wilkinson or Lepsius of our century to read this passage! And how encouraging it is to some of us who, by their labors, have looked with some degree of intelligence upon the monumental records of Egypt, to think that a future generation will prob-ably see much more than we do; —perhaps understanding the genii, and the other mysteries of this tomb, nearly as well as if they had Pythagoras, or some more plainspoken old priest, for a guide.

No part of the illustrations of this tomb is more mysterious than those of the second passage. Kneph, "the Spirit of the Supreme, which moves upon the face of the waters,"[136] has naturally a boat for one of his emblems: the serpent is another. Phthah, his colleague in the work of creation, is the patron of the occupant of this tomb; and their symbols abound. In this second passage we find the boats of Kneph: and a curious series of descending planes, each with a

135   Relation de l'Egypte, par Abdallatif, Livre I., Ch. IV.
136   Wilkinson's Ancient Egyptians, IV. 236.

door upon it, which is supposed to figure the descent to Hades; —the Amenti, or western region of the dead. We meet the serpent here in the shape of the bier, which elsewhere is almost invariably lion-shaped. Here, the serpent has lion's paws, instead of human feet, as usual. The "justifying" goddess stands at the lower end of the descent.

We next come to a small chamber which almost any one but Belzoni would have taken to be the extremity of the excavation. Its walls were all painted, and it had every appearance of completeness: and a deep pit in face of the entrance passage would have been concluded to be the place of burial. This pit, however, was a well: and it was dug there to draw off the waters which would otherwise injure, and which since have injured, the interior chambers. Belzoni filled up this pit; not knowing its purpose. He spied a hole in the wall, and, striking it, found it sounded hollow. He and his companions brought a palm trunk to bear on it, and battered it down; finding immediately that the best part of this wonderful tunnel was before them.

In the chamber to which the pit belongs, the King Osirei is seen making offerings to Osiris, and to some less conspicuous deities. It is in this chamber that an immeasurable serpent of considerable thickness, winds round the walls in a curious and rather elegant involution: and I think it is in the next that a serpent bier extends continuously round nearly half the walls, bearing a series of prostrate mummies. In another place, instead of mummies, the serpent supports human heads, — the headless bodies in some cases remaining near, and in other cases, being absent. The strangest use I saw made of the serpent in any old monument was here, where it was double-headed, and wore the crowns of the two Egypts, —Upper and Lower, —and had two pairs of human legs, walking opposite ways, —a dove being perched in the bend of its body. Sometimes the serpent is winged; and two, uniting their necks to support a disk, wonderfully resembled a caduceus. —In one instance, where an enormous serpent is carried by the gods, Champollion says it is the great Apophis, enemy of the sun, who is overcome and carried away captive; a suggestion which the Greeks were not slow to adopt. And it is impossible to look upon these representations of the serpent; of the tree of life, of which those who ate were made as gods; of the moving spirit of the Creator, and of the universally prevalent ideas of the original spread of water; the separation of the land from the water; the springing of vegetation, and the sudden appearance of animals on the new surface; and the separation of the upper air into regions of abode, without seeing whence was derived the first of the two accounts of the creation given in the Book of Genesis;[137]—that in which, not Jehovah, but the Elohim were engaged, who would be understood by the Egyptian instructors of Moses to be Kneph and

137   Genesis, I.; II., 1, 2, 3.

Phthah; —the Presiding Spirit, and the Forming Intellect of the Supreme. The other, and very different, account[138] has little that is Egyptian in its character, and was probably not learned at Heliopolis or Thebes.

In the hall through the first chamber is the curious group of four kinds of people (four of each) which has excited so much speculation, but which Champollion believed that he understood plainly enough. Ka, the Sun, stands behind the sixteen figures, who are not captives, but dwellers under the sun—inhabitants of the earth. The general legend declares them to be "the inhabitants of Egypt, and those of foreign countries." Four are red, the Egyptian conventional complexion; and their special legend is "the race of men;" which savors of the conceit of primitive patriotism. The next four have primrose-colored skins, and are called "Namou,"—("Asiatics.") The third set are altogether negro, in complexion and feature; and they are called "Nahasi,"— ("Africans.") The fourth group are pale yellow again, and blue-eyed, and dressed in barbaric fashion, with feathers in their hair, but with long flowing robes. These are inscribed. "Tamhou," which Champollion believed to designate a northern people, and probably Europeans.[139] The rest of this hall is chiefly occupied by the reception of the departed king by the gods.

Next we come to an unfinished chamber, where the drawings are made for sculptures which have never been wrought. Here are the bold and free outlines which we cannot but admire now; outlines which were corrected where faulty by the master hand with its red chalk pencil, coming after the pupil with his black one. In one figure the arm was made too long; and the rectification by the master—the red outline over the black, stands as light, fresh, and no doubt effaceable, as in the hour when it was made, —before the Great Ramases was born, or in his childhood.

Then comes another staircase, and then more passages, with their ceremonial paintings: and, at length, the great hall—which yet is not the most interesting of these chambers of the grave. The most remarkable thing in it that meets the eye is the picture of the states through which the soul has to pass, after leaving the lower hemisphere, and entering upon the abodes of the sun. Of these abodes there are twelve, each shown by a door valve, disclosing a mummy, and guarded by a serpent. Each serpent has a name; and all have the legend.[140] "It dwells above this great door, and opens it to the god Sun." One beautiful illustration is of the connection of the deceased with time. The mummy stands with a chain round his neck, which is held by a procession of twenty-four figures, each with a star over its head. These are the Hours; and in

138   Genesis, II. 4-25.
139   Champollion's Lettres sur l'Egypte.
140   Ibid.

another tomb I saw the same company, telling the season of the year by their appearance; those betokening the night being dark, and standing near together; those betokening the day being lighter, and further apart. If Champollion reads the legends of these spheres and spirits in the tombs aright, we have some light as to the expectations of these ancient worshipers. He translates thus, about the inhabitants of two series of abodes: "These hostile souls see not our god when he casts the rays from his disk: they no longer dwell in the terrestrial world; and they hear not the voice of the great god when he traverses their zones." "These have found grace in the eyes of the great god. They dwell in the abodes of glory; those in which the heavenly life is led. The bodies which they have abandoned will repose forever in their tombs, while they will enjoy the presence of the Supreme God."[141]

In the side chambers are devices yet waiting for their interpretation: — flames, heads and headless bodies, men bound, or standing feet upper-most, or lying on their backs—or with their heads just leaving their shoulders; with the scarabaeus in the boat, and other animal symbols which show that these are not, as some have hastily supposed, human sacrifices, (which did not make a part of Egyptian worship,) but were probably a symbolical representation of the process of initiation into the priestly mysteries.

The sarcophagus chamber is wonderfully fine. After exploring it as well as we could with the lights we carried—picking out the devices on the walls, but discerning nothing of the vaulted ceiling at the end where the sarcophagus stood, we enjoyed seeing the whole lighted up by a fire of straw. I never shall forget that gorgeous chamber in this palace of death. The rich colors on the wall, (especially the profusion of deep red,) were brought out by the flame; and the wonderful ceiling whose black vault was all starred with emblems, and peopled with lines of yellow figures—countless, in two vast regiments—this was like nothing earthly. And it is like nothing on the earth. These starry emblems are what has been called the Zodiac. I should not have discovered or supposed them to bear that meaning: but Champollion, who knew more than anybody else about such things, offers his readings of old Egyptian almanacks—quoting the testimony of Diodorus about "the gilded circle of Osymandyas, which gave the hours of the rising of the constellations, with the influences of each." Champollion gives as some of these influences: —as, "Orion influences the left ear. 1st hour: Orion influences the left arm. 2d hour: Sirius influences the heart," and so on.[142] Payne Knight says[143] that Astrology is not expressly mentioned among the pursuits of the ancient Egyptians; but that their creed certainly admitted

141   Ibid.
142   Lettres sur l'Egypte.
143   Payne Knight's "Inquiry into the Symbolical Language," &c.

the principle on which it is founded; —that is, necessity—a derivation of all destinies from the original impulse given by an immutable Creator.

Beyond the sarcophagus chamber, the excavation still descends, by staircases and passages, till the mass of earth, fallen from above, bars further progress.

Such are the places where, as Isaiah says, "the Kings of the nations, even all of them, lie in glory, each in his own house,"[144] and such are the regions supposed by him to be moved at the approach of the tyrant, and to stir up their dead to meet him who has become as weak as they, and must now be brother of the worm, and be brought down to Hades, to the sides of the pit. —From Egypt, this method of burial spread far over the east; and the caverns of the hills contained the successive generations of many people, besides the Hebrews, who had, in their civilization, followed the ideas and methods of Egypt. Happily for the human race, the ideas spread with the forms. After the example of Egypt, men preserved, amidst more or less corruption, the belief in One Supreme God; in a Divine Moral Government; in a future life and retribution; and in the greatest of all truths, that moral good is the highest good, and moral evil the deepest evil. From the lips of this thoughtful people it was that infant nations learned, through a long course of centuries, whatever they held that was most noble, concerning the origin and tendencies of things, and what was most to be desired for the race of man at large, and the soul of every individual man. Many things remained to be learned; and many needed to be unlearned. We find much that was barbaric, coarse, ignorant, and untrue: but the wonder is at the amount of insight, achievement and truth. The ground gained by the human mind was never lost; for out of this Valley of the Nile issued Judaism: and out of Judaism issued, in due time, Christianity.

---

144   Is. xiv. 18.

CHAPTER XVI

THEBES—TOMBS—MUMMIES—MEDEENET HABOO—DAYR EL BAHREE—EL-KARNAC

WE PASSED THE WORKING HOURS of several days among the tombs; and my journal has copious accounts of them: but, remembering how much sooner one wearies of reading of such places than of seeing them, I will say little about them.

One of the most celebrated is the Harpers' Tomb, first mentioned by Bruce, and, therefore, often called by his name. This is the work of two of the Ramases: and a vast work it is, —extending 405 feet into the hill. The entrance passages have small chambers on either hand, whose walls present us with capital pictures of ancient Egyptian life. The kitchen comes first, —on the left-hand side: and there the servants are kneading bread, and carrying to the oven cakes sprinkled with black seeds: and others are making broth, and pastry; and some are drawing off liquor with a syphon; and others slaughtering cattle, and preparing the joints for the cook. Some of the beef is to be boiled, — the joints being put into caldrons over the fire: and an assistant is pounding something in a mortar; and there is a meat-safe, suspended from the ceiling. —The other chambers have boats, furniture, arms, gardens and a fish-pond; fowls, fields and their produce; and so forth. The standards are striking. They bear the hawk, the fox, the ibis, &c. The blade part of the arms is painted blue, which seems to show that they were of steel. —The furniture is so elegant, —the couches, fauteuils, hangings, vases, baskets and lamps, —that it could hardly be surpassed in Greece or Rome at any time, or in Paris and London now. It is very strange to look upon these evidences of in-door luxury, and then to turn to the pictures of savage warfare on the propyla of the palaces. And yet it is only what one knows to be happening even now, within the limits of Christendom. No luxury on earth can exceed that of many houses in New York: and at this moment, while

999

some ladies are passing their days in the midst of it, their husbands are shooting down the Mexicans with a hatred as cordial as any Ramases ever felt for his southern or eastern foes. And if we ourselves have not outgrown warfare, (and it is too soon to declare that we have,) we may present the same humiliating spectacle to the antiquarians of a future age. Our warfare will not be so savage as that of these old heathens; but it will be far more shameful, inasmuch as we call ourselves Christians.

Among the figures in this tomb are two harpers playing before the god Ao, or Hercules. They are clothed in white garments, striped with red: and their harps have each ten strings. Some preceding travelers have declared these harpers to be blind; but there is now too much defacement about the heads to permit this to be seen. The most striking device I observed in this tomb (unless indeed it be the piggish soul returning to earth in charge of the monkeys), was one which related to the death of the occupant of the tomb. The funereal boat is drawn by men who are at a loss about passing the bridge before them. The steep, angular bridge intercepts the rope; but the scarabaeus stoops to help. By its hind legs it hangs to the heaven; while, with its foreclaws it pulls up the rope, allowing the hearse to pass. In this position the scarabaeus signifies the resurrection.

Each of the small apartments having a closed pit, Sir G. Wilkinson supposes[145] that each was the burial-place of that officer of the royal household whose function is illustrated on the walls: —as the cook, the armor-bearer, the gardener, &c. This appears very probable.

In the tomb of the Pharaoh who reigned (it is thought) in right of his wife Taosiri, there is a vaulted chamber in which we could only grope till our dragoman lighted a fire of straw. Its blaze showed us a most striking device, representing the king in his former and present state of being. In the upper hemisphere is the sun, and a living man. Then there is the scarabaeus, head downwards, representing, as before, the resurrection or immortality which connects the two lives of earth and heaven. Beneath is the moon, above the funereal altar, where Isis attends with her protecting wings, and mourners are ranged, —the whole group being inclosed by a half-circle of human-headed birds.

The tomb of Osirei II. is remarkable for being in great part unfinished, though begun with great care and pains. This condition is at once a proof and a consequence of the shortness of his reign. This tomb is remarkably clear and bright looking; but the figures become barer and barer as we proceed, —one sort of lines of illustration after another failing, till we come to blank walls. The sarcophagus chamber is quite rough and rude: but the sculptured figure of the king on the lid of the sarcophagus is fine, —being in relief to the height of nine inches.

145   Modern Egypt and Thebes, II. 209.

The priests took care to preserve their grandeur and rank after death. Their tombs are found where the rock is of the most compact quality, fit to bear extensive excavations, while inferior people must find a where there is more danger of the soil crumbling. We went as far as heat and bats would let us in a priestly tomb which occupies an acre and a quarter of the heart of the rock. The great man who occupied it left other tokens of his wealth; but none could be more striking than this. There is an extraordinary array of niches, pillars and pits: but the covering of almost the whole of the walls with small hieroglyphic writing is the crowning wonder. Will no one go and read this great volume of Egyptian ecclesiastical history?

The tomb of the Pharaoh who pursued the Hebrews to the Red Sea, is extremely interesting. There are five lines of tribute-bearers—black, red, light red, and yellow, —showing how extensive was his dominion. The people of "Pount" bring ivory, apes, leopards, and other tropical wealth. The next bring valuables of an ornamental kind which they declare to be "chosen offerings of the chiefs of the gentiles of Kufa."[146] Next come Ethiopians, "gentiles of the south," with African gifts of beasts, skins and gold. Then come the whites, —red-haired, — dressed in white garments with a blue border, —arms covered (Sir G. Wilkinson saw gloves, but I did not), and bringing, among other offerings, a bear. These must be northern people, surely; —and at the time of the Exodus! Their wives follow with the other women who are collected in the rear; and they are dressed in long gowns which have three flounces. If our upholsterers might study in these tombs, so, it appears, might our dress-makers.

This is the tomb which exhibits to us the Egyptian trades, which it is so interesting to understand. When one looks at the brick-making, one thinks of the Hebrews who were just effecting their escape from that employment. I will abstain from details which may be found fully given elsewhere, mentioning only, as curious, the bellows, the inlaying or joining of wood of different colors with glue, the stone-cutting; and, above all, the carving of the Sphinx, and of two colossal statues, which some suppose to be the Vocal Statue, and the Karnac Colossus. The men are at work on stages, chipping away at the mighty monster, the Sphinx, which here looks as calm and cheerful as afterwards in its own person, among the sands. Such of these tombs as are simple tunnels are airy and lofty. The roof of this one rises towards the inner end, —no one knows why; for the effect is not good in any way. In the sporting tomb we see how the Egyptians excelled in the painting of animals. The animation of action here, and generally where brutes are presented, shows that the stiffness and monotony of their human images were from choice, and not from incapacity for other methods. The animation of their warrior figures indeed shows the same thing.

146   Wilkinson's Modern Egypt and Thebes, II. 235.

We visited, of course, the tombs of the Queens, and explored two, as far as decay and the blackening of the walls would permit. The dominions of these ancient ladies were indicated by masses of red and yellow rock, with large black birds perched upon them. The complexions are somewhat strange and perplexing. The yellow prevails, it being the sign of feminine subjects; but we find pink and blue faces also. The blue is probably appropriated, as elsewhere, to individuals of the priestly caste. Emblematical animals abound here, and a row of apes, not bareheaded, was so astonishingly like a set of Christian judges as to send us into a fit of most profane laughter. These queenly tombs are in a desolate mountain hollow, with rocks towering over head: —a fit place for hiding away the pomps and vanities of the world.

We much enjoyed exploring two recently opened tombs; one discovered about five years ago; the other only a few months before; and by Lepsius. Of the first of these we thought highly, —not only from the good execution of the animals, and the fine effect of a phalanx of men, but because the faces of homage and supplication were admirably given. The colors were very gay, where not spoiled by smoke. The gayest of all was the tomb opened by Lepsius. No picture in this year's exhibition could be brighter. And the stucco was smooth, and the outlines clear as on the day when it was closed. The figures were all women, I believe, in flowing garments of white striped with red. As for the finish of the painting, I observed an ibis which, while duly spirited as a whole, had every feather separately painted, in light gray outlines upon dark gray ground. This was more like a daguerreotype picture than any other work of art I ever saw.

After visiting so many repositories of the dead where every resource had been used to make them secure, and ample and sumptuous, it was strange to pass by spots where the common people of those old days were laid away. It was a doctrine of this ancient nation that all Egyptians were noble: and they applied this so far as to consider every one who was virtuous enough entitled to cross the dark water, and to be laid in the sacred soil of the death region; just as we declare that all men are equal in the presence of God, —that he has no respect of persons, and that in his field, the rich and poor lie down together. But as, with us, the rites of a pauper funeral differ from those of a princely one; as in the United States, the dark-skinned children of God are laid apart from the whites, so here in this metropolis of heathendom, did human weakness come in to mock the profession which human reason had made. Not far from the royal valley of death are pits—hardly to be called catacombs, where undistinguished mummies were laid. One day, our attendants, always on the watch for treasure of one sort or another, saw something which induced them to poke and dig; and next ensued the extraordinary sight of disinterring mummies. These bodies had probably been searched before for valuables; but they had been buried away with some care, and probably for a long time; for it was no easy matter to disengage them from the soil. We partly unrolled two: and even ventured upon removing the bituminous mask which covered the face, which came away, bearing the impression of not uncomely features.

While we were fingering the curly brown hair of one of these mummies, our dragoman cooly wrenched off the head, the throat giving way like a fold of rotten leather. I never remember so strange a sensation as in seeing this; but the thing was done before we could stop it. — People on the spot have no notion of reverence for these remains. Travelers who were at Thebes in 1827 tell us how all the fires wanted by themselves and their attendants were made of the sycamore wood of the mummy-cases. Abdallatif[147] tells us how, in his time (the 12th century) the country people stripped the mummies of whatever was of substance sufficient to make garments; and sold the rags of the mummy cloth to the paper-makers, to make paper for the use of the grocers. He speaks of some of the sycamore wood being then rotten; but some sound, and fit for use. —One extraordinary variety of burial he tells us of, on the word of one on whom he could rely. This friend of his was once searching for treasure with some companions, in the tombs at Geezeh, when they came upon a jar carefully sealed. They opened it, found it contained honey, and began to eat. Presently one of the party perceived a hair sticking to his finger. Drawing it out, he found it belonged to the body of an infant which was preserved in the honey. The body was in good condition, and adorned with jewels and rich ornaments. What care to preserve the earthy frame! and with what a result! The three thousand years of purgatory of many of these Theban sleepers is now about expiring. If their faith was a true one, and they are now returning to resume their bodies, and begin a new cycle, in what a state will they find their sumptuous death-chambers, and their hundred-gated metropolis! Their skulls, stained with bitumen, and indented with the creases of the bandages, are carried away; one to Russia, another to America; one is in a royal palace—another in a Mechanics' Museum: —their coffins are burnt to make an English lady's tea; their cere-cloths are made into paper to wrap up an Arab's tobacco. The spices and unguents were taken from their brains and chests hundreds of years ago, to be melted down, and serve for some other perfuming and embalming. —These things may appear less grave and pathetic at home than on the spot: for mummies are little more respected in Europe than by the ignorant Arabs who pull them up and to pieces, for sale and use. Something is perhaps owing to the name; and something to the dollish oddity of their appearance; but, in its proper place, there is great dignity about a mummy. Reposing in its recess or painted chamber, and bearing the marks of allegiance to Osiris, and of acceptance by him, there is something as solemn in

147   Abdallatif. Relation de l'Egypte, Livre I. Ch. IV.

its aspect as in that of any coffin in an English vault: and this solemnity is not lessened by the thought that in that still breast and sleeping head beat the heart, and wrought the ideas of three thousand years ago. This black pall of oblivion hanging over all gives one, though a mere stranger, something of the mourner feeling which is one of the privileges of the speculative, when bringing speculation to bear on the obliterated past, instead of the unrevealed future.

We had an opportunity of seeing how different is the interment of the present inhabitants of the country from that of the old. Of old, seventy-two days intervened between the death and the burial. Here it was hardly more minutes. A woman in the village near our boat died at one o'clock; and before five, we met the funeral procession. The howl here answers perhaps to the throwing dust on the head, that we see in the sculptures. Both appear painfully barbarous, as all strong outward expressions of grief must ever be. —We learned that, wood being scarce, there was no coffin; but that the woman was buried in new clothes; and that stones would be laid over the grave, so as to secure it perfectly.

On the 23d, we went to Medeenet Haboo, including the great palace temple of Ramases III., and some older buildings, which I will deny myself the pleasure of dwelling on. I must speak presently of Karnac, which is still grander; and I cannot hope that my readers can enter much into the feelings with which Egyptian travelers regard these vast monuments. I find in my journal this remark, which here occurs: — "it is difficult to assign the grounds of the knowledge one gains in these places of the people who lived in them: but it really amounts to much." I must remember that it is difficult to assign the grounds of knowledge, and to convey the impressions received of the living and moving existence of these people, and not carry my readers through too many of those scenes which can be vivified only by the inhabiting spirit of the spot. I will mention only two or three peculiarities of this pile of edifices.

On the wall of the Pavilion of Ramases, we see him among his attendant ladies. He is seated; they are standing. Some are offering flowers; others waving fans; and one is his partner at that game resembling draughts which is painted on older walls than these; —in the caves at Benee Hasan. There is a board with pieces resembling pins or pegs; and the lady's hand is on one which she is about to move.

In another place, we have the coronation; a very grand affair. The king is on his canopied throne or shrine, which is borne by twelve princes, his sons. A great procession follows, of princes, priests, soldiers, and various official personages. A scribe is reading from a scroll; the High-priest burns incense; and the band makes music. — Further on, the king presents offerings to his god; —and the queen looks on from one side. Some of the priestly order bear the statues of the king's ancestors, and a crowd of standards. The hieroglyphic legends tell us that the king has put on the crown of the Upper and Lower countries: and birds are set free, —carrier-pigeons, —to convey the news to the gods of the north, south, east and west. This last was a pretty discovery of Champollion's. Then comes a long invocation, which is written on the wall, above the figure of the reading priest. The king has cut six ears of corn with a sickle; and these are offered to the god by a priest. —They had grand coronations in those days, it is clear.

The war-pictures are very spirited; and, in some respects, very barbarous. There are heaps of severed hands, which the scribes are numbering and noting; each heap being marked 3000. On the outer walls are heaps of tongues, also numbered. We are told that the rows of captives contain one thousand in each line. —We have, on the outer walls, a naval conflict, for the first time, —supposed to have taken place on some Asiatic inland sea, as the enemy appears to be of Asiatic race. The Egyptian galleys are distinguished from those of a foe by a lion's head at the prow. One pretty scene in this foreign country is where the king is attacked by lions, which he kills and puts to flight, —in a marsh. —We have also besieged towns, where the children are lifted in over the ramparts, for safety, and the besiegers fell trees in the neighboring woods. Then we have triumphs, captives, approving gods, &c., as in other places, but with much grandeur. —The predominant impression on one's mind here, as in so many other monumental areas in Egypt, is of the interest to us now of that early stage of the human mind which united with its barbaric aims and pursuits such serene and abstract conceptions of deity, and such a subordination of the present life to the future. Here we have the king and all human beings in intense action, in the Physical Force stage of civilization, while the gods remain the same imperturbable abstractions that we ever find them; and the preparation of the tombs is an object of even more interest to men than the prosecution of their wars. It is curious, and very instructive to see how an age appropriated to the supremacy of Force was no less distinguished by Faith in abstractions.

When Thebes had so far declined as to become a mere collection of villages in the plain, the Christians took possession of Medeenet Haboo, plastering over the sculptures with mud, putting up an altar at the east end of the temple, introducing their little red columns and low roofs among the massy and gorgeous pillars of the heathen courts; and even defacing the architraves to admit their rafters. Their priests took possession of the small apartments of the temple; and their people built mud houses within the precincts. On the approach of the Arabs, the Christians fled to Isna; and here lie their remains, scattered among the outstanding glories of an older time. —I have said how the Christian erections and paintings appeared to us. It may be interesting to know how they appeared to our predecessor in this journey, —the Bagdad physician who saw these places when the crusaders were warring with his faith in Syria. If we remember that he speaks of the Coptic Christians of between six and seven centuries ago, we shall not be apt to take offence, as at an attack on the Christianity of our country and our time. We do not pique ourselves on a fellowship with the Coptic Christians of the 12th century in their country settlements.

Abdallatif says, after extolling the grandeur and beauty of the Egyptian sculptures, "The children of Israel, having been witness of the homage which the Egyptians rendered to these idols, of the profound veneration which they entertained for them, and of the zeal with which they worshiped them, became accustomed, during their long abode among this nation, to see these superstitious ceremonies; and having found in Syria also people delivered over in the same manner to the worship of idols, required of Moses that he should give them such gods as these people had: which drew forth from Moses this reproach, You are a foolish nation. The greater number of Christians, being either Egyptians or Sabeans, have retained the propensities belonging to their origin, and have suffered themselves to slide easily into the ancient habits of their forefathers: —in consequence, they have admitted images into their churches, and into the temples appropriated to the exercise of their worship. They have even pushed matters to an extreme: they have in many ways improved upon the existing abuses of this custom, and have carried their folly so far as to pretend to represent the god whom they adore surrounded by angels. All this was merely a remnant of the customs of their ancestors which had been preserved among them: with this difference, however: that their ancestors, far from representing the deity under any form, had too exalted an idea of him to imagine that He could be apprehended by the sense, or comprehended by the understanding. That which has drawn the Christians into these excesses, and which has emboldened them to adopt such a custom, is the dogma which they profess of the divinity of a creature. —All this," the sober Mohammedan goes on to say, "we have discussed with care in the treatise which we have composed against the Christians."[148] —No enlightened person, of any faith, could help sympathizing with Abdallatif while in sight of the profane daubs which the Christians have left among the sculptures, and which seem put there to give every advantage to the old heathens. They have something of the effect of the ritual of the Greek church, which makes our most religious countrymen feel, in Asia Minor, that they had rather, in case of need, turn Mohammedan than enter it.

Near Medeenet Haboo is an expanse of sunk soil, with alluvial deposits round its edges, which Sir G. Wilkinson believes to have contained the Lake of the Dead, over which the body must be ferried to its tomb.[149]

148   Abdallatif. Relation de l'Egypte, Livre I. Ch. IV.
149   Wilkinson's Modern Egypt and Thebes, II. 187.

Passing over the other edifices on the western bank, I will mention only that on the last day of our abode on this side, we visited the very old temple called Dayr el Bahree, or "the Northern Convent;" so called from its having been appropriated by the Christians for a church and monastery. It is gloriously situated; in the great central perpendicular rock; —excavated in the mountain itself; and once approached by an ascending dromos of great length, and between rows of sphinxes, with pylons and obelisks at intervals, and a succession of terraces at last. This temple is quite unlike any other; and few are more impressive. The crude brick arches of ancient date which are found in many places prove that the Egyptians were acquainted with the principle of the arch; yet here the vaulted chambers showed roofs composed of courses of stone, laid on fiat, and hollowed into an arch afterwards. Some bits of walls and curious corners had been recently laid open to view, —their paintings as vivid as ever. On one wall from which the sand had been shoveled away, we found a splendid lotus plant, on which was a nest of water birds, bending the budded stem which supported it. A rabbit had attacked the young birds: a dog was attacking the rabbit, and an ibis the dog. On another part of the plant were a lizard and two yellow butterflies: and two human hands were plucking blossoms.

This was, as I said, our last day on the western shore. Our guides knew this; and I fancied that my open-faced and obliging donkey-boy felt sorry to part; as I truly did. There could be no exchange of sentiment, however; for the only language we had in common consisted of two words, which we found enough to signify our pleasure by, and that was all. "Bono" and "non bono" was our whole discourse. But my guide's face and close service on this last day seemed to say more. He understood my wish to go once more to the Ramaseum, and look about me when there; —to go once more to the Colossi, and ride round them once and again. He put my donkey to its best canter, that I might accomplish all this. I turned a grateful face upon him, and said "Bono:" and his answer was, with a wise nod, and holding out his hand, "La, la, —bono baksheesh!" He little knew how he had spoiled everything by that one word, —what I might have given him, in cash and character, but for that act of begging at such a moment.

We crossed to the El-Uksur side in the dusk of the evening, and looked forward to spending the next two days in the most magnificent spot in Egypt— among the ruins of El-Karnac.

The 25th was cloudy; —our first cloudy day in Africa. I was surprised to see how the whole landscape, and especially the ruins, suffered by the absence of light, shadow and vivid tint. It was very well to become aware of this; but one would rather it had happened elsewhere. We had planned to ride over in the evening, to see El-Karnac by moonlight; but in the evening, the whole sky was gray. We had not, all this day, one single gleam from sun or moon. We had made such a survey of the ruins, however, as prepared us for a thorough exploring the next day.

On the 26th, the sky was still dull when I looked out; but as I was taking my early walk on the shore, some lustrous gleams touched upon the points of the western mountains, and at length illumined the whole shore, and stole over the river towards us. Before breakfast, we visited first a stuffed crocodile which was offered for sale. It was a hideous creature; but I was glad to have an opportunity for a safe study of it. Then we went down to our old kandjia of the cataracts, which had just arrived with a cargo of slaves for Ibraheem Pasha's hareem. The girls looked as earnest and content as they always do while making cakes, Nubian fashion: but the officer who had charge of them and the boys carried a little whip.

After breakfast, we rode away to El-Karnac, the sun coming out, but the wind rising so as to cover us with dust, and render the examination of the external sculptures less easy than we could have wished. The road from El-Uksur to El-Karnac once lay, as everybody knows, between sphinxes, standing six feet apart, for a mile and a half. Those which remain, headless, encumbered, and extending only a quarter of a mile, are still very imposing. Then come pylons, propyla, halls, obelisks, temples, groves of columns, and masses of ruins, oppressive to see, and much more to remember. I think I must say nothing about them. They must be sacred to the eyes that see them; I mean, incapable to be communicated to any others. Those that have not seen El-Karnac know nearly as much as can be told when they remember that here are the largest buildings, and the most extensive ruins in the known world: and that the great hall is 329 feet by 170, and 85 feet high, containing 134 columns, the 12 central ones of which are 12 feet in diameter, and the others not much smaller; the whole of this forest of columns being gay with colors, and studded with sculptures. Of this hall the central roof is gone, and part of the lateral covering. The columns are falling, and at an accelerated rate. There is saltpetre in the stone; and the occasional damps from the ground cause the corrosion of these mighty masses near the bases. They fall, one by one; and these leaning wrecks, propped up by some accident which, must give way, have a very mournful aspect. We cannot but look forward to the successive fall of these incomparable pillars, as to that of the trees of a forest undermined by springs. These will sink under a waste of sand, as those into the swamp, to be perhaps found again after thousands of years, and traced out curiously, —a fossil forest of the mind.

Nothing was more striking to us than the evidences of the earthquake, to which, and not only to Cambyses and Ptolemy Lathyrus, we attribute the overthrow of gigantic columns in the area, colossal statues, and mountainous masses

of the propyla. If, perplexed by the magnitude of Egyptian achievement altogether, we give up the point whether means existed for the overthrow of such
masses, there still remains the question how huge columns could fall straight, so
as to be shattered in regular order, by any means but such a shaking of the earth
as art cannot be conceived to produce.

One curious incident I must mention. A stone has fallen out, in more
than one place, from the wall of the old Pharaonic propyla; and looking in
at the holes, I saw sculptured and painted blocks, built into the interior; —
remnants of a still earlier time, used as material. These propyla were standing
before Moses was born. The great hall was built by Osirei, the occupant of the
magnificent tomb I have described. But the original buildings of El-Karnac are
of a date beyond our ken. The earliest portions now remaining are a hundred
years older than any other edifices in Thebes. —I have before mentioned that
the only known allusion to the Jews in the monuments of Egypt is on the walls
of El-Karnac. The conqueror Sheshonk (Shishak) holds by the hair a group of
captives, whose race is determined, not only by the face, but by the cities of
Judah being named among the array of tributaries.

The finest view I obtained of the El-Karnac ruins was from a mound just
above the lake. To the left lay the blue lake, —a sheet of still water, fed by the
Nile through the soil, but too salt now for use. Remains of quays and baths
made this look as ancient and forlorn as any other part. To the right lay the
somewhat dreary plain which extends between the ruins and the river. Before
me, filling a circuit of a mile and a half, lay the ruins; obelisks peeping over
roofless temples; statues seen through rows of columns; pylons standing firm
like out posts, while within there is now nothing but wreck to guard: and all
around, wherever we could look or set foot, were mute mourners over the des-
olations of time, —shattered inscriptions, defaced pictures, useless blocks, and
unintelligible fragments.

The finest view I obtained from the ruins was from the top of the mound
heaped up against the face of the propyla which front the river. Here I could
command the plain of tufty coarse grass, strewn with stone, and varied with
palm-clumps: and the remains of the avenue of smaller sphinxes, which used
to extend to the landing-place on this side; then the platform above the quay:
then the river; and beyond it the western plain, with its precipitous mountain
boundary, now drest in rainbow hues. The temple at El-Kurneh was hidden by a
palm- clump: but the Ramaseum, with its wrecked propyla, stood out distinct:
and the recess of the Dayr el Bahree was traceable; and the group at Medeenet Haboo; and, best of all, the Pair were sitting in the bright sunlight, above,
because far beyond, the dark screen of palm groves which hid the modern village. This was my last view of them; and in my parting yearning, I thought it

the best. How inexplicable is the distinctness with which some images impress themselves upon the memorial faculty! I did not see them more distinctly in that African sunshine than I see them now.

The finest impression, or the most memorable, which we obtained of El-Karnac was derived from our moonlight visit, that last evening. There is no questioning of any style of art, if only massive, when its results are seen by moonlight. Then, spaces and distances become what the mind desiderates; and drawbacks are lost in shade. Here, the mournful piles of fragments were turned into masses of shade; and the barbaric coloring disappeared. Some capricious, but exquisite lights were let in through crevices in the roof and walls of the side chambers. Then, there were the falling columns and their shadows in the great hall, and the long vistas ending in ruins; and the profound silence in this shadowy place, striking upon the heart. In the depth of this stillness, when no one moved or spoke, the shadow of an eagle on the wing above fell upon the moonlit aisle, and skimmed its whole length.

It was with heavy hearts, and little inclination to speak that we turned, on our way home, to take a last view of the pylons of Karnac. The moonlit plain lay, with the river in its midst, within the girdle of mountains. Here was enthroned the human intellect when humanity was elsewhere scarcely emerging from chaos. And how was it now? That morning, I had seen the Governor of Thebes, crouching on his haunches on the filthy shore among the dung heaps, feeding himself with his fingers, among a circle of apish creatures like himself.

The next morning, I was glad we were off. I had had as much as, without more knowledge, I could well bear: and it was a delightful holiday to be sitting on deck, reading, and looking at shadoofs and mountains, and wheat and lupins, as we did a month ago.

CHAPTER XVII

MANUFACTURES AT KENNEH—MANNERS OF THE CREW— EXCURSION TO ABYDUS

WE ESCAPED THE DREADED DINING with the old consul at Kenneh. He invited us, when the gentlemen called for their letters; but they pleaded business. The old gentleman then begged our empty bottles of our dragoman, and was made quite happy by them. The cotton manufactory at Kenneh appeared to the gentlemen better than that at Isna, which certainly struck me as the poorest attempt at a manufacture I had ever seen. The machinery there was English, but kept in bad order. It was worked by horse power; and the horses were in poor plight. The thread produced was uneven, and the woven fabric therefore of indifferent quality, from so much of the machinery being worked by hand. One might say that this was as much as could be expected from a factory on the other side of Thebes: but then, what beautiful fabrics the old Thebans wore! and of their own manufacture. And what luxuries they brought into their homes, by exporting their woolen and cotton goods! —At this Kenneh factory, five hundred people were employed, at wages varying, according to their qualifications, from 100 piastres (1l.) per month, with food, to 50 and 30 piastres. The machinery here was superior to that at Isna; the thread more even; and the woven fabric therefore better.

I have before mentioned the Kenneh pottery, and the wide demand for it. As much as possible is still done by hand. There is no mould for the inside. The jar is formed on the ancient potter's wheel; and a piece of copper is used to give the external form, and to mark the outside with the curious scratches which adorn the Kenneh jars. Of course, it is a rare thing to see a jar which stands quite straight, or is not out of shape, one way or another. A man can make one hundred per day of the porous water bottles in common use.

There is a question among students of Egyptian history about some military passes; and a consequent desire to know from those who have been up the Nile, where the mountains approach the river so closely as to make it difficult for armies to pass. Of course, everything must depend upon the season. But, at the season of our voyage, I should say there was no part of the shore where an army could not pass on the one side of the river or the other: and it cannot be conceived that any army, native or invading, could be in the valley without means of crossing the river, which with the inhabitants has always been such a matter of course as it is not seen to be anywhere else. At the high rock of Chenoboscion, and for some way on each side of it, there is only room for a narrow belt of tilled land, at low Nile; but on the opposite shore is a plain of considerable width. Generally speaking, (I might almost say universally,) when the hills approach on one side, they recede on the other; and it is obvious that this must have been the case through all the changes the Nile has certainly made in its course.

We were now about to bid farewell to the doum palm, —a tree which I liked in its place, —its stiffness and angularity rendering it curiously appropriate to the scenery in which it is found. A grove of it between us and the Dendara temple this day looked as well as any tall elms about a cathedral.

The crocodiles abounded now when we were soon to see no more. Some remained asleep on the banks even after the sun had gone down. Near Hou, Mr. E. saw nineteen at one time on the mud banks.

We witnessed more of the doings of the crew now that we were not absent on our temple-haunting all day long. The Buck did not improve in sobriety as time went on; and one morning about this date, he was insufferably noisy, in his elation at being dressed in a grand suit of new clothes; —brown burnoose, yellow slippers and a vast turban, white as muslin can be. On Mrs. Y. complaining of the noise, after the Rais and dragoman had used every kind of remonstrance, Alee quietly went up to him, as he stood in his grandeur by the gun wale, lifted him by the waist, and popped him overboard. We really feared that the weight of his clothes would have sunk him; but Alee knew better. In two minutes I saw him standing by the gunwale again, high and dry, but in his ordinary blue shirt and white skullcap. —One of our quiet Nubians, twenty-five years of age, had already two wives; and by what we heard of his life at home, he might well be content on board the boat. As Alee observed, a rich man may put his wives into different apartments; but the poor man cannot: and the women quarrel fiercely and incessantly. This Nubian had to carry presents for his two wives after every voyage; and if they were not precisely alike, there was no end to the wrangling. —Alee called this permission to have more than one wife a very bad part of his religion. He was not yet married at all; and he did not intend to marry till he

should have obtained money enough by his present employment to enable him
to settle down in a home of his own. One of my friends one day expressed a
hope that he would be careful in the choice of a wife; —so careful in assuring
himself of her temper and goodness as not to be tempted to put her away, as
husbands in Egypt do so lightly and cruelly. Alee did not quite promise this;
but he gave an account of what plan he should pursue, which shows how these
matters are regarded by sensible young men in Egypt. He said he should buy
a white wife, when he wanted to settle. He should tell her what he expected of
her; —viz., to be good-tempered; to make him comfortable; and to take care
of his "boys." If she failed, he should, the first time, tell her his mind "very
strongly." And then, if she got out of temper, or was negligent a second time,
he should "just put her away." This was said with the gesture of Othello at the
words "whistle her down the wind."

The wag Ibraheem was seen to be very sulky to-day, after having passionately thrown some bread overboard, and spat out after it what was in his mouth.
This was because the Rais rebuked him for his shabbiness in eating with the
poor Nubians (the Cairenes having all by this time quarreled) while laying by
his own money for his wife, —he having neither parents nor children to maintain. The way in which this was told to us showed that the maintaining of parents was regarded quite as a matter of course. It is to be feared that the parents'
need of it is too much a matter of course, in the present state of that order of
society in Egypt.

Of the temple of Dendara I will say nothing. The oldest names it bears are
those of Cleopatra and her son Cæsarion; and it has not therefore the interest
of antiquity; while its beauty is of the same kind as that of the Isna temple. At
Dendara, as at Isna, the Pasha has caused the building to be cleared out; for
which the world is obliged to him: and it would have been more so, if he had
not run a mud-brick wall directly up against the middle of the front; so that
no complete view of the portico can be had from any point. However, we must
thankfully accept any conservative aid we can obtain, and hope to remove, in
course of time, any blemishes as manageable as mud-brick walls.

On Saturday, January 23d, we made an excursion of some importance:
—to Abydus, which stood near, if not, as some scholars think, on the spot
where This was built—This, the old capital of Upper Egypt, where sixteen kings
reigned before Thebes was heard of. It will be observed that as we are coming
down the river, we are ascending the stream of Time. Thebes, built chiefly by
monarchs of the Third Period, appeared very ancient when we were there. We
are now (supposing Abydus to be the site of This), carried back to the First
Period. The only other ancient monuments now remaining for us to see were
the Caves at Benee Hasan, whose dates are of the latter part of the First Period;

and the Pyramids, and the cluster of remains about them; which are the very oldest of all, bearing date from the early part of the First Period. If we this day stood on the site of This, we were standing on the buried metropolis of powerful monarchs, who flourished here within a few centuries of the building of the Pyramids; —somewhere between four and five thousand years ago.

We left our boat at Beliane, and were to rejoin it in the evening at Girgeh, a few miles down the river. We rode for above two hours through a rich plain which bore crops of wheat, barley, lupins, vetches, lentils, a little flax, beans and sugar-cane. The barley was turning, in some places, and the beans were in blossom, and some beginning to pod. They grow tall, but are less strong in the stalk than with us. I had a good opportunity to-day of observing the supplies of water in the interior of the country. More than one curious point depends on whether the whole supply of water is derived from the river, or whether there are any springs whatever near the mountains. I should not have doubted the supply being wholly derived from the river, but from the decided declaration of one resident who certainly ought, from his function, to understand the matter. But his declaration that the interior of the country is watered partly by springs, was contradicted by so many —one of these being Linant Bey—as to convince me that it was mistaken. The ponds I saw—this day in considerable number, seven miles from the river—are filled by filtration from the Nile. Linant Bey says that the water of the Nile filters through to any distance where water is found in the valley. From another authority I learned that it penetrates to the Oasis. The ponds I saw to-day were of various depths, shapes and sizes. Some few had clear water in them—the shallower had a mere daub of mud at the bottom, while the sides were green with young wheat—and the deepest were half filled with a green puddle. A large number of men were employed in cleaning out the canal, and some of our party saw others employed upon a new one. The first thought of many, in reading about this filtration of Nile water, will be of the passage in Herodotus about the actual burial place of the king in the Great Pyramid. Speaking of the Second Pyramid, Herodotus says, (Footnote: Herod. II. 127.) "It does not approach the magnitude of that of Cheops (I have measured them both); it has neither subterranean structures nor canal to convey the waters of the Nile; whereas the other, where it is said the tomb of Cheops is placed, is in an island, and is surrounded by the waters of the Nile, which are conducted there by a canal constructed for the purpose." This version, which I translate from Larcher, intimates that the pyramid itself stood in an island, and was surrounded by a canal. But another version of the passage gives a different impression. Sir G. Wilkinson offers the passage thus: "It has neither underground chambers nor any canal flowing into it from the Nile, like the other, where the tomb of its founder is placed in an island surrounded by water." In another passage, Herodotus tells us

(II. 124) that Cheops made "the subterranean structures to serve him for a tomb, in an island formed by the waters of the Nile, which he introduced into it by a canal." There are some who, finding more and more "subterranean structures" the lower they go in the Great Pyramid, and of a very different kind of building from mere foundation—that is, passages leading down and down again, so as to indicate some object lying deeper still, cannot but wonder whether there may not be a royal tomb at the bottom, with a moat of Nile water around it. What a discovery it would be! It must be observed, however, as Larcher points out, that Herodotus does not declare the king to be actually in the pyramid, but only his destined tomb; while Diodorus relates that the kings who built these pyramids were so odious to their subjects that neither of them was actually buried there. The people threatened to snatch the corpses from their graves, and tear them to pieces; so that the monarchs desired their families to inter them secretly in some unknown place.[150] We should like to know, some day, whether the penetrating Nile has been searching out, for all these thousands of years, the secrets of that great prison-house which has permitted access to no other visitor.

One of the most curious sights occurring in the course of an Egyptian country ride, like this of ours to-day, is of the little victories of the Nile over the Desert, in the outskirts of their battle-field. It is worth riding ten miles inland, if it were for nothing else, to see what the soil is where the fertile and barren tracts meet. In the cucumber and melon patches, I saw holes dug which showed a layer of from two to five inches of rich black soil deposited upon the most hopeless yellow sand. We all know that it is so. We all know how the Nile deposits its mud; but it is best witnessed by seeing the crust thus sharply cut through, and perceiving how it lies unmixed upon the sand.

We passed villages, farms, and single dwellings to-day, with their dogs, geese, cattle, and children. The camels removed it further from likeness to country scenes elsewhere than any other feature. We passed the village of Arábat el Matfoon (which means "the buried"), and came out upon the site and ruins of Abydus—a mighty place on its own account, whether it succeeded This or not. The position, for a capital city, is very fine. I doubt whether the situation of Thebes itself is finer, except that there the Nile is nearer, and in full view; whereas, here it is merely traced by its evidences, unless the canals are full. From the south-east to the north-west is an amphitheatre of rocks, guarding the plain from the sands of the Lybian Desert. In the middle of this barrier, due west from the temples, is an opening of great interest. It is the road to the Great Oasis. How many caravans and military processions have moved and glittered along that road from the city, disappearing in that defile of the hills! From those precipitous rocks now descend sandy slopes, as far as the mounds

150   Larcher's note to Herodotus, II. 127.

which lie between the hills and the fertile plain. The temple and palace—now the only coherent remains, are so far elevated as to afford a noble view of the wide area which they ruled. They rose above the city which now no doubt lies buried under these hillocky sands. A very distant range of heights, faint and soft in color, incloses the rest of the land scape; and from them to the temples spreads the rich plain, all variegated with groves and belts of palm and acacia, among which the villages are hid. The airy space and brightness of this scene are not to be conveyed by description.

The remaining temple and palace are mainly the work of Ramases the Great and his father Osirei. The temple is dedicated to Osiris, to whom indeed the whole area is sacred; for this is one of the places where he was believed to have been buried; and where the opulent families of the region all therefore desire to be buried too. This peculiarity, and that of the road to the Great Oasis beginning here, sufficiently account for the grandeur of Abydus, after it had parted with its primitive distinction of being, as This, the capital of Upper Egypt. Meeting Ramases and his father here, we think differently of them from what we do at Thebes. Here, they are comparatively moderns, though living while the Hebrews were driving out the inhabitants of the Holy Land. Ramases and his father were as much younger than the monarchs on whose foundations they built as we are younger than Josephus and the conquering Titus who laid low the temple of Solomon. This temple contained the celebrated tablet, —the tablet of Abydus—on which was cut, by order of Ramases the Great, a list of names of the kings his predecessors. This tablet is now in the British Museum. As far as it goes, it most satisfactorily accords with the memorials on the temples and palaces, and with the names given on the walls of the Ramaseum at Thebes. But the beginning of the list is unhappily broken away; and we thus lose the light we most wanted for the illustration of the earlier periods of Egyptian history.

Ramases lined one chamber of this temple throughout with alabaster. The only part of this building which could be entered when we were there was the hall; and even there we could only creep about among the capitals of the pillars. We could not even count them. I made out that there were two in the width; but I could not penetrate further than the seventh in length; which made fourteen. An Arab, whom we sent in to count the rest, said there were twenty-six in all. If Ramases could have looked forward to the time when his temple would be explored in this way, how he would have mourned for his religion and for mankind! The capitals of these pillars are so large, and the architraves so deep, that the hall, if cleared out, must be very lofty. I saw the cornices of two portals; but there is no saying what lies behind them. Air and light are let in by holes in the roof.

The palace at hand is remarkable for its roof, which is of sandstone, while the walls are of limestone. The blocks which, laid together by their broadest face, form a roof of prodigious weight and solidity, are hollowed out into a vaulted form: —a laborious and primitive method of vaulting for people who certainly understood the principle of the arch. The sculptures on the walls are still clear; and there are strong traces of color. One superb boat caught my attention. The king, and the ape of Thoth, and some other small figures were in it; and one extremity was ornamented with the ram's horns, while the other had two towers, crowned with the moon.

We walked on, about a quarter of a mile, over mounds of broken pottery and sand, to see such forlorn remains of these two great cities as lie above ground, to grieve and tantalize the eye. A limestone gateway, gayly painted, is partly disinterred; and also the corner portion of some place once lined with alabaster, blocks and fragments of which are lying about. There is a good deal of red granite, —some sculpture, and two blocks which appear to be the flanks of a pylon. There were some black stelæ and blocks; and plenty of crude brick. This was all; but I would not, for much, have missed it. Such places are full of interest in any state; for their monuments, if their monuments remain; for their desolation, and the harvest of thoughts yielded by that barren ness, if the sand has spread itself over all.

We rode away from the begging Arabs of Arábat, and found a charming spot whereon to take our rest and luncheon. We passed that rare object, —a round, natural-looking pond of blue water, in a basin of the desert, with palms scattered about it: and then we came to a grove where the palms sprang up, straight and lofty, from an expanse of grass of the vivid green of our April turf. There remained the ride to Girgeh, which occupied three hours and a half. It was all through the same rich plain which we had overlooked from the mounds of Abydus; and the fertility never failed, all the way, except where patches of the coarse grass called halfeh lay here and there between the fields. Girgeh looked fine as we approached it, with its tall minarets, its thick grove behind, and the range of mountains on the other side of the blue line of river. The rocks were red in the sunset, and the ghostly moon was stealing up behind them as we reached the shore. When the afterglow had died away, and the moon had assumed her glory, it was pleasant to sit watching the currents of the river in the trail of golden light she cast.

CHAPTER XVIII

BENEE HASAN—MASGOON—PYRAMIDS OF DASHOOR AND SAKKÁRA—MEMPHIS—MUMMY PITS—CONSECRATION OF BRUTES

I T IS SAFE AND EASY NOW TO VISIT THE CAVES of Benee Hasan; but it was dangerous or impossible a quarter of a century ago. The village now lies apparently roofless and ruined; but it is still inhabited to a certain extent, and by people of good character. It was formerly a pirate village. When no boat on the river was safe from pillage in passing Benee Hasan, and murders became frequent, Ibraheem Pasha took the matter in hand. He brought his troops round the hills, surprised the place in the night, and shot almost every individual in it— man, woman, and child.

The village is seen from a ravine a little above the caves. From this point, the further view is of the rich valley and its winding river; but the near view is wild enough. Down this ravine trotted a very large fox, which, from its size, looked at first like a jackal. Some of the lower strata of the rocks are worn away, leaving the upper parts overhanging. Strange boulders are perched at intervals along the brink of the ravine, some being cut sheer through, like felled trees; and those which were entire exactly resembling (and they were all alike) large petrified sheep without their heads. Similar boulders stood at intervals on either side the great road, easily traceable from the front of the caves, which led up the steep, from the boats to the tombs.

Up this road came the funeral processions, to the caves which are opened in the strata of the rock. We must remember how very long ago this was. We must remember that Josephus, in his national vanity, desired to make out that the Hebrews were descended from the Shepherd Race of invaders, and falsified history for the purpose; and then, we must remember that some of these tombs were sealed up before the Shepherd Kings entered Egypt. As that hated host swept conquering by, and perhaps looked up at these rocks as they passed, some of these tombs were occupied and closed —their walls being covered with the paintings which were before our eyes this day. The tombs I speak of bear date from the latter part of the First Period. They are the oldest known monuments in the country, except the Pyramids.

It is in one of these caves, however, that some people have fancied they have found a procession of Joseph's brethren. It may be natural for those who go from a Christian country, with little other antecedent interest in Egypt than its being the abode of Joseph and his descendants, to look for Hebrew personages on the monuments. But I think such travelers should take some little pains to reflect and observe before they say that they have found them. A very little observation would show that the Egyptians never put on their monuments anything that they were ashamed of. There are no traces of the Shepherd Race. There are certainly none of the Hebrews as a nation—except where the cities of Judah and the captives of Jerusalem come in among the pictures of Sheshonk's conquests. There was no reason for celebrating them while they were neither enemies nor captives, but only the lowest working class in the country. Still less reason was there for representing the brethren of Joseph, who came as individuals or a family, and not as representatives of any nation, or even tribe. It is thus improbable beforehand that the Hebrews should appear on any early monuments.

In the next place, the procession here conjectured to have been one of Hebrew offerers, can be shown, I think, to be a very different set of people indeed. I will presently explain why. But, further, if the discoveries of Lepeius and the conclusions of Bunsen are right, in relation to the dates of the Three great Periods of Egyptian history (and it would take much power and learning to overthrow them), this particular tomb was painted a thousand years before Joseph was born. This tomb bears date in the reign of Osirtasen, who is now believed, on new evidence produced by Dr. Lepsius, to be the Sesortasen of the twelfth dynasty of the Monuments; the Sesonchosis of the same dynasty of Manetho. According to the same evidence, the Shepherd Kings came in in the middle of the thirteenth dynasty, remained 926 years, and were then driven out by the great Pharaohs of the eighteenth dynasty; under one of whom Moses led away the Hebrews. The Septuagint declares their residence in Egypt to have lasted 215 years; the Hebrew Chronology gives 430 years. Whichever be preferred, it is clear that this tomb must have been shut up many hundred years before Joseph was born.

This tomb, —the twenty-ninth from the South, and second from the North, —has a vaulted portico, with two fluted pillars; —beautiful Doric pillars they would have been called, if erected many centuries later. Throughout its chambers, its basement is painted a deep red; and on this basement, and the architraves and everywhere, the hieroglyphics are green; the effect of which is extremely good. —The interior chamber contains the pedestal of a statue. Two longitudinal architraves divide the ceiling of this outer chamber into three portions, which are vaulted, and richly starred. There are three pits in this chamber; and there were four pillars; but they are gone.

It is in this painted chamber that the procession occurs which many have supposed, and all have striven to suppose, might be the arrival of Joseph's brethren. At each end of the row stands a great man. (There is no sitting figure, as some have reported.) The hieroglyphics show that neither of these great men can be Pharaoh or Joseph. The principal figure is named Nefothph; and his parents' names are also given. He is presented as governor of this district, on the east side of the Nile. He is no doubt the owner of the tomb. —The number of persons presented to the king by Joseph was five; and the number who had arrived were seventy: but here we have written up over the heads of the strangers the word "captives," and the number "thirty-seven." The complexions are of the yellow, by which the Egyptians designated the whites; the tint of the men's faces being only a little deeper than that of the women. The men wear beards, tunics, and sandals: the women have their hair long, and bound round the temples. They wear tunics; —one at least with a very handsome Greek border, as we should call it if Greece had existed then; and they are all shod in ankle-boots. Two children's heads emerge from ornamented panniers slung on an ass. The offerings brought are not like what the sons of Jacob would have to give. After a wild goat and gazelle, comes a handsome present of ostriches; —quite a flock of them; and the procession closes with a red man who carries an ibis. Now, it is curious that no account that I have met with of this celebrated procession has mentioned the ostriches; which are precisely the gift of the whole set which Joseph's brethren could not have brought. And there is no pretence that we could see for stopping short at the ostriches, which join on to the rest of the procession without any interval, and, with the man carrying the ibis, finish the subject.

What shall we say to this omission? And what shall we say to a traveler (Mrs. Romer), who coolly reports, without any apparent shame, that she has brought away from Benee Hasan the head and shoulders of a figure which she does not doubt to be that of a Jewish captive; — her dragoman having cleverly detached from the wall this interesting specimen of antiquity! Where are our hopes for the monuments of Egypt, if passing travelers are to allow their servants, (who know no better,) to commit thefts for them in such a way as this? Who will undertake to say what may be the value of any one head and shoulders in a group which may be made unintelligible by its absence! It is mournful enough to see what scientific antiquarians do; —how one saws through the middle of a tablet of inscriptions; and another knocks down one pillar of a series; and another carries away a group, —symbolical and necessary in its own place: but there really seems no hope left if desultory travelers are to pick and steal at their fancy from a repository where everything has its place, and is in its place.

I visited the whole thirty of these tombs; and found twenty-one which may be called commonplace; by which I mean that they contained the ordinary pits for the reception of bodies, a few niches, a few mock door-ways, —which are frequently a form of tablet for inscriptions; — some with remains or traces of pillars; some with small inner chambers; many with slightly vaulted roofs, and usually an architrave to divide the vaulted from the plain part of the ceiling. Where the pillars are gone, the circular bases which are left are so smooth as to perplex one's thought as to what has been done to them: —as smooth as if some dexterous dragoman had sawn through the precious shaft, to indulge his employer with a new toy. The pillars which remain are often very beautiful. In the southern caves, they consist of the stems of four water plants, springing from a large, solid, circular base, and bound together below the capital, which is formed of four lobes of lotus buds. —The polygonal pillars which I have mentioned as being truly Doric have simply a lowly abacus between the shaft and the architrave.

The tombs throughout are not sculptured, except the hieroglyphic inscriptions, but painted on plaster. In many places the plaster seems to have been purposely broken or scraped away, —so hard is the material, and so vivid the painting, in the corners that are left. This ruin was probably wrought by the Christians, who have elsewhere cut their crosses deep into the very figures on the walls. —Considering the early times, the colors here are various. I found a bright scarlet, —I think for the first time. The women are yellow skinned throughout. There are multitudes of pairs of wrestlers in what are called the military pictures; and these pairs are of a darker and lighter red, so as to show distinctly the intertwining of the lithe limbs. The birds, which are very various, rejoice throughout in a prodigiously gay plumage. I will not indulge myself, and weary my readers, with going over the nine tombs which we found remarkable and full of interest. I will only just ask those who read to bear in mind the antiquity of these paintings, while I mention a few particulars of them.

We have here the art of writing as a familiar practice, in the scribes who are numbering the stores on every hand. There are ships which would look handsome in Southampton Water, any sunny day. There are glass-blowers who might be from Newcastle, but for their dress and complexion. There are flax-dressers, spinners, weavers, —and a production of cloth which an English manufacturer would study with interest. There are potters, painters, carpenters and statuaries. There is a doctor attending a patient; and a herdsman physicking cattle. The hunters employ arrows, spears and the lasso. The lasso is as evident as on the

Pampas at this day. —There is the Nile full of fish, and a hippopotamus among the ooze. There is the bastinado for the men; and the flogging of a seated woman. Nothing is more extraordinary than the gymnastics and other games of the women. Their various games of ball are excellent. —The great men are attended by dwarfs and buffoons, as in a much later age; and it is clear that bodily infirmity was treated with contempt; —deformed and decrepit personages appearing in the discharge of the meanest offices. —It was an age when this might be looked for; and when war would be the most prominent occupation, and wrestling the prevailing sport; and probably also the discipline of the soldiery: and when hunting, fishing and fowling would be very important pursuits. But then, —what a power of representation of these things is here! and what luxury co-existing with those early pursuits! Here are harpers with their harps of seven strings; and garments and boat-sails with elegant patterns and borders, where, by the way, angular and regular figures are pointedly preferred; —and the ladies' hair, disordered and flying about in their sports, has tails and tassels, very like what may have been seen in London drawing-rooms in no very remote times. The incident which most reminds one of the antiquity of these paintings is that the name of bird, beast, fish or artificer is written up over the object delineated. It is the resource, —not needed here, however, of the artist who wrote on his picture "this is the man,"— "this is the monkey." Another barbarism is the same that I have mentioned elsewhere; —that the great man, the occupant of the tomb, has his greatness signified by bigness, being a giant among middle-sized people.

We spent four hours in the diligent study of these tombs; and I ran over the note-worthy nine once more, to keep them all distinct in my memory. The wind was so high that we could not leave the bank till after sunset; so we had excellent leisure for noting down on the spot what we had seen.

Our letters had lately told us of snow eighteen feet deep in Yorkshire; and at this date (4th February) I find in my journal that our days were "like August days on Windermere." The thermometer stood at 74° in the shaded cabin in the middle of the day. It had been down to 40°, one cold morning, up the river: but I had never felt any degree of cold that was really uncomfortable; and rarely any heat that could be seriously complained of. The flies were troublesome for some hours in the middle of the day, so as to compel us to sit on deck instead of in the cabin; but they let us alone in the mornings and evenings, which were the only times when I, for one, cared to be in the cabin.

While we stopped at a village for milk, one afternoon, a man came down to us for medical advice. I used to think it one of the prettiest sights we saw when, on such occasions, Mr. E. examined the case with as much care as he would have given to a brother's, and Mr. Y. administered whatever aid could be given. Such offices cannot but abate Mohammedan prejudices against the

Christians; and I trust all who go up the Nile endeavor to do their part, with prudence and earnest kindness. Without much quacking, —without danger of doing real harm, — some little relief may be given by simple medicines, and yet more perhaps by sending away the patient with hope in his heart. Any advice or medicine which he may obtain from English travelers is likely to be safer and better than what he will have at home; and at any rate, he may be granted the cordial of sympathy and good-will.

The wind to-night was high; and it so jostled us against the bank as to destroy sleep. In the morning we passed another foundered vessel, whose masts just showed themselves above the water. The river was now less interesting to us than at any previous time. The crocodiles were absent; and the birds were scarcely more numerous than at home. The water had sunk so much, and the hills had so retreated, that the shores looked very flat. Yet we felt rather heavy at heart when we recognized objects, —as the False Pyramid to-day, — which told us that we were drawing near to Cairo. So far from being "bored to death with the Nile," as we had been often threatened, we heartily enjoyed, to the last moment, our boat life, and felt really melancholy when packing up our books and papers for the Cairo hotel. We had still, however, two more days from the present date to spend on board.

On the evening of the 7th we walked on shore at Masgoon, where we stopped in order to visit, the next day, the Pyramids of Dashoor and Sakkára, and the remains of Memphis. When we had passed the village and groves, we saw in the desert such an array of pyramids as justifies Strabo's description of them as being all along the brow of the hills. The people here look comfortable, though their district is the property of Abbas Pasha, who is not noted for conducing to the comfort of humanity. This village and its lands are a present to him from his grandfather, the Pasha. He gives the people the land, seed, and irrigation, and takes half the produce. Such are the nominal terms, which, in Egypt generally, are something widely different from the actual bargain. The palms here are very fine. The wool, which the people were spinning and reeling, was white; —the first white wool I remember to have seen. The distaffs were clumsy; but both men and women were as heartily busy as they could have been about better work. The children were ludicrously afraid of us; and not even baksheesh could reconcile them. We were to them, no doubt, what the dreaded "black man" is to cottagers' children in England. One little boy fled like the wind from the offer of a five para piece; and he could hardly be persuaded to take it from behind his mother's skirts, where he sought refuge. A large quantity of mud bricks was here laid out to dry. They had an unusual proportion of straw in them; so that I believe they would have burned to ashes if set fire to. This naturally brought to mind the brick-making of the Hebrews, who were from about this time never out of my mind till we reached Damascus. We were on their traces now; and afterwards all through our journeyings in Arabia and Palestine. All the next day I saw them in the plain of Memphis; saw the remains of the heavy works in which they might have toiled; in the brick-fields, and in the cucumber and melon grounds which yielded the food they so longed for in the Desert. When I looked upon those fruitful plots, neatly fenced with millet stalks; and upon the bright verdure which spread like a carpet beneath the palms, —a carpet of the richest clover; —and upon the blue ponds inland, and the noble river flowing gently between its fertile banks, with family groups basking in the evening sun above the stream, or sitting in the checkered shade of the acacia groves, I could understand the longing of the Hebrews for a return to Egypt on any terms. From the midst of such a desert as I had seen at Aswan, what is such a scene as this to the memory, —a sunset among palms, ponds, clover-fields, and acacia groves, near the adored Nile! Might not this contrast make any exile as heart-sick to think of as the image of any country under heaven, — unless going from slavery, he was worthy of the freedom in store for him; which the Hebrews were not, and could not become on a sudden.

While we were on shore this evening, Mrs. Y., who had remained on board, was not without amusement. Our crew, always like children, went to child's play. By Mrs. Y.'s account, it was a capital scene. The Buck took office as Governor; was high and mighty, and had the tax-payers brought before him. There was no end to the bastinado and imprisonment he inflicted on unfortunate debtors, who told such tales of outrageous misfortune as were never heard before. Where our children play school, and naughtiness, and punishment, these men play tax-gathering, mishap, and bastinado.

When we were ready to start, on the morning of the 8th, there was much disputing between Alee and the donkey men: and the sheikh was called to give his opinion. The difficulty was that the men wanted the whole pay (seven piastres per donkey) in advance, which of course Alee was unwilling to give to strangers. He offered half in advance: and I believe it was settled so, at last. The men's plea was that a party of Europeans the day before had agreed to pay seven piastres per donkey; but had at last paid only four, alleging discontent with the animals. I hope this was not true.

We crossed the rich plain, which was very lively from its being market-day. The assemblage of people was considerable; most of them bringing something to market. The women carried loads like those of their husbands; —baskets of charcoal, from the acacia-groves; tow, wool, kids carried on the shoulder, &c. The women's faces were carelessly covered, or not at all; and we were suddenly struck by the lighter shade of complexion here.

We came abruptly upon the Desert, near the two stone Pyramids of Da-shoor. The first, which changes its angle halfway up, is the ugliest building I ever saw, being at once clumsy and decrepit in appearance. I saw a wild cat run up the south-west angle, and hide itself among the stones; and Mr. E. had just before seen a large fox. On every side but the north, the stones were rough and broken. One circumstance became thus apparent, which struck me as worth remembering, —the method of joining the blocks by locking them with a stone-key. A square hole on one side of each block being fitted to the corresponding hole of the other, makes an oblong square hole, of course: and an oblong square of stone fitting into it locks them together in one direction, as dovetailing would in two. —On the north side, though the surface was crusted, there was a smoothness and accurate joining of the stone, which showed what the face must once have been. The entrance is at the north; and we saw the square hole; but there is nothing within, it is understood, to tempt the passing traveler to enter, while so near other pyramids which are worth all the time and effort he has to spare. —The best effect of these pyramids is when one looks up to the glorious sky above them, and sees how sharp and bright they stand out, —the yellow edifice glittering against the blue heaven.

The brick Pyramids of Dashoor are now crumbled down into mere ruin. Yet it is believed by some that the northernmost of these is the one which once bore the proud inscription recorded by Herodotus. The old Pharaoh, of the First Period, Asychis, who built that pyramid (whichever it may be) was proud-er of his brick than of any stone edifice, —whether from its novelty, or from its having had a vaulted roof within, —(a trial of the arch, as Dr. Richardson sug-gests,)—there is no saying now: but this is the account Herodotus gives of the matter. "This prince, wishing to surpass all the kings who had reigned in Egypt before him, left for a monument a pyramid of brick, with this inscription cut upon a stone: 'Despise me not, in comparing me with the pyramids of stone. I am as much above them as Jupiter (Amun) is above the other gods: for I have been built of bricks made of the mud brought up from the bottom of the lake!' This is the most memorable thing Asychis did."[151]

From hence to Sakkára was a ride of about two miles across the Desert. We enjoyed the ride, being aided and braced by a cool wind from the south, which carried us along cheerily. From the first sand-ridge, we saw the white citadel of Cairo, standing finely on its rock, under the Mokuttam range. I was sorry to see it, and to receive its warning that our Nile voyage was just over.

At Sakkára, we found ourselves among the remains of the Necropolis. It was a mournful confusion of whitened skulls, deep pits, mummy rags, and mounds of sand.

151   Herod. II. 136.

It was here that Herodotus rose into his enthusiasm about the grandeur and wisdom of Egypt, and learned most that he knew of its history, and saw the mighty works which glorified the name and memory of Sesostris and other old Pharaohs. It was here that in a later day, — (two-thirds of the centuries which lie between Herodotus and us,) — the learned physician of Bagdad saw what transported him with admiration and astonishment, though he complains with indignation of the mischief wrought by treasure-seekers, who were even parting the stones of the edifices for the sake of the copper used in joining them. He looked upon the place as ruined, and mourned over the disappearance of Memphis. What would he think of it now! —Seven centuries ago, Abdallatif wrote thus of the spot we were on to-day.

"Let us now pass on to other traces of the ancient grandeur of Egypt. I am now speaking of the ruins of the old capital of this country, which was situated in the territory of Geezeh, a little above Fostat. This capital was Memphis: it was there that the Pharaohs resided; and this city was the seat of empire in Egypt. It is of this city that we are to understand the words of God in the Kurán, when he is speaking of Moses: He entered into the city at the moment when the inhabitants were sinking into sleep: and again: Moses then went forth from the city, full of terror, and looking about him. For Moses made his abode in a village of the territory of Geezeh, a little way from the capital; which village was called Dimouh. The Jews have a synagogue there at this day. The ruins of Memphis now occupy a space which is half-a-day's journey every way. This city was flourishing in the time of Abraham, Joseph and Moses, and a long time before them, and a long time after them." … "As for the idols which are found among these ruins, whether one considers their number or their prodigious magnitude, it is a thing beyond all description, and of which no idea can be conveyed; but there is a thing yet more worthy of admiration; and that is the precision of their forms, the justness of their proportions, and their resemblance to nature." And then this anatomist goes on to show what are the requisites to the perfect representation of the human frame, with its muscular niceties, and continues: "There are some of these statues which hold in their hands a kind of cylinder, —probably a roll of writing: and the artist has not forgotten to represent the folds and wrinkles which are formed in the skin of the hand when it is closed, towards the outer part by the little finger. The beauty of the face of these statues, and the perfect proportions which are observed there, are such as the most excellent art of men alone can effect, and the best that such a substance as stone can receive. There is nothing wanting but the flesh and the blood. The figure of the ear, its orifice, and its sinuosities, are given to perfection. — I have seen two lions placed opposite and near to each other: their aspect inspired terror. Notwithstanding their colossal size, so far beyond nature, all the truth of form and proportion

had been preserved. They have been broken, and covered with earth."—
"A man of good sense, seeing all these remains of antiquity, feels disposed to
excuse that error of the vulgar which supposes that men of distant ages lived
much longer than those of our times: that they were of gigantic stature: and that
by means of a wand with which they struck the stones, the stones obeyed their
will, and transported themselves wherever they were desired. We remain indeed
in a sort of stupor when we consider how much of genius, of resolution and of
patience, must have been united with a profound knowledge of geometry, to
execute such works; what different instruments from any that we know of must
have been employed; and what obstinate labor; and to what point these men
have studied the structure of animals and of men."[152]

These are some few particulars of what Abdallatif saw among these ruins of
Memphis, which in his day occupied a space of half-a-day's journey. At the end
of seven centuries, the aspect of the place is this. From the village of Mitrahen-
ny (which now occupies the site), can be seen only palm woods, a blue pond,
rushes, and a stretch of verdant ground, broken into hollows, where lie a single
colossus, a single capital of a column, a half-buried statue of red granite, twelve
feet high, and some fragments of granite strewn among the palms. This is all of
the mighty Memphis!

The colossus is the celebrated Ramases' statue, given to the British Museum
by Signor Caviglia and Mr. Sloane, but left in its grassy hollow on account of
the expense. It is very beautiful. The serene and cheerful face is like that of the
Colossi at Aboo-Simbil, but more beautiful. Each hand holds a scroll, with a
cartouche at the end. There it lies, for the Nile to flow over it every year, and the
grass to grow up round it when the waters have retired. It lies on its face: but by
going down into the hollow, we could obtain a good view of the features, which
are as sharp cut, and almost as delicately finished, as any of Chantrey's works at
home. The upper part of the statue is somewhat corroded; but the under part
retains its polish. If this statue is really the colossus which Herodotus speaks of
as erected in front of the temple of Phthah, what a pity it is that further research
is not made, and that glorious structure laid open to view from beneath the
mounds! Herodotus says that that statue of Sesostris was accompanied by one
of his wife, of similar proportions, and by four smaller ones of his sons.[153] But,
if Lepsius is right in believing Sesostris to be a Pharaoh of the First Period, this
is not the statue. At all events, there it lies in the mud; likely to be, as Sir G.
Wilkinson observes, burned for lime, any day, by the Turks.

The view which I obtained from a ridge in the Necropolis was truly dreary.
It was at the colorless time of day—noon: and there was no relief to the white

152   Relation de l'Egypte, Livre I. Ch. 4.
153   Herod. II. 110.

expanse of waste but black and bristling palm tops in clumps, with a slight glimpse of the green beneath. The citadel of Cairo, white, on its white rock, was about a dozen miles off to the northeast; the white city stretching from it west-wards—a slender belt of black palms dividing it from the desert plain on which I stood. A range of white mounds near almost hid the alluvion, beyond which rose the white Arabian hills. All around, and filling up the whole scene to the west, stretched the glaring Desert, oppressing the sense. Yellow "sand ponds," as they are called in my journal, lay between the mounds. To the northwest stood the sharp-shadowed Pyramids of Geezeh; and nearer, those of Abooseer: and close at hand, that of Sakkára.

This Pyramid is built in degrees or terraces; the spaces between the gra-dations being very wide. Five of these degrees are clearly marked all round; a sixth was traceable by a bit of wall uncovered on the north side: and a deep well was at our feet, on that north side, wherein there is, as we were told, an entrance, probably opening upon a seventh terrace. The sand has hidden a large proportion of this Pyramid: but, making all allowance for that, we saw no great wonder, nor any beauty, thus far.

We next went to the mummy pits; and first into the underground world of ibises. There is no season of Egyptian travel in which one's sensations are more strange than in that spent in mummy pits. Here were underground chambers, pillared, painted, and sculptured, excavated into ornamented recesses, and con-secrated to the gods; and destined for the burial of birds. And then the cats! In a sort of quarry, lay strata of these bodies, the rags fluttering out, and the layers consisting of hosts of cats. The feline population of a whole continent for ages would be required, it seems, to fill these pits. The cats are swathed like the hu-man body; the ibises are inclosed in red pots, like chimney-pots, with the round end cemented on.

I am far from wondering at the feelings of contempt and disgust expressed by most travelers who visit these pits. I was conscious of some tendency to those feelings in myself; but I think it is necessary to remember here, as in all strange positions of the mind, that we ought to understand before we despise, and that, usually, the more we understand the less we despise. Of course I do not, and never shall, pretend to explain, in any degree, the old Egyptian practices with regard to the consecration of animals; but two or three considerations occurred to me on the spot which appeared to be worth revolving.

The most obvious particular of old Egyptian thought and feeling— that which presses upon the traveler's notice everywhere among the monuments, so as to compel him to a reiteration of the fact which must be excused in him—is the sacredness of Life, and therefore of Organization. The evidences of this are sometimes such as our existing morality and taste forbid to be dwelt upon or described to any public, or to any large number who have not been there to witness the simplicity and the solemnity with which this subject is regarded and treated in the monuments; but my own impression is that there is as much work for the philosopher—the religious philosopher—in contemplating the ancient ideas of sacred things as for the antiquarian in interpreting the forms of their conveyance; and it may yet perhaps be found that the speculations of the most devout Christian and the most enlightened of the old heathens have the same root, and a development not so different as the superficial might suppose. It may be seen, sooner or later, that in our reverence for Life, we underrate the facts of Organization as much as the old Egyptians appear to us to have overrated them, in their reverence for Life. The Christian contempt for the body may be found to be an error as great and as mischievous as any heathen worship of it. It may appear that, in considering the animal frame, so "fearfully and wonderfully made," as a carcass, a mere shell for the habitation of the principle of Life, to be despised and disparaged as a mere instrumentality of what we call Mind, we are as wrong as any old heathens could be in striving after a factitious immortality for it. For our contempt of the body—for any species of asceticism—we are, as far as I can see, without any warrant to be found in Christianity or in true philosophy. In our just reverence for the higher part of man's nature, his powers of thought and feeling, we may be found, at length, to have adopted a false supposition of facts, and to have striven after a separation not warranted by nature between those powers and the animal frame. Wherever this separation of treatment has been aimed at, wherever asceticism has been practiced for the good of the soul, the object has failed; and precisely in proportion to men's contempt of the body has been the vitiation of the mind. The whole history of asceticism shows that the mental and moral powers of man sink, or become corrupted, when the bodily frame is treated with indignity and cruelty, quite as certainly as when the animal appetites are unreasonably and unnaturally indulged. And the thoughtful philosopher sees that it must be so. All that we really know is that we know nothing of absolute creation; that we have no evidence of it, and can form no conception of it; that Life itself is an inexplicable fact to us; that we recognize it only through organization; and, that we have no right, and no power, to conceive of it as apart from organization— all our laborious attempts, so to conceive of it, terminating in imaginations of an organization more subtle and refined than Nature has presented to our view. On such a subtle and refined organization a considerable number of men have in all ages fixed their imagination, their hope and their belief; but they have never succeeded in showing any evidence for it, while, in wandering away from the facts of Nature, they have injured their own best powers, and failed of the highest attainments possible to their nature. The highest of human beings, the holiest, and the safest in any event, would be one whose bodily frame was of the highest order originally, the most fully exercised (which includes its being the most perfectly disciplined), and whose functions of brain were therefore performed in the most perfect manner—giving him the highest moral and intellectual elevation possible to humanity. In the reverence for Life which would rest upon such a being, the unsophisticated Christian and the devout old Egyptian would meet. Previous to such an encounter, the one might err in holding to his Platonic or Essene notions of a separate soul, clogged with a contemptible and obstructive body, and spurning the notion of its resurrection; and the other might err in regarding every animal frame as such a manifestation of deity as it would be profane to allow to decay; but in actually meeting with the highest example of existence ever offered to their notice, their common reverence for Life would be gratified to such a degree as to enable each to mend his philosophy, and both to ascertain more carefully than hitherto the ground of fact on which alone true philosophy can be reared. The Platonizing Christians of our time might have sympathy with the ancient philosopher who pointed contemptuously to a dead body, with the words, "See the shell of the flown bird!" but the Corinthian readers of Paul's Epistle would shrink from the saying, as the old Egyptians would; the early Christians from their belief in Paul's doctrine of the Resurrection; and the heathens from their belief that whatever had been gifted with sentient life was forever sacred. And if it came to argument between the two, whether the line of sacredness was to be drawn between Man and Brute, it certainly appears to most people now that in reason the Egyptian would have the advantage. Remembering that the Egyptians grounded their belief in the immortality of life on the constitution of living beings, on the mystery of their existence at all in the absence of any evidence of absolute creation, we must see that they could not draw a line of separation between any classes of beings who had sentient life. Any exclusion of brutes from the reverence entertained towards Life, and from its quality of immortality, is grounded solely on the plea of a divine revelation that Man shall either not die, or shall live again; and there are not a few devout receivers of this revelation who have refused to exclude brute animals from the condition of immortality; not a few Christian philosophers who have shrunk from declaring that beings which enjoy the intellectual and moral powers of the dog, for instance, shall be annihilated at death while Man survives. Such men as some of these are not treated with ridicule or contumely on account of this speculation, and they could hardly treat with ridicule or contumely the Egyptians who in their reverence for the mystery of Life—the ultimate fact in nature to us all —treated with serious care its sole manifestation to them and to us—the organization of sentient beings.

If the Egyptians ventured upon a step further back than the fact of Life, and assumed it to be a divine particle flowing forth from a self-existent and sole eternal Being, to flow back into its centre on the death of the body, it is clear that no line could be drawn between the human being and the brute, as to the reverence in which the sentient frame was to be held. —It is true, the Egyptians worshiped no human beings; and they did pay religious observance to some brutes. They called their monarchs and great men "gods," explaining that by this they meant to dignify men whom the gods favored with intercourse and special protection: but they paid no reverential honors to them, as they did to brutes. This seems to have arisen from their reverence for Instinct; which does truly answer to the original idea of inspiration; and is so acknowledged among all such primitive people as those who hold madness and idiocy sacred. The original idea of inspiration is, exercise of mind without consciousness. Thus, the highest order of genius is with us the nearest approach to inspiration; and among primitive and inexperienced nations, it is the unconscious and involuntary action from ideas which is seen in the idiot Highland child, or the lost Indian Fakeer, or the half-knavish, half-foolish Arabian derweesh; or, in old times, the magnetized utterer of the oracles, or the spontaneously-prophesying seer. The instinct of animals comes under this head, or appears to do so. It appears to be action of mind unattended by consciousness; and it might well, therefore, be taken for inspiration: and every action of the creature would then be watched for guidance, and every incident connected with it be accepted for an omen. It is as easily conceivable that the Egyptians, paying homage to beings above and below Man, actually raised the brute with his instinct above Man with his reason, in that one point of view which regarded his inspiration, as that there are men now who look with greater awe upon an idiot or crazed fanatic than on a rational person. In the old case, it was not the brutality, and in the modern case, it is not the folly, that is reverenced: it is the mysterious working of mental faculty, apart from the will, which appears to those ignorant of the powers and functions of the brain to be the communication of Ulterior Thought through an unconscious medium.

We do not know what the Egyptians did with the bodies of animals which they did not hold sacred. Abdallatif could find no remains of the camel, the horse or the ass: and on his inquiring of the old people in the neighborhood of the Memphis mummy-pits, they hastened to assure him that they had been struck by the absence of all traces of these animals. This absence of all trace is curious in the case of animals which were not eaten. —It is no contradiction of the supposition that the Egyptians reverenced brutes for the possible reasons mentioned above, that they sacrificed some and ate others. In some cases they chose for sacrifice animals which were hated by the particular Deity in question:

as in the case of the red ox. And in eating animals not disliked by the gods, they might have the same idea that lies at the root of cannibalism and human sacrifices, in the South Sea islands, and probably everywhere else. The belief, in such cases, is that the gods wait to imbibe the spirit of the victim; and the idea is that the victim, in passing through the gods, becomes assimilated to their nature, and remains henceforth divine, to the extent of immortality at least, and usually in some other respects. It is thus an honor and blessing to be sacrificed; and the being eaten implies no disrespect to the perishable frame, because the body merely follows the analogy of the spirit's lot; and what is honorable to the one part of the creature cannot be disgraceful to the other. If the nobler part entered into the gods, the meaner might enter into the sons of the gods.

The choice of animals for consecration and preservation was probably determined by the characters of their instinct. Herodotus declines to explain some particulars which were known to him, and which certainly appear to have borne, in his view, a solemn import. —How can we say that it would not have been so with ourselves, if we had stood, with Herodotus, or Plato, or Pythagoras, in the inner apartments of the priests, surrounded by the monuments of their art, and the records of their learning, and favored with their confidence about matters of the nearest and the most general concern! I own that in the absence of priests and papyri, when all around was dumb and desolate, and I had no external aid to knowledge but faded pictures of offerings and fluttering mummy rags, I could not resign myself to feelings of disgust and contempt. If I had been on the banks of some South African river, seeing a poor naked savage at his Fetish worship, I must have tried to learn what idea, however low, was at the bottom of his observance: and here, where I knew that men had read the stars, and compassed in visible truths of geometry, and achieved unaccountable marvels of art, and originated, or transmitted, the theologies of the world, I could not despise them for one set of tenets and observances which remains unexplained. I might lament that analogies have been the mischievous Will-o'-the-wisp to the human intellect that they appear to have been in the valley of the Nile, as in the plains of Asia, and the groves of Greece, and the wilderness of Middle Age scholarship in Europe: but this is a sorrow which one feels in every hour of actual study, in any country of the world. I might lament that aspiration, in its young and irrepressible activity, must make so many flights into a dim world of dreams, and come back perplexed and disheartened before it can learn to fly up to the glorious and unfailing light of Nature, to replenish its life: but this regret is only what one feels every day in exploring the only true history of Man, —the history of Ideas. I might lament that the Egyptians should have so framed and illustrated their faith, as that it must inevitably become corrupted in its diffusion: but this is the regret which attends the contemplation of the spread of every faith by which mankind has yet been guided. The old Egyptian faith deteriorated into worshiping animals; the Jewish into the Pharisaic superstitions and oppressions rebuked throughout the Gospels; and what Christianity has become, among the widest class of its professors, let the temples and congregations of the Greek and Latin churches show. Amidst these natural regrets remains the comfort that the great governing Ideas of mankind, —the guiding lights of the human intellect, — have never failed, and have scarcely suffered eclipse. The great Ideas of Moral Obligation and strict retribution, of the supreme desirableness of moral good, and the eternal "beauty of holiness," pass from system to system, immortalizing all with which they assimilate, and finally annihilating all else, dispensing the best blessings that men have ever received, and promising an increase of them in all time to come.

There was nothing else to be seen about this buried city but a tomb or two—a sarcophagus here—a mummy-case there. On our return to the river, we saw sights which did not tend to raise the spirits after the depressing influence of the aspect of old Memphis. We fell in with a wedding procession which was a sad antic exhibition. We saw a great number of men at work upon the causeway which crosses the plain; and a large portion of their work consisted in carrying soil in frail-baskets, and scooping out the earth with their hands. Such is the state of manners and art on the spot where Herodotus held counsel with the wise men of the world, and where the greatest works of Man's hands were reared by means of science and art of which the world is not now capable!

CHAPTER XIX

VISIT TO THE PYRAMIDS—ASCENT OF THE GREAT PYRAMID— INTERIOR—TRADITIONS AND HISTORY ABOUT THE PYRAMIDS— THE SPHINX—FAREWELL TO ANCIENT EGYPT

THE DAY WAS COME WHICH I DREADED—the day of our expedition to the Great Pyramids. I dreaded it, because I feared a sort of disappointment most difficult to bear—that of failing in the sight-seeing of the day. Since arriving at Thebes, I had not been well; and I had no reason for confidence in my strength, in a place and enterprise so new. I had made up my mind not to be disconcerted if I should have to return without having been either up or into the Pyramid; but I was sorry to open my eyes upon the sunrise that morning. I went over in my mind all the stories I knew of persons who had failed, and felt that I had no better title to success than they. My comfort was in the Sphinx. I should see that, at all events. It did not mend the matter that I found that a messenger was sent to Cairo for our letters. Three of us had had no letters of a later date than the 5th of November; and this was the 9th of February. I knew that the winter at home was a dreadful one—for weather, sickness and distress; and never, I think, was I so anxious about letters from home, or so afraid to receive them. Whatever they might be, however, they would be awaiting me on my return.

We set out for Geezeh at half-past eight, on fine handsome asses, so spirited as to be almost as good to ride as horses. To-day we once more came in sight of that curious sign of civilization —shaven donkeys. Dark rings were left round the legs, and the neck and hind quarters were shaven. The scarlet housings and gay rider made a set-out very unlike what one sees of donkey-riding at home. I was not aware till I came to Egypt how dependent a donkey is on dress.

Our first adventure was being carried on men's shoulders over a muddy pond which stopped the way. We knew that our plague today would be from the multitude of country people who would obtrude their services upon us. At this pond the teasing began. Our dragoman met it vigorously, by trying to throw a pertinacious fellow, bigger than himself, into the water. It was a desperate scuffle, such as would make ladies shriek and fly in England; but it came to nothing, as usual. All the rest of the way, men joined us from the fields on either hand, till, when we arrived at the sand, our train was swelled to forty.

I was surprised to find myself disappointed in the Pyramids now, when it had been precisely the reverse at a distance. Instead of their growing larger as we approached, they became less and less wonderful, till at last they exactly met one's preconception, except in being rougher, and of a brighter tint. The platform on which the largest stands is higher than our reading had given us to suppose; and the Second Pyramid, which at a distance looks as large as the other, here sinks surprisingly. This was to me the strongest evidence of the magnitude of the Great Pyramid. Though I have spoken of disappointment on a near approach, these mighty objects were perfectly absorbing, as a little incident presently proved. One of our party said, on our arrival, "when we were passing the Sphinx," "O! the Sphinx!" cried I. "You don't mean that you have seen the Sphinx!" To be sure they had; and they insisted on it that I had too; that I must have seen it—could not have missed it. I was utterly bewildered. It was strange enough to have forgotten it; but not to have seen it, was inexplicable. However, on visiting it, later in the day, I found I had seen it. Being intent on the Pyramid before me, I had taken the Sphinx for a capriciously-formed rock, like so many that we had passed —forgetting that I should not meet with limestone at Geezeh. I rather doubt whether any traveler would take the Sphinx for anything but a rock unless he was looking for it, or had his eye caught by some casual light. One other anecdote, otherwise too personal for print, will show how engrossing is the interest of the Pyramid on the spot. The most precious articles of property I had with me abroad were two ear-trumpets, because, in case of accident happening to them, I could not supply the loss. I was unwilling to carry my trumpet up the Pyramid—knocking against the stones while I wanted my hands for climbing. So I left it below, in the hands of a trusty Arab. When I joined my party at the top of the Pyramid, I never remembered my trumpet; nor did they; and we talked as usual, during the forty minutes we were there, without my ever missing it. When I came down, I never thought of it; and I explored the inside, came out and lunched, and still never thought of my trumpet, till, at the end of three hours and a half from my parting with it, I saw it in the hands of the Arab, and was reminded of the astonishing fact that I had heard as well without it as with it, all that time. Such a thing never happened before, and probably never will again; and a stronger proof could not be offered of the engrossing interest of a visit to the Pyramid.

The sheikh who met us on the spot, appointed our attendants; — three to each of us. Mr. E. set out first, —waving an adieu to us till we should meet aloft. He mounted with a deliberate, quiet step, such as he could keep up to the end, and reached the summit in seventeen minutes. It took me about five minutes more.

On looking up, it was not the magnitude of the Pyramid which made me think it scarcely possible to achieve the ascent; but the unrelieved succession, —almost infinite, —of bright yellow steps; a most fatiguing image! —Three strong and respectable-looking Arabs now took me in charge. One of them, seeing me pinning up my gown in front, that I might not stumble over it, gave me his services as lady's-maid. He turned up my gown all round, and tied it in a most squeezing knot, which lasted all through the enterprise. We set out from the north east corner. By far the most formidable part of the ascent was the first six or eight blocks. If it went on to the top thus broken and precipitous, the ascent would, I felt, be impossible. Already, it was disagreeable to look down, and I was much out of breath. One of my Arabs carried a substantial camp-stool, which had been given me in London with a view to this very adventure, —that it might divide the higher steps, —some of which, being four feet high, seem impracticable enough beforehand. But I found it better to trust to the strong and steady lifting of the Arabs in such places, and, above everything, not to stop at all, if possible; or, if one must stop for breath, to stand with one's face to the Pyramid. I am sure the guides are right in taking people quickly. The height is not so great, in itself: it is the way in which it is reached that is trying to look back upon. It is trying to some heads to sit on a narrow ledge, and see a dazzling succession of such ledges for two or three hundred feet below; and there, a crowd of diminutive people looking up, to see whether one is coming bobbing down all that vast staircase. I stopped for a few seconds two or three times, at good broad corners or ledges. —When I left the angle, and found myself ascending the side, the chief difficulty was over; and I cannot say that the fatigue was at all formidable. The greater part of one's weight is lifted by the Arabs at each arm; and when one comes to a four feet step, or a broken ledge, there is a third Arab behind. When we arrived at a sort of recess, broken in the angle, my guides sported two of their English words, crying out "Half-way!" with great glee. The last half was easier than the first; and I felt, what proved to be true, that both must be easier than the coming down. I arrived second, and was kindly welcomed to that extraordinary spot by Mr. E. Mrs. Y. appeared presently after; and lastly, Mr. Y.; —all in good spirits.

I was agreeably surprised to find at the top, besides blocks standing up which gave us some shade, a roomy and even platform, where we might sit and write, and gaze abroad, and enjoy ourselves, without even seeing over the edge, unless we wished it. There was only the lightest possible breeze, just enough to fan our faces, without disturbing us. The reason of our ascending the Pyramid first, before going into it, was that we might take advantage of an hour of calm, and avoid the inconvenience of the wind which might spring up at noon. And most fortunate we were in our weather, and in all other particulars. It was a glorious season, —full of new delight, without drawback; —for I now began to think I might perhaps see the inside of the Pyramid too.

Here are my notes of what we saw from the lop; —a height of 480 feet. "Bearings by compass. In a line from us to the North, the hager (sandy plain) joins the fertile land, a blue stream flowing between them, and the line being wavy, and having a sprinkling of palms towards the North. In this northern direction, the green plain extends to the furthest horizon, and over to Cairo eastwards. It is dotted with villages, —clusters of brown houses among palms, —and watered with blue thread-like canals, and showing a faint line of cause-way here and there. —E. by N., stands up the citadel of Cairo, the city stretch-ing north-westwards from it. Behind the city, some way round to the N.N.E., is a low ridge of sandy hills: and the other way, southwards, the Mokuttam range, which looks higher the higher one mounts. Round from hence are sandy hills, with alluvion and canals between them and us, as far as the S.E., where the Nile wanders away, and the Abooseer Pyramids rise. S.S.E. are the Sakkára Pyramids; and from them, round the rest of the landscape, all is desert, —terribly arid and glaring. In the midst of the sand, a train of camels, wonderfully diminutive, is winding along, and a few brown Arab tents are pitched, not far from the foot of the Pyramid. Off our S.W. corner is the Second Pyramid, standing in its sunken area, surrounded by walls, and showing by the casing that is left how much finer these Pyramids must have looked before they were so dismantled. —Beyond this, lies the little one."—This was what we saw; and long we gazed in every direction: —most pathetically perhaps to the South, where we had seen and left so much; or over into the Delta, which we should enter no more, and which lay so rich and lovely between our eyes and the horizon, that it seemed to be melting-away. We began letters to friends at home, drank some water, intrepidly carried up by a little Arab girl; mounted the highest block, lo get as near the sky as we could; and then found that we really must be going down.

The descent was fatiguing; but not at all alarming. Between stepping, jumping, and sliding, with full reliance on the strength and care of the guides, the descent may be easily accomplished in ten minutes; —as far, that is, as the height of the entrance to the Pyramid, which is some way from the bottom. We had bargained before starting that we should not be asked for baksheesh "while going up the Pyramid." Our guides took this literally, and began begging, the moment we put our feet upon the summit. And all the way down, my guides never let me alone, though they knew I had no money about me. They were otherwise extremely kind, giving me the benefit of their other two words of English. On my jumping down a particularly high block, they patted me on the back, crying, with approving nods, "Ah! ah! good morning; good morning!" I joined my party at the beautiful entrance to the Pyramid, where a large assemblage of Arabs was ranged on the rising stones opposite to us, like a hill-side congregation waiting for the preacher.

I resolved that morning not to be induced by any pleasure or triumph of the hour to tell people that it is very easy to go up and into the Pyramid. To determined and practiced people it is easy; but not, probably, to the majority. I would not recommend any one to do it of whose nerve I was not sure. To the tranquil, the inside of the Pyramid is sufficiently airy and cool for the need of the hour. But it is a dreadful place in which to be seized with a panic: and no woman should go who cannot trust herself to put down panic by reason. There is absolutely nothing to fear but from one's self; no danger of bad falls, or of going astray, or of being stifled. The passages are slippery: but there are plenty of notches; and a fall could hardly be dangerous—unless at one place—the entrance upon the passage to the King's Chamber. We knew beforehand that there were air-passages from that chamber to the outside; and when I walked about before examining the place, and questioned my senses, I was surprised to find how little oppressive heat, and how much air there really was. The one danger is from the impression upon the senses of the solidity and vastness of the stone structure in such darkness. Almost any nerves may be excused for giving way under the sight of that passage and that chamber; —the whole, even the roof, being constructed of blocks of dark granite, so joined as that the edge of a penknife could not be inserted between them. The passage runs up, a steep inclined plane, with its lines on either hand, and its notches in front, retiring almost to a vanishing point, other grooves and projections high up the side walls apparently coming down to the same vanishing point, and all closed in by the ponderous ceiling, at such a height as to be well nigh lost in gloom. The torches of the Arabs glare near the eye, and perplex the vision by their fitful shining on the granite walls; and it the same time, the lights in advance or far behind are like waving glow-worm sparks. There is nothing else like it; —no catacomb or cavern in the world; there never was, and surely there never will be. I have spent the greater part of two days in the Mammoth Cave of Kentucky; a place generally considered awful enough: but compared with this, it was like a drawing-room to a cellar. The fantastic character of its walls and roofs takes off from the impression of its vastness and gloom. Here, the symmetry and finish so deepen the gloom as to make this seem like a fit prison-house for fallen angels. Notwithstanding the plain view we obtained in the chamber of the enormous longitudinal blocks of the ceiling, the impression was less tremendous than in the descending passage, from the inferior vastness. There is nothing but the structure itself to be seen, except the sarcophagus near one end. It is sadly broken: but it still rings like a bell, when struck on the side. The granite is blackened by time; but its grain is seen where it has been chipped by those who were in search of the air-holes. The prodigious portcullises of granite in the passage were more visible to us in going down than in ascending: and how they came there was an oppressive speculation in itself. It must be remembered that this structure, with its wonderful art and bewildering grandeur, was the work of the men of five thousand years ago. It dates from the earlier part of the First Period, and is the oldest monument known to exist in the world. If this is, to us, the beginning of the Arts—this, which manifests the existence of so many appliances of art unknown to us now, how are we to speculate on what went before? and how completely do we find ourselves thrown out in all our notions of the duration of the human race!

On returning, two of our party had had enough of Pyramid searching. I and another had not; and we proceeded to the Qtueen's Chamber, along the passage, above which we had ascended to the King's. This passage was not so low as we had expected. It only required us to walk stooping. The chief interest about the Queen's Chamber is from its being under the apex of the Pyramid; which the King's is not. Its ceiling is on this account pointed, like the great entrance. There are also five small, rough chambers above it, evidently put there to lessen the superincumbent weight. Though this chamber is smaller than the King's, it seems to be distinguished by being under the apex; and also by a niche, rather elaborately wrought. A pit has been opened below this niche, by searchers, and the rubbish thrown into a corner. Sir G. Wilkinson wishes that, if further search is made here for the king's body, it should be by looking under this niche. My great desire would be to have the Pyramid explored down to the lowest part where any traces of works could be found. Works carried down so low must have some purpose; and it might be well worth our while to discover what. It is not satisfactory to my mind to suppose the "subterranean structures" intended merely to let the workmen out, after they had closed the upper passage with its granite portcullis. The great difficulty, in exploring the Pyramid—after the expense and toil of getting to work at all—is from the wonderful way in which these ancient builders closed the passages. Their huge granite portcullises, blocking up the way, are almost insuperable. It is hard to distinguish them from other blocks, and to guess when there is a passage behind; and then it is very hard to get round them. I have a strong impression myself that, after all the wonders our pains-taking and disinterested antiquarian travelers have laid open, there is much more behind, and that the exploration of the Pyramid is only just begun. If it be true that some one fired a pocket-pistol within the Pyramid, and that the echoes were countless —the reverberation going on for an astonishing length of time—it seems as if the edifice might be honey-combed with chambers. But for these unmanageable granite portcullises, what might we not learn!

It becomes us, however, to be grateful for what we have learned. Colonel Howard Vyse has laid the world under great obligations by his generous and laborious exertions. He made, among many discoveries, one of inestimable importance. He found inscribed in the Pyramid, in the most antique style, the names of the Pharaohs who raised these edifices: and they turn out to be the same given by Herodotus and Manetho. It is now ascertained, beyond all doubt, that these Pyramids are the work of Pharaohs of the fourth dynasty; — that is, of kings early succeeding Menes, and living near the beginning of the First Period of Egyptian history.

I suppose every one knows the account given by Herodotus of the building of this pyramid; —how Cheops closed the temples, stopped the sacrifices, and made everybody work for him: —how some quarried the stone in the Arabian hills, and others conveyed it to the river and over a bridge of boats; and others drew it to the spot where it was wanted: —and how it could be carried and mounted only by a causeway which of itself took ten years to construct, and which was a fine work, with its polished stones and figures of animals engraved on them: — how 100,000 men were employed at a time, and were relieved by the same number at the end of three months: how, besides the ten years occupied by the causeway, much was required for leveling the rock on which the edifice stands, and twenty years for the building of the pyramid itself: —how a machine, made of short pieces of wood, was placed on every step, as the work proceeded, to raise the stones for the step above; and how the filling in of these gradations, forming the last smooth surface, was begun from the top: —how this surface bore engraved, so that Herodotus himself saw it, an inscription which told the expense of the vegetables eaten by the laborers during the progress of the work; and how confounded the traveler declares himself to be, judging from the sum spent in vegetables, at the thought of the expenditure further necessary for the rest of the food and the clothes of the workmen, and their iron tools, during the long course of years required for the whole series of works, —amongst which, by the way, he includes the " subterranean structures" which he again mentions, as made by the king, "for purpose of sepulture, in an island formed by the waters of the Nile, which he introduced into them by a canal."[154]

All this narrative, thus briefly glanced at, is known to everybody who cares about Egypt: and everybody has no doubt been struck by this testimony to the

154   Herod. II. 124.

use of iron tools, and the existence of polished stones, machinery, writing and engraving, between five and six thousand years ago. —But everybody may not know what evidence we have of the solidity and extraordinary vastness of these works, in the impossibility which has been found of taking them to pieces. This evidence we have through our useful middle age witness, Abdallatif, whose book is so little known that I may be rendering a service by translating some passages relating to his visits to the pyramids in or about A.D. 1190. Abdallatif begins with the same thought which suggested the noble saying, "All things dread Time: but Time dreads the Pyramids." He says—

"The form which has been adopted in the construction of the Pyramids, and the solidity which has been given them are well worthy of admiration. It is to their form that they owe the advantage of having resisted the hostility of centuries: or rather, it seems as if it were Time which has resisted the opposition of these eternal edifices. Indeed, when we meditate deeply on the construction of the Pyramids, we are compelled to acknowledge that men of the greatest genius have here employed in combination their best powers; and that the subtlest minds have exhausted their deepest resources; that the most enlightened souls have exercised in profusion all the abilities that they possessed which could be applied to these constructions; and that the wisest theory of geometry has employed all its means to produce these wonders, as the last point of astonishment which it was possible to reach. Thus we may say that these edifices speak to us now of those who reared them, teach us their history, open to us in an intelligible manner the progress which they had made in the sciences, and the excellence of their abilities: —in a word, they put us in possession of the life and actions of the men of those days."[155] After telling how the Pyramids are placed with a regard to the points of the compass, and how this breaks the force of the wind, and what the gross measurements are, he goes on: —" Their pyramidal figure is truncated; and the summit offers thereby a level of ten cubits every way. Here is a thing which I myself observed. When I visited them, there was in our party an archer, who let fly an arrow in the direction of the perpendicular height of one of these Pyramids, and in that of its thickness (its base): and the arrow fell a little short of midway.[156] We learned that in the neighboring village there were people accustomed to mount the pyramid, who did it without any difficulty. We sent for one of these men; and for a trifle which we gave him, he set off up the pyramid, as we should to mount a staircase, and even quicker, without putting off either his shoes or his garments, which were very ample. I had

155   Relation de l'Egypte, Livre I. Ch. 4.
156   It is well known that the ground covered by the Great Pyramid is equal to the area of Lincoln's Inn Fields, and 50 feet over, every way; —say, Lincoln Inn Fields and the row of surrounding houses.

desired him to measure, with his turban, the area at the top, when he got there. When he came down, we took the measure of his turban, as it answered to that of the area at the summit. We found it to be eleven cubits, by the measure of the original cubit." —It does not seem to have occurred to the grave physician to go up himself. It is a pity that he could not know that ladies would accomplish the feat, seven centuries after him. If he had looked abroad from the summit, what would he have done for words to express his raptures! He goes on to show how much less he dared than we: —

"One of these two pyramids is open, and offers an entrance by which the interior may be visited. This opening leads to narrow passages, to conduits which go down to a great depth, and to wells and precipices, as we are assured by such persons as have courage to explore them: for there are many people who are tempted by a foolish avarice and chimerical hopes into the interior of this edifice. They plunge into deep recesses, and come at last to a place where they find it impossible to penetrate further. As for the most frequented and ordinarily used passage, it is a glacis which leads to the upper part of the pyramid, where there is a square chamber; and in this chamber a sarcophagus of stone."

Up to a recent date, there have been doubts whether the pyramid was open so long ago as this, and whether, therefore, the tradition was true which declares that Caliph Mamoon opened it, somewhere about A.D. 820. It is clear that in Abdallatif's time there was no novelty in its standing open: and there seems no reason to doubt the narrative given by Arab writers of the opening by Caliph Mamoon. One of them, Abdel Hôkm, declares that a statue resembling a man (a mummy-case, no doubt), was found in the sarcophagus; and within the statue, a human body, with a breast-plate of gold and jewels, bearing written characters which no one understood. Abdallatif says—

"The opening by which the interior of the pyramid is reached at this day is not the original entrance; it is a hole begun at random, and made by force. It is said it was the Caliph Mamoon who made it. The greater part of our company entered it, and went up to the higher chamber. When they came down, they gave marvelous accounts of what they had seen; and they said that this passage was so full of bats and their dirt that it was almost stopped up: that the bats were nearly as large as pigeons; and that there were to be seen in the upper part, open spaces and windows which seemed to have been intended to admit air and light. —In another visit which I made to the Pyramids, I entered this interior passage with several persons, and went about two-thirds of the way along it: but having become insensible through the fear which struck me in this ascent, I came down again, half dead.

"These pyramids are constructed of great stones, from ten to twenty cubits long, and two or three cubits in the breadth and thickness. The most admirable particular of the whole is the extreme nicety with which these stones have been prepared and adjusted. Their adjustment is so precise that not even a needle or a hair can be inserted between any two of them. They are joined by a cement laid on to the thickness of a sheet of paper. I cannot tell what this mortar is made of, it being of a substance entirely unknown to me. These stones are covered with writing in that unknown character whose import is at this day wholly unknown. I have not met in Egypt with any person who could say that he knew, even by hearsay, of any one who under stood this character. These inscriptions are so multitudinous, that if those only which are seen on the surface of these two pyramids were copied upon paper, more than ten thousand pages would be filled with them."

For "pages," Pococke here translates "books." When we remember that Abdallatif is telling us what he himself saw, we cannot but admit this particular of his simple narrative. He goes on: "I have read in some books of the ancient Sabeans, that, of these two pyramids, one is the tomb of Agathodemon, and the other that of Hermes. These are, they say, two great prophets; but Agathodemon is the older and greater of the two. They say that from all the countries of the world, people come in pilgrimage to these two pyramids. — In my great work, I have enlarged upon this subject; and I have related what others have said of these edifices. To that account I refer those who desire further details. Here, I limit myself to what I have myself seen.

"When Melic-alaziz Othman-ben-Yousouf had succeeded his father, he let himself be persuaded by some of his courtiers, —foolish people, —to demolish these pyramids: and they began with the red[157] pyramid, which is the third and smallest of the three great pyramids.

"The Sultaun sent there his sappers, miners and quarrymen, under the superintendence of some of the principal officers and first Emirs of his court, and gave them orders to destroy it. To execute these orders, they established their camp near the pyramid: they collected there a multitude of laborers from all quarters, and maintained them at great cost. They remained there eight entire months, occupied, with all their people, in executing their commission, carrying away, each day, after extreme exertion and exhaustion, two or three stones. Some pushed them from above with wedges and levers, while others drew them away from the base with ropes and cables. Whenever one of these stones fell, it made a fearful noise, which echoed far off, shook the earth, and made the hills tremble. By its fall, it was buried in the sand; and then, great efforts were made to remove it; after which the people wrought grooves for the wedges to enter; and thus the stones were split into several pieces: —then each fragment was placed upon a car, to be carried to a mountain a little way off", and thrown out at its foot.

157   So called from its being made of red granite.

"After the company had remained a long time encamped on this spot, when their pecuniary means were all expended, while their trouble and fatigue went on increasing, and their resolution growing weaker, day by day, and their strength was utterly exhausted, they were obliged ignominiously to quit their enterprise. Far from obtaining the result they had anticipated, and succeeding in their design, they ended by doing nothing but spoiling the pyramid, and evidencing their own powerlessness. This passed in the year 593, (A.D. 1196.) When one now looks at the stones brought down in the course of the demolition, one is persuaded that the pyramid has been destroyed from its foundation: but when, on the other hand, one looks up at the pyramid, one believes that it has suffered no injury whatever, and that nothing has happened but the paring off of a portion of the casing on one of its sides.

"Observing one day what extremely heavy work it was to remove a single stone, I addressed one of the superintendents who was directing the workmen, and put this question to him—'If any one offered you a thousand pieces of gold to replace one of these stones, and adjust it as it was before, do you think you could accomplish it?' His answer was that if many times as much was offered, they could not do such a thing; and this he affirmed with an oath."[158]

I fear that all such descriptions are thrown away, in regard to the object of giving to the readers of them any idea of what the Pyramids are. They are useful as records, however, and extremely interesting to travelers in going over the ground. As for the impression, —there is nothing like the momentary sensation of seeing the blue daylight at the top of the entrance passage, when one is on one's way out. More real astonishment is felt at that moment than from reading all the descriptions of all authors.

After resting for luncheon on a block on the east side of the Pyramids, we visited some tombs, very interesting from their extreme antiquity, but too much like those of Benee Hasan to justify description here. The preparations for feasts, numbering stock, &c, go on here as elsewhere, showing that people lived between five and six thousand years ago, much as they do now. It was hereabouts that that precious ring was found which ought to be in the British Museum, but which remains in the hand of Dr. Abbott, at Cairo—the gold ring of Cheops, with his cartouche cut upon it. In Dr. Abbott's possession, too, are some gold ornaments with "Menes" marked upon them. Treasures of such singular value as these should surely be national property.

And now the time was come for visiting the Sphinx. What a monstrous idea was it from which this monster sprang! True as I think Abdallatif's account of it, and just as is his admiration, I feel that a stranger either does not see the Sphinx at all, or he sees it as a nightmare. When we first passed it, I saw it only

158   Relation de l'gypte, Livre I., Ch. 4.

as a strange-looking rock; an oversight which could not have occurred in the olden time, when the head bore the royal helmet or the ram's horns. Now I was half-afraid of it. The full serene gaze of its round face, rendered ugly by the loss of the nose, which was a very handsome feature of the old Egyptian face—this full gaze and the stony calm of its attitude almost turn one to stone. So life-like—so huge—so monstrous—it is really a fearful spectacle. I saw a man sitting in a fold of the neck, as a fly might settle on a horse's mane. In that crease he reposed, while far over his head extended the vast penthouse of the jaw, and above that, the dressed hair on either side the face—each bunch a mass of stone which might crush a dwelling house. In its present state, its proportions cannot be obtained; but Sir G. Wilkinson tells us,[159] "Pliny says it measured from the belly to the highest part of the head sixty-three feet; its length was one hundred and forty-three; and, the circumference of its head round the forehead one hundred and two feet—all cut out in the natural rock, and worked smooth." Fancy the long well-opened eyes, in such proportion as this—eyes which have gazed unwinking into vacancy, while mighty Pharaohs, and Hebrew law-givers, and Persian princes, and Greek philosophers, and Anthony with Cleopatra by his side, and Christian anchorites, and Arab warriors, and European men of science, have been brought hither in succession by the unpausing ages to look up into those eyes—so full of meaning, though so fixed! We have here a record of the Egyptian complexion, or of the Egyptians' own notion of it, as well as of the characteristic features of the race. There is red paint on the face, of the same tint as the complexions in the tombs. The face is (supposing the nose restored) much like the Berber countenance. The long mild eye, the thick but not protuberant lips, (lips like Malibran's, and like no others that I ever saw in Europe,) and the projecting jaw, with the intelligent, gentle expression of the whole face, are very like what one sees in Nubia at every village. That man sitting in the fold of the neck was a happy accident. It enabled one to estimate proportions, when looking up from below, and to learn how it was that religious processions marched up between its paws to the temple sheltered by its breast. I could see how the sanctuary and altar of sacrifice might very well stand there, so towered over by the neck and head as that the savor of the sacrifices might rise straight up into its nostrils. The granite tablet above this altar is visible, peeping out of the sand in the hollow. Thy ridge of the back is above ground, and I walked along it from the neck to the root of the tail. If only the paws could be kept uncovered, it would much improve our conception of this strange work—perhaps, as my journal observes, the strangest object I ever saw.

While riding away, I turned to give a last look, and was struck with the ugliness of the scene. The Pyramids lessened in height from north to south,

159   Modern Egypt and Thebes, I. 356.

and were scattered about without evident plan; tombs yawned in the yellow rocks; the Sphinx lay low, and seemed to belong to nothing; and the whole vast, desolate circuit of monuments was in cumbered by rubbish. This was my last glimpse into the ancient world, except that I had the obelisk at Heliopolis yet to see. This was my last clear view into the times of the vanished race. As I turned my face towards Cairo, the cloud curtain was again drawn over the living and moving scene which I had studied for so long, and anything more that I might learn must be by thought and not by sight.

The amount of what one does learn by the eye is very great—really astonishing in the case of a people whose literature is lost, instead remaining as an indication of what one is to look for, and a commentary on what one sees. What do we not owe to their turn for engraving and painting! Here is a people remaining only, as one may say, in the abstract! —living only in the ideas they have bequeathed to us, and in the undecayed works of their hands. No one of that great race survives; we have their corpses in plenty, but not a breathing man left of them all. We do not know what their complexion was; their language is lost, except as studious men pick it up, word by word, with painful uncertainty, from an obscure cypher. But, phantoms as they are to us, how much do they teach us!

They teach us to be modest and patient in regard to our knowledge of the ancient world, by showing us that while we have been talking confidently of the six thousand years of human existence, and about who was who in the earliest days, we have in reality known nothing about it. They rebuke us sufficiently in showing us that at that time men were living very much as we do, without some knowledge that we have gained, but in possession of some arts which we have not. They confound us by their mute exhibitions of their iron tools and steel armor, their great range of manufactures, and their feasts and sports, so like our own. In their kitchens they decant wine by a syphon, and strew their sweet cakes with seeds, and pound their spices in a mortar. In the drawing-room, they lounge on chaises-lounges, and the ladies knit and net as we do, and darn better than we can. I saw at Dr. Abbott's a piece of mending left unfinished several thousand years ago, which any Englishwoman might be satisfied with or proud of. In the nursery the little girls had dolls—jointed dolls, with bunchy hair and long eyes—as our dolls have blue eyes and fair tresses. And the babies had, not the woolly bow-wow dogs which yelp in our nurseries, but little wooden crocodiles with snapping jaws. In the country we see the agriculturist taking stock, and in the towns the population divided into castes, subject to laws, and living under a theocracy, long before the supposed time of the Deluge. There is enough here to teach us some humility and patience about the true history of the world.

We almost lose sight of the evidences of their ways that they have left us in recognizing the Ideas that they have recorded and transmitted. Here they were, nearly two thousand years before the birth of Abraham, worshiping One Supreme God, and owning him for their king, appointing for his agent and chief servant as their ruler, a priest whom they called his son. They recognized his moral government— always strictly a moral government, through how many hands soever it might be administered—whether those of his personified attributes, or those of his human instruments. The highest objects set before these people were purity of life and rectitude of conduct. Their highest aspirations were directed to the glory and favor of God in this life, and acceptance by him hereafter. Their conceptions of death were that it was a passage to an eternal existence, where a divine benefactor, sent to dispense the mercies of the Supreme, had gone before them, having submitted to death, in order to overcome the power of evil, and who had, therefore, been raised from among the dead, when his probation in Hades was ended, and made the eternal Judge of the living and the dead. Those whom he judged favorably had their names written in the book of Life, and were brought to taste of the tree of Life, which would make them to be as gods; after which they were to enjoy such bliss as it has not entered into men's hearts to conceive. The wicked were meanwhile to undergo shame and anguish till they had expiated the very last sin, or were to be destroyed.

They believed the creation to have taken place as they annually saw re-creation take place. They said that the Spirit of the Supreme moved on the face of the waters; and that the dry land appeared at his bidding, yielding vegetation first, and then animals. They believed in a substantial firmament, wherein the sun and moon were placed, which were privileged to travel, with the spirits of the virtuous in their train, through a long series of Mansions in the great abode of the Supreme. They taught that every mind, whether of man or brute, was an emanation from the Supreme; and that the body was only its abode and instrument; the soul being, from its nature and derivation, immortal.

Such were the Ideas transmitted to other countries and to future races by this very ancient people. That such were their ideas, we know by a far surer medium than tradition—though that also is not wanting. By the hearing of the ear, and the sympathy of the mind, they transmitted these Ideas in their living force. By their sculptures, their paintings and their legends, they immutably recorded them.

All knowledge is sacred. All truth is divine. It is not for us to mix up passion and prejudice with our perception of new facts. We may not like to be perplexed by new knowledge which throws us out of some notions which we took for knowledge before. We are apt to feel our own spiritual privileges lessened by its appearing that they were held for many ages before the time which we had supposed. It might be enough to leave the minds of students of the past to subside and grow tranquil, (as minds always do, sooner or later,) in the sublime presence of facts; but I would just ask whether the great guiding Ideas of mankind are the more or the less venerable for having wrought for some thousands of years longer than we had imagined; and whether it is or is not a testimony to the power of those Ideas that they raised into spiritual light a race which thereby became the greatest in the ancient world, preserved their empire through a longer duration than that of any other known people, and were made the source of enlightenment to nations then and still unborn. If, weak in our partial knowledge, and in the prejudices of our whole lives, we need reconciling to the facts of the Egyptian history of Mind, I think these testimonies to the power and saving character of these venerable Ideas may have a cheering efficacy, and can have no other.

Here, as I said, the volume of ancient Egyptian history was closed to us. We had Cairo before our eyes as we rode away, and found letters from England on board our boat—happy letters which were a rebuke to our anxiety—at least I may say this for myself.

We were not injuriously fatigued by our most successful excursion; rather tired in the evening, and very stiff the next day; but nobody ill, and everybody well satisfied. It was no satisfaction to any of us that our Nile voyage was over; but this was an inevitable misfortune; and we bore it as well as we could.

CHAPTER XX

INUNDATION OF THE NILE—FAMINE IN EGYPT

WE HEAR SO MUCH OF THE REGULARITY of the overflow of the Nile, that we are apt to forget that it may fail, or to contemplate the consequences in such a case. It is true, we read of the seven years of famine in Joseph's time; but we think of that as a kind of miracle, and do not ask whether such a misfortune ever happened again, when a less sagacious and politic minister than Joseph was at the head of affairs. There is some information extant about this; and it maybe of sufficient interest to justify us in dwelling upon it a little.

It is amusing to observe how, according to Herodotus, the Egyptians and Greeks pitied each other for their respective ways of having their lands watered. The priests told Herodotus of a time when a rise of eight cubits sufficed to water the land below Memphis; whereas "now," he says,[160] "if the river does not rise sixteen cubits.[161] or at least fifteen, it does not cover the fields. If the land continues to rise in the same proportion,"—(a proportion which he calculated on mistaken dates, as the event has shown,) "and to receive the same augmentations as hitherto, the Nile no longer covering it with its waters, it seems to me that the Egyptians who dwell below Lake Maris, and in other districts, and especially in what is called the Delta, must continually experience at last the same fate as that with which they suppose the Greeks to be threatened, sooner

---

160   Herod. II. 13.

161   The priests were possibly speaking of a different measure from the cubit of the time of Herodotus. The cubit originally signified the length from the bend of the elbow to the end of the middle finger. It is believed that among Hebrews there were two cubit-measures; — one of 18 inches, and the other of 21 inches. Sir G. Wilkinson gives the cubit at the Nilometer at Elephantine as measuring 1 3/5 ft.—i.e. 19 ½ inches. There were 28 digits in a cubit.

or later; for, having learned that the whole of Greece is watered by rains, and not by the inundation of the rivers, as in their country, they say that if the Greeks should ever be disappointed of their hopes, they would run the risk of perishing miserably by famine. By this they mean to convey that if, instead of raining in Greece, there should come a drought, they would die of hunger, because they have no other resource than the waters of the sky. —This reflection of the Egyptians upon the Greeks is just; but now let us see to what extremity they themselves may be reduced. If it should happen, as I said before, that the region below Memphis, which is that which receives accumulations, should go on rising as it has done hitherto, must it not certainly happen that the Egyptians who inhabit it must experience the horrors of famine, since it does not rain in their country, and the river can no longer overspread their fields? But there is nobody now, in the rest of Egypt, or even in the whole world, who obtains a harvest with less care and toil."—After all these wise and kind apprehensions on each other's account, the people of neither of the two countries have seen the other lapse into desert, or the inhabitants exterminated by a permanent failure of water. Seedtime and harvest have not yet ceased. —In Egypt, however, they have intermitted; and terrible have those seasons been. Abdallatif's account of one of them is dreadful to read, at the end of nearly seven centuries.

One is filled with astonishment at the constancy of the overflow, and the regularity of its amount, when one learns what are the consequences of a small diminution or excess of the ordinary quantity; and perhaps it is as perplexing to men of science as to other people that such regularity should accrue from any such sources as those to which the inundation of the Nile has yet been attributed. If the Messrs. Abbadie should return in safety to Europe, to tell us what they believe they have discovered respecting the fountains of the Nile, we may know something ere long which may relieve our perplexity. Meantime, it appears to us one of the chief wonders of the natural world that the mountains of Abyssinia should so punctually gather the clouds about them, and entice the rains, as to send out streams of the same force, which shall water two thousand miles of country to within a few inches of the same height, and a few hours of the same time, year by year, for as many ages as are known to man.

The highest point reached by the inundation, and very rarely reached, is a little above nineteen cubits. In this case, much cultivable land remains so long submerged that the sowing cannot take place; and it is as barren as a desert for that year, while some spots which are ordinarily dry yield a harvest for once. Of course, there is a great destruction of dwellings and of stock in this case. When the rise reaches eighteen cubits, there is great rejoicing, for the produce is then sufficient for two years' consumption, after the government dues are paid. When it reaches sixteen cubits, there is enough produce for the wants of the year; and this was called, in Abdallatif's time, "the Sultaun's flood," because then the Sultaun claimed his taxes. Below sixteen cubits, there is more or less scarcity. In such a case the south wind has prevailed: and in good years, the north.

The lowest Nile ever known seems to have been that of A.D. 966, when the waters rose only to twelve cubits, seventeen digits: and the next lowest was in A.D. 1199, when it rose only four digits higher. For four centuries before the earliest of these dates, the Nile had only six times failed to reach fourteen cubits; and about twenty times only had it stopped short of fifteen cubits. The inundation begins about the twenty-fifth of June, and reaches its height in three months. It remains stationary about twelve days, and then begins to subside.

Niebuhr gives a full account of popular methods of divination as to what the Nile will be pleased to do that year. The Mohammedans believe, he says, [162] that the fall of a drop of water from heaven upon a place in Abyssinia is the cause of the inundation; and that this drop falls on the night of the 17th and 18th of June. As the Mohammedan months vary, they use the Coptic time for this calculation. On that night, about every second house in Cairo had, in Niebuhr's time, a piece of paste laid out upon the roof; and if it was found heavier in the morning than at night, it was a settled matter that the Drop had fallen in Abyssinia, and that there would be a good Nile. We should suppose this to be owing to a heavy dew: but the people would have it that it was of no consequence whether the paste was laid out within the house or on the roof. Another method was to expose equal weights of dry Nile soil and water; if, in the morning, the earth had sucked up all the water, it would be a sterile year; if any remained, there would be a good flood. Niebuhr tried this experiment repeatedly; and there was always water remaining: whence he drew the conclusion that the soil of the valley will not absorb its own weight of water. Another popular method of divination was to set out on the house-tops at night, little paper-boxes containing a small portion of wheat. Each box was inscribed with the name of a Coptic month; and all were of equal weight. The box which was heaviest in the morning showed in what month the inundation would reach its height. As was natural, the people tried to learn a little more while they were about it; and some fortune-telling was joined with the other experiments. The best informed people laughed at the whole matter as an amusement of the women: but nevertheless, about every other house in Cairo had something laid out upon its roof on the night of the 17th of June. The Christians were in no way behind the Mohammedans in their experiments. They had their paste and their Nile soil, and their calculations of uncertain times, connecting their observances, however, with their

162   Voyage en Arabie, tom. 1. p. 104.

saints' days. They professed a caution greater than their neighbors thought of; declaring that unless three of their experiments yielded the same result, none were to be relied on.

The people dreaded falling stars at this time of year. Learned men said that if they all tended to the same point of the heavens, this indicated only what winds would prevail: and the winds are largely concerned in the inundation. Learned and ignorant seem to have agreed that if these meteors abounded in the whole sky, it was a forewarning of a low Nile; and also of political troubles. In A.D. 902, fiery meteors filled the air: and lo! the Nile rose only to thirteen cubits, and the dynasty of the Tooloonides was overthrown; the last of them reigning only ten days. Again, in A.D. 912, the same signs occurred, and were followed by scarcity and civil war. Abdallatif observes, after quoting the chronicler who tells these things, "These are certainly very strong indications; but they are common to all countries, and not peculiar to Egypt. But we observed the same things in this year (A.D. 1199). At the beginning of the year (Mohammedan) stars darted across the sky; and at the end, the waters were very low: and in this same year, the Sovereign who ruled in Egypt was dethroned by his uncle Melicaladel after they had been at war." He tells us elsewhere, however, that an ambassador from Abyssinia brought to Cairo, in August of that year, a letter from his sovereign, (about appointing a new Patriarch in the place of the one who had just died;) in which letter it was stated that the rains had that season been very moderate; and that this was the reason of the lowness of the Nile.

It is a sign of a bad inundation if the waters of the river have a green tinge and a bad odor at the time of the visible rise of the flood. The aquatic mosses and vegetable fibres which occasion this corrupt state of the water ought to be carried away quickly by the force of the current sweeping through, and washing out, the stagnant pools and nooks of the damp shores. It is a bad sign if the current is so low and lazy as merely to float this corruption. In the first year of dearth of which Abdallatif gives an account, the water was insufferable to the taste and smell; and all who could had recourse to well-water. He boiled the Nile water; but that only made it worse: and when he let a portion stand in a narrow-necked bottle, and then took off the scum, he found the water, though then clear as fetid as ever. This plague lasted, in that terrible year, all through June and July and part of August: and besides the putrid vegetable matter, there were worms and other creatures that swarm in stagnant water. Almost as soon as they were gone, the inundation reached its limit for that year. On the 9th of September, it stood no higher than twelve cubits, twenty-one digits; and it then began to decline. The inhabitants could scarcely have had time to fill their cisterns, which they do when the waters have become red (as they call it) and not before: that is, when they bring down earth in suspension, instead of decayed vegetation. After filtering, or when the earth has subsided, the water of the Nile is the finest conceivable. In the time of Abdallatif, the people sat watching the rise of the waters, as at this day: and terrible must have been the consternation when it appeared, on the 9th of September, that the scanty flood was already subsiding. Many thousands were watching there, who would presently be beyond the reach of mortal hope or fear, listening for the voice of the crier who would never proclaim another inundation. I will give, from Abdallatif, some account of the state of Egypt this year, —believing his to be the only detailed history we have of such a season in Egypt; and certain that every one must feel interest in having presented to him such a proof of the blessing that Joseph was to the nation of his time, in preserving them from such horrors as a single year of drought inevitably brings, when no preparation is made for it. I shall, however, omit the most horrible and disgusting details, as occasioning more pain than they would be worth to us in this place, though they could hardly be spared from their own.

"Under these circumstances," says Abdallatif,[163] "the year presented itself as a monster whose wrath must annihilate all the resources of life, and all the means of subsistence. There was no longer any hope of a further rise of the Nile; and already therefore the price of provisions had risen: the provinces were desolated by drought; the inhabitants foresaw an inevitable scarcity; and the fear of famine excited tumultuous commotions among them. The inhabitants of the villages and country estates repaired to the great provincial towns: large numbers emigrated to Syria, Magreb, Hedjaz, and Yemen, where they dispersed themselves on every hand, as did formerly the descendants of Saba. There was also an infinite number who sought retreat in the towns of Misr[164] and Cairo, where they experienced a frightful famine and mortality; for when the sun had entered Aries, the air had become corrupt, pestilence and a mortal contagion began to be felt; and the poor, pressed by a continually increasing famine, ate carrion, corpses, dogs and the dung of animals. They went further, even devouring little children. It was not an uncommon thing to surprise people with infants roasted or boiled. The commandant of the city caused all who committed this crime to be burned alive, as well as those who ate that meat. I myself saw in a basket an infant that had been roasted. It was brought to the magistrate; and with it a man and woman who were said to be its parents, and whom the magistrate sentenced to be burned alive.

163   Relation de l'Egypte, Livre II. ch. 2.

164   By Misr, Abdallatif throughout means Old Cairo, originally called Fostát. It was built by the Mohammedan conqueror of Egypt (A.D. 638), on the site of the Egyptian Babylon. The founder made it the capital and royal residence, which it continued to be for about two centuries and a half.

"In the month of Ramadhan, a corpse was found at Misr, which had been stripped of its flesh for food, and whose legs were tied, like those of a sheep prepared for cooking. Galen desired in vain to obtain a sight of such a skeleton; and there were no means that he did not attempt for the purpose. This spectacle has been no less sought by all who have devoted themselves to the study of anatomy.

"When the poor began to eat human flesh, the horror and astonishment caused by the practice were such that these crimes were the material of every one's conversation; and the subject seemed inexhaustible: but afterwards people became so accustomed to it, and such a relish began to spread for this detestable food, that some came to make it their ordinary meat, to eat it as a treat, and even to lay in a stock of it: different ways of preparing this flesh were made known: and the use of it being once introduced, the custom extended into the provinces, so that there was no part of Egypt where it might not be met with. Then it no longer caused any surprise; the horror which it bad at first in spired ceased to be felt; and people spoke and heard of it as an indifferent and ordinary thing."

In this indifference lay the best hope of the cessation of the practice; for it is usually found that monstrous practices which arise out of extremity spread like a diabolical fashion; and the distracted minds which are shaken by affliction find a sort of relief in the excitement of desperate practices: and when the strangeness and novelty are over, the habitual disgust and compunction are pretty sure to return. It appears in the later parts of Abdallatif's narrative that it was so in this instance. After citing come atrocious cases, he goes on to say—

"There were children of the poor, some in infancy and some growing up, who had no one to look after them and protect them, spread through all the quarters of the city, and in the narrowest streets, like locusts that are beaten down in the fields. Poor people, men and women, lay in wait for these wretched children, carried them off, and ate them. It was rarely that they could be detected in the very act, and when they were not on their guard. It was generally women who were so caught: a circumstance which, in my opinion, occurred only because women have less ingenuity ('finesse') than men, and cannot fly and hide themselves with so much readiness. In the space of a few days, as many as thirty women were burnt, every one of whom confessed that she had eaten several children. I saw one led before the magistrate, who had a roasted infant suspended from her neck. Two hundred stripes were inflicted upon her, to draw from her an avowal of her crime; but no reply could be wrung from her. It even appeared as if she had lost all the faculties which characterize human nature. Then she was led away by force, and she expired in the street."

Doubtless she was no longer human, but rendered brutish and idiotic by extremity. After telling how the bodies of the burnt criminals were eagerly sought, "as already cooked," and some other atrocities, our physician proceeds to relate the peculiar dangers of his medical brethren—

"Among the abandoned people, there were some who laid every sort of snare to surprise men, and to entrap them into their houses on false pretences. This was what happened to three physicians who were accustomed to visit me... The third was summoned by a man to accompany him to a sick person who lived, he said, in the Schari (the great street). As they went along, the man gave alms of small coin; and he said (out of the Kurán), It is to-day that there will be retribution, and a reward which shall double that that is given away. Let those who act, act in view of such a recompense. This was repeated so often, that the physician began to suspect some foul play. However, the good opinion he had of this man led him on; and besides, the desire of gain actuated him; and therefore he permitted himself to be introduced into a half-ruined mansion. Its appearance increased his alarm; and he stopped upon the staircase, while his guide went before him, and opened the door. A comrade came to meet them, and said, 'After keeping us so long, you have brought us good game, I hope.' These words struck terror into the heart of the physician. He leaped through an open window which he happily perceived, into a stable. The owner of the stable came, and asked him what was the matter: but the physician took good care not to tell him, not venturing to trust him. Then the man said to him, 'I know about your adventure: the people who live here surprise men and kill them.'"

It may be hoped that this was a mauvaise plaisanterie, appropriate to the time. But much that Abdallatif saw was only too real and indubitable. He says:

"If we were to relate all the anecdotes of this kind that we have heard told, or have seen with our own eyes, we should run the risk of being suspected of exaggeration, or accused of a too copious gossip. All the facts which we have related as eye-witnesses, have come under our notice without any design on our part, and without our having gone on purpose to the places where they were likely to happen: chance only made us witnesses of them; for, far from seeking them, we generally avoided the sight of them, so great was our horror of such things. Those, on the other hand, who were in the house of the magistrate, to be present at these tragic scenes, saw cases of this sort, of every kind and degree, all day and all night long."

"This frightful calamity which I have just represented, extended over all Egypt: there was not a single inhabited spot where the practice of eating human flesh did not become extremely common. Syene, Kous, the Faioum, Mahalleh, Alexandria, Damietta, and all other parts of Egypt, were witnesses of these scenes of horror. —A merchant, a friend of mine, a man on whom one may rely, told me, on his return from Alexandria, many facts of the nature of those which I have related, which had passed before his own eyes; and the most remarkable thing that he told me was that he had seen five children's heads in the same boiler, prepared with exquisite spices. And now, here is enough on this part of the subject, upon which, though I have enlarged a good deal, it appears to me that I have been very brief."

He then gives an account of the murders on the river and the roads; and continues:

"As for the number of the poor who perished from hunger and exhaustion, God alone knows what it was. What we shall say of it must be regarded only as a slight sketch which may convey some idea of the fearful excess reached by this mortality. One thing of which I may speak as having seen it myself, at Misr, at Cairo, and in the neighboring places, is that wherever one went, there was not a spot in which one's feet or one's eyes were not encountered by a corpse, or a man in the agonies of death, or even a great number in this dreadful state. Day by day, from one hundred to five hundred dead bodies were taken from Cairo, to be carried to the place where they might have funeral rites. At Misr the number of dead was incalculable. They were not buried, but merely cast out of the town. At last, there were not enough living left to carry away the dead, and they remained in the open air, among the houses and shops, or even in the interior of dwellings. You might see a corpse falling to pieces in the very place where a cook or a baker, or other tradesman, was carrying on his business.

"As for the suburbs and villages, all the inhabitants perished, except a small number, of whom a portion quitted their abodes to go somewhere else. We must scarcely except from what I have now said the capitals of the provinces, and the largest villages… A traveler often passed through a large village without seeing a single living inhabitant. He saw the houses standing open, and the corpses of those who had lived there stretched out opposite one another—some decayed, and some recently dead. Very often, there was a house full of furniture, without any one to take possession of it. What I am now saying has been communicated to me by several persons whose narratives confirmed each other. One of them said as follows: —'We arrived at a village, and there found no living thing, on the earth or in the air. Having entered the houses, the state in which the inhabitants appeared offered us an exact picture of what God says in this passage of the Kurán: We have mowed them all down, and exterminated them. We saw the inhabitants of each house extended dead, the husband, the wife, and the children. From thence we went to another village, where we were told that there had been till now four hundred weaving shops; and it presented to us the same scene of desolation as the first. We saw the weaver dead in his loom-pit, (Footnote: See p. 80.) and all his dead family round him. I was here reminded of that other text of the Kurán: One single cry was heard, and they all perished. We then proceeded,' says the same person, 'to another village, where we found things just in the same state; no creature living, and the inhabitants having all become the prey of death. As we were obliged to remain there, in order to sow the lands, we had to hire people to carry away the bodies, and throw them into the Nile, at the rate of a piece of silver [165] for every ten bodies. At last,' added this person, 'the wolves and hyænas succeeded to the inhabitants, feeding on their carcasses.'

"This is one of the most remarkable things which I myself saw," continues Abdallatif. "As I was one day, in company with several other persons, in a place which overlooked the Nile, there passed before our eyes, in the course of one hour, about ten corpses, swollen and puffed up like water-skins filled with air. We saw them by chance, not having directed our attention that way, and without commanding from our station the whole breadth of the Nile. The next day, being in a boat, we saw on the canal and on all the banks, scattered limbs like— to use a comparison of the poet Amrialkaïs—'the roots of bulbous plants which have been drawn out of the ground.' I have heard of a fisherman of the port of Tennis who saw pass near him, in a single day, four hundred corpses which the waters of the river carried with them to the sea.

"According to the testimony of a great number of witnesses, the road between Egypt and Syria was like a vast field sown with human bodies; or rather, like a plain which has just been swept by the scythe of the mower. It had become as a banquet-hall for the birds and wild beasts which gorged themselves on their flesh; and the very dogs that these fugitives had taken with them, to share their exile, were the first to devour their bodies.

"The inhabitants of the Hauf," (a district to the east of the Nile, below Cairo,) "when they retired into Syria to find pasturage, were the first who perished upon this road; long as it is, it was strewn with their corpses, like locusts which have been broiled" (by the fires lighted to smoke them down); "and to this moment, some are yet perishing there. The emigration transported some to Mosul, to Bagdad, to the countries of Korasan, of the Greek empire, of Africa, and of Yemen; and they were dispersed into all parts. It often happened that, among this crowd of emigrants, a woman slipped away from her children, and thus abandoned the unhappy little creatures, who were tormented by hunger till death put an end to their sufferings."

165   The value of these "pieces" of gold and silver has varied largely; but Mr. Lane, in his notes to the "Arabian Nights," advises us to suppose them to average, —the piece of gold, half a guinea or ten shillings, and the piece of silver about six-pence.

After a dreadful notice of the sale for bread of people of condition, Abdal-latif tells us what he considers the most wonderful thing in the whole history; a thing which to us does not appear wonderful at all; that, notwithstanding such a complexity of woes as distinctly revealed the wrath of God, men continued to adore the idols of their criminal passions without any amendment, and still wallowed in the sea of their sins. He seems to be unaware that the tempting devils of human passions are roused and exasperated and hardened by such hopeless misery as leaves them nothing more to fear from the anger of God, which, in such a season, becomes to them a mere empty name.

He next tells us of the strange appearance of a multitude of dwellings without any one to inhabit them. "I ought not," he says, "to omit noticing the depopulation of towns and villages, and the desertion of the unpeopled houses and shops: —this last trait belongs to the picture which I have undertaken to draw Even at Cairo, the mansions, the houses, and the shops situated in the heart of the town, and in the best quarters, are for the most part, empty or deserted, so that, in the most frequented part of this capital there is a mansion composed of more than fifty apartments which have all remained empty except four, where some people are lodged to take care of the place. The inhabitants of Cairo at the present time use no other fuel for their hearths and ovens than rafters, doors, and posts. —It is, however, a thing well worthy of wonder that, among people who had always before been unfortunate, there are some who have made a fortune this year. Some have amassed wealth by trade in corn; others by coming to rich inheritances: some others have grown wealthy without any one knowing how. Blessed be He who distributes or withholds his gifts according to His good pleasure, and who gives a share of His favors to all creatures!"

As the waters were so low previous to the inundation of this year as to leave the Nilometer completely dry, it is obvious that the flood must be again inadequate, unless a most unusual amount of water came down. And it was inadequate: yet the account of the second year leaves the reader consoled and hopeful; so that I will give a few passages, which are also necessary to the completeness of the narrative.

Not only did the Nile cease to flow at the base of the Nilometer on the Geezeh side; it left a long and broad island, where fragments of ancient constructions were observed. I wish Abdallatif had told us what these ancient constructions appeared to be. If he had, we might have learned some secrets about the bed of the river, and about the changes of its course. The corruption of the water was very great this year. The inundation took place languidly, sometimes stopping; and once, for three days, when the people gave up all for lost, and prepared themselves for total destruction. This was on the 9th of August. But it rose again, at irregular intervals, till the 4th of September, when it reached fifteen cubits, sixteen digits. It began to sink the same day, before the ground could imbibe much of the benefit, and declined so rapidly that not nearly all the districts felt the inundation, and some of those very scantily. Abdallatif observes, "One would have said that it was only the phantom of the inundation which had visited them, like those spectres that we imagine we see in a dream, and which immediately vanish. Only the level lands profited by the inundation: and the lower provinces, as Garbiyyeh and some others, were sufficiently watered: but the villages were entirely emptied of cultivators and laborers. This text of the Kurán might be applied to them, The next morning nothing was seen of them but their habitations. The rich collected their scattered dependents, and brought together the few laborers who remained to them. Laborers and cattle were so rare that a bull in good condition was sold for seventy pieces of gold; and one which was in poor plight for a little less. —In the greater part of the country districts, the waters retired too soon, and before the lands had been duly soaked, because there was no one to shut in the waters, and detain them upon the fields; and this was the reason why such lands remained untitled, though they had partaken of the inundation. Many which had been watered enough remained fallow, because the proprietors could neither provide the seed nor pay the expenses of cultivation. Of the fields which were sown, many were laid waste by the vermin which devoured the seed: and of the seed which escaped this destruction, much gave out only a weak blade which presently perished.

"It is from God that consolation must be looked for: for it is He who, by His goodness and liberality, determines happy events."

Till the middle of the second year, everything continued to grow worse. "Fewer poor perished," says Abdallatif,[166] "not because the cause of their destruction was altered, but only because they were reduced to a small number. —The practice of eating human flesh became less common; and at last we heard no more of it. The provisions exposed for sale in the market were more rarely stolen, because vagabonds had almost disappeared from the town. The price of provisions fell till the ardeb of wheat[167] was sold for three pieces of gold, (it had been five,) "but this abatement of price was owing to the small number of consumers, and not to the abundance of food. The city was relieved by the loss of the greater part of its population; and all that it contained was reduced in the same proportion. People became accustomed to the dearness of provisions; and by dint of enduring famine, they had, as it were, contracted the habit, like that of a natural state of things."

... "I have been assured that there had previously been at Misr nine hundred machines for weaving mats; and that now only fifteen remained. We have

166   Relation de l'Egypte, Livre II. Ch. 3.
167   A little under five bushels.

only to apply the same proportion to the other trades which are carried on in that town; to the shop-keepers, bakers, grocers, shoemakers, tailors and other artisans. The numbers employed in each of these were reduced in the same proportion as the mat weavers; or in a greater.

"Fowls failed altogether, except a few which were brought from Syria. I have heard that an inhabitant of Egypt, seeing himself reduced to indigence, was, as it were, inspired by God to buy a hen, which he caused to be brought from Syria, and for which he paid sixty pieces of gold. He sold it again at Cairo, for eight hundred pieces of gold, to the people whose business is to rear fowls. When the eggs appeared, they were bought for a piece of silver each: —afterwards, two, three, and then four eggs might be had for that money; and this was the price which was sustained. A chicken sold for a hundred pieces of silver; and the price remained for a long time as high as a piece of gold, and more. —The ovens were heated with the wood taken from empty mansions. Those who had ovens bought a mansion for a very low price, and used the partitions and the rafters, which served them for a time to heat their ovens: when this resource was exhausted, they bought another mansion. There were some among them who, regarding only the baseness of their feelings, got into the houses in the night, and took their provision of food, without meeting anybody who could oppose their thievery. —It often happened that a mansion continued empty, nobody remaining there but the proprietor: and for want of finding any one who would purchase it, he himself took the joists, the doors, and all the furniture, which he sold: and then he abandoned the dismantled place. The same was done with houses which were hired, —As for the villages round Cairo, and in the provinces, they are now merely a fearful solitude. One may travel for several days together, and in all directions, without meeting a single living creature; —nothing but corpses. —A great mortality and pestilence happened again in the Faioum, in the province of Garbiyyeh, and at Damietta and Alexandria. It was the time of sowing that this scourge was at the worst; and there were instances where many laborers perished successively at the same plough. It was related to me how the cultivators who sowed the seed were not those who had prepared the land: and that again, it was a different set who gathered the harvest. —I myself saw the sowing done for one of the principal lords: he sent people to do it: then, having found that they were all dead, he sent others: and the greater part of these died also. This happened over and over again, in various districts. —Persons who may be relied on informed me that at Alexandria, on one single Friday, the Imaum had uttered the funeral prayers over seven hundred bodies: and that the same inheritance had passed to fourteen heirs in succession over the course of a month: and also that above twenty thousand inhabitants of that city had left it, had retired to the province of Barka, had established themselves there, and had rendered that region flourishing."

On the 20th of May, "there happened a violent earthquake, which filled every one with terror. Every one leaped from his bed, and uttered cries of supplication to the all-powerful God. The movement remained a long time; the shocks were like the motion of a sieve or riddle, or like that which a bird makes in flapping its wings. There were in all three violent shocks, which shook the buildings, made the doors rattle, and the rafters and roof tremble: and the dwellings which were in bad condition or in a lofty situation seemed doomed to destruction. There were more shocks towards noon of the same day; but they were felt by few persons, because they were gentle and soon over. It has been extremely cold that night, so as to compel us to cover ourselves more warmly than usual: to this temperature succeeded the next day an extreme heat, and an excessive pestilential wind which intercepted respiration, and was positively suffocating. Such an earthquake as this is rarely known in Egypt. We afterwards learned by tidings which arrived from many quarters, that the earthquake was felt at the same hour in distant countries, and in villages a long way off. I consider it certain that at the same moment a great part of the world felt the shock, from Kous to Damietta, Alexandria, the coast of Syria, and indeed the whole of Syria, in all its length and breadth. Many inhabited places disappeared altogether, without any trace whatever being left of them, and an innumerable multitude of people perished. I know of no place in all Syria which suffered less than Jerusalem: that city suffered very little damage. The ravages caused by this event were much greater in the countries inhabited by the Franks than in those occupied by the Mussulmans."

"The following fact is one of the most remarkable of all that I witnessed. Several persons among those who diligently visited me to confer with me on medicine, having got as far as the Treatise on Anatomy (of Galen) found it difficult to understand me, as I found it difficult to make myself understood by them, because there is a great difference between a verbal description and the inspection of the objects themselves. Having learned that there was at Maks a hill on which human remains had accumulated in great quantity, we went there; and we saw a mound of considerable extent composed of the remains of human bodies: there was more of them than of the soil: and we could reckon that there were twenty thousand corpses, and, more that could be perceived by the eye. They might be distinguished into different classes, according to age." And then he proceeds to give an anatomical lecture.

"When from a height we looked down," he continues, "upon the place called the Basin, and which is a considerable hollow, we saw skulls, some white, some black, and others of a deep brown: they were in layers, and heaped up in such a quantity that they covered up the other bones: one would have said that there were only heads without bodies: and one might suppose that one saw

melons which had been gathered, and which were thrown into a pile, as we
heap sheaves upon a granary floor. Some days afterwards I saw them again: the
sun had dried the flesh: the skulls had become white, and I compared them to
ostriches' eggs piled together. When I contemplated on the one hand the solitude which reigned in the streets and markets of Misr, and on the other these
plains and hills which vomited corpses, I represented to myself a caravan which
had quitted the spot where it had encamped, and had removed to another place.
Moreover, this was not the only scene which offered such a spectacle: wherever
one went, the same scene was presented; and often a much more frightful one."

"We will now briefly declare the state of the Nile for this year. The waters
had considerably sunk in the month of January; and they continued to sink
till men and horses could pass the river by fording in several places. It was in
Ramadhan that the river was at its lowest point: its bed was left dry, below
Mikyas, to the distance of about eight hundred cubits. Ebn-Abi'braddad ascertained the height of the water at Mikyas on the 18th of June; it was a cubit and
a half: whereas the year before it stood at two cubits on that day. Last year too,
the river had begun to rise on this day: but now we had to wait till the 19th of
July. In all this interval, the river had risen only four digits; so that there was a
very bad opinion of the inundation for this year; the despair was general; people imagined that something extraordinary had happened to the sources of the
Nile, and in the places through which it passes. However, the river now began
sensibly to rise: so that at the end of Epiphi (July) its height was three cubits.
At this time the waters ceased to rise for two days, which caused extreme terror;
because such a pause was contrary to ordinary experience. But soon after the
waters came in great abundance; they rose by strides, and one might have said
that mountains of water leaped upon one another. In the space of ten days, the
river rose eight cubits, three of which were continuous, without any pause at all.
On the 1st of September the greatest height was reached, which was one digit
under sixteen cubits. After remaining for two days at this height, the waters
began to decline slowly, and to flow away very gradually.

"Here is what I had to say of the circumstances of the horrible scourge
whose history I have narrated. I shall, therefore, finish here this section and the
whole book. Praise be to God, the Sovereign Master of the universe! May God
be favorable to the Prince of his messengers, to Mohammed the Prophet without learning, and to his holy and honorable descendants!"

Such was the dearth of the years A.D. 1199-1202. Such was the temporary victory gained by the pertinacious old Desert over the struggling Nile.
The history suggests many thoughts; —much admiration of the sagacity and
administrative ability of Joseph in saving the Egyptian nation of his day from a
fate as much worse even than the above related, as their numbers were greater

in the ages of the national glory than ever afterwards. Much do we wonder, too, whether Joseph was guided by any precedent; and how far by the prophecies of science. We should like to know whether, as he grew up in his new country, he heard traditionary accounts of the horrors of drought in the valley; and whether, in such a case, he applied himself to learn the premonitory signs of the calamity. Much do we wonder whether the ancient race was ever thus nearly swept away; whether the priestly watchmen ever looked abroad from the top of their propyla over plains sown with human bones instead of sprouting seed, and whether they called together the few survivors to sacrifice to Osiris, to bring him back from his absence or displeasure to his favorite valley. Much should we like to know from what depth of ages the greatest of intermittent springs had regularly gushed forth, to give life to an expecting nation, waiting in hope along a line of two thousand miles. The priests who expressed to Herodotus such anxious fears for the Greeks, because of their dependence upon the clouds could hardly have known of any such drought as could parallel that of A.D. 1300, or they would have moderated their boasting, even if they had concealed the fact. Among the few historical notices which remain appended by Manetho to the names of the kings, such as "During this reign" (first king of the Second Dynasty), "a great landslip took place at Bubastis, and many perished," I am not aware that any relate to a failure of the Nile; or that there is any where a hint of even a tradition of such a famine as Abdallatif witnessed. It is probable that, in the days of high Egyptian civilization, when Egypt was the granary of the world, better precautions were taken than by succeeding races of inhabitants. It seems more probable that men so able as that old Egyptian aristocracy, should have kept ample stores of food in reserve, than that the Nile should never have failed through several thousand years; or than that the memory of a great famine should have been lost in the time of Herodotus.

Here, then, we leave the Nile, which has been the thread of our discourse thus far. It has been before me, with all its antique interest, and all its fresh young beauty, during whatever I have written to this point; and I must hope that my readers have caught some sensations of that interest, and some glimpses of that beauty, as they have followed me. We shall see no more of it now, except as a mere line noticed from the citadel of Cairo, and as a mournful parting vision on the evening of our first encampment in the Desert. — And now, to Cairo!

CHAPTER XXI

CAIRO—STREETS AND BAZAARS—MOSQUES—CITADEL—
FETE OF THE BIRTH OF THE PROPHET—ENTRANCE OF THE
MAHHMIL— THE MAGICIAN—SOCIETY IN CAIRO—MR. LANE

THERE ARE FEW GAYER THINGS IN LIFE, for one who chooses to be gay, than a visit to Cairo. The stranger must use a few precautions against the disturbance of his gayety; and then he may surrender himself to the most wonderful and romantic dream that can ever meet his waking senses. The most wonderful and romantic, —because there is nothing so wonderful and romantic in the whole social world as an Arabian city; and Cairo is the queen of Arabian cities. Damascus is usually ranked with Cairo; but, full of charms as Damascus is, (as we may see by and by,) it is charming for other reasons than its virtues as an Arabian city; on which ground it cannot for a moment stand a comparison with Cairo. The precautions against seriousness which a stranger must take are, first, to forget that he is in Egypt; to avoid looking over westwards to the Pyramids, or too far southwards, lest an array of old Egyptian ghosts should marshal themselves on the horizon, and cast a shadow of solemnity over his thoughts. He must also shake off any considerate humanity which may hang about him, and avoid inquiring what lies beneath what he sees, or thinking of any people but those whom he meets in the bazaars. A butterfly may enjoy a glorious day in hovering about an array of flower-baskets, not caring whether the flowers are growing or stuck into wet sand; and the stranger in Cairo may have a short season of transport, if he will only take up with the shows of things, and forget the roots.

The mere spectacle of the streets I relished more and more to the last. As for the rest, I could not keep my heart and mind in abeyance for many days; and before I left, I felt that there is hardly a spot in what I have seen of the countries of the world where I would not rather live than in Cairo. The more I liked the

Arabs, and the more I admired their gem of a city, the more impossible I felt it would be to live there, for any other reason than a strong call of duty. The mere spectacle of the streets became, however, as I said, more bewitching every day.

After an early cup of coffee, we usually mounted our donkeys for a ride of two hours before the table-d'hôte breakfast. I like donkey-riding in Cairo. I never tried it out of Egypt, except for a few miles in Palestine; but I do not suppose it is the same thing anywhere else.

The creatures are full of activity, and their amble is a pleasant pace in the streets. Side-saddles, more or less tattered, may be hired with Cairo donkeys now. Mrs. Y. took her saddle from England, and I was fortunate enough to buy one, in good repair, on my arrival at Cairo, which would serve for either horse or donkey. The little rogues of donkey-boys were always ready and eager, close by the hotel—hustling each other to get the preference—one displaying his English with "God save the queen ros bif;" another smiling amiably in one's face; and others kicking and cuffing, as people who had a prior right, and must relieve us of encroachers. Then off we went briskly through the Ezbekeeyeh, under the acacias, past the water-carriers, with their full skins on their left shoulder, and the left hand holding the orifice of the neck, from which they could squirt water into the road, or quietly fill a jar at pleasure; past the silent smoking party, with their long chibouques or serpentine nargeelehs; past the barber, shaving the head of a man kneeling and resting his crown on the barber's lap; past the veiled woman with her tray of bread—thin, round cakes; past the red and white striped mosque, where we looked up to the gallery of the minaret, in hope of the muezzin coming out to call the men to prayer; past a handsome house or two, with its rich lattices, its elaborate gate way, and its shade of trees in front, or of shrubs within the court, of which we might obtain a tempting glimpse; past Shepherd's hotel, where English gentlemen might be seen going in and out, or chatting before the door; past a row of artisan dwellings, where the joiner, the weaver, and the maker of slippers were at work, with their oriental tools, and in their graceful Oriental postures—and then into the bazaars. But before I had reached the bazaars, I was generally in a state of vexation with myself for my carelessness about surrounding objects. I hardly know what it is in these Eastern countries which disposes one to reverie; but I verily thought, the whole journey through, and especially at Cairo, that I was losing my observing faculties—so often had I to rouse myself, or to be roused by others, to heed what was before my eyes. I did not find it so on our route to Egypt, nor in crossing France on our return; so, my own experience would lead me to suppose that there is something in the aspect of Oriental life and scenery which meets and stimulates some of one's earliest and deepest associations, and engages some of one's higher mental faculties too much to leave the lower free. The conflict was not agreeable, however; the longing to have for one's own forever every exquisite feature of the scene, and presently the discovery that one had passed through half a dozen alleys without seeing anything at all; and all for pondering something which might be as well thought over at home! By dint of incessant self-flapping and endless rides, however, I arrived at last at knowing and remembering almost every peculiar object in Cairo—of such, I mean, as offer themselves to the eye in the streets. I really do not know how I can convey my own impression of what I saw so well as in the words of my memoranda put down at the time. "Cairo streets are wholly indescribable— their narrowness, antiquity, sharp lights, and arcades of gloom, carved lattices, mat awnings, mixture of hubbub and fatalist quietude in the people, to whom loss of sight appears a matter of course—the modes of buying and selling—all are in my mind, but cannot be set down." Again. "Went with my party to shop—a most amusing affair. I bought a Tuscan straw hat for 4s. 6d., while a common and not large saucepan, copper tinned, was priced 12s. It was awkward waiting while Mr. E. bought brown shoes, —the way was so narrow, and our donkeys were five, and horses and laden camels were continually passing, thrusting us among the very merchandize; and then there was the smart and repeated crack of the courbash which gives warning that a carriage is coming, and that we must plunge into the nearest alley; and then there was a cart or two; and all the while there was some staring, though not much, and clouds of flies from a fruiterer's shop." The tranquil slowness with which the tradespeople (who all looked, to my eyes, like kings and princes in fairy tales) served any one of us gave all the rest many such opportunities of observation. One of the drollest incidents of this kind befell when the gentlemen were in search of some eastern garments for their desert ride. We ladies, with the aid of our dragoman, made our purchases and returned to the tailor's —stood, sat, inquired into the meaning of everything within sight, and wondered at the long delay. It ended in the amusement of finding that the gentle men had obtained nothing but a lesson, and some practice in trying on eastern garments. After a world of effort, and of tying and hooking, and inquiring of prices, it came out that the clothes were second-hand; and they were pulled off much more quickly than they were put on.

Carriages are quite alarming in Cairo, which was not built for the passage of anything so large. They are very peremptory, having no idea of stopping for anybody. Notice of their approach is given by the crack of the courbash of the outrider who precedes them, and any one who does not get out of the way on that signal must take the consequences. On comes the vehicle, jolting and rocking, and filling the narrow way; and young and old, blind and seeing, must squeeze themselves up against the bazaar front; and a loaded camel must meet the shock as it may. It is worse, however, to ride in one than to meet it. In our drive to the hareem which we visited, we were kept in a continual agony, so many were the people we drove against. The keeping of carriages was much on the increase before there was any pro vision for them. A friend of mine found one in his street when he went to live there, four years and a half before my visit; and now there are twenty-four or twenty-five, making the passage of the street very hazardous. Since I left Cairo, a wide street has been begun, extending from the Ezbekeeyeh to the Citadel—a great convenience to the Pasha and the Franks, but a ruinous innovation upon the oriental appearance of the city. The Frank residents, however, now give up the orientalism of Cairo; and I was perpetually told by them that I was looking at a half-European city—but my own impression is that it is as like as possible to the pictures in the Arabian Nights—so that, of all the cities that I have seen, Cairo is the one which may be the most easily imagined at a distance, in a superficial way, provided the notions of a mosque, a bazaar and an eastern house are once obtained from pictures. The one unimaginable circumstance is the atmosphere. No conception of the light, shade, and color can be conveyed; and they are an hourly surprise to the stranger in Cairo, to the last.

The mosques are extremely interesting; partly from their architectural beauty; more so from their purposes, and the pleasure of seeing those purposes fulfilled. Nothing charmed me so much about them as the spectacle of the houseless poor, who find a refuge there. In the noble mosque of Sultaun Hasan, when we had mounted a long flight of steps from the street, and more stairs which led to the barrier where we must put on slippers, we entered a vast court, sacred to all who have hearts, whether they be heathens, Mohammedans or Christians, for the solace and peace which are to be found there. The greater part of this court was open to the sky; its floor was of inlaid marble; and in the centre was the tank where the worshipers perform their ablutions before praying. The steps to the roofed platform at the upper end were matted; and on these steps some men were at prayer. On the platform sat a man making a garment, —spreading out his cloth upon the mat, and running the seams, as much at his ease as if he had been in a home of his own. This was a homeless man; and here he was welcome. Several poor people were sitting talking cheerfully; and under this roof, and on this mat, they were welcome to sleep, if they had no other place of rest. Some children were at play quietly on the marble pavement. We are accustomed to say that there is no respect of persons, and that all men are equal, within the walls of our churches; but I never felt this so strongly in any Christian place of worship as in this Mohammedan one, with its air of freedom, peace, and welcome to all the faithful. I felt myself an intruder there, in a retreat which should be kept sacred for those who go to it, not as a church, but as a religious home. —Still, good as it seems for the people to be there, and happy as appears the provision for them, they are sighing, as people everywhere are always sighing, for the return of their golden age. This reverting propensity seems common to all men; and every race seems to have had its golden age. Our dragoman pointed to a medallion in the interior, three feet in diameter, and told us that in Sultaun Hasan's time, "bread of the size of that was to be had for a para."—We reached this interior from the platform, through a magnificent portal of cast metal of beautiful pattern. In the centre of the vast chamber was the Sultaun's tomb, railed round. On the tomb lay a tattered, but very fine old copy of the Kurán; and some Syrian lamps were beside it. The decorations of the walls and corners must once have been magnificent, some elaborate wood carving remaining which shows traces of gilding and color. The best account of a mosque that I know is that of Mr. Milnes in his "Palm Leaves;" a book, the value and beauty of which can be appreciated only during or after a visit to the East. As his poem of "the Mosque" may not have met the eye, or fixed the attention, of all my readers, I venture to give part of it here. Any one who is acquainted with it will not be sorry to fall in with it again: —

"A simple unpartitioned room, —

Surmounted by an ample dome,
Or, in some lands that favored lie,
With centre open to the sky,
But roofed with arched cloisters round,
That mark the consecrated bound,
And shade the niche to Mekkeh turned,
By which two massive lights are burned;
With pulpit whence the sacred word
Expounded on great days is heard;
With fountains fresh, where, ere they pray,
Men wash the soil of earth away;
With shining minaret, thin and high,
From whose fine trellised balcony,
Announcement of the hours of prayer
Is uttered to the silent air;
Such is the Mosque—the holy place,
Where faithful men of every race,
Meet at their ease arid face to face.

"Not that the power of God is here
More manifest, or more to fear;
Not that the glory of his face

Is circumscribed by any space;
But that, as men are wont to meet
In court or chamber, mart or street,
For purposes of gain or pleasure,
For friendliness or social leisure, —
So for the greatest of all ends
To which intelligence extends,
The Created worship of the Lord, whose will
Created and sustains us still,
And honor of the Prophet's name,
By whom the saving message came,
Believers meet together here,
And hold these precincts very dear.

"The floor is spread with matting neat,
Unstained by touch of shodden feet, —
A decent and delightful seat!
Where after due devotions paid,
And legal ordinance obeyed,
Men may in happy parlance join,
And gay with serious thought combine;
May ask the news from lands away,
May fix the business of today;
Or, with "God willing," at the close,
To-morrow's hopes and deeds dispose.

"Children are running in and out,
With silver-sounding laugh and shout,
No more disturbed in their sweet play,
No more disturbing those that pray,
Than the poor birds that fluttering fly
Among the rafters there on high,
Or seek at times, with grateful hop,
The corn fresh-sprinkled on the top.

"So, lest the stranger's scornful eye
Should hurt this sacred family, —
Lest inconsiderate words should wound
Devout adorers with their sound, —
Lest careless feet should stain the floor
With dirt and dust from out the door, —

Tis well that custom should protect
The place with prudence circumspect,
And let no unbeliever pass
The threshold of the faithful mass;
That as each Muslim his Hareem
Guards even from a jealous dream,
So should no alien feeling scathe
This common home of public faith,
So should its very name dispel
The presence of the infidel."

The Pasha's new mosque at the citadel is a building magnificent for space, and in its position: and I hope he will see it finished before the time comes for him to be laid in it. It is a great enterprise; and this, mosque will henceforth be a striking feature to the stranger in the aspect of Cairo. But I must think the use of alabaster for the interior of the court a great mistake. However beautiful this veined alabaster is in small portions, its effect is not good in the mass. I never looked round that court without being reminded of dirty soap-suds. The streaky and mottled character of the alabaster utterly destroys the impression of grandeur which the architecture would otherwise give. And, what is worse, it is a crumbling material. Little kernels are falling out, and corners are broken off, and the sharpness of edges is gone already, before the work is half done. One might almost as well build a sculptured and pillared hall of chalk. The interior of this mosque is of vast dimensions, and must be truly imposing when finished.

It is from this eminence, —from the terrace of the citadel—that that view is obtained which is by some declared to be unsurpassed by any in the known world. On the whole, I prefer the view of Damascus from the Salaheeyeh to that of Cairo from the terrace of the citadel: but elsewhere I certainly should not know how to find a parallel for it.

I would entreat any stranger to see this view first in the evening, — before sunset. I saw it three times or more. In the morning there was much haze in the distance, and a sameness of color which hurt the eye. At noon there was no color at all: all color being discharged in the middle of the day in Egypt, except in shady places. In the evening the beauty is beyond description. The vastness of the city, as it lies stretched below, surprises every one. It looks a perfect wilderness of flat roofs, cupolas, minarets, and palm tops, with an open space here and there, presenting the complete front of a mosque, and gay groups of people, and moving camels, —a relief to the eye, though so diminished by distance. The aqueduct is a most striking feature, running off for miles. The City of Tombs was beautiful and wonderful, —its fawn-colored domes rising against the somewhat darker sand of the desert. The river gleamed and wound away from the dim south into the blue distance of the north, the green strip of cultivation on its banks delighting the eye amidst the yellow sands. Over to the west, the Pyramids looked their full height, and their full distance, which is not the case from below. The platform of the Great Pyramid is here seen to be a considerable hill of itself; and the fields and causeways which intervene between it and the river lie as in a map, and indicate the true distance and elevation of these mighty monuments. The Lybian hills, dreary as possible, close in the view behind them, as the Mokuttam range does above and behind the citadel. —This view is the great sight of Cairo, and that which the stranger contrives to bring into his plan for almost every day.

Of course we saw the court where the Memlooks were slaughtered, and the wall whence Emin Bey took his leap, and the narrow street below, up which he fled. The wall must have been a good deal raised, even allowing for the rubbish heap which that day lay below; for its height above the street is now not less than eighty feet. No lapse of time or consideration of circumstances can soften one's feelings about that act of treacherous barbarity, or lessen one's compassion for the man who would purchase life and empire (supposing them to have been really in danger) at such a price. If any of my readers should be unaware of this deed of Mohammed Alee's, it may be soon learned. — He wanted to go into Arabia, to drive out the Wahabees who molested the pilgrims: but he was afraid to leave Egypt while the proud Memlooks remained, to accomplish some objects of theirs, adverse to him, in his absence. He invited the whole body of their leaders to the citadel, to witness a fete, treated them with the usual hospitalities, and dismissed them courteously. As the last went out, the doors were securely fastened; and when the guests, who had mounted their horses in the court, reached the gates, they found them closed, and nobody to answer their call to have them opened. As they turned, to gallop back to the Pasha, a murderous fire was directed upon them from above. They could find no one; and they were surrounded by high walls. Men and horses lay heaped together in the agonies of death. Some fled round and round the court till the inevitable ball reached them: and more than one, in rage and agony at such a death being appointed to armed men in their martial strength, drove their heads against the stone walls, or shot out their own brains. One only escaped; —Emin Bey, who made his horse leap the parapet, alighted on a heap of rubbish in the street below, pushed his frantic horse to a gallop through the narrow streets, and took refuge with some Arabs, whose tents were about two miles from the city, and who concealed him till he could reach the sea, and quit the country. The Pasha employed his barbarous Greek soldiers to do this deed, and paid them by a license to plunder the houses of the Memlooks. The slaughter and ravage which ensued were so horrible that the Pasha himself had to parade the city on the second day, to put a stop to the pillage. The massacre took place on the 1st of March, 1811; and the number of Memlooks slain in the citadel is reported to be from 360 to 440. How many more of inferior rank were slain in the city, no one seems to know, the reports varying from 80 to 1200. Of course, the Memlook power was destroyed. The Pasha obtained his object with regard to that. But the memory of this deed interferes fatally with his other great object of being considered to have emancipated himself from the barbarism of the eastern world.

We saw his palace, in which there is nothing remarkable. His bath was yet warm: and his fine, uncomfortable, embroidered towel still wet. His gardener offered flowers to Mrs. Y. and me, in bouquets of a pyramidal form, —as carefully built up, in their way, as the pyramids themselves.

The fete of the Birth of the Prophet happened when we were at Cairo; and we went at noon to see what it was like. The best part of it was the appearance of the city that day, when the people were all dressed in their best; the men with clean turbans and bright purple tunics, and the ladies with gay silks under their floating balloon mantles of black silk. On the spot of the fete, the scene was not unlike that of a fair at home, except of course in regard to the dresses, and that the riders in the swings sat in the oriental fashion. There was a booth with dancing girls: a horrid sight, which we were glad to turn away from. So hideous a creature as the one who was dancing, I never saw; the music was only the ordinary drum, or tom-tom, as it would be called further south in Africa: and the dancing is an observance which we could never understand, —there being neither grace, nor mirth, nor any other merit in it that we could perceive. Whenever we saw it, in this booth, in the hareems, or on our deck, it appeared to us the same disagreeable and foolish wriggle, without activity of limb, or grace of attitude. The rest of the spectacle at this fete was merely swinging, and feeding at the stalls. The Arabs are fond of sucking the sugar-cane, which indeed I think very pleasant myself. We never rode through Cairo without meeting people thus enjoying themselves; and during our voyage, the avidity of the crew, when they could contrive to land in a cane patch, was remarkable. Watchmen would come rushing down, to defend the canes: and we were made seriously uneasy sometimes by seeing what bundles our men carried away under their arms. If we remonstrated, we were told that they had paid for them. Perhaps they might; but I could never, by the sharpest watching, see the payment made: and I did see, now and then, that the country people were very angry.

Of course, the chief interest in these fetes which we saw, and where-ever many people were gathered together, was in observing their faces. The Arab face is very beautiful; and the expression has so much to do with it that the worst set of features is not ugly, as it would be elsewhere. One face, of which I saw a good deal, would appear hideous if drawn in profile or presented in a cast, —with its outrageously thick lips, immense jaw and ugly nose: but I think of that face as almost beautiful. The brown complexion (which, in this case, precisely matched the owner's cinnamon-colored vest) is a kind of veil to English eyes, softening down harshness of features: and then, there are the brilliant teeth, quite universally magnificent, and only injured by the strange practice I have mentioned— of drawing the teeth needful for biting cartridges: —and then, there are the beautiful eyes, soft, clear and intelligent; and the exquisite grace of carriage and gesture, set off to the utmost by the oriental dress. Among these advantages, the ugliness of particular features is almost lost: and the prevailing impression of the observer is that he sees beauty wherever he turns. The pathetic expression of the Arab face, its softness and melancholy; the flowing dress, the slow movement, (in the absence of causes of disturbance.) give the impression of great dignity, it is true, but also of languor and delicacy: but the muscular strength of these pathetic Arabs is very great. It is not only that they can support fatigue and hunger in their journeys, and wrestle vigorously with an opponent, in one of the quarrels they are so fond of falling into: they lift prodigious weights, and carry vast burdens in cool blood. We understood our dragoman's health not to be very good; and I certainly doubted his fitness for his office at first, when it was clear that his lungs were weak; but the daily proofs he gave of muscular strength would have surprised many a stout English servant.

As for accurate knowledge of the health and length of life of the Egyptians, there is none to be had. The distrust existing between the government and the people is a bar to the obtaining of any reliable information about any of their affairs; and the observations of a passing stranger can be worth little. My impression was that of travelers generally. I was surprised to see how dirty and unhealthy-looking children can grow into strong and well-formed men and women: and I was struck by the small proportion of sick that came under my notice throughout the country. On the whole, a stranger would be disposed to conclude that the poorer classes, whom the curse of polygamy scarcely reaches, must be in favorable circumstances in regard to health, —judging from the prevalence of muscular strength, of fine teeth, and of beauty of form and face. Among the richer classes, where a viler polygamy prevails than in almost any country of the world, it is far otherwise.

We were so fortunate as to witness a much more imposing festival than that of the birth of the Prophet: —the return of the Mahhmil.

On the morning of Sunday, the 14th of January, the news flew through the city of the return of the Pilgrims from Mekkeh. This pilgrimage is always subject to so many hardships and dangers, so many lives and fortunes are concerned in it, and there is such an absence of news from the departure of the caravan till its return, that its re-appearance is always an occasion of great excitement: and this year the excitement was unusually strong, from the cholera having committed great ravages among the pilgrims. As soon as this fact was made known in the city by the first comers, early that Sunday morning, crowds poured out to meet the caravan; —crowds of people, each one of whom was in suspense about the life of some relation or friend. We were told by friends who happened to witness this meeting, that it was a very touching sight; and that the joy of some, and the dreadful wailing of others, were indeed quite overpowering. The report in the city throughout the day was that eight thousand out of thirty thousand had perished; but this was a great exaggeration, as we soon found. The caravan consisted of seventy thousand in the whole—Cairo, that is, Egypt, sending out about thirty thousand of these. One-tenth of the whole, seven thousand, were carried off by cholera.

We rode, in the afternoon, to the encampment outside the walls. There was not much to see, the pilgrims having naturally entered the city and gone home, instead of waiting to join the procession of the next morning. Out of the two thousand camels of the morning, we saw only about one hundred and fifty. The tents were to the last degree shabby and sordid-looking; and so were the machines—the canopied-boxes—in which some of the women and children were carried on the backs of camels: but one likes to see the shabbiness which tells of the reality of such a pilgrimage. A governor of the expedition is appointed yearly: and here the governor with his attendants was sitting in his tawdry and faded green tent, smoking, and permitting the gaze of all who came. We saw how the beasts of the caravan are tethered at night, and observed a few groups of the pilgrims, eating or lounging, or tending their children; and that was all.

Accounts differed as to the time when the procession was to enter, the next morning. Alee had hired for us a shop-front in the Turkish bazaar; and there we were seated, by seven o'clock, I think, on a carpet, at the level of the people's shoulders; —in as good a place as could be had. While there, no insult whatever was offered us; and our presence seemed to excite very little notice, except among those who wanted baksheesh. Afterwards, when we were riding after the Mahhmil to the citadel, and when the press of the crowd made the act a safe one, somebody spat a mouthful of chewed sugar-cane at me; and I received a smart slap in the face from a millet-stalk: and one or two oilier persons in the Frank group met with a similar insult. But the good behavior on the whole was wonderful, in comparison with former times. Baké Bey, the ruler of the affairs of the festival, had declared that any rudeness to Europeans should be severely punished.

We had not to wait long for the procession; and the interval was amusing enough. A pair of wrestlers came to show their prowess before us. Never had

I imagined such wrestling. Their bodies, bare to the waist, were slippery with grease; and they took the greatest imaginable care not to hold one another too hard. They seemed to suppose each other made of pie-crust. They looked at each other with a sort of good-humored threatening; shook their heads manfully; slipped their hands round one another's greasy arms; leaned their heads gently against one another's shoulders; strove to pant and be out of breath; and then turned to us for baksheesh. We had seen many a better match on the river-bank, when two of our crew had quarreled about a bit of bread.

There were no pilgrims in the procession. They were gone home, or were entering the city more quickly and quietly by other gates. First, came music, loud and rude: and next a company of foot-soldiers. Then, the governor of the caravan, —the Emir el Hadj, with his officers. Then the Mahhmil: —which is the sort of vehicle or tent in which a royal lady would ride on her camel, if she went on the pilgrimage. The origin of the custom of sending the Mahhmil is, as Mr. Lane tells us,[168] supposed to be that a royal lady did make the pilgrimage, in the thirteenth century, in such a vehicle; that her empty tent was dispatched with the caravan for several years afterwards, as an emblem of royalty; and that princes of other countries sent a similar emblem. Why it is now esteemed so sacred as it is, no one seems able to explain. The Mahhmil was, on this occasion, of square form, with a pyramidal top, surmounted by a gilt ball and crescent. Its covering was of dark purple brocade, richly embroidered, in gold, with various symbolical devices. It was carried by a tall, handsome, light-colored camel, hung over with fringes and tassels, like the Mahhmil itself, and led by a proud driver, who was soon to yield up the rein to no less a personage than Abbas Pasha. This was the final task of the camel, which was never to work more. —Next came the only offensive object in the whole show, —the Sheikh of the camel. This was the old fanatic or knave who has attended the caravan for a quarter of a century, rolling his head all the way to Mekkeh and back, every year. I do not know whether he can now hold up his head: but if his brain is really disordered, I am sure it is no wonder. He was naked, except a little pair of old cotton trowsers; his hair grew bushy and wild; and, as he rolled about on his camel, he looked, of course, perfectly crazy. We were assured, however, that he is a rich and luxurious man, having one of the handsomest hareems in Cairo, and another, no less enviable, at Mekkeh. This fellow is allowed by government two camels, and whatever he wants for the journey. He is keeper of the cats; about which cats we could learn nothing, except that an old woman used to carry a camel load of cats in pilgrimage; and we suppose the Sheikh of the camel has taken them in charge.

The next part of the procession interested me the most. The guard rode two and two. These soldiers were in shabby, sometimes tattered clothing; which was

168   Modern Egyptians, II. 182.

their badge of honor. Their clothing testified to their activity and their hard-ships, during the three months that they had acted as escort to the expedition: and they were now going to the citadel, to receive new dresses. Several camels, adorned with little flags, small tufts of feathers, and housings embroidered with cowries, were among and behind these soldiers: and that was all.

Our asses were held in readiness for us to mount, and follow the procession to the citadel, which we did without difficulty, though the streets were crowded. We fell in with almost all the Frank travelers in Cairo, making a pretty large and very conspicuous group, and a curious rear guard of the procession of the Mahhmil. It was here, when for an instant riding in single file, that I met with the insult I mentioned: and I really did not wonder at it; and could not resent it, putting myself in the place, for the moment, of a devout Mohammedan.

The finest part of the sight was now to come. In the midst of the vast area before the citadel, soldiers were drawn out in three sides of a square; music brayed; cannons were fired; and cavalry dashed about in the way which I had often read of, but had not, up to this moment, seen. Such horsemanship is really a great sight, as I afterwards occasionally felt in the Desert. It is no more like the best riding we see in England than the swiftest run of a greyhound is like the trot of a cat, or the flight of a swallow is like that of a chicken. We have not room for Arabian riding in England, if we had all the other requisites. It is not every horseman who can get access to Salisbury plain, or a race course, or a long stretch of hard and smooth sea-shore. —Amidst the noise of the cannon, the music, and the multitude, Abbas Pasha, the grandson of Mohammed Alee, took the rein of the camel of the Mahhmil, and led it hither and thither and away. It was a spirited and beautiful sight.

I have been so often asked since my return whether I saw the Magician at Cairo, that I suppose I had better say what I know about him, and what I saw him do. —Some gentlemen in our hotel (Hotel d'Orient) told us that they had engaged the Magician for the evening of this Monday, the 22d. It was per-mitted to our party, and to some other English in the hotel, to be present. The Magician did not come: and on being questioned the next morning, he excused himself on various grounds; but it plainly appeared at last that he was afraid to come; —afraid of being browbeaten and laughed at by the Franks, and of having his fee taken from him (he said) by the people in the innyard. He was promised civil treatment and earnest attention while with us, and special pro-tection home after the séance. Moreover, an admirable interpreter was offered to us. Little reliance is to be placed on the interpretation of any dragoman in this case: and Mr. Lane's nephew, Stanley Poole, kindly offered to come and be tongue to both parties. Those who have the pleasure of knowing Mr. Lane's nephews know that wherever they are, there is security for good sense, cheerful kindness, and gentlemanly manners: and on this occasion, my young friend Stanley appeared to satisfy the Magician as much as he pleased everybody else.

All the experiments were failures; —total and ludicrous failures: yet I am glad we saw the Magician; because I have brought away a very clear and strong impression of the whole case: an impression which is shared by some who are qualified like myself to form a judgment upon it.

The Magician, who is rather a good-looking old gentleman, followed his usual and well-known method of preparing and burning charms and incense, and then summoned the Arab boy who had been brought by himself, or some-one not of the English party. When the boy crouched down, close to the Magician and his pan of charcoal, the incense burning was so powerful that three of the English party were presently sound asleep; and some others were drowsy. I, having no sense of smell, and being therefore unaffected by the perfumes, was wide awake, and closely on the watch. As soon as the old man had poured the ink into the boy's hand, and had his own left hand at liberty, he rested the tips of the fingers firmly on the crown of the boy's head, and kept them there. When asked why he did so, he replied that it was to hold the boy's head steady, that he might look fixedly into the ink; but it was observable that he did not touch the head of the others afterwards brought in—nor mine, when I took their place. I saw in the boy that peculiar quivering of the eyelids which is one sign of the presence of mesmeric action.

One specimen of the failures will suffice. I was sitting opposite the boy when he was told to call and look for Harriet Martineau. By degrees he spoke the name; —saw nothing at first; but presently said the person was visible. "What do you see?"— "I see a young lady, dressed in black silk, walking in a garden, leading a little child by the hand."—After a few more failures like this, he was sent away, and kept carefully apart till one of the gentlemen had brought in a boy picked up in the street. He, and another after him, succeeded no better. —By this time I had arrived at the conclusion which I now hold; —that it is an affair of mesmerism, and that the Magician himself probably does not know it. If the truth were understood, I have no doubt it would appear that, in the first instance, a capital clairvoyant did see and tell the things declared, under the influence of the old man's mesmeric power, and when there was accidentally a rapport established between the questioner and the boy. I am disposed to think that there was originally no imposture about the matter at all: that the Magician did not then understand the causes of his success, and does not now understand the causes of his failures. If he continues to take fees without hope of success, of course he is now an impostor: but if he believes that his success or failure depends on the pleasure of spirits whom he propitiates, he may be always hoping for success, and may think it wrong to refuse the chance. It is true, he is meantime taking money for what he does not perform, and is therefore fairly open to any extent of suspicion: but I do not see reason to suppose that it is a case of imposture from end to end. I wish a trial could be made by someone who understands what is known of Mesmerism. If a boy, proved to be susceptible in the inferior degrees, could be subjected to the Magician's charms, and questioned, after being put in rapport with the questioner and the interpreter, I think it probable that he would succeed as well as the original oracle: or, if the first should not prove clairvoyant, a second, third, or fourth might. In my opinion, the experiment would be well worth trying where subjects could be had of a race probably so susceptible of the Mesmeric influence as the Arabs.

Seeing what I saw, and being myself a very good mesmeric subject, I asked one of my friends to tell the old man that I had seen curious things done in England, and knew the truth of such clairvoyance as he professed to show; and that I would take the boy's place. I knew he would refuse, and plead some good reasons against it: but I desired my friend to take no refusal. The old man presently said I might do as I liked; but he did not think it would succeed. —More charms and incense were burned, my hand was duly scored with ink, and the usual pool poured into the palm; and I faithfully gazed into it. In two minutes the sensation came, though there was no hand upon my head. The Magician is a powerful, and, no doubt, unconscious mesmeriser. Presently I began to see such odd things in the pool of ink, —it grew so large before my aching eyes, and showed such strange moving shadows and clear symmetrical figures and intersecting lines, that I felt uncertain how long I could command my thoughts and words; and, considering the number of strangers present, I thought it more prudent to shake off the influence while I could, than to pursue the experiment. The perfumes might have some effect, though I was insensible to them; and so might the dead silence, and my steadfast gazing into the ink. But that there was also a strong mesmeric influence present, I am certain.

I hope it will not be long before some satisfactory course of mesmeric experiment, like that so triumphantly pursued by Dr. Esdaile in India, is instituted in Egypt, or at Jerusalem, with Arabs for subjects.

As far as our knowledge goes (which is but a little way, at present) it appears that the dark-skinned races, —as the Hindoos and the negroes, —are eminently susceptible; and it is a loss to science not to ascertain what they can do. —Nothing mortified me so much, in the course of my journey, as the being obliged to leave unused such an apparent opportunity of inquiry as I had while traveling among the Arabs: but in truth, I had no opportunity. We were always moving from place to place; there was no one who could help me; —and I needed all my own strength to meet the fatigues of traveling. I mesmerized a sick friend at Cairo, and found the exhaustion so great, —so unlike anything I ever experienced from mesmerizing at home, —that I was warned to be prudent, for my party's sake even more than my own. But I wish some few of the many I met abroad who know the truth of mesmerism would unite to institute a course of experiments on Arab subjects. All the naval surgeons I met in the Mediterranean know the truth of Mesmerism as well as I do, and admit its importance: so do some eminent naval officers there; and the Physician of the French Embassy in Egypt; and the gentlemen from India who have witnessed what Dr. Esdaile and the Bengal Government have done; and Mr. Lane, and the Bishop of Jerusalem; and, in short, every man of education, who has really attended to the subject. Among them, there are some who think most of the curative powers of Mesmerism; but there are others who see how infinitely more important and interesting are those of its facts which belong to Mental philosophy, and who feel what an illustrious foreigner expressed to me, in London, not long ago: "It is a shame for your country that it should be behind every other civilized nation, in regard to this portion of science. It is strange that men should be slow to investigate a powerful curative means. But when the same agent shows that man has a new faculty of the mind, —a faculty hitherto not numbered among his powers, — what can one say to indifference to such a discovery as that, —the greatest that Man has ever made, or can ever make! It is a shame for your country!" If others of our countrymen abroad will follow Dr. Esdaile's example in using their opportunities, they may yet redeem us from the disgrace we lie under with the educated classes of every country in Europe, for our want of a true philosophical spirit of inquiry and teachableness in regard to the facts of Mesmerism. However, we are wiser than we were a few years ago: and it is now a rare thing, I believe, to meet an educated person who does not regard the subject with seriousness and candor, and, after inquiry, with undoubting belief to a greater or less extent.

Cairo is indeed a pleasant place to spend a few weeks in, at the season of the year when we were there. Besides the delightful temperature, and its Arabian wonders and beauties, there is some agreeable society. The Hotel d'Orient and Shepherd's Hotel were quite full during our stay: and I believe there is seldom a time when many English do not meet at Cairo, —some coming from home on their way to India, or for traveling objects, and others arriving from India for health or holiday. Then, there are the European Legations, with their hospitalities and agreeable society. And the kindness of Mr. and Mrs. Lieder of the Prussian Mission is known to everybody who has needed a welcome, or aid, or guidance in that strange city, so far from home. There is another privilege, accessible to few, but of inestimable value to the traveler in Egypt, which I was permitted to enjoy; —intercourse with Mr. Lane and his family. There is no need for me, or any one, at this time of day, to say anything of Mr. Lane personally. His opinions and character have long taken their rank; —a rank so high that it is a sort of impertinence for a passing traveler to present them. But I have been so often asked since my return home what it is exactly that Mr. Lane is about at Cairo, and it concerns the best classes of Englishmen so much to know exactly what Mr. Lane is about at Cairo, that I certainly ought to tell, as far as I am capable, how I found him occupied.

Everybody knows Mr. Lane's reputation for Arabic scholarship; but too few know the generosity with which he has devoted himself to the interests of scholarship, to the injury of his private fortunes, and the sacrifice, for some years, of home and country. We are, happily, never without examples of generosity before our eyes; —the generosity of men of honor, the generosity of the poor, and of the philanthropic; and men of science and literature have never been behind others in sacrificing their means, whether of money, time, health, or domestic ease, to the cause of knowledge and human improvement. Among these public benefactors is Mr. Lane; and I wish the nature and extent of his labors and sacrifices were better known than they are. One gentleman has shown his sense of the public obligations to Mr. Lane; —has shown that sense in the best possible way; —by aiding Mr. Lane's object. The present Duke of Northumberland, when Lord Prudhoe, saw at once that Mr. Lane's object was one of vast importance, and that no time must be lost in accomplishing it; and he acted accordingly. It is owing to him that the work has advanced so far as that we may hope for its completion in, I believe, two years.

It is well known to oriental scholars that no good Arabic Lexicon exists: and perhaps none but men of learning can fully understand how important it is to the world that it should have a good Arabic Lexicon; but it is evident enough to ordinary people that it is of consequence to our knowledge of history and ancient literature to have as good a key as can be found to the treasures of Arabic literature. There are, in the Mosques of Cairo, materials essential to the formation of a perfect Lexicon which can be had nowhere else; these MSS. are crumbling to pieces so fast that, if not used now, they will be lost for ever; and Mr. Lane is the only competent man who has access to these materials. He saw the importance of the object, felt the pressure of the time, knew that he was the man for the work, and therefore devoted himself to it, in a generous negligence of his personal interests. He gave up a good literary income in London, the comforts of an English home, and the society of family and friends, and went to live at Cairo, working, to the injury of his health, at an unremunerative labor which he well knew the world would be slow to appreciate. And there he toils, day by day, with his sheikh, poring over the old MSS., which can scarcely be touched without falling to pieces. And there he must toil for two years more, till his work is finished. —And what next? How will our Universities, and the

Government, and the India Company show that they understand the boon which Mr. Lane has conferred upon them? The common notion of welcoming a book is, taking a single copy; or five, or ten copies. Is this what will be done in the case of this rare book, which it is certain the public will never buy? One of the European powers understands the matter better than this; —understands too that tokens of appreciation should be given so timely as that they may cheer the toils of the laborer, and assure him that he is not working in vain. The King of Prussia has been first, as usual, to give encouragement. Since my return, I find that he has sent a commissioner to Egypt, by way of London, to make arrangements for the establishment and diffusion of the work. I rejoice at this: but I feel some shame that a foreign government should first have the honor—after the Duke of Northumberland—of welcoming and fostering the work of an English scholar.

In thinking of Mr. Lane's household, and the happy hours I spent among them, it occurs to me to mention thus publicly (what it would certainly never occur to Mr. Lane and his family that I should mention in relation to them), the idea that struck me there, and many times since, —what a pity it is that such lads as his nephews are not looked to to occupy some such public offices in the East as are at present filled imperfectly from the imperfect oriental education of English youths at home. Here is Stanley Poole, —well educated as an English youth, and trained in a virtuous and religious English home in the heart of the East, —fit, at the same time, to live among the people of the East all his days; —speaking their languages like his mother tongue, seasoned to their climate, habituated to their ways, and familiar with their minds: —what a waste it will be if such a youth should be destined to any occupation in life which might as well be discharged by any other good and clever and accomplished Englishman, when there is such a want of well-qualified diplomatic and consular agents, and (what is more important still) scientific travelers who can make their way freely, and use fully their opportunities in the East! While we keep at work such expensive arrangements as we have at home for the preparation of oriental officers and agents, what a pity it seems not to use the rare chance, when it presents itself, of securing the services of promising youths in whom are united the advantages of an English and an Eastern education! I say this wholly of my own accord, and without consultation with any one: and I shall be very glad if I find that any one who can act in the matter is of my opinion.

CHAPTER XXII

THE HAREEM

I saw two Hareems in the east; and it would be wrong to pass them over in an account of my travels; though the subject is as little agreeable as any I can have to treat. I cannot now think of the two mornings thus employed without a heaviness of heart greater than I have ever brought away from Deaf and Dumb Schools, Lunatic Asylums, or even Prisons. As such are my impressions of hareems, of course I shall not say whose they were that I visited. Suffice it that one was at Cairo and the other at Damascus.

The royal hareems were not accessible while I was in Egypt. The Pasha's eldest daughter, the widow of Defterdar Bey, was under her father's displeasure, and was, in fact, a prisoner in her own house. While her father did not visit her, no one else could: and while she was secluded, her younger sister could not receive visitors: and thus, their hareems were closed. —The one which I saw was that of a gentle man of high rank; and as good a specimen as could be seen. The misfortune was that there was a mistake about the presence of an interpreter. A lady was to have met us who spoke Italian or French: but she did not arrive; and the morning therefore passed in dumb show; and we could not repeat our visit on a subsequent day, as we were invited to do. We lamented this much at the time: but our subsequent experience of what is to be learned in a hareem with the aid of an intelligent and kind interpretess convinced us that we had not lost much.

Before I went abroad, more than one sensible friend had warned me to leave behind as many prejudices as possible; and especially on this subject, on which the prejudices of Europeans are the strongest. I was reminded of the wide extent, both of time and space, in which Polygamy had existed; and that openness of mind was as necessary to the accurate observation of this institution as of every other. I had really taken this advice to heart: I had been struck by the view

1082

taken by Mr. Millies in his beautiful poem of "the Hareem;" and I am sure I did meet this subject with every desire to investigate the ideas and general feelings involved in it. I learned a very great deal about the working of the institution; and I believe I apprehend the thoughts and feelings of the persons concerned in it: and I declare that if we are to look for a hell upon earth, it is where polygamy exists: and that as polygamy runs riot in Egypt, Egypt is the lowest depth of this hell. I always before believed that every arrangement and prevalent practice had some one fair side, —some one redeeming quality: and diligently did I look for this fair side in regard to polygamy: but there is none. The longer one studies the subject, and the deeper one penetrates into it, —the more is one's mind confounded with the intricacy of its iniquity, and the more does one's heart feel as if it would break.

I shall say but little of what I know. If there were the slightest chance of doing any good, I would speak out at all hazards; —I would meet all the danger, and endure all the disgust. But there is no reaching the minds of any who live under the accursed system. It is a system which belongs to a totally different region of ideas from ours: and there is nothing to appeal to in the minds of those who, knowing the facts of the institution, can endure it; and at home, no one needs appealing to and convincing. Any plea for liberality that we meet at home proceeds from some poetical fancy, or some laudable desire for impartiality in the absence of knowledge of the facts. Such pleas are not operative enough to render it worthwhile to shock and sadden many hearts by statements which no one should be required needlessly to endure. I will tell only something of what I saw; and but little of what I thought and know.

At ten o'clock, one morning, Mrs. Y. and I were home from our early ride, and dressed for our visit to a hareem of a high order. The lady to whose kindness we mainly owed this opportunity, accompanied us, with her daughter. We had a disagreeable drive in the carriage belonging to the hotel, knocking against asses, horses and people all the way. We alighted at the entrance of a paved passage leading to a court which we crossed: and then, in a second court, we were before the entrance of the hareem.

A party of eunuchs stood before a faded curtain, which they held aside when the gentlemen of our party and the dragoman had gone forward. Retired some way behind the curtain stood, in a half circle, eight or ten slave girls, in an attitude of deep obeisance. Two of them then took charge of each of us, holding us by the arms above the elbows, to help us upstairs. —After crossing a lobby at the top of the stairs, we entered a handsome apartment, where lay the chief wife, — at that time an invalid. —The ceiling was gayly painted; and so were the walls, —the latter with curiously bad attempts at domestic perspective. There were four handsome mirrors; and the curtains in the doorway were of a beautiful shawl fabric, fringed and tasseled. A Turkey carpet not only covered the whole floor, but was turned up at the corners. Deewáns extended round nearly the whole room, —a lower one for ordinary use, and a high one for the seat of honor. The windows, which had a sufficient fence of blinds, looked upon a pretty garden, where I saw orange trees and many others, and the fences were hung with rich creepers.

On cushions on the floor lay the chief lady, ill and miserable-looking. She rose as we entered; but we made her lie down again: and she was then covered with a silk counterpane. Her dress was, as we saw when she rose, loose trowsers of blue striped cotton under her black silk jacket; and the same blue cotton appeared at the wrists, under her black sleeves. Her head-dress was of black net, bunched out curiously behind. Her hair was braided down the sides of this head-dress behind, and the ends were pinned over her forehead. Some of the black net was brought round her face, and under the chin, showing the outline of a face which had no beauty in it, nor traces of former beauty, but which was interesting to-day from her manifest illness and unhappiness. There was a strong expression of waywardness and peevishness about the mouth, however. She wore two handsome diamond rings; and she and one other lady had watches and gold chains. She complained of her head; and her left hand was bound up: she made signs by pressing her bosom, and imitating the dandling of a baby, which, with her occasional tears, persuaded my companions that she had met with some accident and had lost her infant. On leaving the hareem, we found that it was not a child of her own that she was mourning, but that of a white girl in the hareem: and that the wife's illness was wholly from grief for the loss of this baby; —a curious illustration of the feelings and manners of the place! The children born in large hareems are extremely few: and they are usually idolized, and sometimes murdered. It is known that in the houses at home which morally most resemble these hareems (though little enough externally) when the rare event of the birth of a child happens, a passionate joy extends over the wretched household: —jars are quieted, drunkenness is moderated, and there is no self-denial which the poor creatures will not undergo during this gratification of their feminine instincts. They will nurse the child all night in illness, and pamper it all day with sweetmeats and toys; they will fight for the possession of it, and be almost heart-broken at its loss: and lose it they must; for the child always dies, —killed with kindness, even if born healthy. This natural outbreak of feminine instinct takes place in the too populous hareem, when a child is given to any one of the many who are longing for the gift: and if it dies naturally, it is mourned as we saw, through a wonderful conquest of personal jealousy by this general instinct. But when the jealousy is uppermost, —what happens then? —why, the strangling the innocent in its sleep, —or the letting it slip from the window into the river below, —or the mixing poison with its food; —the mother and the murderess, always rivals and now fiends, being shut up together for life. If the child lives, what then? If a girl, she sees before her from the beginning the nothingness of external life, and the chaos of interior existence, in which she is to dwell for life. If a boy, he remains among the women till ten years old, seeing things when the eunuchs come in to romp, and hearing things among the chatter of the ignorant women which brutalize him for life before the age of rationality comes. But I will not dwell on these hopeless miseries.

A sensible looking old lady, who had lost an eye, sat at the head of the invalid: and a nun-like elderly woman, whose head and throat were wrapped in unstarched muslin, sat behind for a time, and then went away, after an affectionate salutation to the invalid. —Towards the end of the visit, the husband's mother came in, —looking like a little old man in her coat trimmed with fur. Her countenance was cheerful and pleasant. We saw, I think, about twenty more women, —some slaves, —most or all young—some good-looking, but none handsome. Some few were black; and the rest very light: —Nubians or Abyssinians and Circassians, no doubt. One of the best figures, as a picture, in the hareem, was a Nubian girl, in an amber-colored watered silk, embroidered with black, looped up in festoons, and finished with a black bodice. The richness of the gay printed cotton skirts and sleeves surprised us: the finest shawls could hardly have looked better. One graceful girl had her pretty figure well shown by a tight-fitting black dress. Their heads were dressed much like the chief lady's. Two, who must have been sisters, if not twins, had patches between the eyes. One handmaid was barefoot, and several were without shoes. Though there were none of the whole large number who could be called particularly pretty individually, the scene was, on the whole, exceedingly striking, as the realization of what one knew before, but as in a dream. The girls went out and came in. but, for the most part, stood in a half circle. Two sat on their heels for a time: and some went to play in the neighboring apartments.

Coffee was handed to us twice, with all the well-known apparatus of jeweled cups, embroidered tray cover, and gold-flowered napkins. There were chibouques, of course: and sherbets in cut glass cups. The time was passed in attempts to have conversation by signs; attempts which are fruitless among people of the different ideas which belong to different races. How much they made out about us, we do not know: but they inquired into the mutual relationships of the party, and put the extraordinary questions which are always put to ladies who visit the hareems. —A young lady of my acquaintance, of the age of eighteen, but looking younger, went with her mother to a hareem in Cairo (not the one I have been describing), and excited great amazement when obliged to confess that she had not either children or a husband. One of the wives threw her arms about her, entreated her to stay for ever, said she should have any husband she liked, but particularly recommended her own, saying that she was sure he would soon wish for another wife, and she had so much rather it should be my young friend, who would amuse her continually, than anybody else that she could not be so fond of. Everywhere they pitied us European women heartily, that we had to go about traveling, and appearing in the streets without being properly taken care of, —that is, watched. They think us strangely neglected in being left so free, and boast of their spy system and imprisonment as tokens of the value in which they are held.

The mourning worn by the lady who went with us was the subject of much speculation: and many questions were asked about her home and family. To appease the curiosity about her home, she gave her card. As I anticipated, this did not answer. It was the great puzzle of the whole interview. At first the poor lady thought it was to do her head good: then, she fidgeted about it, in the evident fear of omitting some observance; but at last, she understood that she was to keep it. When we had taken our departure, however, an eunuch was sent after us to inquire of the dragoman what "the letter" was which our companion had given to the lady.

The difficulty is to get away, when one is visiting a hareem. The poor ladies cannot conceive of one's having anything to do; and the only reason they can understand for the interview coming to an end is the arrival of sunset, after which it would, they think, be improper for any woman to be abroad. And the amusement to them of such a visit is so great that they protract it to the utmost, even in such a case as ours to-day, when all intercourse was conducted by dumb show. It is certainly very tiresome; and the only wonder is that the hostesses can like it. To sit hour after hour on the deewán, without any exchange of ideas, having our clothes examined, and being plied with successive cups of coffee and sherbet, and pipes, and being gazed at by a half-circle of girls in brocade and shawls, and made to sit down again as soon as one attempts to rise, is as wearisome an experience as one meets with in foreign lands. —The weariness of heart is, however, the worst part of it. I noted all the faces well during our constrained stay; and I saw no trace of mind in any one except in the homely one-eyed old lady. All the younger ones were dull, soulless, brutish, or peevish. How should it be otherwise, when the only idea of their whole lives is that which, with all our interests and engagements, we consider too prominent with us? There cannot be a woman of them all who is not dwarfed and withered in mind and soul by being kept wholly engrossed with that one interest, —detained at that stage in existence which, though most important in its place, is so as a means to ulterior ends. The ignorance is fearful enough; but the grossness is revolting.

At the third move, and when it was by some means understood that we were waited for, we were permitted to go, —after a visit of above two hours. The sick lady rose from her cushions, notwithstanding our opposition, and we were conducted forth with much observance. On each side of the curtain which overhung the outer entrance, stood a girl with a bottle of rose water, some of which was splashed in our faces as we passed out.

We had reached the carriage when we were called back: —his excellency was waiting for us. So we visited him in a pretty apartment, paved with variegated marbles, and with a fountain in the centre. His excellency was a sensible-looking man, with gay, easy and graceful manners. He lamented the mistake about the interpreter, and said we must go again, when we might have conversation. He insisted upon attending us to the carriage, actually passing between the files of beggars which lined the outer passage. The dragoman was so excessively shocked by this degree of condescension, that we felt obliged to be so too, and remonstrated; but in vain. He stood till the door was shut, and the whip was cracked. He is a liberal-minded man; and his hareem is nearly as favorable a specimen as could be selected for a visit; but what is this best specimen? I find these words written down on the same day, in my journal: written, as I well remember, in heaviness of heart. "I am glad of the opportunity of seeing a hareem: but it leaves an impression of discontent and uneasiness which I shall be glad to sleep off. And I am not conscious that there is prejudice in this. I feel that a visit to the worst room in the Rookery in St. Giles' would have affected me less painfully. There are there at least the elements of a rational life, however perverted; while here humanity is wholly and hopelessly baulked. It will never do to look on this as a case for cosmopolitan philosophy to regard complacently, and require a good construction for. It is not a phase of natural early manners. It is as pure a conventionalism as our representative monarchy, or German heraldry, or Hindoo caste; and the most atrocious in the world."

And of this atrocious system, Egypt is the most atrocious example. It has unequaled facilities for the importation of black and white slaves; and these facilities are used to the utmost; yet the population is incessantly on the decline. But for the importation of slaves, the upper classes, where polygamy runs riot, must soon die out, —so few are the children born, and so fatal to health are the arrangements of society. The finest children are those born of Circassian or Georgian mothers; and but for these, we should soon hear little more of an upper class in Egypt. —Large numbers are brought from the south, —the girls to be made attendants or concubines in the hareem, and the boys to be made, in a vast proportion, those guards to the female part of the establishment whose mere presence is a perpetual insult and shame to humanity. The business of keeping up the supply of these miserable wretches, —of whom the Pasha's eldest daughter has fifty for her exclusive service, —is in the hands of the Christians of Asyoot. It is these Christians who provide a sufficient supply, and cause a sufficient mortality to keep the number of the sexes pretty equal: in consideration of which we cannot much wonder that Christianity does not appear very venerable in the eyes of Mohammedans.

These eunuchs are indulged in regard to dress, personal liberty, and often the possession of office, domestic, military, or political. When retained as guards of the hareem, they are in their master's confidence, —acting as his spies, and indispensable to the ladies, as a medium of communication with the world, and as furnishing their amusements, — being at once playmates and servants. It is no unusual thing for the eunuchs to whip the ladies away from a window, whence they had hoped for amusement; or to call them opprobrious names; or to inform against them to their owner: and it is also no unusual thing for them to romp with the ladies, to obtain their confidence, and to try their dispositions. Cases have been known of one of them becoming the friend of some poor girl of higher nature and tendencies than her companions; and even of a closer attachment, which is not objected to by the proprietor of both. It is a case too high for his jealousy, so long as he knows that the cage is secure. It has become rather the fashion to extenuate the lot of the captive of either sex: to point out how the Nubian girl, who would have ground corn and woven garments, and nursed her infants in comparative poverty all her days, is now surrounded by luxury, and provided for for life: and how the Circassian girl may become a wife of the son of her proprietor, and hold a high rank in the hareem: and how the wretched brothers of these slaves may rise to posts of military command or political confidence; but it is enough to see them to be disabused of all impressions of their good fortune. It is enough to see the dull and gross face of the handmaid of the hareem, and to remember at the moment the cheerful, modest countenance of the Nubian girl busy about her household tasks, or of the Nubian mother, with her infants hanging about her as she looks, with face open to the sky, for her husband's return from the field, or meets him on the river bank. It is enough to observe the wretched health and abject, or worn, or insolent look of the guard of the hareem, and to remember that he ought to have been the head of a household of his own, however humble: and in this contrast of what is with what ought to have been, slavery is seen to lie fully as detestable here as anywhere else. These two hellish practices, slavery and polygamy, which, as practices, can clearly never be separated, are here avowedly connected; and in that connection, are exalted into a double institution, whose working is such as to make one almost wish that the Nile would rise to cover the tops of the hills, and sweep away the whole abomination. Till this happens, there is, in the condition of Egypt, a fearful warning before the eyes of all men. The Egyptians

laugh at the marriage arrangements of Europe, declaring that virtual polygamy exists everywhere, and is not improved by hypocritical concealment. The
Europeans may see, when startled by the state of Egypt, that virtual slavery is
indispensably required by the practice of polygamy; virtual proprietorship of
the women involved, without the obligation imposed by actual proprietorship;
and cruel oppression of the men who should have been the husbands of these
women. And again, the Carolina planter, who knows as well as any Egyptian
that polygamy is a natural concomitant of slavery, may see in the state of Egypt
and the Egyptians what his country and his children must come to, if either of
those vile arrangements is permitted which necessitates the other.

It is scarcely needful to say that those benevolent persons are mistaken, who
believe that slavery in Egypt has been abolished by the Pasha, and the importation of slaves effectually prohibited. Neither the Pasha nor any other human
power can abolish slavery while polygamy is an institution of the country, the
proportion of the sexes remaining in Egypt what it is, there and everywhere else.

The reason assigned by Montesquieu for polygamy throughout the East has
no doubt something in it: —that women become so early marriageable that
the wife cannot satisfy the needs of the husband's mind and heart: and that
therefore he must have both a bride and a companion of whom he may make a
friend. How little there is in this to excuse the polygamy of Egypt may be seen
by an observation of the state of things there and in Turkey, where the same
religion and natural laws prevail as in Egypt. In Egypt, the difficulty would be
great of finding a wife of any age who could be the friend of a man of any sense:
and in Turkey, where the wives are of a far higher order, polygamy is rare, and
women are not married so young. It is not usual there to find such disparity
of years as one finds in Egypt between the husband and his youngest wife. The
cause assigned by Montesquieu is true in connection with a vicious state of society: but it is not insuperable, and it will operate only as long as it is wished for.
If any influence could exalt the ideas of marriage, and improve the training of
women in Egypt, it would soon be seen that men would prefer marrying wom-
en of nearly their own age, and would naturally remain comparatively constant:
but before this experiment can be tried, parents must have ceased to become
restless when their daughter reaches eleven years old, and afraid of disgrace if
she remains unmarried long after that.

I was told, while at Cairo, of one extraordinary family where there is not
only rational intercourse and confidence at home, and some relaxation of imprisonment, but the young ladies read! —and read French and Italian! I asked
what would be the end of this: and my informant replied that whether the
young ladies married or not, they would sooner or later sink down, he thought,
into a state even less contented than the ordinary. There could be no sufficient

inducement for secluded girls, who never saw anybody wiser than themselves, to go on reading French and Italian books within a certain range. For want of stimulus and sympathy, they would stop; and then, finding themselves dissatisfied among the nothings which fill the life of other women, they would be very unhappy. The exceptional persons under a bad state of things, and the beginners under an improving system must ever be sufferers—martyrs of their particular reformation. To this they may object less than others would for them, if they are conscious of the personal honor and general blessing of their martyrdom.

The youngest wife I ever saw (except the swathed and veiled brides we encountered in the streets of Egyptian cities) was in a Turkish hareem which Mrs. Y. and I visited at Damascus, I will tell that story now, that I may dismiss the subject of this chapter. I heartily dreaded this second visit to a hareem, and braced myself up to it as one does to an hour at the dentist's, or to an expedition into the city to prove a debt. We had the comfort of a good and pleasant interpreter; and there was more mirth and nonsense than in the Cairo hareem; and, therefore, somewhat less disgust and constraint: but still it was painful enough. We saw the seven wives of three gentlemen, and a crowd of attendants and visitors. Of the seven, two had been the wives of the head of the household, who was dead: three were the wives of his eldest son, aged twenty-two; and the remaining two were the wives of his second son, aged fifteen. The youngest son, aged thirteen, was not yet married; but he would be thinking about it soon. The pair of widows were elderly women, as merry as girls, and quite at their ease. Of the other five, three, were sisters: —that is, we conclude, half-sisters; —children of different mothers in the same hareem. It is evident at a glance what a tragedy lies under this; what the horrors of jealousy must be among sisters thus connected for life; —three of them between two husbands in the same house! And we were told that the jealousy had begun, young as they were, and the third having been married only a week. This young creature, aged twelve, was the bride of the husband of fifteen. She was the most conspicuous person in the place, not only for the splendor of her dress, but because she sat on the deewán, while the others sat or lounged on cushions on the raised floor. The moment we took our seats, I was struck with compassion for this child—she looked so grave, and sad and timid. While the others romped and giggled, pushing and pulling one another about, and laughing at jokes among themselves, she never smiled, but looked on listlessly. I was determined to make her laugh before we went away; and at last she relaxed somewhat—smiling, and growing grave again in a moment: but at length she really and truly laughed; and when we were shown the whole hareem, she also slipped her bare and dyed feet into her pattens inlaid with mother-of-pearl, and went into the courts with us, nestling to us, and seeming to lose the sense of her new position for the time: but there was far less of the gayety of a child about her than in the elderly widows. Her dress was superb; —a full skirt and bodice of geranium-colored brocade, embossed with gold flowers and leaves; and her frill and ruffles were of geranium-colored gauze. Her eyebrows were frightful—joined and prolonged by black paint. Her head was covered with a silk net, in almost every mesh of which were stuck jewels or natural flowers: so that her head was like a bouquet sprinkled with diamonds. Her nails were dyed black; and her feel were dyed black in checkers. Her complexion, called white, was of an unhealthy yellow: and, indeed, we did not see a healthy complexion among the whole company; nor anywhere among women who were secluded from exercise, while pampered with all the luxuries of eastern living.

Besides the seven wives, a number of attendants came in to look at us, and serve the pipes and sherbert; and a few ladies from a neighboring hareem; and a party of Jewesses, with whom we had some previous acquaintance. Mrs. Y. was compelled to withdraw her lace veil, and then to take off her bonnet: and she was instructed that the street was the place for her to wear her veil down, and that they expected to see her face. Then her bonnet went round, and was tried on many heads—one merry girl wearing it long enough to surprise many newcomers with the joke. My gloves were stretched and pulled in all manner of ways, in their attempts to thrust their large, broad brown hands into them, one after another. But the great amusement was my trumpet. The eldest widow, who sat next me, asked for it, and put it to her ear; when I said "Bo!" When she had done laughing, she put it into her next neighbor's ear, and said "Bo!" and in this way it came round to me again. But in two minutes, it was asked for again, and went round a second time—everybody laughing as loud as ever at each "Bo!"—and then a third time! Could one have conceived it! The next joke was on behalf of the Jewesses, four or five of whom sat in a row on the deewán. Almost everybody else was puffing away at a chibouque or a nargeeleh, and the place was one cloud of smoke. The poor Jewesses were obliged to decline joining us; for it happened to be Saturday: they must not smoke on the Sabbath. They were naturally much pitied: and some of the young wives did what was possible for them. Drawing in a long breath of smoke, they puffed it forth in the faces of the Jewesses, who opened mouth and nostrils eagerly to receive it. Thus was the Sabbath observed, to shouts of laughter.

A pretty little blue-eyed girl of seven was the only child we saw. She nestled against her mother; and the mother clasped her closely, lest we should carry her off to London. She begged we would not wish to take her child to London, and said she "would not sell her for much money." One of the wives was pointed out to us as particularly happy in the prospect of becoming a mother: and we were taken to see the room in which she was to lie in, which was all in readiness, though the event was not looked for for more than half a year. She was in the gayest spirits, and sang and danced. While she was lounging on her cushions, I thought her the handsomest and most graceful, as well as the happiest, of the party: but when she rose to dance, the charm was destroyed for ever. The dancing is utterly disgusting. A pretty Jewess of twelve years old danced, much in the same way; but with downcast eyes and an air of modesty. While the dancing went on, and the smoking, and drinking coffee and sherbet, and the singing, to the accompaniment of a tambourine, some hideous old hags came in successively, looked and laughed, and went away again. Some negresses made a good background to this thoroughly Eastern picture. All the while, romping, kissing and screaming, went on among the ladies, old and young. At first, I thought them a perfect rabble; hut when I recovered myself a little, I saw that there was some sense in the faces of the elderly women. In the midst of all this fun, the interpretess assured us that "there is much jealousy every day;" jealousy of the favored wife; that is, in this case, of the one who was pointed out to us by her companions as so eminently happy, and with whom they were romping and kissing, as with the rest. Poor thing! even the happiness of these her best days is hollow: for she cannot have, at the same time, peace in the hareem and her husband's love.

They were so free in their questions about us, and so evidently pleased when we used a similar impertinence about them, that we took the opportunity of learning a good deal of their way of life. Mrs. Y. and I were consulting about noticing the bride's dress, when we found we had put off too long: we were asked how we liked her dress, and encouraged to handle the silk. So I went on to examine the bundles of false hair that some of them wore; the pearl bracelets on their tattooed arms, and their jeweled and inlaid pattens. —In answer to our question what they did in the way of occupation, they said "nothing;" but when we inquired whether they never made clothes or sweetmeats, they replied "yes." —They earnestly wished us to stay always; and they could not understand why we should not. My case puzzled them particularly. I believe they took me for a servant; and they certainly pitied me extremely for having to go about without being taken care of. They asked what I did: and Mrs. Y., being anxious to do me all honor, told them I had written many books: but the information was thrown away, because they did not know what a book was. Then we informed them that I lived in a field among mountains, where I had built a house; and that I had plenty to do; and we told them in what way: but still they could make nothing of it but that I had brought the stones with my own hands, and built the house myself. There is nothing about which the inmates of hareems seem to be so utterly stupid as about women having anything to do. That time should be valuable to a woman, and that she should have any business on her hands, and any engagements to observe, are things quite beyond their comprehension.

The pattens I have mentioned are worn to keep the feet and flowing dress from the marble pavement, which is often wetted for coolness. I think all the ladies here had bare feet. When they left the raised floor on which they sat, they slipped their feet into their high pattens, and went slumping about, rather awkwardly. I asked Dr. Thompson, who has admission as a physician into more houses than any other man could familiarly visit, whether he could not introduce skipping-ropes upon these spacious marble floors. I see no other chance of the women being induced to take exercise. They suffer cruelly from in diges- tion, —gorging themselves with sweet things, smoking intemperately, and pass- ing through life with more than half the brain almost unawakened, and with scarcely any exercise of the limbs. Poor things! our going was a great amusement to them, they said: and they showed this by their entreaties to the last moment that we would not leave them yet, and that we would stay always. — "And these," as my journal says, "were human beings, such as those of whom Christ made friends! —The chief lady gave me roses as a farewell token. —The Jewish ladies, who took their leave with us, wanted us to visit at another house: but we happily had not time. —I am thankful to have seen a hareem under favorable circumstances; and I earnestly hope I may never see another."

I kept those roses, however. I shall need no reminding of the most injured human beings I have ever seen, —the most studiously depressed and corrupt- ed women whose condition I have witnessed: but I could not throw away the flowers which so found their way into my hand as to bespeak for the wrongs of the giver the mournful remembrance of my heart.

CHAPTER XXIII

PRESENT CONDITION OF EGYPT

I FIND IN MY JOURNAL THE FOLLOWING COMPLAINT. "One pregnant fact here is that one can get no reliable information from the most reliable men. About matters on which there ought to be no difference of statement, we meet with strange contradictions; such as the rate and amount of tax, &c. In fact, there are no data; and there is little free communication. Even a census does not help. The present census, we are told, will be a total failure—so many will bribe the officials to omit their names, because of the poll-tax." Thus it is that neither I nor any other traveler can give accounts of any value of the actual material condition of the people of Egypt. But we have a substantial piece of knowledge in this very negation of knowledge. We know for certain that a government is bad, and that the people are unprosperous and unhappy in a country where there is a great ostentation of civilization and improvement, side by side with mystery as to the actual working of social arrangements, and every sort of evasion on the part of the people. We have a substantial piece of knowledge in the fact that men of honor, men of station, men of business, men of courage, who have all the means of information which the place and time permit, dirtier in opinion and statement about every matter of importance on which they converse with inquiring strangers. I saw several such men. They were quite willing to tell me what they knew; and they assigned frankly the grounds of their opinions and statements: but what I obtained was merely a mass of contradictions so extraordinary that I cannot venture to give any details: and if I give any general impressions, it can be only under the guard of a declaration that I am sure of nothing, and can offer only what I suppose on the whole to be an indication of the way in which the government of Mohammed Alee works.

Of the Pasha himself I have little or nothing to say. It is a mere impertinence for a passing traveler to estimate the character of the man. That will be a study for the future historian; and it ought to be a wise historian who will hereafter review the life of the man, from its beginning to its close, estimating his temperament, his position, his intercourses and his opportunities, so as to decide on his personal merits, —to judge him as a man. It may be easier to estimate his relation to his people as a matter of fact, apart from the question of his personal value: but I know of no man in the country who is qualified to do this: and of course no stranger who is anxious not to mislead, will attempt it. —I never saw the Pasha, except once in his carriage. He was gone up the river, to look about him and depose Selim Pasha, when we returned to Cairo. And if it had not been so, we could merely have seen him by meeting him in the gardens at Shoobra, or in some such transient way as would have yielded us no real knowledge about him. —Having thus explained how small were our means of information, I will bring together here the few fragments I could collect of knowledge or probability.

One thing is certain: that, in his endeavors to improve the civilization of his people, Mohammed Alee has omitted the first step, which is essential to all substantial advance. He has given them no security of property or other rights. Moreover, he seems to be unaware that this security is the only ground of improvement. He appears never to have learned that national welfare can arise from no other basis than national industry; and that there can be no reliable national industry where no man is sure of receiving the rewards of his labor. He appears not to see that public works, of whatever magnitude and utility, are merely monumental as long as the people who are to work at them have to be caught like game, marched to the spot, and kept there by companies of soldiers, and paid at his mere will and pleasure; —such of them as are not killed off by his mistakes in the provision of food and labor-saving tools. He appears never to have considered that schools, however grand in expense, and in their appearance on paper, will not enlighten the people at large while parents snatch up their children and hide them, on the mere rumor of the approach of his recruiting parties, or maim the young creatures in time to prevent their being chosen for the schools at all. He seems not to see that the love of knowledge cannot grow among the people while he sets his schooling before them as an evil for which he gives in compensation money, maintenance, and the prospect of a handsome provision in life. He appears not to see that his people cannot become orderly tax-paying subjects while every peasant is liable to ruin whenever his next neighbor fails to pay his dues. The moment the tax-collector is mentioned, the inhabitants of a village will fly to the mountains, and hide there, leaving their crops and goods at the mercy of the government officers: and it does not strike their prince that such a flight is not a step in civilization. He appears to forget that the people will not become more religious while he possesses himself of the endowments of mosques, promising to keep up their condition, but so neglecting to do so as that all go to decay but those which have strong claims on the piety of the Mohammedans. He does not perceive that lands will not be the better tilled for his seizing on them, while the title deeds are carefully concealed, in hope of a favorable change by and by. He does not see that every man is discouraged from improving his condition while the bad faith of the government, through the corruption of its agents, is a matter of course; —the general rule, to which the fellah and the journeyman find no exceptions. The Pasha may, if he can find the means, cover the land with his public works, his schools, his factories, and his cattle from Dongola; but his people will continue to decline in numbers and resources till he can induce a certain portion of them to endeavor to improve their own condition. Among his many enterprises, this, which should have been the first, appears never to have entered his head. That the population is declining, I have myself no doubt. One official gentleman may point to the plague and cholera as the causes of a merely temporary depopulation of particular spots, which indicates nothing of the condition of the whole country; and another may reckon up the new canals made in his time: but these considerations are no set off against the evidence there is of decreasing numbers, and of the extent of land perpetually going out of cultivation. It is clear that the truth will not be learned by means of a census, while the agents take bribes to set down a greater or smaller number, or have to make a guess at the population of a village which they find deserted. If the population be decreasing, the fact may be for a while concealed by stout denial: if it be increasing, the fact must soon show itself, to the satisfaction of everybody, in a country which certainly once contained above three times the number of the present inhabitants, while exporting food to a wide range of neighboring states. In a country where there is so much more than room for everybody, so much fertility ready to every one's hand, an increase of population must be rapid and evident, under circumstances which admit of it at all; and if, in such a country, there is no evident increase, but a general persuasion of its decline, what can be thought of its ruler's boast of advancing civilization!—There was a time when the Nile Valley was regularly inhabited by a population of 8,000,000. The number of settled in habitants is believed to be now not more than 2,500,000; and it is, to all appearance, still declining, as it has been from the beginning of the century.

I cannot say that I saw much during my voyage which could serve as material for an opinion on this subject: but I saw something. I saw one new canal in Upper Egypt; and, to set against this, I saw many and large tracts of land let out of cultivation, showing evident signs of former irrigation and drainage, and sprinkled over, or bordered by ruined cottages or villages. I saw a few factories struggling for existence, while it was evident to English eyes that the only security for their permanency was in the improvement of agriculture; —the natural occupation of the Egyptians, and that to which Nature perpetually invites them, and for which she would reward them, if the tyranny and bad faith of Man did not interfere. But how is agriculture to improve under such arrangements as the following? —The cultivator undertakes to till a certain quantity of land, —all the land, it is understood, being the Pasha's property, except such as he pensions or gratifies certain parties with. Some, I am aware, declare that private property in land, of a much older date than the Pasha's life, does exist to a great extent. Others, whom I think higher authority, say there is little or none, though the title deeds of a large quantity are hidden away, in hope of better times. —And, by the way, what a telling fact it is that there should be any doubt about such a point as this among well-informed men on the spot!—At all events, whether the land is the Pasha's or another's, the cultivator engages, in return for being furnished with all that is needful for its cultivation, to hand over a stipulated amount (not proportion) of the produce, after harvest. He receives, among other requisites, an order for a good and sufficient quantity of seed-corn from the government granary. —When he presents the order, the great official gentleman at the granary directs a subordinate officer to supply the applicant with three-quarters of the specified quantity, he retaining the other quarter for his own fee. The second officer subtracts a second quarter; and the cultivator sows his land with half the proper seed. Of course, when it comes up thin, he considers what he shall do. The probability is that at harvest time, he will go out in the night, and filch from his neighbors' fields, while those neighbors may be in his fields, doing the like. When the day of reckoning comes, one or more of the neighbors (it may be remembered that some of my party saw eight), may be chained and led off to be bastinadoed for nonpayment of dues. Or, as some other friends of mine saw, the Pasha may send a force to seize the land of a whole district, because some of the cultivators may be unable, or be supposed to be unable, to pay their rent. —While such is the state of things, and in the absence of any promise of improvement, the stranger does not see how manufactures should grow out of the agriculture of Egypt, or an increasing population out of either. Nor is it easy to suppose that any circumstances which may lie out of the stranger's sight can neutralize such facts as these.

The state of affairs does not seem to be mended by the Pasha's practice of giving away his villages, —which is the same thing as giving away the people who inhabit them. When, for instance, it is inconvenient to pay to any claimant or favorite five hundred purses a year, the Pasha will give half the money and five or six villages. Then, of course, the uncertainty of the peasant's lot at best is aggravated by new liabilities: he depends on the temper, fortunes and business habits of his new proprietor, while he is not relieved from the corruption of the agents with whom he has to deal. The mischief of the Middleman system exists everywhere, whoever be the proprietor; and while the proprietor may make matters worse than the average, he can hardly lighten the evils of such a system, in any one village. —As might be expected, no such spectacle is ever seen as a native bettering his condition, or attempting to do so. A foreigner, whether he be a slave from Circassia, or a man of science from France, Italy or England, may rise to high honors and great wealth; but if any native born Egyptian can improve his rank and fortunes, I never heard of such; and it is certain that the people generally have no other view, no further hope, than obtaining bare necessaries from season to season; and I might say, in regard to too many, from day to day.

And now, what are we to think of the boasted public works of Egypt! By all means let them proceed, if they aid production and transit. For as much as they are good in themselves, let them proceed. But let it be remembered that public works in Egypt do not arise from a firm foundation of national industry, and that the people who work at them are virtually slaves. The case is just the reverse of that of the public works of Ancient Egypt. The old Pharaohs, natives of the Nile Valley, raised their mighty palaces and temples by the hands of the captives they brought into slavery from foreign lands. Now we see the opposite case of a Greek ruler, his throne surrounded by foreigners, raising the monuments of his reign by the hands of the enslaved nation whom he calls his subjects. Those who can may choose between the two cases for preference. In each case, there is much vain-glory in the enterprise, and much barbarism in the way of carrying it out. The old Pharaoh thought to honor his gods, according to the morality of his time, and made no pretence of benefiting his slave-laborers. The modern Pasha does homage to the morality of his time by professing to aim at the good of his people; but he outrages every right and every interest of the many thousands who are driven to work at his patriotic enterprises. As we have seen, nearly a hundredth part of the whole present population of the country (23,000 out of 2,500,000) were killed off in six months, in the making of the Mahmoudieh canal. After such an experiment as this, the prosecution of other public works by laborers no better fitted and prepared to achieve and desire them, appears to those on the spot a barbarism equal to any that can be charged upon any heathen temple-builder of them all.

As for other laboring classes than the cultivators, —the boatmen are, I am told, the most fortunate, and therefore the most intelligent and prudent. They are sure of the money they earn, and are exempt from the extortion which ruins the fortunes, and breaks the spirit of other classes of laborers. As for the insecurity and extortion, almost all the working classes seem as badly off as the cultivator. Everybody has heard of Ibraheem Pasha's fine garden at Roda. The laborers in that garden are paid nominally a piastre and a quarter per day. Out of this, they have to feed themselves. This they might possibly do, if they really received the money: but they are paid in corn, or some other produce which it is convenient so to dispose of; and this produce is reckoned at a price higher than they can obtain for it.

At the Sugar-refinery, near this garden of Ibraheem Pasha's, the people are paid with molasses, in a similar manner; and, in addition, they have to bribe the measurer of the molasses to give them due measure, —it being an understood thing that he will help himself out of either their purses or their molasses.

While on the subject of the Pasha's public works, it should be remembered, in justice to him, that he is under strong stimulus to prosecute them. I am not, as I said before, attempting to estimate the character of the Pasha, but only to tell the very little I could learn of the condition of his people: but while his public works, with all their ostentation, stand in such mournful contrast with the misery of his people, it would be unjust to him not to mention that he has about him men of various European nations, who endeavor to serve both their national and individual interests by stimulating him to enterprises in which they may be wanted, or their country may be served. However shrewd the old man may be on the whole, however he may amuse himself by receiving flatteries and holding out hopes, and hanging out caprices, he cannot, in his state of crude civilization, be always clear sighted and prudent. He may be easily dazzled by the glory proposed to him of doing something which shall make France and England wonder; something which shall make the whole world think him the most patriotic ruler in it.

At the same time, we see how cautious he can be about matters which he really understands. Some people on the spot, as well as many at a distance, wonder that a man who acted so wisely and well as the Pasha did about our communication with India, when nothing better could have been hoped from him than that he would have closed the passage through Egypt, should not yet have made a canal or railway to the Red Sea, as he is incessantly urged to do. Those who so wonder may be assured that there is more in the matter than has been presented to them. It is a case which the Pasha happens to understand, and about which he chooses to take his time, and to judge for himself. He knows all about the shallows at both ends of the proposed ship canal, and he knows also the precise depth of the interests engaged in the railway scheme. He has amused himself by seeing locomotives run on a little railway before his palace: he looked, and laughed, and stroked his beard, and talked of the devil being in it; and he has some reason to think that the devil would be in it indeed if he should be in a hurry to lay down the rails which, as he knows, lie at hand, wanting to be used. He knows what a devil he would raise among the Bedoueens if he rashly took from them the carriage of persons and goods through the Desert. What could he do with these wild tribes, if he deprived them of their only profitable employment? And how could he compensate them for the loss of the Desert transport by which they now live? If the railway did not interfere with the Bedoueens, being used only for India passengers and their luggage and the mails, it may be asked whether it would answer to the Pasha to make a railroad for this purpose merely, and to receive the proceeds only twice a month. He may think that an inland canal, from the Nile to Suez, would answer better, as it would be in use every day for the transport of corn and other produce. He may think that the whole matter, however important to England, may be so dubious in regard to Egypt as not to be hastily proceeded in at the risk of rousing the Bedoueens to harass the country. If he appears to people in London and Paris as dilatory and uncertain about undertaking either of these works as he has been rash and positive about others, it is clear that there must be a reason for his new slowness and uncertainty: and that reason may be other than one of foreign policy. When I hear that either canal or railroad is certainly begun in earnest, and not merely surveyed for, I shall believe that it may be at work in time. Till then, I am not disposed to think we shall have either during the old man's life. If he goes seriously into the undertaking at all, I think he will make a canal. If he makes a canal, I think it will be an inland one, —from the Nile to Suez. And if he makes a railroad, I think it will not be the English one which has been so earnestly pressed on his attention, both from England and on the spot. The only thing I am sure of, however, is that people at home had better not decide what the Pasha ought to do, and represent the matter as a very plain and simple one. For my own part, —while seeing as distinctly as any one the advantage to my own country of an improved passage across the Isthmus of Suez, and after having learned on the spot all that I could on every side, I see that it is a matter so complicated at present with difficulties of many kinds, that I am glad not to be obliged to form an opinion on what ought to be done.

I really feel very doubtful about sending this chapter through the press, —so meager as it is, and yet so vague. I could have made it much fuller, and far more interesting and distinct, if I had written down what I was told, —or either side of what I was told. But, as I said before, I could not rely on the information, while entirely relying on the honor of those who kindly gave it. I have thought it best to offer only the little that I believe to be true. Of this little I cannot say how much might be modified by facts which may lie behind; and I feel that I know scarcely anything of the modern Egyptian polity but the significant fact that nothing can be certainly known.

CHAPTER XXIV

GARDENS OF RODA AND SHOOBRA—HELIOPOLIS—PETRIFIED FOREST—TOMBS OF THE MEMLOOK KINGS—THE NILOMETER— LEAVING CAIRO

THE ROSES WHICH HANG OVER THE WALL of the garden in the island of Roda are a pleasant sight to the traveler returning from the south. As some of our party had letters to the gentleman who is in charge of the place, we went to see it. The fame of this garden proves how difficult it must be to have a good garden at Cairo. Besides the roses (which were not abundant) we saw a few anemones and violets; and that was nearly all. The fruits are oranges, dates and bananas, excellent; grapes, pretty good; peaches and nectarines not good; melons bad. Neither fruits nor flowers can satisfy one who knows what gardening is in Europe. Sometimes, there is drought; and then again, the river comes up occasionally to destroy everything, —to drown the garden. There is to be a steam-engine to water the place with; and thus the drought will be kept off. —I believe it is the fashion to admire this garden, and to imagine it peopled by the Houris of Ibraheem Pasha's hareem. We were told by the gardener that the ladies had been twice; but that their going was an exceptional event. This gentleman can hardly wish it otherwise if, as I believe is true, these wives of a grey-bearded man behave like disorderly children, doing mischief to the flower-beds in their senseless play. —The only thing that struck me as at all beautiful in any part of the garden was an elegant bamboo, which was a treat to the eye. Everywhere else it was painful to see the attempt at making an English garden of an arid plot, where it seemed as if all the plants had quarreled, and were trying how far apart they could keep.

We were delighted, after this, with the Pasha's garden at Shoobra. It has a character appropriate to the country. It is formal, but exceedingly pretty; studded thick with parterres of roses, geraniums and stocks; and thick set as possible with orange and lemon trees. The Djebel is charming; —the hill ascended by a succession of terraces connected by a trellised ascent, which conducts to a fine point of view. Such a formal and blossomy garden is in strong contrast with scenery round; and the true charm of a garden is there accordingly. We thought it the only place worthy of the name that we had seen in Egypt. —The kiosks round the central fountain are beautiful; and one of them is a truly splendid apartment. If the ordinary gas-lamps were absent, and better glass present in the windows, and more flowers about the fountain, this spot would nearly fulfil our ideas of garden luxury in the East. —I cannot imagine why the Pasha's windows are so badly glazed. In these days of universal plate glass, it is strange to look round the apartments of his palaces, and see his brilliant furniture, and gorgeous bijoux from Paris contrasting with the coarse, greenish, seamed window panes. I would advise the European power which is most anxious to propitiate Mohammed Alee to send him out a freight of plate glass windows. I can assure such European power that a vast commotion of envy and jealousy will be excited in those circles where every present made to the Pasha is regarded as an event in the politics of the world. Come, now! which of the politicians of the world will be quickest to glaze the Pasha's windows?

The ride from Cairo to Shoobra is the pleasantest we found in the neighborhood; I might almost call it the only one. It is under an avenue of picturesque spreading trees, chiefly acacias, through which the tilled lands on either hand show themselves, refreshing the eyes. The Nile, spreading abroad in reaches, or flowing between shoals, is visible also; to-day in a state of singular commotion, from the strength of the wind. The dust flew in clouds, and the river broke in waves over the shoals.

It was just such weather the day (February 19th) we went to that mournful place, —old Heliopolis. We were to have made our first trial of camel-riding that day; but the wind was too high, though it might permit us to ride lowlily, on our asses, through the fenced and cultivated country, which lies between Cairo and the solitary obelisk. Our ride was pleasant enough while it was among fields, and under the shelter of hedges and avenues of acacia. On our return by a different route, we were almost strangled with wind and sand.

The obelisk looks well from a distance, springing from among trees: but as the sole relic of the once brilliant little city, the University of old Egyptian learning, it is a mournful object enough. When one comes near, one finds its very hieroglyphics filled up and plastered over by the wild bees. Round its base there is a hollow, fruitlessly dug to ascertain how deep its platform lies. The surface of the land must have risen very much. Yet the circuit of mounds indicates where the remains of the city lie. This circuit of mounds is what one should come to Heliopolis to see. It is a moment not to be forgotten when one stands at the foot of the obelisk, and looks round through trees and over-stretches of sand at these mounds, and thinks of Joseph coming here to fetch his wife, and celebrating the marriage with all the courtly and priestly pomp of the time; —and of Moses, sitting here at the feet of the priests, nurtured with such care and wisdom as would be given to the education of the son of Pharaoh's daughter: —and of Plato, dwelling within this circuit for thirteen years, as it is said, and almost daily perhaps, in all that time, passing the spot where we are standing now, and looking up at the tapering lines of sculptures, as we are now looking up at the bee-cells with which those sculptures are filled up. This was one glimpse more into the old world of Egypt, after the cloud curtain had seemed to cover all. After yielding this brief glimpse, it closed again, to open no more.

On our return, we were taken to see, in a sort of garden, the tree of Joseph and Mary; a very old sycamore, under which, as Jews and Mohammedans alike believe, the Holy Family reposed when they fled into Egypt, —by this honor rendering the tree immortal, —as one would think it must be, if this be really it.

In this direction lies the (so-called) Petrified Forest; an absurd name, meant probably to convey the fact that the quantity of petrified wood is surprisingly large. The ride to this spot is so interesting that it matters little what lies at the end of it. After threading the narrow ways of the city, we emerged by the fine "gate of Victory,"—the Bab e' Nusr, —into the eastern Desert, in view of the Tombs of the Memlook Kings, past whose courts and domes and minarets we rode in among the sandhills. We had a fine view of the road to Suez, which wound away to our left; and then we entered the region of rock and sand, of heat and drought, where, in a few days, we were to make our home for many weeks. In about an hour, we began to note some odd-looking stones lying about in the sand, and among ordinary looking pebbles. These were pieces of petrified wood. As we advanced, they lay thicker; and before we returned, we had certainly seen an astonishing quantity. Fragments of palm trunks, approaching to the size of logs, were perhaps the commonest kind: but there were several kinds of wood; even the bamboo was there, with its joints distinctly visible.

Of course, we visited the Tombs of the Memlook Kings, —commonly but erroneously called the Tombs of the Caliphs. What a descent from the tombs of the Kings that we had seen up the river! Yet these well repay a visit; and it may be worthwhile to describe one of them, very briefly. These tombs look almost as well when one rides among them as from the terrace of the citadel, where one is so struck with the pale yellow domes and minarets, rising against their ground of darker sand. Now those domes and spires stood up bright and sharp against the cloudless sky. Round the base of the dome of some are inscriptions in colored tiles, white letters on a dark blue or other ground. Some of the walls outside are in courses of yellowish white and red, alternately; the white being the limestone of the neighboring hills, and the red a mere daub of paint upon the stones. These tombs are going to decay so fast, that the next generation of travelers will see but little of them. Some of the walls are slanting to their fall: others show gaping rents; and many stones are carried away by the builders of some new edifice.

The threshold across which we stepped into the enclosure of one of these tombs was of gray granite, split down the very middle of an antique sculptured figure, whose cartouche remained entire. Thus do men go on making for themselves inviolable tombs by violating those of their predecessors! This fractured sculpture was laid down for a door-step over which the kingly pride of this Memlook sultaun might pass to its last repose: and now men cross this threshold, to carry away the stones of the newer edifice—but not to serve for another royal tomb.

Within the court, we found a dry and meager bit of garden, and a well covered with a shattered wooden dome. Along two sides of the court were dwellings; those of one side ruined; those of the other inhabited by tenants who have them free. There is no competition for these almshouses; for the people are becoming fewer in the land, and there is plenty of houseroom. Apartments as good as these, and more convenient for situation, may be had in Cairo for next to nothing; and there is therefore no eagerness to live rent free in this place. On a third side is a wall, with a beautiful minaret at one corner. This minaret is fast going to ruin: but one of the gentlemen made his way to its upper gallery, whence he obtained a fine view—even to the second station on the Suez road. On the fourth side of the court is the Mosque, with the tomb of the sultaun at one end, and that of his hareem at the other, each under a dome. The loftiness of this range was very striking: and indeed I never was in any mosque where I did not wonder afresh at the height of the dome, and the magnificence of the spring of the pillars. The handsome stairs and pulpit of the mosque, and its rich covered and inlaid screens, are rotting away. The sordid decay was a desolate spectacle.

From hence we went to see a Coptic church, which we found altogether disgusting, from its profane altar-piece to the swarms of fleas which inhabit its matting. There was a handsome carved screen; but nothing else that we could bear to look at. The pictures of saints were most audacious; and as for the altar-piece—any Mohammedan who ever saw its central figure would be quite justified in classing these Christians with low idolaters. It may be well to look into these places, to learn to be just towards the originals of other corrupted faiths, whose symbols may no more represent their primitive ideas than these Coptic pictures represent Christianity.

On Saturday the 20th, the weather was suitable for our first attempt at camel-riding; and we went to the Nilometer. We had committed the ordering of the apparatus to those whose business it was, and who were supposed to understand the matter: and they had prepared for Mrs. Y. and me wooden boxes or chairs, instead of saddles. In these we set out from the Hotel d'Orient. The swaying motion, and the being carried as dead weight, were excessively disagreeable, and especially to one so fond of riding as I am. Being carried on a camel is too little like riding at best: but while one is on a saddle, and holds a rein, one may amuse one's self with the semblance: but the being carried in a chair permits no such relief. Moreover, it is impossible so to fasten on the chair as that it shall never slip in the least on one side; and the leaning sensation is intolerable. It seemed very doubtful to me how long; I could support this method of traveling; and I wondered what was to be done if my companion and I should have to protest against it in the middle of the Desert. Happily we were seen by Linant Bey, whom we met at dinner afterwards, at the Consul General's. He has traveled over more miles of desert than almost any civilized man, and knows all about it: and he told us at once that we must leave our chairs behind, and adopt such a method of cushioning our saddles as he would instruct us in. Before dinner was over, he was sent for, to follow the Pasha up the river immediately: but his instructions set us on our camels to the best advantage. I often afterwards rejoiced that he had chanced to see us that day.

We met in this ride two or three sons of Ibraheem Pasha's—gentle manly and lively-looking boys. We crossed by a ferry boat to the island of Roda, to see the Nilometer, which I was surprised to find a very pretty place; —a damp, dim chamber, tufted with water weeds; — steep stairs down into it; and a green pool and mud at the bottom: — in the centre, a graduated pillar: —in the four sides of the chamber, four pointed arches—one filled in with an elegant grating: —round the cornice, and over the arches, Cufic inscriptions; and in two of the niches, within the arches, similar inscriptions. The crypt-like aspect of the chamber, with its aquatic adornments of weeds and mosses—so perfectly in accordance with its purpose—was charming, the charm being aided perhaps by a sense of the unique character of the place. I need not say that we did not see the base of the graduated pillar. We are told that it is never seen, even when the Nile is at the lowest, the yearly nominal cleaning out leaving yet a considerable deposit of mud. We were glad to have seen the Nilometer; and this was our last sight-seeing at Cairo—unless it was the Ezbekeeyeh, the next day.

The great square of the Ezbekeeyeh is always gay on Sundays, when the Franks walk there after church, and the Mohammedans sit smoking in groups to watch them. Some of the returned pilgrims further enlivened it this day. There were a few tents, and some conjurors; and pilgrims walking with a flag and singing: and then they formed into a circle, and one man chanted prayers. The eastern and western groups, —the turbans and burnooses here, and the French bonnets and mantles there, —all among the dark acacias, or crossing the gleams of bright sunshine, make a strange picture, not to be likened to anything I saw afterwards.

Monday, the 22d, was our packing day. I was to carry nothing that would not travel in saddle-bags: so I took care that my saddle-bags should be very large. Having stuffed them with necessaries, —not forgetting plenty of paper and ink, —I put away all finery and delicate articles of dress or use, in trunks which were to meet us at Alexandria, three months afterwards. What kind of appearance I was to make at Jerusalem and Damascus, it was useless to consider now. Saddle bags will not carry bonnets, caps and dresses which will not bear crushing; and all such were therefore left behind. —The hems of our gowns told rather a sad tale of the state of the floors in our hotel. We could only hope that the Desert would prove a cleaner floor. We had done our best by remonstrance here; but the answer to our petition to have our rooms cleaned was decisive: — it would be useless to clean our rooms, as they would be dirty again to-morrow! We had not our remedy in our own hands, as Swift had with his man Ralph; so we were obliged to be patient.

Remembering the scarcity of water which we were about to encounter for some weeks, I washed and dried this day the few things which remained over from the hands of the washerman. The occasion was more strange than the employment; and strangely I felt it. Here we were going to spend weeks in the newest scene and way of life the world could offer us. We were going into the dreariest wastes of the globe, with no means of existence but those which we carried with us. We were going to spend weeks among rocks and sands, wild Arabs, glaring suns, scorching winds, and a poor sprinkling of brackish pools. How should we like it? How should I, for one, bear it? How could I tell beforehand? I had had some experience, in former years, of the hardships of travel in rude countries: but I had never tried anything like this. —More strange still was the thought of what we were going to see. Strange above all, perhaps, was the composure with which I let all the imagery of this extraordinary prospect pass before me. I could not detect in myself any alarm, any surprise, any kind of excitement: and I have little doubt of the same calmness being in the mind of every one of the large company who were this day preparing to set forth through the Desert.

And now—as to where we were going. Before we left England, Mr. Y. had asked me what I thought of our going to Petra. I laughed, not at all supposing that he could be in earnest about English travelers, —and especially women, —going to Petra. In my youth I had read all the books of Arabian travel that I could get hold of; and I was aware of the extreme difficulty and danger of passing through Idumæa in those times, and up to the present day: I never gave a serious thought to the suggestion of going to Petra; nor did I suppose that any one else did.

"Till within a few days of our departure, our plan had been, as a matter of course, to go by El Arish to Hebron and Jerusalem: and again, Mr. Y. had asked me how I should like to go to Petra, if we found we could get there from Hebron; and again I had laughed, not supposing him in earnest. —But a more distinct vision arose when many friends, residents of Cairo, and passing travelers, —I think I may say all our friends, —advised and urged our going to Mount Sinai. This I did most heartily desire; and certainly not the less when it appeared that a large party of travelers, including English, Scotch and Irish, were in hope, —a doubtful and vague hope, but still a hope, —of penetrating to Petra, on their way from Sinai to Jerusalem. If they could do it, so might we. But still, my thoughts barely glanced towards it; and when I was told the good news that we were going to Mount Sinai, I felt this quite enough, and did not yet look further.

The large party I have mentioned, —a company of as kind hearts as one can find in a chance wandering over the world, —wished us to join them. We held off from the junction, feeling that the fatigues of desert traveling would be quite enough for some of us, without any addition from the presence of numbers. As for me, I am a particularly unsociable member of a traveling party; as I suppose every deaf person must be who wishes to profit by the journey. It is impossible for a deaf person to listen from the ridge of a camel, and note the objects of travel at the same time. So my way must be to ride in silence during the traveling hours; and we did not expect to have strength left for any evening sociability. We therefore engaged our own sheikh and escort, and twenty camels, wished our friendly compatriots a good journey, and resolved to go by ourselves.

We were to set out on Tuesday morning, February 23d. On the Monday we bade farewell to our Cairo friends; and Stanley Poole and his brother accompanied me to the terrace of the citadel, for one more enjoyment of that glorious view. —That evening, the mail from England arrived. In the morning, we waited for letters; and Mr. E.'s share detained us till after an early dinner.

For some days our preparations had been very visible in the court yard and environs of our hotel. Mr. Y.'s large tent, which was to house Mrs. Y. and me, had been stoutly lined for warmth at night. — Our sheikh, Bishara, with his bright and genial face, had basked there in the sun every day, and given his advice on our affairs; and our camels had been brought to the spot. All this morning, the cross-grained brutes had been growling and groaning in the yard; and when their loads were put on, their vicious lamentations were horrible to hear. —Before two p.m., we were mounted; and we paced forth in procession through the streets of Cairo. The sheikh wore under his blue burnoose, a brilliant dress of green satinet, striped with red and gold color. The gentlemen were dressed half and half, Eastern and European. Alee and the cook were smoking after the toils of the morning: —my camel-driver kissed my camel repeatedly, and allured the creature to stoop and offer its huge lips to the salute.

From my high seat, I saw more of the deep, dim, wide interiors of the Cairo dwellings, and of the people at their trades, than I ever did before. This last view of the streets was the best: but there was something mournful in passing for the last time those picturesque alleys, and imposing mosques, and busy bazaars, and the captivating groups of oriental figures of which the eye never tires. —We passed out near the citadel, traversed the bazaar or market which was formed outside the gates, and entered upon the sand of the Desert.

I now thought camel riding as easy as sleeping on a feather bed. I found afterwards how little first impressions are worth in such a case; but in this unexpected ease, and in the beauty about me, and the prospect of the journey before me, I was very happy, when lo! at about two miles from the city, there were the green and blue and white tents of the British travelers! —I supposed that they had been delayed, and that we should pass them: but no! —our camels were made to lie down, and we were made to dismount, on reaching the camp. This was Bissateen; and the escort never will go further than Bissateen the first day, that there may be an opportunity of supplying any needful article that may have been forgotten. —Here we were, after all, in junction with the British travelers; —a junction much approved by the escort, as conducing to the safety of all parties. We separated no more till we left Jerusalem, nearly two months afterwards.

We strolled about in the sunset light, bidding many a farewell to Cairo, which stood out clear and bright in the evening glow, —its citadel predominant. The green levels between us and the Nile looked flatter in surface and more vivid in color than ever. Over westward were the Pyramids, glorious against the orange sky; and near us the palm grove belonging to Bissateen, and the wells where the women came with their water-pots and cords. Close at hand was our camp, with the Arabs in groups round the fires, and camels lying about as if they wanted to be sketched. We were not sorry now to have stopped for the night within sight of Cairo and the Pyramids. As I consider this day the last of our Egyptian life, I shall here close my first Part. It is true, we did not pass the Egyptian frontier for some days; but our life in the Desert was so Arabian in its character and interests as to belong to the Arabian section of this book.

Here, then, we take leave of Egypt, —to me by far the most interesting portion of our travels. I believe that some others did not find it so in the experience of their journey; and I hope my readers may not in the retrospect. And yet I should like them to feel with me in regard to the surpassing interest of Egypt, even at the cost of their relishing the latter half of my book less than the first.

END OF PART I

Suggested Reading

Campbell, Ffyona. *On Foot Through Africa*. Orion, 1994.

Edwards, Amelia. *A Thousand Miles up the Nile*. New York City, A.L. Burt, 1891.

Murphy, Dervla. *Full Tilt: Ireland to India with a Bicycle*. Eland Books, 2010.

Murphy, Dervla. *In Ethiopia with a Mule*. John Murray Pubs Ltd., 2003.

Said, Edward W. *Orientalism*. Random House, Inc., 1978.

Spalding, Lavinia, editor. *Best Women's Travel Writing, Volume 11*. Travelers' Tales, 2017.

Stanhope, Hester. *Travels of Lady Hester Stanhope: Forming the Completion of her Memoirs*. London, H. Colburn, 1848.

Works by:
Freya Stark
Dame Rebecca West
Jan Morris

www.ingramcontent.com/pod-product-compliance
Lightning Source LLC
Chambersburg PA
CBHW071554160426
42812CB00093BB/3338/J